Foundation MATHEMATICS for IIT-JEE / Olympiad

disha
Nurturing Ambitions

Includes NCERT & Exemplar Solutions

Class 9

100% useful for Class 9 School Exam

Set of 4 Solved Exercises

- Exercise 1: FIB, T/F, Matching, VSA, SA and LA Questions
- Exercise 2: NCERT, Exemplar and HOTS Questions
- Exercise 3 & 4: MCQs 1 Correct, MCQs ≥ 1 Correct, Passage, Assertion-Reason, Multiple Matching and Integer Type Questions

1050+ FIB, T/F & Subjective Questions

480+ IIT-JEE New Pattern MCQs

260+ Illustrations & Solved Examples

- **Corporate Office :** 45, 2nd Floor, Maharishi Dayanand Marg, Corner Market, Malviya Nagar, New Delhi-110017
  Tel. : 011-26692293 / 26692294

Editor :
D.P. Gupta

Typeset by Disha DTP Team

For further information about the books from DISHA,

Log on to **www.dishapublication.com** or email to **info@dishapublication.com**

INDEX

Chapter 1

Number Systems

INTRODUCTION

We all know the numbers. We are playing with the numbers since our childhood. All the numbers which we studied till now are rational numbers. We also studied the representation of rational numbers on number line and about their basic algebraic operations like addition, subtraction, multiplication, division, L.C.M., H.C.F., etc of rational numbers.

In this chapter, we shall learn a new type of numbers called Irrational numbers. We will also learn the representation of irrational numbers on the number line and basic operations related to irrational numbers. All the rational and irrational numbers taken together are known as Real Numbers.

NUMBER LINE

Representation of various types of numbers on the number line.

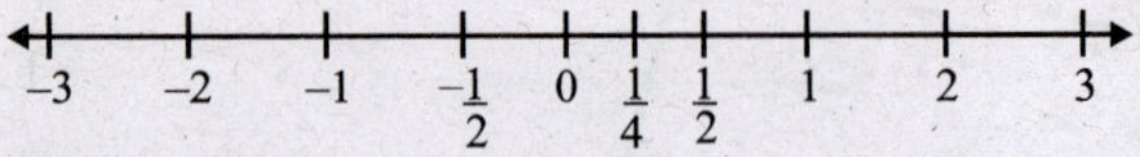

Various Types of Numbers

1. Set of Natural Numbers, N = {1, 2, 3, ...}

representation of N on number line

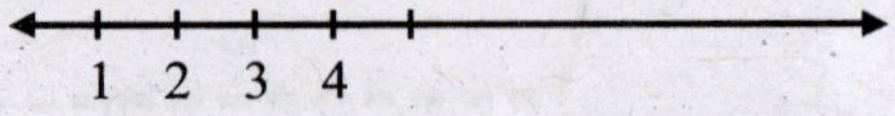

2. Set of whole numbers, W = {0, 1, 2, 3, ...}

number line of W (whole numbers) :

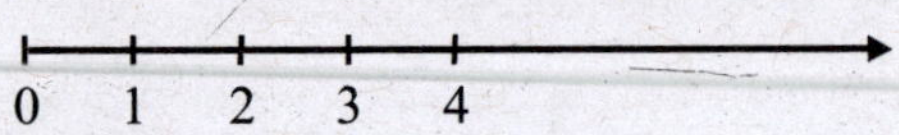

3. Set of integers,
   Z = {..., −3, −2, −1, 0, 1, 2, 3, ... }

number line of Z (integers) :

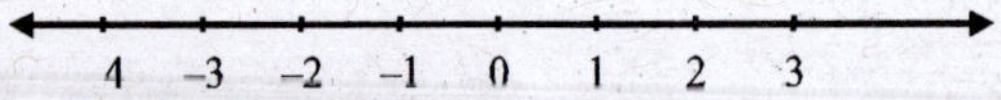

4. Rational numbers : A number 'r' is called a rational number, if it can be written in the form $\frac{p}{q}$, where p and q are integers and $q \neq 0$.

   Rational numbers, $Q = \left\{\frac{p}{q} : p, q \in I, q \neq 0\right\}$

NOTE: The rational numbers also include the natural numbers, whole numbers and integers.

IRRATIONAL NUMBERS

A number 's' is called irrational, if it cannot be written in the form $\frac{p}{q}$, where p and q are integers and $q \neq 0$.

Examples are : $\sqrt{2}, \sqrt{3}, \sqrt{15}$, Π, 0.10110111011110...

NOTE: When we use the symbol $\sqrt{\ }$, we assume that it is the positive square root of the number. So $\sqrt{4} = 2$, though both 2 and − 2 are square roots of 4.

REAL NUMBERS

The set of rational numbers and irrational numbers form a set of real numbers which is denoted by R.

Remark

Every real number is represented by a unique point on the number line. Also, every point on the number line represents a unique real number.

NOTE: (i) All integers are rational numbers.

(ii) The square root of every perfect square number is rational. eg. $\sqrt{4} = 2, \sqrt{9} = 3, \sqrt{16} = 4$ etc. are all rational numbers.

(iii) The square root of any positive number which is not a perfect square is an irrational number.

E.g.: $\sqrt{5}, \sqrt{3}, \sqrt{10}, \sqrt{12}, \sqrt{3.4}, \sqrt{0.748}$ etc.

(iv) π is an irrational number, which is actually the ratio of circumference to the diameter of a circle i.e. $\pi = \frac{c}{d}$, where c and d are the circumference and diameter of a circle. Approximate value of π is taken as $\frac{22}{7}$ or 3.14

FINDING RATIONAL NUMBERS BETWEEN TWO NUMBERS

Method to find two or more rational numbers between two numbers *p* and *q*:

In general, there are infinitely many rational numbers between any two given rational numbers.

If $p < q$, then one of the number be $p < \frac{p+q}{2} < q$ and others will be in continuation as $p < \frac{p+(p+q)/2}{2} < \frac{p+q}{2}$

ILLUSTRATION : 1

Find six rational numbers between $\frac{4}{7}$ and $\frac{1}{7}$.

SOLUTION:

Denominator of both the given rational numbers $\frac{4}{7}$ and $\frac{1}{7}$ are equal. Now the difference of numerator = 4 – 1 = 3, which is not greater than 6 (i.e. the number of rational numbers is to be found out). On multiplying both numerator and denominator of $\frac{4}{7}$ and $\frac{1}{7}$ by 3, we get

$$\frac{4}{7} = \frac{4\times 3}{7\times 3} = \frac{12}{21},\ \frac{1}{7} = \frac{1\times 3}{7\times 3} = \frac{3}{21}$$

Now the difference of numerator of $\frac{12}{21}$ and $\frac{3}{21}$ = 12 – 3 = 9, which is greater than 6.

Also, $\frac{3}{21} < \frac{12}{21}$ therefore $\frac{4}{21}, \frac{5}{21}, \frac{6}{21}, \frac{7}{21}, \frac{8}{21}$ and $\frac{9}{21}$ are one set of six rational numbers between $\frac{4}{7}$ and $\frac{1}{7}$.

DECIMAL REPRESENTATION OF RATIONAL NUMBERS IN THE FORM $\frac{p}{q}$

Every rational number in the form $\frac{p}{q}$ can be expressed to its equivalent decimal form.

For example $\frac{1}{5} = 0.2$, $\frac{1}{3} = 0.333..... = 0.\overline{3}$, etc

Generally, we use long division method to get the decimal form.

For example to get the decimal form of $\frac{13}{7}$, we simply divide 13 by 7 is shown below

$$\begin{array}{r|l} 7 & 13 \quad (1.857142 \\ & \underline{7} \\ & 60 \\ & \underline{56} \\ & 40 \\ & \underline{35} \\ & 50 \\ & \underline{49} \\ & 10 \\ & \underline{7} \\ & 30 \\ & \underline{28} \\ & 20 \\ & \underline{14} \\ & 6 \end{array}$$

$\therefore \frac{13}{7} = 1.857142857142.... = 1.\overline{857142}$

Terminating Decimal Expansions

In this case, the decimal expansion terminates or ends after a finite number of steps. We call such a decimal expansion as terminating.

Non-terminating Recurring Expansions

In this case we have a repeating block of digits in the quotient. We say that this expansion is non-terminating recurring.

CONVERSION OF RATIONAL NUMBER IN DECIMAL FORM TO ITS SIMPLEST $\frac{p}{q}$ FORM

Type-I : Conversion of a Terminating Decimal Number to its Simplest $\frac{p}{q}$ Form.

Step 1 : Obtain the rational number.
Step 2 : Determine the number of digits in its decimal part.
Step 3 : Remove decimal point from the given number and write 1 as its denominator followed by as many zeros as the total number of digits in the decimal part of the given number.
Step 4 : Write the number obtained in step-3 in its simplest form (i.e. the form in which there is no common factor other than 1 in its numerator and denominator).

The number so obtained is the required $\frac{p}{q}$ form.

ILLUSTRATION : 2

Convert rational number 2.348 in simplest $\frac{p}{q}$ form.

SOLUTION :

Given rational number = 2.348
There are three digits in the decimal part.

$\therefore \quad 2.348 = \frac{2348}{1000}$

Now, write $\frac{2348}{1000}$ in its lowest form.

$2.348 = \frac{2348}{1000} = \frac{1174}{500} = \frac{587}{250}$, which is the required form.

Type-II : Conversion of Non-terminating Repeating Decimal Number to its Simplest $\frac{p}{q}$ Form.

Step 1 : Put the given number equal to x and consider it as equation number say (i)
Step 2 : If there are some non-repeating digits after decimal on the right hand side of the equation (i), then count the number of non-repeating digits after the decimal point. Let it be n. Otherwise go to step 4 directly.
Step 3 : Multiply both sides of equation (i) by $(10)^n$, so that on the right hand side of the decimal point only the repeating digit(s) is/are left. Consider the equation so obtained as equation number (ii).
Step 4 : Multiply both sides of the equation (ii) by $(10)^m$, where m is the number of digit(s) which repeats on the right hand side after decimal point. Consider the equation so obtained as equation number (iii).
Step 5 : Subtract the equation (ii) from equation (iii).
Step 6 : Divide both sides of the equation obtained in step-5 by the coefficient of x.
Step 7 : Write the rational number on the right hand side of equation obtained in step-6 in the simplest $\frac{p}{q}$ form. This simplest $\frac{p}{q}$ form is the required form.

ILLUSTRATION : 3

Express 6.48261261261......... in the simplest $\frac{p}{q}$ form.

SOLUTION :

Let x = 6.48261264261......

$\Rightarrow \quad x = 648.\overline{261}$ ...(i)

Since there are two non-repeating digits (48) on the right hand side of equation (i), therefore we multiply both sides of equation (i) by $(10)^2$ i.e. 100, we get

$100\,x = 648.\overline{261}$ ...(ii)

Since there are three repeating digits (261), therefore multiply both sides of equation (ii) by $(10)^3$ i.e. 1000, we get

$100000x = 648261.\overline{261}$ ... (iii)

NOTE: $648.\overline{261}$ can be written as $648.261\overline{261}$ also.

Subtracting equation (ii) from (iii), we get $90900x = 648261 - 648$

$\Rightarrow \quad 90900x = 647613$ ...(iv)

Divide both side of equation (iv) by the coefficient 90900 of x in equation (iv), we get

$$\frac{90900x}{90900} = \frac{647613}{90900} \Rightarrow x = \frac{647613}{90900} \Rightarrow x = \frac{71957}{10100} \text{ (in simplest form)}$$

Hence, $6.48261261261.................. = \frac{71957}{10100}$, which is the required $\frac{p}{q}$ form.

ILLUSTRATION : 4

Express $0.\overline{52}$ in the $\frac{p}{q}$ form.

SOLUTION :

Let $x = 0.\overline{52}$

$x = 0.525252$ ...(i)

There is no non-repeating digit after decimal point on the right hand side in equation (i).

Number of repeating digits after the decimal point on the right hand side of equation (i) is 2. Hence, multiplying both sides of equation (i) by $(10)^2$ i.e. 100, we get

$100\,x = 52.525252.....$ ...(ii)

Subtract (i) from (ii), we get

$100x = 52.5252.....$

$x = 0.525252...$

$99x = 52$

$\frac{52}{99} \quad \therefore \quad 0.\overline{52} = \frac{52}{99}$

ILLUSTRATION : 5

Express 0.2434343......... in the form of $\frac{p}{q}$.

SOLUTION :

Let $x = 0.2434343$ ......

$x = 0.2\overline{43}$ ...(i)

Here, a digit 2 does not repeat after decimal point.

So, we multiply equation (i) by 10, we get

$10x = 2.4343$ ...(ii)

Since there are two repeating digits (43) after decimal point in the right side of equation (ii).

So, multiplying (ii) by $(10)^2$ i.e. 100, we get

$1000x = 243.4343$ ...(iii)

Subtract (ii) from (iii), we get

$1000x = 243.4343......$

$10x = \ \ 2.4343......$

$990x = 241$

$x = \frac{241}{990}$

$\Rightarrow \quad 0.2434343.........= \frac{241}{990}$ is the required $\frac{p}{q}$ form.

REPRESENTATION OF DECIMAL NUMBERS ON NUMBER LINE

(i) Representation of 4.2 on the Number Line

Clearly 4.2 lies between 4 and 5 in fig. (i).

Take a magnified look of the line segment between 4 and 5 and divide it into 10 equal parts and mark each point of division between 4 and 5 as shown in the fig. (ii).

We can see in fig. (ii), 4.2 is represented by the second mark of division after 4 in between 4 and 5.

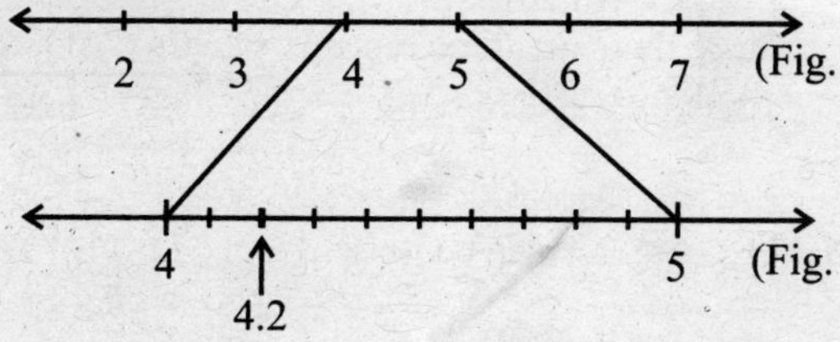

(Fig. i)
(Fig. ii)

(ii) Representation of 4.83 on the Number Line

4.83 will lies in between 4 and 5. In a closer look 4.83 lies in between 4.8 and 4.9 as 4.8 is equal to 4.80 and 4.9 is equal to 4.90 Hence first we draw a number line indicating all integral point on it (fig. (i)). Then after, we find the points on the number line representing 4.8 and 4.9 by dividing the line segment between 4 and 5 in to 10 equal parts using successive magnification (fig. (ii)). Take a magnified look of the line segment between 4.8 and 4.9 and divide it into 10 equal parts. Then third marked point of division shows 4.83 (fig. (iii)).

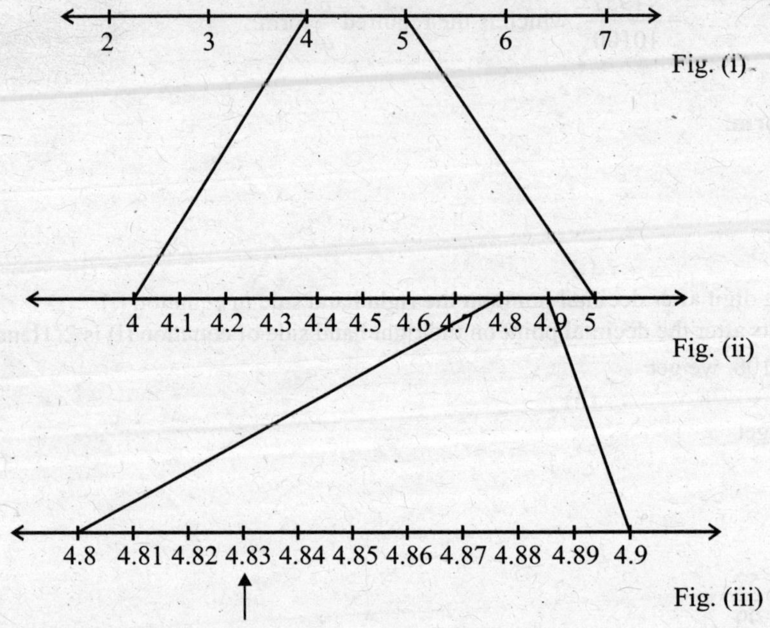

(iii) Representation of 6.328 on the Number Line

We know that 6.328 lies between 6 and 7. We divide the portion between 6 and 7 into 10 equal parts as shown in fig (ii) :

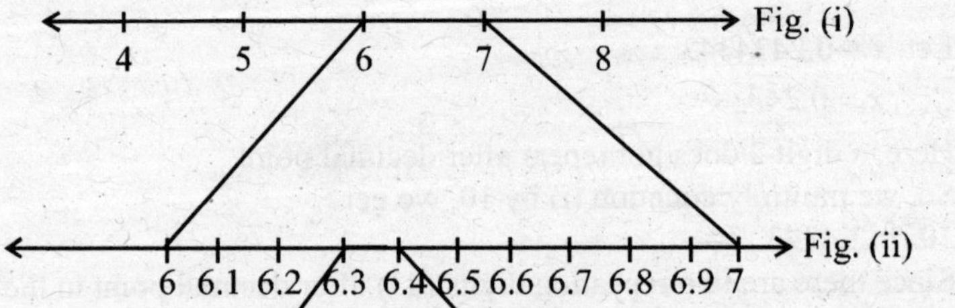

Now, 6.328 lies between 6.3 and 6.4, we divide the portion between 6.3 and 6.4 into 10 equal parts as shown in fig (iii) :

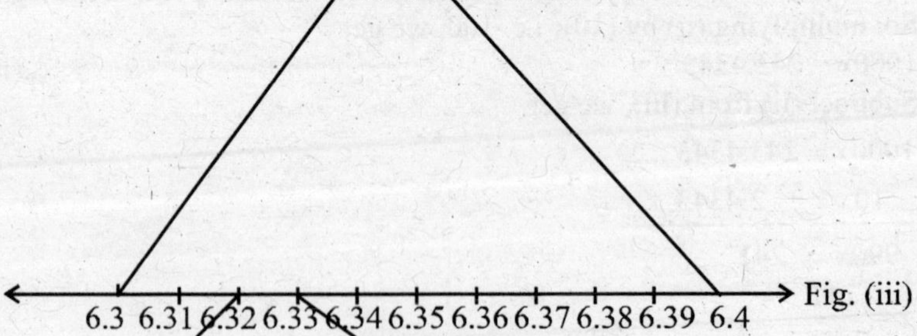

Now, 6.328 lies between 6.32 and 6.33, we divide the portion between 6.32 and 6.33 into 10 equal parts as shown in fig (iv) :

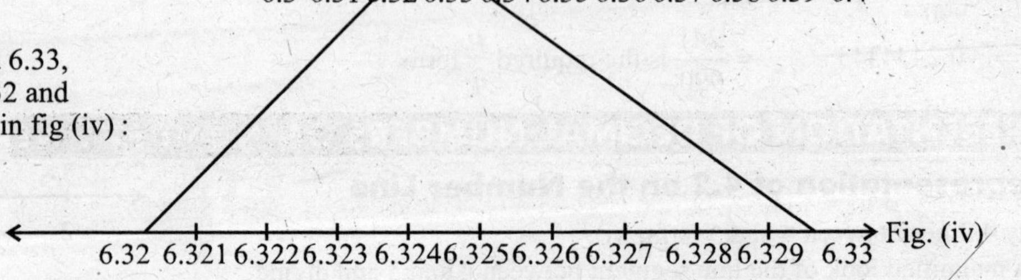

REPRESENTATION OF NON-TERMINATING RECURRING DECIMAL NUMBERS ON NUMBER LINE

Representation of $4.6\overline{2}$ on the Number Line up to Five Decimal Places

$4.6\overline{2} = 4.62222$ (up to 5 decimal places)

we know that $4.6\overline{2}$ lies between 4 and 5. We divide the portion between 4 and 5 into 10 equal parts as shown:

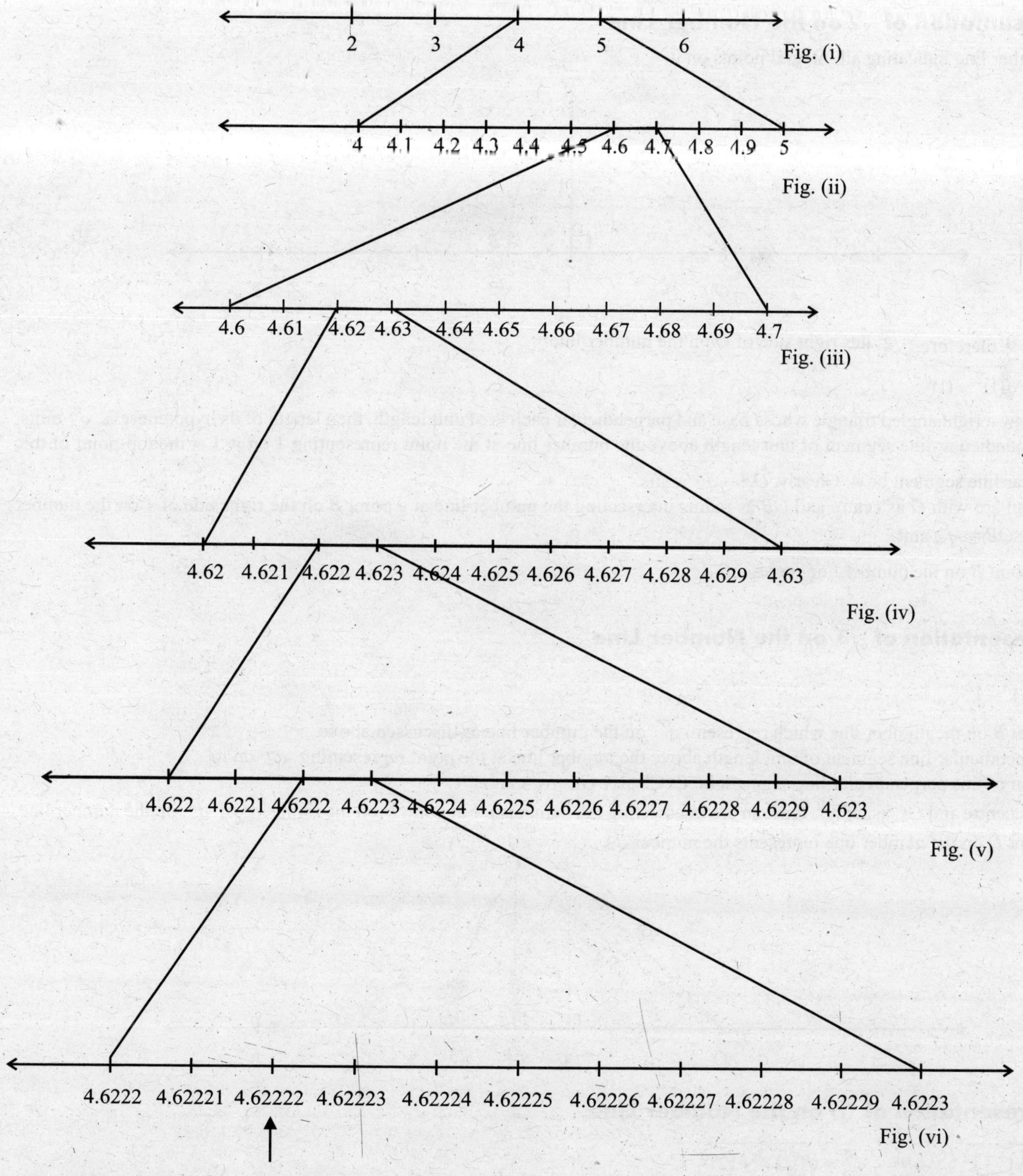

The method of representing a real number in decimal form (up to a certain number of digits) on the number line using the process of magnification is explained above. Now we are able to represent any real number in decimal form (up to a certain number of digits) on the number line using process of successive magnification.

REPRESENTATION OF IRRATIONAL NUMBERS IN THE FORM $\frac{p}{q}$ ON THE NUMBER LINE

To represent an irrational number in the form $\frac{p}{q}$, we use the Pythagoras theorem of a right angle triangle, according to which, in a right angled triangle, the square of the hypotenuse is equal to the sum of the square of the other two sides.
i.e. $(\text{Hypotenuse})^2 = (\text{Base})^2 + (\text{perpendicular})^2$

(i) Representation of $\sqrt{2}$ on the Number Line

Draw a number line indicating all integral points on it.

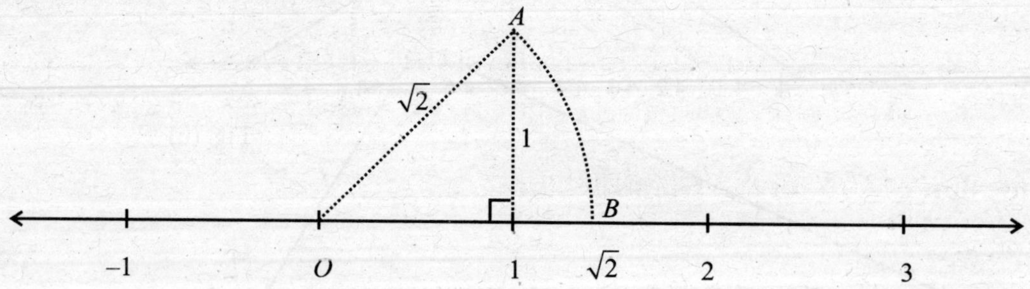

Since $\sqrt{2} > 0$ therefore, $\sqrt{2}$ lies right side of O on the number line.

Now, $\sqrt{2} = \sqrt{(1)^2 + (1)^2}$

So, if we draw a right angled triangle whose base and perpendicular each is of unit length, then length of its hypotenuse is $\sqrt{2}$ units.
Draw a perpendicular line segment of unit length above the number line at the point representing 1 on it. Let the top-point of this perpendicular line segment be A. Clearly, $OA = \sqrt{2}$ units.
Now draw an arc with O as centre and OB as radius intersecting the number line at a point B on the right side of 1 on the number line. Hence, $OB = \sqrt{2}$ unit.

Therefore point B on the number line represent $\sqrt{2}$.

(ii) Representation of $\sqrt{3}$ on the Number Line

$\sqrt{3} = \sqrt{(\sqrt{2})^2 + 1^2}$

Mark a point B on the number line which represent $\sqrt{\ }$ on the number line as discussed above.
Draw a perpendicular line segment of unit length above the number line at the point representing $\sqrt{2}$ on it.
Let top point of this perpendicular line segment be C. Clearly $OC = \sqrt{3}$ units.
Taking O as centre and OC as radius, draw an arc intersecting the number line at point D on the right side of $\sqrt{2}$ on the number line.
Clearly point D on the number line represents the number $\sqrt{3}$.

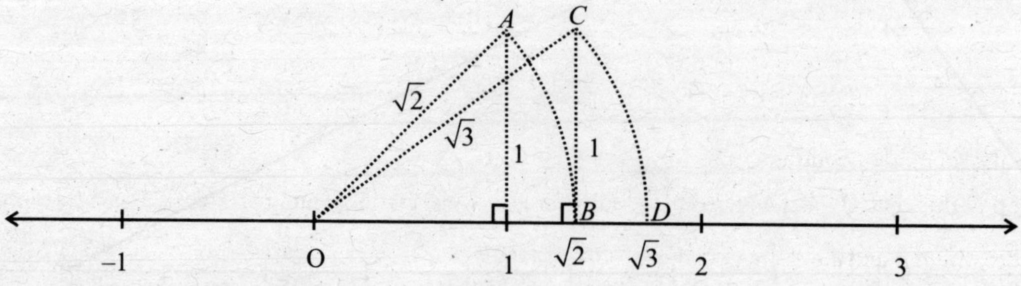

(iii) Representation of $\sqrt{7}$ on the Number Line

$\sqrt{7} = \sqrt{(\sqrt{6})^2 + 1^2}$ or $\sqrt{7} = \sqrt{(\sqrt{3})^2 + (2)^2}$

Take $\sqrt{7} = \sqrt{\left(\sqrt{3}\right)^2 + (2)^2}$

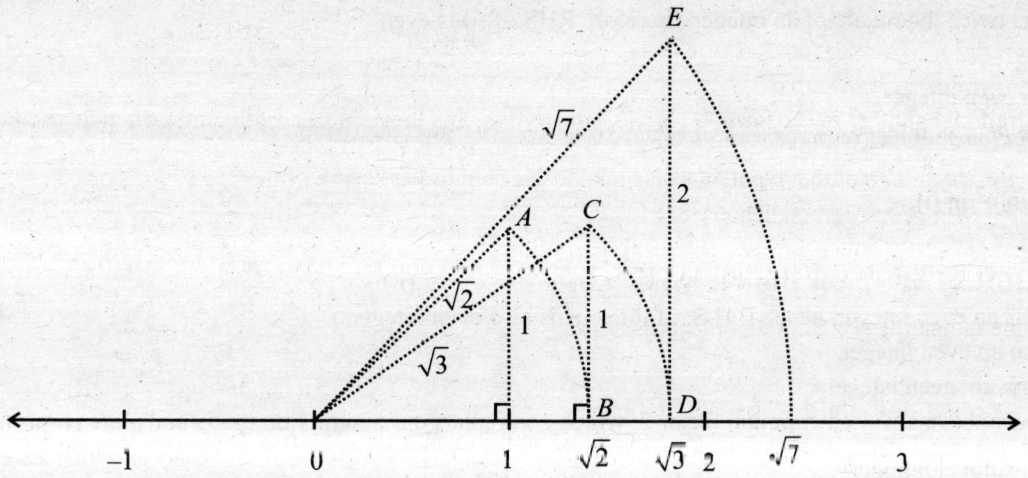

(iv) Representation of $\sqrt{10}$ on the Number Line

$\sqrt{10} = \sqrt{(3)^2 + (1)^2}$

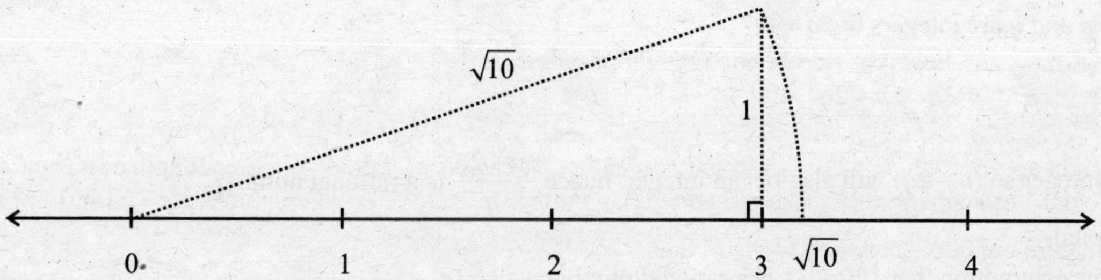

(v) Representation of $\sqrt{13}$ on the Number Line

$\sqrt{13} = \sqrt{3^2 + 2^2}$

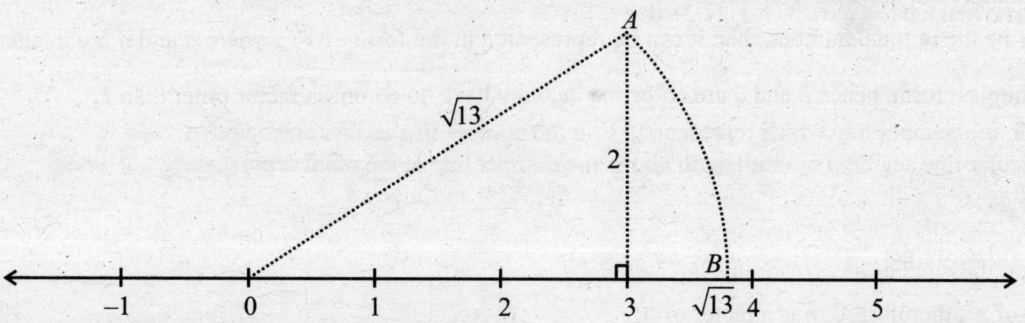

TO PROVE $\sqrt{2}$ IS AN IRRATIONAL NUMBER

This is proved by the method of contradiction.

Let us suppose, if possible that $\sqrt{2}$ is not an irrational number i.e. $\sqrt{2}$ is a rational number. Hence, it can be represented in the form of $\frac{p}{q}$ i.e. $\sqrt{2} = \frac{p}{q}$; where p and q are integers but $q \neq 0$.

Let $\frac{p}{q}$ is in simplest form hence p and q are co-primes i.e. they have no common factor other than 1.

Squaring both the sides, we get $2 = \frac{p^2}{q^2}$

$\Rightarrow \quad p^2 = 2q^2 \qquad$ ...(i)

Since RHS of (i) is twice the square of an integer, therefore RHS of (i) is even

$\Rightarrow$ p^2 is even

Hence p is also an even integer.

Let $p = 2m$, where m is an integer.

$p^2 = 4\,m^2$

Putting the value of p^2 in (i),

$4\,m^2 = 2\,q^2$

$\Rightarrow$ $q^2 = 2m^2$ ...(ii)

Since RHS of (ii) is an even integer, hence L.H.S. of it i.e. q^2 is also even integer.

Therefore, q is also an even integer.

Hence, p and q both are even integers.

But two even integers have always a common factor 2, which contradicts our assumption that p and q are co-primes.

Hence, $\sqrt{2}$ is an irrational number.

TO PROVE $(2+\sqrt{3})$ IS AN IRRATIONAL NUMBER

Let us suppose if possible that $2+\sqrt{3}$ is not an irrational number i.e. $2+\sqrt{3}$ is a rational number, then it can be represented in the form of $\frac{p}{q}$ where p and q are integers but $q \neq 0$.

i.e. $2+\sqrt{3} = \frac{p}{q} \Rightarrow \sqrt{3} = \frac{p}{q} - 2 = \frac{p-2q}{q}$ ...(i)

Since p and q are integer so $(p - 2q)$ will also be, an integer, hence $\frac{p-2q}{q}$ is a rational number.

But $\sqrt{3}$ is an irrational.

This contradicts our assumption that $(2+\sqrt{3})$ is a rational number.

Hence, $(2+\sqrt{3})$ is an irrational number.

TO PROVE $\sqrt{n}$ IS NOT A RATIONAL NUMBER, IF n IS NOT A PERFECT SQUARE

Let n be a whole number but not a perfect square

If possible, let $\sqrt{n}$ be the rational number, then it can be represented in the form of $\frac{p}{q}$, where p and q are integers but $q \neq 0$. Also suppose $\frac{p}{q}$ is in simplest form, hence p and q are co-prime i.e. they have no common factor other than 1.

Now, $\frac{p}{q} = \sqrt{n}$

Squaring both the sides, we get $\frac{p^2}{q^2} = n \Rightarrow \quad p^2 = nq^2$ ...(i)

Since n is a factor of p^2, therefore, n is a factor of p.

Hence, we can suppose that $p = nm$, where m is an integer.

Putting the value of p in equation (i), we get

$n^2m^2 = nq^2 \quad \Rightarrow \quad q^2 = nm^2$

$\therefore$ n is a factor of q^2

$\Rightarrow$ n is a factor of q. ...(ii)

Hence, n is a factor of both p and q. This contradicts our assumption that p and q does not have any common factor.

This means our assumption that $\sqrt{n}$ is a rational number is wrong. Hence $\sqrt{n}$ is an irrational number, where n is not a perfect square.

PROPERTIES OF IRRATIONAL NUMBERS

(i) Negative of an irrational number is also an irrational number.

For example: $-\sqrt{5}$ is an irrational number, because $\sqrt{5}$ is an irrational number.

(ii) The sum or difference of a rational number and an irrational number is an irrational.

For example : $2+\sqrt{3}$, $2-\sqrt{3}$, $\sqrt{3}-2$ are irrational numbers because 2 is a rational number and $\sqrt{3}$ is an irrational number.

(iii) The product or quotient of a non-zero rational number with an irrational number is an irrational.

For example : $2\sqrt{3}, \frac{2}{\sqrt{3}}, \frac{\sqrt{3}}{2}$ are irrational numbers because 2 is a rational number and $\sqrt{3}$ is an irrational number.

(iv) The sum, difference, product and quotient of two irrational numbers may be rational or irrational.

For examples :

(i) $(2+\sqrt{3})$ and $(2-\sqrt{3})$ are two irrational numbers but their sum $= 2+\sqrt{3}+2-\sqrt{3}=4$, is a rational number.

(ii) $(2+\sqrt{3})$ and $(-2+\sqrt{3})$ are two irrational numbers. Their sum $=(2+\sqrt{3})+(-2+\sqrt{3})=2\sqrt{3}$, is an irrational number.

(iii) $(2+\sqrt{3})$ and $(-2+\sqrt{3})$ are two irrational numbers but their difference $=(2+\sqrt{3})-(-2+\sqrt{3})=4$, is a rational number.

(iv) $(2+\sqrt{3})$ and $(2-\sqrt{3})$ are two irrational numbers. Their difference $=(2+\sqrt{3})-(2-\sqrt{3})=2\sqrt{3}$ is also an irrational number.

(v) $\sqrt{2}$ and $\sqrt{8}$ are two irrational numbers but their product $=\sqrt{2}\times\sqrt{8}=\sqrt{16}=4$ or -4, is a rational number.

(vi) $\sqrt{2}$ and $\sqrt{3}$ are two irrational numbers. Their product $=\sqrt{2}\times\sqrt{3}=\sqrt{6}$, is an irrational number.

(vii) $\sqrt{8}$ and $\sqrt{2}$ are irrational numbers but their quotient $=\frac{\sqrt{8}}{\sqrt{2}}=\sqrt{\frac{8}{2}}=\sqrt{4}=2$ is a rational number.

(viii) $(2+\sqrt{3})$ and $(2-\sqrt{3})$ are irrational numbers. Their quotient $=\frac{2+\sqrt{3}}{2-\sqrt{3}}=\frac{(2+\sqrt{3})\times(2+\sqrt{3})}{(2-\sqrt{3})\times(2+\sqrt{3})}=\frac{(2+\sqrt{3})^2}{4-3}\ \frac{4+3+4\sqrt{3}}{1}$

$=7+4\sqrt{3}$, is an irrational number.

> **NOTE:** If a is the rational number and n is a positive integer such that the nth root of a is an irrational number, then $a^{1/n}$ is called a surd eg. $\sqrt{5}, \sqrt{2}$ etc. If $\sqrt[n]{a}$ is a surd then 'n' is known as order of surd and 'a' is known as radicand. Every surd is an irrational number but every irrational number, is not a surd.

SOME IDENTITIES RELATED TO SQUARE ROOTS

Let a and b be positive real numbers. Then

(i) $\sqrt{ab}=\sqrt{a}\sqrt{b}$

(ii) $\sqrt{\frac{a}{b}}=\frac{\sqrt{a}}{\sqrt{b}}$

(iii) $(\sqrt{a}+\sqrt{b})(\sqrt{a}-\sqrt{b})=a-b$

(iv) $(a+\sqrt{b})(a-\sqrt{b})=a^2-b$

(v) $(\sqrt{a}+\sqrt{b})(\sqrt{c}+\sqrt{d})=\sqrt{ac}+\sqrt{ad}+\sqrt{bc}+\sqrt{bd}$

(vi) $(\sqrt{a}+\sqrt{b})^2=a+2\sqrt{ab}+b.$

LAWS OF RATIONAL EXPONENTS

If a & b are positive real numbers and m & n are rational numbers, then

(i) $a^m \times a^n = a^{m+n}$

(ii) $a^m \div a^n = a^{m-n}$

(iii) $(a^m)^n = a^{mn}$

(iv) $a^{-n}=\frac{1}{a^n}$

(v) $a^{\frac{m}{n}}=(a^m)^{\frac{1}{n}}=\left(a^{\frac{1}{n}}\right)^m$ i.e. $a^{\frac{m}{n}}=\sqrt[n]{a^m}=(\sqrt[n]{a})^m$

(vi) $(ab)^m=a^m b^m$

(vii) $\left(\frac{a}{b}\right)^m=\frac{a^m}{b^m}$

ILLUSTRATION : 6

Simplify : $13^{\frac{1}{5}}.17^{\frac{1}{5}}$

SOLUTION :

$13^{\frac{1}{5}}.17^{\frac{1}{5}}=(13\times17)^{\frac{1}{5}}=221^{\frac{1}{5}}=\sqrt[5]{221}$

ILLUSTRATION : 7

Simplify: $\left(\frac{2^a}{2^b}\right)^{a+b}\left(\frac{2^b}{2^c}\right)^{b+c}\left(\frac{2^c}{2^a}\right)^{c+a}$

SOLUTION :

$$\left(\frac{2^a}{2^b}\right)^{a+b}\left(\frac{2^b}{2^c}\right)^{b+c}\left(\frac{2^c}{2^a}\right)^{c+a} = (2^{a-b})^{a+b}\cdot(2^{b-c})^{b+c}\cdot(2^{c-a})^{c+a} = 2^{(a^2-b^2)+(b^2-c^2)+(c^2-a^2)} = 2^0 = 1$$

ILLUSTRATION : 8

Prove that $\frac{x^{a(b-c)}}{x^{b(a-c)}} \div \left(\frac{x^b}{x^a}\right)^c = 1$

SOLUTION :

We have,

$$\frac{x^{a(b-c)}}{x^{b(a-c)}} \div \left(\frac{x^b}{x^a}\right)^c = \frac{x^{ab-ac}}{x^{ba-bc}} \div (x^{b-a})^c = x^{(ab-ac)-(ba-bc)} \times \frac{1}{x^{(b-a)c}}$$

$$= x^{ab-ac-ba+bc} \times \frac{1}{x^{bc-ac}} = x^{ab-ba-ac+ac+bc-bc}, = x^0 = 1$$

RATIONALISING FACTOR

Rationalisation

When the denominator of an expression contains a term with a square root, the procedure of converting it to an equivalent expression whose denominator is a rational number is called rationalising the denominator.

For example :

(i) $(\sqrt{a}+\sqrt{b})$ is the rationalising factor of $(\sqrt{a}-\sqrt{b})$ and vice-versa.

(ii) $(a+\sqrt{b})$ is the rationalising factor of $(a-\sqrt{b})$ and vice-versa.

ILLUSTRATION : 9

Rationalise the denominator of $\frac{1}{7+3\sqrt{2}}$

SOLUTION :

We have,

$$\frac{1}{7+3\sqrt{2}} = \frac{1}{7+3\sqrt{2}} \times \frac{7-3\sqrt{2}}{7-3\sqrt{2}} = \frac{7-3\sqrt{2}}{(7)^2 \quad (3\sqrt{2})^2} = \frac{7-3\sqrt{2}}{49-18} = \frac{7-3\sqrt{2}}{31}$$

ILLUSTRATION : 10

Simplify each of the following by rationalising the denominator $\frac{2\sqrt{3}-\sqrt{5}}{2\sqrt{2}+3\sqrt{3}}$

SOLUTION:

Multiplying both numerator and denominator by the rationalisation factor of the denominator, we have

$$\frac{2\sqrt{3}-\sqrt{5}}{2\sqrt{2}+3\sqrt{3}} = \frac{2\sqrt{3}-\sqrt{5}}{2\sqrt{2}+3\sqrt{3}} \times \frac{2\sqrt{2}-3\sqrt{3}}{2\sqrt{2}-3\sqrt{3}} = \frac{(2\sqrt{3}-\sqrt{5})(2\sqrt{2}-3\sqrt{3})}{(2\sqrt{2}+3\sqrt{3})(2\sqrt{2}-3\sqrt{3})}$$

$$= \frac{2\sqrt{3}\times 2\sqrt{2} - 2\sqrt{3}\times 3\sqrt{3} - \sqrt{5}\times 2\sqrt{2} + \sqrt{5}\times 3\sqrt{3}}{(2\sqrt{2})^2 - (3\sqrt{3})^2} = \frac{4\sqrt{3\times 2} - 6\sqrt{3\times 3} - 2\sqrt{5\times 2} + 3\sqrt{5\times 3}}{4\times 2 - 9\times 3}$$

$$= \frac{4\sqrt{6} - 6\times 3 - 2\sqrt{10} + 3\sqrt{15}}{8-27} = \frac{4\sqrt{6} - 18 - 2\sqrt{10} + 3\sqrt{15}}{-19} = \frac{18 + 2\sqrt{10} - 4\sqrt{6} - 3\sqrt{15}}{19}$$

MISCELLANEOUS SOLVED EXAMPLES

1. Find the value of $2.\overline{6} - 0.\overline{9}$

Sol. Let $x = 2.\overline{6}$ ...(i)

$\therefore \quad 10x = 26.\overline{6}$ ...(ii)

Subtracting (i) from (ii)

$9x = 24$

$\therefore \quad x = \frac{24}{9} = \frac{8}{3}$

Also suppose $y = 0.\overline{9}$ ...(iii)

$\Rightarrow \quad y = 0.9\overline{9}$

$\therefore \quad 10y = 9.\overline{9}$ ...(iv)

Subtracting equation (iii) from (iv), we get

$9y = 9$

$\therefore \quad y = \frac{9}{9} = 1$

$\therefore \quad 2.\overline{6} - 0.\overline{9} = x - y = \frac{8}{3} - 1 = \frac{8-3}{3} = \frac{5}{3}$

2. Show how $\sqrt{5}$ can be represented on the number line.

Sol. Consider a unit square OABC onto the number line with the vertex O which coincides with zero.

Then OB = $\sqrt{1^2 + 1^2} = \sqrt{2}$

Construct BD of unit length perpendicular to OB. Then OD = $\sqrt{(\sqrt{2})^2 + 1^2} = \sqrt{3}$

Construct DE of unit length perpendicular to OD. Then OE = $\sqrt{(\sqrt{3})^2 + 1^2} = \sqrt{4} = 2$

Similarly, construct EF of unit length perpendicular to OE. Then OF = $\sqrt{2^2 + 1^2} = \sqrt{5}$

Using a compass, with centre O and radius OF, draw an arc which intersects the number line in the point R. Then R corresponds to $\sqrt{5}$.

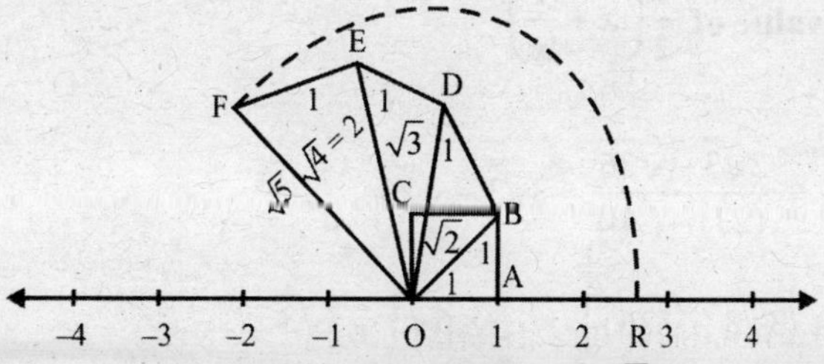

Representation of $\sqrt{5}$

3. Rationalise the denominator and simplify : $\frac{3\sqrt{2}}{\sqrt{3}+\sqrt{6}} - \frac{4\sqrt{3}}{\sqrt{6}+\sqrt{2}} + \frac{\sqrt{6}}{\sqrt{2}+\sqrt{3}}$

Sol. $\frac{3\sqrt{2}}{\sqrt{3}+\sqrt{6}} - \frac{4\sqrt{3}}{\sqrt{6}+\sqrt{2}} + \frac{\sqrt{6}}{\sqrt{2}+\sqrt{3}}$

$$= \frac{3\sqrt{2}}{\sqrt{3}+\sqrt{6}} \times \frac{\sqrt{3}-\sqrt{6}}{\sqrt{3}-\sqrt{6}} - \frac{4\sqrt{3}}{\sqrt{6}+\sqrt{2}} \times \frac{\sqrt{6}-\sqrt{2}}{\sqrt{6}-\sqrt{2}} + \frac{\sqrt{6}}{\sqrt{2}+\sqrt{3}} \times \frac{\sqrt{2}-\sqrt{3}}{\sqrt{2}-\sqrt{3}} = \frac{3\sqrt{2}(\sqrt{3}-\sqrt{6})}{3-6} - \frac{4\sqrt{3}(\sqrt{6}-\sqrt{2})}{6-2} + \frac{\sqrt{6}(\sqrt{2}-\sqrt{3})}{2-3}$$

$$= -\sqrt{2}(\sqrt{3}-\sqrt{6}) - \sqrt{3}(\sqrt{6}-\sqrt{2}) - \sqrt{6}(\sqrt{2}-\sqrt{3}) = -\sqrt{6} + \sqrt{12} - \sqrt{18} + \sqrt{6} - \sqrt{12} + \sqrt{18} = 0$$

4. If $x = \frac{1}{2+\sqrt{3}}$, find the value of $x^3 - x^2 - 11x + 3$

Sol. As $x = \frac{1}{2+\sqrt{3}} = 2 - \sqrt{3}$ (on rationalizing)

$x - 2 = -\sqrt{3}$

Squaring both sides, we get

$(x-2)^2 = (-\sqrt{3})^2 \Rightarrow x^2 + 4 - 4x = 3 \Rightarrow x^2 - 4x + 1 = 0$

Now, $x^3 - x^2 - 11x + 3 = x^3 - 4x^2 + x + 3x^2 - 12x + 3$

$x(x^2 - 4x + 1) + 3(x^2 - 4x + 1) = x \times 0 + 3(0) = 0 + 0 = 0$

5. Show that $\frac{(x^{a+b})^2 (x^{b+c})^2 (x^{c+a})^2}{(x^a x^b x^c)^4} = 1$

Sol. We have $\frac{(x^{a+b})^2 (x^{b+c})^2 (x^{c+a})^2}{(x^a x^b x^c)^4}$

$$= \frac{x^{2(a+b)} x^{2(b+c)} x^{2(c+a)}}{(x^a)^4 . (x^b)^4 (x^c)^4} = \frac{x^{2a+2b} . x^{2b+2c} . x^{2c+2a}}{x^{4a} . x^{4b} . x^{4c}} = \frac{x^{2a+2b+2b+2c+2c+2a}}{x^{4a+4b+4c}} = \frac{x^{4a+4b+4c}}{x^{4a+4b+4c}} = 1$$

6. If $\frac{9^n \times 3^2 (3^{-n/2})^{-2} - (27)^n}{3^{3m} \times 2^3} = \frac{1}{27}$, prove that $m - n = 1$.

Sol. We have, $\frac{9^n \times 3^2 (3^{-n/2})^{-2} - (27)^n}{3^{3m} \times 2^3} = \frac{1}{27}$

$$\Rightarrow \frac{(3^2)^n \times 3^2 \times 3^{-n/2 \times -2} - (3^3)^n}{3^{3m} \times 2^3} = \frac{1}{27}$$

$$\Rightarrow \frac{3^{2n} \times 3^2 \times 3^n - 3^{3n}}{3^{3m} \times 2^3} = \frac{1}{27} \quad \Rightarrow \frac{3^{2n+2+n} - 3^{3n}}{3^{3m} \times 2^3} = \frac{1}{27}$$

$$\Rightarrow \frac{3^{3n}(3^2 - 1)}{3^{3m} \times 2^3} = \frac{1}{27} \Rightarrow \frac{3^{3n}.8}{3^{3m}.8} = \frac{1}{27} \quad \Rightarrow 3^{3n-3m} = \frac{1}{3^3} \quad \Rightarrow 3^{3n-3m} = 3^{-3}$$

On equating the exponent, we get

$3n - 3m = -3 \Rightarrow n - m = -1 \Rightarrow m - n = 1.$

7. If $x = 3\sqrt{3} + \sqrt{26}$, then find the value of $\frac{1}{2}\left(x + \frac{1}{x}\right)$

Sol. Let $x = 3\sqrt{3} + \sqrt{26}$

$$\frac{1}{x} = \frac{1}{3\sqrt{3}+\sqrt{26}} \times \frac{3\sqrt{3}-\sqrt{26}}{3\sqrt{3}-\sqrt{26}} = \frac{3\sqrt{3}-\sqrt{26}}{(27)-(26)} = 3\sqrt{3} - \sqrt{26}$$

$$\therefore \quad \frac{1}{2}\left(x + \frac{1}{x}\right) = \frac{1}{2}\left[(3\sqrt{3}+\sqrt{26}) + (3\sqrt{3}-\sqrt{26})\right] = \frac{1}{2} \times 6\sqrt{3} = 3\sqrt{3}$$

8. If $\left[\left\{\left(\frac{1}{7^2}\right)^{-2}\right\}^{-1/3}\right]^{\frac{1}{4}} = 7^m$, then find the value of m.

Sol. $\left[\left\{\left(\frac{1}{7^2}\right)^{-2}\right\}^{\frac{-1}{3}}\right]^{\frac{1}{4}} = 7^m \quad \Rightarrow \quad \left[\{(7^{-2})^{-2}\}^{-1/3}\right]^{\frac{1}{4}} = 7^m \quad \Rightarrow \left[(7^4)^{-1/3}\right]^{\frac{1}{4}} = 7^m$

$\Rightarrow \quad (7^{-4/3})^{1/4} = 7^m \Rightarrow \quad 7^{-1/3} = 7^m$

$\therefore \quad m = -1/3$

9. Find two irrational numbers between 0.12 and 0.13.

Sol. The two numbers 0.1201001000100001...... and 0.12101001000100001....... are the irrational numbers between 0.12 and 0.13.

10. Find three rational numbers between $\frac{1}{5}$ and $\frac{7}{10}$.

Sol. One rational number between $\frac{1}{5}$ and $\frac{7}{10} = \frac{1}{2}\left(\frac{1}{5}+\frac{7}{10}\right) = \frac{1}{2}\left(\frac{2+7}{10}\right) = \frac{9}{20}$

Second rational number between $\frac{1}{5}$ and $\frac{7}{10} = \frac{1}{2}\left(\frac{1}{5}+\frac{9}{20}\right) = \frac{1}{2}\left(\frac{4+9}{20}\right) = \frac{13}{40}$

Third rational number between $\frac{1}{5}$ and $\frac{7}{10} = \frac{1}{2}\left(\frac{13}{40}+\frac{1}{5}\right) = \frac{1}{2}\left(\frac{13+8}{40}\right) = \frac{21}{80}$

11. Express 1.272727..... = $1.\overline{27}$ in the form $\frac{p}{q}$, where p and q are integers and $q \neq 0$.

Sol. Let $x = 1.272727$.......... Since two digits are repeating, we multiply x by 100 to get

$100x = 127.2727$ ....

So, $100x = 126 + 1.272727$......... $= 126 + x$

Therefore, $100x - x = 126, \Rightarrow 99x = 126 \Rightarrow x = \frac{126}{99} = \frac{14}{11}$

12. Express $0.12\overline{3}$ in $\frac{p}{q}$ form.

Sol. Let $x = 0.12\overline{3}$ i.e. $x = 0.12333$ ... (i)

Multiply both sides of (i) by 100

$100x = 12.333$ ... (ii)

Multiply both sides of (ii) by 10

$1000x = 123.333$ ... (iii)

Subtract (ii) from (iii)

$1000x = 123.333$

$100x = 12.333$

$900x = 111.0$

$\Rightarrow \quad x = \frac{111}{900} = \frac{3 \times 37}{900} = \frac{37}{300}$

13. Prove that $\sqrt{3}$ is an irrational number.

Sol. Let us suppose if possible that $\sqrt{3}$ is not an irrational number i.e. $\sqrt{3}$ is a rational number.

Hence $\sqrt{3}$ can be represented in the form of $\frac{p}{q}$.

i.e. $\sqrt{3} = \frac{p}{q}$, where p and q both are integers but $q \neq 0$.

Let $\frac{p}{q}$ is in simplest form, hence p and q are co-prime i.e. they have no common factor other than 1.

Squaring both sides, we get $3 = \frac{p^2}{q^2} \Rightarrow p^2 = 3q^2$ ...(i)

Since q is an integer, therefore q^2 is also an integer.

$\Rightarrow \quad 3q^2$ is an integral multiple of 3.

$\Rightarrow \quad p^2$ is also an integral multiple of 3.

Hence p is also an integral multiple of 3.

Therefore we can assume that $p = 3m$, where m is an integer.

Now putting the value of p in equation (i), we get

$9m^2 = 3q^2, \Rightarrow q^2 = 3m^2 \Rightarrow q^2$ is an integral multiple of 3.

Hence q is an integral multiple of 3.

Since both p and q are integral multiple of 3, therefore they have a common factor 3, which contradict our assumption that p and q are co-primes. Hence $\sqrt{3}$ is an irrational number.

1 EXERCISE

Fill in the Blanks :

DIRECTIONS: *Complete the following statements with an appropriate word / term to be filled in the blank space(s).*

1. The sum/difference of a rational and an irrational number is _____.
2. 0.578 is ______ number. (rational/irrational)
3. 0.72737475 is ______ number. (rational/irrational)
4. If $x+\sqrt{5}=4+\sqrt{y}$, then $x+y=$ ______. (where x and y are rational)
5. An irrational number between $\frac{2}{5}$ and $\frac{3}{7}$ is
6. Value of a is __________ if $\frac{\sqrt{3}-1}{\sqrt{3}+1}=a+b\sqrt{3}$
7. Two mixed quadratic surds, $a+\sqrt{b}$ and $a-\sqrt{b}$, whose sum and product are rational, are called __________.
8. $\sqrt[4]{\frac{1008}{63}}$ is equal to __________
9. Between two rational numbers, there exist __________ number of rational numbers.
10. Between two real numbers, there exists infinite number of __________ numbers.

True / False :

DIRECTIONS: *Read the following statements and write your answer as true or false.*

1. Every whole number is a natural number.
2. Every rational number is an integer.
3. Every natural number is a whole number.
4. Every integer is a whole number.
5. Every rational number is a whole number.
6. All rational numbers when expressed in decimal form are either terminating decimals or repeating decimals.
7. All rational numbers can be represented by some point on the number line.
8. The sum or difference of a rational number and an irrational number is an irrational.
9. A real number is either rational or irrational.
10. Product of a rational and an irrational number is always irrational.

Match the Columns :

DIRECTIONS: *Each question contains statements given in two columns which have to be matched. Statements (A, B, C, D) in Column-I have to be matched with statements (p, q, r, s, t) in Column-II.*

1.

Column-I	Column-II
(A) 12 is a	(p) prime number
(B) 2,7 are	(q) not a rational number
(C) 2 is a	(r) composite number
(D) $\sqrt{2}$	(s) co-prime numbers

2.

Column-I	Column-II
(A) Decimal expansion of an irrational number is non-terminating and ______	(p) irrational
(B) The sum of two numbers may be a rational number or an irrational number.	(q) $\sqrt{5}$
(C) A number x is called a ____ number, if it can be written in the form $\frac{m}{n}$, where m and n are integers, $n \neq 0$	(r) rational
(D) An irrational number between 2 and 2.5 is	(s) non-repeating
(E) The value of $\frac{}{0.23+0.22}$ is	(t) $0.\overline{45}$

Very Short Answer Questions :

DIRECTIONS: *Give answer in one word or one sentence.*

1. Write the smallest whole number.
2. Write the integer other than 1, which is a reciprocal of itself.
3. Suppose a is a rational number. What is the reciprocal of the reciprocal of a ?
4. Write the repeating decimal for each of the following, and use a bar to show the repetend.

(i) $\frac{4}{3}$ (ii) $\frac{11}{12}$ (iii) $\frac{7}{13}$

5. Classify the following numbers as rational or irrational.

(i) $\sqrt{225}$ (ii) 7.478478......

6. Are the square roots of all positive integers irrational? If not, give an example of the square root of a number that is a rational number.

7. Simplify :

(i) $\left(\frac{1}{3^3}\right)^7$ (ii) $7^{\frac{1}{2}}.8^{\frac{1}{2}}$

8. Simplify :

(i) $(\sqrt{4})^{3/4}$ (ii) $\left(\frac{5}{8}\right)^3\left(\frac{4}{3}\right)^3$

(iii) $\left[\frac{\frac{\sqrt{5}}{3}}{\frac{5}{9}}\right]^6$ (iv) $\left(\frac{5}{3}\right)^3.\left(\frac{9}{2}\right)^4$

(v) $\frac{2^6 \times 8^2}{4^4}$

9. Find two irrational numbers between 0.1 and 0.2.

10. Determine, without actually dividing, which of the following rational numbers can be named, (a) by a terminating decimal, (b) by a repeating decimal.

(i) $\frac{7}{20}$ (ii) $\frac{1}{6}$

(iii) $\frac{1}{12}$ (iv) $3\frac{47}{160}$

11. Write down a fraction which is equivalent to 0.033636363.........

12. Find two rational numbers between 0.222332333233332.... and 0.252552555255552....

13. Which is greatest : $\sqrt[3]{4}$, $\sqrt[4]{5}$ or $\sqrt[4]{3}$?

14. Find four rational numbers between $\frac{1}{4}$ and $\frac{1}{3}$.

Short Answer Questions :

DIRECTIONS: *Give answer in 2-3 sentences.*

1. If $\frac{3+\sqrt{5}}{4-2\sqrt{5}} = p+q\sqrt{5}$, where p and q are rational numbers, find the values of p and q.

2. Simplify:

$$\frac{1}{3-\sqrt{8}}-\frac{1}{\sqrt{8}-\sqrt{7}}+\frac{1}{\sqrt{7}-\sqrt{6}}-\frac{1}{\sqrt{6}-\sqrt{5}}+\frac{1}{\sqrt{5}-2}$$

3. Examine whether the following numbers are rational or irrational :

(i) $(2-\sqrt{3})^2$ (ii) $(3+\sqrt{2})(3-\sqrt{2})$

4. Find the value of 'a' in the following expression.

$$\frac{6}{3\sqrt{2}-2\sqrt{3}} = 3\sqrt{2}-a\sqrt{3}$$

5. Simplify : $\left[5\left(8^{\frac{1}{3}}+27^{\frac{1}{3}}\right)^3\right]^{\frac{1}{4}}$

6. Examine whether the number is rational or irrational $\frac{(2+\sqrt{2})(3-\sqrt{5})}{(3+\sqrt{5})(2-\sqrt{2})}$.

7. Given that $\sqrt{3} = 1.732$ find the value of $\sqrt{75}+\frac{1}{2}\sqrt{48}-\sqrt{192}$

8. Simplify and express the result in simplest form

$$\frac{\sqrt{x^2-y^2}+x}{\sqrt{x^2+y^2}+y} \div \frac{\sqrt{x^2+y^2}-y}{x-\sqrt{x^2-y^2}}$$

9. Find x^2, if $x = \frac{\sqrt{\sqrt{5}+2}+\sqrt{\sqrt{5}-2}}{\sqrt{\sqrt{5}+1}}$

Long Answer Questions :

DIRECTIONS: *Give answer in four to five sentences.*

1. Express $0.6+0.\overline{7}+0.4\overline{7}$ in the form $\frac{p}{q}$, where p and q are integers and $q \neq 0$

2. If $x = \frac{\sqrt{3}+\sqrt{2}}{\sqrt{3}-\sqrt{2}}$ and $y = \frac{\sqrt{3}-\sqrt{2}}{\sqrt{3}+\sqrt{2}}$.

Then find the value of $x^2 + y^2$.

3. Express with a rational denominator :

$$\frac{15}{\sqrt{10}+\sqrt{20}+\sqrt{40}-\sqrt{5}-\sqrt{80}}$$

4. Simplify : $\frac{7\sqrt{3}}{\sqrt{10}+\sqrt{3}}-\frac{2\sqrt{5}}{\sqrt{6}+\sqrt{5}}-\frac{3\sqrt{2}}{\sqrt{15}+3\sqrt{2}}$

5. Represent $\sqrt{9.3}$ on number line.

6. If $x = \frac{\sqrt{a+2b}+\sqrt{a-2b}}{\sqrt{a+2b}-\sqrt{a-2b}}$ prove that $b^2x^2 - abx + b^2 = 0$.

7. If $\frac{\sqrt{7}-1}{\sqrt{7}+1}-\frac{\sqrt{7}+1}{\sqrt{7}-1} = a+b\sqrt{\ }$, find the values of a and b

2 EXERCISE

Text-Book Exercise :

1. Is zero a rational number? Can you write it in the form $\frac{p}{q}$, where p and q are integers and $q \neq 0$?
2. Find five rational numbers between $\frac{3}{5}$ and $\frac{4}{5}$.
3. State whether the following statements are true or false? Give reasons for your answers.
   (i) Every natural number is a whole number.
   (ii) Every integer is a whole number.
   (iii) Every rational number is a whole number.
4. State whether the following statements are true or false. Justify your answers.
   (i) Every irrational number is a real number.
   (ii) Every point on the number line is of the form $\sqrt{m}$, where m is a natural number.
   (iii) Every real number is an irrational number.
5. Are the square roots of all positive integers irrational ? If not, give an example of the square roots of a number that is a rational number.
6. Write the following in decimal form and say what kind of decimal expansion each has :
   (i) $\frac{36}{100}$ (ii) $4\frac{1}{8}$
   (iii) $\frac{2}{11}$
7. You know that $\frac{1}{7} = 0.\overline{142857}$. Can you predict what the decimal expansions of $\frac{2}{7}, \frac{3}{7}, \frac{4}{7}, \frac{5}{7}, \frac{6}{7}$ are, without actually doing the long division? If so, how?
   [**Hint :** Study the remainders while finding the value of $\frac{1}{7}$ carefully.]
8. Express 0.99999 ..... in the form $\frac{p}{q}$. Are you surprised by your answer?
   With your teacher and classmates discuss why the answer makes sense.
9. Write three numbers whose decimal expansions are non-terminating non-recurring.
10. Classify the following numbers as rational or irrational :
    (i) $\sqrt{23}$ (ii) 7.478478.......
11. Visualise $4.\overline{26}$ on the number line, up to 4 decimal places.
12. Classify the following numbers as rational or irrational :
    (i) $2 - \sqrt{5}$ (ii) $\frac{2\sqrt{7}}{7\sqrt{7}}$
    (iii) 2π.
13. Simplify each of the following expressions :
    (i) $(3 + \sqrt{3})(2 + \sqrt{2})$ (ii) $(\sqrt{5} + \sqrt{2})^2$
14. Find : $125^{1/3}$
15. Find :
    (i) $32^{2/5}$ (ii) $125^{-1/3}$
16. Simplify :
    (i) $2^{\frac{2}{3}} . 2^{\frac{1}{5}}$ (ii) $\left(\frac{1}{3^3}\right)^7$
    (iii) $\frac{11^{1/2}}{11^{1/4}}$

Exemplar Questions :

1. Simplify the following :
   (i) $3\sqrt{3} + 2\sqrt{27} + \frac{7}{\sqrt{3}}$
   (ii) $\sqrt[4]{81} - 8\sqrt[3]{216} + 15\sqrt[5]{32} + \sqrt{225}$
2. Locate $\sqrt{10}$ on the number line.
3. Find the value of:
   $$\frac{4}{(216)^{\frac{-2}{3}}} + \frac{1}{(256)^{\frac{-3}{4}}} + \frac{2}{(243)^{\frac{-1}{5}}}$$
4. Rationalise the denominator of the following:
   (i) $\frac{3\sqrt{5} + \sqrt{3}}{\sqrt{5} - \sqrt{3}}$ (ii) $\frac{4\sqrt{3} + 5\sqrt{2}}{\sqrt{48} + \sqrt{18}}$
5. Find the value of a in the following:
   $$\frac{3 - \sqrt{5}}{3 + 2\sqrt{5}} = a\sqrt{5} - \frac{19}{11}$$
6. If $a = 2 + \sqrt{3}$, then find the value of $a - \frac{1}{a}$
7. Simplify:
   (i) $\left(\frac{3}{5}\right)^4 \left(\frac{8}{5}\right)^{-12} \left(\frac{32}{5}\right)^6$
   (ii) $\frac{9^{\frac{1}{3}} \times 27^{-\frac{1}{2}}}{3^{\frac{1}{6}} \times 3^{-\frac{2}{3}}}$

HOTS Questions :

1. Find three different irrational numbers between the rational numbers $\frac{5}{7}$ and $\frac{9}{11}$.
2. Express 2.5434343... in the form p/q where p and q are integers and $q \neq 0$
3. If $x = \frac{1}{7+4\sqrt{3}}, y = \frac{1}{7-4\sqrt{3}}$, find the value of $5x^2 - 7xy - 5y^2$.
4. If $\frac{9^n \times 3^2 (3^{-n/2})^{-2} - (27)^n}{3^{3m} \times 2^3} = \frac{1}{27}$, prove that $m - n = 1$.
5. If $a = \frac{\sqrt{2}+1}{\sqrt{2}-1}$ and $b = \frac{\sqrt{2}-1}{\sqrt{2}+1}$ then find the value of $a^2 + b^2 - 4ab$.
6. If $2^a = 3^b = 6^c$ then show that $c = \frac{ab}{a+b}$.
7. If $x = 2 + 3\sqrt{2}$, then find the value of $\left(x + \frac{14}{x}\right)$.

3 EXERCISE

Single Option Correct :

DIRECTIONS: *This section contains multiple choice questions. Each question has 4 choices (a), (b), (c) and (d) out of which ONLY ONE is correct.*

1. The value of x, when $(2)^{x+4}.(3)^{x+1} = 288$ is
   (a) 1 (b) –1
   (c) 0 (d) None
2. The value of 0.423 is
   (a) $\frac{423}{1000}$ (b) $\frac{423}{100}$
   (c) $\frac{423}{990}$ (d) $\frac{419}{990}$
3. If $a = 2+\sqrt{3}$ and $b = 2-\sqrt{3}$, then $\frac{1}{a^2} - \frac{1}{b^2}$ is equal to,
   (a) 14 (b) – 14
   (c) $8\sqrt{3}$ (d) $-8\sqrt{3}$
4. Value of x satisfying $\sqrt{x+3} + \sqrt{x-2} = 5$, is
   (a) 6 (b) 7
   (c) 8 (d) 9
5. A rational number equivalent to a rational number $\frac{7}{19}$ is
   (a) $\frac{17}{119}$ (b) $\frac{14}{57}$
   (c) $\frac{21}{38}$ (d) $\frac{21}{57}$
6. Rationalizing factor of $(2+\sqrt{3})$=
   (a) $2-\sqrt{3}$ (b) $\sqrt{3}$
   (c) $2+\sqrt{3}$ (d) $3+\sqrt{3}$
7. Rationalizing factor of $1+\sqrt{2}+\sqrt{3}$
   (a) $1+\sqrt{2}-\sqrt{3}$ (b) 2
   (c) 4 (d) $1+\sqrt{2}+\sqrt{3}$
8. Value of $\frac{2^{n+2} - 2(2^n)}{2^{(2n+2)}}$ when simplified is
   (a) $1-2(2^n)$ (b) $2^{n+3} - \frac{1}{4}$
   (c) $\frac{1}{2^{n+1}}$ (d) $\frac{1}{2^{n-1}}$
9. Which of the following statement is not true?
   (a) Between two integers, there exist infinite number of rational numbers
   (b) Between two rational numbers, there exist infinite number of integers
   (c) Between two rational numbers, there exist infinite number of rational numbers
   (d) Between two real numbers, there exists infinite number of real numbers
10. Four rational numbers between 3 and 4 are:
    (a) $\frac{3}{5}, \frac{4}{5}, 1, \frac{6}{5}$ (b) $\frac{13}{5}, \frac{14}{5}, \frac{16}{5}, \frac{17}{5}$
    (c) 3.1, 3.2, 4.1, 4.2 (d) 3.1, 3.2, 3.8, 3.9

More Than One Option Correct :

DIRECTIONS: *This section contains multiple choice questions. Each question has 4 choices (a), (b), (c) and (d) out of which ONE OR MORE may be correct.*

1. Which of the following is irrational?
   (a) $\sqrt{17}$ (b) $\frac{\sqrt{12}}{\sqrt{3}}$
   (c) $\sqrt{7}$ (d) $\sqrt{81}$

2. Value of $\sqrt[4]{(81)^{-2}}$ is

(a) $\frac{1}{9}$ (b) $\frac{1}{3}$

(c) 9 (d) 3

3. Which of the following is equal to x ?

(a) $x^{\frac{12}{7}} - x^{\frac{5}{7}}$ (b) $\sqrt[12]{(x^4)^{\frac{1}{3}}}$

(c) $(\sqrt{x^3})^{\frac{2}{3}}$ (d) $x^{12/19} + x^{7/19}$

4. Which of the following is/are not correct ?
   (a) Every whole number is a natural number.
   (b) Every integer is a rational number
   (c) Every rational number is an integer
   (d) Every rational number is a whole number

5. Which of the following is/are correct ?
   (a) There are infinitely many rational numbers between any two given rational numbers.
   (b) Every point on the number line represents a unique real number.
   (c) The decimal expansion of an irrational number is non-terminating non-recurring.
   (d) A number whose decimal expansion is non-terminating non-recurring is rational.

Assertion & Reason :

DIRECTIONS: *Each of these questions contains an Assertion followed by Reason. Read them carefully and answer the question on the basis of following options. You have to select the one that best describes the two statements.*

(a) If both **Assertion** and **Reason** are **correct** and Reason is the **correct explanation** of Assertion.

(b) If both **Assertion** and **Reason** are correct, but Reason **is not the correct explanation** of Assertion.

(c) If **Assertion** is **correct** but **Reason** is **incorrect**.

(d) If **Assertion** is **incorrect** but **Reason** is **correct**.

1. **Assertion :** Every integer is a rational number
   Reason : Every integer 'm' can be expressed in the form $\frac{m}{1}$.

2. **Assertion :** $\sqrt{2}$ is an irrational number.
   Reason : A number is called irrational, if it cannot be written in the form $\frac{p}{q}$, where p and q are integers and $q \neq 0$.

3. **Assertion :** $17^2 . 17^5 = 17^3$
   Reason : If $a > 0$ be a real number and p and q be rational numbers. Then $a^p . a^q = a^{p+q}$.

4. **Assertion :** $2 + \sqrt{6}$ is an irrational number.
   Reason : Sum of a rational number and an irrational number is always an irrational number.

5. **Assertion :** A rational number between $\frac{1}{3}$ and $\frac{1}{2}$ is $\frac{5}{12}$.
   Reason : Rational number between two numbers a and b is $\sqrt{ab}$.

Multiple Matching Question :

DIRECTIONS : *Following question has four statements (A, B, C and D) given in Column-I and four statements (p, q, r, s) in Column-II. Any given statement in Column-I can have correct matching with one or more statement(s) given in Column-II.*

1.

Column-I	Column-II
(A) $\frac{1}{2+\sqrt{3}}$	(p) Irrational
(B) $64^{1/2}$	(q) $\sqrt{56}$
(C) $16^{3/4}$	(r) 8
(D) $7^{1/2}\, 8^{1/2}$	(s) $2-\sqrt{3}$

Integer Type Questions :

DIRECTIONS : *Answer the following questions. The answer to each of the question is a single digit integer, ranging from 0 to 9.*

1. If $\frac{\sqrt{7}-1}{\sqrt{7}+1} - \frac{\sqrt{7}+1}{\sqrt{7}-1} = a + b\sqrt{7}$, find the product of a and b.

2. If $x = \frac{\sqrt{p+2q}+\sqrt{p-2q}}{\sqrt{p+2q}-\sqrt{p-2q}}$ and $q \neq 0$, then find $qx^2 - px + q$

3. If $x = 9 + 4\sqrt{5}$ and $xy = 1$, then $\frac{1}{322}\left(\frac{1}{x^2} + \frac{1}{y^2}\right)$ is

4. The value of x, if $5^{x-3} . 3^{2x-8} = 225$ is

5. If $a^2bc^3 = 25$ and $ab^2 = 5$, then abc equals

6. If $x + 1/x = 3$, then $x^2 + 1/x^2$ is equal to

SOLUTIONS

Brief Explanations of Selected Questions

1 EXERCISE

FILL IN THE BLANKS :

1. irrational 2. rational 3. irrational

4. 9 5. $\sqrt{\dfrac{6}{35}}$ 6. 2

7. conjugate 8. $\left(\dfrac{1008}{63}\right)^{1/4} = (16)^{1/4} = (2^4)^{1/4} = 2$

9. infinite 10. real

TRUE/FALSE :

1. False 2. False 3. True 4. False
5. False 6. True 7. True 8. True
9. True 10. True

MATCH THE COLUMNS :

1. (A) → (r); (B) → (s); (C) → (p); (D) → (q);
   (A) $12 = 3 \times 4$ is a composite no.
   (B) g.c.d (2,7) = 1
   (C) $\sqrt{2}$ is not a rational no.
2. (A) → (s); (B) → (p); (C) → (r); (D) → (q); (E) → (t)

VERY SHORT ANSWER QUESTIONS :

1. 0 2. –1 3. *a*
4. (i) $-1.\overline{3}$ (ii) $0.91\overline{6}$ (iii) $0.\overline{538461}$
5. (i) rational (ii) rational
6. No, for example $\sqrt{4} = 2$ is a rational number.
7. (i) 3^{-21} (ii) $56^{1/2}$
8. (i) $2^{\frac{3}{4}}$ (ii) $\dfrac{125}{216}$
   (iii) $\dfrac{729}{125}$ (iv) $\dfrac{30375}{16}$
   (v) 2^4
9. 0.10101001000100001 and 0.11001001000100001
10. (i) terminating (ii) repeating
    (iii) repeating (iv) terminating
11. 37/1100 12. 0.25 and 0.2525
13. $\sqrt[3]{4}$ is the greatest 14. $\dfrac{7}{24}, \dfrac{13}{48}, \dfrac{15}{48}, \dfrac{31}{96}$

SHORT ANSWER QUESTIONS :

1. $p = -11/2,\ q = -5/2$ 2. 5
3. (i) irrational (ii) rational
4. $$\frac{6}{3\sqrt{2}-2\sqrt{3}} = \frac{6}{3\sqrt{2}-2\sqrt{3}} \times \frac{3\sqrt{2}+2\sqrt{3}}{3\sqrt{2}+2\sqrt{3}}$$
$$= \frac{6(3\sqrt{2}+2\sqrt{3})}{(3\sqrt{2})^2-(2\sqrt{3})^2} = \frac{6(3\sqrt{2}+2\sqrt{3})}{18-12}$$
$$= \frac{6(3\sqrt{2}+2\sqrt{3})}{6} = 3\sqrt{2}+2\sqrt{3}$$
Therefore, $3\sqrt{2}+2\sqrt{3} = 3\sqrt{2} - a\sqrt{3}$
$\Rightarrow\ a = -2$
5. $$\left[5\left(8^{\frac{1}{3}}+27^{\frac{1}{3}}\right)^3\right]^{\frac{1}{4}} = \left[5\left((2^3)^{\frac{1}{3}}+(3^3)^{\frac{1}{3}}\right)^3\right]^{\frac{1}{4}}$$
$$= \left[5(2+3)^3\right]^{\frac{1}{4}} = \left[5(5)^3\right]^{\frac{1}{4}} = \left[5^4\right]^{\frac{1}{4}} = 5$$
6. On rationalizing the denominator, we get
$$\frac{(2+\sqrt{2})(3-\sqrt{5})}{(3+\sqrt{5})(2-\sqrt{2})} = \frac{(2+\sqrt{2})(3-\sqrt{5})}{(3+\sqrt{5})(2-\sqrt{2})} \times \frac{(3-\sqrt{5})(2+\sqrt{2})}{(3-\sqrt{5})(2+\sqrt{2})}$$
$$= \frac{(2+\sqrt{2})^2(3-\sqrt{5})^2}{(3^2-(\sqrt{5})^2)(2^2-(\sqrt{2})^2)} = \frac{(4+2+4\sqrt{2})(9+5-6\sqrt{5})}{(9-5)(4-2)}$$
$$= \frac{(6+4\sqrt{2})(14-6\sqrt{5})}{4\times 2} = \frac{84-36\sqrt{5}+56\sqrt{2}-24\sqrt{10}}{8}$$
Hence irrational.
7. $$\sqrt{75}+\frac{1}{2}\sqrt{48}-\sqrt{192} = 5\sqrt{3}+\frac{4}{2}\sqrt{3}-8\sqrt{3} = \sqrt{3}(5+2-8)$$
$= -1.732$
8. $$\frac{\sqrt{x^2-y^2}+x}{\sqrt{x^2+y^2}+y} \times \frac{x-\sqrt{x^2-y^2}}{\sqrt{x^2+y^2}-y} = \frac{x^2-(\sqrt{x^2-y^2})^2}{(\sqrt{x^2+y^2})^2-y^2}$$
$$= \frac{x^2-(x^2-y^2)}{(x^2+y^2)-y^2} = \frac{y^2}{x^2}$$
9. $$x^2 = \frac{\sqrt{5}+2+\sqrt{5}-2+2\sqrt{(\sqrt{5})^2-2^2}}{\sqrt{5}+1}$$
$$= \frac{2\sqrt{5}+2}{\sqrt{5}+1} = \frac{2(\sqrt{5}+1)}{\sqrt{5}+1} = 2$$

LONG ANSWER QUESTIONS :

1. $0.6+0.\bar{7}+0.4\bar{7}$

Let $x=0.\bar{7}\,;\, y=0.4\bar{7}$

$\Rightarrow\quad 9x=7.\bar{7}\,;10y=4.\bar{7}$

$\Rightarrow\quad 9x=7\,;100y=47.\bar{7}$

$\Rightarrow\quad x=\dfrac{7}{9}\,;\,90y=43\Rightarrow y=\dfrac{43}{90}$

$\therefore$ Required expression $=\dfrac{6}{10}+\dfrac{7}{9}+\dfrac{43}{90}$

2. 98

3. $\sqrt{10}+\sqrt{20}+\sqrt{40}-\sqrt{5}-\sqrt{80}$

$=\sqrt{10}+\sqrt{4\times5}+\sqrt{4\times10}-\sqrt{5}-\sqrt{16\times5}$

$=\sqrt{10}+2\sqrt{5}+2\sqrt{10}-\sqrt{5}-4\sqrt{5}$

$=3\sqrt{10}-3\sqrt{5}=3(\sqrt{10}-\sqrt{5})$

$\therefore$ Given expression

$$=\frac{15}{3(\sqrt{10}-\sqrt{5})}=\frac{5}{\sqrt{10}-\sqrt{5}}=\frac{5}{\sqrt{10}-\sqrt{5}}\times\frac{\sqrt{10}+\sqrt{5}}{\sqrt{10}+\sqrt{5}}$$

$$=\frac{5(\sqrt{10}+\sqrt{5})}{10-5}=\sqrt{10}+\sqrt{5}$$

4. Let $I=\dfrac{7\sqrt{3}}{\sqrt{10}+\sqrt{3}}-\dfrac{2\sqrt{5}}{\sqrt{6}+\sqrt{5}}-\dfrac{3\sqrt{2}}{\sqrt{15}+3\sqrt{2}}=A-B-C$

where $A=\dfrac{7\sqrt{3}}{\sqrt{10}+\sqrt{3}}\times\dfrac{\sqrt{10}-\sqrt{3}}{\sqrt{10}-\sqrt{3}}=\dfrac{7\sqrt{3}(\sqrt{10}-\sqrt{3})}{10-3}$

$$=\frac{7\sqrt{30}-7\times3}{7}=\frac{7(\sqrt{30}-3)}{7}=\sqrt{30}-3$$

$$B=\frac{2\sqrt{5}}{\sqrt{6}+\sqrt{5}}\times\frac{\sqrt{6}-\sqrt{5}}{\sqrt{6}-\sqrt{5}}=\frac{2\sqrt{30}-2\times5}{6-5}=2\sqrt{30}-10$$

$$C=\frac{3\sqrt{2}}{\sqrt{15}+3\sqrt{2}}\times\frac{\sqrt{15}-3\sqrt{2}}{\sqrt{15}-3\sqrt{2}}=\frac{3\sqrt{30}-18}{15-18}=\frac{3\sqrt{30}-18}{-3}$$

$=-\sqrt{30}+6$

Now, $I=A-B-C$

$=(\sqrt{30}-3)-(2\sqrt{30}-10)-(-\sqrt{30}+6)$

$=\sqrt{30}-3-2\sqrt{30}+10+\sqrt{30}-6$

$=2\sqrt{30}-2\sqrt{30}-3+10-6=1$

5.

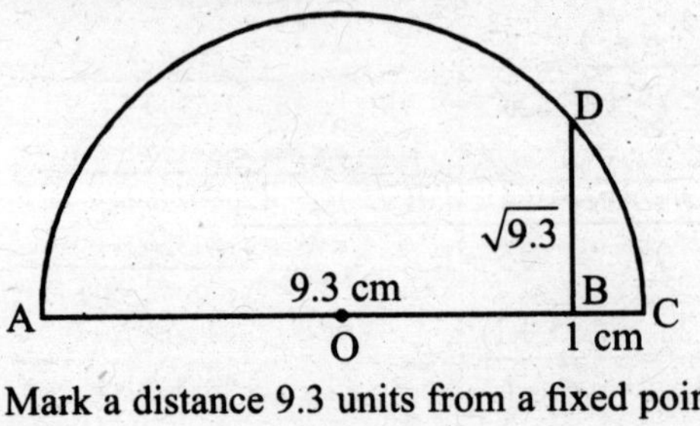

Mark a distance 9.3 units from a fixed point A on a given line to obtain a given point B such that AB = 9.3 units. From B mark a distance of 1 unit and call the new point as C. Find the mid point of AC and call that point as O. Draw a semi circle with centre O and radius OC = 5.15 units. Draw a line perpendicular to AC passing through B cutting the semi-circle at D.

Then, BD = $\sqrt{9.3}$ = 3.05 units.

6. $x=\dfrac{(\sqrt{a+2b}+\sqrt{a-2b})}{(\sqrt{a+2b}-\sqrt{a-2b})}\times\dfrac{(\sqrt{a+2b}+\sqrt{a-2b})}{(\sqrt{a+2b}+\sqrt{a-2b})}$

$$\Rightarrow\quad x=\frac{(\sqrt{a+2b}+\sqrt{a-2b})^2}{(a+2b)-(a-2b)}$$

$$=\frac{a+2b+a-2b+2\sqrt{(a+2b)(a-2b)}}{4b}$$

$$\Rightarrow\quad x=\frac{a+\sqrt{a^2-4b^2}}{2b}$$

$\Rightarrow\quad 2bx=a+\sqrt{a^2-4b^2}$

$\Rightarrow\quad 2bx-a=\sqrt{a^2-4b^2}$

Squaring both sides, we get

$(2bx-a)^2=\left(\sqrt{a^2-4b^2}\right)^2$

$\Rightarrow\quad 4b^2x^2+a^2-4abx=a^2-4b^2$

$\Rightarrow\quad 4b^2x^2-4abx+4b^2=0$

$\Rightarrow\quad b^2x^2-abx+b^2=0$

7. L.H.S. $=\dfrac{\sqrt{7}-1}{\sqrt{7}+1}-\dfrac{\sqrt{7}+1}{\sqrt{7}-1}=\dfrac{(\sqrt{7}-1)^2-(\sqrt{7}+1)^2}{(\sqrt{7}+1)\,(\sqrt{7}-1)}$

$$=\frac{(7+1-2\sqrt{7})-(7+1+2\sqrt{7})}{(\sqrt{7})^2-(1)^2}$$

$$=\frac{8-2\sqrt{7}-8-2\sqrt{7}}{7-1}$$

$$=-\frac{4\sqrt{7}}{6}=\frac{-2}{3}\sqrt{7}$$

$\therefore\ -\dfrac{2}{3}\sqrt{7}=a+b\sqrt{7}$

$\Rightarrow\ 0.a-\dfrac{2}{3}\sqrt{7}=a+b\sqrt{7}\quad\Rightarrow\ a=0$ and $b=-\dfrac{2}{3}$

2 EXERCISE

TEXT-BOOK EXERCISE :

1. Yes! zero is a rational number. We can write zero in the form $\dfrac{p}{q}$, as follows :

$0=\dfrac{0}{1}=\dfrac{0}{2}=\dfrac{0}{3}$ ......so on., q can be negative integer also.

2. $\frac{3}{5}=\frac{3\times10}{5\times10}=\frac{30}{50}$, $\frac{4}{5}=\frac{4\times10}{5\times10}=\frac{40}{50}$, therefore, five rational numbers between $\frac{3}{5}$ and $\frac{4}{5}$ are $\frac{31}{50},\frac{32}{50},\frac{33}{50},\frac{34}{50},\frac{35}{50}$.

3. (i) True, since the collection of whole numbers contains all natural numbers.
   (ii) False, because, -3 is not a whole number.
   (iii) False, $\because$ $\frac{1}{2}$ is not a whole number.

4. (i) True, ($\because$ real numbers are collection of rational and irrational numbers.)
   (ii) False
   (iii) False, (2 is real but not irrational.)

5. No, the square roots of all positive integers are not irrational. For example, $\sqrt{16}=4$ is a rational number.

6. (i) Given $\frac{36}{100}=0.36$. Hence, the decimal expansion is terminating.

   (ii) Consider $4\frac{1}{8}=4+\frac{1}{8}=\frac{33}{8}$

   $\therefore$ 8) 33.000 (4.125
   32
   10
   8
   20
   16
   40
   40
   ×

   Thus, from the divison, we get $4\frac{1}{8}=4.125$

   Hence, The decimal expansion of $4\frac{1}{8}$ is terminating.

   (iii) Consider $\frac{2}{11}$
   11) 2.0000 (0.1818......
   11
   90
   88
   20
   11
   90
   88
   2

   On dividing by 11, we get

   $\frac{2}{11}=0.1818.....=0.\overline{18}$.

   So, the decimal expansion of $\frac{2}{11}$ is non-terminating repeating.

7. Yes! we can predict the decimal expansions of $\frac{2}{7},\frac{3}{7},\frac{4}{7},\frac{5}{7},\frac{6}{7}$ without actually doing the long division as follows :

$$\frac{2}{7}=2\times\frac{1}{7}=2\times0.\overline{142857}=0.\overline{285714}$$

$$\frac{3}{7}=0.\overline{428571}$$

Similarly,

$$\frac{4}{7}=0.\overline{571428}$$

$$\frac{5}{7}=0.\overline{714285}$$

$$\frac{6}{7}=0.\overline{857142}.$$

8. Let $x=0.99999........$

   Multiplying both sides by 10 (since one digit is repeating), we get

$$10x=9.9999.....$$

$$\Rightarrow\ 10x=9+0.99999.....\qquad\Rightarrow\ 10x=9+x$$

$$\Rightarrow\ x=\frac{9}{9}=1$$

   Thus, $0.99999.....=1=\frac{1}{1}$

   Which is in the form $\frac{p}{q}$,

   where, $p=1$
   $q=1\ (q\neq0)$

   Since 0.99999........goes on for ever, so there is no gap between 1 and 0.99999...... end. Hence they are equal.

9. 0.01001 0001 00001.........,
   0.20 2002 20003 200002........,
   0.003000300003..............,

10. (i) $\sqrt{23}$

	4.795831523
4	23.00 00 00 00 00 00 00 00 00
	16
87	700
	609
949	9100
	8541
9585	55900
	47925
95908	797500
	767264
959163	3023600
	2877489
9591661	14611100
	9591661
95916625	501943900
	479583125
959166302	2236077500
	1918332604
9591663043	31774489600
	28774989129
	2999500471

Thus, $\sqrt{23} = 4.795831523........$

$\sqrt{23}$ is an irrational number.

$\therefore$ The decimal expansion is non-terminating non-recurring.

(ii) $7.478478.....= 7.\overline{478}$

Since, the decimal expansion is non- terminating recurring.

$\therefore$ 7.478478......... is a irrational number.

11. $4.2\overline{6} = 4.262626......$

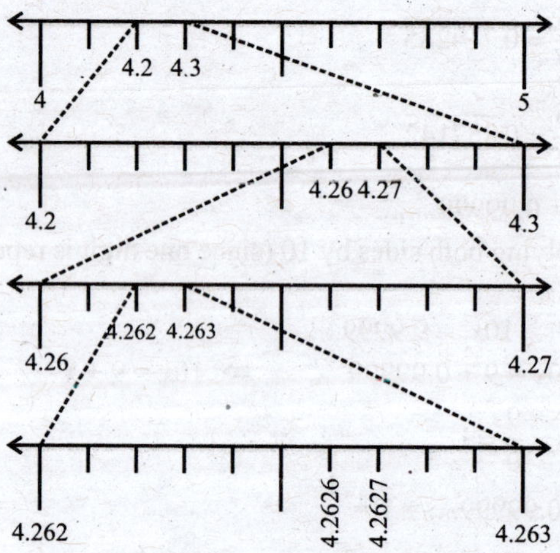

12. (i) $2 - \sqrt{5}$ is an irrational number as 2 is a rational number and $\sqrt{5}$ is an irrational number.

($\because$ The difference of a rational number and an irrational number is irrational.)

(ii) Consider

$$\frac{2\sqrt{7}}{7\sqrt{7}} = \frac{2}{7}$$

which is a rational number.

$$\left(\frac{p}{q}, q \neq 0 \text{ form}\right)$$

where $p = 2, q = 7\ (\neq 0)$

(iii) Since, the product of a non-zero rational number with an irrational number is irrational.

$\therefore$ 2π is an irrational number.

13. (i) Consider

$(3 + \sqrt{3})(2 + \sqrt{2})$

$= (3)(2) + 3\sqrt{2} + (\sqrt{3})(2) + (\sqrt{3})(\sqrt{2})$

$= 6 + 3\sqrt{2} + 2\sqrt{3} + \sqrt{(3)(2)} \left(\because \sqrt{a}\sqrt{b} = \sqrt{ab}\right)$

$= 6 + 3\sqrt{2} + 2\sqrt{3} + \sqrt{6}.$

(ii) Consider

$(\sqrt{5} + \sqrt{2})^2 = (\sqrt{5})^2 + 2\sqrt{5}\sqrt{2} + (\sqrt{2})^2$

$= 5 + 2\sqrt{10} + 2 \left(\because \sqrt{a}\sqrt{b} = \sqrt{ab}\right)$

$= 7 + 2\sqrt{10}.$

14. Consider $125^{1/3} = (5^3)^{1/3} = 5^{3\times1/3} = 5^1 = 5.$

15. (i) Consider $32^{2/5} = (2^5)^{2/5} = 2^{5\times2/5} = 2^2 = 4.$

(ii) Consider $125^{-1/3} = (5^3)^{-1/3} = 5^{3\times(-1/3)} = 5^{-1} = \frac{1}{5}$

16. (i) Consider $2^{\frac{2}{3}} \cdot 2^{\frac{1}{5}} = 2^{2/3 + 1/5}$

$= 2^{\frac{10+3}{15}} = 2^{13/15}.$

(ii) Consider $\left(\frac{1}{3^3}\right)^7 = \frac{1^7}{(3^3)^7} = \frac{1}{3^{21}} = 3^{-21}$

(iii) Consider $\frac{11^{1/2}}{11^{1/4}} = 11^{1/2-1/4} = 11^{1/4}.$

EXEMPLAR QUESTIONS :

1. (i) $3\sqrt{3} + 2\sqrt{3\times3\times3} + \frac{7}{\sqrt{3}}$

$= 3\sqrt{3} + 2\sqrt{3\times3\times3} + \frac{7}{\sqrt{3}}$

$= 3\sqrt{3} + 6\sqrt{3} + \frac{7}{\sqrt{3}}$

$= \frac{3\sqrt{3}\times\sqrt{3} + 6\sqrt{3}\times\sqrt{3} + 7}{\sqrt{3}}$

$= \frac{9+18+7}{\sqrt{3}} = \frac{34}{\sqrt{3}} \times \frac{\sqrt{3}}{\sqrt{3}} = \frac{34\sqrt{3}}{3}$

(ii) $\sqrt[4]{81} - 8\sqrt[3]{216} + 15\sqrt[5]{32} + \sqrt{225}$

$= \sqrt[4]{3\times3\times3\times3} - 8\sqrt[3]{6\times6\times6}$

$+ 15\sqrt[5]{2\times2\times2\times2\times2} + \sqrt{15\times15}$

$= 3 - 8\times6 + 15\times2 + 15$

$= 3 - 48 + 30 + 15$

$= -45 + 45$

$= 0$

2. We write 10 as the sum of the squares of two natural numbers.

$10 = 9 + 1 = 3^2 + 1^2$

Take OA = 3 units, on the number line

Draw BA = 1 unit, perpendicular to OA. Join OB

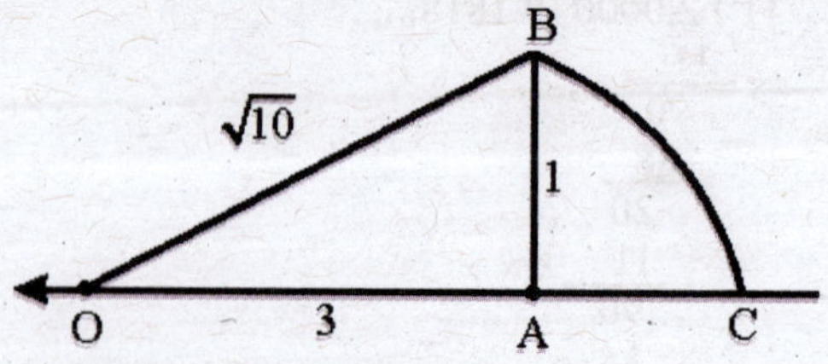

Now, by Pythagoras theorem.

$OB^2 = AB^2 + OA^2$

$OB^2 = 1^2 + 3^2 = 10$

$\Rightarrow OB = \sqrt{10}$

Taking O as centre and OB as a radius, draw an arc which intersects the number line at point C. Clearly, C corresponds to $\sqrt{10}$ on the number line.

3. $\dfrac{4}{(216)^{\frac{-2}{3}}}+\dfrac{1}{(256)^{\frac{-3}{4}}}+\dfrac{2}{(243)^{\frac{-1}{5}}}$

$=4(216)^{\frac{2}{3}}+(256)^{\frac{3}{4}}+2(243)^{\frac{1}{5}}$

$=4\left(6^3\right)^{\frac{2}{3}}+\left(4^4\right)^{\frac{3}{4}}+2\left(3^5\right)^{\frac{1}{5}}$

$=4\times 6^{\frac{6}{3}}+4^{\frac{12}{4}}+2\times 3^{\frac{5}{5}}=4\times 6^2+4^3+2\times 3$

$=4\times 36+64+6=144+64+6=214$

4. (i) $\dfrac{3\sqrt{5}+\sqrt{3}}{\sqrt{5}-\sqrt{3}}=\dfrac{3\sqrt{5}+\sqrt{3}}{\sqrt{5}-\sqrt{3}}\times\dfrac{\sqrt{5}+\sqrt{3}}{\sqrt{5}+\sqrt{3}}$

$=\dfrac{3\sqrt{5}\left(\sqrt{5}+\sqrt{3}\right)+\sqrt{3}\left(\sqrt{5}+\sqrt{3}\right)}{\left(\sqrt{5}\right)^2-\left(\sqrt{3}\right)^2}$

$=\dfrac{3\times 5+3\sqrt{5}\times\sqrt{3}+\sqrt{3}\times\sqrt{5}+\sqrt{3}\times\sqrt{3}}{5-3}$

$=\dfrac{15+3\sqrt{15}+\sqrt{15}+3}{2}$

$=\dfrac{18+4\sqrt{15}}{2}=9+2\sqrt{15}$

(ii) $\dfrac{4\sqrt{3}+5\sqrt{2}}{\sqrt{48}+\sqrt{18}}=\dfrac{4\sqrt{3}+5\sqrt{2}}{\sqrt{48}+\sqrt{18}}\times\dfrac{\sqrt{48}-\sqrt{18}}{\sqrt{48}-\sqrt{18}}$

$=\dfrac{4\sqrt{3}\times\sqrt{48}+5\sqrt{2}\times\sqrt{48}-4\sqrt{3}\times\sqrt{18}-5\sqrt{2}\times\sqrt{18}}{\left(\sqrt{48}\right)^2-\left(\sqrt{18}\right)^2}$

$=\dfrac{4\sqrt{3\times 3\times 4\times 4}+5\sqrt{2\times 2\times 2\times 2\times 2\times 3}-4\sqrt{3\times 3\times 6}-5\sqrt{2\times 3\times 3\times 2}}{48-18}$

$=\dfrac{4\times 3\times 4+5\times 2\times 2\sqrt{6}-4\times 3\sqrt{6}-5\times 3\times 2}{30}$

$=\dfrac{48-30+20\sqrt{6}-12\sqrt{6}}{30}$

$=\dfrac{18+8\sqrt{6}}{30}=\dfrac{9+4\sqrt{6}}{15}$

5. We have $\dfrac{3-\sqrt{5}}{3+2\sqrt{5}}=a\sqrt{5}-\dfrac{19}{11}$

Consider,

$\dfrac{3-\sqrt{5}}{3+2\sqrt{5}}=\dfrac{3-\sqrt{5}}{3+2\sqrt{5}}\times\dfrac{3-2\sqrt{5}}{3-2\sqrt{5}}$

$=\dfrac{9-3\sqrt{5}-6\sqrt{5}+10}{(3)^2-\left(2\sqrt{5}\right)^2}$

$=\dfrac{19-9\sqrt{5}}{9-20}=\dfrac{19-9\sqrt{5}}{-11}$

$=-\dfrac{19}{11}+\dfrac{9}{11}\sqrt{5}=a\sqrt{5}-\dfrac{19}{11}$

Comparing the coefficient of $\sqrt{5}$, we get

$a=\dfrac{9}{11}$

6. We have, $a=2+\sqrt{3}$

$\dfrac{1}{a}=\dfrac{1}{2+\sqrt{3}}$

$=\dfrac{2-\sqrt{3}}{\left(2+\sqrt{3}\right)\left(2-\sqrt{3}\right)}$

$=\dfrac{2-\sqrt{3}}{(2)^2-\left(\sqrt{3}\right)^2}$

$=\dfrac{2-\sqrt{3}}{4-3}=2-\sqrt{3}$

$\therefore\quad a-\dfrac{1}{a}=2+\sqrt{3}-\left(2-\sqrt{3}\right)$

$2+\sqrt{3}-2+\sqrt{3}=2\sqrt{3}$

$\therefore\ a-\dfrac{1}{a}=2\sqrt{3}$

7. (i) $\left(\dfrac{3}{5}\right)^4\left(\dfrac{8}{5}\right)^{-12}\left(\dfrac{32}{5}\right)^6$

$=\dfrac{3^4\times 8^{-12}\times 32^6}{5^4\times 5^{-12}\times 5^6}=\dfrac{3^4\times(2)^{-36}\times(2)^{30}}{5^{4-12+6}}$

$=\dfrac{3^4\times(2)^{-36+30}}{5^{-2}}=\dfrac{3\times 3\times 3\times 3\times 2^{-6}}{5^{-2}}$

$=\dfrac{81\times 5\times 5}{2\times 2\times 2\times 2\times 2\times 2}=\dfrac{2025}{64}$

(ii) $\dfrac{9^{\frac{1}{3}}\times 27^{-\frac{1}{2}}}{3^{\frac{1}{6}}\times 3^{-\frac{2}{3}}}=\dfrac{(3)^{2\times\frac{1}{3}}\times(3)^{3\times-\frac{1}{2}}}{(3)^{\frac{1}{6}}\times 3^{-\frac{2}{3}}}$

$=\dfrac{3^{\frac{2}{3}}\times 3^{\frac{-3}{2}}}{3^{\frac{1}{6}}\times 3^{\frac{-2}{3}}}=\dfrac{3^{\frac{2}{3}-\frac{3}{2}}}{3^{\frac{1}{6}-\frac{2}{3}}}=\dfrac{3^{\frac{-5}{6}}}{3^{\frac{-1}{2}}}$

$=3^{\frac{-5}{6}+\frac{1}{2}}=3^{-\frac{1}{3}}$

HOTS QUESTIONS :

1. Consider the rational number $\frac{5}{7}$. On dividing by 7, we get,

$$\begin{array}{l} 7\,)\,5.000000\,(0.714285\ldots\ldots \\ \underline{49} \\ \ \ 10 \\ \ \ \underline{\ 7} \\ \ \ 30 \\ \ \ \underline{28} \\ \ \ \ 20 \\ \ \ \ \underline{14} \\ \ \ \ \ 60 \\ \ \ \ \ \underline{56} \\ \ \ \ \ \ 40 \\ \ \ \ \ \ \underline{35} \\ \ \ \ \ \ \ 5 \end{array}$$

Thus, $\frac{5}{7} = 0.714285\ \ldots\ldots = 0.\overline{714285}$

Now, consider $\frac{9}{11}$.

On dividing by 11, we get

$$\begin{array}{l} 11)\,9.0000\,(0.8181\ldots\ldots \\ \ \ \underline{88} \\ \ \ \ 20 \\ \ \ \ \underline{11} \\ \ \ \ \ 90 \\ \ \ \ \ \underline{88} \\ \ \ \ \ \ 20 \\ \ \ \ \ \ \underline{11} \\ \ \ \ \ \ \ 9 \end{array}$$

Thus, $\frac{9}{11} = 0.8181\ldots\ldots = 0.\overline{81}$

Three different irrational numbers between the rational numbers $\frac{5}{7}$ and $\frac{9}{11}$ can be

0.75 075007500075000075.......,

0.7670767000767........... and

0.808008000800008...........

2. Let $x = 2.5434343$

$\Rightarrow x = 2.5\overline{43}$

Multiplying both sides by 10 we get

$10x = 25.\overline{43}$ … (i)

Again multiplying equation (i) by 100

$1000x = 2543.\overline{43}$

On subtracting

$1000x - 10x = 2543.\overline{43} - 25.\overline{43}$

$990x = 2518$

$x = \frac{2518}{990}$

$x = \frac{1259}{495}$

Hence, $2543.\overline{43} - 25.\overline{43} = \frac{1259}{495}$

3. $-7\left[1+80\sqrt{3}\right]$

4. We have $\frac{9^n \times 3^2 (3^{-n/2})^{-2} - (27)^n}{3^{3m} \times 2^3} = \frac{1}{27}$

$\Rightarrow \frac{(3^2)^n \times 3^2 \times 3^{-n/2 \times -2} - (3^3)^n}{3^{3m} \times 2^3} = \frac{1}{27}$

$\Rightarrow \frac{3^{2n} \times 3^2 \times 3^n - 3^{3n}}{3^{3m} \times 2^3} = \frac{1}{27}$

$\Rightarrow \frac{3^{2n+2+n} - 3^{3n}}{3^{3m} \times 2^3} = \frac{1}{27}$

$\Rightarrow \frac{3^{3n}(3^2 - 1)}{3^{3m} \times 2^3} = \frac{1}{27} \Rightarrow \frac{3^{3n}.8}{3^{3m}.8} = \frac{1}{27}$

$\Rightarrow 3^{3n-3m} = \frac{1}{3^3}$

$\Rightarrow 3^{3n-3m} = 3^{-3}$

On equating the exponent, we get

$\Rightarrow 3n - 3m = -3 \Rightarrow n - m = -1 \Rightarrow m - n = 1.$

5. Here, $a = \frac{\sqrt{2}+1}{\sqrt{2}-1} = \frac{\sqrt{2}+1}{\sqrt{2}-1} \times \frac{\sqrt{2}+1}{\sqrt{2}+1} = \frac{(\sqrt{2}+1)^2}{(\sqrt{2})^2 - 1^2}$

$\frac{(\sqrt{2})^2 + 1 + 2\sqrt{2}}{2-1} = \frac{2+1+2\sqrt{2}}{1} = 3 + 2\sqrt{2}$

$\therefore\ a = 3 + 2\sqrt{2}$ ...(i)

$b = \frac{\sqrt{2}-1}{\sqrt{2}+1} = \frac{\sqrt{2}-1}{\sqrt{2}+1} \times \frac{\sqrt{2}-1}{\sqrt{2}-1} = \frac{(\sqrt{2}-1)^2}{(\sqrt{2})^2 - 1}$

$= \frac{(\sqrt{2})^2 + 1^2 - 2\sqrt{2}}{2-1} = \frac{2+1-2\sqrt{2}}{1} = 3 - 2\sqrt{2}$

$\therefore\ b = 3 - 2\sqrt{2}$ ... (ii)

From equations (i) and (ii)

$a + b = 3 + 2\sqrt{2} + 3 - 2\sqrt{2} = 6$

$ab = (3+2\sqrt{2})(3-2\sqrt{2}) = 3^2 - \left(2\sqrt{2}\right)^2$

$= 9 - 4 \times 2 = 9 - 8 = 1$

$a^2 + b^2 - 4ab = a^2 + b^2 + 2ab - 6ab$

$= (a+b)^2 - 6ab$

$= 6^2 - 6 \times 1 = 36 - 6 = 30.$

6. Let $2^a = 3^b = 6^c = k$

So, $2^a = k$

$\Rightarrow k^{1/a} = 2$ …(i)

Similarly, $k^{1/b} = 3$ …(ii)

$k^{1/c} = 6$ …(iii)

Now, we know that $6 = 2 \times 3$

Putting the values of 6, 2 and 3 from (i), (ii) and (iii), we get:

$k^{1/c} = k^{1/a} \times k^{1/b} \Rightarrow k^{1/c} = k^{1/a + 1/b}$

$\Rightarrow \frac{1}{c} = \frac{1}{a} + \frac{1}{b} \Rightarrow \frac{1}{c} = \frac{b+a}{ab} \Rightarrow c = \frac{ab}{a+b}$

7. $x = 2 + 3\sqrt{2}$

$\frac{1}{x} = \frac{1}{2+3\sqrt{2}}$

By rationalising, we get:

$\frac{1}{x} = \frac{2-3\sqrt{2}}{2^2-(3\sqrt{2})^2} = \frac{2-3\sqrt{2}}{4-18} = \frac{3\sqrt{2}-2}{14}$

Now,

$\left(x+\frac{14}{x}\right) = 2 + 3\sqrt{2} + 14\left(\frac{3\sqrt{2}-2}{14}\right)$

$= 2 + 3\sqrt{2} + 3\sqrt{2} - 2$

$= 6\sqrt{2}$

3 EXERCISE

SINGLE OPTION CORRECT :

1. (a) $2^{x+4} . 3^{x+1} = 2^5 . 3^2 \Rightarrow x = 1$

2. (a) **3.** (d)

4. (a) $x = 6$ satisfies the given equation

5. **(d)** Simplest form of $\frac{17}{119} = \frac{17}{119}$

Simplest form of $\frac{14}{57} = \frac{14}{57}$

Simplest form of $\frac{21}{38} = \frac{21}{38}$

Simplest form of $\frac{21}{57} = \frac{7}{19}$

6. (a) **7.** (a) **8.** (c) **9.** (b)

10. (d) To find four rational numbers between 3 and 4.

$\frac{3\times 5}{5}$ and $\frac{4\times 5}{5}$

$\Rightarrow \frac{15}{5}$ and $\frac{20}{5}$

Between $\frac{15}{5}$ and $\frac{20}{5}$ lies $\frac{16}{5}, \frac{17}{5}, \frac{18}{5}, \frac{19}{5}$

Now, from the given options (a) and (b) does not contain rational number between 3 and 5.

(c) has 4.1 and 4.2 that does not lie between 3 and 4.

MORE THAN ONE OPTION CORRECT :

1. (a) and (c) **2.** (b)

3. (c) **4.** (a), (c) and (d)

5. (a), (b) and (c)

ASSERTION AND REASON :

1. (a)

2. (a)

3. (d) $17^2 . 17^5 = 17^{2+5} = 17^7$

4. (a)

5. (c) $\frac{1}{2}\left(\frac{1}{3}+\frac{1}{2}\right) = \frac{5}{12}$

MULTIPLE MATCHING QUESTIONS :

1. (A) → (p, s); (B) → (r) ; (C) → (r); (D) → (q)

INTEGER TYPE QUESTIONS :

1. **Ans : 0**

$\text{L.H.S.} = \frac{\sqrt{7}-1}{\sqrt{7}+1} - \frac{\sqrt{7}+1}{\sqrt{7}-1} = \frac{(\sqrt{7}-1)^2-(\sqrt{7}+1)^2}{(\sqrt{7}+1)(\sqrt{7}-1)}$

$= \frac{(7+1-2\sqrt{7})-(7+1+2\sqrt{7})}{(\sqrt{7})^2-(1)^2}$

$= \frac{8-2\sqrt{7}-8-2\sqrt{7}}{7-1}$

$= -\frac{4\sqrt{7}}{6} = -\frac{2}{3}\sqrt{7}$

$\therefore -\frac{2}{3}\sqrt{7} = a + b\sqrt{7}$

$\Rightarrow a = 0$ and $b = -\frac{2}{3}$

$\Rightarrow a - b = 0$

2. **Ans : 0**

$\frac{x}{1} = \frac{\sqrt{p+2q}+\sqrt{p-2q}}{\sqrt{p+2q}-\sqrt{p-2q}}$

$\frac{x+1}{x-1} = \frac{2\sqrt{p+2q}}{2\sqrt{p-2q}}$ (By componendo and dividendo)

On squaring both sides, we get

$\frac{(x^2+1)+2x}{(x^2+1)-2x} = \frac{p+2q}{p-2q}$

On again applying componendo and dividendo.

we have,

$\frac{2(x^2+1)}{2.2x} = \frac{2.p}{2.2q}$

$qx^2 + q = px$

Then, $qx^2 - px + q = 0.$

3. Ans : 1

$x = 9 + 4\sqrt{5}$

$$y = \frac{1}{x} = \frac{1}{9+4\sqrt{5}} = \frac{9-4\sqrt{5}}{(9)^2 - (4\sqrt{5})^2} = 9 - 4\sqrt{5}$$

$$\therefore \quad \frac{1}{322}\left(\frac{1}{x^2} + \frac{1}{y^2}\right)$$

$$= \frac{1}{322}[(9-4\sqrt{5})^2 + (9+4\sqrt{5})^2]$$

$$= \frac{2(81+80)}{322} = \frac{2(161)}{322} = \frac{322}{322} = 1$$

4. Ans : 5

$5^{x-3}\,3^{2x-8} = 225 \Rightarrow 5^{x-3}.3^{2x-8} = 5^2.3^2$

By comparing $x - 3 = 2 \Rightarrow x = 3 + 2 = 5.$

5. Ans : 5

$a^2bc^3 = 25$ ......(i)

$ab^2 = 5$ ......(ii)

Multiplying (i) & (ii), we get $a^3\ b^3\ c^3 = 125$

$abc = (125)^{1/3} = 5$

6. Ans : 7

$x + \frac{1}{x} = 3$ (given)

Squaring both sides $x^2 + \frac{1}{x^2} + 2 = 9$

$\Rightarrow \quad x^2 + \frac{1}{x^2} = 7.$

Chapter 2

Polynomials

INTRODUCTION

In earlier classes, you have studied constants, variables, algebraic expressions, terms and some basic algebraic operations (addition, subtraction and multiplication) of polynomials. You have also studied to factorise simple algebraic expressions and use of simple algebraic identities in the factorization of algebraic expressions.

In this chapter, you will study the polynomial which is a particular type of algebraic expression and various terminology related to it. You will also study the Division of Polynomials, Remainder Theorem, Factor Theorem, some more Algebraic Identities and their uses.

POLYNOMIAL

An algebraic expression in which the variable involved has only non-negative integral power, when the variable in any term is in numerator, is called a polynomial. For example: $3x^4 - 5x^2 + x - 10$, $5x + 3$, $x^2 + 2x - 5$, $x^3 - \frac{5}{2}x + \sqrt{7}$, $2\sqrt{3}x^4 - \frac{5}{6}x$ etc.

But $3x^3 + 2\sqrt{x} - 7$, $5x^4 - \frac{2}{x^2} + 2\sqrt{3}$, $7x^3 - 5x^{\frac{3}{2}} + 3$ and $x^5 + 2x^{-4} + x - 1$ are not the polynomials, because

(i) in $3x^3 + 2\sqrt{x} - 7$, $2\sqrt{x}$ is a term. $2\sqrt{x}$ means $2x^{\frac{1}{2}}$, hence the power of x is not a non-negative integer.

(ii) in $5x^4 - \frac{2}{x^2} + 2\sqrt{3}$, $-\frac{2}{x^2}$ is a term. $-\frac{2}{x^2}$ means $-2x^{-2}$, hence the power of x is not a non-negative integer.

(iii) in $7x^3 - 5x^{\frac{3}{2}} + 3$, $-5x^{\frac{3}{2}}$ is a term. The power of x is $\frac{3}{2}$, which is not a non-negative integer.

(iv) in $x^5 + 2x^{-4} + x - 1$, $2x^{-4}$ is a term. The power of x is -4, which is not a non-negative integer.

STANDARD FORM OF POLYNOMIAL

The standard form of the polynomial in any variable x is $a_nx^n + a_{n-1}x^{n-1} + a_{n-2}x^{n-2} + \ldots a_3x^3 + a_2x^2 + a_1x + a_0$. Here $a_0, a_1, a_2, \ldots a_n$ are real numbers and all the index (or power) of x are non-negative integers $a_n, a_{n-1}, a_{n-2}, \ldots, a_3, a_2, a_1$ are called coefficients of $x^n, x^{n-1}, x^{n-2}, \ldots, x^3, x^2$ and x. a_0 is called constant term.

In the standard form of the polynomial in any one variable, terms are written in decreasing order of indices of x. The highest index n if $a_n \neq 0$, is called the degree of the polynomial. In particular, if $a_0 = a_1 = a_2 = a_3 = \ldots, = a_n = 0$ (all the constants). We get the zero polynomial, which is denoted by O. The degree of zero polynomial is not defined. A polynomial may has one or more terms.

If a polynomial has only one term, which is a non-zero constant, then the degree of this non-zero constant polynomial is zero. For example 5, $\sqrt{3}$, $-\frac{7}{2}$ are constant polynomial of degree zero, because 5, $\sqrt{3}$ and $-\frac{7}{2}$ can be written as $5x^0$, $\sqrt{3}\,x^0$ and $-\frac{7}{2}x^0$ respectively.

NOTE : (i) If a polynomial involves two or more variables, then in standard form terms are written in decreasing order of indices of the variable which comes earlier in alphabatic order.

(ii) To find the degree of such type of polynomial, sum of the power of all the variables in each term is taken up. The highest sum so obtained is the degree of the polynomial. For example : $5x^4y^2 - 7x^3y^2 + \sqrt{5}y^4$ and $7x^5y - 3\sqrt{2}xy^6 + 8$ are polynomials in two variables x and y in standard form. The degree of the first polynomial is 6 and the degree of the second polynomial is 7.

TYPES OF POLYNOMIALS ON THE BASIS OF THEIR DEGREE

(i) Linear Polynomial

A polynomial of degree one is called a linear polynomial. The general form of a linear polynomial is $ax + b$, where a and b are any real constants and $a \neq 0$.

Example: $3x + 5$ is a linear polynomial.

(ii) Quadratic Polynomial

A polynomial of degree two is called a quadratic polynomial. The general form of quadratic polynomial is $ax^2 + bx + c$, where $a \neq 0$.

Example: $2y^2 + 3y - 1$ is a quadratic polynomial.

(iii) Cubic Polynomial

A polynomial of degree three is called a cubic polynomial. The general form of a cubic polynomial is $ax^3 + bx^2 + cx + d$, where $a \neq 0$.

Example: $6x^3 - 5x^2 + 2x + 1$ is a cubic polynomial.

(iv) Biquadratic Polynomial

A polynomial of degree four is called a biquadratic polynomial. The general form of a biquadratic polynomial is $ax^4 + bx^3 + cx^2 + dx + e$ where $a \neq 0$.

Example: $x^4 - 2x^2 + \sqrt{3}x + 2$ is a biquadratic polynomial.

> **NOTE :** A polynomial of degree five or more than five does not have any particular name. Such a polynomial usually called a polynomial of degree five or six or .... etc.

TYPES OF POLYNOMIALS ON THE BASIS OF NUMBER OF TERMS OF THE POLYNOMIAL

On the basis of the number of terms of the polynomial, the polynomial is named as follows:

(i) Monomial

A polynomial is said to be a monomial if it has only one term.

For Example: $-3x^2$, $5x^3$, $10x$ are monomials.

(ii) Binomial

A polynomial is said to be a binomial if it contains two terms.

For Example: $2x^2 + 5$, $3x^3 - 7$, $6x^2 + 8x$ are binomials.

(iii) Trinomial

A polynomial is said to be a trinomial if it contains three terms.

For Example: $3x^3 - 8x + \frac{5}{2}$, $\sqrt{7}x^{10} + 8x^4 - 3x^2$, $5 - 7x + 8x^9$, etc, are trinomials.

There is no specific name of the polynomial which has more than 3 terms.

ILLUSTRATION 1 :

Which of the following expressions is/are polynomial(s)?

(a) $5x^2 - 3x + 9$ **(b)** $\frac{4}{3}x^7 - 5x^4 + 3x^2 - 1$ **(c)** $\frac{5}{4}x^{-3} + 2x - 1$ **(d)** $\sqrt{2}x^4 + x^{\frac{3}{4}} - 7$

SOLUTION :

(*a*) and (*b*) are polynomials.

ILLUSTRATION 2 :

Write down the degree of the following polynomials.

(a) $3x + 5$ **(b)** $3t^2 - 5t + 9t^4$ **(c)** $2 - y^2 - y^3 + 2y^8$

SOLUTION :

(a) The highest power term is $3x$ and its exponent is 1.

$\therefore$ degree of $3x + 5 = 1$

(b) The highest power term is $9t^4$ and exponent of t is 4. So, degree of the given polynomial is 4.

(c) The highest power of the variable is 8. So, the degree of the polynomial is 8.

ILLUSTRATION 3 :

Write the following polynomials in standard form:

(a) $x^6 - 3x^4 + \sqrt{2}x + \frac{5}{2}x^2 + 7x^5 + 4$ **(b)** $5x^4 - 2x + 5 + \sqrt{3}x$

SOLUTION :

The given polynomials in standard form are:

(a) $x^6 + 7x^5 - 3x^4 + \frac{5}{2}x^2 + \sqrt{2}x + 4$ (b) $5x^4 + (\sqrt{3} - 2)x + 5$

VALUE OF A POLYNOMIAL

A polynomial in any variable x is symbolically may be repersented by $p(x), f(x), \ldots$, (etc.)

The value of a polynomial $p(x)$ at $x = \alpha$ is obtained by substituting $x = \alpha$ in the given polynomial and is denoted by $p(\alpha)$.

For e.g. : Consider the polynomial $p(x) = 5x^3 - 2x^2 + 3x - 2$

If we replace x by 1 everywhere in $p(x)$, we get

$$p(1) = 5 \times (1)^3 - 2 \times (1)^2 + 3 \times (1) - 2$$
$$= 5 - 2 + 3 - 2 = 4$$

So, we say that the value of $p(x)$ at $x = 1$ is 4.

ZEROE(S) OR ROOT(S) OF A POLYNOMIAL

If value of a polynomial $p(x)$ at $x = \alpha$ is 0 i.e., $p(\alpha) = 0$, then α is called the zero of the polynomial $p(x)$.

Let $f(x) = 2x^2 - x - 1$ is a polynomial

Now, $f(1) = 2 \times (1)^2 - (1) - 1 = 0$

Hence, $x = 1$ is a zero or root of the polynomial $f(x)$.

NOTE : (a) Every real number is a zero of the zero polynomial
(b) A non-zero constant polynomial has no zero.
(c) Every linear polynomial in one variable has a unique zero.
(d) Every quadratic polynomial in one variable has two zeroes.
(e) Every cubic polynomial in one variable has three zeroes.

How to Find the Zero(es) of a Polynomial

To find the zero(es) of any polynomial (except zero polynomial and constant polynomial) put the polynomial equal to zero and solve them.

ILLUSTRATION 4 :

If $x = \frac{4}{3}$ is a root of the polynomial $f(x) = 6x^3 - 11x^2 + kx - 20$, then find the value of k.

SOLUTION :

$f(x) = 6x^3 - 11x^2 + kx - 20$

Put $f\left(\frac{4}{3}\right) = 0 \Rightarrow f\left(\frac{4}{3}\right) = 6\left(\frac{4}{3}\right)^3 - 11\left(\frac{4}{3}\right)^2 + k\left(\frac{4}{3}\right) - 20 = 0$

$$\Rightarrow 6\left(\frac{64}{27}\right) - 11\left(\frac{16}{9}\right) + \frac{4k}{3} - 20 = 0 \Rightarrow 128 - 176 + 12k - 180 = 0$$

$$\Rightarrow 12k + 128 - 356 = 0 \Rightarrow 12k = 228 \Rightarrow k = 19$$

REMAINDER THEOREM

Let $p(x)$ be any polynomial of degree greater than or equal to one and a be any real number. If $p(x)$ is divided by the linear polynomial $x - a$, then the remainder is equal to $p(a)$.

Remark :

If a polynomial $p(x)$ is divided by $(x + a)$, $(ax - b)$, $(ax + b)$, $(b - ax)$, then the remainder is the value of $p(x)$ at $x = -a, \frac{b}{a}, -\frac{b}{a}, \frac{b}{a}$

i.e., $p\left(\frac{b}{a}\right), p\left(-\frac{b}{a}\right), p\left(\frac{b}{a}\right)$ are remainders respectively.

ILLUSTRATION 5 :

Find the values of a and b so that the polynomial $x^3 + 10x^2 + ax + b$ is exactly divisible by $(x - 1)$ as well as $(x + 2)$.

SOLUTION :

Let $p(x) = x^3 + 10x^2 + ax + b$

Now, $(x - 1)$ is a factor of $p(x) \Rightarrow p(1) = 0$ and $(x + 2)$ is a factor of $p(x) \Rightarrow p(-2) = 0$

Now, $p(1) = 1^3 + 10 \times 1^2 + a \times 1 + b = 11 + a + b$ and $p(-2) = (-2)^3 + 10 \times (-2)^2 + a(-2) + b = 32 - 2a + b$

So, we must have

$11 + a + b = 0$ ... (i) and $32 - 2a + b = 0$ ... (ii)

Subtracting (ii) from (i), we get $3a - 21 = 0$ or $a = 7$

Putting $a = 7$ in (i), we get $b = -18$

$\therefore$ $a = 7$ and $b = -18$

FACTORIZATION OF A QUADRATIC POLYNOMIAL BY SPLITTING THE MIDDLE TERM

To Factorize Quadratic Polynomial: $ax^2 + bx + c$

(i) Take the product of the constant term and the coefficient of x^2 i.e., ac.

(ii) Now this product ac is to split into two factors m and n such that $m + n$ is equal to the coefficient of x i.e., b.

(iii) Then we pair one of them, say mx, with x^2 and the other nx, with c and factorize.

ILLUSTRATION 6 :

Factorize $2x^2 + 5x - 3$ by splitting the middle term.

SOLUTION :

Here, $2 \times (-3) = -6 = 6 \times (-1)$ and $6 + (-1) = 5$

$\therefore$ $2x^2 + 5x - 3 \quad = 2x^2 + 6x - x - 3$

$= 2x(x + 3) - 1(x + 3)$

$= (x + 3)(2x - 1)$

FACTOR THEOREM

Let $p(x)$ be a polynomial of degree greater than or equal to 1 and 'a' be a real number such that $p(a) = 0$, then $(x - a)$ is a factor of $p(x)$.

Conversly : If $(x - a)$ is a factor of $p(x)$, then $p(a) = 0$.

Remarks :

(i) $(x + a)$ is a factor of a polynomial $p(x)$ iff $p(-a) = 0$

(ii) $(ax - b)$ is a factor of a polynomial $p(x)$ iff $p\left(\frac{b}{a}\right) = 0$.

(iii) $(x - a)(x - b)$ is a factor of a polynomial $p(x)$ iff $p(a) = 0$ and $p(b) = 0$

ILLUSTRATION 7 :

Use the factor theorem to factorize $x^3 + x^2 - 4x - 4$ completely.

SOLUTION :

Let $f(x) = x^3 + x^2 - 4x - 4$

The constant term in $f(x)$ is -4. Its factors are $1, -1, 2, -2, 4$ and -4

Now, $f(2) = 2^3 + 2^2 - 4 \times 2 - 4 = 0$ $\therefore$ $(x - 2)$ is a factor of $f(x)$

On dividing $f(x)$ by $(x - 2)$, we get

$$\begin{array}{r|l|l} x-2 & x^3 + x^2 - 4x - 4 & x^2 + 3x + 2 \\ & x^3 - 2x^2 & \\ & -\quad + & \\ \hline & 3x^2 - 4x - 4 & \\ & 3x^2 - 6x & \\ & -\quad + & \\ \hline & 2x - 4 & \\ & 2x - 4 & \\ & -\quad + & \\ \hline & 0 & \end{array}$$

$f(x) = (x - 2)(x^2 + 3x + 2) = (x - 2)[x^2 + x + 2x + 2]$

$= (x - 2)[x(x + 1) + 2(x + 1)] = (x - 2)(x + 2)(x + 1)$

ALGEBRAIC IDENTITIES

Some important Algebraic Identities, which are used in factorization, simplification and to find the product of polynomials are given below:

(i) $(x+y)^2 = x^2 + 2xy + y^2$

(ii) $(x-y)^2 = x^2 - 2xy + y^2$

(iii) $x^2 - y^2 = (x+y)(x-y)$

(iv) $(x+a)(x+b) = x^2 + (a+b)x + ab$

(v) $(x+y+z)^2 = x^2 + y^2 + z^2 + 2xy + 2yz + 2zx$

(vi) $(x+y)^3 = x^3 + y^3 + 3xy(x+y) = x^3 + y^3 + 3x^2y + 3xy^2$

(vii) $(x-y)^3 = x^3 - y^3 - 3xy(x-y) = x^3 - y^3 - 3x^2y + 3xy^2$

(viii) $x^3 + y^3 + z^3 - 3xyz = (x+y+z)(x^2+y^2+z^2-xy-yz-zx)$

Special Case :

If $x + y + z = 0$, then $x^3 + y^3 + z^3 = 3xyz$

ILLUSTRATION 8 :

Use a suitable identity to factorise each of the following :

(a) $4x^2 + 4xy + y^2$ **(b)** $25p^2 - 36q^2$ **(c)** $x^2 - y^2 + 2x + 1$ **(d)** $4a^2 - 4b^2 + 4a + 1$

SOLUTION :

(a) Consider $4x^2 + 4xy + y^2 = (2x)^2 + 2(2x)(y) + (y)^2$

$= (2x + y)^2 = (2x+y)(2x+y)$ (Using Identity (i))

(b) Consider $25p^2 - 36q^2 = (5p)^2 - (6q)^2$

$= (5p + 6q)(5p - 6q)$ (Using Identity (iii))

(c) $x^2 - y^2 + 2x + 1 = x^2 + 2x + 1 - y^2$

$= (x+1)^2 - (y)^2 = (x+1+y)(x+1-y)$ (Using Identities (i) and (iii))

(d) $4a^2 - 4b^2 + 4a + 1 = (4a^2 + 4a + 1) - 4b^2$

$= \{(2a)^2 + 2(2a)(1) + (1)^2\} - (2b)^2$

$= (2a+1)^2 - (2b)^2 = (2a+1+2b)(2a+1-2b)$. (Using Identities (i) and (iii))

ILLUSTRATION 9 :

Simplify : $(a+b)^3 + (a-b)^3 + 6a(a^2-b^2)$

SOLUTION :

Consider $(a+b)^3 + (a-b)^3 + 6a(a^2-b^2)$

$= (a+b)^3 + (a-b)^3 + 3(2a)(a+b)(a-b)$. (Using Identity (iii))

$= (a+b)^3 + (a-b)^3 + 3(a+b)(a-b)\{(a+b)+(a-b)\}$

$= \{(a+b)+(a-b)\}^3$

$= (2a)^3 = 8a^3$ (Using Identity vi)

ILLUSTRATION 10 :

Factorise : $(a+b-c)^3 + (a-b+c)^3 - 8a^3$

SOLUTION :

$(a+b-c)^3 + (a-b+c)^3 - 8a^3 = (a+b-c)^3 + (a-b+c)^3 + (-2a)^3$

$= 3(a+b-c)(a-b+c)(-2a)$ $[\because (a+b-c)+(a-b+c)+(-2a) = 0]$

$= -6a(a+b-c)(a-b+c)$

ILLUSTRATION 11 :

Evaluate each of the following using suitable identities :

(i) $(104)^3$ **(ii)** $(999)^3$

SOLUTION :

(i) We have

$(104)^3 = (100+4)^3 = (100)^3 + (4)^3 + 3(100)(4)(100+4)$ (Using Identity (vi))

$= 1000000 + 64 + 124800 = 1124864$

(ii) We have

$(999)^3 = (1000-1)^3 = (1000)^3 - (1)^3 - 3(1000)(1)(1000-1)$ (Using Identity (vii))

$= 1000000000 - 1 - 2997000 = 997002999$

CONNECTING TOPIC

Division of a Polynomial by a Polynomial

To divide a polynomial by other polynomial, the degree of the dividend will be either equal or greater than the degree of the divisor.

Division of a Polynomial by a Non-zero, Non-constant Monomial

To divide a polynomial by a monomial, divide each term of the polynomial by the monomial

ILLUSTRATION 12 :

Divide $12x^4 - 15x^3 + 6\sqrt{3}.x$ by $3x$

SOLUTION :

$$\frac{12x^4 - 15x^3 + 6\sqrt{3}x}{3x} = \frac{12x^4}{3x} - \frac{15x^3}{3x} + \frac{6\sqrt{3}x}{3x} = 4x^3 - 5x^2 + 2\sqrt{3}$$

Division of a Polynomial by a Polynomial (Non-monomial)

Factorization Method

To divide one polynomial by other polynomial (non-monomial), factorize the polynomial to be divided so that one of the factors is equal the polynomial by which we want to divide.

ILLUSTRATION 13 :

Divide $6x^2 + x - 12$ by $2x + 3$

SOLUTION :

$$\frac{6x^2 + x - 12}{2x + 3} = \frac{6x^2 + 9x - 8x - 12}{2x + 3} = \frac{3x(2x+3) - 4(2x+3)}{2x+3} = \frac{(2x+3)(3x-4)}{2x+3} = 3x - 4$$

MISCELLANEOUS SOLVED EXAMPLES

1. Find α and β if $x + 1$ and $x + 2$ are factors of $p(x) = x^3 + 3x^2 - 2\alpha x + \beta$.

Sol. Put $x + 1 = 0$ or $x = -1$ and $x + 2 = 0$ or $x = -2$ in $p(x)$

Then, $p(-1) = (-1)^3 + 3(-1)^2 - 2\alpha(-1) + \beta = 0$

$\Rightarrow -1 + 3 + 2\alpha + \beta = 0$

$\Rightarrow \beta = -2\alpha - 2$ ... (i)

$p(-2) = (-2)^3 + 3(-2)^2 - 2\alpha(-2) + \beta = 0$

$\Rightarrow -8 + 12 + 4\alpha + \beta = 0$

$\Rightarrow \beta = -4\alpha - 4$ ... (ii)

By equalising both of the above equation

$-2\alpha - 2 = -4\alpha - 4$

$\Rightarrow 2\alpha = -2 \Rightarrow \alpha = -1$

put $\alpha = -1$ in eq. (i) $\Rightarrow \beta = -2(-1) - 2 = 2 - 2 = 0$.

Hence, $\alpha = -1, \beta = 0$

2. What must be subtracted from $x^3 - 6x^2 - 15x + 80$, so that the result is exactly divisible by $x^2 + x - 12$.

Sol. In $p(x) = x^3 - 6x^2 - 15x + 80$ we subtracted $ax + b$ so that it is exactly divisible by $x^2 + x - 12$.

$\therefore \quad s(x) = x^3 - 6x^2 - 15x + 80 - (ax + b)$

$= x^3 - 6x^2 - (15 + a)x + (80 - b)$

Dividend = Divisor × quotient + remainder

But remainder will be zero.

$\therefore$ Dividend = Divisor × quotient

$\Rightarrow s(x) = (x^2 + x - 12) \times$ quotient

$\Rightarrow s(x) = x^3 - 6x^2 - (15 + a)x + (80 - b)$

$= x(x^2 + x - 12) - 7(x^2 + x - 12)$

$= x^3 + x^2 - 7x^2 - 12x - 7x + 84$

$= x^3 - 6x^2 - 19x + 84$

Hence, $x^3 - 6x^2 - 19x + 84 = x^3 - 6x^2 - (15 + a)x + 80 - b \Rightarrow -15 - a = -19 \Rightarrow a = +4$

and $80 - b = 84 \Rightarrow b = -4$

Hence, if from $p(x)$, we subtract $4x - 4$ (= $ax + b$) then it is exactly divisible by $x^2 + x - 12$

3. Find the value of $(99)^2$.

Sol. $(99)^2 = (100 - 1)^2$

$= 100^2 - 2(100)(1) + (1)^2 = 10000 - 200 + 1 = 9801$

4. Factorize $6x^2 - 5xy - 4y^2 + x + 17y - 15$.

Sol. $6x^2 - 5xy - 4y^2 + x + 17y - 15$

$= 6x^2 + x[1 - 5y] - [4y^2 - 12y - 5y + 15]$

$= 6x^2 + x[1 - 5y] - [4y(y - 3) - 5(y - 3)]$

$= 6x^2 + x[1 - 5y] - (4y - 5)(y - 3)$

$= 6x^2 + 3(y - 3)x - 2(4y - 5)x - (4y - 5)(y - 3)$

$= 3x(2x + y - 3) - (4y - 5)(2x + y - 3)$

$= (2x + y - 3)(3x - 4y + 5)$

5. Solve : $0.645 \times 0.645 + 2 \times 0.645 \times 0.355 + 0.355 \times 0.355$

Sol. $0.645 \times 0.645 + 2 \times 0.645 \times 0.355 + 0.355 \times 0.355$

$= (0.645)^2 + 2 \times (0.645)(0.355) + (0.355)^2$

$= (0.645 + 0.355)^2 = (1)^2 = 1$

6. **Factorize : $x^2 - x\left(\frac{a^2-1}{a}\right) - 1$.**

Sol. $x^2 - x\left(\frac{a^2-1}{a}\right) - 1 = x^2 - x\left(a - \frac{1}{a}\right) - 1 = x^2 - ax + \frac{x}{a} - 1 = x(x-a) + \frac{1}{a}(x-a) = (x-a)\left(x + \frac{1}{a}\right)$

7. **Solve : $\frac{0.73 \times 0.73 - 0.27 \times 0.27}{0.73 - 0.27}$**

Sol. $\frac{0.73 \times 0.73 - 0.27 \times 0.27}{0.73 - 0.27} = \frac{(0.73)^2 - (0.27)^2}{0.73 - 0.27} = \frac{(0.73 + 0.27)(0.73 - 0.27)}{(0.73 - 0.27)} = 0.73 + 0.27 = 1$

8. **Factorize : $x^6 - 7x^3 - 8$**

Sol. $x^6 - 7x^3 - 8 = y^2 - 7y - 8$, where $x^3 = y$

$= y^2 - 8y + y - 8$

$= y(y-8) + 1(y-8)$

$= (y-8)(y+1)$

$= (x^3 - 8)(x^3 + 1)$ $\quad [\because \ y = x^3]$

$= (x^3 - 2^3)(x^3 + 1^3)$

$= (x-2)(x^2 + 2x + 4)(x+1)(x^2 - x + 1)$

9. **Using remainder theorem, find the remainder when $x^3 + x^2 - 2x + 1$ is divided by $x - 3$.**

Sol. Let $p(x) = x^3 + x^2 - 2x + 1$

By remainder theorem, we know that $p(x)$ when divided by $(x - 3)$ gives a remainder equal to $p(3)$

Now, $\quad p(3) = [3^3 + 3^2 - 2 \times 3 + 1] = (27 + 9 - 6 + 1) = 31$

Hence, the remainder is 31.

10. **Factorize $8x^3 + 27y^3 + 36x^2y + 54xy^2$**

Sol. The given expression can be written as

$(2x)^3 + (3y)^3 + 3(4x^2)(3y) + 3(2x)(9y^2)$

$= (2x)^3 + (3y)^3 + 3(2x)^2(3y) + 3(2x)(3y)^2$

$= (2x + 3y)^3 = (2x + 3y)(2x + 3y)(2x + 3y)$

11. **Factorize : $x^3 - 23x^2 + 142x - 120$**

Sol. Let $p(x) = x^3 - 23x^2 + 142x - 120$

We shall now look for all the factors of – 120.

Some of these are $\pm 1, \pm 2, \pm 3, \pm 4, \pm 5, \pm 6, \pm 8, \pm 10, \pm 12, \pm 15, \pm 20, \pm 24, \pm 30, \pm 60$

By trial, we find that $p(1) = 0$. So $x - 1$ is a factor of $p(x)$.

Now we see that $x^3 - 23x^2 + 142x - 120 = x^3 - x^2 - 22x^2 + 22x + 120x - 120$

$= x^2(x-1) - 22x(x-1) + 120(x-1)$

$= (x-1)(x^2 - 22x + 120)$ $\quad$ [Taking $(x - 1)$ common]

We could have also got this by dividing $p(x)$ by $x - 1$

Now, $x^2 - 22x + 120$ can be factorized either by splitting the middle term or by using the factor theorem. By splitting the middle term, we have :

$x^2 - 22x + 120 = x^2 - 12x - 10x + 120$

$= x(x-12) - 10(x-12)$

$= (x-12)(x-10)$

So, $x^3 - 23x^2 + 142x - 120 = (x-1)(x-10)(x-12)$

12. **Find the value of p and q, if $(x + 3)$ and $(x - 4)$ are factors of $x^3 - px^2 - qx + 24$.**

Sol. Let $f(x) = x^3 - px^2 - qx + 24$.

Since, $(x + 3)$ is a factor of $f(x)$, so by factor theorem, $f(-3) = 0$

$\therefore \quad f(-3) = (-3)^3 - p(-3)^2 - q(-3) + 24 = 0$

$\Rightarrow \quad -27 - 9p + 3q + 24 = 0$

$\Rightarrow \quad -3p + q - 1 = 0 \qquad \ldots (i)$

Similarly, if $(x-4)$ is a factor of $f(x)$, then $f(4)=0$

$\therefore\quad (4)^3 - p(4)^2 - q(4) + 24 = 0$

$\Rightarrow\quad 64 - 16p - 4q + 24 = 0$

$\Rightarrow\quad -4p - q + 22 = 0$ ... (ii)

Solving eqs. (i) and (ii) we get

$-7p + 21 = 0, \quad \therefore\ p = 3$

Substituting, $p = 3$ in eq. (i), we get $-3(3) + q - 1 = 0 \therefore q = 10 \therefore p = 3$ and $q = 10$

SOLVED EXAMPLES BASED ON CONNECTING TOPIC

13. Divide : $3x^4 + 2x^3 - 5x^2 + 3x + 1$ by $2x$

Sol.

$$2x \,\big)\, 3x^4 + 2x^3 - 5x^2 + 3x + 1 \,\big(\, (3/2)x^3 + x^2 - (5/2)x + (3/2)$$

$$\begin{array}{r} 3x^4 + 2x^3 - 5x^2 + 3x + 1 \\ 3x^4 \\ \hline 2x^3 - 5x^2 + 3x + 1 \\ 2x^3 \\ \hline -5x^2 + 3x + 1 \\ -5x^2 \\ \hline 3x + 1 \\ 3x \\ \hline 1 \\ \hline \end{array}$$

$\therefore\quad$ Quotient $= \left(\frac{3}{2}x^3 + x^2 - \frac{5}{2}x + \frac{3}{2}\right)$ and remainder $= 1$

14. Divide : $4x^2 + 7x - 15$ by $x + 3$

Sol.

$$x + 3 \,\big)\, 4x^2 + 7x - 15 \,\big(\, 4x - 5$$

$$\begin{array}{r} 4x^2 + 7x - 15 \\ 4x^2 + 12x \\ (-) \quad (-) \\ \hline -5x - 15 \\ -5x - 15 \\ \hline \times \\ \hline \end{array}$$

15. Divide $18x^8 - 15x^3 + 24x^2 + 9x$ by $3x$.

Sol. $\dfrac{18x^8 - 15x^3 + 24x^2 + 9x}{3x}$

$= 6x^7 - 5x^2 + 8x + 3$

1 EXERCISE

Fill in the Blanks :

DIRECTIONS: *Complete the following statements with an appropriate word/term to be filled in the blank space(s).*

1. A polynomial of one term is called a ....
2. A polynomial of three terms is called a ....
3. $11x^2 - 88x^3 + 14x^4$ is called a .... polynomial.
4. The degree of the polynomial $7x^3 y^{10} z^2$ is ....
5. A polynomial of degree one is called a .... polynomial
6. A polynomial of degree three is called a .... polynomial.
7. If $a + b + c = 0$, then $a^3 + b^3 + c^3 =$ ....
8. Factors of $x^6 - y^6$ is ....
9. $x - a$ is a factor of the polynomial $p(x)$, if $p(a) =$ ....
10. The remainder obtained when $80x^3 + 55x^2 + 20x + 172$ is divided by $x + 2$ is ....
11. The quotient of $8x^3 - 7x^2 + 5x$ when divided by $2x$ is ....
12. The factors of $a^3 + b^3 + c^3 - 3abc$ are ....

True / False :

DIRECTIONS: *Read the following statements and write your answer as true or false.*

1. $5x^3 - 4x^2 + 2x + 3$ is a polynomial over integers.
2. $3x^2 - 5x + 6$ is a polynomial of degree 2.
3. $7x^3 - 3x^2 + \sqrt{2}x + 5$ is a polynomial.
4. When $x^3 - 6x^2 + 9x + 7$ is divided by $(x - 1)$ remainder is 11.
5. The degree of a constant polynomial is 1.
6. Every binomial is a polynomial of degree 2.
7. Every polynomial is a binomial.
8. $\sqrt{3}x^2 + 11x + 6\sqrt{3} = (x + 3\sqrt{3})(\sqrt{3}x + 2)$
9. A polynomial may have more than one zero.
10. The number of zeroes of a polynomial is the degree of the polynomial.

Match the Columns :

DIRECTIONS: *Each question contains statements given in two columns which have to be matched. Statements (A, B, C, D) in Column-I have to be matched with statements (p, q, r, s) in Column-II.*

1. Column-II gives remainder when $x^3 + 3x^2 + 3x + 1$ is divided by expression given in Column-I.

Column- I	Column- II
(A) $x + 1$	(p) 27/8
(B) x	(q) –27/8
(C) $x - \frac{1}{2}$	(r) 1
(D) $5 + 2x$	(s) 0

2. Column- II gives value of k for polynomials given in Column- I when it is divided by $x - 1$.

Column- I	Column- II
(A) $kx^2 - 3x + k$	(p) -2
(B) $x^2 + x + k$	(q) 3/2
(C) $2x^2 + kx + \sqrt{2}$	(r) $\sqrt{2} - 1$
(D) $kx^2 - \sqrt{2}x + 1$	(s) $-(2 + \sqrt{2})$

3. Column-II gives factors for expression given in Column-I.

Column- I	Column- II
(A) $9x^2 + 6xy + y^2$	(p) $(2x + 3y - 4z)(2x + 3y - 4z)$
(B) $4x^2 + 9y^2 + 16z^2 + 12xy - 24yz - 16xz$	(q) $\left(x + \frac{y}{10}\right)\left(x - \frac{y}{10}\right)$
(C) $27x^3 + y^3 + z^3 - 9xyz$	(r) $(3x + y + z)(9x^2 + y^2 + z^2 - 3xy - yz - 3zx)$
(D) $x^2 - \frac{y^2}{100}$	(s) $(3x + y)(3x + y)$

Very Short Answer Questions :

DIRECTIONS: *Give answer in one word or one sentence.*

1. Check whether –2 and 2 are zeroes of the polynomial $x + 2$.
2. Write the following polynomial in standard form: $m^7 + 8m^5 + 4m^6 + 6m - 3m^2 - 11$
3. Factorize : $49a^2 + 70ab + 25b^2$
4. Factorize : $25x^2 + 60xy + 36y^2$
5. Factorize : $xy - 3z + xz - 3y$
6. Factorize : $axb + axc + 3aby + 3acy - 5b - 5c$
7. Find the value of 49^2
8. Factorize : $(a - 2b)^3 - a + 2b$
9. Factorize : $x^2 - y^2 - 4xz + 4z^2$

10. Factorise the following using appropriate identities : $9x^2 + 6xy + y^2$

11. Expand the following using suitable identities : $(-2x + 3y + 2z)^2$

12. Factorize $a^5b - ab^5$.

13. Use the Factor Theorem to determine whether $q(x)$ is a factor of $p(x)$: $p(x) = 2\sqrt{2}x^2 + 5x + \sqrt{2}, q(x) = x + \sqrt{2}$

Short Answer Questions :

DIRECTIONS: *Give answer in 2-3 sentences.*

1. Evaluate the following products without multiplying directly:
   (i) 103×107 (ii) 104×96

2. Factorize : $2x(a - b) + 3y(5a - 5b) + 4z(2b - 2a)$

3. Factorize: $6a^2b^2x - 48abx + 96x$

4. Factorize: $\frac{a^2}{4b^2} - \frac{1}{3} + \frac{b^2}{9a^2}$, $a \neq 0, b \neq 0$

5. Factorize: $4x^2 - 4\sqrt{3}x + 3$

6. Factorize : $3.7 \times 3.7 + 3.7 \times 2.6 + 1.3 \times 1.3$

7. Factorize : $\frac{0.564 \times 0.564 - 0.436 \times 0.436}{0.564 - 0.436}$

8. Factorize : $12(a + 1)^2 - 25(a + 1)(b + 2) + 12(b + 2)^2$

9. Find the value of $a^3 + b^3 + c^3 - 3abc$, given that $a + b + c = 10$ and $a^2 + b^2 + c^2 = 83$.

10. If $A = x^3$, $B = 4x^2 + x - 1$, $C = x + 1$, then find $(A - B)(A - C)$.

11. Factorize : $(a - b)^3 + (b - c)^3 + (c - a)^3$

12. If $x = \frac{4}{3}$ is a root of the polynomial $f(x) = 6x^3 - 11x^2 + kx - 20$ then find the value of k.

13. Check whether $7 + 3x$ is a factor of $3x^3 + 7x$.

Long Answer Questions :

DIRECTIONS: *Give answer in four to five sentences.*

1. Solve $2(x + 3)^2 + 9(x + 3) + 9$

2. Given $f(x) = x^3 + 5x^2 + 2x - 8$.
   Find (i) $f(1)$ (ii) $f(-2)$ (iii) $f(-4)$.
   Hence find all the factors of $f(x)$.

3. Show that $(3x - 2)$ is a factor of $(3x^3 + x^2 - 20x + 12)$

4. For what values of a is $2x^3 + ax^2 + 11x + a + 3$ exactly divisible by $(2x - 1)$?

5. If both $(x - 2)$ and $\left(x - \frac{1}{2}\right)$ are factors of $px^2 + 5x + r$, show that $p = r$.

6. If $f(x) = x^4 - 2x^3 + 3x^2 - ax + b$ is a polynomial such that when it is divided by $x - 1$ and $x + 1$, the remainders are respectively 5 and 19. Determine the remainder when $f(x)$ is divided by $(x-2)$

7. Find the value of $\frac{1}{27}r^3 - s^3 - s^3 + 125t^3 + 5rst$, when $s = \frac{r}{3} + 5t$.

2 EXERCISE

Text-Book Exercise :

1. Give one example each of a binomial of degree 35, and of a monomial of degree 100.

2. Classify the following as linear, quadratic and cubic polynomials:
   (i) $x^2 + x$ (ii) $x - x^3$
   (iii) $y + y^2 + 4$ (iv) $1 + x$
   (v) $3t$ (vi) r^2
   (vii) $7x^3$.

3. Verify whether the following are zeroes of the polynomial, indicated against them.
   (i) $p(x) = 3x + 1, x = -\frac{1}{3}$
   (ii) $p(x) = x^2 - 1, x = 1, -1$
   (iii) $p(x) = lx + m, x = -\frac{m}{l}$
   (iv) $p(x) = 2x + 1, x = \frac{1}{2}$

4. Find the zero of the polynomial in each of the following cases :

(i) $p(x) = 2x + 5$ (ii) $p(x) = 3x$

(iii) $p(x) = cx + d$, $c \neq 0$, c, d are real numbers.

5. Use the factor theorem to determine whether $g(x)$ is a factor of $p(x)$ in each of the following cases:

(i) $p(x) = 2x^3 + x^2 - 2x - 1$, $g(x) = x + 1$

(ii) $p(x) = x^3 - 4x^2 + x + 6$, $g(x) = x - 3$

6. Find the value of k, if $x - 1$ is a factor of $p(x)$ in each of the following cases:

(i) $p(x) = 2x^2 + kx + \sqrt{2}$ (ii) $p(x) = kx^2 - 3x + k$

7. Use suitable identities to find the following products:

(i) $(3x + 4)(3x - 5)$ (ii) $\left(y^2 + \frac{3}{2}\right)\left(y^2 - \frac{3}{2}\right)$

8. Evaluate the following products without multiplying directly :

(i) 103×107 (ii) 95×96

9. Factorise the following using appropriate identities:

(i) $9x^2 + 6xy + y^2$ (ii) $4y^2 - 4y + 1$

(iii) $x^2 - \frac{y^2}{100}$

10. Expand each of the following using suitable identities :

(i) $(x + 2y + 4z)^2$ (ii) $(3a - 7b - c)^2$

(iii) $\left[\frac{1}{4}a - \frac{1}{2}b + 1\right]^2$

11. Factorise :

(i) $4x^2 + 9y^2 + 16z^2 + 12xy - 24yz - 16xz$

(ii) $2x^2 + y^2 + 8z^2 - 2\sqrt{2}\,xy + 4\sqrt{2}\,yz - 8zx$.

12. Factorise each of the following :

(i) $8a^3 + b^3 + 12a^2b + 6ab^2$

(ii) $64a^3 - 27b^3 - 144a^2b + 108ab^2$

(iii) $27p^3 - \frac{1}{216} - \frac{9}{2}p^2 + \frac{1}{4}p$.

13. Verify that $x^3 + y^3 + z^3 - 3xyz$

$= \frac{1}{2}(x + y + z)[(x - y)^2 + (y - z)^2 + (z - x)^2]$.

14. If $x + y + z = 0$ show that $x^3 + y^3 + z^3 = 3xyz$.

15. Without actually calculating the cubes, find the value of each of the following :

(i) $(-12)^3 + (7)^3 + (5)^3$

(ii) $(28)^3 + (-15)^3 + (-13)^3$

16. Give possible expressions for the length and breadth of each of the following rectangles, in which their areas are given :

(i) Area : $25a^2 - 35a + 12$

(ii) Area : $35y^2 + 13y - 12$

17. What are the possible expressions for the dimensions of the cuboids whose volumes are given below?

(i) Volume : $3x^2 - 12x$

(ii) Volume : $12ky^2 + 8ky - 20k$

Exemplar Questions :

1. For the polynomial

$\frac{x^3 + 2x + 1}{5} - \frac{7}{2}x^2 - x^6$, write

(i) the degree of the polynomial

(ii) the coefficient of x^3

(iii) the coefficient of x^6

(iv) the constant term

2. If $p(x) = x^2 - 4x + 3$, evaluate: $p(2) - p(-1) + p\left(\frac{1}{2}\right)$

3. Find the zeroes of the polynomial:

$p(x) - (x - 2)^2 - (x - 2)^2$

4. If $x + 2a$ is a factor of $x^5 - 4a^2x^3 + 2x + 2a + 3$, find a.

5. If the polynomials $az^3 + 4z^2 + 3z - 4$ abd $z^3 - 4z + a$ leave the same remainder when divided by $z - 3$, find the value of a.

HOTS Questions :

1. Factorise : $x^3 - 23x^2 + 142x - 120$.

2. If $x + y = 12$ and $xy = 27$, find the value of $x^3 + y^3$.

3. If the polynomials $(2x^3 + ax^2 + 3x - 5)$ and $(x^3 + x^2 - 2x + a)$ leave the same remainder when divided by $(x - 2)$, find the value of a. Also, find the remainder in each case.

4. Without actual division, prove that $(2x^4 - 6x^3 + 3x^2 + 3x - 2)$ is exactly divisible by $(x^2 - 3x + 2)$.

5. Find the value of $x^3 - 8y^3 - 36xy - 216$ when $x = 2y + 6$.

6. If $z^2 + \frac{1}{z^2} = 14$, find the value of $z^3 + \frac{1}{z^3}$.

7. If the polynomials $az^3 + 4z^2 + 3z - 4$ and $z^3 - 4z + a$ leave the same remainder when divided by $z - 3$, find the value of a.

3 EXERCISE

Single Option Correct :

DIRECTIONS: *This section contains multiple choice questions. Each questions has 4 choices (a), (b), (c) and (d), out of which ONLY ONE is correct.*

1. Factors of polynomial $x^3 - 3x^2 - 10x + 24$ are
(a) $(x-2)(x+3)(x-4)$ (b) $(x+2)(x+3)(x+4)$
(c) $(x+2)(x-3)(x-4)$ (d) $(x-2)(x-3)(x-4)$

2. The values of a and b so that the polynomial $x^3 - ax^2 - 13x + b$ is divisible by $(x+1)$ and $(x-3)$ are
(a) $a = 15, b = 3$ (b) $a = 0, b = -12$
(c) $a = -3, b = 15$ (d) $a = -12, b = 0$

3. Factors of $a^2 - b + ab - a$ are
(a) $(a-b)(a+1)$ (b) $(a+b)(a-1)$
(c) $(a-b)(a-1)$ (d) $(a+b)(a+1)$

4. Expansion of $\left(x+\frac{1}{x}\right)^2$ is
(a) $x^2+2x+\frac{1}{x^2}$ (b) $x^2-2x+\frac{1}{x^2}$
(c) $x^2+2+\frac{1}{x^2}$ (d) $x^2-2+\frac{1}{x^2}$

5. If $x^2 - x - 42 = (x+k)(x+6)$, then the value of k is
(a) 6 (b) -6
(c) 7 (d) -7

6. If $\left(x-\frac{1}{x}\right)^2 = x^2+x+\frac{1}{x^2}$, then the value of x is
(a) -2 (b) 2
(c) $2x$ (d) $-2x$

7. If one factor of $5 + 8x - 4x^2$ is $(2x+1)$, then the second factor is
(a) $(5+2x)$ (b) $(2x-5)$
(c) $(5-2x)$ (d) $-(5+2x)$

8. Factors of $x^2 - 7x + 12$ are
(a) $(x-3)(x+4)$ (b) $(x-3)(x-4)$
(c) $(x+3)(x-4)$ (d) $(x+3)(x+4)$

9. If $x = 2, y = -1$, then the value of $x^2 + 4xy + 4y^2$ is
(a) 0 (b) 1
(c) -1 (d) 2

10 If one factor of $a(x+y+z) + bx + by + bz$ is $(x+y+z)$, then the second factor is
(a) $ax + ay + az$ (b) $bx + by + bz$
(c) $bx + by - bz$ (d) $a + b$

11. Factors of $36+11\left(z-\frac{y}{3}+x\right)-12\left(z-\frac{y}{3}+x\right)^2 + \left(4z-\frac{4}{3}y+4x-9\right)(5+3z-y+2x)$ are
(a) $(1-x)\left(4z-\frac{4y}{3}+4x-9\right)$
(b) $(1+x)\left(4z-\frac{4y}{3}+4x-9\right)$
(c) $(1-x)\left(4z+\frac{4y}{3}+4x-9\right)$
(d) $(1+x)\left(4z+\frac{4y}{3}+4x+9\right)$

12. The polynomials $ax^2 + 3x^2 - 3$ and $2x^3 - 5x + a$ when divided by $(x-4)$ leaves remainders R_1 and R_2 respectively, then value of a if $2R_1 - R_2 = 0$, is
(a) $-\frac{18}{127}$ (b) $\frac{18}{32}$
(c) $\frac{17}{127}$ (d) $-\frac{17}{31}$

13. If $2x^2 + xy - 3y^2 + x + ay - 10 = (2x + 3y + b)(x - y - 2)$, then the values of a and b are
(a) 11 and 5 (b) 1 and -5
(c) -1 and -5 (d) -11 and 5

More Than One Option Correct :

DIRECTIONS: *This section contains multiple choice questions. Each question has 4 choices (a), (b), (c) and (d), out of which ONE or MORE may be correct.*

1. Factors of polynomial $12x^2 - 7x + 1$ are
(a) $(3x-1)(4x-1)$ (b) $(4x+1)(3x-1)$
(c) $12\left(x-\frac{1}{3}\right)\left(x-\frac{1}{4}\right)$ (d) $12\left(x+\frac{1}{4}\right)\left(x-\frac{1}{3}\right)$

2. Which of the following polynomials has a degree 3 ?
(a) $2x^3 - 5x^2 + ax + b = 0$ (b) $6x^3 - 11x^2 + kx = 20$
(c) $3x + 8 = 4$ (d) $\sqrt[3]{x^2} = x$

3. Which of the following is/are not false?
(a) Highest power of the variable in a polynomial is the degree of polynomial.

(b) Degree of zero polynomial is always defined.

(c) A polynomial of degree one is called a linear polynomial.

(d) A polynomial of degree two is called a constant polynomial.

4. Zeroes of the polynomial $x(x + 7)$ is /are

(a) -7 (b) 7

(c) 0 (d) None of these

5. Which of the following is/are cubic polynomials?

(a) $x - x^3$ (b) $2x^2 + x^{3/2}$

(c) $x^3 - x^{1/2}$ (d) $8x^2 + \frac{5}{2}x - 6x^3$

6. Expansion of $(x - y)^3$ is

(a) $x^3 + y^3 - 3xy(x - y)$ (b) $x^3 - y^3 - 3x^2y - 3xy^2$

(c) $x^3 - y^3 - 3x^2y + 3xy^2$ (d) $x^3 - y^3 - 3xy(x - y)$

7. If $a + b + c = 0$, then $a^3 + b^3 + c^3$ is equal to

(a) $4abc = abc$ (b) $2abc$

(c) $abc + (abc)^0$ (d) $3abc$

8. Which of the following is/are a polynomial?

(a) $x^3 - 4x^2 + 5\sqrt{x} + 1$ (b) $x^3 + 5x^2 + 2$

(c) $x^{-2} + 4$ (d) x

Passage Based Questions :

DIRECTIONS: *Study the given paragraph(s) and answer the following questions.*

PASSAGE

$f(x) = 2x^3 - 9x^2 + x + 12$

1. The degree of the given polynomial is

(a) 2 (b) 3

(c) 0 (d) 1

2. Zeroes of the given polynomial is

(a) (1, 3/2) (b) (–1, –3/2)

(c) (–1, 3/2) (d) (1, 3/2)

3. If $f(x)$ is divided by $\left(x - \frac{3}{2}\right)$, then the remainder is

(a) 1 (b) $\frac{3}{2}$

(c) 0 (d) None of these

Assertion & Reason :

DIRECTIONS: *Each of these questions contains an Assertion followed by Reason. Read them carefully and answer the question on the basis of following options. You have to select the one that best describes the two statements.*

(a) If both **Assertion** and **Reason** are **correct** and Reason is the **correct explanation** of Assertion.

(b) If both **Assertion** and **Reason** are correct, but Reason **is not the correct explanation** of Assertion.

(c) If **Assertion** is **correct** but **Reason** is **incorrect**.

(d) If **Assertion** is **incorrect** but **Reason** is **correct**.

1. **Assertion :** If $f(x) = 3x^7 - 4x^6 + x + 9$ is a polynomial, then its degree is 7.

Reason : Degree of a polynomial is the highest power of the variable in it.

2. **Assertion :** If $p(x) = ax + b$, $a \neq 0$ is a linear polynomial, then $x = \frac{-b}{a}$ is the only zero of $p(x)$.

Reason : A linear polynomial has one and only one zero.

3. **Assertion :** If $f(x) = x^4 + x^3 - 2x^2 + x + 1$ is divided by $(x - 1)$, then its remainder is 2.

Reason : If $p(x)$ be a polynomial of degree greater than or equal to one, divided by the linear polynomial $x - a$, then the remainder is $p(-a)$.

4. **Assertion :** $(x + 2)$ is a factor of $x^3 + 3x^2 + 5x + 6$ and of $2x + 4$.

Reason : If $p(x)$ be a polynomial of degree greater than or equal to one, then $(x - a)$ is a factor of $p(x)$, if $p(a) = 0$

5. **Assertion :** If $(x + 1)$ is a factor of $f(x) = x^2 + ax + 2$, then $a = -3$.

Reason : If $(x - a)$ is a factor of $p(x)$, then $p(a) = 0$.

Multiple Matching Question :

DIRECTIONS : *Following question has four statements (A, B, C and D) given in Column- I and statements (p, q, r, s and t) in Column- II. Any given statement in Column- I can have correct matching with one or more statement(s) given in Column- II.*

1.

Column-I (Degree)	Column-II (Polynomial)
(A) 1	(p) $6 - y^3 + 4y^6 + y^2$
(B) 6	(q) $7x - \sqrt{3}$
(C) 3	(r) $2 + x^2$
(D) 2	(s) $x^2 + 5x^3 + 3$
	(t) $8x^2 - 4x + 6$

Integer Type Questions :

DIRECTIONS : *Answer the following questions. The answer to each of the question is a single digit integer, ranging from 0 to 9.*

1. If $x - a$ is a factor of $x^3 - 3x^2a + 2a^2x + b$, then the value of 'b' is

2. If $x^{140} + 2x^{151} + k$ is divisible by $x + 1$, then the value of 'k' is

3. One factor of $x^4 + x^2 - 20$ is $x^2 + 5$. The other factor is $x^2 - a$. Find the value of 'a'.

4. If $x + 2$ is a factor of $x^2 + mx + 14$, then m is equal to

5. If $x + a$ is a factor of $x^4 - a^2x^2 + 3x - 6a$, then the value of 'a' is

4 ADVANCE EXERCISE
BASED ON CONNECTING TOPICS

DIRECTIONS (Qs 1–4): *This section contains multiple choice questions. Each question has 4 choices (a), (b), (c) and (d) out of which only one is correct.*

1. Let R_1 and R_2 are the remainders when the polynomials $x^3 + 2x^2 - 5ax - 7$ and $x^3 + ax^2 - 12x + 6$ are divided by $x + 1$ and $x - 2$ respectively. If $2R_1 + R_2 = 6$, find the value of a.

(a) -3 (b) 2
(c) 4 (d) 5

2. Which of the following polynomial $p(x) = 2x^3 - 9x^2 + x + 12$ is a multiple of $2x - 3$?

(a) $2x - 3$ (b) $x + 3$
(c) $2x + 3$ (d) None of these

3. If $ax^3 + bx^2 + x - 6$ has $x + 2$ as a factor and leaves a remainder 4 when divided by $(x - 2)$, find the values of a and b.

(a) 0, –2 (b) 2, 3
(c) –2, 3 (d) 0, 2

4. Determine the value of a for which the polynomial $2x^4 - ax^3 + 4x^2 + 2x + 1$ is divisible by $1 - 2x$.

(a) 26 (b) 25
(c) 24 (d) 0

SOLUTIONS

Brief Explanations of Selected Questions

1 EXERCISE

FILL IN THE BLANKS :

1. monomial 2. trinomial 3. biquadratic
4. 15 5. linear 6. cubic
7. $a^3 + b^3 + c^3 = 3abc$
8. $(x - y)(x + y)(x^2 + y^2 - xy)(x^2 + y^2 + xy)$
9. 0 10. – 288
11. $4x^2 - \frac{7}{2}x + \frac{5}{2}$
12. $(a + b + c)(a^2 + b^2 + c^2 - ab - bc - ca)$

TRUE/FALSE :

1. True 2. True 3. True 4. True
5. False 6. False 7. False 8. True
9. True 10. True

MATCH THE COLUMNS :

1. (A) → (s); (B) → (r); (C) → (p); (D) → (q)
2. (A) → (q); (B) → (p); (C) → (s); (D) → (r)
3. (A) → (s); (B) → (p); (C) → (r); (D) → (q)

VERY SHORT ANSWER QUESTIONS :

1. Let $r(x) = x + 2$.
Then $r(2) = 2 + 2 = 4$, $r(-2) = -2 + 2 = 0$
Therefore, -2 is a zero of the polynomial $x + 2$, but 2 is not.
2. $m^7 + 4m^6 + 8m^5 - 3m^2 + 6m - 11$
3. $(7a + 5b)(7a + 5b)$
4. $(5x + 6y)^2$ 5. $(y + z)(x - 3)$
6. $(b + c)(ax + 3ay - 5)$
7. 2401
8. $(a - 2b)(a - 2b + 1)(a - 2b - 1)$
9. $(x + y - 2z)(x - y - 2z)$
10. $9x^2 + 6xy + y^2 = (3x)^2 + 2(3x)(y) + (y)^2$
$= (3x + y)^2 = (3x + y)(3x + y)$
11. $(-2x + 3y + 2z)^2 = (-2x)^2 + (3y)^2 + (2z)^2$
$+ 2(-2x)(3y) + 2(3y)(2z) + 2(2z)(-2x)$
$= 4x^2 + 9y^2 + 4z^2 - 12xy + 12yz - 8zx.$
12. $ab(a^2 + b^2)(a + b)(a - b)$
13. The zero of $q(x)$ is $-\sqrt{2}$
Now, $p(-\sqrt{2}) = 2\sqrt{2}(-\sqrt{2})^2 + 5(-\sqrt{2}) + \sqrt{2}$
$= 4\sqrt{2} - 5\sqrt{2} + \sqrt{2} = 0$
∴ By factor thm, $q(x)$ is a factor of $p(x)$.

SHORT ANSWER QUESTIONS :

1. (i) 11021 (ii) 9981
2. $(a - b)(2x + 15y + 8z)$
3. $6x(ab - 4)^2$
4. $\left(\frac{a}{2b} - \frac{b}{3a}\right)^2$ 5. $(2x - \sqrt{3})^2$
6. 25 7. 1
8. $(4a - 3b - 2)(3a - 4b - 5)$
9. 745
10. $x^6 - 4x^5 - 2x^4 + 4x^3 + 5x^2 - 1$
11. $3(a - b)(b - c)(c - a)$
12. $f(x) = 6x^3 - 11x^2 + kx - 20$

$$f\left(\frac{4}{3}\right) = 6\left(\frac{4}{3}\right)^3 - 11\left(\frac{4}{3}\right)^2 + k\left(\frac{4}{3}\right) - 20 = 0$$

$$\Rightarrow \quad -6.\frac{64}{9.3} - 11.\frac{16}{9} + \frac{4k}{3} - 20 = 0$$

$\Rightarrow$ $128 - 176 + 12k - 180 = 0$
$\Rightarrow$ $12k + 128 - 356 = 0$
$\Rightarrow$ $12k = 228 \Rightarrow k = 19$

13. $7 + 3x$ will be a factor of $3x^3 + 7x$ only if $7 + 3x$ divides $3x^3 + 7x$ leaving no remainder.
Let $p(x) = 3x^3 + 7x$
put $7 + 3x = 0 \Rightarrow x = -\frac{7}{3}$

$$\therefore \quad \text{Remainder} = p\left(-\frac{7}{3}\right) = 3\left(-\frac{7}{3}\right)^3 + 7\left(-\frac{7}{3}\right)$$

$$= -\frac{343}{9} - \frac{49}{3} = -\frac{490}{9} \neq 0$$

∴ $7 + 3x$ is not a factor of $3x^3 + 7x$.

LONG ANSWER QUESTIONS :

1. $2(x + 3)^2 + 9(x + 3) + 9$
$= 2a^2 + 9a + 9$ (where $(x + 3) = a$)
$= 2a^2 + 6a + 3a + 9 = (2a^2 + 6a) + (3a + 9)$
$= 2a(a + 3) + 3(a + 3) = (a + 3)(2a + 3)$
$= (x + 3 + 3)\{2(x + 3) + 3\}$, (substituting the value of a)
$= (x + 6)(2x + 9)$
2. (i) $f(1) = (1)^3 + 5(1)^2 + 2(1) - 8 = 1 + 5 + 2 - 8 = 0$
(ii) $f(-2) = (-2)^3 + 5(-2)^2 + 2(-2) - 8$
$= -8 + 20 - 4 - 8 = 0$

(iii) $f(-4) = (-4)^3 + 5(-4)^2 + 2(-4) - 8$

$= -64 + 80 - 8 - 8 = 0$

Since, $f(1) = 0$ $\therefore$ $(x - 1)$ is a factor of $f(x)$

$f(-2) = 0$ $\therefore$ $(x + 2)$ is a factor of $f(x)$

$f(-4) = 0$ $\therefore$ $(x + 4)$ is a factor of $f(x)$

Hence all the factors of $f(x)$ are

$(x - 1)$, $(x + 2)$ and $(x + 4)$

3. Let $f(x) = 3x^3 + x^2 - 20x + 12$.

Now, $3x - 2 = 0 \Rightarrow x = \frac{2}{3}$.

$(3x - 2)$ is a factor of $f(x) = 3x^3 + x^2 - 20x + 12$

If and only if $f\left(\frac{2}{3}\right) = 0$

Now, $f\left(\frac{2}{3}\right) = \left[3\times\left(\frac{2}{3}\right)^3 + \left(\frac{2}{3}\right)^2 - 20\times\left(\frac{2}{3}\right) + 12\right]$

$= \left(\frac{8}{9} + \frac{4}{9} - \frac{40}{3} + 12\right) = 0$

Hence, $(3x - 2)$ is a factor of the given polynomial $f(x)$.

4. Let $p(x) = 2x^3 + ax^2 + 11x + a + 3$ be the given polynomial. If $p(x)$ is exactly divisible by $2x - 1$, then $(2x - 1)$ is a factor of $p(x)$.

$\therefore$ $p\left(\frac{1}{2}\right) = 0$ $\quad [\because 2x - 1 = 0 \Rightarrow x = \frac{1}{2}]$

$\Rightarrow 2\times\left(\frac{1}{2}\right)^3 + a\times\left(\frac{1}{2}\right)^2 + 11\times\frac{1}{2} + a + 3 = 0$

$\Rightarrow \frac{1}{4} + \frac{a}{4} + \frac{11}{2} + a + 3 = 0$

$\Rightarrow \frac{1 + a + 22 + 4n + 12}{4} = 0 \Rightarrow \frac{5a + 35}{4} = 0$

$\Rightarrow 5a + 35 = 0 \Rightarrow a = -7$

Thus the given polynomial is divisible by $2x - 1$, if $a = -7$.

5. Let $f(x) = px^2 + 5x + r$

As $(x - 2)$ is a factor of $f(x)$, so $f(2) = 0$

$p \times 2^2 + 5 \times 2 + r = 0$

$\Rightarrow 4p + 10 + r = 0$ ....(i)

Also, $\left(x - \frac{1}{2}\right)$ is a factor of $f(x)$, so $f\left(\frac{1}{2}\right) = 0$

$p\left(\frac{1}{2}\right)^2 + 5.\frac{1}{2} + r = 0 \Rightarrow \frac{p}{4} + \frac{5}{2} + r = 0$

$p + 10 + 4r = 0$ ...(ii)

From equations (i) and (ii), we have

$4p + 10 + r = p + 10 + 4r$

$4p - p + 10 = 4r + 10 - r \Rightarrow 3p = 3r$

$\Rightarrow p = r$

6. When $f(x)$ is divided by $x - 1$ and $x + 1$ the remainders are 5 and 19 respectively.

$\therefore$ $f(1) = 5$ and $f(-1) = 19$

$(1)^4 - 2\times(1)^3 + 3\times(1)^2 - a(1) + b = 5$ and

$\Rightarrow (-1)^4 - 2\times(-1)^3 + 3\times(-1)^2 - a\times(-1) + b = 19$

$\Rightarrow 1 - 2 + 3 - a + b = 5$ and $1 + 2 + 3 + a + b = 19$

$\Rightarrow 2 - a + b = 5$ and $6 + a + b = 19$

$\Rightarrow -a + b = 3$ and $a + b = 13$

Adding these two equations, we get

$(-a + b) + (a + b) = 3 + 13 \Rightarrow 2b = 16 \Rightarrow b = 8$

Putting $b = 8$ in $-a + b = 3$, we get

$-a + 8 = 3 \Rightarrow -a = -5 \Rightarrow a = 5$

Putting the values of a and b in

$f(x) = x^4 - 2x^3 + 3x^2 - 5x + 8$

The remainder when $f(x)$ is divided by $(x - 2)$ is equal to $f(2)$.

So, remainder $= f(2) = 2^4 - 2\times2^3 + 3\times2^2 - 5\times2 + 8$

$= 16 - 16 + 12 - 10 + 8 = 10$

7. $\frac{1}{27}r^3 - s^3 + 125t^3 + 5rst$

$= \frac{1}{3^3}r^3 + (-s)^3 + 5^3t^3 + 5rst$

$= \left(\frac{r}{3}\right)^3 + (-s)^3 + (5t)^3 - 3\left(\frac{r}{3}\right)(-s)(5t)$

$= \left(\frac{r}{3} + (-s) + 5t\right)$

$\left[\left(\frac{r}{3}\right)^2 + (-s)^2 + (5t)^2 - \frac{r}{3}.(-s) - (-s)(5t) - \frac{r}{3}(5t)\right]$

$= \left(\frac{r}{3} - s + 5t\right)\left(\frac{r^2}{9} + s^2 + 25t^2 + \frac{rs}{3} + 5st - \frac{5rt}{3}\right)$

Now, $s = \frac{r}{3} + 5t$ (Given)

$\Rightarrow \frac{r}{3} - s + 5t = 0$

$\therefore \frac{1}{27}r^3 - s^3 + 125t^3 + 5rst$

$= 0 \times \left(\frac{r^2}{9} + s^2 + 25t^2 + \frac{rs}{3} + 5st - \frac{5rt}{3}\right) = 0$

2 EXERCISE

TEXT-BOOK EXERCISE :

1. Binomial of degree 35 is $2x^{35} + 4$. One example of a monomial of degree 100 is y^{100}.

2. (i) quadratic (ii) cubic

(iii) quadratic (iv) linear

(v) linear (vi) quadratic

(vii) cubic

3. (i) Given $p(x) = 3x + 1,\ x = -\frac{1}{3}$

Now, $p\left(-\frac{1}{3}\right) = 3\left(-\frac{1}{3}\right) + 1 = -1 + 1 = 0$

$\therefore\ -\frac{1}{3}$ is a zero of $p(x)$.

(ii) Given $p(x) = x^2 - 1,\ x = 1, -1$

Now, $p(1) = (1)^2 - 1 = 1 - 1 = 0$

$p(-1) = (-1)^2 - 1 = 1 - 1 = 0$

$\therefore$ 1, – 1 are zeros of $p(x)$.

(iii) Given $p(x) = lx + m,\ x = -\frac{m}{l}$

$p\left(-\frac{m}{l}\right) = l\left(-\frac{m}{l}\right) + m = -m + m = 0$

$\therefore\ -\frac{m}{l}$ is a zero of $p(x)$.

(iv) Given $p(x) = 2x + 1,\ x = \frac{1}{2}$

$p\left(\frac{1}{2}\right) = 2\left(\frac{1}{2}\right) + 1 = 1 + 1 = 2 \neq 0$

$\therefore\ \frac{1}{2}$ is not a zero of $p(x)$

4. (i) $p(x) = 2x + 5$

$p(x) = 0$

$\Rightarrow\ 2x + 5 = 0 \Rightarrow 2x = -5 \Rightarrow x = -\frac{5}{2}$

$\therefore\ -\frac{5}{2}$ is a zero of the polynomial $p(x)$.

(ii) $p(x) = 3x$

$p(x) = 0$

$\Rightarrow\ 3x = 0 \Rightarrow x = 0$

$\therefore$ 0 is a zero of the polynomial $p(x)$.

(iii) $p(x) = cx + d,\ c \neq 0,\ c,\ d$ are real numbers.

$p(x) = 0$

$\Rightarrow\ cx + d = 0 \Rightarrow cx = -d \Rightarrow x = -\frac{d}{c}$

$\therefore\ -\frac{d}{c}$ is a zero of the polynomial $p(x)$.

5. (i) Given $p(x) = 2x^3 + x^2 - 2x - 1$, and $g(x) = x + 1$,

put $g(x) = 0 \Rightarrow x = -1$

$\therefore$ Zero of $g(x)$ is – 1.

Now,

$p(-1) = 2(-1)^3 + (-1)^2 - 2(-1) - 1$

$= -2 + 1 + 2 - 1 = 0$

$\therefore$ By factor theorem, $g(x)$ is a factor of $p(x)$.

(ii) Given $p(x) = x^3 - 4x^2 + x + 6$, and $g(x) = x - 3$

By putting $g(x) = 0$, we get $x = 3$

$\therefore$ Zero of $g(x)$ is 3.,

Now, $p(3) = (3)^3 - 4(3)^2 + 3 + 6$

$= 27 - 36 + 3 + 6 = 0$

$\therefore$ By factor theorem, $g(x)$ is a factor of $p(x)$.

6. (i) Given, $p(x) = 2x^2 + kx + \sqrt{2}$

since, $x - 1$ is a factor of $p(x)$,

$\therefore\ p(1) = 0,$ [By Factor Theorem]

$\Rightarrow\ 2(1)^2 + k(1) + \sqrt{2} = 0$

$\Rightarrow\ 2 + k + \sqrt{2} = 0 \Rightarrow k = -(2 + \sqrt{2}).$

(ii) Given $p(x) = kx^2 - 3x + k$ since, $x - 1$ is a factor of $p(x)$,

$\therefore$ By Factor Theorem $p(1) = 0$

$\Rightarrow\ k(1)^2 - 3(1) + k = 0 \Rightarrow 2k - 3 = 0$

$\Rightarrow\ k = \frac{3}{2}.$

7. (i) Consider $(3x + 4)(3x - 5)$

$= (3x)^2 + \{4 + (-5)\}(3x) + (4)(-5)$

$= 9x^2 - 3x - 20.$

(ii) Consider $\left(y^2 + \frac{3}{2}\right)\left(y^2 - \frac{3}{2}\right) = y^2 - \left(\frac{3}{2}\right)^2$

$= y^4 - \frac{9}{4}.$

8. (i) Consider 103×107

$= (100 + 3) \times (100 + 7)$

$= (100)^2 + (3 + 7)\,100 + (3)(7)$

$= 10000 + 1000 + 21 = 11021.$

Aliter: $103 \times 107 = (105 - 2) \times (105 + 2)$

$= (105)^2 - (2)^2$

$= (100 + 5)^2 - 4$

$= (100)^2 + 2(100)(5) + (5)^2 - 4$

$= 10000 + 1000 + 25 - 4 = 11021.$

(ii) Consider $95 \times 96 = (90 + 5) \times (90 + 6)$

$= (90)^2 + (5 + 6)(90) + (5)(6)$

$= 8100 + 990 + 30 = 9120.$

Aliter: $95 \times 96 = (100 - 5) \times (100 - 4)$

$= \{100 + (-5)\}\{100 + (-4)\}$

$= (100)^2 + \{(-5) + (-4)\}(100) + (-5)(-4)$

$= 10000 - 900 + 20 = 9120.$

9. (i) Consider $9x^2 + 6xy + y^2$

$= (3x)^2 + 2(3x)(y) + (y)^2$

$= (3x + y)^2 = (3x + y)(3x + y)$

(ii) Consider $4y^2 - 4y + 1$

$= (2y)^2 - 2(2y)(1) + (1)^2$

$= (2y - 1)^2$

$= (2y - 1)(2y - 1)$

(iii) Consider $x^2 - \frac{y^2}{100}$

$= (x)^2 - \left(\frac{y}{10}\right)^2 = \left(x + \frac{y}{10}\right)\left(x - \frac{y}{10}\right).$

10. (i) Consider $(x + 2y + 4z)^2 = (x)^2 + (2y)^2 + (4z)^2 + 2(x)(2y) + 2(2y)(4z) + 2(4z)(x)$

$= x^2 + 4y^2 + 16z^2 + 4xy + 16yz + 8zx$

(ii) Consider $(3a - 7b - c)^2$

$= \{3a + (-7b) + (-c)\}^2$

$= (3a)^2 + (-7b)^2 + (-c)^2 + 2(3a)(-7b) + 2(-7b)(-c) + 2(-c)(3a)$

$= 9a^2 + 49b^2 + c^2 - 42ab + 14bc - 6ca$

(iii) Consider $\left[\frac{1}{4}a-\frac{1}{2}b+1\right]^2$

$=\left[\frac{1}{4}a+\left(-\frac{1}{2}b\right)+1\right]^2$

$=\left(\frac{1}{4}a\right)^2+\left(-\frac{1}{2}b\right)^2+(1)^2+2$

$=\left(\frac{1}{4}a\right)\left(-\frac{1}{2}b\right)+2\left(\frac{1}{4}a\right)\left(-\frac{1}{2}b\right)$

$+2\left(-\frac{1}{2}b\right)(1)+2(1)\left(\frac{1}{4}a\right)$

$=\frac{1}{16}a^2+\frac{1}{4}b^2+1-\frac{1}{4}ab-b+\frac{1}{2}a.$

11. (i) Consider $4x^2+9y^2+16z^2+12xy-24yz-16xz$

$=(2x)^2+(3y)^2+(-4z)^2+2(2x)(3y)$

$+2(3y)(-4z)+2(-4z)(2x)$

$=\{2x+3y+(-4z)\}^2=(2x+3y-4z)^2$

$=(2x+3y-4z)(2x+3y-4z)$

(ii) Given $2x^2+y^2+8z^2-2\sqrt{2}\,xy+4\sqrt{2}\,yz-8zx$

$=\left(-\sqrt{2}x\right)2+y3+\left(2\sqrt{2}z\right)2+2\left(-\sqrt{2}x\right)y+2y\left(2\sqrt{2}z\right)$

$+2(2\sqrt{2}z)(-\sqrt{2}x)$

$=(-\sqrt{2}x+y+2\sqrt{2}z)^2$

$=(-\sqrt{2}x+y+2\sqrt{2}z)\ (-\sqrt{2}x+y+2\sqrt{2}z)$

12. (i) Consider $8a^3+b^3+12a^2b+6ab^2$

$=(2a)^3+(b)^3+3\ (2a)(b)(2a+b)$

$=(2a+b)^3$

$=(2a+b)(2a+b)(2a+b)$

(ii) Consider $64a^3-27b^3-144a^2b+108ab^2$

$=(4a)^3-(3b)^3-3(4a)(3b)(4a-3b)$

$=(4a-3b)^3=(4a-3b)(4a-3b)(4a-3b)$

(iii) Consider $27p^3-\frac{1}{216}-\frac{9}{2}p^2+\frac{1}{4}p.$

$=(3p)^3-\left(\frac{1}{6}\right)^3-3(3p)\left(\frac{1}{6}\right)\left(3p-\frac{1}{6}\right)$

$=\left(3p-\frac{1}{6}\right)^3$

$=\left(3p-\frac{1}{6}\right)\left(3p-\frac{1}{6}\right)\left(3p-\frac{1}{6}\right)$

13. L.H.S. $=x^3+y^3+z^3-3xyz$

$=(x+y+z)(x^2+y^2+z^2-xy-yz-zx)$

$=\frac{1}{2}(x+y+z)\{2(x^2+y^2+z^2-xy-yz-zx)\}$

$=\frac{1}{2}(x+y+z)(2x^2+2y^2+2z^2-2xy-2yz-2zx)$

$=\frac{1}{2}(x+y+z)\{(x^2-2xy+y^2)$

$+(y^2-2yz+z^2+(z^2-2zx+x^2)\}$

$=\frac{1}{2}(x+y+z)[(x-y)^2+(y-z)^2+(z-x)^2]$

14. We know that $x^3+y^3+z^3-3xyz$

$=(x+y+z)(x^2+y^2+z^2-xy-yz-zx)$

$=(0)(x^2+y^2+z^2-xy-yz-zx)$ $(\because x+y+z=0)$

$=0$

15. (i) Consider

$(-12)^3+(7)^3+(5)^3=3(-12)(7)(5)=-1260$

$(\because (-12)+(7)+(5)=0)$

(ii) Consider $(28)^3+(-15)^3+(-13)^3$

$=3(28)(-15)(-13)=16380$

$(\because (28)+(-15)+(-13)=0)$

16. (i) $25a^2-35a+12=25a^2-20a-15a+12$

$=5a(5a-4)-3(5a-4)$

$=(5a-4)(5a-3)$

$\therefore$ The one possible expression for the length and breadth of the rectangle is $5a-3$ and $5a-4$

(ii) $35y^2+13y-12-35y^2+28y-15y-12$

$=7y(5y+4)-3(5y+4)$

$=(5y+4)(7y-3)$

$\therefore$ The one possible expression for the length and breadth of the rectangle is $7y-3$ and $5y+4$.

17. (i) $3x^2-12x=3x(x-4)$

$\therefore$ The one possible expression for the dimensions of the cuboid is 3, x and $x-4$.

(ii) $12ky^2+8ky-20k=4k(3y^2+2y-5)$

$=4k(3y^2+5y-3y-5)$

$=4k\{y(3y+5)-1(3y+5)\}$

$=4k(3y+5)(y-1)$

$\therefore$ The one possible expression for the dimensions of the cuboid is $4k$, $3y+5$ and $y-1$.

EXEMPLAR QUESTIONS:

1. (i) Degree is 6

(ii) Coefficient of x^3 is $\frac{1}{5}$

(iii) Coefficient of x^6 is -1

(iv) the constant term is $\frac{1}{5}$

2. $p(x)=x^2-4x+3$

$p(2)=(2)^2-4(2)+3$

$=4-8+3=-1$

$p(-1)=(-1)^2-4(-1)+3=1+4+3=8$

$p\left(\frac{1}{2}\right)=\left(\frac{1}{2}\right)^2-4\left(\frac{1}{2}\right)+3$

$=\frac{1}{4}-2+3=\frac{5}{4}$

$\therefore$ $p(2)-p(-1)+p\left(\frac{1}{2}\right)=-1-8+\frac{5}{4}$

$=-9+\frac{5}{4}=-\frac{31}{4}$

3. $p(x)=(x-2)^2-(x+2)^2$

$=x^2+4-4x-(x^2+4+4x)$

$=x^2+4-4x-x^2-4-4x$

$p(x)=-8x$

$p(x)=0$

$\therefore$ $-8x=0\Rightarrow x=0$

$x=0$ is the zero of $p(x)$

4. $p(x)=x^5-4a^2x^3+2x+2a+3$

$r(x)=x+2a$ is a zero of $p(x)$

$\therefore$ $p(-2a)=0$

$\Rightarrow \quad p(-2a) = (-2a)^5 - 4(-2a)^3 \times a^2 + 2(-2a) + 2a + 3$
$= -32a^5 + 32a^5 - 4a + 2a + 3$
$p(-20) = -2a + 3 = 0$

$\Rightarrow \quad -2a + 3 = 0 \Rightarrow a = \frac{3}{2}$

5. Consider,
$p(z) = az^3 + 4z^2 + 3z - 4$
$q(z) = z^3 - 4z + a$ and $r(z) = z - 3$
$z = 3$ is the root of both p(z) and q(z)
$p(3) = a(3)^3 + 4(3)^2 + 3(3) - 4$
$p(3) = 27a + 36 + 9 - 4$
$p(3) = 27a + 41$ and $q(3) = (3)^3 - 4(3) + a$
$= 27 - 12 + a$
$q(3) = 15 + a$
$\therefore \quad 27a + 41 = 15 + a$
$27a - a = 15 - 41$
$26a = -26 \Rightarrow a = -1$

HOTS QUESTIONS:

1. Let $r(x) = x^3 - 23x^2 + 142x - 120$
Some of the factors of – 120 are ±1, ±2, ±3, ±4, ±5, ±6, ±8, ±10, ±12, ±15, ±20, ±24, ±30, ±60.

By trial, we find that $r(1) = 0$. So $x - 1$ is a factor of $r(x)$.
Now, $x^3 - 23x^2 + 142x - 120$
$= x^3 - x^2 - 22x^2 + 22x + 120x - 120$
$= x^2(x-1) - 22x(x-1) + 120(x-1) = (x-1)(x^2 - 22x + 120)$
[Taking $(x - 1)$ common]

We could have also got this by dividing $r(x)$ by $x - 1$.
Now, $x^2 - 22x + 120$ can be factorised either by splitting the middle term or by using the Factor theorem. By splitting the middle term, we have :
$x^2 - 22x + 120 = x^2 - 12x - 10x + 120$
$= x(x - 12) - 10(x - 12)$
$= (x - 12)(x - 10)$
So, $x^3 - 23x^2 - 142x - 120 = (x - 1)(x - 10)(x - 12)$.

2. $x^3 + y^3 = (x + y)(x^2 - xy + y^2)$
$= (x + y)[(x + y)^2 - 3xy] = 12[12^2 - 3 \times 27]$
$= 12 \times 63 = 756$

3. Let $f(x) = 2x^3 + ax^2 + 3x - 5$ and $g(x) = x^3 + x^2 - 2x + a$.
When $f(x)$ is divided by $(x - 2)$, remainder $= f(2)$.
When $g(x)$ is divided by $(x - 2)$, remainder $= g(2)$.
Now, $f(2) = (2 \times 2^3 + a \times 2^2 + 3 \times 2 - 5) = (17 + 4a)$.
And, $g(2) = (2^3 + 2^2 - 2 \times 2 + a) = (8 + a)$.
Since, both the polynomials leave the same remainder when divided by $(x - 2)$
$\therefore \quad 17 + 4a = 8 + a \Rightarrow 3a = -9 \Rightarrow a = -3$.
Hence, $a = -3$.
Remainder in each case = (8 – 3) = 5

4. Let $f(x) = 2x^4 - 6x^3 + 3x^2 + 3x - 2$
Let $g(x) = (x^2 - 3x + 2) = x^2 - 2x - x + 2$.
$= x(x - 2) - 1(x - 2) = (x - 2)(x - 1)$
Now, $f(x)$ will be exactly divisible by $g(x)$ if it is exactly divisible by $(x - 2)$ as well as $(x - 1)$.
For this, we must have $f(2) = 0$ and $f(1) = 0$
Now, $f(2) = (2 \times 2^4 - 6 \times 2^3 + 3 \times 2^2 + 3 \times 2 - 2)$
$= (32 - 48 + 12 + 6 - 2) = 0$
And, $f(1) = (2 \times 1^4 - 6 \times 1^3 + 3 \times 1^2 + 3 \times 1 - 2)$
$= (2 - 6 + 3 + 3 - 2) = 0$
$\therefore f(x)$ is exactly divisible by $(x - 2)$ as well as $(x - 1)$.
So, $f(x)$ is exactly divisible by $(x - 2)(x - 1)$.
Hence, $f(x)$ is exactly divisible by $(x^2 - 3x + 2)$.

5. $x^3 - 8y^3 - 216 - 36xy = x^3 + (-2y)^3 + (-6)^3 - 3x(-2y)(-6)$
$= (x - 2y - 6)(x^2 + 4y^2 + 36 + 2xy - 12y + 6x)$
$= 0 \times (x^2 + 4y^2 + 36 + 2xy - 12y + 6x)$
$[\because x = 2y + 6 \Rightarrow x - 2y - 6 = 0]$
$= 0$

6. We have,
$$\left(z+\frac{1}{z}\right)^2 = z^2+\frac{1}{z^2}+2z\frac{1}{z}$$
$$\Rightarrow \left(z+\frac{1}{z}\right)^2 = z^2+\frac{1}{z^2}+2 \quad \Rightarrow \left(z+\frac{1}{z}\right)^2 = 14+2 = 16$$
$$\Rightarrow \left(z+\frac{1}{z}\right)^2 = 4^2 \quad \Rightarrow \quad + - =$$
$$\Rightarrow \left(z+\frac{1}{z}\right)^2 = 4^2$$
$$\Rightarrow z^3+\frac{1}{z^3}+3\times z\times\frac{1}{z}\left(z+\frac{1}{z}\right) = 64$$
$$\Rightarrow z^3+\frac{1}{z^3}+3\times 4 = 64 \quad \Rightarrow z^3+\frac{1}{z^3} = 64-12$$
$$\Rightarrow z^3+\frac{1}{z^3} = 52$$

7. Let $p(z) = az^3 + 4z^2 + 3z - 4$ and $q(z) = z^3 - 4z + a$
When $p(z)$ is divided by $z - 3$ the remainder is given by,
$p(3) = a \times 3^3 + 4 \times 3^2 + 3 \times 3 - 4 = 27a + 36 + 9 - 4$
$p(3) = 27a + 41$ ...(i)
When $q(z)$ is divided by $z - 3$ the remainder is given by,
$q(3) = 3^3 - 4 \times 3 + a = 27 - 12 + a$
$q(3) = 15 + a$ (ii)
According to question $p(3) = q(3)$
$\Rightarrow \quad 27a + 41 = 15 + a \quad \Rightarrow 27a - a = -41 + 15$
$\Rightarrow \quad 26a = -26$
$\Rightarrow \quad a = \frac{-26}{26} \Rightarrow a = -1$

3 EXERCISE

SINGLE OPTION CORRECT :

1. (a)	**2.** (b)	**3.** (b)	**4.** (c)
5. (d)	**6.** (a)	**7.** (c)	**8.** (b)
9. (a)	**10.** (d)	**11.** (a)	**12.** (b)
13. (d)			

MORE THAN ONE OPTION CORRECT :

1. (a, c) 2. (a, b, d) 3. (a, c) 4. (a, c)
5. (a, d) 6. (c, d) 7. (a, d) 8. (b, d)

PASSAGE BASED QUESTIONS :

1. (b) 2. (c) 3. (c)

ASSERTION & REASON :

1. (a) 2. (a) 3. (c) 4. (a)
5. (d)

MULTIPLE MATCHING QUESTIONS :

1. (A) → (q); (B) → (p); (C) → (s); (D) → (r), (t)

INTEGER TYPE QUESTIONS :

1. **Ans : 0**
Since $x - a$ is a factor
$\therefore \quad (a)^3 - 3(a)^2 . a + 2a^2(a) + b = 0$
$\Rightarrow \quad a^3 - 3a^3 + 2a^3 + b = 0 \Rightarrow b = 0$

2. **Ans : 1**
Put $x = -1$ in the given expression, we get
$(-1)^{140} + 2(-1)^{151} + k = 0$
$\Rightarrow \quad 1 - 2 + k = 0 \Rightarrow k = 1$

3. **Ans : 4**
Consider $x^4 + x^2 - 20 = 0$
$\Rightarrow \quad (x^2)^2 + x^2 - 20 = 0$ ....(i)
Put $x^2 = t$ in the eqn (i),
$t^2 + t - 20 = 0 \Rightarrow t^2 + 5t - 4t - 20 = 0$
$\Rightarrow \quad t(t + 5) - 4(t + 5) = 0$
$\Rightarrow \quad (t - 4)(t + 5) = 0$
$\Rightarrow \quad (x^2 - 4)(x^2 + 5) = 0$
Thus, other factor is $x^2 - 4$. Hence, $a = 4$

4. **Ans : 9**
Since $x + 2$ is a factor of $x^2 + mx + 14$
therefore put $x = -2$ in given quadratic equation, we get
$(-2)^2 + m(-2) + 14 = 0 \Rightarrow -2m = -18 \Rightarrow m = 9$

5. **Ans : 0**
Since $x + a$ is a factor of given expression
$\therefore$ put $x = -a$ in the given polynomial, we get
$(-a)^4 - a^2(-a)^2 + 3(-a) - 6a = 0$
$\Rightarrow \quad a^4 - a^4 - 3a - 6a = 0$
$\Rightarrow \quad -9a = 0 \Rightarrow a = 0$

4 ADVANCED EXERCISE
BASED ON CONNECTING TOPICS

1. **(b)** Let $p(x) = x^3 + 2x^2 - 5ax - 7$ and
$q(x) = x^3 + ax^2 - 12x + 6$ be the given polynomials.
Now,
R_1 = Remainder when $p(x)$ is divided by $x + 1$
$\Rightarrow \quad R_1 = p(-1)$
$\Rightarrow \quad R_1 = (-1)^3 + 2(-1)^2 - 5a \times (-1) - 7$
$\Rightarrow \quad R_1 = -1 + 2 + 5a - 7$
$\Rightarrow \quad R_1 = 5a - 6$
And, R_2 = Remainder when $q(x)$ is divided by $x - 2$
$\Rightarrow \quad R_2 = q(2)$
$\Rightarrow \quad R_2 = (2)^3 + a \times 2^2 - 12 \times 2 + 6$
$\Rightarrow \quad R_2 = 8 + 4a - 24 + 6$
$\Rightarrow \quad R_2 = 4a - 10$
Substituting the values of R_1 and R_2 in $2R_1 + R_2 = 6$, we get
$2(5a - 6) + (4a - 10) = 6$
$\Rightarrow \quad 10a - 12 + 4a - 10 = 6$
$\Rightarrow \quad 14a = 28 \Rightarrow a = 2$

2. **(a)** The polynomial $p(x)$ will be a multiple of $2x - 3$ if $(2x - 3)$ divides $p(x)$ completely.
Now, $2x - 3 = 0 \Rightarrow x = \frac{3}{2}$
Also, $p\left(\frac{3}{2}\right) = 2\left(\frac{3}{2}\right)^3 - 9\left(\frac{3}{2}\right)^2 + \frac{3}{2} + 12$
$= 2 \times \frac{27}{8} - 9 \times \frac{9}{4} + \frac{3}{2} + 12$
$= \frac{54}{8} - \frac{81}{4} + \frac{3}{2} + 12$
$= \frac{54 - 162 + 12 + 96}{8} = \frac{162 - 162}{8} = 0$
As $(2x - 3)$ divides $p(x)$ completely, therefore $p(x)$ is a multiple of $(2x - 3)$.

3. **(d)** Let $p(x) = ax^3 + bx^2 + x - 6$ be the given polynomial.
Now $(x + 2)$ is a factor of $p(x)$.
$\Rightarrow \quad p(-2) = 0 \quad [\because x + 2 = 0 \Rightarrow x = -2]$
$\Rightarrow \quad a(-2)^3 + b(-2)^2 + (-2) - 6 = 0$
$\Rightarrow \quad -8a + 4b - 2 - 6 = 0$
$\Rightarrow \quad -2a + b = 2$ ...(i)
It is given that $p(x)$ leaves the remainder 4 when it is divided by $(x - 2)$.
$\therefore \quad p(2) = 4 \quad [x - 2 = 0 \Rightarrow x = 2]$
$\Rightarrow \quad a(2)^3 + b(2)^2 + 2 - 6 = 4$
$\Rightarrow \quad 8a + 4b = 8 \Rightarrow 2a + b = 2$ ...(ii)
Adding (i) and (ii), we get
$2b = 4 \Rightarrow b = 2$
Putting $b = 2$ in (i), we get
$-2a + 2 = 2 \Rightarrow a = 0$
Hence, $a = 0$ and $b = 2$

4. **(b)** Let $p(x) = 2x^4 - ax^3 + 4x^2 + 2x + 1$. If the polynomial $p(x)$ is divisible by $(1 - 2x)$, then $(1 - 2x)$ is a factor of $p(x)$.
$\therefore \quad p\left(\frac{1}{2}\right) = 0$
$\Rightarrow 2\left(\frac{1}{2}\right)^4 - a\left(\frac{1}{2}\right)^3 + 4\left(\frac{1}{2}\right)^2 + 2 \times \frac{1}{2} + 1 = 0$
$\Rightarrow \quad 2\left(\frac{1}{16}\right) - a\left(\frac{1}{8}\right) + 4\left(\frac{1}{4}\right) + \frac{2}{2} + 1 = 0$
$\Rightarrow \quad \frac{1}{8} - \frac{a}{8} + 1 + 1 + 1 = 0 \quad \Rightarrow \frac{25}{8} = \frac{a}{8} \quad \Rightarrow a = 25$

Chapter 3

CO-ORDINATE GEOMETRY

INTRODUCTION

Co-ordinate geometry is the branch of mathematics which deals with the unification of algebra. You have already studied the number line and know how to locate the position of a number on the number line. In this chapter you will learn how to locate the position of a point or any thing in a plane which will be further used to draw various type of graph.

NUMBER LINE

On the number line, distances from a fixed point are marked at equal distances taken positively in one direction and negatively in other direction. The point from which the distances are marked is called the origin denoted by O.

TO LOCATE THE POSITION OF A POINT IN A PLANE

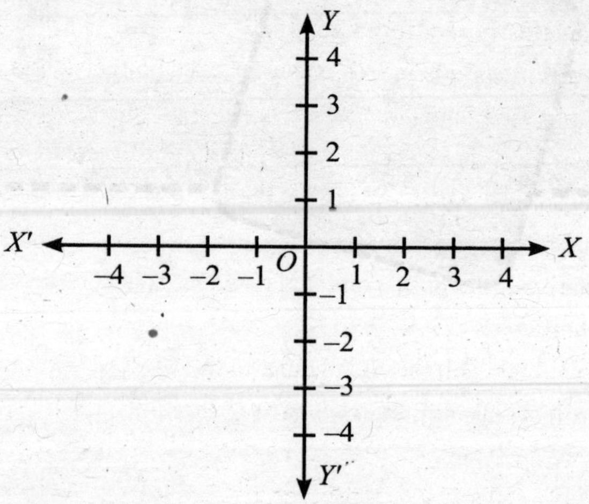

To locate a point on a plane we require two such number lines, both perpendicular to each other and meeting each other at origin. One number line is kept horizontal marked XX' and other perpendicular marked YY'.

Numbers are written on both of them just as written on number line. XX' is called X-axis and YY' is called Y-axis.

From the figure, it is clear that positive numbers lies on OX and OY. OX and OY are called positive direction of X-axis and Y-axis respectively. Similarly OX' and OY' are called negative direction of X-axis and Y-axis respectively because negative numbers lies on OX' and OY'.

QUADRANTS

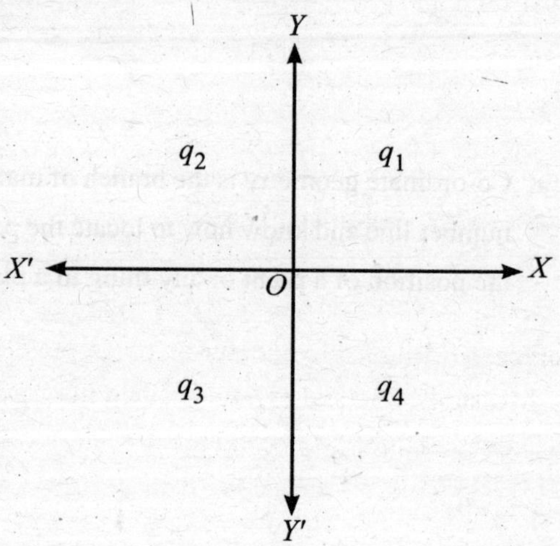

Here we see that the two axis divide the plane into four parts, these parts are called quadrants denoted by q_1, q_2, q_3 and q_4 as shown in the figure.

CARTESIAN PLANE

The entire plane consists of the two axis and four quadrants. We call this plane as XY-plane or Cartesian plane or co-ordinate plane. The two axes (plural of axis) are called co-ordinate axes.

CO-ORDINATES OF A POINT

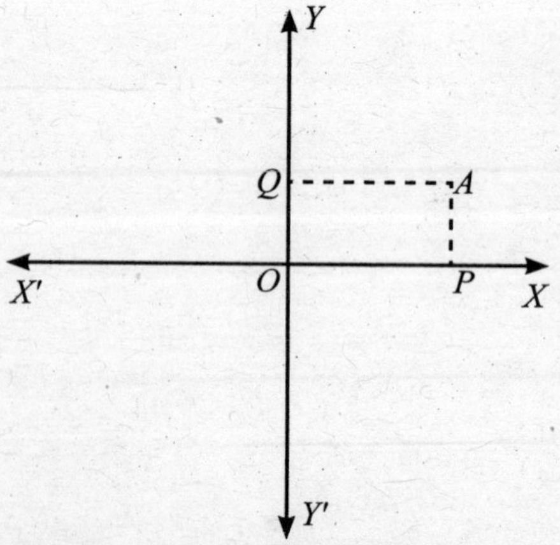

Let us take a point A in XY-plane as shown in figure and draw two perpendiculars AP and AQ on X and Y-axis respectively.

Distance $AQ = OP$, is called x-co-ordinate or abscissa of point A and distance $AP = OQ$, is called y-co-ordinate or ordinate of point P.

Actually in XOY plane, x-co-ordinate of a point is the distance of the point from Y-axis and y-co-ordinate of the point is the distance of the point from x-axis.

The abscissa and ordinate of a point taken together is known as co-ordinate of a point. Thus, if $OP = x$ and $OQ = y$, then (x, y) is co ordinates of point A. Now, we know about the co-ordinates of a point.

> **NOTE :** (i) In the co-ordinate of a point, first entry is always x-co-ordinate and second entry is always y-co-ordinate. Hence $(x, y) \neq (y, x)$.
>
> (ii) The order of x and y in (x, y) are important. So (x, y) is an ordered pair.

SIGN OF A POINT

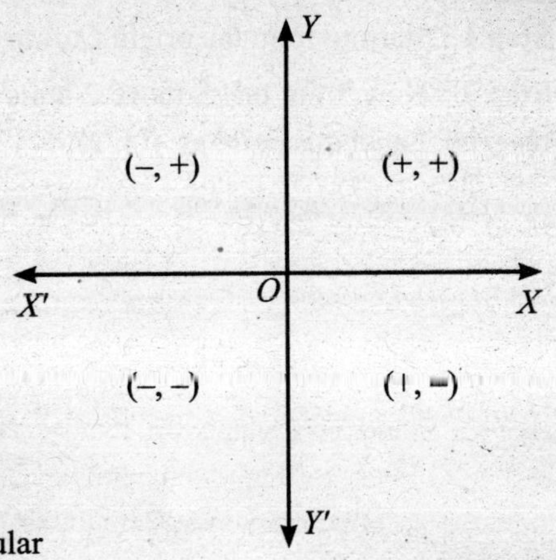

The figure shows the sign of the co-ordinates of a point in different quadrants.
We can clearly see from figure that

(a) All the points in first quadrant have both abscissa and ordinate positive.

(b) In second quadrant abscissa is negative and ordinate is positive.

(c) In third quadrant both abscissa and ordinate are negative.

(d) In fourth quadrant abscissa is positive and ordinate is negative.

All the points which lie on x-axis have zero-ordinate as their distance from x-axis is zero.
Similarly all the points on y-axis have zero abscissa as their distance from y-axis is zero.

In other words :

Let (x, y) is a point in the plane and Q_1, Q_2, Q_3, and Q_4 are the four quadrants of rectangular co ordinate system, then we have four results

1. If $x > 0$ and $y > 0$, then $(x, y) \in Q_1$
2. If $x < 0$ and $y > 0$, then $(x, y) \in Q_2$
3. If $x < 0$ and $y < 0$, then $(x, y) \in Q_3$
4. If $x > 0$ and $y < 0$, then $(x, y) \in Q_4$

CO-ORDINATES OF ORIGIN

Origin is the point of inter-section of x-axis and y-axis. Now the distance of origin from any of the axes is zero, so origin has zero abscissa and zero ordinate. Therefore the co-ordinates of origin is (0, 0).

PLOTING OF A POINT WHOSE CO-ORDINATES ARE KNOWN

A point can be plotted by measuring its proper distances from the axes. Thus any point (h, k) can be plotted as follows:

(i) Measure OM equal to h units along the x-axis.

(ii) Now measure PM perpendicular to OM at M and equal to k units.

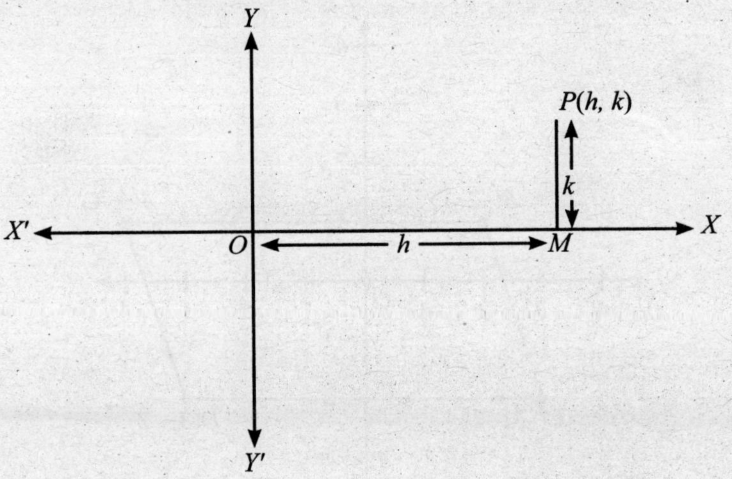

ILLUSTRATION : 1

Plot the point $A(4, 2)$ on a graph paper.

SOLUTION :

On a graph paper, draw the co-ordinate axes XOX' and YOY' intersecting at origin O. With proper scale, mark the numbers on the two co-ordinate axes. For plotting any point, two steps are to be adopted.

Step 1 : Starting from the origin *O*, move 4 units along the positive direction of *X*-axis i.e. to the right of the origin *O*.

Step 2 : Now, from there, move 2 units up (i.e., parallel and towards the positive direction of *y*-axis) and place a dot at the point reached. Label this point as *A*(4, 2)

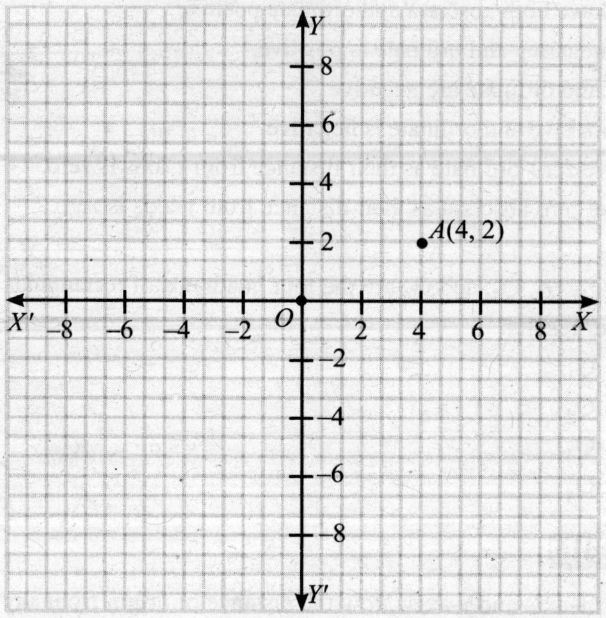

ILLUSTRATION : 2

Plot the points *A*(4, 1), *B*(−2, 1), *C*(−3, −2) and *D*(3, −2). Name the figure *ABCD*. Find its area.

SOLUTION :

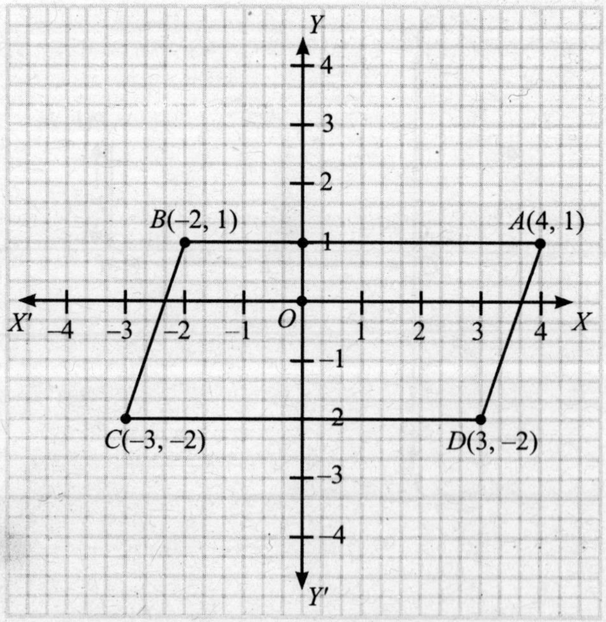

Points *A*, *B*, *C*, *D* are marked in the above figure. It is clear from the diagram that it is a parallelogram.

Area = base × height = 6 units × 3 units = 18 square units

ILLUSTRATION : 3

Using the adjoining diagram, write down the co-ordinates of the points *A, B, C, D* and *E*.

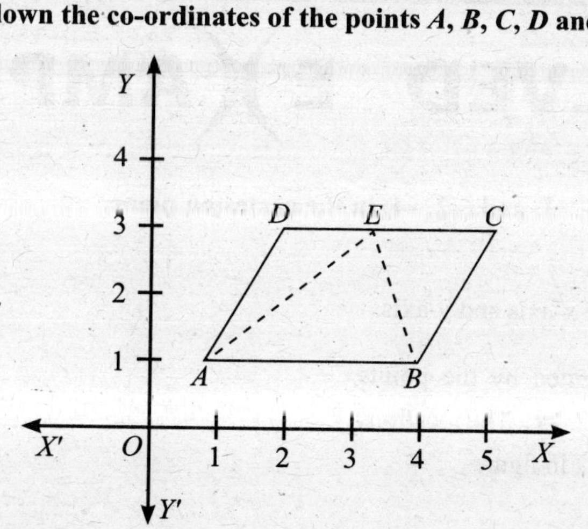

(i) Name the figure *ABCD* and find its area.

(ii) Name the figure *ABE* and find its area.

(iii) Is area of the figure *ABCD* twice the area of the figure *ABE* ?

What conclusion can you derive from the above result ?

SOLUTION :

Clearly from the diagram, we have

$A(1, 1), B(4, 1), C(5, 3), D(2, 3), E(3, 3)$.

(i) *ABCD* is a parallelogram, since $AB = DC = 3$ units, and *AB* is parallel to *DC*.

Area = base × height = $3 \times 2 = 6$ sq. units

(ii) *ABE* is a triangle, since, it is a three-sided figure.

Area = $\frac{1}{2}$ × base × height = $\frac{1}{2} \times 3 \times 2 = 3$ sq. units

(iii) Yes, Area of parallelogram *ABCD* = 2 (Area of triangle *ABE*)

Conclusion : The area of parallelogram is twice the area of a triangle on the same base and between the same parallels.

MISCELLANEOUS SOLVED EXAMPLES

1. Locate the points (5, 2), (0, 4), (5, –3) and (–2, –4) in the cartesian plane.

Sol. Taking 1 cm = 1 unit, we draw the x-axis and y-axis.

The given points can be represented by the points A(5, 2), B(0, 4), C(5, –3) and D(–2, –4). The locations of the points are shown by the dots in figure

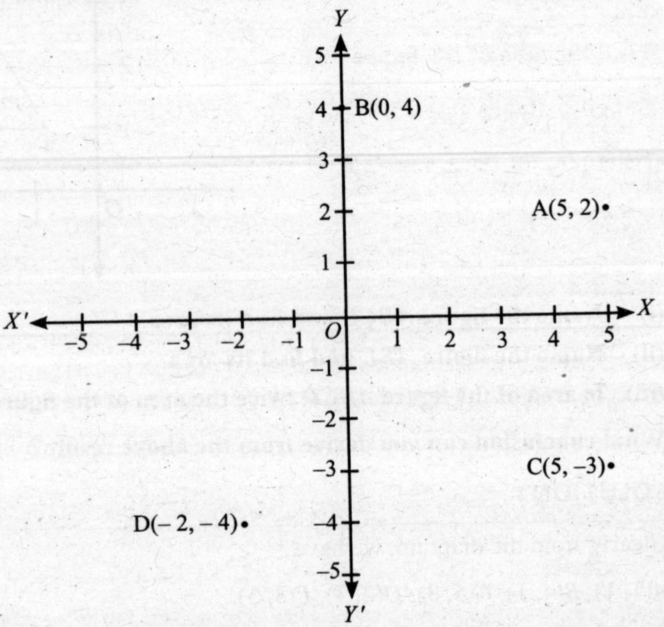

2. Plot the following ordered pair of numbers (x, y) as points in the Cartesian plane. Use the scale 1 cm = 1 unit on the axes.

x	–2	0	1	2	–3	+2
y	5	3.5	3	2	–4	–2

Sol.

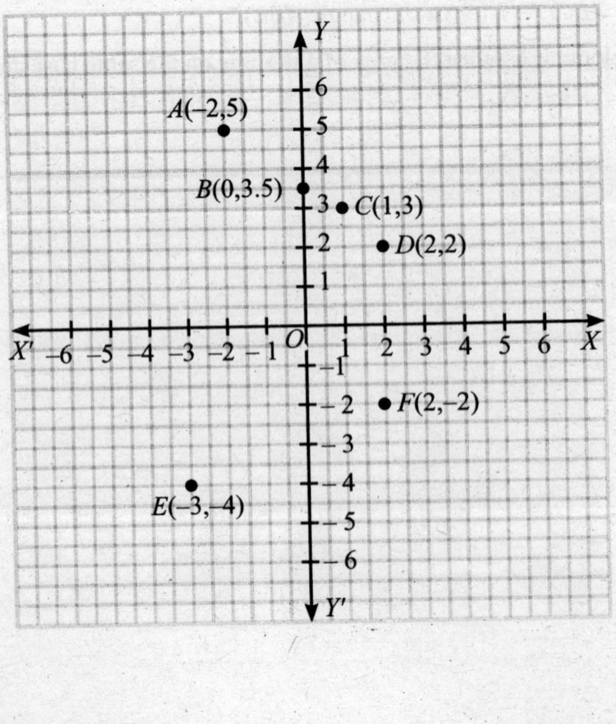

3. Write the co-ordinates of a point

(i) Above *x*-axis and lying on *y*-axis at a distance of 3 units.

(ii) Below *x*-axis and on *y*-axis at a distance of 8 units.

(iii) Right of origin and on *x*-axis at a distance of 2 units.

(iv) Left of *y*-axis and on *x*-axis at a distance of 4 units.

Sol. (i) The co-ordinates of the point are (0, 3) (ii) The co-ordinates of the point are (0, –8)

(iii) (2, 0) (iv) (–4, 0)

4. Find the area of the figure formed by joining the points (5, 0), (0, 0), (0, 6).

Sol. Let given points are $A(5, 0)$, $B(0, 0)$, and $C(0, 6)$.

After plotting the points A, B, C, we get (figure)

ΔABC is a right-triangle in which $\angle ABC = 90°$, $AB = 5$ units

and $BC = 6$ units.

$\therefore$ Area of right $\Delta\, ABC = \frac{1}{2}$ base × height $= \frac{1}{2} \times 5 \times 6$

$\therefore$ ar $(\Delta\, ABC) = 15$ sq. units.

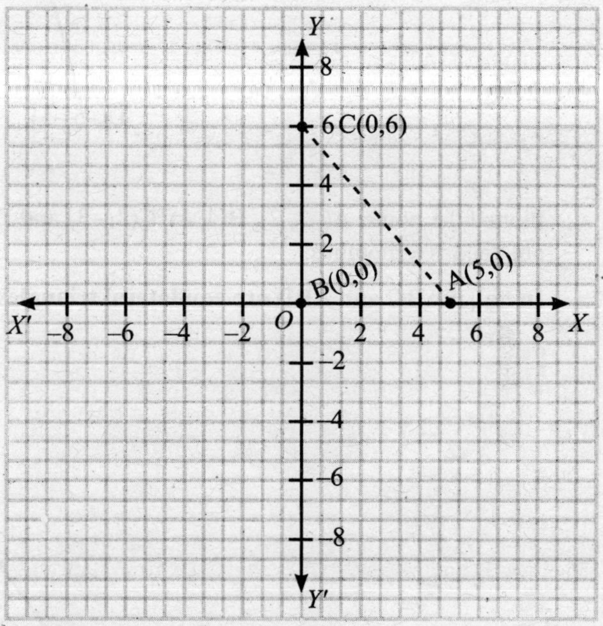

5. Plot the points (2, 0), (2, 3), (0, 6), (–2, 3) and (–2, 0) and join them in order. Find the type of figure thus formed

Sol. Let the given points are $A(2, 0)$, $B(2, 3)$, $C(0, 6)$, $D(–2, 3)$ and $E(–2, 0)$. After plotting and joining, we get the figure. After plotting A, B, C, D and E and joining, we get a 'Pentagon.'

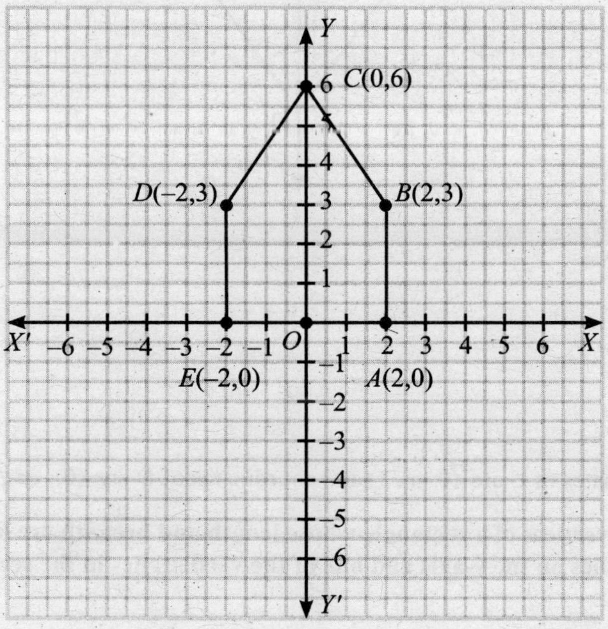

6. Show that the points (–3, 2), (–5, –5), (2, –3) and (4, 4) are vertices of a rhombus.

Sol.

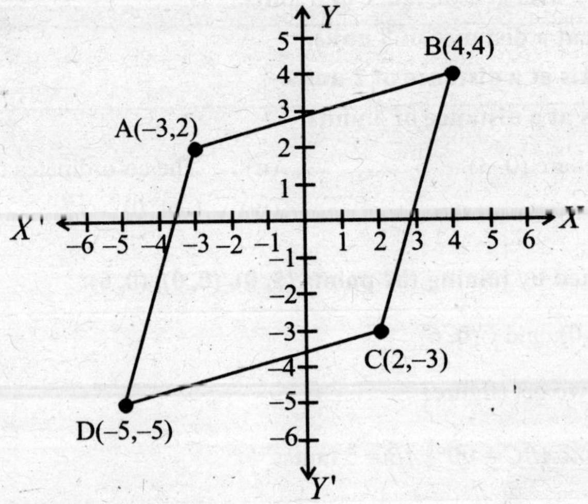

Plotted the points A(–3, 2), B(4, 4), C(2, –3) and D(–5, –5), and joined the lines AB, BC, CD and AD. The figure ABCD so obtained is a rhombus.

7. In fig., if ABC and ABD are equilateral triangles, then find the coordinates of C and D.

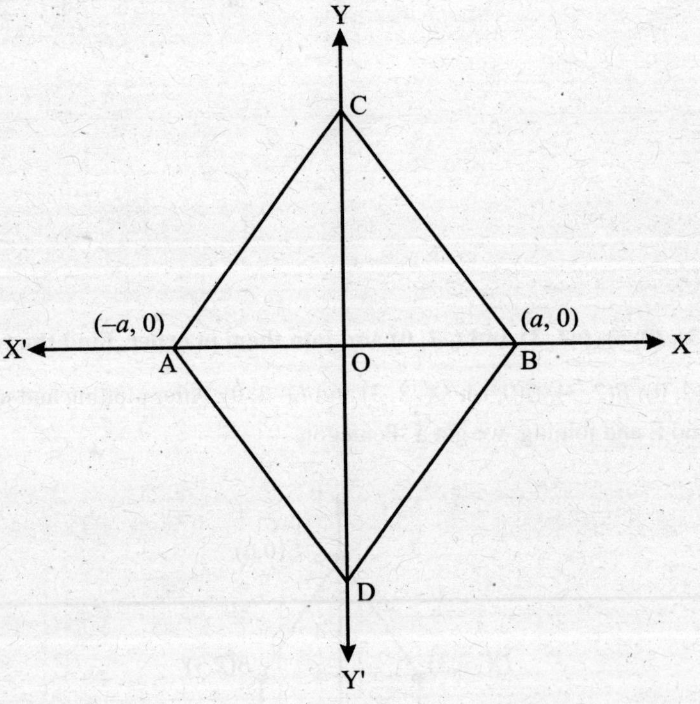

Sol. Here, $AC = 2a$ and $AO = a$

$$OC^2 = AC^2 - AO^2$$
$$= 4a^2 - a^2$$
$$= 3a^2$$

$\Rightarrow$ $OC = a\sqrt{3}$

Therefore, coordinates of C are $(0, a\sqrt{3})$ and coordinates of D are $(0, -a\sqrt{3})$.

8. Write the coordinates of the vertices of a rectangle whose length and breadth are 6 and 3 units respectively, one vertex at the origin, the longer side lies on the y-axis and one of the vertices lies in the second quadrant.

Sol. Given one vertex of the rectangle is at origin (0,0), and one vertex lies in the second quadrant. As longer side lies on the y-axis and is 6 units long. Thus, one coordinate would be (0, 6).

As shorter side lies on the x-axis and is 3 units long. Thus, one coordinate would be (–3, 0).

On plotting the points O(0,0), A(0,6), C(–3,0) and B(–3,6) on the graph and joining these points we get rectangle ABCO.

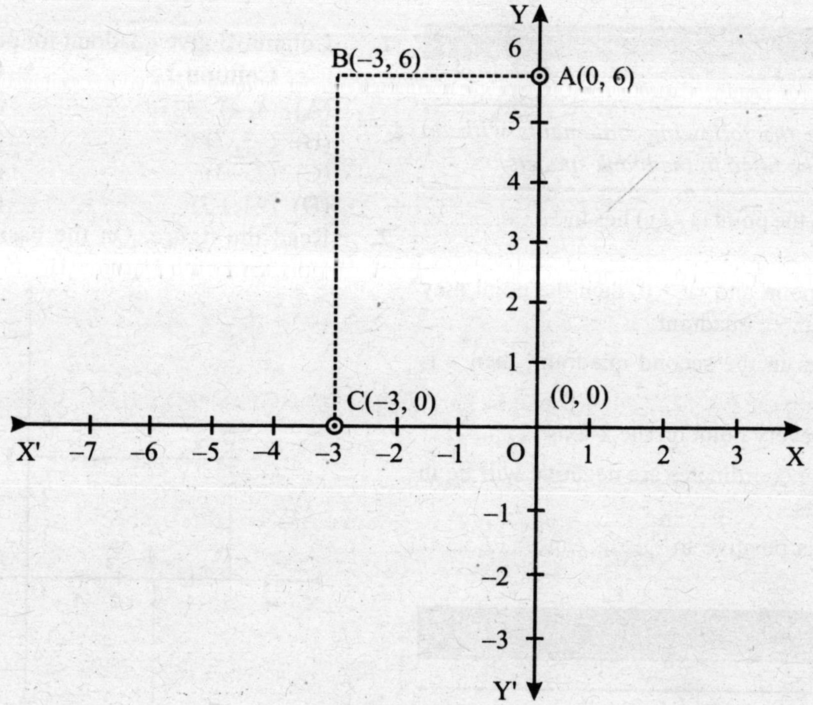

1 EXERCISE

Fill in the Blanks :

DIRECTIONS: *Complete the following statements with an appropriate word / term to be filled in the blank space(s).*

1. If $x > 0$ and $y < 0$, then the point $(x, -y)$ lies in .... quadrant.
2. If (x, y) represents a point and $xy > 0$, then the point may lie in .... or .... quadrant.
3. If the point (x, y) lies in the second quadrant, then x is .... and y is ....
4. The y-co-ordinate of every point on the x-axis is ....
5. A point both of whose coordinates are negative will lie in .... quadrants.
6. Abscissa of a point is positive in .... and .... quadrants.

True / False :

DIRECTIONS: *Read the following statements and write your answer as true or false.*

1. The ordinate of a point is its x-co-ordinate.
2. The point (a, b) lies on y-axis if $b = 0$.
3. The origin lies in the first quadrant.
4. If the ordinate of a point is equal to its abscissa, then the point lies either in the first quadrant or in the second quadrant.
5. The y-axis is the vertical number line.
6. Every point is located in one of the four quadrant.
7. The point $(-2, 0)$ lies on the y-axis.
8. The point $(0, -4)$ lies on the y-axis.
9. The point $(-1, 2)$ lies below the x-axis.
10. The point $(3, -2)$ lies below the x-axis.
11. The point $(-1, -1)$ lies on the x-axis.
12. The point $(4, -5)$ lies in the third quadrant.

Match the Columns :

DIRECTIONS: *Each question contains statements given in two columns which have to be matched. Statements (A, B, C, D) in Column-I have to be matched with statements (p, q, r, s...) in Column-II.*

1. Column-II give quadrant for points given in Column-I.

Column-I	Column-II
(A) (4, 4)	(p) I quadrant
(B) (–3, 7)	(q) II quadrant
(C) (2, –3)	(r) III quadrant
(D) (–1, –3)	(s) IV quadrant

2. Read the figure. On the basis of this figure match the Column-I with Column-II.

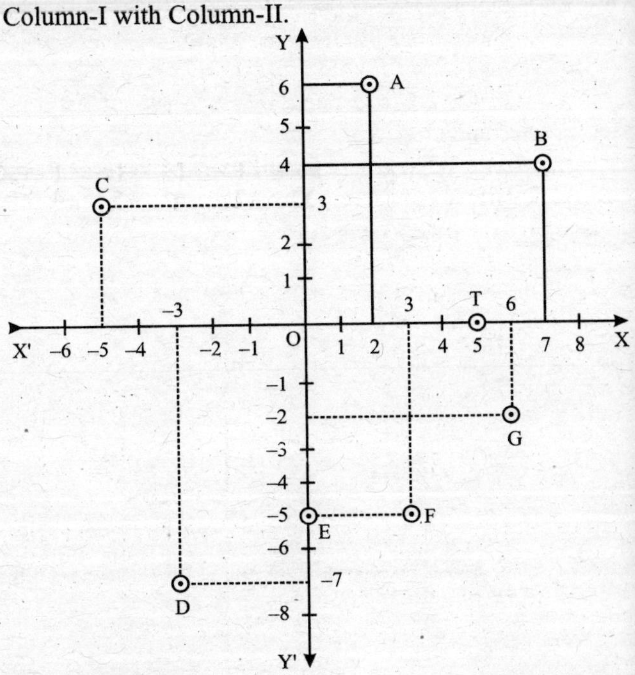

Column-I	Column-II
(A) Co-ordinates of point C is	(p) –5
(B) The abscissa of point E is	(q) (0, 0)
(C) The ordinate of the point F is	(r) 6
(D) Co-ordinates of point O is	(s) 7
(E) The perpendicular distance of the point A from the x-axis is	(t) 0
(F) The perpendicular distance of the point B from the y-axis is	(u) (–5, 3)

Very Short Answer Questions :

DIRECTIONS: *Give answer in one word or one sentence.*

1. What are the coordinates of the origin?
2. In which quadrant do the point $(-2, -5)$ lies?
3. If $x > 0$ and $y < 0$, then $(x, -y)$ lies in which quadrant?
4. Find the coordinate of the point whose abscissa is 5 and which lies on x-axis.
5. If a point lies on both x and y axes, then write the name and coordinate of that point.

6. Write the ordinate and abscissa of the point whose coordinates are (4, –3).
7. Do the points (–5, 0) and (0, –4) lie in quadrant or not?
8. On the graph paper sketch the parallelogram whose vertices are P(0, –3), Q(5, –3), R(8, 1) and S(3, 1).

Short Answer Questions :

DIRECTIONS: *Give answer in 2-3 sentences.*

1. Find the distance of the point (3, 4) from y-axis.
2. A point lies on the *x*-axis at a distance of 7 units from the *y*-axis. What are its co-ordinates? What will be the coordinates if it lies on *y*-axis at a distance of –7 units from *x*-axis?
3. In fig. AB is a line parallel to the y-axis at a distance of 2 units.
   (i) What are the coordinates of the points P, R and Q?
   (ii) What is the difference between the abscissa of the point A and B?

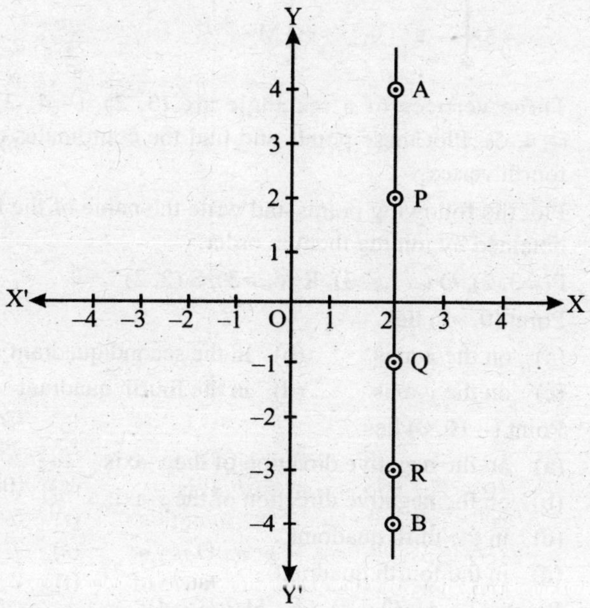

4. Write the coordinates of the vertices of a rectangle whose length and breadth are 7 and 4 units respectively, one vertex at the origin, the longer side lies on the x-axis and one of the vertices lies in the third quadrant.

Long Answer Questions :

DIRECTIONS: *Give answer in four to five sentences.*

1. Plot the following points on a graph paper.
   (a) (2, 4) (b) (–5, 3) (c) (–1, –3)
   (d) (2, –1) (e) (2, 0) (f) (–3, 0)
   (g) (0, 4) (h) (0, 2)
2. Plot the points A(2, 0), B(2, 2), C(0, 2) and draw the line segments OA, AB, BC and CO. Which figure do you obtain?
3. Plot the points A(4, 4) and B(–4, 4) and join the lines OA, OB and BA. Which figure do you obtain?
4. In the figure OAB is an equilateral triangle. Find the co-ordinate of vertex .

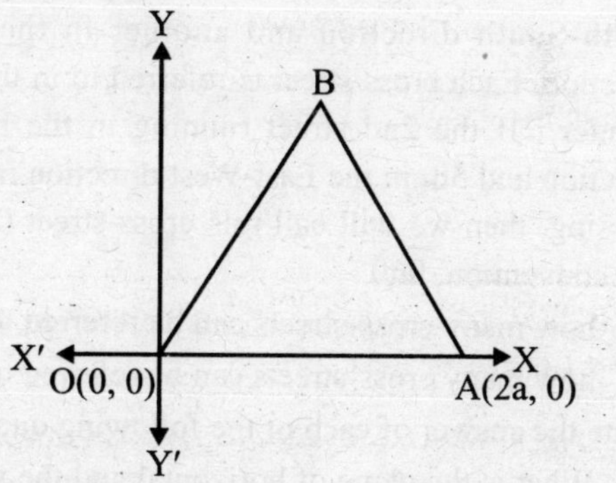

2 EXERCISE

Text-Book Exercise :

1. How will you describe the position of a table lamp on your study table to another person?
2. (Street Plan) : A city has two main roads which cross each other at the centre of the city. These two roads are along the North-South direction and East-West direction. All the other streets of the city run parallel to these roads and are 200m apart. There are about 5 streets in each direction. Using 1 cm = 200m, draw a model of the city on your notebook, represent the roads/streets by single lines.
   There are many cross-streets in your model. A particular cross-street is made by two streets, one running in the North-South direction and another in the East-West direction. Each cross street is referred to in the following manner : If the 2nd street running in the North-South direction and 5th in the East-West direction meet at some crossing, then we will call this cross-street (2, 5). Using this convention, find :
   (i) how many cross-streets can be referred to as (4, 3)
   (ii) how many cross-streets can be referred to as (3, 4)
3. Write the answer of each of the following questions:
   (i) What is the name of horizontal and the vertical lines drawn to determine the position of any point in the Cartesian plane?
   (ii) What is the name of each part of the plane formed by these two lines?
   (iii) Write the name of the point where these two lines intersect.
4. In which quadrant or on which axis do each of the points (– 2, 4), (3, – 1), (– 1, 0) (1, 2) and (– 3, – 5) lie? Verify your answer by locating them on the Cartesian Plane.
5. Plot the points (x, y) given in the following table on the plane, choosing suitable units of distance on the axes.

x	–2	–1	0	1	3
y	8	7	–1.25	3	–1

Exemplar Questions :

1. In which quadrant or on which axis each of the following points lie?
   (– 3, 5), (4, – 1), (2, 0), (2, 2), (– 3, – 6)
2. In fig., LM is a line parallel to the y-axis at a distance of 3 units.
   (i) What are the coordinates of the points P, R and Q ?
   (ii) What is the difference between the abscissa of the points L and M ?

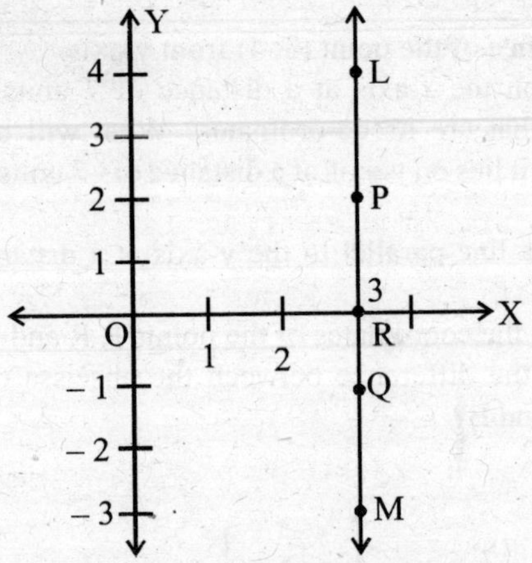

3. Three vertices of a rectangle are (3, 2), (– 4, 2) and (– 4, 5). Plot these points and find the coordinates of the fourth vertex.
4. Plot the following points and write the name of the figure obtained by joining them in order:
   P(– 3, 2), Q (– 7, – 3), R (6, – 3), S (2, 2)
5. Point (0, –7) lies
   (a) on the x-axis (b) in the second quadrant
   (c) on the y-axis (d) in the fourth quadrant
6. Point (– 10, 0) lies
   (a) on the negative direction of the x-axis
   (b) on the negative direction of the y-axis
   (c) in the third quadrant
   (d) in the fourth quadrant
7. Points (1, –1), (2, –2), (4, –5), (–3, –4)
   (a) lie in II quadrant
   (b) lie in III quadrant
   (c) lie in IV quadrant
   (d) do not lie in the same quadrant
8. Abscissa of a point is positive in
   (a) I and II quadrants
   (b) I and IV quadrants
   (c) I quadrant only
   (d) II quadrant only
9. The point which lies on y-axis at a distance of 5 units in the negative direction of y-axis is
   (a) (0, 5) (b) (5, 0)
   (c) (0, –5) (d) (–5, 0)

3 EXERCISE

Single Option Correct :

DIRECTIONS: *This section contains multiple choice questions. Each question has 4 choices (a), (b), (c) and (d) out of which ONLY ONE is correct.*

1. The distance of the point (3, 4) from y-axis is
(a) 1 (b) 4
(c) 2 (d) 3

2. The distance of the point (5, –2) from x-axis is
(a) 5 (b) –2
(c) 3 (d) 4

See Graph for (Qs. 3 to 6)

3. In the given figure, find Coordinate of A

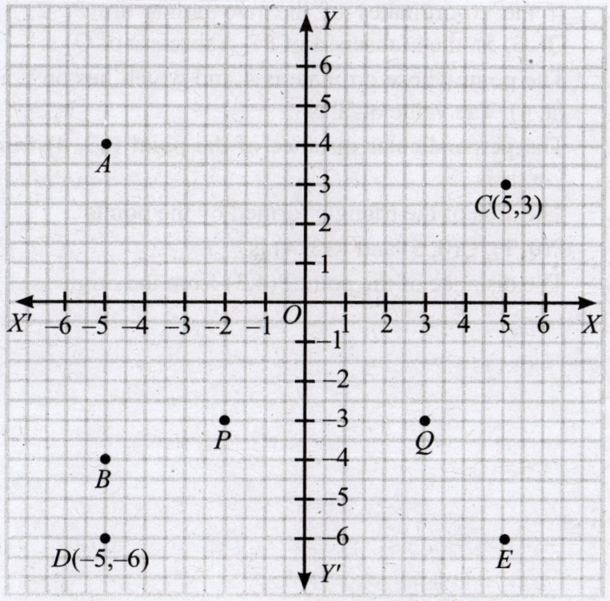

(a) (–5, 4) (b) (5, 4)
(c) (–5, – 4) (d) (4, 5)

4. In the given figure, points identified by the coordinates (–2, –3)
(a) P (b) Q
(c) A (d) C

5. In the given figure, find Abscissa of C
(a) 4 (b) 5
(c) 6 (d) 7

6. In the given figure, find co-ordinate of the point E
(a) (1, 2) (b) (5, –6)
(c) (5, 6) (d) (–5, –6)

See Graph for (Qs. 7 to 10)

7. In the figure, the coordinates of B is

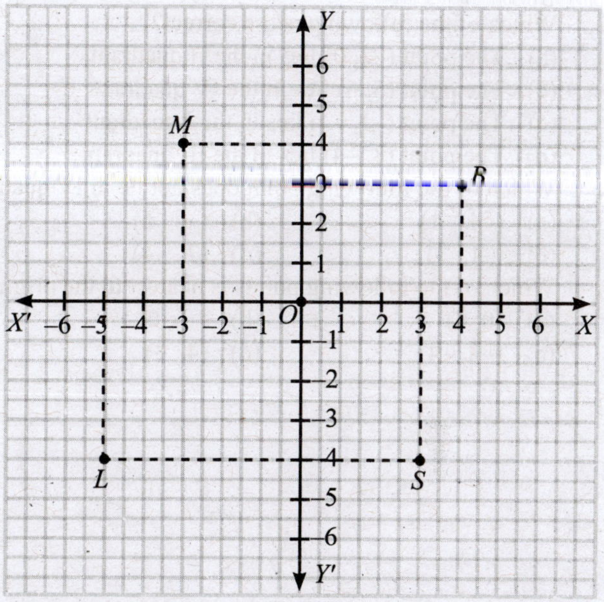

(a) (–3, 4) (b) (4, 3)
(c) (–5, –4) (d) (3, – 4)

8. In the figure, the co-ordinates of M are
(a) (–3, 4) (b) (4, 3)
(c) (–5, – 4) (d) (3, – 4)

9. In the figure, the co-ordinates of L are
(a) (–3, 4) (b) (4, 3)
(c) (–5, –4) (d) (3, – 4)

10. In the figure, the co-ordinates of S are
(a) (–3, 4) (b) (4, 3)
(c) (–5, –4) (d) (3, – 4)

11. The point (3, – 4) lies in the quadrant
(a) 1st (b) II nd
(c) III rd (d) IV th

12. The abscissa of a point is –7 and the ordinate is 2, then the point is
(a) (2, –7) (b) (–7, 2)
(c) (–2, 7) (d) (7, –2)

13. The point (0, 5) lies
(a) on the x-axis (b) on the y-axis
(c) in the IInd quadrant (d) in the Ist quadrant

More Than One Option Correct :

DIRECTIONS: *This section contains multiple choice questions. Each question has 4 choices (a), (b), (c) and (d) out of which ONE or MORE may be correct.*

1. Which of the following point does not lie in IIIrd quadrant?
(a) (–1, 2) (b) (6, 3)
(c) (–1, –2) (d) (–6, –3)

2. Which of the following is/are correct?
(a) The point (–2, 0) lies in the II quadrant.
(b) The point (5, 6) lies in the IV quadrant
(c) The point (–1, –4) lies in the I quadrant
(d) The point (3, –4) lies in the III quadrant

3. Which of the following point does not lie in IV quadrant ?
(a) (–4, –1) (b) (–2, 6)
(c) (–1, 3) (d) (2, –4)

4. Which of the following points is nearest to the origin?
(a) (0, 6) (b) (–6, 0)
(c) (–3, –4) (d) (4, 3)

Multiple Matching Question :

DIRECTIONS : *Following question has four statements (A, B, C and D) given in Column - I and four statements (p, q, r, ...) in Column - II. Any given statement in Column - I can have correct matching with one or more statement(s) given in Column - II.*

1.

Column - I	Column - II
(A) Ist quadrant	(p) (–1, –4)
(B) IVth quadrant	(q) (5, –1)
(C) IInd quadrant	(r) (0, 6)
(D) IIIrd quadrant	(s) (–3, 2)
	(t) (–3, –2)
	(u) (4, 1)

Integer Type Questions :

DIRECTIONS : *Answer the following questions. The answer to each of the question is a single digit integer, ranging from 0 to 9.*

1. If the co-ordinates of the two points are P(–2, 3) and Q(–3, 5), then (abscissa of P) – (abscissa of Q) is

2. The point whose ordinate is 4 and which lies on y-axis is (a, 4). The value of 'a' is

3. The perpendicular distance of the point P(3, 4) from the y-axis is

4. The area of the triangle formed by the points P(0, 1), Q(0, 5) and R(3, 4) is

5. The distance of the point P(4,3) from the origin is

SOLUTIONS

Brief Explanations of Selected Questions

1 EXERCISE

FILL IN THE BLANKS :

1. I
2. the first or third quadrant
3. (– ve, + ve)
4. 0
5. third
6. first and fourth

TRUE/FALSE :

1. False 2. False 3. False 4. False
5. True 6. False 7. False 8. True
9. False 10. True 11. False 12. False

MATCH THE COLUMNS :

1. (A) → (p); (B) → (q); (C) → (s); (D) → (r)
2. (A) → (u); (B) → (t); (C) → (p); (D) → (q); (E) → (r); (F) → (s)

VERY SHORT ANSWER QUESTIONS :

1. (0, 0)
2. The point (–2, –5) lies in the third quadrant.
3. $y < 0 \Rightarrow -y > 0$
   $\therefore$ The point $(x, -y)$ lies in first quadrant.
4. (5, 0)
5. Origin (0, 0) is the only point that lies on both x and y-axes. It lies at their point of intersection.
6. Ordinate = –3 and Abscissa = 4
7. No. These lie on axes. Point (–5, 0) lies on the x-axis since its ordinate is 0 and point (0, –4) lies on the y-axis since its abscissa is 0.
8.

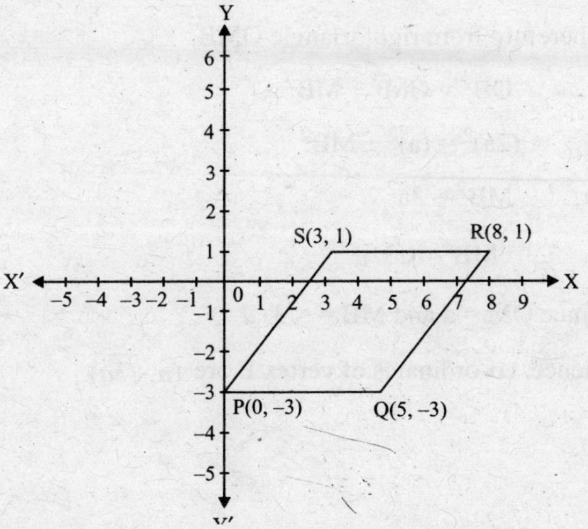

SHORT ANSWER QUESTIONS :

1. Let us plot the point P(3, 4) on the XY-plane.

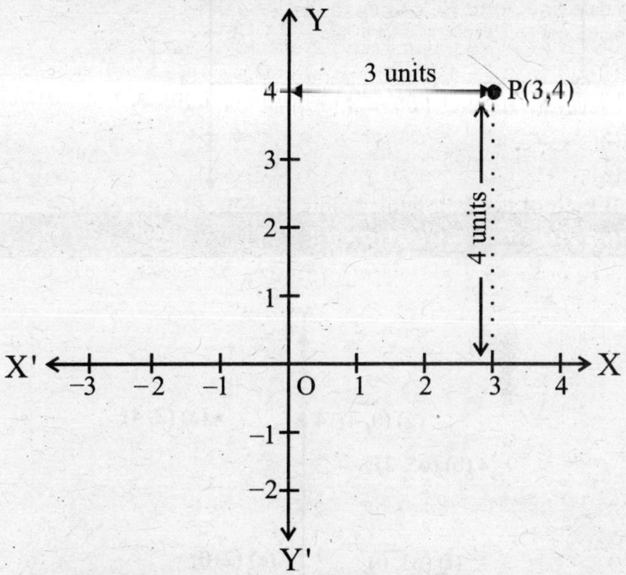

The perpendicular distance of the point P from y-axis is equal to its x-coordinate = 3 units.
The perpendicular distance of the point P from x-axis is equal to its y-coordinate = 4 units.

2. Any point that lies on x-axis has its ordinate 0. Since the point is at a distance of 7 units from y-axis, therefore coordinate of the point will be (7, 0). If the point lies on the y-axis its abscissa will be 0. Since the point is at a distance of –7 units from x-axis, therefore, coordinate of point will be (0, –7).
3. (i) Coordinates of the points P, Q and R are
   P = (2, 2), Q = (2, –1), R = (2, –3)
   (ii) Abscissa of point A is 4 and of point B is –4.
   Difference between their abscissa = 4 –(–4) = 8.
4. Given, one vertex of the rectangle is at origin O(0,0), and one vertex lies in third quadrant. As longer side lies on x-axis and is 7 units long. Thus, one coordinate would be (–7, 0). As shorter side lies on y-axis and is 4 units long. Thus, one coordinate would be (0, –4). On plotting the points O(0, 0), B(–7, 0), C(0, –4) and A(–7, –4) on the graph we get rectangle ABOC.

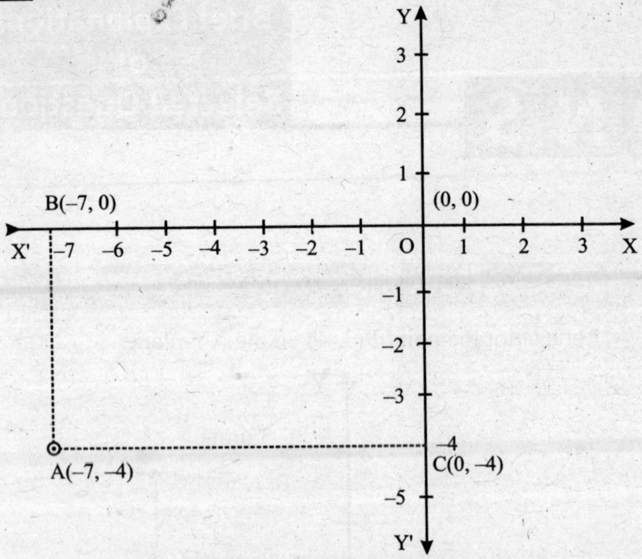

LONG ANSWER QUESTIONS :

1.

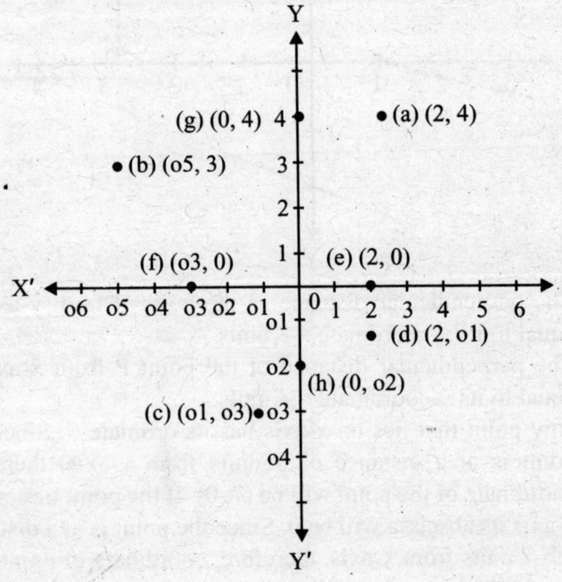

2.

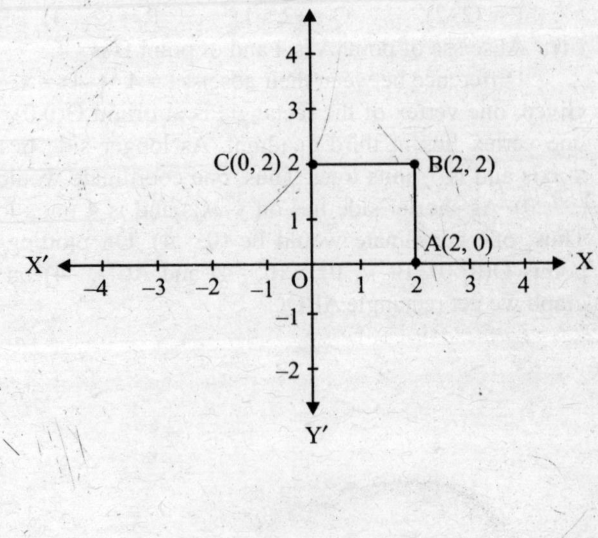

On joining OA, AB, BC and CO, we get a square OABC of each side of 2 units.

3.

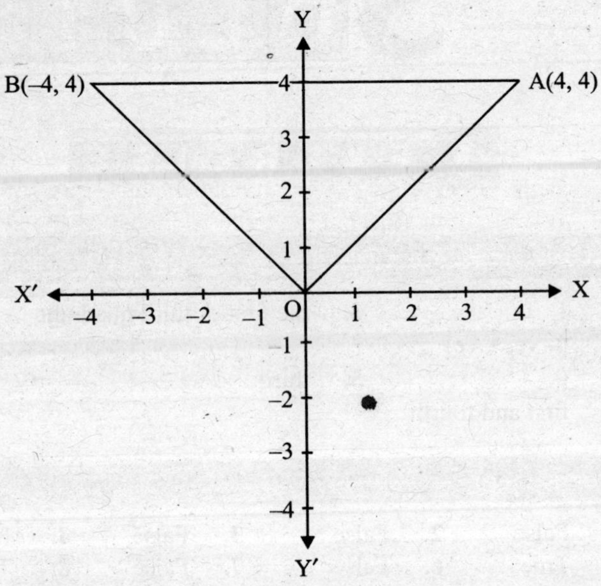

On joining OA, OB and BA, we get an isosceles triangle OAB.

4. In Figure

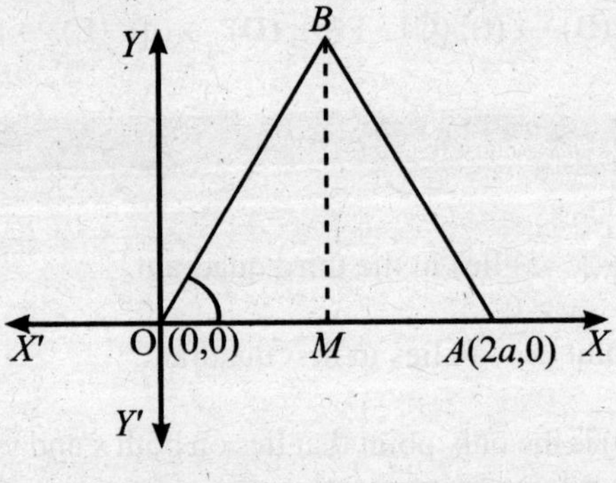

OAB is an equilateral triangle of length 2a units.

$\therefore \quad OA = AB = OB = 2a$

Now, from the point B, draw BM perpendicular on OA.

$\therefore \quad OM = MA = a$

Therefore from right triangle OMB,

$$OB^2 = OM^2 + MB^2$$

or, $\quad (2a)^2 = (a)^2 + MB^2$

or, $\quad MB^2 = 3a^2$

$\therefore \quad MB = \sqrt{3} \cdot a$

Since OM = a and MB = $\sqrt{3} \cdot a$

Hence, co-ordinates of vertex B are $(a, \sqrt{3}a)$.

2 EXERCISE

TEXT-BOOK EXERCISE :

1. In order to locate the position of the lamp, we take a fixed point (i.e. corner of the table) for reference. Let lamp be a point and table as plane. Draw perpendicular from the lamp point of two edges (perpendicular from the lamp point to each other) of the table and measure the distance of these perpendiculars from the fixed point (i.e. corner of the table). Let these distances are 26 cm. and 32 cm.

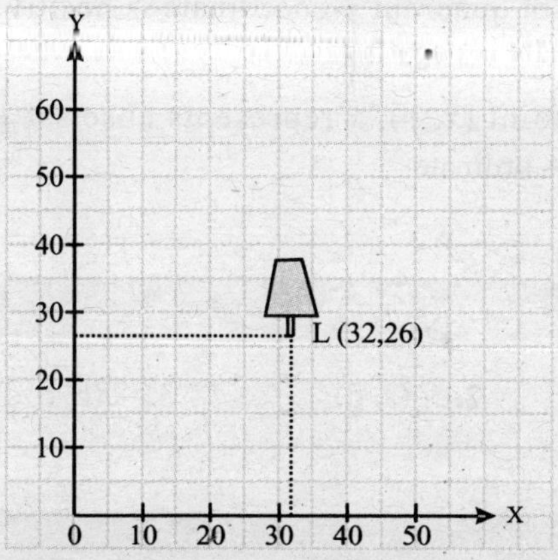

Then position of lamp can be written as L (32,26) with respect to origin i.e. fixed point i.e. corner of table. (see figure).

2. The street plane is shown below:

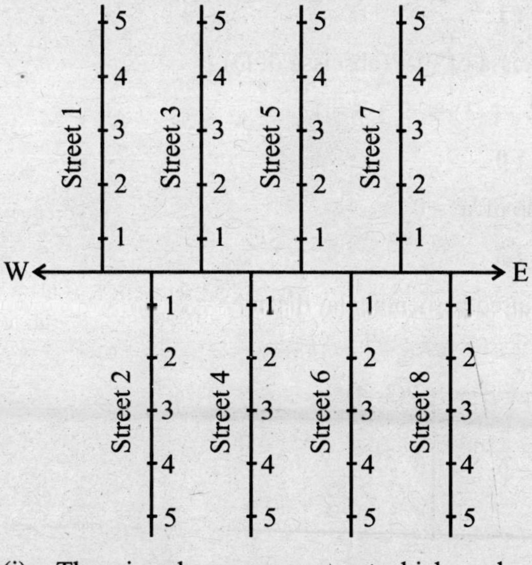

(i) There is only one cross-street which can be referred to as (4,3)

(ii) There is only one cross-street which can be referred to as (3,4)

3. (i) Horizontal line is the x-axis and vertical line is the y-axis.

(ii) Part of the plane formed by these two lines is called quadrants.

(iii) The origin.

4.

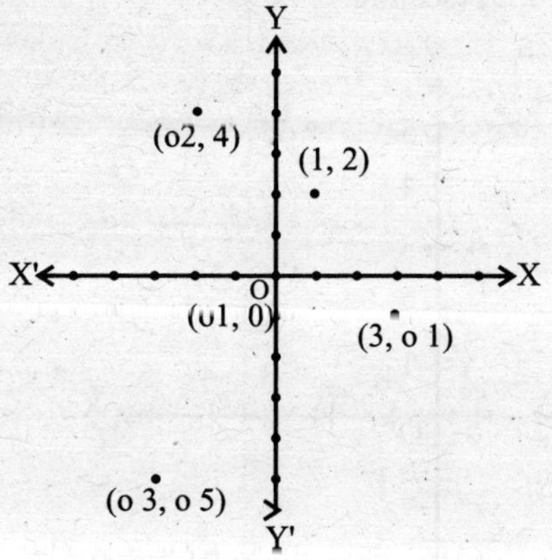

The point (– 2, 4) lies in the II quadrant.
The point (3, – 1) lies in the IV quadrant.
The point (– 1, 0) lies on the negative x-axis.
The point (1, 2) lies in the I quadrant.
The point (– 3, – 5) lies in the III quadrant.

5.

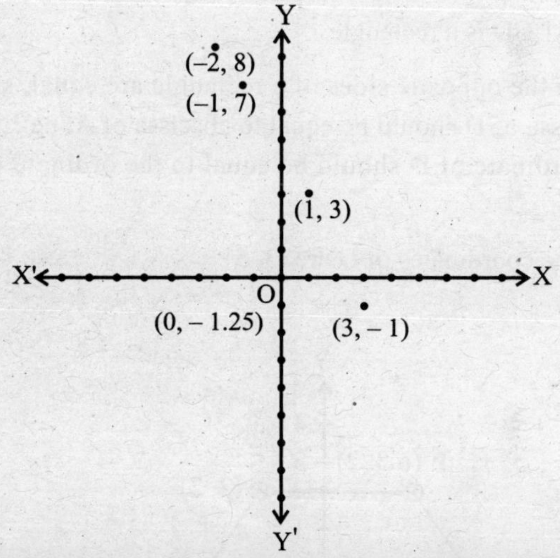

EXEMPLAR QUESTIONS:

1. (– 3, 5) lie in II quadrant
(4, – 1) lie in IV quadrant
(2, 0) on x-axis
(2, 2) lie in I quadrant
(– 3, – 6) lie in III quadrant

2. (i) Coordinates of P: (3, 2)
Coordinates of R: (3, 0)
Coordinates of Q: (3, – 1)

(ii) Difference between the abscissa of points L (3, 4) and M (3, – 3) is 3 – 3 = 0

3. Plot the three vertices of the rectangle as A(3, 2), B (– 4, 2), C (– 4, 5) (see Fig.)

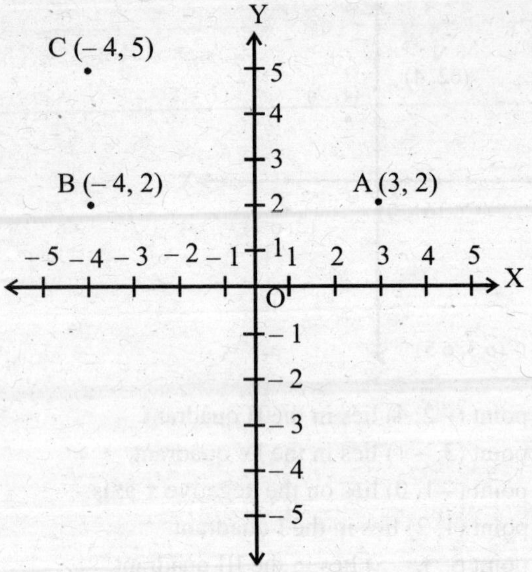

We have to find the coordinates of the fourth vertex D so that ABCD is a rectangle.

Since the opposite sides of a rectangle are equal, so the abscissa of D should be equal to abscissa of A, i.e., 3 and the ordinate of D should be equal to the ordinate of C, i.e., 5.

So, the coordinates of D are (3, 5)

4.

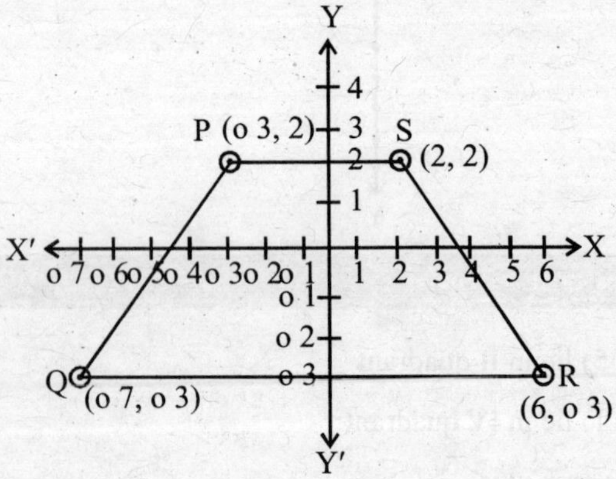

The figure obtained is a trapezium

i.e., PQRS is a trapezium.

5. (c) Point (0, – 7) lies on the y-axis.

6. (a) Point (–10, 0) lies on the negative direction of x-axis.

7. (d) Given points do not lie in the same quadrant.

8. (b) Abscissa of a point is positive in I and IV quadrants

9. (c)

3 EXERCISE

SINGLE OPTION CORRECT :

1. (d) 2. (b) 3. (a) 4. (a) 5. (b)
6. (b) 7. (b) 8. (a) 9. (c) 10. (d)

11. (d) As in IVth quadrant x-coordinate is positive and y-coordinate is negative.

12. (b) As for point (x, y), x represents abscissa and y represents ordinate

13. (b)

MORE THAN ONE OPTION CORRECT :

1. (a, b) 2. (a, d) 3. (b, c, d)
4. (c, d)

MULTIPLE MATCHING QUESTIONS :

1. (A) → (r, u); (B) → (p, t); (C) → (s); (D) → (q)

INTEGER TYPE QUESTIONS :

1. **Ans : 1**

(abscissa of P) – (abscissa of Q)

$= -2 - (-3) = -2 + 3 = 1$

2. **Ans : 0**

Value of 'a' = 0

3. **Ans : 3**

Required perpendicular distance = 3

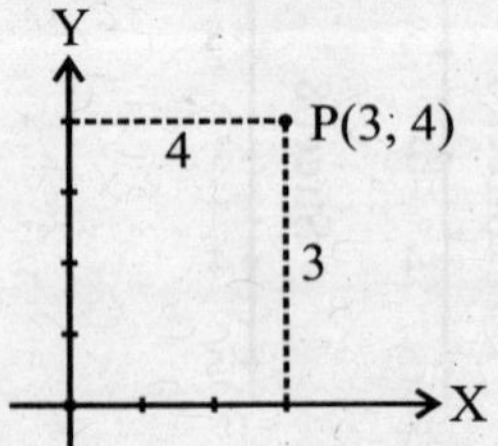

4. **Ans : 6**

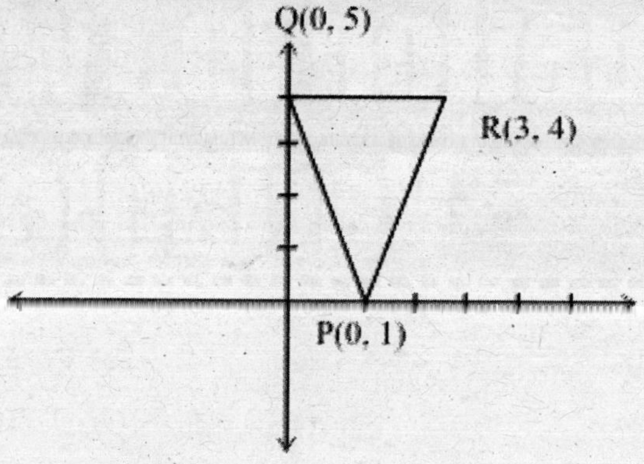

Area of $\Delta PQR = \frac{1}{2} \times 3 \times 4$ sq. units

= 6 sq. units

5. **Ans : 5**

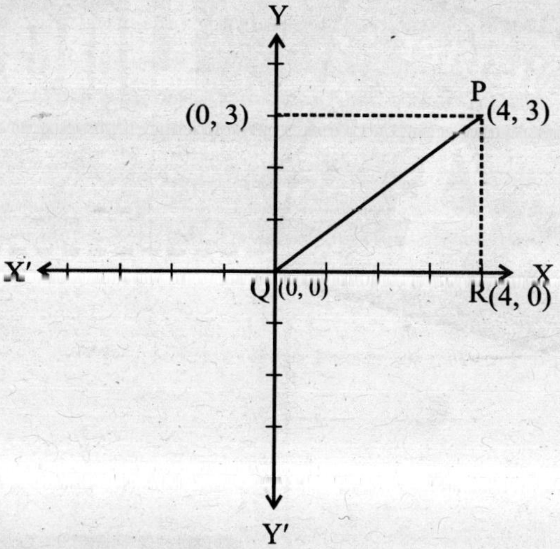

QP = $\sqrt{QR^2 + PR^2} = \sqrt{(4)^2 + (3)^2}$

$= \sqrt{16+9} = \sqrt{25} = 5$

Chapter 4

Linear Equation In Two Variables

INTRODUCTION

Many times in mathematics, we have to find the value of an unknown. In this case we represent the unknown by using some letters like p, q, r, x, y etc. These letters are then called as the variable representations of the unknown quantity.

In earlier classes, you have studied linear equation in one variable. You know that standard form of a linear equation in one variable is $ax + b = 0$, $(a \neq 0)$. Its solution $x = -\frac{b}{a}$, is unique. In this chapter, you will study the linear equation in two variables like $5x - y + \frac{7}{2} = 0$, $x - 2y + 1 = 0$, etc. A polynomial equation having two unknowns of degree one is called the linear equation in two variables. You will see that a linear equation in two variables has infinite many solutions. You will also study, how to draw the graph of a linear equation in two variables in a graph paper.

LINEAR EQUATION IN TWO VARIABLES

An equation of the form $ax + by + c = 0$ where a, b, c are real numbers ($a, b \neq 0$) and x, y are variables, is called a linear equation in two variables.

Here 'a' is called coefficient of x, b is called coefficient of y and c is called constant term.

eg. $6x + 2y + 5 = 0$, $5x - 2y + 3 = 0$, etc.

In the linear equation in two variables, index (power) of each of the variable is 1.

SOLUTION OF A LINEAR EQUATION

Let $ax + by + c = 0$, where a, b, c are real numbers such that $a \neq 0$ and $b \neq 0$. Then any pair of values of x and y which satisfies the equation $ax + by + c = 0$, is called a solution of it.

TO FIND THE SOLUTION(S) [OR ROOT(S)] OF A LINEAR EQUATION IN TWO VARIABLES ALGEBRICALLY

Standard form of a linear equation in two variables : $ax + by + c = 0 \quad (a, b \neq 0)$

Express any one variable y in terms of other variable say x as

$$y = -\frac{ax + c}{b} \qquad \ldots(i)$$

Now by putting any real value of x in above equation (i), you will get the corresponding real value of y. The value of x and its corresponding value of y is one set of solution of the given linear equation in two variables. In the same way by putting another real value of x in the above equation (i), you will get another value of y. Thus you will get another set of solution. In this way, you will get infinite sets of solution.

ILLUSTRATION : 1

Find any three sets of solution of $-x + 2y = 4$

SOLUTION :

Consider $-x + 2y = 4$

$\Rightarrow \quad x = 2y - 4 \qquad \ldots(i)$

Put $y = 0$ in equation (i), then $x = 2 \times 0 - 4 = -4$

Hence, one set of solution : $x = -4, y = 0$

Put $y = 1$ in equation (i), then $x = 2 \times 1 - 4 = 2 - 4 = -2$

Hence, second set of solution : $x = -2, y = 1$

Put $y = 2$ in equation (i), then $x = 2 \times 2 - 4 = 0$

Hence, third set of solution : $x = 0, y = 2$

Thus, three sets of solution are $(-4, 0)$, $(-2, 1)$ and $(0, 2)$

GRAPH OF A LINEAR EQUATION IN TWO VARIABLES

To draw the graph of a linear equation $ax + by + c = 0$; $a, b \neq 0$; we may follow the following steps:

(i) Obtain the linear equation : $ax + by + c = 0$

(ii) Express any one variable y in terms of other variable x as $y = -\dfrac{ax + c}{b}$

(iii) Put any three values x_1, x_2, x_3 for x one by one in the equation obtained in step (ii) and calculate the corresponding values y_1, y_2, y_3 of y. Thus you obtained three solution sets, (x_1, y_1) (x_2, y_2) and (x_3, y_3)

(iv) Plot points (x_1, y_1), (x_2, y_2) and (x_3, y_3) on a graph paper.

(v) Join the points marked in step (iv).

You will see that the three points lie on a straight line. The straight line passing through these three points is the graph of the linear equation in two variables, because coordinates of each point on the line satisfy the linear equation in two variables and hence coordinates of each point on the line is a set of solution of the equation.

NOTE : The graph of a linear equation in two variable is always a straight line.

ILLUSTRATION : 2

Draw the graph of the equation $y - x = 2$.

SOLUTION :

We have, $y - x = 2 \Rightarrow y = x + 2$

When $x = 1$, we have $y = 1 + 2 = 3$

When $x = 3$, we have $y = 3 + 2 = 5$

Thus, we have the following table exhibiting the abscissae and ordinates of points on the line represented by the given equation.

x	1	3
y	3	5

Plotting the points (1, 3) and (3, 5) on the graph paper and drawing a line joining them, we obtain the graph of the line represented by the given equation as shown in the Figure.

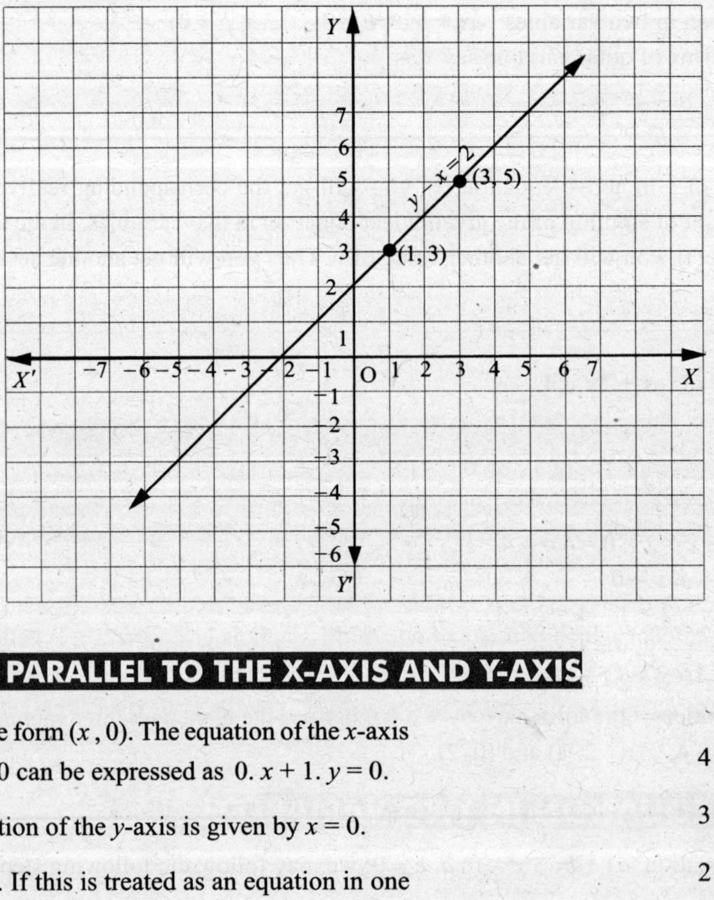

EQUATIONS OF LINES PARALLEL TO THE X-AXIS AND Y-AXIS

Every point on the x-axis is of the form $(x, 0)$. The equation of the x-axis is given by $y = 0$. Note that $y = 0$ can be expressed as $0.x + 1.y = 0$.

Similarly, observe that the equation of the y-axis is given by $x = 0$.

Consider the equation $x - 2 = 0$. If this is treated as an equation in one variable x only, then it has the unique solution $x = 2$, which is a point on the number line.

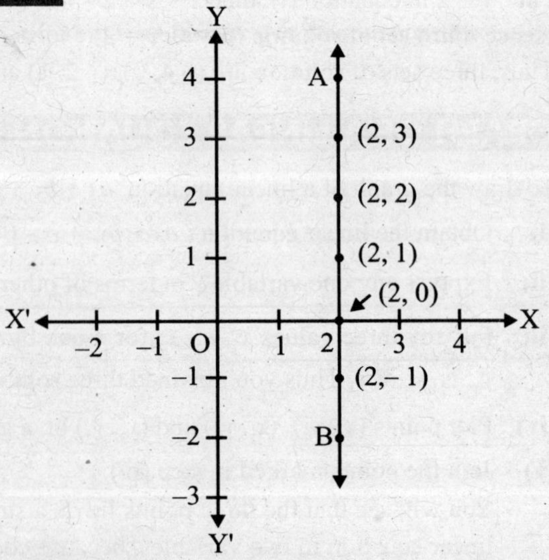

NOTE : (i) The graph of $x = a$ is a straight line parallel to the y-axis

(ii) The graph of $y = a$ is a straight line parallel to the x-axis.

ILLUSTRATION : 3

Draw the graph of the equation $x - y + 3 = 0$. Use it to find some solution of the equations and check from the graph that $x = 0$ and $y = 3$ is a solution.

SOLUTION:

The given equation is $x - y + 3 = 0$

To draw the graph we use the table of corresponding values of x and y.

x	2	–6	3
y	1	–3	6

We have drawn the graph of $x - y + 3 = 0$ by plotting the points (– 2, 1), (– 6, – 3) and (3, 6). As shown in the figure some of the other solutions of $x - y + 3 = 0$ are : $x = 1, y = 4$; $x = -1, y = 2$

The point $x = 0$ and $y = 3$ is on the graph. Hence, $x = 0, y = 3$ is a solution of the equation

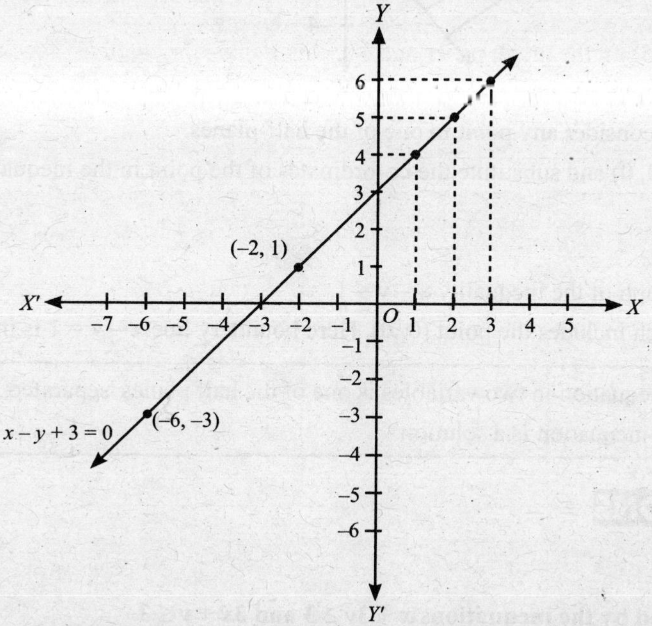

CONNECTING TOPIC

INEQUATION : An open sentence which consists of one of the symbols viz, >, <, ≥, ≤ is called an inequation.

LINEAR INEQUATIONS IN TWO VARIABLES :

Linear equation of two variables of the form ax + by + c = 0 divides the plane into three mutually disjoint sets of points.

(a) Points lying on the line ax + by + c = 0.

(b) Points lying on one side of the line ax + by + c = 0.

(c) Points lying on the other side of the line ax + by + c = 0.

⇒ The line $ax + by + c = 0$ divides the plane into two half-planes and they are represented by $ax + by + c < 0$ and $ax + by + c > 0$.

ILLUSTRATION : 4

Draw the graph $x - y \leq 1$ in the cartesian plane.

SOLUTION:

First draw the line x – y = 1 i.e., y = x – 1

x	1	0	–1
y	0	–1	–2

As a first step, plot the ordered pairs (1, 0), (0, – 1), (–1, –2) and then join them with a line.

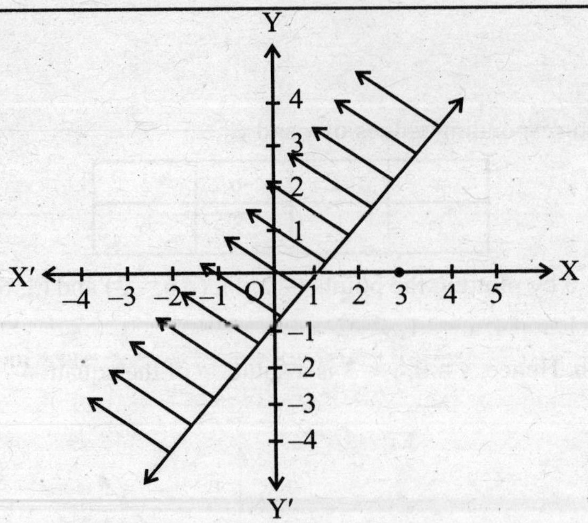

For shading the region we consider any point in one of the half-planes.

Let us consider the point (0, 0) and substitute the co-ordinates of the point in the inequation $x - y \le 1$

$\Rightarrow 0 - 0 \le 1 \Rightarrow 0 \le 1$

Which is true.

$\therefore$ (0, 0) belongs to the graph of the inequality $x - y \le 1$.

Now shade the region which includes the point (0, 0). Here boundary line $x - y = 1$ is included.

NOTE : The graph of a linear inequation in two variables is one of the half planes 'separated by the boundary line. Any ordered pair which satisfies the inequation is a solution.

SYSTEM OF INEQUATIONS

ILLUSTRATION : 5

Construct the region represented by the inequations $x + 3y \ge 3$ and $3x + y \le 3$.

SOLUTION:

1. Consider $x + 3y = 3 \Rightarrow y = \dfrac{3-x}{3}$

x	0	3
y	1	0

Substitute (0, 0) in $x + 3y \ge 3$.

$\Rightarrow$ $0 + 0 \ge 3$

$\Rightarrow$ $0 \ge 3$ which is false.

$\therefore$ $x + 3y \ge 3$ does not contain (0, 0)

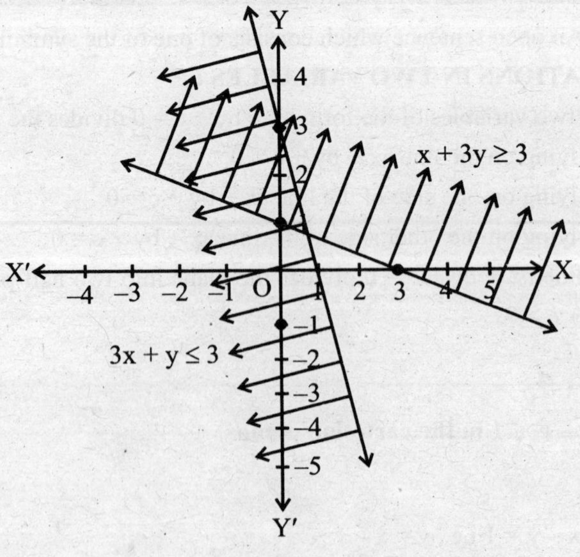

2. Consider $3x + y = 3$

x	1	0
y	0	3

Substitute (0, 0) in the inequation

$3x + y \le 3$.

$\Rightarrow \quad 0 + 0 \leq 3$ which is true.

$\therefore \quad 3x + y \leq 3$ contains (0, 0).

The region common to the two half-planes is the graph of the given system of inequations.

Interval Notation

The set of all real numbers between *a* and *b* (where $a < b$) excluding *a* and *b* is represented as (*a*, *b*) read as "the open interval *a*, *b*".

[*a*, *b*] read as "the closed interval *a*, *b*" means all real numbers between *a* and *b* including *a* and *b* ($a < b$). [*a*, *b*) means all numbers between *a* and *b*, with a being included and *b* excluded ($a < b$).

ILLUSTRATION : 6

Find the solution set of $\frac{1}{2x-4} < 0$.

SOLUTION:

$$\frac{1}{2x-4} < 0$$

$\Rightarrow \quad 2x - 4 < 0$

$\Rightarrow \quad x < 2$

The solution set is $\{x/x < 2\}$ or $(-\infty, 2)$

MISCELLANEOUS SOLVED EXAMPLES

1. Express y in terms of x, given that $2y - 4x = 7$. Check whether $(-1, -1)$ is a solution of the line.

Sol. Given equation is $2y - 4x = 7 \Rightarrow 2y = 7 + 4x \Rightarrow y = \frac{7+4x}{2}$

Now substituting $x = -1$, $y = -1$ in the equation, we get

$-1 = \frac{7+4(-1)}{2} \Rightarrow -1 = \frac{7-4}{2} \Rightarrow -1 = \frac{3}{2}$ which is not true

$\therefore$ LHS $\neq$ RHS

Therefore point $(-1, -1)$ does not lie on the line $2y - 4x = 7$

2. Draw the graph of the equation $2x - y + 3 = 0$. Using the graph, find the value of y, when $x = -2$.

Sol. $2x - y + 3 = 0 \Rightarrow y = 2x + 3$ ...(i)

When $x = 0$, then $y = 2 \times 0 + 3 = 3$

When $x = 1$, then $y = 2 \times 1 + 3 = 5$

Thus, we have the table :

x	0	1
y	3	5

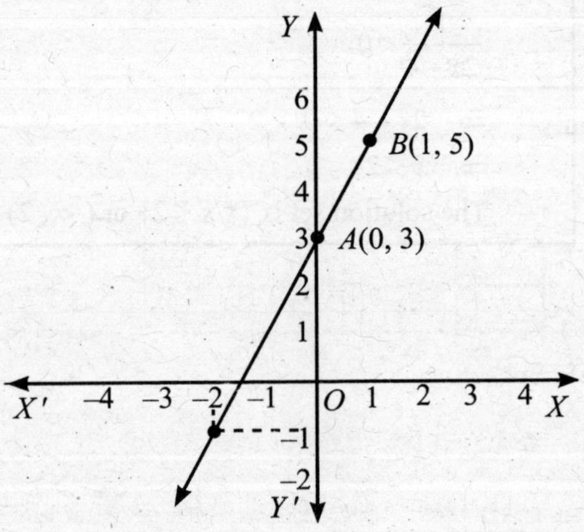

Now, plot the points A (0, 3) and B (1, 5) on a graph paper

Join AB and extend it in both the directions.

Then, the line AB is the required graph of $2x - y + 3 = 0$

From the graph it is clear when $x = -2$, then $y = -1$

3. Draw the graph of the equation $2x + 3y = 11$. From your graph, find the value of y, when $x = -2$.

Sol. $2x + 3y = 11 \Rightarrow y = \frac{(11-2x)}{3}$ ...(i)

When $x = 1$, then $y = \frac{(11-2\times1)}{3} = \frac{9}{3} = 3$

When $x = 4$, then $y = \frac{(11-2\times1)}{3} = \frac{9}{3} = 3$

Thus, we have the following table :

x	1	4
y	3	1

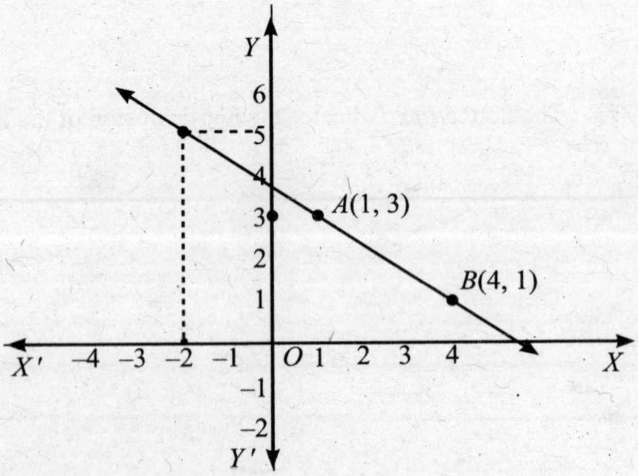

Now, plot the points $A(1, 3)$ and $B(4, 1)$ on a graph paper.

Join AB and extend it in both the directions. Line AB is the required graph of $2x + 3y = 11$

From the graph, it is clear that when $x = -2$, then $y = 5$.

4. Find four different solutions of the equation $x + 2y = 6$.

Sol. When $x = 2$, then $2 + 2y = 6 \Rightarrow 2y = 4, \Rightarrow y = 2$

Now, let us choose $x = 0$. With this value of x, the given equation reduces to $2y = 6$ which has the unique solution $y = 3$.

So $x = 0, y = 3$ is also a solution of $x + 2y = 6$.

Similarly, taking $y = 0$, the given equation reduces to $x = 6$. So, $x = 6, y = 0$ is a solution of $x + 2y = 6$ as well.

Finally let us take $y = 1$. The given equation now reduces to $x + 2 = 6$, whose solution is given by $x = 4$. Therefore, $x = 4$, $y = 1$ is also a solution of the given equation.

So four of the infinitely many solutions of the given equation are : (2, 2), (0, 3), (6, 0) and (4, 1).

5. Given the point (1, 2), find the equation of a line on which it lies. How many such equations are there?

Sol. Here (1, 2) is a solution of a linear equation. So, you are looking for any line passing through the point (1, 2). One example of such a linear equation is $x + y = 3$. Others are $y - x = 1$, $y = 2x$, since they are also satisfied by the coordinates of the point (1, 2). In fact, there are infinitely many linear equations which are satisfied by the coordinates of the point (1, 2).

SOLVED EXAMPLES BASED ON CONNECTING TOPIC

6. Draw graph of $x < -y$

Sol.

(i) Draw $x = -y$

X	–1	0	1
Y	1	0	–1

(ii) Substitute (1, 1) in $x < -y$

$\Rightarrow 1 < -1$ which is not true.

$\therefore$ (1, 1) does not belong to the graph represented by $x < -y$

(iii) Now shade the region (half plane) which does not contain the point (1, 1)

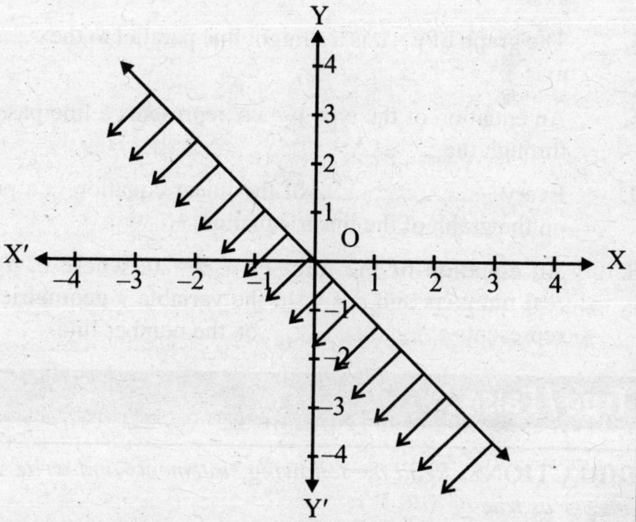

NOTE : The dotted line indicates the non-inclusion of the line $x = -y$ in the graph

1 EXERCISE

Fill in the Blanks :

DIRECTIONS: *Complete the following statements with an appropriate word / term to be filled in the blank space(s).*

1. A linear equation in two variables has .... solutions.

2. The graph of every linear equation in two variables is a ....

3. $x = 0$ is the equation of the ....axis and $y = 0$ is the equation of the .... axis.

4. The graph of $x = a$ is a straight line parallel to the .... axis.

5. The graph of $y = a$ is a straight line parallel to the .... axis

6. An equation of the type $y = mx$ represents a line passing through the ....

7. Every .... of the linear equation is a point on the graph of the linear equation.

8. An equation of the form $cy + d = 0$, where c, d are real numbers and $c \neq 0$, in the variable y geometrically represents a..........................on the number line.

True / False :

DIRECTIONS: *Read the following statements and write your answer as true or false.*

1. An equation of the form $ax + by + c = 0$, where a, b and c are real numbers, such that a and b are both zero, is called a linear equation in two variables.

2. $y = 3x + 5$ has a unique solution.

3. $(0, 2)$ is a solution for $x - 2y = 4$

4. $\left(2, \frac{1}{2}\right)$ is a solution for $x = 4y$

5. The solution of a linear equation is not affected when the same number is added to both the sides of the equation.

6. All the points $(2, 0)$, $(-3, 0)$, $(4, 2)$ and $(0, 5)$ lie on the x-axis.

7. The line parallel to the y-axis at a distance 4 units to the left of y-axis is given by the equation $x = -a$.

8. The graph of the equation $y = mx + c$ passes through the origin.

Match the Columns :

DIRECTIONS: *Each question contains statements given in two columns which have to be matched. Statements (A, B, C, D) in Column-I have to be matched with statements (p, q, r, s) in Column-II.*

1.

Column-I (Equations)	Column-II (Solutions)
(A) $2x + y = 7$	(p) $(0, 9)$
(B) $x - 2y = 4$	(q) $(1, 5)$
(C) $x - 4y = 0$	(r) $(0, 0)$
(D) $px + y = 9$	(s) $(4, 0)$

2.

Column-I	Column-II
(A) $x = a$	(p) x-axis
(B) $y = a$	(q) st. line parallel to x-axis
(C) $y = mx$	(r) st. line parallel to y-axis
(D) $y = 0$	(s) st. line passing through origin.

Very Short Answer Questions :

DIRECTIONS: *Give answer in one word or one sentence.*

1. Express the linear equation $y - 2 = 0$ in the form $ax + by + c = 0$ and indicate the values of a, b and c

2. Determine the whether the $x = 2$, $y = -1$ is a solution of equation $3x + 5y - 2 = 0$.

3. Find two solutions for $3y + 4 = 0$

4. Find the value of k, if $x = 2$, $y = 1$ is a solution of the equation $2x + 3y = k$.

5. Give the equations of two lines passing through (2, 14). How many more such lines are there, and why?

6. Find four different solutions of the equation $x + 2y = 6$.

7. The sum of the ages of Mrs. Meenu Goyal and Dr. H.K. Goyal is 80. Write a linear equation in two variables to represent the statement.

8. Show that $x = 2$, $y = 3$ satisfy the linear equation $3x - 4y + 6 = 0$.

9. Find the value of k if the line on $2x + y = k$ passes through the point (3, 5).

10. Write the equation of the line parallel to the x-axis at distance 3 units above x-axis.

Short Answer Questions :

DIRECTIONS: *Give answer in 2-3 sentences.*

1. (a) Verify 3 is solution of $5x - 8 = 7$.
(b) Check $x = 2$ is a solution of $5x + 7 = 3$.

2. Given the point (2, 11), find the equation of a line on which it lies. How many such equations are there?

3. Write each of the following as an equation in two variables:
(i) $x = -5$ (ii) $y = 2$
(iii) $2x = 3$ (iv) $5y = 2$.

4. Find four different solutions of the equation $x + 2y = 6$.

5. Express y in terms of x in the equation $2x + 3y = 11$. Find the point where the line represented by the equation $2x + 3y = 11$ cuts the y-axis.

6. Find the points where the graph of the equation $3x + 4y = 12$ cuts the x-axis and the y-axis.

7. At what point does the graph of the linear equation $x + y = 5$ meet a line which is parallel to the y-axis, at a distance 2 units from the origin and in the positive direction of x-axis?

8. Determine the point on the graph of the equations $2x + 5y = 20$ whose x-coordinate is $\frac{5}{2}$ times its ordinate.

9. Write any two solutions of the linear equation $3x + 2y = 9$.

10. Solve for x : $5(4x + 3) = 3(x - 2)$.

11. Solve for x : $\frac{3}{x-1} + \frac{1}{x+1} = \frac{4}{x}$, where $x \neq 0,\ x \neq 1, x \neq -1$.

12. Solve for x : $(5x + 1)(x + 3) - 8 = 5(x + 1)(x + 2)$.

Long Answer Questions :

DIRECTIONS: *Give answer in four to five sentences.*

1. Draw the graph of $2x + 3y = 9$. Using the graph, check whether (3, 1) and (–1, 2) are solutions of the given equation.

2. Draw the graph of the linear equation $2x + 3y = 12$. At what points, the graph of the equation cuts the x-axis and the y-axis?

3. Draw the graph of each of the following linear equations in two variables :
(i) $x + y = 4$ (ii) $x - y = 2$

4. Draw the graph of the equation $2x - y + 3 = 0$. Using the graph, find the value of y, when $x = -2$.

5. Solve the equation $2x + 1 = x - 3$, and represent the solution(s) on
(i) the number line,
(ii) the Cartesian plane.

6. Give the geometric representations of $2x + 9 = 0$ as an equation
(i) in one variable (ii) in two variables.

7. Alka and Noori, two students of class IX, together contribute ₹ 500 towards Prime Minister's Relief fund to help the earthquake victims. Write a linear equation which satisfies this data and draw the graph of the same.

8. Draw the graph of the linear equation $3x + 4y = 12$. At what points does, the graph cut the x-axis and the y-axis?

2 EXERCISE

Text-Book Exercise :

1. The cost of a notebook is twice the cost of a pen. Write a linear equation in two variables to represent this statement. (Take the cost of a notebook to be ₹ x and that of a pen to be ₹ y)

2. Express the following linear equations in the form $ax + by + c = 0$ and indicate the values of a, b and c in each case :
(i) $-2x + 3y = 6$ (ii) $x = 3y$ (iii) $2x = -5y$

3. Which one of the following options is true, and why? $y = 3x + 5$ has
(i) a unique solution (ii) only two solutions,
(iii) infinitely many solutions.

4. Write four solutions for each of the following equations:
(i) $2x + y = 7$ (ii) $x = 4y$

5. Check which of the following are solutions of the equation $x - 2y = 4$ and which are not :
(i) (0, 2) (ii) (4, 0)
(iii) $\sqrt{2}, 4\sqrt{2}$

6. Find the value of k, if $x = 2, y = 1$ is a solution of the equation $2x + 3y = k$.

7. Draw the graph of each of the following linear equations in two variables :
(i) $x + y = 4$ (ii) $y = 3x$

8. Give the equations of two lines passing through (2, 14). How many more such lines are there, and why?

9. The taxi fare in a city is as follows : For the first kilometre, the fare is ₹ 8 and for the subsequent distance it is ₹ 5 per km. Taking the distance covered as x km and total fare as ₹ y, write a linear equation for this information, and draw its graph.

10. Yamini and Fatima, two students of Class IX of a school, together contributed ₹ 100 towards the Prime Minister's Relief Fund to help the earthquake victims. Write a linear equation which satisfies this data. (You may take their contributions as ₹ x and ₹ y.) Draw the graph of the same.

11. In countries like USA and Canada, temperature is measured in Fahrenheit, where as in countries like India, it is measured in Celsius. Here is a linear equation that converts Fahrenheit to Celsius.

$$F = \left(\frac{9}{5}\right) C + 32$$

(i) Draw the graph of the linear equation above using Celsius for x-axis and Fahrenheit for y-axis.

(ii) If the temperature is 30°C, what is the temperature in Fahrenheit?

(iii) If the temperature is 95°F, what is the temperature in Celsius?

(iv) If the temperature is 0°C, what is the temperature in Fahrenheit and if the temperature is 0°F, what is the temperature in Celsius?

(v) Is there a temperature which is numerically the same in both Fahrenheit and Celsius? If yes, find it.

Exemplar Questions :

1. If (2, 0) is a solution of the linear equation $2x + 3y = k$, then the value of k is
   (a) 4 (b) 6
   (c) 5 (d) 2

2. The graph of the linear equation $2x + 3y = 6$ cuts the y-axis at the point
   (a) (2, 0) (b) (0, 3)
   (c) (3, 0) (d) (0, 2)

3. The linear equation $3x - y = x - 1$ has :
   (a) A unique solution
   (b) Two solutions
   (c) Infinitely many solutions
   (d) No solution

4. Any point on the line $y = x$ is of the form
   (a) (a, a) (b) (0, a)
   (c) (a, 0) (d) (a, – a)

5. Find the points where the graph of the equation $3x + 4y = 12$ cuts the x-axis and the y-axis.

6. At what point does the graph of the linear equation $x + y = 5$ meet a line which is parallel to the y-axis, at a distance 2 units from the origin and in the positive direction of x-axis ?

7. Determine the point on the graph of the equation $2x + 5y = 20$ whose x-coordinate is $\frac{5}{2}$ times its ordinate.

8. Draw the graph of the equation represented by the straight line which is parallel to the x-axis and is 4 units above it.

HOTS Questions :

1. From the choices given below, choose the equation whose graphs are given in Fig.(1) and Fig. (2).

For Fig. 1	For Fig. 2
(i) $y = x$	(i) $y = x + 2$
(ii) $x + y = 0$	(ii) $y = x - 2$
(iii) $y = 2x$	(iii) $y = -x + 2$
(iv) $2 + 3y = 7x$	(iv) $x + 2y = 6$

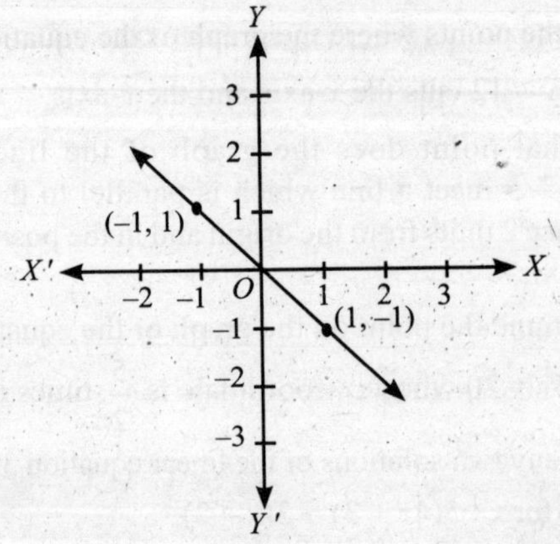

Fig. 1

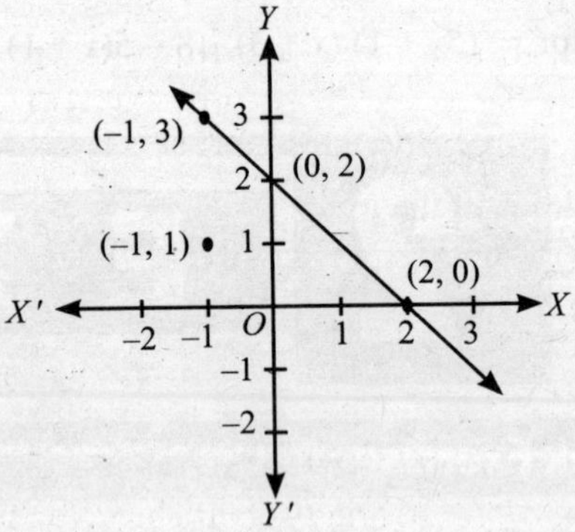

Fig. 2

2. Draw the graph of each of the following equations:
   (i) $x = 0$ (ii) $y = 0$ (iii) $x = 4$ (iv) $y = 3$
   (v) $y + 4 = 0$ (vi) $x + 2 = 0$

3. The autorikshaw fare in a city is charged ₹ 10 for the first kilometer and @ ₹ 4 per kilometer for subsequent distance covered. Write the linear equation to express the above statement. Draw the graph of the linear equation.

4. If the graph of the equation $4x + 3y = 12$ cuts the coordiante axes at A and B, then find the length of the hypotenuse of right triangle AOB.

3 EXERCISE

Single Option Correct :

DIRECTIONS: *This section contains multiple choice questions. Each questions has 4 choices (a), (b), (c) and (d) out of which ONLY ONE is correct.*

1. The linear equation $2x - 5y = 7$ has
(a) A unique solution
(b) Two solutions
(c) Infinitely many solutions
(d) No solution

2. The equation $2x + 5y = 7$ has a unique solution, if x, y, are:
(a) Natural numbers (b) Positive real numbers
(c) Real numbers (d) Rational numbers

3. If $(3, -2)$ is a solution of the equation $3x - py - 7 = 0$, then the value of p is
(a) -1 (b) 1
(c) $-\frac{13}{3}$ (d) 2

4. The value of x for which $y = -4$ is a solution of the linear equation $5x - 8y = 47$ is
(a) -3 (b) 3
(c) $\frac{79}{5}$ (d) $-\frac{79}{5}$

5. A solution of the equation $2x + 5y - 3 = 0$ is
(a) $(5, -2)$ (b) $(-5, 2)$
(c) $(-1, 1)$ (d) $(1, -1)$

6. Any solution of the linear equation $2x + 0y + 9 = 0$ in two variables is of the form
(a) $\left(-\frac{9}{2}, m\right)$ (b) $\left(n, -\frac{9}{2}\right)$
(c) $\left(0, -\frac{9}{2}\right)$ (d) $(-9, 0)$

7. The equation $x = 7$, in two variables, can be written as
(a) $1.x + 1.y = 7$ (b) $1.x + 0.y = 7$
(c) $0.x + 1.y = 7$ (d) $0.x + 0.y = 7$

8. Which of the following equations represents a line parallel to x-axis?
(a) $3x + 2 = 0$ (b) $3y + 2 = 0$
(c) $3x + 2y = 0$ (d) $3x - 2y = 0$

9. Which of the following equations represents a line parallel to y-axis?
(a) $2y = 5x$ (b) $2y = 5$
(c) $2x = 5$ (d) $2x + 3y = 5$

10. Which of the following equations has a graph shown in the figure?

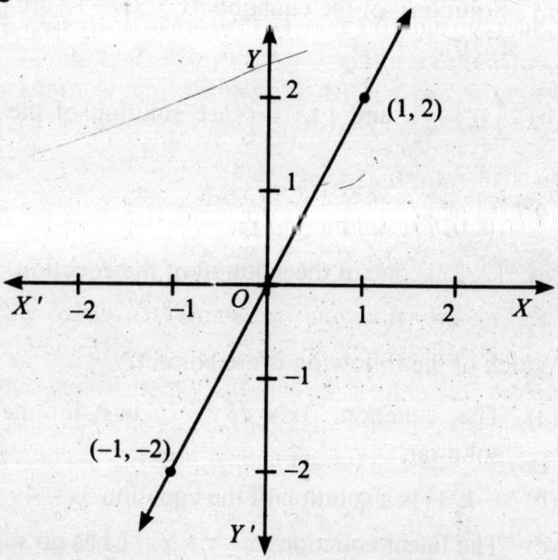

(a) $2x + y = 0$ (b) $2x - y = 0$
(c) $x + 2y = 0$ (d) $x - 2y = 0$

11. The graph of $y = 6$ is a line
(a) parallel to x-axis at a distance 6 units from the origin
(b) parallel to y-axis at a distance 6 units from the origin
(c) making an intercept 6 on the x-axis.
(d) making an intercept 6 on both the axes.

12. If a linear equation has solutions $(-2, 2)$, $(0, 0)$ and $(2, -2)$, then it is of the form
(a) $y - x = 0$ (b) $x + y = 0$
(c) $-2x + y = 0$ (d) $-x + 2y = 0$

13. The positive solutions of the equation $ax + by + c = 0$ always lie in the
(a) 1st quadrant (b) 2nd quadrant
(c) 3rd quadrant (d) 4th quadrant

14. The graph of the linear equation $2x + 3y = 6$ is a line which meets the x-axis at the point
(a) $(0, 2)$ (b) $(2, 0)$
(c) $(3, 0)$ (d) $(0, 3)$

15. The point of the form (a, a) always lies on :
(a) x-axis (b) y-axis
(c) on the line $y = x$ (d) on the line $x + y = 0$

More Than One Option Correct :

DIRECTIONS: *This section contains multiple choice questions. Each question has 4 choices (a), (b), (c) and (d) out of which ONE OR MORE may be correct.*

1. Which of the following is/are correct?

(a) Solutions of the equation $4x + 3y = 12$ are (0, 4) and (3, 0).

(b) $\left(0, -\frac{4}{3}\right)$ and $\left(1, -\frac{4}{3}\right)$ are solution of the equation $3y + 4 = 0$.

(c) (0, 0) is a solution of the equation $2x + 5y = 0$

(d) (2, 3) is one of the solution of the equation $x + 2y = 6$.

2. Which of the following is/are correct?

(a) The equation $3x = \sqrt{5}y - 7$ has infinitely many solutions.

(b) (–1, 1) is a solution of the equation $3x - 4y + 7 = 0$

(c) The linear equation $3x - y = x - 1$ has no solution.

(d) $x = 5$, $y = 2$ is a solution of the linear equation $x + 2y = 7$.

3. Which of the following statement(s) is/are not correct?

(a) Any point on the *y*-axis is of the form (*x*, 0)

(b) The equation of *x*-axis is of the form $x + y = 0$

(c) Any point on the *x*-axis is of the form (0, *y*)

(d) The equation $y + 3 = 0$ represents a line.

4. Which of the following is/are not the solutions of the equation $x - 2y = 4$?

(a) (4, 0) (b) $(\sqrt{2}, 4\sqrt{2})$

(c) (1, 1) (d) (2, 0)

5. Which of the following statement(s) is/are false statement?

(a) The solution of a linear equation is affected when the same number is added to (or subtracted from) both the sides of the equation.

(b) $x - 4 = 3\sqrt{y}$ is a linear equation in two variables.

(c) Geometrical representation of $ax + by + c = 0$ is a straight line

(d) Every solution of the linear equation is a point on the graph of the linear equation.

6. Check which of the following are solutions of the equation $2x - y = 4$?

(a) $x = 0, y = -4$ (b) $x = 3, y = 2$

(c) $x = 1, y = 1$ (d) $y = 0, x = 2$

Passage Based Questions :

DIRECTIONS: *Study the given paragraph(s) and answer the following questions.*

PASSAGE-I

If the temperature of a liquid can be measured in Kelvin units as *x*°K or in Fahrenheit units as *y*°F, the relation between the two systems of measurement of temperature is given by the linear equation

$$y = \frac{9}{5}(x - 273) + 32$$

1. The temperature of the liquid in Fahrenheit if the temperature of the liquid is 313°K, is

(a) 105°F (b) 104°F

(c) 343°F (d) 100°F

2. If the temperature is 158°F, then the temperature in Kelvin is.

(a) 105°K (b) 104°K

(c) 343°K (d) 100°K

PASSAGE-II

The linear equation that converts Fahrenheit (F) to Celsius (C) is given by the relation

$$C = \frac{5F - 160}{9}$$

3. If the temperature is 35°C, then the temperature in Fahrenheit is

(a) 95°F (b) 96°F

(c) 98°F (d) 94°F

4. The numerical value of the temperature which is same in both the scales, is

(a) 40 (b) – 40

(c) 50 (d) – 50

Assertion & Reason :

DIRECTIONS: *Each of these questions contains an Assertion followed by Reason. Read them carefully and answer the question on the basis of following options. You have to select the one that best describes the two statements.*

(a) If both **Assertion** and **Reason** are **correct** and **Reason** is the **correct explanation** of **Assertion**.

(b) If both **Assertion** and **Reason** are correct, but **Reason** is **not the correct** explanation of **Assertion**.

(c) If **Assertion** is **correct** but **Reason** is **incorrect**.

(d) If **Assertion** is **incorrect** but **Reason** is **correct**.

1. **Assertion :** A linear equation $2x + 3y = 5$ has a unique solution.

Reason : A linear equation in two variables has infinitely many solutions

2. **Assertion :** All the points (1, 0), (–1, 0), (2, 0) and (5, 0) lie on the x-axis.
Reason : Equation of the x-axis is $y = 0$

3. **Assertion :** The point (0, 3) lies on the graph of the linear equation $3x + 4y = 12$.
Reason : (0, 3) satisfies the equation $3x + 4y = 12$.

4. **Assertion :** The graph of every linear equation in two variables need not be a line.
Reason : Graph of a linear equation in two variables is always a line.

5. **Assertion :** The graph of the equation $3x + y = 0$ is a line passing through the origin.
Reason : An equation of the form $ax + by + c = 0$, where a, b, c are real numbers is called a linear equation in x and y.

Multiple Matching Question :

DIRECTIONS : *Following question has four statements (A, B, C and D) given in Column-I and statements (p, q, r, s, ...) in Column-II. Any given statement in Column I can have correct matching with one or more statement(s) given in Column-II.*

1.

Column-I (Equation)	Column-II (Solutions)
(A) $x + y = 0$	(p) (3/2, 3)
(B) $y - 2x = 0$	(q) (–5, 5)
(C) $3x + 5y = 0$	(r) (5, –2)
(D) $2x - y = 12$	(s) (0, 0)
	(t) (–5, 3)
	(u) (5, –3)

Integer Type Questions :

DIRECTIONS: *Answer the following questions. The answer to each of the question is a single digit integer, ranging from 0 to 9.*

1. If $x = k^2$ and $y = k$ is a solution of the equation $x - 5y + 6 = 0$, then the sum of the values of k is
2. For equation $x + y = 8$, ordered pair (5, a) lies on its graph. The value of 'a' is
3. If the points A(3, 5) and B (1, 4) lie on the graph of the line $ax + by = 7$, then the sum of values of 'a' and 'b' is
4. The distance between the graphs of the equations $y = -1$ and $y = 3$ is
5. The graph of the linear equation $2x - y = 4$ cuts x- axis at (a, 0). The value of 'a' is
6. If $(2k - 1, k)$ is a solution of the equation $10x - 9y = 12$, then the value of 'k' is

4 ADVANCED EXERCISE
BASED ON CONNECTING TOPICS

DIRECTIONS (Qs 1–4): *This section contains multiple choice questions. Each question has 4 choices (a), (b), (c) and (d) out of which only one is correct.*

1. The number of common integral solutions of the inequations $x > -5$ and $x < 5$ is
(a) 6 (b) 8 (c) 9 (d) 5

2. Solution set for the inequation $\frac{1}{x+1} > 0$ is
(a) $\{x : x > 1\}$ (b) $\{x : x > -1\}$
(c) $\{x : x < 1\}$ (d) $\{x : x < -1\}$

3. Any line in a plane divides the plane into ______ disjoint parts.
(a) one (b) two
(c) three (d) four

4. If $x + y \le 7$ and $x - y \le 3$ then
(a) $x \le 4$ (b) $x \le 7$
(c) $x \le 3$ (d) $x \le 5$

5. Boundary line for the region $y \le x + 4$ is
(a) $y = x + 4$ (b) $y > x + 4$
(c) $y \ge x + 4$ (d) $y = x - 4$

6. If $0 < x < 5$ and $1 < y < 2$, then which of the following is true?
(a) $x + y < 0$ (b) $-3 < 2x - 3y < 4$
(c) $-6 < 2x - 3y < 7$ (d) $-3 < 3x - y < 2$

7. Inequation that represents the following graph is

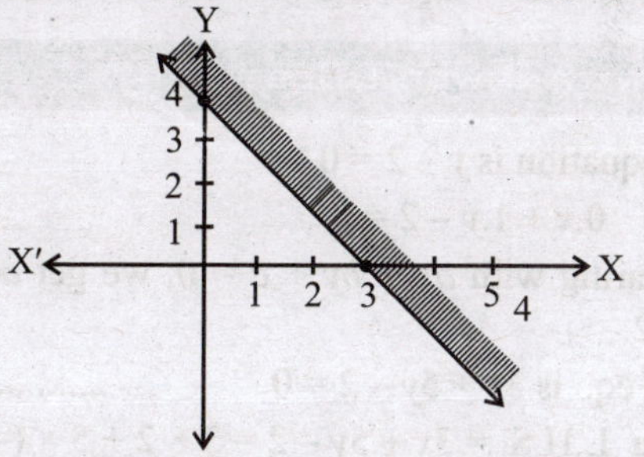

(a) $4x + 3y \ge 12$ (b) $4x + 3y \le 12$
(c) $4x + 3y - 12 \ge 12$ (d) $4x + 3y - 12 \le 12$

8. Which of the following is the solution set of $|2x - 3| < 7$
(a) $\{x : -5 < x < 2\}$ (b) $\{x : -5 < x < 5\}$
(c) $\{x : -2 < x < 5\}$ (d) $\{x : x < -5 \text{ or } x > 2\}$

9. $|x^2 - 4x| < 5$
(a) $-1 \le x \le 5$ (b) $1 \le x \le 5$
(c) $-1 < x < 5$ (d) $1 < x < 5$

10. If $x > 5$ and $y < -1$, then which of the following statements is true?
(a) $(x + 4y) > 1$ (b) $x > -4y$
(c) $-4x < 5y$ (d) None of these

SOLUTIONS

Brief Explanations of Selected Questions

1 EXERCISE

FILL IN THE BLANKS :

1. infinitely many
2. straight line
3. y, x
4. y
5. x
6. origin.
7. solution
8. point

TRUE/FALSE :

1. False
2. False
3. False
4. True
5. True
6. False, the points (2, 0), (–3, 0) lie on the x-axis. The point (4, 2) lies in the first quadrant. The point (0, 5) lies on the y-axis.
7. True, since the line parallel to y-axis at a distance a units to the left to y-axis is given by the equation $x = -a$
8. False, because $x = 0, y = 0$ does not satisfy the equation.

MATCH THE COLUMNS :

1. (A) → (q); (B) → (s); (C) → (r); (D) → (p)
2. (A) → (r); (B) → (q); (C) → (s); (D) → (p)

VERY SHORT ANSWER QUESTIONS

1. Given equation is $y - 2 = 0$

   $\Rightarrow \quad 0.x + 1.y - 2 = 0$

   Comparing with $ax + by + c = 0$, we get $a = 0$, $b = 1$, $c = -2$.
2. Given eq. is $3x + 5y - 2 = 0$ .... (i)

   Taking L.H.S. $= 3x + 5y - 2 = 3 \times 2 + 5 \times (-1) - 2$
   $= 6 - 5 - 2 = -1 \neq 0$

   Here L.H.S. ≠ R.H.S. therefore $x = 2$, $y = -1$ is not a solution of given equation.
3. Writing the equation $3y + 4 = 0$ as $0.x + 3y + 4 = 0$, we will find that $y = -\frac{4}{3}$ for any value of x. Thus, two solutions can be given as $\left(0, -\frac{4}{3}\right)$ and $\left(1, -\frac{4}{3}\right)$
4. Since, $x = 2$, $y = 1$ is a solution of the equation $2x + 3y = k$, therefore these values will satisfy the equation. So, we put $x = 2$ and $y = 1$ in the equation, we get

   $2(2) + 3(1) = k \Rightarrow k = 7$.
5. The equations of two lines passing through (2, 14) can be taken as

   $x + y = 16$ and $7x - y = 0$.

   So, There are infinitely many such lines because through a point an infinite number of lines can be drawn.
6. (2, 2), (0, 3), (6, 0) and (4, 1).
7. $x + y = 80$
8. Substituting $x = 2$, $y = 3$ in the given equation, we get

   LHS $= 3 \times 2 - 4 \times 3 + 6 = 0 =$ RHS.

   $\therefore x = 2, y = 3$ satisfy $3x - 4y + 6 = 0$
9. $2x + y = k$

   $\Rightarrow \quad 2 \times 3 + 5 = k \Rightarrow k = 11$
10. The equation of any line parallel to x-axis at a distance b units is given by $y = b$.

    Here, $b = 3$ (above x-axis represent positive direction)

    ⇒ Required equation is $y = 3$.

SHORT ANSWER QUESTIONS :

1. (a) $5x - 8 = 7$

   L.H.S. $= 5x - 8 = 5 \times 3 - 8$, (on putting $x = 3$)
   $= 15 - 8 = 7$

   and R.H.S. = 7

   ∴ On putting $x = 3$, we find that L.H.S. = R.H.S.

   Hence, the solution of the given equation is $x = 3$.

   (b) $x = 2$ is not a solution of $5x + 7 = 3$ as we substituting $x = 2$ in the equation.

   L.H.S. $= 5 \times 2 + 7 = 17 \neq$ R.H.S.
2. Given point (2, 11) i.e. $x = 2$ and $y = 11$

   By addition, we get $x + y = 2 + 11 = 13$

   By subtraction, we get $x - y = 2 - 11 = -9$

   Hence $x + y = 13$ and $x - y = -9$ are two lines passing through (2, 11). Infinite number of lines may be drawn through the point (2, 11).
3. (i) $1.x + 0.y + 5 = 0$

   (ii) $0x + 1y - 2 = 0$

   (iii) $2x + 0y - 3 = 0$

   (iv) $0x + 5y - 2 = 0$.
4. When $x = 2$, then $2 + 2y = 6 \Rightarrow 2y = 4, \Rightarrow y = 2$

   Now, let us choose $x = 0$. With this value of x, the given equation reduces to $2y = 6$ which has the unique solution $y = 3$. So $x = 0$, $y = 3$ is also a solution of $x + 2y = 6$.

   Similarly, taking $y = 0$, the given equation reduces to $x = 6$.

So, $x = 6, y = 0$ is a solution of $x + 2y = 6$ as well.

Finally let us take $y = 1$. The given equation now reduces to $x + 2 = 6$, whose solution is given by $x = 4$. Therefore, $x = 4, y = 1$ is also a solution of the given equation.

So four of the infinitely many solutions of the given equation are : (2, 2), (0, 3), (6, 0) and (4, 1).

5. $y = \frac{11-2x}{3}, \left(0, \frac{11}{3}\right)$

6. The graph of the linear equation $3x + 4y = 12$ cuts the x-axis at the point where $y = 0$. On putting $y = 0$ in the linear equation, we have $3x = 12$, which gives $x = 4$. Thus, the required point is (4, 0).

The graph of the linear equation $3x + 4y = 12$ cuts the y-axis at the point where $x = 0$. On putting $x = 0$ in the given equation, we have $4y = 12$, which gives $y = 3$. Thus, the required point is (0, 3).

7. The co-ordinates of the points lying on the line parallel to the y-axis, at a distance 2 units from the origin and in the positive direction of the x-axis are of the form $(2, a)$. Putting $x = 2, y = a$ in the equation $x + y = 5$, we get $a = 3$. Thus, the required point is (2, 3)

8. As the x-coordinate of the point is $\frac{5}{2}$ times its ordinate, therefore, $x = \frac{5}{2}y$.

Now putting $x = \frac{5}{2}y$ in $2x + 5y = 20$, we get $5y = 10$.

Therefore, $x = 5$. Thus, the required point is (5, 2)

9. Given equation is $3x + 2y = 9$.

$\Rightarrow \quad y = \frac{9-3x}{2}$

When $x = 1$, $y = \frac{9-3}{2} = \frac{6}{2} = 3$

When $x = -1$, $y = \frac{9+3}{2} = \frac{12}{2} = 6$

$\therefore$ Two solutions of the given equation are (1, 3), (– 1, 6).

10. $5(4x + 3) = 3(x - 2)$

$\Rightarrow \quad 20x + 15 = 3x - 6$

$\Rightarrow \quad 20x - 3x = -6 - 15$

$\Rightarrow \quad 17x = -21 \Rightarrow x = \frac{-21}{17}$

11. $\frac{3}{x-1} + \frac{1}{x+1} = \frac{4}{x}$

$\Rightarrow \quad \frac{3(x+1)+1(x-1)}{(x-1)(x+1)} = \frac{4}{x} \quad \Rightarrow \quad \frac{3x+3+x-1}{x^2-1} = \frac{4}{x}$

$\Rightarrow \quad \frac{4x+2}{x^2-1} = \frac{4}{x} \quad \Rightarrow \quad x(4x+2) = 4(x^2-1)$

$\Rightarrow \quad 4x^2 + 2x = 4x^2 - 4 \Rightarrow 2x = -4 \Rightarrow x = -2$

12. $(5x + 1)(x + 3) - 8 = 5(x + 1)(x + 2)$

$\Rightarrow \quad (5x^2 + 15x + x + 3) - 8 = 5(x^2 + 2x + x + 2)$

$\Rightarrow \quad 5x^2 + 16x + 3 - 8 = 5(x^2 + 3x + 2)$

$\Rightarrow \quad 5x^2 + 16x - 5 = 5x^2 + 15x + 10$

$\Rightarrow \quad 16x - 15x = 15 \Rightarrow x = 15$

LONG ANSWER QUESTIONS :

1.

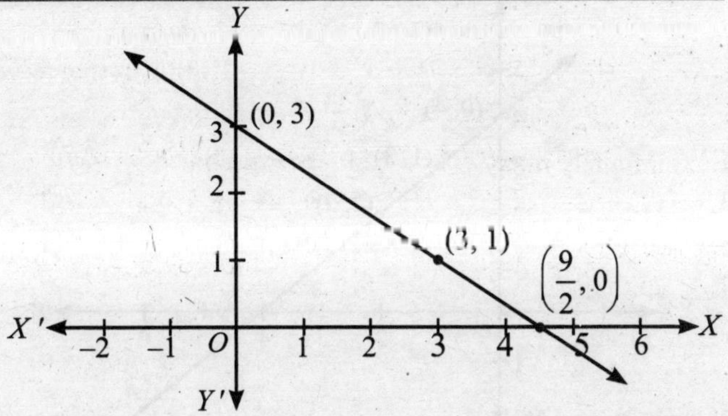

2. The given equation is $2x + 3y = 12$. To draw the graph of this equation, we need at least two points lying on the graph.

From the equation, we have $y = \frac{12-2x}{3}$

For $x = 0, y = 4$, therefore, (0, 4) lies on the graph.

For $y = 0, x = 6$, therefore, (6, 0) lies on the graph.

Now plot the points $A(0, 4)$ and $B(6, 0)$ and join them (see Fig.), to get the line AB. Line AB is the required graph.

You can see that the graph (line AB) cuts the x-axis at the point (6, 0) and the y-axis at the point (0, 4).

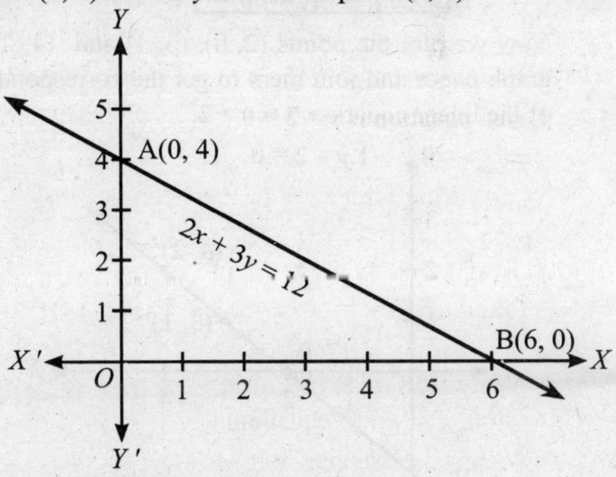

3. (i) Given equation is $x + y = 4$ or $y = 4 - x$

Now, we take certain values of x and find their corresponding values of y

For $x = 0, y = 4 - 0 = 4$

$x = 1, y = 4 - 1 = 3$

$x = 2, y = 4 - 2 = 2$

∴ Table is given below:

x	0	1	2
y	4	3	2

Now, we plot the points (0, 4), (1, 3) and (2, 2) on the graph and join them to get the straight line which represents the linear equation $x + y = 4$.

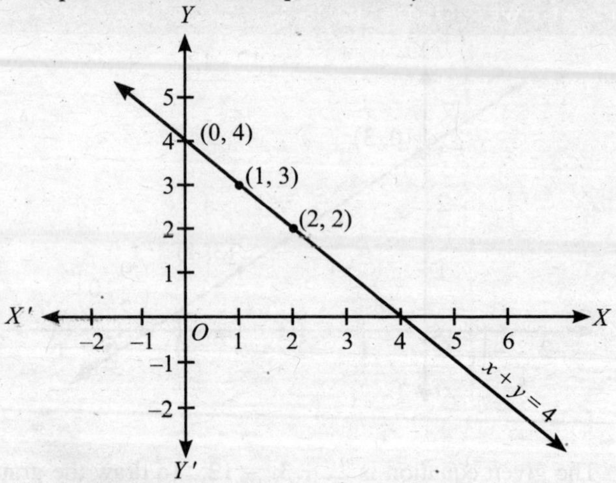

(ii) Given equation is $x - y = 2$

$\Rightarrow \quad x = 2 + y$

Now take certain values of y and find their corresponding values of x.

For $y = 0, x = 2$

$y = 1, x = 3$

$y = 2, x = 4$

∴ The corresponding table is

x	2	3	4
y	0	1	2

Now we plot the points (2, 0), (3, 1) and (4, 2) on the graph paper and join them to get the corresponding line of the linear equation $x - y = 2$.

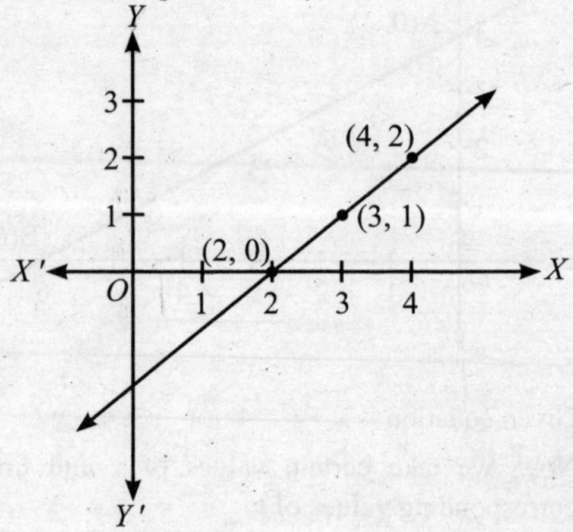

4. $2x - y + 3 = 0 \Rightarrow y = 2x + 3$

When $x = 0$, then $y = 2 \times 0 + 3 = 3$

When $x = 1$, then $y = 2 \times 1 + 3 = 5$

Thus, we have the following table :

x	0	1
y	3	5

Now, plot the points A (0, 3) and B (1, 5) on a graph paper Join AB and extend it in both the directions.

Then, the line AB is the required graph of $2x - y + 3 = 0$

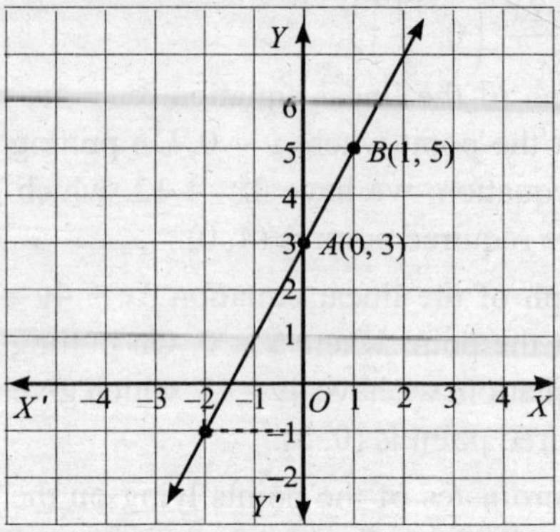

From the graph it is clear when $x = -2$, then $y = -1$

5. We solve $2x + 1 = x - 3$,

$\Rightarrow \quad 2x - x = -3 - 1$

i.e., $x = -4$

(i) The representation of the solution on the number line is shown in below given fig. where $x = -4$ is treated as an equation in one variable.

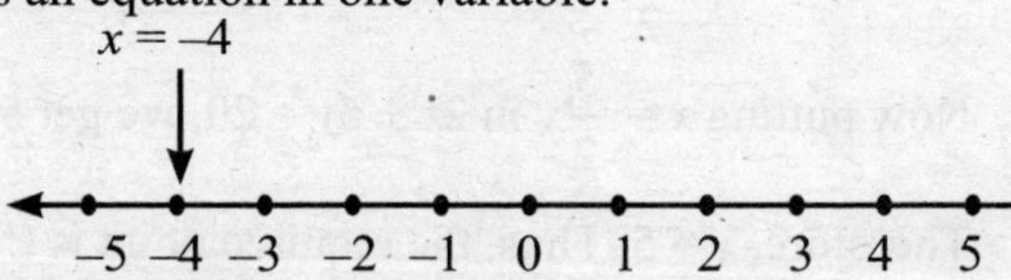

(ii) We know that $x = -4$ can be written as $x + 0.y = -4$, which is a linear equation in two variables x and y. Now all the values of y are permissible because $0.y$ is always 0. However, x must satisfy the equation $x = -4$. Hence, two solutions of the given equation are $x = -4, y = 0$ and $x = -4, y = 2$.

The graph of $x + 0.y = -4$ is the straight line AB parallel to the y-axis and at a distance of 4 units to the left of it.

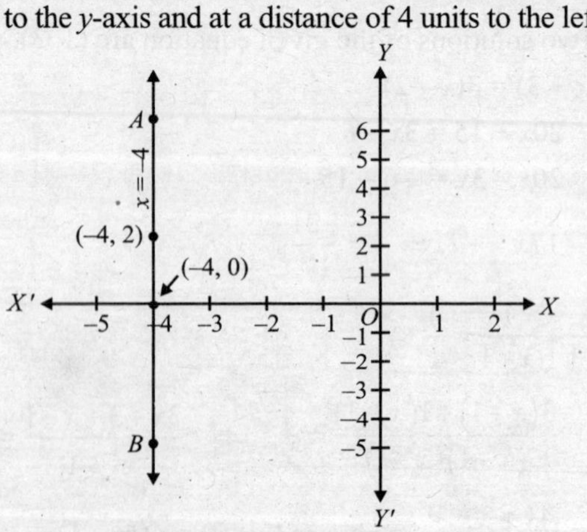

Similarly, you can obtain a line parallel to the x-axis corresponding to equations of the type $y = 3$ or $0.x + 1.y = 3$.

6. The given equation is $2x + 9 = 0$

(i) **In one variable**

$2x + 9 = 0 \Rightarrow x = -\frac{9}{2}$

The representation of $2x + 9 = 0$ on the number line is as shown below:

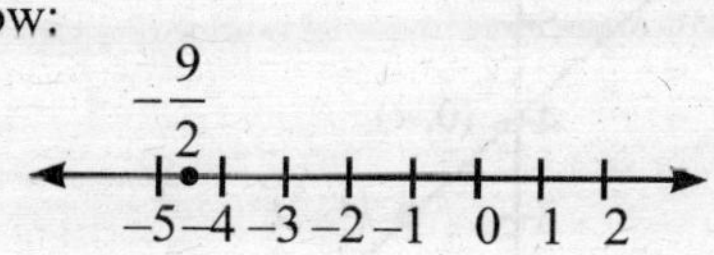

(ii) **In two variables**

$2x + 9 = 0$ can be written as $2x + 0.y + 9 = 0$

It is a linear equation in two variables x and y. This is represented by a line. All the values of y are permissible because $0y$ is always 0. However, x must satisfy the relation $2x + 9 = 0$.

i.e., $x = -\frac{9}{2}$.

Hence, two solution of the given equation are $x = -\frac{9}{2}, y = 0$ and $x = -\frac{9}{2}, y = 2$.

The graph AB is a line parallel to the y-axis and at a distance of $\frac{9}{2}$ units to the left of it.

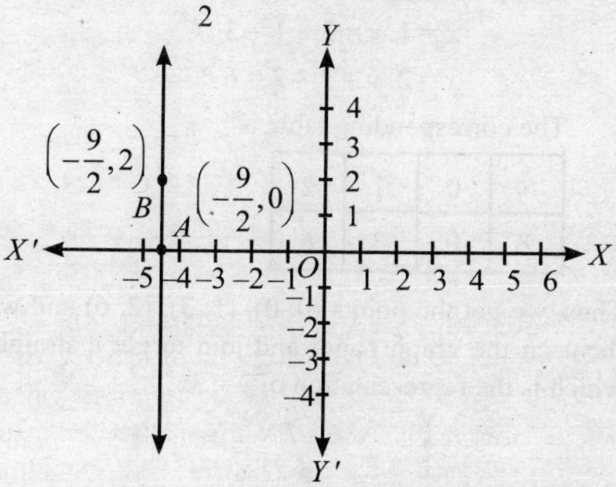

7. Let Alka and Noori contribute ₹ x and ₹ y respectively, then the linear equation satisfying the given data is $x + y = 500$.

Let 1 cm represent ₹ 100 on both axes. The graph of the **linear equation** is shown in the adjoining figure.

Note that as the values of x or y cannot be negative, the graph of the given data is the line segment AB.

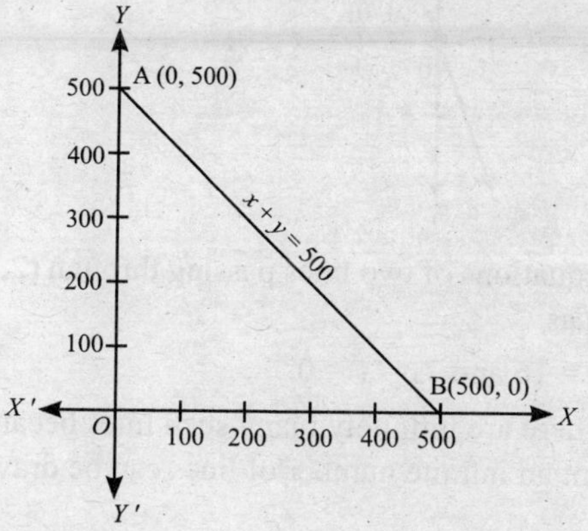

8. $3x + 4y = 12 \Rightarrow 4y = 12 - 3x$

$\Rightarrow \quad y = \frac{12 - 3x}{4}$

Putting $x = 4$, $y = \frac{12 - 3(4)}{4} = \frac{12 - 12}{4} = \frac{0}{4}$

$y = 0$

Putting $x = 0$, $y = \frac{12 - 3 \times 0}{4} = \frac{12}{4}$

$y = 3$

Putting $x = -4$, $y = \frac{12 - 3 \times -4}{4} = \frac{12 + 12}{4}$

$y = 6$

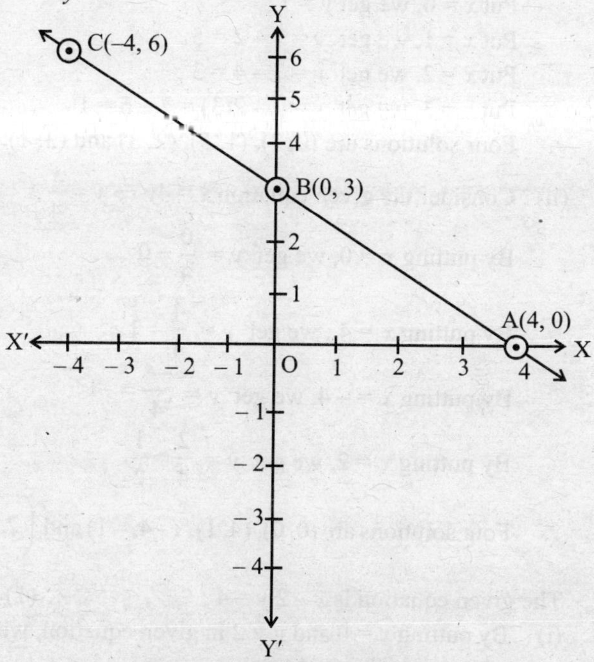

x	4	0	–4
y	0	3	6

Clearly, the graph (line AB) cuts the x-axis at the point (4, 0) and the y-axis at the point (0, 3).

2 EXERCISE

TEXT-BOOK EXERCISE :

1. Let the cost of a note book be ₹ x and the cost of a pen be ₹ y.

According to the question, $x = 2y \Rightarrow x - 2y = 0$ which is the required linear equation in two variables.

2. (i) Given equation is $-2x + 3y = 6$

$\Rightarrow \quad -2x + 3y - 6 = 0$

Comparing with $ax + by + c = 0$,

we get $a = -2$, $b = 3$, $c = -6$.

(ii) Given equation is $x = 3y$

$\Rightarrow \quad x - 3y = 0$

Comparing with $ax + by + c = 0$,

we get $a = 1$, $b = -3$, $c = 0$.

(iii) Given equation is $2x = -5y$

$\Rightarrow \quad 2x + 5y = 0$

Comparing with $ax + by + c = 0$,

we get $a = 2$, $b = 5$, $c = 0$.

3. $y = 3x + 5$ has infinitely many solution, because for every value of x, there is a corresponding value of y and vice versa.

So, option (iii) is true.

4. (i) Consider $2x + y = 7$

$\Rightarrow \quad y = 7 - 2x$

Put $x = 0$, we get $y = 7$

Put $x = 1$, we get $y = 7 - 2 = 5$

Put $x = 2$, we get $y = 7 - 4 = 3$

Put $x = 3$, we get $y = 7 - 2(3) = 7 - 6 = 1$

$\therefore$ Four solutions are (0, 7), (1, 5), (2, 3) and (3, 1).

(ii) Consider the given equation $x = 4y \Rightarrow y = \frac{x}{4}$

By putting $x = 0$, we get $y = \frac{0}{4} = 0$

By putting $x = 4$, we get $y = \frac{4}{4} = 1$

By putting $x = -4$, we get $y = \frac{-4}{4} = -1$

By putting $x = 2$, we get $y = \frac{2}{4} = \frac{1}{2}$

$\therefore$ Four solutions are (0, 0), (4, 1), (–4, – 1) and $\left(2, \frac{1}{2}\right)$

5. The given equation is $x - 2y = 4$ ...(1)

(i) By putting $x = 0$ and $y = 2$ in given equation, we get $-4 = 4$, which is not true.

$\therefore$ (0, 2) is not a solution of given equation.

(ii) By putting $x = 4$ and $y = 0$ in (1), we get $4 = 4$ which is true

$\therefore$ (4, 0) is a solution of (1).

(iii) By putting $x = \sqrt{2}$, $y = 4\sqrt{2}$ in (1), we get $\sqrt{2} - 2(4\sqrt{2}) = \sqrt{2} - 8\sqrt{2} = -7\sqrt{2} \neq 4$.

$\therefore$ $(\sqrt{2}, 4\sqrt{2})$ is not a solution of (1).

6. Since, $x = 2$, $y = 1$ is a solution of the equation $2x + 3y = k$, therefore these values will satisfy the equation.

So, we put $x = 2$ and $y = 1$ in the equation, we get

$2(2) + 3(1) = k \Rightarrow k = 7$.

7. (i) Given equation is $x + y = 4$ or $y = 4 - x$

Now we take certain values of x and find their corresponding values of y

For $x = 0, y = 4 - 0 = 4$

$x = 1, y = 4 - 1 = 3$

$x = 2, y = 4 - 2 = 2$

$\therefore$ Table is given below :

x	0	1	2
y	4	3	2

Now we plot the points (0, 4), (1, 3) and (2, 2) on the graph and join them to get the straight line which represents the linear equation $x + y = 4$.

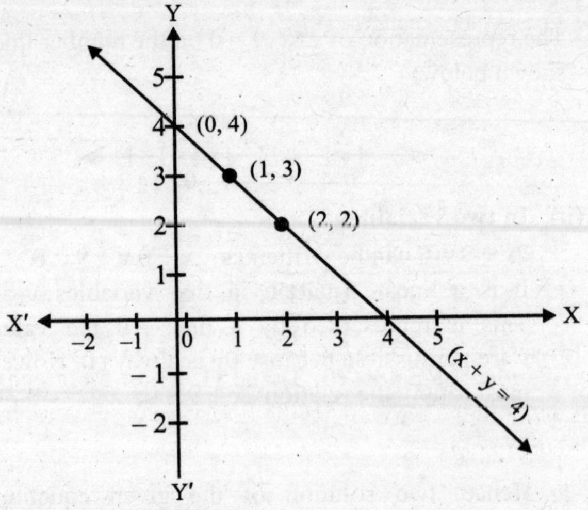

(iii) Given equation is $y = 3x$

Now we take certain values of x and find the corresponding values of y.

When $x = 0, y = 3 \times 0 = 0$

$x = 1, y = 3 \times 1 = 3$

$x = 2, y = 3 \times 2 = 6$

The corresponding table is

x	0	1	2
y	0	3	6

Thus, we get the points (0, 0), (1, 3), (2, 6) and we plot them on the graph paper and join to get a straight line which is the representation of $y = 3x$.

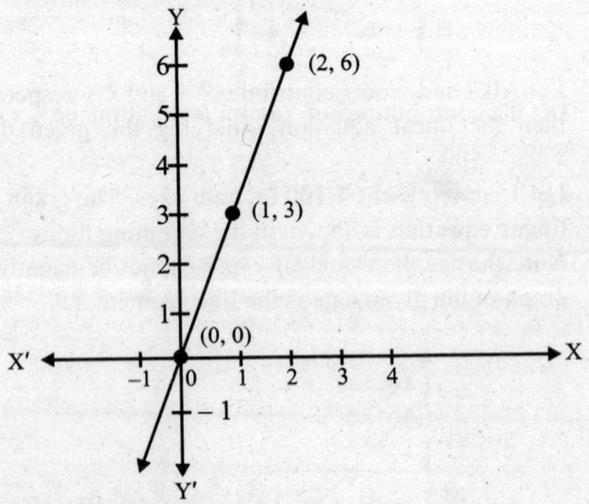

8. The equations of two lines passing through (2, 14) can be taken as

$x + y = 16$ and $7x - y = 0$.

So, There are infinitely many such lines because through a point an infinite number of lines can be drawn.

9. Total distance covered = x km
Total fare = ₹ y
Fair for the first kilometre = ₹ 8
Subsequent distance = (x – 1) km
Fair for the subsequent distance = ₹ 5(x – 1)
According to the question,

$y = 8 + 5(x-1)$

$\Rightarrow \quad y = 8 + 5x - 5$

$\Rightarrow \quad y = 5x + 3$

Table of solution is

x	0	1
y	3	8

We plot the points (0, 3) and (1, 8) on the graph paper and join the same to get the line which is the graph of the equation y = 5x + 3.

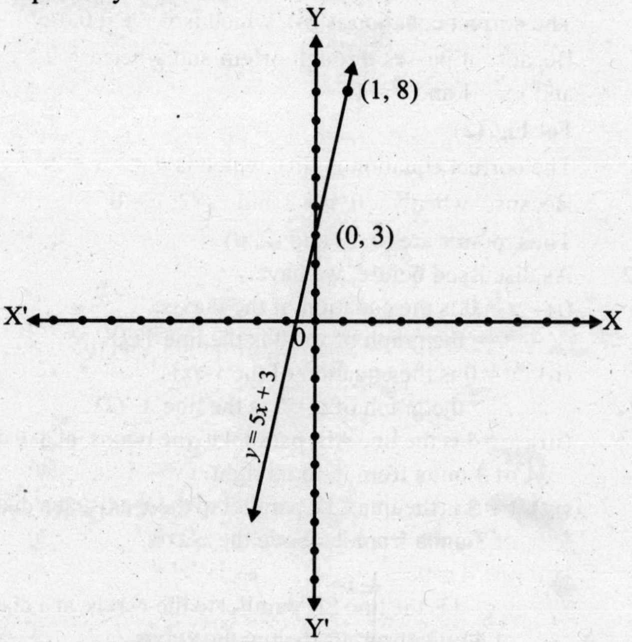

10. Let the contributions of Yamini and Fatima be ₹ x and ₹ y respectively.
Then according to the question
$x + y = 100$
This is the required linear equation which satisfies the given data
Now, we consider certain value of x and find corresponding values of y.
For $x = 0, y = 100$
For $x = 50, y = 50$

x	0	50
y	100	50

We plot the points (0, 100) and (50, 50) on the graph paper and join the same to get the line which is the graph of the equation $x + y = 100$.

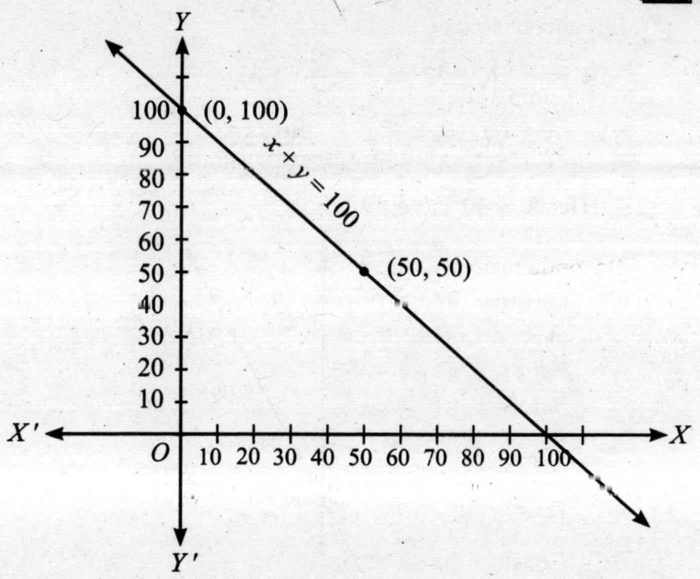

11. Given linear equation is $F = \left(\frac{9}{5}\right)C + 32$

(i) Let the value of C is represented on x-axis and the value of F is represented on y-axis.
So, we can consider $C = x$ and $F = y$

$\therefore$ Given equation becomes $y = \frac{9}{5}x + 32$

Now, we consider certain values of x and find the corresponding values of y.

For $x = 5$, $y = \frac{9}{5} \times (5) + 32 = 41$

For $x = 10$, $y = \frac{9}{5} \times (10) + 32 = 50$

For $x = 15$, $y = \frac{9}{5} \times (15) + 32 = 59$

Now, we plot the points $A(0, 32)$, $B(5, 41)$, $C(10, 50)$ and $D(15, 59)$ on the graph paper.

(ii) For $C = 30°$, $F = \frac{9}{5} \times 30° + 32° = 86°$

Required temperature = 86° Fahrenheit.

(iii) For $F = 95°$ we have $95 = \frac{9}{5} \times C + 32°$

$\Rightarrow \quad 95° - 32° = \frac{9}{5}C \Rightarrow \frac{9}{5}C = 63°$

$\Rightarrow \quad C = 35°$ Fahrenheit

(iv) For $C = 0$, $F = \frac{9}{5} \times 0 + 32° = 32°$ and

For $F = 0°$ Fahrenheit we have $0 = \frac{9}{5} \times C + 32°$

$\Rightarrow \quad C = \frac{-32° \times 5}{9} = \frac{-160°}{9}$

(v) Let the temperature be $x°$ numerically.
-i.e. $x°$ F = $x°$ C

$\therefore \quad F = \left(\frac{9}{5}\right)C + 32 \Rightarrow x = \frac{9}{5}x + 32$

$\Rightarrow \quad -32 = \frac{9x - 5x}{5} \quad \Rightarrow x = \frac{-32 \times 5}{4} = -40°$

Hence, – 40°F = – 40°C.

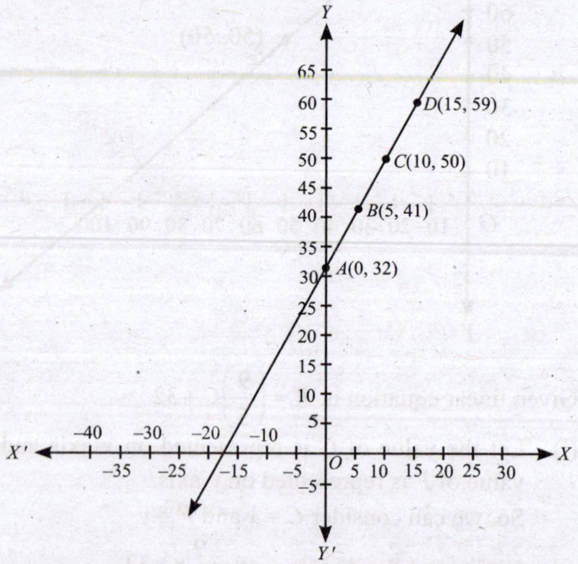

EXEMPLAR QUESTIONS:

1. (a) $2(2) + 3(0) = k \Rightarrow k = 4$
2. (d) By putting $x = 0$ in $2x + 3y = 6$, we get $y = 2$.
   Hence, graph of $2x + 3y = 6$ cuts the y-axis at (0, 2)
3. (c) Given equation is $3x - y = x - 1$
   $\Rightarrow \quad 2x - y = -1$
   It has infinitely many solutions
4. Any point on the line $y = x$ is of the form (a, a)
5. The graph of the linear equation 3x + 4y = 12 cuts the x-axis at the point where y = 0. On putting y = 0 in the linear equation, we have 3x = 12, which gives x = 4. Thus, the required point is (4, 0).
   The graph of the linear equation 3x + 4y = 12 cuts the y-axis at the point where x = 0. On putting x = 0 in the given equation, we have 4y = 12, which gives y = 3. Thus, the required point is (0, 3).
6. The coordinates of the points lying on the line parallel to the y-axis, at a distance 2 units from the origin and in the positive direction of the x-axis are of the form (2, a). Putting x = 2, y = a in the equation x + y = 5, we get a = 3. Thus, the required point is (2, 3).
7. As the x-coordinate of the point is $\frac{5}{2}$ times its ordinate, therefore, $x = \frac{5}{2}y$.
   Now putting $x = \frac{5}{2}y$ in 2x + 5y = 20, we get, y = 2.
   Therefore, x = 5. Thus, the required point is (5, 2).
8. Any straight line parallel to x-axis is given by y = k, where k is the distance of the line from the x-axis. Here k = 4. Therefore, the equation of the line is y = 4. To draw the graph of this equation, plot the points (1, 4) and (2, 4) and join them. This is the required graph

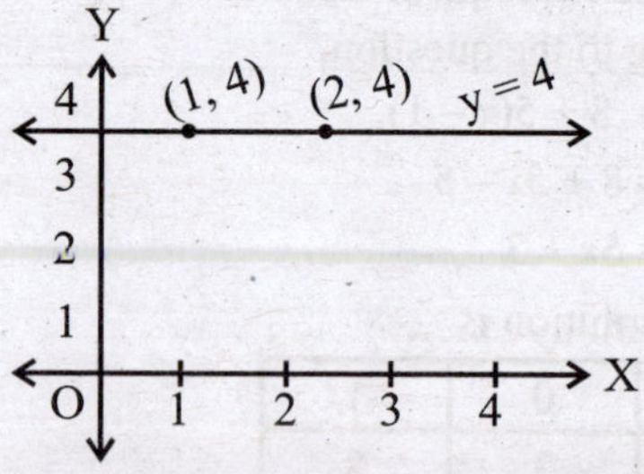

HOTS QUESTIONS:

1. **For Fig. (1)**
   The correct equation is (ii), which is $x + y = 0$.
   Because it passes through origin and when $x = 1$, $y = -1$ and $x = -1$ and $y = 1$
   For Fig. (2)
   The correct equation is (iii), which is $y = -x + 2$.
   Because, when $x = 0$, $y = 2$ and $x = 2$, $y = 0$
   Thus, points are (0, 2) and (2, 0)
2. As discussed before, we have:
   (i) $x = 0$ is the equation of the y-axis.
   $\therefore$ the graph of $x = 0$ is the line YOY'
   (ii) $y = 0$ is the equation of the x-axis.
   $\therefore$ the graph of $y = 0$ is the line $X'OX$.
   (iii) $x = 4$ is the line AB, parallel to the y-axis, at a distance of 4 units from it, to its right.
   (iv) $y = 3$ is the line CD, parallel to the x-axis, at a distance of 3 units from it, above the x-axis.
   (v) $y + 4 = 0 \Rightarrow y = -4$.
   $y = -4$ is the line EF, parallel to the x-axis, at a distance of 4 units from its, below the x-axis.
   (vi) $x + 2 = 0 \Rightarrow x = -2$.
   $x = -2$ is the line GH, parallel to the y-axis, at a distance of 2 units from it, to its left.

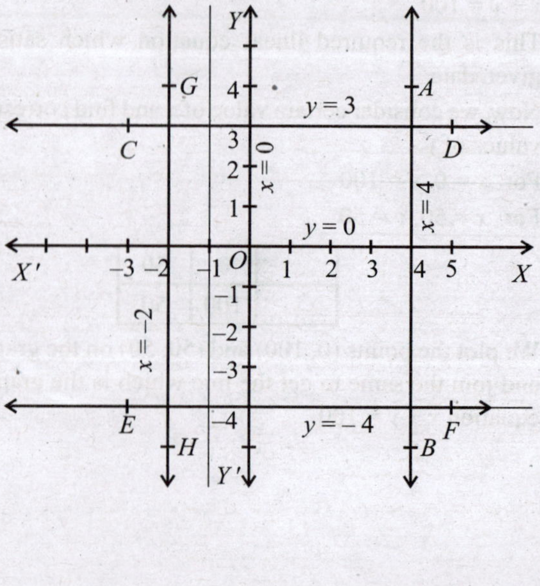

3. Let the total distance covered be x km and the fare charged ₹ y. Then for the first km, fare charged is ₹ 10 and for remaining $(x-1)$ km fare charged is ₹ $4(x-1)$
Therefore, $y = 10 + 4(x-1) = 4x + 6$
The required equation is $y = 4x + 6$.
Now, when $x = 0, y = 6$ and when $x = -1, y = 2$.
The graph is given in fig.

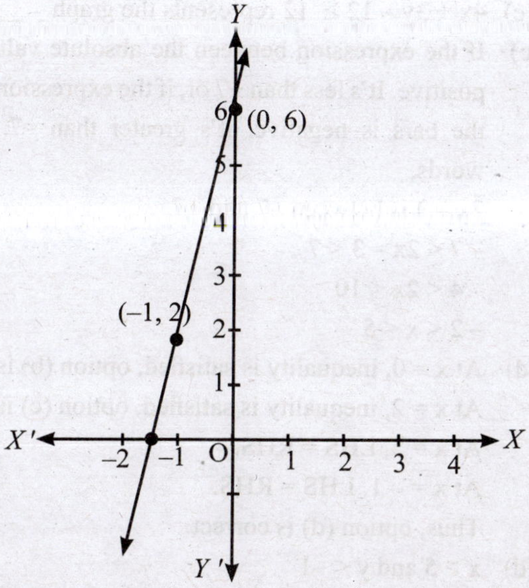

4. y-coordinate of the point A where graph (i.e. line) of the equation $4x + 3y = 12$ cuts the x-axis is 0 i.e. $y = 0$.
On putting $y = 0$ in equation $4x + 3y = 12$, we get
$4x = 12 \Rightarrow x = 3$
Hence, co-ordiantes of the point A where the graph (i.e. line) of the equation cuts the x-axis is (3, 0).
Now x-coordinate of the point B where graph (i.e. line) of the equation $4x + 3y = 12$ cuts the y-axis is 0 i.e. $x = 0$.
On putting $x = 0$ in equation $4x + 3y = 12$, we get
$3y = 12 \Rightarrow y = 4$
Hence, coordinate of the point B where graph (i.e. line) of the equation $4x + 3y = 12$ cuts the y-axis is (0, 4).

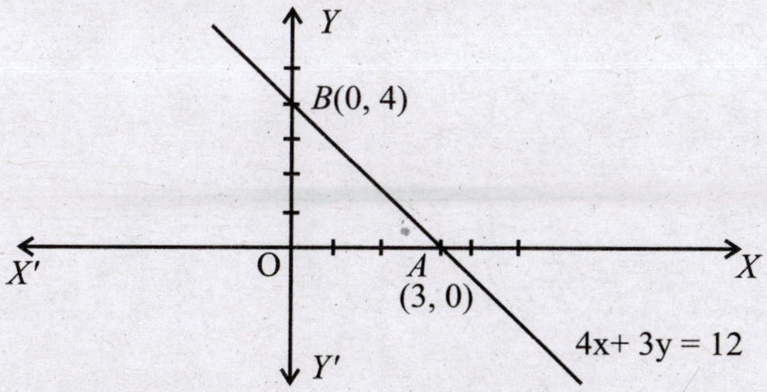

In the diagram, AOB is a triangle right angled at O.
In right ΔAOB,
$AB^2 = OA^2 + OB^2 = (3)^2 + (4)^2 = 9 + 16 = 25$
$\therefore$ AB = 5 units
Hence, length of hypotenuse AB = 5 units

3 EXERCISE

SINGLE OPTION CORRECT :

1. (c) Given linear equation has infinitely many solution.
2. (a)
3. (a) $3(3) - p(-2) - 7 = 0 \Rightarrow 2 + 2p = 0 \Rightarrow p = -1$
4. (b) As $y = -4$ is a solution of $5x - 8y = 47$

$\therefore \; 5x - 8(-4) = 47 \Rightarrow 5x + 32 = 47$

$\Rightarrow 5x = 15 \Rightarrow x = 3$

5. (c) (–1, 1) satisfies the equation $2x + 5y - 3 = 0$
6. (a) 7. (b)
8. (b) $3y + 2 = 0 \Rightarrow y = -\frac{2}{3}$
It is the line parallel to x-axis.
9. (c) Line $2x = 5 \Rightarrow x = \frac{5}{2}$ which is parallel to y-axis
10. (b)
11. (a) 12. (b)
13. (a) 14. (c)
15. (c)

MORE THAN ONE OPTION CORRECT :

1. (a), (b), (c) 2. (a), (b)
3. (a, b, c) 4. (b, c, d)
5. (a, b)
6. (a, b) $(x = 0, y = -4), (x = 3, y = 2)$

PASSAGE BASED QUESTIONS :

1. (b) 104°F 2. (c) 343°K
3. (a) 95° F 4. (b) –40

ASSERTION & REASON :

1. (d) 2. (a)
3. (a) 4. (d)
5. (b)

MULTIPLE MATCHING QUESTION :

1. (A) → (q, s); (B) → (p); (C) → (t), (u); (D) → (r)

INTEGER TYPE QUESTIONS :

1. **Ans : 5**
Given $x = k^2$ and $y = k$ is a solution
$\therefore$ we have
$k^2 - 5k + 6 = 0 \Rightarrow k^2 - 3k - 2k + 6 = 0$
$\Rightarrow (k-3)(k-2) = 0 \Rightarrow k = 3, 2$
Sum = 3 + 2 = 5
2. **Ans : 3**
Since (5, a) lies on $x + y = 8$,
$\therefore \; 5 + a = 8 \Rightarrow a = 8 - 5 = 3$

3. **Ans : 1**

Since A(3, 5) and B(1, 4) lies on the graph ax + by = 7

Therefore we have

$3a + 5b = 7$ ...(i)

and $a + 4b = 7$ ...(ii)

On solving these, we get

$a = -1$ and $b = 2$.

$a + b = -1 + 2 = 1$

4. **Ans : 4**

Required distance $= 3 - (-1)$

$= 4$

5. **Ans : 2**

Since $2x - y = 4$ cuts x-axis at (a, 0) therefore

$2(a) - 0 = 4 \Rightarrow 2a = 4 \Rightarrow a = 2$

6. **Ans : 2**

Since (2k – 1, k) is a solution of $10x - 9y = 12$ therefore

$10(2k - 1) - 9(k) = 12 \Rightarrow 20k - 10 - 9k = 12$

$\Rightarrow 11k = 22 \Rightarrow k = 2$

4 ADVANCED EXERCISE
BASED ON CONNECTING TOPICS

1. (c) Common integral solutions are – 4, – 3, –2, –1, 0, 1, 2, 3, 4.

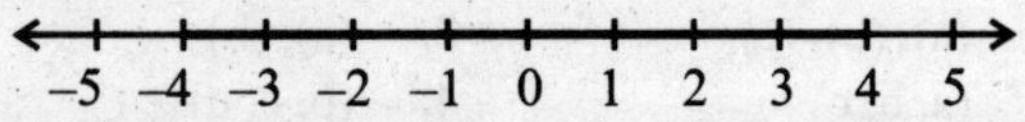

2. (b) $\frac{1}{x+1} > 0 \Rightarrow x + 1 > 0 \Rightarrow x > -1$

$\therefore$ Solution set $= \{x : x > -1\}$

3. (c)

4. (d) On solving both the equations simultaneously, we get $x \leq 5$

5. (a) Required boundary line is $y = x + 4$

6. (c) $0 < x < 5$ ...(1)

$0 < 2x < 10$ ...(2) (multiply (1) by 2)

$1 < y < 2$ ...(3)

$-6 < -3y < -3$ ...(4) (multiply (3) by –3)

Subtracting (4) from (2)

$0 - 6 < 2x - 3y < 10 - 3$ i.e., $-6 < 2x - 3y < 7$.

7. (c) $4x + 3y - 12 \geq 12$ represents the graph.

8. (c) If the expression between the absolute value bars is positive. It's less than +7 or, if the expression between the bars is negative, it's greater than –7. In other words,

2x – 3 is between –7 and +7

$-7 < 2x - 3 < 7$

$-4 < 2x < 10$

$-2 < x < 5$

9. (d) At x = 0, inequality is satisfied, option (b) is rejected.

At x = 2, inequality is satisfied, option (c) is rejected.

At x = 5, LHS = RHS.

At x = – 1, LHS = RHS.

Thus, option (d) is correct.

10. (d) $x > 5$ and $y < -1$

(i) $x > 5$ and $4y < -4$ so $x + 4y < 1$

(ii) Let $x > -4y$ be true $4y < -4$ or $-4y > 4$

So, $x > 4$, which is not true as given $x > 5$.

So, is not necessarily true.

(iii) $x > 5 \Rightarrow -4x < -20$ and $5y < -5$

It is not necessary that $-4x < 5y$ as $-4x$ can be greater than $5y$, since $5y < -5$.

Hence, none of the options is true.

Chapter 5

Introduction to Euclid's Geometry

INTRODUCTION

The word 'Geometry' comes from the Greek. The ancient people faced several practical problems like measurement of land, computing volumes of granaries, construction of pyramid, construction of altars (or vedis) and fire places for performing vedic rites. So the geometry was studied in various forms in every ancient civilisation, in Egypt, Babylonia, China, India, Greece, etc.

Euclid (325 BC – 265 BC), a teacher of mathematics at Alexandra in Egypt, collected all the known work and arranged it in his famous treatise, called 'Elements'. He divided the 'Elements' into thirteen chapters, each called a book. Euclid's Elements form one of the most beautiful and influential works of mathematics. These books influenced the whole world's understanding of geometry. In this chapter, we shall discuss Euclid's approach of geometry and shall try to link it with the present day geometry.

Euclid began his exposition by listing 23 definitions in Book-1 of the 'Elements'.

23 DEFINITIONS FROM BOOK-1

Definition 1

A point is that which has no part.

Definition 2

A line is breadthless length.

Definition 3

The ends of a line are points.

Definition 4

A straight line is a line which lies evenly with the points on itself.

Definition 5

A surface is that which has length and breadth only.

Definition 6

The edges of a surface are lines.

Definition 7

A plane surface is a surface which lies evenly with the straight lines on itself.

Definition 8

A plane angle is the inclination to one another of two lines in a plane which meet one another and do not lie in a straight line.

Definition 9

When the lines containing the angle are straight, the angle is called rectilinear.

Definition 10

When a straight line standing on a straight line makes the adjacent angles equal to one another, each of the equal angles is right, and the straight line standing on the other is called a perpendicular to that on which it stands.

Definition 11

An obtuse angle is an angle greater than a right angle.

Definition 12

An acute angle is an angle less than a right angle.

Definition 13

A boundary is that which is an extremity of anything.

Definition 14

A figure is that which is contained by any boundary or boundaries.

Definition 15

A circle is a plane figure contained by one line such that all the straight lines falling upon it from one point among those lying within the figure equal one another.

Definition 16

The point within the circle from which all the straight lines falling on it are equal is called the centre of the circle.

Definition 17

A diameter of the circle is any straight line drawn through the centre and terminated in both directions by the circumference of the circle, and such a straight line also bisects the circle.

Definition 18

A semicircle is the figure contained by the diameter and the circumference cut off by it. And the center of the semicircle is the same as that of the circle.

Definition 19

Rectilinear figures are those which are contained by straight lines, trilateral figures being those contained by three, quadrilateral those contained by four, and multilateral those contained by more than four straight lines.

Definition 20

Of trilateral figures, an equilateral triangle is that which has its three sides equal, an isosceles triangle is that which has two of its sides alone equal, and a scalene triangle is that which has its three sides unequal.

Definition 21

Further, of trilateral figures, a right-angled triangle is that which has a right angle, an obtuse-angled triangle is that which has an obtuse angle, and an acute-angled triangle is that which has its three angles acute.

Definition 22

Of quadrilateral figures, a square is that which is both equilateral and right-angled; a rectangle is that which is right-angled but not equilateral; a rhombus is that which is equilateral but not right-angled; and a rhomboid is that which has its opposite sides and angles equal to one another but is neither equilateral nor right-angled and the quadrilaterals other than these be called trapezia.

Definition 23

Parallel straight lines are straight lines which being in the same plane and being produced indefinitely in both directions, do not meet one another in either direction.

UNDEFINED TERMS

If you carefully study these definitions, you find that some of the terms like part, breadth, length, evenly, etc. need to be further explained clearly. So, to define one thing, you need to defined many other things, and may get a long chain of definitions without an end. For such reasons, mathematicians agree to leave some geometric terms undefined. However, we have an institutional feeling of these undefined terms. In Euclid's geometry a point, a line and a plane are taken as undefined. But we can represent them intuitivly and explain them with the help of 'Physical models'.

EUCLID'S POSTULATE AND COMMON NOTIONS (OR AXIOMS)

Starting with his definitions, Euclid assumed certain properties, which were not to be proved. These assumptions are actually 'obvious universal truths'. He divided them into two types: postulates and common notions (or axioms). He used the term **'postulate'** for the assumptions that were specific to geometry. Common notions often called **axioms**, on the other hand, were assumptions used throughout mathematics and not specifically linked to geometry.

Some of Euclid's notions (or axioms), not in his order, are given below:

Euclid's Axioms

1. Things which equal the same thing also equal one another.
   [Note that, this common notion can be apply to plane figures only.]
2. If equals are added to equals, then the wholes are equal.
   [Note that, magnitude of only same kind can be added.]
3. If equals are subtracted from equals, then the remainders are equal.
   [Note that, magnitude of only same kind can be subtracted from larger one.]
4. Things which coincide with one another are equal one another.
   [Note that, if two things are identical, then they are equal.]
5. The whole is greater than the part.
6. Things which are double of the same things are equal to one another.
7. Things which are halves of the same things are equal to one another.

POSTULATES

Euclid's five postulates are given below:

Postulate 1

A straight line may be drawn from any one point to any other point.

This first postulate says that for given any two points such as A and B, there is a unique line AB whose end points are A and B.

Postulate 2

A terminated line can be produced indefinitely.

Euclid's terminated line is now called line segment. So, according to the present day terms, the second postulate say that a line segment can be extended on either side to form a line.

Postulate 3

A circle can be drawn with any centre and any radius.

Postulate 4

All right angles equal one another.

Postulate 5

If a straight line falling on two straight lines makes the interior angles on the same side of it taken together less than two right angles, then the two straight lines, if produced indefinitely, meet on that side on which the sum of the angles is less than the two right angles.

For example, in the figure, the line PQ falls on lines AB and CD such that the sum of the interior angles 1 and 2 is less than 180° on the left side of PQ. Therefore, the lines AB and CD will eventually intersect on the left side of PQ, if the produced infinitely.

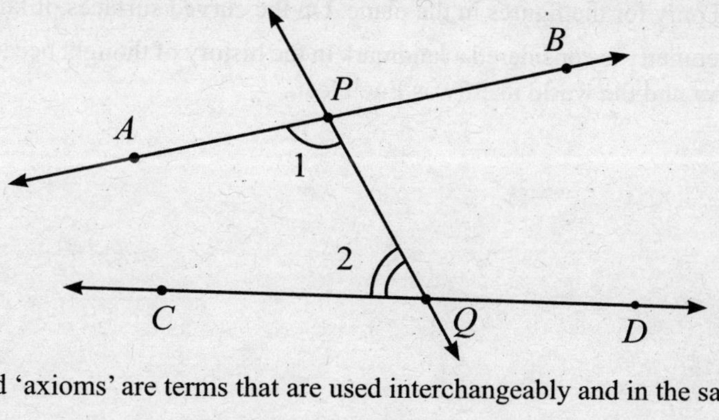

Now-a-days, 'postulates' and 'axioms' are terms that are used interchangeably and in the same sense.

Equivalent Versions of Euclid's Fifth Postulate

Euclid's fifth postulate is very significant in the history of mathematics. There are several equivalent versions of this postulate. One of them is 'Playfair's Axiom' (given by a Scottish mathematician John Playfair in 1729), as stated below:

'For every line ℓ and for every point P not lying on ℓ, there exists a unique line m passing through P and parallel to line ℓ'.

From figure you can see that of all the lines passing through the point P, only line m is parallel to line ℓ.

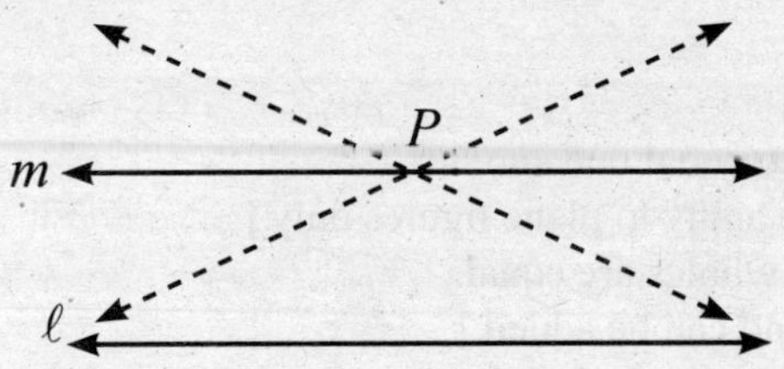

This result can also be stated in the following form:

Two distinct intersecting lines cannot be parallel to the same line.

CONSISTENT SYSTEM OF AXIOMS

A system of axioms is called **consistent** if it is impossible to deduce from these axioms a statement that contradicts any axiom or previously proved statement.

PROPOSITIONS OR THEOREMS

After Euclid stated his postulates and axioms, he used them to prove other results. Then using these results, he proved some more results by applying deductive reasoning. The statements that were proved are called **propositions** or **theorems**.

Euclid deduced 465 propositions in a logical chain using his axioms, postulates, definitions and theorems proved earlier in the chain.

Now, we prove a theorem, which is frequently used in different results:

Theorem

Two distinct lines cannot have more than one point in common.

Proof

For the time being, let us suppose that the two lines intersect in two distinct points, say P and Q. So, you have two lines passing through two distinct points P and Q. But this assumption clashes with the axiom that only one line can pass through two distinct points. So, the assumption that we started with, that two lines can pass through two distinct points is wrong.

Therefore, we conclude that two distinct lines cannot have more than one point in common.

NON-EUCLIDEAN GEOMETRY

All the attempts to prove Euclid's fifth postulate using first 4 postulates failed. But they led to the discovery of several other geometries, called non-Euclidean Geometries.

Euclidean Geometry is valid only for the figures in the plane. On the curved surfaces, it fails.

Creation of non-Euclidean geometry is considered a landmark in the history of thought because till then every one had believed that Euclid's was the only geometry and the world itself was Euclidean.

MISCELLANEOUS SOLVED EXAMPLES

1. **If A, B and C are three points on a line, and B lies between A and C (Fig.), then prove that $AB + BC = AC$.**

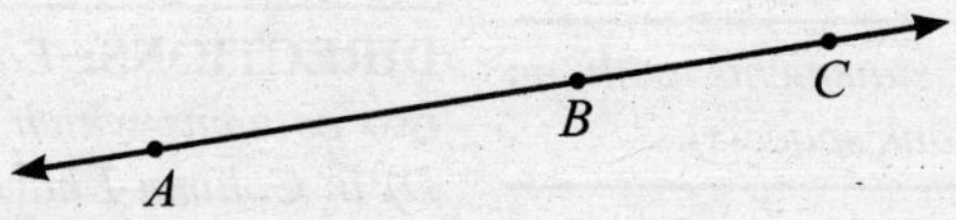

Sol. In the figure given above, AC coincides with $AB + BC$.

Also, Euclid's Axiom (4) says that things which coincide with one another are equal to one another. So, it can be deduced that $AB + BC = AC$.

Note that in this solution, it has been assumed that there is a unique line passing through two points.

2. **Consider the following statement : There exists a pair of straight lines that are everywhere equidistant from one another. Is this statement a direct consequence of Euclid's fifth postulate? Explain.**

Sol. Take any line ℓ and a point P not on ℓ. Then, by Playfair's axiom, which is equivalent to the fifth postulate, we know that there is a unique line m through P which is parallel to ℓ.

Now, the distance of a point from a line is the length of the perpendicular from the point to the line. This distance will be the same for any point on m from ℓ and any point on ℓ from m. So, these two lines are everywhere equidistant from one another.

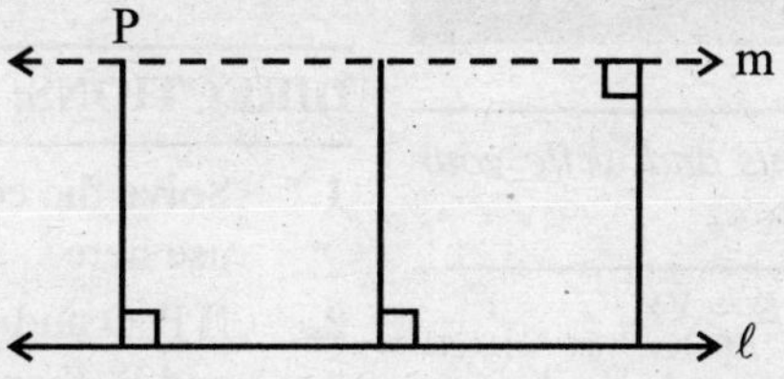

3. **If ℓ and m are intersecting lines, $\ell \parallel p$ and $m \parallel q$, show that p and q also intersect.**

Sol. Since ℓ and m are intersecting and $\ell \parallel p$

$\Rightarrow$ m and p intersect.

Now, m and p intersect and $m \parallel q$.

$\Rightarrow$ p and q intersect.

1 EXERCISE

Fill in the Blanks :

DIRECTIONS: *Complete the following statements with an appropriate word/term to be filled in the blank space(s).*

1. .... are the assumptions which are obvious universal truths.
2. Things which are equal to the same thing are .... to one another.
3. If equals are subtracted from equals, the remainder are ....
4. Things which are double of the same things are .... one another.
5. Two distinct intersecting lines cannot be .... to the same line.
6. 'For every line l and for every point P not lying on l, there exists a unique line m passing through P and parallel to ......
7. Lines which are parallel to the same line are .... to each other.

True / False :

DIRECTIONS: *Read the following statements and write your answer as true or false.*

1. In fig., if $AB = PQ$ and $PQ = XY$, then $AB = XY$.

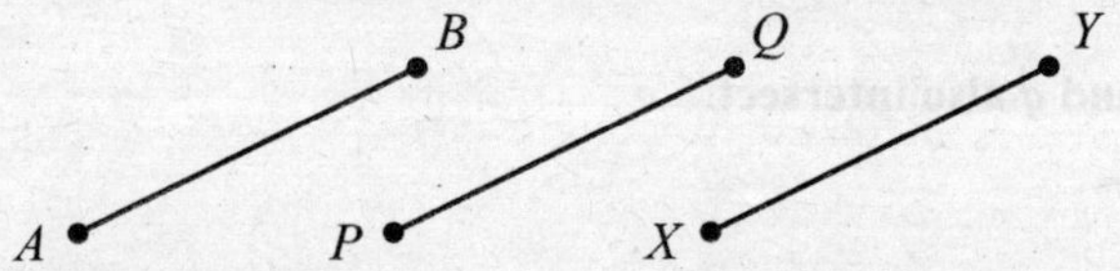

2. Only one line can pass through a single point.
3. If two circles are equal, then their radii are equal.
4. A terminated line can be produced indefinitely on both the sides.
5. There are an infinite number of lines which pass through two distinct points.
6. A line segment has one end-point only.

Match the Columns :

DIRECTIONS: *Each question contains statements given in two columns which have to be matched. Statements (A, B, C, D) in Column-I have to be matched with statements (p, q, r, s) in Column-II.*

1.

Column-I	Column-II
(A) Postulate 1	(p) A terminated line can be produced indefinitely.
(B) Postulate 2	(q) All right angles are equal to one another.
(C) Postulate 3	(r) A straight line may be drawn from any one point to any other point.
(D) Postulate 4	(s) A circle can be drawn with any centre and any radius.

Very Short Answer Questions :

DIRECTIONS: *Give answer in one word or one sentence.*

1. Solve the equation $u - 5 = 15$ and state the axiom that you use here.
2. If P, Q and R are three points on a line and Q is between P and R, then prove that $PR - QR = PQ$.
3. What are the three basic concepts in geometry?
4. What is the least number of distinct points which determine a unique line?

Short Answer Questions :

DIRECTIONS: *Give answer in 2-3 sentences.*

1. It is known that $x + y = 10$ and that $x = z$. Show that $z + y = 10$.
2. Two salesmen make equal sales during the month of August. In September, each salesman doubles his sale of the month of August. Compare their sale in month September.
3. Look at the fig. show that the length AH > sum of lengths of AB + BC + CD.

2 EXERCISE

Text-Book Exercise :

1. Which of the following statements are true and which are false? Give reasons for your answers.
   (i) Only one line can pass through a single point.
   (ii) There are an infinite number of lines which pass through two distinct points.
   (iii) A terminated line can be produced indefinitely on both the sides.
   (iv) If two circles are equal, then their radii are equal.
   (v) If AB = PQ and PQ = XY, then AB = XY.

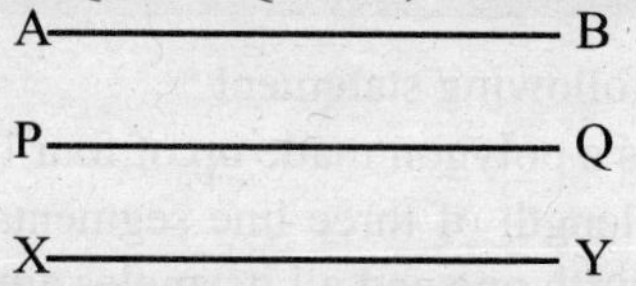

2. Give a definition for each of the following terms. Are there other terms that need to be defined first? What are they, and how might you define them?
   (i) parallel lines
   (ii) perpendicular lines
   (iii) line segment
   (iv) radius of a circle
   (v) square
3. Consider two 'postulates' given below:
   (i) Given any two distinct points A and B, there exists a third point C which is in between A and B.
   (ii) There exist at least three points that are not on the same line.
   Do these postulates contain any undefined terms? Are these postulates consistent?
   Do they follow from Euclid's postulates? Explain.
4. If a point C lies between two points A and B such that AC = BC, then prove that AC = AB/2.
5. In Question 4, point C is called a mid-point of line segment AB. Prove that every line segment has one and only one mid-point.
6. If AC = BD, then prove that AB = CD.

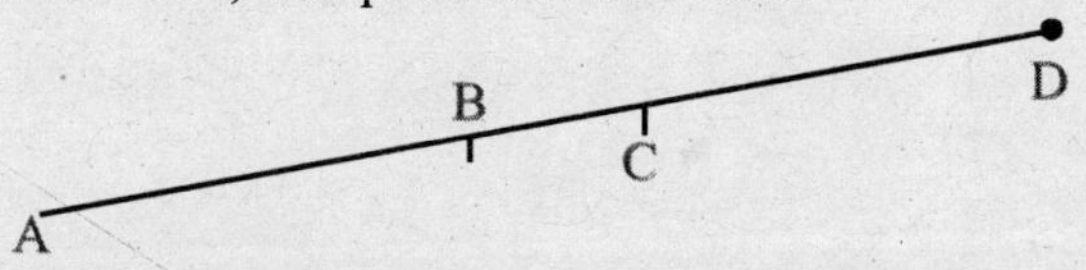

7. Why is axiom 5, in the list of Euclid's axioms, considered a 'universal truth'? (Note that the question is not about the fifth postulate).
8. How would you rewrite Euclid's fifth postulate so that it would be easier to understand?
9. Does Euclid's fifth postulate imply the existence of parallel lines? Explain.

Exemplar Questions :

1. In the figure, we have
   X and Y are the mid-points of AC and BC and AX = CY.
   Show that AC = BC

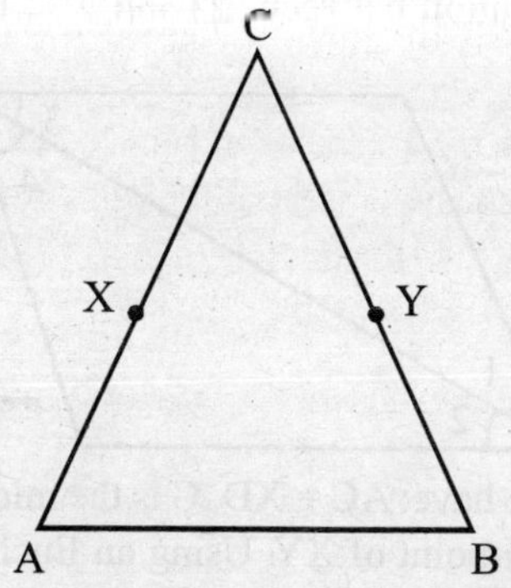

2. In the figure, if OX $-$XY , PX = $\frac{1}{2}$XZ and OX = PX,
   show that XY = XZ.

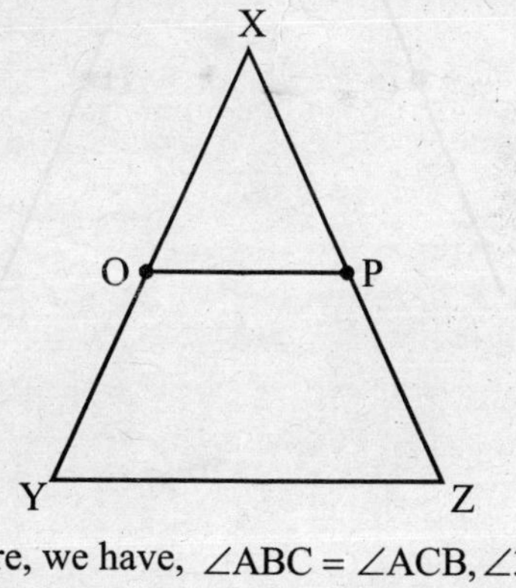

3. In the figure, we have, $\angle ABC = \angle ACB$, $\angle 3 = \angle 4$.
   Show that $\angle 1 = \angle 2$

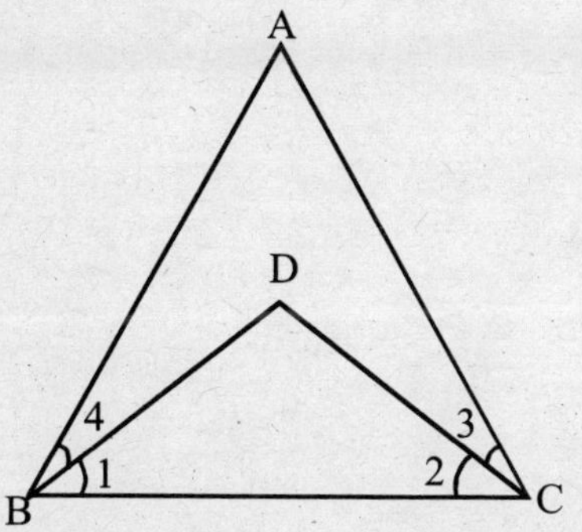

4. In the figure, we have AB = BC, BX = BY. Show that AX = CY.

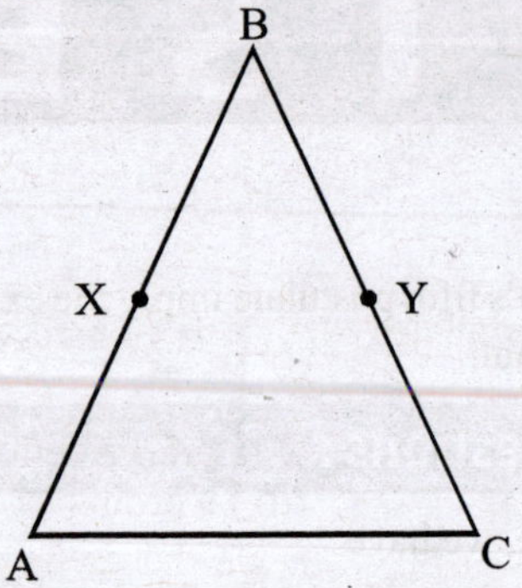

5. In the figure, if $\angle 1 = \angle 3, \angle 2 = \angle 4$ and $\angle 3 = \angle 4$, write the relation between $\angle 1$ and $\angle 2$, using an Euclid's axiom.

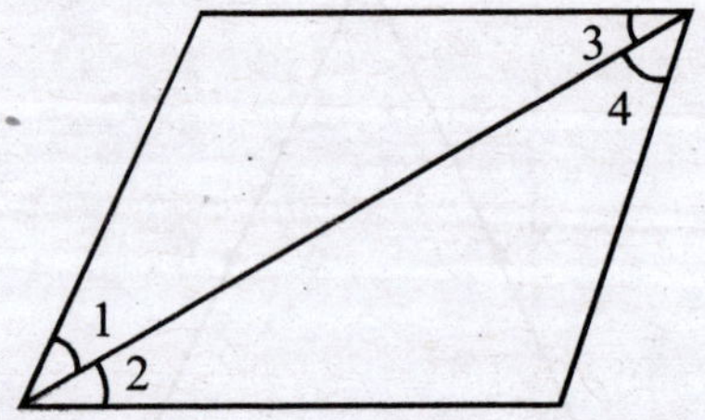

6. In figure, we have: AC = XD, C is the mid-point of AB and D is the mid-point of XY. Using an Euclid's axiom, show that AB = XY.

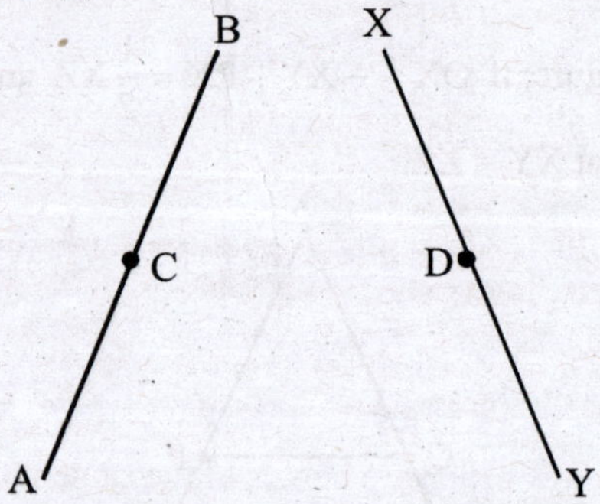

7. The number of dimensions, a solid has :
(a) 1 (b) 2
(c) 3 (d) 0

8. The number of dimensions, a surface has :
(a) 1 (b) 2
(c) 3 (d) 0

9. The number of dimensions, a point has :
(a) 0 (b) 1
(c) 2 (d) 3

10. Euclid divided his famous treatise "The elements" into :
(a) 13 chapters (b) 12 chapters
(c) 11 chapters (d) 9 chapters

11. The total number of propositions in the elements are :
(a) 465 (b) 460
(c) 13 (d) 55

HOTS Questions :

1. Read the following statement :
"A square is a polygon made up of four line segments, out of which , length of three line segments are equal to the length of fourth one and all its angles are right angles". Define the terms used in this definition which you feel necessary. Are there any undefined terms in this? Can you justify that all angles and sides of a square are equal?

2. Prove that every line segment has one and only one mid-point.

3. If a point O lies between two points P and R such that PO $\frac{1}{2}$ = OR, then prove that PO = PR.

3 EXERCISE

Single Option Correct :

DIRECTIONS: *This section contains multiple choice questions. Each questions has 4 choices (a), (b), (c) and (d) out of which ONLY ONE is correct.*

1. The word geometry comes from the Greek word 'geo' and 'meterrion' which means
   (a) 'Geography' and 'meter'
   (b) 'Globe' and 'meter'
   (c) 'Go' and 'to measure'
   (d) 'Earth' and 'to measure'
2. The first known proof that 'the circle is bisected by its diameter' was given by
   (a) Pythagoras (b) Thales
   (c) Euclid (d) None of these
3. A point is defined as
   (a) that which has no length no breadth no height
   (b) small part of a line with no length
   (c) no dimension, but represented by dot only
   (d) undefined term, represented by a dot
4. Difference between 'postulate' and 'axiom' is
   (a) there is no difference
   (b) few statements are termed as axioms and other as postulates
   (c) 'postulates' are the assumptions used specially for geomerty and 'axioms' are the assumptions used throughout mathematics.
   (d) None of these
5. For every line 'l' and a point P not lying on it, the number of lines that pass through P and parallel to 'l' are
   (a) 2 (b) 1
   (c) no line (d) 3
6. Greeks emphasised on:
   (a) deductive reasoning
   (b) inductive reasoning
   (c) practical use of geometry
   (d) infinitely many solutions
7. Which of the following needs a proof?
   (a) Axiom (b) Theorem
   (c) Postulate (d) Definition
8. Axioms are assumed:
   (a) universal truths in all branches of mathematics
   (b) theorems
   (c) definitions
   (d) universal truths specific to geometry
9. 'Lines are parallel if they do not intersect' is stated in the form of.
   (a) a postulate (b) a definition
   (c) an axiom (d) a proof
10. It is known that if $x + y = 10$, then $x + y + z = 10 + z$. The Euclid's axiom that illustrates this statement is:
    (a) first axiom (b) second axiom
    (c) third axiom (d) fourth axiom

More Than One Option Correct :

DIRECTIONS: *This section contains multiple choice questions. Each question has 4 choices (a), (b), (c) and (d) out of which ONE or MORE may be correct.*

1. Which of the following is/are correct?
   (a) A plane surface is a surface which lies evenly with the straight line on itself.
   (b) A surface is that which has length and breadth only.
   (c) A line is breadthless length.
   (d) A point is that which has no part.
2. Which of the following is/are Euclid's axioms?
   (a) Things which are equal to the same thing are never equal to one another.
   (b) If equals are added to equals, the wholes are equal.
   (c) The whole is greater than the part.
   (d) Things which are halves of the same things are equal to one another.
3. Which of the following is/are Euclid's postulates?
   (a) A straight line may be drawn from any one point to any other point.
   (b) A circle can be drawn with any centre and any radius.
   (c) A terminated line cannot be produced indefinitely.
   (d) All right angles are never equal to one another.
4. Which of the following is/are incorrect?
   (a) A triangle whose sides are equal, is called a scalene triangle.
   (b) A triangle, each of whose angle is less than 90°, is called an acute triangle.
   (c) If all sides of a polygon are different, it is called a regular polygon.
   (d) A triangle with one of its angles greater than 90°, is known as an obtuse triangle.

SOLUTIONS

Brief Explanations of Selected Questions

1 EXERCISE

FILL IN THE BLANKS :

1. Axioms 2. equal 3. equal 4. equal
5. parallel 6. l 7. parallel

TRUE/FALSE :

1. True 2. False 3. True 4. True
5. False 6. False

Match the Columns :

1. (A) → (q); (B) → (p); (C) → (s); (D) → (r)

VERY SHORT ANSWER QUESTIONS :

1. $u - 5 = 15$

On adding 5 to both sides, we have

$u - 5 + 5 = 15 + 5$

(Euclid's second axiom, when equals are added to equals, the wholes are equal)

or $u = 20$

2. 

In the above figure PQ coincides with PR – QR

So, according to axiom, "things" which coincide with one another are equal to 'one another'. We have,

$$PR - QR = PQ$$

3. The three basic concepts in geometry are:
   - Point
   - Line
   - Plane

4. Two distinct points determine a unique points.

SHORT ANSWER QUESTIONS :

1. The given equation is:

$x + y = 10$ ...(i)

and, $x = z$ ...(ii)

Subtracting (ii) from (i)

$x + y - x = 10 - z$

[∵ If equals are subtracted from equals, the remainders are equal]

∴ $y = 10 - z$

⇒ $y + z = 10$

[∵ If equals are added to equals, the wholes are equal]

2. Let sale of salesman A in August = x

and, sale of salesman B in August = y

Given, $x = y$ ...(i)

In September, each salesman doubles his sale

∴ Sale of salesman A in September = 2x

and, sale of salesman B in September = 2y

From Euclid's second postulate, if equals are added to equals, then the wholes are equal.

∴ $2x = 2y$

Thus, their sales in month of September are equal.

3. $AH = AB + BC + CD + DE + EF + FG + GH$

Now, $AB + BC + CD = AD$

Since AD is a part (fraction) of AH, therefore $AH > AD$ or $AH > AB + BC + CD$

(Axiom 6: Whole is greater than any one of the part).

2 EXERCISE

TEXT-BOOK EXERCISE :

1. (i) False. As we know that there are various points in a plane such that A, B, C, D and E. Now by first postulate.

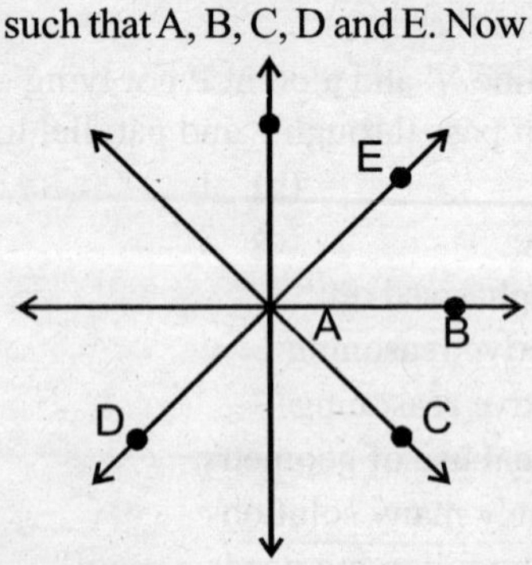

We can draw a line from A to B, A to C, A to E and A to D. It proves that many lines can pass through point A.

Similarly, we conclude that infinite lines can pass through a single point.

(ii) False

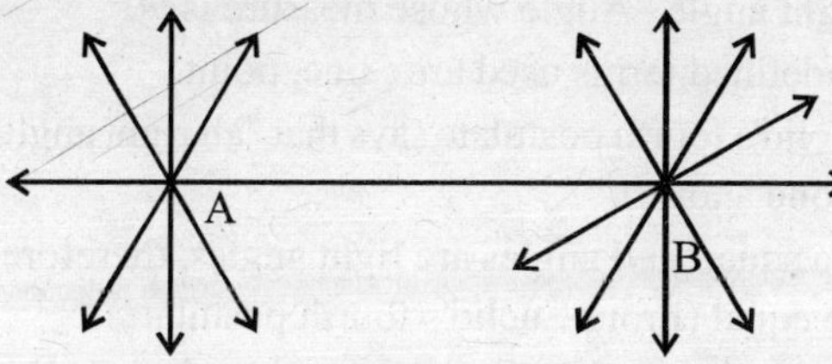

Mark two points A and B on the plane of paper. Fold the paper so that a crease passes through A. Again fold the paper so that a line passes through B. Clearly infinite number of lines can pass through B. Now fold the paper in such a way that a line passes through both A and B. We observe that there is just only one line passes through both A and B.

(iii) True.

In geometry, by a line, we mean the line in its totality and not a portion of it. Since a line extends indefinitely in both the directions.

So it cannot be drawn whole on paper. In practice, only a portion of a line is drawn and arrowheads are marked at its two ends indicating that it extends indefinitely in both directions.

(iv) True.

On superimposing the region bounded by one circle on the other if the circles coincides. Then, their centres and boundaries coincide. Therefore, their radii will be equal.

(v) True.

As we know things which are equal to the same thing, are equal to one another.

2. (i) Lines which do not intersect anywhere are called **parallel lines**.

(ii) Two lines which are at a right angle to each other are called **perpendicular lines**.

(iii) <u>**Line Segment :**</u> It is a terminated line.

(iv) **Radius of a circle:** The length of the line-segment joining the centre of a circle to any point on its circumference.

(v) A quadrilateral with all the four sides equal and all the four angles of measure 90° each is called a **square**.

3. There are several undefined terms which should be list. These postulates are consistent.

(i) says that the given two points A and B, there is a point C lying on the line in between them;

(ii) says that given A and B, we can take C not lying on the line through A and B.

These 'postulates' do not follow from Euclid's postulates However, they follow from axiom stated as given two distinct points there is a unique line that passes through them.

4.

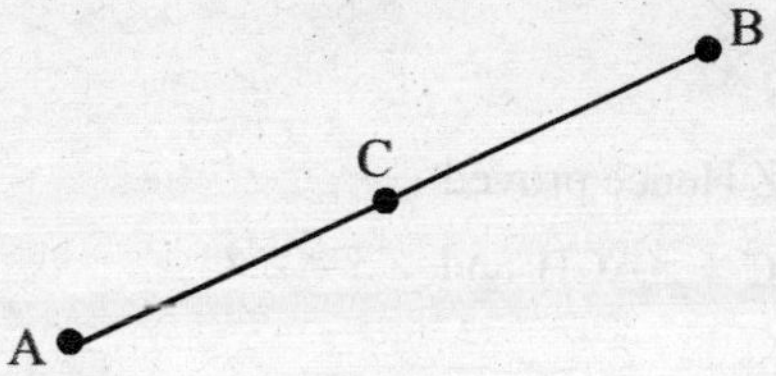

AC = BC

$\Rightarrow$ AC + AC = BC + AC

[Equals are added to equals]

$\Rightarrow$ 2AC = AB $\Rightarrow$ AC = AB/2

5. **Given:** C is mid-point of AB .

To Prove: C is the only mid-point of AB.

Let a line AB have two mid-points, say, C and D. Then,

$AC = \frac{1}{2}AB$ and ....(i)

$AD = \frac{1}{2}AB$ ....(ii)

From (i) and (ii)

AC = AD. ($\because$ Things which are equal to the same thing are equal to one another)

6. AC = BD ... (i)

AC = AB + BC [B lies between A and C] ... (ii)

BD = BC + CD [C lies between B and D] ... (iii)

Substituting (ii) and (iii) in (i), we get

AB + BC = BC + CD

$\Rightarrow$ AB = CD [Subtracting equals from equal]

7. This is true for any thing in any part of the world, this is a universal truth.

8. The two facts about the axioms are

(i) There is a line through P which is parallel to ℓ.

(ii) There is only one such line.

9. If a straight line ℓ falls on two straight lines m and n such that the sum of the interior angles on one side of ℓ is two right angles, then by Euclid's fifth postulate the lines will not meet on this side of ℓ. Next, we know that the sum of the interior angles on the other side of line ℓ will also be two right angles. Therefore, they will not meet on the other side also. So, the lines m and n never meet and are, therefore, parallel.

EXEMPLAR QUESTIONS :

1. Given: AX = CY

Also, AX = CX (X and Y are mid points of AC and CB) and CY = BY

AX = CY = BY = CX

AX = CY $\Rightarrow$ AX + CX = CY + CX

AX + CX = CY + BY

AC = BC (Hence proved)

2. Given: $OX = \frac{1}{2}XY$, $PX = \frac{1}{2}XZ$ and OX = PX

$\Rightarrow \frac{1}{2}XY = \frac{1}{2}XZ$

$\Rightarrow$ XY = XZ Hence proved

3. Given: $\angle ABC = \angle ACB$ and $\angle 3 = \angle 4$

We have,

$\angle ABC = \angle 1 + \angle 4$

$\angle ACB = \angle 2 + \angle 3$

$\angle 1 + \angle 4 = \angle 2 + \angle 3$

$\angle 1 + \angle 3 = \angle 2 + \angle 3$

$\Rightarrow \angle 1 = \angle 2$. Hence proved.

4. Given, AB = BC, and BX = BY

AB = BC

AB – BX = BC – BX

AB – BX = BC – BY

AX = CY

Hence proved

5. Here, $\angle 3 = \angle 4$, $\angle 1 = \angle 3$ and $\angle 2 = \angle 4$. Euclid's first axiom says, the things which are equal to equal thing are equal to one another.

So, $\angle 1 = \angle 2$

6. AB = 2AC (C is the mid-point of AB)

XY = 2XD (D is the mid-point of XY)

Also, AC = XD (Given)

Therefore, AB = XY, because things which are double of the same things are equal to one another.

7. (c) 8. (b)

9. (a) 10. (a)

11. (a)

HOTS Questions :

1. The terms need to be defined are :

Polygon : A simple closed figure made up of three or more line segments.

Line segment : Part of a line with two end points.

Line : Undefined term

Point : Undefined term

Angle : A figure formed by two rays with a common initial point.

Ray : Part of a line with one end point.

Right angle : Angle whose measure is 90°

Undefined terms used are : line, point.

Euclid's fourth postulate says that "all right angles are equal to one another."

In a square, all angles are right angles, therefore, all angles are equal (From Euclid's fourth postulate).

Three line segments are equal to fourth line segment (Given).

Therefore, all the four sides of a square are equal. (by Euclid's first axiom "things which are equal to the same thing are equal to one another.")

2. **Proof:** Let us prove this statement by contradiction method. Let us assume that the line segment *PT* has two midpoints *R* and *S*.

$\Rightarrow PR = \frac{1}{2}PT$

and, $PS = \frac{1}{2}PT$

($\because$ *R* and *S* are mid-points according to assumption)

$\Rightarrow PR = PS$

But this is possible only if *R* and *S* coincide.

3. **Proof:** From fig., $PO + OR = PR$ ...(i)

$PO = OR$ (given) ...(ii)

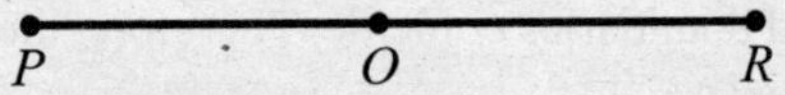

$PO + PO = PR$ [using (ii) in (i)]

$2PO = PR$

$PO = \frac{1}{2} PR$

3 EXERCISE

Single Option Correct :

1. (d) 2. (b) 3. (d) 4. (c)
5. (b) 6. (c) 7. (c) 8. (a)
9. (a) 10. (b)

More than One Option Correct :

1. (a, b, c, d)
2. (b, c, d)
3. (a, b)
4. (a, c)

Chapter 6

Lines & Angles

INTRODUCTION

Knowledge of lines and angles is critical in the study of geometry. In the geometry the lines and angles are important tools. We see all sorts of angles on an everyday basis. The way a ladder rests against a house and the inclination of a hill all have angles that can be measured.

In this chapter, you will learn about the different properties of lines, angles and their measures.

BASIC TERMS AND DEFINITIONS

Line

Line is a set of infinite points that has no end point. If A and B are any two points on line l, then we denote the line as $\overleftrightarrow{AB}$ and is represented as

We also denote the line by a single small English Alphabet say l and represented as

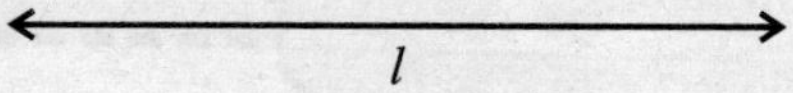

Line Segment

Line segment is a part of a line that has two end points. It is of finite length and cannot be extended further. Line segment is denoted as AB where A, B are at its end points and is represented as

Ray

Ray is a part of a line with one end point. It can be extended infinitely on one side. Ray is denoted as $\overrightarrow{AB}$ where A is the end point and B is any other point on the ray. It is represented as

Here B is not the end point
We can extend the ray towards B from A infinitely.

Collinear Points

Three or more points are said to be collinear if there is a line which contains all of them.

Angle

Two rays which have common end point form an angle. The rays making an angle are called arms of the angle. OR
An angle is the union of two non-collinear rays with a common initial point. The common initial point is called the vertex of the angle and the two rays are called the 'arms' of the angle.

TYPES OF ANGLES

(i) Acute angle : An angle whose measuring is less than 90° is called an acute angle.

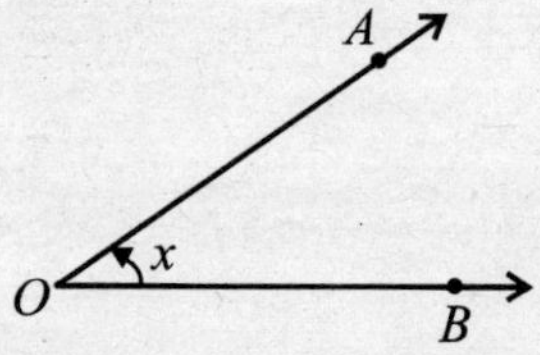

$\angle AOB = x$, $0° < x < 90°$

(ii) Right angle : An angle whose measure is 90° is called a right angle.

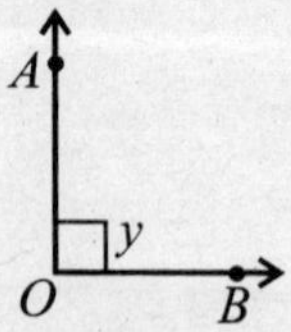

$\angle AOB = y$, $y = 90°$

(iii) Obtuse angle: An angle whose measure is more than 90° but less than 180° is called an obtuse angle.

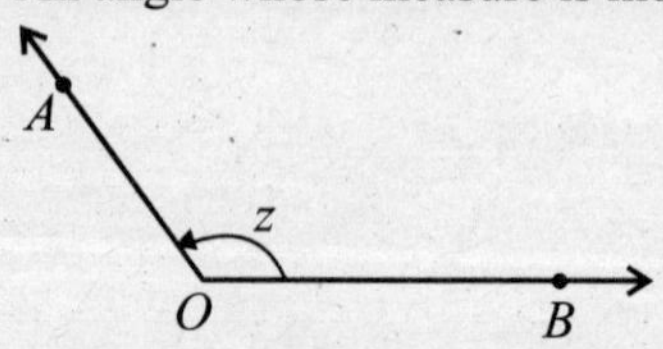

$\angle AOB = z$, $90° < z < 180°$

(iv) Straight angle: An angle whose measure is 180° is called a straight angle.

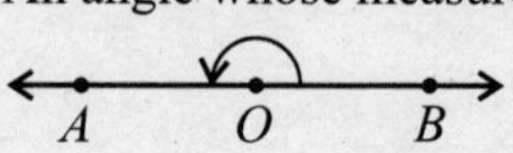

$\angle AOB = 180°$

(v) Reflex angle: An angle whose measure is more than 180° is called a reflex angle.

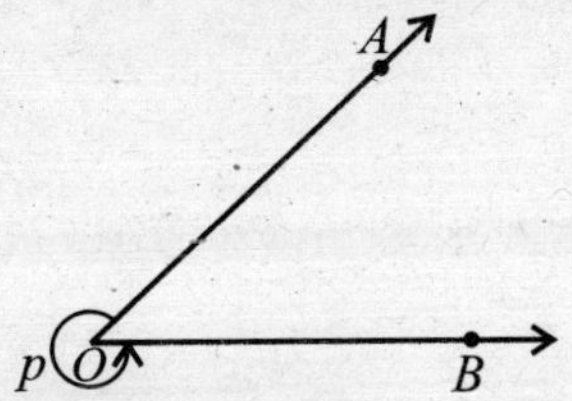

Reflex $\angle AOB = 360° - \angle AOB = p$, $180° < p < 360°$

SPECIAL TYPE OF ANGLES

Adjacent angles

Two angles are called adjacent angles, if

(i) they have the same vertex

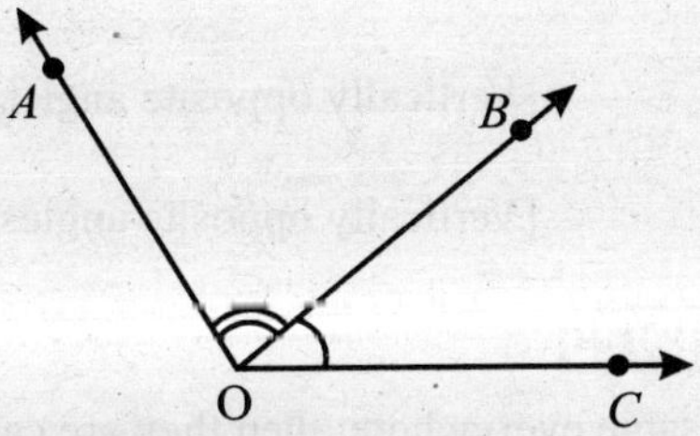

$\angle AOB$ and $\angle BOC$ are adjacent angles.

(ii) they have a common arm and

(iii) non-common arms are on either side of the common arm.

Axiom 1 : If a ray stands on a line, then the sum of two adjacent angles so formed is 180°.

Axiom 2 : If the sum of two adjacent angles is 180°, then the non-common arms of the angles are in a straight line.

Complimentary and supplementary angles

If sum of two angles is 90°, then they are complimentary angles and if sum of two angles is 180°, then they are supplementary angles.

Linear pair of angles

If the sum of two adjacent angles is 180°, they are said to form a linear pair.

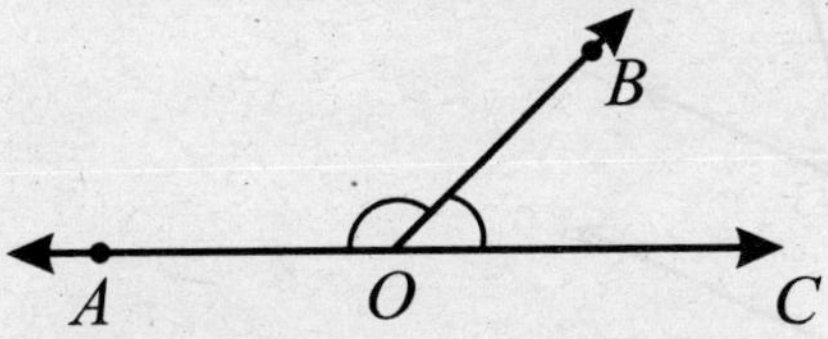

$\angle AOB$ and $\angle BOC$ are linear pair of angles and their sum is 180°.

i.e., $\angle AOB + \angle BOC = 180°$

Vertically opposite angles

If two lines AB and CD intersects each other at point O, then four angles are formed.

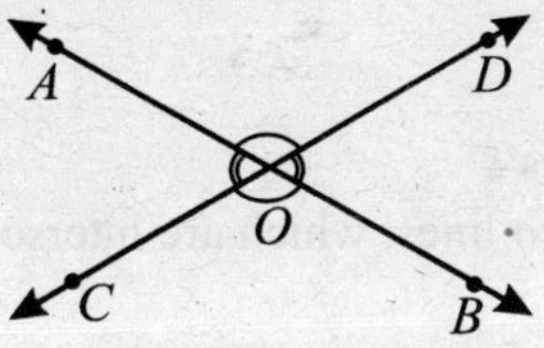

$\angle AOD$, $\angle BOC$ are vertically opposite angles and are equal.

Similarly, $\angle BOD$ and $\angle AOC$ are vertically opposite angles and are equal

i.e., $\angle AOD = \angle BOC$

$\angle AOC = \angle BOD$

THEOREM 1 :

If two lines intersect each other, then the vertically opposite angles are equal.

ILLUSTRATION : 1

In the given figure lines PQ and RS intersect each other at point O. If $\angle POR : \angle ROQ = 7 : 11$, find all the other angles.

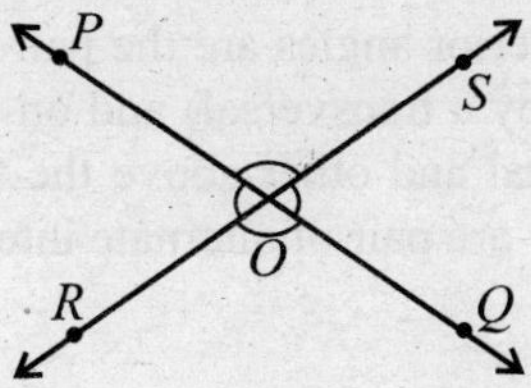

SOLUTION :

Here

$\angle POR + \angle ROQ = 180°$

Let $\angle POR = 7x$ and $\angle ROQ = 11x$ [As their ratio are given]

So, $7x + 11x = 180 \Rightarrow 18x = 180 \Rightarrow x = 10$

$\Rightarrow \angle POR = 7 \times 10 = 70°$, $\angle ROQ = 11 \times 10 = 110°$

$\angle SOQ = \angle POR = 70°$ [Vertically opposite angles]

$\angle POS = \angle ROQ = 110°$ [Vertically opposite angles]

PARALLEL AND INTERSECTING LINES

If the distance between two lines in a plane are same everywhere, then they are called parallel lines. Otherwise called intersecting lines. The distance between two intersecting lines is zero. If two or more lines parallel to the same line, then all the lines are parallel to each other.

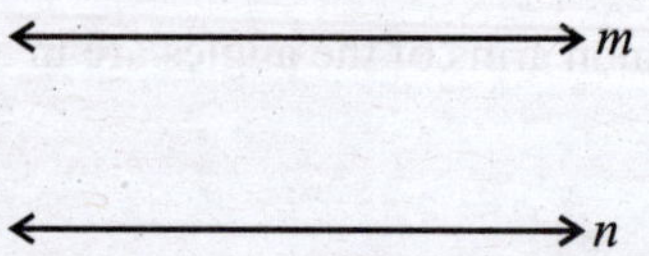

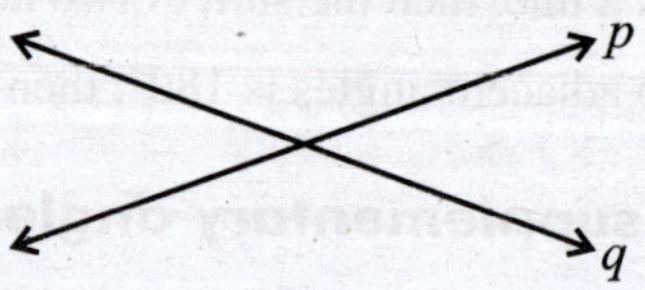

m and *n* are parallel lines. *p* and *q* are intersecting lines. If two lines *m* and *n* are parallel then we can write it as $m \parallel n$. If two lines *p* and *q* are intersecting lines, then we can write it as $m \neq n$.

TRANSVERSAL LINE

A straight line intersecting two or more straight lines in distinct points is known as a transversal to the two given lines.

In the figure, the line *l* is a transversal which intersects two lines *m* and *n* forming eight angles, $\angle 1, \angle 2, \angle 3, \angle 4, \angle 5, \angle 6, \angle 7$ and $\angle 8$.

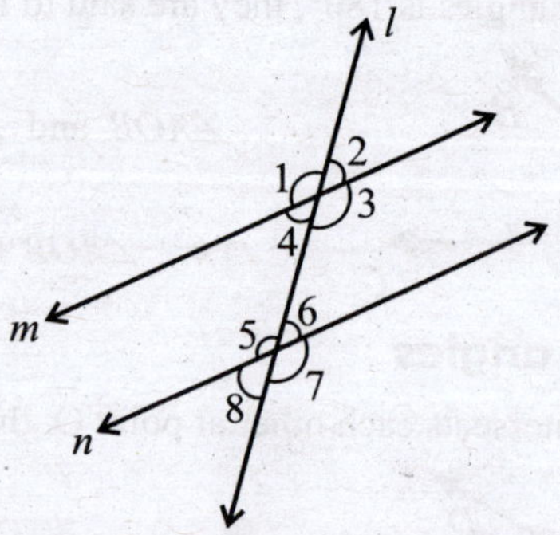

Related Terms

(i) Exterior angles : Exterior angles are the angles lying outside the region between the two lines, which are intersected by a transversal. In the given figure $\angle 1, \angle 2, \angle 7$ and $\angle 8$ are exterior angles.

(ii) Interior angles : Interior angles are the angles lying inside the region between the two lines, which are intersected by a transversal. In the given figure $\angle 3, \angle 4, \angle 5$ and $\angle 6$ are interior angles.

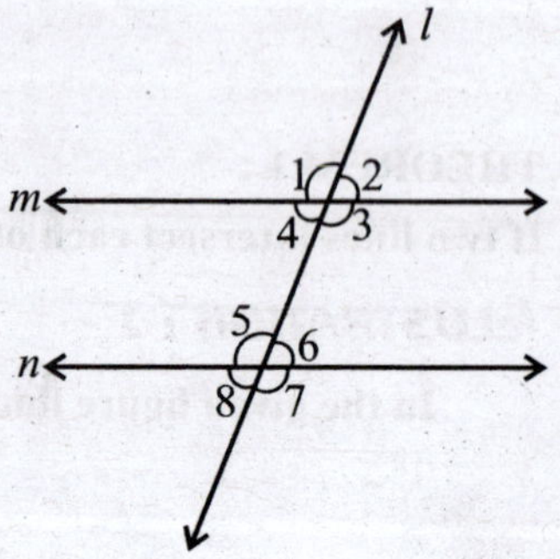

(iii) Corresponding angles : Corresponding angles are the pair of angles lying on the same side of the transversal, both of which either lie above the two lines or below the two lines intersected by a transversal. In the given figure $\angle 1$ & $\angle 5$, $\angle 2$ & $\angle 6$, $\angle 3$ & $\angle 7$, $\angle 4$ & $\angle 8$ are pair of corresponding angles.

(iv) Alternate interior angles : Alternate interior angles are the pair of angles lying in the region between the two lines (intersected by a transversal) and on the opposite sides of the transversal but one below the transversal and other above the transversal. In the adjoining figure ($\angle 4$ & $\angle 6$) and ($\angle 3$ & $\angle 5$) are pair of alternate interior angles.

(v) Alternate exterior angles : Alternate exterior angles are the pair of angles lying outside the region between the two lines (intersected by a transversal) and on the opposite sides of the transversal but one below the transversal and other above the transversal. In the given figure $(\angle 1 \& \angle 7)$ and $(\angle 2 \& \angle 8)$ are pair of alternate exterior angles.

Axiom 3 : If a transversal intersects two parallel lines, then each pair of corresponding angles is equal.

Axiom 4 : If a transversal intersects two lines, such that a pair of corresponding angles is equal, then the two lines are parallel to each other.

Special Case

If lines m and n are parallel i.e. $m \parallel n$ and 'ℓ' is a transversal, then

(i) Corresponding angles are equal i.e.
$\angle 1 = \angle 5, \angle 2 = \angle 6, \angle 3 = \angle 7$ and $\angle 4 = \angle 8$

(ii) Alternate interior angles are equal i.e.
$\angle 4 = \angle 6$ and $\angle 3 = \angle 5$

(iii) Alternate exterior angles are equal i.e.
$\angle 1 = \angle 7$ and $\angle 2 = \angle 8$

(iv) Exterior angles on the same side of the transversal are supplementary i.e.
$\angle 1 + \angle 8 = 180°$ and $\angle 2 + \angle 7 = 180°$

(v) Interior angles on the same side of the transversal are supplementary i.e.
$\angle 4 + \angle 5 = 180°$ and $\angle 3 + \angle 6 = 180°$

ILLUSTRATION : 2

In the given figure if $AB \parallel CD$, $\angle APQ = 50°$ and $\angle PRD = 127°$, find a and b

SOLUTION :

In the given figure,

$\angle APQ = \angle PQR$ {alternate interior opposite angles}

$\Rightarrow a = 50°$

Also $\angle APR = \angle PRD$ {alternate interior opposite angles}

$50 + b = 127$

$b = 127 - 50 = 77°$

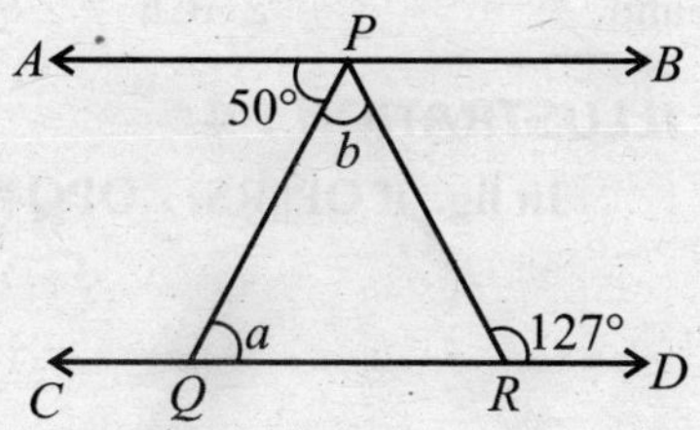

THEOREM 2 :

Prove that the sum of the three angles of a triangle is 180°.

Given: A triangle ABC.

To prove: $\angle A + \angle B + \angle C = 180°$.

Construction: Through A, draw a line DE parallel to BC

Proof : Since $DE \parallel BC$, therefore,

	$\angle 2 = \angle 4$	...(i)	[Alternate angles]
and	$\angle 3 = \angle 5$	...(ii)	[Alternate angles]
$\therefore$	$\angle 2 + \angle 3 = \angle 4 + \angle 5$	...(iii)	[Adding (i) and (ii)]

Adding $\angle 1$ to both sides of (iii), we have

$\angle 1 + \angle 2 + \angle 3 = \angle 1 + \angle 4 + \angle 5$ ...(iv)

But $\angle 4 + \angle 1 + \angle 5 = 180°$ ...(v) [Linear Pair Axiom]

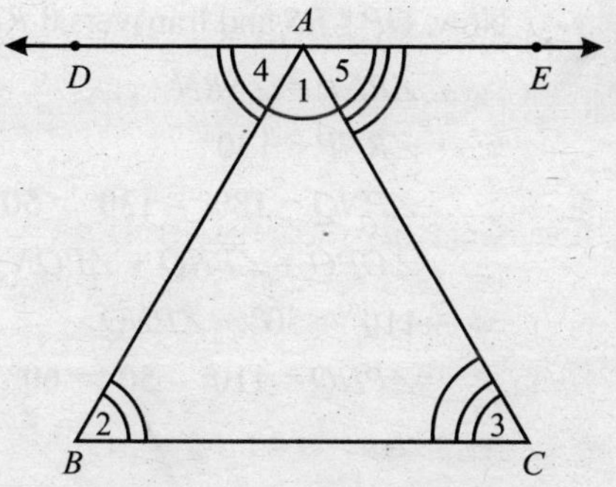

From (iv) and (v), we have

$\angle 1 + \angle 2 + \angle 3 = 180°$, i.e., $\angle A + \angle B + \angle C = 180°$

Thus, the sum of the three angles of a triangle is 180°.

ILLUSTRATION : 3

If the ratio of three angles of a triangle is 1 : 2 : 3, find the angles.

SOLUTION :

Ratio of three angles of a triangle = 1 : 2 : 3

Let the angles be x, $2x$ and $3x$.

$x + 2x + 3x = 180°$

$\therefore \quad 6x = 180° \qquad \therefore \; x = 30°$

Hence, the first angle = x = 30°

The second angle = $2x$ = 60°

The third angle = $3x$ = 90°

THEOREM 3 :

If a side of a triangle is produced, then the exterior angle so formed is equal to the sum of the two interior opposite angles.

Given : A triangle ABC of which sides AB, BC and CA are produced.

To prove : $\angle BAF = \angle ABC + \angle ACB$

$\angle CBD = \angle BAC + \angle ACB$

and $\angle ACE = \angle BAC + \angle ABC$

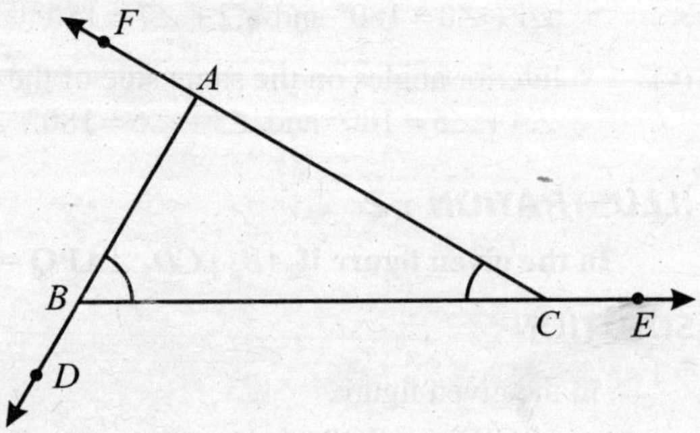

Proof : $\angle BAF + \angle BAC = 180°$ ...(i) [Linear pair axiom]

In ΔABC, $\angle BAC + \angle ABC + \angle ACB = 180°$ ...(ii)

From equations (i) and (ii), we get

$\angle BAF + \angle BAC = \angle BAC + \angle ABC + \angle ACB$

$\Rightarrow \quad \angle BAF = \angle ABC + \angle ACB$

Similarly we can prove that

$\angle CBD = \angle BAC + \angle ACB$

and $\angle ACE = \angle BAC + \angle ABC$

ILLUSTRATION : 4

In fig., if OP||RS, ∠OPQ = 110° and ∠QRS = 130°, then determine ∠PQR.

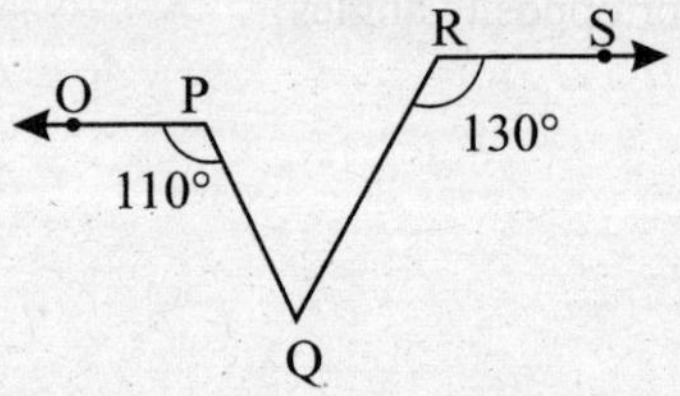

SOLUTION :

Produce OP to intersect RQ at point N such that $PQ = QN$.

Now, $OP \parallel RS$ and transversal RN intersects them at N and R respectively.

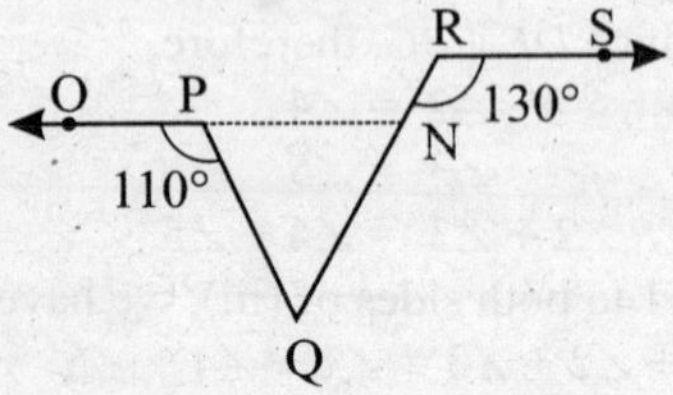

$\therefore \quad \angle RNP = \angle SRN$ (Alternate interior angles)

$\Rightarrow \quad \angle RNP = 130°$

$\therefore \quad \angle PNQ = 180° - 130° = 50°$ (Linear pair)

$\angle OPQ = \angle PNQ + \angle PQN$ (Exterior angle property)

$\Rightarrow \quad 110° = 50° + \angle PNQ$

$\angle PNQ = 110° - 50° = 60° = \angle PQR \quad [\because PQ = QN \Rightarrow \angle PQR = \angle PNQ]$

MISCELLANEOUS SOLVED EXAMPLES

1. The side BC of a triangle ABC is produced to D. The bisector of the $\angle A$ meets BC in L. Prove that $\angle ABC + \angle ACD = 2\angle ALC$

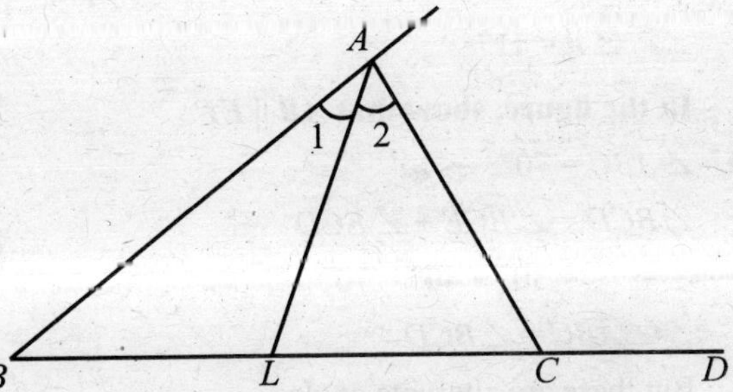

Sol. $\angle ALC = \angle 1 + \angle B$

$\Rightarrow \quad 2\angle ALC = 2\angle 1 + 2\angle B$

$\Rightarrow \quad 2\angle ALC = \angle A + 2\angle B$

$\Rightarrow \quad 2\angle ALC = (\angle ACD - \angle B) + 2\angle B \qquad (\because \quad \angle ACD = \angle A + \angle B)$

$\Rightarrow \quad 2\angle ALC = \angle ACD + \angle B = \angle ACD + \angle ABC$

2. In the adjoining figure, find the value of $x°$.

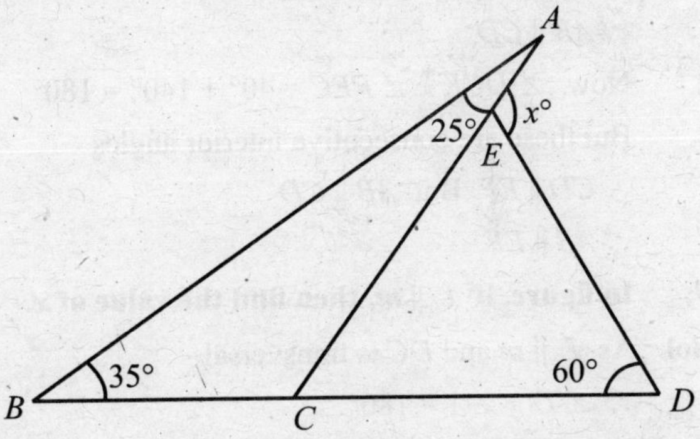

Sol. In the ΔABC, $\angle A + \angle B + \angle ACB = 180°$

$\Rightarrow \quad 25° + 35° + \angle ACB = 180°$

$\Rightarrow \quad \angle ACB = 120°$

Now, $\angle ACB + \angle ACD = 180°$ (linear pair)

or $\quad 120° + \angle ACD = 180°$

or $\quad \angle ACD = 60° = \angle EDC$

Again in the $\Delta\ CDE$, CE is produced to A.

Hence, $\angle AED = \angle ECD + \angle EDC \quad \Rightarrow x = 60° + 60° = 120°$

3. In the given adjoining figure, find the value of $x°$.

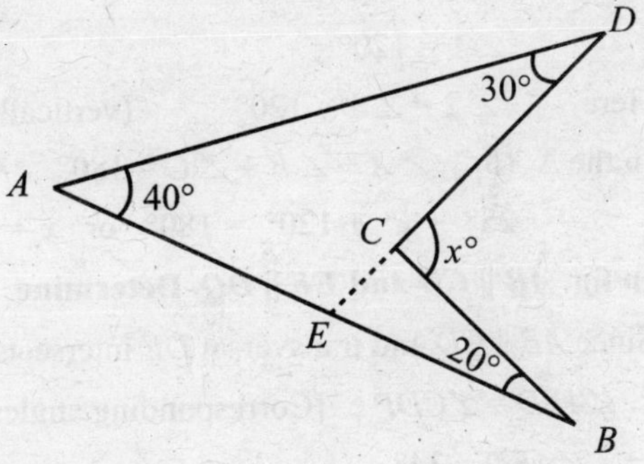

Sol. Produce DC such that it meets AB in E

Now in the $\Delta\ AED$,

Side AE is produced to B

$\therefore \quad \angle DEB = \angle EDA + \angle DAE$ (Ext. angle of a triangle)

$\angle DEB = 30° + 40° = 70° = \angle CEB$

Now in the $\Delta\ BEC$,

Side EC is produced to D

$\therefore \quad \angle DCB = \angle CEB + \angle CBE$ (Ext. angle of a triangle)

$\therefore \quad \angle DCB = 70° + 20° = 90° \quad \Rightarrow x° = 90°$

4. OA, OB, OC, OD and OE (Fig.) have common starting point O. Show that $\angle AOB + \angle BOC + \angle COD + \angle DOE + \angle EOA = 360°$

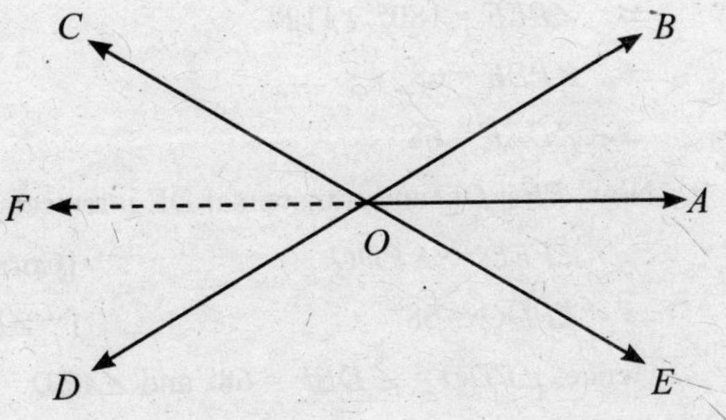

Sol. Draw a ray OF opposite to the ray OA (Fig.)

$\therefore \quad \angle AOB + \angle BOC + \angle COF = 180°$ .... (i)

and $\angle FOD + \angle DOE + \angle EOA = 180°$ .... (ii)

Adding (i) and (ii), we get

$\angle AOB + \angle BOC + \angle COF + \angle FOD + \angle DOE + \angle EOA$

$= 180° + 180° = 360°$

$\therefore \quad \angle AOB + \angle BOC + \angle COD + \angle DOE + \angle EOA = 360°$

5. In the figure, lines l and m intersect at O. If $\angle x = 63°$, then find the values of y, z and n.

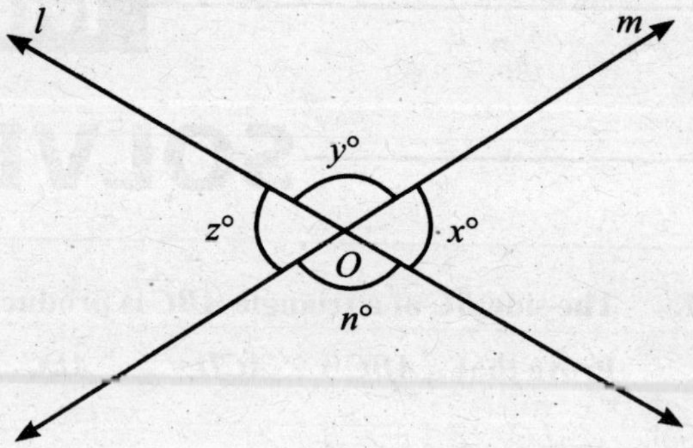

Sol. $\angle x = 63°$

Now, $\angle x = \angle z$ (vertically opposite angles)

$\therefore \quad \angle z = 63°$

As $\angle x + \angle y = 180°$

$63° + \angle y = 180°$

$\angle y = 117°$

Now, $\angle y = \angle n$ (vertically opposite angles)

$\therefore \quad \angle n = 117°$

6. In the figure, show that $AB \parallel EF$

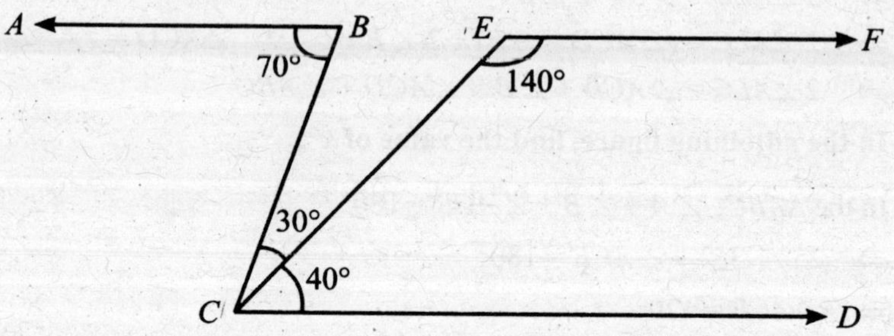

Sol. $\angle ABC = 70°$

$\angle BCD = \angle BCE + \angle ECD$

$= 30° + 40° = 70°$

$\therefore \angle ABC = \angle BCD$

But these are alternate angles

$\therefore AB \parallel CD$

Now, $\angle DCE + \angle FEC = 40° + 140° = 180°$

But these are consecutive interior angles

$\therefore CD \parallel EF$ But $AB \parallel CD$

$\therefore AB \parallel EF$

7. In figure, if $\ell \parallel m$, then find the value of x.

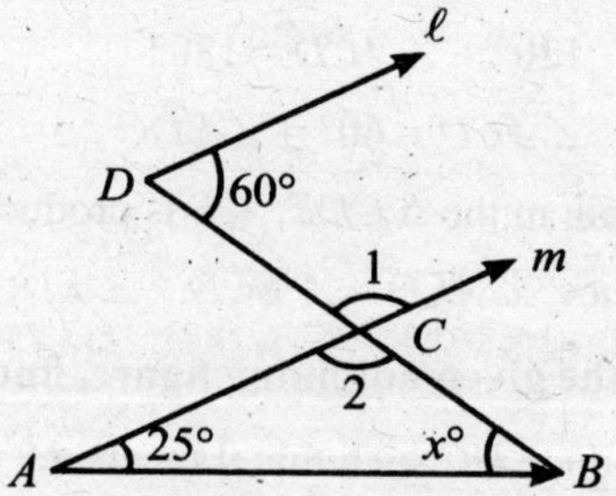

Sol. As $\ell \parallel m$ and DC is transversal

$\therefore \angle D + \angle 1 = 180°$

$60° + \angle 1 = 180°$

$\angle 1 = 120°$

Here $\angle 2 = \angle 1 = 120°$ (vertically opposite angles)

In the ΔABC, $\angle A + \angle B + \angle C = 180°$

$25° + x° + 120° = 180°$ or $x = 35°$

8. In fig. $AB \parallel CD$ and $EF \parallel DQ$. Determine $\angle PDQ$, $\angle AED$ and $\angle DEF$.

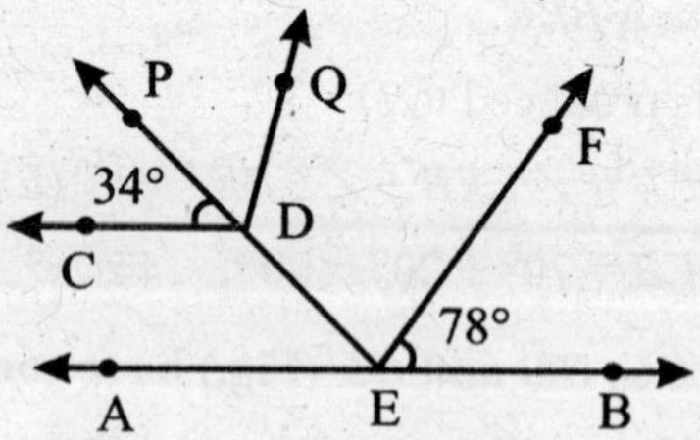

Sol. Since $AB \parallel CD$ and transversal DE intersects them at E and D respectively.

$\therefore \angle AED = \angle CDP$ [Corresponding angles]

$\Rightarrow \angle AED = 34°$ ... (i)

Now, ray EF stands on AB at E.

$\therefore \quad \angle AEF + \angle BEF = 180°$

$\Rightarrow \angle AEP + \angle PEF + \angle BEF = 180°$ [$\because \angle AEF = \angle AEP + \angle PEF$]

$\Rightarrow 34° + \angle PEF + 78° = 180°$ [$\because \angle AEP = \angle AED = 34°$ from (i)]

$\Rightarrow \angle PEF = 180° - 112°$

$\Rightarrow \angle PEF = 68°$ ...(ii)

$\Rightarrow \angle DEF = 68°$

Now, $EF \parallel DQ$ and transversal DE intersects them at E and D respectively.

$\therefore \quad \angle FED = \angle PDQ$ [Corresponding angles]

$\Rightarrow \angle PDQ = 68°$ [$\because \angle FED = \angle PEF = 68°$ from (ii)]

Hence, $\angle PDQ = \angle DEF = 68°$ and $\angle AED = 34°$

9. In fig. if $AB \parallel CD$, $\angle APQ = 50°$ and $\angle PRD = 127°$, find x and y.

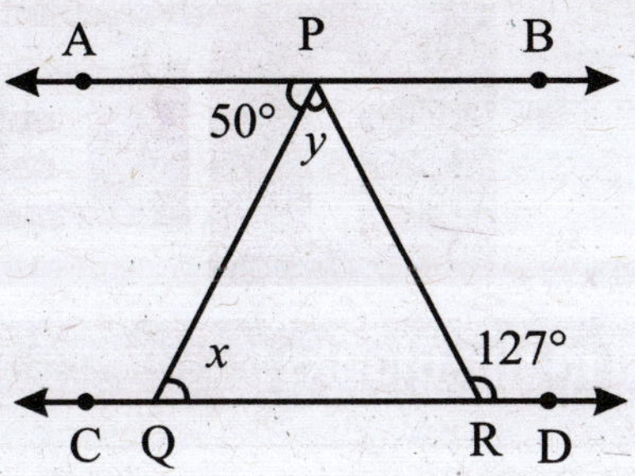

Sol. We have,

$\angle APR = \angle PRD$ [Alternate angles]

$\Rightarrow$ $50° + y = 127°$

$\Rightarrow$ $y = 127° - 50° = 77°$

Also, $\angle APQ = \angle PQR$ [Alternate angles]

$\Rightarrow$ $50° = x$

Hence, $x = 50°$ and $y = 77°$

10. In fig. $AB \parallel CF$ and $BC \parallel ED$. Prove that $\angle ABC = \angle FDE$.

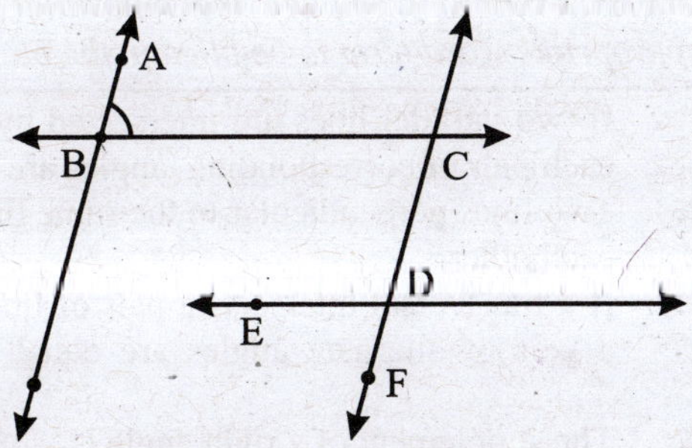

Sol. We have

$AB \parallel CF$ ...(i)

$\Rightarrow$ $\angle ABC = \angle BCF$ [Alternate $\angle$s] ...(ii)

Also, $BC \parallel ED$ [Given]

$\Rightarrow$ $\angle BCF = \angle FDE$ [Corresponding $\angle$'s] (iii)

From (i) and (ii), we get

$\angle ABC = \angle FDE$

11. Let OA, OB, OC and OD be the rays in the anticlockwise direction starting from OA such that $\angle AOB = \angle COD = 100°$, $\angle BOC = 82°$ and $\angle AOD = 78°$. Is it true that AOC and BOD are straight lines ? Justify your answer.

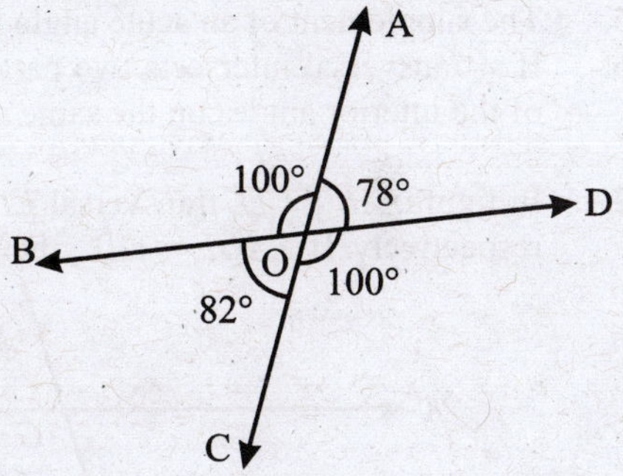

Sol. No, AOC and BOD are not straight lines.

$\angle AOB + \angle COB = 100° + 82° = 182° \neq 180°$

$\Rightarrow$ AOC is not a straight line

Similarly, $\angle AOD + \angle COD = 78° + 100° = 178° \neq 180°$

$\Rightarrow$ BOD is not a straight line

[If the sum of two adjacent angles is 180°, then the ray stands on a line (i.e., the non-common arms form a line)]

12. In figure, if $AB \parallel CD$, then find the measure of x.

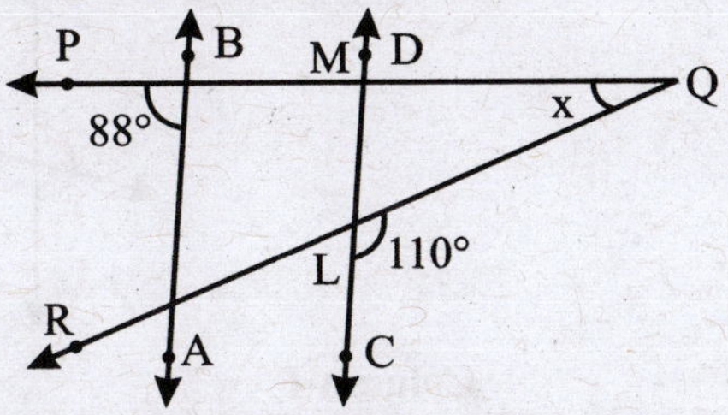

Sol. Since $AB \parallel CD$ and PQ is a transversal, therefore

$88° = \angle PML$ …(i)

Since the ray CD stands on PQ, therefore

$\angle PML + \angle QML = 180°$ [Adjacent $\angle$s]

$\Rightarrow$ $88° + \angle QML = 180°$ [using (i)]

$\Rightarrow$ $\angle QML = 180° - 88° = 92°$ …(ii)

Since the ray QR stands on the line CD, therefore

$\angle QLM + \angle QLC = 180°$ [Sum of adjacents $\angle$s = 180°]

$\Rightarrow$ $\angle QLM + 110° = 180°$ [$\because \angle QLC = 110°$ (given)]

$\Rightarrow$ $\angle QLM = 180° - 110°$

$\Rightarrow$ $\angle QLM = 70°$ …(iii)

In ΔQML, we have

$\angle QML + \angle QLM + x = 180°$ [Angle sum property of a Δ]

$\Rightarrow$ $92° + 70° + x = 180°$ [using (ii) and (iii)]

$\Rightarrow$ $162° + x = 180°$

$\Rightarrow$ $x = 180° - 162°$

$\Rightarrow$ $x = 18°$

1 EXERCISE

Fill in the Blanks :

DIRECTIONS: *Complete the following statements with an appropriate word/term to be filled in the blank space(s).*

1. If two parallel lines are intersected by a transversal, then each pair of corresponding angles are ....
2. Two lines perpendicular to the same line are .... to each other.
3. If a transversal intersects a pair of lines in such way that a pair of alternate angles are equal, then the lines are ....
4. The supplement of a right angle is ....
5. The supplement of an acute angle is ....
6. If a transversal intersects two parallel lines, then the sum of the interior angles on the same side of the transversal is ....
7. In figure, $AB \parallel CD$, transversal EF cuts them at G and H respectively. If $\angle AGE = 110°$, then $\angle GHD =$ ....

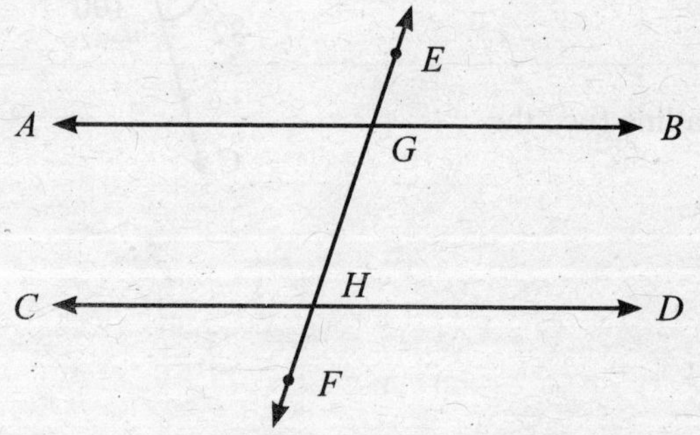

8. In figure, a transversal PQ intersects two parallel line AB and CD at L and M respectively. If $\angle 1 = 95°$, then $\angle 2 =$ ....

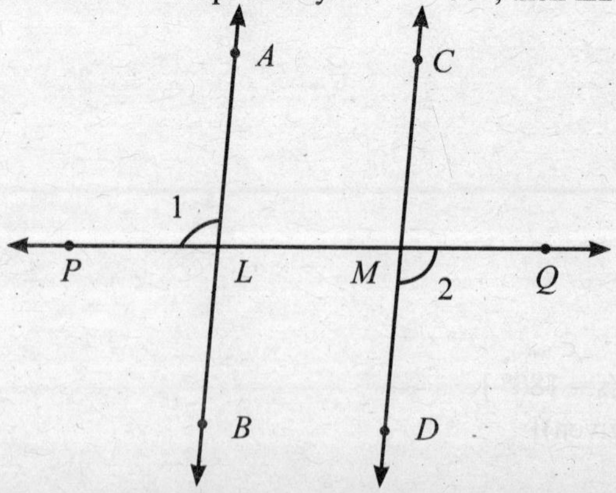

True / False :

DIRECTIONS: *Read the following statements and write your answer as true or false.*

1. If a transversal intersects two parallel lines, then each pair of alternate interior angles are equal.
2. Two adjacent angles are said to form a linear pair of angles, if their non-common arms are two opposite rays.
3. An angle is the union of two non-collinear rays with a common initial point.
4. Three lines are concurrent if they have a common point.
5. A segment has no length.
6. Three points will be collinear only when they lie on a line.
7. A ray has a finite length.
8. Two lines will meet in one point only when they are parallel.

Match the Columns:

DIRECTIONS: *Each question contains statements given in two columns which have to be matched. Statements (A, B, C, D) in Column-I have to be matched with statements (p, q, r, s) in Column-II.*

1.

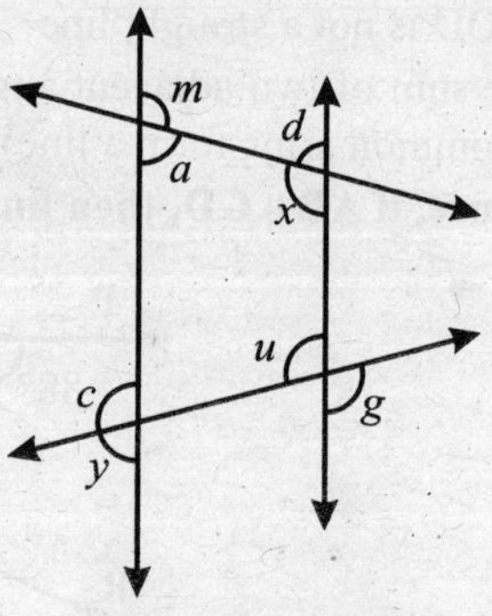

Column-I	Column-II
(A) angles m and y	(p) alternate exterior pair
(B) angles a and d	(q) alternate interior pair
(C) angles d and u	(r) corresponding pair
(D) angles u and g	(s) vertical pair

2. For the figure shown, match column I with II correctly

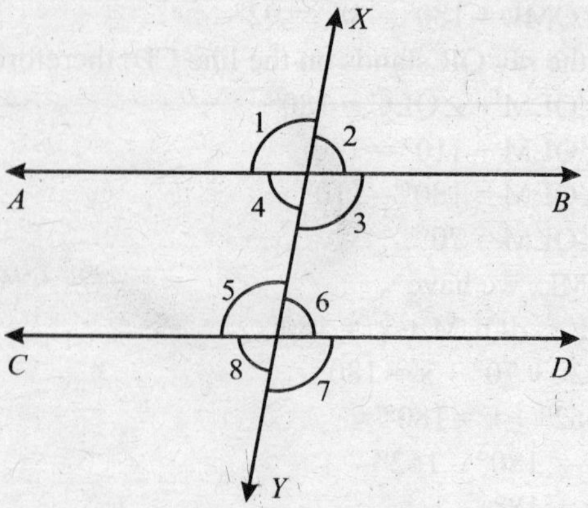

Column-I	Column-II
(A) Corresponding angles	(p) 1 and 5
(B) Alternate interior angles	(q) 4 and 6
(C) Alternate exterior angles	(r) 1 and 7
(D) Interior angles on same side of the transversal	(s) 4 and 5

Very Short Answer Questions :

DIRECTIONS: *Give answer in one word or one sentence.*

1. An angle is 16° more than its complement. What is its measure ?

2. Two parallel lines are cut by a transversal such that one of the interior angle is 57°. Find each of the other interior angles.

3. In the given figure, *AB*, *CD* and *EF* are parallel. If $\angle z = 70°$, find the value of x and y.

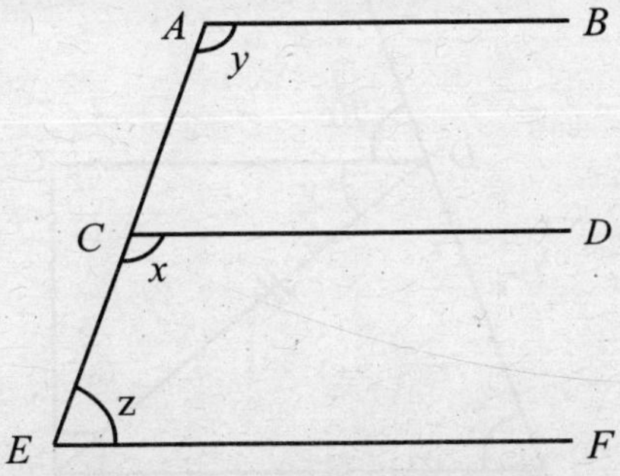

4. For what value of $x + y$ in the given figure, will *ABC* be a line ? Justify your answer.

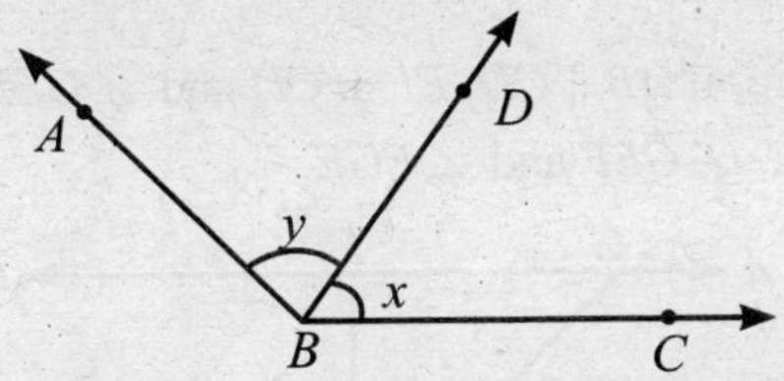

5. Can a triangle have all angles less than 60°? Give reason for your answer.

6. In the given figure, find the value of x for which the lines l and m are parallel.

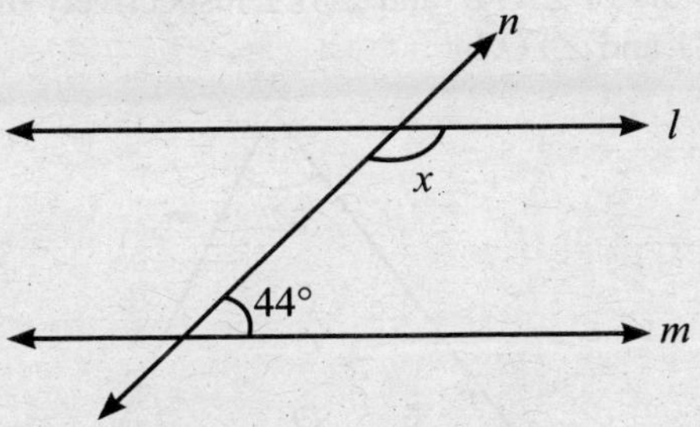

7. In ΔABC, $\angle B = 105°$, $\angle C = 50°$. Find $\angle A$.

8. Define complementary angles.

9. Define vertically opposite angles.

10. Define the term 'transversal'.

11. In the given figure, find the value of x.

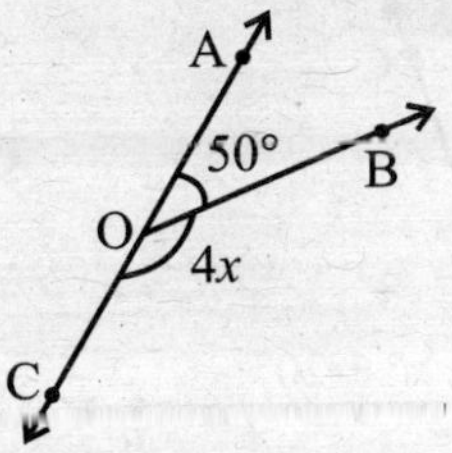

12. Angles 'a' and 'b' form a linear pair of angles and $a - 2b = 30°$, then find the value of 'a'.

13. In the given figure, find the value of 'b'.

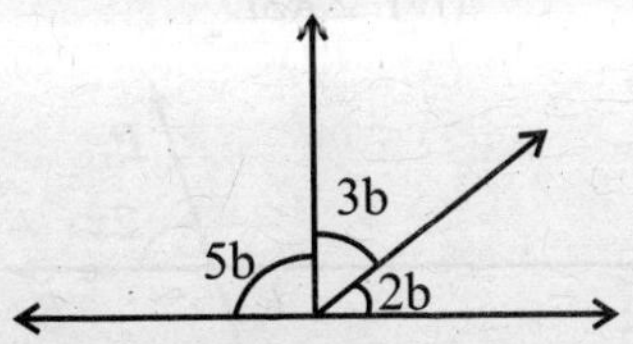

Short Answer Questions:

DIRECTIONS: *Give answer in 2-3 sentences.*

1. The supplement of an angle is one-fifth of itself. Determine the angle and its supplement.

2. In figure if $l \parallel m$, $n \parallel p$, and $\angle 1 = 85°$, then find $\angle 2$.

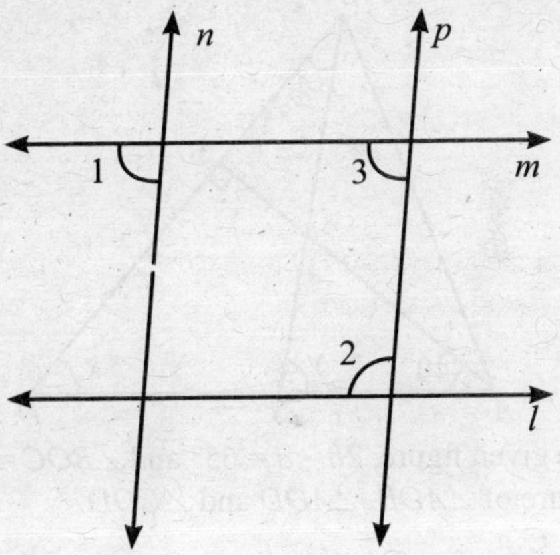

3. From the given diagram, calculate $\angle x$, $\angle y$, $\angle z$ and $\angle w$.

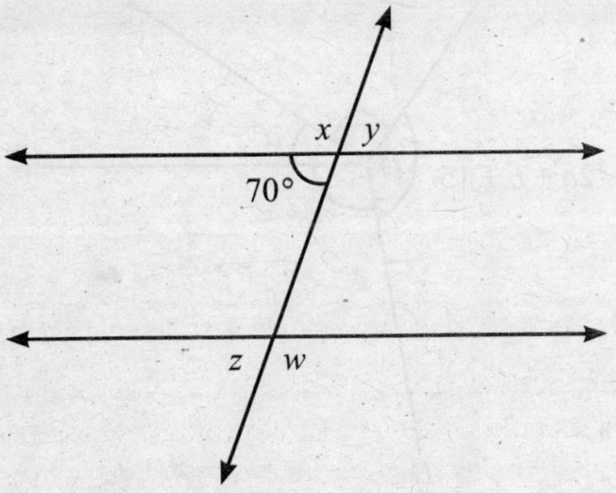

4. In the following figure, find $\angle x$. Further find $\angle BOC$, $\angle COD$ and $\angle AOD$.

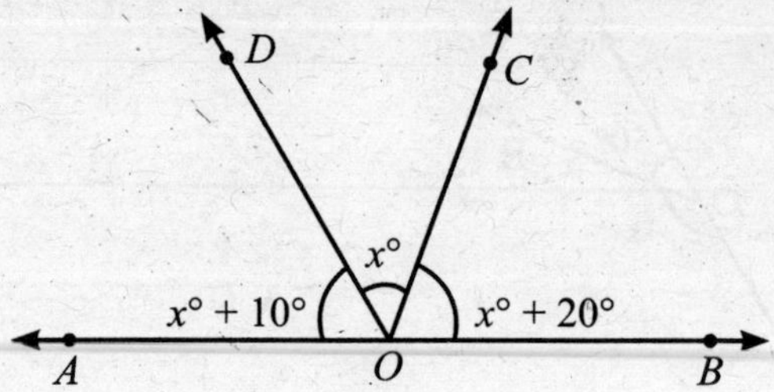

5. In the figure, find the values of

(i) x (ii) $\angle GHS$

(iii) $\angle PRG$ (iv) $\angle RSD$

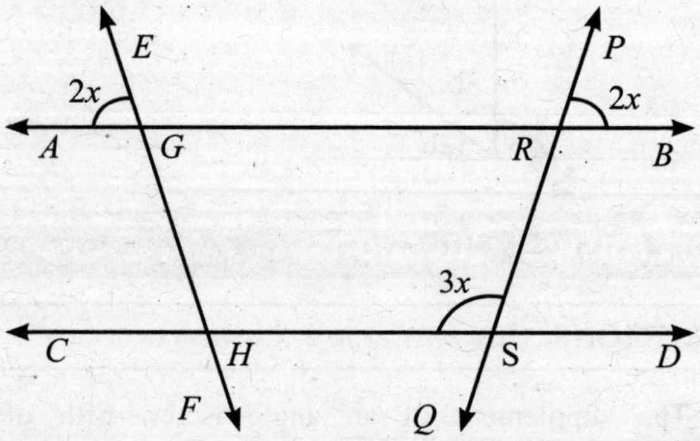

6. In figure, if $AB \perp CD$, $\angle BAD = 40°$ and $\angle SCD = 30°$, find x and y.

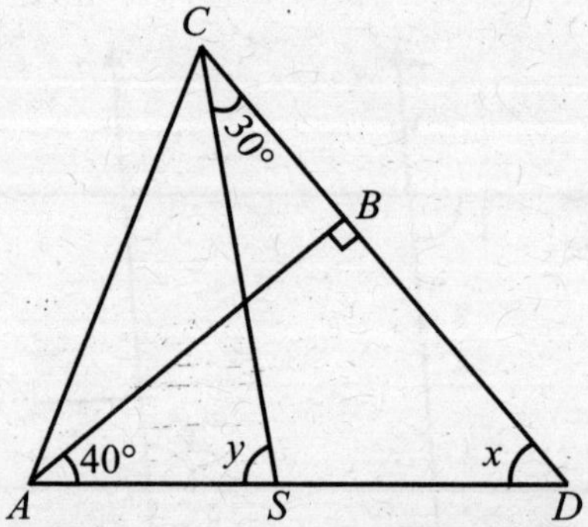

7. In the given figure, $2b - a = 65°$ and $\angle BOC = 90°$, find the measure of $\angle AOB$, $\angle AOD$ and $\angle COD$.

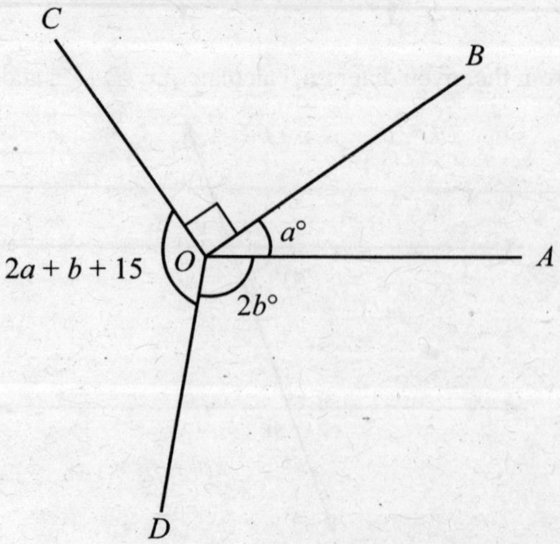

Long Answer Questions:

DIRECTIONS: *Give answer in four to five sentences.*

1. In figure, $\angle POR$ and $\angle QOR$ form a linear pair. If $a - b = 80°$, find the values of a and b.

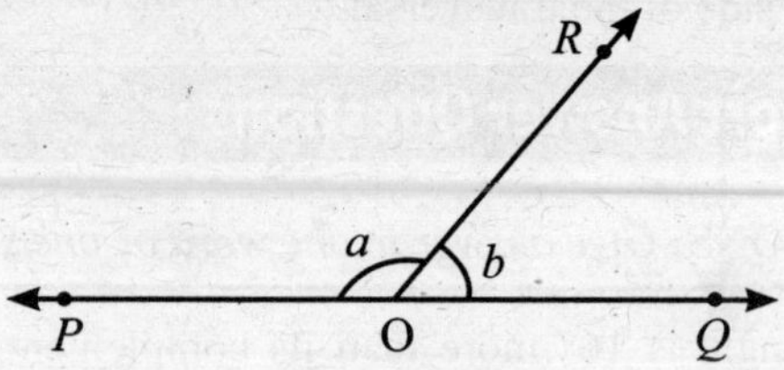

2. It is given that $\angle XYZ = 64°$ and XY is produced to point P. Draw a figure from the given information. If ray YQ bisects $\angle ZYP$, find $\angle XYQ$ and reflex $\angle QYP$.

3. From the adjoining diagram $AB \parallel DC$, calculate

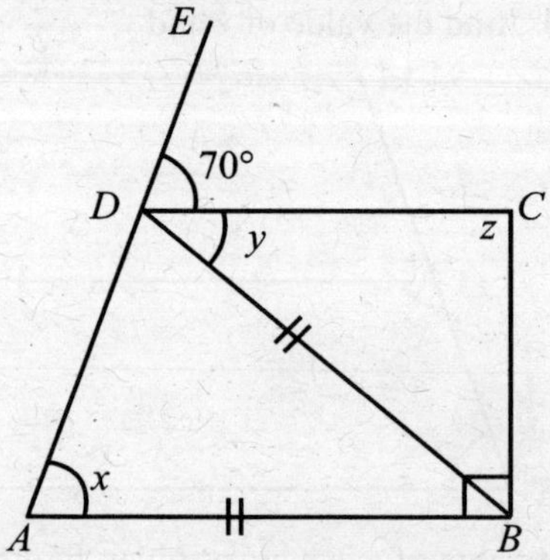

(i) $\angle x$ (ii) $\angle y$ (iii) $\angle z$

4. In figure, if $AB \parallel CD$, $EF \perp CD$ and $\angle GED = 126°$, find $\angle AGE$, $\angle GEF$ and $\angle FGE$.

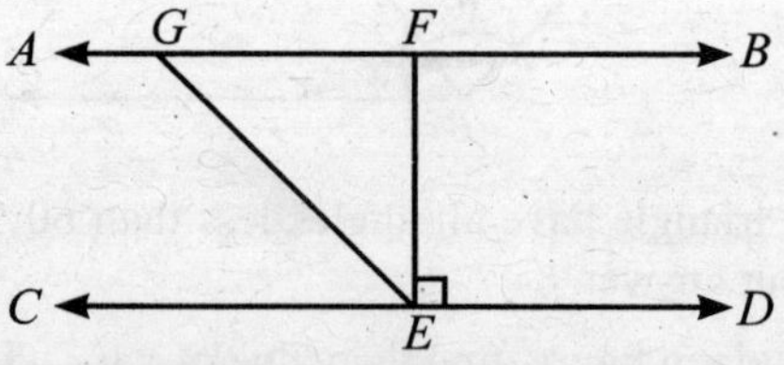

5. In figure, $\angle X = 62°$, $\angle XYZ = 54°$. If YO and ZO are the bisectors of $\angle XYZ$ and $\angle XZY$ respectively of ΔXYZ, find $\angle OZY$ and $\angle YOZ$.

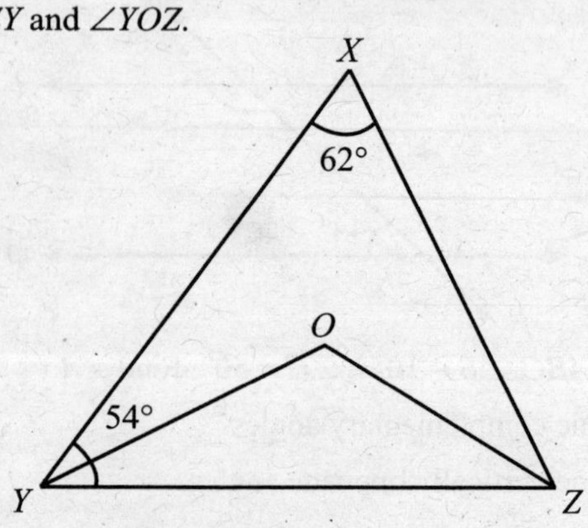

6. In figure, if $PQ \perp PS$, $PQ \parallel SR$, $\angle SQR = 28°$ and $\angle QRT = 65°$, then find the values of x and y.

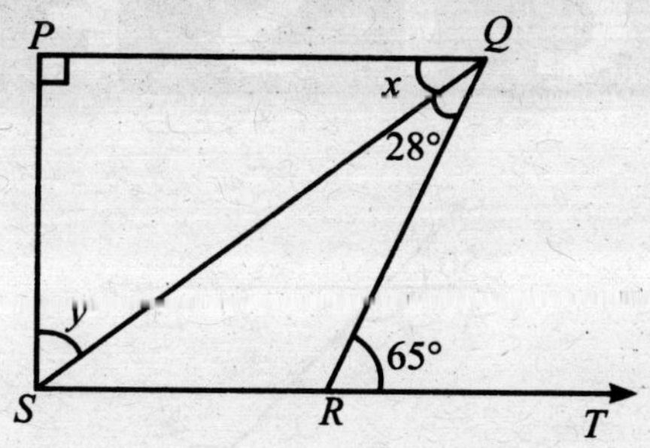

7. In fig. AB||CD. Find the value of x.

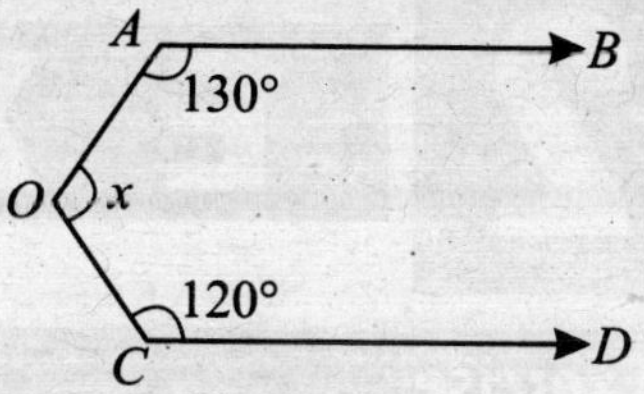

2 EXERCISE

Text-Book Exercise :

1. In figure, lines AB and CD intersect at O.

If $\angle AOC + \angle BOE = 70°$ and $\angle BOD = 40°$, find $\angle BOE$ and reflex $\angle COE$.

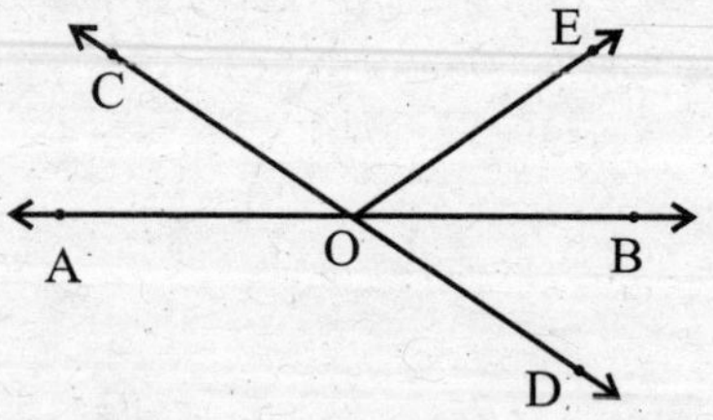

2. In figure, $\angle PQR = \angle PRQ$, then prove that $\angle PQS = \angle PRT$.

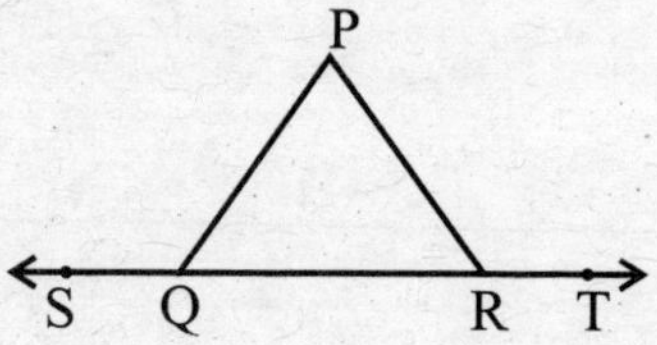

3. In figure, if $x + y = w + z$, then prove that AOB is a line.

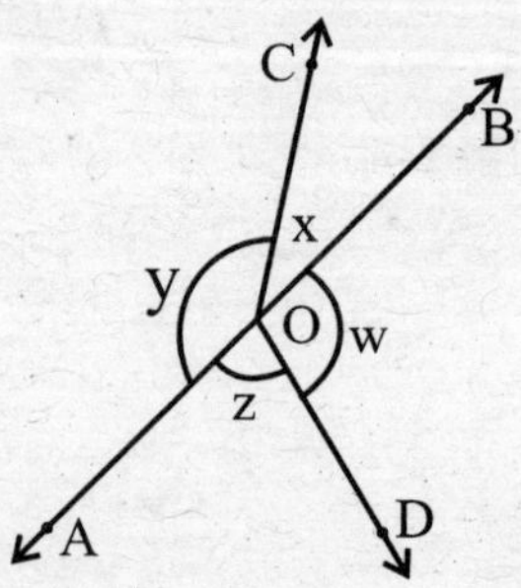

4. In figure, POQ is a line. Ray OR is perpendicular to line PQ. Also, OS is another ray lying between rays OP and OR. Prove that

$$\angle ROS = \frac{1}{2}(\angle QOS - \angle POS)$$

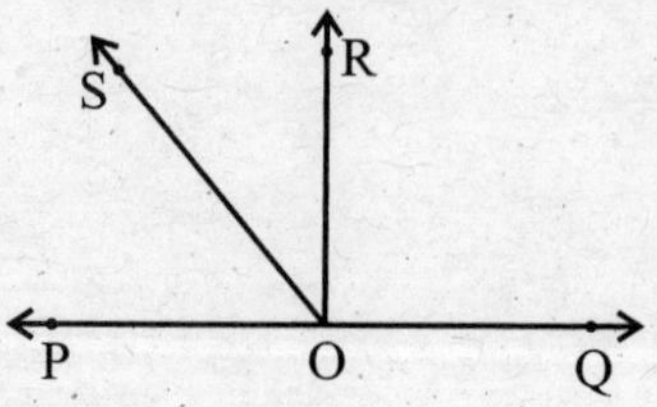

5. In figure, find the values of x and y and then show that AB || CD.

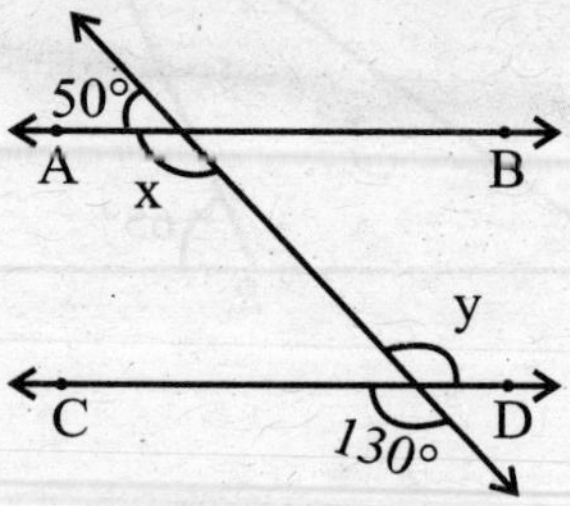

6. In figure, if AB || CD, CD || EF and $y : z = 3 : 7$, find x.

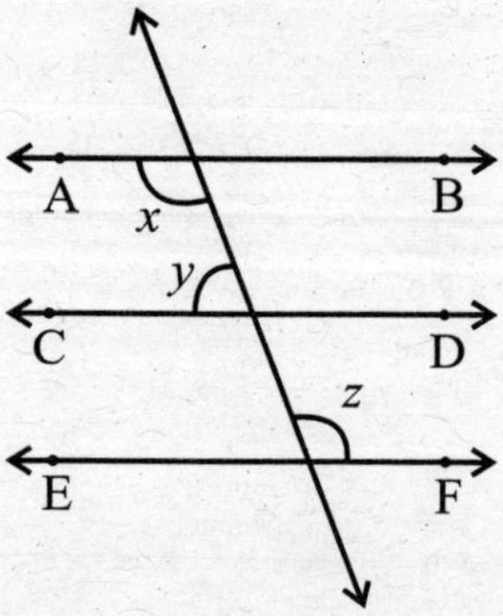

7. In figure, sides QP and RQ of ΔPQR are produced to points S and T respectively. If $\angle SPR = 135°$ and $\angle PQT = 110°$, find $\angle PRQ$.

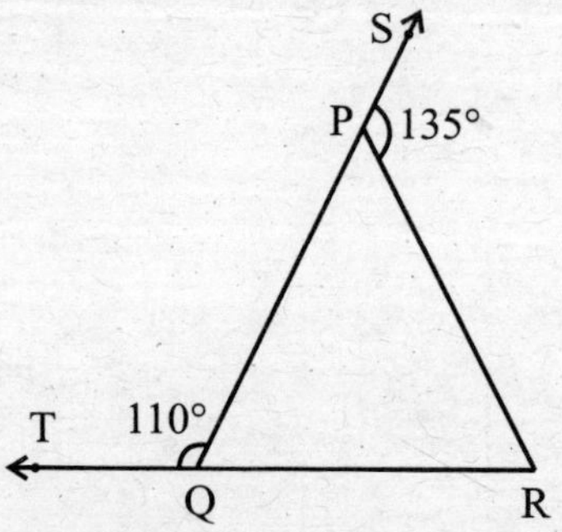

8. In figure, if $AB \parallel DE$, $\angle BAC = 35°$ and $\angle CDE = 53°$, find $\angle DCE$.

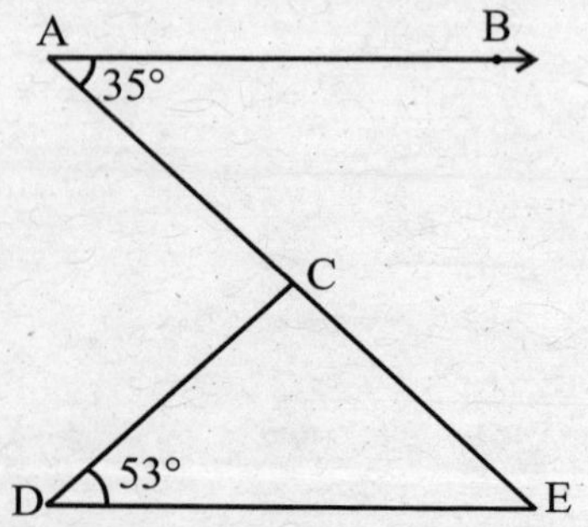

9. In figure, the side QR of ΔPQR is produced to a point S. If the bisectors of $\angle PQR$ and $\angle PRS$ meet at point T, then prove that $\angle QTR = \frac{1}{2}\angle QPR$

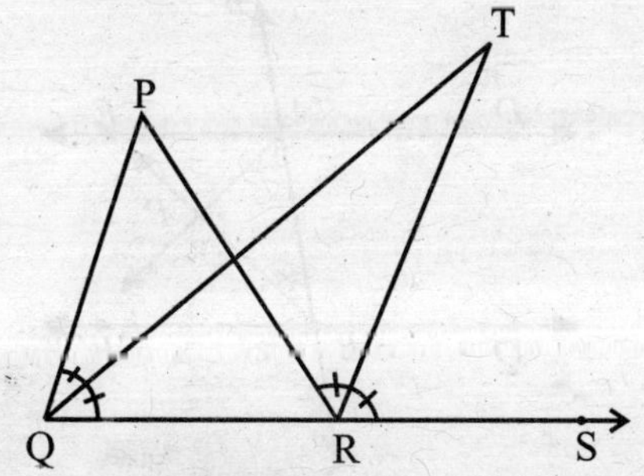

Exemplar Questions :

1. In figure, find the value of x for which the lines l and m are parallel.

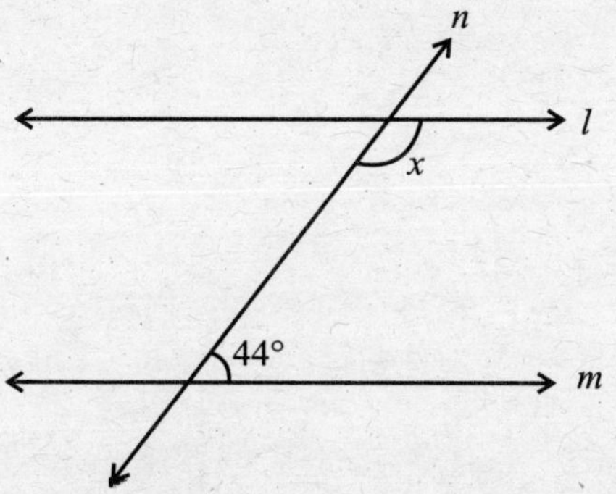

2. How many triangles can be drawn having its angles as 45°, 64° and 72°? Give reason for your answer.
3. In figure, $x = y$ and a = b. Prove that $l \parallel$ n.

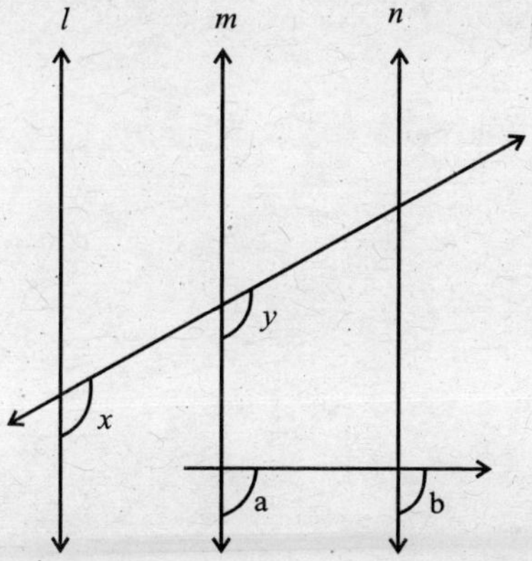

4. Bisectors of angles B and C of a triangle ABC intersect each other at the point O.

   Prove that $\angle BOC - 90° + \frac{1}{2}\angle A$

5. In figure $\angle Q > \angle R$, PA is the bisector of ∠QPR and PM $\perp QR$. Prove that $\angle APM = \frac{1}{2}(\angle Q - \angle R)$

6. In fig. if AB || CD || EF, PQ || RS, ∠RQD = 25° and ∠CQP = 60°, then ∠QRS is equal to

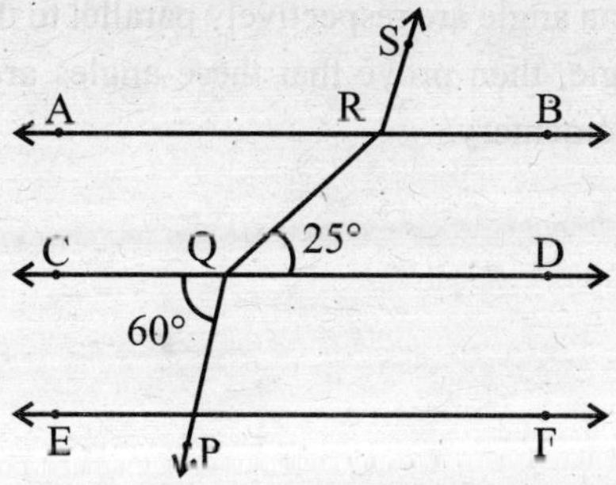

   (a) 85° (b) 135°
   (c) 145° (d) 110°

7. If one angle of a triangle is equal to the sum of the other two angles, then the triangle is
   (a) an isosceles triangle
   (b) an obtuse triangle
   (c) an equilateral triangle
   (d) a right triangle
8. An exterior angle of a triangle is 105° and its two interior opposite angles are equal. Each of these equal angle is

   (a) $37\frac{1}{7}°$ (b) $52\frac{1}{2}°$

   (c) $72\frac{1}{2}°$ (d) 75°
9. The angles of a triangle are in the ratio 5 : 3 : 7. The triangle is
   (a) an acute angled triangle
   (b) an obtuse angled triangle
   (c) a right triangle
   (d) an isosceles triangle
10. If one of the angles of a triangle is 130°, then the angle between the bisectors of the other two angles can be
    (a) 50° (b) 65°
    (c) 145° (d) 155°

HOTS Questions :

1. The sides BC, CA and AB of a ΔABC are produced in order, forming exterior angles $\angle ACD$, $\angle BAE$ and $\angle CBF$. Show that $\angle ACD + \angle BAE + \angle CBF = 360°$.
2. Find $\angle ADC$ from the given figure.

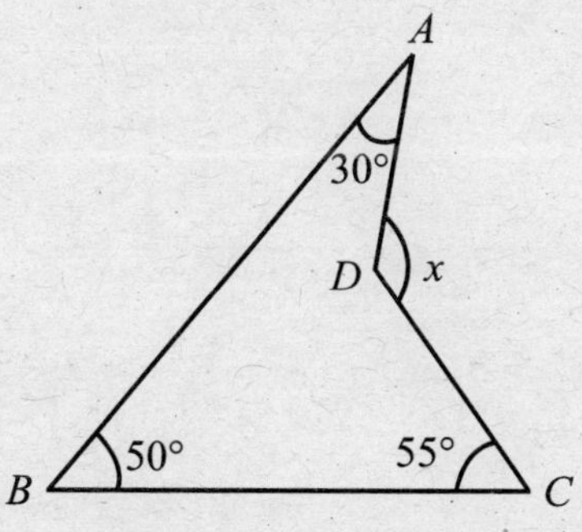

3. If the sides of an angle are respectively parallel to the sides of another angle, then prove that these angles are either equal or supplementary.

4. In fig., $DE || QR$ and AP and BP are bisectors of ∠EAB and ∠RBA respectively. Find ∠APB.

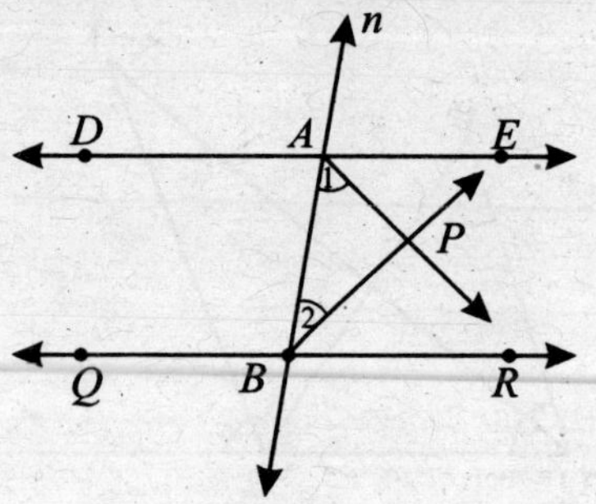

3 EXERCISE

Single Option Correct :

DIRECTIONS: *This section contains multiple choice questions. Each questions has 4 choices (a), (b), (c) and (d) out of which ONLY ONE is correct.*

1. If two lines intersected by a transversal, then each pair of corresponding angles so formed is

(a) Equal (b) Complementary
(c) Right angle (d) None of these

2. An angle is 14° more than its complementary angle then angle is

(a) 38° (b) 52°
(c) 50° (d) None of these

3. If one angle of triangle is equal to the sum of the other two then triangle is

(a) acute a triangle (b) obtuse triangle
(c) right triangle (d) None of these

4. In the figure, angle a is

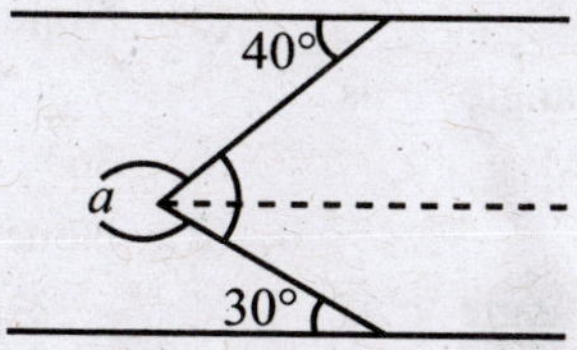

(a) 290° (b) 70°
(c) 105° (d) 45°

5. Value of $\angle x =$

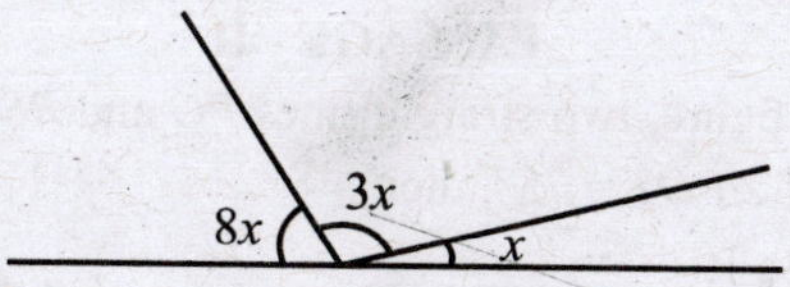

(a) 270° (b) 70°
(c) 15° (d) 45°

6. Value of $\angle x =$

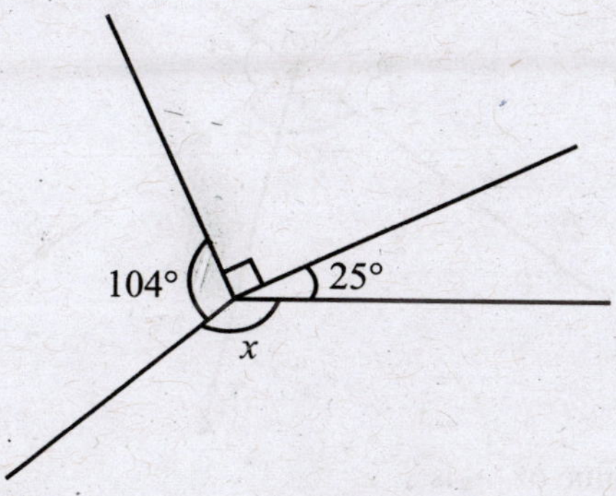

(a) 141° (b) 70°
(c) 105° (d) 45°

7. In the given figure, if lines l and m are parallel, then x =

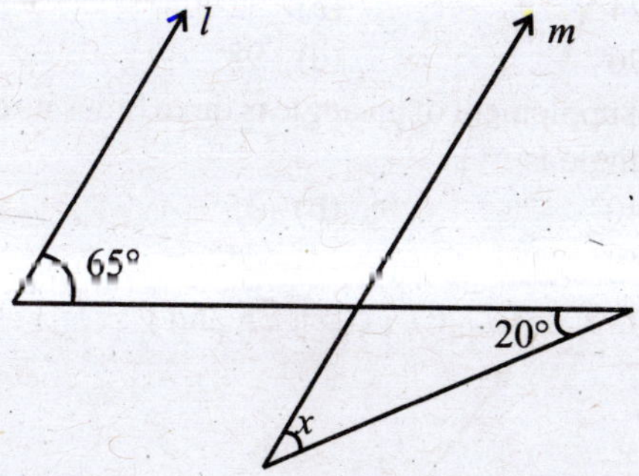

(a) 65° (b) 85°
(c) 45° (d) 20°

8. In figure, if $l \parallel m$, what is the value of x ?

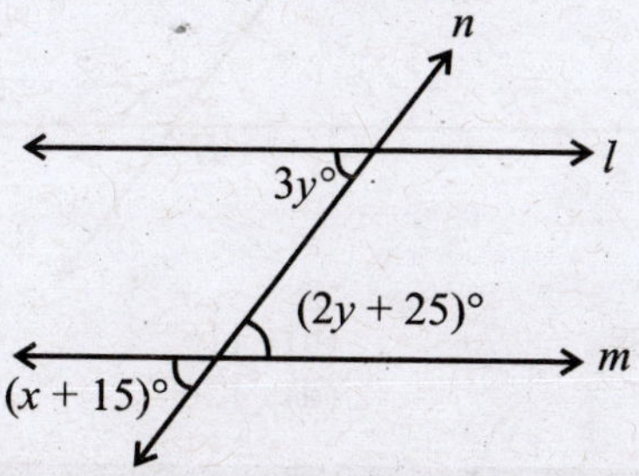

(a) 50° (b) 30°
(c) 45° (d) 60°

9. In figure, if $l \parallel m$, what is the value of y ?

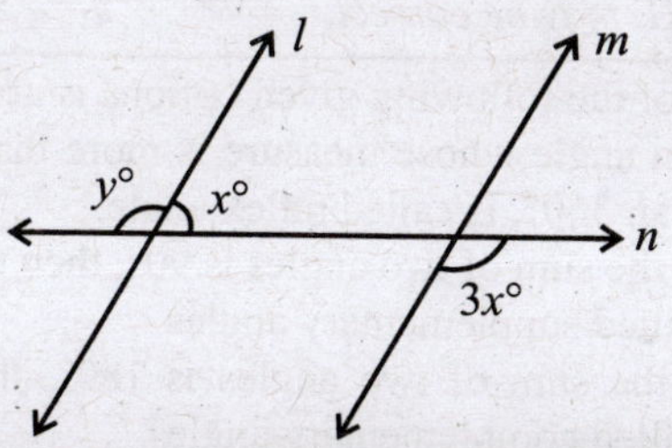

(a) 135° (b) 120°
(c) 100° (d) 150°

10. If angle with measure x and y form a complementary pair, then angles with which of the following measures will form a supplementary pair?

(a) $(x + 47°), (y + 43°)$
(b) $(x - 23°), (y + 23°)$
(c) $(x - 43°), (y - 47°)$
(d) No such pair is possible

11. In adjoining figure, if $\angle A = (3x + 2)°$, $\angle B = (x - 3)°$, $\angle ACD = 127°$, then $\angle A =$

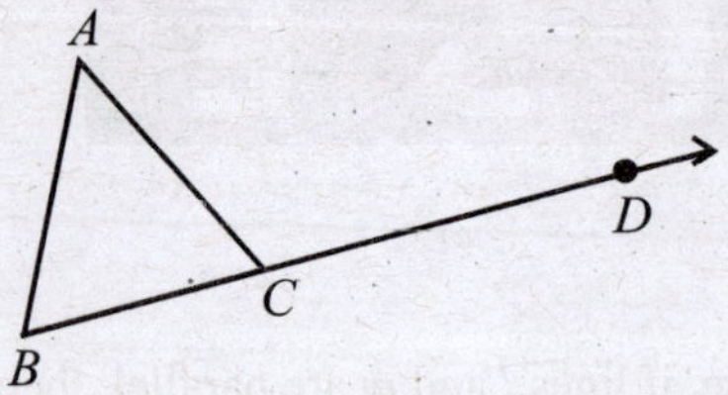

(a) 24° (b) 32°
(c) 96° (d) 98°

12. If the supplement of an angle is three times its complement, then angle is
(a) 40° (b) 35°
(c) 50° (d) 45°

13. In figure, if $AB \parallel CD$, $CD \parallel EF$ and $y : z = 3 : 7$, $x = ?$

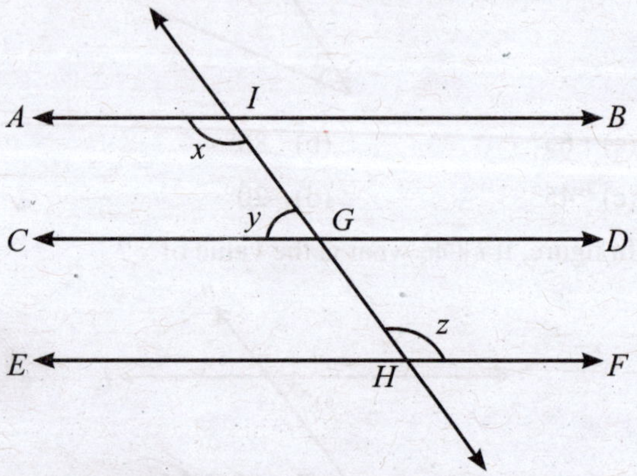

(a) 112° (b) 116°
(c) 96° (d) 126°

More Than One Option Correct :

DIRECTIONS: *This section contains multiple choice questions. Each question has 4 choices (a), (b), (c) and (d) out of which ONE or MORE may be correct.*

1. Which of the following given options is/are correct?
(a) An angle whose measure is more than 180, but less than 360°, is called reflex angle.
(b) If the sum of two angles is 90°, then these angles are called supplementary angles.
(c) If the sum of two angles is 180°, these angles are called complementary angles.
(d) The sum of angles forming a linear-pair is 360°.

2. Which of the following is/are correct?
(a) Angles forming a linear pair are supplementary.
(b) If angles forming a linear pair are equal, then each of these angles is of measure 90°.
(c) If two adjacent angles are equal, then each angle measure 90°.
(d) Angles forming a linear pair can both be acute angles.

3. Which of the following is/are false?
(a) Angles forming a linear pair can both be acute angles.
(b) If two lines are intersected by a transversal, then corresponding angles are equal.
(c) The supplementary angles have their sum equal to 360°.
(d) Two angles are complementary if their sum is 90°.

Passage Based Questions :

DIRECTIONS: *Study the given paragraph(s) and answer the following questions.*

PASSAGE - I

In figure, lines XY and MN intersect at O. If $\angle POY = 90°$ and $a : b = 2 : 3$, then

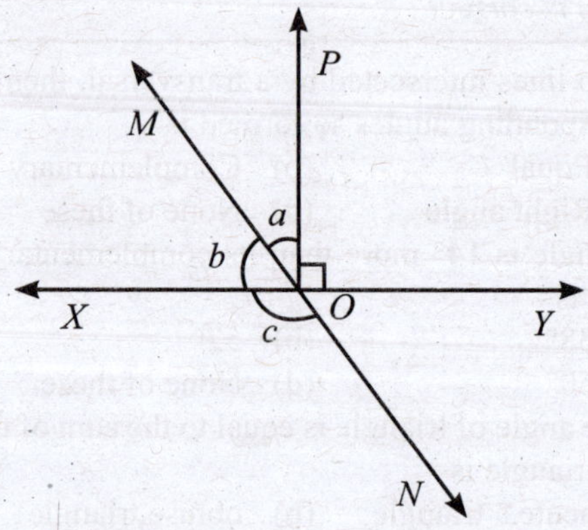

1. Measure of angle 'a' is
(a) 54° (b) 36°
(c) 126° (d) None of these

2. Measure of angle 'b' is
(a) 126° (b) 36°
(c) 54° (d) None of these

3. Measure of angle 'c' is
(a) 36° (b) 126°
(c) 54° (d) None of these

PASSAGE - II

In the given figure, two straight lines PQ and RS intersect each other at O. If $\angle POT = 75°$, then

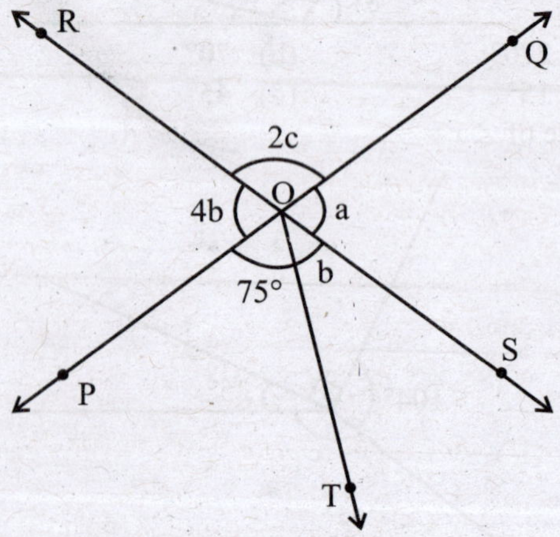

4. the value of 'a' is
(a) 105° (b) 48°
(c) 84° (d) 21°

5. the value of 'b' is
(a) 105° (b) 48°
(c) 84° (d) 21°

6. the value of 'c' is
(a) 105° (b) 48°
(c) 84° (d) 21°

Assertion & Reason :

DIRECTIONS: *Each of these questions contains an Assertion followed by Reason. Read them carefully and answer the question on the basis of following options. You have to select the one that best describes the two statements.*

(a) If both **Assertion** and **Reason** are **correct** and Reason is **the correct explanation** of Assertion.
(b) If both **Assertion** and **Reason** are correct, but Reason is **not the correct explanation** of Assertion.
(c) If **Assertion** is **correct** but **Reason** is **incorrect**.
(d) If **Assertion** is **incorrect** but **Reason** is **correct**.

1. **Assertion :** Sum of the pair of angles (like 120°, 60°) is supplementary.
Reason : Two angles, the sum of whose measures is 180°, are called supplementary angles.
2. **Assertion :** If an angle formed by two intersecting lines is 60°, then its vertically opposite angle is 60°
Reason : If two lines intersect each other, then the vertically opposite angles are equal.
3. **Assertion :** If angles '*a*' and '*b*' form a linear pair of angles and $a = 40°$, then $b = 150°$.
Reason : Sum of linear pair of angles is always 180°.
4. **Assertion :** A triangle can have two obtuse angles.
Reason : Sum of the three angles in a triangle is always 180°.
5. **Assertion :** If two internal opposite angles of a triangle are equal and external angle is given to be 110°, then each of the equal internal angle is 55°.
Reason : A triangle with one of its angle 90°, is called a right triangle.

Multiple Matching Question :

DIRECTIONS : *Following question has four statements (A, B, C and D) given in Column - I and statements (p, q, r, s, ...) in Column - II. Any given statement in Column - I can have correct matching with one or more statement(s) given in Column - II.*

1.

Column - I	Column - II
(A) Complementary angle	(p) $180° < \theta < 360°$
(B) Reflex angle	(q) $\theta = 100°$
(C) Obtuse triangle	(r) $0 < \theta < 90°$
(D) supplementary angle	(s) (35°, 55°)
	(t) $\theta = 240°$
	(u) (140°, 40°)

Integer Type Questions :

DIRECTIONS: *Answer the following questions. The answer to each of the question is a single digit integer, ranging from 0 to 9.*

1. In the given figure, find the value of $\frac{y}{2}$.

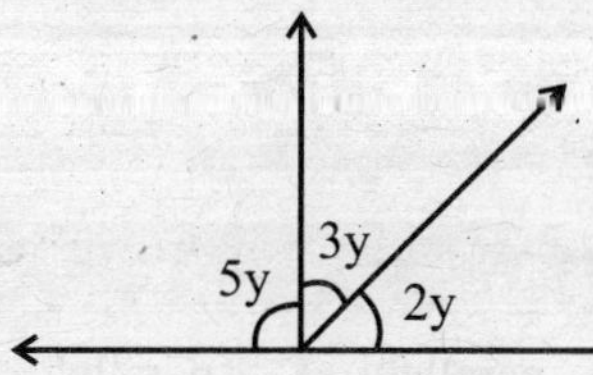

2. In the given figure, AB, CD and PQ are three lines concurrent at O. If $\angle AOP = 3x$, $\angle QOD = 2x$ and $\angle BOC = 5x$, find the value of $\frac{x}{3}$.

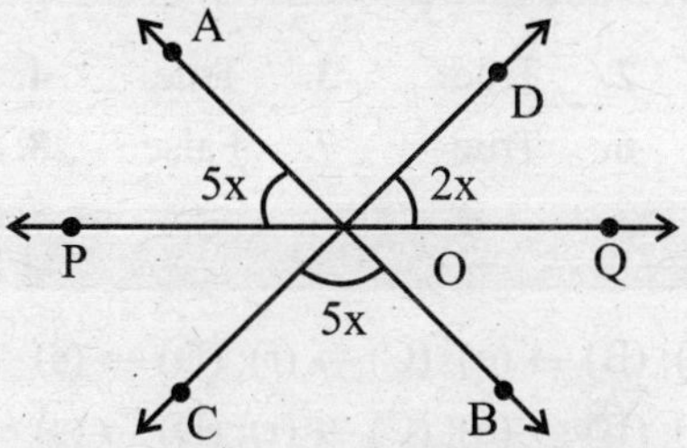

3. In the given figure, ∠AOC and ∠BOC form a linear pair. If $x - 2y = 30°$, then find the value of $\frac{x+y}{90}$.

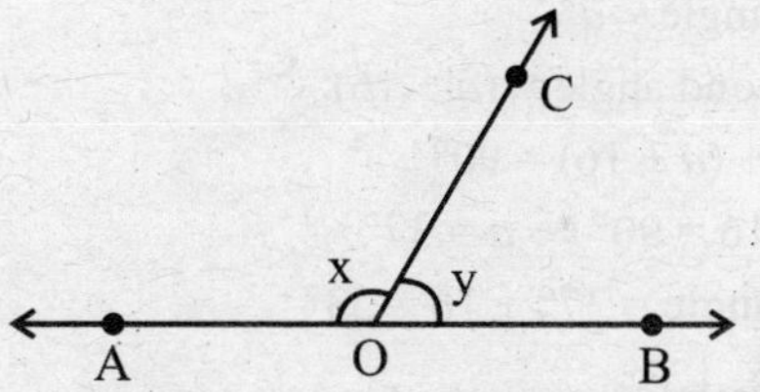

4. In the given figure, AOC is a line. Find the value of $\frac{x}{5}$.

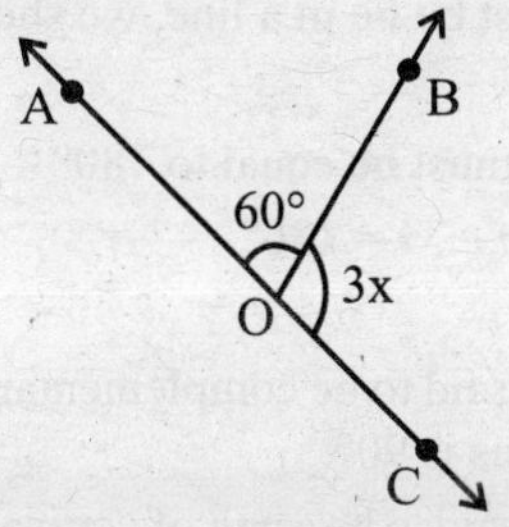

5. In the given figure, two straight lines *PQ* and *RS* intersect each other at O. If ∠POT = 75°, then find the value of $\frac{b}{3}$.

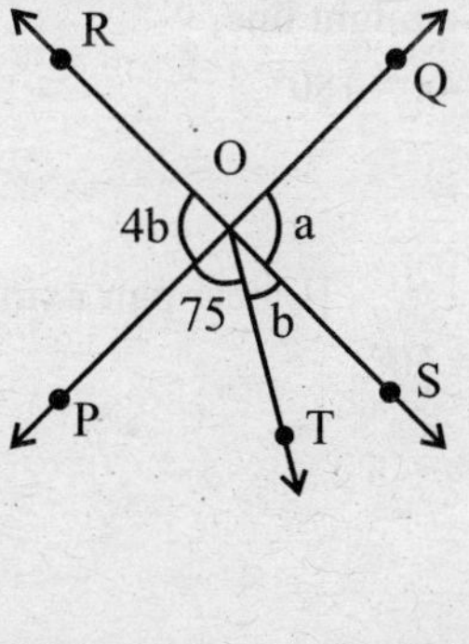

SOLUTIONS

Brief Explanations of Selected Questions

1 EXERCISE

FILL IN THE BLANKS :

1.	equal	**2.**	parallel	**3.**	parallel
4.	right	**5.**	obtuse.	**6.**	$180°$
7.	$70°$	**8.**	$25°$		

TRUE/FALSE :

1.	True	**2.**	True	**3.**	True	**4.**	True
5.	False	**6.**	True	**7.**	False	**8.**	False

MATCH THE COLUMNS :

1. (A) $\rightarrow$ (p); (B) $\rightarrow$ (q); (C) $\rightarrow$ (r); (D) $\rightarrow$ (s)

2. (A) $\rightarrow$ (p); (B) $\rightarrow$ (q); (C) $\rightarrow$ (r); (D) $\rightarrow$ (s)

VERY SHORT ANSWER QUESTIONS :

1. Let one angle $= a°$

Then second angle $= (a + 16)°$

Now, $a + (a + 16) = 90°$

$\Rightarrow 2a + 16 = 90° \Rightarrow a = 37°$

Second angle $= 37° + 16 = 53°$

2. $123°, 57°, 123°$

3. $x = y = 110°$

4. For A, B, C must be lie in a line, we should have $x + y = 180°$.

5. No, angle sum must be equal to $180°$

6. $x + 44° = 180°$ *i.e.*, $x = 136°$.

7. $25°$

8. Two angles are said to be complementary angles if the sum of their measures is $90°$.

9. Two angles are said to be a pair of vertically opposite angles, if their arms form two pairs of opposite rays.

10. A line which intersects two or more given lines at distinct points, is called a transversal of the given lines.

11. Since AOC is a straight line,

therefore $50° + 4x = 180°$

$\Rightarrow 4x = 130°$

$x = 32.5°$

12. $a + b = 180°$ [Linear pair axiom]

Given : $a - 2b = 30°$

On solving both, we get

$3b = 150 \Rightarrow b = 50°$ and $a = 130°$

13. $5b + 3b + 2b = 180°$

$\Rightarrow 10b = 180°$

$\Rightarrow b = 18°$

SHORT ANSWER QUESTIONS :

1. Let the measure of the angle be $x°$, then the measure of its supplementary angle is $180° - x°$.

It is given that $180 - x = \frac{1}{5}x$

$\Rightarrow 5(180° - x) = x$

$\Rightarrow 900 - 5x = x \Rightarrow 900 = 5x + x$

$\Rightarrow 900 = 6x \Rightarrow x = \frac{900}{6} = 150$

2. $\because n \parallel p$ and m is transversal

$\therefore \angle 1 = \angle 3 = 85°$ (Corresponding angles)

Also, $m \parallel l$ & p is transversal

$\therefore \angle 2 + \angle 3 = 180°$ ($\because$ Consecutive interior angles)

$\Rightarrow \angle 2 + 85° = 180°$

$\Rightarrow \angle 2 = 180° - 85°$

$\Rightarrow \angle 2 = 95$

3. $\angle y = 70°$ ..... (vertical opp. angle)

$\angle x + 70 = 180°$

.... (adjacent angles on a st. line or linear pair)

$\therefore \angle x = 180 - 70 = 110°$

$\angle z = 70°$ .....(corresponding angles)

$\angle z + \angle w = 180°$

..... (adjacent angles on a st. line or linear pair)

$\therefore 70 + \angle w = 180°$

$\therefore \angle w = 180° - 70° = 110°$

4. $x + 10 + x + x + 20 = 180 \Rightarrow 3x + 30 = 180 \Rightarrow x + 10 = 60$

$\Rightarrow x = 50$

Hence, $\angle x = 50°$ and other angles are $70°$ and $60°$

5. (i) $36°$ (ii) $72°$

(iii) $108°$ (iv) $108°$

6. In ΔABD, $90° + 40° + x = 180°$

$\Rightarrow x = 50°$

In ΔSDC, $30° + 50° + \angle CSD = 180°$

$\Rightarrow \angle CSD = 100$

Hence, $y = 180° - 100° = 80°$ (linear pair)

7. $35°, 100°, 135°$

LONG ANSWER QUESTIONS :

1. Since, $\angle POR$ and $\angle QOR$ form a linear pair

$\therefore$ $\angle POR + \angle QOR = 180°$ (Linear pair axiom)

or $a + b = 180°$ .... (i)

But $a - b = 80°$ [Given] .... (ii)

Adding eqs (i) and (ii), we get

$2a = 260°$ $\therefore$ $a = \frac{260}{2} = 130°$

Substituting the value of a in (i), we get

$130° + b = 180°$

$b = 180° - 130° = 50°$

2. $\angle XYZ + \angle ZYP = 180°$

(Linear Pair Axiom and YZ stands on line PX)

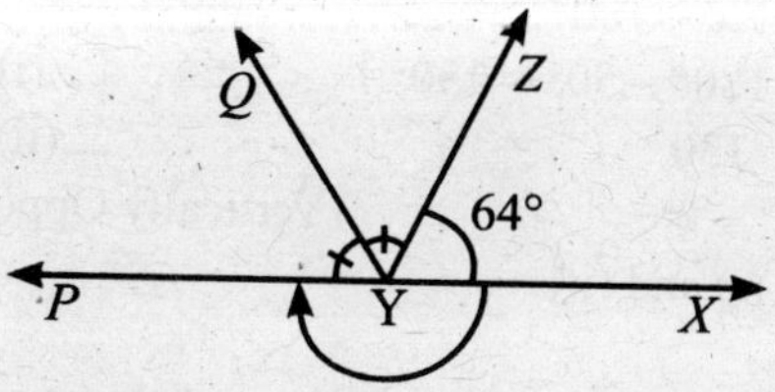

Given, $\angle XYZ = 64°$

$\therefore$ $64° + \angle ZYP = 180°$

$\Rightarrow$ $\angle ZYP = 116°$ ...(i)

Also, Ray YQ bisects $\angle ZYP$

$\therefore$ $\angle PYQ = \angle ZYQ = \frac{1}{2}$ $\angle ZYP$

$= \frac{1}{2}(116°) = 58°$ (Using (i)) ...(ii)

$\therefore$ Reflex $\angle QYP = 360° - 58° = 302°$

($\because$ The sum of all the angles around a point is equal to 360°)

Again, $\angle XYQ = \angle XYZ + \angle ZYQ$

$= 64° + 58°$

$= 122°$.

($\because \angle XYZ = 64°$ (given) and $\angle ZYQ = 58°$ [From (ii)])

3. $\angle x = \angle EDC = 70°$ (corresponding angles)

Now, $\angle ADB = x = 70°$ [$\because AB = DB$]

In ΔABD, $\angle ABD = 180 - \angle x - \angle x$

$= 180 - 70 - 70 = 40°$

$\Rightarrow$ $\angle BDC = \angle ABD = 40°$ (alternate angles)

$\Rightarrow$ $\angle y = 40°$

Since, $AB \parallel DC$

$\Rightarrow$ $\angle z + 90 = 180°$

$\Rightarrow$ $\angle z = 180 - 90 = 90°$

4. (i) $\angle AGE = \angle GED = 126°$ (Alternate Interior Angles)

(ii) We have $\angle GED = 126°$

$\angle GEF + \angle FED = 126°$.

$\Rightarrow \angle GEF + 90° = 126°$ (From the figure, $\angle FED = 90°$)

$\Rightarrow \angle GEF = 126° - 90° = 36°$

(iii) Since, CD is a line

$\therefore$ By linear sum property, we have

$\angle GEC + \angle GEF + \angle FED = 180°$

$\Rightarrow$ $\angle GEC + 36° + 90° = 180°$

$\Rightarrow$ $\angle GEC = 180° - 126° = 54°$

Now, $\angle FGE = \angle GEC = 54°$(Alternate Interior Angles)

5. From ΔXYZ, we have

$\angle XYZ + \angle YZX + \angle ZXY = 180°$

(By Δ's angle sum property)

$\Rightarrow$ $54° + \angle YZX + 62° = 180°$

$\Rightarrow$ $\angle YZX = 180° - 116° = 64°$ ...(i)

Given YO is the bisector of $\angle XYZ$

$\therefore$ $\angle XYO = \angle OYZ = \frac{1}{2}\angle XYZ = \frac{1}{2}(54°) = 27°$ ...(ii)

Similarly

$\angle XZO = \angle OZY = \frac{1}{2}$ $\angle YZX = \frac{1}{2}(64)° = 32°$ ... (iii)

($\because ZO$ is the bisector of $\angle YZX$)

Now, consider ΔOYZ, which gives

$\angle OYZ + \angle OZY + \angle YOZ = 180°$ (By angle sum property)

$\Rightarrow$ $27° + 32° + \angle YOZ = 180°$ [Using (ii) and (iii)]

$\Rightarrow$ $\angle YOZ = 180° - 59° = 121°$.

6. As we know the exterior angle is equal to the sum of the two interior opposite angles

$\therefore$ $\angle QRT = \angle RQS + \angle QSR$

$\Rightarrow$ $65° = 28° + \angle QSR$

$\Rightarrow$ $\angle QSR = 65° - 28° = 37°$

Also given $PQ \perp SP$

$\therefore$ $\angle QPS = 90°$

Also, $PQ \parallel SR$ gives

$\angle QPS + \angle PSR = 180°$

($\because$ The sum of consecutive interior angles on the same side of the transversal is 180°)

$\angle PSR = 90°$

$\Rightarrow$ $\angle PSQ + \angle QSR = 90° \Rightarrow y + 37° = 90°$

$\Rightarrow$ $y = 90° - 37° = 53°$

Now, from ΔPQS, we have

$\angle PQS + \angle QSP + \angle QPS = 180°$

(By angle sum property of a Δ)

$\Rightarrow$ $x + y + 90° = 180°$

$\Rightarrow$ $x + 53° + 90° = 180°$

$\Rightarrow$ $x = 180° - 143° = 37°$.

7. Through O, draw a line POQ parallel to AB [Fig.]

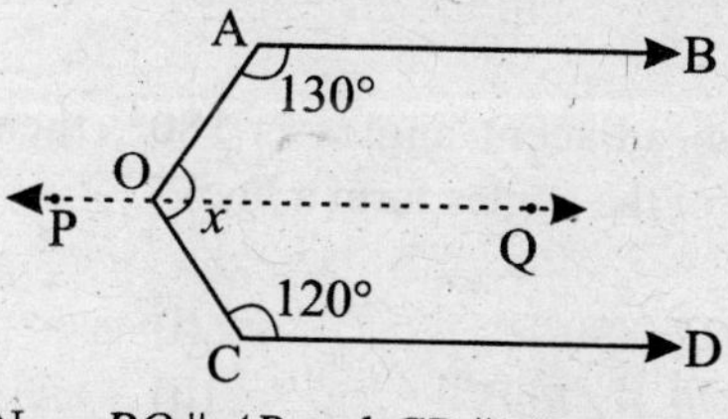

Now $PQ \parallel AB$ and $CD \parallel AB$

So, $CD \parallel PQ$

We have,

$AB \parallel PQ$ and AO is a transversal

$\therefore \angle AOQ + \angle OAB = 180°$

(Cointerior angles are supplementary)

$\Rightarrow \angle AOQ + 130° = 180°$

$\Rightarrow \angle AOQ = 180° - 130° = 50°$

Similarly, $PQ \parallel CD$ and OC is a transversal

$\therefore \angle QOC + \angle DCO = 180°$

$\Rightarrow \angle QOC + 120° = 180°$

$\Rightarrow \angle QOC - 180° - 120° - 60°$

$\therefore \angle AOC = \angle AOQ + \angle QOC$

$= 50° + 60° = 110°$

2 EXERCISE

TEXT-BOOK EXERCISE :

1. $\angle AOC = \angle BOD$ (Vertically Opposite Angles)

But Given $\angle BOD = 40°$ ...(i)

$\therefore \angle AOC = 40°$ (Alternate angle)...(ii)

Now, Given $\angle AOC + \angle BOE = 70°$

$\Rightarrow \angle BOE = 70° - 40°$ (from ii)

$\Rightarrow \angle BOE = 30°$

Again, Reflex $\angle COE = \angle COD + \angle BOD + \angle BOE$

$\because$ Ray OA stands on line CD

$= \angle COD + 40° + 30°$ (Using (i) and (ii))

$= 180° + 40° + 30°$

$= 250°$ ($\because$ Ray OA stands on line CD)

2. By linear pair axiom we have

$\angle PQS + \angle PQR = 180°$ ...(i)

Also, Ray RP stands on line ST

$\therefore \angle PRQ + \angle PRT = 180°$ ...(ii)

(Linear Pair Axiom)

From (i) and (ii), we obtain

$\angle PQS + \angle PQR = \angle PRQ + \angle PRT$

Now, Given $\angle PQR = \angle PRQ$

$\therefore \angle PQS = \angle PRT.$

3. $x + y = w + z$ ...(i) (Given)

$\because$ The sum of all the angles round a point is equal to 360°

$\therefore x + y + w + z = 360°$

$\Rightarrow x + y + x + y = 360°$ (Using (i))

$\Rightarrow 2(x + y) = 360°$

$\Rightarrow x + y = \dfrac{360°}{2}$

$\Rightarrow x + y = 180°$

$\therefore$ AOB is a line.

(If the sum of two adjacent angles is 180°, then the non-common arms of the angles form a line)

4. Since $OR \perp PQ$

$\therefore \angle QOR = \angle POR = 90°$ ...(i)

and $\angle QOS = \angle QOR + \angle ROS$ ...(ii)

Also, $\angle POS = \angle POR - \angle ROS$ ...(iii)

Subtracting (ii) and (iii),

$\Rightarrow \angle QOS - \angle POS =$

$(\angle QOR - \angle POR) + 2\angle ROS = 2\angle ROS$ (Using (i))

$\Rightarrow \angle ROS = \dfrac{1}{2}(\angle QOS - \angle POS)$

5. Since, line AE cuts line GH

$\therefore \angle AEG + \angle AEH = 180°$ (Linear Pair property)

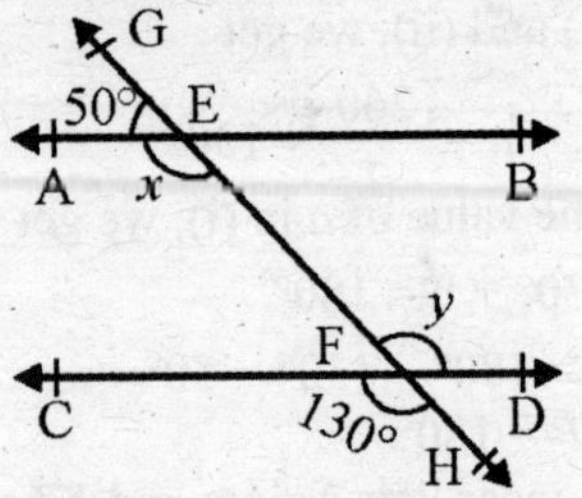

$\Rightarrow 50° + x = 180°$

$\Rightarrow x = 180° - 50° = 130°$ ....(i)

Now, $y = 130°$ ....(ii)

(Vertically Opposite Angles)

$\therefore$ From (i) and (ii)

$x = y$

But x and y are alternate interior angles and equal.

So, we can say that AB ∥ CD

6.

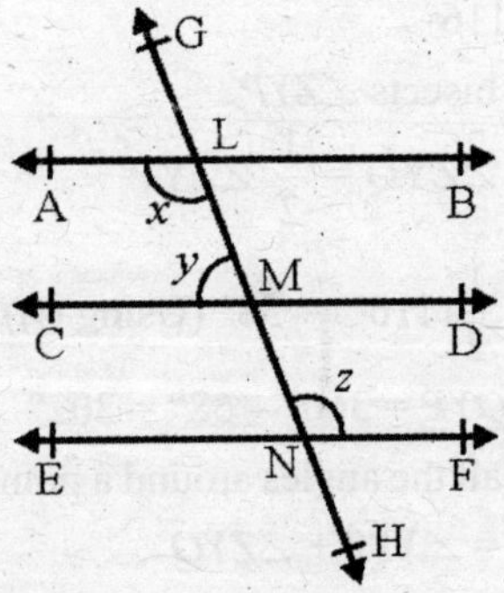

Since, AB ∥ CD and CD ∥ EF (Lines parallel to the same line are parallel to each other) ....(i)

therefore, AB ∥ EF

$\therefore x = z$ (Alternate Interior Angles) ....(ii)

$x + y = 180°$

(Consecutive interior angles on the same side of the transversal GH to parallel lines AB and CD)

From (i) and (ii),

$z + y = 180°$

Given $y : z = 3 : 7$

Now, sum of the ratios = 3 + 7 = 10

$\therefore y = \dfrac{3}{10} \times 180° = 54°$ and $z = \dfrac{7}{10} \times 180° = 126°$

Since $x = z$

$\therefore x = 126°.$

7. $\angle PQT + \angle PQR = 180°$ ...(linear pair)

$\Rightarrow 110° + \angle PQR = 180°$

$\Rightarrow \angle PQR = 180° - 110° = 70°$ ...(i)

Again, $\angle SPR + \angle QPR = 180°$

$135° + \angle QPR = 180°$ ($\because QS$ is a line)

$\Rightarrow \angle QPR = 180° - 135° = 45°$ ...(ii)

In ΔPQR,

$\angle PQR + \angle QPR + \angle PRQ = 180°$(By Δ's angle sum property)

From (i) and (ii)

$70° + 45° + \angle PRQ = 180°$

$\Rightarrow \angle PRQ = 180° - 115° = 65°$

8. Since, AB || DE therefore,

$\angle DEC = \angle BAC = 35°$ ...(i)

(Alternate Interior Angles)

and $\angle CDE = 53°$ (Given) ...(ii)

∴ From ΔCDE, we have

$\angle CDE + \angle DEC + \angle DCE = 180°$

(By angle sum property)

$\Rightarrow 53° + 35° + \angle DCE = 180°$ [Using (i) & (ii)]

$\Rightarrow \angle DCE = 180° - 88° = 92°$.

9. Since , $\angle TRS$ is an exterior angle of ΔTQR

$\therefore \angle TRS = \angle TQR + \angle QTR$ ...(i)

(∵ The exterior angle is equal to sum of the two interior opposite angles)

Again $\angle PRS$ is an exterior angle of ΔPQR

$\therefore \angle PRS = \angle PQR + \angle QPR$ ...(ii)

$\Rightarrow 2\angle TRS = 2\angle TQR + \angle QPR$

(∵ QT is the bisector of $\angle PQR$ and RT is the bisector of $\angle PRS$)

$\Rightarrow 2(\angle TRS - \angle TQR) = \angle QPR$ ...(iii)

From (i),

$\angle TRS - \angle TQR = \angle QTR$ ...(iv)

From (iii) and (iv), we obtain

$2\angle QTR = \angle QPR$

$\Rightarrow \angle QTR = \frac{1}{2}\angle QPR$

EXEMPLAR QUESTIONS :

1. If l || m, then

$x + 44 = 180$

$x = 180 - 44$

$x = 136°$

2. By angle sum property

$45° + 64° + 72° = 180°$

but sum is 181°

∴ No triangle can be formed

3. x = y (Given)

Therefore, l | | m (corresponding angles) ...(i)

Also, a = b (Given)

Therefore, n | | m (Corresponding angles) ...(ii)

From (i) and (ii) , l | | n (Lines parallel to the same line)

4.

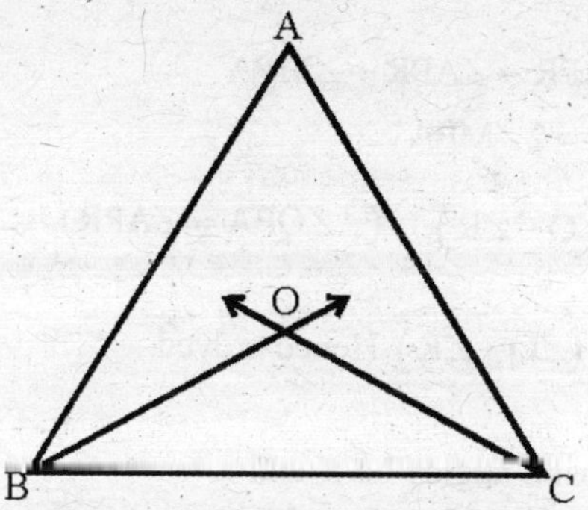

Let us draw the figure as shown in Figure

$\angle A + \angle ABC + \angle ACB = 180°$

(Angle sum property of a triangle)

Therefore,

$\frac{1}{2}\angle A + \frac{1}{2}\angle ABC + \frac{1}{2}\angle ACB = \frac{1}{2} \times 180° = 90°$

i.e., $\frac{1}{2}\angle A + \angle OBC + \angle OCB = 90°$

(Since BO and CO are bisectors of $\angle B$ and $\angle C$) ...(i)

But $\angle BOC + \angle OBC + \angle OCB = 180$ (Angle sum property) ...(ii)

Subtracting (i) from (ii), we have

$\angle BOC - \frac{1}{2}\angle A = 180° - 90°$

i.e., $\angle BOC = 90° + \frac{1}{2}\angle A$

5. Since PA is the bisector of $\angle QPR$

$\therefore \angle QPA = \angle APR$ ...(i)

In ΔPQM, We have

$\angle PQM + \angle PMQ + \angle QPM = 180°$

$\angle PQM + 90° + \angle QPM = 180°$

$\angle PQM + \angle QPM = 90°$

$\angle PQM = 90° - \angle QPM$

$\angle Q = 90° - \angle QPM$ ...(ii)

In ΔPMR, we have

$\angle PRM + \angle MPR + \angle PMR = 180°$

$\angle PRM + \angle MPR = 90°$

$\angle PRM = 90° - \angle MPR$

$\angle R = 90° - \angle MPR$ ...(iii)

Subtracting (iii) from (ii), we get

$\angle Q - \angle R = (90° - \angle QPM) - (90° - \angle MPR)$

$= -\angle QPM + \angle MPR$

$= \angle MPR - \angle QPM$

$\angle Q - \angle R = (\angle MPA + APR) - (\angle QPA - MPA)$

$= \angle MPA + \angle APR - \angle APR + \angle MPA$

$\Rightarrow \quad \angle Q - \angle R = 2\angle MPA$

$\angle MPA = \frac{1}{2}(\angle Q - \angle R) \quad (\because \angle QPA = \angle APR)$

i.e $\angle APM = \frac{1}{2}(\angle Q - \angle R)$ Hence proved

6. (c) , 7. (d)

8. (b) Let opposite angles be x and x
So, $x + x = 105 \Rightarrow x = 52\frac{1}{2}°$

9. (a) We have $5x + 3x + 7x = 180$
$\Rightarrow 15x = 180 \Rightarrow x = 12$
$\therefore$ All the three angles are 60°, 36° and 84°
Hence, triangle is an acute angled triangle.

10. (d)

HOTS QUESTIONS :

1. $\angle ACD + \angle z = 180°$

$\angle BAE + \angle x = 180°$

$\angle CBF + \angle y = 180°$

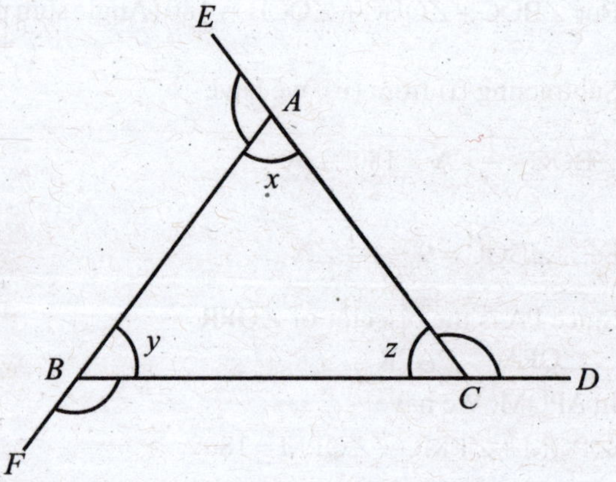

$\angle ACD + \angle BAE + \angle CBF + \angle x + \angle y + \angle z = 540°$ ..(i)

Now put, $\angle x + \angle y + \angle z = 180°$ in eqn. (i)

We get $\angle ACD + \angle BAE + \angle CBF = 360°$

2. Construction: Join BD

Now in, ΔABD

$\angle x + \angle ADB + 30° = 180°$ ...(i)

In ΔBDC, $\angle y + \angle BDC + 55° = 180°$ ...(ii)

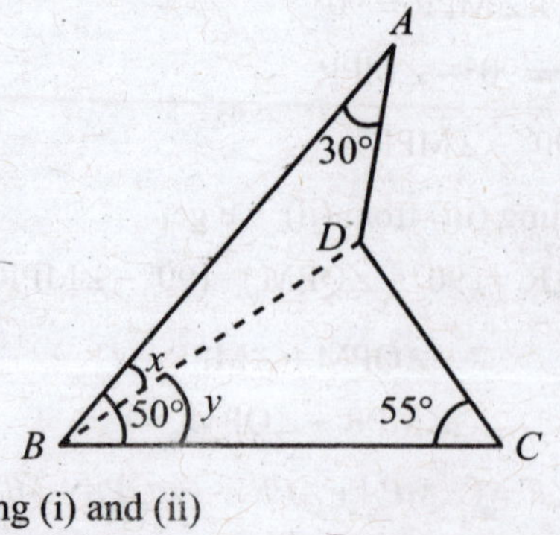

By adding (i) and (ii)

$\angle x + \angle ADB + 30° + \angle y + \angle BDC + 55° = 360°$

Also, $\angle x + \angle y = 50°$

Then $\angle ADB + \angle BDC + 135° = 360°$

$\Rightarrow \quad \angle ADB + \angle BDC = 225°$

i.e., $x = \angle ADC = 135°$

3. **Case I :**

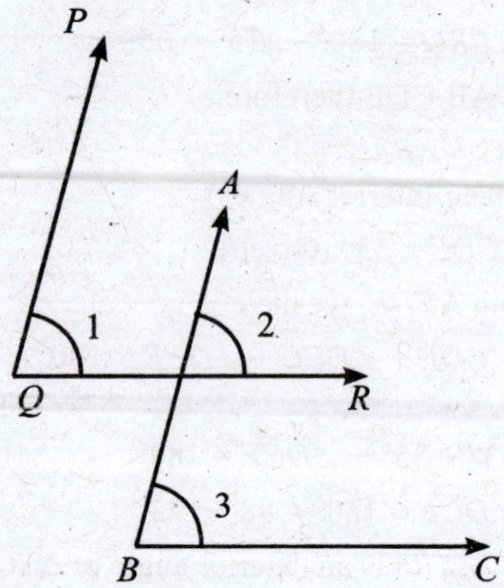

As $QR \parallel BC$

$\therefore \angle 2 = \angle 3$ and $PQ \parallel AB$

Then $\angle 1 = \angle 2$

Hence, $\angle 1 = \angle 2 = \angle 3$

Case II:

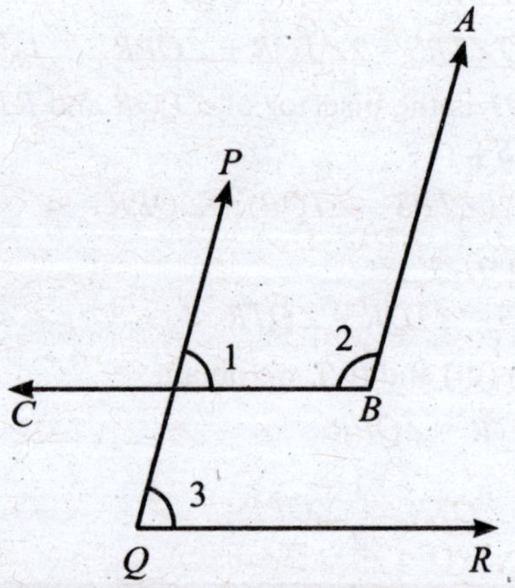

As $QR \parallel CB$

$\therefore \quad \angle 1 = \angle 3$

but $\angle 1 + \angle 2 = 180°$ then

$\angle 3 + \angle 2 = 180°$ (supplementary).

$(\because \angle 1 = \angle 3)$

4. Since interior angles on the same side of transversal are supplementary,

$\therefore \quad \angle EAB + \angle RBA = 180°$

$\Rightarrow \frac{1}{2}\angle EAB + \frac{1}{2}\angle RBA = \frac{1}{2} \times 180°$ ...(i)

As AP and BP are bisectors of $\angle EAB$ and $\angle RBA$ respectively,

$\therefore \angle 1 = \frac{1}{2}\angle EAB$ and $\angle 2 = \frac{1}{2}\angle RBA$ ...(ii)

From (i) and (ii), we get

$\angle 1 + \angle 2 = 90°$ ...(iii)

In ΔAPB, we have

$\angle 1 + \angle 2 + \angle APB = 180°$

$\Rightarrow$ $90° + \angle APB = 180°$ [using (iii)]

$\Rightarrow$ $\angle APB = 180° - 90°$

$\therefore$ $\angle APB = 90°$

3 EXERCISE

SINGLE OPTION CORRECT :

1. (d) 2. (b) 3. (c) 4. (a)

5. (c) $8x + 3x + x = 180°$

$\Rightarrow 12x = 180°$

$\Rightarrow x = \frac{180°}{12} = \frac{60°}{4} = 15°$

6. (a) $104 + 90 + 25 + x = 360°$

$219 + x = 360°$

$x = 360 - 219$

$x = 141°$.

7. (c)

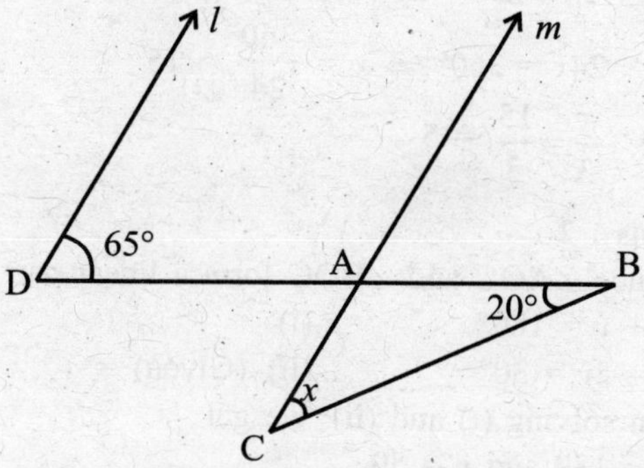

Since l and m are parallel and DB is transversal

$\therefore \angle D = \angle DAC = 65°$

Now, $\angle DAC + \angle CAB = 180°$ (Linear pair)

$\Rightarrow \angle CAB = 180° - 65° = 115°$

Now, $115° + 20° + x = 180° \Rightarrow x = 180° - 135° = 45°$

(Angle sum property of Δ)

8. (d) Since l and m are parallel lines and n is transversal

$\therefore 3y = 2y + 25 \Rightarrow y = 25°$

Similarly, $2y + 25 = x + 15$

$\Rightarrow x + 15 = 50 + 25 = 75$

$\Rightarrow x = 75 - 15 = 60°$

9. (a) Since l and m are parallel and n is transversal

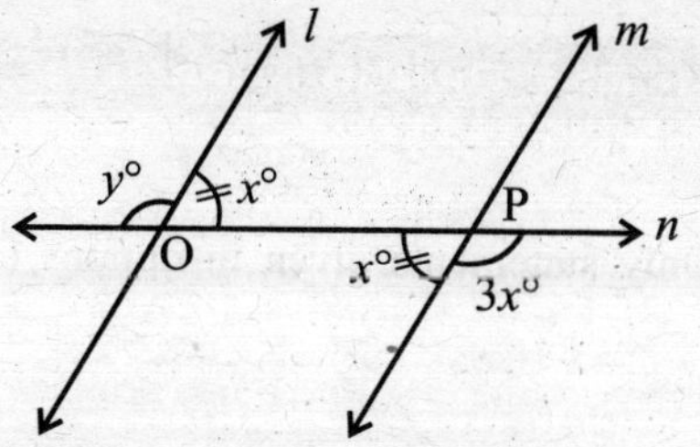

$\therefore y + x = 180°$ (Linear pair)

$x + 3x = 180°$ (Linear pair)

$4x = 180°$

$x = 45°$

$\Rightarrow y = 180° - 45° = 135°$

10. (a) x and y forms a complementary pair

$\Rightarrow x + y = 90°$

Now $x + 47° + y + 43° = x + y + 47° + 43°$

$= x + y + 90° = 90° + 90° = 180°$

$\therefore (x + 47°)$ and $(y + 43°)$ form a supplementary pair.

11. (d) In ΔABC

$\angle ACD = \angle A + \angle B$

[By exterior angle property of a Δ]

$\Rightarrow$ $127° = 3x + 2° + x - 3° \Rightarrow 127° = 4x - 1°$

$\Rightarrow$ $128° = 4x$

$\Rightarrow$ $x = 32°$

$\therefore$ $\angle A = (3x + 2°) = 3 \times 32 + 2°$

$= 96° + 2° = 98°$

12. (d) Let the angle be x

Complement of $x = 90° - x$

Supplement of $x = 180° - x$

Given that, $180° - x = 3\,(90° - x)$

$\Rightarrow$ $180° - x = 270° - 3x$

$\Rightarrow$ $2x = 270° - 180°$

$\Rightarrow$ $2x = 90° \Rightarrow x = 45°$.

13. (d) Given CD || EF

$\Rightarrow$ $\angle CGH = \angle FHG$ [Alternate interior angles]

$\Rightarrow$ $\angle CGH = z$

Also,

$\angle CGI + \angle CGH = 180°$ [Linear pair] ...(i)

$\Rightarrow$ $y + z = 180°$

Given

$y : z = 3 : 7$

$\Rightarrow$ $y = 3k$ and $z = 7k$ for some $k \in R$

Substituting in (i)

$3k + 7k = 180°$

$\Rightarrow$ $k = 18$

$\therefore$ $z = 7k = 7(18) = 126°$

Also, $\because$ AB || CD

$\therefore$ $\angle x = \angle CGH$ [Corresponding angles]

$\Rightarrow$ $\angle x = 126°$.

MORE THAN ONE OPTION CORRECT :

1. (b, c, d)
2. (a, b) Only statements given in options (a) and (b) are correct.
3. (a, b, c)

PASSAGE BASED QUESTIONS :

For (1–3)

Since Ray OP stands on line XY and form Linear Pair Axiom

$\therefore \quad \angle POX + \angle POY = 180°$

Given $\angle POY = 90°$

$\Rightarrow \quad \angle POX = 90°$

$\Rightarrow \quad \angle POM + \angle XOM = 90°$

$\Rightarrow \quad a + b = 90°$ (from figure) ...(i)

Now, we have

$a : b = 2 : 3$

$\Rightarrow \quad \frac{a}{b} = \frac{2}{3} \Rightarrow \frac{a}{2} = \frac{b}{3} = k \text{ (say)} \Rightarrow a = 2k \text{ and } b = 3\text{ k}$

Putting the values of a and b in (i), we get

$2k + 3k = 90°$

$\Rightarrow \quad k = 18°$

$\therefore \quad \left.\begin{array}{l} a = 2k = 2(18°) = 36° \\ b = 3k = 3(18°) = 54° \end{array}\right\}$ ...(ii)

Again, Ray OX stands on Line MN

$\therefore \quad \angle XOM + \angle XON = 180°$ (Linear Pair Axiom)

$\Rightarrow \quad b + c = 180°$

$\Rightarrow \quad 54° + c = 180°$ (Using (ii))

$\Rightarrow \quad c = 180° - 54°$

$\Rightarrow \quad c = 126°$

1. (b) $\angle a = 36°$ 2. (c) $\angle b = 54°$
3. (b) $\angle c = 126°$

For (4–6)

Since OR and OS are in the same line.

$\therefore \angle ROP + \angle POT + \angle TOS = 180°$

$\Rightarrow 4b° + 75° + b° = 180°$

$\Rightarrow 5b° + 75° = 180°$

$\Rightarrow 5b° = 105° \Rightarrow b = 21°$

Since PQ and RS intersect at O. Therefore,

$\angle QOS = \angle POR$ [Vertically opp. angles]

$\Rightarrow a = 4b$

$\Rightarrow a = 4 \times 21 = 84$ [$\because b = 21$]

Now, OR and OS are in the same line. Therefore.

$\angle ROQ + \angle QOS = 180°$ [Linear pair]

$\Rightarrow 2c + a = 180°$

$\Rightarrow 2c + 84 = 180°$ [$\because a = 84$]

$\Rightarrow 2c = 96 \Rightarrow c = 48$

Hence, $a = 84$, $b = 21$ and $c = 48$

4. (c) 5. (d) 6. (b)

ASSERTION & REASON :

1. (a) 2. (a) 3. (d)
4. (d) 5. (b)

MULTIPLE MATCHING QUESTIONS :

1. (A) → (s); (B) → (p, t); (C) → (q); (D) → (u)

INTEGER TYPE QUESTIONS :

1. **Ans : 9**

We have

$5y + 3y + 2y = 180°$

$\Rightarrow \quad 10y = 180°$

$\Rightarrow \quad y = 18$

Thus, $\frac{y}{2} = \frac{18}{2} = 9.$

2. **Ans : 5**

$\angle AOP = \angle BOQ = 5x$

$\angle QOD = \angle COP = 2x$

$\angle BOC = \angle AOD = 5x$

On adding, we get

$5x + 5x + 2x + 2x + 5x + 5x = 360°$

$\Rightarrow \quad 24x = 360° \Rightarrow x = \frac{360}{24} = 15$

$\Rightarrow \quad \frac{x}{3} = \frac{15}{3} = 5$

3. **Ans : 2**

Since $\angle AOC$ and $\angle BOC$ form a linear pair therefore

$x + y = 180°$ ...(i)

$x - 2y = 30°$ ...(ii) (Given)

On solving (i) and (ii), we get

$x = 130$ and $y = 50$

Hence, $\frac{x+y}{90} = \frac{180}{90} = 2$

4. **Ans : 8**

Since AOC is a line therefore $\angle AOB$ and $\angle BOC$ forms a linear pair.

$\therefore \quad 60 + 3x = 180 \Rightarrow 3x = 120 \Rightarrow x = 40$

Hence, $\frac{x}{5} = \frac{40}{5} = 8.$

5. **Ans : 7**

Since ROC is a straight line therefore

$\angle ROP$, $\angle POT$ and $\angle TOS$ forms a linear pair

$\therefore \quad 4b + 75 + b = 180°$

$\Rightarrow \quad 75 + 5b = 180$

$\Rightarrow \quad 5b = 180 - 75 = 105$

$\Rightarrow \quad b = 21$

Hence, $\frac{b}{3} = \frac{21}{3} = 7$

Chapter 7

Triangles

INTRODUCTION

A triangle is a closed figure formed by three intersecting lines. 'Tri' means 'three'. A triangle has three sides, three angles and three vertices. The point of intersection of any two sides of a triangle is called a vertex.

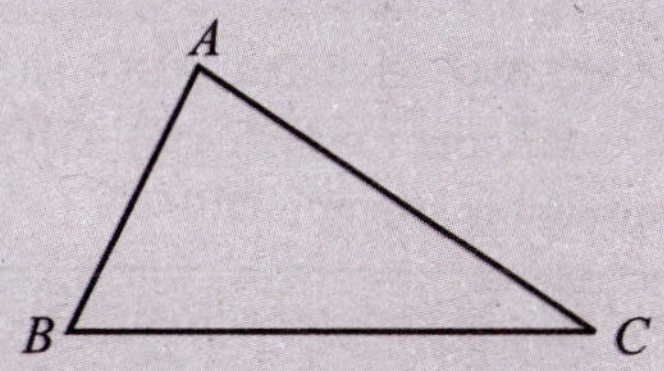

In this chapter, we shall study about a plane figure formed by three non-parallel lines in plane.

Also, in this chapter, we shall study about the congruence of triangles, some more properties of triangles and inequality in a triangle.

CONGRUENCY OF TWO PLANE GEOMETRICAL FIGURES (OR SHAPES)

Two geometrical figures or shapes are said to be congruent, if they have same size and same shape i.e. exactly overlap each other. For examples :

(i) Two line segments are congruent if and only if their lengths are equal.

(ii) Two angles are congruent if and only if their measures are equal.

CONGRUENCY OF TWO TRIANGLES

Two triangles are said to be congruent if three sides and three angles of a triangle are respectively equal to the corresponding sides and angles of other triangle.

In other words, two triangles are congruent if and only if there exists a correspondence between their vertices such that the corresponding angles of the two triangles are equal or congruent.

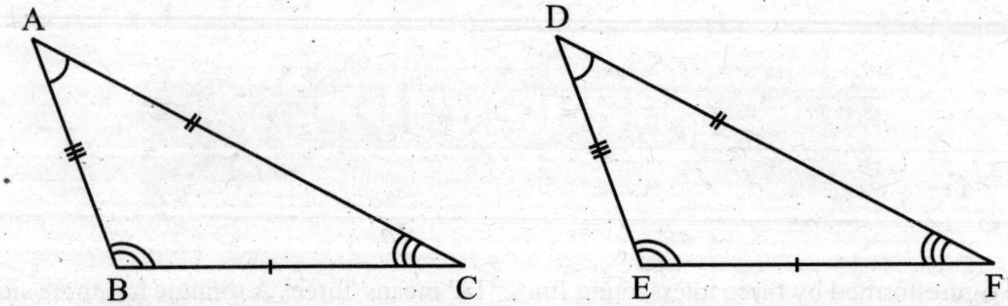

In fig., two triangles ABC and DEF are shown, where AB = DE, BC = EF, AC = DF, $\angle A = \angle D$, $\angle B = \angle E$ and $\angle C = \angle F$, then ΔABC and ΔDEF are congruent and we write $\Delta ABC \cong \Delta DEF$. $\Delta ABC \cong \Delta DEF$ is read as "triangle ABC is congruent to triangle DEF".

> **NOTE :** In congruent triangles corresponding parts are equal and we write in short 'CPCT' for corresponding parts of congruent triangles.

SUFFICIENT CONDITIONS (OR RULE OR CRITERIA) FOR CONGRUENCE OF TRIANGLES

The followings are the sufficient conditions for congruency of two triangles.

(i) Side-Angle-Side (ii) Angle-Side-Angle (iii) Angle-Angle-Side

(iv) Side-Side-Side and (v) Right Angle-Hypotenuse-Side

Let us now discuss these three conditions (or criteria) which ensure the congruence of two triangles.

(i) Side-Angle-Side (SAS) Rule for Congruency of Two Triangles

If two sides and the included angle of one triangle are equal to two sides and the included angle of the other, then the triangles are congruent.

Given : ΔABC and ΔDEF in which $AB = DE$, $AC = DF$ and $\angle A = \angle D$

To Prove : $\Delta ABC \cong \Delta DEF$

Proof : Place ΔABC over ΔDEF such that A falls on D and AB falls along DE.

Since $AB = DE$, so B falls on E.

Since, $\angle A = \angle D$, so AC will fall along DF.

Also, $AC = DF$

$\therefore$ C will fall on F.

Thus, AC will coincide with DF.

And, therefore, BC will coincide with EF.

$\therefore$ ΔABC coincides with ΔDEF.

Hence, $\Delta ABC \cong \Delta DEF$

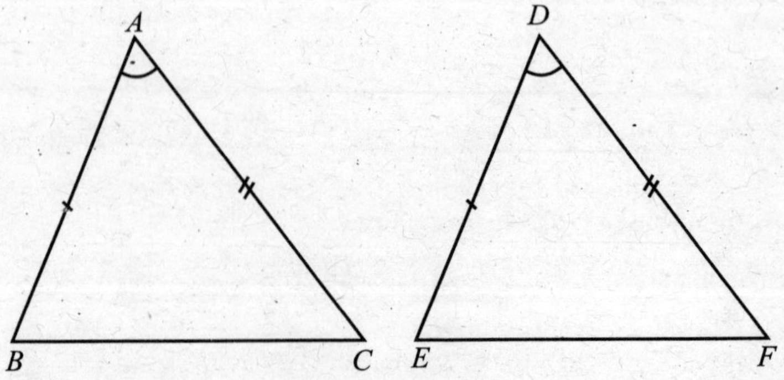

ILLUSTRATION 1 :

l and m are two parallel lines intersected by another pair of parallel lines p and q. Show that $\Delta ABC \cong \Delta CDA$.

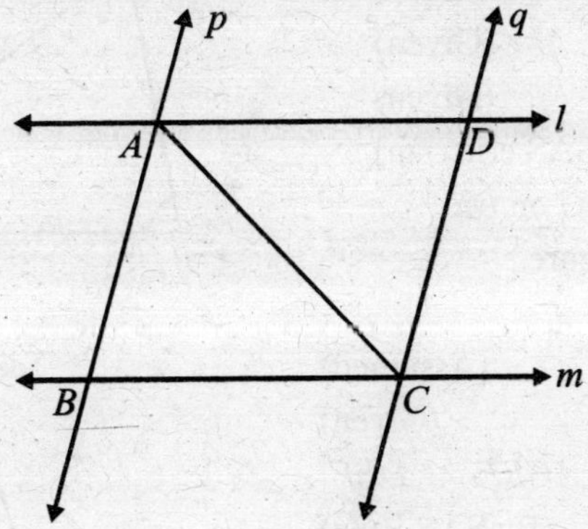

SOLUTION :

Since l & m and p & q are parallel lines,
therefore $AB \parallel DC$ and $AD \parallel BC$
$\therefore$ Quadrilateral $ABCD$ is a parallelogram.
($\because$ A quadrilateral is a parallelogram if both the pairs of opposite sides are parallel)
Since, $ABCD$ is ||gm
$\therefore$ $BC = AD$ ....(i)
and $AB = CD$ ....(ii) (Opposite sides of a || gm are equal)
and $\angle ABC = \angle CDA$ ....(iii) (Opposite angles of a || gm are equal)
Thus, In ΔABC and ΔCDA, we get
$AB = CD$ (From (ii))
$BC = DA$ (From (i))
$\angle ABC = \angle CDA$ (From (iii))
$\therefore$ $\Delta ABC \cong \Delta CDA$ (SAS Rule)

ILLUSTRATION 2 :

In figure, $AE = EC$ and $DE = BE$. Prove that

(i) $\angle AED = \angle CEB$ **(ii) $\angle A = \angle C$**

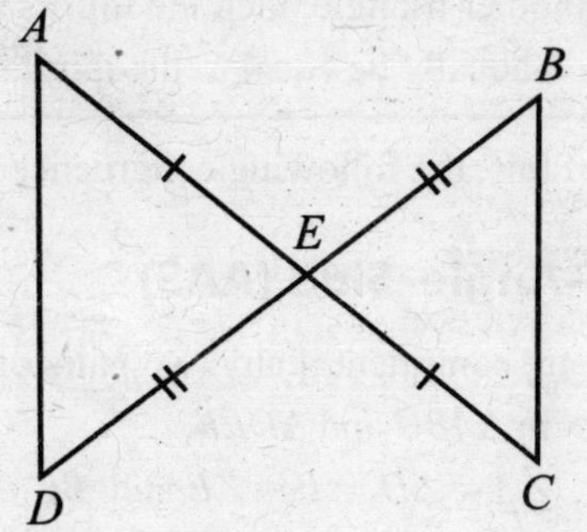

SOLUTION :

Given that as in figure
$AE = EC$
$DE = BE$
In ΔAED and ΔBEC
$AE = EC$ (Given)
$\angle AED = \angle CEB$ (Vertically opposite angles)
$DE = EB$ (Given)
Then by SAS Rule
$\Delta AED \cong \Delta CEB$
Hence, $\angle A = \angle C$ and $\angle D = \angle B$ (By CPCT)

(II) Angle-Side-Angle (ASA) Rule for Congruency of Two Triangles

Two triangles are congruent if any two angles and the included side of one triangle are equal to the two angles and the included side of the other triangle.

Given : ΔABC and ΔDEF, in which
$\angle ABC = \angle DEF$, $\angle ACB = \angle DFE$ and $BC = EF$

To Prove : $\Delta ABC \cong \Delta DEF$

Proof : On comparing the sides AB and DE of ΔABC and ΔDEF, there are three possibilities :

(i) $AB = DE$ (ii) $AB < DE$ and (iii) $AB > DE$

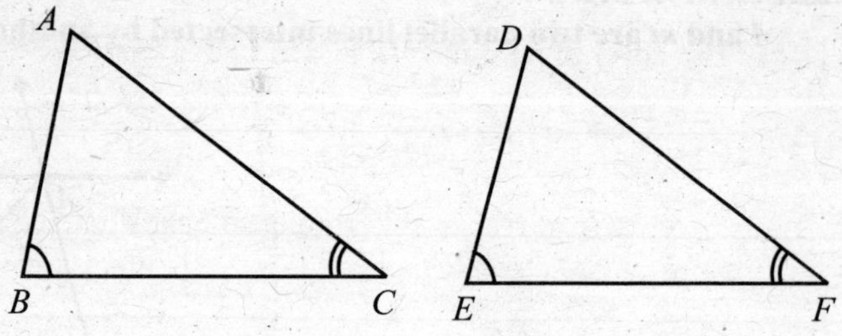

Case (i) : When $AB = DE$, then in ΔABC and ΔDEF

$AB = DE$ (Assumed)

$\angle ABC = \angle DEF$ (Given)

$BC = EF$ (Given)

Hence, $\Delta ABC \cong \Delta DEF$ [By SAS criterian]

Case (ii) : When $AB < DE$, then we take point G on DE such that $AB = GE$ and join GF as shown in figure.

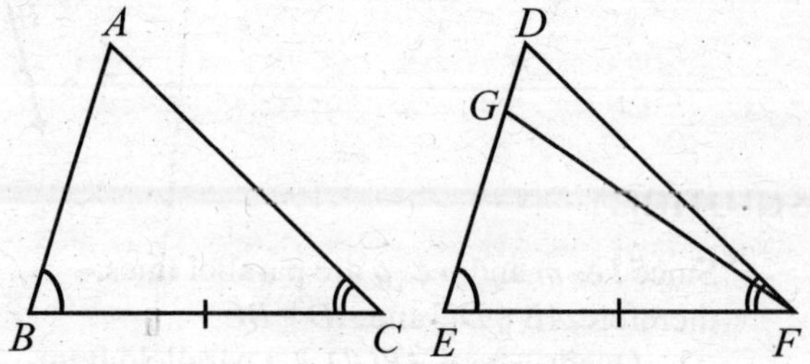

Now in ΔABC and ΔGEF

$AB = GE$ (Assumed)

$BC = EF$ (Given)

$\angle ABC = \angle GEF$ (Given) [$\because \angle GEF = \angle DEF$]

$\therefore$ $\Delta ABC \cong \Delta GEF$ (By SAS Rule)

Hence $\angle ACB = \angle GFE$ .... (i)

But $\angle ACB = \angle DFE$ (Given) .... (ii)

Therefore from (i) and (ii), we have

$\angle DFE = \angle GFE$

which is impossible unless GF coincide with DF and hence G coincides with D.

$\therefore$ $AB = DE$

Hence, $\Delta ABC \cong \Delta DEF$ [By SAS criterion]

Case (iii) : When $AB > DE$, then we take a point G on AB such that $BG = DE$ and show as in case (ii) that G must coincide with A, i.e., $AB = DE$ and hence, $\Delta ABC \cong \Delta DEF$ (SAS rule)

Hence in all three cases $\Delta ABC \cong \Delta DEF$

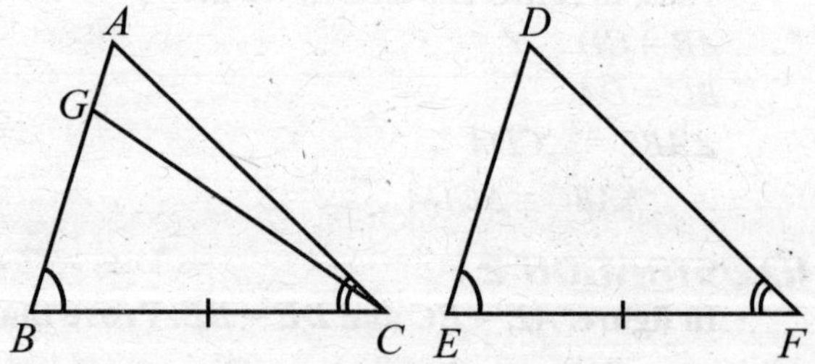

> **NOTE :** Since the sum of the three interior angles of a triangle is 180°, therefore if two angles of one triangle are equal to the two angles of another triangle, then the third angle of the first triangle will automatically be equal to the third angle of the second triangle.

On the basis of this, the following congruence rule arise.

(III) Angle-Angle-Side (AAS)

Two triangles are congruent if any two pairs of angles and one pair of corresponding sides are equal.

Given : In ΔABC and ΔDEF,

$\angle A = \angle D$, $\angle B = \angle E$ and $BC = EF$

To Prove : $\Delta ABC \cong \Delta DEF$

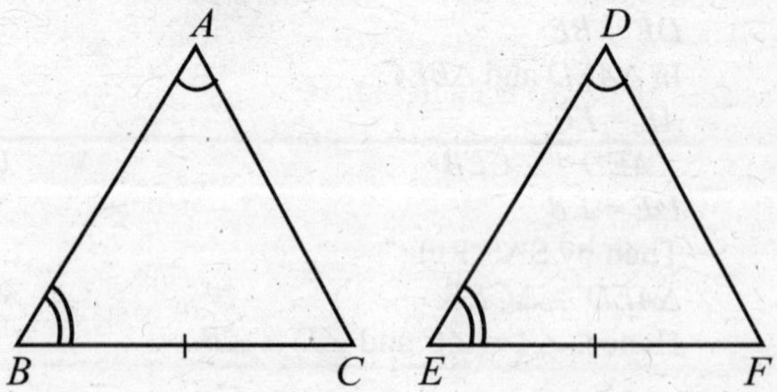

Proof : The sum of three interior angles of a triangle is 180°, then

$\angle A + \angle B + \angle C = 180°$ .....(i)

$\angle D + \angle E + \angle F = 180°$ .....(ii)

From (i) and (ii),

$\angle A + \angle B + \angle C = \angle D + \angle E + \angle F$ .....(iii)

$\angle B = \angle E$ (Given)

$\angle A = \angle D$ (Given)

Hence, $\angle C = \angle F$ [By (iii)] ...(iv)

Now in ΔABC and ΔDEF

$\angle B = \angle E$ (Given)

$BC = EF$ (Given)

$\angle C = \angle F$ [By (iv)]

Hence, $\Delta ABC \cong \Delta DEF$ (By ASA rule)

ILLUSTRATION : 3

In the adjoining figure, $AB = AC$. Prove that $BM = CN$

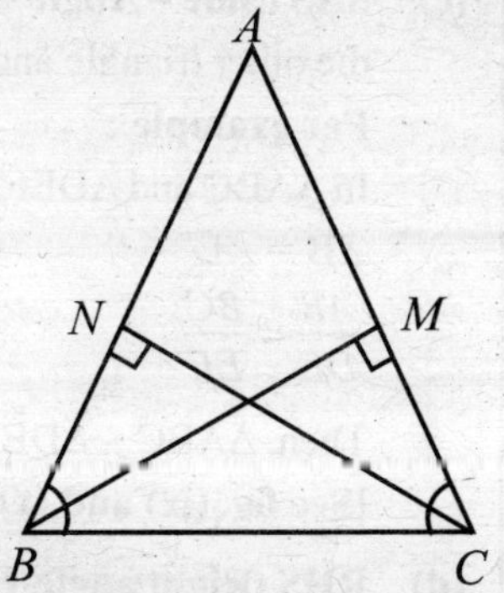

SOLUTION :

In ΔABC, $AB = AC$ (given)

$\therefore$ $\angle ABC = \angle ACB$ (angles opposite to equal sides are equal)

In Δs BCM and CBN,

$\angle N = \angle M$ (each = 90°)

$\angle ABC = \angle ACB$ (from above)

$BC = BC$ (common)

$\therefore$ $\Delta BCM \cong \Delta CBN$ (A.A.S. rule of congruency)

$\Rightarrow$ $BM = CN$ (CPCT)

CONNECTING TOPIC

SIMILARITY OF TWO TRIANGLES

Two triangles are said to similar, if

(i) all the corresponding angles are equal and

(ii) all the corresponding sides are in same ratio (or proportion).

In ΔABC and ΔDEF, if

$\angle A = \angle D$

$\angle B = \angle E$

$\angle C = \angle F$

and $\frac{AB}{DE} = \frac{BC}{EF} = \frac{CA}{FD}$ **[See fig. (i) and (ii)]**

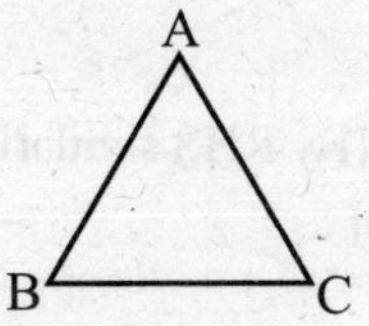

(i)

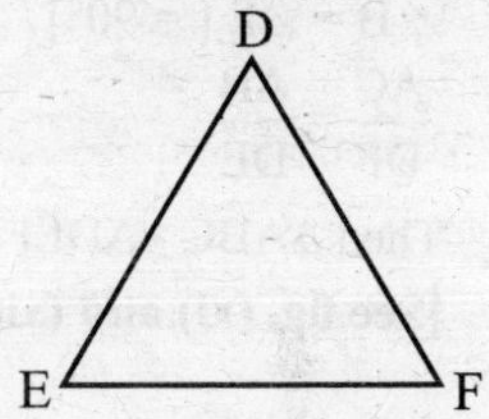

(ii)

Then $\Delta ABC \sim \Delta DEF$, (Read as triangle ABC is similar to triangle DEF).

Conditions of similarity :

There are four conditions of similarity of two triangles.

(a) AAA (Angle – Angle – Angle) Similarity : Two triangles are said to be similar, if their all corresponding angles are equal.

For example :

In ΔABC and ΔDEF, if

$\angle A = \angle D$

$\angle B = \angle E$

$\angle C = \angle F$

Then $\Delta ABC \sim \Delta DEF$ [By AAA Similarity]

[See fig. (iii) and (iv)]

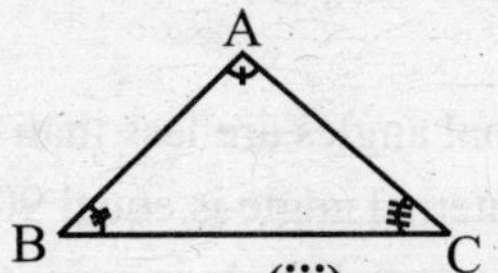

(iii)

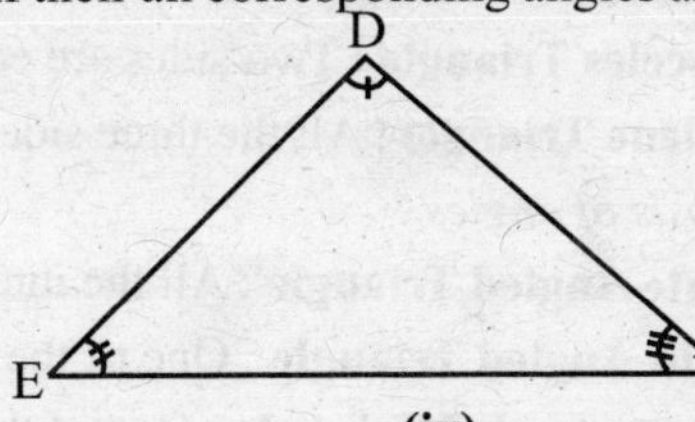

(iv)

Corollary :

A A (Angle – Angle) Similarity: If two angles of one triangle are respectively equal to two angles of another triangles, then two triangles are similar.

In ΔABC and ΔDEF, if

$\angle A = \angle D$

$\angle B = \angle E$

then $\Delta ABC \sim \Delta DEF$ [By AA Similarity]

[See fig. (v) and (vi)]

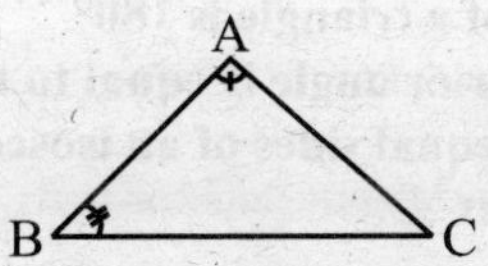

(v)

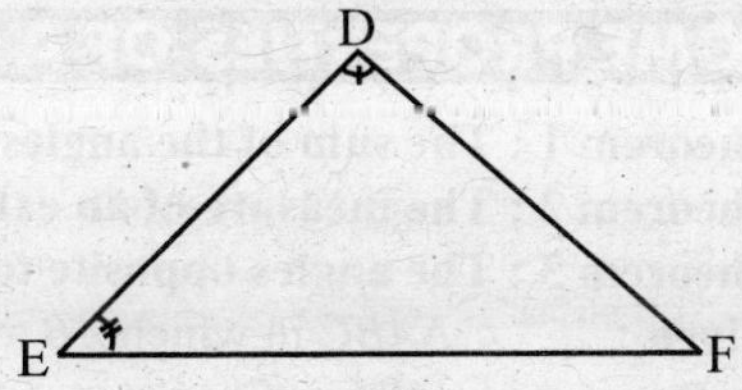

(vi)

(b) SSS (Side–Side–Side) Similarity : Two triangles are said to be similar, if sides of one triangles are proportional to (or in the same ratio of) the side of the other triangle:

For example :

In ΔABC and ΔDEF, if

$\frac{AB}{DE} = \frac{BC}{EF} = \frac{CA}{FD}$

Then $\Delta ABC \sim \Delta DEF$ [By SSS Similarity]

[See fig. (vii) and (viii)]

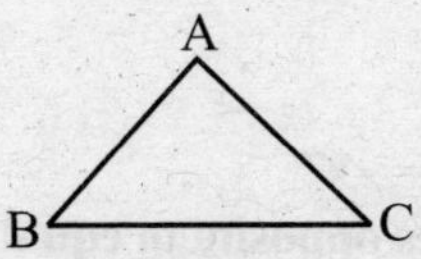

(vii)

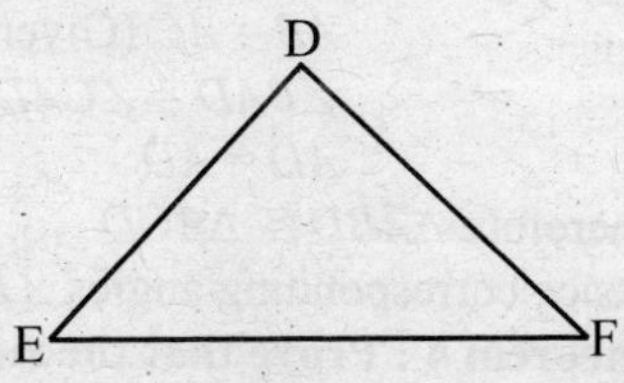

(viii)

(c) **SAS (Side – Angle – Side) Similarity :** Two triangles are said to similar if one angle of a triangle is equal to one angle of the other triangle and the sides including these angles are proportional.

For example :

In ΔABC and ΔDEF, if

$\angle B = \angle E$

$\frac{AB}{DE} = \frac{BC}{EF}$

Then, $\Delta ABC \sim \Delta DEF$ [By SSS Similarity]

[See fig. (ix) and (x)]

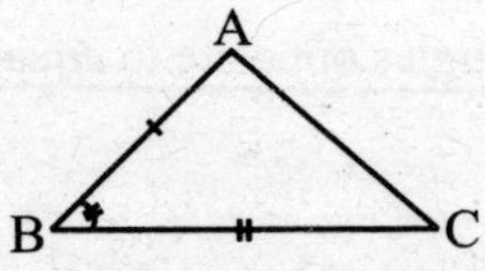

(ix)

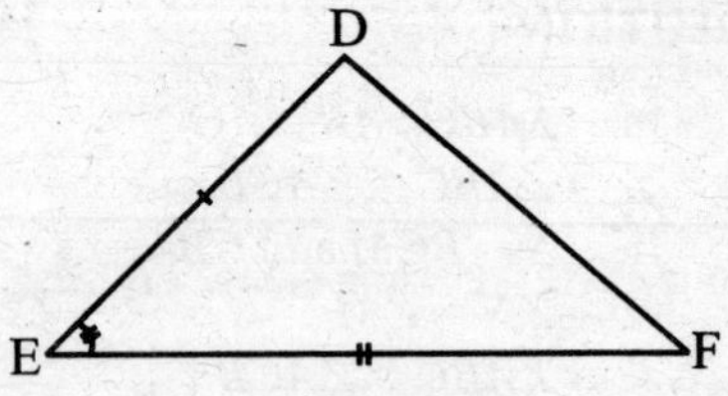

(x)

(d) **RHS (Right angle-Hypotenuse-Side) Similarity :** Two triangles are said to be similar if one angle of both triangle is right angle and hypotenuse of both triangles are proportional to any one another side of both triangles respectively.

In ΔABC and ΔDEF, if

$\angle B = \angle E\ [= 90°]$

$\frac{AC}{DF} = \frac{AB}{DE}$

Then $\Delta ABC \sim \Delta DEF$ [By RHS similarity]

[See fig. (xi) and (xii)]

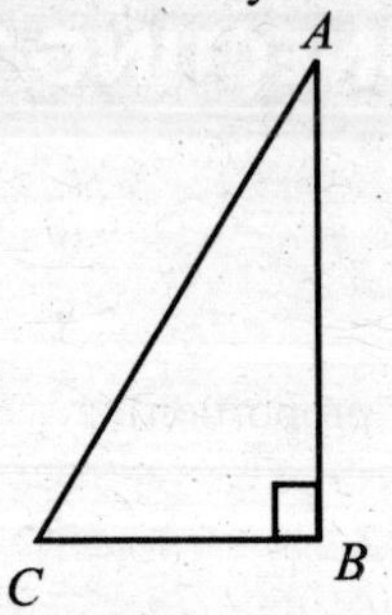

(xi)

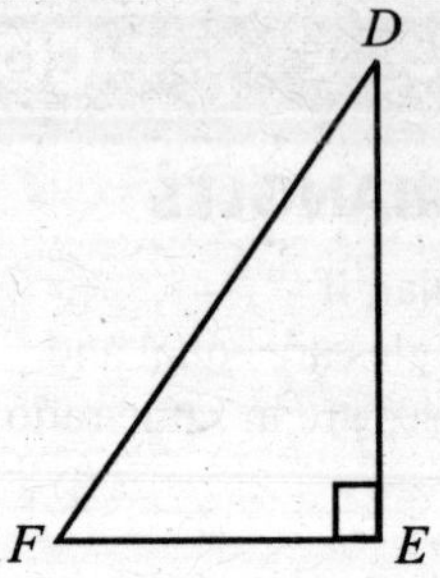

(xii)

CLASSIFICATION OF TRIANGLES

Triangles can be classified on the basis of their sides or angles.

On the basis of sides :

(a) **Equilateral Triangle** : All the three sides are equal

(b) **Isosceles Triangle** : Two sides are equal

(c) **Scalene Triangle** : All the three sides are unequal.

On the basis of angles :

(a) **Acute Angled Triangle** : All the internal angles are less than 90°

(b) **Right Angled Triangle** : One of the internal angle is equal 90°

(c) **Obtuse Angled Triangle** : One of the internal angle is more than 90°.

A triangle is represented by the symbol Δ.

SOME PROPERTIES OF A TRIANGLE

Theorem 1 : The sum of the angles of a triangle is 180°.

Theorem 2 : The measure of an exterior angle is equal to the sum of the measure of its two interior opposite angles.

Theorem 3 : The angles opposite to equal sides of an isosceles triangle are equal.

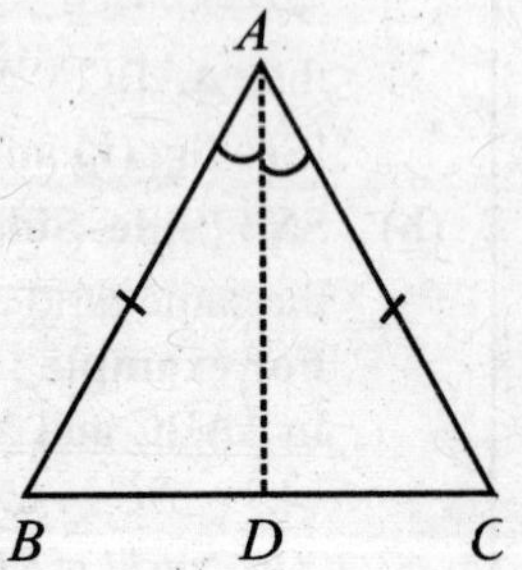

Given : ΔABC in which $AB = AC$.

To Prove : $\angle B = \angle C$

Construction : Draw AD, bisector of angle $\angle BAC$ which meets BC at D.

Proof : In ΔABD and ΔACD

$AB = AC$ (Given)

$\angle BAD = \angle CAD$ (By construction)

$AD = AD$ (Common side)

Therefore $\Delta ABD \cong \Delta ACD$ (By SAS Rule)

Hence corresponding angles $\angle B = \angle C$

Theorem 4 : Prove that the sides opposite to equal angles of a triangles are equal.

Given : ΔABC, in which $\angle B = \angle C$

To prove : $AB = AC$

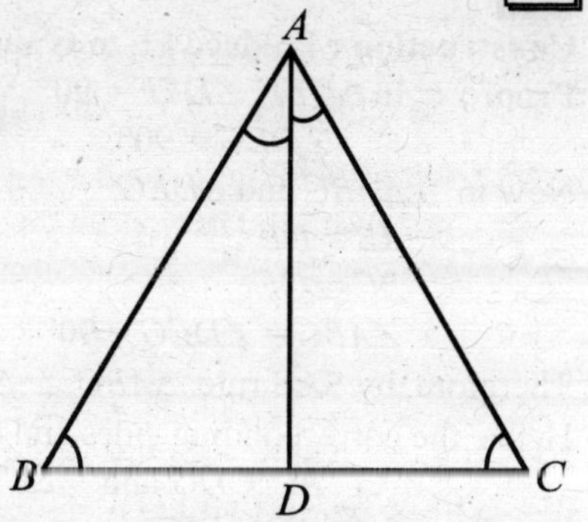

Construction : Draw AD, the bisector of angle $\angle BAC$ which meets BC at D.

Proof : In ΔABD and ΔACD

$\angle B = \angle C$ (Given)

$AD = AD$ (Common side)

$\angle BAD = \angle CAD$ (By construction)

Therefore $\Delta ABD \cong \Delta ACD$ (By ASA)

Hence corresponding sides, $AB = AC$

Some More Criteria for Congruence of Triangles

(iv) Side-Side-Side (SSS) Rule for Congruency of Two Triangles

Two triangles are congruent if the three sides of one triangle are equal to the three sides of the other triangle.

Given : ΔABC and ΔDEF in which

$AB = DE,\ BC = EF$ and $AC = DF$

To Prove: $\Delta ABC \cong \Delta DEF$

Construction : Draw a line segment EG at the other side of ED with respect to EF such that $EG = AB$ and $\angle ABC = \angle FEG$ then join GF and DG.

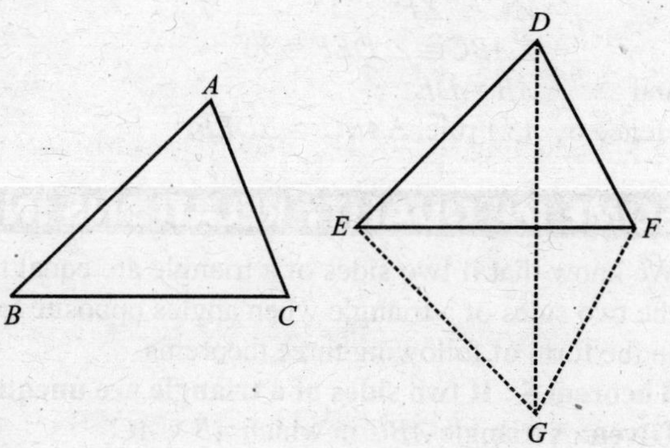

Proof : In ΔABC and ΔGEF

$AB = GE$ (By construction)

$\angle ABC = \angle GEF$ (By construction)

$BC = EF$ (Given)

Hence by SAS rule,

$\Delta ABC \cong \Delta GEF$

Hence the corresponding sides and angles are equal

$\therefore\ \angle A = \angle EGF, AC = GF$ .... (i)

Now $AB = EG$ (By construction)

$AB = DE$ (Given)

$\therefore\ GE = DE$ .... (ii)

Similarly $AC = GF$ [From (i)]

and $AC = DF$ (Given)

$\therefore\ GF = DF$ .... (iii)

Now in ΔEDG the opposite angle of equal sides EG and DE are equal

$\therefore\ \angle EDG = \angle EGD$ .... (iv)

Similarly in ΔFDG the opposite angle of equal sides GF and DF are equal

$\angle GDF = \angle DGF$ .... (v)

Adding equations (iv) and (v), we get

$\angle EDG + \angle GDF = \angle EGD + \angle DGF$

$\Rightarrow$ $\angle EDF = \angle EGF$ .... (vi)

From eq. (i), $\angle A = \angle EGF$ .... (vii)

Hence, from (vi) and (vii), we have

$\angle A = \angle EDF$ .... (viii)

In ΔABC and ΔDEF

$AB = DE$ (Given)

$\angle A = \angle EDF$ [By (viii)]

$AC = DF$ (Given)

By SAS rule, $\Delta ABC \cong \Delta DEF$

(v) Right-Angle-Hypotenuse-Side (RHS) Rule for Congruency of Two Triangles

Two right triangles are congruent if the hypotenuse and a side of one triangle are equal to hypotenuse and a side of the other triangle respectively.

Given : Two right triangles ΔABC and ΔDEF, in which

$\angle B = \angle E = 90°$

Hypotenuse AC = Hypotenuse DF and Side AB = Side DE

To prove : $\Delta ABC \cong \Delta DEF$

Construction : Produce FE to G such that $GE = BC$ and join G and D.

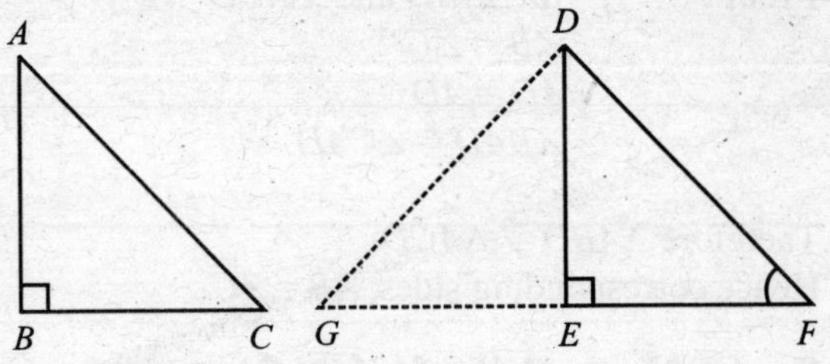

Proof : In ΔDEF, $\angle DEF = 90°$

$\therefore \quad \angle DEG = 90°$ .... (i)

Now in ΔABC and ΔDEG

$AB = DE$ (Given)

$BC = GE$ (By construction)

$\angle ABC = \angle DEG = 90°$ [By (i)]

Therefore, by SAS rule, $\Delta ABC \cong \Delta DEG$

Hence the corresponding sides and angles are equal

$\therefore \quad AC = DG$ and $\angle C = \angle G$ .... (ii)

But given that $AC = DF$ .... (iii)

From (ii) and (iii) $DG = DF$ .... (iv)

$\because$ Angles opposite to the equal sides DG and DF of ΔDGF are equal

Hence $\angle G = \angle F$ .... (v)

Therefore, from (ii) and (v)

$\angle C = \angle F$ .... (vi)

Now in ΔABC and ΔDEF

$\angle C = \angle F$ [From (vi)]

$\angle ABC \cong \angle DEF = 90°$ (Given)

and $AB = DE$ (Given)

Hence by ASA rule, $\Delta ABC \cong \Delta DEF$

SOME INEQUALITY RELATIONS IN A TRIANGLE

We know that if two sides of a triangle are equal then the angles opposite to them are also equal and vice-versa. What happens to the two sides of a triangle when angles opposite to them are unequal and vice-versa ? We get the answer of such type of questions in the form of following three theorems.

Theorem 5 : If two sides of a triangle are unequal, then the angle opposite to the longer side is larger (or greater).

Given: A triangle ABC in which $AB > AC$

To Prove: $\angle C > \angle B$

Construction: Take a point D on AB such that $AC = AD$ join CD.

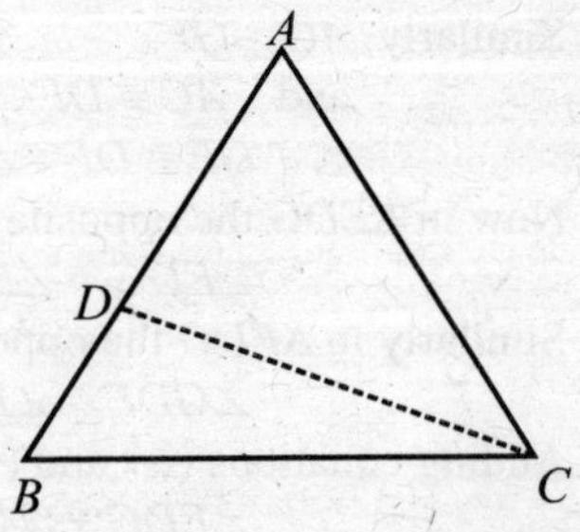

Proof : In ΔACD, $AC = AD$

Therefore, $\angle ACD = \angle ADC$ .... (i)

But $\angle ADC$ is an exterior angle of ΔBDC

$\therefore \quad \angle ADC > \angle B$ .... (ii)

From (i) and (ii), we have

$\angle ACD > \angle B$ .... (iii)

By figure, $\angle ACB > \angle ACD$ .... (iv)

From (iii) and (iv), we have

$\angle ACB > \angle ACD > \angle B$

$\Rightarrow \quad \angle ACB > \angle B$

$\Rightarrow \quad \angle C > \angle B$

Theorem 6 : In any triangle, the side opposite to the larger (greater) angle is longer.

Given: A triangle ABC in which $\angle B > \angle C$

To Prove: $AC > AB$

Proof: We have the following three possibilities for sides AB and AC of ΔABC.

(i) $AC = AB$ (ii) $AC < AB$ and (iii) $AC > AB$

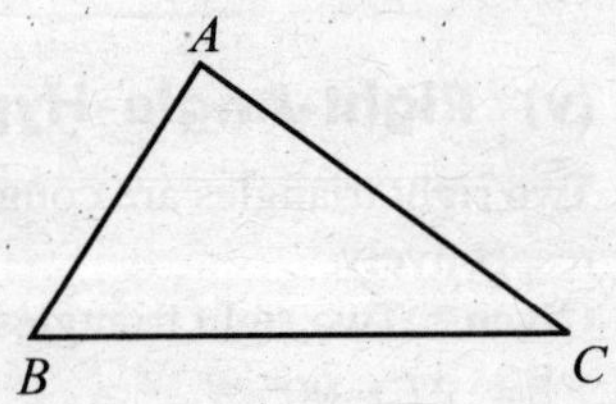

Case (i) : If $AC = AB$:

Since $AC = AB$, then opposite angles of equal sides are equal. Hence, $\angle B = \angle C$.

But it is given that $\angle B > \angle C$

Hence $AC \neq AB$

Case (ii) : If $AC < AB$:

We know that the angle opposite to longer side is larger.

$\therefore \quad AC < AB \Rightarrow \angle C > \angle B$,

which is also contrary to given $\angle B > \angle C$

Hence, $AC \nless AB$

Case (iii) :If $AC > AB$:

We are left only this possibility which must be true.

Hence, $AC > AB$.

Theorem 7 : The sum of any two sides of a triangle is greater than the third side.

Given : A triangle ABC.

To Prove :

(i) $AB + BC > AC$

$BC + AC > AB$

$AC + AB > BC$

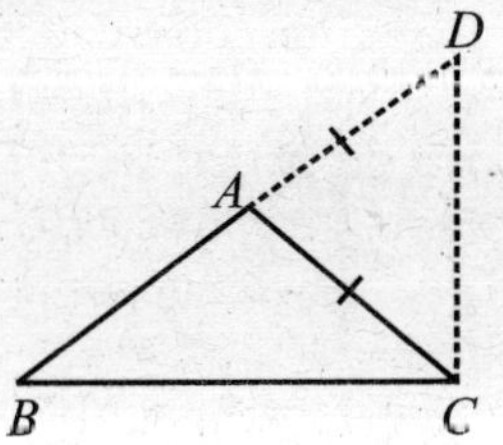

Construction : Produce BA to D, such that $AD = AC$ and join DC.

Proof : In ΔADC, by construction $AD = AC$, then opposite angles are equal,

$\therefore$ $\angle ACD = \angle ADC$ .... (i)

Now, $\angle BCD > \angle ACD$ .... (ii)

From (i) and (ii), we have

$\angle BCD > \angle ACD = \angle ADC$

Therefore, $BD > BC$ [side opposite to larger angle in a triangle is longer]

$\Rightarrow$ $BA + AD > BC$ [$\because BD = BA + AD$]

$\Rightarrow$ $BA + AC > BC$ [By construction $AD = AC$]

$\Rightarrow$ $AB + AC > BC$

Similarly, we can show that

$AB + BC > AC$

$BC + AC > AB$

ILLUSTRATION : 4

In figure, $\angle DBA = 132°$ and $\angle EAC = 120°$. Show that $AB > AC$

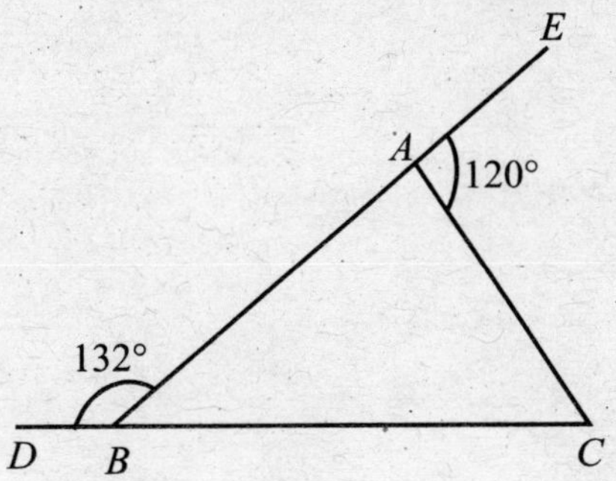

SOLUTION :

As DBC is a straight line,

$132° + \angle ABC = 180°$

$\Rightarrow$ $\angle ABC = 180° - 132° = 48°$

For ΔABC, $\angle EAC$ is an exterior angle

$120° = \angle ABC + \angle BCA$ (Ext. angle = sum of two opp. int. angles)

$\Rightarrow$ $120° = 48° + \angle BCA$

$\Rightarrow$ $\angle BCA = 120° - 48° = 72°$

Thus, we find that $\angle BCA > \angle ABC$

$\Rightarrow$ $AB > AC$ (side opposite to greater angle is greater)

ILLUSTRATION : 5

In quadrilateral $ABCD$, AB is the shortest side and DC is the longest side. Prove that : (i) $\angle B > \angle D$ (ii) $\angle A > \angle C$

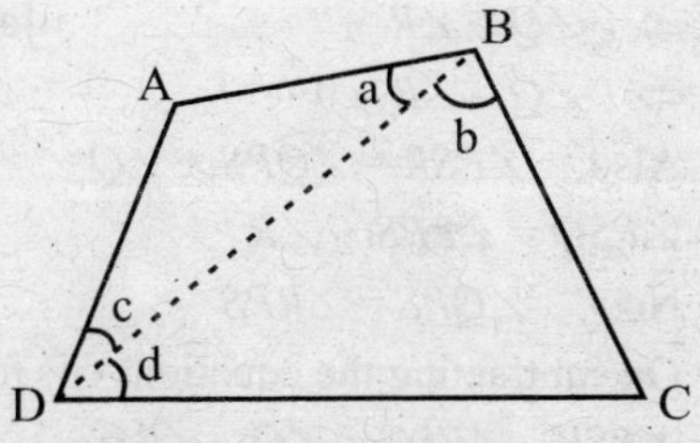

SOLUTION :

Join B and D

In ΔABD, $AD > AB$ (given, AB is the shortest side)

$\therefore$ $\angle a > \angle c$ .... (i) (angle opposite to greater side is greater)

In ΔBCD, $CD > BC$ (given, CD is the longest side)

$\therefore$ $\angle b > \angle d$ .... (ii) (angle opposite to greater side is greater)

$\therefore \quad \angle a + \angle b > \angle c + \angle d$ (Adding (i) and (ii))

$\Rightarrow \quad \angle B > \angle D$

Similarly, by joining AC, it can be proved that $\angle A > \angle C$.

ILLUSTRATION : 6

In figure, $ABCD$ is a quadrilateral. Show that

(i) $AB + BC + CD + DA > 2AC$

(ii) $AB + BC + CD + DA > AC + BD$

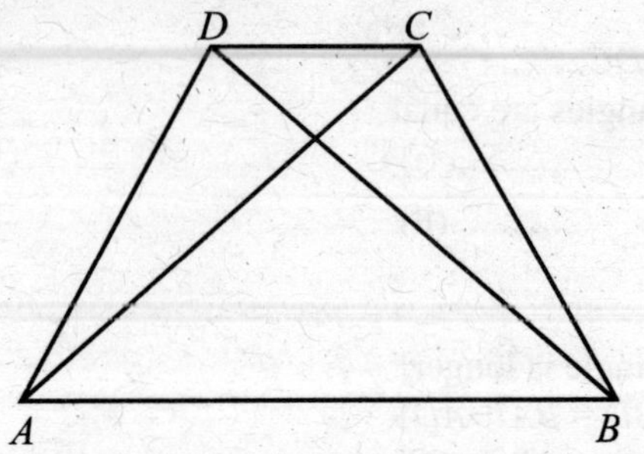

SOLUTION :

We know that the sum of the two sides of a triangle is greater than its third side.

In ΔABC, $AB + BC > AC$ .... (i)

In ΔADC, $AD + DC > AC$ .... (ii)

In ΔABD, $AB + AD > BD$ .... (iii)

In ΔBCD, $BC + CD > BD$ .... (iv)

Adding (i) and (ii), we get

$AB + BC + AD + CD > 2\,AC$

Again adding (i), (ii), (iii) and (iv), we get

$2\,(AB + BC + DO + AD) > 2\,(AC + BD)$

$\Rightarrow \quad AB + BC + DC + AD > AC + BD$

ILLUSTRATION 7 :

In the given figure, $PR > PQ$ and PS bisects $\angle QPR$.

Prove that : $\angle PSR > \angle PSQ$.

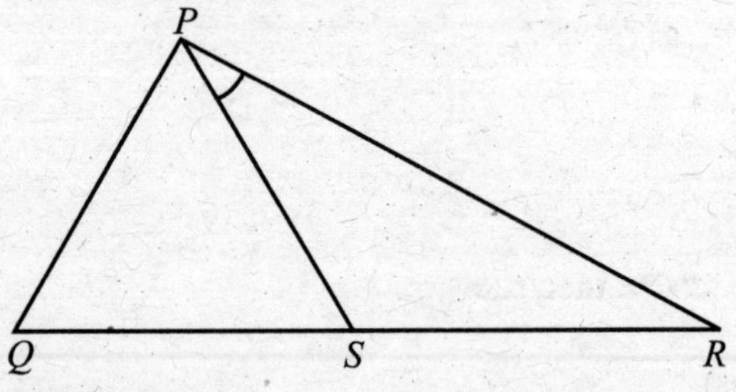

SOLUTION :

In ΔPQR

$PR > PQ$ (given)

$\Rightarrow \quad \angle Q > \angle R$ [angle opposite to larger side is greater]

$\Rightarrow \quad \angle Q - \angle R > 0$

Also, $\angle PSR = \angle QPS + \angle Q$ .... (i)

$\angle PSQ = \angle RPS + \angle R$ .... (ii) [exterior angle is equal to sum of interior opposite angles]

Now, $\angle QPS = \angle RPS$ [PS bisects $\angle QPR$]

On subtracting the equations (ii) from (i), we get

$\angle PSR - \angle PSQ = \angle Q - \angle R$

$\Rightarrow \quad \angle PSR - \angle PSQ > 0$

$\Rightarrow \angle PSR > \angle PSQ$

MISCELLANEOUS

SOLVED EXAMPLES

1. In figure, $AD = BC$ and $BD = CA$. Prove that $\angle ADB = \angle BCA$ and $\angle DAB = \angle CBA$

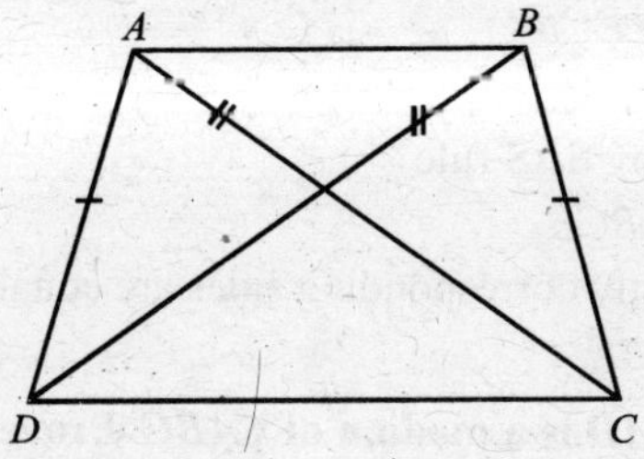

Sol. Given that $AD = BC$ and $BD = CA$

In ΔABD and ΔABC,

$\left.\begin{array}{l} AD = BC \\ BD = CA \end{array}\right\}$ (Given)

$AB = AB$ (Common)

Therefore by SSS rule,

$\Delta ABD \cong \Delta BAC$

Hence corresponding angles are equal,

i.e. $\angle ADB = \angle BCA$ and $\angle DAB = \angle CBA$

2. In figure, $AB = AC$. D is a point in the interior of ΔABC such that $\angle DBC = \angle DCB$. Prove that AD bisects $\angle BAC$.

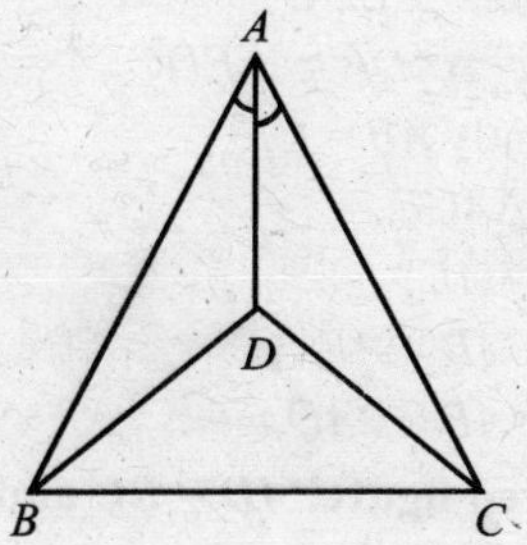

Sol. In ΔBDC, $\angle DBC = \angle DCB$, then the opposite sides are equal.

i.e. $CD = BD$ ...... (i)

Now in ΔABD and ΔACD

$BD = CD$ [by (i)]

$AD = AD$ (common side)

$AB = AC$ (Given)

Therefore by SSS rule,

$\Delta ABD \cong \Delta ACD$

Consequently, $\angle BAD = \angle CAD$

$\Rightarrow$ AD bisects $\angle BAC$

3. In figure, $ABCD$ is a quadrilateral in which $BC = AD$ and $\angle ADC = \angle BCD$, then show that

(i) $AC = BD$ (ii) $\angle ACD = \angle CDB$

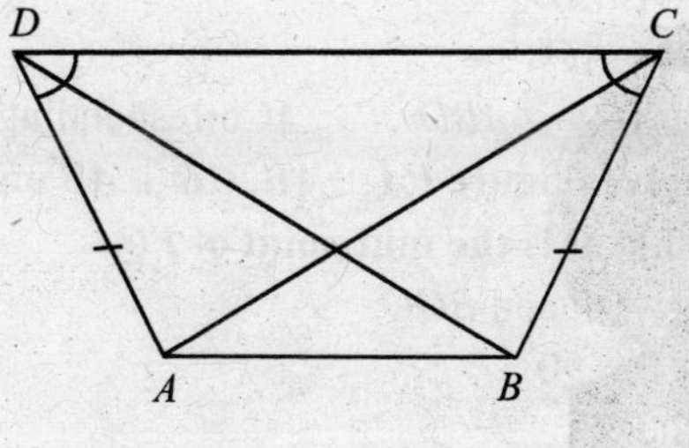

Sol. In figure, it is given that

$BC = AD$ and $\angle ADC = \angle BCD$

Hence in ΔADC and ΔBCD

$AD = BC$ (Given)

$CD = CD$ (common)

$\angle ACD = \angle BCD$ (Given)

Therefore, by SAS rule, $\Delta ADC \cong \Delta BCD$

Hence corresponding sides and angles are equal.

i.e., $AC = BD$ and $\angle ACD = \angle CDB$

4. In figure, $ABCD$ is a square and Δ CDE is an equilateral triangle.

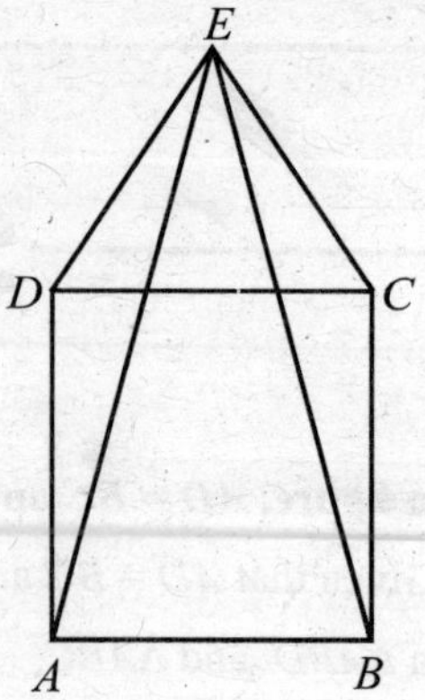

Prove that $AE = BE$.

Sol. ΔCDE is a equilateral triangle.

$CD = DE = CE$ .... (i)

$\angle DEC = \angle EDC = \angle DCE = 60°$ .... (ii)

and $ABCD$ is a square

$\angle ADC = \angle BCD = 90°$

On adding $\angle EDC$ to both sides

$\angle ADC + \angle EDC = \angle BCD + \angle EDC$

$\therefore$ $\angle EDA = \angle ECB$ ($\because \angle EDC = \angle DCE$) .... (iii)

Now in ΔADE and ΔBCE

$AD = BC$ (sides of the square)

$\angle EDA = \angle ECB$ [by (iii)]

$DE = EC$ [by (i)]

Therefore by SAS rule

$\Delta ADE \cong \Delta BCE$

Consequently corresponding sides are equal,

i.e., $AE = BE$.

5. In figure, AD is a median of ΔABC. Prove that $AB + AC > 2AD$.

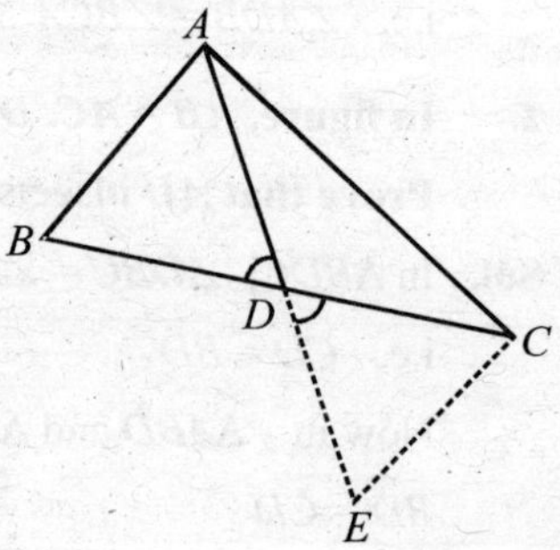

Sol. Produce AD to E such that $AD = DE$ and join CE.

In ΔADB and ΔEDC

$AD = DE$ (By construction)

$BD = DC$ (Given)

and $\angle ADB = \angle EDC$ (Vertically opposite angle)

Therefore, $\Delta ADB \cong \Delta EDC$ (By SAS rule)

Consequently $AB = CE$

Now in ΔACE

$AC + CE > AE$

$\Rightarrow$ $AC + AB > AE$ [$\because CE = AB$]

$\Rightarrow$ $AC + AB > 2AD$ [$\because AE = 2AD$]

6. In the given figure, $AD = BC$ and $\angle DAB = \angle CBA$, Prove that:

(i) $AC = BD$ (ii) $\angle BAC = \angle ABD$

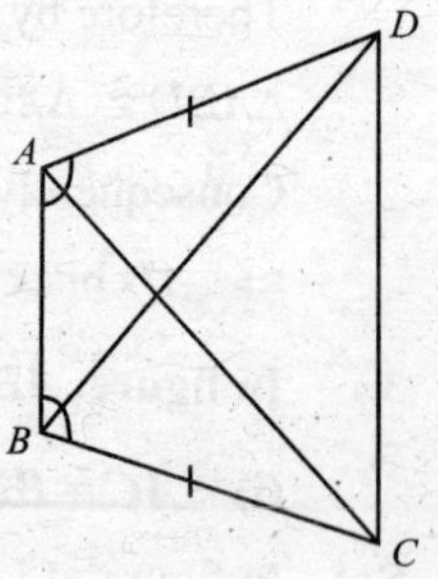

Sol. In Δs ABC and BAD,

$BC = AD$ (given)

$\angle ABC = \angle BAD$ (given)

$AB = AB$ (common)

So, by SAS rule,

$\Delta ABC \cong \Delta BAD$,

$\therefore$ $BD = AC$

and $\angle BAC = \angle ABD$ [Corresponding parts of congruent triangles are equal]

7. In the given figure $PA \perp AB$, $QB \perp AB$ and $OA = OB$.

Show that O is the mid point of PQ.

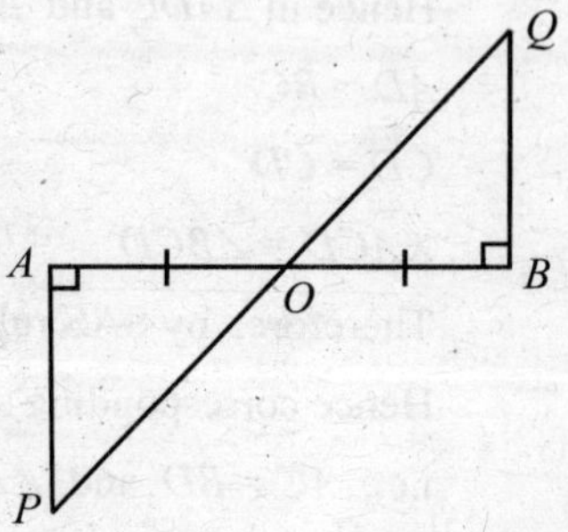

Sol. In Δs AOP and BOQ,

$\angle A = \angle B = 90°$

$AO = BO$ (given)

$\angle AOP = \angle BOQ$ (vertically opposite angles)

$\Rightarrow$ By ASA rule

$\Delta AOP \cong \Delta BOQ$

$\therefore$ $PO = QO$ [Corresponding parts of congruent triangles are equal]

$\Rightarrow$ O is the mid point of PQ.

8. In a triangle ABC, BE and CF are two equal altitudes.
Using RHS congruency rule, prove that ΔABC is isosceles.

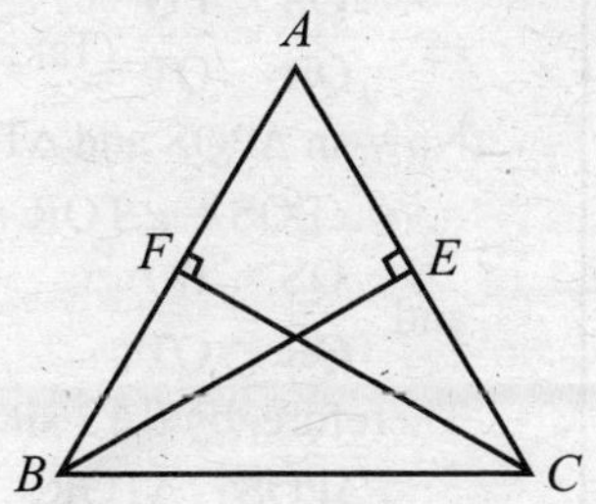

Sol. In right Δs BCE and CBF

$BC = BC$ (common hypotenuse)
$BE = CF$ (given)
So, by RHS property
$\Delta CBE \cong \Delta BCF$
$\Rightarrow \angle BCE = \angle CBF$ [CPCT]
$\Rightarrow AB = AC$ [sides opposite to equal angles of a triangle are equal]
Hence, ΔABC is isosceles.

9. In the adjoining figure, ABC and BAD are two triangles on the same base AB such that $BC = AD$ and $\angle ABC = \angle BAD$. Prove that : (i) AC = BD (ii) $\angle$ACB = $\angle$BDA (iii) CO = DO

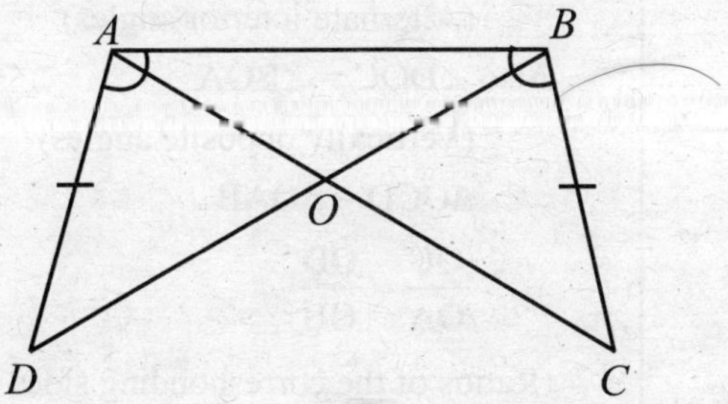

Sol. In Δs ABC and BAD, we have :
$AB = BA$ (Common)
$BC = AD$ (Given)
$\angle ABC = \angle BAD$ (Given)
$\therefore \Delta ABC \cong \Delta BAD$ (SAS rule)
$\therefore AC = BD$ and $\angle ACB = \angle BDA$ and therefore, $\angle OCB = \angle ODA$
Again, in Δs, BOC and AOD, we have :
$BC = AD$ (Given)
$\angle OCB = \angle ODA$ (Proved)
and $\angle BOC = \angle AOD$ (Vertically opposite angles)
$\therefore \Delta BOC \cong \Delta AOD$ (AAS rule)
Hence, $CO = DO$.

SOLVED EXAMPLES BASED ON CONNECTING TOPIC

10. In fig., ABC and AMP are two right triangles, right angled at B and M, respectively. Prove that:
(i) $\Delta ABC \sim \Delta AMP$
(ii) $\frac{CA}{PA} = \frac{BC}{MP}$

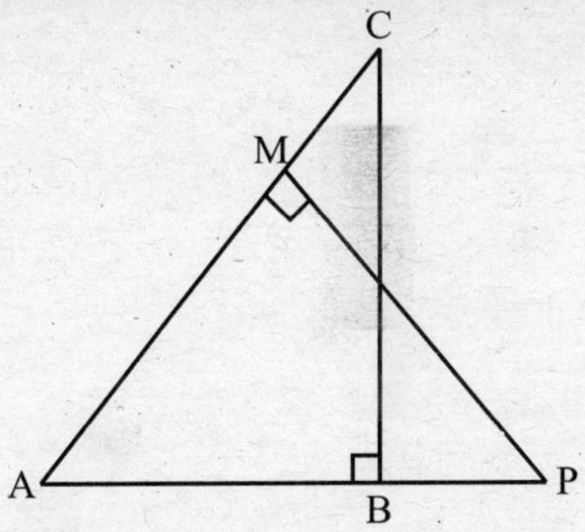

Sol. In figure, we have
$\angle ABC = \angle AMP$ (Each = 90°)
Because the Δs ABC and AMB are right angled at B and M, respectively.
Also $\angle BAC = \angle PMA$ (Each = $\angle$A)
$\Rightarrow \Delta ABC \sim \Delta AMP$ (By AA similarity criterion)
$\Rightarrow \frac{AC}{AP} = \frac{BC}{MP}$
(Ratio of the corresponding sides of similar triangles)
$\Rightarrow \frac{CA}{PA} = \frac{BC}{MP}$

11. In figure, $\frac{QR}{QS} = \frac{QT}{PR}$ and $\angle 1 = \angle 2$. Show that $\Delta PQS \sim \Delta TQR$.

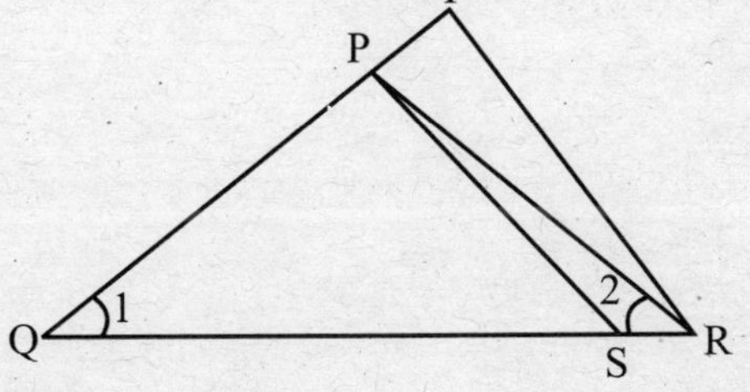

Sol. In figure, $\angle 1 = \angle 2$ (Given)
$\Rightarrow PQ = PR$
(Sides opposite to equal angles of ΔPQR)
We are given that
$\frac{QR}{QS} = \frac{QT}{PR} \Rightarrow \frac{QR}{QS} = \frac{QT}{PR}$ ($\because$ PQ = PR proved)

$\Rightarrow \frac{QS}{QR} = \frac{PQ}{QT}$ (Taking reciprocals) ...(i)

Now, in ΔPQS and ΔTQR, we have

$\angle PQS = \angle TQR$ (Each = ∠1)

and $\frac{QS}{QR} = \frac{PQ}{QT}$ (By (1))

Therefore, by SAS similarity criterion, we have

$\Delta PQS \sim \Delta TQR$.

12. Diagonals AC and BD of a trapezium ABCD with AB || DC intersect each other at the point O. Using a similarity criterion for two triangles, show that $\frac{OA}{OC} = \frac{OB}{OD}$.

Sol. In figure, AB || DC

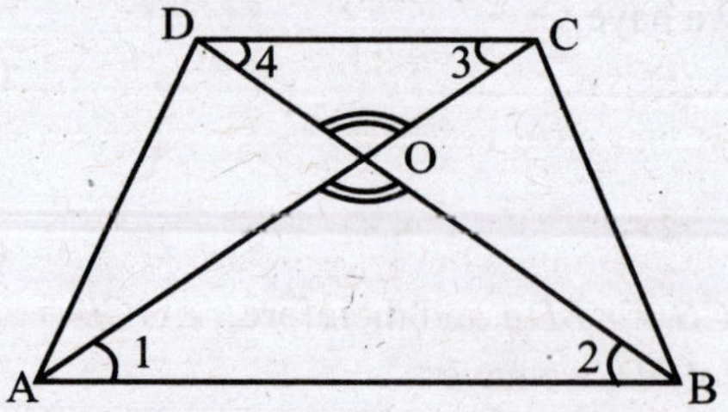

$\Rightarrow \angle 1 = \angle 3, \angle 2 = \angle 4$

(Alternate interior angles)

Also $\angle DOC = \angle BOA$

(Vertically opposite angles)

$\Rightarrow \Delta OCD \sim \Delta OAB$

$\Rightarrow \frac{OC}{OA} = \frac{OD}{OB}$

(Ratios of the corresponding sides of the similar triangles)

$\Rightarrow \frac{OA}{OC} = \frac{OB}{OD}$ (Taking reciprocals)

1 EXERCISE

Fill in the Blanks :

DIRECTIONS: *Complete the following statements with an appropriate word / term to be filled in the blank space(s).*

1. In ΔABC, $\angle A > \angle B$ and $\angle B > \angle C$, then smallest side is ....
2. If $\angle C$ is right angle in ΔABC, then larger side is .....
3. The angles opposite of equal sides of a triangle are ....
4. If two angles and the included side of one triangle are equal to two angles and the included side of the other triangle, then the two triangles are ....
5. In a triangle, angle opposite to the longer side is ....
6. Sum of any two sides of a triangle is greater than the .... side.
7. If $\Delta PQR \cong \Delta EFD$, then $\angle E$ = ...
8. If $\Delta PQR \cong \Delta EFD$, then ED = ...
9. If $\Delta ABC \cong \Delta ACB$, then ΔABC is isosceles with AB = ...
10. If $\Delta ABC \cong \Delta LKM$, then side of ΔLKM equal to side AC of ΔABC is ....

True / False :

DIRECTIONS: *Read the following statements and write your answer as true or false.*

1. If two sides of a triangle are unequal, the greater side has the greater angle opposite to it.
2. Scalene triangle may be an acute-angled triangle.
3. An isosceles triangle may be a right angled triangle.
4. An obtuse angled triangle may be an equilateral triangle.
5. A right angled triangle may be a scalene triangle.
6. The angles of a triangle are in the ratio 2 : 1 : 3. Triangle is a right angled triangle.
7. A triangle can have two right angles.
8. All the angles of a triangle can be less than 60°.
9. All the angles of a triangle can be equal to 60°.
10. A triangle can have at most one obtuse angle.

Match the Columns :

DIRECTIONS: *Each question contains statements given in two columns which have to be matched. Statements (A, B, C, D) in Column-I have to be matched with statements (p, q, r, s) in Column-II.*

1. In right triangle *ABC*, right angled at *C*, *M* is the mid-point of hypotenuse *AB*. *C* is joined to *M* and produced to a point *D* such that *DM* = *CM*. Point *D* is joined to point *B*.

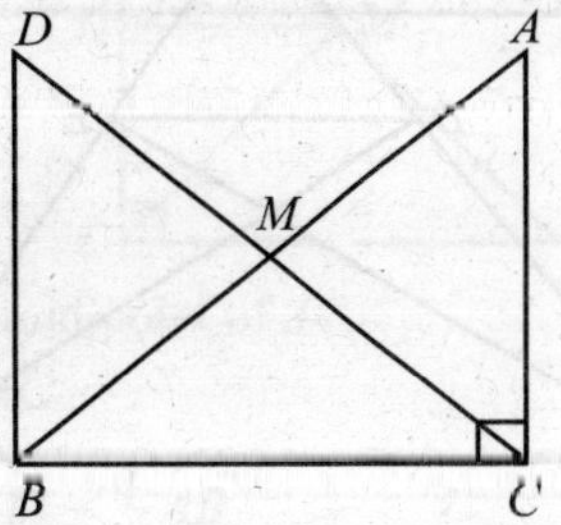

Column-I	Column-II
(A) ΔAMC	(p) congruent ΔBMD
(B) $\angle DBC$	(q) a right angle
(C) ΔDBC	(r) congruent ΔACB
(D) *CM*	(s) (1/2) *AB*

2. **Column-I (Triangles)** **Column-II (Congruency Rule)**

(A)

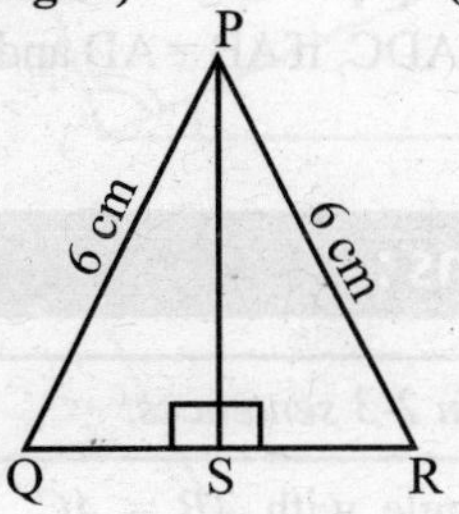

(p) SAS rule

(B)

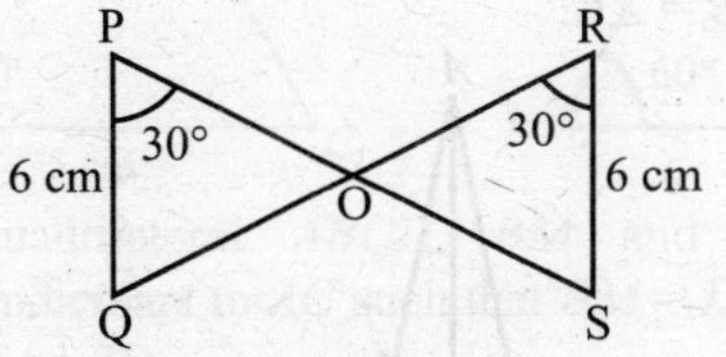

(q) RHS rule

(C)

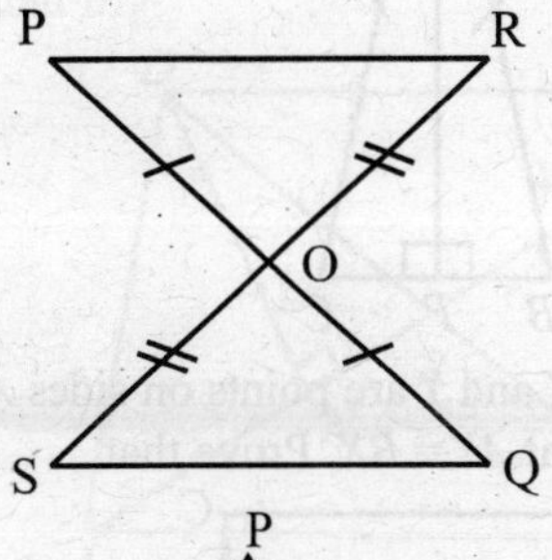

(r) SSS rule

(D)

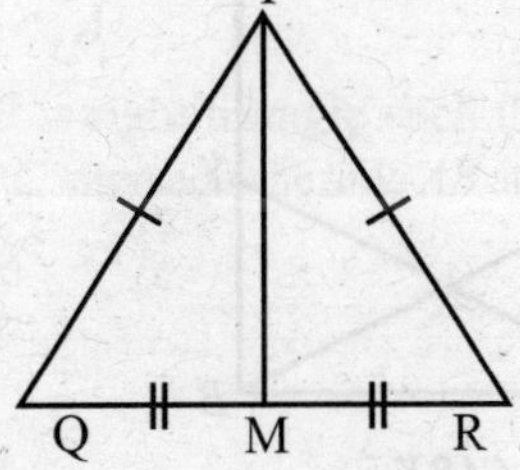

(s) AAS rule

2. In triangle ABC, points M and N on sides AB and AC respectively are taken so that $AM = \frac{1}{4}AB$ and $AN = \frac{1}{4}AC$. Prove that $MN = \frac{1}{4}BC$

3. P and Q are respectively the mid-points of sides AB and BC of a triangle ABC and R is the mid-point of AP. Show that :

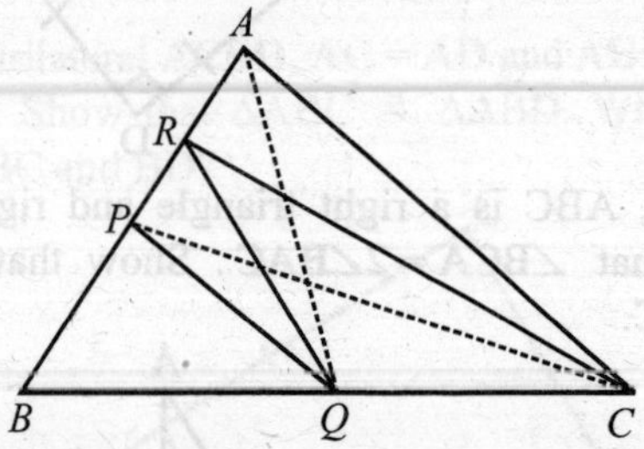

(i) ar (ΔPRQ) = $\frac{1}{2}$ ar(ΔARC)

(ii) ar (ΔRQC) = $\frac{3}{8}$ ar (ΔABC)

4. ABC is a triangle in which $\angle B = 2\angle C$. D is a point on side BC such that AD bisects $\angle BAC$ and $AB = CD$. Prove that $\angle BAC = 72°$.

5. Prove that sum of any two sides of a triangle is greater than twice the medians with respect to the third side.

6. Prove that in a triangle, other than an equilateral triangle, angle opposite the longest side is greater than $\frac{2}{3}$ of a right angle.

3 EXERCISE

Single Option Correct :

DIRECTIONS: *This section contains multiple choice questions. Each questions has 4 choices (a), (b), (c) and (d) out of which ONLY ONE is correct.*

1. In ΔABC, $BD \perp AC$ and $CE \perp AB$. If BD and CE intersect at O, then $\angle BOC =$

(a) $\angle A$ (b) $90 + A$
(c) $180 + \angle A$ (d) $180 - \angle A$

2. If D is any point on the side BC of a ΔABC, then

(a) $AB + BC + CA > 2AD$
(b) $AB + BC + CA < 2AD$
(c) $AB + BC + CA > 3AD$
(d) None

3. In a right angled triangle, one acute angle is double the other then the hypotenuse is

(a) Equal to smallest side
(b) Double the smallest side
(c) Triple the smallest side
(d) None of these

4. Each angle of an equilateral triangle is

(a) 60° (b) 45°
(c) 90° (d) 30°

5. In a triangle ABC, $\angle A + \angle B = 144°$ and $\angle A + \angle C = 124°$ then $\angle B =$

(a) 56° (b) 60°
(c) 65° (d) 45°

6. In an isosceles triangle $AB = AC$ and BA is produced to D, such that $AB = AD$ then $\angle BCD$ is

(a) 70° (b) 90°
(c) 60° (d) 45°

7. In the given figure, S is any point on the side QR of ΔPQR. What can you say about $PQ + QR + RP$?

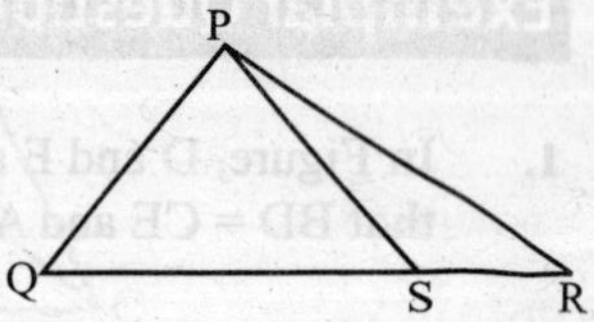

(a) $PQ + QR + RP > 2PS$
(b) $PQ + QR + RP < 2PS$
(c) $PQ + QR + RP = 2PS$
(d) None of these

8. If $\Delta ABC \cong \Delta PQR$ and ΔABC is not congruent to ΔRPQ, then which of the following is not true?

(a) $BC = PQ$ (b) $AC = PR$
(c) $AB = PQ$ (d) $QR = BC$

9. In triangles ABC and PQR, $AB = PQ$ and $\angle B = \angle Q$. The two triangles will be congruent by SAS axiom if

(a) $BC = QR$ (b) $AC = PR$
(c) $AB = QR$ (d) None of these

10. In ΔABC, if $\angle C > \angle B$, then

(a) $BC > AC$ (b) $AB > AC$
(c) $AB < AC$ (d) $BC < AC$

11. In the given figure, the ratio $\angle ABD : \angle ACD$ is

(a) 1 : 1
(b) 2 : 1
(c) 1 : 2
(d) 2: 3

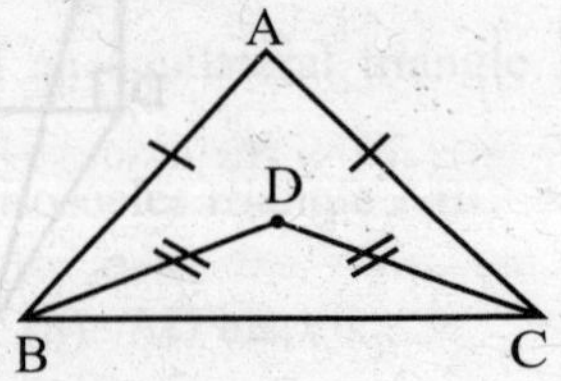

12. In the given figure if $BE = CF$, then
(a) $\Delta ABE \cong \Delta ACF$ (b) $\Delta ABE \cong \Delta AFC$
(c) $\Delta ABE \cong \Delta CAF$ (d) $\Delta AEB \cong \Delta AFC$

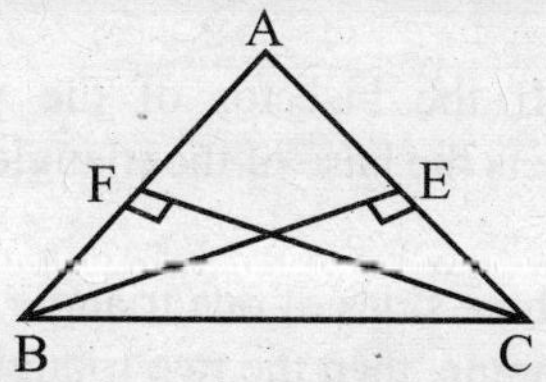

13. If the three altitudes of a triangle are equal then triangle is
(a) isosceles (b) equilateral
(c) right angled (d) none

14. In the given figure, the congruency rule used in proving $\Delta ACB \cong \Delta ADB$ is
(a) ASA (b) SAS
(c) AAS (d) RHS

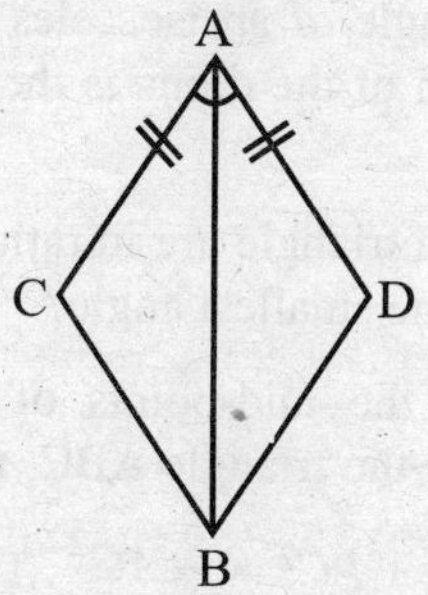

15. In the given figure
(a) $x = 70°, y = 37°$ (b) $x = 37°, y = 70°$
(c) $x + y = 107°$ (d) $x - y = 57°$

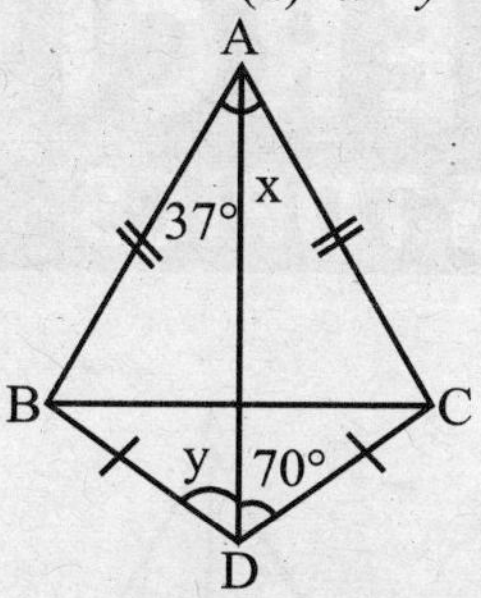

More Than One Option Correct :

DIRECTIONS: *This section contains multiple choice questions. Each question has 4 choices (a), (b), (c) and (d) out of which ONE OR MORE may be correct.*

1. Which of the following is/are correct?
(a) If two sides of a triangle are unequal, the larger side has the greater angle opposite to it.
(b) The sum of any two sides of a triangle is greater than its third side.
(c) If all the line segments that can be drawn to a given line from an external point, the perpendicular line segment is the shortest.
(d) If all the three sides of a triangle are equal, it is called a scalene triangle.

2. Which of the following is/are correct?
(a) Angles opposite to two equal sides of a triangle are equal.
(b) The medians of an equilateral triangle are equal.
(c) The medians of an equilateral triangle are different.
(d) A triangle is isosceles if and only if any two altitudes are equal.

3. Which of the following definitions is/are correct?
(a) A triangle having all sides equal is called an equilateral triangle.
(b) A triangle having two sides equal is called an isosceles triangle.
(c) A triangle in which all the sides are of different lengths is called a scalene triangle.
(d) None of these

4. Which of the following statement(s) is/are correct?
(a) Two geometrical figures are congruent if they have exactly the same shape and size
(b) Two triangles are congruent if and only if their corresponding sides and the corresponding angles are equal.
(c) If the bisector of the vertical angle of a triangle bisects the base then the triangle is isosceles.
(d) None of these

Passage Based Questions :

DIRECTIONS: *Study the given paragraph(s) and answer the following questions.*

PASSAGE

In any triangle, the sides opposite to the greater angle is longer.

1. In figure, AB > AC, PB and PC are bisectors of ∠B and ∠C respectively.

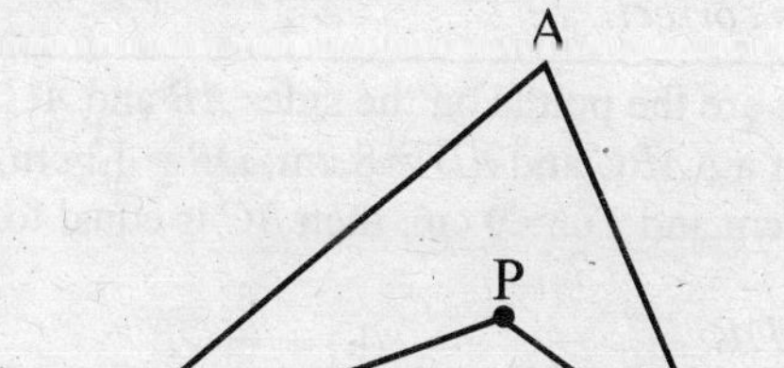

(a) PC < PB (b) PC > PB
(c) PC = PB (d) None of these

2. In ΔABC if ∠C > ∠B, then
(a) BC > AC (b) AB > AC
(c) AB < AC (d) BC < AC

Assertion & Reason :

DIRECTIONS: *Each of these questions contains an Assertion followed by Reason. Read them carefully and answer the question on the basis of following options. You have to select the one that best describes the two statements.*

(a) If both **Assertion** and **Reason** are **correct** and Reason is the **correct explanation** of Assertion.

(b) If both **Assertion** and **Reason** are correct, but Reason **is not the correct explanation** of Assertion.

(c) If **Assertion** is **correct** but **Reason** is **incorrect**.

(d) If **Assertion** is **incorrect** but **Reason** is **correct**.

1. **Assertion :** If the base and the altitude of a triangle are 4 cm and 8 cm respectively, then its area is 36 cm^2.
Reason : Area of a triangle $= \frac{1}{2} \times$ base $\times$ altitude.

2. **Assertion :** If $\Delta ABC \cong \Delta PQR$ and area $(\Delta ABC) = 10$ sq. units, then area $(\Delta PQR) = 20$ sq. units.
Reason : Two congruent figures have equal areas.

3. **Assertion:** When two triangles are congruent then their corresponding angles are equal.
Reason: Two triangles are congruent if their shapes and size are not same.

4. **Assertion:** Angles opposite to equal sides of a triangle are equal.
Reason: Sides opposite to equal angles of a triangle are not equal.

5. **Assertion:** If the bisector of the vertical angle of a triangle bisects the base of the triangle, then the triangle is equilateral.
Reason: If three sides of one triangle are equal to three of the other triangle, then the two triangles are congruent.

Integer Type Questions :

DIRECTIONS : *Answer the following questions. The answer to each of the question is a single digit integer, ranging from 0 to 9.*

1. The vertical angle of an isosceles triangle is 110°. What is value of sum of the digits is the measure of one of the equal angle ?

2. The angles of a triangle are in ratio 7 : 6 : 2. What is unit place digit of the smallest angle?

3. P and Q are the mid-points of the side AB and BC respectively of the triangle ABC, right angled at B. Then prove that $AQ^2 + PC^2 = \frac{5}{k} AC^2$. The value of k is

4 ADVANCED EXERCISE
BASED ON CONNECTING TOPICS

DIRECTIONS: *This section contains multiple choice questions. Each questions has 4 choices (a), (b), (c) and (d) out of which ONLY ONE is correct.*

1. D and E are the points on the sides AB and AC respectively of a ΔABC and $AD = 8$ cm, $DB = 12$ cm, $AE = 6$ cm and $EC = 9$ cm, then BC is equal to

(a) $\frac{2}{5} DE$ (b) $\frac{5}{2} DE$

(c) $\frac{3}{2} DE$ (d) $\frac{2}{3} DE$

2. In a right angled ΔABC in which $\angle A = 90°$. If $AD \perp BC$, then the correct statement is

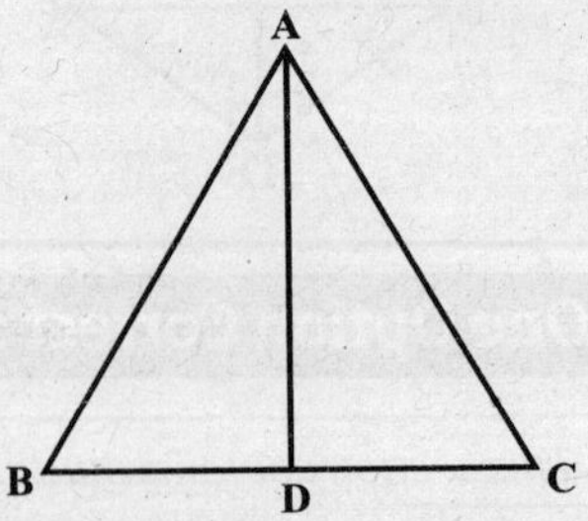

(a) $AB^2 = BD \times DC$ (b) $AB^2 = BD \times AD$

(c) $AB^2 = BC \times DC$ (d) $AB^2 = BC \times BD$

3. From the adjoining diagram, we have

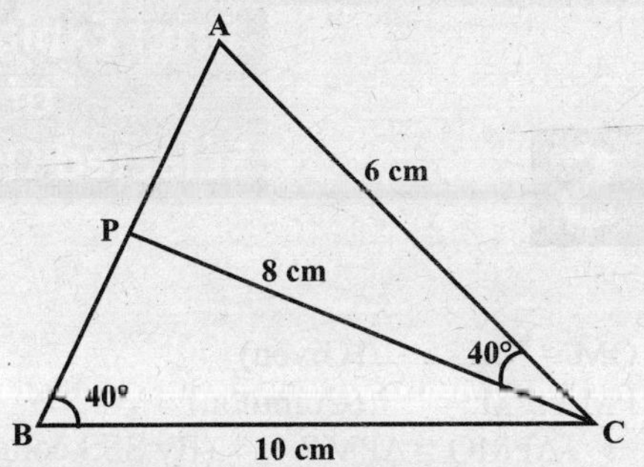

(a) AB = 7.5 cm, AP = 8.4 cm
(b) AB = 5.7 cm, AP = 4.8 cm
(c) AB = 7.5 cm, AP = 4.8 cm
(d) AB = 4.8 cm, AP = 7.5 cm

4. In the adjoining figure, DE || BC and AD : DB = 4 : 3

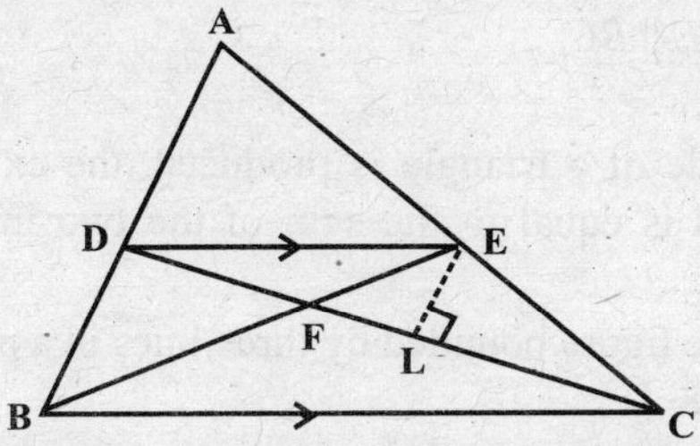

Value of $\frac{AD}{AB}$ and then $\frac{DE}{BC}$ is

(a) $\frac{4}{7}, \frac{4}{7}$ (b) $\frac{7}{4}, \frac{7}{4}$
(c) $\frac{4}{3}, \frac{4}{3}$ (d) $\frac{3}{4}, \frac{3}{4}$

5. In the given figure, DE parallel to BC. If AD = 2 cm, DB = 3 cm and AC = 6 cm, then AE is

(a) 2.4 cm (b) 1.2 cm
(c) 3.4 cm (d) 4.8 cm

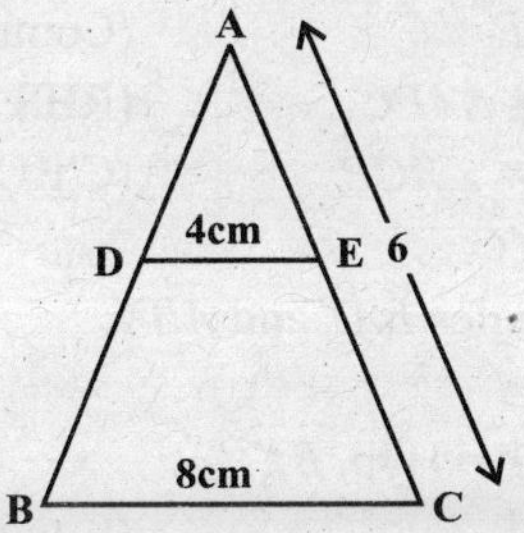

6. The perimeters of two similar triangles *ABC* and *PQR* are 36 cm, and 24 cm, respectively. If *PQ* = 10 cm, then the length of AB is :

(a) 16 cm (b) 12 cm
(c) 14 cm (d) 15 cm

7. In ΔABC, AD is the bisector of $\angle A$ if $AC = 4.2$ cm., $DC = 6$ cm., $BC = 10$ cm., find AB.

(a) 2.8 cm (b) 2.7 cm
(c) 3.4 cm (d) 2.6 cm

DIRECTIONS: *This section contains multiple choice questions. Each question has 4 choices (a), (b), (c) and (d) out of which ONE OR MORE may be correct.*

8. Which of the following statement(s) is/are correct ?

(a) Two triangles are said to be similar, if their all corresponding angles are equal.
(b) Two triangles are said to be similar, if sides of one triangle are proportional to the sides of the other triangle.
(c) When two triangles are similar, then all the corresponding angles are equal.
(d) None of these

DIRECTIONS: *Each of these questions contains an Assertion followed by Reason. Read them carefully and answer the question on the basis of following options. You have to select the one that best describes the two statements.*

(a) If both **Assertion** and **Reason** are **correct** and Reason is the **correct explanation** of Assertion.
(b) If both **Assertion** and **Reason** are correct, but Reason **is not the correct explanation** of Assertion.
(c) If **Assertion** is **correct** but **Reason** is **incorrect**.
(d) If **Assertion** is **incorrect** but **Reason** is **correct**.

9. **Assertion :** Two triangles are said to be similar, if their all corresponding angles are equal
Reason : Condition of similarity of two triangles given in assertion is known as Angle-Side-Angle criteria.

10. **Assertion :** If the area of two similar triangles are equal, they are equal.
Reason : If two triangles are equiangular, then they are similar.

11. **Assertion :** Two triangles are similar iff they are equiangular.
Reason : If the corresponding sides of two triangles are proportional, then they are similar.

SOLUTIONS

Brief Explanations of Selected Questions

1 EXERCISE

FILL IN THE BLANKS :

1. AB
2. AB
3. Equal
4. Congruent
5. larger
6. third
7. $\angle E = \angle P$
8. PR
9. AC
10. LM

TRUE/FALSE :

1. True
2. True
3. True
4. False
5. True
6. True
7. False
8. False
9. True
10. True

MATCH THE COLUMNS :

1. (A) → (p); (B) → (q); (C) → (r); (D) → (s)
2. (A) → (q); (B) → (s); (C) → (p); (D) → (r)

(A) In ΔPQS and ΔPRS

$PQ = PR = 6$ cm

$PS = PS$

$\angle PSQ = \angle PSR$ (= 90°)

$\Rightarrow$ $\Delta PQS \cong \Delta PRS$ (By R.H.S congruency)

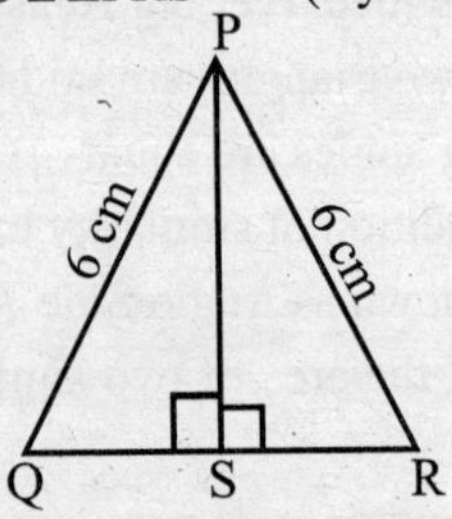

(B) In ΔPOQ and ΔROS,

$PQ = RS$ (= 6 cm)

$\angle QPO = \angle SRO$ (= 30°)

$\angle POQ = \angle ROS$ (Vertically opp. angles)

$\Rightarrow$ $\Delta POQ \cong \Delta ROS$ (By AAS congruency)

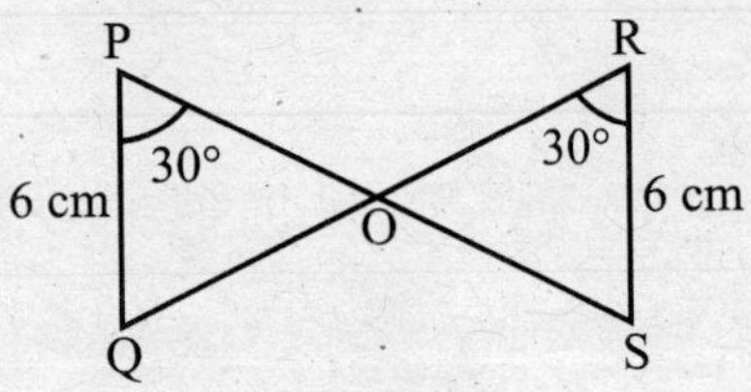

(C) Similarly, we can prove

$\Delta POR \cong \Delta QOS$ (By SAS congruency)

(D) In ΔPMQ and ΔPMR,

$PQ = PR$ (Given)

$QM = RM$ (Given)

$PM = PM$ (Common)

$\Rightarrow$ $\Delta PMQ \cong \Delta PMR$ (By SSS congruency)

VERY SHORT ANSWER QUESTIONS :

1. Since, ΔDBC and ΔEBC are on the same base BC and have equal areas.

   $\therefore$ Their altitudes must be the same.

   $\therefore$ $DE \parallel BC$.

2. 180°.
3. If a side of a triangle is produced, the exterior angle so formed is equal to the sum of the two interior opposite angles.
4. A plane figure bounded by three lines in a plane is called a triangle.
5. Let the smallest angle be x°.

   Other two angles are 2x° and 3x°.

   So, $x + 2x + 3x = 180 \Rightarrow x = \frac{180}{6} = 30$.

6. $\angle A = \angle D$; $\angle B = \angle E$; $\angle C = \angle F$
7. Yes

SHORT ANSWER QUESTIONS :

1. In right triangle APB and right triangle APC,

   Given Hyp. AB = Hyp. AC

   $AP = AP$ (Common)

   $\therefore$ $\Delta APB \cong \Delta APC$ (RHS Rule)

   $\therefore$ $\angle ABP = \angle ACP$ (C.P.C.T.)

   $\Rightarrow$ $\angle B = \angle C$.

2. In right triangles BAY and ABX,

   Given that

   Hyp. AY = Hyp. BX

   $AB = AB$ (Common)

   $\therefore$ $\Delta BAY \cong \Delta ABX$ (R.H.S. Axiom)

   $\therefore$ $BY = AX$

   and $\angle BAY = \angle ABX$. (C.P.C.T.)

3. In ΔABC,

   $AB = AC$ (Given)

   $\therefore$ $\angle ACB = \angle ABC$ ....(i)

   (Angles opposite to equal sides of a triangle)

   $\therefore$ $\angle ACB > \angle CBS$

   $\therefore$ $BS > CS$ (Side opposite to greater angle is longer)

   $\therefore$ $CS < BS$

4. In ΔABC, $AB = AC$ (given)

$\therefore \angle ABC = \angle ACB$ (angles opposite equal sides are equal)

In Δs BCM and BCN, $\angle N = \angle M$ (each = 90°)

$\angle ABC = \angle ACB$ (from above)

$BC = BC$ (common)

$\therefore \Delta BCM \cong \Delta CBN$ (A.A.S. axiom of congruency)

$\Rightarrow BM = CN$ (C.P.C.T.)

5. Since, AD is the bisector of $\angle BAC$ therefore, in ΔCAQ and ΔBAQ,

$\angle CAQ = \angle BAQ$

Given that $\angle CQD = \angle BQD$ (Given)

$\Rightarrow 180° - \angle CQD = 180° - \angle BQD$

$\Rightarrow \angle AQC = \angle AQB$ (Common)

$AQ = AQ$ (ASA Axiom)

$\therefore \Delta CAQ \cong \Delta BAQ$ (C.P.C.T.)

$\therefore CQ = BQ$

6. From ΔPQT, we have given

$PQ = PT$

Since, Angles opposite to equal sides

$\therefore \angle PTQ = \angle PQT$ ....(i)

Now, In ΔPST and ΔPRQ,

We have

$PT = PQ$ and $\angle TPS = \angle QPR$

$\therefore$ From (i)

$\angle PTQ = \angle PQT$

$\Rightarrow \angle PTS = \angle PQR$

$\therefore \Delta PST \cong \Delta PRQ$ (ASA Axiom)

and by C.P.C.T

$PS = PR$

$\Rightarrow \Delta PRS$ is isosceles.

7. ΔADB and ΔADC gives us that

$\angle ADB = \angle ADC$ (Each = 90°)

($\because$ AD is the perpendicular bisector of BC)

$\therefore DB = DC$

$AD = AD$ (Common)

$\therefore \Delta ADB \cong \Delta ADC$ (By SAS Rule)

$\therefore AB = AC$ (C.P.C.T)

Hence proved.

8. (i) In ΔABE and ΔACF, we have given

$BE = CF$

$\angle BAE = \angle CAF$ (Common)

$\angle AEB = \angle AFC$ (Each = 90°)

$\therefore \Delta ABE = \Delta ACF.$ (By AAS Rule)

(ii) From (i) $\Delta ABE \cong \Delta ACF$

$\therefore AB = AC$ (C.P.C.T.)

$\therefore \Delta ABC$ is an isosceles triangle.

9. $DR = CS$

$\Rightarrow DR + RQ = CS + RS$ ....(i)

$\Rightarrow DS = CR$

In right triangles ADS and BCR,

Hyp. AS = Hyp. BR

$DS = CR$

$\therefore \Delta ADS \cong \Delta BCR$ (R.H.S. Axiom)

$\therefore \angle DAS = \angle CBR.$ (C.P.C.T.)

10. Let PQR be a right angled triangle in which $\angle Q = 90°$

Then, $\angle P + \angle R = 90°$ (By angle sum property)

$\therefore \angle Q = \angle P + \angle R$

$\Rightarrow \angle Q > \angle P$

and $\angle Q > \angle R$

$\therefore PR > QR$ ($\because$ Side opposite to greater angle is longer)

Similarly $PR > PQ$

$\therefore$ PR is the longest side, i.e., hypotenuse is the longest side.

11. Since, AD is a median in ΔABC which divides it into two triangles of equal areas.

$\therefore$ ar (ΔABD) = ar (ΔACD) ....(i)

Similarly, ar (ΔEBD) = ar(ΔECD) ....(ii)

($\because$ ED is a median in ΔEBC)

Subtracting (ii) from (i), we get

ar (ΔABD) – ar(ΔEBD) = ar(ΔACD) – ar(ΔECD)

$\Rightarrow$ ar(ΔABE) = ar(ΔACE).

LONG ANSWER QUESTIONS :

1. In ΔAPC and ΔBPD,

$\angle ACP = \angle BDP$ (Given)

$\angle APC = \angle BPD$ (Vertically Opposite Angles)

$\therefore$ Third $\angle A$ = Third $\angle B$

($\because$ The sum of the three angles of a Δ is 180°)

In ΔACD and ΔBDC,

$CD = CD$ (Common)

$\angle A = \angle B$ (Prove above)

$\angle BCD = \angle ADC$ (Given)

$\angle ACB = \angle BDA$ (Given)

Adding, we get

$\angle BCD + \angle ACB = \angle ADC + \angle BDA$

$\Rightarrow \angle ACD = \angle BDC$

$\therefore \Delta ACD \cong \Delta BDC$ (ASS. Axiom)

$\therefore AD = BC$ (C.P.C.T.)

2. (i) In ΔABC, Which is right angled at B, we have

$BC^2 = AC^2 - AB^2$

$= (15)^2 - (9)^2 = 225 - 81$

$= 144$

$\Rightarrow BC = \sqrt{144} = 12\text{cm}.$

(ii) Since, D and E are the mid-points of AB and AC respectively in ΔABC

$\therefore DE \parallel BC$

and $DE = \frac{1}{2}BC = \frac{1}{2}(12) = 6\text{ cm}$

$AD = BD = \frac{1}{2}AB = \frac{1}{2}(9) = \frac{9}{2}\text{cm}$

$\because$ $DE \parallel BC$ and AB intersects them.

$\therefore$ $\angle ADE = \angle ABC = 90°$ (Corresponding angles)

$\Rightarrow$ ΔADE is a right angled triangle

$\therefore$ Area of ΔADE

$$= \frac{(AD)(DE)}{2} = \frac{9}{2}.\frac{6}{2} = \frac{27}{2} = 13.5\,\text{cm}^2.$$

3. (i) In ΔACB, since, M is the mid-point of AB and $MD \parallel BC$.

$\therefore$ D is the mid-point of AC.

(By converse of mid-point theorem)

(ii) $\angle ADM = \angle ACB$ (Corresponding angles)

($\because$ $MD \parallel BC$ and AC intersects them)

But we have given $\angle ACB = 90°$

$\therefore$ $\angle ADM = 90° \Rightarrow MD \perp AC$

(iii) Now, $\angle ADM + \angle CDM = 180°$

(Linear Pair Axiom)

$\therefore$ $\angle ADM = \angle CDM = 90°$

In ΔADM and ΔCDM, in which

$AD = CD$ ($\because$ D is the mid-point of AC)

$\angle ADM = \angle CDM$ (Each measures 90°)

$DM = DM$ (Common)

$\therefore$ $\Delta ADM \cong \Delta CDM$ (SAS Rule)

$\therefore$ $MA = MC$ (C.P.C.T.)

But we know M is the mid-point of AB

$\therefore$ $MA = MB = \frac{1}{2}AB$

$\therefore$ $MA = MC = \frac{1}{2}AB$

$\Rightarrow$ $CM = MA = \frac{1}{2}AB$.

4. In ΔAPC and ΔBPD,

$\angle ACP = \angle BDP$ (Given)

$\angle APC = \angle BPD$ (Vertically Opposite Angles)

Third $\angle A$ = Third $\angle B$

($\because$ The sum of the three angles of a Δ is 180°)

In ΔACD and ΔBDC,

$CD = CD$ (Common)

$\angle A = \angle B$ (Prove above)

$\angle BCD = \angle ADC$ (Given) ...(i)

$\angle ACB = \angle BDA$ (Given) ...(ii)

Adding (i) and (ii) we get

$\angle BCD + \angle ACB = \angle ADC + \angle BDA$

$\Rightarrow$ $\angle ACD = \angle BDC$

$\therefore$ $\Delta ACD \cong \Delta BDC$ (AAS. Axiom)

$\therefore$ $AD = BC$ (C.P.C.T.)

5. In ΔABC and $\Delta A'B'C'$

$AB = A'B' = 6$ cm

$BC = B'C' = 5$ cm

$\angle B = \angle B' = 60°$

Hence by SAS criterion

$\Delta ABC \cong \Delta A'B'C'$

$\therefore$ $\angle A = \angle A'$ [By CPCT]

$\Rightarrow$ $3x = 2x + 20°$

$\Rightarrow$ $x = 20°$

$\therefore$ $\angle B'A'C' = x = 20°$

6. Consider ΔDNR and ΔBMR

$DN = BM$

$\angle DNR = \angle BMR$ [Each = 90°]

$\angle DRN = \angle BRM$ (Vertically Opposite Angles)

$\therefore$ $\Delta DNR \cong \Delta BMR$ (AAS criterion of congruency)

$\therefore$ $DR = BR$ (CPCT)

$\therefore$ $BD = 2BR$

$\therefore$ $BD = 2 \times 8 = 16$ cm

7. Let $AB = AC = x$

By Pythagoras theorem

$$BC = \sqrt{AB^2 + AC^2} = \sqrt{x^2 + x^2}$$

$$BC = \sqrt{2}x$$

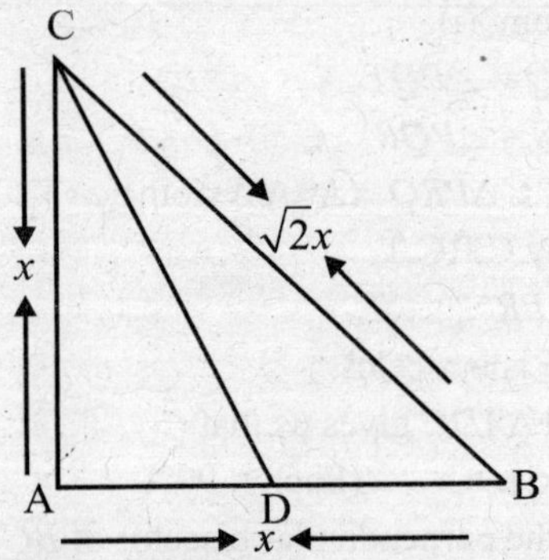

Again by Bisector theorem

$$\frac{AC}{BC} = \frac{AD}{BD} \Rightarrow \frac{BC}{AC} = \frac{BD}{AD}$$

$$\Rightarrow \frac{BC}{AC} + 1 = \frac{BD}{AD} + 1$$

$$\Rightarrow \frac{BC + AC}{AC} = \frac{BD + AD}{AD}$$

$$\Rightarrow \frac{BC + AC}{AC} = \frac{AB}{AD} \Rightarrow \frac{\sqrt{2}x + x}{x} = \frac{x}{AD}$$

$$\Rightarrow \frac{\sqrt{2} + 1}{1} = \frac{x}{AD} \Rightarrow AD = \frac{x}{\sqrt{2} + 1}$$

$$\therefore AC + AD = x + \frac{x}{\sqrt{2}+1} = \frac{\sqrt{2}x + x + x}{\sqrt{2}+1} = \frac{\sqrt{2}x + 2x}{\sqrt{2}+1}$$

$$= \frac{\sqrt{2}x(1+\sqrt{2})}{(\sqrt{2}+1)} = \sqrt{2}x = BC$$

2 EXERCISE

TEXT-BOOK EXERCISE :

1. We have a quadrilateral ACBD in which AC = AD and AB bisects ∠A.
We have to Prove : ΔABC ≅ ΔABD
Proof : In ΔABC and ΔABD,
Given AC = AD
AB = AB (Common)
Since, AB bisects angle A
∴ ∠CAB = ∠DAB
Thus, ΔABC ≅ ΔABD (SAS Rule)
BC = BD (CPCT)

2. **Given :** AD and BC are equal perpendiculars to a line segment AB.
To Prove : CD bisects AB.
Proof : From ΔOAD and ΔOBC we have given
AD = BC
∠OAD = ∠OBC (Each = 90°)
∠AOD = ∠BOC (Vertically Opposite Angles)
∴ By AAS rule, ΔOAD ≅ ΔOBC
∴ By CPCT, OA = OB
Thus CD bisects AB.

3. We have given that *l* and *m* are two parallel lines which are intersected by another pair of parallel lines *p* and *q*.
Prove that : ΔABC ≅ ΔCDA.
Proof : Since , *l* and m & p and q are parallel lines therefore AB || DC and AD || BC
∴ Quadrilateral ABCD is a parallelogram.
(∵ A quadrilateral is a parallelogram if both the pairs of opposite sides are parallel)
Since, ABCD is ||gm
∴ BC = AD ....(i)
and AB = CD ....(ii)
(∵ Opposite sides of a ||gm are equal)
and ∠ABC = ∠CDA ....(iii)
(∵ Opposite angles of a ||gm are equal)
Thus, In ΔABC and ΔCDA we get
AB = CD (From (ii))
BC = DA (From (i))
∠ABC = ∠CDA (From (iii))
∴ ΔABC ≅ ΔCDA (SAS Rule)

4. From the given figure, AC = AE, AB = AD and ∠BAD = ∠ EAC.
Prove that : BC = DE.
Proof : In ΔABC and ΔADE,
Given AB = AD,
AC = AE
and ∠BAD = ∠EAC
⇒ ∠BAD + ∠DAC = ∠DAC + ∠EAC
(Adding ∠DAC to both sides)
⇒ ∠BAC = ∠DAE
∴ By SAS rule
ΔABC ≅ ΔADE
⇒ BC = DE. (CPCT)

5. **Given** : AB is a line segment and P is its mid-points. D and E are points on the same side of AB such that ∠BAD = ∠ABE and ∠EPA = ∠DPB.
Prove that : (i) ΔDAP ≅ ΔEBP
(ii) AD = BE
Proof : (i) Since, P is the mid-point of the line segment AB
∴ from ΔDAP and ΔEBP,
AP = BP
Also, given ∠DAP = ∠EBP and ∠EPA = ∠DPB
Adding ∠EPD to both sides
⇒ ∠EPA + ∠EPD = ∠EPD + ∠DPB
⇒ ∠APD = ∠BPE
Thus, by ASA rule
ΔDAP ≅ ΔEBP
(ii) Since, ΔDAP ≅ ΔEBP (From above)
∴ AD = BE (CPCT)

6. Given an isosceles triangle ABC, in which AB = AC, and the bisectors of ∠B and ∠C intersect each other at O. Let us join A to O.
We have to Prove : (i) OB = OC
(ii) AO bisects A.
Proof : (i) Given AB = AC
∴ ∠B = ∠C (∵Angles opposite to equal sides of a triangle are equal)

$$\therefore \quad \frac{1}{2}\angle B = \frac{1}{2}\angle C$$

Since, BO and CO are the bisectors of ∠B and ∠C respectively
∴ ∠OBC = ∠OCB
Also, sides opposite to equal angles of a triangle are equal

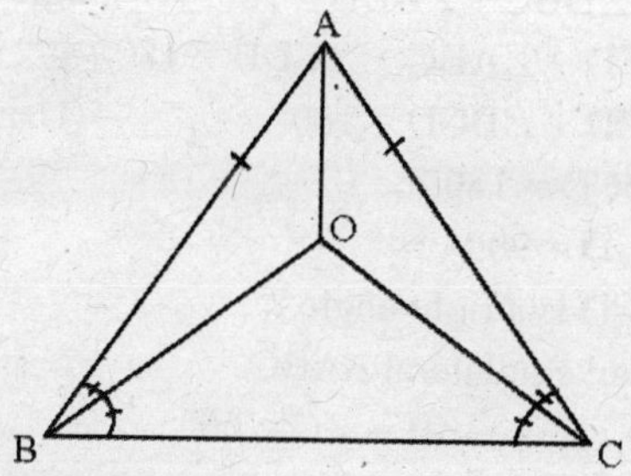

∴ OB = OC
(ii) In ΔOAB and ΔOAC, we have given
AB = AC
Also, from (i) OB = OC
∴ ∠B = ∠C
(Angles opposite to equal sides of a triangle are equal)

$\therefore \quad \frac{1}{2}\angle B = \frac{1}{2}\angle C$

($\because$ BO and CO are the bisectors of $\angle B$ and $\angle C$ respectively)

$\therefore \quad \angle ABO = \angle ACO$

$\therefore$ By SAS Rule, $\Delta OAB \cong \Delta OAC$

$\therefore \quad \angle OAB = \angle OAC$ (C.P.C.T.)

$\therefore$ AO bisects $\angle A$.

7. **Given :** An isosceles ΔABC in which altitudes BE and CF are drawn to sides AC and AB respectively.

To Prove : BE = CF

Proof : ΔABC is an isoscele triangle

$\therefore \quad AB = AC$

Also, Angles opposite to equal sides of a traingle are equal

$\therefore \quad \angle ABC = \angle ACB$ ....(i)

Thus, In ΔBEC and ΔCFB

$\angle BEC = \angle CFB$ (Each = 90°)

BC = CB (Common)

$\angle ECB = \angle FBC$ (From (i))

$\therefore$ By ASA rule, $\Delta BEC \cong \Delta CFB$

$\therefore$ By C.P.C.T

BE = CF.

8. Given a ΔABC which is isosceles with AB = AC. Side BA is produced to D such that AD = AB.

To Prove : $\angle BCD$ is a right angle.

Proof : Since, ΔABC is an isosceles

$\therefore \quad \angle ABC = \angle ACB$ ....(i)

AC = AD ($\because$ AB = AC and AD = AB)

$\therefore$ In ΔACD,

$\angle CDA = \angle ACD$

(Angles opposite to equal sides of a triangle are equal)

$\angle CDB = \angle ACD$ ....(ii)

By adding (i) and (ii), we get

$\angle ABC + \angle CDB = \angle ACB + \angle ACD$

$\Rightarrow \quad \angle ABC + \angle CDB = \angle BCD$ ....(iii)

Now, In ΔBCD,

$\angle BCD + \angle DBC + \angle CDB = 180°$ (By angle sum property)

$\Rightarrow \quad \angle BCD + \angle ABC + \angle CDB = 180°$

$\Rightarrow \quad \angle BCD + \angle BCD = 180°$ (Using (iii))

$\Rightarrow \quad 2\angle BCD = 180°$

$\Rightarrow \quad \angle BCD = 90°$

$\Rightarrow \quad \angle BCD$ is a right angle.

9. We have an equilateral ΔABC.

To Prove : $\angle A = \angle B = \angle C = 60°$

Proof : Since, ABC is an equilateral triangle.

$\therefore$ All the three sides are equal

ie AB = BC = CA ....(i)

Consider AB = BC

$\Rightarrow \quad \angle A = \angle C$ ....(ii)

(Angles opposite to equal sides of a triangle are equal)

Consider BC = CA

$\therefore \quad \angle A = \angle B$ ....(iii)

(Angles opposite to equal sides of a triangles are equal)

From (ii) and (iii), we obtain

$\angle A = \angle B = \angle C$ ....(iv)

Also, In ΔABC,

$\angle A + \angle B + \angle C = 180°$ ....(v)

(By angle sum property)

Let $\angle A = y°$. Then, $\angle B = \angle C = y°$ From (iv)

$\therefore$ From (v),

$y° + y° + y° = 180°$

$3y° = 180° \quad \Rightarrow \quad y° = 60°$

$\Rightarrow \quad \angle A = \angle B = \angle C = 60°$.

10. **Given :** AD is an altitude of an isosceles ΔABC such that AB = AC.

To Prove : (i) AD bisects BC

(ii) AD bisects $\angle A$.

Proof : (i) Given in right ΔADB and right ΔADC,

Hyp. AB = Hyp. AC

AD = AD (Common)

$\therefore \quad \Delta ADB \cong \Delta ADC$ (R.H.S. Rule)

$\therefore$ By C.P.C.T

BD = CD

$\Rightarrow$ AD bisects BC.

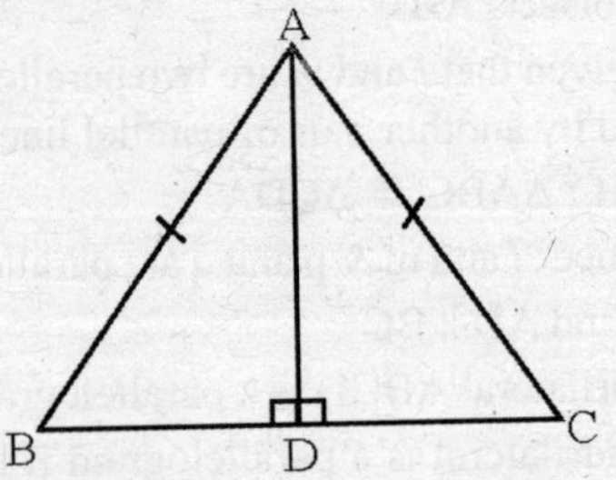

(ii) From the (i) part $\Delta ADB \cong \Delta ADC$

$\therefore \quad \angle BAD = \angle CAD$ (C.P.C.T.)

$\Rightarrow$ AD bisects $\angle A$.

11. We have given a ΔABC, in which BE and CF are two equal altitudes

To Prove : ΔABC is isosceles.

Proof : From right ΔBEC and right ΔCFB, we have

BE = CF

Hyp. BC = Hyp. CB (Common)

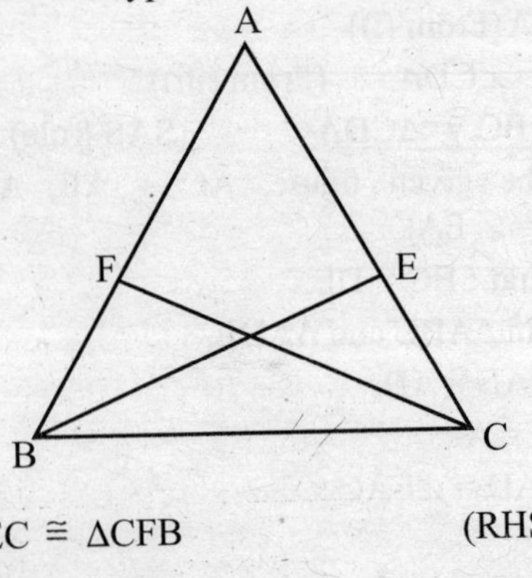

$\therefore \quad \Delta BEC \cong \Delta CFB$ (RHS Rule)

$\therefore \quad \angle BCE = \angle CBF$ (C.P.C.T)

Since, Side opposite to equal angles of a triangle are equal

$\therefore \quad AB = AC$

$\therefore \quad \Delta ABC$ is isosceles.

12. Let PQR be a right angled triangle in which $\angle P = 90°$

Then, $\angle P + \angle R = 90°$ (By angle sum property)

$\therefore \quad \angle Q = \angle P + \angle R$

$\Rightarrow \quad \angle Q > \angle P$

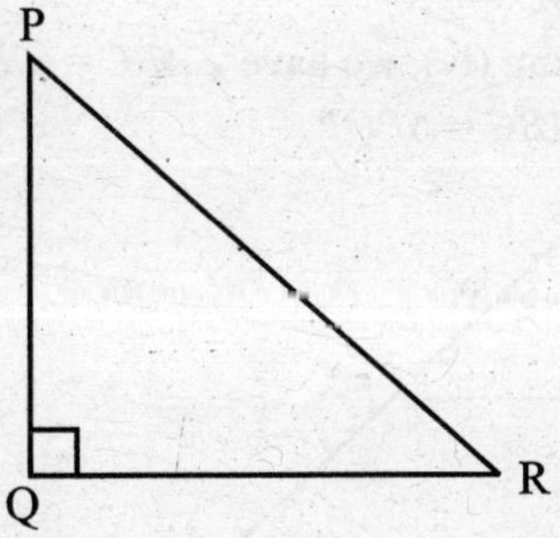

and $\angle Q > \angle R$

$\therefore \quad PR > QR$ ($\because$ Side opposite to greater angle is longer)

and $PR > PQ$

$\therefore \quad PR$ is the longest side, *i.e.*, hypotenuse is the longest side.

13. From the figure, we have $\angle B < \angle A$ and $\angle C < \angle D$.

We have to show that $AD < BC$

Proof : Since $\angle B < \angle A$

i.e $\angle A > \angle B$

$\therefore \quad OB > OA$ ....(i)

($\because$ Side opposite to greater angle is longer)

Also $\angle C < \angle D$ (Given)

i.e. $\angle D > \angle C$

$\Rightarrow \quad OC > OD$ ....(ii)

($\because$ Side opposite to greater angle is longer)

Hence, from (i) and (ii), we get

$OB + OC > OA + OD$

$\Rightarrow \quad BC > AD$

$\Rightarrow \quad AD < BC$.

14. **Given :** $PR > PQ$ and PS bisects $\angle QPR$.

To Prove : $\angle PSR > \angle PSQ$

Proof : Given in ΔPQR, $PR > PQ$

Since, Angle opposite to longer side is greater

$\therefore \quad \angle PQR > \angle PRQ$ ....(i)

Also, PS bisects $\angle QPR$

$\therefore \quad \angle QPS = \angle RPS$ ....(ii)

$\therefore$ In ΔPQS, by angle sum property, we have

$\angle PQR + \angle QPS + \angle PSQ = 180°$ ....(iii)

Similarly, In ΔPRS

$\angle PRS + \angle SPR + \angle PSR = 180°$ ....(iv)

From (iii) and (iv),

$\angle PQR + \angle QPS + \angle PSQ = \angle PRS + \angle SPR + \angle PSR$

$\Rightarrow \quad \angle PQR + \angle PSQ = \angle PRS + \angle PSR$

$\Rightarrow \quad \angle PRS + \angle PSR = \angle PQR + \angle PSQ$

$\Rightarrow \quad \angle PRS + \angle PSR > \angle PRQ + \angle PSQ$

(From (i))

$\Rightarrow \quad \angle PRQ + \angle PSR > \angle PRS + \angle PSQ$

($\because \quad \angle PRQ = \angle PRS$)

$\Rightarrow \quad \angle PSR > \angle PSQ$.

15. Construct the perpendicular bisectors of two sides of ABC. Their point of intersection is the required point.

16. Draw the angle bisectors of any two angles of the triangle. Their point of intersection is the required point.

EXEMPLAR QUESTIONS :

1. Given: $BD = CE$ and $AD = AE$

In ΔADE

$AD = AE$

$\Rightarrow \angle AED = \angle ADE$

Now, $\angle ADE + \angle ADB = 180°$ (linear pair)

$\angle ADB = 180° - \angle ADE$ ...(i)

also, $\angle AED + \angle AEC = 180°$ (linear pair)

$\angle AEC = 180° - \angle AED$

$= 180° - \angle ADE$ ...(ii)

$\therefore$ from (i) & (ii)

$\angle ADB = \angle AEC$

Consider,

ΔABD and ΔACE

$AD = AE$ (given)

$\angle ADB = \angle AEC$ (proved)

$BD = EC$ (given)

$\therefore \Delta ABD \cong \Delta ACE$ (By S.A.S)

2. Given: ΔCDE is an equilateral triangle

$\angle ADC = \angle BCD$ (each 90°)

$\angle EDC = \angle ECD$ (each 60°)

$\angle ADC + \angle EDC = \angle BCD + \angle ECD$

$\Rightarrow \angle ADE = \angle BCE$

Consider

ΔADE and ΔBCE

$AD = BC$ (Sides of square ABCD).

$\angle ADE = \angle BCE$ (Proved)

$DE = CE$ (Sides of equilateral triangle)

$\therefore \Delta ADE \cong \Delta BCE$ (By SAS)

3. Given $BA = DE$ and $BF = EC$.

Consider,

$BF = CE$

$BF + CF = CE + CF$

$BC = EF$

Consider, ΔABC and ΔDEF

$\angle CAB = \angle FDE$ (each 90°)

$AB = DE$ (given)

$BC = EF$ (proved)

$\therefore \Delta ABC \cong \Delta DEF$ (By RHS)

4. Produce CB at a point D such that BC = BD and join AD.

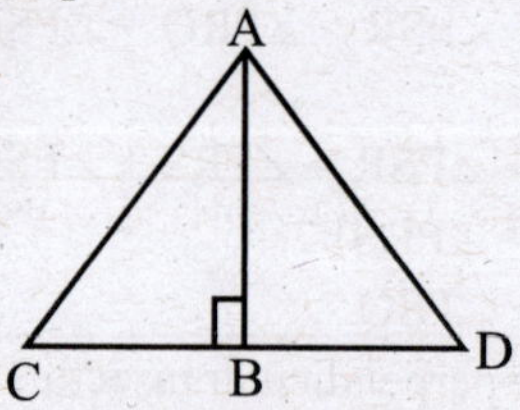

In ΔABC and ΔABD, we have

$BC = BD$ (By construction)

$AB = AB$ (Same side)

$\angle ABC = \angle ABD$ (Each of 90°)

Therefore, $\Delta ABC \cong \Delta ABD$ (SAS)

So, $\left.\begin{array}{l}\angle CAB = \angle DAB\\ AC = AD\end{array}\right\}$ (CPCT) ...(ii)

and

Thus, $\angle CAD = \angle CAB + \angle BAD = x + x = 2x$ [From (i)]

and $\angle ACD = \angle ADB = 2x$ [From (ii), AC = AD]

That is, ΔACD is an equilateral triangle.

or AC = CD, i.e., AC = 2 BC (Since BC = BD).

5. Produce QS to intersect PR at T (See Fig.).

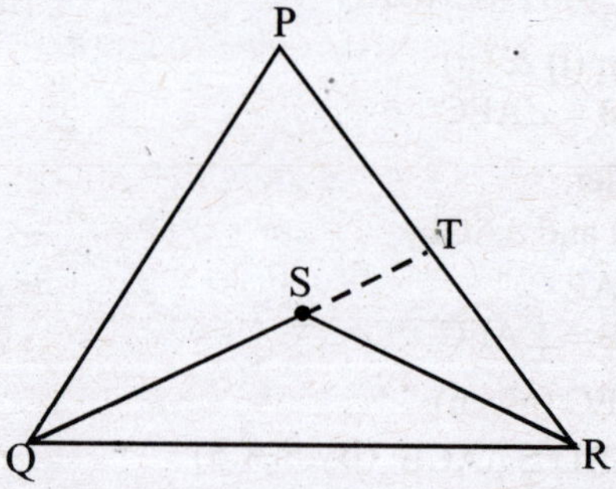

From ΔPQT, we have

$PQ + PT > QT$ (Sum of any two sides is greater than the third side)

i.e., $PQ + PT > SQ + ST$ ...(i)

From ΔTSR, we have

$ST + TR > SR$ ...(ii)

Adding (i) and (ii), we get

$PQ + PT + ST + TR > SQ + ST + SR$

i.e., $PQ + PT + TR > SQ + SR$

i.e., $PQ + PR > SQ + SR$

or $SQ + SR < PQ + PR$

HOTS QUESTIONS :

1. (i) In ΔABM and ΔPQN

$AB = PQ$ ....(i)

$AM = PN$ ....(ii) (Given)

and $BC = QR$ (Given)

Since, M and N are the mid-points of BC and QR respectively

$\therefore 2BM = 2QN$

$\Rightarrow BM = QN$ ....(iii)

From, (i), (ii) and (iii)

$\Delta ABM = \Delta PQN$ (SSS Rule)

(ii) From (i) part $\Delta ABM \cong \Delta PQN$

$\therefore$ By C.P.C.T.

$\angle ABM = \angle PQN$

$\Rightarrow \angle ABC = \angle PQR$ ....(iv)

Now, in ΔABC and ΔPQR, we have given

$AB = PQ$

and $BC = QR$

$\therefore$ From (iv), we have $\angle ABC = \angle PQR$

$\therefore \Delta ABC = \Delta PQR.$ (SAS Rule)

2.

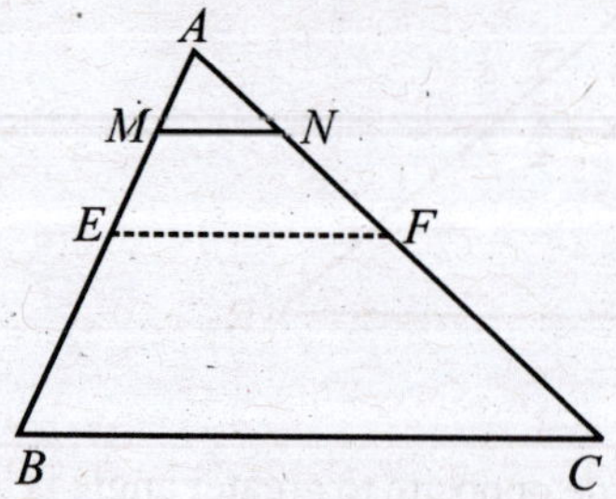

We construct a line EF where E and F are the middle points of AB and AC respectively.

$EF \parallel BC$ and $EF = \frac{1}{2}BC$ ... ...(i)

($\because$ E and F are mid points)

Now, $AE = \frac{1}{2}AB$ and $AM = \frac{1}{4}AB$

$\therefore \quad AM = \frac{1}{2}AE$

Similarly, $AN = \frac{1}{2}AF$

$\Rightarrow$ M and N are the mid-points of AE and AF respectively.

$\therefore \quad MN \parallel EF$ and

$MN = \frac{1}{2}EF = \frac{1}{2}\left(\frac{1}{2}AE\right)$ [From (i)]

$= \frac{1}{4}BC$

3. We join AQ and CP.

(i) ar (ΔPRQ) = ar(ΔARQ)

$= \frac{1}{2}$ ar (ΔAPQ) $= \frac{1}{2}$ ar (ΔBPQ)

$= \frac{1}{2}$ ar (ΔCPQ) $= \frac{1}{2}\cdot\frac{1}{2}$ ar (ΔBPC)

$= \frac{1}{4}$ ar (ΔBPC) $= \frac{1}{4}\cdot\frac{1}{2}$ ar (ΔABC)

$= \frac{1}{8}$ ar (ΔABC) ....(1)

Also, $\frac{1}{2}$ ar(ΔARC) $= \frac{1}{2}\cdot\frac{1}{2}$ ar(ΔAPC)

$= \frac{1}{4}$ ar $(\Delta APC) = \frac{1}{4} \cdot \frac{1}{2}$ ar (ΔABC)

$= \frac{1}{8}$ ar (ΔABC) ....(2)

From (1) and (2), we have,

ar$(\Delta PRQ) = \frac{1}{2}$ ar (ΔARC)

(ii) ar $(\Delta RQC) =$ ar (ΔRBQ)
$=$ ar $(\Delta PRQ) +$ ar (ΔBPQ)

$= \frac{1}{8}$ ar $(\Delta ABC) + \frac{1}{2}$ ar (ΔPBC) [Using(i)]

$= \frac{1}{8}$ ar $(\Delta ABC) + \frac{1}{2} \cdot \frac{1}{2}$ ar (ΔABC)

$= \frac{1}{8}$ ar $(\Delta ABC) + \frac{1}{4}$ ar $(\Delta ABC) = \frac{3}{8}$ ar (ΔABC)

4. **Given:** $\angle B = 2\angle C$ ...(i)

AD is angle bisector of $\angle$A and $AB = DC$

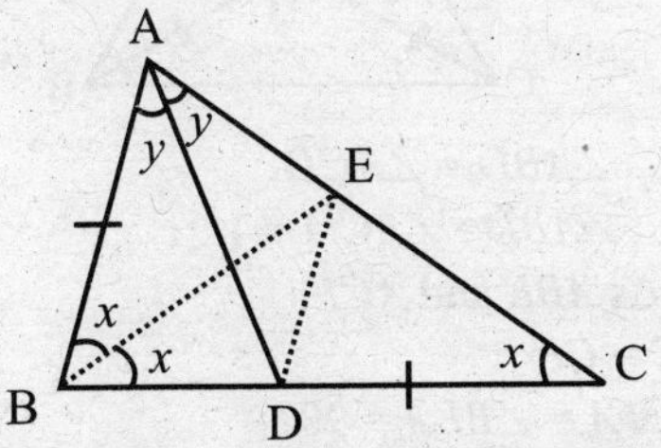

Construction: Draw BE as angle bisector of $\angle B$. Join DE.

If $\angle C = x \Rightarrow \angle ABE = \angle EBC = x$.

Proof: Since AD is bisector of $\angle A$,

Let $\angle BAD = \angle CAD = y$.

Now, $\angle EBC = \angle ECB = x$

$\Rightarrow$ EB = EC

ΔEBC is an isosceles triangle

Consider $\Delta ABE \cong \Delta DCE$ (By SAS Congruency)

$\Rightarrow \angle EDC = 2y$ [C.P.C.T.]....(i)

and $EA = ED$ [.C.P.C.T.]

Consider isosceles ΔAED as $EA = ED$

$\angle EDA = \angle EAD = y$. ... (ii)

From (i) and (ii)

$\angle ADC = y + 2y = 3y$ ...(iii)

Also, $\angle ADC = 2x + y$ ... (iv)

[Exterior angles of ΔABD]

From (iii) and (iv)

$3y = 2x + y$

$\Rightarrow x = y$ ... (v)

Now consider ΔABC,

$\angle A + \angle B + \angle C = 180°$

$2y + 2x + x = 180°$

$\Rightarrow 5y = 180°$ [*As x = y from* (v)]

$\Rightarrow 2y = 72°$

$\Rightarrow \angle A = 72°$

5. **Given :** A ΔABC in which AD is a median.

To Prove: $AB + AC > 2AD$

Construction: Produce AD to E such that $AD = DE$. Join EC

Proof: In triangle ADB and EDC, we have

$AD = DE$ (By construction)

$BD = DC$ ($\because$ AD is the median)

and, $\angle ADB = \angle EDC$ (Vertically opposite angles)

$\therefore \Delta ADB \cong \Delta EDC$ (SAS congruence criterion)

$\Rightarrow AB = EC$ (CPCT) ...(i)

In ΔAEC, we have

$AC + EC > AE$ ...(ii)

[As sum of the two sides of a triangle is greater than the third side]

Also, $AE = 2AD$ (by constructions) ...(iii)

Using (i) and (iii) in (ii), we get

$AC + AB > 2AD$

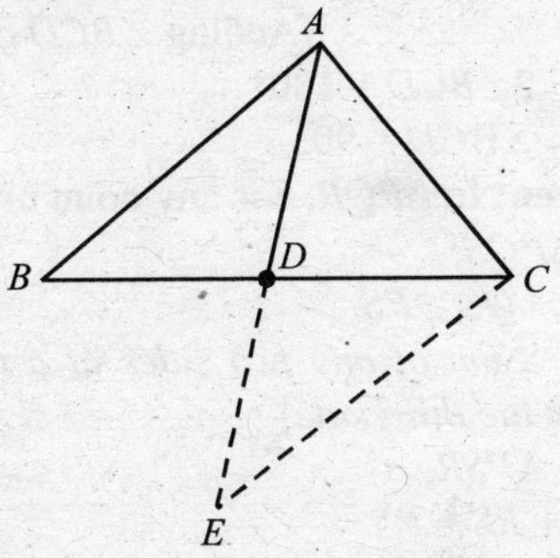

6. Let ΔABC be a triangle in which AC is longest side.

$\Rightarrow \angle B$ is largest angle

$\Rightarrow \angle B > \angle A$ ...(i)

and $\angle B > \angle C$ ...(ii)

Adding (i) and (ii), we get

$\angle B + \angle B > \angle A + \angle C$

$\Rightarrow 2\angle B > \angle A + \angle C$

$\Rightarrow 2\angle B + \angle B > \angle A + \angle B + \angle C$

$\Rightarrow 3\angle B > 180° \Rightarrow \angle B > 60°$

$\Rightarrow \angle B > \frac{2}{3} \times$ right angle. [**Note:** $60° = \frac{2}{3} \times 90°$]

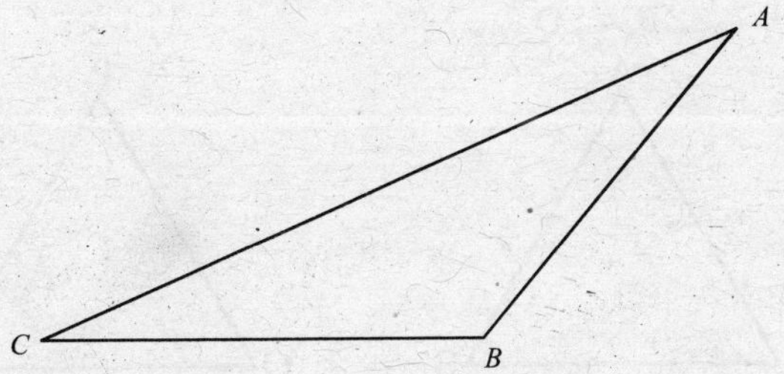

3 EXERCISE

SINGLE OPTION CORRECT :

1. (d) **2.** (a) **3.** (b) **4.** (a)

5. (a)

6. (b) Given, $AB = AC$ and $AD = AB$

Now, as we know that angles opposite to equal sides are equal.

Thus, $\angle ABC = \angle ACB$ ...(i)

and, $\angle ADC = \angle ACD$ ...(ii)

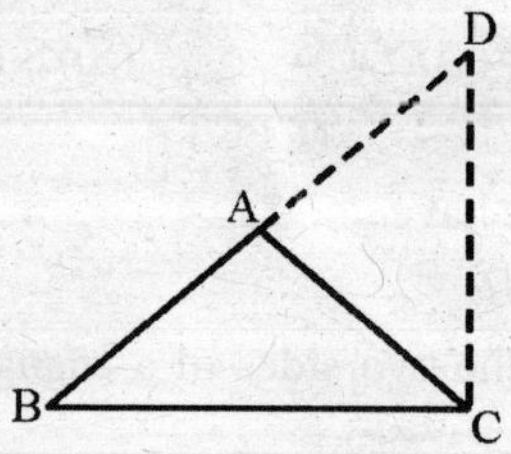

Adding (i) and (ii), we get

$\angle ABC + \angle ADC = \angle ACB + \angle ACD$

$\Rightarrow \angle BCD = \angle ABC + \angle ADC$

$\Rightarrow \angle BCD + \angle BCD = \angle ABC + \angle ADC + \angle BCD$

[Adding $\angle BCD$ on both sides]

$\Rightarrow 2\angle BCD = 180°$

$\Rightarrow \angle BCD = 90°$

7. **(a)** **Given:** In ΔPQR, S is any point on the side QR.

In ΔPQS,

$PQ + QS > PS$ ...(i)

[$\because$ *Sum of any two sides of a triangle is greater than the third side*]

In ΔPSR,

$PR + RS > PS$ ...(ii)

[$\because$ *Sum of any two sides of a triangle is greater than the third side*]

Adding (i) and (ii),

$(PQ + QS) + (PR + RS) > 2PS$

$PQ + (QS + RS) + PR > 2PS$

or $PQ + QR + RP > 2PS$

8. **(a)** If $\Delta ABC \cong \Delta PQR$, then their respective congruent sides and angles will be as follows

$AB = PQ$, $\angle A = \angle P$

$BC = QR$, $\angle B = \angle Q$

$AC = PR$, $\angle C = \angle R$

Thus, only (a) is not true.

9. **(a)** Given, $AB = PQ$

$\angle B = \angle Q$

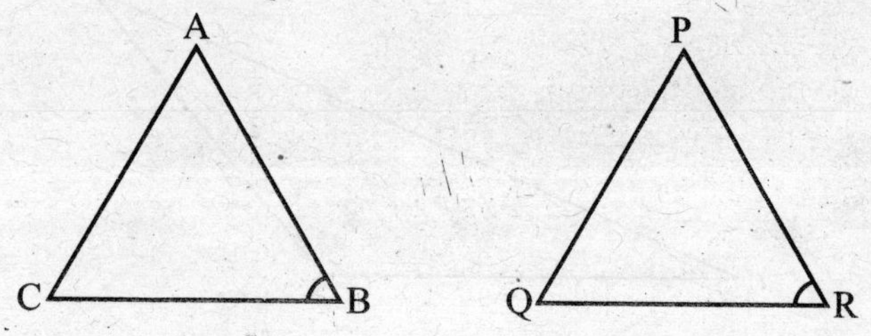

In order for ΔABC to be congruent to ΔPQR by SAS axiom corresponding sides BC and QR should be equal.

10. **(b)** In ΔABC

Given, $\angle C > \angle B$

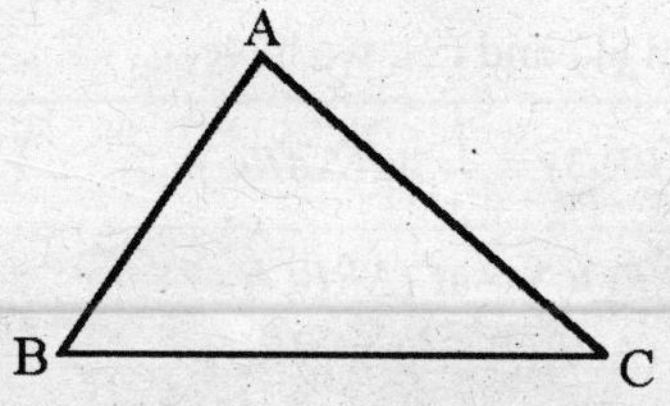

We know that in a triangle the greater angle has the longer side opposite to it.

Thus, $AB > AC$

11. **(a)** Join A to D,

then $\Delta ABD \cong \Delta ACD$ [SSS Criterion]

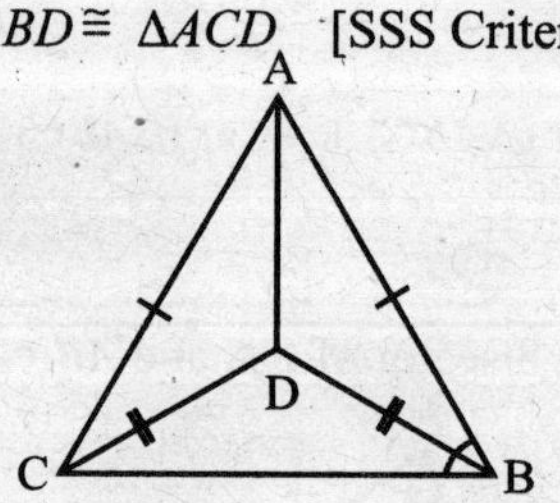

$\Rightarrow \angle ABD = \angle ACD$ [CPCT]

$\therefore \angle ABD : \angle ACD = 1 : 1$

12. **(a)** In Δs ABE and ACF,

$BE = CF$

$\angle CFA = \angle BEA = 90°$

$\angle A$ is common.

Hence, $\Delta ABE \cong \Delta ACF$ [AAS Criterion]

13. **(b)** In right triangles BEC and BFC, we have

Hyp. BC = Hyp. BC (Common)

$BE = CF$ (Given)

So, by *RHS* criterion of congruence

$\Delta BEC \cong \Delta BFC$

$\Rightarrow \angle B = \angle C$ [C.P.C.T.]

$\Rightarrow AC = AB$ ...(i)

Similarly, $\Delta ABD \cong \Delta ABE$

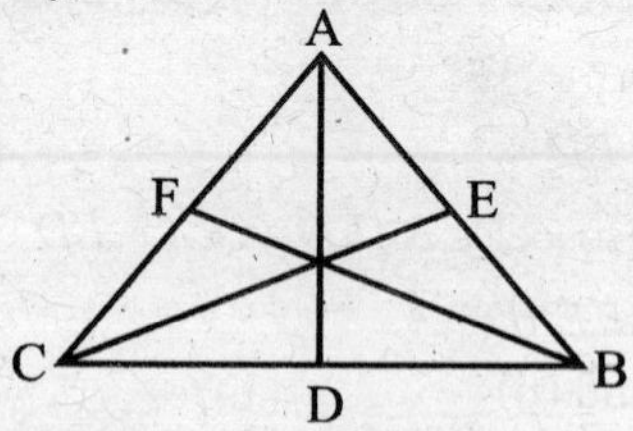

$\Rightarrow \angle B = \angle A$ [C.P.C.T.]

and $AC = BC$ ...(ii)

From (i) and (ii), we get

$AB = BC = AC$

Hence, ΔABC is an equilateral triangle.

14. **(b)** In ΔACB and ΔADB

$AC = AD$ [Given]

$\angle CAB = \angle DAB$ [Given]

$AB = AB$ [Common]

$\therefore \Delta ACB \cong \Delta ADB$ [SAS]

15. (b) In ΔABD and ΔACD

$AB = AC$ [Given]

$BD = CD$ [Given]

$AD = AD$ [Common]

$\therefore \Delta ABD \cong \Delta ACD$ [SSS congruency criterion]

$\therefore \angle BAD = \angle CAD$ [CPCT]

$\Rightarrow x = 37^\circ$

and, $\angle BDA = \angle CDA$ [CPCT]

$\Rightarrow y - 70^\circ$

MORE THAN ONE OPTION CORRECT :

1. (a, b, c)
2. (a, b, d)
3. (a, b, c) All the definitions given in options (a), (b) and (c) are correct.
4. (a, b, c) All the given statements are correct.

PASSAGE BASED QUESTIONS ;

1. (a) In ΔABC, AB > AC

$\Rightarrow \angle C > \angle B$ [Greater side has greater angle opp. to it]

$\Rightarrow \frac{1}{2}\angle C > \frac{1}{2}\angle B$

$\Rightarrow \angle PCB > \angle PBC$

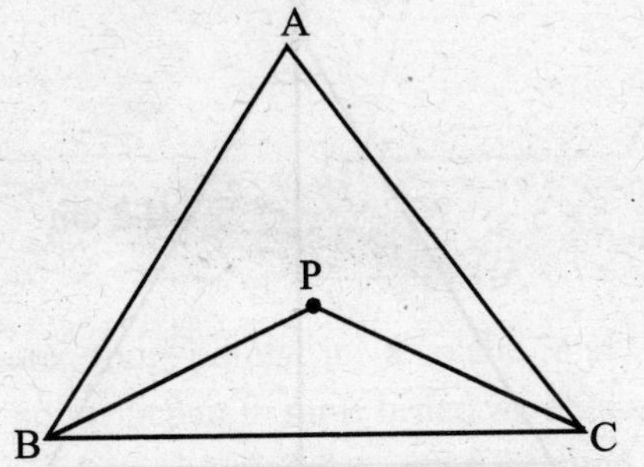

$\left\{ \angle PCB - \frac{1}{2}\angle C \text{ and } \angle PCB - \frac{1}{2}\angle B \right.$ as PB and PC are bisector of ∠B and ∠C$\left. \right\}$

In ΔPBC, ∠PCB > ∠PBC

$\Rightarrow$ PB > PC

2. (b) We have

$\angle C > \angle B$

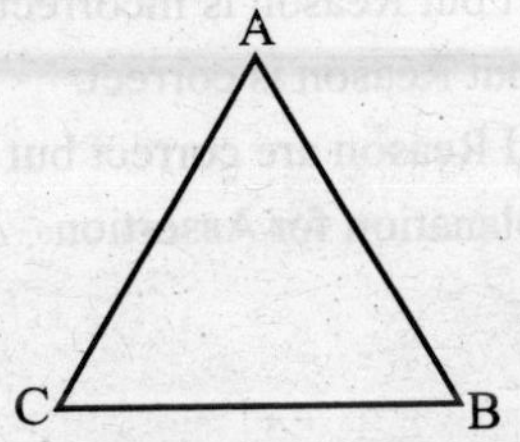

$\Rightarrow$ AB > AC [Greater angle has longer side opp. to it]

ASSERTION AND REASON :

1. (d)
2. (d)
3. (c) Assertion is correct and Reason is incorrect.
4. (c) Assertion is correct and Reason is incorrect.
5. (d) Assertion is incorrect but Reason is correct.

INTEGER TYPE QUESTIONS :

1. Ans : 8

$x + x + 110^\circ = 180^\circ$

$\Rightarrow 2x = 70^\circ \Rightarrow x = 35^\circ$

So, sum of digit = 8

2. Ans : 4

Let angles be 7x, 6x and 2x.

$7x + 6x + 2x = 180^\circ \Rightarrow 15x = 180^\circ$

$\therefore x = 12^\circ$

$\therefore$ Smallest angle $= 2 \times 12 = 24^\circ$.

3. Ans : 4

In rt. ΔABQ

$AQ^2 = AB^2 + BQ^2$

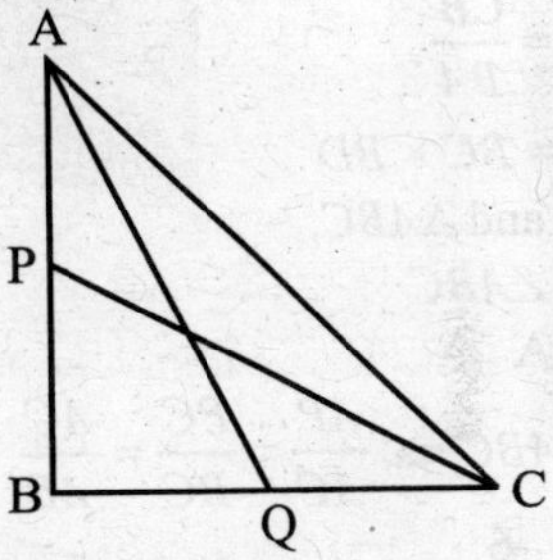

$= AB^2 + \left(\frac{BC}{2}\right)^2$

$= AB^2 + \frac{BC^2}{4}$ ...(i)

In rt. ΔPBC

$PC^2 = BP^2 + BC^2$

$= \left(\frac{AB}{2}\right)^2 + BC^2$

$= \frac{AB^2}{4} + BC^2$ ...(ii)

Adding (i) and (ii)

$AQ^2 + PC^2 = AB^2 + BC^2 + \frac{AB^2 + BC^2}{4}$

$= AC^2 + \frac{AC^2}{4} = \frac{5AC^2}{4}$

4 ADVANCED EXERCISE
BASED ON CONNECTING TOPICS

1. (b) As in ΔADE ans ΔABC

$\frac{AD}{AB} = \frac{8}{20} = \frac{2}{5}, \frac{AE}{AC} = \frac{6}{15} = \frac{2}{5}$

So, $\frac{AD}{AB} = \frac{AE}{EC}$

⇒ $BP = CR$

Also, $AP = PB$ [As, P is mid-point of AB]

∴ $CR = AP$

$AB \parallel CR$ and AC is transversal, ⇒ $\angle PAQ$ = alternate $\angle RCQ$

$AB \parallel CR$ and PR is transversal, ⇒ $\angle APQ$ = alternate $\angle CRQ$

In ΔAPQ and ΔCRQ

$AP = CR$, $\angle PAQ = \angle RCQ$ and $\angle APQ = \angle CRQ$

⇒ $\Delta APQ \cong \Delta CRQ$ (A.S.A rule)

⇒ $AQ = CQ$ (CPCT)

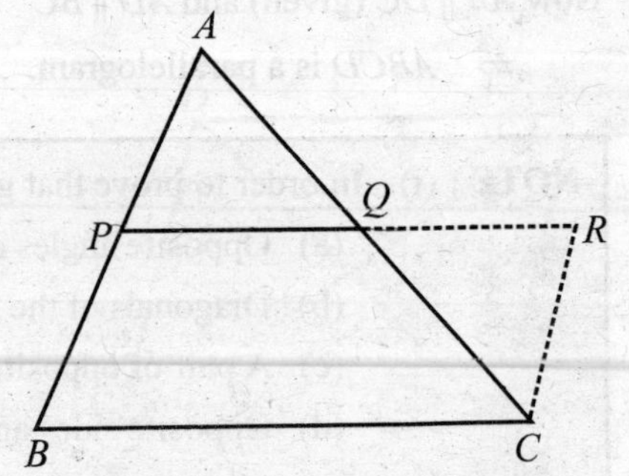

Theorem 11 : If there are three or more parallel lines and the intercepts made by them on a transversal are equal, then the corresponding intercepts on any other transversal are also equal.

Given : Three parallel lines ℓ, m and n i.e., $\ell \parallel m \parallel n$.

A transversal p meets these parallel lines at points A, B and C respectively such that $AB = BC$.

Another transversal q also meets these parallel lines at ℓ, m and n at points D, E and F respectively.

To Prove : $DE = EF$

Construction : Through point A, draw a line parallel to DEF ; which meets BE at point P and CF at point Q.

Proof : In ΔACQ, B is mid-point of AC and BP is parallel to CQ and we know that the line through the mid-point of one side of a triangle and parallel to another side bisects its third side.

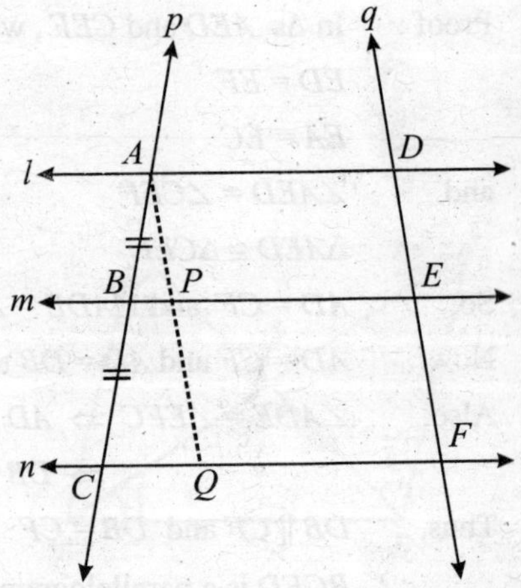

∴ $AP = PQ$ .... (i)

∵ $AP \parallel DE$ and $AD \parallel PE$ [By construction]

⇒ $APED$ is a parallelogram.

∴ $AP = DE$ .... (ii)

and $PQ \parallel EF$ and $PE \parallel QF$ [By construction]

⇒ $PQFE$ is a parallelogram

⇒ $PQ = EF$ .... (iii)

From (i), (ii) and (iii) we get, $DE = EF$

ILLUSTRATION : 2

In ΔABC, D, E and F are respectively the mid-points of sides AB, BC and CA. Show that ΔABC is divided into four congruent triangles by joining D, E and F.

SOLUTION :

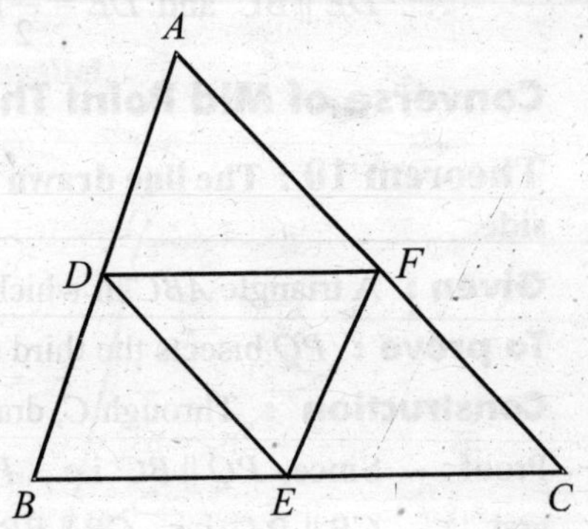

As D and E mid-points of sides AB and BC respectively of the triangle ABC.

∴ $DE \parallel AC$

Similarly, $DF \parallel BC$ and $EF \parallel AB$

Therefore, $ADEF$, $BDFE$ and $DFCE$ are all parallelograms.

Now, DE is a diagonal of the parallelogram $BDFE$,

therefore, $\Delta BDE \cong \Delta FED$

Similarly, $\Delta DAF \cong \Delta FED$

and $\Delta EFC \cong \Delta FED$

So, all the four triangles are congruent.

MISCELLANEOUS SOLVED EXAMPLES

1. Prove that the quadrilateral formed by joining the mid points of the adjacent sides of a quadrilateral is a parallelogram.

Sol. Consider a quadrilateral $ABCD$, in which P, Q, R and S are the mid points of sides respectively.

Join AC

In ΔABC, P and Q are the mid-points of the sides AB and BC respectively. Since we know that the line drawn through the mid-point of one side of a triangle parallel to another side bisects the third side

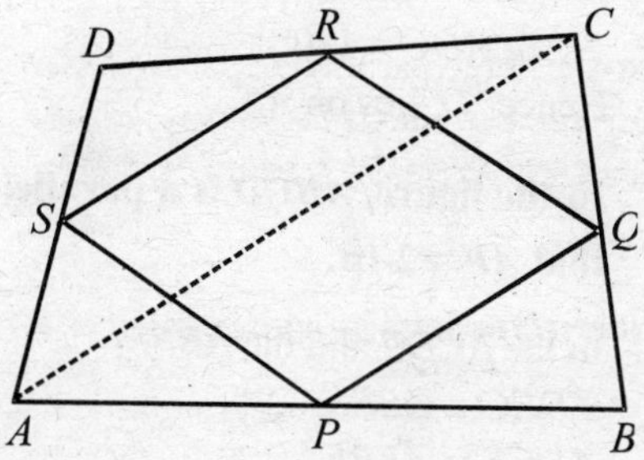

So, $PQ \parallel AC$ and $PQ = \frac{1}{2} AC$ .....(i)

Similarly, S and R are the mid points of the sides AD and DC respectively.

$\therefore$ $SR \parallel AC$ and $SR = \frac{1}{2} AC$ .....(ii)

From (i) and (ii), we get

$PQ \parallel SR$ and $PQ = SR = \frac{1}{2} AC$

Therefore $PQRS$ is a parallelogram.

2. In the adjoining kite, diagonals intersect at O. If $\angle ABO = 32°$ and $\angle OCD = 40°$, find

(i) $\angle ABC$ (ii) $\angle ADC$ (iii) $\angle BAD$

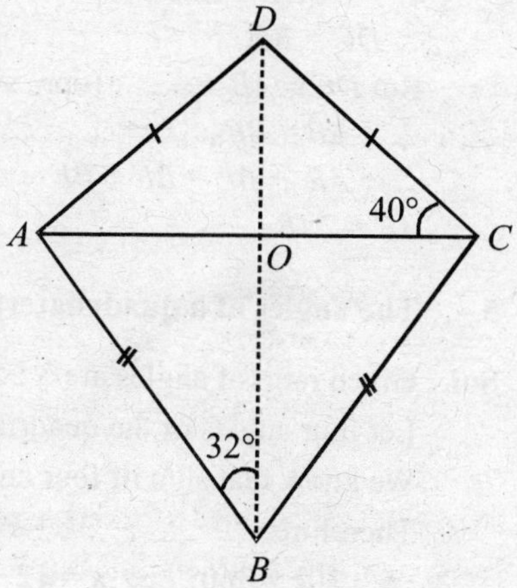

Sol. Given, $ABCD$ is a kite.

(i) As diagonal BD bisects $\angle ABC$,

$\angle ABC = 2\angle ABO = 2 \times 32° = 64°$

(ii) $\angle DOC = 90°$ [diagonals intersect at right angles]

$\angle ODC + 40° + 90° = 180°$ [sum of angles in ΔOCD]

$\Rightarrow$ $\angle ODC = 180° - 40° - 90° = 50°$

As diagonal BD bisects $\angle ADC$,

$\angle ADC = 2\angle ODC = 2 \times 50° = 100°$

(iii) As diagonal BD bisects $\angle ABC$

$\angle OBC = \angle ABO = 32°$

$\angle BOC = 90°$ [diagonals intersect at right angles]

$\angle OCB + 90° + 32° = 180°$ [sum of angles in ΔOBC]

$\Rightarrow$ $\angle OCB = 180° - 90° - 32° = 58°$

$\angle BCD = \angle OCD + \angle OCB = 40° + 58° = 98°$

$\therefore$ $\angle BAD = \angle BCD = 98°$ [In kite $ABCD$, $\angle A = \angle C$]

3. In a quadrilateral (kite) $ABCD$ there is a point 'O' inside it such that $OB = OD$. Prove that 'O' lies on AC.

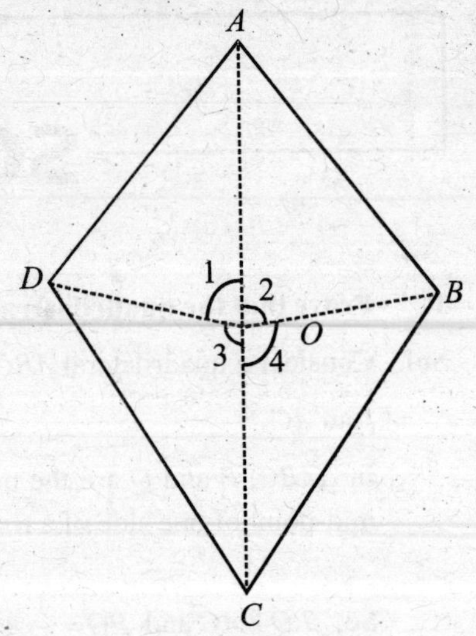

Sol. In the ΔAOD and the ΔAOB.

$AD = AB$ (given)

$OD = OB$ (given)

$OA = OA$ (common)

$\therefore \quad \Delta AOD \cong \Delta AOB$

$\therefore \quad \angle 1 = \angle 2$ .... (i) (C.P.C.T.)

Similarly in the ΔCDO and ΔCBO

$\angle 3 = \angle 4$ .... (ii)

Adding eqs (i) and (ii), we get

$\angle 1 + \angle 3 = \angle 2 + \angle 4$

But $\angle 1 + \angle 2 + \angle 3 + \angle 4 = 360°$

$\therefore \quad 2(\angle 1 + \angle 3) = 360°$

$\Rightarrow \quad \angle 1 + \angle 3 = 180°$

$\therefore \quad \angle AOC = 180°$

Hence 'O' lies on AC.

4. In the figure, $ABCD$ is a parallelogram. E is the mid-point of BC. Also DE and AB, when produced meet at F. Prove that $AF = 2AB$.

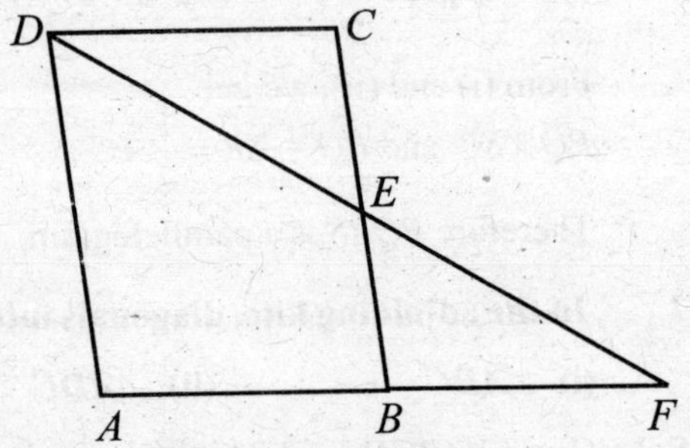

Sol. In the ΔCDE and the ΔBFE,

$\angle DEC = \angle BEF$ (vert. opp. angles)

$\angle DCE = \angle EBF$ (alt. angles)

$CE = EB$

$\therefore \quad \Delta CDE \cong \Delta BFE$

$\therefore DC = BF$

But $DC = AB$ (opp. sides of a parallellogram)

$\therefore \quad AB = BF$

$\therefore \quad AB + BF = BF + BF = AB + AB$ $(\because AB = BF)$

$AF = 2AB$

5. The angles of a quadrilaterals are in the ratio 3 : 5 : 9 : 13. Find all the angles of the quadrilaterals.

Sol. Given ratio of angles are 3 : 5 : 9 : 13

Let four angles of the quadrilateral be $3k$, $5k$, $9k$ and $13k$.

We know that sum of four angles of a quadrilateral is 360°

Therefore, $\quad 3k + 5k + 9k + 13k = 360°$

$\Rightarrow \quad 30k = 360° \Rightarrow k = 12$

Therefore four angles are $(3 \times 12)°$, $(5 \times 12)°$, $(9 \times 12)°$ and $(13 \times 12)°$ or 36°, 60°, 108°, 156°.

6. ABC is an isosceles in which $AB = AC$. AD bisects exterior angle PAC and $CD \parallel AB$. Show that

(i) $\angle DAC = \angle BCA$ and (ii) $ABCD$ is a parallelogram.

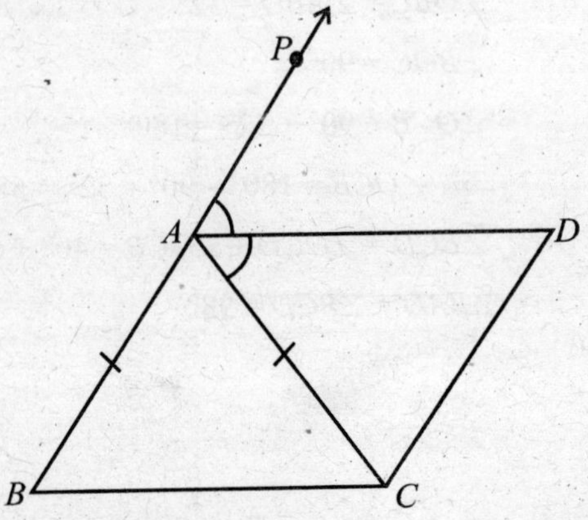

Sol. (i) ΔABC is an isosceles in which $AB = AC$ (Given)

So, $\angle ABC = \angle ACB$ (angles opposite to equal sides)

Also, $\angle PAC = \angle ABC + \angle ACB$ (Exterior angle of a triangle)

or $\angle PAC = 2\angle ACB$ .... (i)

Now, AD bisects $\angle PAC$

So, $\angle PAC = 2\angle DAC$ .... (ii)

Therefore, $2\angle DAC = 2\angle ACB$ [From (i) and (ii)]

or $\angle DAC = \angle ACB$

(ii) Now, these equal angles form a pair of alternate angles because line segments BC and AD are intersected by a transversal AC.

So, $BC \parallel AD$

Also, $BA \parallel CD$ (Given)

Now, both pairs of opposite sides of quadrilateral $ABCD$ are parallel.

So, $ABCD$ is a parallelogram.

7. Show that the bisectors of angles of a parallelogram form a rectangle.

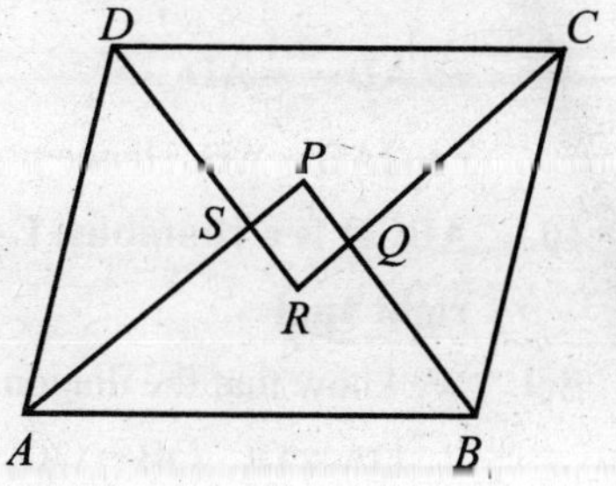

Sol. Let P, Q, R and S be the points of intersection of the bisectors of $\angle A$ and $\angle B$, $\angle B$ and $\angle C$, $\angle C$ and $\angle D$, and $\angle D$ and $\angle A$ respectively of parallelogram $ABCD$

Since DS bisects $\angle D$ and AS bisects $\angle A$, therefore,

$$\angle DAS + \angle ADS = \frac{1}{2}\angle A + \frac{1}{2}\angle D$$

$$= \frac{1}{2}(\angle A + \angle D) = \frac{1}{2} \times 180^\circ = 90^\circ \quad (\because \angle A \text{ and } \angle D \text{ are interior angles on the same side of the transversal})$$

Also, $\angle DAS + \angle ADS + \angle DSA = 180°$

or $90° + \angle DSA = 180°$

or $\angle DSA = 90°$

or $\angle PSR = \angle DSA = 90°$ (Being vertically opposite to $\angle DSA$)

Similarly, it can be shown that

$\angle SPQ = \angle PQR = \angle QRS = 90°$

So, $PQRS$ is a rectangle.

8. $ABCD$ is a trapezium in which $AB \parallel DC$, BD is a diagonal and E is the mid-point of AD. A line is drawn through E parallel to AB intersecting BC at F (as shown). Prove that F is the mid-point of BC.

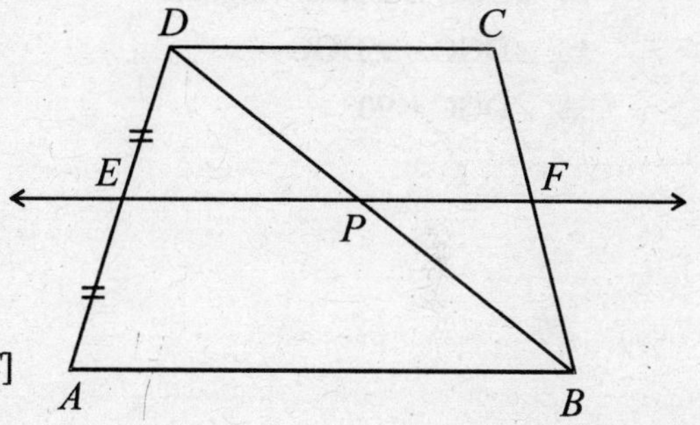

Sol. Given line EF is parallel to AB and $AB \parallel DC$

i.e. $EF \parallel AB \parallel DC$.

In ΔABD, E is the mid-point of AD

EP is parallel to AB (As $EF \parallel AB$)

$\therefore$ P is mid-point of side BD. [Since, the line through the mid-point of a side of a triangle and parallel to the other side, bisects the third side]

Now, in ΔBCD, P is mid-point of BD and, PF is parallel to DC [As $EF \parallel DC$]

$\therefore$ F is mid-point of BC

9. In a parallelogram $ABCD$, the bisector of $\angle A$ also bisects BC at X. Prove that $AD = 2AB$.

Sol.

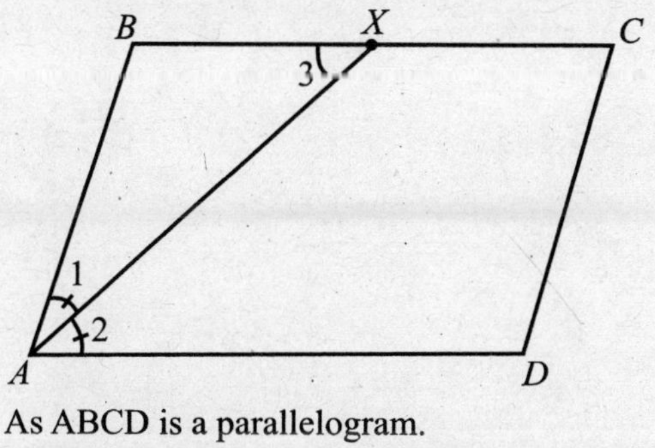

As ABCD is a parallelogram.

$\therefore$ AD || BC

Also, AX is a transversal

$\therefore \angle 3 = \angle 2$ (Alternate angles)

$\angle 1 = \angle 2$ (... AX is bisector of $\angle$A)

$\Rightarrow \angle 1 = \angle 3$

In ΔABX, we have

$\angle 1 = \angle 3$ (Proved above)

$\Rightarrow AB = BX$ (Sides opposite to equal angles are equal)

$\Rightarrow AB = \frac{1}{2}BC$ (X is the mid-point of BC)

Also, $AD = BC$ (Opposite sides of parallelogram are equal)

$\Rightarrow AB = \frac{1}{2}AD$

$\Rightarrow 2AB = AD$. Hence proved

10. ABCD is a rhombus, EABF is a straight line such that EA = AB = BF. Prove that ED and FC when produced meet at right angles.

Sol. We know that the diagonals of a rhombus are perpendicular bisector of each other.

$\therefore$ $OA = OC$, $OB = OD$, $\angle AOD = \angle COD = 90°$

and, $\angle AOB = \angle COB = 90°$

In ΔBDE, A and O are mid-points of BE and BD respectively.

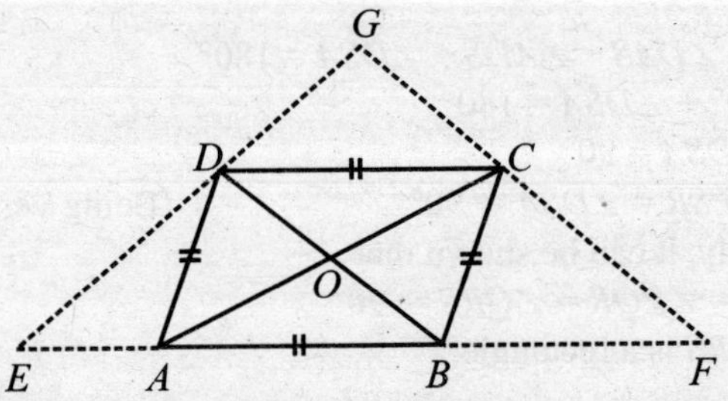

$\therefore$ $OA \parallel DE$

$\Rightarrow OC \parallel DG$

In ΔCFA, B and O are mid-points AF and AC respectively

$\therefore$ $OB \parallel CF$

$\Rightarrow OD \parallel GC$

Thus, in quadrilateral DOCG, we have

$OC \parallel DG$ and $OD \parallel GC$

$\Rightarrow$ DOCG is a parallelogram.

$\therefore$ $\angle DGC = \angle DOC$

$\Rightarrow \angle DGC = 90°$

1 EXERCISE

Fill in the Blanks :

DIRECTIONS: *Complete the following statements with an appropriate word / term to be filled in the blank space(s).*

1. A quadrilateral is a parallelogram if and only if its pair of opposite sides are ....
2. Sum of the angles of a .... is 360°
3. The diagonals of a quadrilateral bisect each other if and only if it is a ....
4. The diagonals of a rhombus bisect each other at ....
5. If the diagonals of a parallelogram are equal, it is a ....
6. If in a quadrilateral only one pair of opposite sides are parallel, the quadrilateral is a ....
7. The triangle formed by joining the mid-point of the side of an isosceles triangles is ....
8. The triangle formed by joining the mid-points of the sides of a right triangle is ....
9. The figure formed by joining the mid-points of the consecutive sides of a quadrilateral is ....
10. If the diagonals of a parallelogram are equal, then it is a ....

True / False :

DIRECTIONS: *Read the following statements and write your answer as true or false.*

1. In a parallelogram ABCD, sum of angles A and B is 180°.
2. The figure formed by joining the mid-points of the adjacent sides of a quadrilateral is a parallelogram.
3. Diagonals necessarily bisect opposite angles in a square.
4. We get a rhombus by joining the mid-points of the sides of a rectangle.
5. In a parallelogram, the diagonals are equal.
6. In a parallelogram, the diagonals intersect at right angles.
7. If all angles of a quadrilateral are equal, it is a parallelogram.
8. Every square is a rectangle.
9. Every rectangle is a parallelogram.
10. The sum of the interior angles of a quadrilateral is 180°.
11. If the diagonals of a quadrilateral divide it into four triangles which are equal in area, then the quadrilateral must be a parallelogram.

Match the Columns :

DIRECTIONS: *Each question contains statements given in two columns which have to be matched. Statements (A, B, C, D) in Column I have to be matched with statements (p, q, r, s) in Column II.*

1.

Column-I	Column-II
(A) In a parallelogram ABCD, if $\angle D = 115°$, then the measure of $\angle A$ is	(p) 68°
(B) *PQRS* is a square such that *PR* and *SQ* intersect at *O*. The measure of $\angle POQ$ is	(q) 58°
(C) The diagonals of a rectangle ABCD meet at O. If $\angle BOC = 44°$, then the measure of $\angle OAD$ is	(r) 90°
(D) If ABCD is a rectangle with $\angle BAC = 32°$, then the measure of $\angle DBC$ is	(s) 65°

2.

Column-I	Column-II
(A) Square, rectangle and rhombus are	(p) quadrilateral
(B) Kite and trapezium are	(q) parallelograms
(C) All squares are	(r) not parallelograms
(D) All parallelograms are	(s) rectangles

Very Short Answer Questions :

DIRECTIONS: *Give answer in one word or one sentence.*

1. ABCD is a trapezium in which AB || DC, BD is a diagonal and E is the mid-point of AD. A line is drawn through E parallel to AB intersecting BC at F. Show that F is the mid-point of BC.

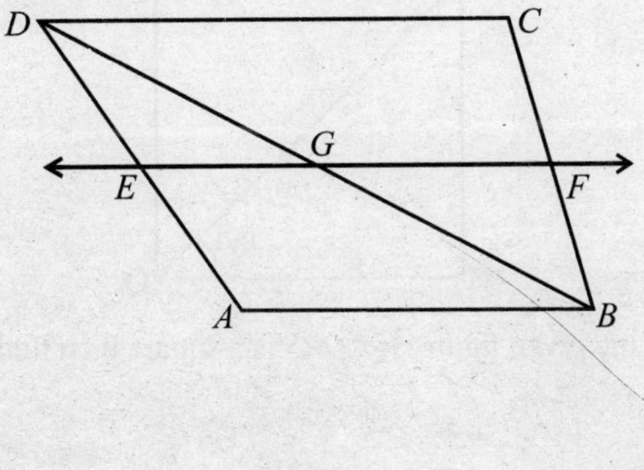

2. In fig, ABCD and AEFG are two parallelograms. If $\angle C = 50°$, determine $\angle F$.

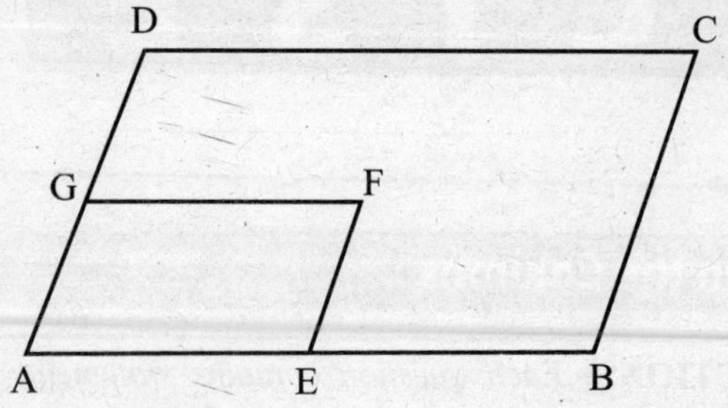

3. In quadrilateral ABCD, bisectors of angles A and B intersect at O such that $\angle AOB = 75°$, then find the value of $\angle C + \angle D$.

4. If ABCD is a rhombus with $\angle ABC = 56°$, then find the measure of $\angle ACD$.

5. In parallelogram ABCD, if $\angle A = (3x - 20)°$, $\angle B = (y + 15)°$, $\angle C = (x + 40)°$, then find the values of x and y.

6. If measures of opposite angles of a parallelogram are $(60 - x)°$ and $(3x - 4)°$, then find the measures of angles of the parallelogram.

7. The figure formed by joining the mid-points of the adjacent sides of a rhombus is known as ________

8. Find all the other three angles of a parallelogram, if one of its angles is given to be

(i) 70° (ii) 135°

(iii) 95°

Short Answer Questions :

DIRECTIONS: *Give answer in 2-3 sentences.*

1. ΔABC is an isosceles triangle in which $AB = AC$. AD bisects exterior angle PAC and $CD \parallel AB$. Show that

(i) $\angle DAC = \angle BCA$ and (ii) ABCD is a parallelogram.

2. In a parallelogram ABCD, bisectors of two adjacent angles A and B meet at O. Find the measure of the angle AOB.

3. In the given figure, PQRS is a square. Find the measure of $\angle SQR$.

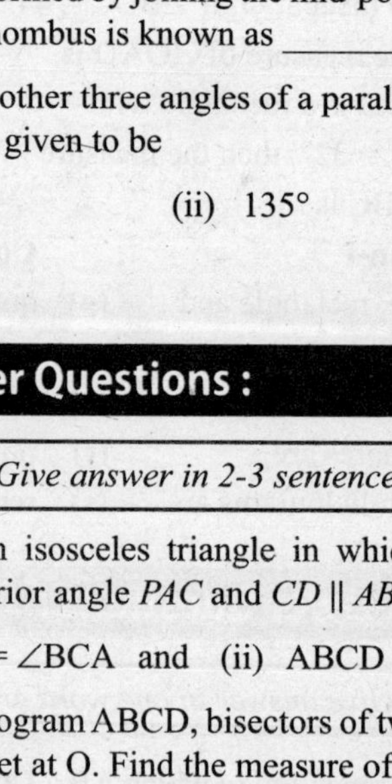

4. In the given figure, if $PQRS$ is a square then find the value of x.

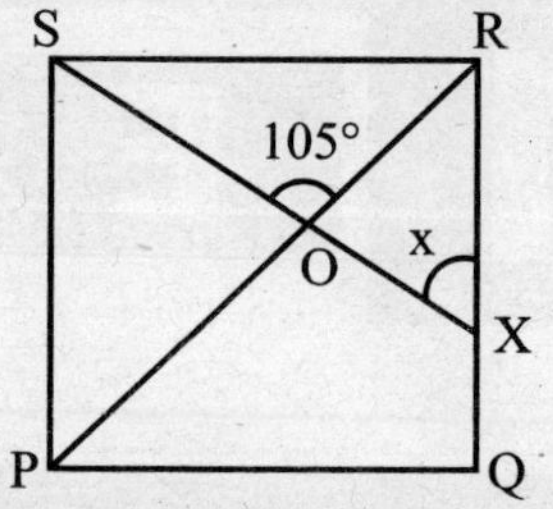

5. If the sides BA and DC of quadrilateral ABCD are produced as shown in the figure, then prove that $x + y = a + b$.

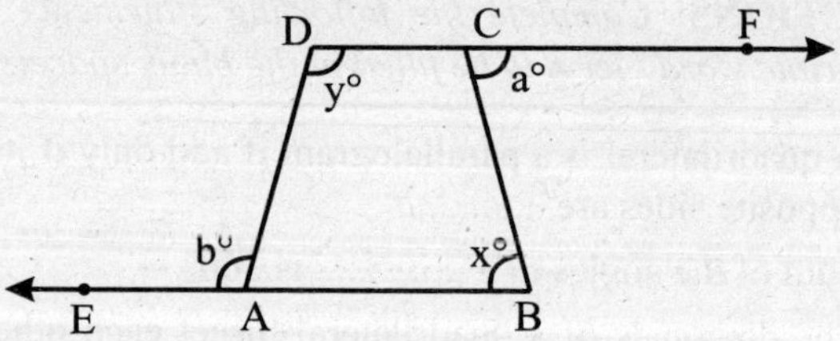

6. In a parallelogram ABCD, diagonals AC and BD intersect at O and AC = 12.8 cm and BD = 7.6 cm. Find the measure of OC and OD.

7. The length and breadth of a rectangle are in the ratio 4 : 3. If the diagonal measures 25 cm, then find the perimeter of the rectangle.

8. In the given figure, $ABCD$ is a quadrilateral, the line segments bisecting $\angle C$ and $\angle D$ meet at E. Then find the value of $2\angle CED$

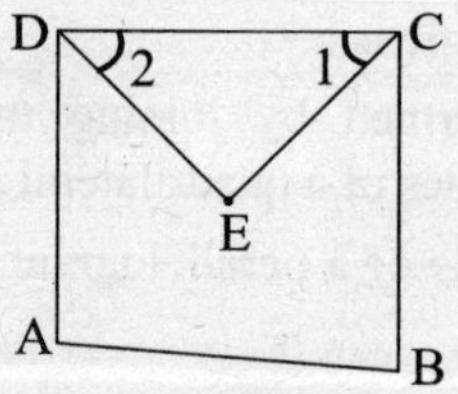

9. ABC and DBC are two isosceles triangles on the same base BC. (See figure) Show that $\angle ABD = \angle ACD$.

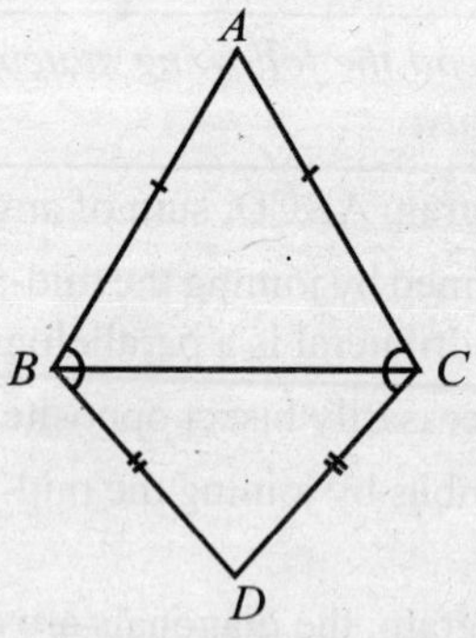

10. In figure $PQRS$ and $ABRS$ are parallelograms and X is any point on side BR. Show that :

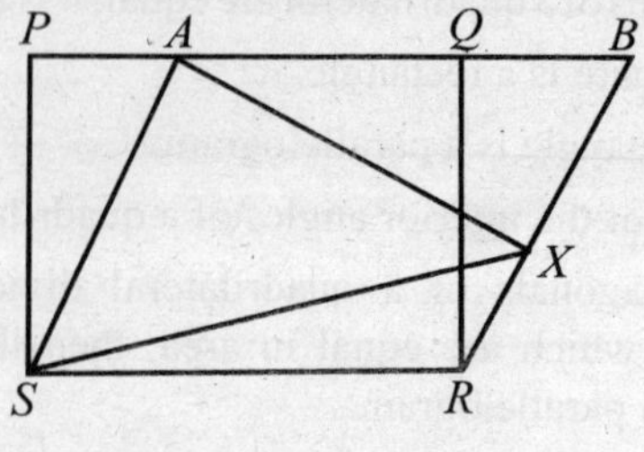

(i) ar (parallelogram $PQRS$) = ar (parallelogram $ABRS$)

(ii) ar (ΔAXS) = $\frac{1}{2}$ ar (parallelogram $PQRS$).

Long Answer Questions :

DIRECTIONS: *Give answer in four to five sentences.*

1. l and m are two parallel lines intersected by another pair of parallel lines p and q. Show that $\Delta ABC \cong \Delta CDA$.

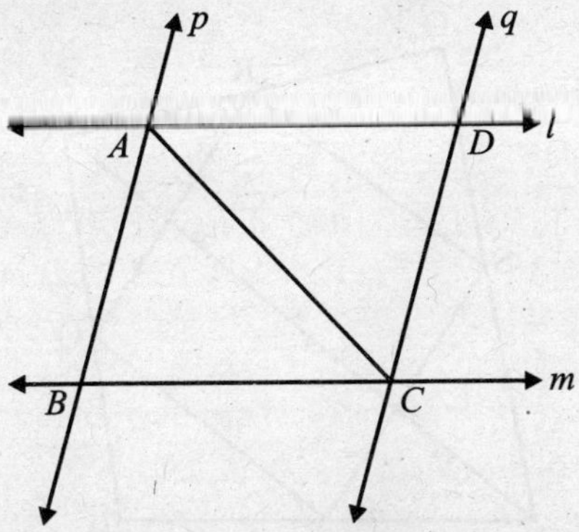

2. Show that the line segments joining the mid-points of the opposite sides of a quadrilateral bisect each other.

3. $ABCD$ is a quadrilateral and BD is one of its diagonals as shown in the following figure. Show that quadrilateral $ABCD$ is a parallelogram and find its area.

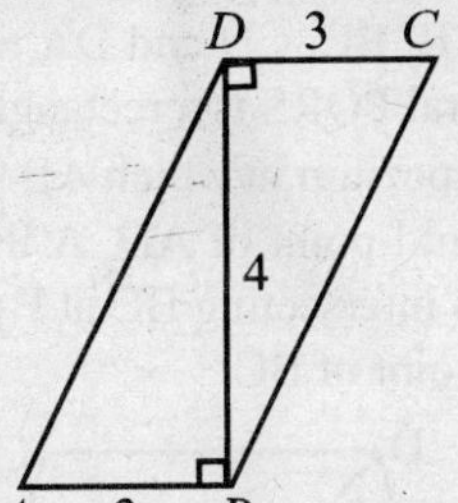

4. In figure, $ABCD$ is a parallelogram, $AE \perp DC$ and $CF \perp AD$. If AB = 16 cm, AE = 8 cm and CF = 10 cm, find AD.

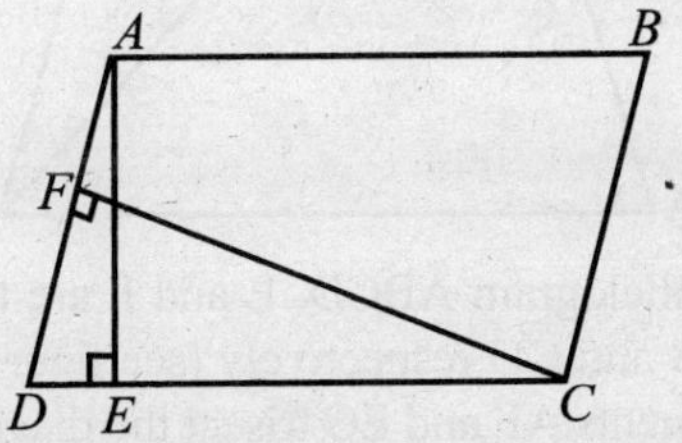

5. In figure P is a point in the interior of a parallelogram $ABCD$. Show that

(i) ar (ΔAPB) + ar (ΔPCD) = $\frac{1}{2}$ ar ($ABCD$)

(ii) ar (ΔAPD) + ar (ΔPBC) = ar (ΔAPB) + ar (ΔPCD)

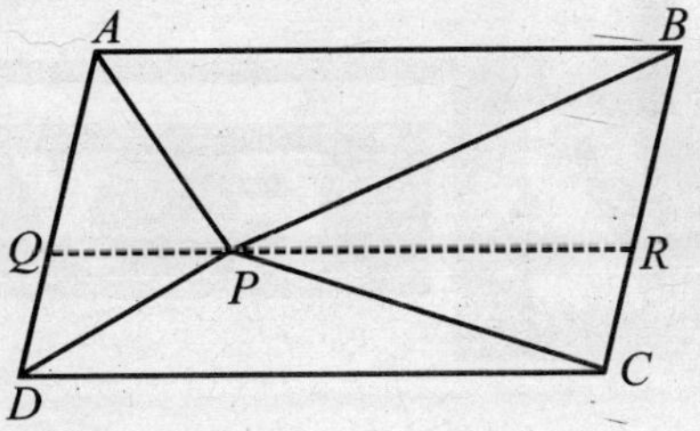

(**Hint** : Through P, draw a line parallel to AB)

6. D, E and F are respectively the mid-points of the sides BC, CA and AB of a ΔABC. Show that :

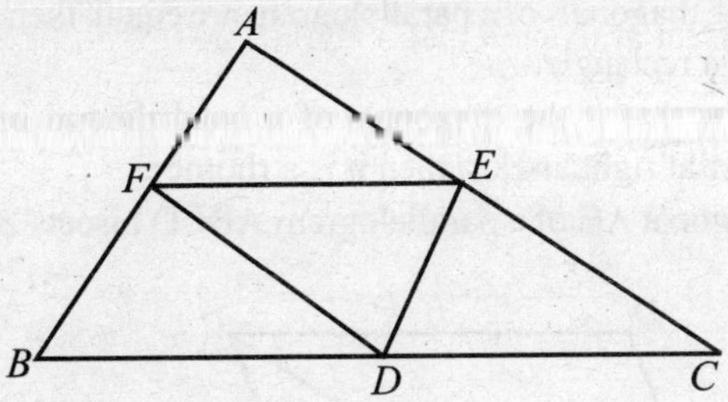

(i) $BDEF$ is a parallelogram

(ii) ar (ΔDEF) = $\frac{1}{4}$ ar (ΔABC)

(iii) ar (BDEF) = $\frac{1}{2}$ ar (ΔABC).

7. In figure, diagonals AC and BD of quadrilateral $ABCD$ intersect at O such that $OB = OD$. If $AB = CD$, then show that :

(i) ar (ΔDOC) = ar (ΔAOB)

(ii) ar (ΔDCB) = ar (ΔACB)

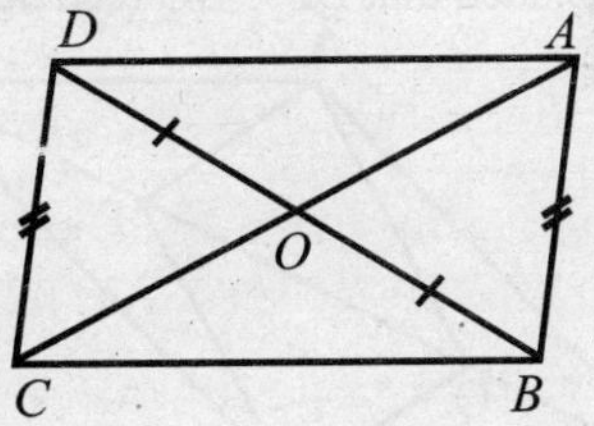

(iii) $DA \parallel CB$ or $ABCD$ is a parallelogram.

[**Hint**. From D and B, draw perpendiculars to AC.]

8. P is the mid-point of side AB of a parallelogram ABCD. A line through B parallel to PD meets DC at Q and AD produced at R. Prove that

(i) AR = 2 BC (ii) BR = 2BQ

2 EXERCISE

Text-Book Exercise :

1. If the diagonals of a parallelogram are equal, then show that it is a rectangle.
2. Show that if the diagonals of a quadrilateral bisect each other at right angles, then it is a rhombus.
3. Diagonal AC of a parallelogram ABCD bisects ∠A. Show that

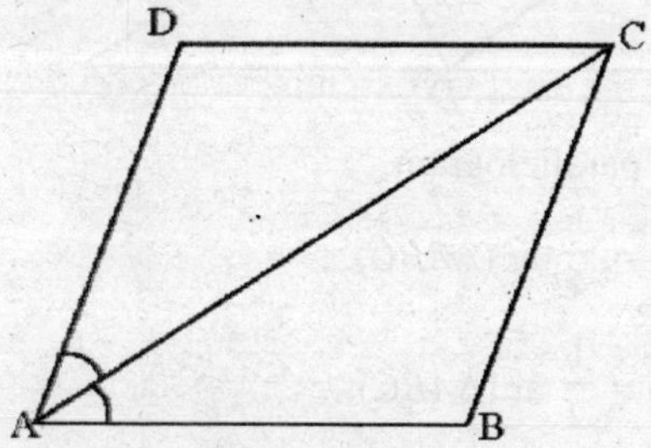

(i) it bisects ∠ C also,
(ii) ABCD is a rhombus.

4. ABCD is a rhombus. Show that diagonal AC bisects ∠ A as well as ∠C and diagonal BD bisects ∠ B as well as ∠D.
5. In parallelogram ABCD, two points P and Q are taken on diagonal BD such that DP = BQ (see figure). Show that:

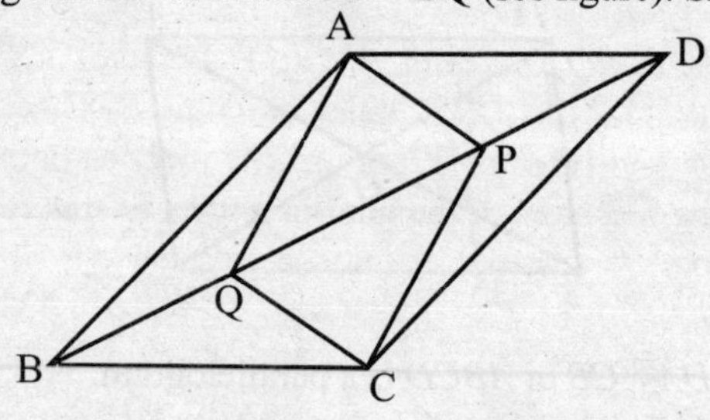

(i) Δ APD ≅ Δ CQB (ii) AP = CQ
(iii) Δ AQB ≅ Δ CPD (iv) AQ = CP
(v) APCQ is a parallelogram

6. ABCD is a parallelogram and AP and CQ are perpendiculars form vertices A and C on diagonal BD respectively (see figure). Show that
(i) Δ APB ≅ Δ CQD (ii) AP = CQ

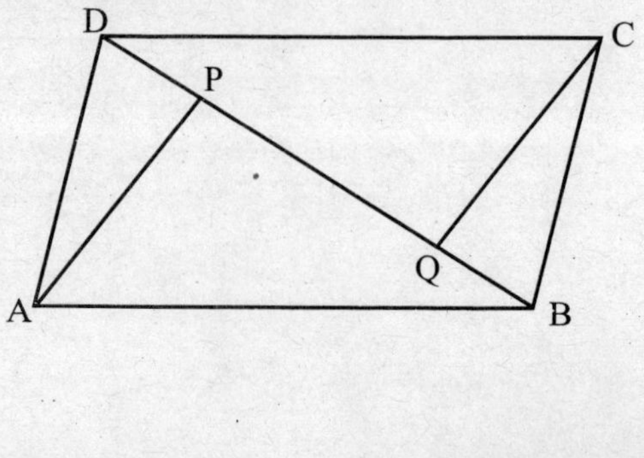

7. ABCD is a quadrilateral in which, P, Q, R and S are mid- points of the sides AB, BC, CD and DA (see figure) AC is a diagonal. Show that

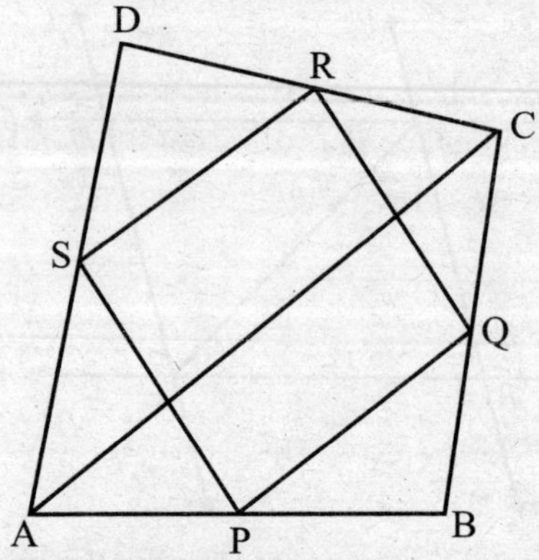

(i) SR || AC and $SR = \frac{1}{2}AC$
(ii) PQ = SR
(iii) PQRS is a parallelogram.

8. ABCD is a rhombus and P, Q, R and S are the mid-points of the sides AB, BC, CD and DA respectively. Show that the quadrilateral PQRS is a rectangle.
9. ABCD is a trapezium in which AB || DC, BD is a diagonal and E is the mid-point of AD. A line is drawn through E parallel to AB intersecting BC at F (see figure). Show that F is the mid-point of BC.

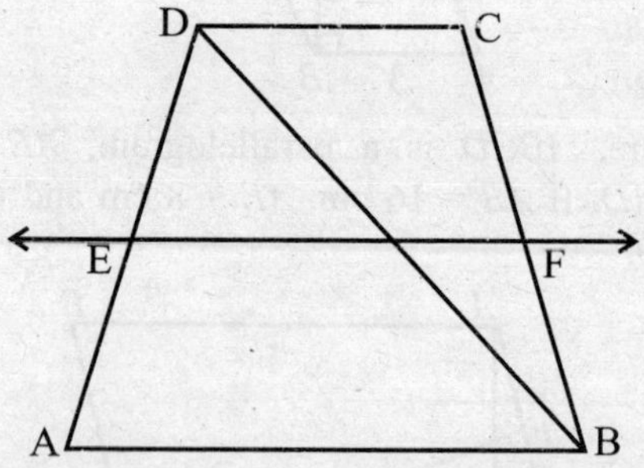

10. In a parallelogram ABCD, E and F are the mid-points of sides AB and CD respectively (see figure). Show that the line segments AF and EC trisect the diagonal BD.

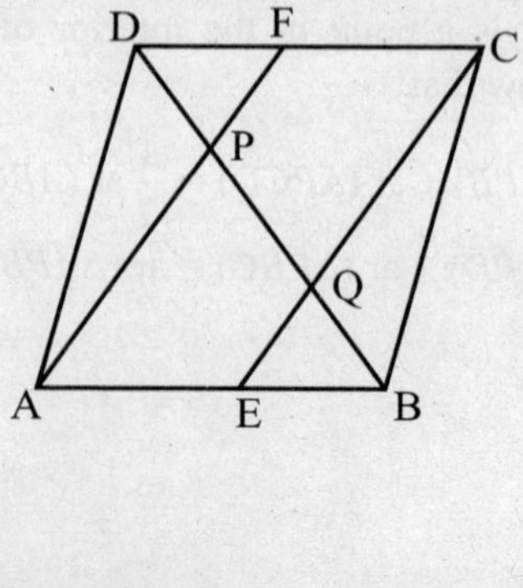

11. ABC is a triangle right angled at C. A line through the mid-point M of hypotenuse AB and parallel to BC intersects AC at D. Show that
(i) D is the mid- point of AC
(ii) $MD \perp AC$
(iii) $CM = MA = \frac{1}{2}AB$

Exemplar Questions :

1. Diagonals of a rhombus are equal and perpendicular to each other. Is this statement true? Give reason for your answer.
2. In fig, AX and CY are respectively the bisectors of the opposite angles A and C of a parallelogram ABCD. Show that AX || CY

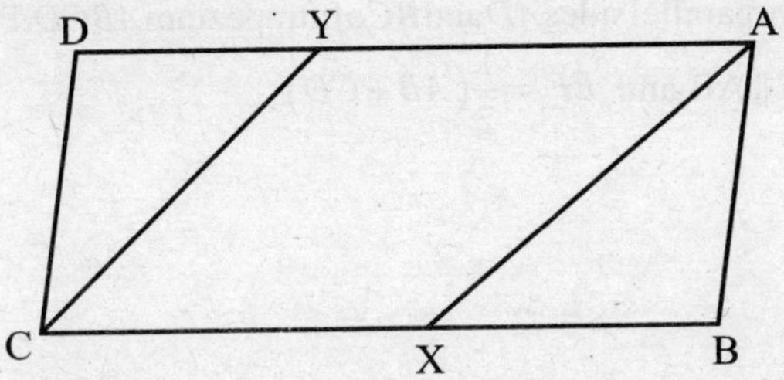

3. A diagonal of a parallelogram bisects one of its angle. Prove that it will bisect its opposite angle also.
4. Diagonals AC and BD of a quadrilateral ABCD intersect each other at O such that OA : OC = 3 : 2. Is ABCD a parallelogram ? Why or why not ?
5. Three angles of a quadrilateral are 75°, 90° and 75°. The fourth angle is
(a) 90°
(b) 95°
(c) 105°
(d) 120°
6. ABCD is a rhombus such that $\angle ACB = 40°$. Then $\angle ADB$ is
(a) 40°
(b) 45°
(c) 50°
(d) 60°
7. The quadrilateral formed by joining the mid-points of the sides of a quadrilateral PQRS, taken in order, is a rectangle, if
(a) PQRS is a rectangle
(b) PQRS is a prallelogram
(c) diagonals of PQRS are perpendicular
(d) diagonals of PQRS are equal
8. The quadrilateral formed by joining the mid-points of the sides of a quadrilateral PQRS, taken in order, is a rhombus, if
(a) PQRS is a rhombus
(b) PQRS is a parallelogram
(c) diagonals of PQRS are perpendicular
(d) diagonals of PQRS are equal
9. If APB and CQD are two parallel lines, then the bisectors of the angles APQ, BPQ, CQP and PQD form
(a) a square
(b) a rhombus
(c) a rectangle
(d) any other parallelogram

HOTS Questions :

1. A point *P* is taken inside an equilateral four-sided figure *ABCD* such that its distances from the vertices *D* and *B* are equal. Show that *AP* and *PC* are in one and the same straight line.

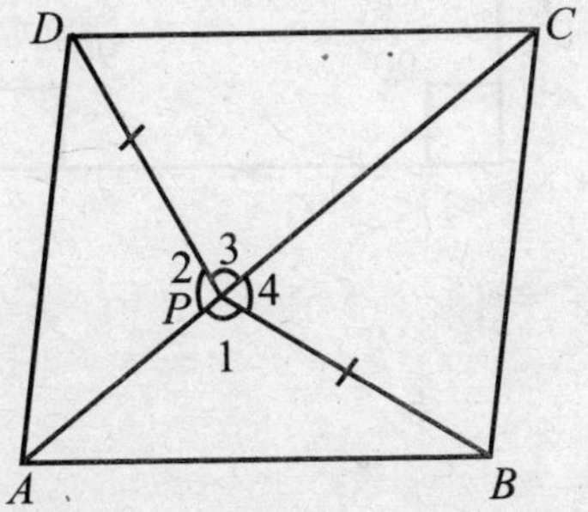

2. *PQ* and *RM* are two parallel lines and a transversal *l* intersects *PQ* at *X* and *RM* at *Y*. Bisector *XS* of $\angle PXY$, bisector *YS* of $\angle XYR$ meet at point *S*. Bisector *XT* of $\angle QXY$ and bisector *YT* of $\angle XYM$ meet at point *T*. Prove that the bisectors of the interior angles form a rectangle.

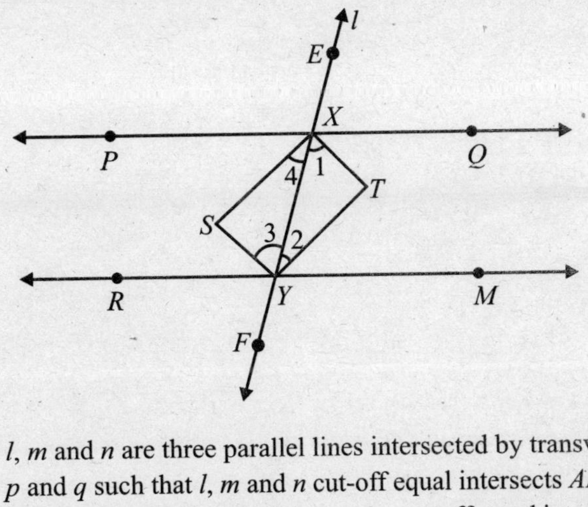

3. *l*, *m* and *n* are three parallel lines intersected by transversal *p* and *q* such that *l*, *m* and *n* cut-off equal intersects *AB* and *BC* on *p* (Fig.). Show that *l*, *m* and *n* cut-off equal intercepts *DE* and *EF* on *q* also.

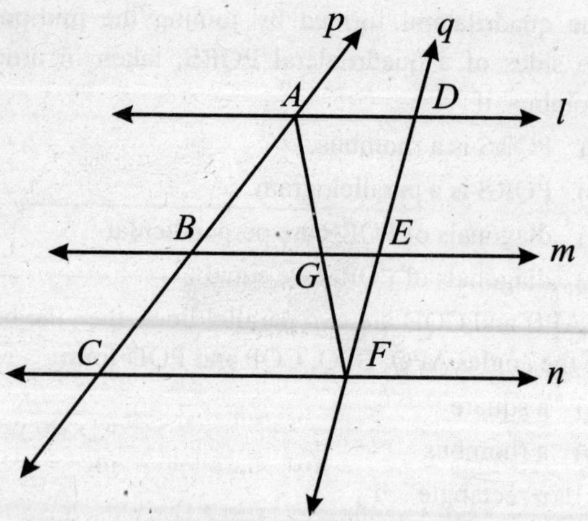

4. Explain why each interior angle of a square is 90°

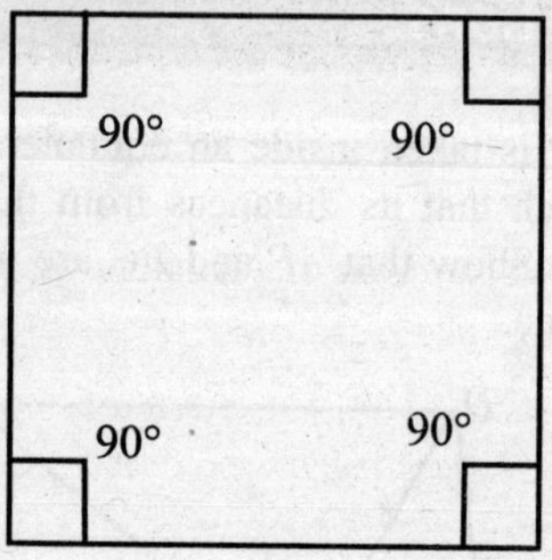

5. In fig, $BE \perp AC$. AD is any line from A to BC intersecting BE in H. P, Q and R are respectively the mid-points of AH, AB and BC. Prove that $\angle PQR = 90°$

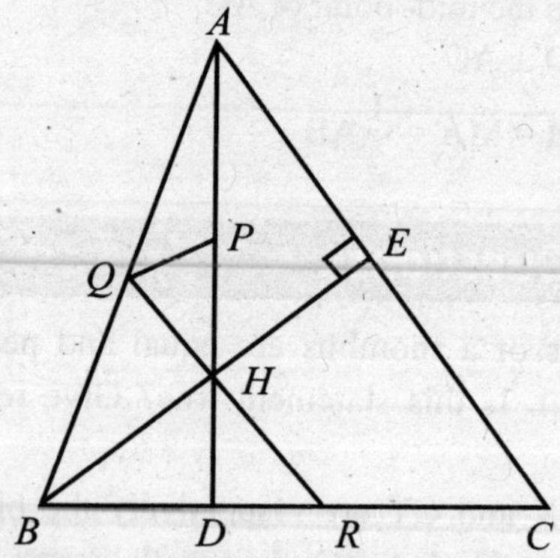

6. E and F are respectively the mid-points of the non-parallel sides AD and BC of a trapezium $ABCD$. Prove that $EF \parallel AB$ and $EF = \frac{1}{2}(AB + CD)$

3 EXERCISE

Single Option Correct :

DIRECTIONS: *This section contains multiple choice questions. Each questions has 4 choices (a), (b), (c) and (d) out of which ONLY ONE is correct.*

1. In a parallelogram *ABCD* diagonals *AC* and *BD* intersects at *O* and *AC* = 12.8 cm and *BD* = 7.6 cm, then the measure of *OC* and *OD* respectively equal to

(a) 1.9 cm and 6.4 cm (b) 3.8 cm and 3.2 cm
(c) 3.8 cm, 3.8 cm (d) 6.4 cm and 3.8 cm

2. *ABCD* is a rhombus with $\angle ABC = 56°$, then $\angle ACD$ will be

(a) 56° (b) 124°
(c) 62° (d) 34°

3. *LMNO* is a trapezium with $LM \parallel NO$. If *P* and *Q* are the mid-points of *LO* and *MN* respectively and *LM* = 5 cm and ON = 10 cm then *PQ* =

(a) 2.5 cm (b) 5 cm
(c) 7.5 cm (d) 15 cm

4. In the given figure, *AP* and *BP* are angle bisector of $\angle A$ and $\angle B$ which meets at *P* on the parallelogram *ABCD*. Then $2\angle APB$ =

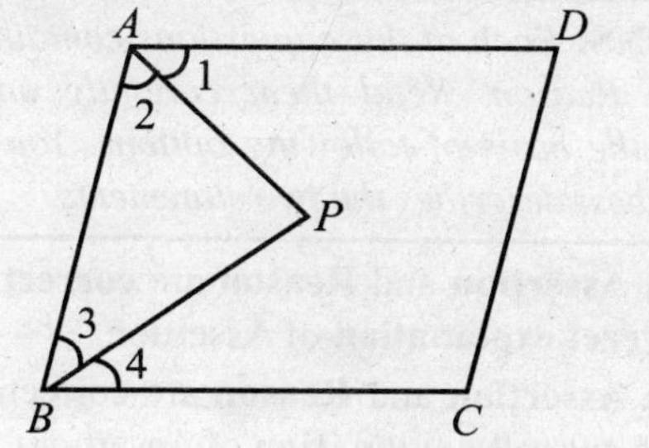

(a) $\angle C + \angle D$ (b) $\angle A + \angle C$
(c) $\angle B + \angle D$ (d) $2\angle C$

5. In the figure *ABCD*, the angles *x* and *y* are

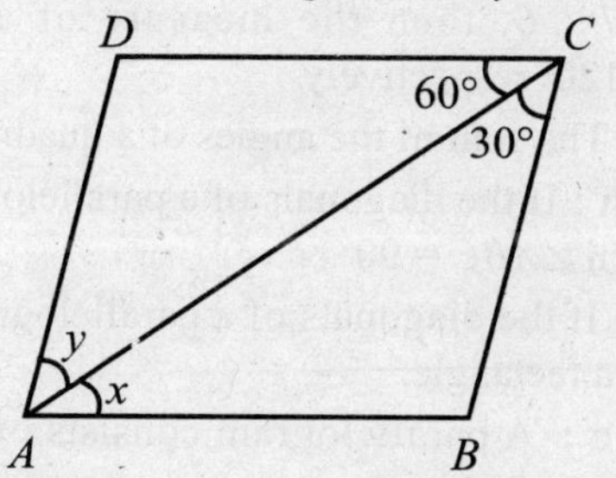

(a) 60°, 30° (b) 30°, 60°
(c) 45°, 45° (d) 90°, 90°

6. Quadrilateral whose four sides are equal but angles are not equal is

(a) square (b) quadrilateral
(c) rectangle (d) parallelogram

7. *ABCD* is quadrilateral. If *AC* and *BD* are its diagonals then the

(a) sum of the squares of the sides of the quadrilateral is equal to the sum of the squares of its diagonals.
(b) perimeter of the quadrilateral is equal to the sum of the diagonals
(c) perimeter of the quadrilateral is less than the sum of the diagonals
(d) perimeter of the quadrilateral is greater than the sum of the diagonals

8. In quadrilateral ABCD, BM and DN are drawn perpendiculars to AC such that BM = DN. If BR = 8 cm, then BD is

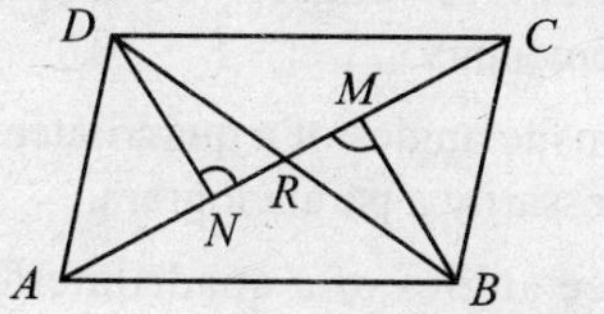

(a) 4 cm (b) 2 cm
(c) 12 cm (d) 16 cm

9. In the given figure is a parallelogram, find the values of *x* and *y*.

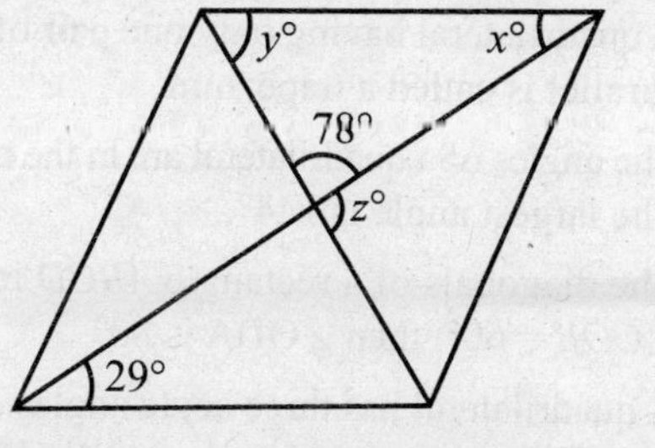

(a) 29°, 73° (b) 23°, 78°
(c) 23°, 23° (d) 29°, 78°

10. ABCD is a parallelogram, if the two diagonals are equal, find the measure of $\angle$ABC.

(a) 70° (b) 80°
(c) 90° (d) 100°

11. In fig. *X* is a point in the interior of square *ABCD*. *AXYZ* is also a square. If *DY* = 3 cm and *AZ* = 2 cm, then *BY* =

(a) 5 cm (b) 6 cm
(c) 7 cm (d) 8 cm

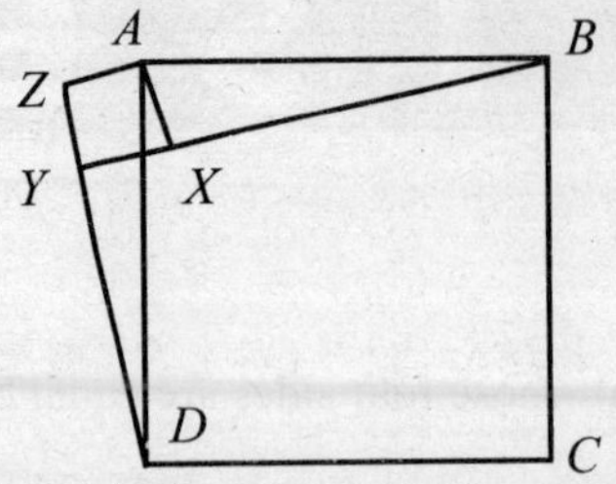

More Than One Option Correct :

DIRECTIONS: *This section contains multiple choice questions. Each question has 4 choices (a), (b), (c) and (d) out of which ONE OR MORE may be correct.*

1. Which of the following statement(s) is/are incorrect ?
   (a) A trapezium is a quadrilateral, having one pair of opposite sides parallel.
   (b) A parallelogram is a quadrilateral with both pairs of opposite sides parallel.
   (c) A rhombus is a quadrilateral, whose all the sides are equal and each angle is 90°.
   (d) A square is a quadrilateral, whose all sides are equal
2. Which of the following statement(s) is/are correct?
   (a) Consecutive angles of a parallelogram are supplementary.
   (b) If opposite angles of a quadrilateral are equal, then it is necessarily a parallelogram.
   (c) If three angles of a quadrilateral are equal, it is a parallelogram.
   (d) If three sides of a quadrilateral are equal, it is a parallelogram.
3. Which of the following statement(s) is/are correct?
   (a) A quadrilateral having only one pair of opposite sides parallel is called a trapezium.
   (b) The angles of a quadrilateral are in the ratio 1 : 2 : 3 : 4. The largest angle is 144°.
   (c) The diagonals of a rectangle *ABCD* intersect at *O*. If $\angle COB = 60°$, then $\angle ODA$ is 80°
   (d) A quadrilateral has three acute angles each measuring 70°. The measure of fourth angle is 150°

Passage Based Question :

DIRECTIONS: *Study the given paragraph(s) and answer the following questions.*

PASSAGE - I

The sum of the four angles of a quadrilateral is 360°

1. In a quadrilateral ABCD, $\angle A + \angle C = 180°$, then $\angle B + \angle D =$
   (a) 360° (b) 180°
   (c) 80° (d) 100°
2. The angle of a quadrilateral are respectively 100°, 98°, 92°. The measure of fourth angle is
   (a) 70° (b) 290°
   (c) 98° (d) 92°

PASSAGE - II

In a parallelogram *ABCD*, the sum of any two consecutive angles is 180°.

3. In a parallelogram *ABCD*, $\angle D = 115°$, determine the measure of $\angle A$ and $\angle B$.
   (a) $\angle A = 85°, \angle B = 115°$
   (b) $\angle A = 65°, \angle B = 65°$
   (c) $\angle A = 65°, \angle B = 115°$
   (d) $\angle A = 75°, \angle B = 105°$
4. In the given figure, find $\angle A$ in the parallelogram *ABCD*.

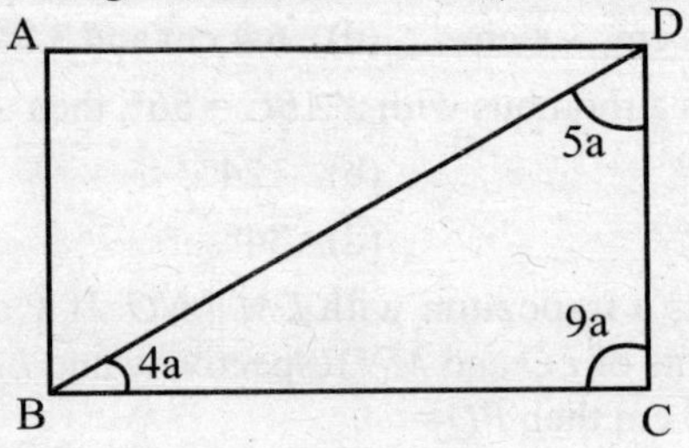

   (a) 90° (b) 60°
   (c) 30° (d) 110°

Assertion & Reason :

DIRECTIONS: *Each of these questions contains an Assertion followed by Reason. Read them carefully and answer the question on the basis of following options. You have to select the one that best describes the two statements.*

(a) If both **Assertion** and **Reason** are **correct** and Reason is the **correct explanation** of Assertion.
(b) If both **Assertion** and **Reason** are correct, but Reason **is not the correct explanation** of Assertion.
(c) If **Assertion** is **correct** but **Reason** is **incorrect**.
(d) If **Assertion** is **incorrect** but **Reason** is **correct**.

1. **Assertion :** If the angles of a quadrilateral are in the ratio 2 : 3 : 7 : 6, then the measure of angles are 40° 60°,140°,120° respectively.
   Reason : The sum of the angles of a quadrilateral is 360°.
2. **Assertion :** If the diagonals of a parallelogram *ABCD* are equal, then $\angle ABC = 90°$.
   Reason : If the diagonals of a parallelogram are equal, it becomes a rectangle.
3. **Assertion :** A parallelogram consists of two congruent triangles.
   Reason : Diagonal of a parallelogram divides it into two congruent triangles.

4. **Assertion :** The angles of a quadrilateral are $x°$, $(x - 10)°$, $(x + 30)°$ and $(2x)°$, the smallest angle is equal to 58°.

   Reason : Sum of the angles of a quadrilateral is 360°.

5. **Assertion :** The consecutive sides of a quadrilateral have one common point.

   Reason : The opposite sides of a quadrilateral have two common point.

Integer Type Questions :

DIRECTIONS: *Answer the following questions. The answer to each of the question is a single digit integer, ranging from 0 to 9.*

1. In the given figure, *ABCD* is a parallelogram. Compute the value of $x - y$.

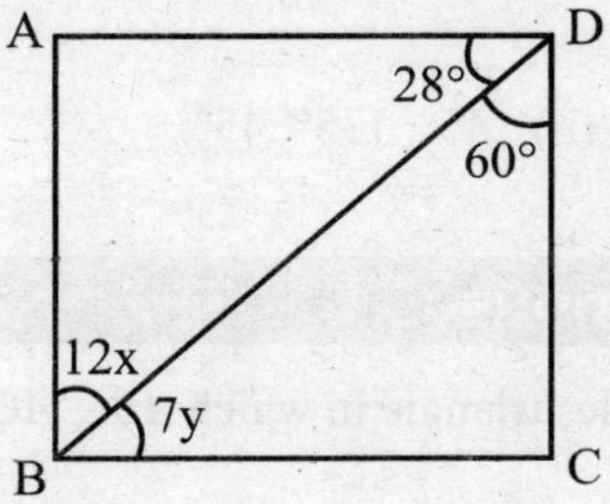

2. *PQRS* is a square. Determine $\frac{\angle SRP}{5}$.

3. *P* is the mid-point of side *AB* of a parallelogram *ABCD*. A line through *B* parallel to *PD* meets *DC* at *Q* and *AD* produced at *R*. Prove that $AR = m\,BC$. The value of m is

4. In a square *PQRS*, $PQ = (4x + 3)$ cm and $QR = (5x - 6)$ cm. Then the value of *x* is

5. In a rhombus *ABCD*, $\angle A = 60°$ and $AB = 6$ cm. The length of the diagonal *BD* is equal to

6. Using the information given in figure, calculate the value of $\frac{x}{34}$.

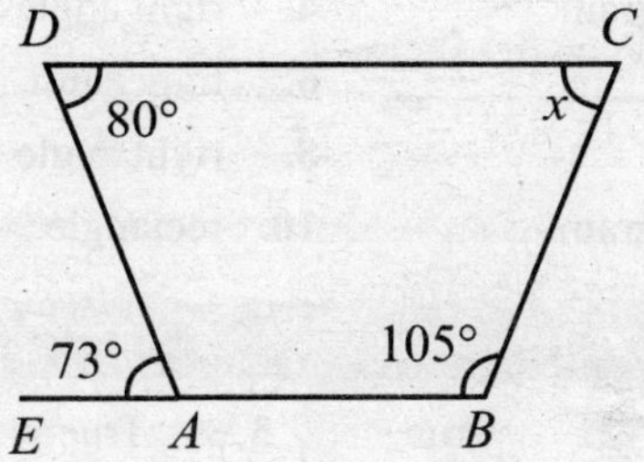

SOLUTIONS

Brief Explanations of Selected Questions

1 EXERCISE

FILL IN THE BLANKS :

1. equal
2. quadrilateral
3. parallelogram
4. right angles
5. rhombus
6. trapezium
7. Isosceles
8. right angle triangle
9. parallelogram.
10. rectangle

TRUE/FALSE :

1. True 2. True 3. True. 4. True
5. False 6. False 7. True 8. True
9. True 10. False 11. True

MATCH THE COLUMNS :

1. (A) → (s); (B) → (r); (c) → (p); (D) → (q)

   (A) $\angle A = 180 - 115 = 65$

   (B) $\angle POQ = 90°$

   (C) $\angle OAD = 68°$

   (D) $\angle DBC = 58°$

2. (A) → (q); (B) → (r); (c) → (s); (D) → (p)

VERY SHORT ANSWER QUESTIONS :

1. Let DB intersect EF at G. i.e., G is the mid-point of BD. Since, E is the mid-point of DA and $EG \parallel AB$. Hence, G is the mid-point of DB. (By converse of mid-point theorem)

   Similarly, now G is the mid-point of BD and $GF \parallel AB \parallel DC$ by converse of mid-point theroem, F is the mid-point of BC.

2. Since, the opposite angles of a parallelogram are equal.

   ∴ In parallelogram $ABCD$

   $\angle A = \angle C$

   ∴ $\angle A = 50°$

   Similarly, in parallelogram $AEFG$

   $\angle A = \angle F$

   ∴ $\angle F = 50°$

3. $\angle C + \angle D = 150°$

4. $\angle ACD = 62°$

5. $\angle A = \angle C$

   ⇒ $3x - 20 = x + 40$

   ⇒ $2x = 60$ ⇒ $x = 30°$

   Also, $\angle A + \angle B = 180$ ⇒ $(90 - 20) + y + 15 = 180$

   ⇒ $y + 85 = 180$ ⇒ $y = 95°$

6. $60 - x = 3x - 4$

   ⇒ $4x = 64$ ⇒ $x = 16$

   Hence, all four angles are

   $(60 - 16)°, (48 - 4)°, (180 - 48 + 4)°, (180 - 60 + 16)°$.

   $= 44°, 44°, 136°, 136°$.

7. Rectangle

8. (i) 110°, 70°, 110° (ii) 45°, 135°, 45°

   (iii) 85°, 95°, 85°

SHORT ANSWER QUESTIONS :

1. (i) ΔABC is an isosceles triangle in which $AB = AC$ (Given)

   So, $\angle ABC = \angle ACB$ (angles opposite to equal sides)

   Also, $\angle PAC = \angle ABC + \angle ACB$ (exterior angle of a triangle)

   or $\angle PAC = 2\angle ACB$ .... (i)

   Now, AD bisects $\angle PAC$

   So, $\angle PAC = 2\angle DAC$ .... (ii)

   Therefore, $2\angle DAC = 2\angle ACB$ [From (i) and (ii)]

   or $\angle DAC = \angle ACB$

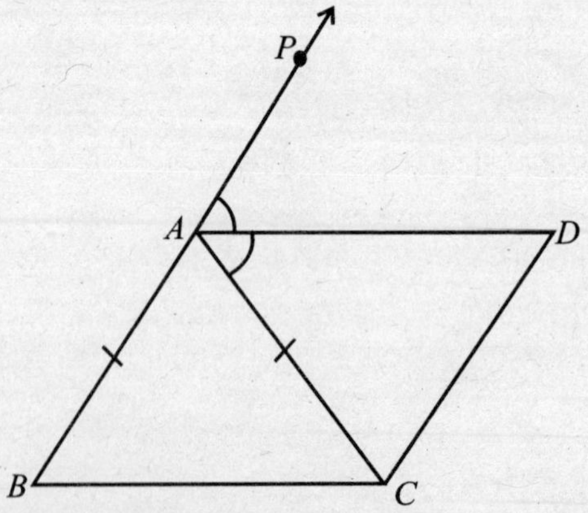

   (ii) Now, these equal angles form a pair of alternate angles because line segments BC and AD are intersected by a transversal AC.

   So, $BC \parallel AD$

   Also, $BA \parallel CD$ (Given)

   Now, both pairs of opposite sides of quadrilateral $ABCD$ are parallel.

   So, $ABCD$ is a parallelogram.

2. Since adjacent angles are supplementary

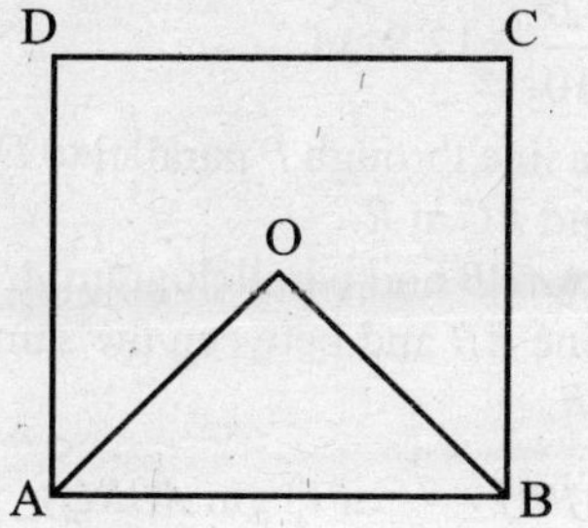

$\therefore \quad \angle A + \angle B = 180°$

$\Rightarrow \quad \frac{1}{2}(\angle A + \angle B) = 90°$

In ΔAOB, $\frac{1}{2}(\angle A + \angle B) + \angle AOB = 180°$

$\Rightarrow \quad \angle AOB = 90°$

3. $\angle PQR = 90°$

$\Rightarrow \quad \angle PQS + \angle SQR = 90° \Rightarrow \angle SQR = 90 - 48 = 42°$

4. The angles of a square are bisected by the diagonals.

$\therefore \quad \angle ORX = 45°$

Now, $\angle ROS + \angle ROX = 180°$ (Linear pair)

$\Rightarrow \quad \angle ROX = 180 - 105 = 75°$

In ΔROX,

$45° + 75° + x = 180° \quad \Rightarrow x = 180 - 120 = 60°$

5. Join BD.

In ΔABD we have

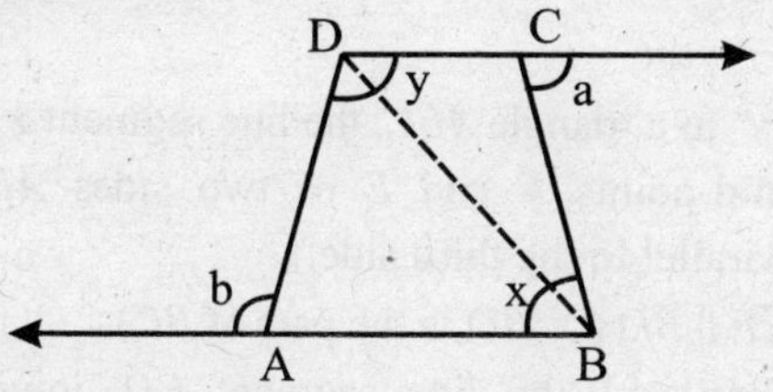

$\angle ABD + \angle ADB = b \quad$ ...(i)

In ΔCBD, we have

$\angle CBD + \angle CDB = a \quad$ ...(ii)

Adding (i) and (ii), we get

$(\angle ABD + \angle CBD) + (\angle ADB + \angle CDB) = a + b$

$\Rightarrow \quad x + y = a + b$

6. The diagonal of a ||gm bisect each other.

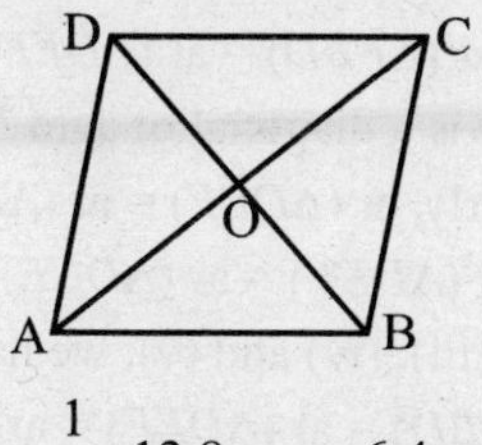

$\therefore \quad OC = \frac{1}{2} AC = \frac{1}{2} \times 12.8$ cm $= 6.4$ and

$OD = \frac{1}{2} BD = \frac{1}{2} \times 7.6$ cm $= 3.8$ cm

7. Let the length and breadth of the rectangle be $4x$ and $3x$.

$(4x)^2 + (3x)^2 = (25)^2 \quad$ [By Pythagoras theorem]

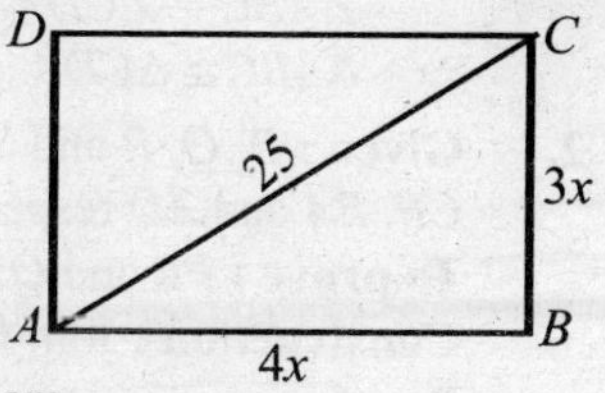

$\Rightarrow \quad 16x^2 + 9x^2 = 625$

$\Rightarrow \quad 25x^2 = 625$

$\Rightarrow \quad x^2 = 25 \Rightarrow x = 5$

Length of rectangle $= 4x = 20$ cm

Breadth of rectangle $= 3x = 15$ cm

Perimeter of rectangle $= 2(l + b) = 2(35) = 70$ cm

8. $\angle 1 = \frac{1}{2}\angle C$ and $\angle 2 = \frac{1}{2}\angle D$

In ΔDEC, $\angle 1 + \angle 2 + \angle CED = 180°$

$\Rightarrow \quad \angle CED = 180° - (\angle 1 + \angle 2) \quad$ ...(i)

Also, $\angle A + \angle B + \angle C + \angle D = 360°$

$\Rightarrow \quad \angle A + \angle B = 360° - (\angle C + \angle D)$

$\Rightarrow \quad \frac{1}{2}(\angle A + \angle B) = 180° - \frac{1}{2}\angle C - \frac{1}{2}\angle D$

$\Rightarrow \quad \frac{1}{2}(\angle A + \angle B) = 180° - (\angle 1 + \angle 2) \quad$ ...(ii)

From (i) and (ii), we get $\angle A + \angle B = 2\angle CED$

9. Since ΔABC is an isosceles triangle on the base BC

$\therefore \quad \angle ABC = \angle ACB \quad$ ...(i)

Similarly, ΔDBC is an isosceles triangle on the base BC

$\therefore \quad \angle DBC = \angle DCB \quad$ ...(ii)

Adding the corresponding sides of (i) and (ii), we get

$\angle ABC + \angle DBC = \angle ACB + \angle DCB$

$\Rightarrow \quad \angle ABD = \angle ACD.$

10. (i) ar $(PQRS)$ = ar $(ABRS)$ ...(i)

($\because$ Parallelograms $PQRS$ and $ABRS$ are on the same base SR and between the same parallels SR and PB.)

(ii) ar $(\Delta AXS) = \frac{1}{2}$ ar $(ABRS)$ ...(ii)

($\because$ ΔAXS and ||gm $ABRS$ are on the same base AS and between the same parallels AS and RB)

From (i) and (ii), we get, ar $(\Delta AXS) = \frac{1}{2}$ ar $(PQRS)$.

LONG ANSWER QUESTIONS :

1. Since, l and m and p and q are parallel lines therefore, $AB \parallel DC$ and $AD \parallel BC$

$\therefore$ Quadrilateral $ABCD$ is a parallelogram.

($\because$ A quadrilateral is a parallelogram if both the pairs of opposite sides are parallel)

Since, $ABCD$ is ||gm

$\therefore \quad BC = AD \quad$ ...(i)

and $AB = CD \quad$ ...(ii)

(Opposite sides of a || gm are equal)

and $\angle ABC = \angle CDA \quad$ ...(iii)

(Opposite angles of a || gm are equal)

Thus, In ΔABC and ΔCDA we get

$AB = CD \quad$ (From (ii))

$BC = DA \quad$ (From (i))

$\angle ABC = \angle CDA$ (From (iii))

$\therefore$ $\Delta ABC \cong \Delta CDA$ (SAS Rule)

2. **Given :** P, Q, R and S are the mid-points of the sides DC, CB, BA and AD respectively in a quadrilateral $ABCD$.

To prove : PR and QS bisect each other.

Construction : Join PQ, QR, RS, SP, AC and BD.

Proof :

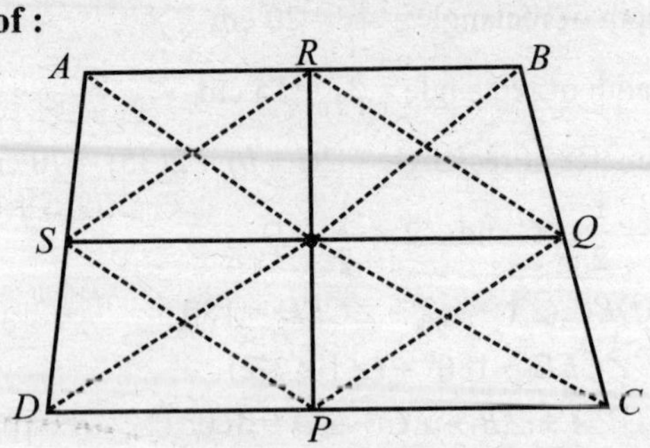

Since, R and Q are the mid-points of AB and BC respectively. in ΔABC

$\therefore$ $RQ \parallel AC$ and $RQ = \frac{1}{2} AC$

Similarly, P and S are the mid-points of AD and DC respectively

$\therefore$ we have

$PS \parallel AC$ and $PS = \frac{1}{2} AC$

$\therefore$ $RQ \parallel PS$ and $RQ = PS$.

Thus a pair of opposite sides of a quadrilateral $PQRS$ are parallel and equal.

$\therefore$ Quadrilateral $PQRS$ is a parallelogram.

Since the diagonals of a parallelogram bisect each other.

$\therefore$ PR and QS bisect each other.

3. From the figure it is clear that

$\angle CDB = \angle ABD = 90°$

But these angles form a pair of alternate equal angles.

$\therefore$ $DC \parallel AB$

Also, $DC = AB = 3$ units (From figure)

Now, we know that A quadrilateral is a parallelogram if a pair of opposite sides is parallel and is of equal length.

$\therefore$ Quadrilateral $ABCD$ is a parallelogram.

Now, area of the $\parallel$ gm $ABCD$

= Base × Corresponding altitude

= $AB \times BD$

= 3×4 square units ($\because AB = 3, BD = 4$)

= 12 square units

4. Since, $ABCD$ is a parallelogram in which $AB \parallel DC$

$\therefore$ $AB = DC$

$\Rightarrow$ Base $DC = 16$ cm

Height $AE = 8$ cm. (Given)

Area of $\parallel$ gm = Base × Corresponding Altitude

$\therefore$ Area of $\parallel$ gm $ABCD$

$= DC \times AE = 16 \times 8 = 128 \text{ cm}^2$ ....(i)

Again by considering AD as the base and height as $CF = 10$ cm.

$\therefore$ Area of $\parallel$ gm $ABCD = AD \times CF$

$= AD \times 10 = (10\, AD) \text{ cm}^2$

Clearly $10.\, AD = 128$ (By using (i))

$\Rightarrow AD = \frac{128}{10} = 12.8$ cm.

5. (i) Draw a line through P parallel to DC which meets AD at Q and BC at R.

Since ΔAPB and parallelogram $ABRQ$ have the same base line AB and between the same parallels line AB and QR.

$\therefore$ ar $(\Delta APB) = \frac{1}{2}$ ar ($\parallel$ gm $ABRQ$) ....(i)

Similarly,

ΔPCD and $\parallel$gm $DCRQ$ have the same base DC and between the same parallel lines DC and QR.

$\therefore$ ar $(\Delta PCD) = \frac{1}{2}$ ar ($\parallel$ gm $DCRQ$) ....(ii)

From (i) and (ii), we get,

ar (ΔAPB) + ar (ΔPCD)

$= \frac{1}{2}$ ar ($\parallel$ gm $ABRQ$) + $\frac{1}{2}$ ar ($\parallel$ gm $DCRQ$)

Hence, ar (ΔAPB) + ar $(\Delta PCD) = \frac{1}{2}$ ar ($\parallel$ gm $ABCD$)

(ii) Similarly, ar (ΔAPD) + ar (ΔPBC)

$= \frac{1}{2}$ ar ($\parallel$ gm $ABCD$)

Hence, ar (ΔAPB) + ar (ΔPCD)

= ar (ΔAPD) + ar (PBC)

6. (i) $EF \parallel BC$

($\because$ In a triangle ABC, the line segment FE joining the mid-points F and E of two sides AB and AC is parallel to the third side.)

$\Rightarrow$ $EF \parallel BD$ ($\because$ BD is the part of BC) ....(i)

Similarly, the line segment ED, joining the mid-points E and D of two sides CA and CB is parallel to the 3rd side.

$\therefore$ $ED \parallel BF$ ....(ii)

From (i) and (ii),

$BDEF$ is a parallelogram.

(ii) From (i), we can have

$AFDE$ and $FDCE$ are parallelograms.

Now, ar (ΔFBD) = ar (ΔDEF) ....(iii)

($\because$ FD is a diagonal of $\parallel$gm $BDEF$.)

Similarly, ar (ΔDEF) = ar (ΔFAE) ....(iv)

and, ar (ΔDEF) = ar (ΔDCE) ....(v)

From (iii), (iv) and (v), we have

ar (ΔFBD) = ar (ΔDEF) = ar (ΔFAE)

= ar (ΔDCE) ....(vi)

Since, ΔABC is divided into four triangles ΔFBD, ΔDEF, ΔFAE and ΔDCE.

$\therefore$ ar (ΔABC) = ar (ΔFBD) + ar (ΔDEF) + ar (ΔFAE)

$+ \text{ar}(\Delta DCE) = 4 \text{ ar}(\Delta DEF)$ [From (vi)]

$\Rightarrow \text{ar}(\Delta DEF) = \frac{1}{4} \text{ ar}(\Delta ABC)$ ....(vii)

(iii) Consider

$\text{ar}(BDEF) = \text{ar}(\Delta FBD) + \text{ar}(\Delta DEF)$

$= \text{ar}(\Delta DEF) + \text{ar}(\Delta DEF)$ [From (iii)]

$= 2 \text{ ar}(\Delta DEF)$ [From (vii)]

$= 2.\frac{1}{4} \text{ ar}(\Delta ABC)$

$= \frac{1}{2} \text{ ar}(\Delta ABC).$

7.

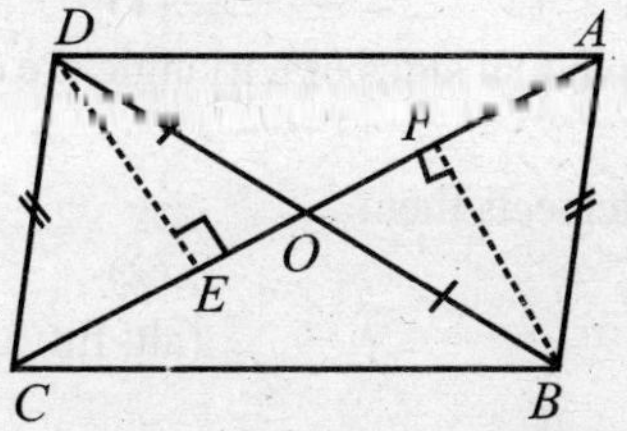

(i) Draw $DE \perp AC$ and $BF \perp AC$

In ΔADB, AO is a median

$\therefore \text{ar}(\Delta AOD) = \text{ar}(\Delta AOB)$ ....(i)

($\because$ A median of a triangle divides it into two triangles of equal areas)

Similarly, in ΔCBD, CO is a median.

$\therefore \text{ar}(\Delta COD) = \text{ar}(\Delta COB)$ ....(ii)

Adding (i) and (ii), we get

$\text{ar}(\Delta AOD) + \text{ar}(\Delta COD) = \text{ar}(\Delta AOB) + \text{ar}(\Delta COB)$

$\Rightarrow \text{ar}(\Delta ACD) = \text{ar}(\Delta ACB)$

$$\Rightarrow \frac{(AC)(DE)}{2} = \frac{(AC)(BF)}{2}$$

$$\left(\because \text{Area of a triangle} = \frac{\text{Base} \times \text{Corresponding altitude}}{2}\right)$$

$\Rightarrow DE = BF$ ....(iii)

In right Δs DEC and BFA,

Hyp. DC = Hyp. BA

$DE = BF$ (From (iii))

$\therefore \Delta DEC \cong \Delta BFA$ (R.H.S. Rule)

$\therefore \angle DCE = \angle BAF$ (C.P.C.T.)

But these angles form a pair of equal alternate interior angles.

$\therefore DC \parallel AB$ ....(iv)

Since, $DC = AB$ and $DC \parallel AB$

$\therefore$ ABCD is a parallelogram

($\because$ A quadrilateral is a parallelogram if a pair of opposite sides is parallel and equal)

$\therefore DA \parallel CB$

($\because$ Opposite sides of a ||gm are parallel)

(ii) Since, $ABCD$ is a || gm

$\therefore OC = OA$ ....(v)

$$\text{ar}(\Delta DOC) = \frac{OC \times DE}{2}$$

$$\text{ar}(\Delta AOB) = \frac{OA \times BE}{2}$$

$\text{ar}(\Delta DOC) = \text{ar}(\Delta AOB).$

($\because DE = BF$ and $OC = OA$)

(iii) $\text{ar}(\Delta DOC) = \text{ar}(\Delta AOB)$ [From (i)]

$\Rightarrow \text{ar}(\Delta DOC) + \text{ar}(\Delta OCB)$

$= \text{ar}(\Delta AOB) + \text{ar}(\Delta OCB)$

(Adding same areas on both sides)

$\Rightarrow \text{ar}(\Delta DCB) = \text{ar}(\Delta ACB).$

8. (i) Consider ΔARB. In ΔARB,

P is the mid-point of AB and $PD \parallel BR$ (Given)

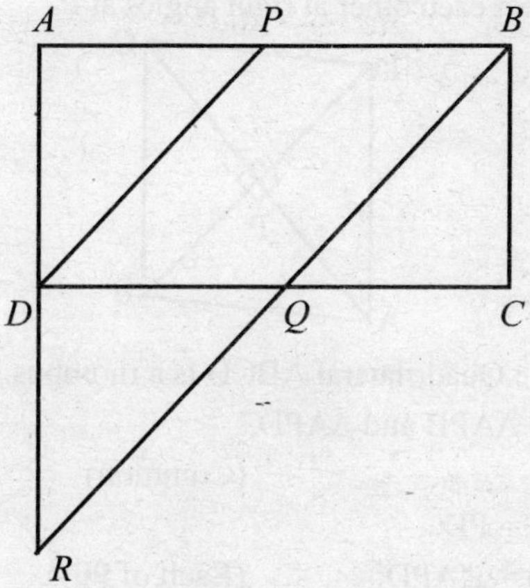

$\therefore$ D is the mid-point of AR

$\Rightarrow$ $AR = 2AD$

$\Rightarrow$ $AR = 2BC$ $\left[\because ABCD \text{ is a } \|^{gm} \therefore AD = BC\right]$

(ii) ABCD is a ||gm

$\Rightarrow$ $DC \parallel AB$

$\Rightarrow$ $DQ \parallel AB$

Thus, in ΔRAB, D is the mid-point of AR and $DQ \parallel AB$.

$\therefore$ Q is the mid-point of RB

$\Rightarrow$ $BR = 2BQ$

2 EXERCISE

TEXT-BOOK EXERCISE :

1. Consider a parallelogram $ABCD$, in which diagonals are equal i.e., $AC = BD$.

To show : Parallelogram $ABCD$ is a rectangle.

Proof : Consider ΔACB and ΔBDA, in which

$AC = BD$ (Given)

$AB = BA$ (Common)

$BC = AD$ ($\because$ Opposite sides of ||gm are equal.)

$\therefore$ By SSS rule, $\Delta ACB \cong \Delta BDA$

$\therefore$ $\angle ABC = \angle BAD$ (C.P.C.T.) ...(i)

Again since $AD \parallel BC$ and transversal AB intersects them.

$\therefore$ $\angle BAD + \angle ABC = 180°$ ...(ii)

($\because$ Sum of consecutive interior angles on the same side of the transversal is 180°)

From (i) and (ii), we have

$\angle BAD = \angle ABC = 90°$

$\therefore$ $\angle A = 90°$

$\Rightarrow$ Parallelogram ABCD is a rectangle.

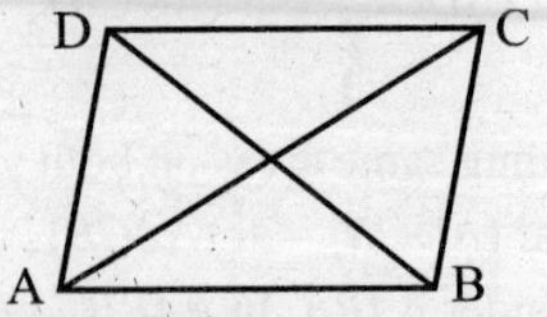

2. Consider quadrilateral ABCD in which diagonals AC and BD intersect each other at right angles at P.

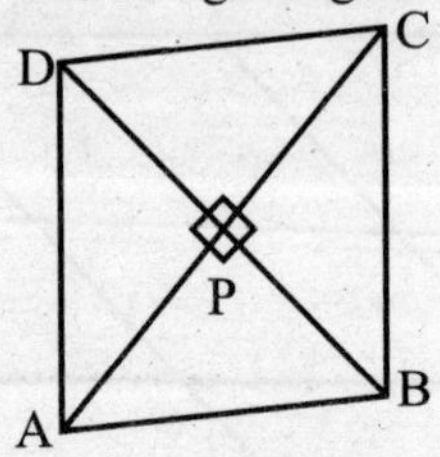

To prove : Quadrilateral ABCD is a rhombus.

Proof : In ΔAPB and ΔAPD,

AP = AP (Common)

Given PB = PD

$\angle APB = \angle APD$ (Each of 90°)

$\therefore$ By SAS rule

$\Delta APB \cong \Delta APD$

$\therefore$ AB = AD ...(i) (C.P.C.T.)

Similarly, we can prove that

AB = BC ...(ii)

BC = CD ...(iii)

and CD = AD ...(iv)

From (i), (ii), (iii) and (iv), we get

AB = BC = CD = DA

Thus, Quadrilateral ABCD is a rhombus.

3. Given a ||gm ABCD whose diagonal AC bisects $\angle A$.

To prove :(i) AC bisects $\angle C$ also

(ii) ABCD is a rhombus.

Proof :

(i) Consider ΔADC and ΔCBA.

AD = CB (Opp. sides of || gm)

CA = CA (Common)

DC = BA (Opp. sides of || gm ABCD)

$\therefore$ By SSS rule, $\Delta ADC \cong \Delta CBA$

$\therefore$ $\angle ACD = \angle CAB$

and $\angle DAC = \angle BCA$ (C.P.C.T.)

But given $\angle CAB = \angle DAC$

$\therefore$ $\angle ACD = \angle BCA$

$\Rightarrow$ AC bisects $\angle C$.

(ii) From (i) part,

$\angle ACD = \angle CAD$

$\therefore$ AD = CD

(Opposite sides of equal angles of a triangle are equal)

$\therefore$ AB = BC = CD = DA ($\because$ ABCD is a ||gm)

Thus, ABCD is a rhombus.

4. **Given :** ABCD is a rhombus.

To show :

(i) Diagonal AC bisects $\angle A$ as well as $\angle C$.

(ii) Diagonal BD bisects $\angle B$ as well as $\angle D$.

Proof : (i) Since, it is given that ABCD is a rhombus

$\therefore$ AD = CD

$\angle DAC = \angle DCA$ ......(1)

(Angles opposite to equal sides of a triangle are equal)

Also, CD || AB

and transversal AC intersects them

$\therefore$ $\angle DAC = \angle BCA$ ......(2)

(alt. Int. angles)

From (1) and (2)

$\angle DCA = \angle BCA$

$\Rightarrow$ AC bisects $\angle C$

Similarly AC bisects $\angle A$.

(ii) Proceeding in similar manner as in (i) above, we can show that diagonal BD bisects $\angle B$ as well as $\angle D$.

5. We have given two points P and Q on diagonal BD of a ||gm ABCD such that DP = BQ.

To Show :

(i) $\Delta APD \cong \Delta CQB$

(ii) AP = CQ

(iii) $\Delta AQB \cong \Delta CPD$

(iv) AQ = C P

(v) APCQ is a parallelogram.

We construct a line AC by joining A to C intersect BD at O.

Proof :

(i) In ΔAPD and ΔCQB,

Since, AD || BC

(Opp. sides of parallelogram ABCD and a transversal BD intersects them)

$\therefore$ $\angle ADB = \angle CBD$ (Alternate angles)

$\Rightarrow$ $\angle ADP = \angle CBQ$ ....(i)

and DP = BQ ....(ii)

AD = CB ....(iii)

(Opposite sides of ||gm)

From (i), (ii) and (iii)

$\Delta APD \cong \Delta CQB$ (By SAS rule)

(ii) Now, we have from (i) $\Delta APD \cong \Delta CQB$

$\therefore$ By C.P.C.T

AP = CQ

(iii) From ΔAQB and ΔCPD,

AB || CD (Opp. sides of ||gm ABCD and a transversal BD intersects them)

$\therefore$ $\angle ABD = \angle CDP$ (Alternate angles)

$\Rightarrow$ $\angle ABQ = \angle CDP$

and $AQ = CP$

$QB = PD$ (Given)

$\Rightarrow$ $AB = CD$

(Opp. sides of || gm ABCD)

$\therefore$ $\Delta AQB \cong \Delta CPD$ (SAS Rule)

(iv) From (iii) part we have $\Delta AQB \cong \Delta CPD$

$\therefore$ $AQ \cong CP$ (C.P.C.T.)

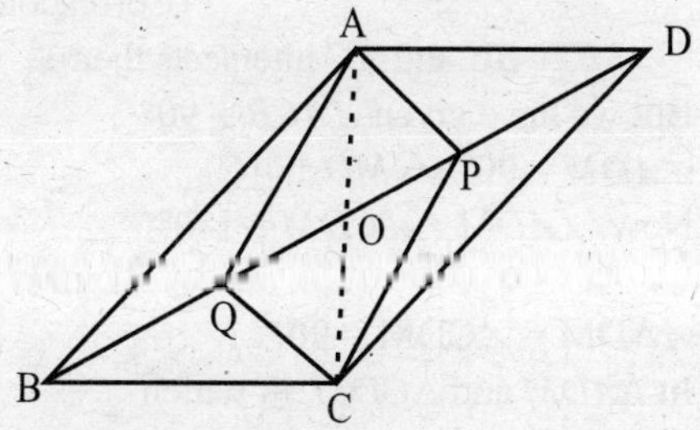

(v) Given, $BQ = DP$ and The diagonals of a parallelogram bisect each other.

$\therefore$ $OB = OD$

$\therefore$ $OB - BQ = OD - DP$

$\therefore$ $OQ = OP$ ....(i)

Also, $OA = OC$ ....(ii)

From (i) and (ii), $APCQ$ is a parallelogram.

6. **Given :** A parallelogram $ABCD$ in which AP and CQ are perpendiculars from vertices A and C on diagonal BD respectively.

To Show :

(i) $\Delta APB \cong \Delta CQD$

(ii) $AP = CQ$.

Proof :

(i) Since opposite sides of ||gm are equal

$\therefore$ In ΔAPB and ΔCQD,

$AB = CD$

and $\angle ABP = \angle CDQ$ ($\because$ $AB = DC$ and transversal BD intersects them)

Now, $\angle APB$ and $\angle CQD$ are of 90°

$\therefore$ $\angle APB = \angle CQD$

$\therefore$ $\Delta APB \cong \Delta CQD$ (By AAS Rule)

(ii) From (i), $\Delta APB \cong \Delta CQD$

$\therefore$ $AP = CQ$. (C.P.C.T.)

7. **Given :** A quadrilateral ABCD in which P, Q, R and S are mid-points of the sides AB, BC, CD and DA and AC is a diagonal.

To show :

(i) $SR \parallel AC$ and $SR = \frac{1}{2} AC$

(ii) $PQ = SR$

(iii) PQRS is a parallelogram.

Proof :

(i) Mid-point theorem: The line segment joining the mid-points of two sides of a triangle is parallel to the third side in ΔDAC, we have given S is the mid-point of DA and R is the mid-point of DC

$\therefore$ $SR \parallel AC$ and $SR = \frac{1}{2} AC$

(By above given mid-point theorem)

(ii) In similar manner, consider ΔBAC, in which P is the mid-point of AB and Q is the mid-point of BC

$\therefore$ Again by Mid-point theorem

$PQ \parallel AC$ and $PQ = \frac{1}{2} AC$

But from (i), we have $SR = \frac{1}{2} AC$

$\therefore$ $PQ = SR$

(iii) From (ii) and (i) we have $PQ \parallel AC$

$SR \parallel AC$

$\therefore$ $PQ \parallel SR$

(Two lines parallel to the same line are parallel to each other)

Also, $PQ = SR$ (From (ii))

$\therefore$ PQRS is a parallelogram.

(A quadrilateral is a parallelogram if a pair of opposite sides is parallel and is of equal length)

8. **Given :** $ABCD$ is a rhombus and P, Q, R, S are the mid-points of AB, BC, CD, DA respectively. Join PQ, QR, RS and SP.

To prove : Quadrilateral $PQRS$ is a rectangle.

Join the diagonals AC and BD.

Proof : In ΔRDS and ΔPBQ.

$DS = QB$ and $DR = PB$

($\because$ Halves of opposite sides of || gm $ABCD$ are equal)

Also, $\angle SDR = \angle QBP$ (Opposite angles of || gm $ABCD$ are equal)

$\therefore$ By SAS rule

$\Delta RDS \cong \Delta PBQ$

$\therefore$ $SR = PQ$ (C.P.C.T.)

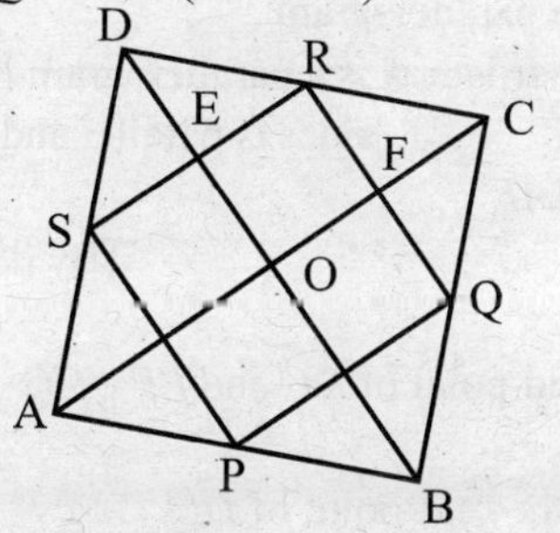

Silmlarly, From ΔRCQ and ΔPAS,

$RC = AP$ and $CQ = AS$

$\angle RCQ = \angle PAS$

(Opposite angles of || gm $ABCD$ are equal)

$\therefore$ By SAS congruence rule

$\Delta RCQ \cong \Delta PAS$

$\therefore$ $RQ = SP$ (C.P.C.T.)

$\therefore$ Quadrilateral $PQRS$, gives us

$SR = PQ$ and $RQ = SP$

$\Rightarrow$ Quadrilateral PQRS is a parallelogram,

In ΔCDB,

R and Q are the mid-points of DC and CB respectively.

$\therefore \quad RQ \parallel DB \Rightarrow RF \parallel EO$.

Similarly, $RE \parallel FO$

Thus, $OFRE$ is a ||gm

$\therefore \quad \angle R = \angle EOF = 90°$

(Opposite angles of a || gm are equal and diagonals of a rhombus intersect at 90°)

Thus quadrilateral $PQRS$ is a rectangle.

9. **Given :** A trapezium $ABCD$ in which we have $AB \parallel DC$, BD is a diagonal and E is the mid-point of AD. A line is drawn through E parallel to AB intersecting BC at F.

We have to show that : F is the mid-point of BC.

Proof : Let DB intersect EF at G. ie - G is the mid-point of BD

Since, E is the mid-point of DA and $EG \parallel AB$ in ΔDAB, G is the mid-point of DB (By converse of mid-point theorem)

Similarly,

$\therefore$ G is the mid-point of BD and $GF \parallel AB \parallel DC$ in ΔBDC,

$\therefore$ By converse of mid-point theorem.

F is the mid-point of BC.

10. **Given :** Two mid-point E and F of sides AB and CD respectively in a parallelogram $ABCD$

Show that : Line segments AF and EC trisect the diagonal BD.

Proof : In parallelogram $ABCD$, $AB \parallel DC$

$\Rightarrow \quad AE \parallel FC$ ....(i)

Since, $AB = DC$ (Opp. sides of ||gm $ABCD$)

$\therefore \quad \frac{1}{2} AB = \frac{1}{2} DC$

$\Rightarrow$ AE = CF ....(ii)

From (i) and (ii),

AECF is a parallelogram

($\because$ quadrilateral is a parallelogram if a pair of opposite sides is parallel and is of equal length)

$\therefore \quad EC \parallel AF$ ....(iii)

(By defn of || gm AECF)

In ΔDBC,

F is the mid-point of DC and $FP \parallel CQ$

($\because$ EC || AF)

$\therefore \quad P$ is the mid-point of DQ

(By converse of mid-point theorem)

$\Rightarrow \quad DP = PQ$ ....(iv)

Similarly, in ΔBAP,

$BQ = PQ$ ....(v)

From (iv) and (v), we obtain

$DP = PQ = BQ$

$\Rightarrow$ Line segments AF and EC trisect the diagonal BD.

11. **Given :** A right triangle ABC right angled at C. A line through the mid-point M of hypotenuse AB and parallel to BC which intersects AC at D.

To prove : (i) D is the mid-point of AC.

(ii) $MD \perp AC$

(iii) $CM = MA = \frac{1}{2} AB$.

Proof :

(i) In ΔACB, Since, M is the mid-point of AB and $MD \parallel BC$.

$\therefore$ D is the mid-point of AC. (By converse of mid-point theorem)

(ii) $\therefore \angle ADM = \angle ACB$

(Corresponding angles)

($\because$ $MD \parallel BC$ and AC intersects them)

But we have given $\angle ACB = 90°$

$\therefore \quad \angle ADM = 90° \Rightarrow MD \perp AC$

(iii) Now, $\angle ADM + \angle CDM = 180°$

(Linear Pair Axiom)

$\therefore \quad \angle ADM = \angle CDM = 90°$

In ΔADM and ΔCDM, in which

$AD = CD$ ($\because$ D is the mid-point of AC)

$\angle ADM = \angle CDM$ (Each measures 90°)

$DM = DM$ (Common)

$\therefore \quad \Delta ADM \cong \Delta CDM$ (SAS Rule)

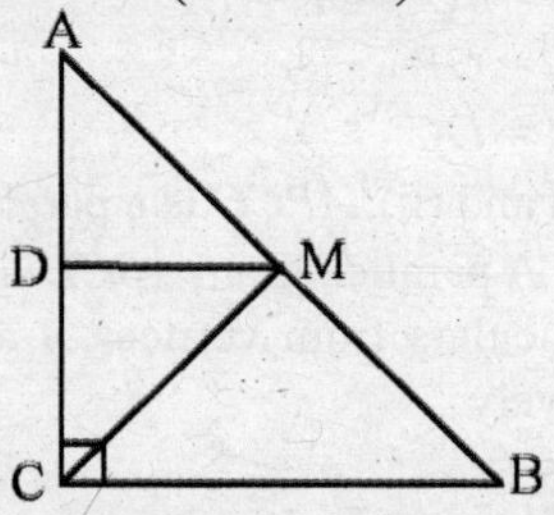

$\therefore \quad MA = MC$ (C.P.C.T.)

But we know M is the mid-point of AB

$\therefore \quad MA = MB = \frac{1}{2} AB$

$\therefore \quad MA = MC = \frac{1}{2} AB$

$\Rightarrow \quad CM = MA = \frac{1}{2} AB$.

EXEMPLAR QUESTIONS :

1. This statement is false, because diagonals of a rhombus are perpendicular but not equal to each other.

2. $\angle A = \angle C$

(Opposite angles of parallelogram ABCD)

Therefore, $\frac{1}{2}\angle A = \frac{1}{2}\angle C$

i.e., $\angle YAX = \angle YCX$ ...(i)

Also, $\angle AYC + \angle YCX = 180°$ (Because $YA \parallel CX$) ...(ii)

Therefore, $\angle AYC + \angle YAX = 180°$ [From (i) and (ii)]

So, $AX \parallel CY$

(As interior angles on the same side of the transversal are supplementary)

3. Let us draw the figure as per given condition (Fig.) In it, AC is a diagonal which bisects $\angle BAD$ of the parallelogram $ABCD$, i.e., it is given that $\angle BAC = \angle DAC$. We need to prove that $\angle BCA = \angle DCA$

$AB \parallel CD$ and AC is a transversal.

Therefore, $\angle BAC = \angle DCA$ (Alternate angles) ...(i)

Similarly, $\angle DAC = \angle BCA$ (From $AD \parallel BC$) ...(ii)

But it is given that $\angle BAC = \angle DAC$ ...(iii)

Therefore, from (i) and (iii), we have $\angle BCA = \angle DCA$

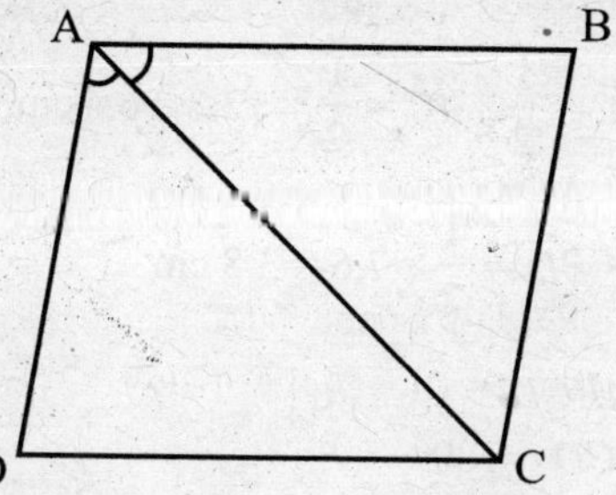

4. ABCD is not a parallelogram, because diagonals of a paralellogram bisect each other.
Here OA ≠ OC

5. (d) Fourth angle is $360° - (75 + 90 + 75°)$
$= 360° - (240) = 120°$.

6. (c) $\angle DAC = \angle ACB = 40°$
$\angle AOD = 90°$

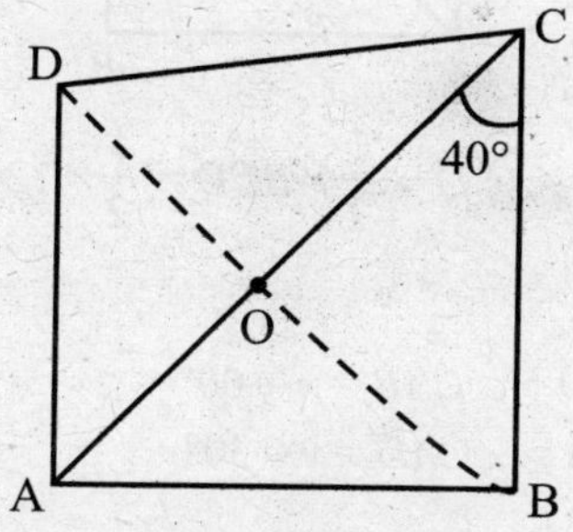

$\therefore \angle ADO = 180° - (90 + 40)$
$= 180° - 130° = 50°$

7. (c)
8. (d)
9. (c)

HOTS QUESTIONS :

1 In ΔAPD and ΔAPB, we have
$AD = AB$
$AP = AP$ (Common)
and given
$PD = PB$
$\therefore$ By SSS rule
$\Delta APD \cong \Delta APB$
$\therefore \angle 1 = \angle 2$ (C.P.C.T)
Similarly, $\Delta DPC \cong \Delta BPC$
$\therefore \angle 3 = \angle 4$ (C.P.C.T.)
But $\angle 1 + \angle 2 + \angle 3 + \angle 4 = 360°$
($\because$ Sum of all the angles round a point = 360°)
$\Rightarrow 2\angle 2 + 2\angle 3 = 360°$ ($\because \angle 1 = \angle 2$ and $\angle 3 = \angle 4$)
$\Rightarrow \angle 2 + \angle 3 = 180°$
$\Rightarrow$ AP and PC are in one and the same straight line (Linear Pair Axiom)

2. Since $PQ \parallel RM$ and EF intersects them
$\therefore \angle QXY = \angle RYX$ (Alternate angles)
$\Rightarrow \frac{1}{2}\angle QXY = \frac{1}{2}\angle RYX$
$\Rightarrow \angle 1 = \angle 3$
But these angles form a pair of equal alternate angles for lines XT and SY and a transversal XY.
$\therefore XT = SY$ ....(i)
Similarly, we can have
$SX \parallel YT$ ....(ii)
From (i) and (ii), and fact that a quadrilateral is a parallelogram if both pairs of its opposite sides are parallel $SYTX$ is a parallelogram
Now, $\angle QXY + \angle MYX = 180°$ (Consecutive interior angles)
$\Rightarrow \frac{1}{2}\angle QXY + \frac{1}{2}\angle MYX = 90°$
$\Rightarrow \angle 1 + \angle 2 = 90°$
But $\angle 1 + \angle 2 + \angle XTY = 180°$ (Angle sum property of a Δ)
$\Rightarrow 90° + \angle XTY = 180°$
$\Rightarrow \angle XTY = 90°$
$\Rightarrow \angle YSX = 90°$
and $\angle SXT = 90$
($\because$ Consecutive interior angles are supplementary)
Now, $\angle SXT = 90° \Rightarrow \angle SYT = 90°$
(Opposite angles of a ||gm are equal)
Thus each angle of the parallelogram $SYTX$ is 90°. Hence parallelogram $SYTX$ is a rectangle.

3. We are given that $AB = BC$ and have to prove that $DE = EF$
Let us join A to F intersecting m at G.
The trapezium $ACFD$ is divided into two triangles; namely ΔACF and ΔAFD
In ΔACF, it is given that B is the mid-point of AC ($AB = BC$)
and $BG \parallel CF$ (Since $m \parallel n$)
So, G is the mid-point of AF
(By the converse of Mid-point Theorem)
Now, in ΔAFD, we can apply the same argument as G is the mid-point of AF, $GE \parallel AD$ so E is the mid-point of DE.
i.e., $DE = EF$
In other words l, m and n cut-off equal intercepts on q also.

4. Square is a parallelogram. In a parallelogram sum of the interior angles is 180°, and since square has all its angles equal.

$\therefore \quad \angle A + \angle B = 180°$

$\angle A + \angle A = 180° \quad \Rightarrow 2\angle A = 180°$

$\angle A = 90°$

$\angle A = \angle B = \angle C = \angle D = 90°$

5. In ΔABC, Q and R are the mid-points of AB and BC respectively.

$\therefore \quad QR \parallel AC \quad$ ....(i)

In ΔABH, Q and P are the mid-points of AB and AH respectively.

$\therefore \quad QP \parallel BH \Rightarrow QP \parallel BE \quad$ ....(ii)

But $AC \perp BE$. Therefore, from (i) and (ii) we have

$QP \perp QR \Rightarrow \angle PQR = 90°$

6.

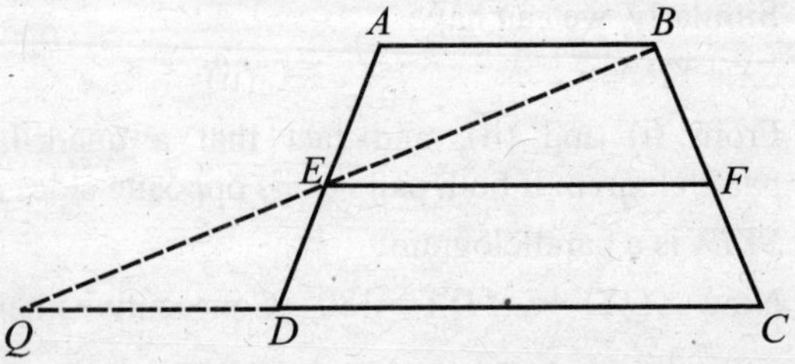

Given: $AB \parallel CD$ and E, F are the mid-points of sides AD and BC respectively.

To prove: $EF \parallel AB$, $EF = \frac{1}{2}(AB + CD)$

Construction: Join BE and produce it to meet CD produced at Q.

Proof: In ΔBQC

Since E and F are the mid-points of sides BQ and BC respectively.

$\therefore$ By Mid-point Theorem,

$EF \parallel QC$ and $EF = \frac{1}{2}QC \quad$ ...(i)

$\Rightarrow \quad FE \parallel DC$

But $CD \parallel AB$ (Given)

$\Rightarrow \quad EF \parallel AB$

Now, In ΔAEB and ΔDEQ, we have

$\angle AEB = \angle DEQ$ (Vertically opposite angles)

$AE = ED$ (E is the mid-point of AD)

$\angle BAE = \angle EDQ$ (Alternate interior angles)

$\therefore \quad \Delta AEB \cong \Delta DEQ$ (By ASA congruence criterion)

$\Rightarrow \quad AB = QD$ (CPCT) $\quad$ ...(ii)

From (i), $EF = \frac{1}{2}QC = \frac{1}{2}(QD + DC) = \frac{1}{2}(AB + CD)$

[Using (ii)]

Hence, $EF = \frac{1}{2}(AB + CD)$

3 EXERCISE

SINGLE OPTION CORRECT :

1. (d) Since diagonals of a parallelogram bisect each other.

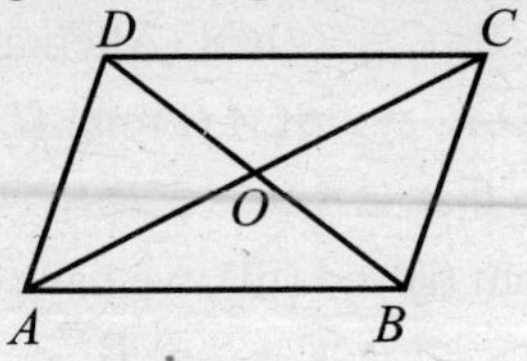

Thus, $\quad OC = \frac{1}{2} \times AC = \frac{1}{2} \times 12.8 = 6.4$ cm

$OD = \frac{1}{2} \times BD = \frac{1}{2} \times 7.6 = 3.8$ cm

2. (c) In rhombus $ABCD$

$\angle ABC + \angle BCD = 180°$

$\angle BCD = 180 - 56 = 124°$

As, diagonals of a rhombus bisect the angles.

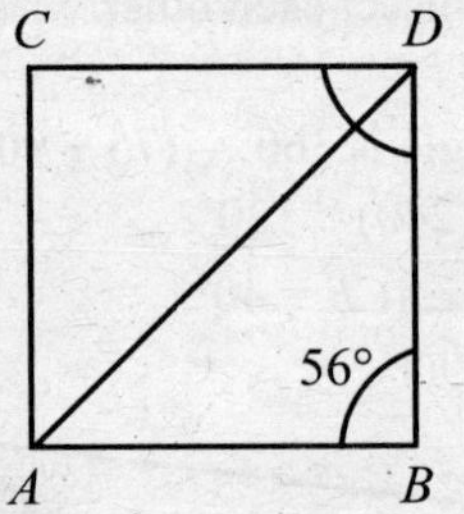

Thus, $\angle ACD = \frac{1}{2} \times BCD = \frac{1}{2} \times 124 = 62°$

3. (c) 4. (a)

5. (a) $\angle ACD = \angle CAB = x = 60°$ (Alternate angles)

$\angle BCA = \angle CAD = y = 30°$ (Alternate angles)

6. (b) 7. (d)

8. (d) Consider Δs, DNR and BMR

$DN = BN$ (Given)

$\angle DNR = \angle BMR = 90°$ (Each)

$\angle DRN = \angle BRM$ [Vertically opposite angles]

$\therefore \Delta DNR \cong \Delta BMR$ [AAS Congruency]

$\therefore DR = BR$

$\therefore BD = 2BR$

$\therefore BD = 2 \times 8 = 16$ cm

9. (a) $\angle x = 29°$ [Alternate Angle]

In triangle,

$\angle x + \angle y + 78° = 180°$

$29 + \angle y + 78 = 180°$

$\angle y = 180° - 107° = 73°$

10. (c) Since $ABCD$ is a parallelogram. Therefore, $AB = CD$ and $AD = BC$

[$\because$ Opposite sides of a parallelogram are equal]

Thus, in Δs ABD and ACB, we have

$AD = BC$ [As proved above]

$BD = AC$ [Given]

and, $AB = AB$ [Common]

So, by SSS criterion of congruence, we have

$\angle BAD = \angle ABC$ [c.p.c.t.] ...(i)

Now, AD || BC and transversal AB intersects them at A and B respectively.

$\therefore$ ∠BAD + ∠ABC = 180°

[Sum of the interior angles on the same side of a transversal is 180°]

$\Rightarrow \angle ABC + \angle ABC = 180°$ [Using (i)]

$\Rightarrow 2\angle ABC = 180°$

$\Rightarrow \angle ABC = 90°$

Hence, the measure of $\angle ABC$ is 90°.

11. (c) Since quadrilateral $AXYZ$ is a square

$\therefore$ $YZ = AZ = 2$ cm

Now $DZ = DY + YZ = 3$ cm + 2cm = 5 cm

In right angled ΔAZD,

$AD^2 = AZ^2 + DZ^2 = 4\text{cm}^2 + 25\text{ cm}^2 = 29\text{ cm}^2$

Since $ABCD$ is a square,

$\therefore$ $AB = AD \Rightarrow AB^2 = AD^2 = 29\text{ cm}^2$

In right angled ΔBAX,

$AB^2 = AX^2 + BX^2$

$29 = 4 + BX^2$

$\Rightarrow$ BX = 5 cm

Since $AXYZ$ is a square

$\therefore$ $XY = AZ = 2$ cm

Now $BY = BX + XY = 5$ cm + 2 cm = 7 cm

More Than One Option Correct :

1. (c, d)

2. (a, b)

Only statements given in option 'a' and 'b' are correct.

3. (a, b, d)

(b) $x + 2x + 3x + 4x = 360° \Rightarrow x = 36°$

Fourth angle = $4x = 4(36) = 144°$

(d) Fourth angle = 360° – 210 = 150°

Passage Based Questions :

1. (b) By angle sum property of quadrilateral.

2. (a) $100 + 98 + 92 + x = 360°$

where x = fourth angle

$\Rightarrow x = 360 - 290 = 70°$

3. **(c)** Since the sum of any two consecutive angles of a parallelogram is 180°. Therefore,

$\angle A + \angle D = 180°$ and $\angle A + \angle B = 180°$

Now, $\angle A + \angle D = 180°$

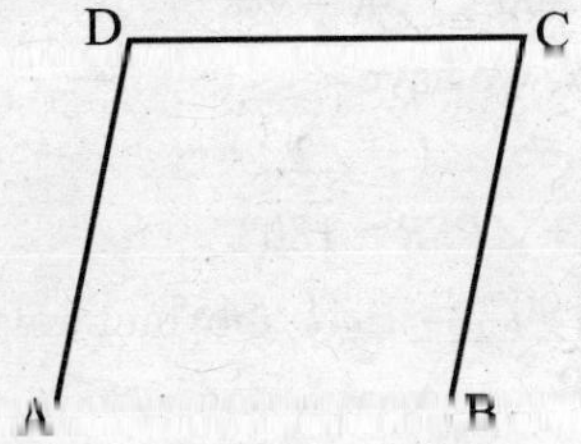

$\Rightarrow$ $\angle A + 115° = 180°$

$\Rightarrow$ $\angle A = 65°$ and $\angle A + \angle B = 180°$

$\Rightarrow$ $65° + \angle B = 180° \Rightarrow \angle B = 115°$

Thus, ∠A = 65° and ∠B = 115°

4. **(a)** In ΔBCD, we have

$\angle BDC + \angle DCB + \angle CBD = 180°$

$\Rightarrow$ $5a + 9a + 4a = 180°$

$\Rightarrow$ 18a = 180° $\Rightarrow a = 10°$

$\therefore$ ∠C = 9 × 10° = 90°

Since opposite angles are equal in a parallelogram. Therefore,

∠A = ∠C ⇒ ∠A = 90°

Assertion and Reason :

1. (a) **2.** (a) **3.** (a)

4. (a) Both Assertion and Reason are correct. Reason is the correct explanation of Assertion.

5. (c) Assertion is correct but Reason is incorrect.

Integer Type Questions :

1. **Ans : 1**

Since $ABCD$ is a parallelogram

$\therefore$ $AB \parallel DC$ and $AD \parallel BC$.

Now, AB || DC and transversal BD intersect them.

$\therefore$ ∠ABD = ∠$BDC \Rightarrow 12x = 60 \Rightarrow x = 5$

Similarly, $AD \parallel BC$ and transversal BD intersects them

$\therefore$ $\angle DBC = \angle ADB$

$\Rightarrow$ $7y = 28 \Rightarrow y = 4$

Hence, $x - y = 5 - 4 = 1$

2. **Ans : 9**

Since $PQRS$ is a square

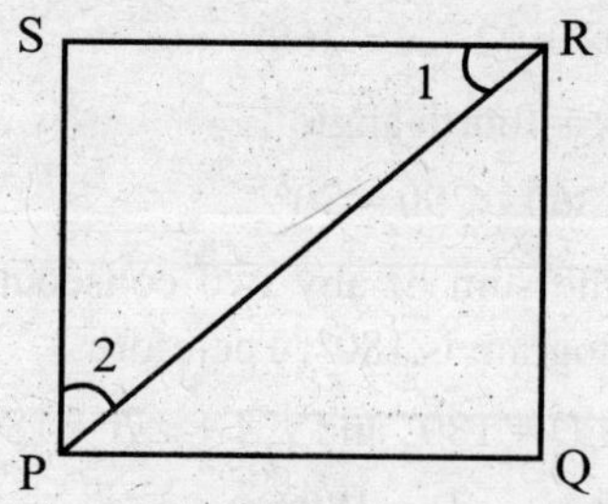

$\therefore \quad PS = SR$ and $\angle PSR = 90°$

Now, in ΔPSR, we have

$PS = SR \Rightarrow \angle 1 = \angle 2$

But $\angle 1 + \angle 2 + \angle PSR = 180°$

$\Rightarrow \quad (2\angle 1) = 90° \Rightarrow \angle 1 = 45°$

Hence, $\dfrac{\angle SRP}{5} = \dfrac{45}{5} = 9$

3. **Ans : 2**

Consider ΔARB.

In ΔARB,

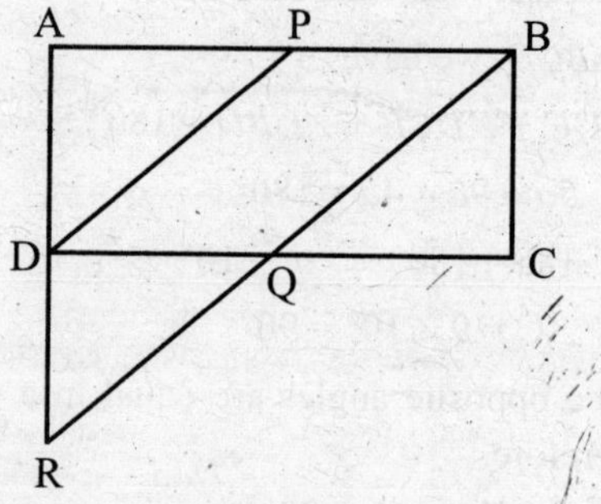

P is the mid-point of AB and $PD \parallel BR$.

$\therefore \quad D$ is the mid-point of AR.

$\Rightarrow \quad AR = 2AD$

$\Rightarrow \quad AR = 2BC \qquad (\because ABCD$ is a $\parallel$ gm)

Hence $m = 2$

4. **Ans : 9**

Since sides of the square are equal therefore,

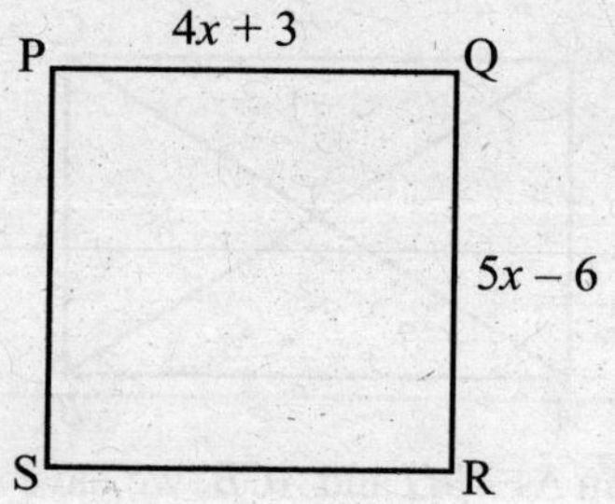

$4x + 3 = 5x - 6 \Rightarrow x = 9$

5. **Ans : 6**

Since all the sides of a rhombus are equal.

$\therefore \quad AB = AD$

$\Rightarrow \quad \angle ABD = \angle ADB$

In ΔABD,

$60° + \angle ABD + \angle ADB = 180°$

$\Rightarrow \quad \angle ABD = 60° = \angle ADB$

Since ΔABD is equilateral

$\therefore \quad BD = 6$ cm

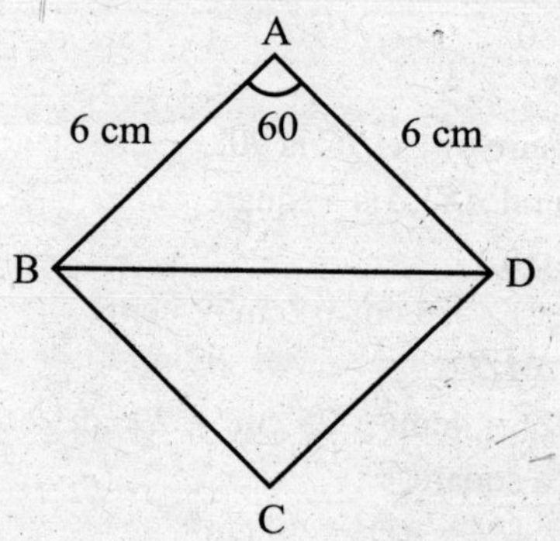

6. **Ans : 2**

Since, EAB is a straight line

$\therefore \quad \angle DAE + \angle DAB = 180°$

$\Rightarrow \quad 73° + \angle DAB = 180°$

i.e., $\angle DAB = 180° - 73° = 107°$

Since, the sum of the angles of quadrilateral $ABCD$ is 360°

$\therefore \quad 107° + 105° + x + 80° = 360°$

$\Rightarrow \quad 292° + x = 360°$

and, $x = 360° - 292° = 68°$

Hence $\dfrac{x}{34} = \dfrac{68}{34} = 2$

Chapter 9

Area of Parallelograms & Triangles

INTRODUCTION

You may recall that the part of the plane enclosed by a simple closed figure is called a planar region corresponding to that figure. The magnitude or measure of this planar region is called its area. Area of a figure is a number in some unit associated with the part of the plane enclosed by the figure. You are also familiar with the concept of congruent figures.

In this chapter, you will learn to find the areas of different plane figures, such as triangle, rectangle, parallelogram, etc. by studying some relationship between the areas of these figures under the condition when they lie on the same base and between the same parallel lines.

FIGURES ON THE SAME BASE AND BETWEEN THE SAME PARALLEL LINES

Two figures are said to be on the same base and between the same parallel lines, if they have a common base (or side) and their vertices opposite to the common base lie on a same line parallel to the base. Look at the figures:

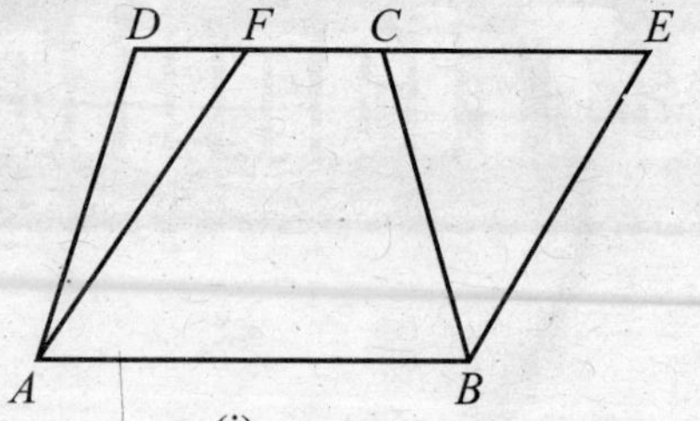

(i)

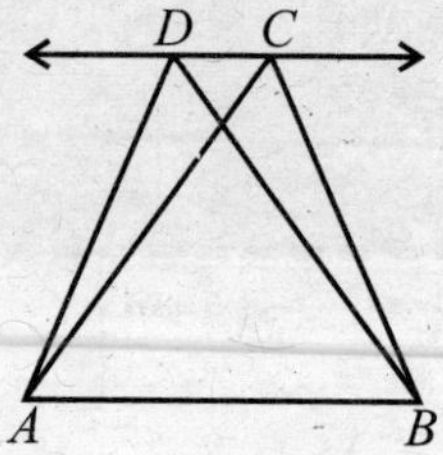

(ii)

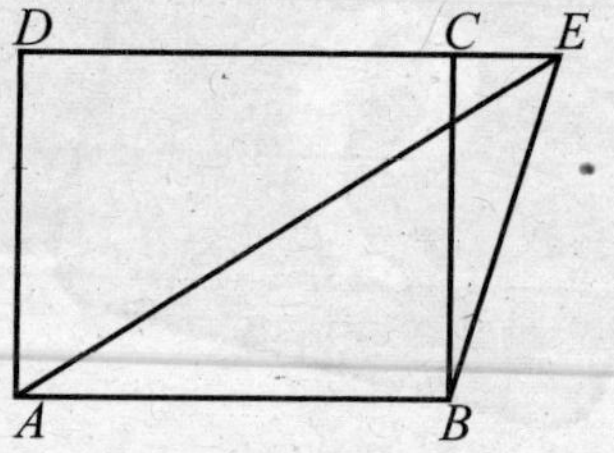

(iii)

In fig (i) trapezium *ABCD* and parallelogram *ABEF* are on the same base *AB*. Besides these, the vertices *C* and *D* of trapezium *ABCD* opposite to base *AB* and the vertices *E* and *F* of parallelogram *ABEF* opposite to base *AB* lie on a line *DE* parallel to *AB*. So we can say that trapezium *ABCD* and parallelogram *ABEF* are on the same base *AB* and between the same pair of parallel lines *AB* and *DE*. Similarly in fig.(ii), triangle *ABC* and *ABD* are on the same base *AB* and lie between the same parallel lines *AB* and *CD*. Also in fig. (iii) parallelogram *ABCD* and triangle *ABE* are on the same base *AB* and between the same parallel lines *AB* and *DE*.

Now ΔABC and ΔADB in fig (iv) have no common base. Also in fig. (v) ΔABC and parallelogram. *PQRS* are not on the same base.

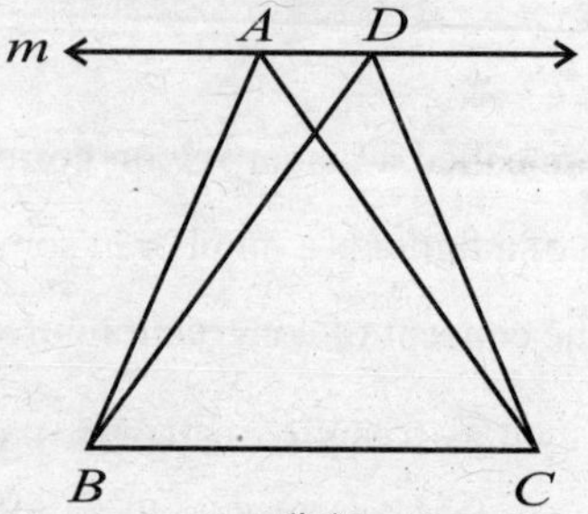

(iv)

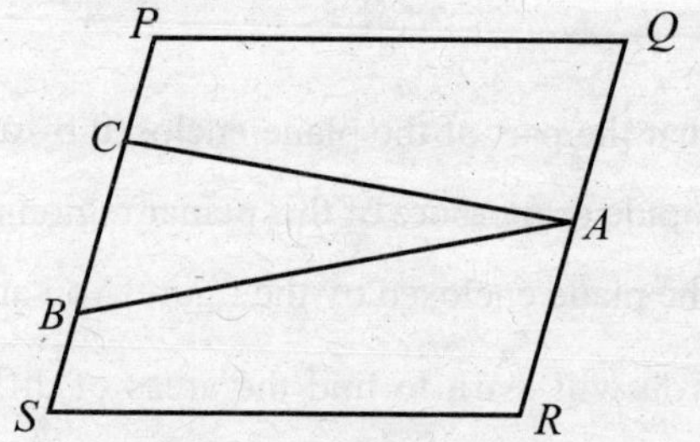

(v)

PARALLELOGRAMS ON THE SAME BASE AND BETWEEN THE SAME PARALLELS

Base

A base of a parallelogram is any side of it.

Altitude

For each base of a parallelogram, the corresponding altitude is the line segment from a point on the base, perpendicular to the line containing the opposite side.

ILLUSTRATION : 1

The diagonals of a parallelogram *ABCD* intersect at *O*. *A* line through *O* meets *AB* in *X* and *CD* in *Y*. Show that ar(□AXYD) $= \frac{1}{2}$ (ar || gm *ABCD*).

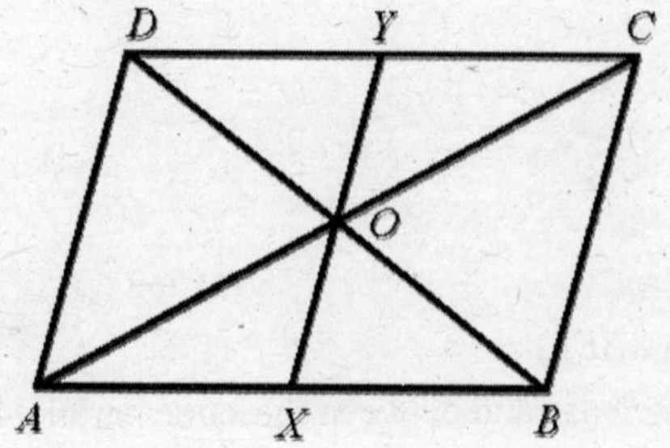

SOLUTION :

Since a diagonal of a parallelogram divides it into two triangles of equal area, therefore diagonal *AC* of || gm ABCD divides it into two triangles of equal area.

$\therefore \quad ar(\Delta ACD) = \frac{1}{2} ar(\|gm\ ABCD)$ ...(i)

In Δs AOX and COY, we have

$\angle AOX = \angle COY$ [$\because$ Vertically opposite angles are equal]

$AO = CO$ $\left[\begin{array}{l}\because \text{Diagonals of a } \| \text{gm bisect each other} \\ \therefore O \text{ is the mid-point of } AC\end{array}\right]$

and $\angle OAX = \angle OCY$ $\left[\begin{array}{l}\because AB \parallel DC \text{ and transversal } AC \text{ cuts them} \\ \therefore \angle CAB = \angle ACD \Rightarrow \angle OAX = \angle OCY\end{array}\right]$

So, by ASA criterion of congruence, we have

$\Delta AOX \cong \Delta COY$

$\Rightarrow$ ar(ΔAOX) = ar(ΔCOY) [By Congruent area axiom]

$\Rightarrow$ ar(ΔAOX) + ar($\square AOYD$) = ar(ΔCOY) + ar($\square AOYD$) [Adding ar($\square AOYD$) on both sides]

$\Rightarrow \quad ar(\square AXYD) = ar(\Delta ACD)$ ...(ii)

From (i) and (ii), we get

$ar(\square AXYD) = \frac{1}{2} ar(\|gm\ ABCD)$

Theorem 1 : A diagonal of parallelogram divides it into two triangles of equal area.

Given : A parallelogram $ABCD$ in which BD is one of its diagonals, side $AB \parallel CD$ and $BC \parallel AD$.

To Prove : Area of ΔABD = area of ΔBCD

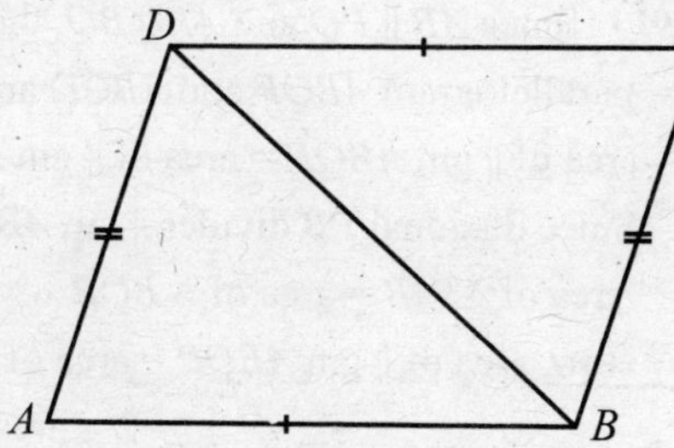

Proof : In ΔABD and ΔBCD,

$AB = CD$ (opp. sides of a $\|$ gm)

$AD = CB$ (opp. sides of a $\|$ gm)

$BD = BD$ (common side)

$\therefore$ $\Delta ABD \cong \Delta CDB$ [By SSS congruent Rule]

$\therefore$ area of ΔABD = area of ΔBCD [congruent area Axiom]

Theorem 2 : Parallelograms on the same (or equal) base and between the same parallel lines are equal in area.

Given : Two parallelograms $ABCD$ and $ABEF$, which have the same base AB and which are between the same parallel lines AB and FC.

To Prove : Area of $\|$ gm $ABCD$ = area of $\|$ gm $ABEF$

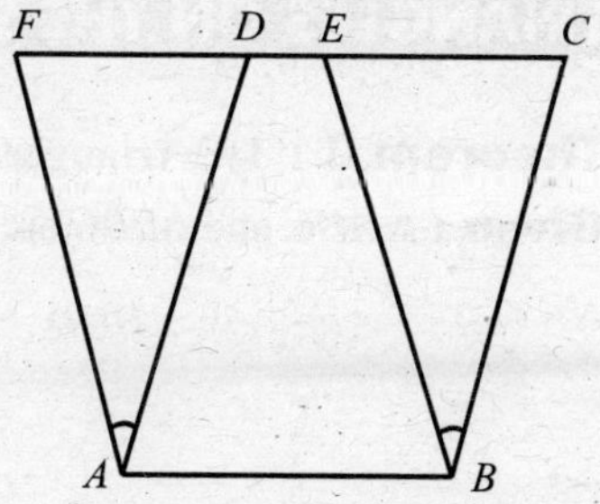

Proof : In ΔADF and ΔBCE,

$AD = BC$ [opp. sides of a $\|$ gm]

$AF = BE$ [opp. sides of a $\|$gm]

Also, $AD \parallel BC$ and $AF \parallel BE$

So the angle between AD and AF is equal to the angle between BC and BE.

i.e. $\angle DAF = \angle CBE$

$\therefore$ $\Delta ADF \cong \Delta BCE$ [By SAS congruent Rule]

$\therefore$ area (ΔADF) = area (ΔBCE) [By congruent area Axiom] ...(i)

Now, area $\|$ gm $ABCD$ = area ($\square ABED$) + (ΔBCE)

= area ($\square ABED$) + area (ΔADF) [Using (i)]

area ($\|$ gm $ABCD$) = area ($\|$ gm $ABEF$)

Corollary : (i) A parallelogram and a rectangle on the same base and between the same parallel lines are equal in area.

(ii) Area of a parallelogram = base $\times$ height

Given : A parallelogram ABCD in which AB is the base and AQ is the corresponding height.

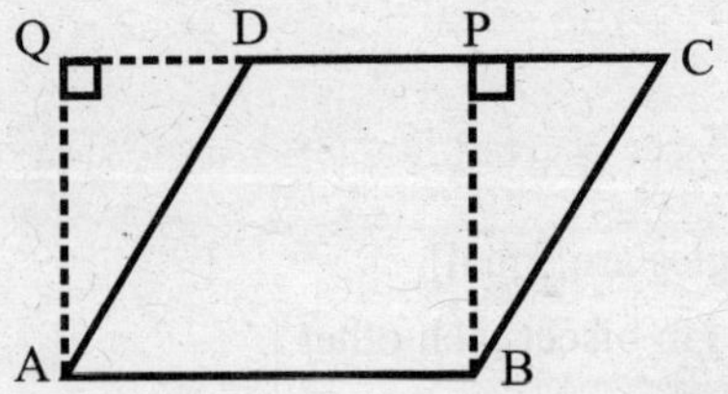

Construction : Draw $BP \perp DC$, so that rectangle $ABPQ$ is formed.

To Prove : Since parallelogram $ABCD$ and rectangle $ABPQ$ are on the same base AB and between the same parallel lines AB and PQ.

$\therefore$ area (|| gm $ABCD$) = ar (rect. $ABPQ$)

$= AB \times AQ$

$\therefore$ area of || gm = base × height.

ILLUSTRATION : 2

If a triangle and a parallelogram are on the same (or equal) base and between the same parallel lines, then prove that area of the triangle is equal to half the area of the parallelogram.

SOLUTION :

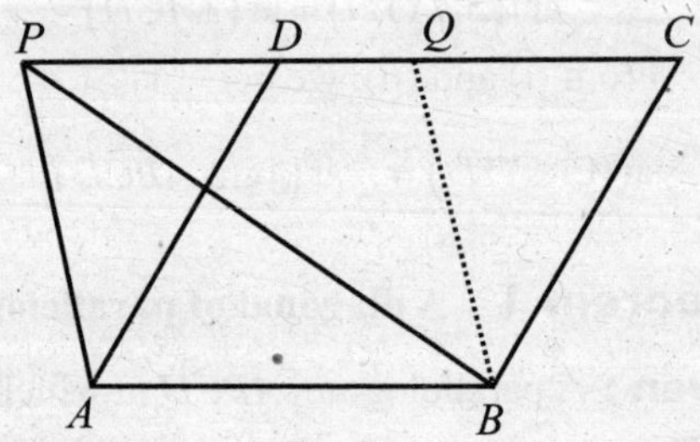

Given : ΔABP and || gm $ABCD$ be on the same base AB and between the same parallel lines AB and PC (See fig.)

To Prove : Area of $\Delta PAB = \frac{1}{2}$ area of || gm $ABCD$

Construction : From B, draw $BQ \parallel AP$

Proof : Since $AB \parallel PQ$ and $AP \parallel BQ$, therefore $ABQP$ is parallelogram.

Now, parallelogram $ABQP$ and $ABCD$ are on the same base AB and between the same parallels AB and PC.

$\therefore$ area of || gm $ABQP$ = area of || gm $ABCD$ ...(i)

Since diagonal PB divides || gm $ABQP$ into two triangles of equal areas (Theorem-2).

$\therefore$ Area of ΔPAB = area of ΔBQP ...(ii)

$\therefore$ Now, area of || gm $ABQP$ = area of ΔPAB + area of ΔBQP

$= 2 \times$ area of ΔPAB [from (ii)]

$\therefore$ Area of $\Delta PAB = \frac{1}{2}$ area of || gm $ABQP$

$\Rightarrow$ area of $\Delta PAB = \frac{1}{2}$ area of || gm $ABCD$

TRIANGLES ON THE SAME BASE AND BETWEEN THE SAME PARALLELS

Theorem 3 : Two triangles on the same base (or equal bases) and between the same parallels are equal in area.

Given : ΔABC and ΔPBC are on the same base BC and between the same parallel lines BC and AP.

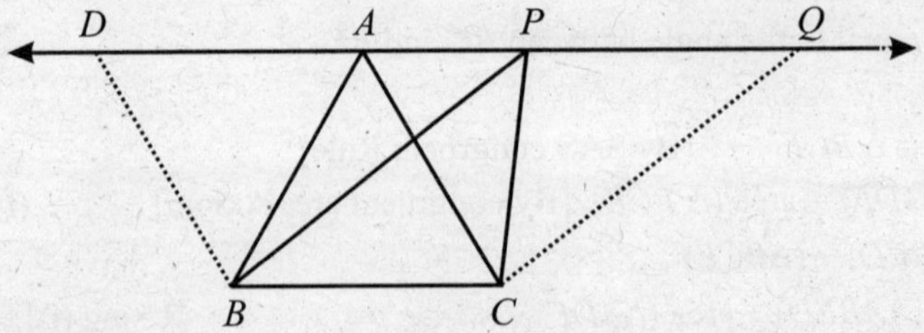

To Prove : Area of ΔABC = area of ΔPBC

Construction : Through B, draw $BD \parallel CA$ intersecting PA produced at D and through C, draw $CQ \parallel BP$ intersecting AP produced in Q.

Proof : We have

$BD \parallel CA$ [By construction]

$BC \parallel DA$ [Given]

∴ $BCAD$ is a parallelogram.

Similarly, $BCQP$ is a parallelogram.

Now, || gm $BCQP$ and $BCAD$ are on the same base BC and lie between the same parallel lines BC and DQ,

∴ area of (|| gm $BCQP$) = area of (|| gm $BCAD$) ...(i)

We know that the diagonals of a || gm divides it into two triangles of equal area. [By theorem-1]

∴ Area of ($\Delta\ PBC$) = $\frac{1}{2}$ area of (|| gm $BCQP$) ...(ii)

and area of ($\Delta\ ABC$) = $\frac{1}{2}$ area of (|| gm $BCAD$) ...(iii)

Now area of (|| gm $BCQP$) = area of (|| gm $BCAD$) [from (i)]

∴ $\frac{1}{2}$ area of (|| gm $BCQP$) = $\frac{1}{2}$ area of (|| gm $BCAD$)

∴ area of ΔABC = area of ΔPBC [From (ii) and (iii)]

> **NOTE :** (i) Two triangles with same base (or equal bases) and equal areas will have equal corresponding altitudes.
> (ii) The area of a triangle is half the product of any of its sides and the corresponding altitude.

Theorem 4 : Two triangles having the same base (or equal bases) and equal areas lie between the same parallels.

ILLUSTRATION : 3

Show that a median of a triangle divides it into two triangles of equal areas.

SOLUTION :

Let ABC be a triangle and let AD be one of its medians (see in Figure).

Show that ar(ABD) = ar (ACD).

Since the formula for area involves altitude, let us draw AN ⊥ BC.

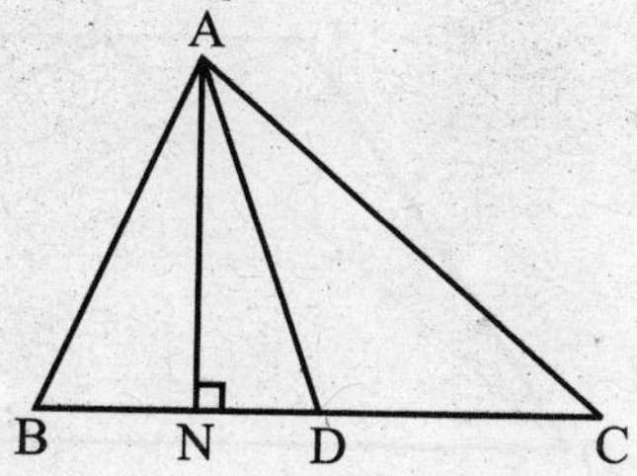

Now, area(ABD) = $\frac{1}{2}$ × base × altitude (of ΔABD)

$= \frac{1}{2} \times BD \times AN$

$= \frac{1}{2} \times CD \times AN$ (as BD = CD)

$= \frac{1}{2}$ × base × altitude (of ΔACD)

= ar(ACD)

> **NOTE :** The area of a trapezium is half the product of its height and the sum of parallel sides.

MISCELLANEOUS SOLVED EXAMPLES

1. Prove that the area of an equilateral triangle is equal to $\frac{\sqrt{3}}{4}a^2$, where *a* is the side of the triangle.

Sol. Draw $AD \perp BC$

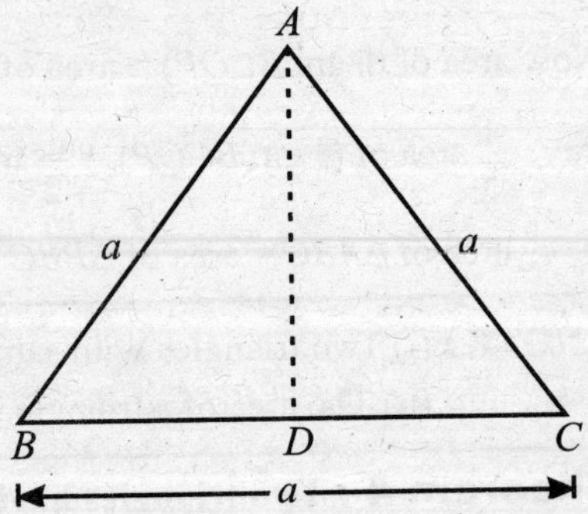

$\Delta ABD \cong \Delta ACD$ (By R.H.S.)

$\therefore BD = DC$ (CPCT)

$\because BC = a$

$\therefore BD = DC = \frac{a}{2}$

In right angled ΔABD

$$AD^2 = AB^2 - BD^2 = a^2 - \left(\frac{a}{2}\right)^2 = a^2 - \frac{a^2}{4} = \frac{3a^2}{4} \Rightarrow AD = \frac{\sqrt{3}a}{2}$$

$$\text{Area of } \Delta ABC = \frac{1}{2}BC \times AD = \frac{1}{2}a\frac{\sqrt{3}a}{2} = \frac{\sqrt{3}a^2}{4}$$

2. ABCD is a trapezium with AB || DC. A line parallel to AC intersects AB at X and BC at Y. Prove that ar(ΔADX) = ar(ΔACY).

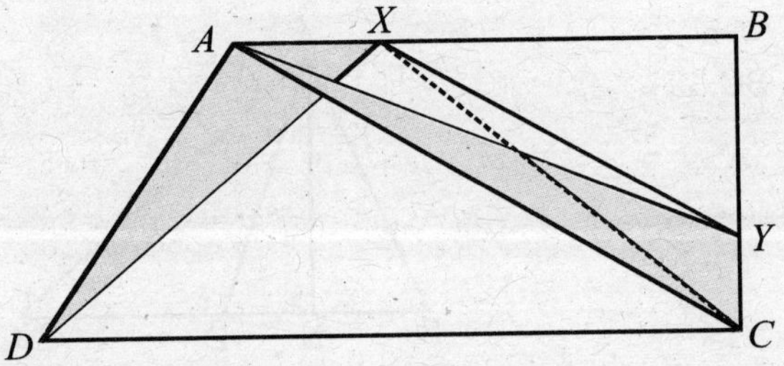

Sol. We have a trapezium ABCD such that AB || DC.

XY || AC meets AB at X and BC at Y.

Let us join CX.

AB || DC [Given]

and ΔADX and ΔACX are on the same base AX and between the same parallels AB and DC.

$\therefore$ ar(ΔADX) = ar(ΔACX) ...(i)

Also, AC || XY [Given]

and ΔACX and ΔACY are on the same base AC and between the same parallels AC and XY.

$\therefore$ ar(ΔACX) = ar(ΔACY) ...(ii)

From (i) and (ii), we have ar(ΔADX) = ar(ΔACY)

3. What is the area of a trapezium whose parallel sides are 55 cm, 40 cm and non-parallel sides are 20 cm and 25 cm respectively?

Sol. In figure, *ABCD* is a trapezium in which parallel sides *AB* = 55 cm, *DC* = 40 cm and non-parallel sides *AD* = 20 cm and *BC* = 25 cm.

Draw AD || EC and CF ⊥ AB

Therefore, $EB = AB - AE = 55 - 40 = 15$ cm and $EC = 20$ cm.

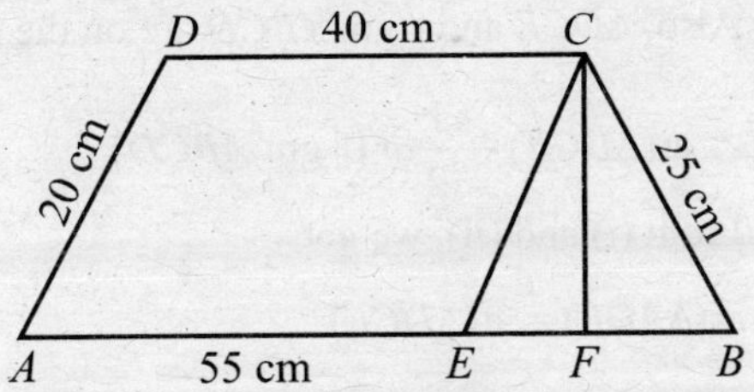

where $s = \dfrac{15+20+25}{2} = 30$ cm.

$\therefore$ Area of ΔBCE

$= \sqrt{30\times(30-15)\times(30-20)\times(30-25)}$

$= \sqrt{30\times15\times10\times5} = \sqrt{22500} = 150$ sq.cm.

Area of $\Delta BCE = \dfrac{1}{2}\times BE\times CF$

$\Rightarrow CF = \dfrac{2\times150}{15} = 20$ cm.

Area of parallelogram $AECD = AE \times CF = 40 \times 20 = 800$ sq. cm.

$\therefore$ Area of the trapezium $ABCD$ = Area of parallelogram $AECD$ + Area of $\Delta EBC = 800 + 150 = 950$ sq. cm.

4. In fig., $AP \,||\, BQ \,||\, CR$. Prove that ar(ΔAQC) = ar(ΔPBR).

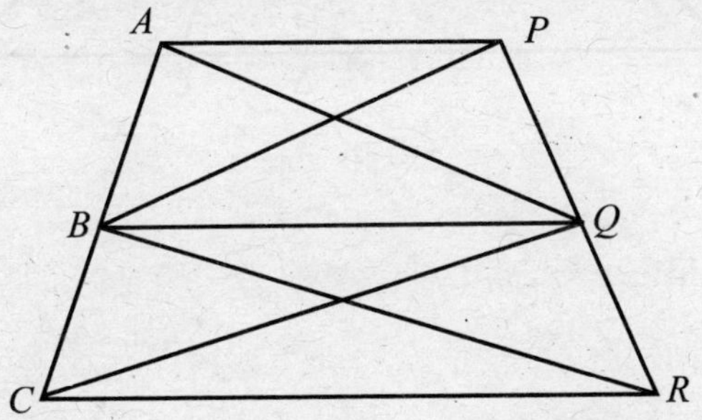

Sol. Since ΔABQ and ΔPBQ are on the same base BQ and between the same parallels AP and BQ.

$\therefore$ ar (ΔABQ) = ar (ΔPBQ) ...(i)

Similarly, ΔBCQ and ΔBRQ are on the same base BQ and between the same parallels BQ and CR.

$\therefore$ ar (ΔBCQ) = ar (ΔBRQ) ...(ii)

Adding (i) and (ii), we get

ar (ΔABQ) + ar (ΔBCQ) = ar (ΔPBQ) + ar (ΔBRQ)

$\Rightarrow$ ar (ΔAQC) = ar (ΔPBR)

5. In a parallelogram, ABCD, E and F are any two points on the sides AB and BC respectively. Show that ar(ΔADF) = ar(ΔDCE).

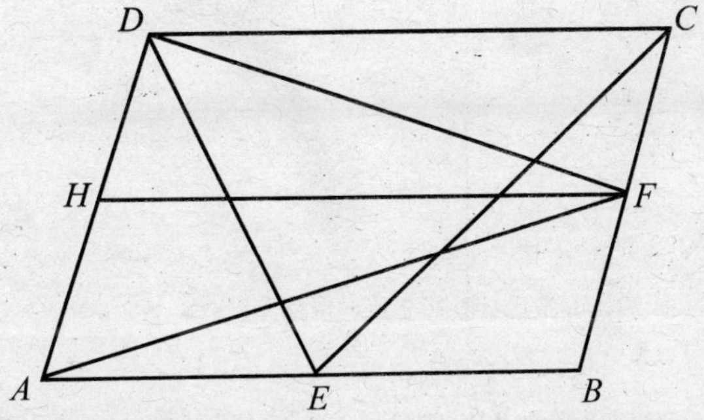

Sol. Since ΔADF and parallelogram $ABCD$ are on the same base AD and between the same parallels AD and BC.

$\therefore$ ar(ΔADF) $= \dfrac{1}{2} ar$ (|| gm $ABCD$) ...(i)

Also, ΔDCE and || gm $ABCD$ are on the same base DC and between the same parallels DC and AB.

$\therefore$ ar(ΔDCE) = $\frac{1}{2} ar(\| \text{gm } ABCD)$ ...(ii)

From (i) and (ii), we get

ar(ΔADF) = ar(ΔDCE)

6. $ABCD$ is a trapezium in which $AB \parallel DC$. DC is produced to E such that $CE = AB$, prove that ar(ΔABD) = ar(ΔBCE).

Sol. Produce BA to M such that $DM \perp AB$ and draw $BN \perp DC$.

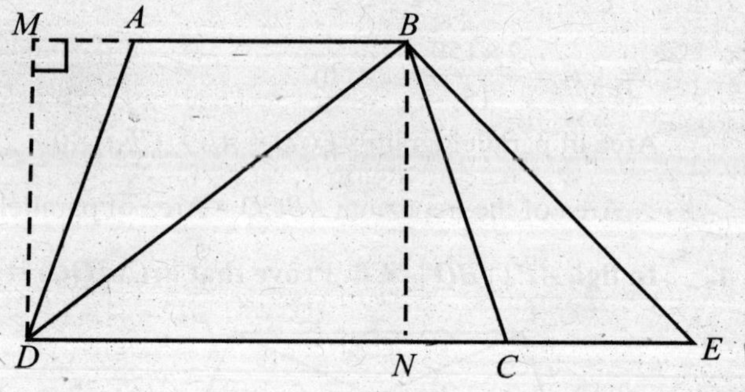

Now, ar(ΔABD) = $\frac{1}{2}(AB \times DM)$ ...(i)

ar(ΔBCE) = $\frac{1}{2}(CE \times BN)$ ...(ii)

Since, triangles ABD and BCE are between the same parallels,

Therefore,

$DM = BN$ ...(iii)

Also, $AB = CE$ (Given) ...(iv)

From (iii) and (iv), we get

$\frac{1}{2}(AB \times DM) = \frac{1}{2}(CE \times BN)$

$\Rightarrow$ ar(ΔABD) = ar(ΔBCE) (Using (i) and (ii))

1 EXERCISE

Fill in the Blanks :

DIRECTIONS: *Complete the following statements with an appropriate word/term to be filled in the blank space(s).*

1. Two triangles having the same base and equal area lie between the same_____________.
2. A diagonal of a parallelogram divides it into two triangles of equal_____________.
3. The area of a parallelogram is the product of its base and the corresponding_____________.
4. A _____________of a triangle divides it into two triangles of equal area.
5. The area of parallelogram is the _____________ of its base and the corresponding altitude.

True / False :

DIRECTIONS: *Read the following statements and write your answer as true or false.*

1. If two triangles have a common vertex and their bases lie on the same line, then their areas are proportional to the lengths of their bases.
2. A median of a triangle divides it into two triangles of equal areas.
3. The area of a triangle = 2 × base × height
4. Parallelograms on the same base and between the same parallels are different in area.
5. Any side of a parallelogram can be said its base.
6. The length of the line segment which is perpendicular to the base from the opposite vertex is called the altitude of the parallelogram corresponding to the given base.
7. The area of a trapezium is half of the product of its height and the sum of parallel sides.
8. The area of a parallelogram $ABCD$ is equal to $AB \times CE$, where CE is the altitude from C to AD.
9. The base of a triangle is 13 cm and height is 6 cm, so its area is 78 sq cm.

Match the Columns :

DIRECTIONS: *Following given question contains statements in two columns which have to be matched. Statements (A, B, C, D, ...) in Column - I have to be matched with statements (p, q, r, s, ...) in Column - II.*

1.

Column-I	Column-II
(A) The area of a rhombus if the lengths of diagonals are 16 cm and 24 cm, is	(p) 9.6 cm
(B) The area of a trapezium whose parallel sides are 9 cm & 16 cm and the distance between these sides is 8 cm, is	(q) 8 cm
(C) The area of a rhombus is 20 cm^2. If one of its diagonals is 5 cm, the other diagonal is	(r) 192 cm^2
(D) In a parallelogram ABCD, AB = 12 cm and the altitude corresponding to AB is 8 cm. If AD = 10 cm, then the altitude corresponding to AD is equal to	(s) 100 cm^2

Very Short Answer Questions :

DIRECTIONS: *Give answer in one word or one sentence.*

1. State formula for evaluating the area of a rhombus.
2. The diagonal of a square is 10 cm. Find its area.
3. BD is one of the diagonals of a quadrilateral ABCD. AM and CN are the perpendiculars from A and C, respectively, on BD. Show that ar(quad. ABCD) = $\frac{1}{2}BD.(AM+CN)$
4. What is rectangular region?
5. What is polygonal region?
6. If ABC and BDE are two equilateral triangles such that D is the mid-point of BC, then find ar (ΔABC) : ar (ΔBDE)
7. In figure, ABCD is a rectangle in which CD = 6 cm, AD = 8 cm. Find the area of parallelogram CDEF.

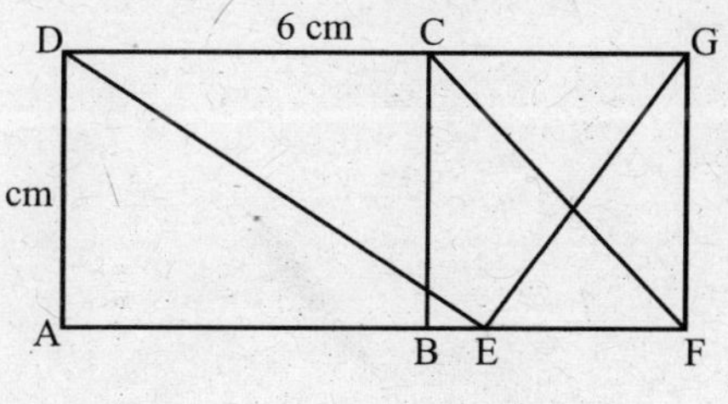

8. In above figure, find the area of ΔGEF.

Short Answer Questions :

DIRECTIONS: *Give answer in 2-3 sentences.*

1. *ABCD* is a quadrilateral and *BD* is one of its diagonals as shown in the following figure. Show that quadrilateral *ABCD* is a parallelogram and find its area.

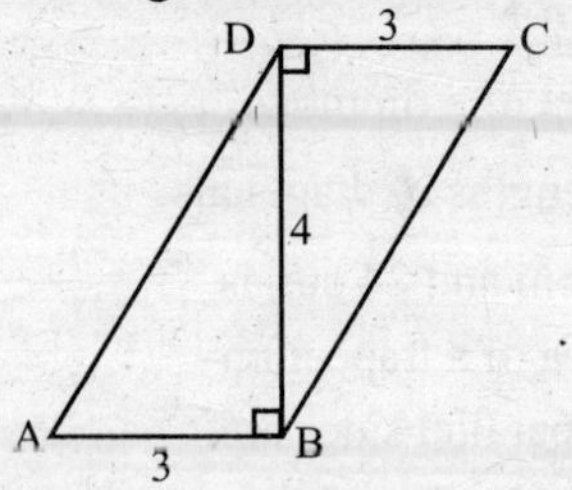

2. In fig., *X* and *Y* are points on the side *LN* of the triangle *LMN* such that $LX = XY = YN$. Through *X*, a line is drawn parallel to *LM* to meet *MN* at *Z*. Prove that $ar(\Delta LZY) = ar(MZYX)$.

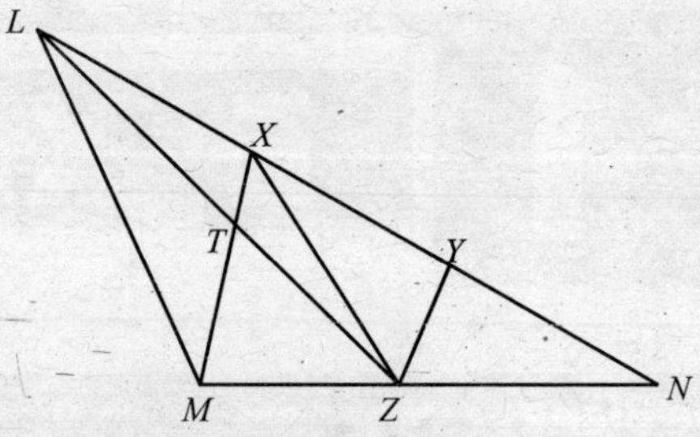

3. In the given figure, *ABCD* is a ||gm. *O* is any point on *AC*. $PQ \parallel AB$ and $LM \parallel AD$. Prove that ar (|| gm *DLOP*) = ar(|| gm *BMOQ*).

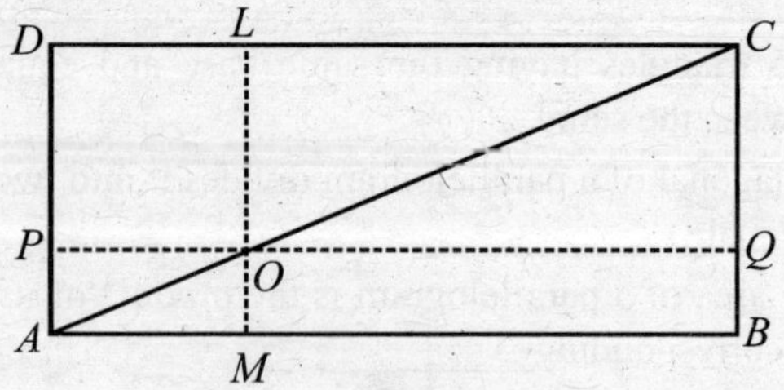

2 EXERCISE

Text-Book Exercise :

1. In figure, ABCD is a parallelogram, AE ⊥ DC and CF ⊥ AD. If AB = 16 cm, AE = 8 cm and CF = 10 cm, find AD.

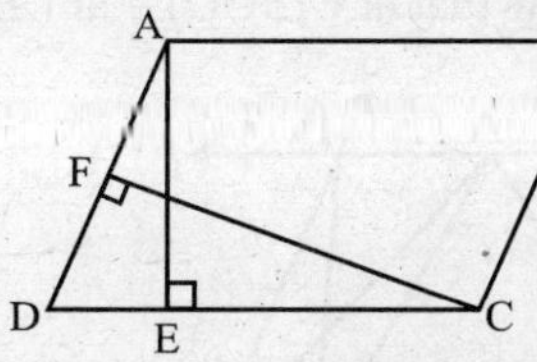

2. P and Q are any two points lying on the sides DC and AD respectively of a parallelogram ABCD. Show that : ar (APB) = ar (BQC).

3. In figure PQRS and ABRS are parallelograms and X is any point on side BR. Show that :

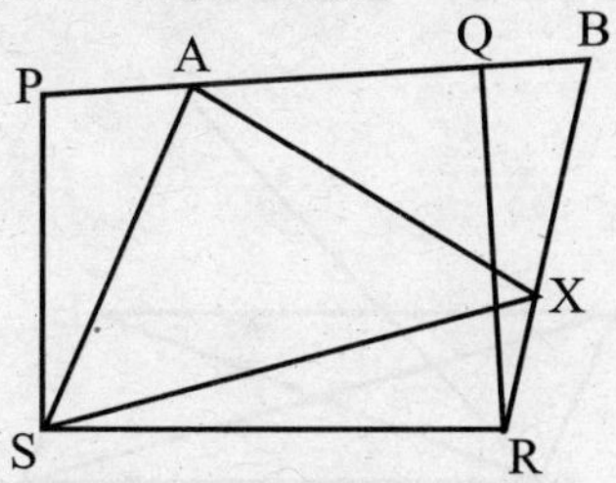

(i) ar (PQRS) = ar (ABRS)

(ii) ar (AXS) = $\frac{1}{2}$ ar (PQRS).

4. In figure, E is any point on median AD of a ΔABC. Show that ar(ABE) = ar (ACE).

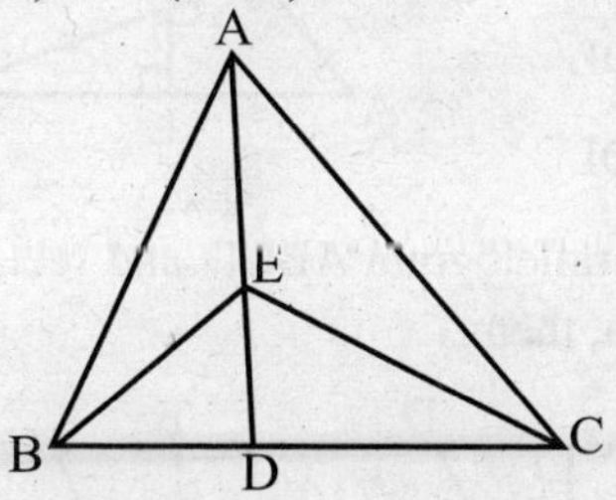

5. In a triangle ABC, E is the mid-point of median AD. Show that ar(BED) = $\frac{1}{4}$ ar (ABC).

6. In figure, ABC and ABD are two triangles on the same base AB. If line segment CD is bisected by AB at O. Show that ar (ABC) = ar (ABD).

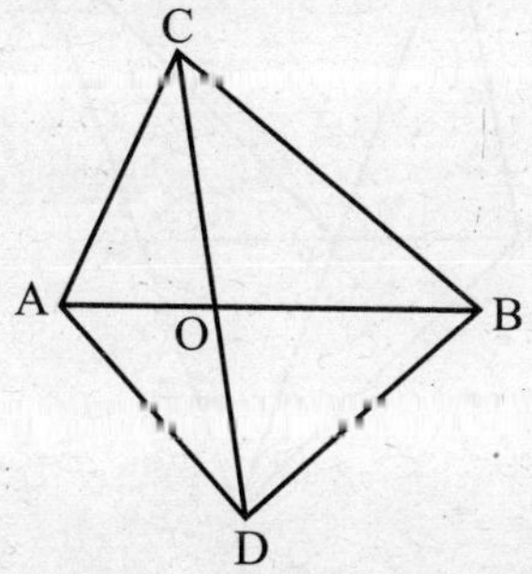

7. D and E are points on sides AB and AC respectively of ΔABC such that ar(ΔDBC) = ar(ΔEBC). Prove that DE || BC.

8. The side AB of a parallelogram ABCD is produced to any point P. A line through A and parallel to CP meets CB produced at Q and then parallelogram PBQR is completed. Show that ar(ABCD) = ar(PBQR).

[**Hint:** Join AC and PQ. Now compare ar(ACQ) and ar(APQ)]

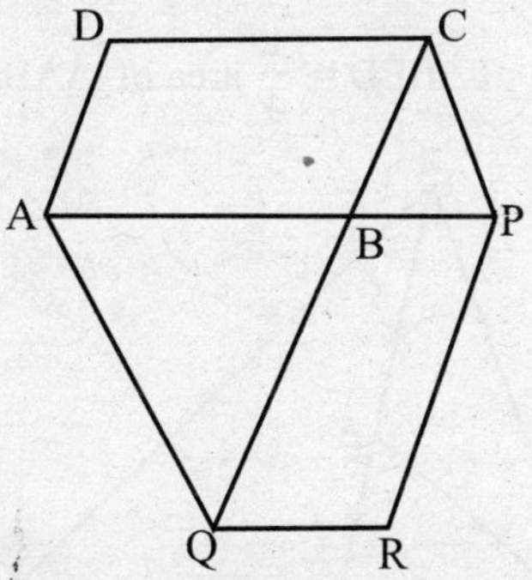

9. In figure, ABCDE is a pentagon. A line through B parallel to AC meets DC produced at F. Show that:

(i) ar(ACB) = ar(ACF)

(ii) ar(AEDF) = ar(ABCDE).

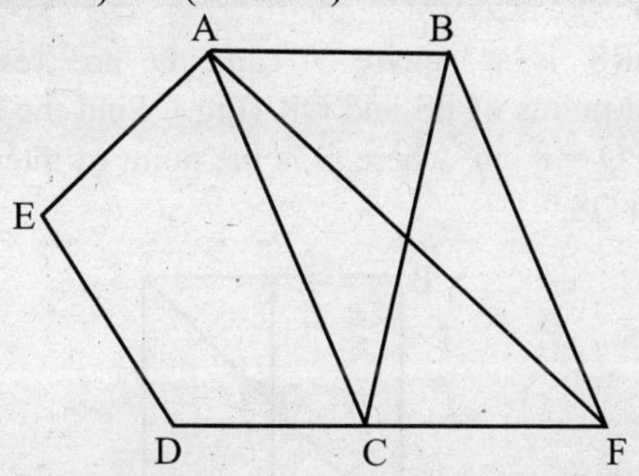

10. Diagonals AC and BD of a quadrilateral ABCD intersect at O in such a way that ar(AOD) = ar(BOC). Prove that ABCD is a trapezium.

11. Parallelogram ABCD and rectangle ABEF are on the same base AB and have equal areas. Show that the perimeter of the parallelogram is greater than that of the rectangle.

12. In figure, ABCD is a parallelogram and BC is produced to a point Q such that AD = CQ.
If AQ intersect DC at P, show that ar (BPC) = ar (DPQ).

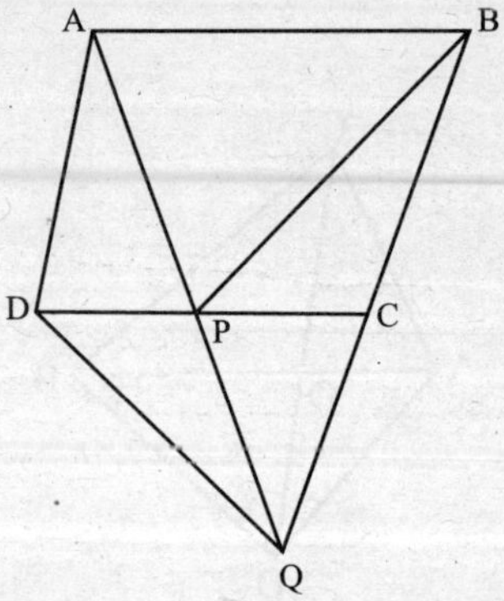

[**Hint.** Join AC.]

13. Diagonals AC and BD of a quadrilateral ABCD intersect each other at P. Show that
ar (ΔAPB) × ar(ΔCPD) = ar (ΔAPD) × ar (ΔBPC).
[**Hint.** From A and C, draw perpendiculars to BD.]

14. A park, in the shape of a quadrilateral ABCD, has ∠C = 90°, AB = 9 m, BC = 12 m, CD = 5 m, and AD = 8 m. How much area does it occupy?

15. In a triangle ABC, E is the mid-point of median AD. Prove that the area of ΔBED = $\frac{1}{4}$ area of ΔABC.

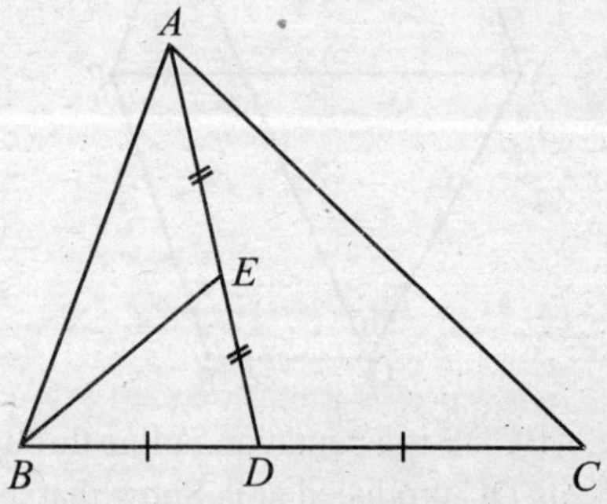

Exemplar Questions :

1. PQRS is a square. T and U are respectively, the mid-points of PS and QR (Fig.). Find the area of ΔOTS, if PQ = 8 cm, where O is the point of intersection of TU and QS.

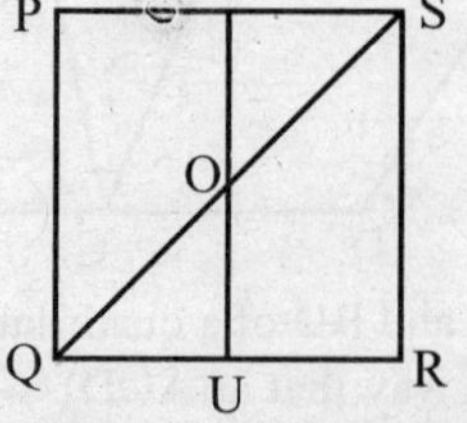

2. ABCD is a parallelogram and BC is produced to a point Q such that AD = CQ (Fig.) If AQ intersects DC at P, show that ar (BPC) = ar (DPQ)

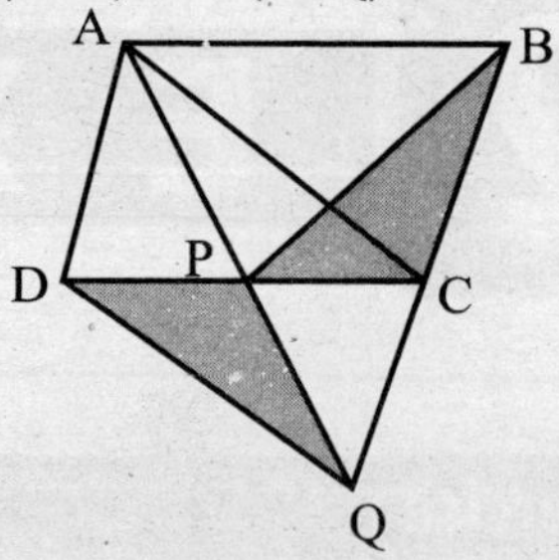

3. In fig. *l*, *m*, *n* are straight lines such that *l* ∥ *m* and *n* intersects *l* at *P* and *m* at *Q*. *ABCD* is a quadrilateral such that its vertex *A* is on *l*. The vertices *C* and *D* are on *m* and *AD* ∥ *n*. Show that ar (*ABCQ*) = ar (*ABCDP*)

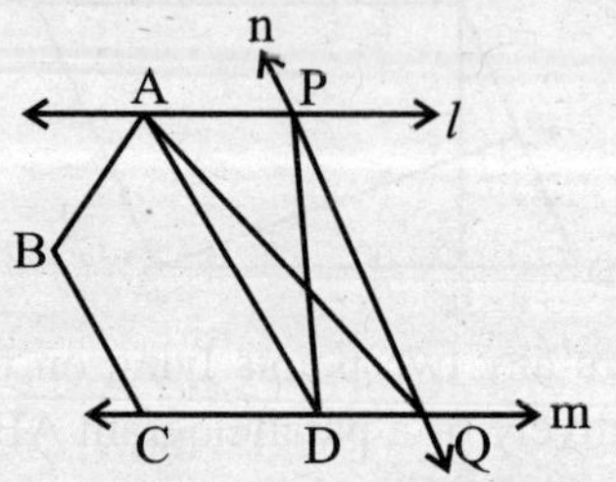

4. In fig. BD ∥ CA, E is mid-point of CA and BD = $\frac{1}{2}$CA. Prove that ar (ABC) = 2 ar (DBC)

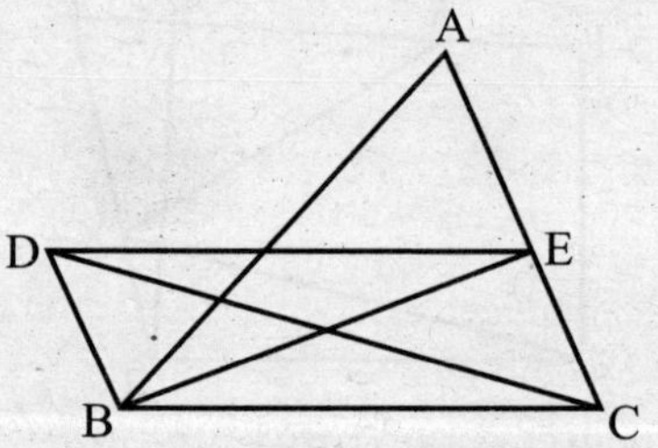

5. In fig., the area of parallelogram ABCD is :

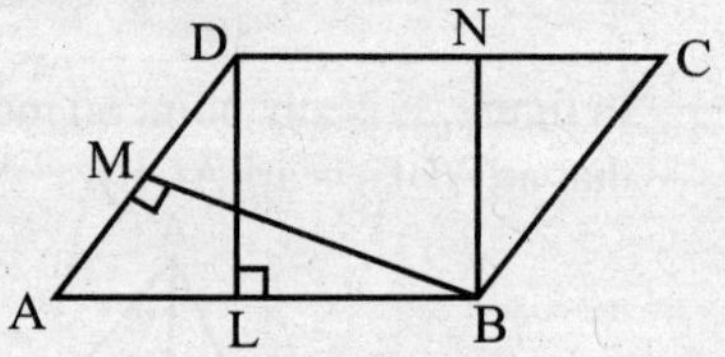

(a) AB × BM
(b) BC × BN
(c) DC × DL
(d) AD × DL

6. In fig., if parallelogram ABCD and rectangle ABEM are of equal area, then :

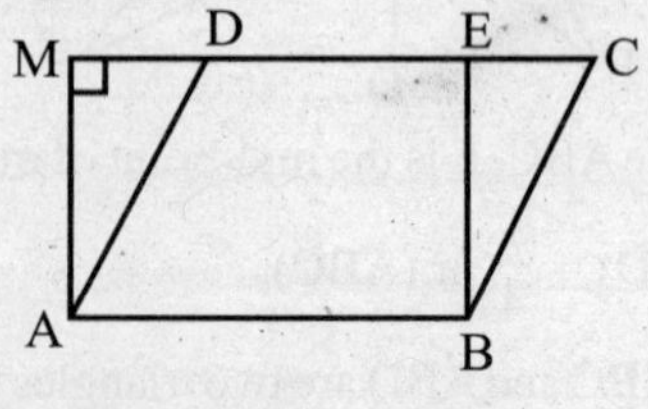

(a) Perimeter of ABCD = Perimeter of ABEM
(b) Perimeter of ABCD < Perimeter of ABEM
(c) Perimeter of ABCD > Perimeter of ABEM
(d) Perimeter of ABCD = $\frac{1}{2}$ (Perimeter of ABEM)

7. The median of a triangle divides it into two
   (a) triangles of equal area
   (b) congruent triangles
   (c) right triangles
   (d) isosceles triangles

8. Two parallelograms are on equal bases and between the same parallels. The ratio of their areas is
   (a) 1 : 2
   (b) 1 : 1
   (c) 2 : 1
   (d) 3 : 1

9. ABCD is a quadrilateral whose diagonal AC divides it into two parts, equal in area, then ABCD
   (a) is a rectangle
   (b) is always a rhombus
   (c) is a parallelogram
   (d) need not be any of (a), (b) or (c)

HOTS Questions :

1. In figure, *ABCDE* is any pentagon. *BP* drawn parallel to *AC* meets *DC* produced at *P* and *EQ* drawn parallel to *AD* meet *CD* produced at *Q*. Prove that ar (*ABCDE*) = ar (*APQ*)

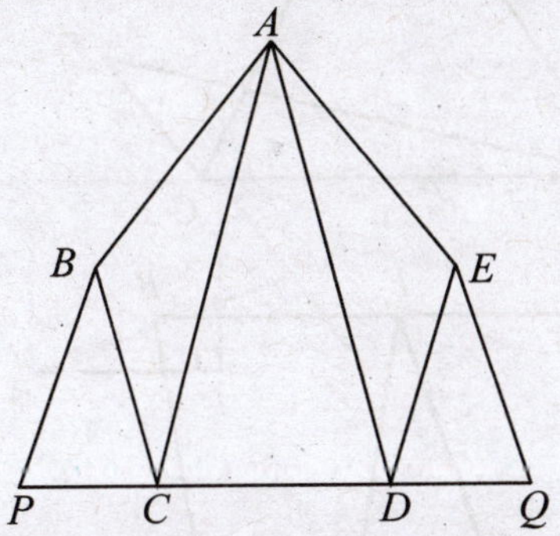

2. In fig., *X* and *Y* are the mid-points of *AC* and *AB* respectively, *QP* || *BC* and *CYQ* and *BXP* are straight lines. Prove that *ar* (ΔABP) = *ar* (ΔACQ).

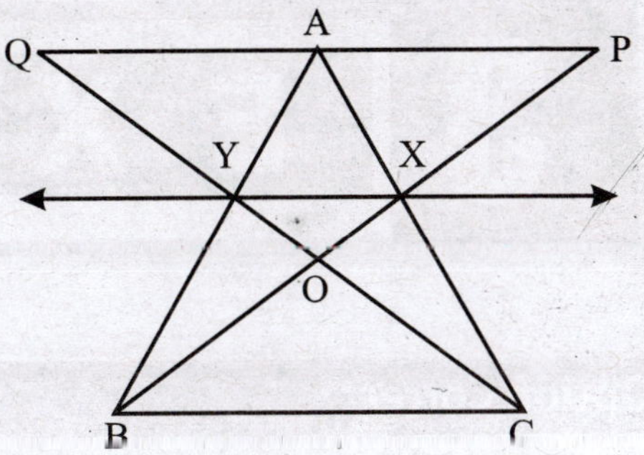

3. In fig., *CD* || *AE* and *CY* || *BA*.
   (i) Prove that *ar* (Δ*ZDE*) = *ar* (Δ*CZA*)
   (ii) Prove that *ar* (*BCZY*) = *ar* (Δ*EDZ*)

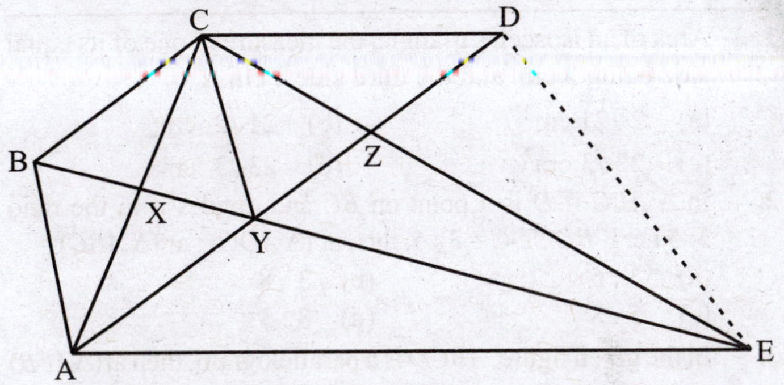

4. In fig., ABCD and AEFD are two parallelograms. Prove that ar (ΔPEA) = ar (ΔQFD).

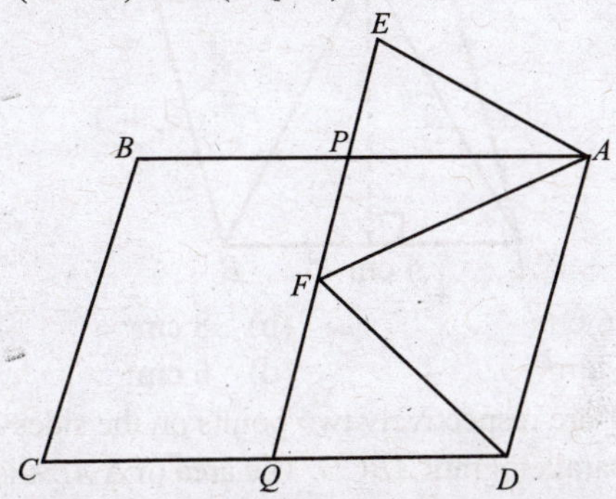

5. In fig., PSDA is a parallelogram in which PQ = QR = RS and AP || BQ || CR || DS. Prove that ar (ΔPQE) = ar (ΔCFD)

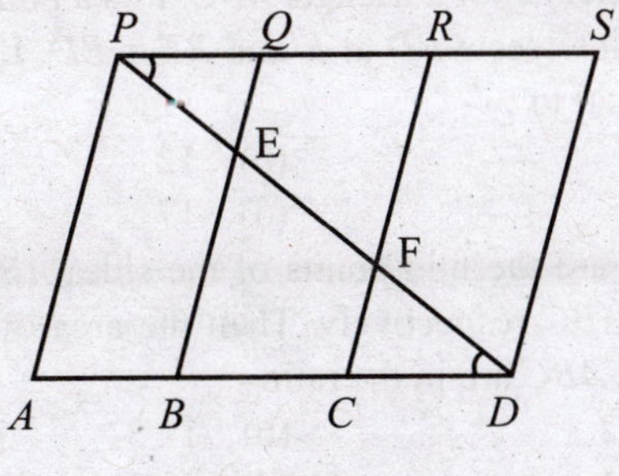

3 EXERCISE

Single Option Correct :

DIRECTIONS: *This section contains multiple choice questions. Each questions has 4 choices (a), (b), (c) and (d) out of which ONLY ONE is correct.*

1. Area of an isosceles triangle, the measure of one of its equal side being 5 cm. and the third side 4 cm is

(a) $2\sqrt{21}$ cm^2 (b) $21\sqrt{2}$ cm^2
(c) $22\sqrt{3}$ cm^2 (d) $23\sqrt{3}$ cm^2

2. In Δ *ABC* if *D* is a point on *BC* and divides it in the ratio 3: 5 i.e. if *BD* : *DC* = 3 : 5, then ar (Δ *ADC*) : ar (Δ *ABC*) =

(a) 3 : 5 (b) 3 : 8
(c) 5 : 8 (d) 8 : 3

3. In the given figure, *ABCD* is a parallelogram, then ar(Δ*AFB*) is

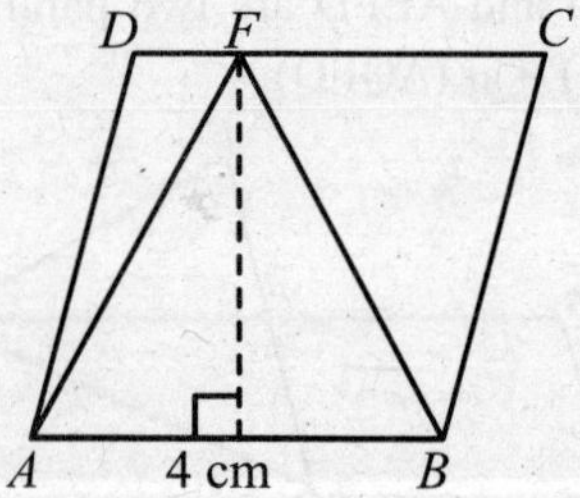

(a) 16 cm^2 (b) 8 cm^2
(c) 4 cm^2 (d) 6 cm^2

4. *X* and *Y* are respectively two points on the sides *DC* and *AD* of the parallelogram *ABCD*. The area of Δ *ABX* is equal to :

(a) 1/3 × area of Δ *BYC* (b) area of Δ *BYC*
(c) 1/2 × area of Δ *BYC* (d) 2 × area of Δ *BYC*

5. *BD* is a median of a triangle *ABC*. *F* is a point on *AB* such that *CF* intersects *BD* at *E* and *BE* = *ED*. If *BF* = 5 cm, *BA* is equal to :

(a) 10 (b) 12
(c) 15 (d) 17

6. *D* and *E* are the mid points of the sides *AB* and *AC* of a triangle *ABC* respectively. Then the area of the triangles *ADE* and *ABC* are in the ratio

(a) 1 : 2 (b) 1 : 3
(c) 1 : 4 (d) 2 : 3

7. In the parallelogram *ABCD*, the side *AB* is produced to point *X*, so that *BX* = *AB*. The line *DX* cuts *BC* at *E*.
Area of Δ *AED* =

(a) 2 × area (Δ *CEX*) (b) 1/2 × area (Δ *CEX*)
(c) area (Δ *CEX*) (d) 1/3 × area (Δ *CEX*)

8. Which of the following figures lie on the same base and between the same parallels?

(a)

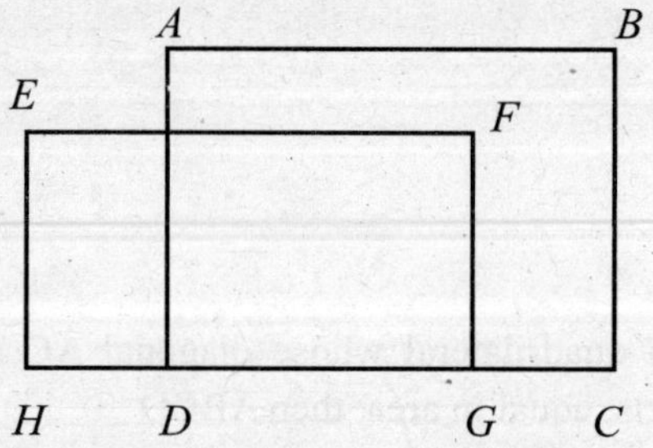

(b)

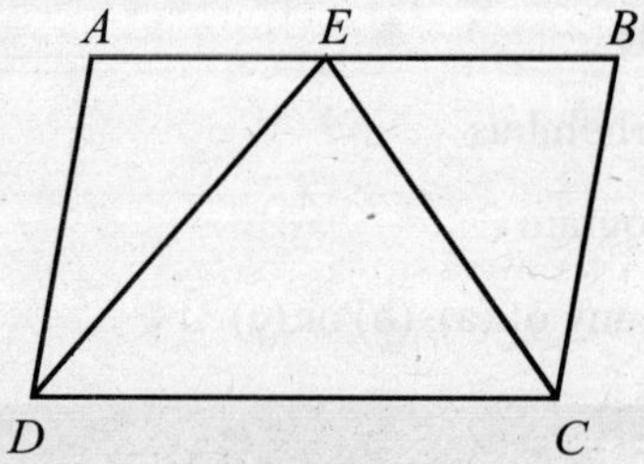

(c)

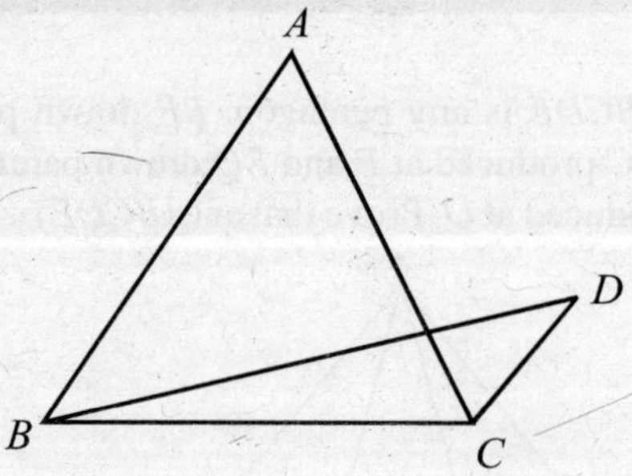

(d)

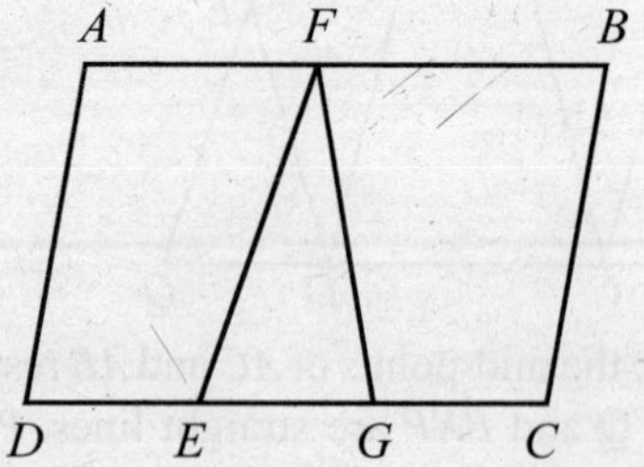

9. ABCD is a trapezium with parallel sides *AB* = *a* cm and *DC* = *b* cm. E and F are the mid-points of the non-parallel sides. The ratio of ar (*ABFE*) and ar (*EFCD*) is

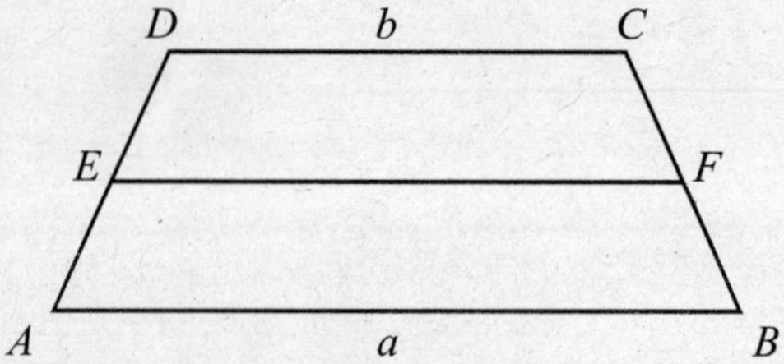

(a) $a : b$ (b) $(3a + b) : (a + 3b)$
(c) $(a + 3b) : (3a + b)$ (d) $(2a + b) : (3a + b)$

10. In parallelogram PQRS, PQ = 10 cm. The altitudes corresponding to the sides PQ and SP are 6 cm and 8 cm respectively, then SP is.
(a) 2.5 cm (b) 5 cm
(c) 7.5 cm (d) 10 cm

11. In fig. *ABCD* and *AEFD* are two parallelograms, then the ratio of ar (ΔPEA) to the ar (ΔQFD).

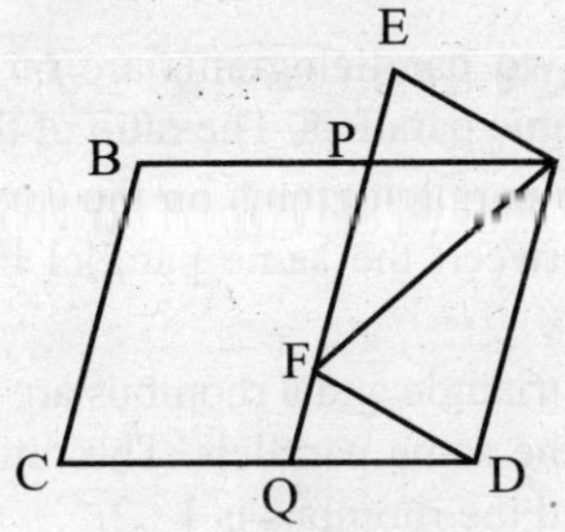

(a) 1 : 4 (b) 1 : 3
(c) 1 : 2 (d) 1 : 1

12. In ΔABC if D is a point in BC and divides it in the ratio 3 : 5 then ar (ΔADC) : ar (ΔABC) =
(a) 3 : 5 (b) 3 : 8
(c) 5 : 8 (d) 8 : 3

13. Sides AB and AC of triangle ABC are trisected at D and E then ΔADE and trapezium $DECB$ have their areas in the ratio of
(a) 1 : 4 (b) 1 : 8
(c) 1 : 9 (d) 1 : 2

14. X and Y are respectively two points on the sides DC and AD of the parallelogram $ABCD$. The area of ΔABX is equal to
(a) 1/3 × area of ΔBYC
(b) area of ΔBYC
(c) 1/2 × area of ΔBYC
(d) 2 × area of ΔBYC

15. The base BC of triangle ABC is divided at D so that $ED = \frac{1}{2} DC$. Area of ΔABD =
(a) 1/3 of the area of ΔABC
(b) 1/2 of the area of ΔABC
(c) 1/4 of the area of ΔABC
(d) 1/6 of the area of ΔABC

More Than One Option Correct :

DIRECTIONS: *This section contains multiple choice questions. Each question has 4 choices (a), (b), (c) and (d) out of which ONE or MORE may be correct.*

1. In parallelogram ABCD, AB = 10 cm. The altitudes corresponding to the sides AB and AD are respectively 7cm and 8 cm. Then
(a) ar(||gm ABCD) = 70 cm^2.
(b) length of AD = 8.75 cm.
(c) ar(||gm ABCD) = (AD × 8) cm^2.
(d) Length of AD = 7 cm

2. ABC is a triangle in which E is mid-point of median AD. Then
(a) area of $\Delta BED = \frac{1}{4}$ area of ΔABC
(b) area of ΔBED = ar (ΔBAE)
(c) area of ΔABD = area of ΔADC
(d) area of $\Delta BED = \frac{1}{2}$ area of ΔABC

3. In the given figure, ABCD is a trapezium in which AB || DC. DC is produced to E such that CE = AB, then

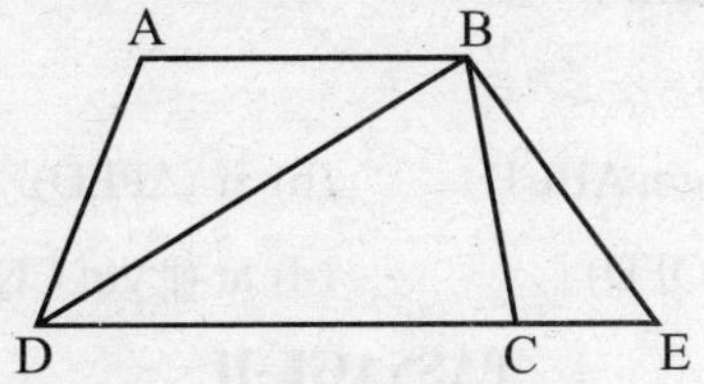

(a) AB = ΔE
(b) ar(ΔBCE) = $\frac{1}{2}$(CE × BN)
(c) ar(ΔABD) = ar (ΔBCE)
(d) None of these

4. Choose the correct statements among the following given options.
(a) Area of a parallelogram is the product of any of its sides and the corresponding altitude.
(b) The area of a triangle is half the product of any of its sides and the corresponding altitude.
(c) The area of a trapezium is half the product of its height and the sum of the parallel sides.
(d) A diagonal of a parallelogram divides it into two triangles of distinct areas.

Passage Based Questions :

DIRECTIONS: *Study the given paragraph(s) and answer the following questions.*

PASSAGE -I

In the given figure, ABCD and AEFD are two parallelograms.

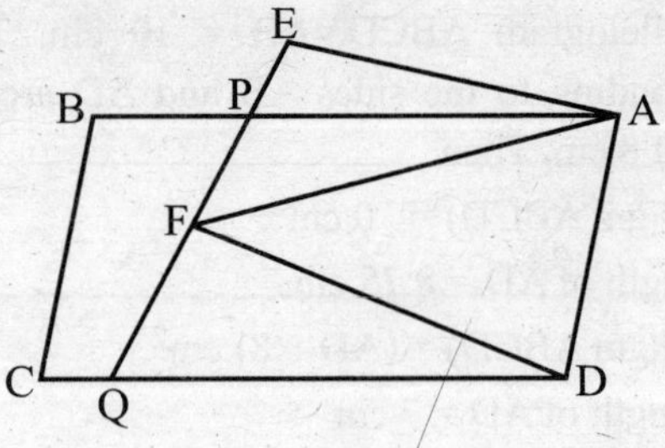

1. PE =

(a) BP (b) FQ

(c) AP (d) CQ

2. $\frac{ar(\Delta APE)}{ar(\Delta PFA)} =$

(a) $\frac{ar(\Delta QFD)}{ar(\Delta PFD)}$ (b) $\frac{ar(\Delta AEF)}{ar(\Delta PFD)}$

(c) $\frac{ar(\Delta QFD)}{ar(\Delta AEF)}$ (d) None of these

3. ar (ΔPEA) =

(a) ar (|| gm ABCD) (b) ar (ΔPFD)

(c) ar (ΔQFD) (d) ar (|| gm CQPB)

PASSAGE-II

In ΔABC, if *L* and M are points on AB and AC respectively such that LM || BC. Then

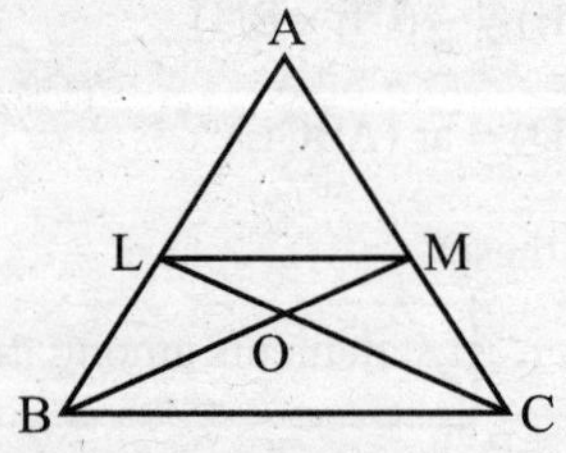

4. ar (ΔLCM) is equal to

(a) ar (ΔLBM) (b) ar (ΔMBC)

(c) ar(ΔMOC) (d) ar (ΔACL)

5. ar (ΔLBC) is equal to

(a) ar (ΔLBM) (b) ar (ΔMBC)

(c) ar (ΔMOC) (d) ar (ΔACL)

6. ar (ΔABM) is equal to

(a) ar (ΔLBM) (b) ar (ΔMBC)

(c) ar (ΔMOC) (d) ar (ΔACL)

Assertion & Reason :

DIRECTIONS: *Each of these questions contains an Assertion followed by Reason. Read them carefully and answer the question on the basis of following options. You have to select the one that best describes the two statements.*

(a) If both **Assertion** and **Reason** are **correct** and Reason is the **correct explanation** of Assertion.

(b) If both **Assertion** and **Reason** are correct, but Reason is **not the correct explanation** of Assertion.

(c) If **Assertion** is **correct** but **Reason** is **incorrect**.

(d) If **Assertion** is **incorrect** but **Reason** is **correct**.

1. **Assertion:** The area of an equilateral triangle is $16\sqrt{3}$ cm^2 whose each side is 8 cm.

Reason: Area of an equilateral triangle is given by $\frac{\sqrt{3}}{4}(\text{side})^2$.

2. **Assertion :** Two parallelograms are on equal bases and between the same parallels. The ratio of their areas is 1 : 1.

Reason : Two parallelograms on the same base (or equal bases) and between the same parallel lines are equal in area.

3. **Assertion :** A triangle and a rhombus are on the same base and between the same parallels. The ratio of the areas of the triangle and the rhombus is 1 : 2.

Reason : The area of a triangle is half of the area of a parallelogram on the same base and between the same parallels.

Integer Type Questions :

DIRECTIONS : *Answer the following questions. The answer to each of the question is a single digit integer, ranging from 0 to 9.*

1. In the given figure, ABCD is a parallelogram, then ar(ΔAFB) is

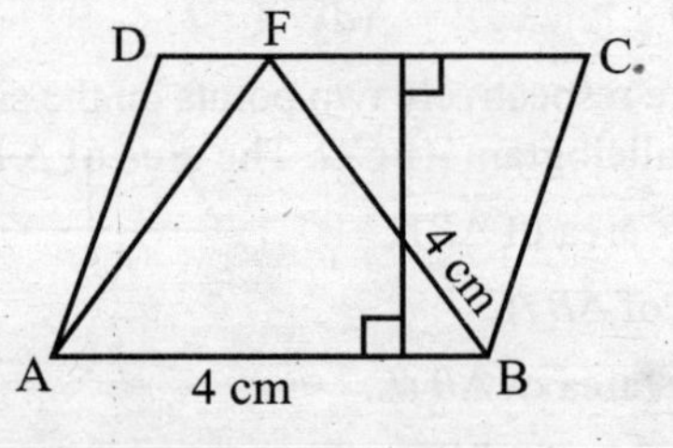

2. If E, F, G, H are respectively the mid-points of the sides of a parallelogram ABCD and ar(EFGH) = 40 cm^2, then the value of $\frac{ar(ABCD)}{40}$ is

3. If AD is the median of a triangle ABC and area of triangle ADC = 15 cm^2, then $\frac{ar(\Delta ABC)}{15}$ is

4. In the given figure, ABCD is a trapezium in which AB = 7cm, AD = BC = 5 cm, DC = x cm and distance between AB and DC is 4 cm. The area of trapezium ABCD is *l* sq cm. Find *l*/8.

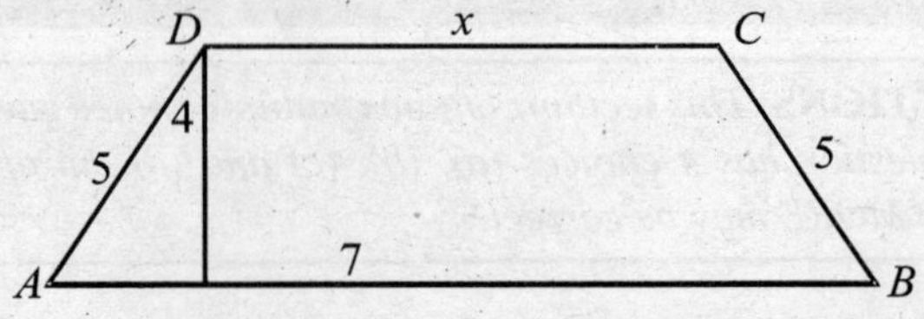

SOLUTIONS

Brief Explanations of Selected Questions

1 EXERCISE

FILL IN THE BLANKS :

1.	parallels	2.	area	3.	altitude
4.	median	5.	product		

TRUE/FALSE :

1.	True	2.	True	3.	False
4.	False	5.	True.	6.	True
7.	True	8.	False	9.	False

MATCH THE COLUMNS :

1. (A) → (r); (B) → (s); (C) → (q); (D) → (p);

(A) Area of rhombus = $\frac{1}{2} \times d_1 \times d_2$

$= \frac{1}{2} \times 16 \times 24 = 192 \text{ cm}^2$

(B) Area of trapezium ABCD = $\frac{1}{2}$ [AB + CD] × AE

$= \frac{1}{2}(16 + 9) \times 8$

$= 100 \text{ cm}^2$

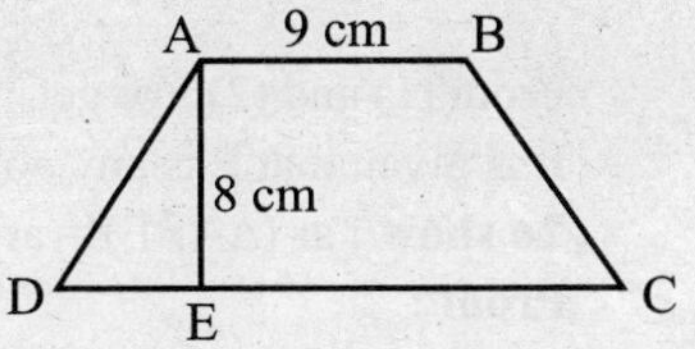

(C) Area of rhombus = $\frac{1}{2} \times d_1 \times d_2$

$20 = \frac{1}{2} \times 5 \times d_2 \Rightarrow d_2 = 8$ cm

(D) Area of || gm = Base × Height

∴ Area of ABCD = $(12 \times 8) \text{ cm}^2$ … (i)

Also, area of ABCD = AD × BN

= BN × 10 … (ii)

From (i) and (ii), we get

12 × 8 = BN × 10

⇒ BN = 9.6 cm

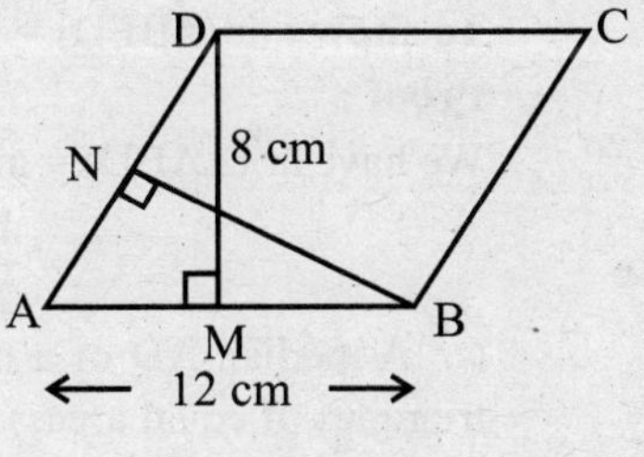

VERY SHORT ANSWER QUESTIONS :

1. Area of rhombus = $\frac{1}{2} \times d_1 \times d_2$ where

d_1 = Length of one diagonal

d_2 = Length of another diagonal

2. Diagonal of a square = $\sqrt{2}a$

$\Rightarrow 10 = \sqrt{2}a \Rightarrow a = \frac{10}{\sqrt{2}}$

Area of the square = $a^2 = \left(\frac{10}{\sqrt{2}}\right)^2 = \frac{100}{2} = 50 \text{ cm}^2$

3. We have

ar (quad. ABCD) = ar (ΔABD) + ar (ΔBCD)

⇒ ar (quad.ABCD) = $\frac{1}{2}$(BD × AM) + $\frac{1}{2}$(BD × CN)

⇒ ar (quad. ABCD) = $\frac{1}{2}$BD × [(AM + CN)]

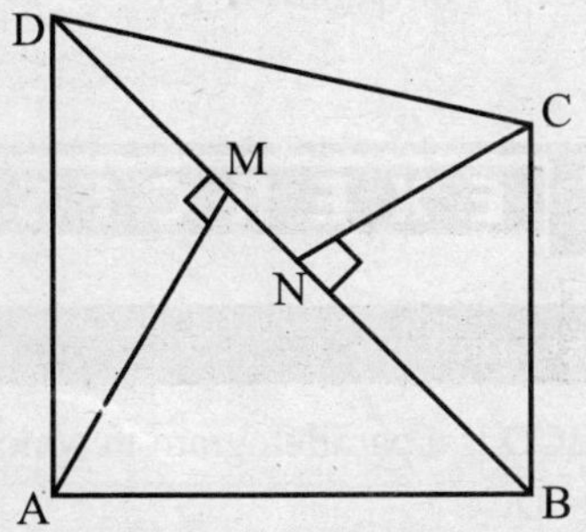

4. The part of the plane enclosed by a rectangle is called the interior of a rectangle and the union of a rectangle and its interior is called a rectangular region.

5. The part of the plane enclosed by a polygon is called the interior of a polygon and the union of a polygon and its interior is called a polygonal region.

6. 4 : 1

7. 48 cm^2

8. 24 cm^2

SHORT ANSWER QUESTIONS :

1. From the figure it is clear that

$\angle CDB = \angle ABD = 90°$

But these angles form a pair of alternate equal angles.

∴ $DC \parallel AB$

Also, $DC = AB = 3$ units (From figure)

Now, we know that a quadrilateral is a parallelogram if a pair of opposite sides is parallel and is of equal length.

∴ Quadrilateral *ABCD* is a parallelogram.

Now, area of the || gm *ABCD*

= Base × Corresponding altitude

= *AB* × *BD*

= 3 × 4 square units (∵ *AB* = 3 and *BD* = 4)

= 12 square units

2. Since, ΔLXZ and ΔMXZ lie on the same base *XZ* and between the same parallels *XZ* and *LM*.

∴ $ar(\Delta LXZ) = ar(\Delta MXZ)$

Adding $ar(\Delta XYZ)$ to both sides, we get

$ar(\Delta LXZ) + ar(\Delta XYZ) = ar(\Delta MXZ) + ar(\Delta XYZ)$

$ar(\Delta LYZ) = ar(MZYX)$

3. Since diagonals of a parallelogram divides it into two triangles of equal area.

∴ ar (ΔADC) = ar (ΔABC)

⇒ ar (ΔAPO) + ar (||gm*DLOP*) + ar (ΔOLC)

= ar (ΔAOM) + ar (||gm*BMOQ*) + ar (ΔOQC) ....(i)

Since *AO* and *OC* are diagonals of parallelograms *AMOP* and *OQCL* respectively

∴ ar (ΔAPO) = ar (ΔAMO) ...(ii)

and ar (ΔOLC) = ar (ΔOQC) ...(iii)

Subtracting (ii) and (iii) from (i), we get

ar (||gm*DLOP*) = ar (||gm*BMOQ*)

2 EXERCISE

TEXT-BOOK EXERCISE :

1. Since, ABCD is a parallelogram in which AB ||DC

∴ AB = DC

⇒ Base DC = 16 cm

Height AE = 8 cm. (Given)

Area of || gm = Base × Corresponding Altitude

∴ Area of || gm ABCD = DC × AE

$= 16 \times 8 = 128 \text{ cm}^2$. ...(i)

Again by considering AD as the base and height as CF = 10 cm.

∴ Area of || gm ABCD = AD × CF

= AD × 10

= 10 AD cm^2

Clearly 10. AD = 128 (By using (i))

⇒ $AD = \frac{128}{10} = 12.8$ cm.

2. Given two points P and Q are lying on DC and AD respectively in a parallelogram ABCD. Also by joining BP, BQ, QC and PA, we form ΔBCQ and ΔABP.

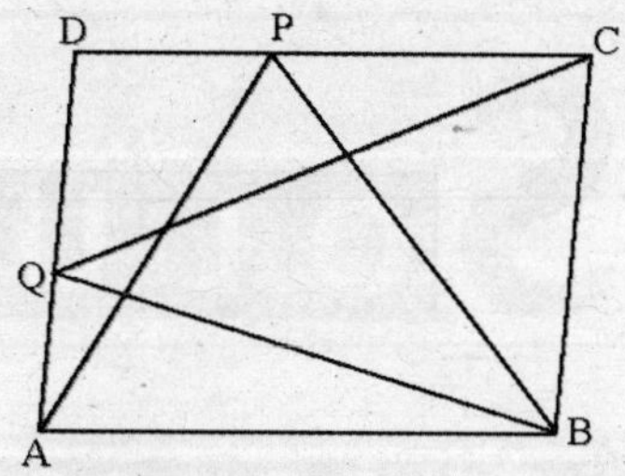

To show : ar (APB) = ar (BQC)

Proof : Since, ΔAPB and || gm ABCD are on the same base AB and between the same parallels line AB and DC.

∴ ar (APB) = $\frac{1}{2}$ ar (ABCD) ....(i)

Similarly, ΔBCQ and || gm ABCD have the same base and between same parallel lines .

∴ ar (BCQ) = $\frac{1}{2}$ ar (ABCD) ....(ii)

From (i) and (ii), we get ar (APB) = ar (BCQ)

3. **Given :** Two parallelograms PQRS and ABRS and X is any point on side BR.

To prove : (i) ar(PQRS) = ar (ABRS)

(ii) ar (AXS) = $\frac{1}{2}$ ar (PQRS).

Proof : (i) ar (PQRS) = ar (ABRS) ....(1)

(∵ Parallelograms PQRS and ABRS are on the same base SR and between the same parallels SR and PB.)

(ii) ar (AXS) = $\frac{1}{2}$ ar (ABRS) ....(2)

(∵ ΔAXS and ||gm ABRS are on the same base AS and between the same parallels AS and RB)

From (1) and (2), we get, ar (AXS) = $\frac{1}{2}$ ar (PQRS).

4. It is given that E is any point on median AD in a ΔABC.

To show : ar (ΔABE) = ar(ΔACE)

Proof :

Since, AD is a median in ΔABC which divides it into two triangles of equal areas.

∴ ar (ΔABD) = ar (ΔACD) ....(i)

Similarly, ar (ΔEBD) = ar(ΔECD) ....(ii)

(∵ ED is a median in ΔEBC)

Subtracting (ii) from (i), we get

ar (ΔABD) –ar (ΔEBD) = ar (ΔACD) – ar (ΔECD)

⇒ ar(ΔABE) = ar(ΔACE).

5. From the given information, we have E is the mid-point of median AD in a triangle ABC.

To show : ar (ΔBED) = $\frac{1}{4}$ ar(ΔABC).

Proof :

We have ar (ΔABD) = ar (ΔACD)

= $\frac{1}{2}$ ar(ΔABC) ...(i)

(∵ A median AD of a triangle ABC divides it into two triangles of equal areas)

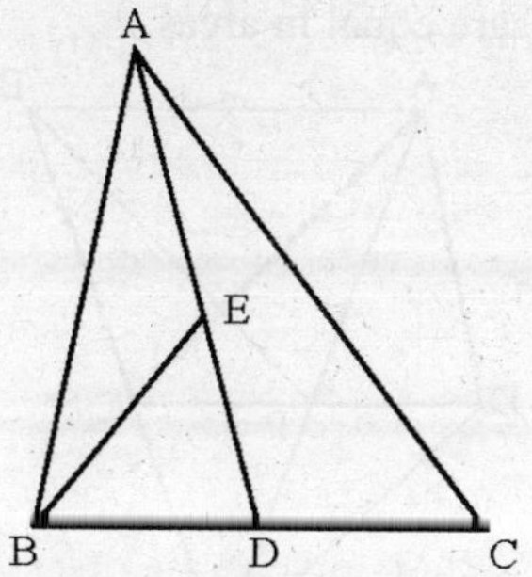

Similarly, ar (ΔBED) = ar (ΔBEA) = $\frac{1}{2}$ ar(ΔABD)
(∵ BE is a median in ΔABD)

⇒ ar (ΔBED) = $\frac{1}{2}$ ar(ΔABD)

= $\frac{1}{2} \cdot \frac{1}{2}$ ar (ΔABC) (From (i))

= $\frac{1}{4}$ ar (ΔABC).

6. We have two triangles ΔABC and ΔABD on the same base AB and a line segment CD which is bisected by AB at O.
To show : ar (ΔABC) = ar (ΔABD).
Proof :
OC = OD (∵ Line segment CD is bisected by AB at O.)
∴ BO is a median of ΔBCD and AO is a median of ΔACD.
Now, ar (ΔOBC) = ar (ΔOBD) ....(i)
(∵ A median BO of a triangle BCD divides it into two triangles of equal areas)
Similarly, ar (ΔOAC) = ar (ΔOAD) ....(ii)
(∵ A median AO of a triangle ACD divides it into two triangles of equal areas)
Adding (i) and (ii), we get
ar (ΔOBC) + ar (ΔOAC) = ar (ΔOBD) + ar (ΔOAD)
⇒ ar (ΔABC) = ar (ΔABD)

7. D and E are points on sides AB and AC respectively of ΔABC such that ar (ΔDBC) = ar(ΔEBC). (Given)

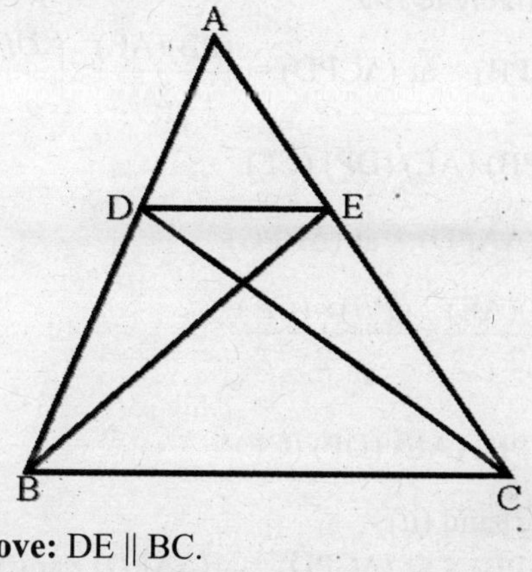

To Prove: DE || BC.
Proof : Since, ΔDBC and ΔEBC are on the same base BC and have equal areas.
∴ Their altitudes must be the same.
∴ DE || BC.

8. **To Prove:** ar(ABCD) = ar(PBQR).
We construct two diagonals AC and PQ of ABCD and BPQR respectively by joining A, C and P, Q.

Proof : ar(ΔABC) = $\frac{1}{2}$ ar(|| gm ABCD) ...(i)
(∵ AC is a diagonal of || gm ABCD)

Similarly, ar(ΔBPQ) = $\frac{1}{2}$ ar(|| gm BQRP) ...(ii)
as PQ is a diagonal

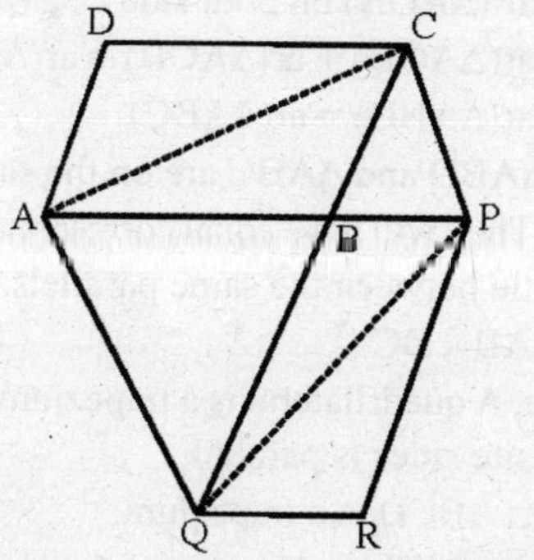

Since, ΔACQ and ΔAPQ have the same base AQ and between the same parallels AQ and CP.
∴ ar(ΔACQ) = ar(ΔAPQ)
By subtracting the same areas from both sides, we get
ar(ΔACQ) – ar(ΔABQ) = ar(ΔAPQ) – ar(ΔABQ)
⇒ ar(ΔABC) = ar(ΔBPQ)

⇒ $\frac{1}{2}$ ar(|| gm ABCD) = $\frac{1}{2}$ ar(|| gm PBQR)
(From (i) and (ii))
⇒ ar (|| gm ABCD) = ar (|| gm. PBQR).
Hence proved.

9. Given a pentagon ABCDE and a line BC through B which is parallel to AC meets DC produced at F.
To show :
(i) ar(ΔACB) = ar(ΔACF)
(ii) ar(□AEDF) = ar(ABCDE).
Proof :
(i) We know Two triangles on the same base (or equal bases) and between the same parallels are equal in area in the given ques, we have ΔACB and ΔACF are on the same base AC and between the same parallels AC and BF.
∴ ar(ΔACB) = ar(ΔACF)
(ii) ar(ΔACB) = ar(ΔACF) (Proved above)
(Adding the same areas on both sides)
ar(ΔACB) + ar(□AEDC) = ar(ΔACF) + ar(□AEDC)
⇒ ar(ABCDE) = ar(□AEDF)
Hence proved.

10. **Given:** In quadrilateral ABCD, two diagonals AC and BD which intersect at O in such a way that
ar (ΔAOD) = ar(ΔBOC).
We have to prove that quadrilateral ABCD is a trapezium.

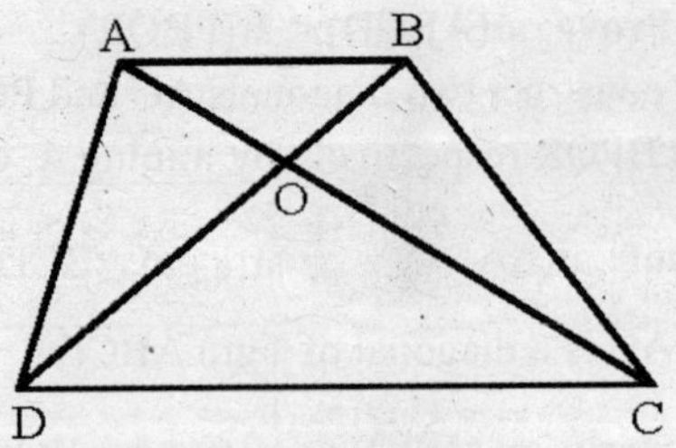

Proof: Given ar(ΔAOD) = ar(ΔBOC)
Add ar (ΔAOB) on both side
⇒ ar(ΔAOD) + ar(ΔAOB) = ar(ΔBOC) + ar(ΔAOB)
⇒ ar(ΔABD) = ar(ΔABC)
But ΔABD and ΔABC are on the same base AB.
∴ They will have equal corresponding altitudes and will lie between the same parallels.
∴ AB || DC
Since, A quadrilateral is a trapezium if exactly one pair of opposite sides is parallel
∴ ▫ABCD is a trapezium.

11. **To Prove:** The perimeter of the parallelogram ABCD is greater than that of rectangle ABEF.

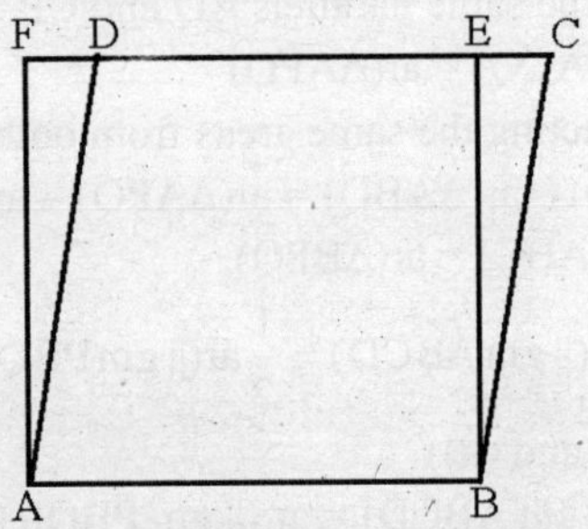

Proof: Consider parallelogram ABCD and rectangle ABEF have same base AB and between the same parallels AB and FC. Now, perimeter of the parallelogram
ABCD = 2(AB + AD)
perimeter of the rectangle ABEF = 2(AB + AF).
Since, ∠AFD = 90° in ΔADF
∴ By Angle sum property of a triangle
∠ADF is an acute angle. (< 90°)
∠AFD > ∠ADF
∴ AD > AF
(Side opposite to greater angle of a triangle is longer)
∴ AB + AD > AB + AF (By adding AB on both sides)
∴ 2(AB + AD) > 2(AB + AF)
∴ Perimeter of the parallelogram ABCD > Perimeter of the rectangle ABEF.

12. **Given:** ABCD is a parallelogram and BC is produced to a point Q such that AD = CQ.
AQ intersects DC at P.
To Prove: ar(ΔBPC) = ar(ΔDPQ)
Proof: Join AC.
ar(ΔQAC) = ar(ΔQDC) ...(i)
(∵ Two triangles QAC and QDC are on the same base QC (or equal bases) and between the same parallels AD and BC are equal in areas.)

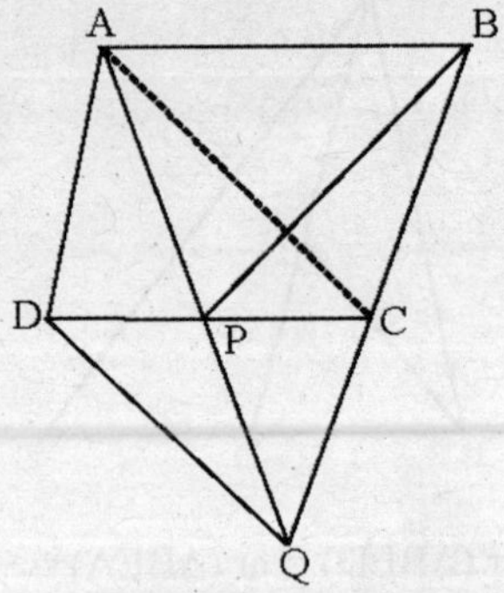

⇒ ar(ΔQAC) – ar(ΔQPC) = ar(ΔQDC) – ar(ΔQPC)
(Subtracting the same areas from both sides)
⇒ ar(ΔPAC) = ar(ΔQDP) ...(ii)
Similarly, ar(ΔPAC) = ar(ΔPBC) ...(iii)
(∵ Two triangles PAC and PBC are on the same base PC (or equal bases) and between the same parallels AB and DC are equal in areas)
From (ii) and (iii),
ar(ΔPBC) = ar(ΔQDP)
⇒ ar(ΔBPC) = ar(ΔDPQ)

13. **Given :** In a quadrilateral ABCD, diagonals AC and BD intersect each other at P.
To Prove :
ar (ΔAPB) × ar(ΔCPD) = ar(ΔAPD) × ar (ΔBPC).

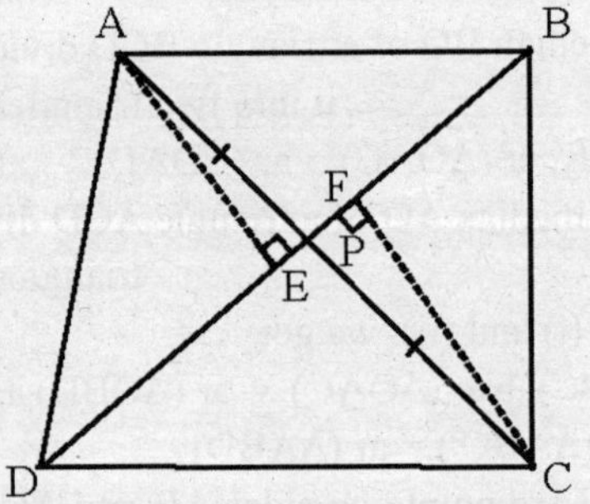

Proof : From A and C, draw perpendiculars AE and CF respectively to BD.

$$\text{ar}(\Delta APB) \times \text{ar}(\Delta CPD) = \frac{(PB)(AE)}{2} \times \left(\frac{DP \times CF}{2}\right)$$

$$= \frac{1}{4}(PB)(AE)(DP)(CF) \qquad \text{....(i)}$$

and ar(ΔAPD) × ar (ΔBPC)

$$= \frac{(DP)(AE)}{2} \times \frac{(PB) \times (CF)}{2}$$

$$= \frac{1}{4}(PB)(AE)(DP)(CF) \qquad \text{....(ii)}$$

From (i) and (ii)
ar (ΔAPB) × ar (ΔCPD) = ar(ΔAPD) ×ar (ΔBPC).
Hence proved.

14. Given, a quadrilateral *ABCD* in which *AB* = 9m, *BC* = 12 m, *CD* = 5m, and *AD* = 8m.

We divide the quadrilateral in two triangular region *ABD* and *BCD*.

Now, In Δ *BCD*, right angle at *C*. We have

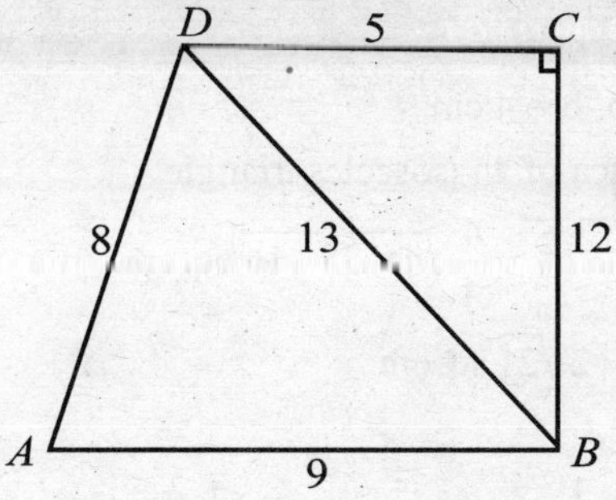

$BD^2 = BC^2 + CD^2$ [By Pythagoras theorem]

$= 5^2 + 12^2 = 25 + 144 = 169 \text{ m}^2$

$BD = \sqrt{169} = 13\text{m}$

$\therefore$ Area of $\Delta\, BCD = \frac{1}{2} \times \text{base} \times \text{height} = \frac{1}{2} \times 5 \times 12$

$= 30 \text{ m}^2$

15. **Given :** A ΔABC in which *E* is the mid-point of median *AD*.

To prove : ar (Δ *BED*) = $\frac{1}{4}$ ar (ΔABC)

Proof : *AD* is a median of ΔABC

ar (ΔABD) = ar (ΔADC)

($\because$ Median of a Δ divides it into two Δs of equal area)

$= \frac{1}{2}$ ar (Δ *ABC*)

Again, BE is a median of Δ *ABD*,

$\therefore$ ar (Δ *BEA*) = ar (Δ *BED*)

($\because$ Median of a Δ divides it into two Δs of equal area)

area of $\Delta BED = \frac{1}{2}(\frac{1}{2}$ area of $\Delta ABC) = \frac{1}{4}$ (area of ΔABC)

EXEMPLAR QUESTIONS :

1. PS = PQ = 8 cm and TU || PQ

$ST = \frac{1}{2} PS = \frac{1}{2} \times 8 = 4 \text{ cm}$

PQ = TU = 8 cm

$OT = \frac{1}{2} TU = \frac{1}{2} \times 8 = 4 \text{ cm}$

Area of triangle OTS

$= \frac{1}{2} \times ST \times OT$ [Since OTS is a right angled triangle]

$= \frac{1}{2} \times 4 \times 4 \text{ cm}^2 = 8 \text{ cm}^2$

2. ar (ACP) = ar (BCP) ...(i)

[Triangles on the same base and between same parallels]

ar (ADQ) = ar (ADC) ...(ii)

ar (ADC) – ar (ADP) = ar (ADQ) – ar (ADP)

ar (APC) = ar (DPQ) ...(iii)

From (i) and (iii), we get

ar (BCP) = ar (DPQ)

3. ar (APD) = ar (AQD) ...(i)

[Have same base AD and also between same parallels AD and n].

Adding ar (ABCD) on both sides in (i), we get

ar (APD) + ar (ABCD) = ar (AQD) + ar (ABCD)

or ar (ABCDP) = ar (ABCQ)

4. Join DE. Here BCED is a parallelogram, since

BD = CE and BD || CE

ar (DBC) = ar (EBC) ...(i)

[Have the same base BC and between the same parallels]

In ΔABC, BE is the median,

So, ar (EBC) = $\frac{1}{2}$ ar (ABC)

Now, ar (ABC) = ar (EBC) + ar (ABE)

Also, ar (ABC) = 2 ar (EBC), therefore,

ar (ABC) = 2 ar (DBC).

5. (c) Area of ||gm ABCD = DC × DL

6. (c) Perimeter of ABCD is greater than the perimeter of ABEM.

7. (a) The median of a triangle divides it into two triangles of equal area.

8. (b) Required ratio of their areas is 1 : 1.

9. (d)

HOTS QUESTIONS :

1. As *BP* || *AC* and *AD* || *EQ*

$\therefore$ ar(ΔABC) = ar(ΔAPC) ... (i)

[Δs on the same base and between the same parallels]

AD || *EQ* [Given]

$\therefore$ ar(ΔADE) = ar(ΔADQ) ...(ii)

[Δs on the same base and between the same parallels]

$\therefore$ ar(ΔACD) = ar(ΔACD) ...(iii)

Adding (i), (ii) and (iii)

ar(ΔABC) + ar(ΔADE) + ar(ΔACD)

= ar(ΔAPC) + ar(ΔADQ) + ar(ΔACD)

ar($\Delta ABCD$) = ar(ΔAPQ)

Hence proved.

2. As X and Y are the mid-points of AC and AB respectively.

$\therefore$ $XY || BC$

Since ΔBYC and ΔBXC are on the same base BC and between the same parallels XY and BC.

$\therefore$ $ar(\Delta BYC) = ar(\Delta BXC)$

$\Rightarrow$ $ar(\Delta BYC) - ar(\Delta BOC) = ar(\Delta BXC) - ar(\Delta BOC)$

$\Rightarrow$ $ar(\Delta BOY) = ar(\Delta COX)$

$\Rightarrow$ $ar(\Delta BOY) + ar(\Delta XOY) = ar(\Delta COX) + ar(\Delta XOY)$

$\Rightarrow$ $ar(\Delta BXY) = ar(\Delta CXY)$ ...(i)

Since quadrilaterals $XYAP$ and $XYQA$ are on the same base XY and between the same parallels XY and PQ.

$\therefore$ $ar(XYAP) = ar(XYQA)$ ...(ii)

Adding (i) and (ii), we get

$ar(\Delta BXY) + ar(XYAP) = ar(\Delta CXY) + ar(XYQA)$

$ar(\Delta ABP) = ar(\Delta ACQ)$

3. (i) Triangles ADE and ACE are on the same base AE and between the same parallels AE and CD.

$\therefore$ $ar(\Delta ADE) = ar(\Delta ACE)$

$\Rightarrow$ $ar(\Delta ADE) - ar(\Delta AZE) = ar(\Delta ACE) - ar(\Delta AZE)$

$\Rightarrow$ $ar(\Delta ZDE) = ar(\Delta ACZ)$

(ii) Triangles ACY and BCY are on the same base CY and between the same parallels CY and BA.

$\therefore$ $ar(\Delta ACY) = ar(\Delta BCY)$ ..... (i)

Now, $ar(\Delta ACZ) = ar(\Delta ZDE)$

$\Rightarrow$ $ar(\Delta ACY) + ar(\Delta CYZ) = ar(\Delta EDZ)$

$\Rightarrow$ $ar(\Delta BCY) + ar(\Delta CYZ) = ar(\Delta EDZ)$ [Using (i)]

$\Rightarrow$ $ar(\text{quad. } BCZY) = ar(\Delta EDZ)$

4. In triangles PEA and QFD, we have

$\angle APE = \angle DQF$ (Corresponding angles)

$AE = DF$ (Opposite sides of ||gm $AEFD$)

$\angle AEP = \angle DFQ$ (Corresponding angles)

$\therefore$ (AAS congruence criterion)

As congruent triangles have equal area,

$\therefore$ ar (ΔPEA) = ar (ΔQFD)

5. Since, $AP || BQ || CR || DS$.

$\therefore PQ = CD$ ...(i)

In ΔBED, C is the mid-point of BD and $CF || BE$.

$\therefore F$ is the mid-point of ED

$\Rightarrow$ $EF = FD$

Similarly, $EF = PE$

$\therefore$ $PE = FD$ ...(ii)

In Δ's PQE and CFD, we have

$PE = FD$

$\angle EPQ = \angle FDC$

and, $PQ = CD$. [Alternate angles]

So, by SAS congruence criterion, we have

$\Delta PQE \cong \Delta DCF$

$\Rightarrow$ ar (ΔPQE) = ar (ΔDCF)

3 EXERCISE

SINGLE OPTION CORRECT :

1. (a) Let a = 5 cm, b = 4 cm.

Therefore area of an isosceles triangle

$= \frac{b}{4} \times \sqrt{4a^2 - b^2} = \frac{4}{4}\sqrt{4 \times 25 - 16}$ sq. cm.

$= \sqrt{84}$ cm. $= 2\sqrt{21}$ sq. cm.

2. (c)

3. (b) ar(ΔAFB) $= \frac{1}{2}$ ar(|| gm $ABCD$) $= \frac{1}{2} \times 4 \times 4$

$= 8$ cm^2

4. (b) **5.** (c) **6.** (c) **7.** (a)

8. (b) Common base = DC and two parallels are AB and DC.

Thus, $DEDC$ and parallelogram $ABCD$ are on same base DC and between same parallel lines AB and DC.

9. (c) Since E and F are mid-points of the sides AD and BC, therefore height of both of the trapezium ABFE and $EFCD$ will be same.

$$\Rightarrow \frac{\text{ar. of trapezium } ABFE}{\text{ar. of trapezium } EFCD} = \frac{\frac{1}{2}(EF + CD) \times h}{\frac{1}{2}(EF + AB) \times h} = \frac{EF + b}{EF + a}$$

EF is parallel to both AB and CD and EF $= \frac{a+b}{2}$

$$\Rightarrow \frac{\text{ar. of } ABFE}{\text{ar. of } EFCD} = \frac{\frac{a+b}{2} + b}{\frac{a+b}{2} + a} = \frac{a+3b}{3a+b}$$

10. (c) Area of parallelogram = base × height

$\therefore$ ar (||gm $PQRS$) = $PQ \times SM$

$= 10 \times 6 = 60$ cm^2 ...(i)

Also, ar (||gm $PQRS$) = $SP \times QN$

$=$ SP × 8 ....(ii)

From (i) and (ii), we have

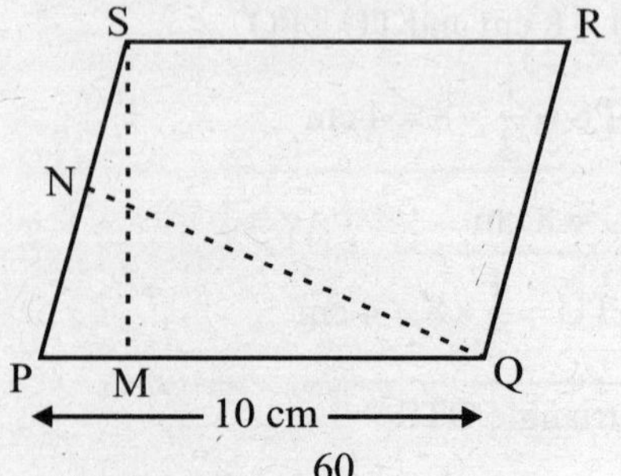

$60 = SP \times 8 \Rightarrow$ SP $= \frac{60}{8} = 7.5$ cm

11. (d) In triangles PEA and QFD, we have

$\angle$APE = $\angle$DQF (Corresponding angles)

$AE = DF$ (Opposite sides of ||gm $AEFD$)

$\angle AEP = \angle DFQ$ (Corresponding angles)

$\therefore \Delta PEA \cong \Delta QFD$ (ASA congruence criterion)

As congruent triangles have equal area,

$\therefore$ ar (ΔPEA) = ar (ΔQFD) $\therefore \dfrac{\text{ar}(\Delta PEA)}{\text{ar}(\Delta QFD)} = \dfrac{1}{1} = 1:1$

12. (c) **13.** (a) **14.** (b) **15.** (a)

MORE THAN ONE OPTION CORRECT :

1. (a, b, c)

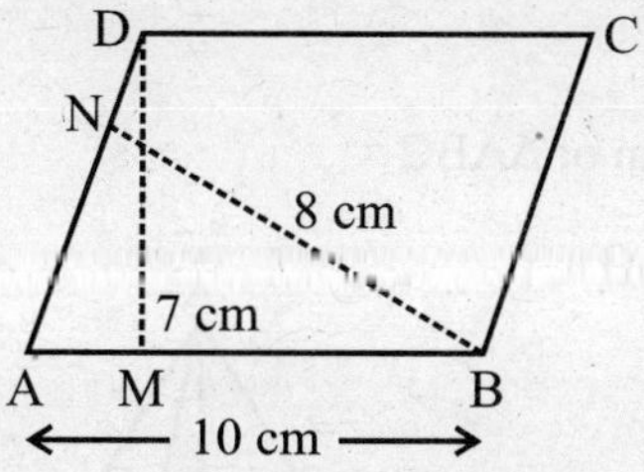

Area of || gm = Base × Height

$\therefore$ ar (|| gm ABCD) = AB × DM

= 10 × 7

= 70 cm^2

Also, area (|| gm ABCD) = AD × BN

= (AD × 8) cm^2

Thus, 10 × 7 = AD × 8

$\Rightarrow$ AD = $\dfrac{35}{4}$ = 8.75 cm

2. (a, b, c)

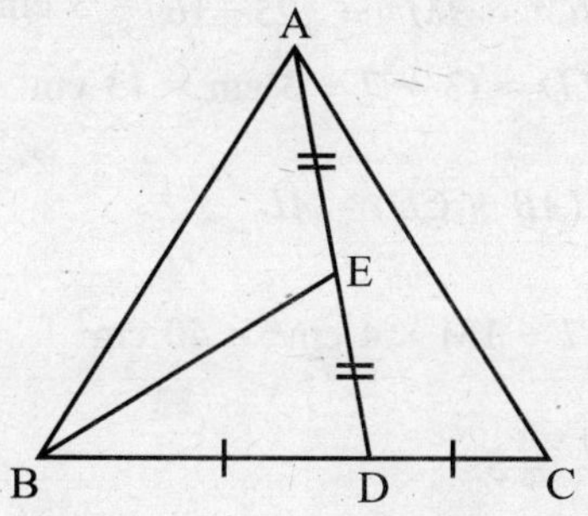

Since AD is a median of ΔABC and median divides a triangle into two triangle of equal area.

$\therefore$ ar (ΔABD) = ar (ΔADC)

$\Rightarrow$ ar (ΔABD) = $\dfrac{1}{2}$ ar (ΔABC)

In ΔABD, BE is the median

$\therefore$ ar (ΔBED) = ar (ΔBAE)

$\Rightarrow$ ar(ΔBED) = $\dfrac{1}{2} \times \dfrac{1}{2}$ × ar (ΔABC)

$\Rightarrow$ ar (ΔBED) = $\dfrac{1}{4}$ ar (ΔABC)

3. (b, c)

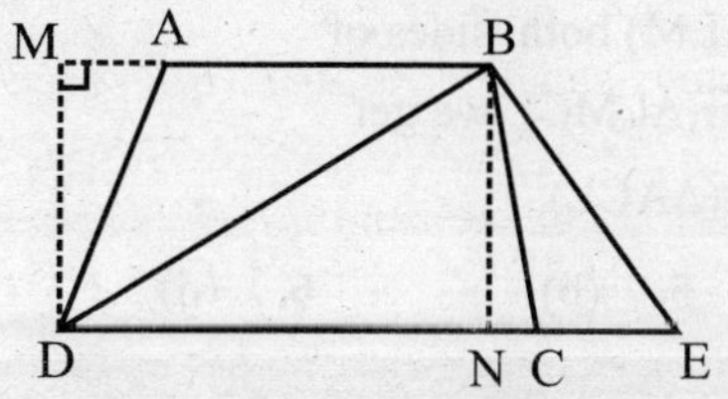

We have ar(ΔABD) = $\dfrac{1}{2}$(AB × DM)

ar(ΔBCE) = $\dfrac{1}{2}$(CE × BN)

Since triangles ABD and BCE are between the same parallel, so their heights are equal i.e. DM = BN

Also, AB = CE

$\therefore$ $\dfrac{1}{2}$(AB × DM) = $\dfrac{1}{2}$(CE × BN)

$\Rightarrow$ ar (ΔABD) = ar (ΔBCE)

4. (a, b, c)

PASSAGE BASED QUESTIONS :

1. (b) Consider triangles *APE* and *DQF*. In these two triangles, we have $\angle APE = \angle DQF$

[$AP \parallel DQ$ and PQ is transversal

$\therefore \angle APE$ and $\angle DQF$ are corresponding angles]

$AE = DF$ [$\because$ *AEFD* is a || gm]

$\angle AEP = \angle DFQ$

$\Delta APE \cong \Delta DQF$ [By AAS congruency]

$\Rightarrow PE = QF$ [By c.p.c.t]

and ar(ΔAPE) = ar(ΔDQF) ...(i)

2. (a) Clearly, triangles *PFA* and *PFD* are on the same base *PF* and between the same parallels *PQ* and *AD*.

$\therefore$ ar(ΔPFA) = ar (ΔPFD) ...(ii)

From (i) and (ii), we get

$$\frac{\text{ar}(\Delta APE)}{\text{ar}(\Delta PFA)} = \frac{\text{ar}(\Delta DQF)}{\text{ar}(\Delta PFD)}$$

3. (c) Already proved in (1)

For (4 – 6)

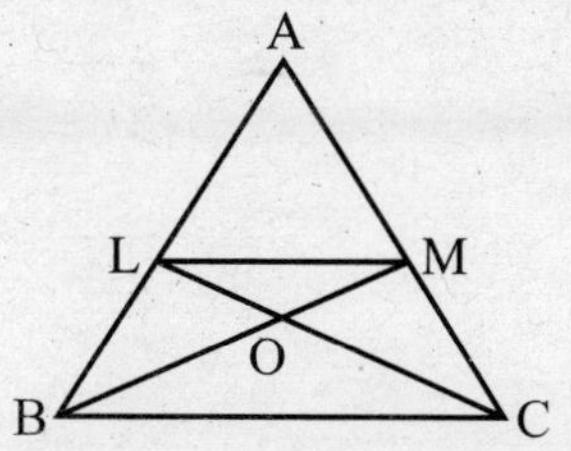

Clearly, triangles LMB and LMC are on the same base LM and between the same parallels LM and BC.

$\therefore$ ar (ΔLMB) = ar (ΔLMC)

Triangles LBC and MBC are on the same base BC and lie between the parallels LM and BC.

$\therefore$ ar (ΔLBC) = ar (ΔMBC)

Adding ar(ΔALM) both sides of ar(ΔLMB) = ar(ΔLMC), we get ar(ΔABM)=ar(ΔACL)

4. (a) **5.** (b) **6.** (d)

ASSERTION & REASON :

1. (a) Area of triangle $= \frac{\sqrt{3}}{4}(8)^2\ cm^2$

$= \frac{\sqrt{3}}{4} \times 8 \times 8 = 16\sqrt{3}\ cm^2.$

2. (a) Both assertion and reason is correct. Also, reason is the correct explanation for assertion.

3. (a) **Assertion:** Area of $\Delta = \frac{1}{2}$ area of rhombus

$\Rightarrow \frac{\text{Area of } \Delta}{\text{Area of rhombus}} = \frac{1}{2} \equiv 1:2$

INTEGER TYPE QUESTIONS :

1. **Ans : 8**

$ar(\Delta AFB) = \frac{1}{2} ar(ABCD)$

$= \frac{1}{2} \times 4 \times 4 = 8\ cm^2$

2. **Ans : 2**

We join G and E.

Now, DG = AE and DG || AE (∵ AB || CD)

∴ AEGD is a parallelogram.

∴ $ar(\Delta HEG) = \frac{1}{2} ar(AEGD)$ ....(i)

Similarly, $ar(\Delta EFG) = \frac{1}{2} ar(EBCG)$ ....(ii)

On adding (i) and (ii), we get

$ar(EFGH) = \frac{1}{2} ar(ABCD)$

$\Rightarrow ar(ABCD) = 80\ cm^2$

Hence, $\frac{ar(ABCD)}{40} = \frac{80}{40} = 2$

3. **Ans : 2**

Since, AD is the median of ΔABC

∴ $ar(\Delta ABD) = ar(\Delta ADC)$

$= \frac{1}{2} ar(\Delta ABC)$

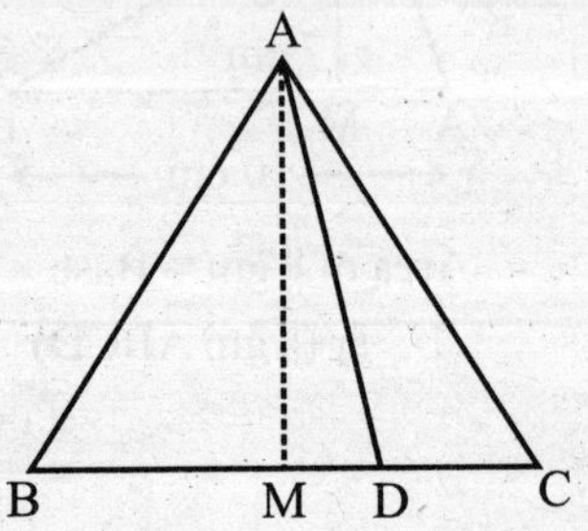

$\Rightarrow \frac{1}{2} ar(\Delta ABC) = 15$

$\Rightarrow \frac{ar(\Delta ABC)}{15} = 2$

4. **Ans : 5**

$AL = BM = 4$ cm and $LM = 7$ cm

In ΔADL, we have $AD^2 = AL^2 + DL^2$

$\Rightarrow 25 = 16 + DL^2$

$\Rightarrow DL = 3$ cm

Similarly, $MC = \sqrt{BC^2 - BM^2} = \sqrt{25-16} = 3$ cm

$CD = CM + ML + LD = (3 + 7 + 3)\text{cm} = 13$ cm

$ar(\text{trap.}ABCD) = \frac{1}{2}(AB + CD) \times AL$

$= \frac{1}{2}(7 + 13) \times 4\ cm^2 = 40\ cm^2$

The value of $\frac{l}{8} = \frac{40}{8} = 5.$

Chapter 10

Circles

INTRODUCTION

See the dial of a clock. You might have observed that the second's hand goes round the dial of the clock rapidly and its tip moves in a round path. This traced path by the tip of the second's hand is called a circle. Also, you may have come across many objects in daily life, which are round (circle) in shape like wheels of a vehicle, bangles, dials of many clocks, buttons of shirts, etc. In this chapter, you will study about circles, terms related to circles and properties of circles and some theorem related to circles.

Clock

CIRCLE

Circle is a set of point or collection of point in a plane which are at a fixed distance from a fixed point. The fixed point is called the centre of the circle. In the given diagram '*O*' is the centre of the circle. The fixed distance is called the radius. In the diagram, *OP* is the radius of the circle.

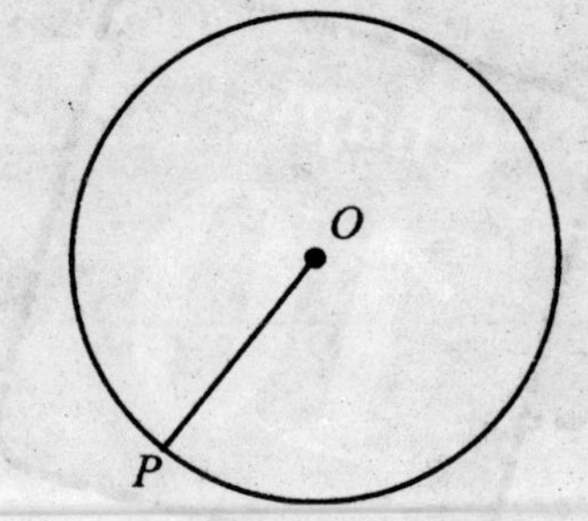

Circle

A circle divides the plane in which it lies into three parts.

These three parts are

(i) Inside the circle which is called the interior of the circle.

(ii) The circle

(iii) Outside the circle which is called the exterior of the circle.

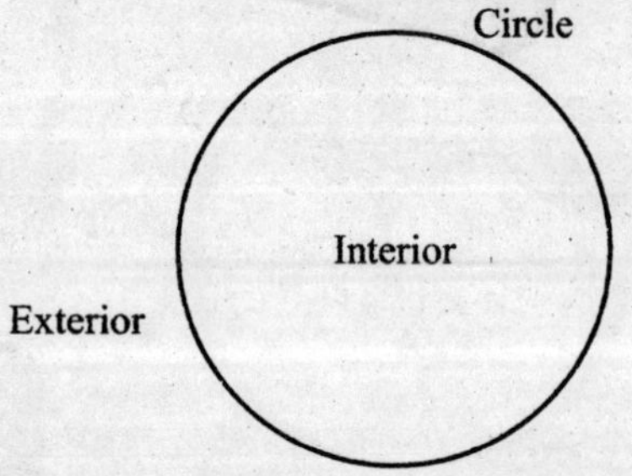

NOTE : The circle and its interior make up the circular region.

Chord

A line segment whose end points lie on the circle is called a chord of the circle. In the given diagram *AB* is a chord.

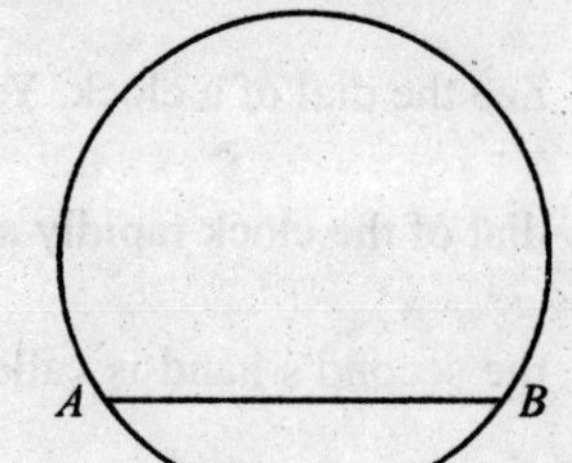

Diameter

A chord which passes through the centre of the circle is called the diameter of the circle.

The length of the diameter is twice the length of the radius. In the given diagram, *AB* is the diameter.

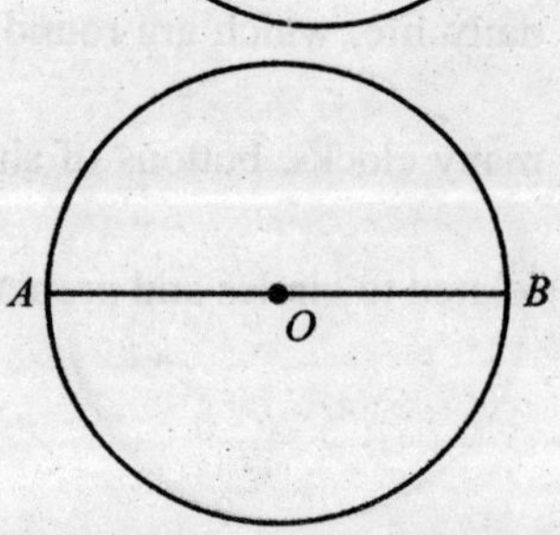

NOTE : The diameter is the longest chord of the circle.

Arcs and Semicircle

Arcs: A piece of a circle between two points is called an arc.

Consider two points M and N on the circle. We find that there are two pieces of circle between M and N. One is longer and other is smaller. The longer piece is called major arc and smaller piece is called minor arc

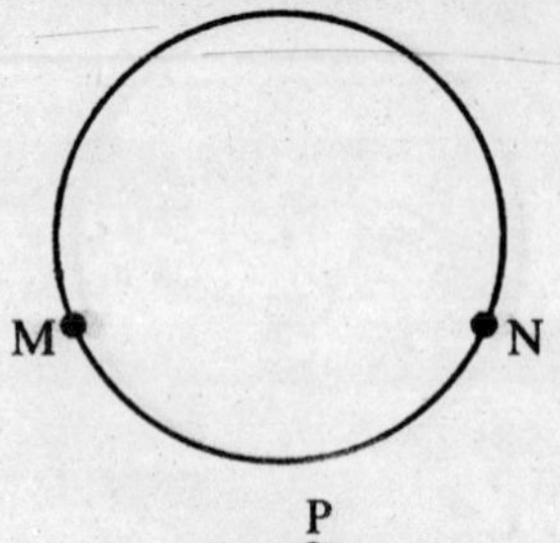

Major arc is denoted by $\overparen{MPN}$ and minor arc is denoted by $\overparen{MQN}$.

When M and N are ends of a diameter then both the arcs are equal and both are called semicircle.

In other words,

A diameter of the circle divides the circle into two equal parts. Each part is called as semi-circle.

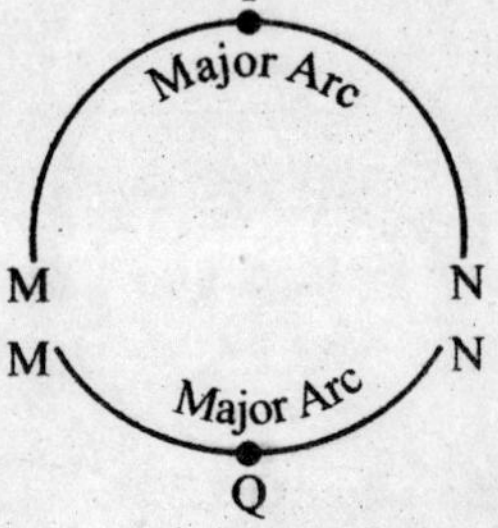

Circumference

The length of the complete circle is called its circumference.

Example : If a circular wire cut from a point and then re-open as a straight piece of wire. The length of this straight piece of wire is the circumference of the circular wire.

Segment

The region between a chord and an arc of a circle is called a segment.

There are two segments corresponding to two arcs, major segment and minor segment. Major segment is the segment enclosed by major arc. Centre of the circle lies in the major segment. Minor segment is the segment enclosed by minor arc. Centre of the circle does not lie in the minor segment.

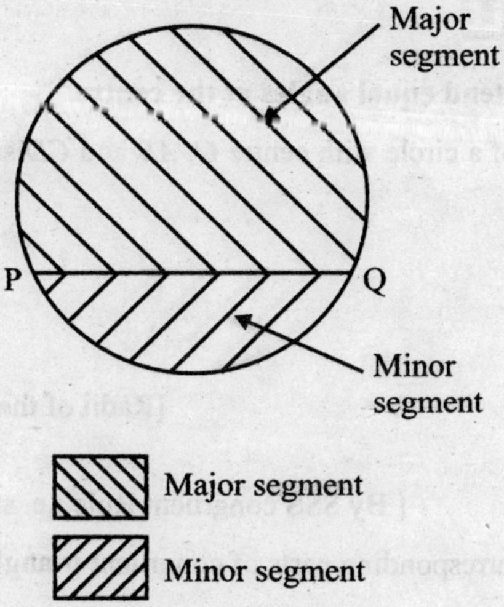

If two arcs are equal, then both segments are semi-circles.

Sector

The region between an arc and the two radii joining the centre to the end point of the arc is called a sector. There are two sectors Minor and Major Sectors.

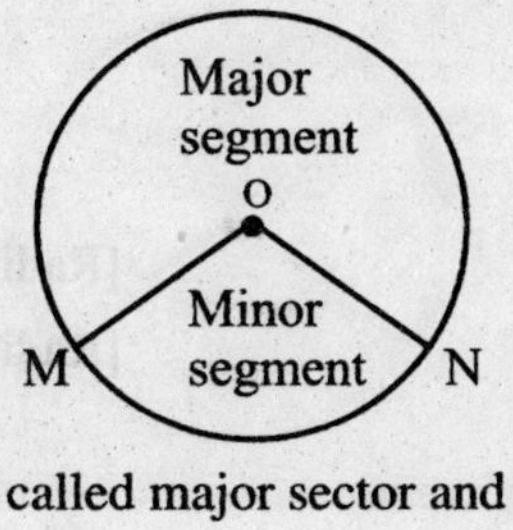

The sector which is larger than semicircular region is called major sector and the region less than the semicircular region is called minor sector.

If both sectors are equal, then each sector is a semi-circle.

CENTRAL ANGLE – ANGLE SUBTENDED BY AN ARC OR CHORD AT THE CENTRE

An angle formed, by an arc of a circle at the centre of the circle is called the central angle. In the given diagram $\angle AOB$ is the central angle made by the minor arc AB.

And the angle subtended by the major arc AB at the centre O of the circle is reflex $\angle AOB$.

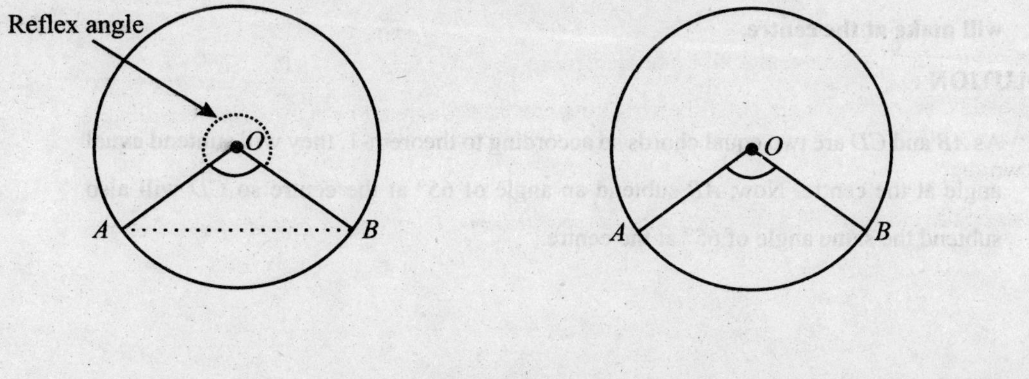

ANGLES IN THE SAME SEGMENT OF A CIRCLE

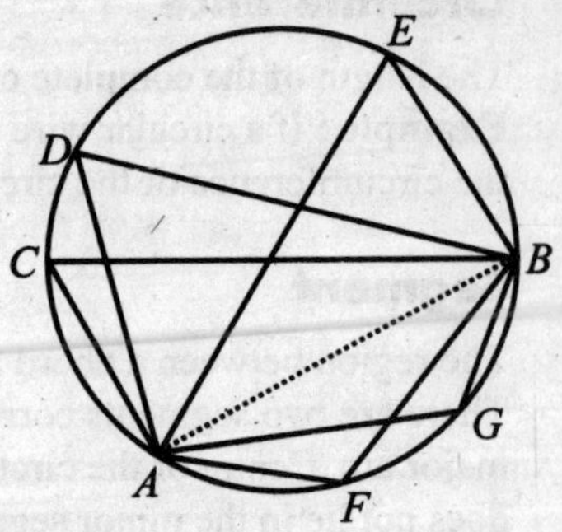

Any chord of a circle divides the circle in two segments. Angles made by any chord at different points (lie on the same side of the chord) on the circle are called angles in the same segment of the circle.

In the figure $\angle ACB$, $\angle ADB$ and $\angle AEB$ are the angles in the same segment of a circle. Also $\angle AFB$ and $\angle AGB$ are the angles in the same segment of a circle.

THEOREMS RELATED TO CIRCLE

Theorem 1 : Equal chords of a circle subtend equal angles at the centre.

Given : AB and CD are two equal chords of a circle with centre O. AB and CD subtends an angle $\angle AOB$ and $\angle COD$ at the centre O respectively.

To Prove : $\angle AOB = \angle COD$

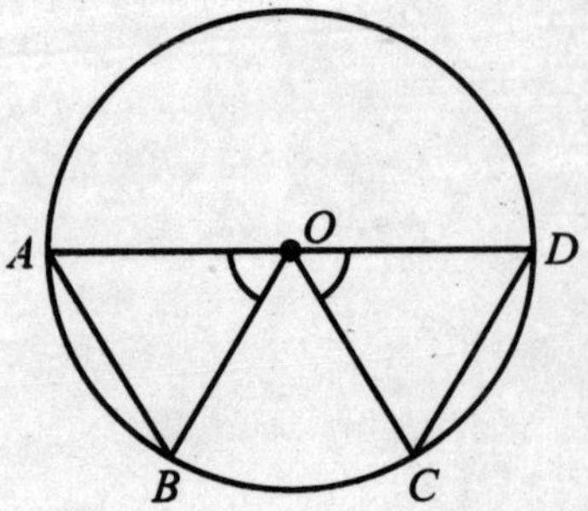

Proof : In ΔAOB and ΔCOD,

$AB = CD$ [Given]

$OA = OC$ [Radii of the same circle]

$OB = OD$

$\therefore$ $\Delta AOB \cong \Delta COD$ [By SSS congruent Rule i.e. side side side]

$\therefore$ $\angle AOB = \angle COD$ [Corresponding parts of congruent triangles are equal]

Theorem 2 : (Converse of the Theorem 1)

If the angles subtended by the chords of a circle at the centre are equal, then the chords are equal.

Given : AB and CD are two chords of a circle with centre O. Chords AB and CD subtend equal angle $\angle AOB$ and $\angle COD$ at the centre respectively.

To Prove : $AB = CD$

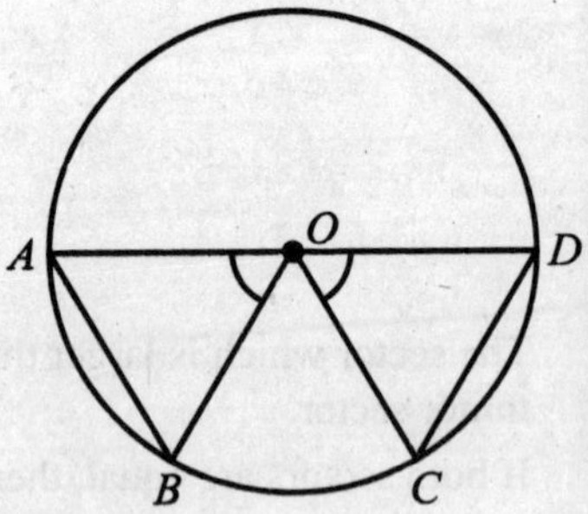

Proof : In ΔAOB and ΔCOD,

$OA = OC$ [Radii of the same circle]

$OB = OD$ [Radii of the same circle]

$\angle AOB = \angle COD$ [Given]

$\therefore$ $\Delta AOB \cong \Delta COD$ [By Side-Angle-Side congruent rule]

$\therefore$ $AB = CD$ [Corresponding parts of congruent triangle are equal]

ILLUSTRATION : 1

AB and CD are two chords each of length 10 cm of a circle whose centre is O and chord AB makes an angle of 65° at the centre. Find the angle which the chord CD will make at the centre.

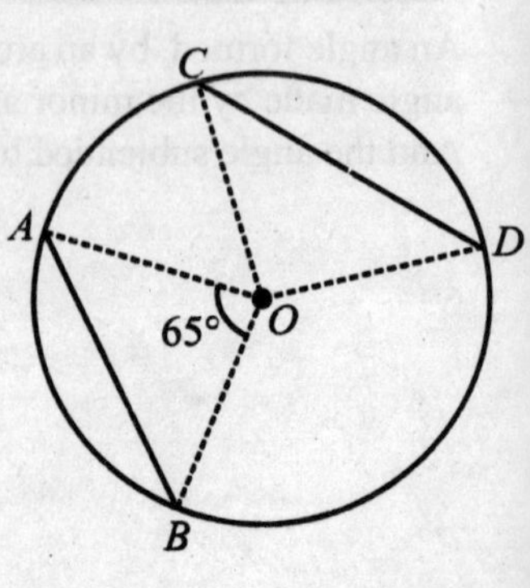

SOLUTION :

As AB and CD are two equal chords so according to theorem-1, they will subtend equal angle at the centre. Now, AB subtend an angle of 65° at the centre so CD will also subtend the same angle of 65° at the centre.

Theorem 3 : The perpendicular from the centre of a circle to a chord bisects the chord.

Given : AB is a chord of a circle with centre O. OM be the perpendicular from O to chord AB.

To Prove : OM bisects AB i.e. $AM = MB$

Construction : Join OA and OB

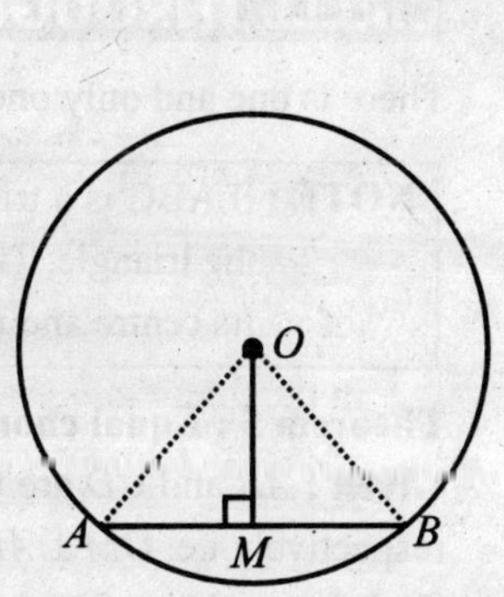

Proof : In ΔAOM and ΔBOM

$OA = OB$ [Radii of the same circle]

$OM = OM$ [Common]

$\angle OMA = \angle OMB = 90°$

$\therefore$ $\Delta OAM \cong \Delta OBM$ [By RHS congruent rule]

$\therefore$ $AM = BM$ [Corresponding parts of two congruent triangles are equal]

Theorem 4 : (Converse of the Theorem 3)

The line drawn through the centre of a circle to bisect a chord is perpendicular to the chord.

OR

The line joining the centre of a circle to the mid-point of a chord is perpendicular to the chord.

Given : AB is a chord of a circle whose centre is O. M is the mid-point of the chord AB. i.e. $AM = MB$.

To Prove : OM is perpendicular to AB i.e. $OM \perp AB$

Construction : Join OA and OB.

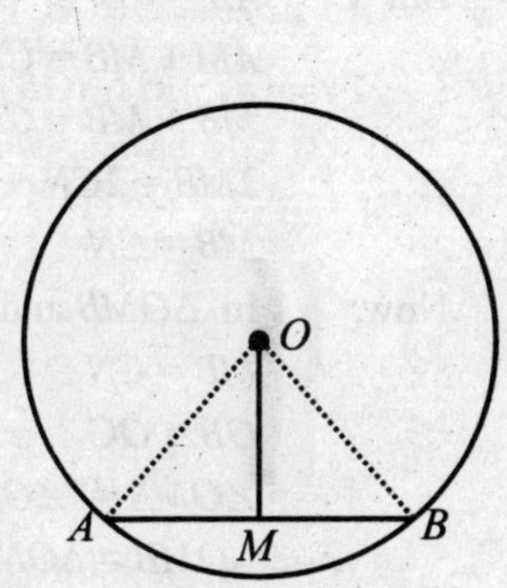

Proof : In ΔAOM and ΔBOM

$OA = OB$ [Radii of the same circle]

$OM = OM$ [Common side]

$AM = MB$ [Given]

$\therefore$ $\Delta AOM \cong \Delta BOM$ [By SSS congruent rule]

$\therefore$ $\angle AMO = \angle BMO$ ....(i) [Corresponding part of two congruent triangles are equal]

Now, $\angle AMO + \angle BMO = 180°$ [Linear pair angles]

But $\angle AMO = \angle BMO$ [from (i)]

$\therefore$ $\angle AMO + \angle AMO = 180°$

$2\angle AMO = 180°$

$\angle AMO = \frac{180°}{2} = 90°$

So, $OM \perp AB$

ILLUSTRATION : 2

The radius of the circle is 5 cm and the perpendicular distance of a chord from the centre is 4 cm. Find the length of the chord.

SOLUTION :

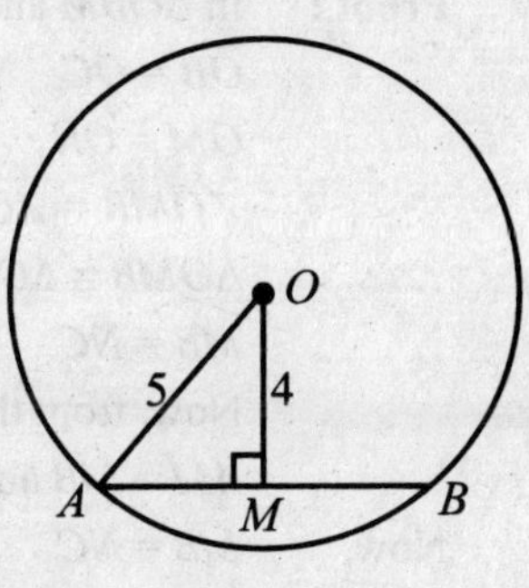

Let AB be the chord whose length is to be found.

Now, OA = radius = 5 cm

OM = perpendicular distance of AB from the centre is 4 cm.

In right angle triangle AOM,

$OA^2 = OM^2 + AM^2$ [By Pythagoras theorem]

$\therefore$ $AM^2 = OA^2 - OM^2 = 5^2 - 4^2 = 25 - 16 = 9$

$\therefore$ $AM = \sqrt{9} = 3$ cm

Now, from theorem 3, the perpendicular from centre to a chord bisect the chord. So M is the mid-point of AB.

$\therefore$ $AB = 2\,AM = 2 \times 3 = 6$ cm.

NOTE : Perpendicular distance of a line from a point is the shortest distance of the line from the point.

CIRCLE THROUGH THREE POINTS

There is one and only one circle passing through three given non-collinear points.

NOTE : If ABC is a triangle then by above statement, there is a unique circle passing through the three vertices A, B and C of the triangle. This circle is called the circumcircle of the ΔABC.
Its centre and radius are called respectively the circumcentre and the circumradius of the triangle.

Theorem 5 : Equal chords of a circle (or of congruent circles) are equidistant from the centre (or centres).

Given : AB and CD are two equal chords of a circle having centre O. OM and ON are the distance of AB and CD from centre O respectively i.e. $OM \perp AB$ and $ON \perp CD$.

To Prove : $OM = ON$

Construction : Join OB and OC.

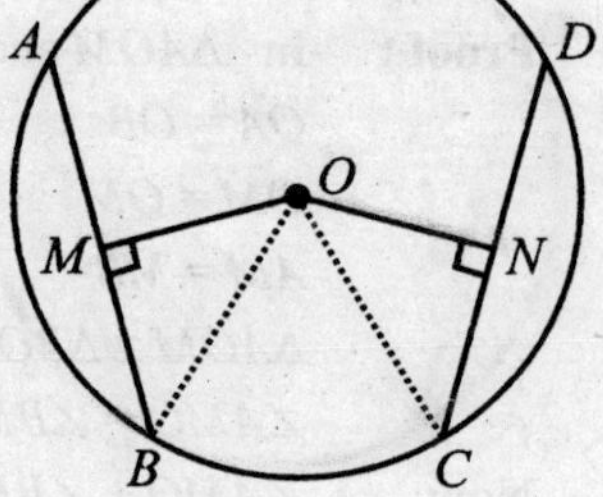

Proof : From theorem-3, perpendicular from centre to chord bisects the chord, so, OM bisect AB and ON bisects CD.

$\therefore$ $AM = MB$ ...(i)

And $CN = ND$ ...(ii)

But $AB = CD$ [Given]

$AM + MB = CN + ND$

$MB + MB = CN + CN$ [from (i) and (ii)]

$\therefore$ $2MB = 2CN$

$MB = CN$ ...(iii)

Now, In ΔOMB and ΔONC

$MB = CN$ [from (iii)]

$\therefore$ $OB = OC$ [Radii of the same circle]

$\therefore$ $\angle OMB = \angle ONC = 90°$ [$OM \perp AB$, $ON \perp CD$]

$\Delta OMB \cong \Delta ONC$ [By RHS congruent rule]

$\therefore$ $OM = ON$ [Corresponding parts of congruent triangles are equal]

Theorem 6 : (Converse of the Theorem 5)

Chords equidistant from the centre of a circle are equal in length.

Given : AB and CD are two chords of a circle having centre O, whose distances of AB and CD from centre O are OM and ON respectively are equal in length i.e. $OM = ON$.

To Prove : $AB = CD$

Construction : Join OB and OC.

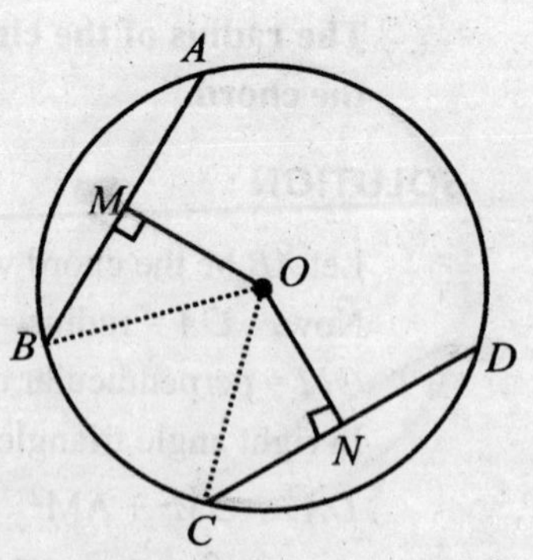

Proof : In ΔOBM and ΔOCN

$OB = OC$ [Radii of the same circle]

$OM = ON$ [Given]

$\angle OMB = \angle ONC = 90°$

$\therefore$ $\Delta OMB \cong \Delta ONC$ [By RHS congruent rule]

$\therefore$ $MB = NC$ ...(i) [Corresponding parts of a congruent triangles are equal]

Now, from theorem-3, perpendicular from centre to a chord bisects the chord

$\therefore$ $AM = MB$ and $CN = ND$

Now, $MB = NC$ [from (i)]

$2MB = 2NC$ [Multiplying both sides by 2]

$MB + MB = NC + NC$

$AM + MB = CN + ND$ [$\because AM = MB$ and $CN = ND$]

$\therefore$ $AB = CD$

Remarks :

(i) If two chords of a circle are equal, then their corresponding arcs are congruent and conversly, if two arcs are congruent, then their corresponding chords are equal.

(ii) Congruent arcs (or equal arcs) of a circle subtend equal angles at the centre.

Theorem 7 : The angle subtended by an arc at the centre is double the angle subtended by it at any point on the remaining part of the circle.

Given : AB is an arc of a circle subtending angles AOB at the centre O and APB at a point P on the remaining part of the circle.

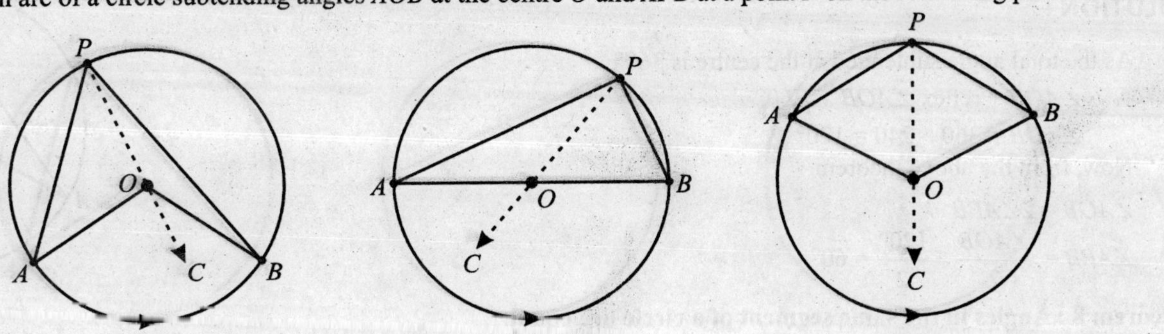

(i) (ii) (iii)

To Prove : $\angle AOB = 2\angle APB$ (if arc AB is minor)

$180° = 2\angle APB$ (if arc AB is semi-circle)

Reflex $\angle AOB = 2\ \angle APB$ (if arc AB is major arc)

Construction : Join P to O and extends it to point C.

We consider the three cases as shown in the above figure (i) arc AB is minor (ii) arc AB is a semicircle and (iii) arc AB is major.

Proof : In all the three cases $\angle AOC$ is the exterior angle of ΔAOP.

$\therefore$ $\angle AOC = \angle APO + \angle OAP$ ...(i) [Exterior angle of a triangle is equal to the sum of the two interior opposite angles]

Now, In ΔOAP

$OP = OA$ [Radii]

$\therefore$ $\angle APO = \angle OAP$ [Angles opp. equal sides in a triangle are equal]

$\therefore$ $\angle AOC = \angle APO + \angle APO$

$\angle AOC = 2\angle APO$ ...(ii)

Similarly, $\angle BOC = 2\angle OPB$ ...(iii)

Case-I : Adding (ii) & (iii), we get

$\angle AOC + \angle BOC = 2\,[\angle APO + \angle OPB]$

$\angle AOB = 2\angle APB$

Case-II : Angle subtended by semicircle at the centre of the circle is 180°.

Adding (ii) and (iii), we get

$\angle AOC + \angle BOC = 2\angle APO + 2\angle OPB$

$\Rightarrow 180° = 2(\angle APO + \angle OPB)$

$\Rightarrow 180° = 2\angle APB$

Case-III : Angle subtended by the major arc AB at the centre of the circle is the reflex angle $\angle AOB$.

Adding (ii) and (iii), we get

$\angle AOC + \angle BOC = 2\angle APO + 2\angle OPB$

$\Rightarrow$ Reflex $\angle AOB = 2(\angle APO + \angle OPB)$

$\Rightarrow$ Reflex $\angle AOB = 2\angle APB$

> **NOTE:** In case (II) $\angle AOB = 2\angle APB$, but $\angle AOB = 180°$ [$\because$ AB is the diameter]
>
> $\therefore$ $\angle APB = \dfrac{180°}{2} = 90°$
>
> This proves the property that the angle in the semi-circle is a right angle.

ILLUSTRATION : 3

In the given figure, the reflex $\angle AOB$ is 240°. Find the $\angle APB$.

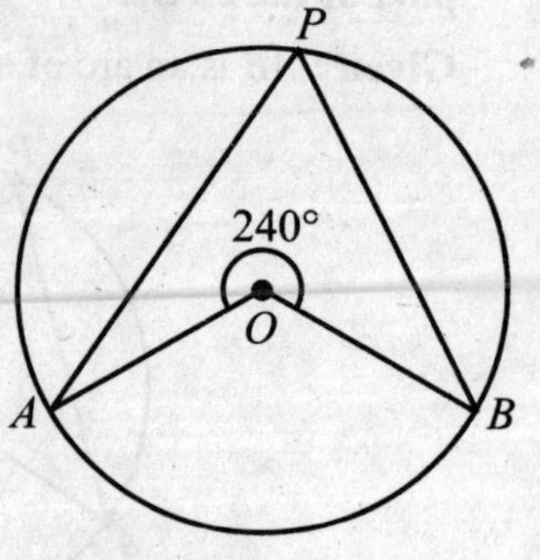

SOLUTION :

As the total angle subtended at the centre is 360°

$\therefore \quad \angle AOB + \text{reflex } \angle AOB = 360°$

$\therefore \quad \angle AOB = 360 - 240 = 120°$

Now, from the above theorem

$\angle AOB = 2\angle APB$

$\angle APB = \dfrac{\angle AOB}{2} = \dfrac{120°}{2} = 60°$

Theorem 8 : Angles in the same segment of a circle are equal.

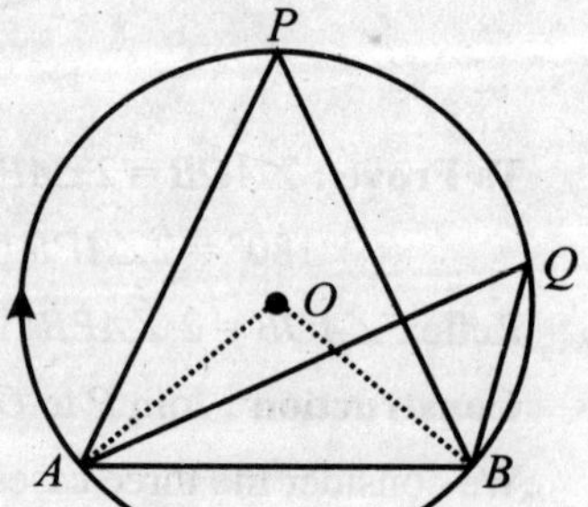

Given : $\angle APB$ and $\angle AQB$ are two angles in the same segment $APQBA$ of a circle with centre O.

To Prove : $\angle APB = \angle AQB$

Construction : Join centre O to A and B.

Proof : From theorem-7,

$\angle AOB = 2\angle APB$ ...(i)

and $\angle AOB = 2\angle AQB$ ...(ii)

$\therefore$ from (i) and (ii), we get

$\angle APB = \angle AQB$

Theorem 9 : (Converse of the Theorem 8)

If a line segment joining two points subtends equal angles at two other points lying on the same side of the line containing the line segment, the four point lie on a circle (i.e. they are concyclic)

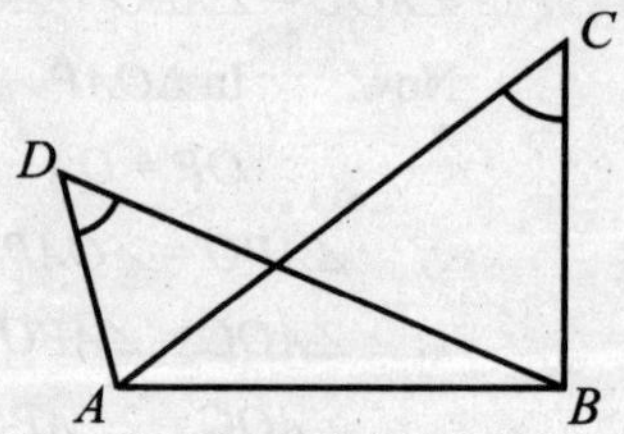

Fig. (i)

Given : A, B, C and D are four points such that point C and D lie on the same side of the line containing the line segment AB.

Also $\angle ACB = \angle ADB$. (Fig. (i))

To Prove : The four points A, B, C, D lie on a circle i.e. they are concyclic.

Construction : Draw a circle through the three non-collinear points A, B and D. Because one and only one circle passes through three non-collinear points.

Proof : This is proved by contradiction.

Let the circle does not pass through the point C.

Then two cases arises:

(i) The circle intersect AC at E. see fig. (ii)

(ii) The circle intersect AC produced at E'. see fig. (iii)

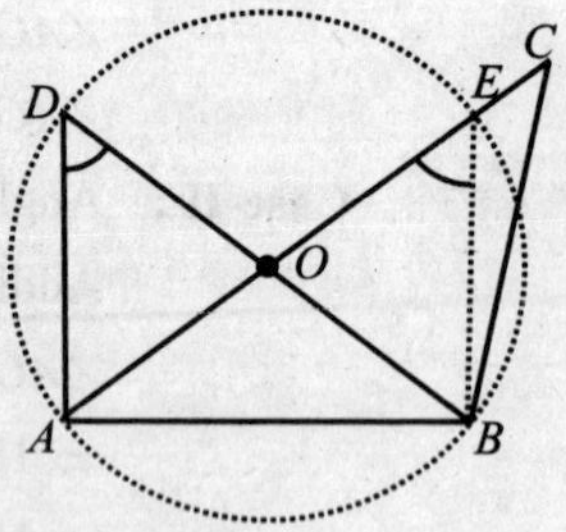

Fig. (ii)

Case (i) : When A, B, E and D lie on a circle [fig. (ii)], join EB.

$\angle ADB = \angle AEB$ ....(i) [$\because$ Angle in the same segment of a circle are equal]

$\angle ACB = \angle ADB$ ...(ii) [Given]

From (i) and (ii), we get

$\angle AEB = \angle ACB$

This can be possible only when E and C coincides.

So, the circle passes through A, B, C and D.

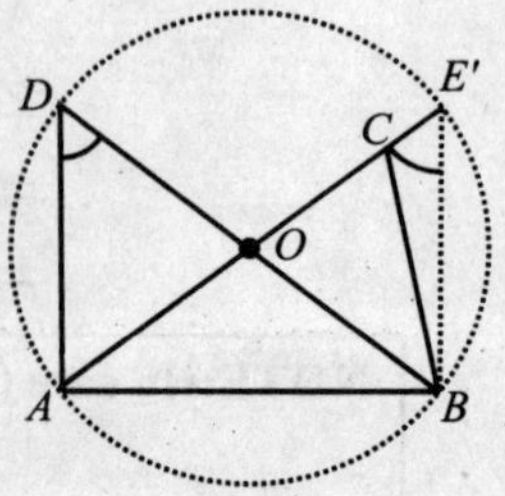

Fig. (iii)

Case (ii) : When A, B, E' and D lie on the circle [fig. (iii)], join $E'B$.

$\therefore \quad \angle ADB = \angle AE'B$ ....(iii) [$\because$: Angle in the same segment of a circle are equal]

$\angle ACB = \angle ADB$ ...(iv) [Given]

From (iii) and (iv),

$\angle ACB = \angle AE'B$

This can be possible only when E' and C coincides. So, the circle passes through A, B, C and D.

Hence, the four points A, B, C and D are concyclic.

CYCLIC QUADRILATERAL

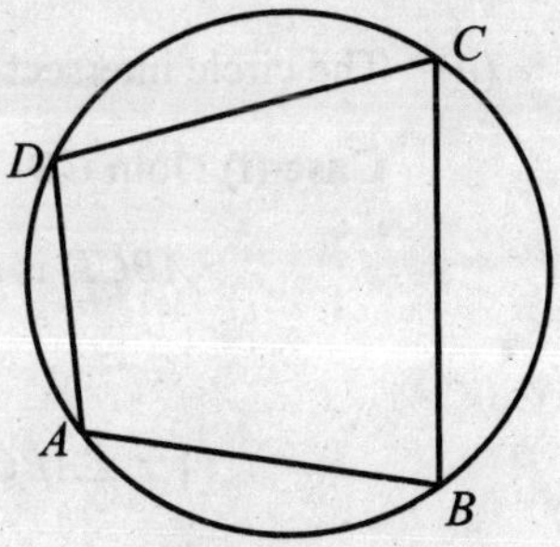

A quadrilateral is called cyclic, if all the four vertices of it lie on a circle. In the figure, $ABCD$ is a cyclic quadrilateral because its all four vertices lie on a circle.

Theorem 10 : The sum of either pair of opposite angles of a cyclic quadrilateral is 180°.

OR

The opposite angles of a cyclic quadrilateral are supplementary.

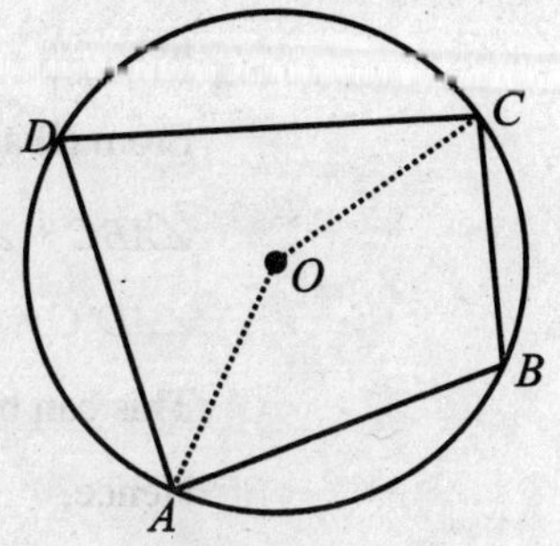

Given : $ABCD$ is a cyclic quadrilateral whose vertices A, B, C and D lie on a circle having centre O.

To prove : (i) $\angle ABC + \angle ADC = 180°$

(ii) $\angle BAD + \angle BCD = 180°$

Construction : Join O to A and C.

Proof : Since, the angle subtended by an arc at the centre of a circle is twice the angle subtended by the arc at any point on the remaining part of the circle.

$\therefore$ $\angle AOC = 2\angle ADC$

Similarly, Reflex $\angle AOC = 2\angle ABC$

Also, $\angle AOC +$ Reflex $\angle AOC = 360°$ [Sum of all the angles at a point is 360°]

$2\angle ADC + 2\angle ABC = 360°$

$$\angle ABC + \angle ADC = \frac{360°}{2} = 180° \quad \ldots(i)$$

In quadrilateral $ABCD$,

$\angle BAD + \angle ABC + \angle BCD + \angle ADC = 360°$ [Sum of all the angles of a quadrilateral is 360°]

$\Rightarrow$ $\angle BAD + \angle BCD + (\angle ABC + \angle ADC) = 360°$

$\Rightarrow$ $\angle BAD + \angle BCD + 180° = 360°$ [From equation (i), $\angle ABC + \angle ADC = 180°$]

$\Rightarrow$ $\angle BAD + \angle BCD = 180°$

Theorem 11 : (Converse of the above Theorem)

If the sum of any pair of opposite angles of a quadrilateral is 180°, then the quadrilateral is cyclic.

Given : A quadrilateral $ABCD$ in which $\angle B + \angle D = 180°$

To prove : $ABCD$ is a cyclic quadrilateral.

Proof : This is proved by contradiction method. Let $ABCD$ is not a cyclic quadrilateral. Draw a circle passing through three non-collinear points A, B and C.

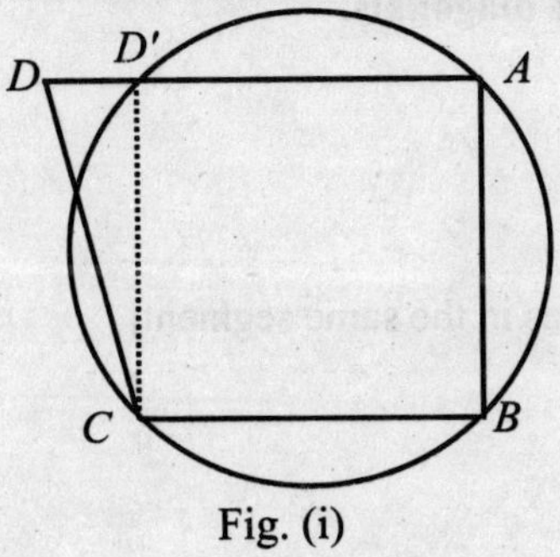

Fig. (i)

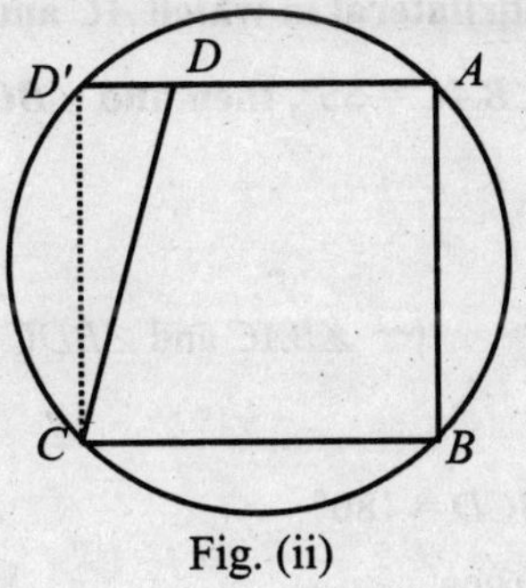

Fig. (ii)

Then two cases arises :

(i) The circle intersect AD at D', see fig (i)

(ii) The circle intersect AD produced at D', see fig. (ii)

Case-(i) : Join CD'

$ABCD$ is a cyclic quadrilateral [fig. (i)]

$\therefore \quad \angle ABC + \angle AD'C = 180°$ ...(i)

[$\because$ $\angle ABC$ and $\angle AD'C$ are opposite angles of a cyclic quadrilateral $ABCD'$]

But, $\angle B + \angle D = 180°$ [Given]

i.e., $\angle ABC + \angle ADC = 180°$ ...(ii)

From (i) and (ii), we get

$\angle ABC + \angle AD'C = \angle ABC + \angle ADC$

$\angle AD'C = \angle ADC$

This can be possible only when D and D' coincides. So the circle passes through A, B, C and D.

Hence, $ABCD$ is a cyclic quadrilateral.

Case-(ii) Join CD'

A, B, C and D' lie on the circle [fig (ii)]

$\therefore \quad \angle ABC + \angle AD'C = 180°$ ...(iii)

[$\because$ $\angle ABC$ and $\angle AD'C$ are opposite ang'es of a cyclic quadrilateral $ABCD'$]

But $\angle B + \angle D = 180°$ [Given]

i.e. $\angle ABC + \angle ADC = 180°$ ...(iv)

From (iii) and (iv), we get

$\angle ABC + \angle AD'C = \angle ABC + \angle ADC$

$\angle AD'C = \angle ADC$

This can be possible only when D and D' coincides. So, the circle passes through A, B, C and D.

Hence, $ABCD$ is a cyclic quadrilateral.

ILLUSTRATION : 4

$ABCD$ is a cyclic quadrilateral in which AC and BD are diagonals.

If $\angle DBC = 65°$ and $\angle BAC = 55°$, then find $\angle BCD$

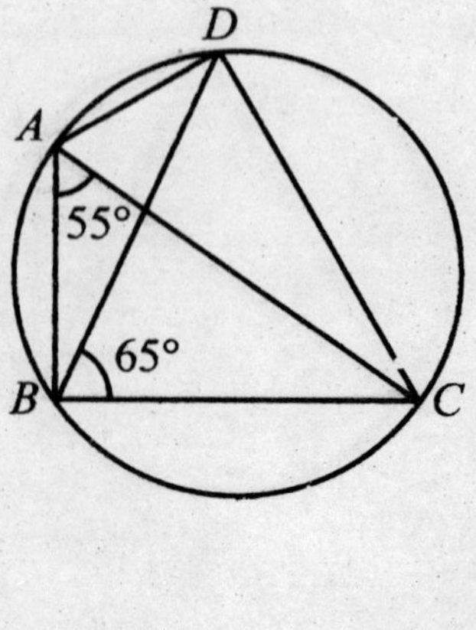

SOLUTION :

$\angle BAC = \angle BDC = 55°$ [$\because$ $\angle BAC$ and $\angle BDC$ are angles in the same segment]

In ΔBDC,

$\angle BDC + \angle DBC + \angle BCD = 180°$

$55° + 65° + \angle BCD = 180°$

$\angle BCD = 180° - 120° = 60°$.

CONNECTING TOPIC

LOCUS

The locus of a point is the path traced out by a moving point under given geometrical condition. Alternatively, the locus is the set of all those points which satisfy the given geometrical condition.
The plural of locus is loci and is read as 'Losai'.

The locus of a point in different conditions :

(i) The locus of a point which is equidistant from two fixed points is the perpendicular bisector of the line segment joining the two fixed points.

(ii) The locus of a point which is equidistant from two intersecting straight lines is a pair of straight lines which bisect the angles between the two given lines.

(iii) The locus of a point equidistant from two given parallel straight lines is a straight line parallel to the given straight lines and midway between them.

(iv) The locus of a point which is equidistant from a fixed point in a plane is a circle.

(v) The locus of a point, which is at a given distance from a given straight line, is a pair of straight lines parallel and either side to the given line and at a given distance from it.

(vi) The locus of the centre of a wheel moving on a straight horizontal road, is a straight line parallel to the road and at a distance equal to the radius of the wheel.

(vii) The locus of midpoints of all parallel chords in a circle, is the diameter of the circle which is perpendicular to the given parallel chords.

(viii) The locus of a point which is equidistant from two concentric circles is the circumference of the circle concentric with the given circles and midway between them.

(ix) If A and B are two fixed points, then the locus of a point P such that $\angle APB = 90°$, is the circle with AB as diameter.

(x) The locus of a midpoints of all equal chords in a circle is the circumference of the circle concentric with the given circle and radius equal to the distance of equal chords from the centre of the given circle.

MISCELLANEOUS SOLVED EXAMPLES

1. In the given figure, *ABC* is an isosceles triangle in which *AB* = *AC* and $\angle ABC = 50°$, find $\angle BDC$.

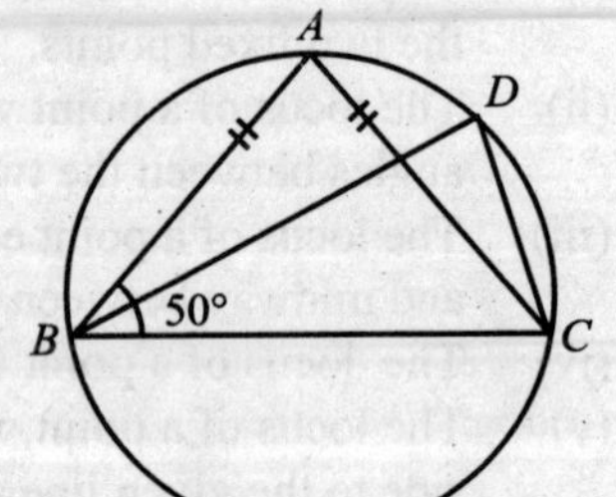

Sol. $AB = AC, \therefore \angle ABC = \angle ACB = 50°$

$\therefore$ In ΔABC,

$\angle ABC + \angle ACB + \angle BAC = 180°$

$50° + 50° + \angle BAC = 180°$

$\angle BAC = 180° - 100° = 80°$

Now, $\angle BAC = \angle BDC$ [$\because$ Angle in the same segment of a circle are equal]

$\therefore \angle BDC = 80°$

2. Two chords *AB* and *CD* of lengths 6 cm, 12 cm respectively of a circle are parallel. If the perpendicular distance between *AB* and *CD* is 3 cm, find the radius of the circle.

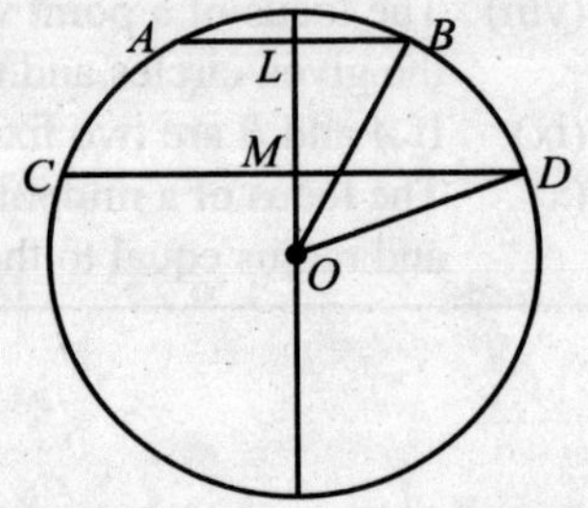

Sol. Here $AB = 6\text{cm} \Rightarrow AL = LB = 3$ cm

$CD = 12$ cm $\Rightarrow CM = MD = 6$ cm

Also $LM = 3$cm. Let $OM = x$

In right triangle *OLB*,

$OL^2 + LB^2 = OB^2$ (By pythagoras theorem)

$\Rightarrow (3+x)^2 + 3^2 = OB^2$ ...(i)

Now in right ΔOMD,

$OM^2 + MD^2 = OD^2$

$\Rightarrow x^2 + 6^2 = OB^2$ .....(ii) (since $OD = OB$ = radius)

Form (i) & (ii), $(3+x)^2 + 3^2 = x^2 + 6^2$

$\Rightarrow 9 + 6x = 36 - 9$ or $x = 3$.

From (i), $OB^2 = (3+3)^2 + 3^2 = 36 + 9 = 45$

$OB = \sqrt{45}$ cm $= 3\sqrt{5}$ cm

Hence radius $= 3\sqrt{5}$ cm

3. In the given figure, *O* is the centre of a circle and *AB* is a diameter. If $\angle EOF = 40°$, find $\angle EDF$.

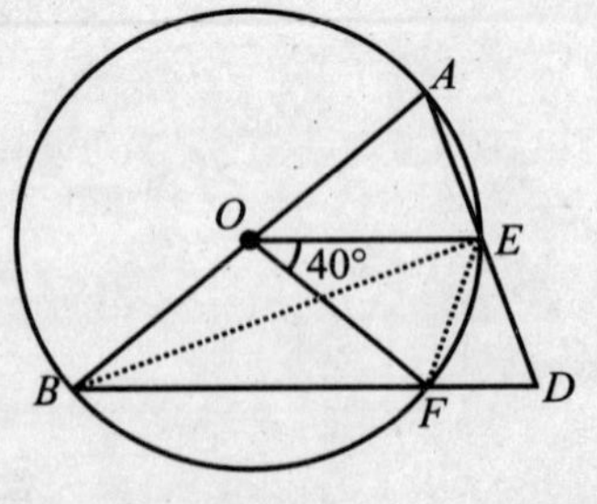

Sol. Join *BE* and *EF*.

Since *AB* is the diameter of the circle

$\angle AEB = 90°$ [Angle in the semi-circles is 90°]

$\angle EBF = \frac{1}{2}\angle EOF = \frac{40°}{2} = 20°$

[Angle made by a chord at any point on the circumference is half the angle made by the chord at the centre of the circle.]

$\therefore \angle BED = 180° - 90° = 90°$

In ΔBED,

$\angle BED + \angle EBD + \angle EDB = 180°$

$90° + \angle EBF + \angle EDB = 180°$ [$\because \angle EBD = \angle EBF$]

$90° + 20° + \angle EDB = 180°$

$\angle EDB = 180° - 110° = 70°$

i.e. $\angle EDF = 70°$

4. In figure, ABCD is a cyclic quadrilateral in which AC and BD are its diagonals. If $\angle DBC = 55°$ and $\angle BAC = 45°$, find $\angle BCD$.

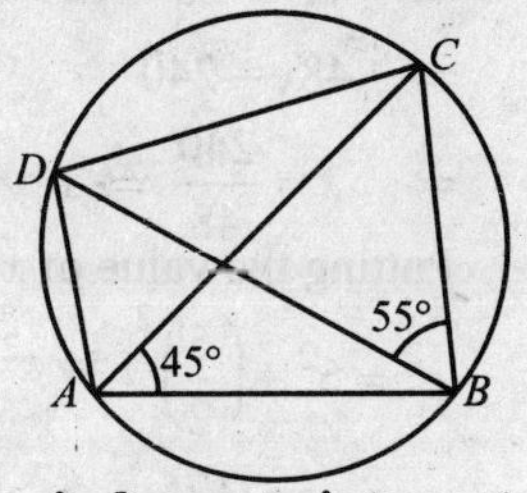

Sol. Given $\angle DBC = 55°$ and $\angle BAC = 45°$.

$\angle BAC = \angle BDC = 45°$ ...(i) [Angle in the same segment of a circle are equal]

Now, in ΔBCD,

$\angle BDC + \angle DBC + \angle BCD = 180°$

$45° + 55° + \angle BCD = 180°$ [from i]

$\angle BCD = 180° - 100° = 80°$

5. In the given figure, PQR is a triangle in which PQ = PR and M is a point on PR. Through R a line is drawn to intersect QM produced at S such that $\angle PQS = \angle PRS$. Prove that $\angle PSR = 90° + \frac{1}{2}\angle QPR$.

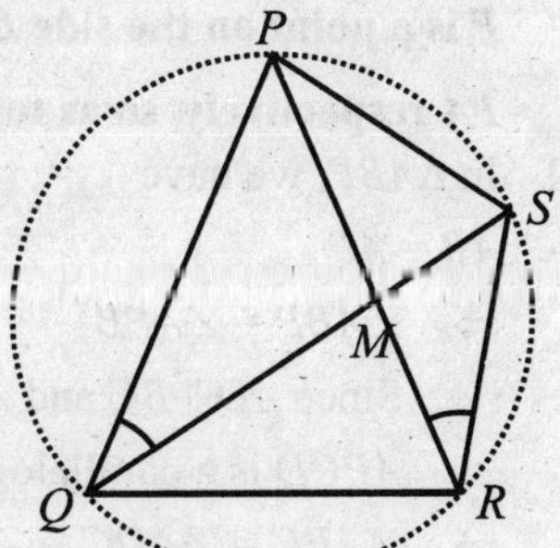

Sol. Given $\angle PQS = \angle PRS$

Since $\angle PQS$ and $\angle PRS$ are equal, therefore P, Q, R, S are concyclic points.

In ΔPQR,

$\angle PQR + \angle PRQ + \angle QPR = 180°$

But $PQ = PR$ [Given]

$\therefore \quad \angle PQR = \angle PRQ$

$\therefore \quad \angle QPR + 2\angle PQR = 180°$

$$\angle PQR = \frac{180° - \angle QPR}{2} = 90° - \frac{1}{2}\angle QPR \quad ...(i)$$

Now, In ΔPSR

$\angle PSR + \angle PQR = 180°$ [$\because$ PQRS is a cyclic quadrilateral whose sum of opposite angles is 180°]

$\therefore \quad \angle PSR = 180° - \angle PQR$

$$= 180° - \left[90° - \frac{1}{2}\angle QPR\right] \quad \text{[from (i)]}$$

$$= 90° + \frac{1}{2}\angle QPR$$

6. Two chords AB and CD of lengths 5 cm and 11 cm respectively of a circle are parallel to each other and are on opposite sides of its centre. If the distance between AB and CD is 6 cm, find the radius of the circle.

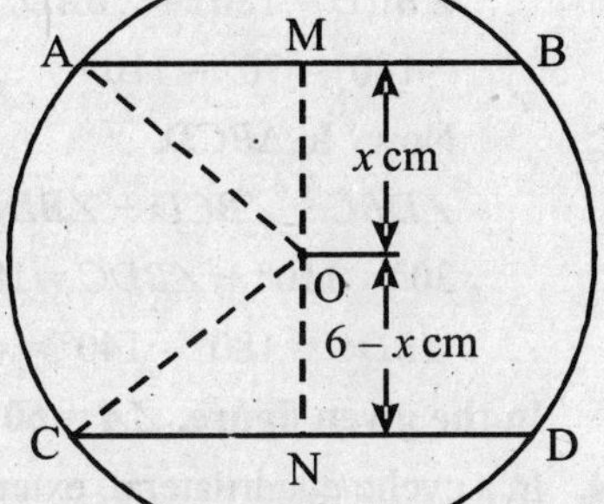

Sol. Let, r be the radius of given circle and its centre be O.

Draw $OM \perp AB$ and $ON \perp CD$

Since, $OM \perp AB$, $ON \perp CD$ and $AB \parallel CD$

Therefore, points M, O and N are collinear, So, MN = 6 cm

Let, OM = x cm. Then, ON = (6 – x) cm.

Join OA and OC. Then OA = OC = r

As the perpendicular from the centre to a chord of the circle bisects chord.

$$\therefore AM = BM = \frac{1}{2}AB = \frac{1}{2}\times 5 = 2.5 \text{ cm}$$

$$CN = DN = \frac{1}{2}CD = \frac{1}{2}\times 11 = 5.5 \text{ cm}$$

In right triangles OAM and OCN, we have

$OA^2 = OM^2 + AM^2$ and $OC^2 = ON^2 + CN^2$

$$r^2 = x^2 + \left(\frac{5}{2}\right)^2 \quad ...(i)$$

$$r^2 = (6-x)^2 + \left(\frac{11}{2}\right)^2 \quad ...(ii)$$

From (i) and (ii), we have

$$x^2 + \left(\frac{5}{2}\right)^2 = (6-x)^2 + \left(\frac{11}{2}\right)^2$$

$$x^2 + \frac{25}{4} = 36 + x^2 - 12x + \frac{121}{4}$$

$\Rightarrow \quad 4x^2 + 25 = 144 + 4x^2 - 48x + 121$

$\Rightarrow \quad 48x = 240$

$\Rightarrow \quad x = \dfrac{240}{48} \Rightarrow x = 5$

Putting the value of x in equation (i), we get

$r^2 = 5^2 + \left(\dfrac{5}{2}\right)^2 \Rightarrow r^2 = 25 + \dfrac{25}{4}$

$\Rightarrow \quad r^2 = \dfrac{125}{4} \Rightarrow r = \dfrac{5\sqrt{5}}{2}$ cm

7. *P* is a point on the side *BC* of a triangle *ABC* such that *AB* = *AP*. Through *A* and *C*, lines are drawn parallel to *BC* and *PA* respectively, so as to intersect at *D* as shown in the figure. Show that *ABCD* is a cyclic quadrilateral.

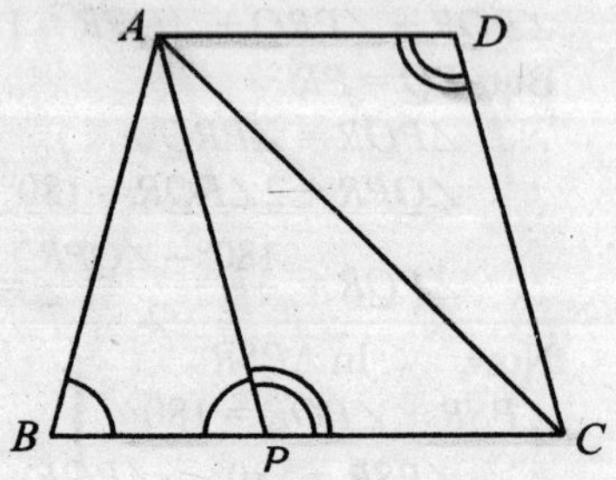

Sol. In ΔABP, we have

$AB = AP$

$\Rightarrow \quad \angle ABP = \angle APB$

Since $AD \parallel BC$ and $AP \parallel DC$.

$\therefore \quad APCD$ is a parallelogram.

$\Rightarrow \quad \angle APC = \angle ADC$

But $\angle APB + \angle APC = 180°$ [Linear pair axiom]

$\Rightarrow \quad \angle ABP + \angle ADC = 180°$ [$\because \angle APB = \angle ABP$ and $\angle APC = \angle ADC$]

$\Rightarrow \quad ABCD$ is a cyclic quadrilateral.

8. In the given figure *AB* is the diameter, $\angle BAD = 70°$ and $\angle DBC = 30°$. Find $\angle BDC$.

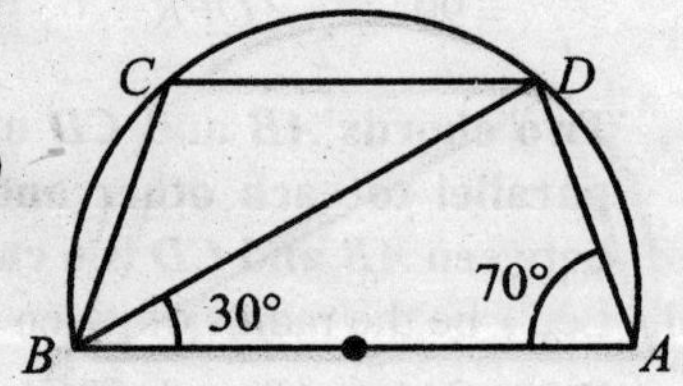

Sol. *ABCD* is a cyclic quadrilateral

$\therefore \quad \angle BAD + \angle BCD = 180°$ [Sum of opposite angles of a cyclic quadrilateral is 180°]

$\angle BCD = 180° - \angle BAD$

$= 180° - 70° = 110°$ [$\because \angle BAD = 70°$, Given] …(i)

Now, In ΔBCD.

$\angle DBC + \angle BCD + \angle BDC = 180°$

$30° + 110° + \angle BDC = 180°$ [$\because \angle DBC = 30°, \quad \angle BCD = 110°$]

$\therefore \quad \angle BDC = 180° - 140° = 40°$

9. In the given figure, $\angle A = 60°$ and $\angle ABC = 80°$, find $\angle DPC$ and $\angle BQC$.

Sol. In a cyclic quadrilateral, exterior angle is equal to opposite interior angle. So, in cyclic quadrilateral *ABCD*, we have

$\angle PDC = \angle ABC$ and $\angle DCP = \angle A$

$\Rightarrow \quad \angle PDC = 80°$ and $\angle DCP = 60°$ [$\because \angle ABC = 80°$ and $\angle A = 60°$]

In ΔDPC, we have

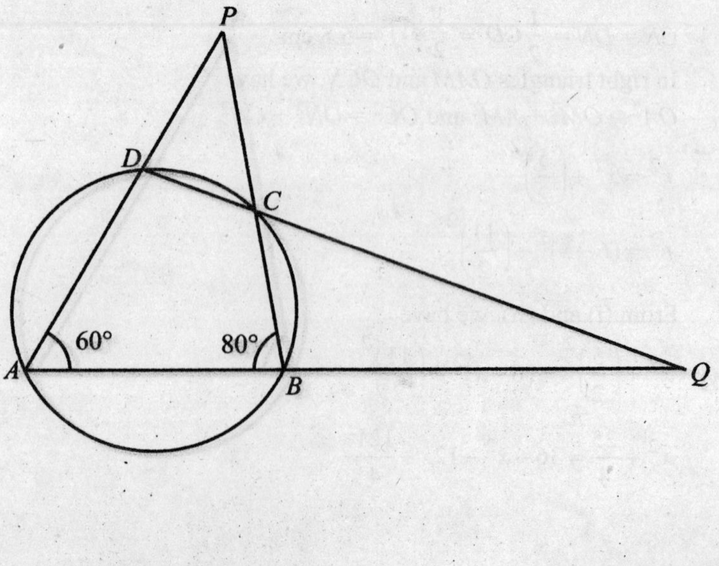

$\angle DPC = 180° - (\angle PDC + \angle DCP)$

$\Rightarrow \quad \angle DPC = 180° - (80° + 60°) = 40°$

Similarly, we have

$\angle QBC = \angle ADC$ and $\angle BCQ = \angle A$

$\Rightarrow \quad \angle QBC = 180° - \angle ABC$ and $\angle BCQ = 60°$

[$\because \angle ADC + \angle ABC = 180°$ and $\angle A = 60°$]

$\Rightarrow \quad \angle QBC = 180° - 80° = 100°$ and $\angle BCQ = 60°$

Now, in ΔBQC, we have

$\angle BQC = 180° - (\angle QBC + \angle BCQ)$

$= 180° - (100° + 60°) = 20°$

10. Three girls Reshma, Salma and Mandeep are playing a game by standing on a circle of radius 5 cm drawn in a park. Reshma throws a ball to Salma, Salma to Mandeep, Mandeep to Reshma, If the distance between Reshma and Salma and between Salma and Mandeep is 6 m each, what is the distance between Reshma and Mandeep?

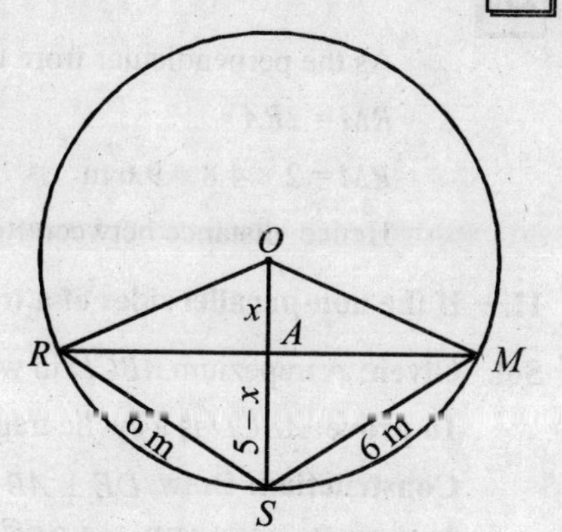

Sol. Let R, S and M represent the position of Reshma, Salma and Mandeep respectively.

Clearly ΔRSM is an isosceles triangle as

$RS = SM = 6$ m

Join OS which intersect RM at A.

In ΔROS and ΔMOS

$OR = OM$ (Radii of the same circle)

$OS = OS$ (Common)

$RS = SM$ (Each 6 cm)

$\therefore \quad \Delta ROS \cong \Delta MOS$ (By SSS congruence criterion)

$\because \quad \angle RSO = \angle MSO$ (CPCT)

In ΔRAS and ΔMAS

$AS = AS$ (Common)

$\therefore \quad \angle RSA = \angle MSA$ $(\because \angle RSO = \angle MSO)$

$RS = MS$ (Given)

$\therefore \quad \Delta RAS \cong \Delta MAS$ (By SAS congruence criterion)

$\therefore \quad \angle RAS = \angle MAS$ (CPCT)

$\because \quad \angle RAS + \angle MAS = 180°$ (Linear pair)

$\Rightarrow \quad \angle RAS = \angle MAS = 90°$

Let $OA = x$ m $\Rightarrow AS = (5 - x)$ m

In right triangle RAS,

$RS^2 = RA^2 + AS^2$

$\Rightarrow \quad 6^2 = RA^2 + (5 - x)^2$

$\Rightarrow \quad RA^2 = 6^2 - (5 - x)^2$ ...(i)

In right triangle RAO,

$RO^2 = RA^2 + OA^2$

$\Rightarrow \quad 5^2 = RA^2 + x^2$

$\Rightarrow \quad RA^2 = 5^2 - x^2$ ...(ii)

From equations (i) and (ii), we get

$6^2 - (5 - x)^2 = 5^2 - x^2$

$6^2 - 5^2 = (5 - x)^2 - x^2$

$36 - 25 = 25 + x^2 - 10x - x^2$

$11 = 25 - 10x \Rightarrow 10x = 14$

$\Rightarrow \quad x = 1.4$m

From equation (ii), we have

$RA^2 = 5^2 - (1.4)^2 = 25 - 1.96$

$RA^2 = 23.04 \Rightarrow RA = \sqrt{23.04}$

$RA = 4.8$ m

As the perpendicular from the centre of a circle bisects the chord.

$\therefore$ $RM = 2RA$

$RM = 2 \times 4.8 = 9.6$ m

Hence, distance between Reshma and Mandeep is 9.6 m

11. If the non-parallel sides of a trapezium are equal, prove that it is cyclic.

Sol. Given: A trapezium $ABCD$ in which $AB \parallel CD$ and $AD = BC$.

To prove: $ABCD$ is a cyclic trapezium.

Construction: Draw $DE \perp AB$ and $CF \perp AB$

In right triangles AED and BFC, we have

$AD = BC$ (Given)

$\angle DEA = \angle CFB$ (Each equal to 90°)

and $DE = CF$ (Distance between two parallel lines)

$\Rightarrow$ $\Delta DEA \cong \Delta CFB$ (RHS congruence criterion)

$\Rightarrow$ $\angle A = \angle B$ (CPCT)

$\angle ADE = \angle BCF$ (CPCT)

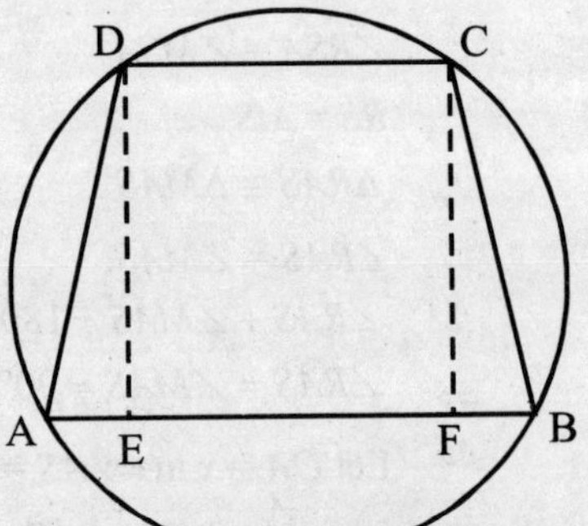

$\Rightarrow$ $\angle C = \angle BCF + 90° = \angle ADE + 90° = \angle ADC$

$\angle C = \angle D$

Now, in quadrilateral $ABCD$, we have

$\angle A = \angle B$ and $\angle C = \angle D$

Now, $\angle A + \angle B + \angle C + \angle D = 360°$

$\Rightarrow$ $2\angle A + 2\angle C = 360°$

$\Rightarrow$ $\angle A + \angle C = 180°$

Hence, quadrilateral $ABCD$ is cyclic.

SOLVED EXAMPLES BASED ON CONNECTING TOPIC

12. Define locus of a point.

Sol. The locus of a point is the path traced out by a moving point under given geometrical condition.

13. What is the locus of a point which is equidistant from a fixed point ?

Sol. Circle with fixed point as centre and radius equal to the distance of the point whose locus is to be find from the fixed point.

14. What is the locus of mid points of all parallel chords in a circle ?

Sol. The locus of mid points of all parallel chords in a circle, is the diameter of the circle which is perpendicular to the given parallel chords.

1 EXERCISE

Fill in the Blanks :

DIRECTIONS: *Complete the following statements with an appropriate word/term to be filled in the blank space (s).*

1. A radius of a circle is a line segment with one end point at the .... and the other end on the ....
2. A diameter of a circle is a chord that passes through the .... of the circle.
3. The centre of a circle lies in the .... of the circle.
4. An arc is a .... when its ends are the ends of a diameter.
5. A point, whose distance from the centre of a circle is greater than its radius, lies on the .... of the circle.
6. The longest chord of a circle is a .... of the circle.
7. Segment of a circle is the region between an arc and the related .... of the circle.
8. Angles in the same segment of a circle are ....
9. The sum of either pair of opposite angles of a cyclic quadrilateral is ....
10. The .... bisectors of two chords to a circle intersect at the centre.
11. The chords of a circle which are .... from the centre are equal.

True / False :

DIRECTIONS : *Read the following statements and write your answer as true or false.*

1. Diameter is the longest chord of the circle.
2. A diameter of a circle divides the circular region into two parts. Each part is called a semi-circular region.
3. Every circle has a unique centre and it lies inside the circle.
4. Line segment joining the centre to any point on the circle is a radius of the circle.
5. A circle is a plane figure.
6. If a circle is divided into three equal arcs, each is a major arc.
7. Sector is the region between the chord and its corresponding arc.
8. A circle has only a finite number of equal chords.
9. A chord of a circle which is twice as long as its radius is a diameter of the circle.
10. Equal chords subtend equal angles at the centre.
11. Chords of congruent circles which are equidistant from the corresponding centres are equal.
12. A cyclic trapezium is always isoscele.

Match the Columns :

DIRECTIONS: *Following given question contains statements in two columns which have to be matched. Statements (A, B, C, D) in Column-I have to be matched with statements (p, q, r, s, t) in Column-II.*

1. **Column-I** | **Column-II**

(A) In the given figure, $\angle ADC =$ | (p) 120

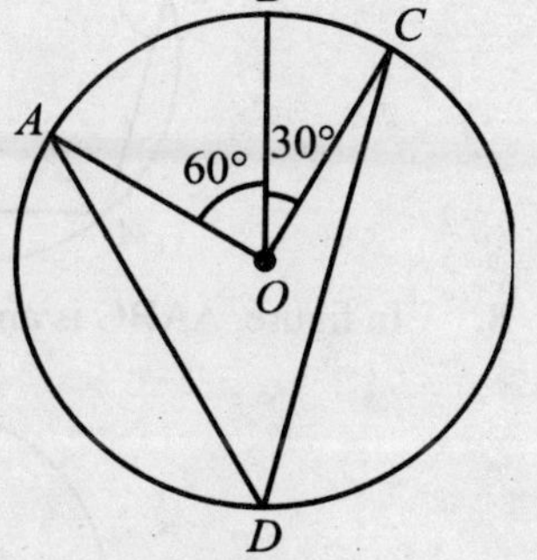

(B) Distance of a chord AB of a circle from the centre is 12 cm and length of the chord is 10cm. The diameter of the circle is .... cm. | (q) 75

(C) In the figure given below, O is the centre of the circle. If $AB = BC$ and $\angle AOB = 70°$ then $\angle OBC$ is equal to — (r) 45

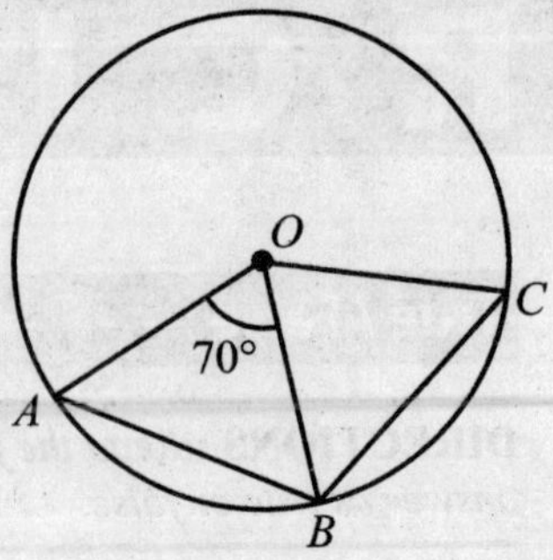

(D) In the given figure, the points A, B, C and D lie on a circle. If $\angle ACB = 75°$, then $\angle ADB$ is equal to — (s) 55

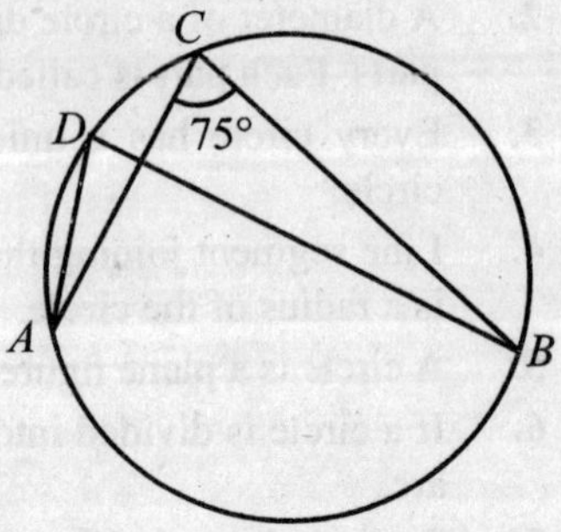

(E) If an equilateral triangle PQR is inscribed in a circle with centre O, then $\angle QOR$ is equal to — (t) 26

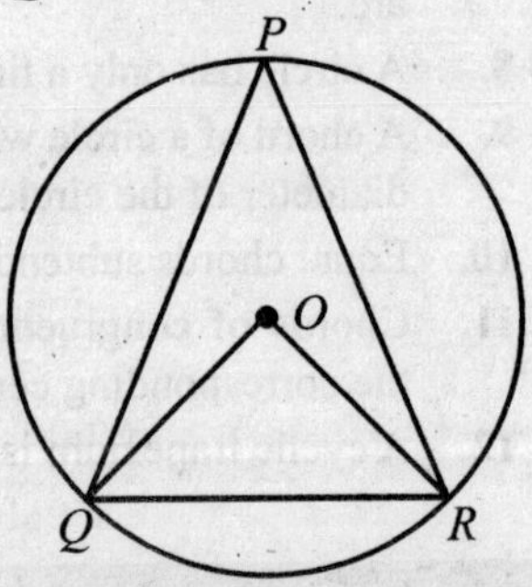

Very Short Answer Questions :

DIRECTIONS: *Give answer in one word or one sentence.*

1. Define the term cyclic quadrilateral.
2. How many circles can be drawn passing through three given non-collinear points?
3. What is the sum of either pair of opposite angles of a cyclic quadrilateral?
4. In the given figure, $\angle ABC = 45°$ prove that $OA \perp OC$.

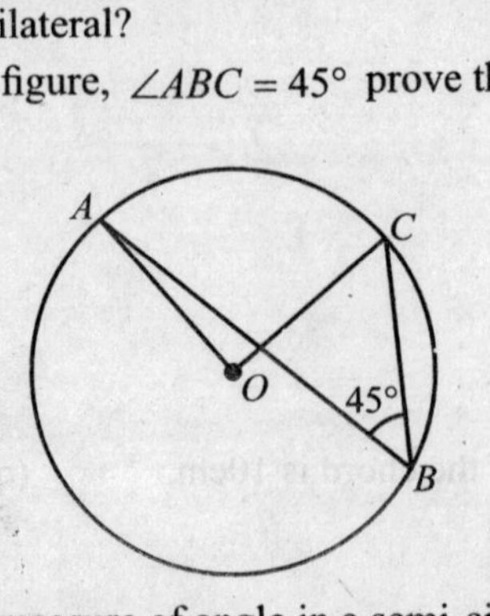

5. What is the measure of angle in a semi-circle?
6. How many circles can be drawn passing through
   (i) one point? (ii) two points ?
   (iii) three collinear points?
7. In the figure, $\angle ADC = 110°$, then find $\angle CBE$.

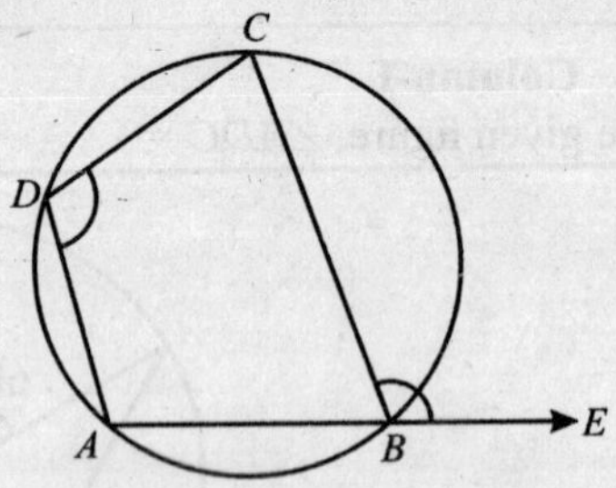

8. In figure, ΔABC is an equilateral triangle. Find m∠BEC.

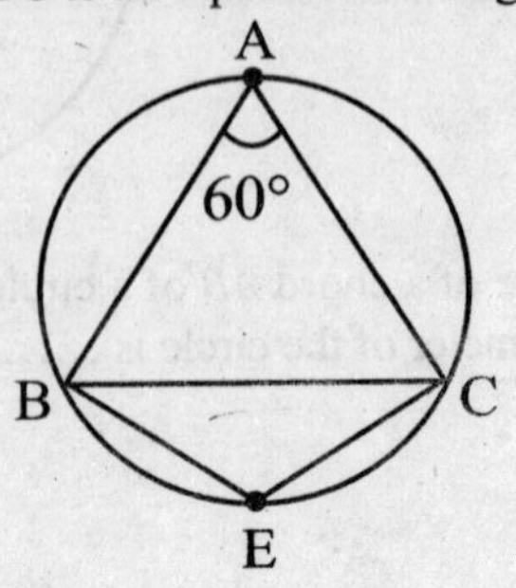

9. In figure, O is the centre of the circle, find ∠CBD.

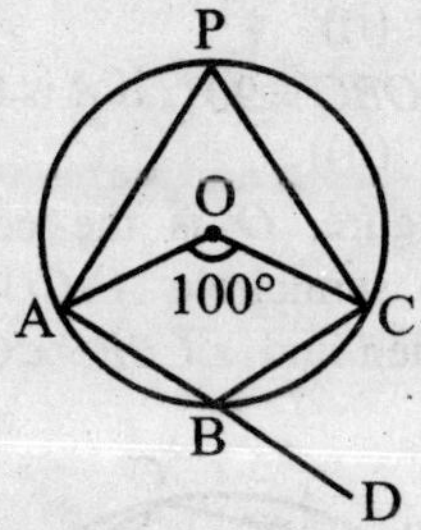

10. In a cyclic quadrilateral ABCD, if m∠A= 3 [m ∠C]. Find m ∠A.

11. In figure, ∠BAD = 78°, ∠DCF = x° and ∠DEF = y°. Find the values of x and y

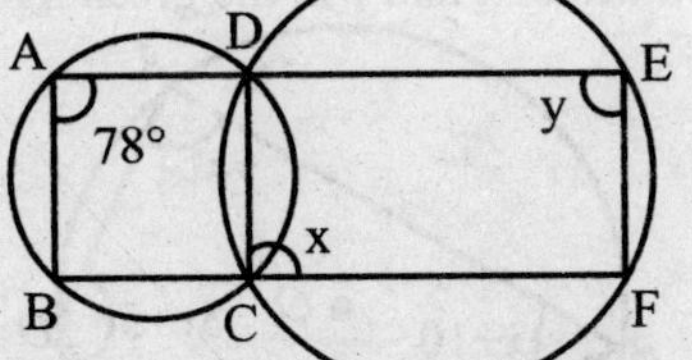

Short Answer Questions :

DIRECTIONS: *Give answer in 2-3 sentences.*

1. A quadrilateral *ABCD* is inscribed in a circle such that *AB* is a diameter and ∠*ADC* = 130°. Find ∠*BAC*.

2. In the given figure chords *AB* and *CD* are parallel and *BC* is a diameter of the circle with centre *O*. Show that *AB* = *CD*

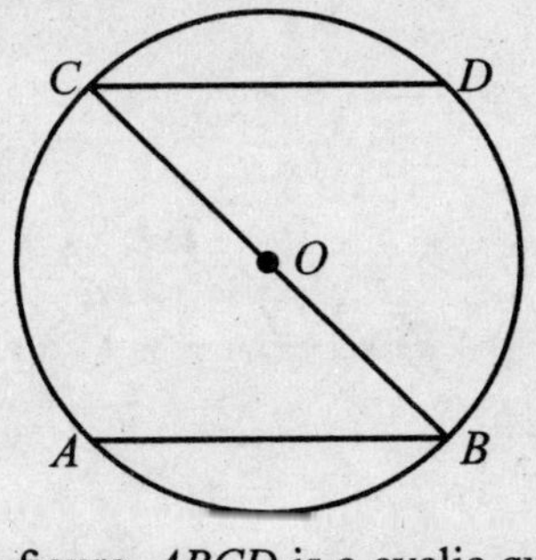

3. In the given figure, *ABCD* is a cyclic quadrilateral whose side *AB* is a diameter of the circle. If ∠*ADC* = 120°, find ∠*BAC*.

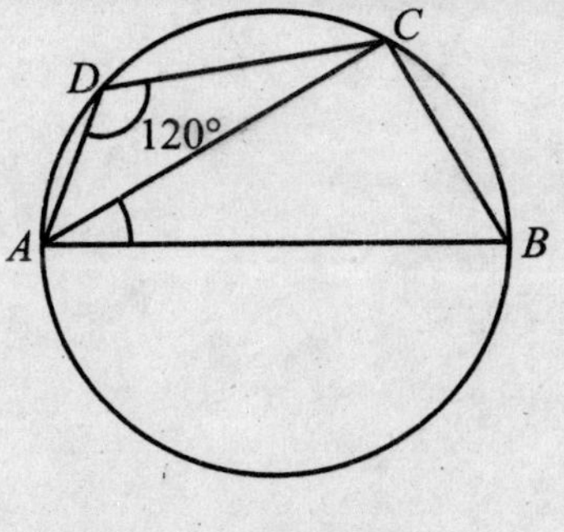

4. PQRS is a cyclic quadrilateral. Find the measure of each of its angles.

5. In the given figure, points *A*, *B*, *C* and *D* lie on a circle. If $\angle CAB = 40°$ and $\angle ABC = 85°$ then find $\angle ADB$.

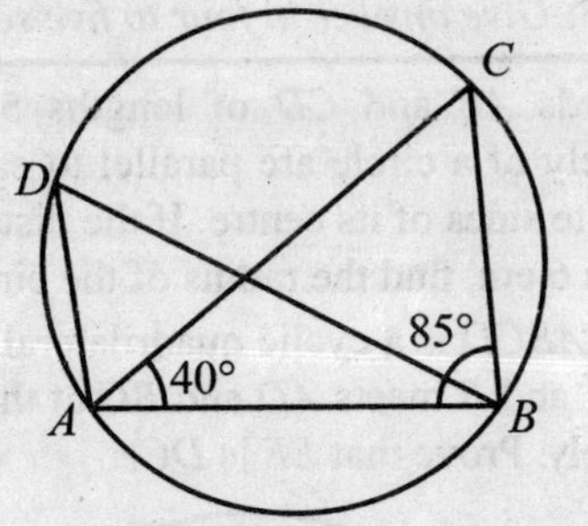

6. In the given figure, *ABCD* is a cyclic quadrilateral. If $\angle BAD = 105°$ and $\angle CBD = 65°$, then find the value of *x*.

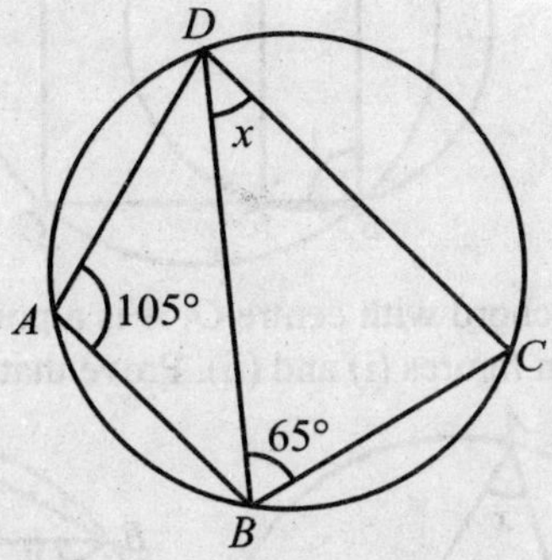

7. In figure, *AB* and *CD* are equal chords of a circle whose centre is *O*. If *OM* ⊥ AB and *ON* ⊥ *CD*. Prove that ∠*OMN* = ∠*ONM*

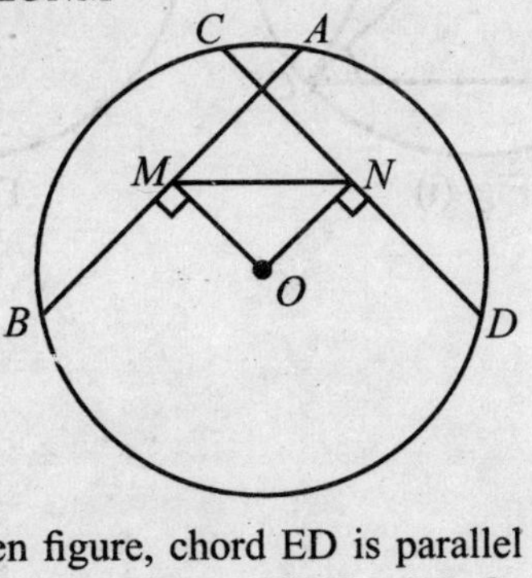

8. In the given figure, chord ED is parallel to the diameter AC of the circle. Given, ∠CBE = 65°, find ∠DEC.

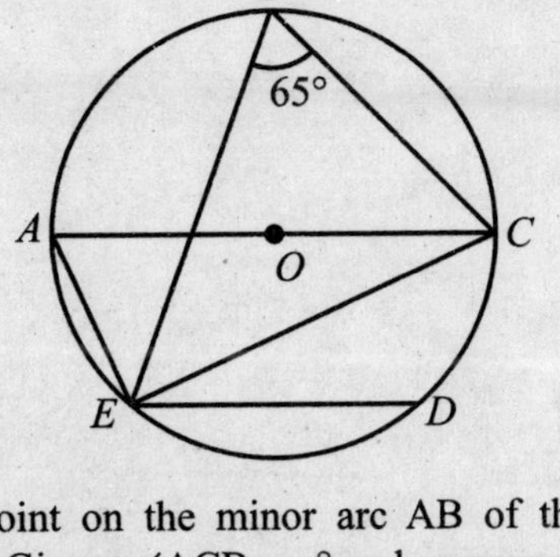

9. C is a point on the minor arc AB of the circle, with centre O. Given ∠ACB = x° and express y in terms of x. Calculate x, if ACBO is a parallelogram.

Long Answer Questions :

DIRECTIONS: *Give answer in four to five sentences.*

1. Two chords AB and CD of lengths 5 cm and 11 cm respectively of a circle are parallel to each other and are on opposite sides of its centre. If the distance between AB and CD is 6 cm, find the radius of the circle.

2. In figure, $ABCD$ is a cyclic quadrilateral. A circle passing through A and B meets AD and BC at the points E and F, respectively. Prove that $EF \parallel DC$.

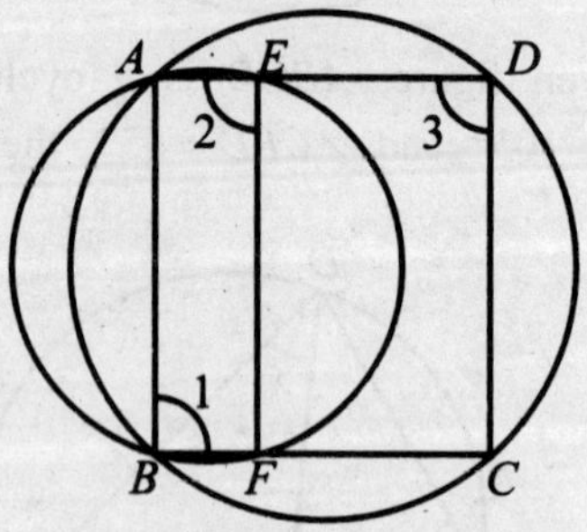

3. BC is a chord with centre O. A is a point on an arc BC as shown in figures (i) and (ii). Prove that

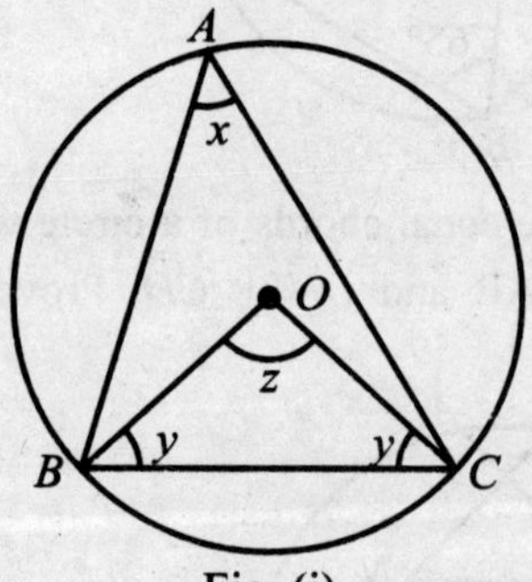

Fig. (i)

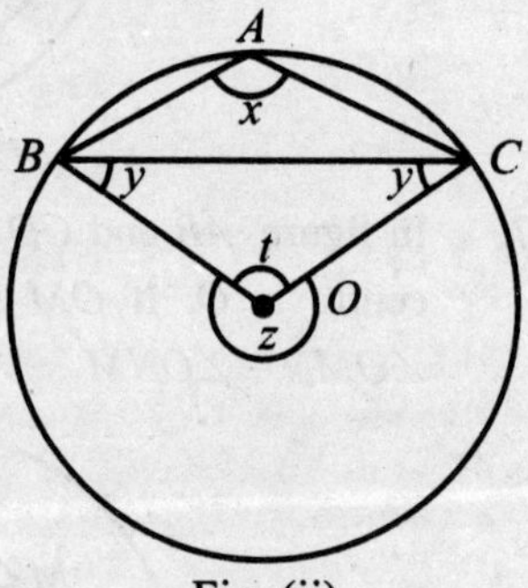

Fig. (ii)

(i) $\angle BAC + \angle OBC = 90°$, if A is the point on the major arc. (see fig. (i))

(ii) $\angle BAC - \angle OBC = 90°$, if A is the point on the minor arc. (see fig. (ii))

4. In the given figure, O is the centre and AE is the diameter of the semicircle $ABCDE$. If $AB = BC$ and $\angle AEC = 50°$, then find $\angle CBE$, $\angle CDE$, $\angle AOB$ and also prove BO || CE.

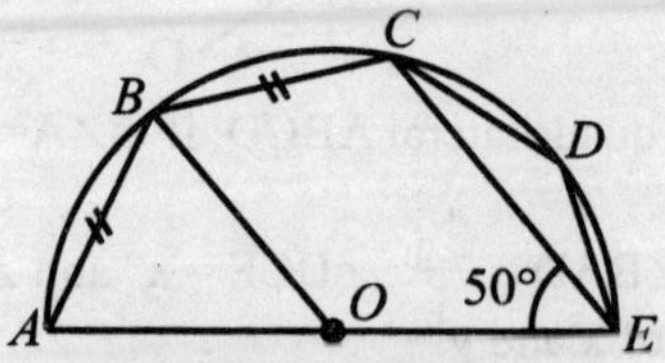

5. Find the values of x and y in the given figure.

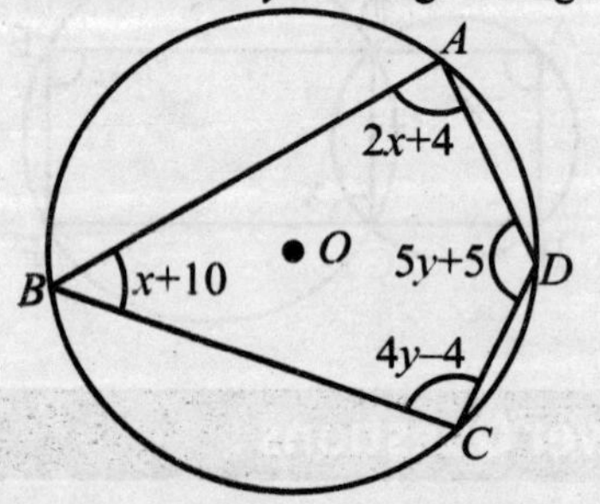

6. A circle has radius $\sqrt{2}$ cm. It is divided into two segments by a chord of length 2 cm. Prove that the angle subtended by the chord at a point in major segment is 45°.

2 EXERCISE

Text-Book Exercise :

1. Write True or False : Give reasons for your answers.
   (i) Line segment joining the centre to any point on the circle is a radius of the circle.
   (ii) A circle has only finite number of equal chords.
   (iii) If a circle is divided into three equal arcs each is a major arc.
   (iv) A chord of a circle, which is twice as long as its radius is a diameter of the circle.
   (v) Sector is the region between the chord and its corresponding arc.
   (vi) A circle is a plane figure.
2. If two circles intersect at two points, prove that their centres lie on the perpendicular bisector of the common chord.

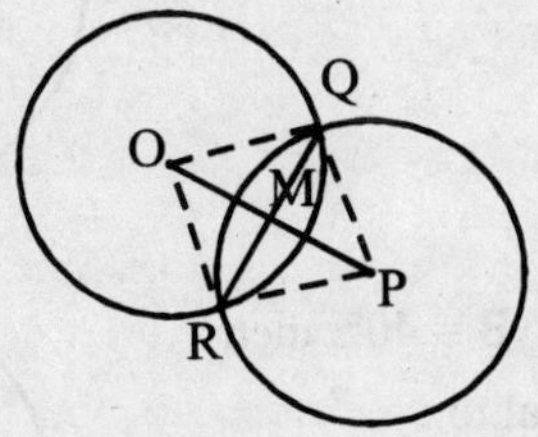

3. If two equal chords of a circle intersect within the circle, prove that the segments of one chord are equal to corresponding segments of the other chord.
4. If a line intersects two concentric circles (circles with the same centre) with centre O at A, B, C and D, prove that AB = CD (see Fig).

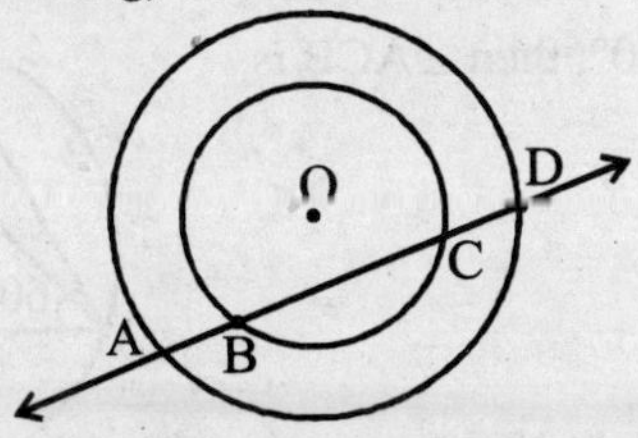

5. A circular park of radius 20m is situated in a colony. Three boys Ankur, Syed and David are sitting at equal distance on its boundary each having a toy telephone in his hands to talk each other. Find the length of the string of each phone.
6. In figure, A, B and C are three points on a circle with centre O such that $\angle BOC = 30°$ and $\angle AOB = 60°$. If D is a point on the circle other than the arc ABC, find $\angle ADC$.

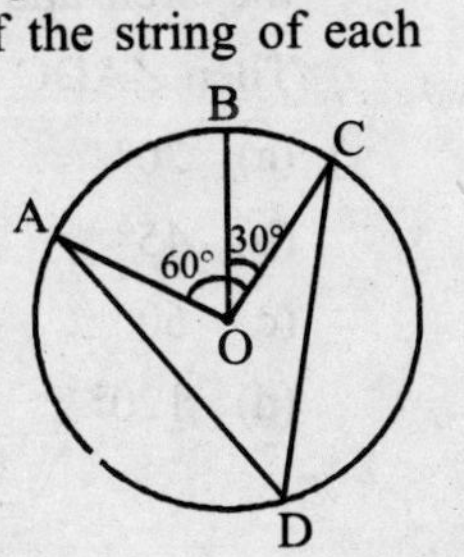

7. A chord of a circle is equal to the radius of the circle. Find the angle subtended by the chord at a point on the minor arc and also at a point on the major arc.
8. In figure, $\angle PQR = 100°$, where P, Q and R are points on a circle with centre O. Find $\angle OPR$.

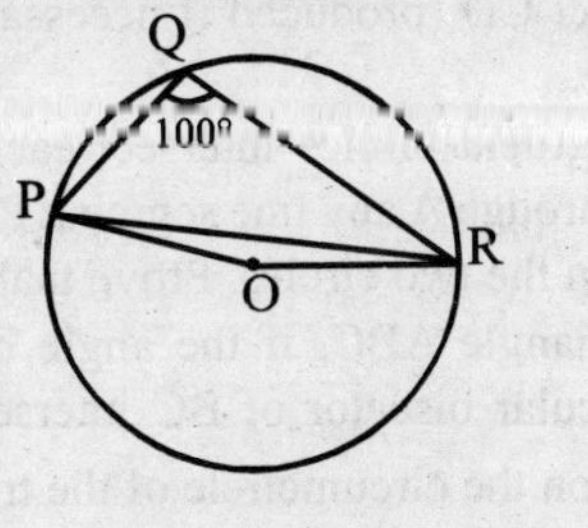

9. In figure, $\angle ABC = 69°$, $\angle ACB = 31°$, find $\angle BDC$.

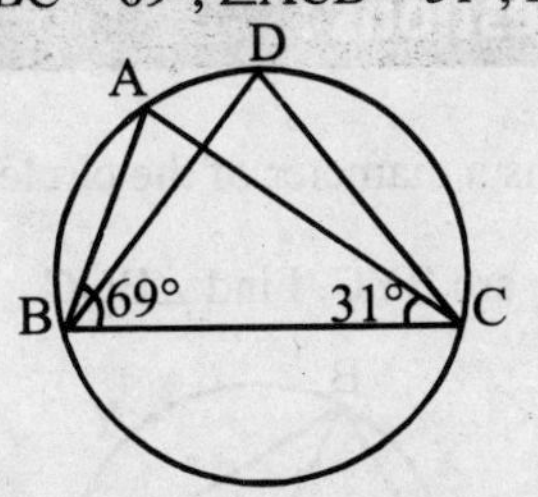

10. In figure, A, B, C and D are four points on a circle. AC and BD intersect at a point E such that $\angle BEC = 130°$ and $\angle ECD = 20°$. Find $\angle BAC$.

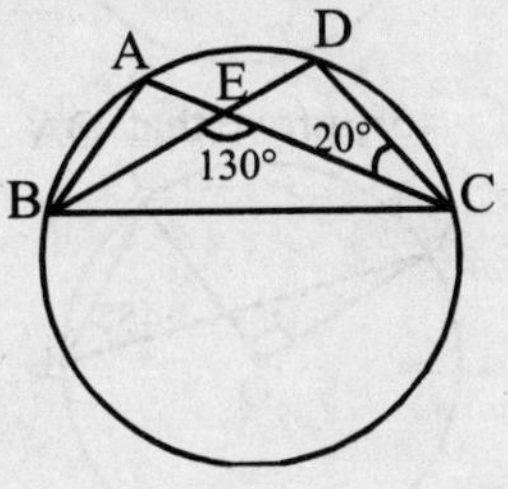

11. ABCD is a cyclic quadrilateral whose diagonals intersect at a point E. If $\angle DBC = 70°$, $\angle BAC$ is 30°, find $\angle BCD$. Further, if AB = BC, find $\angle ECD$.
12. If diagonals of a cyclic quadrilateral are diameters of the circle through the vertices of the quadrilateral, prove that it is a rectangle.
13. If the non-parallel sides of a trapezium are equal, prove that it is cyclic.
14. Two circles intersect at two points B and C. Through B, two line segments ABD and PBQ are drawn to intersect the circles at A, D and P, Q respectively (see figure). Prove that $\angle ACP = \angle QCD$.

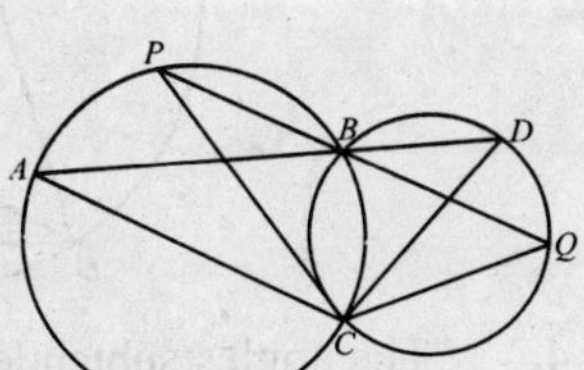

15. If circles are drawn taking two sides of a triangle as diameters, prove that the point of intersection of these circles lie on the third side.
16. ABC and ADC are two right triangles with common hypotenuse AC. Prove that $\angle CAD = \angle CBD$.
17. Prove that a cyclic parallelogram is a rectangle.
18. Prove that the line of centres of two intersecting circles subtends equal angles at the two points of intersection.
19. Prove that the circle drawn with any side of a rhombus as diameter, passes through the point of intersection of its diagonals.
20. ABCD is a parallelogram. The circle through A, B and C intersect CD (produced if necessary) at E. Prove that AE = AD.
21. Two congruent circles intersect each other at points A and B. Through A any line segment PAQ is drawn so that P, Q lie on the two circles. Prove that BP = BQ.
22. In any triangle ABC, if the angle bisector of $\angle A$ and perpendicular bisector of BC intersect, prove that they intersect on the circumcircle of the triangle ABC.

Exemplar Questions :

1. In fig., AOC is a diameter of the circle and arc AXB $= \frac{1}{2}$ arc BYC. Find $\angle BOC$.

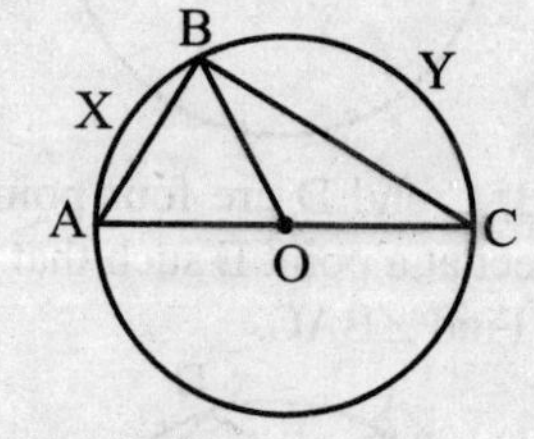

2. In fig., $\angle ABC = 45°$, prove that $OA \perp OC$

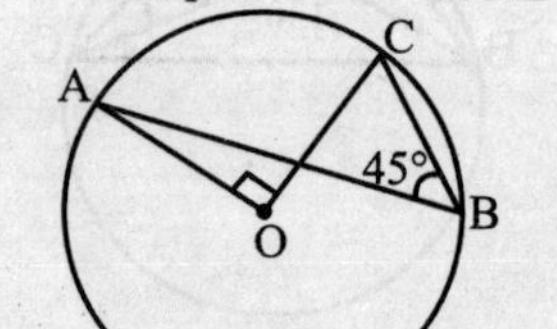

3. In figure, O is the centre of the circle, $\angle BCO = 30°$. Find x and y.

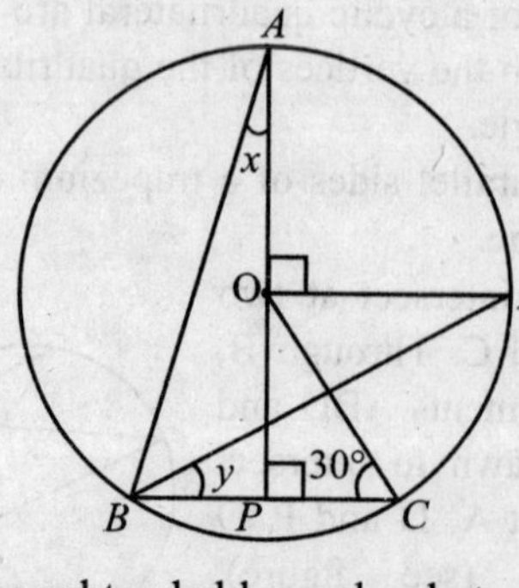

4. "The angles subtended by a chord at any two points of a circle are equal." Is this statement true?

5. "Two chords of a circle of lengths 10 cm and 8 cm are at the distance 8.0 cm and 3.5 cm, respectively from the centre." Is this statements true ?

6. In fig., if OA = 5 cm, AB = 8 cm and OD is perpendicular to AB, then CD is equal to :

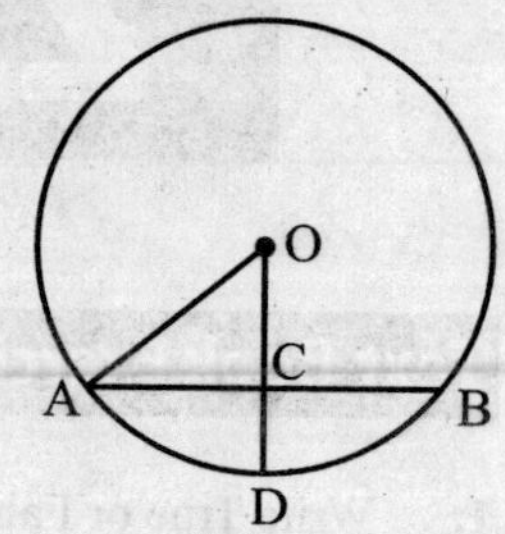

(a) 2 cm
(b) 3 cm
(c) 4 cm
(d) 5 cm

7. In fig., if $\angle ABC = 20°$, then $\angle AOC$ is equal to :

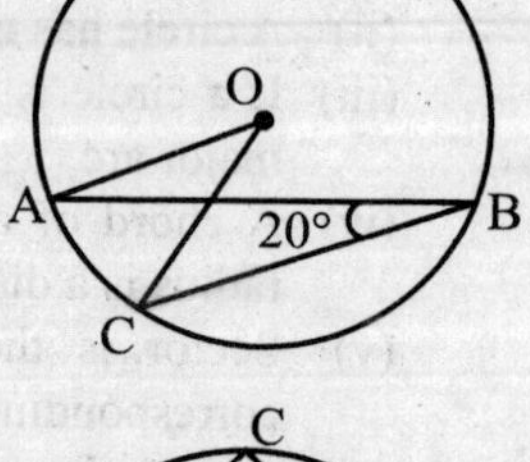

(a) 20°
(b) 40°
(c) 60°
(d) 10°

8. In fig., if AOB is a diameter of the circle and AC = BC, then $\angle CAB$ is equal to :

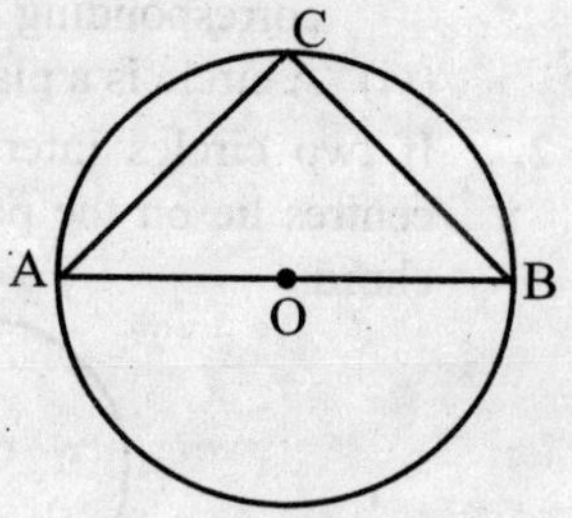

(a) 30°
(b) 60°
(c) 90°
(d) 45°

9. In fig., if $\angle OAB = 40°$, then $\angle ACB$ is equal to :

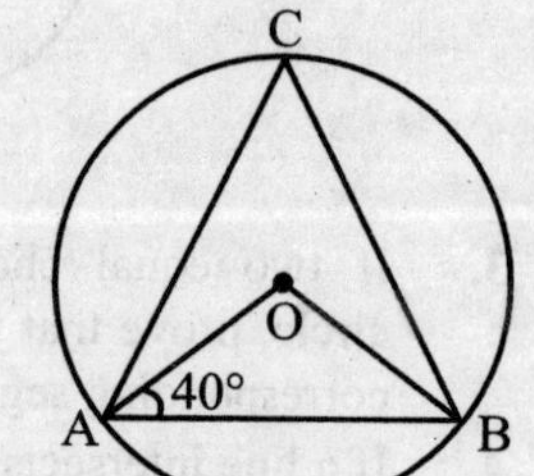

(a) 50°
(b) 40°
(c) 60°
(d) 70°

10. In fig., if $\angle DAB = 60°$, $\angle ABD = 50°$, then $\angle ACB$ is equal to :

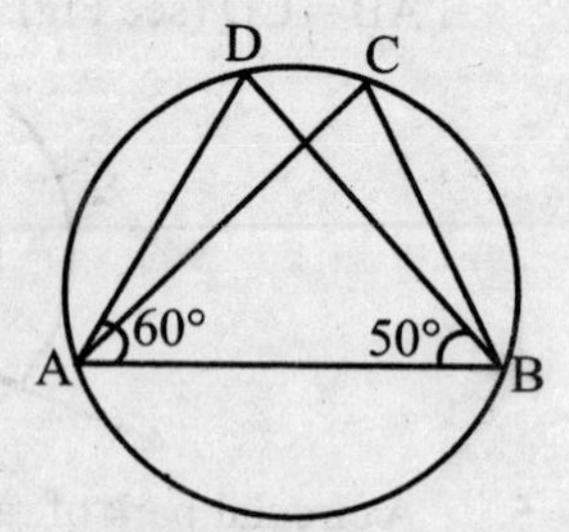

(a) 60°
(b) 50°
(c) 70°
(d) 80°

11. In fig., BC is a diameter of the circle and $\angle BAO = 60°$. Then $\angle ADC$ is equal to :

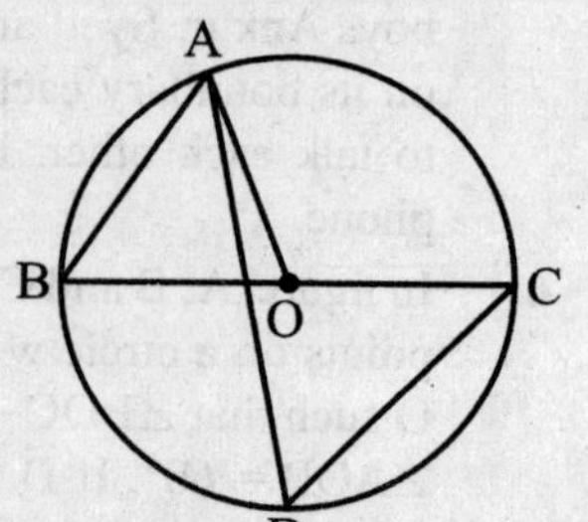

(a) 30°
(b) 45°
(c) 60°
(d) 120°

HOTS Questions :

1. $ABCD$ is a parallelogram. The circle through A, B and C intersects CD produced at E. If $AB = 10$ cm, $BC = 8$ cm, $CE = 14$ cm. Find AE.
2. In the given figure, P and Q are centres of two circles, intersecting at B and C. ACD is a straight line. If $\angle APB = 150°$ and $\angle BQD = x$, find the value of x.

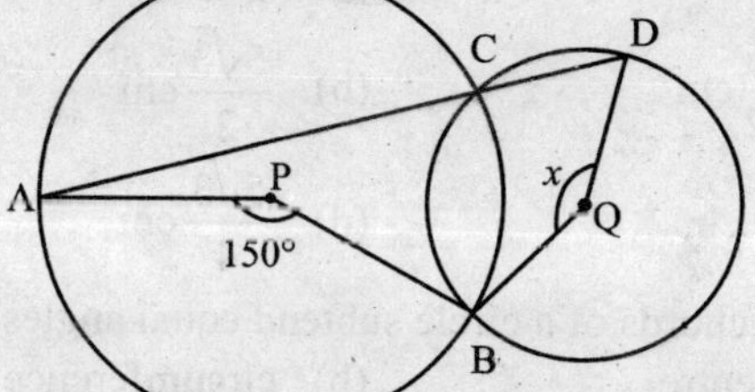

3. In the adjoining figure, AC is the diameter of a circle with centre O and chord $BD \perp AC$ intersecting each other at E. Find the values of p, q, r in terms of x.

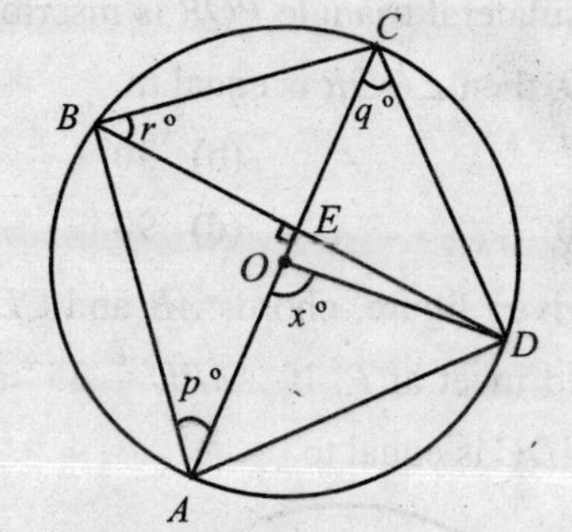

4. AB and AC are two chords of a circle of radius r such that $AB = 2AC$. If p and q are the distances of AB and AC from the centre, prove that $4q^2 = p^2 + 3r^2$.

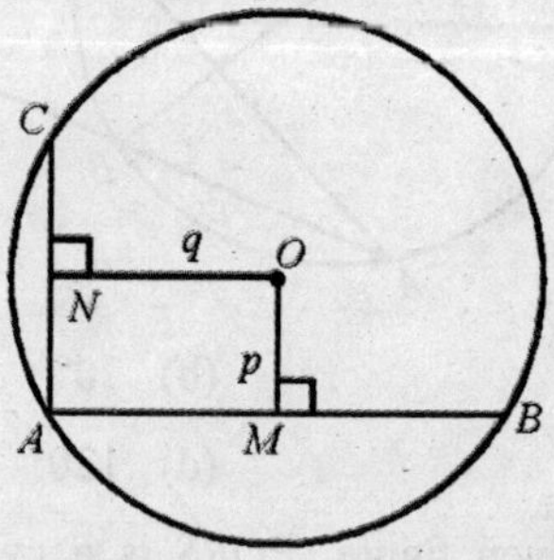

3 EXERCISE

Single Option Correct :

DIRECTIONS: *This section contains multiple choice questions. Each questions has 4 choices (a), (b), (c) and (d), out of which ONLY ONE is correct.*

1. The region between a chord and either of the arcs is called
   (a) an arc (b) a sector
   (c) a segment (d) a semicircle
2. Diagonals of a cyclic quadrilateral are the diameters of that circle, then quadrilateral is a
   (a) parallelogram (b) square
   (c) rectangle (d) trapezium
3. In the given figure, O is the centre of the circle. The value of x is

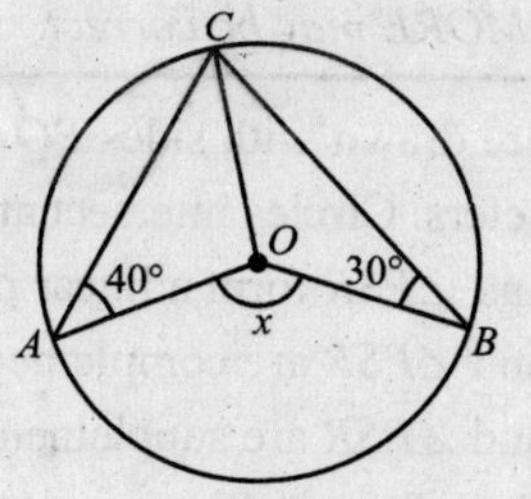

   (a) 140° (b) 70°
   (c) 290° (d) 210°
4. When two circles intersect at points A and B with AC and AD being the diameters of the first and second circle then the points B, C and D are
   (a) concurrent (b) circumcentre
   (c) orthocentre (d) collinear
5. In the given figure, O is the centre of a circle. AB and CD are its two chords. If $OM \perp$ AB, ON $\perp$ CD and $OM = ON$, then

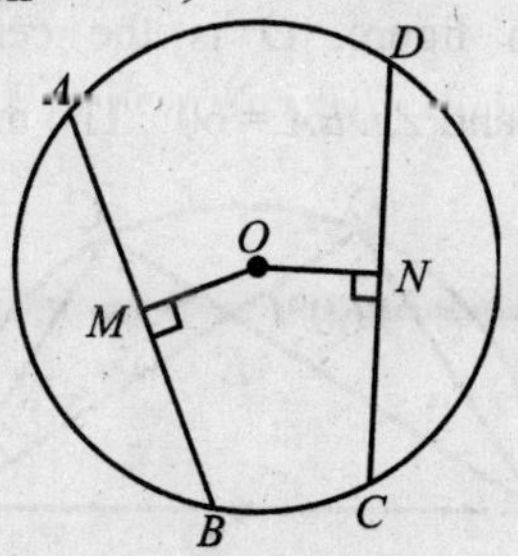

   (a) $AB \neq CD$ (b) $AB < CD$
   (c) $AB > CD$ (d) $AB = CD$
6. If PQ is a chord of a circle with radius r units and R is a point on the circle such that $\angle PRQ = 90°$, then the length of PQ is
   (a) r units (b) $2r$ units
   (c) $\frac{r}{2}$ units (d) $4r$ units

7. If an equilateral triangle PQR is inscribed in a circle with centre O, then $\angle QOR$ is equal to

(a) 60° (b) 30°
(c) 120° (d) 90°

8. In the given figure, chords AB and CD of a circle when produced meet at P. If $\angle APD = 35°$ and $\angle BCD = 25°$, then $\angle ADC$ is equal to

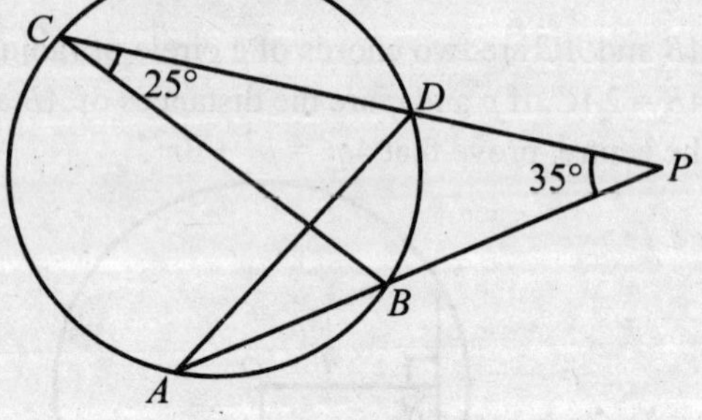

(a) 60° (b) 70°
(c) 50° (d) 120°

9. In the given figure, $PQRS$ is a cyclic quadrilateral. If $\angle SPR = 25°$ and $\angle PRS = 60°$, then the value of x is

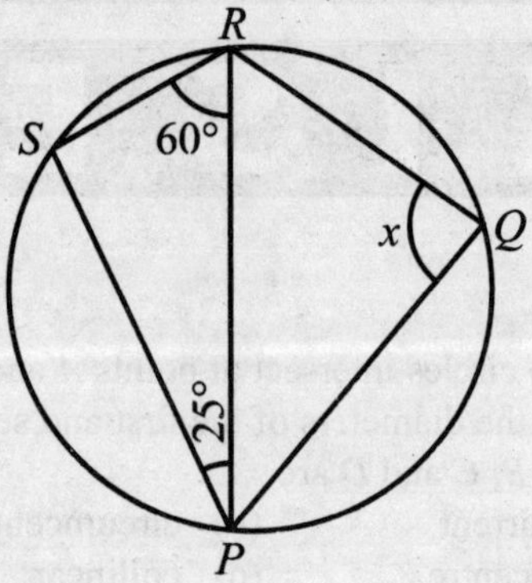

(a) 105° (b) 95°
(c) 115° (d) 85°

10. In the given figure, O is the centre of the circle, $\angle CBE = 25°$ and $\angle DEA = 60°$. The measure of $\angle ADB$ is

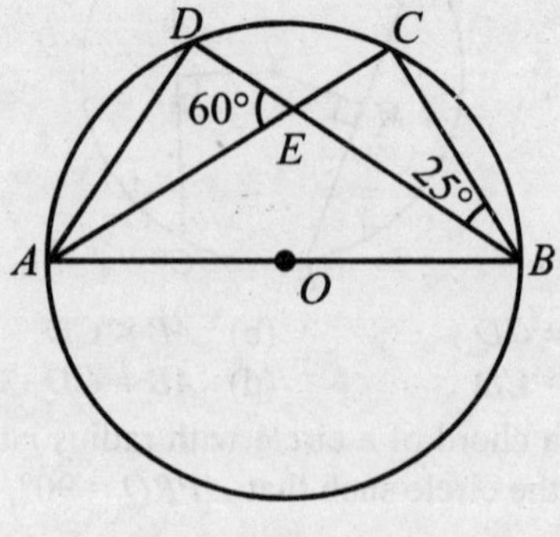

(a) 90° (b) 85°
(c) 95° (d) 120°

11. In the given figure, chord AB subtends $\angle AOB$ equal to 60° at the centre of the circle. If $OA = 5$ cm, then length of AB (in cm) 0 is

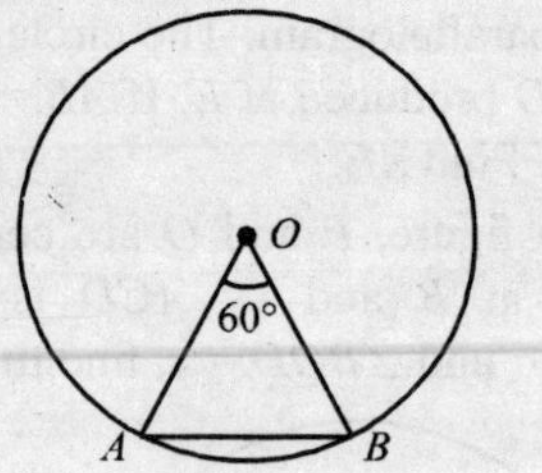

(a) $\frac{5}{2}$ cm (b) $\frac{5\sqrt{3}}{2}$ cm
(c) 5 cm (d) $\frac{5\sqrt{3}}{4}$ cm

12. Equal chords of a circle subtend equal angles at
(a) centre (b) circumference
(c) both (a) and (b) (d) None of these

13. The line joining the centre of a circle to the mid-point of a chord is always
(a) parallel to the chord
(b) perpendicular to chord
(c) equal to the chord
(d) tangent to the chord

14. There is one and only one circle passing through three given ______ points
(a) collinear (b) non-collinear
(c) far-off (d) nearest

15. Which of the following statement is true for the longest chord of a circle?
(a) It is equal to radius.
(b) It is two times of radius.
(c) It is never equal to diameter.
(d) It is two times of diameter.

16. When two chords of a circle bisect each other, then which of the following statements is true?
(a) Both chords are perpendicular to each other.
(b) Both chords are parallel to each other.
(c) Both chords are unequal.
(d) Both are diameters of the circle.

More Than One Option Correct :

DIRECTIONS: *This section contains multiple choice questions. Each question has 4 choices (a), (b), (c) and (d), out of which ONE OR MORE may be correct.*

1. Two circles are drawn with sides PQ and PR of a triangle PQR as diameters. Circles intersect at a point S. Then
(a) $\angle PSQ$ and $\angle PSR$ form a linear pair angles.
(b) $\angle PSQ$ and $\angle PSR$ are complementary angles.
(c) $\angle PSQ$ and $\angle PSR$ are supplementary angles.
(d) Points Q, S, R are collinear points.

2. In the given figure, $\angle R = \angle S = 30°$, then the four points P, Q, R, S

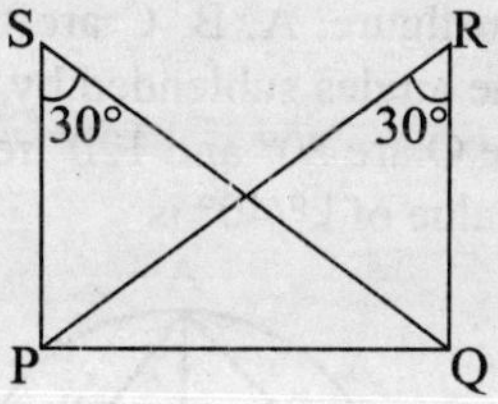

(a) are concyclic (b) are collinear
(c) are not collinear (d) lie on the same circle

3. Which of the following is/are correct?
(a) The perpendicular drawn from the centre of the circle to a chord bisects the chord.
(b) Congruent arcs of a circle subtend equal angles at the centre.
(c) Congruent arcs of a circle subtend right angles at the centre.
(d) Chords equidistant from the centre of a circle are equal in length.

4. Which of the following is/are incorrect?
(a) A circle has only finite number of equal chords.
(b) A circle is not a plane figure.
(c) Sector is the region between the diameter and its arc.
(d) A chord of a circle, which is twice as long is its radius is a diameter of the circle.

5. Which of the following is/are incorrect ?
(a) A continuous piece of a circle is arc of the circle.
(b) Segment of a circle is the region between an arc and radius of the circle.
(c) A circle divides the plane, on which it lies, in two parts.
(d) Circles having the same centre and different radii are called congruent circles.

Passage Based Questions :

DIRECTIONS: *Study the given paragraph(s) and answer the following questions.*

PASSAGE - I

In the given figure, AB is the diameter of a circle with centre O. If $\angle PAB = 55°$, $\angle PBQ = 25°$ and $\angle ABR = 50°$, then

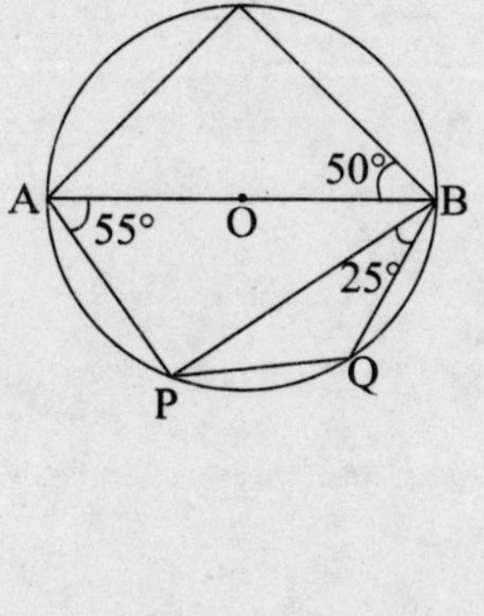

1. The value of $\angle PBA$ is
(a) 35° (b) 40°
(c) 30° (d) 50°

2. The value of $\angle BPQ$ is
(a) 35° (b) 40°
(c) 30° (d) 50°

3. The value of $\angle BAR$ is
(a) 35° (b) 40°
(c) 30° (d) 50°

PASSAGE - II

In the given figure, if $\angle ACE = 43°$ and $\angle EAC = 62°$, then

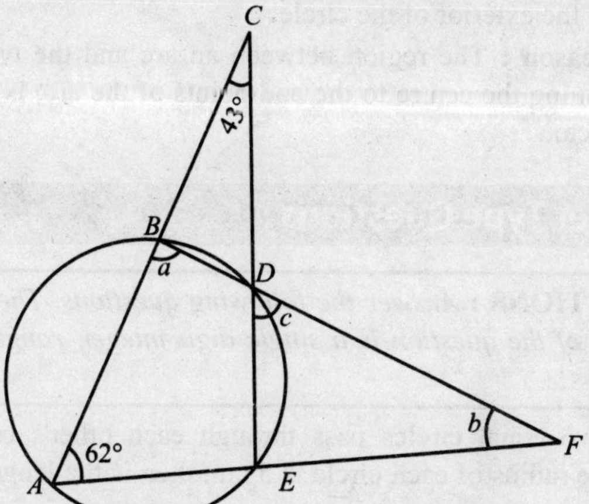

4. The value of a is
(a) 62 (b) 105
(c) 13 (d) 118

5. The value of b is
(a) 62 (b) 105
(c) 13 (d) 118

6. The value of c is
(a) 62 (b) 105
(c) 13 (d) 118

Assertion & Reason :

DIRECTIONS: *Each of these questions contains an Assertion followed by Reason. Read them carefully and answer the question on the basis of following options. You have to select the one that best describes the two statements.*

(a) If both **Assertion** and **Reason** are **correct** and Reason is the **correct explanation** of Assertion.
(b) If both **Assertion** and **Reason** are correct, but Reason **is not the correct explanation** of Assertion.
(c) If **Assertion** is **correct** but **Reason** is **incorrect.**
(d) If **Assertion** is **incorrect** but **Reason** is **correct.**

1. **Assertion:** The circumference of a circle must be a positive real number.
Reason: If r (> 0) is the radius of the circle, then its circumference $2\pi r$ is a positive real number.

2. **Assertion:** If P and Q are any two points on a circle, then the line segment PQ is called a chord of the circle.

Reason: Equal chords of a circle subtend equal angles at the centre.

3. **Assertion:** The sum of either pair of opposite angles of a cyclic quadrilateral is 180°.
Reason: Two or more circles are called concentric circles if and only if they have different centre and radii.

4. **Assertion:** A diameter of a circle is the longest chord of the circle and all diameters have equal length.
Reason: Length of a diameter = radius.

5. **Assertion :** Given a circle of radius r and with centre O. A point P lies in a plane such that $OP > r$ then point P lies on the exterior of the circle.
Reason : The region between an arc and the two radii, joining the centre to the end points of the arc, is called a sector.

Integer Type Questions :

DIRECTIONS : *Answer the following questions. The answer to each of the question is a single digit integer, ranging from 0 to 9.*

1. Two equal circles pass through each other's centre. If the radius of each circle is 5 cm, then is the length of the common chord is $a\sqrt{3}$. Find the value of 'a'.

2. In the adjoining figure, $ABCD$ is a cyclic quadrilateral. If AB is a diameter, $BC = CD$ and $\angle ABD = 40°$, then the measure of $\angle DBC \div 5$ is

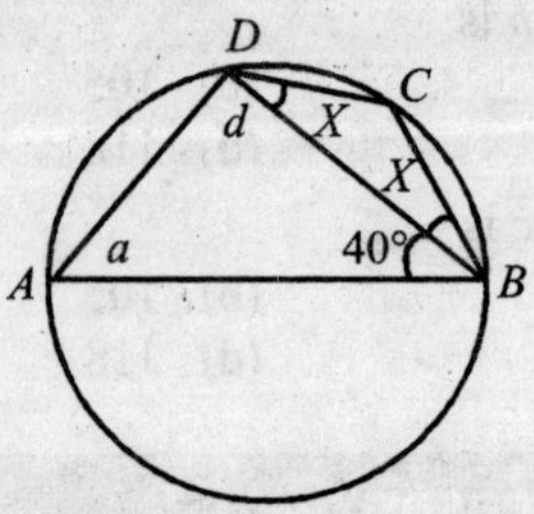

3. In the cyclic quadrilateral $ABCD$, $\angle BCD = 120°$, m (arc DZC) = 7°, then $\angle DAB \div 60$ is 'a' and also m (arc CXB) is $a \times 25$. Find the value of 'a'

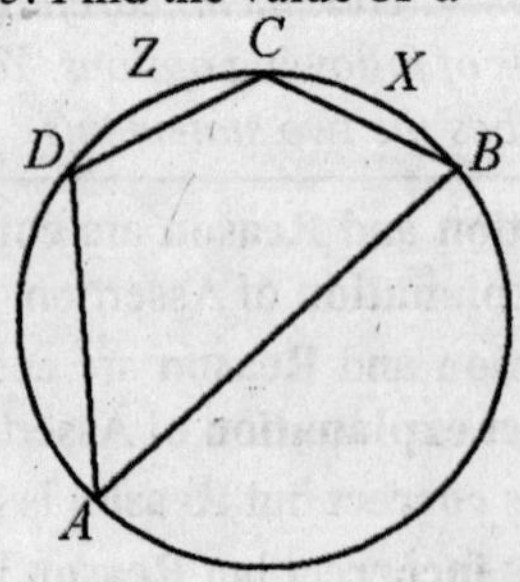

4. The distance between two parallel chords of length 8 cm each in a circle of diameter 10 cm is

5. In the given figure, A, B, C are three points on a circle such that the angles subtended by the chords AB and AC at the centre O are 80° and 120° respectively. The $\angle BAC$ is k°. The value of k°/40° is

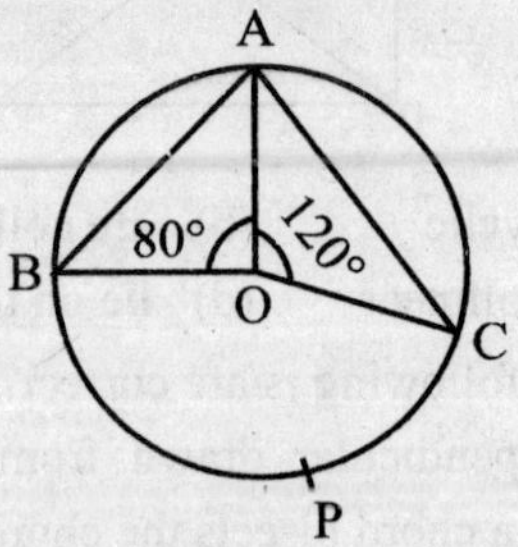

6. In the given figure, ABCD is a cyclic quadrilateral. The value of $\frac{x°}{50}$ is

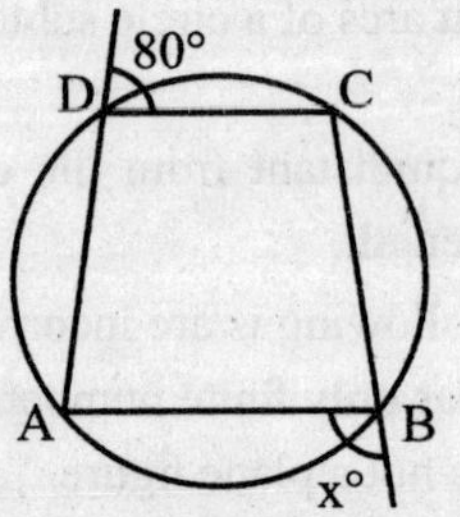

7. In the given figure, the length of AB, if OA = 5 cm and OC = 3 cm is

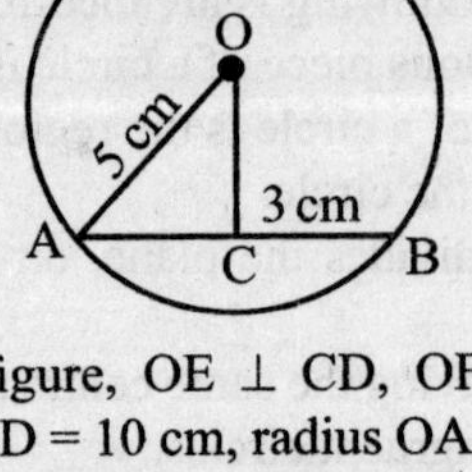

8. In the given figure, OE ⊥ CD, OF ⊥ AB, AB ∥ CD, AB = 24 cm, CD = 10 cm, radius OA = 13 cm. The length of OF is

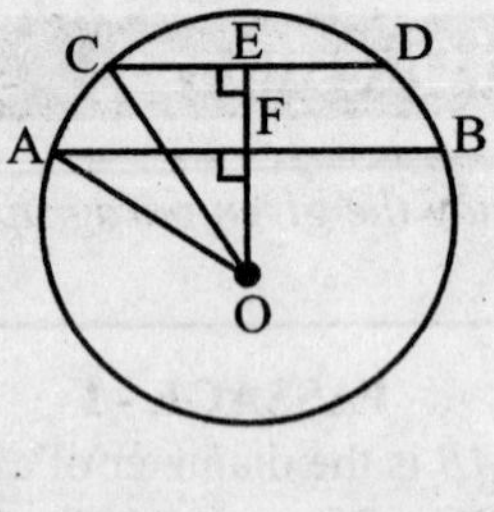

4 ADVANCED EXERCISE
BASED ON CONNECTING TOPICS

DIRECTIONS (Qs 1–4): *This section contains multiple choice questions. Each question has 4 choices (a), (b), (c) and (d) out of which only one is correct.*

1. The locus of point equidistant from three fixed points is a single point. The three points are
   (a) Collinear (b) Non-collinear
   (c) Concurrent (d) None of these
2. The locus of the centre of the circle which touch the given circle internally is
   (a) Circle (b) Straight line
   (c) Any Curve (d) None of these
3. The locus of the centre of a wheel rolling on a straight road is
   (a) Circle (b) Curved path
   (c) Straight line (d) None of these
4. The locus of a point which in equidistant from the three lines determined by the sides of a triangle is
   (a) Circumcentre (b) Incentre
   (c) Orthocentre (d) None of these
5. The locus of a point which is equidistant from two non-intersecting lines *l* and *m* is a
   (a) Straight line parallel to the line '*l*'
   (b) Straight line parallel to the line '*m*'
   (c) Straight line parallel to lines *l* and *m* and mid way between them
   (d) None of these.

DIRECTIONS: *This section contains multiple choice questions. Each question has 4 choices (a), (b), (c) and (d) out of which ONE OR MORE may be correct.*

6. Which of the following is/are correct ?
   (a) Semicircle is one of the sector whose central angle is 180°
   (b) Length of the Arc $= \dfrac{\theta}{360°} \times 2\pi r$
   (c) Circle can be divided into four equal sectors whose angle is 90°
   (d) Area of the sector $= \dfrac{360}{\theta \times \pi r^2}$

DIRECTIONS: *Study the given paragraph(s) and answer the following questions.*

PASSAGE

The locus of a point which moves in a plane such that its distance from a fixed point is always constant is called circle. Each diameter of the circle divides the circle into two segments, each segment is called semicircle. A sector is a part of a circle enclosed by two radii and the arc lying between them.

7. The fixed point is called
   (a) radius (b) centre
   (c) diameter (d) chord
8. The constant distance is called the
   (a) radius (b) centre
   (c) diameter (d) chord
9. The angle in semicircle is
   (a) 180° (b) 360°
   (c) 90° (d) 270°

SOLUTIONS

Brief Explanations of Selected Questions

1 EXERCISE

FILL IN THE BLANKS :

1. centre, circle
2. centre
3. interior
4. semicircle
5. exterior
6. diameter
7. chord
8. equal
9. 180º
10. perpendicular
11. equidistant

TRUE/FALSE :

1.	True	**2.**	True	**3.**	True	**4.**	True
5.	True	**6.**	False	**7.**	False	**8.**	False
9.	True	**10.**	True	**11.**	True	**12.**	True

MATCH THE COLUMNS :

1. A → (r) ; B → (t) ; C → (s) ; D → (q) ; E → (p)

(A) $\angle ADC = \frac{1}{2}\angle AOC = \frac{1}{2}\times 90° = 45°$

(∵ Angle subtended by an arc at the centre is double the angle formed by it on the remaining part of the circle)

(B) The perpendicular from the centre to the chord bisects the chord. $AL = 5$cm and $OL = 12$ cm,

$AO = \sqrt{(12)^2 + (5)^2} = \sqrt{169} = 13$ cm

Radius = 13cm, Diameter = 26 cm.

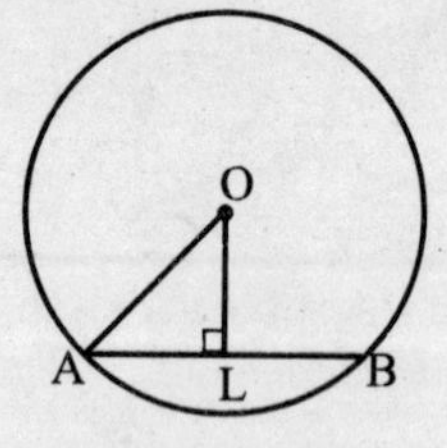

(C) $\angle BOC = 70º$ (∵ equal chords of a circle subtend equal angles at the centre).

$\Rightarrow \angle OBC + \angle OCB = 180° - 70° = 110°$

$\therefore \angle OBC = 55º$

$(\because OB = OC \Rightarrow \angle OBC = \angle OCB)$

(D) Since angles in the same segment of a circle are equal

$\therefore \angle ADB = \angle ACB = 75º$

(E) Since PQR is an equilateral triangle inscribed in a circle,

$\therefore \angle QPR = 60º$

$\therefore \angle QOR = 2 \times \angle QPR = 120º$

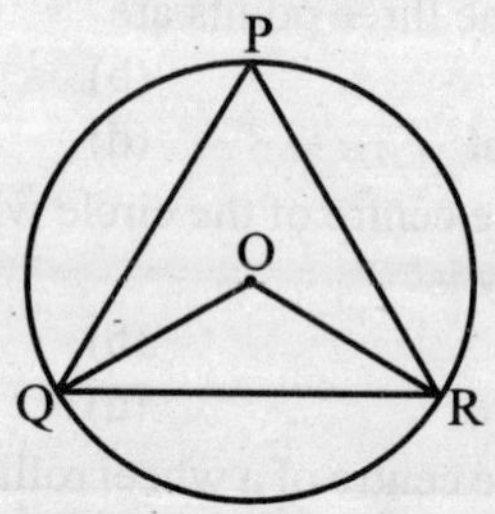

VERY SHORT ANSWER QUESTIONS :

1. A quadrilateral is called a cyclic quadrilateral if its all vertices lie on a circle.

2. There is one and only one circle can passes through three given non-collinear points.

3. 180°

4. $\angle ABC = \frac{1}{2}\angle AOC$

i.e., $\angle AOC = 2\angle ABC$

$= 2 \times 45° = 90°$

$\Rightarrow OA \perp OC$

5. Angle in a semicircle is a right angle.

6. (i) infinitely many (ii) infinitely many (iii) None

7. $\angle CBE = \angle ADC = 110°$

8. Since ΔABC is equilateral

$\therefore \angle A = \angle B = \angle C = 60°$

Now, ABEC is a cyclic quadrilateral

$\therefore \angle A + \angle E = 180° \Rightarrow \angle BEC = 120°$

9. $\angle APC = \frac{1}{2}\angle AOC = 50°$

$\angle APC + \angle ABC = 180°$

$\Rightarrow \angle ABC = 130° \Rightarrow \angle CBD = 50°$

10. $\angle A + \angle C = 180°$ (∵ ABCD is a cyclic quadrilateral)

$\Rightarrow 3\angle C + \angle C = 180° \Rightarrow \angle C = 45°$

$\therefore \angle A = 3 \times 45 = 135°$

11. Since ABCD is a cyclic quadrilateral

$\therefore x = 78° \Rightarrow y = 180 - 78 = 102°$

SHORT ANSWER QUESTIONS :

1. $\angle B = 180° - 130° = 50°$ ($\because$ *ABCD* is a cyclic quadrilateral)

$\angle ACB = 90°$ (Angle in the semi-circle)

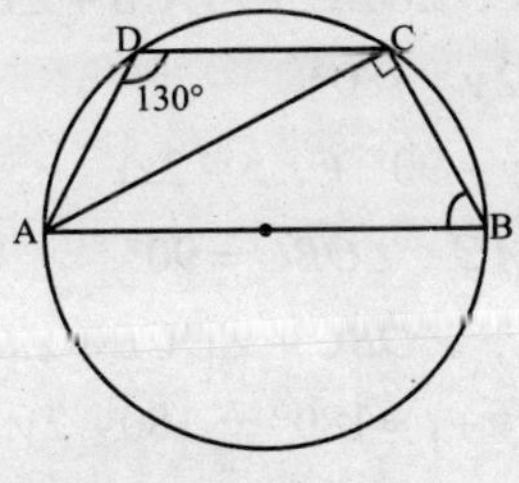

$\angle BAC = 180° - (90° + 50°)$

$= 40.$

2. From O, draw $OM \perp AB$ and $ON \perp CD$

In Δ *OMB* and Δ*ONC*

$OB = OC$ (radii of same circle)

$\angle M = \angle N$ (each = 90°, by construction)

$\angle OBM = \angle OCN$ (Alternate angles)

$\therefore$ $\Delta OMB \cong \Delta ONC$ (By AAS rule)

$\therefore$ OM = ON (c.p.c.t)

$\therefore$ AB = CD ($\because$ Chords which are equidistant from the centre of a circle are equal).

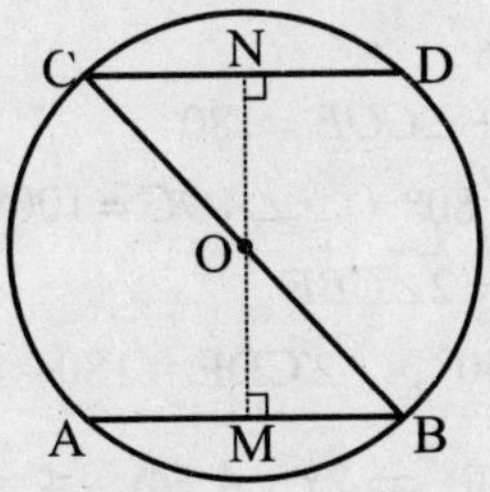

3. ABCD is a cyclic quadrilateral,

$\therefore$ $\angle ABC + \angle ADC = 180°$

($\because$ Opposite angles of a cyclic quadrilateral are supplementary.)

$\Rightarrow$ $\angle ABC + 120° = 180°$

$\Rightarrow$ $\angle ABC = 180° - 120° = 60°$

Also, $\angle ACB = 90°$ (angle in a semi-circle)

Now, in ΔABC

$\angle BAC + \angle ABC + \angle ACB = 180°$ (By angle sum property)

$\Rightarrow$ $\angle BAC + 60° + 90° = 180°$

$\Rightarrow$ $\angle BAC = 180° - 150° = 30°.$

4. Since sum of the opposite pairs of angles in a cyclic quadrilateral is 180°

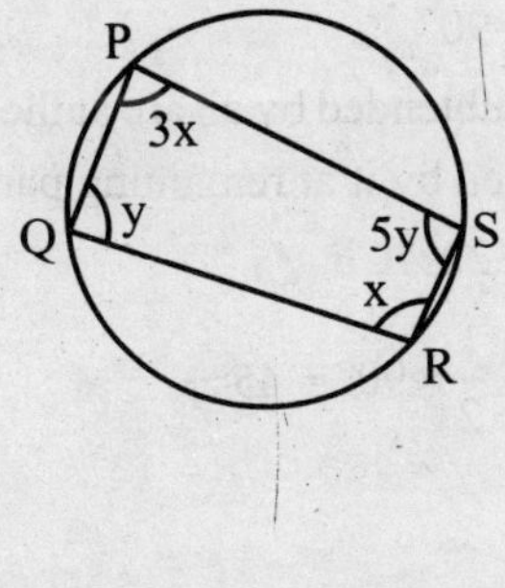

$\therefore$ $\angle P + \angle R = 180°$ and $\angle Q + \angle S = 180°$

$\Rightarrow$ $3x + x = 180°$ and $y + 5y = 180°$

$\Rightarrow$ $4x = 180°$ and $6y = 180°$

$\Rightarrow$ $x = 45°$ and $y = 30°$

$\therefore$ $\angle P = 3x = (3 \times 45°) = 135°$

$\angle Q = y = 30°$, $\angle R = x = 45°$

and, $\angle S = 5y = (5 \times 30°) = 150°$

5. In Δ *ABC*

$\angle ACB + 40° + 85° = 180°$

$\Rightarrow \angle ACB = 180° - 40° - 85° = 55°$

Now, $\angle ADB = \angle ACB = 55°$

($\because$ angles in the same segment of a circle)

6. $\angle BCD + \angle BAD = 180°$

(Sum of the opp. angles of a cyclic quad.)

$\Rightarrow \angle BCD + 105° = 180° \Rightarrow \angle BCD = 75°$

In ΔBCD, $x + 65° + 75° = 180° \Rightarrow x = 40°$

7. Since Chord *AB* = Chord *CD*

$\therefore$ $OM = ON$ ... (i)

($\because$ Equal chords of a circle are equidistant from the centre of the circle)

In ΔOMN,

$OM = ON$ [From (i)]

$\therefore$ $\angle OMN = \angle ONM$ (Angles opp. to equal sides)

8. $\angle CAE = \angle CBE$

($\because$ angles in the same segment of arc *CDE*)

$\Rightarrow$ $\angle CAE = 65°$ ($\because$ $\angle CBE = 65°$)

Since, *AC* is the diameter and the angle in a semi-circle is a right angle.

$\therefore$ $\angle AEC = 90°$

Now, in ΔACE,

$\angle ACE + \angle AEC + \angle CAE = 180°$

$\Rightarrow$ $\angle ACE = 180° - (90 + 65°) = 25°$

Since, $AC \parallel DE$ $\therefore$ $\angle DEC$ and $\angle ACE$ are alternate angles.

$\Rightarrow$ $\angle DEC = \angle ACE = 25°$

9. Clearly, major arc BA subtends x° angle at a point on the remaining part of the circle.

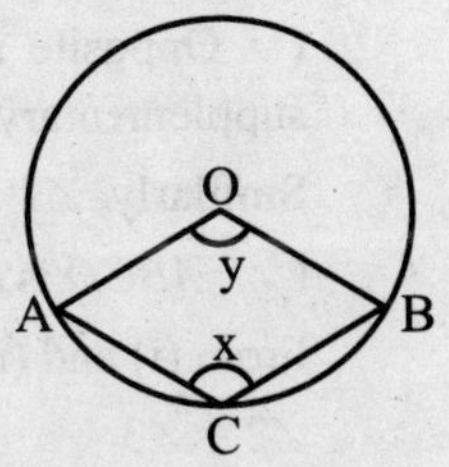

$\therefore$ Reflex $\angle AOB = 2x$

$\Rightarrow$ $360 - y = 2x$

$\Rightarrow$ $y = 360 - 2x$

Thus, $y = 360 - 2x$

Since ACBO is a parallelogram.

$\therefore$ $x = y$

$\Rightarrow$ $x = 360 - 2x$

$\Rightarrow$ $3x = 360$ $\Rightarrow$ $x = 120$

LONG ANSWER QUESTIONS :

1. Let the radius of the circle be r cm. Let $OM = x$ cm.
Then $ON = (6 - x)$ cm.
M is the mid-point of CD. $(\because OM \perp CD)$

$\therefore \quad MD = MC = \frac{1}{2}CD = \frac{1}{2}(11) \text{ cm} = \frac{11}{2} \text{ cm}$

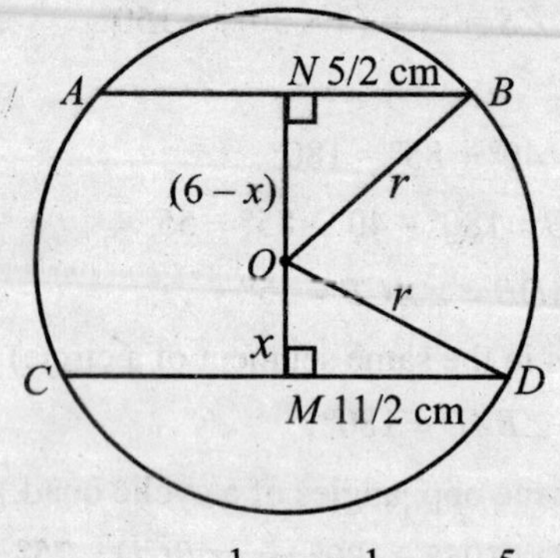

Similarly, $NB = AN = \frac{1}{2}AB = \frac{1}{2}(5) = \frac{5}{2}$ cm

$(\because N$ is the mid-point of AB and $ON \perp AB)$

In right ΔONB,

$OB^2 = ON^2 + NB^2$ (By Pythagoras theorem)

$\Rightarrow \quad r^2 = (6-x)^2 + \left(\frac{5}{2}\right)^2$ ... (i)

Similarly, in right ΔOMD, $OD^2 = OM^2 + MD^2$

(By Pythagoras theorem)

$\Rightarrow \quad r^2 = x^2 + \left(\frac{11}{2}\right)^2$ .. (ii)

From (i) and (ii), we get, $(6-x)^2 + \left(\frac{5}{2}\right)^2 = x^2 + \left(\frac{11}{2}\right)^2$

$\Rightarrow \quad 36 - 12x + x^2 + \frac{25}{4} = x^2 + \frac{121}{4} \Rightarrow x = \frac{12}{12} = 1$

Putting x = 1 in (ii), we get ,

$r^2 = (1)^2 + \left(\frac{11}{2}\right)^2 = 1 + \frac{121}{4} = \frac{125}{4} \Rightarrow r = \frac{5\sqrt{5}}{2}$

Hence, the radius of the circle is $\frac{5\sqrt{5}}{2}$ cm.

2. $\angle 1 + \angle 2 = 180°$ ... (i)

$(\because$ Opposite angles of a cyclic quadrilateral $ABFE$ are supplementary.)

Similarly, $\angle 1 + \angle 3 = 180°$ ... (ii)

$(\because$ $ABCD$ is a cyclic quadrilateral.)

From (i) and (ii),

$\angle 2 = \angle 3$

But these angles form a pair of equal corresponding angles.

$\therefore$ EF || DC.

3. The arc BC makes $\angle BOC = z$ at the centre and $\angle BAC = x$ at a point on circumference

$\therefore \; z = 2x$

(i) In $\Delta\, OBC$, $\angle OBC + \angle OCB + \angle BOC = 180°$

$\Rightarrow \quad z + 2y = 180°$

$\Rightarrow \quad x + y = 90° \; (\because z = 2x)$

$\Rightarrow \quad \angle BAC + \angle OBC = 90°$

(ii) In ΔOBC, $\angle OBC + \angle OCB + \angle BOC = 180°$

$\Rightarrow \quad y + y + t = 180° \Rightarrow 180 - 2y = t$

Now, $z = 360° - t = 360° - (180 - 2y)$

$\Rightarrow \quad 2x - 2y = 180° \Rightarrow x - y = 90°$

$\Rightarrow \quad \angle BAC - \angle OBC = 90°$

4. Join OC and BE

$2\angle AEC = \angle AOC \Rightarrow \angle AOC = 100° \; (\because \angle AEC = 50°)$

In $\Delta\, AOB$ and ΔBOC, $AB = BC$, $AO = OC$ and $OB = OB$

$\therefore \quad \Delta AOB \cong \Delta BOC$

$\therefore \; \angle BOA = \angle BOC$

$\Rightarrow \angle BOA = 50°$ and $\angle BOC = 50°$

$\Rightarrow \angle BOA = \angle CEO$ (each 50°)

$\therefore \; BO \parallel CE$

Now, $\angle AOC + \angle COE = 180°$

$\therefore \quad \angle COE = 80° \; (\because \angle AOC = 100°)$

Also, $\angle COE = 2\angle CBE$

$\Rightarrow \angle CBE = 40°$, $\quad \angle CDE = 180 - 40 = 140°$

5. $\angle A + \angle C = 180° \Rightarrow 2x + 4 + 4y - 4 = 180$

$\Rightarrow x + 2y = 90°$ ... (i)

$\angle B + \angle D = 180° \Rightarrow x + 10 + 5y + 5 = 180°$

$\Rightarrow x + 5y = 165°$ ... (ii)

On subtracting (i) from (ii), we get

$3y = 75 \Rightarrow y = 25°$

Also, $x = 40°$

6. **Given:** A chord AB of length 2 cm and radius of the circle is $\sqrt{2}$ cm.

To prove: $\angle ACB = 45°$

Proof: In ΔAOB,

$OA^2 + OB^2 = (\sqrt{2})^2 + (\sqrt{2})^2 = 2 + 2 = 4 = AB^2$

$\Rightarrow \quad \Delta AOB$ is a right triangle right angled at O.

i.e. $\quad \angle AOB = 90°$

As the angle subtended by an arc at the centre is double the angle subtended by it at remaining part of the circle.

$\therefore \quad \angle AOB = 2\angle ACB$

$\Rightarrow \quad \angle ACB = \frac{1}{2} \times 90° = 45°$

2 EXERCISE

TEXT-BOOK EXERCISE :

1. (i) *True* because all points on the circle are equidistant from its centre.
(ii) *False* because there are infinitely many points on the circle. So for each point on the circle, a point can be determined on the circle at a given distance from that point resulting into greatly many equal chords.
(iii) *False* because for each arc, the remaining arc will have greater length.
(iv) *True* because of definition of diameter.
(v) *False* by virtue of its definition.
(vi) *True* as it is a part of a plane.

2. We have, Two circles with centres O and P intersecting at Q and R.
To Prove : OP is the perpendicular bisector of QR.
Construction : Join OQ, OR, PQ and PR. Let OP intersect QR at M.
Proof : In ΔOQP and ΔORP,
OQ = OR
PQ = PR (Radii of a circle)
OP = OP (Common)
$\therefore$ $\Delta OQP \cong \Delta ORP$ (SSS Rule)
$\therefore$ $\angle QOP = \angle ROP$ (C.P.C.T.)
$\Rightarrow$ $\angle QOM = \angle ROM$ ... (i)
In ΔQOM and ΔROM,
OQ = OR (Radii of a circle)
$\angle QOM = \angle ROM$ (From (i))
OM = OM (Common)
$\therefore$ $\Delta QOM \cong \Delta ROM$ (SSS Rule)
$\therefore$ QM = RM ... (ii) (C.P.C.T.)
and $\angle QMO = \angle RMO$ ... (iii) (C.P.C.T.)
But $\angle QMO + \angle RMO = 180°$ (Linear pair axiom)
$\therefore$ $\angle QMO = \angle RMO = 90°$ ... (iv)
$\therefore$ OM, i.e., OP is perpendicular bisector of QR. (From (ii) and (iv))

3. Let us consider a circle with centre O with two equal chords PQ and CD intersect at E.
To prove : PE = DE and CE = QE
Draw OM $\perp$ PQ and ON $\perp$ CD. and Join OE.
Proof : Since, Equal chords of a circle are equidistant from the centre therefore
In ΔOME and ΔONE,
OM = ON
OE = OE (Common)
$\therefore$ $\Delta OME \cong \Delta ONE$ (R.H.S.)
$\therefore$ ME = NE (C.P.C.T.)
$\Rightarrow$ PM + ME = DN + NE
($\because$ $PM = DN = \frac{1}{2}PQ = \frac{1}{2}CD$)
$\Rightarrow$ PE = DE
$\Rightarrow$ PQ – PE = PQ – DE
$\Rightarrow$ PQ – PE = CD – DE ($\because$ PQ = CD)
$\Rightarrow$ QE = CE

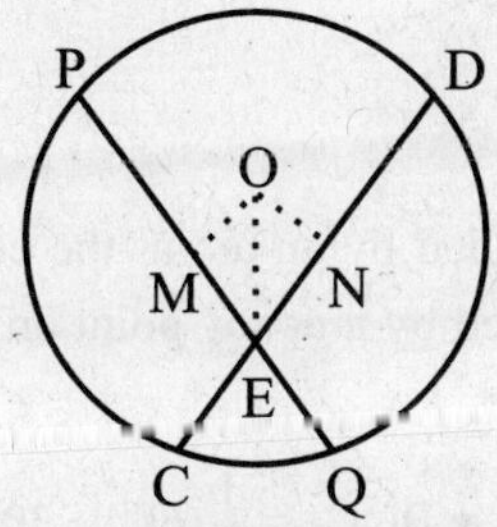

4. We have given two concentric circles with the same centre O and given a line which intersects both the circles at A, B, C and D.
To prove : AB = CD
Let us draw a perpendicular OM to BC.
Proof : Since, we know that the perpendicular drawn from the centre of a circle to a chord bisects the chord.
$\therefore$ AM = DM ... (i)
and BM = CM ... (ii)
By subtracting (ii) from (i), we get
AM – BM = DM – CM
$\Rightarrow$ AB = CD.

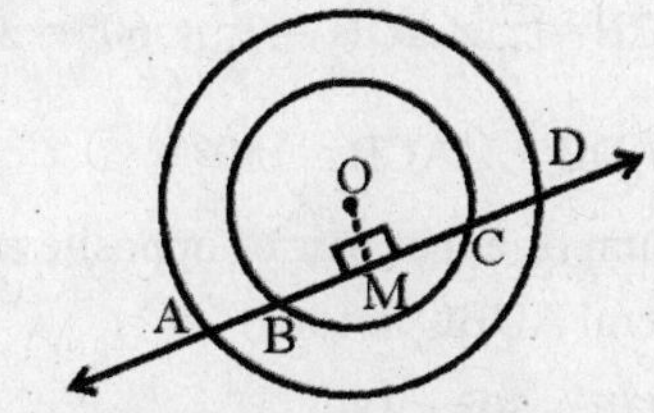

5. Given a circular park with radius 20 m and center O. Let us draw perpendiculars AM on BC and CN on AB i.e., AM $\perp$ BC and CN $\perp$ AB.
To find : AB = BC = CA
Proof :
Since, ΔABC is equilateral. So, AM and CN are median. They intersect at O where O is the centre of the circle.
Also, AO = 2OM = 20
$\Rightarrow$ OM = 10 m ($\because$ OA = radius)
$\Rightarrow$ AM = OA + OM = 20 + 10 = 30 m
Let BM = x
Then, BM = MC = x
$\therefore$ $BM = \frac{1}{2}BC$
$\Rightarrow$ BC = 2x
Similarly, AB = 2x

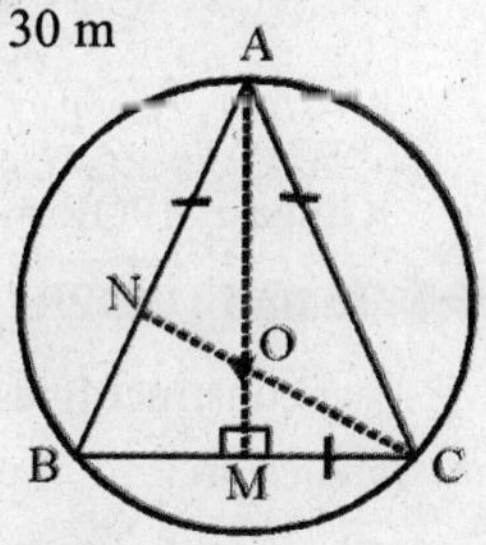

In right triangle AMB,
$AB^2 = AM^2 + BM^2$ (By Pythagoras theorem)
$\Rightarrow$ $(2x)^2 = (30)^2 + x^2$
$\Rightarrow$ $4x^2 - x^2 = 900$
$\Rightarrow$ $3x^2 = 900$
$\Rightarrow$ $x = \sqrt{300} = 10\sqrt{3}$
$\Rightarrow$ $AB = 2x = 2(10\sqrt{3})$
Hence, the length of the string of each phone is $20\sqrt{3}$ m.

6. Given three points A,B and C on a circle with centre O.
Also, $\angle BOC = 30°$ and $\angle AOB = 60°$

To find : $\angle ADC$.

$\angle ADC = \frac{1}{2}\angle AOC$

(Angle subtended by an arc at the centre is double the angle subtended by it at any point on the remaining part of the circle)

$= \frac{1}{2}(\angle AOB + \angle BOC) = \frac{1}{2}(60° + 30°) = \frac{1}{2}(90°) = 45°$

7. Given a chord which is equal to the radius of the circle.
Since, in ΔOAB all the three sides are equal
ie OA = OB = AB (Given)

$\therefore$ ΔOAB is equilateral.

$\therefore$ $\angle AOB = 60°$

Now, Since Angle subtended by an arc at the centre is double the angle subtended by it at any point on the remaining part of the circle.

$\therefore$ $\angle ACB = \frac{1}{2}\angle AOB = \frac{1}{2} \times 60° = 30°$

Now, $\angle ADB + \angle ACB = 180°$

($\therefore$ The sum of either pair of opposite angles of a cyclic quadrilateral ADBC is 180°)

$\Rightarrow$ $\angle ADB + 30° = 180°$

$\Rightarrow$ $\angle ADB = 150°$

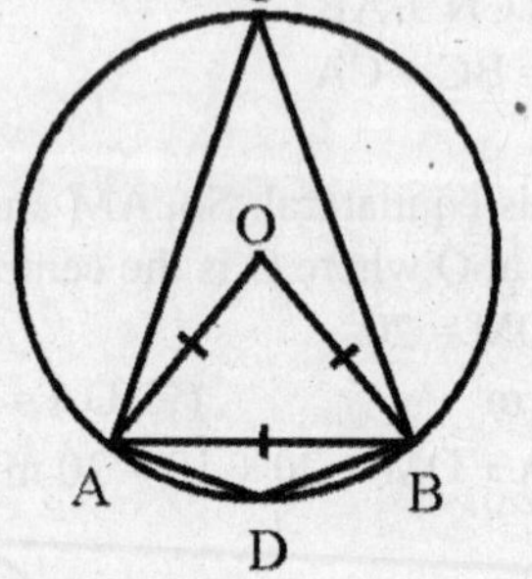

8. **Given :** $\angle PQR = 100°$

To find : $\angle OPR$

we construct lines PT and RT by taking a point T in the major arc.
Since, the sum of either pair of opposite angles of a cyclic quadrilateral PQRT is 180°

$\therefore$ $\angle PQR + \angle PTR = 180°$

$\Rightarrow$ $100° + \angle PTR = 180°$

$\Rightarrow$ $\angle PTR = 80°$ ... (i)

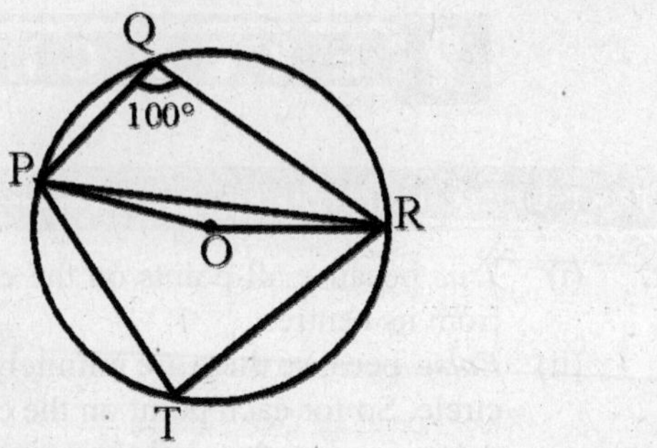

($\because$ The angle subtended by an arc at the centre is double the angle subtended by it at any point on the remaining part of the circle)

$\therefore$ $\angle POR = 2\angle PTR$ (Using (i))

$= 2 \times 80° = 160°$ ... (ii)

In ΔOPR,

$\because$ OP = OR (Radii of a circle)

$\therefore$ $\angle OPR = \angle ORP$ ... (iii)

(Angles opposite to equal sides of a triangle are equal)

Again, in ΔOPR, by angle sum property

$\angle OPR + \angle ORP + \angle POR = 180°$

$\Rightarrow$ $\angle OPR + \angle OPR + 160° = 180°$

$\Rightarrow$ $2\angle OPR = 180° - 160° = 20°$

$\Rightarrow$ $\angle OPR = 10°$

9. **Given :** $\angle ABC = 69°$, $\angle ACB = 31°$

To find : $\angle BDC$

From the angle Sum property in ΔABC,

$\angle BAC + \angle ABC + \angle ACB = 180°$

$\Rightarrow$ $\angle BAC + 69° + 31° = 180°$ (Given)

$\Rightarrow$ $\angle BAC + 100° = 180°$

$\Rightarrow$ $\angle BAC = 80°$

Since, Angles in the same segment of a circle are equal

$\therefore$ $\angle BDC = \angle BAC = 80°$ (Using (i))

10. Given four points A,B,C and D which lie on a circle.
Also, $\angle BEC = 130°$
$\angle ECD = 20°$

To find : $\angle BAC$

We have $\angle CED + \angle BEC = 180°$ (Linear Pair Axiom)

$\Rightarrow$ $\angle CED + 130° = 180°$

$\Rightarrow$ $\angle CED = 180° - 130° = 50°$ ... (i)

and $\angle ECD = 20°$ (Given) ... (ii)

From ΔCED

$\angle CED + \angle ECD + \angle CDE = 180°$ (By angle sum property)

$\Rightarrow$ $50° + 20° + \angle CDE = 180°$ (Using (i) and (ii))

$\Rightarrow$ $\angle CDE = 180° - 70°$

$\Rightarrow$ $\angle CDE = 110°$ ... (iii)

Now, $\angle BAC = \angle CDE = 110°$ ...(Using (iii))

(Angles in the same segment of a circle are equal)

11. Given a cyclic quadrilateral ABCD whose diagonals AC and BD intersects at E.

Also, $\angle DBC = 70°$

$\angle BAC = 30°$

To find : $\angle BCD$ and $\angle ECD$.

Since, angles in the same segment of a circle are equal therefore $\angle CDB = \angle BAC = 30°$ ... (i)

$\angle DBC = 70°$ (Given) ... (ii)

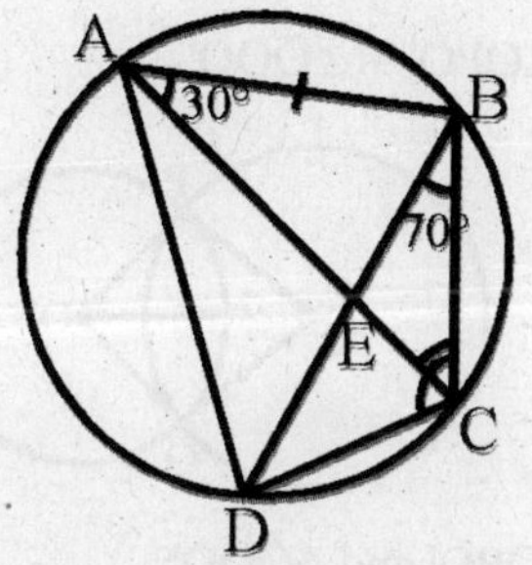

In ΔBCD,

$\angle BCD + \angle DBC + \angle CDB = 180°$

(By angle sum property)

$\Rightarrow \angle BCD + 70° + 30° = 180°$ (Using (i) and (ii))

$\Rightarrow \angle BCD = 80°$ ... (iii)

Now, In ΔABC,

$AB = BC$

$\therefore \angle BCA = \angle BAC$

$= 30°$ ... (iv) ($\because \angle BAC = 30°$ (given))

Now, $\angle BCD = 80°$ (From (iii))

$\Rightarrow \angle BCA + \angle ECD = 80°$

$\Rightarrow 30° + \angle ECD = 80°$

$\Rightarrow \angle ECD = 50°$

12. Given in cyclic quadrilateral ABCD, two diagonals AC and BD are the diameters of circle.

Prove that quadrilateral ABCD is a rectangle.

Proof : In ΔOAB and ΔOCD,

$OA = OC$ and

$OB = OD$ (Radii of a circle)

$\angle AOB = \angle COD$ (Vert. Opp. Angles)

$\therefore$ By (SAS Rule), $\Delta OAB \cong \Delta OCD$

$\therefore AB = CD$ (C.P.C.T.)

$\Rightarrow$ Arc AB = Arc CD ... (i)

Similarly, we can have

Arc AD = Arc CB ... (ii)

By adding (i) and (ii), we get

Arc AB + Arc AD = Arc CD + Arc CB

$\Rightarrow$ Arc BAD = Arc BCD

$\Rightarrow$ BD divides the circle into two equal parts

$\therefore \angle A = 90°, \angle C = 90°$ (Angle of a semi-circle is 90°)

Similarly, $\angle B = 90°, \angle D = 90°$

$\therefore \angle A = \angle B = \angle C = \angle D = 90°$

$\therefore$ ABCD is a rectangle.

13. **Given :** A trapezium PQRS whose two non-parallel sides PS and QR are equal.

To prove : Trapezium PQRS is a cyclic.

Draw QE || PS.

Proof : By construction PS || QE ($\because$ PQ || SE)

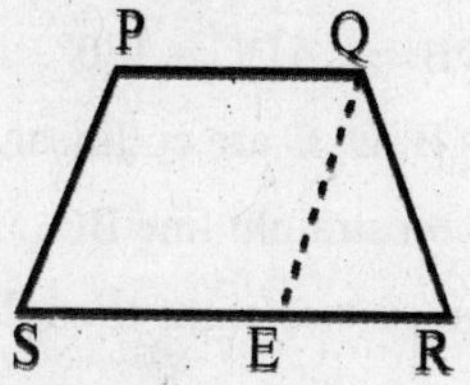

$\therefore \angle QPS = \angle QES$ ... (i)

(Opp. angles of a ||gm)

and $PS = QE$ ... (ii)

(Opp. sides of a || gm)

But $PS = QR$ ... (iii) (Given)

From (ii) and (iii),

$QE = QR$

$\therefore \angle QER = \angle QRE$ ... (iv)

(Angles opposite to equal sides)

$\angle QER + \angle QES = 180°$ (Linear Pair Axiom)

$\Rightarrow \angle QRE + \angle QPS = 180°$ (From (iv) and (i))

$\Rightarrow$ Trapezium PQRS is cyclic.

($\because$ If a pair of opposite angles of a quadrilateral is 180°, then the quadrilateral is cyclic)

14. We have two circles intersect at B and C. Through B, two line segments ABD and PBQ are drawn to intersect the circles at A, D and P, Q respectively.

To prove : $\angle ACP = \angle QCD$

Proof : $\angle ACP = \angle ABP$ ... (i)

and $\angle QCD = \angle QBD$ ... (ii)

(Angles in the same segment of a circle are equal)

$\angle ABP = \angle QBD$ ... (iii)

(Vertically Opposite Angles)

From (i), (ii) and (iii),

$\angle ACP = \angle QCD$

15. Given two sides AB and AC of a triangle ABC. Taking these two sides as diameters we draw a circle which intersect at A and D.

To prove : D lies on the third side BC of ΔABC.

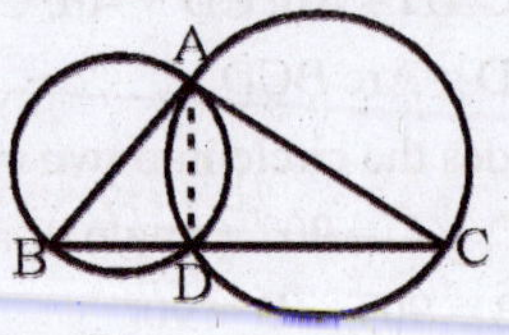

Proof : Join AD.

$\angle ADB = 90°$ ...(i) (Angle in a semi-circle)

But $\angle ADB + \angle ADC = 180°$(Linear Pair Axiom)

$\therefore$ $\angle ADC = 90°$ (From (i))

Hence, the circle described on AC as diameter must pass through D.

Thus, the two circles intersect in D.

Now, $\angle ADB + \angle ADC = 180°$.

$\Rightarrow$ Points B, D, C are collinear.

$\Rightarrow$ D lies on straight line BC.

16. We have given two right triangles ABC and ADC with common hypotenuse AC.

To prove : $\angle CAD = \angle CBD$.

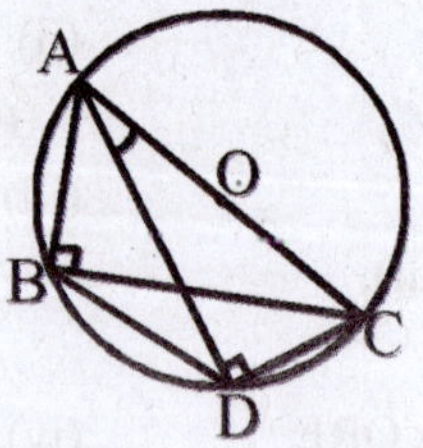

Proof : $\angle ABC = 90° = \angle ADC$

($\because$ AC is the common hypotenuse of both the triangles.)

$\Rightarrow$ Both the triangles are in the same semi-circle.

$\Rightarrow$ Points A, B, D and C are cyclic.

Since, DC is chord and Angles in the same segment are equal

$\therefore$ $\angle CAD = \angle CBD$

17. Let PQRS be a cyclic parallelogram.

To show that PQRS is a rectangle.

Proof : Since, Opposite angles of a cyclic quadrilateral are supplementary

$\therefore$ $\angle PSR + \angle PQR = 180°$ ... (i)

($\because$ PQRS is a cyclic quadrilateral)

Given PQRS is a parallelogram.

$\therefore$ $\angle PSR = \angle PQR$ ... (ii)

(opp. angles of a ||gm) From (i) and (ii),

$\angle PSR = \angle PQR = 90°$

$\therefore$ ||gm PQRS is a rectangle.

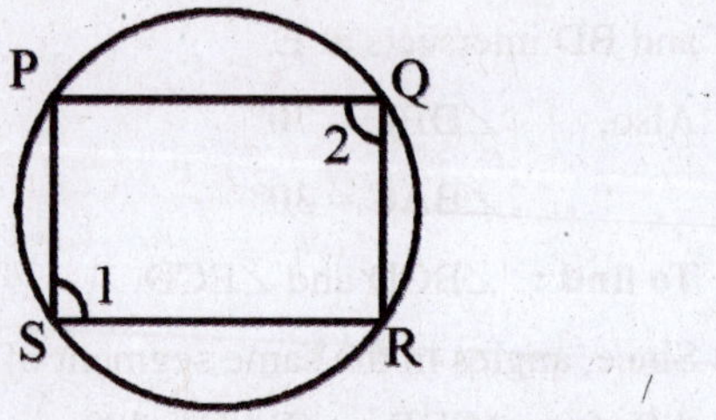

18. We have two circles with centres O and O' intersecting at P and Q.

To prove : $\angle OPO' = \angle OQO'$.

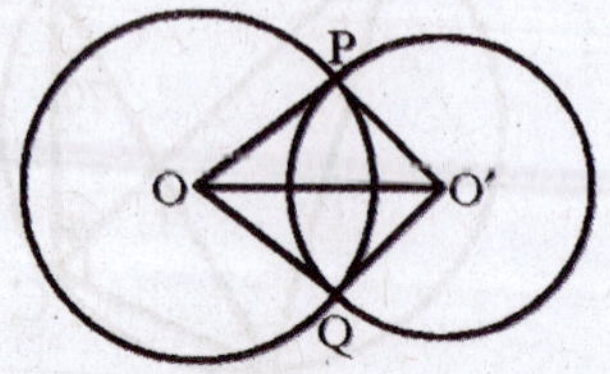

Proof : In $\Delta OPO'$ and $\Delta OQO'$,

OP = OQ and

O'P = O'Q (Radii of a circle)

OO' = OO' (Common)

$\therefore$ $\Delta OPO' \cong \Delta OQO'$ (SSS Rule)

$\therefore$ $\angle OPO' = \angle OQO'$ (C.P.C.T)

19. We know that the diagonals of a rhombus bisect each other at right angles.

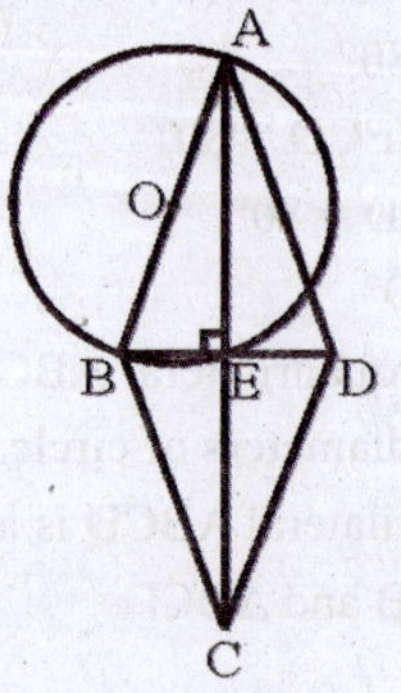

$\therefore$ we have the circle drawn with one side AB as diameter will pass through the mid-point E of BD which is the point of intersection of the diagonals.

20. **Given :** ABCD is a parallelogram. The circle through A, B, and C intersects CD (produced, if necessary) at E.

To prove : AE = AD.

Proof : We have $\angle AED + \angle ABC = 180°$ ...(i)

($\because$ Opposite angles of a cyclic quadrilateral ABCE are supplementary.)

Also, $\angle ADE + \angle ADC = 180°$ (Linear Pair Axiom)

But $\angle ADC = \angle ABC$ (Opposite angles of a ||gm)

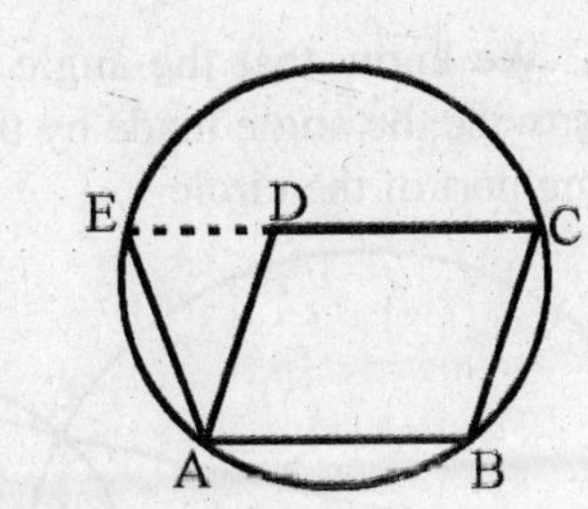

$\therefore \quad \angle ADE + \angle ABC = 180°$ ...(ii)

From (i) and (ii), we have

$\angle AED + \angle ABC = \angle ADE + \angle ABC$

$\Rightarrow \quad \angle AED = \angle ADE$

$\therefore$ In ΔADE, $AE = AD$

($\because$ Sides opposite to equal angles of a triangle are equal.)

21. We have given two congruent circles intersect each other at points A and B and a line through A meets the circles in P and Q.

To prove : BP = BQ

Proof : Since, AB is the common chord of the two congruent circles

$\therefore \quad \angle APB = \angle AQB$

Since, Angles subtended by equal chords are equal

$\therefore \quad BP = BQ$ (Sides opposite to equal angles are equal)

22.

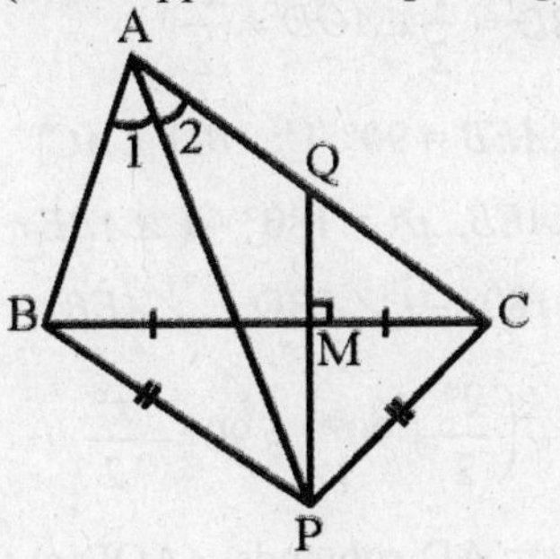

To prove : P lies on the circumcircle of the ΔABC where AP is the bisector of $\angle A$ and PQ is perpendicular bisector of BC.

We can draw the circle through three non-collinear points A, B and P.

Proof : $\angle BAP = \angle CAP$

$\Rightarrow \quad \overset{\frown}{BP} = \overset{\frown}{CP}$

$\Rightarrow$ chord BP = chord CP

From ΔBMP and ΔCMP,

BM = CM and

BP = CP

MP = MP (Common)

$\therefore \quad \Delta BMP \cong \Delta CMP$ (SSS Axiom)

$\therefore \quad \angle BMP = \angle CMP$ (C.P.C.T.)

But $\angle BMP + \angle CMP = 180°$ (Linear Pair Axiom)

$\therefore \quad \angle BMP = \angle CMP = 90°$

$\Rightarrow$ PM is the right bisector of BC.

EXEMPLAR QUESTIONS :

1. As arc AXB = $\frac{1}{2}$ arc BYC,

$\angle AOB = \frac{1}{2} \angle BOC$

Also $\angle AOB + \angle BOC = 180°$

Therefore, $\frac{1}{2} \angle BOC + \angle BOC = 180°$

or $\angle BOC = \frac{2}{3} \times 180° = 120°$

2. $\angle ABC = \frac{1}{2} \angle AOC$

i.e., $\angle AOC = 2\angle ABC = 2 \times 45° = 90°$

or OA OC

3. In $\Delta\, OCP$,

$\angle OPC = 90°$

$\therefore \quad AP \perp BC$

$\angle OCP = 30°$

$\therefore \quad \angle POC = 90° - 30° = 60°$

$DO \perp AP$,

$\therefore \quad \angle DOP = 90°$

$\therefore \quad \angle COD = 90° - 60° = 30°$

$\angle CBD = \frac{1}{2} \angle COD$ [Angle subtended theorem]

$\therefore \quad y = \frac{1}{2} \times 30° = 15° \Rightarrow y = 15°$

$\angle AOD = 90°$

$\therefore \angle ABD = \frac{1}{2} \angle AOD$ [Angle subtended theorem]

$\angle ABD = \frac{1}{2} \times 90° = 45°$

In $\Delta\, ABP$,

$x + 45° + y + 90° = 180°$

$x + 45° + 15° + 90 = 180°$

$x = 180° - 150° = 30°$

4. False. If two points lie in the same segment (major or minor) only, then the angles will be equal otherwise they are not equal.

5. False. As the larger chord is at smaller distance from the centre.

6. (a) $OA = 5$ cm, $AB = 8$ cm

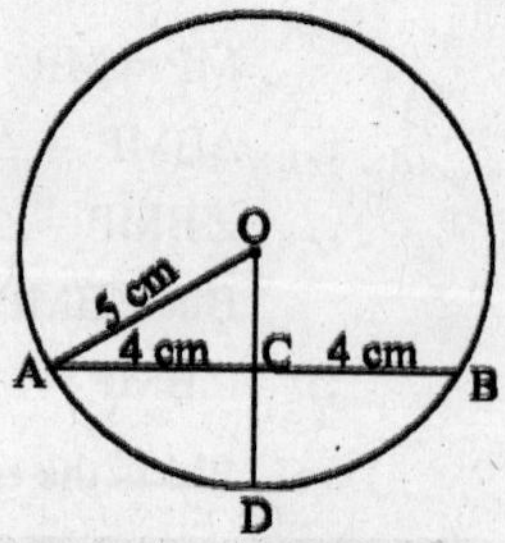

$OC = \sqrt{5^2 - 4^2}$

$OC = \sqrt{25-16} = \sqrt{9} = 3\text{cm}$

$CD = OD - OC$

$CD = 5 - OC$

$CD = 5 - 3 = 2$ cm

7. (b) $\angle AOC = 40°$ ($\because$ the angle subtended by an arc at the centre is double the angle subtended by it at any point on the remaining part of the circle.)

8. (d) $\angle ACB = 90°$ (Angle in semi-circle)

since AC = BC

therefore $\angle CAB = \angle CBA = x$ (say)

Now, $\angle ACB + \angle CAB + \angle CBA = 180°$

(Angle sum property of a triangle)

$90° + x + x = 180°$

$\Rightarrow \ 2x = 90° \Rightarrow x = 45°$

9. (a) Since OA = OB

therefore $\angle OAB = \angle OBA = 40°$

Now, $\angle AOB = 180 - (40 + 40) = 100°$

(By angle sum property of a triangle)

$\Rightarrow \ \angle ACB = 50°$

10. (c) In ΔADB,

$\angle A + \angle B + \angle D = 180°$

$\Rightarrow \ 60° + 50° + \angle D = 180°$

$\Rightarrow \ \angle D = 180 - 110 = 70°$

Now, $\angle ACB = 70°$

($\because$ Angles in the same segment of the circle are equal.)

11. (c) **Given:** $\angle BAO = 60°$

since OA = OB (radius)

therefore $\angle OAB = \angle OBA = 60°$

Now, $\angle OBA = \angle ADC = 60°$

($\because$ Angles in the same segment of the circle are equal)

HOTS QUESTIONS :

1. $\angle 4 = \angle 3$ [Opposite angles of a || gm] ... (i)

$\angle 4 + \angle 1 = 180°$ [Cyclic quadrilateral]

$\therefore \angle 3 + \angle 1 = 180°$ [Using (i)] ... (ii)

Also $\angle 2 + \angle 3 = 180°$ [Linear pair angles] ... (iii)

From eqs. (ii) and (iii)

$\angle 3 + \angle 1 = \angle 2 + \angle 3$

$\Rightarrow \ \angle 1 = \angle 2$

$\Rightarrow \ AE = AD$

Also $AD = BC$

(opp. sides of a ||gm)

$BC = 8$ cm

$\therefore \ AE = 8$ cm

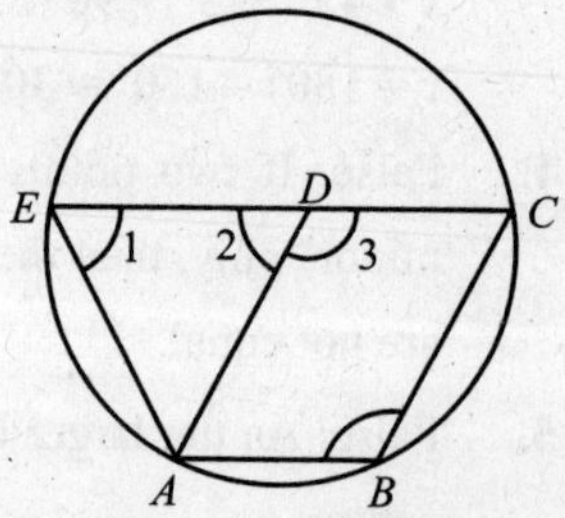

2. Join BC. We know that the angle made by an arc at the centre is twice the angle made by this arc at a point on the remaining part of the circle.

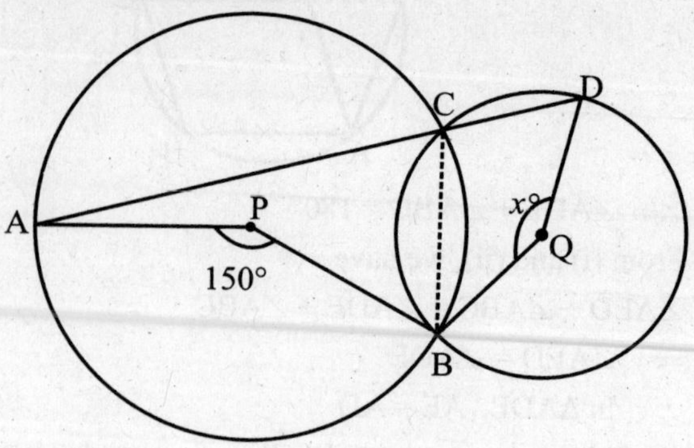

$\therefore \angle ACB = \frac{1}{2}\angle APB = \frac{1}{2}\times 150° = 75°$

Now, ACD being a straight line, we get

$\angle ACB + \angle BCD = 180°$ [Linear pair]

$\angle BCD = 180° - \angle ACB = 180° - 75° = 105°$

Similarly, for second circle.

$\angle BCD = \frac{1}{2}$ reflex $\angle BQD$

$\Rightarrow 105° = \frac{1}{2}(360° - x) \Rightarrow x = 150°$

Hence, $x = 150°$

3. Arc AD subtends $\angle AOD$ at the centre and $\angle ABD$ at a point B on the remaining part of the circle.

$\therefore \angle ABD = \frac{1}{2}\angle AOD = \frac{x°}{2}$

Now, $\angle AEB = 90°$ [$\because BD \perp AC$]

From ΔAEB, $p° = 180° - (\angle ABE + \angle AEB)$

$\therefore p° = 180° - (\angle ABD + \angle AEB)$

$= 180° - \left(\frac{x°}{2} + 90°\right) = 90° - \frac{x°}{2}$

Again, arc AD subtends $\angle AOD$ at the centre and $\angle ACD$ at a point C of the circle.

$\therefore \angle ACD = \frac{1}{2}\angle AOD = \frac{x°}{2} \Rightarrow q = \frac{x°}{2}$

Now $\angle ABC = 90°$ [Angle in a semicircle]

$\Rightarrow \angle ABE + \angle CBE = 90°$

$\Rightarrow \angle ABD + \angle CBE = 90°$

$\Rightarrow \frac{x°}{2} + \angle CBE = 90° \Rightarrow \angle CBE = 90° - \frac{x°}{2}$

$\Rightarrow r° = 90° - \frac{x°}{2}$

Hence, $p° = q° = \frac{x°}{2}$ and $r° = 90° - \frac{x°}{2}$

4. Join OA.

In right ΔOAM,

$OA^2 = OM^2 + AM^2$

$\Rightarrow r^2 = p^2 + \left(\frac{1}{2}AB\right)^2$

($\because OM \perp AB, \therefore OM$ bisects AB)

$\Rightarrow \frac{1}{4}AB^2 = r^2 - p^2$ or $AB^2 = 4r^2 - 4p^2$ ...(i)

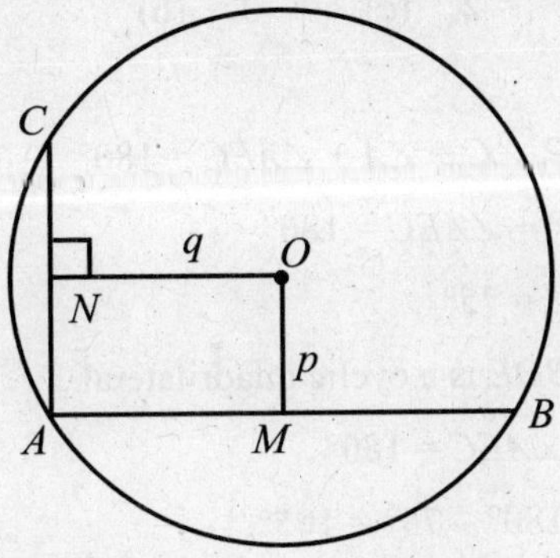

In right ΔOAN

$OA^2 = ON^2 + AN^2$

$\Rightarrow r^2 = q^2 + \left(\frac{1}{2}AC\right)^2$ ($\because ON \perp AC, \therefore ON$ bisects AC)

$\Rightarrow \frac{1}{4}AC^2 = r^2 - q^2$

or $\frac{1}{4}\left(\frac{1}{2}AB\right)^2 = r^2 - q^2$ ($\because AB = 2AC$)

$\Rightarrow \frac{1}{16}AB^2 = r^2 - q^2$ or $AB^2 = 16r^2 - 16q^2$ ...(ii)

From (i) and (ii), we have

$4r^2 - 4p^2 = 16r^2 - 16q^2$

or $r^2 - p^2 = 4r^2 - 4q^2$

or $4q^2 = 3r^2 + p^2$

3 EXERCISE

SINGLE OPTION CORRECT :

1. (c) a segment.
2. (c) rectangle
3. (a) In ΔOAC

as, $OA = OC$ = radius of circle

$\therefore \angle OAC = \angle OCA = 40°$

Similarly, in ΔOBC

$\angle OBC = \angle OCB = 30°$

We know that angle subtended at the arc is half of the angle subtended at the centre.

$\therefore \angle ACB = \frac{1}{2}\angle AOB$

$\Rightarrow \angle AOB = 2(\angle ACB) = 2(70) = 140°$.

4. (d) B, C and D are collinear
5. (d) Chords of a circle which are equidistant from the centre of the circle are equal.
6. (b) Since PQ is a chord of a circle and R is a point on the circle such that $\angle PRQ = 90°$, therefore, the arc PRQ is a semicircle $\Rightarrow PQ$ is a diameter.

$\therefore$ Length of $PQ = 2 \times$ radius $= 2r$ units

7. (c) As PQR is an equilateral triangle inscribed in a circle,

$\angle QPR = 60°$,

$\therefore \angle QOR = 2 \times \angle QPR = 2 \times 60° = 120°$

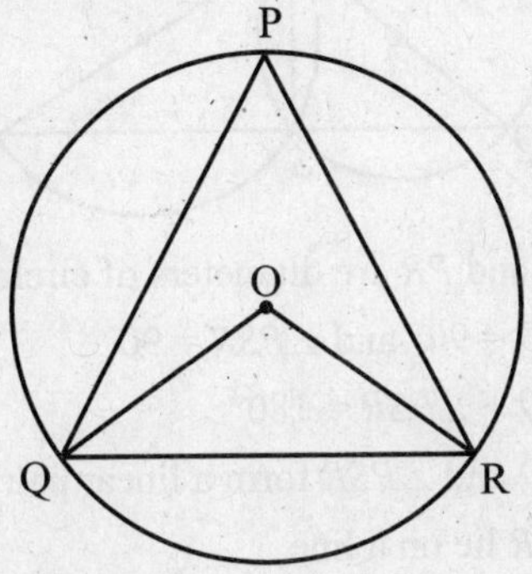

8. (a) $\angle BAD = \angle BCD$

(angles in the same segment of a circle)

$\Rightarrow \angle PAD = \angle BAD = 25°$ ($\because \angle BCD = 25°$, given)

Now, $\angle ADC = \angle PAD + \angle APD$ (ext. angle of a Δ = sum of two int. opp. angles)

$\Rightarrow \angle ADC = 25° + 35° = 60°$.

9. (d) In ΔPRS, $\angle PSR + 25° + 60° = 180°$

$\Rightarrow \angle PSR = 95°$

Now $\angle PQR + \angle PSR = 180°$

(sum of opp. angles of a cyclic quad. is 180°)

$\Rightarrow x + 95° = 180° \Rightarrow x = 85°$.

10. (c) $\angle DEA = \angle BEC$ (Vertic. opp. angles)

$\Rightarrow 60° = \angle BEC$

Now, in ΔBEC,

$\angle E + \angle B + \angle C = 180°$

$\Rightarrow 60 + 25 + \angle C = 180°$

$\Rightarrow \angle C = 95°$

Also, $\angle C = \angle D$

$\Rightarrow \angle D = 95°$

11. **(c)** $OA = OB$ (radius of circle)

$\Rightarrow 5 = OB$

Thus, $\angle A = \angle B$ $(\because OA = OB)$

Thus, in ΔOAB

$\angle A + \angle B + \angle O = 180^\circ$

$\Rightarrow 2\angle A + 60^\circ = 180^\circ$

$\Rightarrow \angle A = 60^\circ$

Hence, $\angle A = \angle B = \angle O = 60^\circ \Rightarrow \Delta OAB$ is an equilateral triangle.

12. (c) **13.** (b) **14.** (b) **15.** (b)
16. (d)

MORE THAN ONE OPTION CORRECT :

1. (a, c, d)

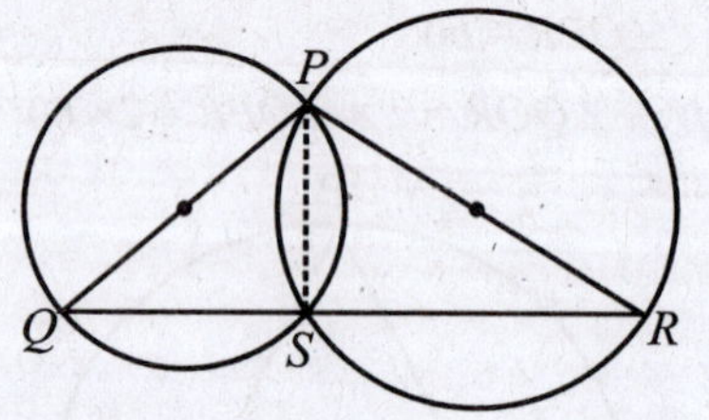

Since, PQ and PR are diameters of circle

$\therefore \angle PSQ = 90^\circ$ and $\angle PSR = 90^\circ$

$\Rightarrow \angle PSQ + \angle PSR = 180^\circ$

$\Rightarrow \angle PSQ$ and $\angle PSR$ form a linear pair angles.

$\Rightarrow Q, S, R$ lie on a line

$\Rightarrow S$ lies on QR.

2. (a, d) **3.** (a, b,d)
4. (a,b,c) **5.** (b,c,d)

PASSAGE BASED QUESTIONS :

For (1-3)

$\angle ARB = 90^\circ$ (Angle in semi-circle is right angle)

Since, $ARBP$ is a cyclic quadrilateral

$\therefore \angle ARB + \angle APB = 180^\circ$

$\Rightarrow \angle APB = 180^\circ - 90^\circ = 90^\circ$

Now, in ΔAPB,

$\angle PAB + \angle ABP + \angle BPA = 180^\circ$

$\Rightarrow 55 + \angle ABP + 90^\circ = 180^\circ$

$\Rightarrow \angle ABP = 180 - 145 = 35^\circ$ ... (i)

Since, $ABQP$ is a cyclic quadrilateral

$\therefore \angle PAB + \angle PQB = 180^\circ$

$\Rightarrow \angle PQB = 180 - 55 = 125^\circ$

Now, In ΔPQB,

$\angle BPQ + \angle PQB + \angle QBP = 180^\circ$

$\Rightarrow \angle BPQ + 125^\circ + 25^\circ = 180^\circ$

$\Rightarrow \angle BPQ = 180^\circ - 150^\circ = 30^\circ$ ... (ii)

In ΔBRA,

$\angle BRA + \angle RAB + \angle ABR = 180^\circ$

$\Rightarrow 90^\circ + \angle RAB + 50^\circ = 180^\circ$

$\Rightarrow \angle RAB = 180^\circ - 140^\circ = 40^\circ$ ... (iii)

From (i), (ii) and (iii)

1. (a) **2.** (c) **3.** (b)

For (4-6)

In ΔCAE, $\angle C + \angle A + \angle AEC = 180^\circ$

$43^\circ + 62^\circ + \angle AEC = 180^\circ$

$\Rightarrow \angle AEC = 75^\circ$

Since, $ABDE$ is a cyclic quadrilateral.

$\therefore a + \angle AEC = 180^\circ$

$\Rightarrow a = 180^\circ - 75^\circ = 105^\circ$ ... (i)

Now, $\angle A + \angle EDB = 180^\circ$

$\Rightarrow \angle EDB = 180^\circ - 62^\circ = 118^\circ$

Now, $c + \angle EDB = 180^\circ$ (Linear pair)

$\therefore c = 180^\circ - 118^\circ = 62^\circ$ ... (ii)

Also, $\angle AED + \angle DEF = 180^\circ$ (linear pair)

$\Rightarrow \angle DEF = 180^\circ - 75^\circ = 105^\circ$

In ΔDEF

$b + c + \angle DEF = 180^\circ$

$b = 180^\circ - (62^\circ + 105^\circ) = 13^\circ$ ... (iii)

So, from (i), (ii) and (iii)

4. (b) **5.** (c) **6.** (a)

ASSERTION & REASON :

1. (a) Both Assertion and Reason are correct and Reason is correct explanation for Assertion.

2. (b) Both Assertion and Reason are correct but reason is not correct explanation for Assertion.

3. (c) Assertion is correct. But Reason is not correct. Two or more circles are called concentric circles if and only if they have same centre but different radii.

4. (c) Assertion is correct but Reason is false.

5. (b) Both Assertion and Reason is correct.

INTEGER TYPE QUESTIONS :

1. Ans : 5

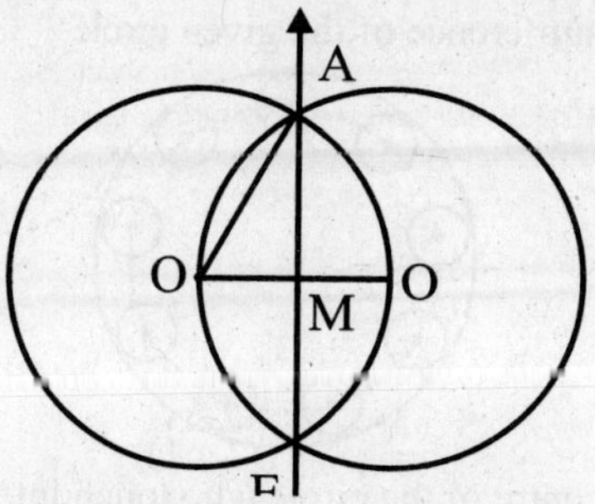

Given, distance between the centres of two circle = 5 cm

$\therefore$ OO' = 5 cm

$OM = \frac{5}{2}$ cm

In ΔOAM,

$OA^2 = OM^2 + AM^2$

$(5)^2 = \left(\frac{5}{2}\right)^2 + AM^2$

$AM = \sqrt{25 - \frac{25}{4}} = \frac{5\sqrt{3}}{2}$ cm

$\therefore$ The length of common chord, AB = 2 × AM

$= 2 \times \frac{5\sqrt{3}}{2} = 5\sqrt{3}$ cm

Hence, $a = 5$

2. Ans : 5

In ΔBCD, $BC = CD$, $\angle BDC = \angle CBD = x$

In cyclic quadrilateral $ABCD$,

$\angle ABC + \angle ADC = 180°$

$40° + x + 90° + x = 180° \Rightarrow x = 25°$.

Hence, measure of $\frac{\angle DBC}{5} = \frac{25}{5} = 5$

3. Ans : 2

$m \angle DAB + 180° - 120° = 60°$

(Opposite angles of a cyclic quadrilateral)

m (arc BCD) = 2m $\Rightarrow \angle DAB = 120°$.

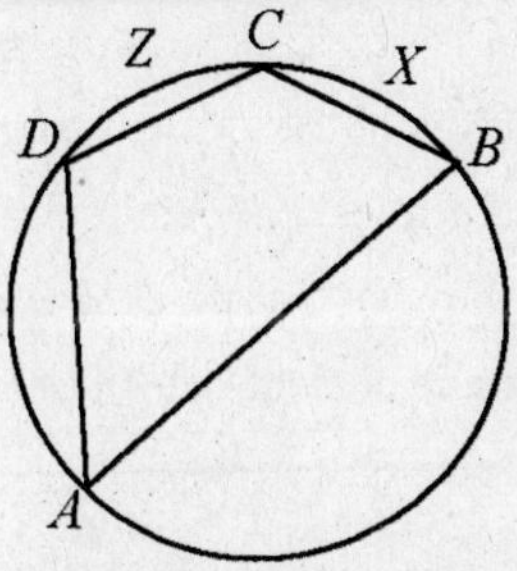

$\therefore m$ (arc CXB) = m (BCD) – m (arc DZC)

= 120° – 70° = 50°.

4. Ans : 6

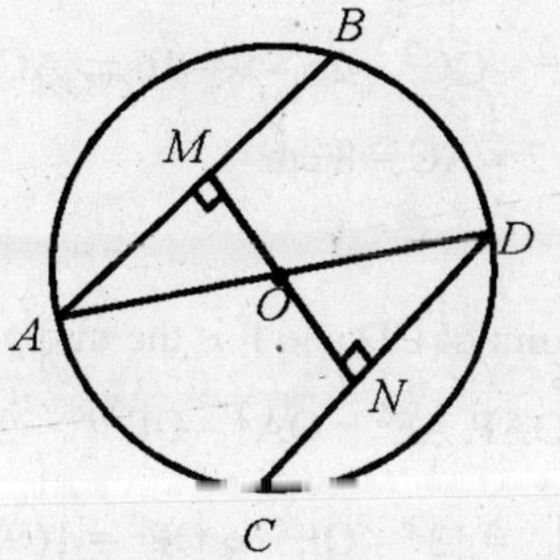

Two parallel chords AB & CD & $AB = CD = 8$ cm

Diameter of circle = AD = 10 cm.

$\therefore$ radius = $AO = OD = \frac{10}{2} = 5$ cm

$AM = MB = \frac{AB}{2} = 4$ cm.

ΔAOM is right angle Δ,

$AO^2 = AM^2 + OM^2$

$5^2 = 4^2 + OM^2$

$OM^2 = 25 - 16 = 9$

$\Rightarrow$ $OM = 3$ cm.

Similarly,

$OM = ON = 3$ cm

$\therefore$ Distance between parallel chords = MN

$= OM + ON$

$= 3 + 3 = 6$ cm

5. Ans : 2

Since arc BPC makes $\angle BOC$ at the centre and $\angle BAC$ at a point on the remaining part of the circle.

$\therefore$ $\angle BAC = \frac{1}{2} \angle BOC$

Now, $\angle BOC = 360° - (120° + 80°) = 160°$

$\therefore$ $\angle BAC = \frac{1}{2} (\angle BOC)$

$\Rightarrow$ $\angle BAC = \frac{1}{2} \times 160° = 80° = k°$

The value of $\frac{k}{40°} = 2$

6. Ans : 2

We have, $\angle CDA = 180° - 80° = 100° = 180°$

and $\angle ABC + x = 180°$

Now, $\angle CDA + \angle ABC = 180°$

$\Rightarrow$ $100° + 180° - x = 180° \Rightarrow x = 100°$

$\therefore$ $\frac{x}{50°} = \frac{100°}{50°} = 2.$

7. **Ans : 8**

$AC^2 = OA^2 - OC^2 = 25 - 9 = 16 \Rightarrow AC = 4$ cm

$\Rightarrow AB = 2 \times AC = 8$ cm

8. **Ans : 5**

E is mid point of CD and F is the mid point of AB.

Now, in ΔOAF, $AF^2 = OA^2 - OF^2$

$\Rightarrow \left(\frac{24}{2}\right)^2 = 13^2 - OF^2 \Rightarrow OF^2 = 169 - 144$

$\Rightarrow OF = 5$ cm

4 ADVANCE EXERCISE
BASED ON CONNECTING TOPICS

1. (b) Let lines l_1 and l_2 are perpendicular bisector of line segments joining the points A and B, B and C respectively.

We know that locus of a point equidistant from two points is the perpendicular bisector of the line segment joining these two given points.

Hence line l_1 is the locus of a point equidistant from two points A and B. Also line l_2 is the locus of a point equidistant from two points B and C.

Therefore locus of a point which is equidistant from three points A, B and C in a plane is the common point(s) of line l_1 and l_2. But the line l_1 and l_2 have only one common point in the case when the three points A, B and C are non-collinear.

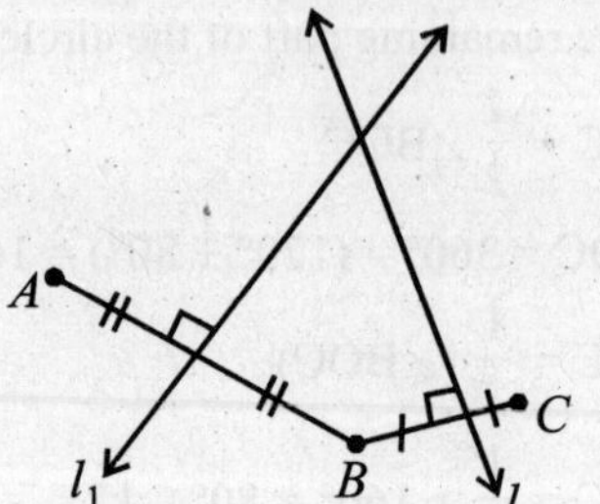

2. (a) Centre of the circle which touch the given circle internally always remains equidistant from the circumference of the given circle.

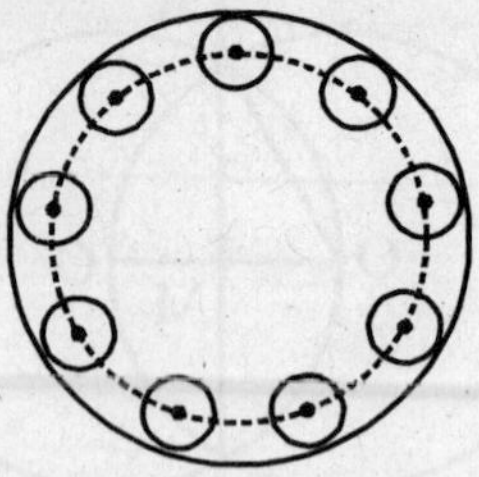

So centre of the circle who touch internally the given circle lies on a circle.

3. (c)

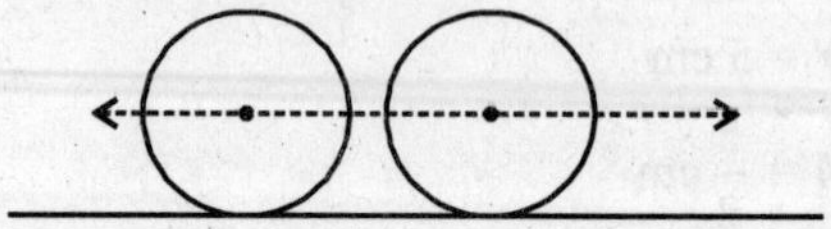

Centre of the wheel rolling on a straight road always remains equidistant from the road. Hence centre of the wheel always lie on a straight line parallel to the road.

4. (b) Incentre (obviously)
5. (c) Two non-intersecting lines l and m means two parallel lines l and m.

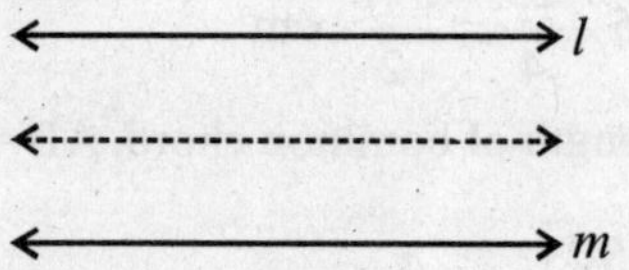

If a point remains equidistant from two parallel lines l and m. Then the point always lie on a straight line parallel to lines l and m and midway between them.

6. (a, b, c)
7. (b)
8. (a)
9. (c)

Chapter 11

Constructions

INTRODUCTION

The diagrams, which were necessary to prove theorems or solving the problems were not necessarily very accurate. They were drawn only to give you a feeling for the situation and as an add for proper reasoning. But many times, we need to draw accurate figures. For examples to draw road map of a city, to draw layout plan of a building to draw a design of a vehicle etc. To draw such accurate figures, we must have some basic knowledge of geometrical constructions, which is a process of drawing a geometrical figure using some geometrical instruments like graduated ruler, protector, compass, a pair of set-squares.

In earlier classes, you have learned some simple geometrical constructions like drawing a line segment of a given measurement, making an angle with the help of protector etc. In this chapter, you will learn some more basic geometrical constructions using ruler and compass with reasoning behind it, why these constructions are valid.

TO CONSTRUCT THE BISECTOR OF AN ANGLE

Bisecting an angle means drawing a ray in the interior of the angle, with its initial point at the vertex of the angle such that it divides the angle into two equal parts.

Given an angle *AOB*.

To construct bisector of $\angle AOB$ follow the steps given below.

Steps of Construction

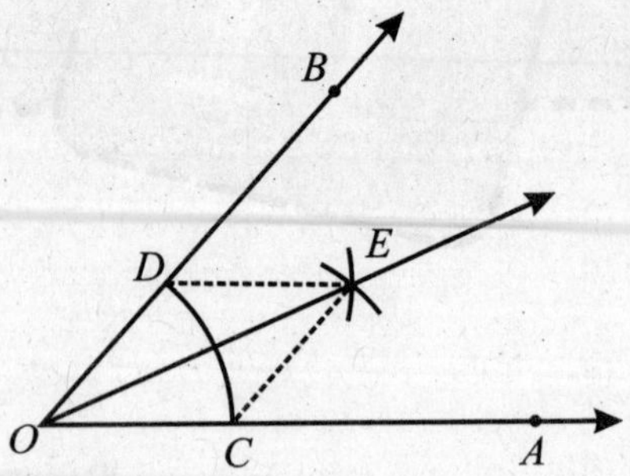

(i) Taking O as centre and any suitable radius draw an arc as shown in the figure, which intersect the ray *OA* and *OB* at *C* and *D* respectively

(ii) Taking *C* as centre and any suitable radius (> ½*CD*), draw an arc.

(iii) Taking *D* as centre and same radius as in step-(ii), draw an arc intersecting the arc drawn in step (ii) at point *E*.

(iv) Draw ray *OE*, which is required bisector of $\angle AOB$.

Justification :

Join *CE* and *DE*

In ΔOCE and ΔODE,

$OC = OD$ (radii of the same arc)

$CE = DE$ (arcs of equal radii)

$OE = OE$ (common)

$\therefore$ $\Delta OCE \cong \Delta ODE$ (by SSS rule of congruency)

$\therefore$ $\angle COE = \angle DOE$ (CPCT)

Hence, OE is the bisector of $\angle$ AOB.

TO CONSTRUCT THE PERPENDICULAR BISECTOR OF A GIVEN LINE SEGMENT

Given a line segment *AB*. To construct perpendicular bisector of AB follow the steps given below.

Steps of Construction

(i) Taking *A* as centre and any suitable radius (> ½ *AB*), draw two arcs, one on each side of *AB*.

(ii) Taking *B* as centre and same radius as in step (i), draw two more arcs, one on each side of *AB* intersecting the previous arcs at *P* and *Q* respectively.

(iii) Join *PQ* which intersects *AB* at *M*. Then the line *PQ* is the required perpendicular bisector of line segment *AB*.

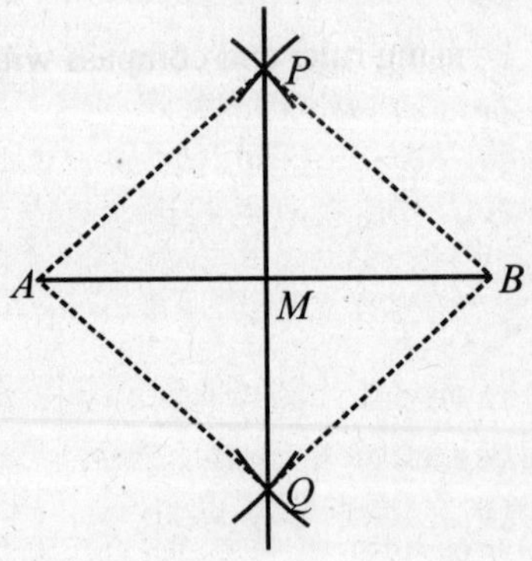

Justification :

Join *AP*, *BP*, *AQ* and *BQ*.

In ΔAPQ and ΔBPQ

$AP = BP$ (arcs of equal radii)

$AQ = BQ$ (arcs of equal radii)

$PQ = PQ$ (common)

$\therefore$ $\Delta APQ \cong \Delta BPQ$ (by SSS rule of congruency)

$\therefore$ $\angle APM = \angle BPM$ (C.P.C.T.)

In ΔAMP and ΔBMP

$AP = BP$ (arcs of equal radii)

$MP = MP$ (common)

$\angle APM = \angle BPM$ (proved above)

$\therefore$ $\Delta AMP \cong \Delta BMP$ (by SAS rule of congruency)

$\therefore$ $AM = BM$ (C.P.C.T.)

And $\angle AMP = \angle BMP$ (C.P.C.T.)

Now $\angle AMP + \angle BMP = 180°$ (linear pair)

$2\angle AMP = 180°$

$\Rightarrow \angle AMP = 90°$

$\Rightarrow MP \perp AM \Rightarrow PQ \perp AB.$

Therefore, the line PQ is the perpendicular bisector of the line segment AB.

TO CONSTRUCT AN ANGLE OF 60° AT THE INITIAL POINT OF A GIVEN RAY

Given a ray AB, we want to construct another ray AC such that $\angle CAB = 60°$.

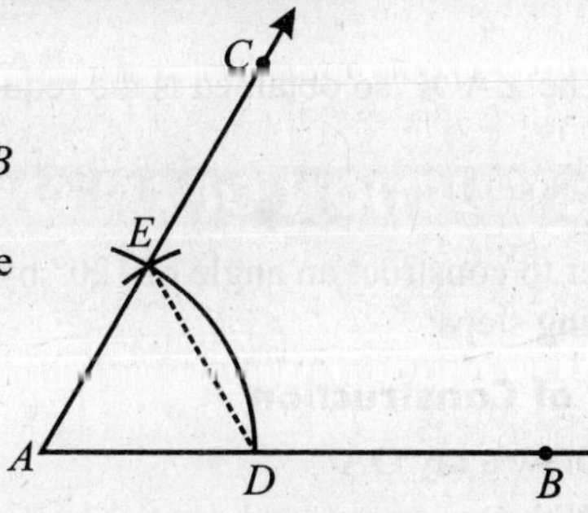

Steps of Construction

(i) Taking A as centre and any suitable radius, draw an arc to intersect the ray AB at D.

(ii) Taking D as centre and same radius as in step (i), draw another arc to intersect the previous arc at E.

(iii) Join AE and produce it to obtain ray AC. Then $\angle CAB$ so obtained is the angle of measure 60°.

Justification :

Join DE.

Then $AD = AE = DE$

$\therefore$ ΔADE is equilateral $\Rightarrow \angle EAD = 60°$

$\therefore$ $\angle CAB = 60°$

CONSTRUCTION OF AN ANGLE OF 30°

In order to construct an angle of 30° with the help of ruler and compasses, we follow the following steps:

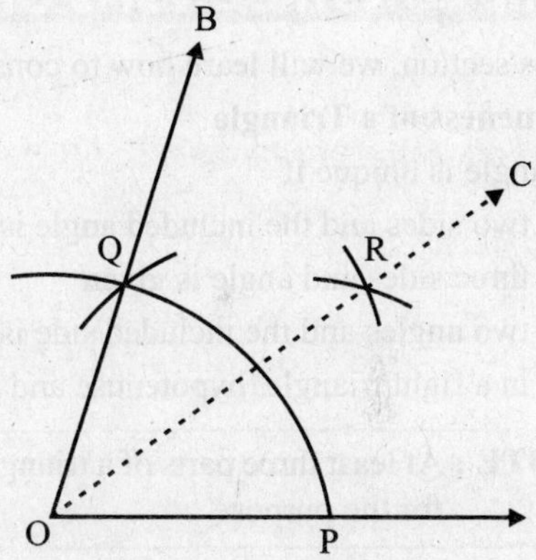

Steps of Construction

(i) Draw ∠AOB = 60° by using the steps mentioned above.

(ii) With centre O and any convenient radius draw an arc cutting OA and OB at P and Q respectively.

(iii) With centre P and radius more than $\frac{1}{2}$ (PQ), draw an arc in the interior of ∠AOB.

(iv) With centre Q and the same radius, as in step (iii(, draw another arc intersecting the arc in step (iii) at R.

(v) Join OR and produce it to any point C.

(vi) The ∠AOC is the angle of measure 30°.

CONSTRUCTION OF AN ANGLE OF 90°

In order to construct an angle of measure 90°, we follow the following steps :

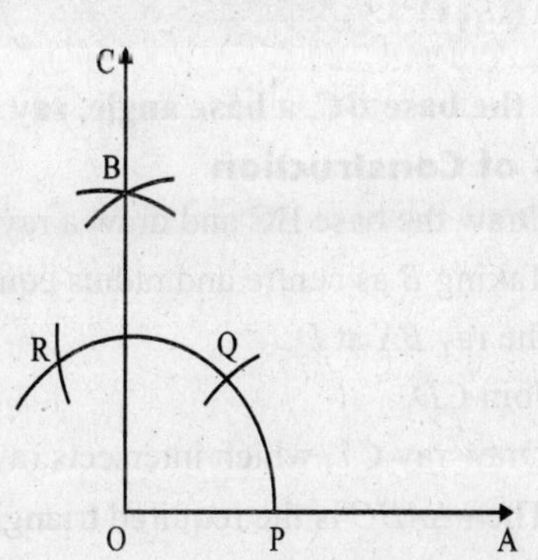

Steps of Construction

(i) Draw a ray OA.

(ii) With O as centre and any convenient radius, draw an arc, cutting OA at P.

(iii) With P as centre and the same radius, draw an arc cutting the arc drawn in step (ii) at Q.

(iv) With Q as centre and the same radius as in steps (ii) and (iii), draw an arc, cutting the arc drawn in step (iii) at R.

(v) With Q as centre and the same radius, drawn an arc, cutting the arc drawn in step v at B.

(vi) With R as centre and the same radius, drawn an arc, cutting the arc drawn in step v at B.

(vii) Draw OB and produce it to C. ∠AOC is the angle of measure 90°.

CONSTRUCTION OF AN ANGLE OF 45°

In order to construct an angle of 45°, we follow the following steps :

Steps of Construction

(i) Draw ∠AOB = 90° by following the steps given above.

(ii) Draw OC, the bisector of ∠AOB.

The ∠AOC so obtained is the required angle of measure 45°.

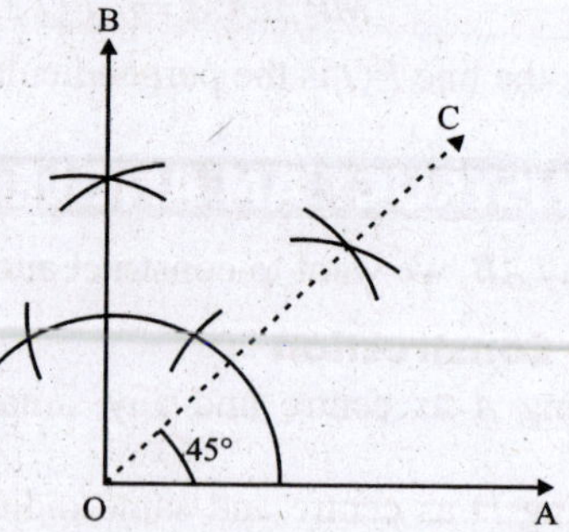

CONSTRUCTION OF AN ANGLE OF 120°

In order to construct an angle of 120° by using ruler and compasses only, we follow the following steps:

Steps of Construction

(i) Draw a ray OA

(ii) With O as centre and any convenient radius, draw an arc cutting OA at P.

(iii) With P as centre and the same radius draw an arc, cutting the first arc at Q.

(iv) With Q as centre and the same radius, draw an arc, cutting the arc drawn in step II at R.

(v) Join OR and produce it to any point C.

∠AOC so obtained is the angle of measure 120°

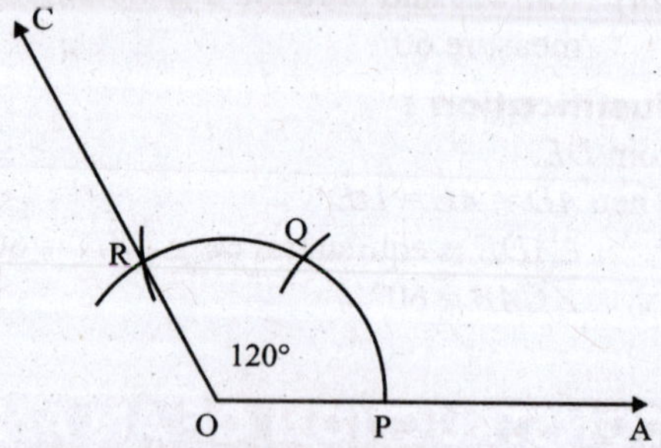

SOME CONSTRUCTIONS OF TRIANGLES

In this section, we will learn how to construct triangles by using the constructions discussed in earlier classes.

Uniqueness of a Triangle

A triangle is unique if

(i) two sides and the included angle is given

(ii) three sides and angle is given

(iii) two angles and the included side is given and,

(iv) in a right triangle, hypotenuse and one side is given.

NOTE : At least three parts of a triangle have to be given for constructing it but not all combinations of three parts are sufficient for the purpose.

TO CONSTRUCT A TRIANGLE GIVEN ITS BASE, A BASE ANGLE AND SUM OF OTHER TWO SIDES

Given the base *BC*, a base angle, say ∠*B* and the sum (*AB* + *AC*). We want to construct Δ*ABC*.

Steps of Construction

(i) Draw the base BC and draw a ray *BX* such that ∠*CBX* equal to given angle.

(ii) Taking *B* as centre and radius equal to (*AB* + *AC*), draw an arc intersecting the ray *BX* at *D*.

(iii) Join *CD*.

(iv) Draw ray *CY*, which intersects ray *AX* at *A* such that ∠*ACD* = ∠*ADC*

Then Δ*ABC* is the required triangle

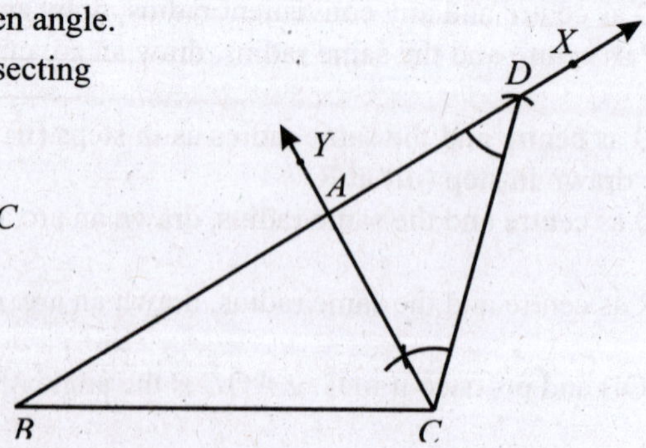

Justification

Base *BC* and ∠*B* are drawn as given

Now in Δ*ACD*,

∠*ACD* = ∠*ADC* (By construction)

$\therefore \quad AC = AD$ (Sides opposite to equal angles in a triangle are equal)

Now $AB = BD - AD$

$= BD - AC$

$\Rightarrow \quad AB + AC = BD$

Alternative Method of Construction

Follow the first three steps of construction given above.

Then draw perpendicular bisector PQ of CD to intersect BD at a point A.

Join AC. Then ΔABC is the required triangle.

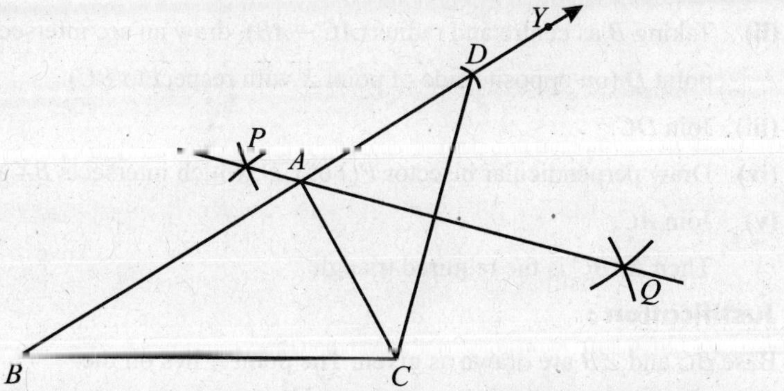

Justification :

Since A lies on the perpendicular bisector of CD,

Therefore $AC = AD$.

$\Rightarrow \quad AB + AC = BD$

NOTE: The construction of any triangle is not possible if sum of its any two sides is equal or less than the third remaining side.

ILLUSTRATION : 1

Construct ΔABC such that $BC = 3.5$ cm, $AB + AC = 5.2$ cm and $\angle B = 60°$.

SOLUTION :

Steps of Construction

(i) Draw $BC = 3.5$cm

(ii) At B, construct $\angle CBP = 60°$

(iii) From ray BP, cut off $BD = 5.2$cm

(iv) Join CD and draw its perpendicular bisector to intersect BD at A.

(v) Join AC. Then, ABC is the required triangle.

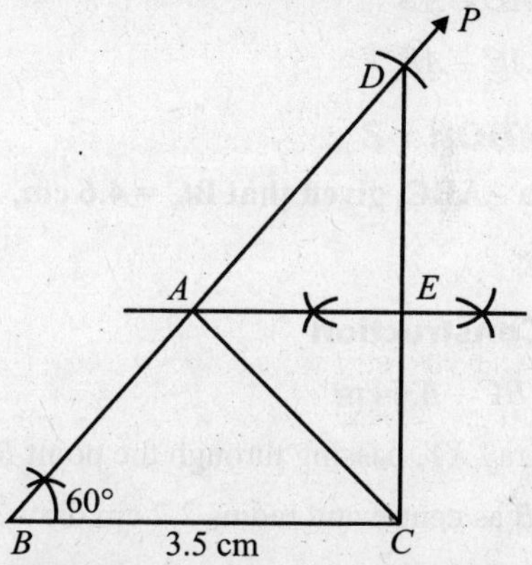

TO CONSTRUCT A TRIANGLE GIVEN ITS BASE, A BASE ANGLE AND THE DIFFERENCE OF THE OTHER TWO SIDES

Given the base BC, a base angle, say $\angle B$ and the difference of other two sides $AB - AC$ or $AC - AB$, we want to construct the ΔABC.

Case-I : ***Let $AB > AC$ that is $AB - AC$ is given.***

Steps of Construction

(i) Draw the base BC and a ray BX such that $\angle CBX$ equal to the given angle.

(ii) Taking B as centre and radius equal to $(AB - AC)$, draw an arc intersecting the ray BX at point D.

(iii) Join DC

(iv) Draw the perpendicular bisector PQ of line segment CD, which intersects the ray BX at A.

(v) Join AC.

Then ΔABC is the required triangle.

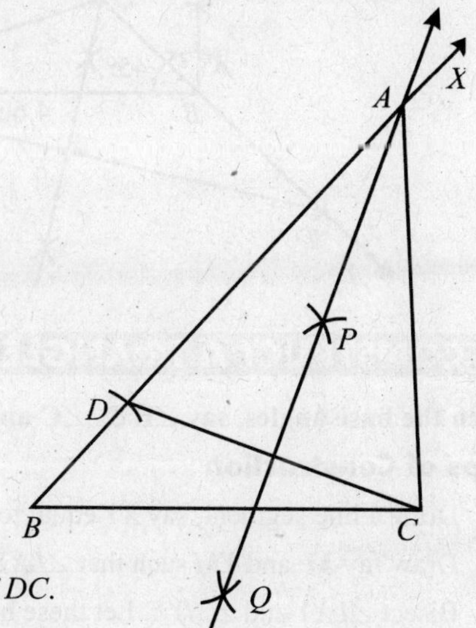

Justification :

Base BC and $\angle CBX$ are drawn as given. The point A lies on the perpendicular bisector of DC.

$\therefore \quad AC = AD$

Now $BD = AB - AD$

$\Rightarrow \quad BD = AB - AC$ $[\because AC = AD]$

Case-II : *Let AB < AC that is AC – AB is given.*

Steps of Construction

(i) Draw base BC and a line XY passing through the point B as shown in the figure. such that $\angle CBX$ is equal to the given angle.

(ii) Taking B as centre and radius $(AC - AB)$, draw an arc intersecting the ray BY at point D (on opposite side of point X with respect to BC).

(iii) Join DC.

(iv) Draw perpendicular bisector PQ of CD, which intersects BX at A.

(v) Join AC.

Then ΔABC is the required triangle.

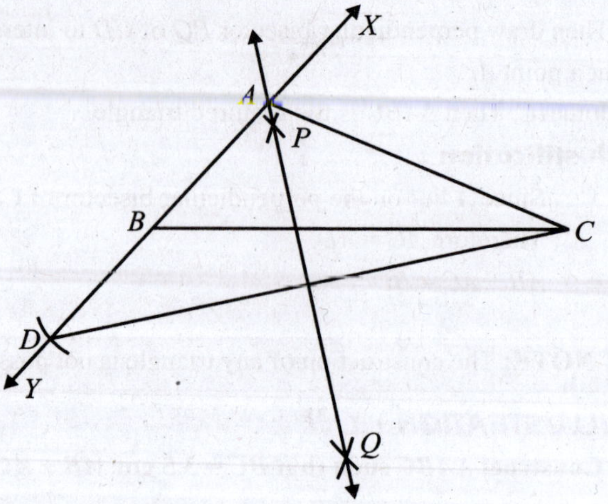

Justification :

Base BC and $\angle B$ are drawn as given. The point A lies on the perpendicular bisector of CD.

$\therefore \quad AC = AD$

Now $BD = AD - AB$

$\Rightarrow \quad BD = AC - AB$

ILLUSTRATION : 2

Construct a ΔABC, given that BC = 4.6 cm, AC – AB = 2.2 cm and ∠B = 45°

SOLUTION :

Steps of Construction

(i) Draw $BC = 4.6$ cm.

(ii) Draw ray XY, passing through the point B as shown, such that $\angle CBX = 45°$

(iii) With B as centre and radius 2.2 cm draw an arc to intersect ray BY at D.

(iv) Join DC and draw its perpendicular bisector to intersect ray BX at A.

(v) Join CA. Then, ABC is the required triangle.

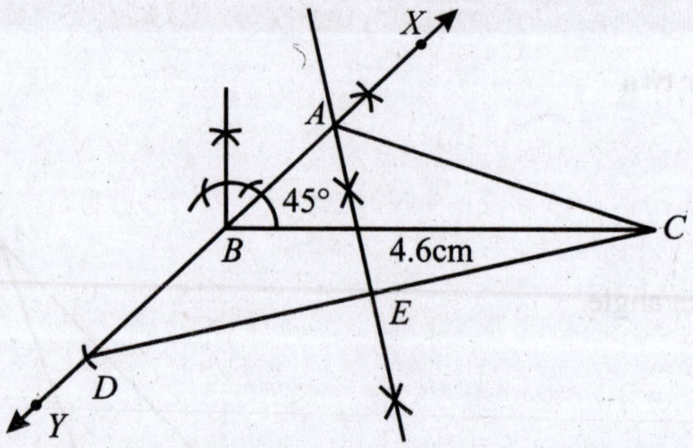

TO CONSTRUCT A TRIANGLE, GIVEN ITS PERIMETER AND ITS TWO BASE ANGLES

Given the base angles, say ∠B & ∠C and AB + BC + CA, we want to construct the triangle ABC.

Steps of Construction

(i) Draw a line segment, say XY equal to $AB + BC + CA$.

(ii) Draw ray XL and YM such that $\angle LXY$ equal to $\angle B$ and $\angle MYX$ equal to $\angle C$.

(iii) Bisect $\angle LXY$ and $\angle MYX$. Let these bisectors intersect at a point A.

(iv) Draw perpendicular bisectors PQ of AX and RS of AY.

(v) Let PQ intersect XY at B and RS intersect XY at C. Join AB and AC.

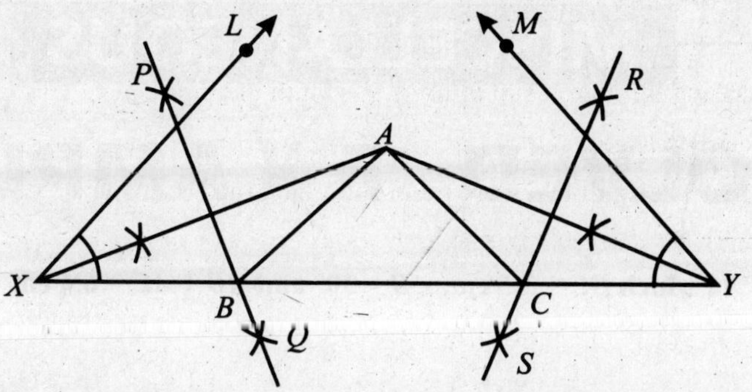

Then ABC is the required triangle.

Justification :

B lies on the perpendicular bisector PQ of AX.

Therefore, $XB = AB$ and similarly, $CY = AC$.

This gives $BC + CA + AB = BC + XB + CY = XY$.

Again $\angle BAX = \angle AXB$ (As in $\Delta\, AXB$, $AB = XB$) and $\angle ABC = \angle BAX + \angle AXB = 2\, \angle AXB = \angle LXY$

Similarly, $\angle ACB = \angle MYX$ as required.

ILLUSTRATION : 3

Construct a ΔABC such that $\angle B = 60°$, $\angle C = 45°$ and its perimeter = 11.5 cm. Justify your construction.

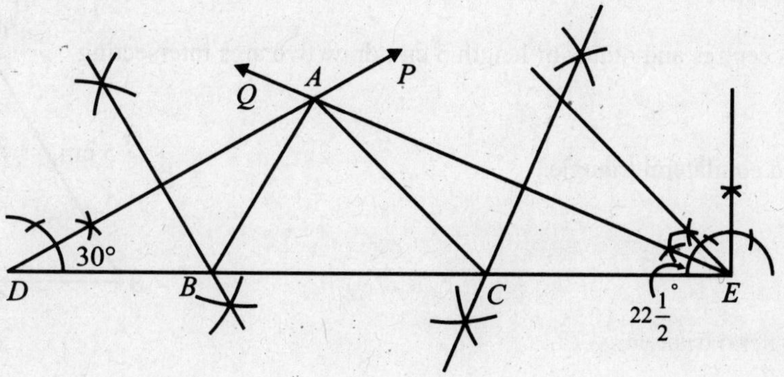

SOLUTION :

Steps of Construction

(i) Draw $DE = 11.5$ cm

(ii) At D, construct $\angle EDP = ½$ of $60° = 30°$ and at E, construct $\angle DEQ = ½$ of $45° = 22½°$.

(iii) Let rays DP and EQ meet at A.

(iv) Draw perpendicular bisector of AD which meets DE at B.

(v) Draw perpendicular bisector of AE which meets DE at C.

(vi) Join AB and AC. Then, ABC is the required triangle.

MISCELLANEOUS SOLVED EXAMPLES

1. Construct a triangle ABC, in which $BC = 3.5$ cm, $\angle B = 30°$ and $AB + AC = 6.4$ cm

Sol. Steps of Construction :

(i) Draw $BC = 3.5$ cm.

(ii) Draw $\angle CBX = 30°$

(iii) From ray BX, cut-off line segment BD equal to $AB + AC$ i.e. 6.4 cm.

(iv) Join CD.

(v) Draw the perpendicular bisector of CD meeting BD at A.

(vi) Join CA to obtain the required triangle ABC.

Hence, ΔABC is the required triangle.

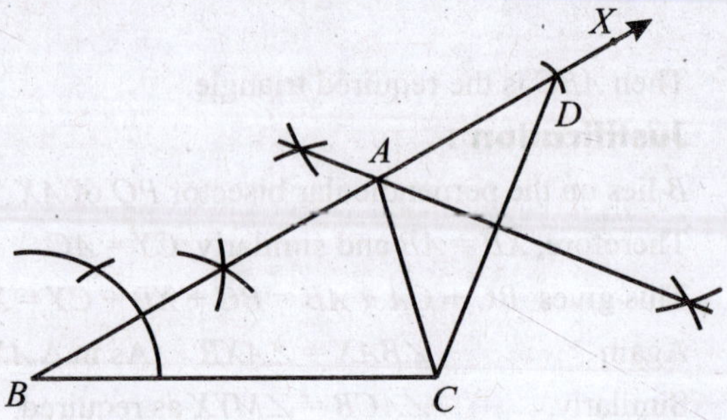

2. Construct an equilateral triangle, given its side 5 cm and justify the construction.

Sol. Steps of Construction :

(i) Draw $BC = 5$ cm

(ii) Taking B and C as centres and radius of length 5 cm, draw two arcs intersecting each other at A.

(iii) Join AB and AC

$\therefore$ ΔABC is the required equilateral triangle.

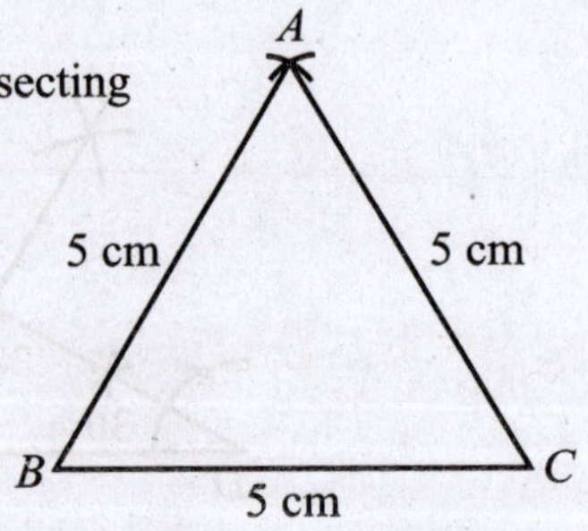

Justification :

Since the three sides

$AB = BC = CA = 5$ cm

Thus ΔABC is an equilateral triangle.

3. Construct a right triangle when one side is 3.5 cm and the sum of the other side and hypotenuse is 5.5. cm.

Sol. Steps of Construction :

(i) Draw BC of length 3.5 cm.

(ii) At B, construct $\angle CBX = 90°$

(iii) From BX, cut off BM of length 5.5 cm.

(iv) Join C to M

(v) Draw perpendicular bisector of CM, let the bisector meet BM at A.

(vi) Join A to C.

Thus ΔABC is the required right triangle.

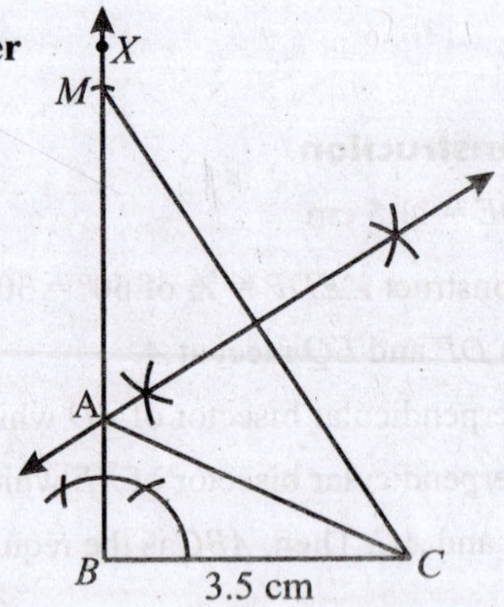

4. Construct a right triangle with perimeter 13 cm and one angle of 30°.

Sol. Steps of Construction :

(i) Draw XY of length 13 cm.

(ii) Draw $\angle PXY = 30°$ and $\angle XYQ = 90°$

(iii) Draw bisectors of $\angle PXY$ and $\angle XYQ$ meeting each other at A.

(iv) Draw right bisectors of AX and AY which meets XY at B and C respectively.

(v) Join AB and AC.

$\therefore$ ΔABC is the required triangle.

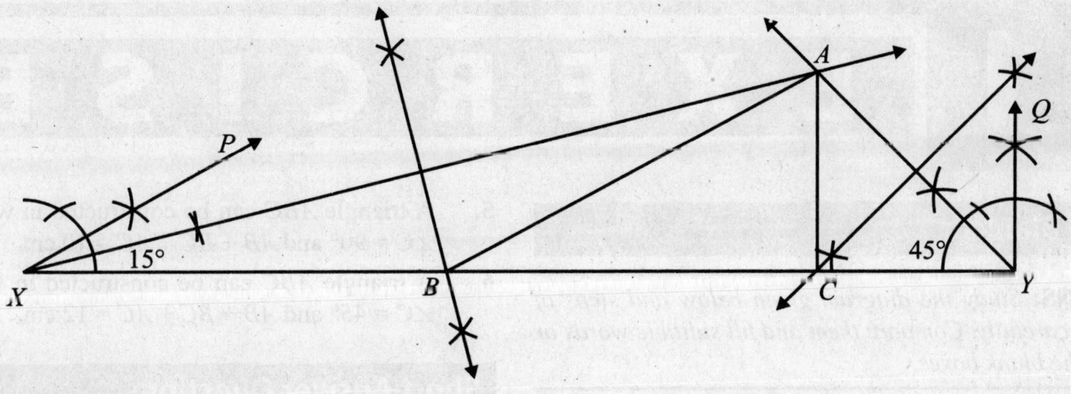

5. **Construct an equilateral triangle with perimeter 16 cm.**

Sol. Steps of Construction :

(i) Draw XY of length 16 cm.

(ii) Draw $\angle PXY = 60°$ and $\angle XYQ = 60°$

(iii) Draw bisectors of $\angle PXY$ and $\angle XYQ$ meeting each other at A.

(iv) Draw right bisectors of AX and AY meeting XY at B and C respectively.

(v) Join AB and AC

$\therefore$ ΔABC is the required equilateral triangle.

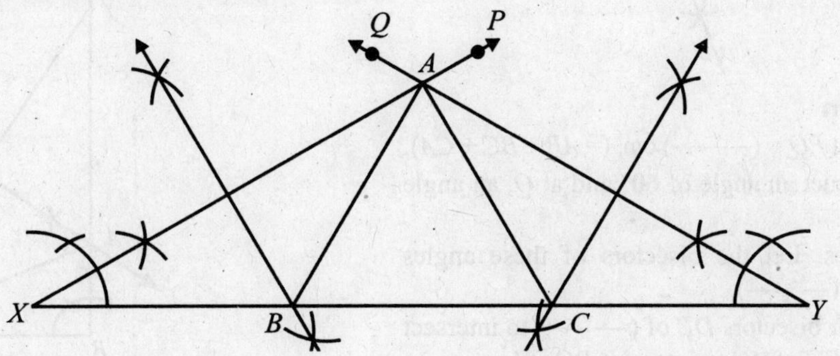

1 EXERCISE

Fill in the Blanks :

DIRECTIONS: *Study the diagram given below and steps of construction carefully. Compare them and fill suitable words or numbers in the blank boxes.*

Construction of a triangle ABC in which $\angle B = 60°$, $\angle C = 45°$ and perimeter = 11 cm.

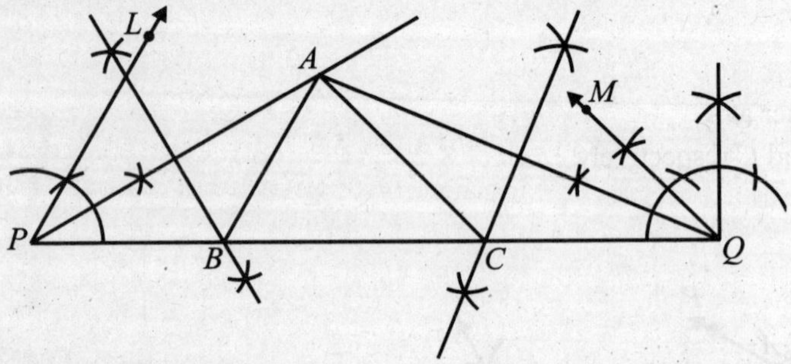

Steps of Construction

1. Draw a line seqment PQ = (———) cm. (= $AB + BC + CA$).
2. At (———) construct an angle of 60° and at Q, an angle of (———).
3. Bisect these angles. Let the bisectors of these angles intersect at a point (———).
4. Draw perpendicular bisectors DE of (———) to intersect (———) at B and FG of AQ to intersect PQ at (———).
5. Join (———) and (———). Thus, (———) is the required triangle.

True / False :

DIRECTIONS: *Read the following statements and write your answer as true or false.*

1. An angle of 52.5° can be constructed.
2. An angle of 42.5° can be constructed.
3. A triangle ABC can be constructed in which AB = 5 cm, $\angle A = 45°$ and $BC + AC$ = 5 cm.
4. A triangle ABC can be constructed in which BC = 6 cm, $\angle C = 30°$ and $AC - AB$ = 4 cm.
5. A triangle ABC can be constructed in which $\angle B = 105°$, $\angle C = 90°$ and $AB + BC + AC$ = 10 cm.
6. A triangle ABC can be constructed in which $\angle B = 60°$, $\angle C = 45°$ and $AB + BC + AC$ = 12 cm.

Short Answer Questions :

DIRECTIONS: *Give answer in 2-3 sentences.*

1. Construct ΔABC where BC = 4.5 cm, AB = 3.5 cm and $\angle B = 45°$.
2. Construct a right triangle whose base is 12 cm and sum of its hypotenuse and other side is 18 cm.

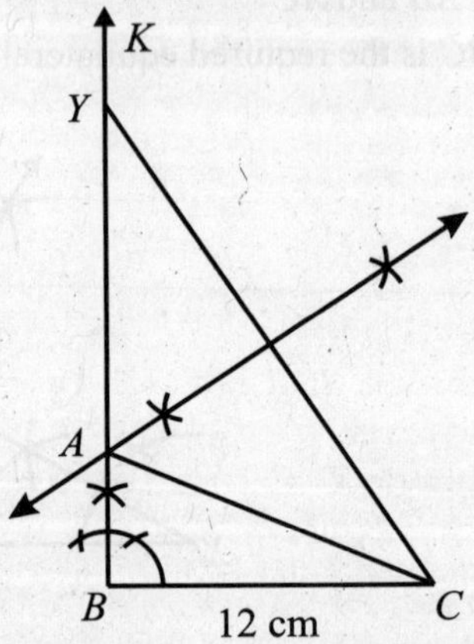

Long Answer Questions :

DIRECTIONS: *Give answer in four to five sentences.*

1. Construct a perpendicular bisector of a line segment of length 6 cm. Write the steps of construction and also justify your construction.
2. Construct a triangle ABC where base BC = 6 cm, $\angle ABC$ = 60° and $AB + AC$ = 7 cm. Justify your construction.
3. Construct a triangle ABC in which AB = 5.8 cm, $BC + CA$ = 8.4 cm and $\angle B = 60°$. Justify your construction.

2 EXERCISE

Text-Book Exercise :

1. Construct an angle of 90° at the initial point of a given ray and justify your construction.
2. Construct the angles of the following measurements:
   (a) 30°
   (b) 22 ½°
   (c) 15°
3. Construct an angle of 45° at the initial point of a given ray and justify the construction.
4. Construct the following angles and verify by measuring them by a protractor.
   (a) 75°
   (b) 105°
   (c) 135°
5. Construct an equilateral triangle, given its side and justify the construction.
6. Construct a triangle ABC in which BC = 7 cm, ∠B = 75° and AB + AC = 13 cm.
7. Construct a triangle ABC in which BC = 8 cm, ∠B = 45° and AB – AC = 3.5 cm.
8. Construct a triangle PQR in which QR = 6 cm, ∠Q = 60° and PR – PQ = 2 cm.
9. Construct a triangle XYZ in which ∠Y = 30°, ∠Z = 90° and XY + YZ + ZX = 11 cm.
10. Construct a right triangle whose base is 12 cm and sum of its hypotenuse and other side is 18 cm.

Exemplar Questions :

1. With the help of a ruler and a compass, it is possible to construct an angle of:
   (a) 35°
   (b) 40°
   (c) 37.5°
   (d) 47.5°.
2. The construction of a triangle ABC in which AB = 4 cm, ∠A = 60° is not possible when difference of BC and AC is equal to:
   (a) 3.5 om
   (b) 4.5 cm
   (c) 3 cm
   (d) 2.5 cm
3. With the help of a ruler and a compass it is not possible to construct an angle of:
   (a) 37.5°
   (b) 40°
   (c) 22.5°
   (d) 67.5°
4. The construction of a triangle ABC, given that BC = 6cm, ∠B = 45° is not possible when difference of AB and AC is equal to:
   (a) 6.9 cm
   (b) 5.2 cm
   (c) 5.0 cm
   (d) 4.0 cm
5. The construction of a triangle ABC, given that BC = 3 cm, ∠C = 60° is possible when difference of AB and AC is equal to:
   (a) 3.2 cm
   (b) 3.1 cm
   (c) 3 cm
   (d) 2.8 cm
6. Construct an equilateral triangle if its altitude is 6 cm. Give justification for your construction.

HOTS Questions :

1. Construct a triangle, whose perimeter is 12 cm and the ratio between its sides are 3 : 4 : 5.
2. Construct a ΔABC in which BC = 5.6 cm, AC – AB = 1.6 cm and ∠B = 45°. Justify your construction.
3. Construct a right triangle in which one side is 3.5 cm and sum of the other side and hypotenuse is 5.5 cm.

3 EXERCISE

Single Option Correct :

1. To construct a right triangle whose base is 12 cm and sum of its hypotenuse and other side is 18 cm. We draw line segment AB of 12 cm. Draw a ray AX making 90° with AB. The next step is :
   (a) Cut a line segment AD of 18 cm on AX
   (b) Cut a line segment BD of 18 cm
   (c) Cut a line segment AD of 18 cm on AB
   (d) Cut a line segment BD of 18 cm on AB
2. By following these steps of construction, (i) Draw a line segment PQ = 11 cm (ii) At P construct an angle of 60° and at Q, an angle of 45°. (iii) Bisect these angles. Let the bisectors of these angles intersect at a point A. (iv) Draw perpendicular bisectors DE of AP to intersect PQ at B and FG of AQ to intersect PQ at C. (v). Join AB and AC. Triangle ABC has been obtained. In this ΔABC,
   (a) $AB + BC + CA = 11$ cm (b) $AB + BC = 11$ cm
   (c) $BC + CA = 11$ cm (d) $AB + BC + CA > 11$ cm
3. In the construction of the bisector of a given angle, as shown in the figure below.

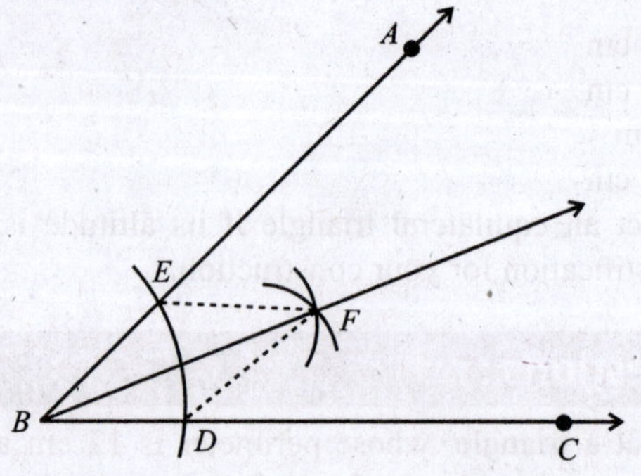

   $\Delta BEF \cong \Delta BDF$ by which congruence criterion?
   (a) SSS (b) SAS
   (c) AAS (d) RHS
4. In the construction of the perpendicular bisector of a given line segment, as shown in the figure below

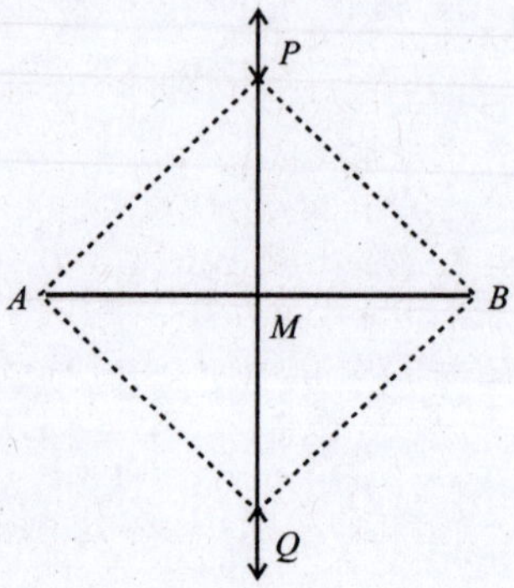

   $\Delta PMA \cong \Delta PMB$ by which congruence criterion?
   (a) SSS (b) SAS
   (c) AAS (d) RHS
5. On a ray AB with initial point A, taking A as centre and some radius, draw an arc of a circle, which intersects AB, say at a point D. Taking D as centre and with the same radius as before, draw an arc intersecting the previously drawn arc, say at a point E. Draw the ray AC passing through E. Then, the measure of $\angle CAB$ is
   (a) 45° (b) 30°
   (c) 15° (d) 60°
6. A triangle can be constructed when the lengths of its three sides are
   (a) 7 cm, 3 cm, 4 cm (b) 3.6 cm, 11.5 cm, 6.9 cm
   (c) 5.2 cm, 7.6 cm, 4.7 cm (d) 33 mm, 8.5 cm, 49 mm
7. A unique triangle cannot be constructed if its
   (a) three angles are given
   (b) two angles and one side is given
   (c) three sides are given
   (d) two sides and the included angle is given
8. If the lengths of two sides of an isosceles triangle are 4 cm and 10 cm, then the length of the third side is
   (a) 4 cm (b) 10 cm
   (c) 7 cm (d) 14 cm
9. The construction of a triangle ABC, given that BC = 6 cm, $\angle B = 45°$ is not possible when difference of AB and AC is equal to:
   (a) 6.9 cm (b) 5.2 cm
   (c) 5.0 cm (d) 4.0 cm
10. The construction of a triangle ABC, given that BC = 3cm, $\angle C = 60°$ is possible when difference of AB and AC is equal to:
   (a) 3.2 cm (b) 3.1 cm
   (c) 3 cm (d) 2.8 cm

SOLUTIONS

Brief Explanations of Selected Questions

1 EXERCISE

FILL IN THE BLANKS :

1. 11
2. P, 45°
3. A
4. AP, PQ, C
5. AB, AC, ABC

TRUE/FALSE :

1. True. As $52.5° = \frac{210°}{4}$ and 210° = 180° + 30° which can be constructed.
2. False. As 42.5° = ½ × 85° and 85° cannot be constructed.
3. False. As BC + AC must be greater than AB which is not so.
4. True. As AC – AB < BC, i.e., AC < AB + BC.
5. False. As ∠B + ∠C = 105° + 90° = 195° > 180°
6. True. As ∠B + ∠C = 60° + 45° = 105° < 180°

SHORT ANSWER QUESTIONS :

1. **Steps of Construction :**

(i) Draw *BC* = 4.5 cm.

(ii) At the point *B*, draw ray *BX*, such that ∠*CBX* = 90°

(iii) Draw the bisector BD of ∠*CBX*.

(iv) With *B* as centre and taking a radius of 3.5 cm, draw an arc, intersecting *BD* at A.

(v) Join *BA* and *AC*.

ABC is the required triangle.

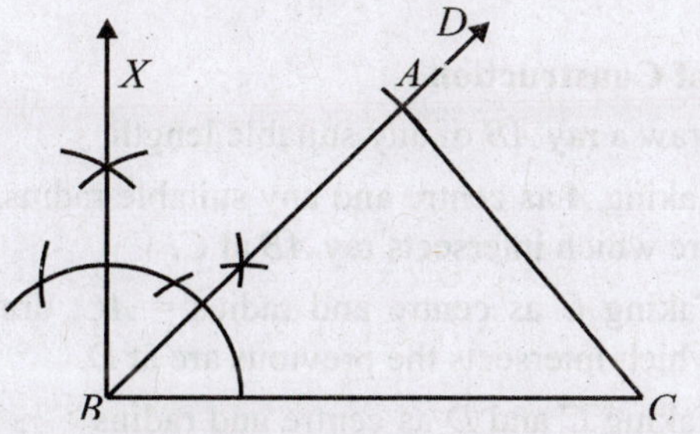

2. **Steps of Construction :**

(i) Draw *BC* of length 12 cm.

(ii) At *B*, draw ∠*CBK* = 90°

(iii) Along *BK*, cut off *BY* of length 18 cm. Join *C* to *Y*.

(iv) Draw the right bisectors of *CY*, which meet *BY* at *A*.

(v) Join *A* and *C*.

Δ*ABC* is the required triangle.

LONG ANSWER QUESTIONS :

1. **Steps of Construction :**

(i) Draw a line segment *AB* of length 6 cm.

(ii) Taking *A* and *B* as centres and radius more than ½*AB*, draw arcs on both sides of the line segment *AB* (to intersect each other).

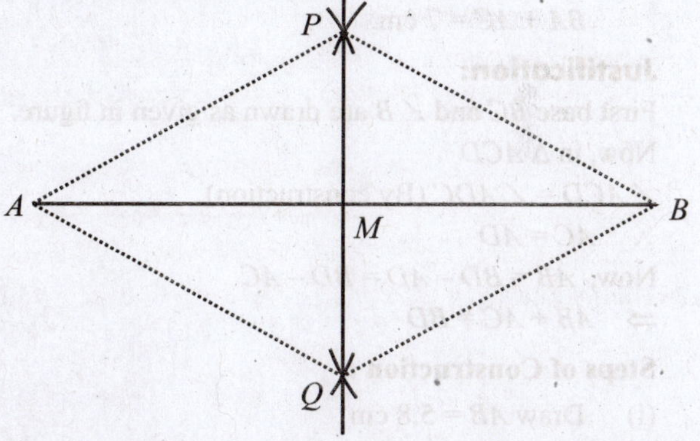

(iii) Let these arcs intersect each other at *P* and *Q*. Join *PQ*.

(iv) Let *PQ* intersect *AB* at the point *M*. Then line *PMQ* is the required perpendicular bisector of *AB*.

Justification:

Join *A* and *B* to both *P* and *Q* to form *AP*, *AQ*, *BP* and *BQ*.

In triangles *PAQ* and *PBQ*,

AP = *BP* (Arcs of equal radii)

AQ = *BQ* (Arcs of equal radii)

PQ = *PQ* (common)

Therefore, Δ*APQ* ≅ Δ*BPQ* (SSS rule)

So, ∠*APQ* = ∠*BPQ*

or ∠*APM* = ∠*BPM* (C.P.C.T.)

Now in triangles *PMA* and *PMB*,

AP = *BP* (As before)

PM = *PM* (Common)

∠*APM* = ∠*BPM* (Proved above)

Therefore, Δ*PMA* ≅ Δ*PMB* (SAS rule)

So, *AM* = *BM* and ∠*AMP* = ∠*BMP* (C.P.C.T.)

As ∠*AMP* + ∠*BMP* = 180° (Linear pair axiom)

we get ∠*AMP* + ∠*AMP* = 180°

⇒ ∠*AMP* = 90°

Therefore, *PM*, that is *PMQ* is the perpendicular bisector of *AB*.

2. **Steps of Construction :**

(i) Draw the base $BC = 6$ cm.

(ii) Using ruler and compass, draw an angle YBC of 60° at B.

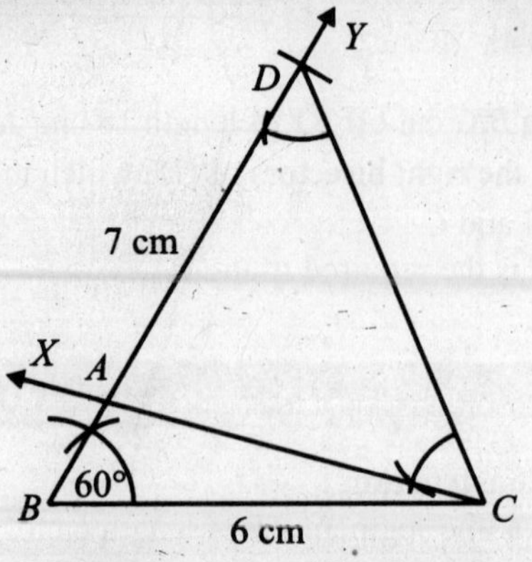

(iii) Cut BD equal to $BA + AC = 7$ cm from the ray BY.

(iv) Join DC and make an angle DCX equal to BDC.

(v) Let CX intersect BY at A.

(vi) Thus ABC is the required triangle where $BA + AC = 7$ cm.

Justification:

First base BC and $\angle B$ are drawn as given in figure.

Now, in ΔACD

$\angle ACD = \angle ADC$ (By construction)

$\therefore \quad AC = AD$

Now, $AB = BD - AD = BD - AC$

$\Rightarrow \quad AB + AC = BD$

3. **Steps of Construction :**

(i) Draw $AB = 5.8$ cm

(ii) Draw $\angle ABX = 60°$

(iii) From ray BX, cut off line segment $BD = BC + CA = 8.4$ cm.

(iv) Join AD

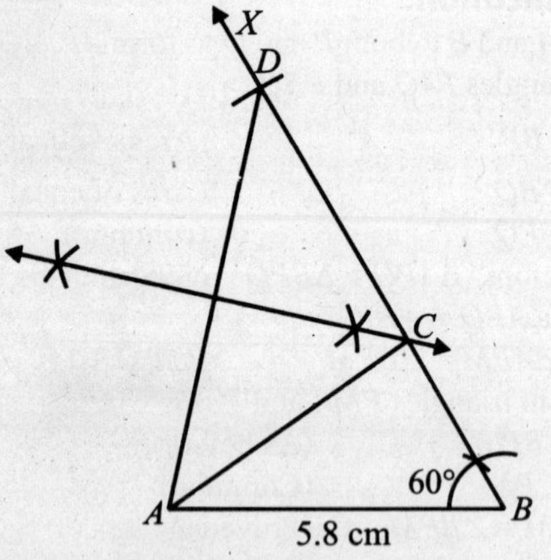

(v) Draw the perpendicular bisector of AD meeting BD at C.

(vi) Join AC to obtain the required triangle ABC.

Justification:

Clearly, C lies on the perpendicular bisector of AD.

$\therefore \quad CA = CD$

Now, $BD = 8.4$ cm

$\Rightarrow \quad BC + CD = 8.4$ cm

$\Rightarrow \quad BC + CA = 8.4$ cm

Hence, ΔABC is the required triangle.

2 EXERCISE

TEXT-BOOK EXERCISE :

1. **Steps of Construction :**

(i) Draw a ray AB.

(ii) Taking A as centre and any convenient radius, draw an arc as shown intersecting AB at C.

(iii) Taking C as centre and radius = AC, draw an arc intersecting the arc drawn in step (ii) at D.

(iv) Again taking D as centre and same radius = AC, draw an arc intersecting the first arc at E.

(v) Again taking D and E as centres and radius > ½ DE, draw two arcs intersecting each other at K.

(vi) Join AK.

(vii) $\angle BAK = 90°$

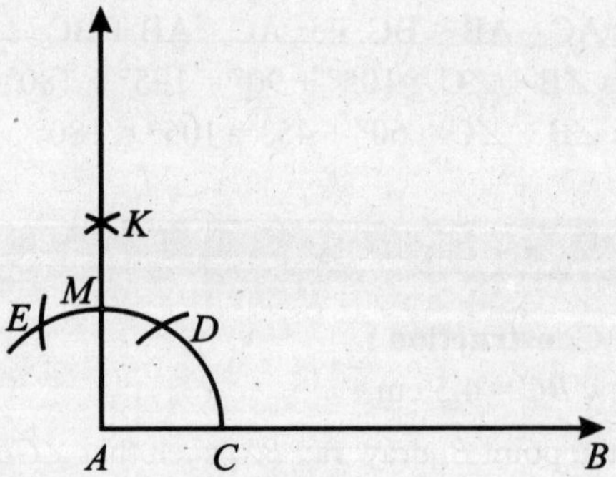

Justification :

Clearly arc CD makes an angle of 60° at A and arc DE also makes an angle of 60° at A. Since M is the mid-point of ED.

$\therefore \quad MD$ makes an angle of 30° at A.

Hence, $\angle BAK = 90°$.

2.

(a) Steps of Construction :

(i) Draw a ray AB of any suitable length.

(ii) Taking A as centre and any suitable radius, draw an arc which intersects ray AB at C.

(iii) Taking C as centre and radius = AC, draw an arc which intersects the previous arc at D.

(iv) Taking C and D as centre and radius > ½ CD draw two arcs intersecting each other at K.

Now $\angle BAK = 30°$

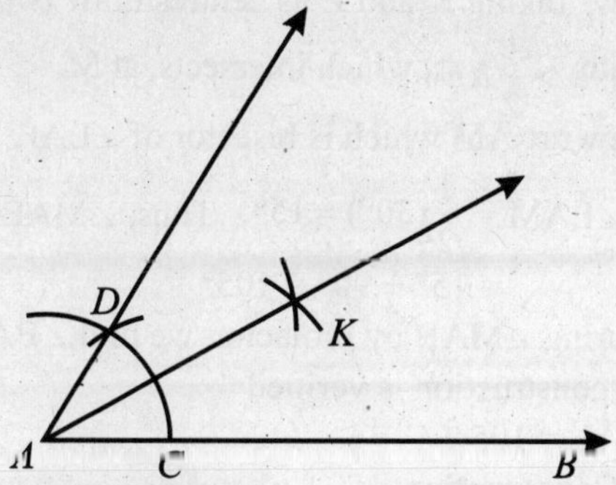

(b) Steps of Construction :

(i) Draw a ray *AB*.

(ii) Taking *A* as centre and with any suitable radius draw an arc intersecting *AB* at *C*.

(iii) Taking *C* as centre and radius = *AC*, draw an arc such that it intersects the previous arc at *D*.
Now $\angle BAD = 60°$

(iv) Taking *C* and *D* as centres and radius > ½ *CD* draw two arcs intersecting each other at P. Join AP, which intersects the arc *CD* at *E*.
Now $\angle BAP = 30°$

(v) Taking *D* and *E* as centres and radius > ½ *ED* draw two arcs intersecting each other at *Q*. Join *AQ*, which intersects arc *CD* at *F*.

(vi) Taking *C* and *F* as centres and radius > ½ *CF* draw two arcs intersecting each other at *R*. Join *AR*.
Now $\angle BAR = 22½°$.

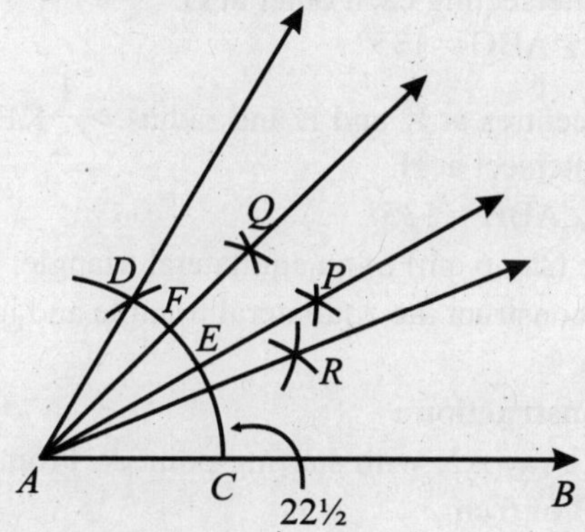

(c) Steps of Construction :

(i) Draw a ray *AB*.

(ii) Taking *A* as centre and with any convenient radius draw an arc intersecting ray *AB* at *C*.

(iii) Taking *C* as centre and radius = *AC*, draw an arc such that it intersects the previous arc at *D*.
Now $\angle BAD = 60°$

(iv) Taking *C* and *D* as centres and radius > ½ *CD* draw two arcs intersecting each other at *P*. Join AP, which intersects the arc *CD* at *E*.

Now, $\angle BAP = 30°$

(v) With *C* and *E* as centres and radius > ½ *CE* draw two arcs intersecting each other at *Q*. Join *AQ*.
Now, $\angle BAQ = 15°$

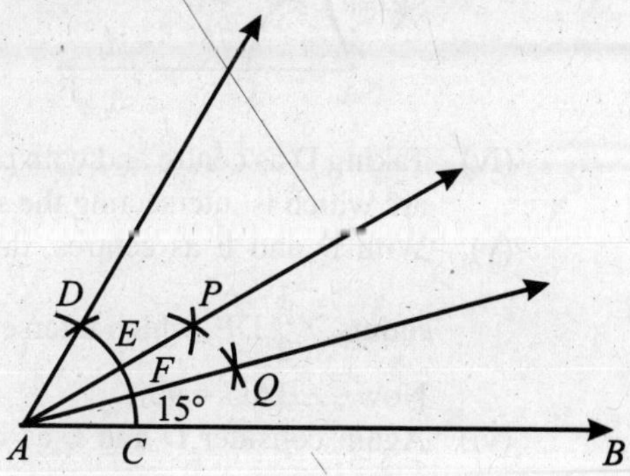

3. Steps of Construction :

(i) First we draw a line BA

(ii) Take B as centre and any radius we draw an arc which is intersecting AB at C.

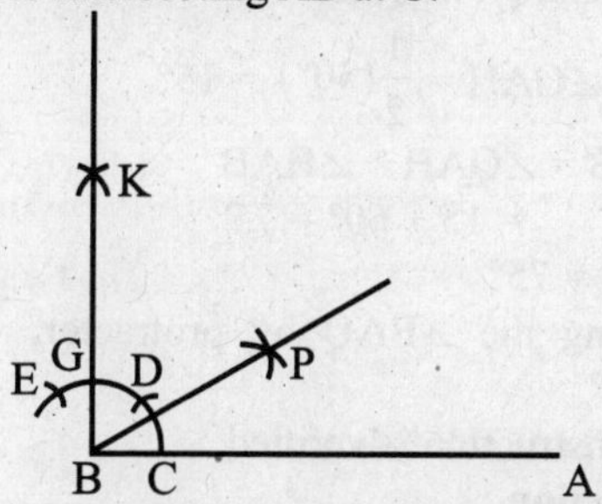

(iii) Again take C as centre and radius = BC we draw an arc which is intersecting the previous arc at D.

(iv) Again repeating the process and take D as centre and radius as BC we draw an arc intersecting the first arc at E.

(v) Now with D and E as centres and radius > ED, draw two arcs which are intersecting each other at K. Also let BK intersect the arc ED at G.
Now $\angle ABK = 90°$

(vi) Take G and C as centre, and radius $> \frac{1}{2}CG$, draw two arcs which are intersecting each other at P. Now,
$\angle ABP = 45°$.
Proof. We have $\angle ABK = 90°$ and BP is its bisector.
$\therefore \angle ABP = 45°$.

4. (a) Steps of Construction :

(i) Draw a ray AB of 5 cm.

(ii) Taking A as centre and any radius, we draw an arc which intersects AB at C.

(iii) Next, Consider C as centre and with radius AC, draw an arc which is intersecting the previous arc drawn in step (ii) at D.

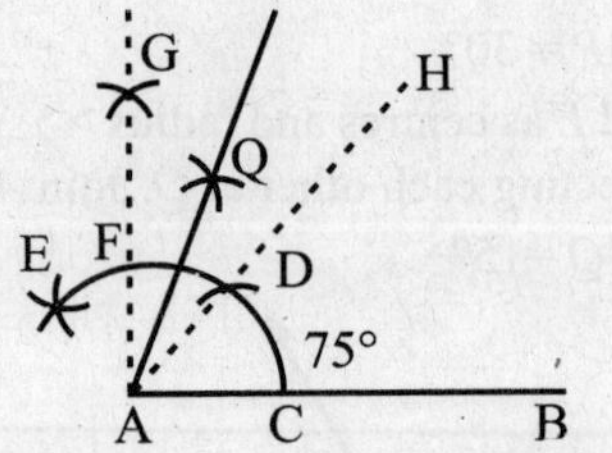

(iv) Taking D as centre and with radius AC, draw an arc which is intersecting the same arc at E.

(v) With D and E as centres, draw two arcs with radius $> \frac{1}{2}$ DE, which intersect at G.
Now , ∠BAG = 90°.

(vi) Again consider D and F as centres and radius $> \frac{1}{2}$ FD, draw two arcs which are intersecting each other at Q.

(vii) Join AQ. which is bisector of angle GAH.
i.e.,- ∠GAQ = ∠QAH

$= \angle GAH = \frac{1}{2}(30°) = 15°$

Thus, ∠QAB = ∠QAH + ∠HAB
= 15 + 60° = 75°
Now ∠BAQ = 75°
On measuring the ∠BAQ by protractor, we find ∠BAQ = 75°
Thus, the construction is verified.

(b) **Steps of Construction :**

(i) Draw a ray AB of 5 cm.

(ii) Consider A as centre and any radius, draw an arc which intersects AB at C.

(iii) Taking C as centre and radius AC as before draw an arc intersecting the previous arc at D.

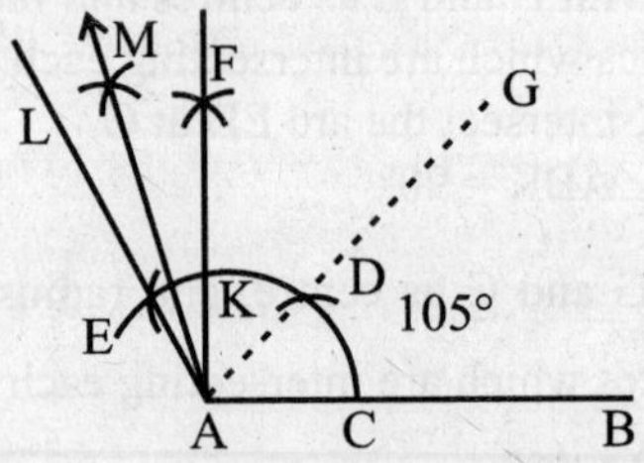

(iv) Consider D as centre and radius as before, draw an arc intersecting the same arc at E.

(v) Draw ray AG which is passing through D such that ∠GAB = 60°

(vi) Draw ray AL which is passing through E such that ∠LAG = 60°

(vii) With D and E as centres, draw two arcs with radius $> \frac{1}{2} DE$, which intersect at F and previous arc at K.
Ray AF is the bisector of ∠LAG.

$\therefore \angle LAF = \angle GAF = \frac{1}{2}\angle LAG = \frac{1}{2}(60°) = 30°$

Thus, ∠FAB = ∠FAG + ∠GAB = 30° + 60° = 90°

(viii) Now, Taking K and E as centres draw two arcs with radius $> \frac{1}{2} KE$, which intersects, at M.
Draw ray AM which is bisector of ∠LAF.

$\therefore \angle LAM = \frac{1}{2}(30°) = 15°$ Thus, ∠MAB
= 15° + 90° = 105°

On measuring ∠MAB by protractor, we find ∠BAL = 105°
Thus, the construction is verified
Now ∠BAL = 105°.

(c) **Steps of Construction :**

(i) Draw BA = 5 cm.

(ii) With B as centre and any radius, draw an arc which intersects BA at C.

(iii) Now with C as centre and radius BC draw an arc which intersects the previous arc at D.

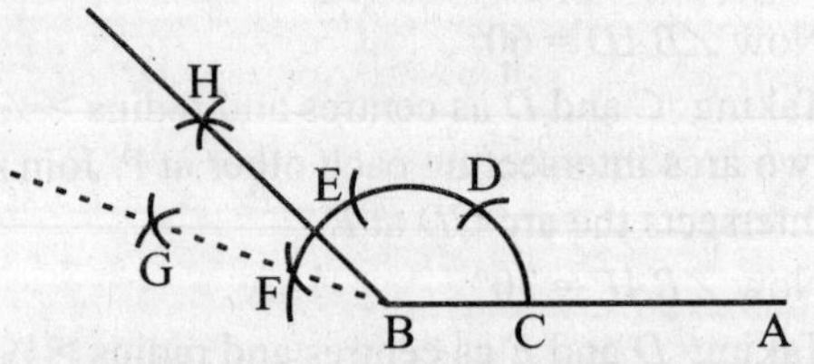

(iv) Again with D as centre and radius as before, draw an arc which intersects the same arc at E.

(v) Again with E as centre and same radius as before, draw another arc which cuts the same arc at F.

(vi) With centres at E and F and radius $> \frac{1}{2} EF$, draw two arcs intersecting each other at G.
Thus ∠ABG = 135°

(vii) With centres at K and E and radius $> \frac{1}{2}$KE, draw 2 arcs intersect at H.
Now ∠ABH = 135°.

5. Given a side (say 6 cm) of an equilateral triangle.
We have to construct the equilateral triangle and justify the construction.

Steps of Construction :

(i) Draw a ray AX with starting point A. From AX, cut off AB of 6 cm.

(ii) Consider A as centre and radius (= 6 cm), draw an arc, which intersects the ray AX, at B.

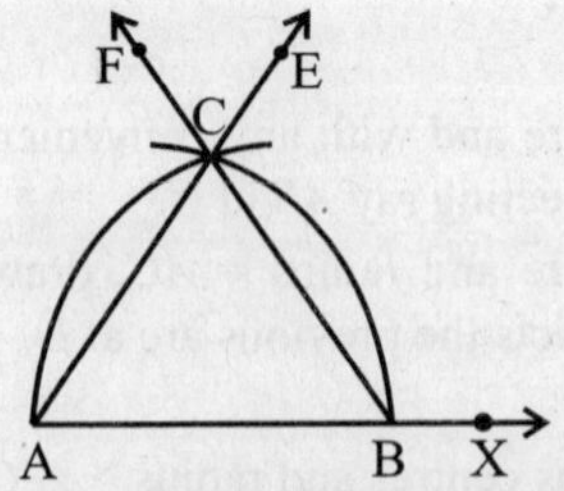

(iii) Now, consider B as centre and with the radius as before, draw an arc which is intersecting the previous arc, at C.
Draw the ray AE passing through C.

(iv) Next, taking B as centre and radius (= 6 cm), draw an arc, which intersects AX, at A.

(v) Taking A as centre and with the same radius as before, draw an arc intersecting the previously drawn arc, at C.
Draw the ray BF passing through C.

(vi) Then ΔABC is the required triangle with side 6 cm.

Justification :

$AB = BC$ [By construction]
$AB = AC$ [By construction]
$\therefore$ $AB = BC = CA$
$\therefore$ ABC is an equilateral triangle.
$\therefore$ The construction is justified.

6. Given : In ΔABC, $BC = 7$ cm, $\angle B = 75°$ and $AB + AC = 13$ cm.
We have to construct the triangle ABC.

Steps of Construction:

(i) Draw the base BC of 7 cm.
(ii) Make an $\angle XBC$ of 75° at the point B.
(iii) From the ray BX cut a line segment BD equal to $AB + AC$ (= 13 cm).
Join the ray DC.

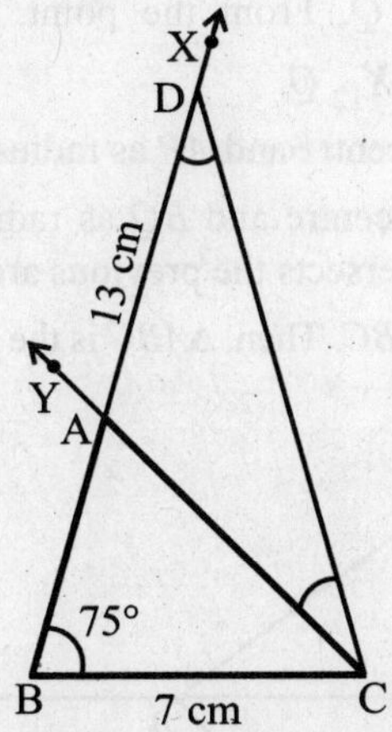

(iv) Make an angle DCY which is equal to $\angle BDC$. where CY intersect the ray BX at A.
Thus, ABC is the required triangle.

7. Given : In ΔABC, $BC = 8$ cm, $\angle B = 45°$ and $AB - AC = 3.5$ cm.
We have to construct the triangle ABC.

Steps of Construction:

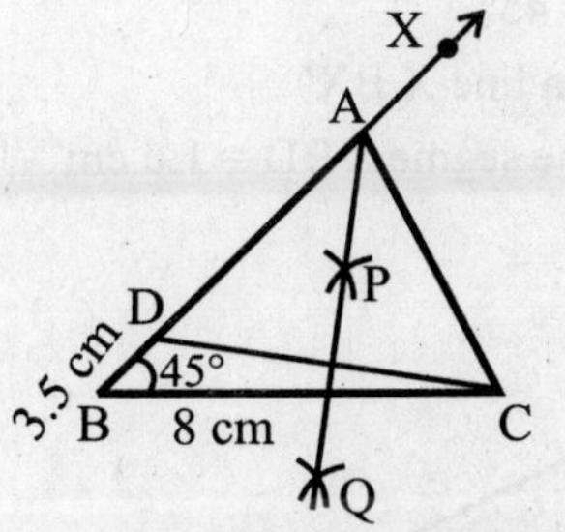

(i) Draw the base BC of 8 cm.
(ii) From the point B, draw a ray BX and make an $\angle XBC = 45°$ at the point B
(iii) Cut the line segment BD equal to $AB - AC$ (= 1 cm) from the ray BX.
Join DC.
(iv) Draw the perpendicular bisector, say PQ of DC. which intersect the ray BX at a point A.
(v) Join AC.
Thus, ABC is the required triangle.

8. Given : In ΔPQR, $QR = 6$ cm, $\angle Q = 60°$ and $PR - PQ = 2$ cm.
We have to construct the ΔPQR.

Steps of Construction:

(i) Draw the base QR of 6 cm.
(ii) Make an angle $XQR = 60°$ at the point Q.

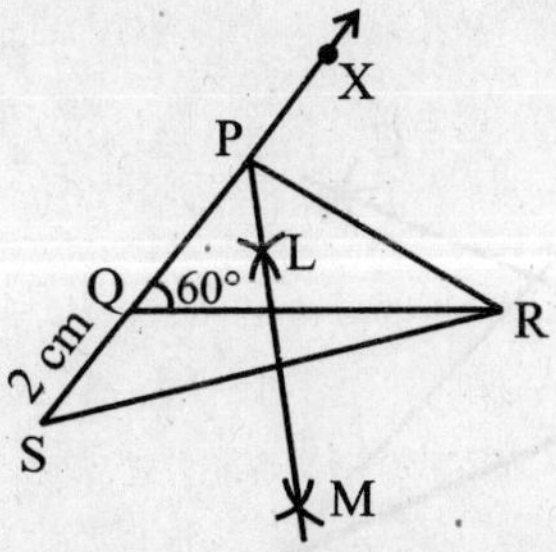

(iii) From the line QX extended on opposite side of line segment QR,
Cut line segment $QS = PR - PQ$ (= 2 cm).
(iv) Join SR and Draw the perpendicular bisector LM of SR.
(v) Now, we assume LM intersect the ray QX at a point P.
Now, we Join PR.
Thus, PQR is the required triangle.

9. Given : In triangle XYZ, $\angle Y = 30°$, $\angle Z = 90°$ and $XY + YZ + ZX = 11$ cm.
We have to construct the ΔXYZ.

Steps of Construction:

(i) Draw a line segment $AB = XY + YZ + ZX$ (= 11 cm).
(ii) Make $\angle LAB = \angle Y$ (= 30°) and $\angle MBA = \angle Z$ (= 90°).
(iii) Let bisect the angle LAB and angle MBA. and these bisectors meet at a point X.

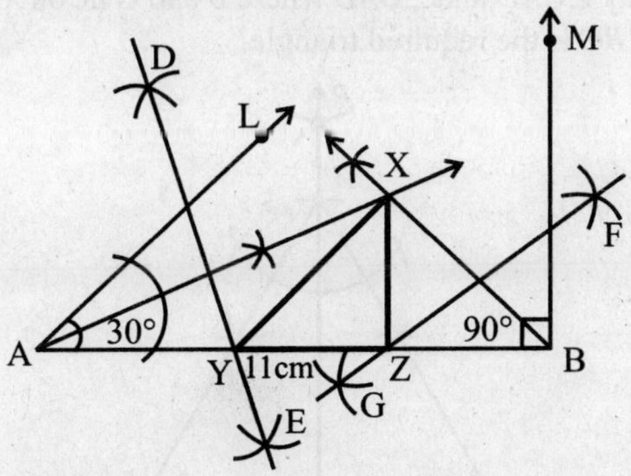

(iv) Draw perpendicular bisectors DE of XA and FG of XB.
(v) Let DE intersect AB at Y and FG intersect AB at Z.
Finally we Join XY and XZ.

Thus, XYZ is the required triangle.

10. Given : In right ΔABC, base $PQ = 12$ cm, $\angle P = 90°$ and $AP + AQ = 18$ cm.
We have to construct the right triangle APQ.

Steps of Construction:

(i) Draw the base PQ of 12 cm.

(ii) Draw the ray PX and make an angle XPQ of 90° at the point P.

(iii) Cut a line segment $PD = AP + AQ$ (= 18 cm) from the ray PX.
Join DQ.

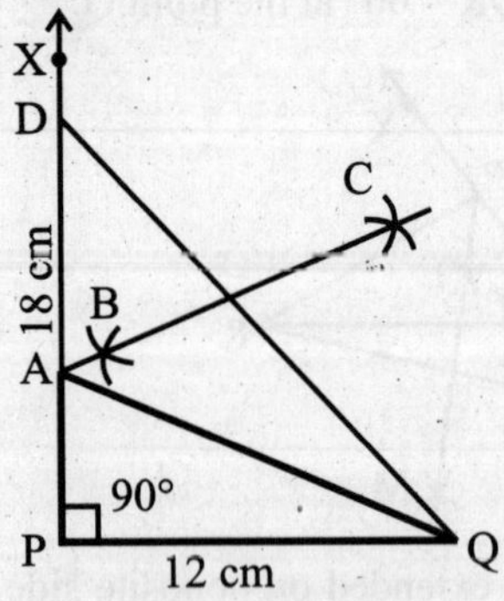

(iv) Draw the perpendicular bisector BC of QD to intersect PD at a point A.
Join AQ.
Then, APQ is the required right triangle.

EXEMPLAR QUESTIONS :

1. (c)
2. (b)
3. (b)
4. (a)
5. (d)
6. (i) Draw a line *XY*.
   (ii) Take any point *D* on this line.
   (iii) Construct perpendicular *PD* on *XY*.
   (iv) Cut a line segment *AD* from *D* equal to 6 cm.
   (v) Make angles equal to 30° at *A* on both sides of *AD*, say $\angle CAD$ and $\angle BAD$ where *B* and *C* lie on *XY*. Then *ABC* is the required triangle.

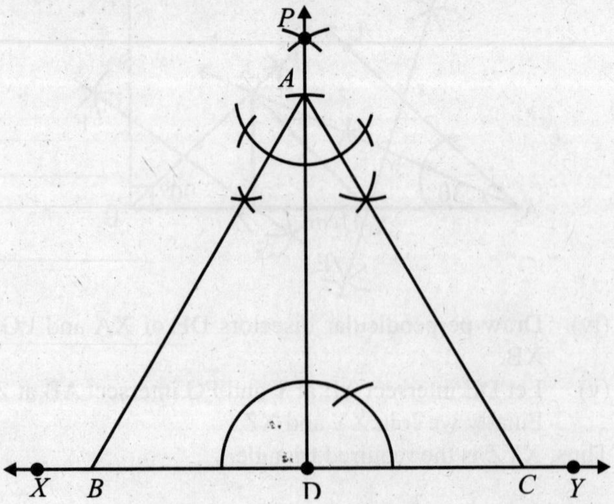

Justification:

Since $\angle BAC = 30° + 30° = 60°$ and $AD \perp BC$. In ΔABD,
$\angle BAD = 30$ and $\angle ADB = 90°$
$\therefore \angle ABD = 60°$, i.e. $\angle ABC = 60°$
Similarly $\angle ACB = 60°$
Hence ΔABC is an equilateral triangle with altitude $AD = 6$ cm.

HOTS QUESTIONS :

1. Steps of Construction:

(i) Draw a line-segment *PQ* of length 12 cm.

(ii) From *P*, draw a ray *PX* making an acute angle with *PQ*.

(iii) Sum of the ratio = 3 + 4 + 5 = 12.

(iv) Mark points $X_1, X_2, X_3, \ldots\ldots\ldots, X_{12}$ on ray *PX*; such that $PX_1 = X_1X_2 = X_2X_3 = \ldots\ldots\ldots\ldots = X_{11}X_{12}$

(v) Join X_{12} to *Q*. From the point X_7 and X_3 draw $X_7B \parallel X_3A \parallel X_{12}Q$.

(vi) Taking *A* as centre and *AP* as radius, draw an arc.

(vii) Taking *B* as centre and *BQ* as radius, draw another arc which intersects the previous arc of step (vi) at *C*.

(viii) Join *AC* and *BC*. Then, ΔABC is the required triangle.

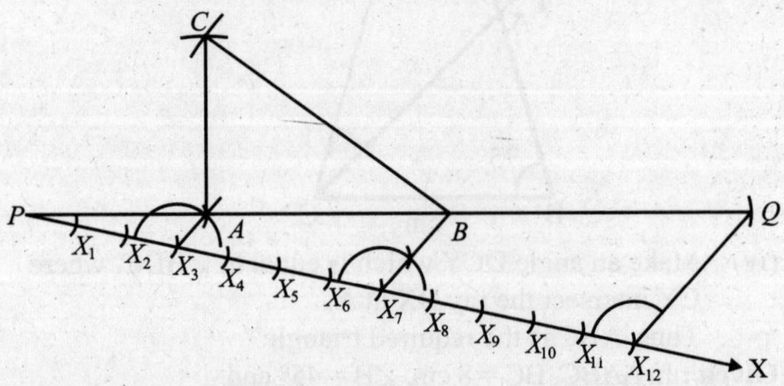

2. Steps of Construction:

(i) Draw BC = 5.6 cm.

(ii) At B, construct $\angle CBX = 45°$.

(iii) Produce XB to X′ to form line X BX′

(iv) From ray BX′, cut-off line segment BD = 1.6 cm

(v) Join CD

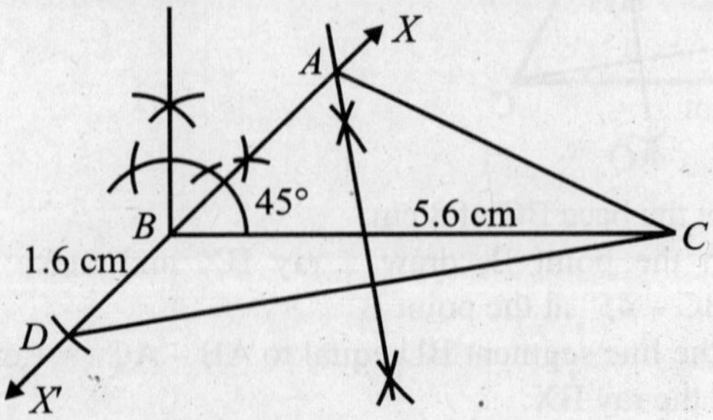

3. Given one side = 3.5 cm and sum of other side and hypotenuse = 5.5 cm.

Steps of Construction:

(i) Draw line segment BC = 3.5 cm.

(ii) Construct ∠CBY = 90°.

(iii) From BY cut off a line segment BD = 5.5 cm.

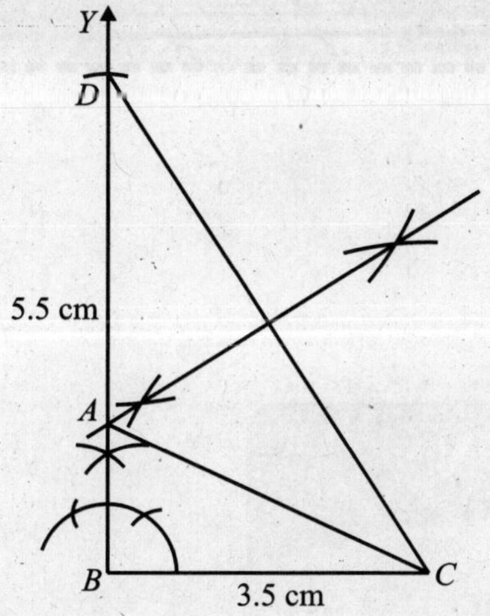

(iv) Join CD.

(v) Draw the perpendicular bisector of CD intersecting BD at a point A.

(vi) Join AC.

So, ΔABC is the required triangle.

3 EXERCISE

SINGLE OPTION CORRECT :

1. **(a)** Next step is to take A as centre and radius equal to (sum of other two sides), draw an arc intersecting AX at D.

2. **(a)** Line segment PQ is equal to the perimeter of triangle i.e., $AB + BC + CA = 11$ cm.

3. **(b)** In ΔBEF and ΔBDF

$BE = BD$ [By construction]

$\angle BEF = \angle BDF$ [By construction]

$BF = BF$ [Common]

$\therefore \Delta BEF \cong \Delta BDF$ [SAS]

4. **(b)** In ΔPMA and ΔPMB

$PM = PM$ [Common]

$\angle PMA = \angle PMB$ [each 90°]

$MA = MB$ [PM being bisector of AB]

$\therefore \Delta PMA \cong \Delta PMB$ [SAS]

5. **(d)**

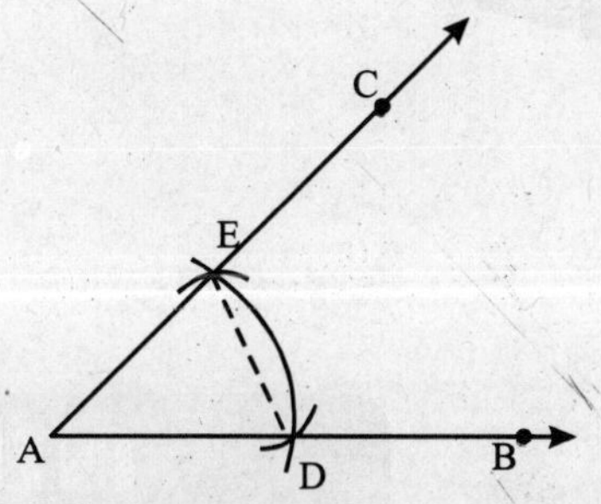

6. **(c)** As sum of two sides of a triangle is always greater than the third side.

7. **(a)** Since many similar triangles can be constructed if measure of three angles are given.

8. **(b)** 10 cm.

As triangle is isosceles, thus two of its sides must be equal. If the length of third side is taken to be 4cm, then sum of two sides that is (4 + 4 = 8) will be less than third side which is not possible. Thus, third side must be 10 cm.

9. **(a)** It is not possible to construct triangle whose difference of two side is more than the third side.

10. **(d)** A triangle can be constructed when difference of two of its sides is less than the third side.

Chapter 12

Heron's Formula

INTRODUCTION

Heron was a Greek Mathematician. Heron gave the famous formula for finding the area of a triangle in terms of its three sides and when you know all three sides. The formula given by him is known as Heron's formula. In this chapter, you will study the Heron's formula. This formula is helpful to calculate the area of any quadrilateral and the area of cyclic quadrilateral.

Also, area of a quadrilateral whose sides and one diagonal are given can also calculated by dividing the quadrilateral into two triangles and by using Heron's formula.

AREA

If a figure does not intersect itself then it is called a simple figure. The region enclosed within a simple closed figure is called its area.

Area of Triangles

We have learned that the perimeter of the triangle is the sum of length of its three sides and area of a triangle = $\frac{1}{2} \times \text{Base} \times \text{Height}$. Using this formula.

(i) Base of Triangle = $\frac{2 \times \text{Area}}{\text{Height}}$

(ii) Height of Triangle = $\frac{2 \times \text{Area}}{\text{Base}}$

Unit of measurement for area of any plane figure is taken as square metre (m^2) or square centimetre (cm^2) etc.

> **NOTE :** When the triangle is right angled, we can directly apply the formula by using two sides containing the right angle as base and height.

AREA OF A RIGHT ANGLED TRIANGLE

The area of a triangle = $\frac{1}{2} \times$ base $\times$ height (or altitude)

AREA OF AN EQUILATERAL TRIANGLE

Area of equilateral triangle of side 'a' = $\frac{\sqrt{3}}{4} a^2$ sq. unit

AREA OF AN ISOSCELES TRIANGLE

Area of an isosceles triangle with base 'a' and equal sides 'b' = $\frac{a}{4}\sqrt{4b^2 - a^2}$

HERON'S FORMULA

In some cases, length of each side of the triangle are given but height of the triangle is neither given nor we are able to find in any way, then to find the area of such type of triangle, we use Heron's formula which is given below.

Area of a triangle = $\sqrt{s(s-a)(s-b)(s-c)}$

where a, b, c are length of the sides of a triangle and s is the semi-perimeter of the triangle i.e. $s = \frac{a+b+c}{2}$

Remark:
This formula is applicable to all types of triangles whether it is right angle triangle or equilateral triangle.

ILLUSTRATION : 1

Find the area of a triangle, length of whose sides are 3 cm, 4 cm, and 5 cm.

SOLUTION :

We have $a = 3$ cm, $b = 4$ cm, $c = 5$ cm

$$s = \frac{a+b+c}{2} = \frac{3+4+5}{2} = 6$$

$$\therefore ar(\Delta ABC) = \sqrt{s(s-a)(s-b)(s-c)} = \sqrt{6 \times (6-3)(6-4)(6-5)} = \sqrt{6 \times 3 \times 2 \times 1}\ \text{cm}^2 = \sqrt{36} = 6\ \text{cm}^2$$

ILLUSTRATION : 2

Find the area of an equilateral triangle having each side's length 4 cm.

SOLUTION :

$a = b = c = 4$ cm and $s = \frac{a+b+c}{2} = \frac{4+4+4}{2} = 6$

Area of a triangle by Heron's formula

$$= \sqrt{s(s-a)(s-b)(s-c)}$$

$$= \sqrt{6(6-4)(6-4)(6-4)} = \sqrt{6\times2\times2\times2} = \sqrt{48} = \sqrt{4\times4\times3} = 4\sqrt{3}\text{ cm}^2$$

APPLICATION OF HERON'S FORMULA IN FINDING AREAS OF QUADRILATERALS

To find the area of a quadrilateral we divide it in triangular parts and then use the formula for area of the triangle. We add the area of divided triangle to get the area of whole quadrilateral.

ILLUSTRATION : 3

Find the area of a quadrilateral *ABCD* in which *AB* = 3 cm, *BC* = 4 cm, *CD* = 4 cm, *DA* = 5 cm and *AC* = 5 cm.

SOLUTION :

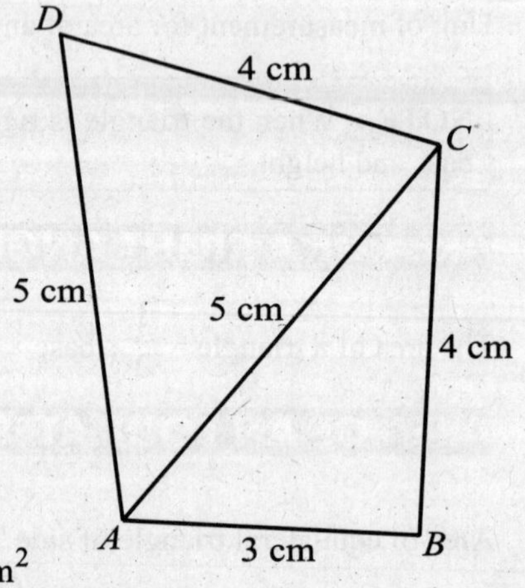

We divide the quadrilateral *ABCD* in two triangle *ABC* and *ACD*.

For ΔABC, $a = 3$, $b = 4$, $c = 5$ and $s = \dfrac{3+4+5}{2} = 6$

$$\text{Area }(\Delta ABC) = \sqrt{s(s-a)(s-b)(s-c)}$$

$$= \sqrt{6(6-3)(6-4)(6-5)} = \sqrt{6\times3\times2\times1} = 6\text{ cm}^2$$

Similarly, for ΔACD,

$$a = 5\text{ cm},\ b = 5\text{ cm},\ c = 4\text{ cm and } s = \frac{5+5+4}{2} = 7$$

$$\text{Area }(\Delta\, ACD) = \sqrt{s(s-a)(s-b)(s-c)} = \sqrt{7(7-5)(7-5)(7-4)} = \sqrt{7\times2\times2\times3} = 2\sqrt{21}\text{ cm}^2$$

$\therefore$ Area of quadrilateral *ABCD* = Area of triangle *ABC* + Area of triangle *ACD* = $6\text{ cm}^2 + 2\sqrt{21}\text{ cm}^2$

MISCELLANEOUS SOLVED EXAMPLES

1. Find the area of a triangle, two of its sides are of length 6 cm and 12 cm and the perimeter is 26 cm.

Sol. Here, $a = 6$ cm, $b = 12$ cm

and Perimeter = 26 cm

Let c be the length of third side

Now, Perimeter = $a + b + c$

$$26 = 6 + 12 + c$$

$$c = 26 - 18 = 8 \text{ cm}$$

$$s = \frac{a+b+c}{2} = \frac{6+12+8}{2} = 13 \text{ cm}$$

$$\text{Area of } \Delta ABC = \sqrt{s(s-a)(s-b)(s-c)}$$

$$= \sqrt{13(13-6)(13-8)(13-12)} = \sqrt{13 \times 7 \times 5 \times 1}$$

$$= \sqrt{13 \times 35} = \sqrt{455} \text{ cm}^2$$

2. The sides of a triangular plot are in the ratio 3 : 5 : 7 and its perimeter is 300 m. Find its area.

Sol. The sides are in the ratio 3 : 5 : 7. So let the sides be $3x$, $5x$ and $7x$ respectively.

Now perimeter = 300 m

$\Rightarrow$ $3x + 5x + 7x = 300$

$15x = 300$

$$x = \frac{300}{15} = 20$$

So the sides are 60m, 100m and 140m

$a = 60$ m, $b = 100$ m, $c = 140$ m

$$\therefore \quad s = \frac{a+b+c}{2} = \frac{300}{2} = 150 \text{ m}$$

$$\therefore \quad \text{Area of } \Delta ABC = \sqrt{s(s-a)(s-b)(s-c)}$$

$$= \sqrt{150(150-60)(150-100)(150-140)}$$

$$= \sqrt{150 \times 90 \times 50 \times 10} = 1500\sqrt{3} \text{ m}^2$$

3. Find the area of the quadrilateral *ABCD in* which *AB* = 12 cm, *BC* = 6 cm, *CD* = 7 cm, *BD* = 9 cm and *AD* = 15 cm.

Sol. In the quadrilateral $ABCD$ diagonal BD divides it into two triangles ABD and BCD.

$\therefore$ Area of quadrilateral $ABCD$ = Area of ΔABD + Area of ΔBCD ...(i)

For ΔABD,

$a = 12$ cm, $b = 9$ cm $c = 15$ cm

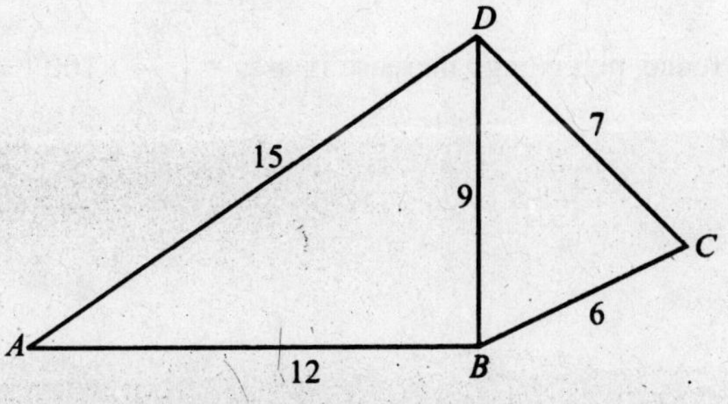

$$s = \frac{a+b+c}{2} = \frac{12+9+15}{2} = 18\text{cm}$$

Applying Heron's formula for ΔABD

$$\text{Area} = \sqrt{s(s-a)(s-b)(s-c)}$$

$$= \sqrt{18(18-12)(18-9)(18-15)}$$

$$= \sqrt{18 \times 6 \times 9 \times 3} = 18 \times 3 = 54 \text{ cm}^2$$

For ΔBCD,

$a = 6$ cm, $b = 7$ cm, $c = 9$ cm

$$s = \frac{6+7+9}{2} = 11\text{cm}$$

Applying Heron's formula for $\Delta\, BCD$.

$$\text{Area} = \sqrt{s(s-a)(s-b)(s-c)}$$

$$= \sqrt{11(11-6)(11-7)(11-9)} = \sqrt{11 \times 5 \times 4 \times 2}$$

$$= \sqrt{440} = 20.98 \text{ cm}^2$$

$\therefore$ Area of Quadrilateral $ABCD = 54 + 20.98 = 74.98$ cm^2 [from (i)]

4. The adjacent sides of a || gm *ABCD* are 34 cm, and 20 cm and the diagonal *AC* is 42 cm. Find the area of the || gm.

Sol. || gm *ABCD* can be divided into two triangles *ABC* and *ACD*.

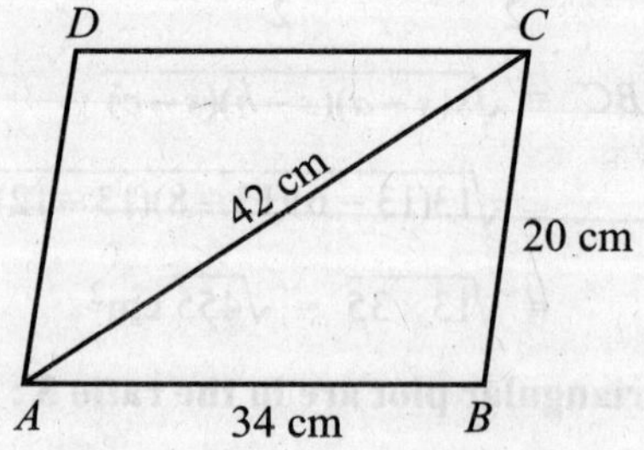

Now, *ABCD* is a || gm

So, $AB = CD = 34$ cm

$BC = DA = 20$ cm

In $\Delta\, ABC$,

$a = 34$ cm, $b = 20$ cm, $c = 42$ cm

$$s = \frac{a+b+c}{2} = \frac{34+20+42}{2} = 48 \text{ cm}$$

Applying Heron's formula

$$\text{Area of } \Delta\, ABC = \sqrt{s(s-a)(s-b)(s-c)} = \sqrt{48(48-34)(48-20)(48-42)} = 48 \times 7 = 336$$

Area of || gm $ABCD = 2 \times$ Area of $\Delta\, ABC$

$= 2 \times 336 = 672$ sq. unit.

5. Find the percentage increase in the area of a triangle if its each side is doubled.

Sol. Let *a*, *b*, *c*, be the sides of the old triangle and *s* be its semi-perimeter. Then,

$$s = \frac{1}{2}(a+b+c)$$

The sides of the new triangle are 2*a*, 2*b* and 2*c*. Let s′ be its semi-perimeter. Then,

$$s' = \frac{1}{2} \times (2a+2b+2c) = a+b+c = 2s$$

Let Δ and Δ' be the areas of the old and new triangles respectively. Then,

$$\Delta = \sqrt{s(s-a)(s-b)(s-c)} \text{ and } \Delta' = \sqrt{s'(s'-2a)(s'-2b)(s'-2c)}$$

$$\Rightarrow \Delta' = \sqrt{2s(2s-2a)(2s-2b)(2s-2c)} \quad [\because s' = 2s]$$

$$\Rightarrow \Delta' = \sqrt{s(s-a)(s-b)(s-c)} = 4\Delta$$

$\therefore$ Increase in the area of the triangle $= \Delta' - \Delta = 4\Delta - \Delta = 3\Delta$

Hence, percentage increase in area $= \left(\frac{3\Delta}{\Delta} \times 100\right) = 300\%$.

1 EXERCISE

True / False :

DIRECTIONS: *Read the following statements and write your answer as true or false.*

1. Area of a quadrilateral whose sides and one diagonal are given, can be calculated by dividing the quadrilateral into two triangles and using the Heron's formula.
2. Sides of a triangle are in the ratio of 12 : 17 : 25 and its perimeter is 540 cm. Its area is 8000 cm^2.
3. Area of a triangle whose sides are 13 cm, 14 cm and 15 cm is 84 cm^2.
4. Area of a quadrilateral *ABCD* in which *AB* = 3 cm, *BC* = 4cm, *CD* = 4 cm, *DA* = 5 cm and *AC* = 5 cm is 15 cm^2.
5. Area of the triangle whose two sides are 8m and 11m and perimeter is 32 m, is $8\sqrt{30}\ m^2$.
6. The sides of a quadrilateral taken in order are 5m, 12m, 14m and 15m. If the angle between the first two sides be 90°, its area 114m^2.
7. Heron's formula cannot be use to calculate area of quadrilaterals.
8. If the adjacent angles of a rhombus of side 10 cm are 120° and 60°, then its area is $25\sqrt{3}\ cm^2$.
9. If P is any point in the interior of a rectangle ABCD, then Area (Δ *PAB*) + Area (Δ *PCD*) = Area (Δ *PBC*) + Area (Δ*PDA*).

Match the Columns :

DIRECTIONS: *Each question contains statements given in two columns which have to be matched. Statements (A, B, C, D, ...) in Column - I have to be matched with statements (p, q, r, s, ...) in Column - II.*

1.

Column-I	Column-II
(A) The sides of a triangle are 35 cm, 54 cm and 61 cm. The length of the longest altitude is	(p) 612
(B) If the side of a rhombus is 10 cm and one diagonal is 16 cm, then area of the rhombus is	(q) 96
(C) The cost of levelling the ground in the form of triangle having sides 51 m, 37 m and 20 m at the rate of ₹ 2 per m^2 is	(r) $24\sqrt{5}$

2.

Column-I	Column-II
(A) The area of a triangle with base 4 cm and height 6 cm is	(p) $\frac{5}{4}\sqrt{11}\,cm^2$
(B) If the perimeter of the isosceles triangle is 11 cm and the base is 5 cm then the area of the isosceles triangle is	(q) $16\sqrt{3}\,cm^2$
(C) The area of the equilateral triangle, whose each side is 8 cm, is	(r) 12 cm^2

Short Answer Questions:

DIRECTIONS: *Give answer in 2-3 sentences.*

1. An isosceles triangle has perimeter 30 cm and each of the equal sides is 12 cm. Find the area of the triangle.
2. Find the area of an equilateral triangle, of each side 2 a units.
3. Two sides of a triangle are 8 cm and 11 cm and perimeter of triangle is 32 cm. Find the value of (s).
4. Find the area of a triangle ABC, in which AB = AC = 4 cm and ∠A = 90°
5. Reema is given three sticks of lengths 12 cm, 6 cm and 4 cm respectively. She is asked to make a triangle and find the area of the triangle formed.

Long Answer Questions :

DIRECTIONS: *Give answer in four to five sentences.*

1. The sides of a triangle are 4, 5 and 6 cm. Find the area of the triangle.
2. One side of an equilateral triangle is 6 cm. Find its area by using Heron's formula. Find its altitude also.
3. The lengths of two adjacent sides of a parallelogram are respectively 40 cm and 50 cm. One of its diagonals is 20 cm. Find the area of the parallelogram.

2 EXERCISE

Text-Book Exercise :

1. A park, in the shape of a quadrilateral ABCD, has $\angle C = 90^\circ$, AB = 9 m, BC = 12 m, CD = 5 m, and AD = 8 m. How much area does it occupy?

2. An umbrella is made by stitching 10 triangular pieces of cloth of two different colours (See Fig.), each piece measuring 20 cm, 50 cm and 50 cm. How much cloth of each colour required for the umbrella?

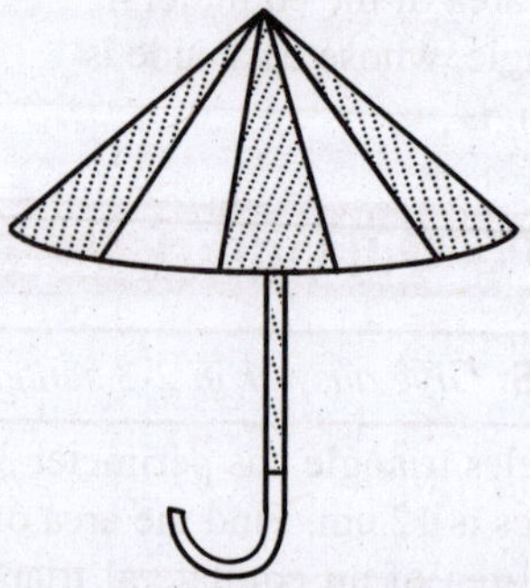

3. A kite in the shape of a square with a diagonal 32 cm and an isosceles triangle of base 8 cm and sides 6 cm each is to be made of three different shades as shown in figure. How much paper of each shade has been used in it?

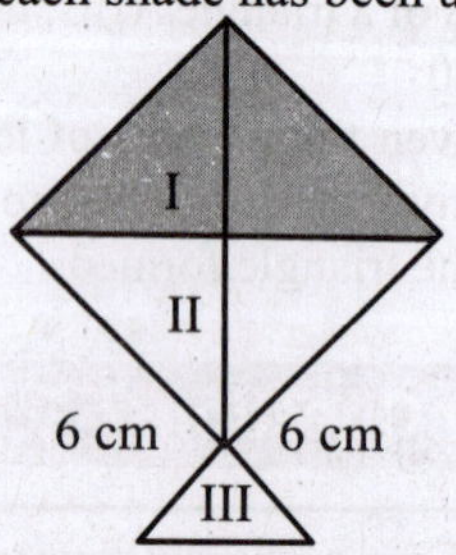

4. A floral design on a floor is made up of 16 tiles which are triangular, the sides of the triangle being 9 cm, 28 cm and 35 cm(see fig). Find the cost of polishing the tiles at the rate of 50 p per cm^2.

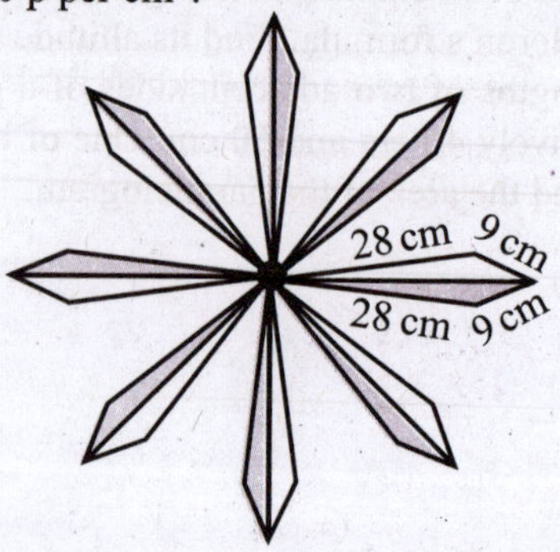

5. A traffic signal board, indicating 'SCHOOL AHEAD' is an equilateral triangle with side's length ***a***. Find the area of the signal board, using Heron's Formula. If its perimeter is 180 cm, what will be the area of the signal board?

6. The triangular side walls of a flyover have been used for advertisements. The sides of the walls are 122 m, 22 m and 120 m (see figure). The advertisements yield an earning of ₹ 5000 per m^2 per year. A company hired one of its walls for 3 months. How much rent did it pay?

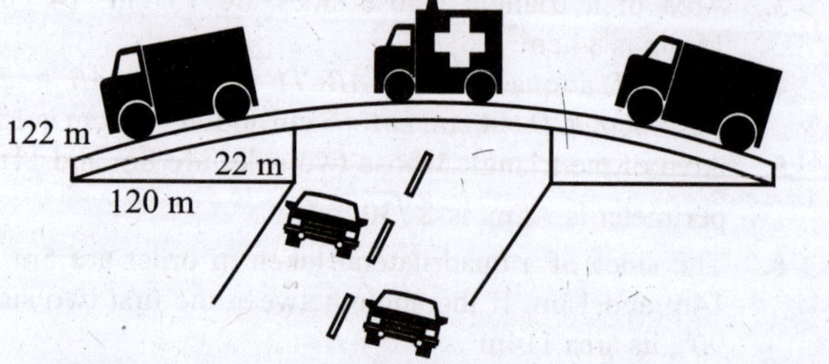

7. There is a slide in a park. One of its side walls has been painted in some colour with a message "KEEP THE PARK GREEN AND CLEAN" (see fig.). If the sides of the wall are 15 m, 11 m and 6 m, find the area painted in colour.

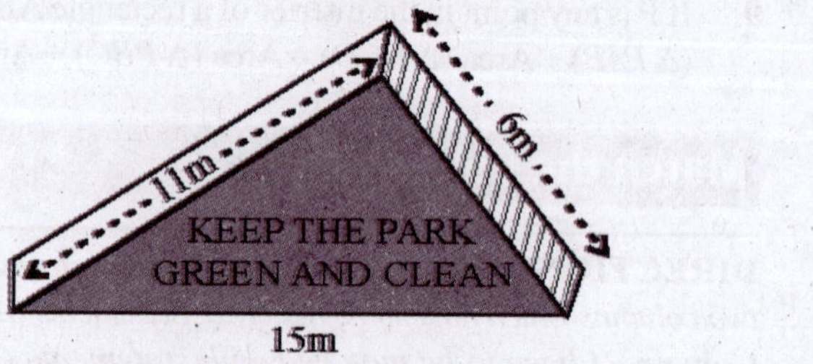

8. An isosceles triangle has perimeter 30 cm and each of the equal sides is 12 cm. Find the area of the triangle.

9. A triangle and a parallelogram have the same base and the same area. If the sides of the triangle are 26 cm, 28 cm and 30 cm, and the parallelogram stands on the base 28 cm, find the height of the parallelogram.

10. A field is in the shape of a trapezium whose parallel sides are 25 m and 10 m. The non-parallel sides are 14 m and 13 m. Find the area of the field.

Exemplar Questions :

1. How much paper of each shade is needed to make a kite given in fig. in which *ABCD* is a square with diagonal 44 cm.

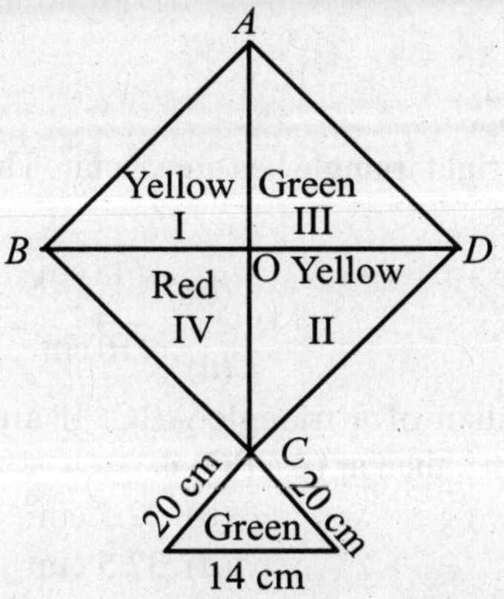

2. The triangular side walls of a flyover have been used for advertisements. The sides of the walls are 13 m, 14 m and 15 m. The advertisements yield an earning of ₹ 2000 per m^2 a year. A company hired one of its walls for 6 months. How much rent did it pay?
3. The perimeter of an isosceles triangle is 32 cm. The ratio of the equal side to its base is 3 : 2. Find the area of the triangle.
4. A field in the form of a parallelogram has sides 60 m and 40 m and one of its diagonals is 80 m long. Find the area of the parallelogram.

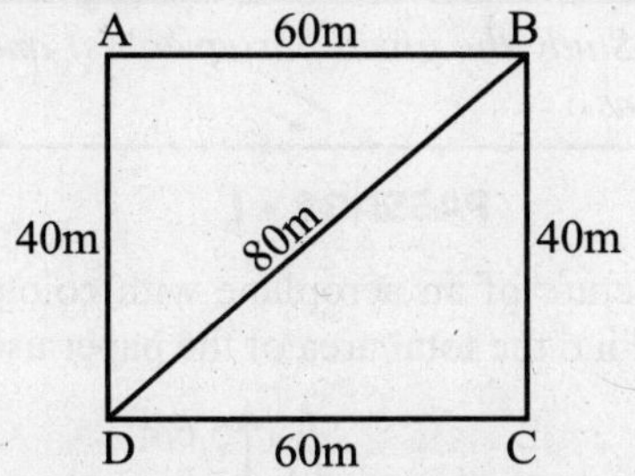

5. The area of trapezium is 475 cm^2 and the height is 19 cm. Find the lengths of its two parallel sides if one side is 4 cm greater than the other.
6. In the figure ΔABC has sides AB = 7.5 cm, AC = 6.5 cm and BC = 7 cm. On base BC a parallelogram DBCE of same area as that of ΔABC is constructed. Find the height DF of the parallelogram.

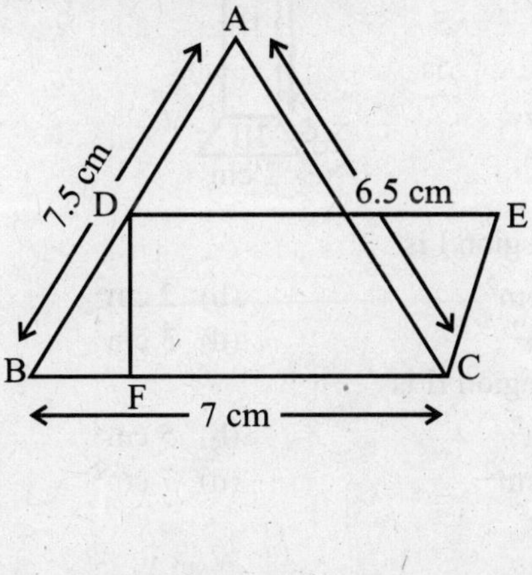

7. The perimeter of an equilateral triangle is 60 m. The area is
   (a) $10\sqrt{3}\ m^2$ (b) $15\sqrt{3}\ m^2$
   (c) $20\sqrt{3}\ m^2$ (d) $100\sqrt{3}\ m^2$
8. The area of an equilateral triangle with side $2\sqrt{3}$ cm is
   (a) 5.196 cm^2 (b) 0.866 cm^2
   (c) 3.496 cm^2 (d) 1.732 cm^2
9. If the area of an equilateral triangle is $16\sqrt{3}\ cm^2$, then the perimeter of the triangle is
   (a) 48 cm (b) 24 cm
   (c) 12 cm (d) 36 cm
10. The edges of a triangular board are 6 cm, 8 cm and 10 cm. The cost of painting it at the rate of 9 paise per cm^2 is
   (a) ₹ 2.00 (b) ₹ 2.16
   (c) ₹ 2.48 (d) ₹ 3.00

HOTS Questions :

1. Find the area of the quadrilateral *ABCD* whose diagonal *AC* = 15 cm. and sides *AB* = 7 cm, *BC* = 12 cm, *CD* = 12 cm and *DA* = 9 cm
2. Find the area of a trapezium whose parallel sides are 55 cm, 40 cm and non-parallel sides are 20 cm and 25 cm respectively.
3. Two identical circle with same inside design as shown in figure are to be made at the entrance. The identical triangular leaves are to be painted red and the remaining area green. Find the total area to be painted red.

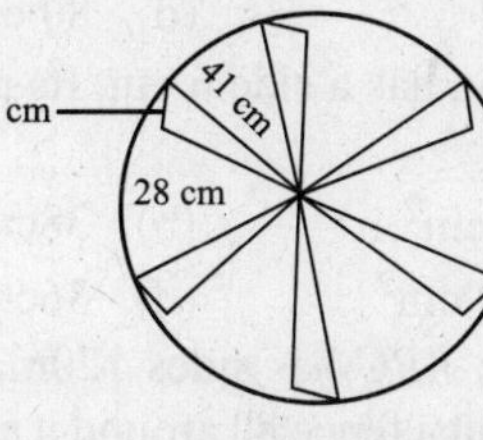

4. The dimensions of a rectangle ABCD are 51 cm × 25 cm. A trapezium PBCQ with its parallel sides QC and PB in the ratio 9 : 8, is cut off from the rectangle as shown in the fig. If the area of the trapezium PBCQ is $\frac{5}{6}$th part of the area of the rectangle, find the lengths of QC and PB.

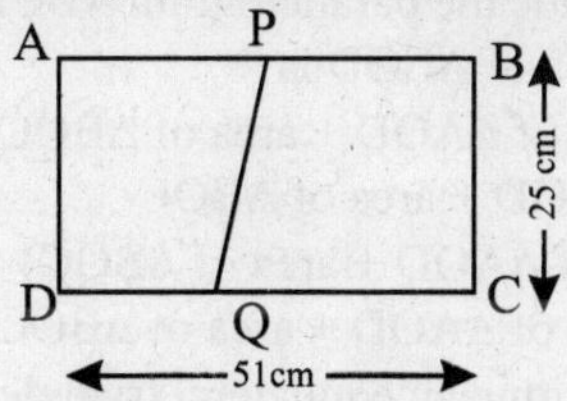

3 EXERCISE

Single Option Correct :

DIRECTIONS: *This section contains multiple choice questions. Each question has 4 choices (a), (b), (c) and (d) out of which only one is correct.*

1. Area of the triangle whose sides are 13 cm, 9 cm and 6 cm is
(a) 23.6 cm^2 (b) 26.3 cm^2
(c) 36.34 cm^2 (d) 23.66 cm^2

2. The sides of a triangular plot are in the ratio of 3 : 5 : 7 and its perimeter is 300m. Its area is
(a) $1500\sqrt{2}$ cm^2 (b) $1500\sqrt{3}$ cm^2
(c) $1425\sqrt{2}$ cm^2 (d) 1500 cm^2

3. The length of two adjacent sides of a parallelogram are 5 cm and 3.5 cm. One of its diagonals is 6.5 cm long. Area of the parallelogram is
(a) $13\sqrt{10}$ cm^2 (b) $23\sqrt{5}$ cm^2
(c) $10\sqrt{5}$ cm^2 (d) $10\sqrt{3}$ cm^2

4. The base of a right triangle is 8 cm and hypotenuse is 10 cm. Its area will be
(a) 24 cm^2 (b) 40 cm^2
(c) 48 cm^2 (d) 80 cm^2

5. A regular hexagon has a side 6 cm. Its perimeter and area are
(a) 35cm, $8\sqrt{3}$ cm^2 (b) 38cm, $10\sqrt{2}$ cm^2
(c) 40cm, $11\sqrt{2}$ cm^2 (d) 36cm, $54\sqrt{3}$ cm^2

6. A triangular park *ABC* has sides 120m, 80m and 50m. A gardener has to put a fence all around it and also plant grass inside. Area of garden and cost of fencing the garden with barbed wire at the rate of ₹ 20 per metre leaving a space 3m wide for a gate on one side are
(a) $375\sqrt{15}$ m^2, ₹ 4940 (b) $357\sqrt{10}$ m^2, ₹ 9440
(c) $573\sqrt{8}$ m^2, ₹ 4944 (d) $683\sqrt{10}$ m^2, ₹ 5490

7. O is a point inside the parallelogram ABCD. Then the area of ΔAOB + area of ΔCOD is
(a) 1/3 × (area of ΔAOD + area of ΔBOC)
(b) area of ΔAOD + area of ΔBOC
(c) 2 × (area of ΔAOD + area of ΔBOC)
(d) 2/3 × (area of ΔAOD + area of ΔBOC)

8. From a point within an equilateral triangle, perpendiculars are drawn to its sides. The length of these perpendiculars are 6m, 7m and 8m. The area of the triangle is
(a) 160 sq. m (b) $147\sqrt{3}$ sq.m.
(c) $210\sqrt{3}$ sq.m. (d) $27\sqrt{3}$ sq.m.

9. An isosceles right triangle has area 8 cm^2. The length of its hypotenuse is
(a) $\sqrt{32}$cm (b) $\sqrt{48}$ cm
(c) $\sqrt{24}$cm (d) $\sqrt{16}$ cm

10. AD is a median of a triangle ABC. If area of triangle ADC = 15 cm^2, then ar (ΔABC) is
(a) 15 cm^2 (b) 22.5 cm^2
(c) 30 cm^2 (d) 37.5 cm^2

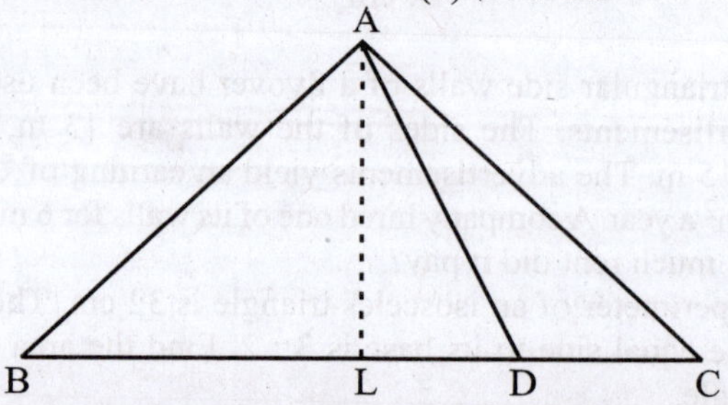

Passage Based Questions :

DIRECTIONS: *Study the given paragraph(s) and answer the following questions.*

PASSAGE - I

Radha made a picture of an aeroplane with coloured paper as shown in figure. Find the total area of the paper used.

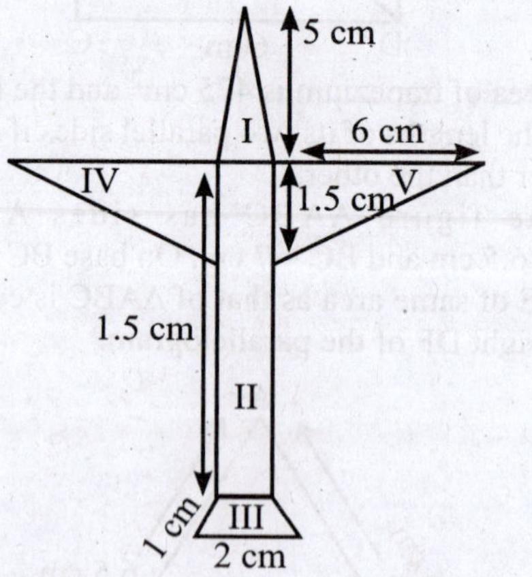

1. Area of region I is
(a) 2.5 cm^2 (b) 2 cm^2
(c) 5 cm^2 (d) 3 cm^2

2. Area of region II is
(a) 6 cm^2 (b) 5 cm^2
(c) 6.5 cm^2 (d) 7 cm^2

3. Area of region III is
(a) $1\ cm^2$ (b) $3\ cm^2$
(c) $2\ cm^2$ (d) $1.3\ cm^2$

PASSAGE - II

A park, in the shape of a quadrilateral ABCD, has $\angle C = 90°$, AB = 9m, BC = 12 m, CD = 5 m and AD = 8 m.

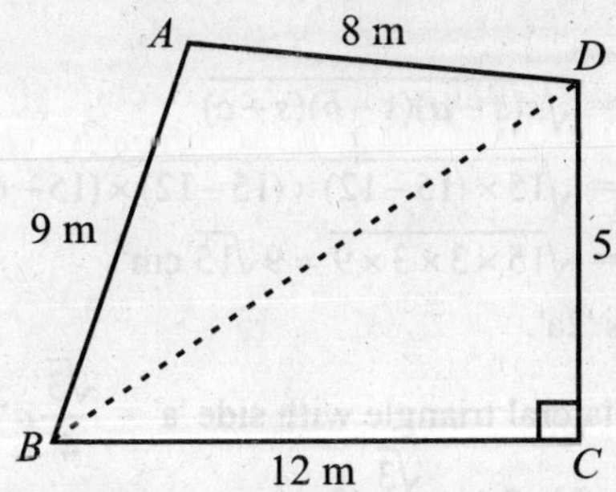

4. Length of BD is
(a) 10 m (b) 11 m
(c) 12 m (d) 13 m

5. Area of Δ ABD is
(a) $35.5\ m^2$ (b) $37\ m^2$
(c) $35\ m^2$ (d) $34\ m^2$

6. Area of quadrilateral ABCD is
(a) $62\ m^2$ (b) $64\ m^2$
(c) $65.5\ m^2$ (d) $66\ m^2$

Assertion & Reason :

DIRECTIONS: *Each of these questions contains an Assertion followed by Reason. Read them carefully and answer the question on the basis of following options. You have to select the one that best describes the two statements.*

(a) If both **Assertion** and **Reason** are **correct** and Reason is the **correct explanation** of Assertion.
(b) If both **Assertion** and **Reason** are correct, but Reason **is not the correct explanation** of Assertion.
(c) If **Assertion** is **correct** but **Reason** is **incorrect**.
(d) If **Assertion** is **incorrect** but **Reason** is **correct**.

1. **Assertion :** The side of an equilateral triangle is 6 cm then the height of the triangle is 9 cm

Reason : The height of an equilateral triangle is $\frac{\sqrt{3}}{2}a$

2. **Assertion :** The sides of a triangle are 3 cm, 4 cm and 5 cm. Its area is $6\ cm^2$.

Reason : If 2s =(a + b + c), where a, b, c are the sides of a triangle, then area $=\sqrt{(s-a)(s-b)(s-c)}$

3. **Assertion :** The sides of a triangle are in the ratio of 25 : 14 : 12 and its perimeter is 510 m. Then the greatest side is 250 cm

Reason : Perimeter of a triangle = a + b + c, where a, b, c are sides of a triangle.

4. **Assertion :** The height of the triangle is 18 cm and its area is $72\ cm^2$. Its base is 8 cm.

Reason : Area of a triangle = $\frac{1}{2}\times$ base × height

Integer Type Questions :

DIRECTIONS: *Answer the following questions. The answer to each of the question is a single digit integer, ranging from 0 to 9.*

1. The lengths of the sides of a triangle are 5 cm, 12 cm and 13 cm. The length of perpendicular from the opposite vertex to the side whose length is 13 cm, is $\frac{m}{13}$. Find the value of $m \div 10$.
2. A triangle and a parallelogram have the same base and the same area. If the sides of the triangle are 26 cm, 28 cm and 30 cm, and the parallelogram stands on the base 28 cm, then the height of the parallelogram is h. Find the value of $h - 10$.
3. A square and an equilateral triangle have equal perimeters. If the diagonal of the square is $12\sqrt{2}$ cm, then area of the triangle is $64\sqrt{p}\ cm^2$. Find the value of 'p'.
4. The length of each side of an equilateral triangle of area $4\sqrt{3}\ cm^2$, is
5. The lengths of the sides of Δ ABC are consecutive integers. If Δ ABC has the same perimeter as an equilateral triangle with a side of 9 cm, then find the length of the shortest side of Δ ABC.

SOLUTIONS

Brief Explanations of Selected Questions

1 EXERCISE

TRUE/FALSE :

1. True 2. False 3. True 4. False
5. True 6. True 7. False 8. False
9. True

MATCH THE COLUMNS :

1. (A) → (r); (B) → (q) ; (C) → (p)

(A) Area of triangle = $420\sqrt{5}$ cm²

$\therefore$ Longest altitude = $\frac{2\times 420\sqrt{5}}{35}$ cm

(B) Area of rhombus = 2 × area of Δ

Now, area of triangle = $\sqrt{18(8)(8)(2)}$

$= 2\times 2\times 2\times 2\times 3 = 48$

Hence, area of rhombus = 2 × 48 = 96 cm²

(C) Area of the triangle = 306 m²

$\therefore$ cost at the rate of ₹ 2 per m² = 306 × 2 = 612

2. (A) → (r); (B) → (p); (C) → (q)

(A) Area of triangle = $\frac{1}{2}\times$ base × height

$= \frac{1}{2}\times 4\times 6 = 12\ \text{cm}^2$

(B) Perimeter of isoscele triangle = 11

$\Rightarrow x + x + 5 = 11 \Rightarrow 2x = 6 \Rightarrow x = 3$

Area of isoscele triangle = $\frac{5}{4}\sqrt{36-25}\ \text{cm}^2$

$= \frac{5}{4}\sqrt{11}\ \text{cm}^2$

(C) Area of equilateral triangle = $\frac{\sqrt{3}}{4}a^2 = \frac{\sqrt{3}}{4}(8)(8)$

$= 16\sqrt{3}\ \text{cm}^2$

SHORT ANSWER QUESTIONS :

1. Let the length of unequal side be x cm.
Then perimeter = 30 cm.

$\Rightarrow \quad x + 12 + 12 = 30$

$\Rightarrow \quad x + 24 = 30$

$\Rightarrow \quad x = 6$ cm

We have, $2s = 30$ cm

$\therefore \quad s = 15$ cm

Hence, area = $\sqrt{s(s-a)(s-b)(s-c)}$

$= \sqrt{15\times(15-12)\times(15-12)\times(15-6)}$

$= \sqrt{15\times 3\times 3\times 9} = 9\sqrt{15}\ \text{cm}^2$

2. Given side is '2a'.

Area of equilateral triangle with side 'a' = $\frac{\sqrt{3}}{4}a^2$ sq. units.

$\therefore$ Area with side 2a = $\frac{\sqrt{3}}{4}(2a)^2$ sq. units

$= \sqrt{3}a^2$ sq. units

3. Perimeter (2s) = 32 cm

$\Rightarrow$ s = 16 cm

4. Δ ABC is a right angled at A

$\therefore$ ar(ΔABC) = $\frac{1}{2}.AB.AC = \frac{1}{2}\times 4\times 4 = 8\ \text{cm}^2$

5. With sticks of given lengths Reema will not be able to form a triangle.
($\because$ for a triangle sum of any two sides must be greater than the third side.)

LONG ANSWER QUESTIONS :

1. We have, $a = 4$ cm, $b = 5$ cm, $c = 6$ cm.

Semi perimeter (s) = $\frac{a+b+c}{2} = \frac{4+5+6}{2} = \frac{15}{2}$ cm

Area of triangle = $\sqrt{s(s-a)(s-b)(s-c)}$

$= \sqrt{\frac{15}{2}\left(\frac{15}{2}-4\right)\left(\frac{15}{2}-5\right)\left(\frac{15}{2}-6\right)} = \frac{15}{4}\sqrt{7}\text{cm}^2$

2. $a = 6$ cm, $b = 6$ cm, $c = 6$ cm

$\therefore \quad s = \frac{a+b+c}{2} = \frac{6+6+6}{2} = 9$ cm

$\therefore$ Area of the equilateral triangle

$= \sqrt{s(s-a)(s-b)(s-c)}$

$= \sqrt{9(9-6)(9-6)(9-6)}$

$= \sqrt{9(3)(3)(3)} = 9\sqrt{3}\ \text{cm}^2$

Area = $\frac{1}{2}$ × Base × Altitude

$\Rightarrow \quad 9\sqrt{3} = \frac{1}{2}\times 6\times \text{Altitude} \Rightarrow 9\sqrt{3} = 3\times \text{Altitude}$

$\Rightarrow \quad \text{Altitude} = \frac{9\sqrt{3}}{3} = 3\sqrt{3}\text{cm}.$

3. Side of ΔABC are given as $a = 50$ cm, $b = 20$ cm, $c = 40$ cm

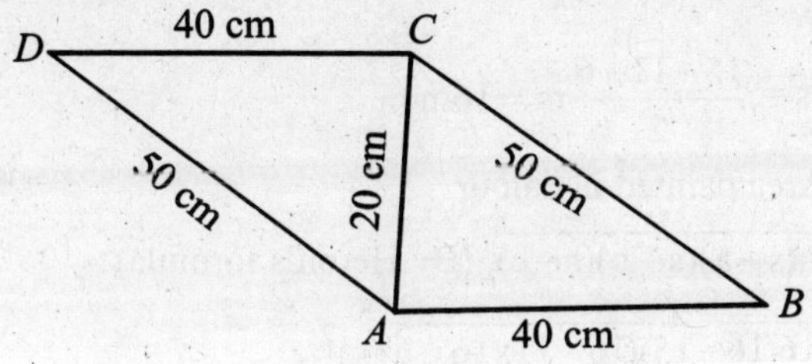

Now, $s = \dfrac{a+b+c}{2}$

$\Rightarrow s = \dfrac{50+20+40}{2} = \dfrac{110}{2} = 55$ cm

$\therefore$ Area of $\Delta ABC = \sqrt{s(s-a)(s-b)(s-c)}$

$= \sqrt{55(55-50)(55-20)(55-40)} = \sqrt{55(5)(35)(15)}$

$= 5\sqrt{5775}$ cm^2

$\therefore$ Area of the parallelogram $ABCD = 2$ Area of ΔABC

$= 2 \times 5\sqrt{5775} = 10\sqrt{5775}$ cm^2

2 EXERCISE

TEXT-BOOK EXERCISE :

1. Given, a quadrilateral $ABCD$ in which $AB = 9$m, $BC = 12$ m, $CD = 5$m, and $AD = 8$m.

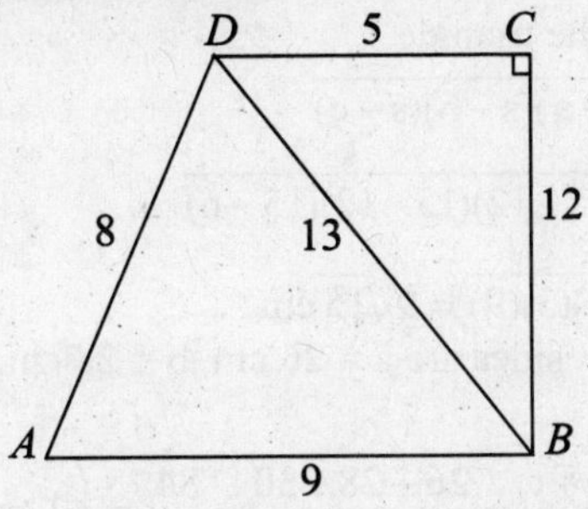

We divide the quadrilateral in two triangular region ABD and BCD.

Now, In ΔBCD right angle at C. We have

$BD^2 = BC^2 + CD^2$ [By pythagoras theorem]

$= 5^2 + 12^2 = 25 + 144 = 169$ m^2

$BD = \dfrac{336}{28}$

$\therefore$ Area of $\Delta BCD = \dfrac{1}{2} \times$ base $\times$ height

$= \dfrac{1}{2} \times 5 \times 12 = 30$ m^2

Note : This area can also be find out using Heron's formula. Now, for triangle ABD, we have

$a = 9$ m, $b = 13$m, $c = 8$m

$s = \dfrac{a+b+c}{2} = \dfrac{9+13+8}{2} = 15\ m$

$\therefore$ Area of $\Delta ABD = \sqrt{s(s-a)(s-b)(s-c)}$

$= \sqrt{15\times 6\times 2\times 7}$

$= \sqrt{3\times 5\times 2\times 3\times 2\times 7}$

$= 3\times 2\ \sqrt{5\times 7} = 6\sqrt{35}$ m^2

$\therefore$ Area of quadrilateral $ABCD$ = Area of ΔBCD + area of $\Delta ABD = (30 + 6\sqrt{35})$ m^2

2. Sides of one triangular piece of cloth are of lengths $a = 20$ cm, $b = 50$ cm and $c = 50$ cm.

Let s be the semi-perimeter of the triangular piece. Then,

$2s = a + b + c \Rightarrow 2s = 20 + 50 + 50 \Rightarrow s = 60$

$\therefore$ $\Delta =$ Area of one triangular piece

$= \sqrt{s(s-a)(s-b)(s-c)}$

$\Rightarrow \Delta = \sqrt{60\times(60-20)\times(60-50)\times(60-50)}$ cm^2

$\Rightarrow \Delta = \sqrt{60\times 40\times 10\times 10}$ cm^2

$= \sqrt{6\times 4\times 10\times 10\times 10\times 10}$ cm^2

$= 200\sqrt{6}$ cm^2

$\therefore$ Area of cloth of each colour $= 5 \times 200\sqrt{6}$ cm^2

$= 1000\sqrt{6}$ cm^2

3. Area of paper of shade I $= \dfrac{1}{2}\left[\dfrac{1}{2}d_1 d_2\right]$ where d_1 and d_2 denotes the diagonals

$= \dfrac{1}{2}\left(\dfrac{1}{2}\times 32\times 32\right) = 256$ cm^2

Area of paper of shade II = 256 cm^2

For paper of shade III, sides are given as $a = 8$ cm, $b = 6$ cm, $c = 6$ cm

$\therefore \dfrac{1}{2}\left(\dfrac{1}{2}\times 32\times 32\right) = 256$ cm^2

$\therefore$ Area of paper of shade III

$= \sqrt{s(s-a)(s-b)(s-c)}$

$= \sqrt{10(10-8)(10-6)(10-6)}$

$= \sqrt{10(2)(4)(4)} = 8\sqrt{5} = 17.92$ cm^2

4. Let the sides of one tile are given as $a = 9$ cm, $b = 28$ cm, $c = 35$ cm

we know $s = \dfrac{a+b+c}{2} = \dfrac{9+28+35}{2} = 36$ cm

$\therefore$ Area of one tile $= \sqrt{s(s-a)(s-b)(s-c)}$

(By Heron's formula)

$= \sqrt{36(36-9)(36-28)(36-35)} = \sqrt{36(27)(8)(1)}$

$= 6 \times 3 \times 2\sqrt{6} = 36\sqrt{6}\ cm^2$

$\therefore$ Area of 16 tiles $= 36\sqrt{6} \times 16 = 576\sqrt{6}\ cm^2$

$\therefore$ cost of polishing the tiles at the rate of 50 paise per cm^2.

$= 576\sqrt{6} \times 50 p = ₹\frac{576\sqrt{6} \times 50}{100}$

$= ₹\ 288\sqrt{6} = ₹\ 705.60$

5. The traffic signal is in the form of an equilateral triangle having side's length '*a*' cm.

$\therefore\ s = \frac{a+a+a}{2} = \frac{3}{2}a$

$\therefore$ Area of triangle using Heron's Formula

$= \sqrt{s(s-a)(s-b)(s-c)}$

$= \sqrt{\frac{3}{2}a\left(\frac{3}{2}a-a\right)\left(\frac{3}{2}a-a\right)\left(\frac{3}{2}a-a\right)}$

$= \sqrt{\frac{3}{2}a \times \frac{a}{2} \times \frac{a}{2} \times \frac{a}{2}} = \frac{\sqrt{3}}{4}a^2$

If perimeter of triangle is 180 cm i.e. $a + a + a = 180$

$\therefore\ a = \frac{180}{3} = 60$ cm

$\therefore$ Area of triangle $= \frac{\sqrt{3}}{4} \times 60 \times 60$

$= \sqrt{3} \times 15 \times 60 = 900\sqrt{3}\ cm^2$

6. Let the sides of the wall be a, b and c.

$\therefore$ a = 122 m, b = 22 m, c = 120 m

Now, we know,

$s = \frac{a+b+c}{2} = \frac{122+22+120}{2} = 132$

$\therefore$ Area of the wall

$= \sqrt{s(s-a)(s-b)(s-c)}$ (By Heron's formula)

$= \sqrt{132(132-122)(132-22)(132-120)}$

$= \sqrt{132(10)(110)(12)} = (12)(11)(10)\ m^2$

$= 1320\ m^2$

Now, 1 year = 12 months

Given, Rent for 12 months per m^2 = ₹ 5000

$\therefore$ Rent for 1 month per $m^2 = ₹\frac{5000}{12}$

$\therefore$ Rent for 3 months per $m^2 = ₹\frac{5000}{12} \times 3 = ₹1250$

$\therefore$ Rent for 3 months of 1320 m^2 = ₹ (1250 × 1320)

= ₹ 1650000.

7. Let the sides of the wall be a, b and c.

$\therefore$ a = 15 m

b = 11 m

c = 6 m

We know $s = \frac{a+b+c}{2}$

$\Rightarrow s = \frac{15+11+6}{2} m = 16m$

$\therefore$ Area painted in colour

$= \sqrt{s(s-a)(s-b)(s-c)}$ (By Heron's formula)

$= \sqrt{16(16-15)(16-11)(16-6)}\ m^2$

$= \sqrt{16(1)(5)(10)}\ m^2 = 20\sqrt{2}\ m^2$

8. Let a, b, c be the sides of isosceles triangle.

Given, a = 12 cm, b = 12 cm

Perimeter = 30 cm

$\Rightarrow a + b + c = 30 \quad \Rightarrow 12 + 12 + c = 30$

$\Rightarrow c = 30 - 24$

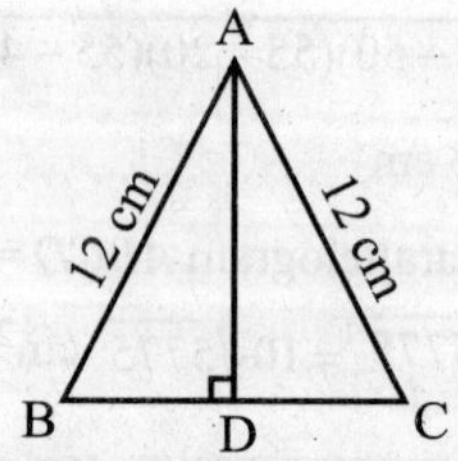

$\Rightarrow c = 6$ cm

Now, $s = \frac{a+b+c}{2} = \frac{12+12+6}{2}$

$\Rightarrow s = \frac{30}{2} cm = 15 cm$

$\therefore$ Area of the triangle

$= \sqrt{s(s-a)(s-b)(s-c)}$

$= \sqrt{15(15-12)(15-12)(15-6)}$

$= \sqrt{15(3)(3)(9)} = 9\sqrt{15}\ cm^2$.

9. For triangle, sides are a = 26 cm, b = 28 cm, c = 30 cm

$\therefore s = \frac{a+b+c}{2} = \frac{26+28+30}{2} = \frac{84}{2} = 42$ cm

$\therefore$ Area of the triangle

$= \sqrt{s(s-a)(s-b)(s-c)}$ (By Heron's formula)

$= \sqrt{42(42-26)(42-28)(42-30)}$

$= \sqrt{42(16)(14)(12)} = \sqrt{(6 \times 7)16(7 \times 2)(6 \times 2)}$

$= 6 \times 4 \times 7 \times 2 = 336\ cm^2$

Let the height of the parallelogram be x cm.

Then, area of the parallelogram = Base × Height $= 28 \times x\ cm^2$

Since, triangle and parallelogram have the same area

$\therefore\ 28x = 336 \Rightarrow x = \frac{336}{28} \Rightarrow x = 12$ cm

10. Let the trapezium be ABCD such that AB = 25 m, CD = 10 m, BC = 13 m and AD = 14 m.
From D, draw DE || BC meeting AB at E.
Also, draw DF ⊥ AB.

$\therefore$ DE = BC = 13 m

AE = AB – EB = AB – DC ($\because$ EB = DC)

= 25 – 10 = 15 m

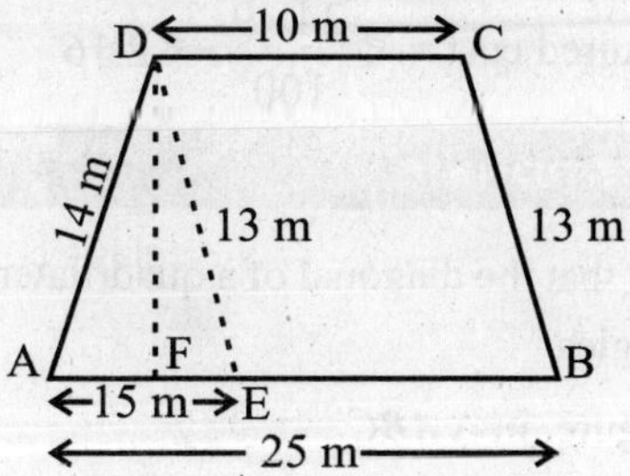

Let the sides of ΔAED are given as

a = 14 m

b = 13 m

c = 15 m

We know $s = \frac{a+b+c}{2}$

$\Rightarrow s = \frac{14+13+15}{2} = \frac{42}{2} = 21$ m

$\therefore$ Area of ΔAED = $\sqrt{s(s-a)(s-b)(s-c)}$

$= \sqrt{21(21-14)(21-13)(21-15)}$

$= \sqrt{21(7)(8)(6)} = \sqrt{(7\times3)7(4\times2)(2\times3)}$

$= 7 \times 3 \times 2 \times 2 = 84$ m^2

Also, area of ΔAED = $\frac{1}{2}$ × Base × altitude

$\Rightarrow \frac{1}{2} \times AE \times DF = 84 \Rightarrow \frac{1}{2} \times 15 \times DF = 84$

$\Rightarrow DF = \frac{84\times2}{15} = \frac{56}{5}$ m

$\therefore$ Area of parallelogram EBCD = Base × Height

$= EB \times DF = 10 \times \frac{56}{5} = 112$ m^2

$\therefore$ Area of the field = Area of ΔAED + Area of parallelogram EBCD = 84 m^2 + 112 m^2 = 196 m^2

EXEMPLAR QUESTIONS :

1. Area of square $= \frac{1}{2} \times 44 \times 44 = 968 \text{cm}^2$

$\therefore$ Area of red portion $= \frac{968}{4} = 242 \text{cm}^2$

Area of yellow portion $= \frac{968}{2} = 484 \text{cm}^2$

$\therefore$ Area of green portion $= \frac{968}{4} = 242$ cm^2

For area of tail of kite, $s = \frac{20+20+14}{2}$

$\Rightarrow$ s = 27 cm

$\therefore$ Area $= \sqrt{27(27-20)(27-20)(27-14)}$

$= \sqrt{27\times7\times7\times13}$

$= 7\times3\sqrt{39} = 21\sqrt{39}\text{cm}^2$

$= 21 \times 6.24 = 131.04$ cm^2

$\therefore$ Total area of green portion = 242 + 131.4

= 373.4 cm^2

2. Sides of the triangular walls are 'a' = 13 m, 'b' = 14 m and 'c' = 15 m

Here, $s = \frac{a+b+c}{2} = \frac{13+14+15}{2} = \frac{42}{2} = 21$ m

Area of the wall

$= \sqrt{21(21-13)(21-14)(21-15)}$

$= \sqrt{21\times8\times7\times6}$

$= \sqrt{3\times7\times2\times2\times2\times7\times3\times2}$

$= 3 \times 7 \times 2 \times 2 = 84$ m^2

Rent paid by the company

$= \frac{2000\times84\times6}{12} = ₹\,84{,}000$

3. Perimeter of an isosceles triangle = 32 cm

Ratio = 3 : 2

3x + 3x + 2x = 32

8x = 32

x = 4

Sides of triangle are a = 12 cm, b = 12 cm, c = 8 cm

Here, s = 16 cm

Area of the triangle $= \sqrt{s(s-a)(s-b)(s-c)}$

$= \sqrt{16(16-12)(16-12)(16-8)}$

$= \sqrt{16\times4\times4\times8}$

$= \sqrt{8\times2\times4\times4\times8}$

$= 32\sqrt{2}$ cm^2

4. Area of parallelogram ABCD

= Area of (ΔABD + ΔBCD)

area of ΔABD = area of ΔBCD

In ΔABD

AB = 'a' = 60 m, BD = 'b' = 80 m, AD = 'c' = 40 m

$s = \frac{60+40+80}{2} = 90$ m

Area of ΔABD $= \sqrt{s(s-a)(s-b)(s-c)}$

$= \sqrt{90\times30\times10\times50}$

$= 300\sqrt{15}$ m^2

Area of parallelogram = 2 × area of ΔABD

$= 2\times300\sqrt{15} = 600\sqrt{15}\ m^2$

5. Area of a trapezium = 475 cm^2
height = 19 cm
Let 'a' and 'b' be the lengths of its parallel sides.
We have
$a = b + 4$ ...(i)
Area of trapezium = 475

$\Rightarrow a + b = \frac{475\times2}{19}$

$\Rightarrow a + b = 50$ ...(ii)

From (i) and (ii), we get
$b + 4 + b = 50$
$\Rightarrow b = 23$ cm
and a = 27 cm
Length of parallel sides of the trapezium are 23 cm and 27 cm

6. In ΔABC
AB = a = 7.5 cm, BC = b = 7 cm, CA = c = 6.5 cm

$s = \frac{a+b+c}{2} = \frac{7.5+7+6.5}{2} = \frac{21}{2} = 10.5$ cm

Area of ΔABC $= \sqrt{s(s-a)(s-b)(s-c)}$

$= \sqrt{(10.5)(3)\times(3.5)\times4}$

$= \sqrt{5\times3\times0.7\times3\times0.7\times5\times2\times2}$

Area of ΔABC = 21 cm^2
Area of parallelogram (trapezium)
= area of ΔABC

$\therefore \frac{1}{2}\times(ED+CB)\times DF = 21$

$\Rightarrow \frac{1}{2}(7+7)\times DF = 21$

$DF = \frac{21\times2}{14} = 3cm$

DF = 3 cm
The height of the parallelogram is 3 cm.

7. (d) Let side of equilateral triangle be 'a' m.
$\therefore a + a + a = 60 \Rightarrow a = 20$ m

Area $= \frac{\sqrt{3}}{4}(20)(20)m^2 = 100\sqrt{3}$

8. (a) Required Area $= \frac{\sqrt{3}}{4}[2\sqrt{3}]^2\ cm^2$

$= 3\sqrt{3}\ cm^2 = 5.196\ cm^2$

9. (b) Given, $\frac{\sqrt{3}}{4}a^2 = 16\sqrt{3}$

$\Rightarrow a^2 = 64 \Rightarrow a = 8$ cm

Perimeter of triangle = 24 cm

10. (b) Let a = 6cm, b = 8 cm, c = 10 cm

$s = \frac{a+b+c}{2} = \frac{6+8+10}{2} = 12$

Area of triangular board $= \sqrt{12(6)(4)(2)}$
$= 24\ cm^2$

Required cost = ₹$\frac{24\times9}{100}$ = ₹2.16

HOTS QUESTIONS :

1. We know that the diagonal of a quadrilateral divides it into two triangles.

As per figure, in Δ *ABC*
AB = 7 cm, *BC* = 12 cm, *AC* = 15 cm
Therefore semi perimeter

$s = \frac{7+12+15}{2} = 17$ cm

Area of Δ *ABC*

$= \sqrt{17\times(17-7)\times(17-12)\times(17-15)}$

$= \sqrt{17\times10\times5\times2}$ sq. cm.

$= 10\sqrt{17}$ sq. cm. = 10 × 4.12 = 41.2 sq. cm.

Similarly for Δ *ACD*, *AC* = 15 cm, *CD* = 12 cm and *DA* = 9 cm

Therefore $s = \frac{15+12+9}{2} = \frac{36}{2} = 18$ cm.

Area of Δ *ACD*

$= \sqrt{18\times(18-15)\times(18-12)\times(18-9)}$

$= \sqrt{18\times3\times6\times9} = 54$ sq. cm.

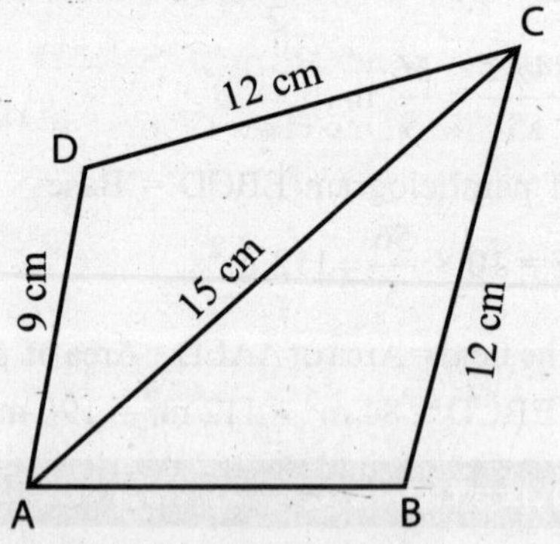

Area of quadrilateral *ABCD*
= Area of Δ *ABC* + Area of Δ *ACD*
= 41.2 + 54 = 95.2 sq. cm.

2. In figure, *ABCD* is a trapezium in which parallel sides *AB* = 55 cm, *DC* = 40 cm and non-parallel sides *AD* = 20 cm and *BC* = 25 cm.

Draw *AD* || *EC* and *CF* ⊥ *AB*
Therefore, *EB* = *AB* – *AE* = 55 – 40 = 15 cm and *EC* = 20 cm.

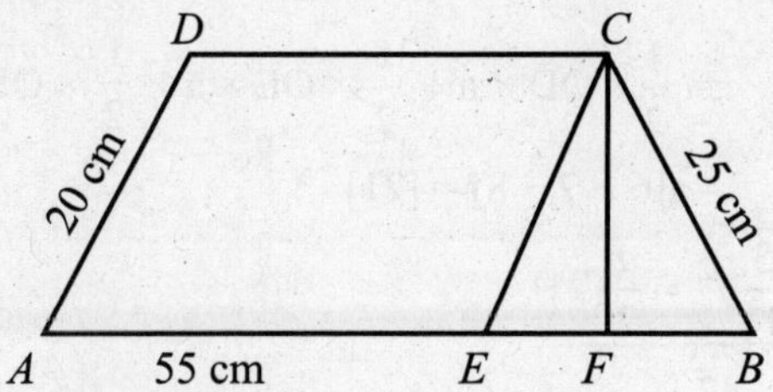

$\therefore$ Area of ΔBCE

$= \sqrt{30\times(30-15)\times(30-20)\times(30-25)}$

where $s = \dfrac{15+20+25}{2} = 30$ cm.

$= \sqrt{30\times15\times10\times5} = \sqrt{22500} = 150$ sq. cm.

Area of ΔBCE

$= \dfrac{1}{2}\times BE\times CF$

$\Rightarrow CF = \dfrac{2\times150}{15} = 20$ cm.

Area of parallelogram $AECD = AE \times CF = 40 \times 20$
$= 800$ sq. cm.

$\therefore$ Area of the trapezium $ABCD$
= Area of parallelogram $AECD$ + Area of ΔEBC
$= 800 + 150 = 950$ sq. cm.

3. Area of one triangular leaf $= \sqrt{s(s-a)(s-b)(s-c)}$

$s = \dfrac{41+28+15}{2} = \dfrac{84}{2} = 42$

Area of a triangle $= \sqrt{42(42-41)(42-28)(42-15)}$

$= \sqrt{42\times1\times14\times27}$

$= 126\text{ cm}^2$

Area of 6 such triangular leaf $= 126 \times 6 = 756\text{ cm}^2$

Since two such circles are there,

Thus, area to be painted red $= 756 \times 2 = 1512\text{ cm}^2$

4. Area of rectangle ABCD = AB × BC = 51 × 25 = 1275 cm^2

Area of trapezium PBCQ $= \dfrac{5}{6}\times1275 = \dfrac{6375}{6}\text{ cm}^2$

Let QC = $9x$ cm and PB = $8x$ cm

$\therefore$ Area of trapezium PBCQ $= \dfrac{1}{2}(\text{QC} + \text{PB}) \times \text{BC}$

$\Rightarrow \dfrac{6375}{6} = \dfrac{1}{2}(9x+8x)\times25$

$\Rightarrow \dfrac{17x\times25}{2} = \dfrac{6375}{6} \Rightarrow x = \dfrac{6375}{6}\times\dfrac{2}{17\times25}$

$\Rightarrow x = 5$

$\therefore$ QC = 9 × 5 cm = 45 cm and PB = 8 × 5 cm = 40 cm

3 EXERCISE

SINGLE OPTION CORRECT :

1. (d) The sides of the triangle are $a = 13$ cm, $b = 9$ cm and $c = 6$ cm.

$s = \dfrac{a+b+c}{2} = \dfrac{13+9+6}{2} = 14$ cm.

$\therefore$ Area of the triangle

$= \sqrt{s(s-a)(s-b)(s-c)}$ [Heron's formula]

$= \sqrt{14\,(14-13)\,(14-9)\,(14-6)}\text{ cm}^2$

$= \sqrt{14\times1\times5\times8}\text{ cm}^2 = \sqrt{560}\text{ cm}^2$

$= 23.66\text{ cm}^2$

2. (b) Suppose that the sides, in metres, are $3x$, $5x$ and $7x$
Then, we know that $3x + 5x + 7x = 300$
(perimeter of the triangle)
Therefore, $15x = 300$, which gives $x = 20$.
So the sides of the triangle are 3 × 20 m, 5 × 20 m and 7 × 20 m
i.e., 60 m, 100 m and 140 m

We have $s = \dfrac{60+100+140}{2}\text{m} = 150\text{ m}$, and area will be $\sqrt{150\,(150-60)\,(150-100)\,(150-140)}\text{ m}^2$

$= \sqrt{150\times90\times50\times10}\text{ m}^2 = 1500\sqrt{3}\text{ m}^2$

3. (d) Area of the parallelogram $ABCD$
= 2 × (Area of ΔABC)
In ΔABC, $AB = 5$ cm, $BC = 3.5$ cm and $AC = 6.5$ cm.

So its perimeter $s = \dfrac{5+3.5+6.5}{2} = 7.5$ cm.

$\because$ Area of ΔABC (By Heron's formula)
$= \sqrt{s(s-a)(s-b)(s-c)}$
$= \sqrt{7.5\times(7.5-5)\times(7.5-3.5)\times(7.5-6.5)}$ sq. cm.
$= \sqrt{7.5\times2.5\times4\times1}$ sq. cm. $= \sqrt{75}$ sq. cm. $= 5\sqrt{3}$ sq.cm.
Area of parallelogram
$= 2\times5\sqrt{3}$ sq. cm. $= 10\sqrt{3}$ sq.cm.

4. (a) Third side $= \sqrt{(\text{Hypotenuse})^2 - (\text{Base})^2}$

$= \sqrt{100-64} = 6$ cm

$s = \dfrac{10+8+6}{2}$ cm = 12 cm

Area $= \sqrt{s(s-a)(s-b)(s-c)}$

$= \sqrt{12(12-10)(12-8)(12-6)}$

$= \sqrt{12\times2\times4\times6}\text{ cm}^2 = 24\text{ cm}^2$

5. (d) Side = 6 cm
$\therefore$ Perimeter of regular hexagon = 6 × 6 = 36 cm
$ABCDEF$ is a regular hexagon. Join diagonals AD, BE and CF. The three diagonal divides the hexagonal in

six. congruent equilateral triangle with side 6cm.

Area of one such triangle

$= \sqrt{s(s-a)(s-b)(s-c)}$

$= \sqrt{9(9-6)(9-6)(9-6)} = \sqrt{9 \times 3 \times 3 \times 3} = 9\sqrt{3}$

$\therefore$ Area of the regular hexagon

= 6 × Area of equilateral triangle *OAB*

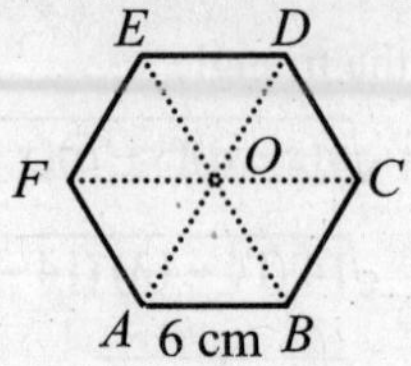

$= 6 \times 9\sqrt{3} = 54\sqrt{3}\ \text{cm}^2$.

6. (a) For area of the park, we have

$2s = 50\text{m} + 80\text{m} + 120\text{ m} = 250\text{ m}$.

$s = 125$ m

i.e., $s - a = (125 - 120)$ m = 5 m,

$s - b = (125 - 80)$ m = 45 m,

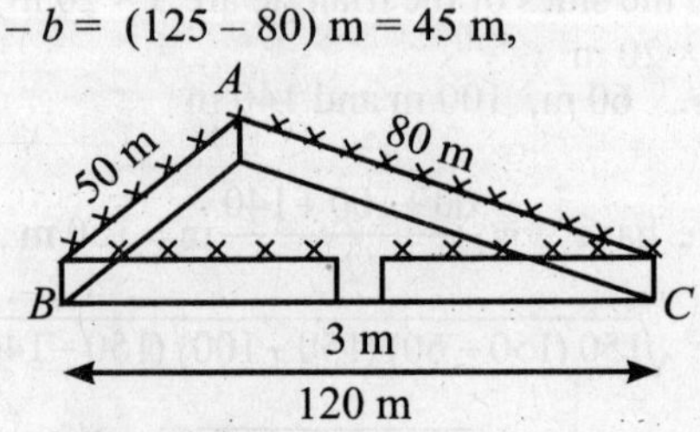

$s - c = (125 - 50)$ m = 75 m.

Therefore, area of the park

$= \sqrt{s(s-a)(s-b)(s-c)}$

$= \sqrt{125 \times 5 \times 45 \times 75}\ \text{m}^2 = 375\sqrt{15}\text{m}^2$

Also, perimeter of the park = *AB* + *BC* + *CA* = 250 m

Therefore, length of the wire needed for fencing

= 250 m – 3 m (to be left for gate) = 247 m

And so the cost of fencing = ₹20 × 247 = ₹4940

7. (b) Since we know that area of

ΔAOB = ar. of ΔCOD = ar. of ΔAOD = ar. of ΔBOC.

Thus, area of ΔAOB + area of ΔCOD

= ar. of ΔAOD + ar. of ΔBOC.

8. (b) Area of $\Delta ABC = \frac{\sqrt{3}}{4}a^2$

and, also

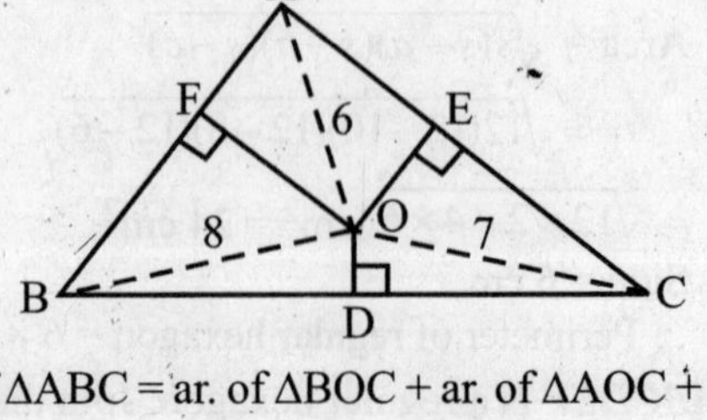

area of ΔABC = ar. of ΔBOC + ar. of ΔAOC + ar. of ΔAOB

$\Rightarrow \frac{1}{2} \times OD \times a + \frac{1}{2} \times OE \times a + \frac{1}{2} \times OF \times a$

$= a[6 + 7 + 8] = [21]$

$\frac{\sqrt{3}}{4}a^2 = \frac{a}{2}(21)$

$a = \frac{42}{\sqrt{3}} \Rightarrow a = 14\sqrt{3}$

Area of $\Delta ABC = \frac{\sqrt{3}}{4} \times (14\sqrt{3})^2 = 147\sqrt{3}\ \text{m}^2$

9. (a) Area of right triangle $= \frac{1}{2} \times b \times h$

Since its an isosceles right triangle

$\therefore\ b = h$

$\Rightarrow \frac{1}{2} \times b^2 = 8 \Rightarrow b^2 = 16 \Rightarrow b = 4$

Hypotenuse $= \sqrt{\text{base}^2 + \text{height}^2}$

$= \sqrt{4^2 + 4^2} = \sqrt{32}$ cm

10. (c) AD is median of ΔABC.

$\Rightarrow$ ar (ΔABD) = ar (ΔADC) $= \frac{1}{2}$ ar (ΔABC)...(i)

Now, ar (ΔADC) = 15 cm^2 (given)

$\therefore$ From (i), $15 = \frac{1}{2}$ ar (ΔABC) $\Rightarrow$ 30 = ar (ΔABC)

$\therefore$ ar (ΔABC) = 30 cm^2

PASSAGE BASED QUESTIONS :

PASSAGE - I

1. (a) **2.** (c) **3.** (d)

1-3. For triangular area I, we have

$a = 5$ cm, $b = 5$ cm, $c = 1$ cm

as the sides of the triangle

$\therefore\quad s = \frac{a+b+c}{2} = \frac{5+5+1}{2} = \frac{11}{2} = 5.5\text{cm}$

$\therefore$ Area of shaded region I $= \sqrt{s(s-a)(s-b)(s-c)}$,

$= \sqrt{5.5(5.5-5)(5.5-5)(5.5-1)}$

$= \sqrt{5.5(.5)(.5)(4.5)} = (.5)\sqrt{(5.5)(4.5)}$

$= (.5)\sqrt{(.5)(11)(.5)(9)} = (.5)(.5)(3)\sqrt{11}$

$= 0.75\sqrt{11} = 0.75(3.3)$ (approx.)

= 2.5 cm^2 (approx.),

Area of shaded region II = Area of rectangle

= 6.5 × 1 = 6.5 cm^2

For Area of shaded region III, draw the figure

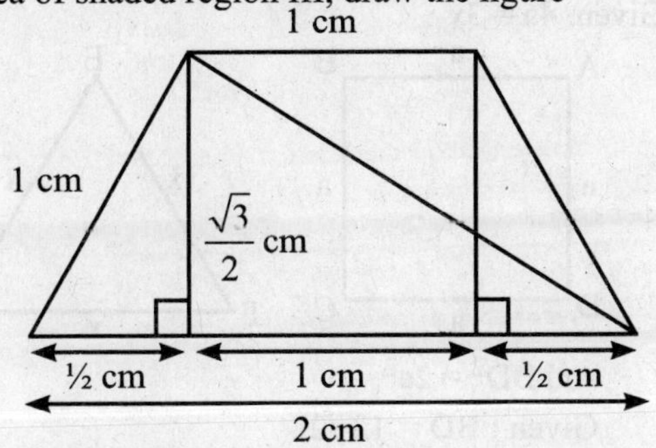

Area of region III

$= \frac{1}{2} \times 2 \times \frac{\sqrt{3}}{2} + \frac{1}{2} \times 1 \times \frac{\sqrt{3}}{2} = \frac{\sqrt{3}}{2} + \frac{\sqrt{3}}{4}$

$= \frac{3\sqrt{3}}{4} = \frac{3 \times 1.732}{4}$ (Approx.)

$= \frac{5.196}{4} = 1.3 \text{ cm}^2$ (approx.)

Thus, area of region IV = Area of right angled Δ

$= \frac{6 \times 1.5}{2} = 4.5 \text{ cm}^2$

Similarly, Area $V = \frac{6 \times 1.5}{2} = 4.5 \text{ cm}^2$

∴ Total area of the paper used

= Area I + Area II + Area III + Area IV + Area V

$= 2.5 \text{ cm}^2 + 6.5 \text{ cm}^2 + 1.3 \text{ cm}^2 + 4.5 \text{ cm}^2 + 4.5 \text{ cm}^2$

$= 19.3 \text{ cm}^2$. (approx)

4. (d) **5.** (a) **6.** (c)

4–6 Let us join B and D, such that Δ BCD is a right-angled triangle.

We have area of Δ BCD $= \frac{1}{2} \times$ base × altitude

$= \frac{1}{2} \times 12 \times 5 \text{ m}^2 = 30 \text{ m}^2$

Now, to find the area of Δ ABD, we need the length of BD.

∴ In right angled Δ BCD,

$BD^2 = BC^2 + CD^2$ [Pythagoras theorem]

⇒ $BD^2 = 12^2 + 5^2$

⇒ $BD^2 = 144 + 25 = 169 \Rightarrow BD = 13$ m

Now, for Δ ABD, we have

a = 9 m, b = 8 m, c = 13 m

$s = \frac{a+b+c}{2} = \frac{9+8+13}{2} = \frac{30}{2} = 15$ m

∴ Area of Δ ABD $= \sqrt{s(s-a)(s-b)(s-c)}$

$= \sqrt{15(15-9)(15-8)(15-13)} \text{ m}^2 = \sqrt{15 \times 6 \times 7 \times 2} \text{ m}^2$

$= \sqrt{3 \times 5 \times 3 \times 2 \times 7 \times 2} \text{ m}^2 = \sqrt{3^2 \times 2^2 \times 5 \times 7} \text{ m}^2$

$= 3 \times 2\sqrt{35} \text{ m}^2$

$= 6 \times 5.916 \text{ m}^2$ (approx) $= 35.5 \text{ m}^2$ (approx)

∴ Area of quadrilateral ABCD = area of Δ BCD + area of Δ ABD

$= 30 \text{ m}^2 + 35.5 \text{ m}^2 = 65.5 \text{ m}^2$ (approx)

ASSERTION AND REASON :

1. (d) The height of the triangle, $h = \frac{\sqrt{3}}{2}a$

$\Rightarrow 9 = \frac{\sqrt{3}}{2}a \Rightarrow a = \frac{9 \times 2}{\sqrt{3}} = \frac{18}{\sqrt{3}} \times \frac{\sqrt{3}}{\sqrt{3}}$

$= \frac{18\sqrt{3}}{3} = 6\sqrt{3}$ cm

2. (c) $s = \frac{a+b+c}{2} \Rightarrow s = \frac{3+4+5}{2} = 6$ cm

Area $= \sqrt{s(s-a)(s-b)(s-c)}$

$= \sqrt{(6)(6-3)(6-4)(6-5)}$

$= \sqrt{(6)(3)(2)(1)} = 6 \text{ cm}^2$

Assertion is true but Reason is false.

3. (a) $510 = a + b + c \Rightarrow 510 = 25x + 14x + 12x$

$\Rightarrow 510 = 51x \Rightarrow x = 10$

Three sides of the triangle are

$25x = 25 \times 10 = 250$ cm, $14x = 14 \times 10 = 140$ cm and $12x = 12 \times 10 = 120$ cm.

4. (a) Assertion and Reason both are correct. Reason is the correct explanation.

Assertion : Area of $\Delta = \frac{1}{2} \times$ base × height

$72 = \frac{1}{2} \times 18 \times b$

$\Rightarrow b = \frac{72 \times 2}{18} = 8$ cm

INTEGER TYPE QUESTIONS :

1. **Ans : 6**

Here, $a = 5$, $b = 12$ and $c = 13$.

∴ $s = \frac{1}{2}(a+b+c) = \frac{1}{2}(5+12+13) = 15$

Let A be the area of the given triangle.

Then,

$A = \sqrt{s(s-a)(s-b)(s-c)} = \sqrt{15(15-5)(15-12)(15-13)}$

$\Rightarrow A = \sqrt{15 \times 10 \times 3 \times 2} = 30 \text{ cm}^2$

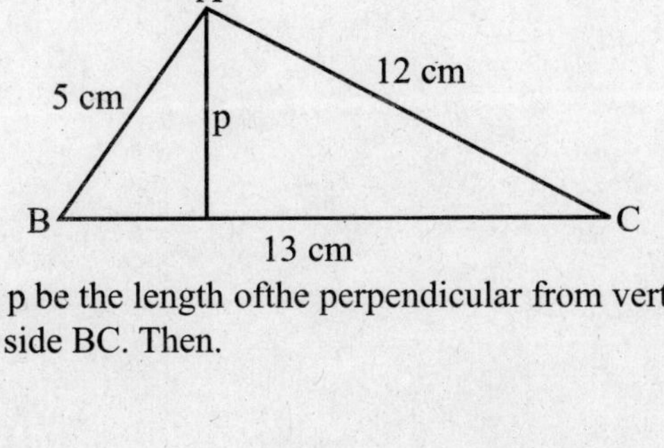

Let p be the length ofthe perpendicular from vertex A on the side BC. Then.

$A=\frac{1}{2}\times(13)\times p$

From (i) and (ii) we get

$\frac{1}{2}\times(13)\times p=30\Rightarrow p=\frac{60}{13}$cm

Hence $m \div 10 = 60 \div 10 = 6$

2. Ans : 2

Let s be the semi-perimeter of the triangle. Then,

$s=\frac{26+28+30}{2}=42$cm

∴ Area of the triangle

$=\sqrt{42\times(42-26)\times(42-28)\times(42-30)}$ cm^2

$=\sqrt{42\times16\times14\times12}$ $cm^2 = 336$ cm^2

Let h be the height of the parallelogram.

It is given that the triangle and the parallelogram have the same base and between the same parallels have the same area.

∴ Area of the parallelogram = 336 cm^2

⇒ Base × Height 336 cm^2

⇒ 28 × h = 336 cm

⇒ $h=\frac{336}{28}$ cm = 12cm.

3. Ans : 3

Given, 4a = 3x

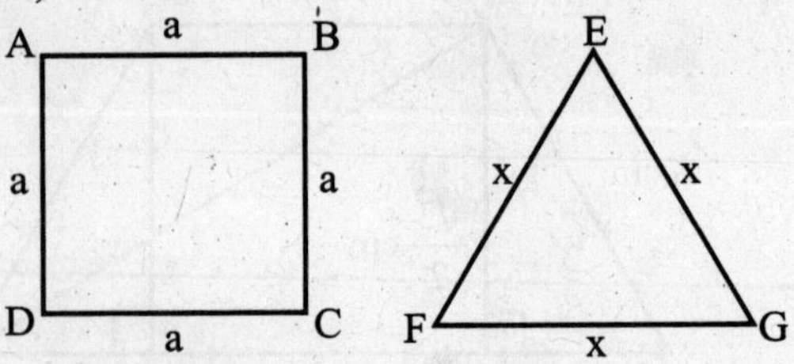

and $BD^2 = 2a^2$

Given : $BD = 12\sqrt{2}$

$\Rightarrow 2a^2 = 144\times 2 \Rightarrow a = 12$ cm

$\Rightarrow x=\frac{4}{3}\times12=16$ cm

So, area of triangle = $\frac{\sqrt{3}}{4}\times16\times16$ cm^2

$=64\sqrt{3}$ $cm^2 \Rightarrow p = 3$

4. Ans : 5

Given : $\frac{\sqrt{3}}{4}a^2=4\sqrt{3}$

$\Rightarrow a^2 = 16 \Rightarrow a = 4$ cm

5. Ans : 8

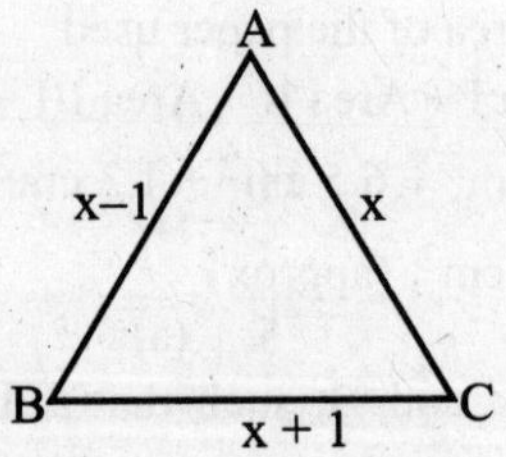

Given : (x – 1) + (x) + (x + 1) = 27

⇒ 3x = 27 ⇒ x = 9

Length of shortest side = 9 – 1 = 8 cm.

Chapter 13

Surface Areas and Volume of Solids

INTRODUCTION

Wherever we look, in our day to day life, we come across several figures that can be easily drawn on our notebooks or blackboards figures which are drawn in 2-dimensional space length wise and breadth wise are called plane figures. Rectangles, squares and circles are some example of plane figures. If we cut out many of these plane figures of the same shape, we shall obtain some solid figures like cuboid, cylinder, etc.

Measuring jars, cylindrical pillars, circular pipes, a garden roller are some example of solid shapes. In this chapter we shall learn about finding the surface areas and volumes of these solid shapes and extend this study to some other solids.

Surfaces is known as the faces which bound a solid and volume is the amount of space occupied by the bounding surfaces of a solid.

In this part of the chapter, you will study about some solids: cuboid, cube, cylinder, cone, sphere, hemisphere and the formula to the surface area and volume of these solids.

CUBOID

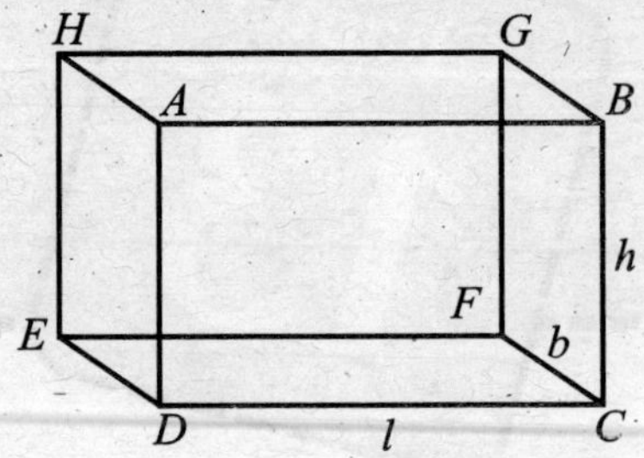

It is a solid bounded by a six rectangular plane regions (or surfaces).

A cuboid is also called a rectangular parallelopiped.

Faces : Cuboid *ABCDEFGH* is bounded by six rectangular plane regions namely *ABCD, EFGH, ADEH, BCFG, ABGH* and *CDEF*.

These six rectangular plane regions are six faces of the cuboid *ABGH* and *CDEF* are the top and bottom faces respectively. Hence a cuboid has six faces.

Edges : Any two adjacent faces of a cuboid meet in a line segment, which is called an edge of the cuboid. in the above fig. *AB, AD, AH, HD, HE, HG, GF, BG, FE, BC, CF, DE* and *CD* are 12 edges of the cuboid. Hence a cuboid has 12 edges.

Vertices : The point of intersection of three edges of a cuboid is called a vertex of the cuboid. In the fig. We have 8 vertices which are *A, B, C, D, E, F, G* and *H*.

Lateral Faces : All the faces except the top and bottom faces are called the lateral faces of a cuboid.

Surface Area of a Cuboid

Consider a cuboid of length l cm, breadth b cm and height h cm.

Total surface area of a cuboid, is equal to the sum of area of all the six faces of the cuboid.

Total surface area of a cuboid = Area of face *ABCD* + Area of face *EFGH* + area of face *DCFE* + area of face *ABGH* + area of face *FCBG* + area of face *AHED*

$= (l \times h) + (l \times h) + (l \times b) + (l \times b) + (b \times h) + (b \times h)$

$= 2\,(lh + bh + lb) = 2\,(lb + bh + hl)$

= 2 [length × breadth + breadth × height + height × length]

Lateral surface of a cuboid = Area of face *ABCD* + Area of face *EFGH* + Area of *FCBG* + Area of *AHED*

$= (l \times h) + (l \times h) + (b \times h) + (b \times h)$

$= 2\,(l \times h + b \times h) = 2\,(l + b) \times h$

= 2 (length + breadth) × height

Diagonal of the Cuboid and Cube

AF, HC, BE, GD are the diagonals of the cuboid

$AF^2 = AD^2 + DF^2$

$= h^2 + l^2 + b^2$

$AF = \sqrt{l^2 + b^2 + h^2}$

Similarly, length of each diagonal = $\sqrt{l^2 + b^2 + h^2}$

Volume of a Cuboid

As we know that the volume of a solid object is the measure of the space occupied by it and the capacity of an object is the volume of the substance that can accomodate in its interior.

Volume of a cuboid = space occupied by the cuboid

= Area of the base × height

$= (l \times b) \times h = lbh$

Volume of the cuboid = length × breadth × height

> **NOTE:** Surface area of any object is measured in 'square units' Volume of any object is measured in 'cube units'

ILLUSTRATION : 1

Find the surface area of a chalk box whose length, breadth and height are 16 cm, 8 cm and 6 cm, respectively.

SOLUTION :

Clearly, A chalk box is in the form of a cuboid.

Here, $l = 16$cm, $b = 8$ cm and $h = 6$ cm

Surface area of the cuboid $= 2\,(lb + bh + lh) = 2\,(16 \times 8 + 8 \times 6 + 16 \times 6)$ cm^2

$= 2\,(128 + 48 + 96)\ cm^2 = 544$ cm^2

CUBE

A cuboid whose edges are equal i.e. its length, breadth and height are equal is called a cube. Each face of cube is a square and area of these squares are equal.

For a cube, $l = b = h$

$\therefore$ Total surfaces area of a cube $= 2\,(l \times l + l \times l + l \times l) = 6\,l^2 = 6 \times (\text{Edge})^2$

Lateral surface of a cube $= 2\,(l \times l + l \times l) = 2\,(l^2 + l^2) = 4l^2 = 4\,(\text{Edge})^2$

Length of a diagonal of the cube $= \sqrt{l^2 + l^2 + l^2} = \sqrt{3}\,l$

Volume of the cube $= l \times l \times l = l^3 = (\text{Edge})^3$

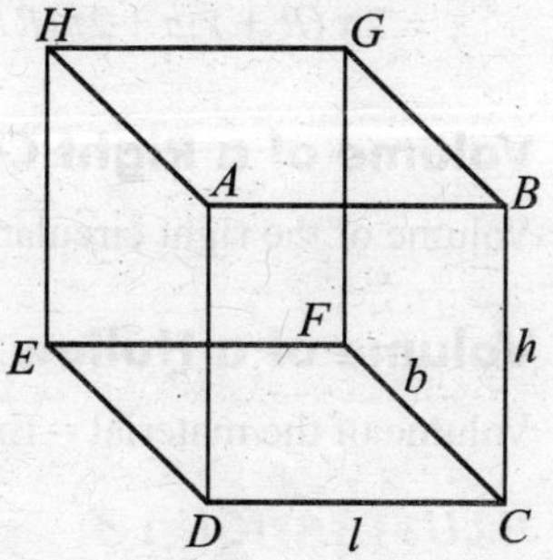

ILLUSTRATION : 2

Find the surface area of a cube whose edge is 11 cm

SOLUTION :

We know that the surface area of a cube $= 6\,(\text{Edge})^2$

Here, edge = 11 cm

$\therefore$ Surface area of the given cube $= 6 \times (11)^2$ cm^2 $= (6 \times 121)$ cm^2 $= 726$ cm^2

RIGHT CIRCULAR CYLINDER

A solid like measuring jars, circular pillars, circular pipes etc., whose cross section is uniform and circular, are examples of circular cylinder. Cylinders have a curved (lateral) surface with congruent circular ends. Some times lower circular end is called the base of the cylinder and upper circular end is called the top of the cylinder. The line joining the centres of the circular ends of a cylinder is called its axis. In figure, OO' is the axis of the cylinder. If the axis is perpendicular to the circular ends then cylinder is called right circular cylinder. Here you will study about right circular cylinder only. Hence a right circular cylinder is simply called cylinder.

A right circular cylinder may also be considered as a solid generated by the revolution of a rectangle about one of its sides.

Thus, if a rectangle $OO'BA$ revolves about its side OO' and completes one revolution to arrive at its initial position, a right circular cylinder will be generated whose axis is OO' and radius $AO = BO' = $ r (say). The length of the axis OO' between the centres is called the length or the height (h) of the cylinder.

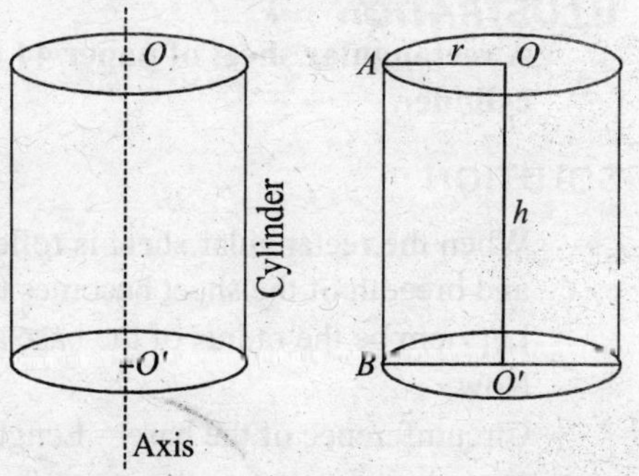

SURFACE AREA OF A RIGHT CIRCULAR CYLINDER

Consider a right circular cylinder of height 'h' and radius 'r'.

We can form curved surface of a right circular cylinder by folding a rectangular sheet as given below:

The area of the sheet gives us the curved surface area of the cylinder. Note that the length (l) of the sheet is equal to the circumference of the circular base which is equal to $2\pi r$.

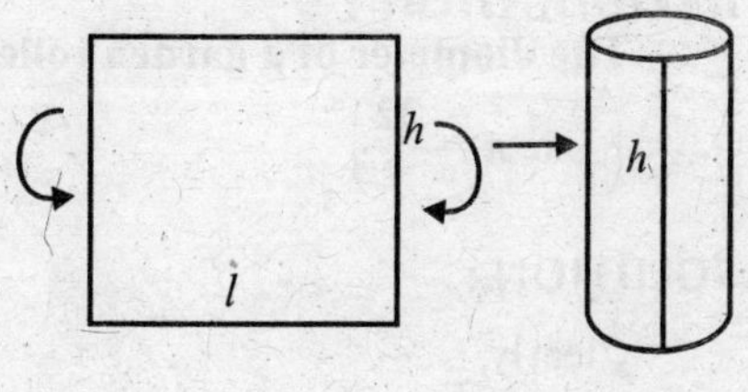

So, curved surface area of the cylinder = Area of the rectangular sheet

$= l \times h =$ perimeter of the base of cylinder $\times h$

$= 2\pi r \times h = 2\pi rh$

Curved surface area of a cylinder $= 2\pi rh$

Total surface area of the cylinder = curved surface + Area of two circular ends

$= 2\pi rh + 2\pi r^2 = 2\pi r\,(h + r)$

Surface Area of A Right Circular Hollow Cylinder

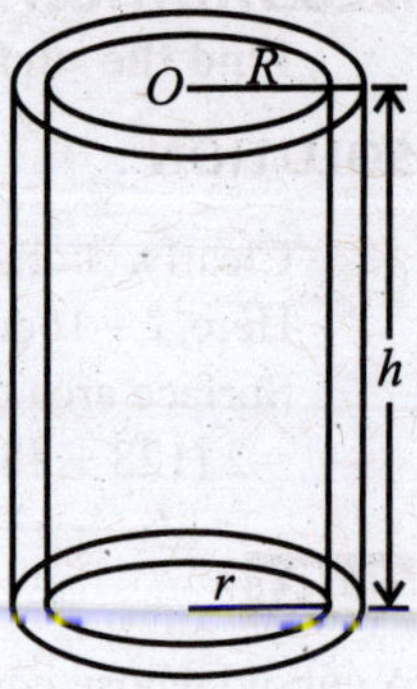

A solid bounded by two coaxial cylinders of the same height and different radii is called a hollow cylinder.

Examples : Iron pipes, rubber tubes, etc.

Let we have a hollow cylinder as shown in the figure having internal and external radii as r and R respectively. h is the height of this cylinder.

Base area $= \pi R^2 - \pi r^2 = \pi(R^2 - r^2)$

curved (lateral) surface area = external surface area + internal surface area

$= 2\pi Rh + 2\pi rh = 2\pi h(R + r)$

Total Surface Area = curved surface area +2 (area of base)

$= 2\pi Rh + 2\pi rh + 2\pi(R^2 - r^2)$

$= 2\pi (R + r)h + 2\pi(R - r)(R + r) = 2\pi (R + r)(h + R - r)$

Volume of a Right Circular Cylinder

Volume of the right circular cylinder = Area of the base × height $= (\pi r^2) \times h = \pi r^2 h$

Volume of a Hollow Cylinder

Volume of the material = Exterior volume – Interior volume $= \pi R^2 h - \pi r^2 h = \pi(R^2 - r^2)h$

ILLUSTRATION : 3

The curved surface area of a right circular cylinder of height 14 cm is 88 cm². Find the diameter of the base of the cylinder.

SOLUTION :

Let r be the radius and h be the height of the cylinder. Then,

$2\pi rh = 88$ and $h = 14 \Rightarrow 2 \times \frac{22}{7} \times r \times 14 = 88$

$\Rightarrow \quad 88r = 88 \Rightarrow r = 1$

$\therefore$ Diameter of the base $= 2r = 2$ cm

ILLUSTRATION : 4

A rectangular sheet of paper 44 cm × 18 cm is rolled along its length and a cylinder is formed. Find the radius of the cylinder.

SOLUTION :

When the rectangular sheet is rolled along its length, we find that the length of the sheet forms the circumference of its base and breadth of the sheet becomes the height of the cylinder.

Let r cm be the radius of the base and h cm be the height. Then, $h = 18$ cm

Now,

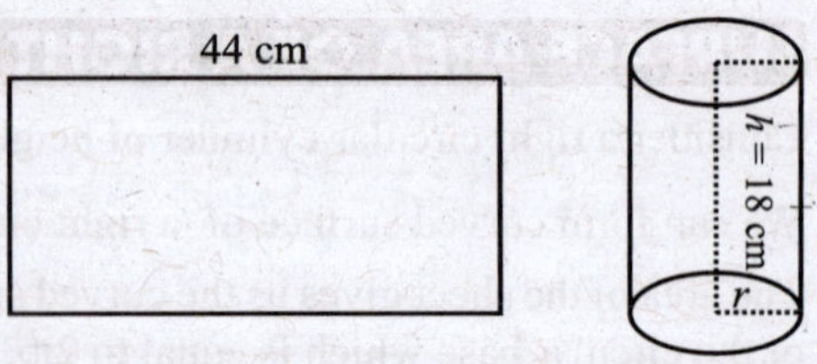

Circumference of the base = Length of the sheet

$\Rightarrow \quad 2\pi r = 44 \Rightarrow 2 \times \frac{22}{7} \times r = 44 \Rightarrow r = 7$cm

Hence, radius of the cylinder is 7 cm.

ILLUSTRATION : 5

The diameter of a garden roller is 1.4 m and it is 2 m long. How much area will it cover in 5 revolutions ? $\left(\text{Use } \pi = \frac{22}{7}\right)$

SOLUTION :

Clearly,

Area covered = Curved surface × Number of revolutions

Here, $r = \frac{1.4}{2}$ m = 0.7m and h = 2m.

$\therefore$ Curved surface = $2\pi rh$ m^2 = $2 \times \frac{22}{7} \times 0.7 \times 2 = 8.8$m^2

Hence, Area covered = Curved surface × No. of revolutions = (8.8 × 5) m^2 = 44m^2

ILLUSTRATION : 6

Find the volume of a right circular cylinder, if the radius (*r*) of its base and height (*h*) are 7 cm and 15 cm, respectively

SOLUTION :

We know that :

Volume of a cylinder = $\pi r^2 h$

$\therefore$ Volume of the cylinder = $\frac{22}{7} \times (7)^2 \times 15$cm^3 $[\because \pi = \frac{22}{7}]$

= 22 × 7 × 15 cm^3 = 2310 cm^3

ILLUSTRATION : 7

The thickness of a hollow wooden cylinder is 2 cm. It is 35 cm long and its inner radius is 12 cm. Find the volume of the wood required to make the cylinder, assuming it is open at either end.

SOLUTION :

We have,

r = Inner radius of the cylinder = 12 cm

Thickness of the cylinder = 2 cm

$\therefore$ R = Outer radius of the cylinder = (12 + 2) cm = 14 cm

h = Height of the cylinder = 35 cm

$\therefore$ Volume of the wood = $\pi (R^2 - r^2) h$

$= \frac{22}{7} \times \{(14)^2 - (12)^2\} \times 35\text{cm}^3$

$= \frac{22}{7} \times (14+12) \times (14-12) \times 35\text{cm}^3$

= 22 × 26 × 2 × 5 cm^3 = 5720 cm^3

RIGHT CIRCULAR CONE

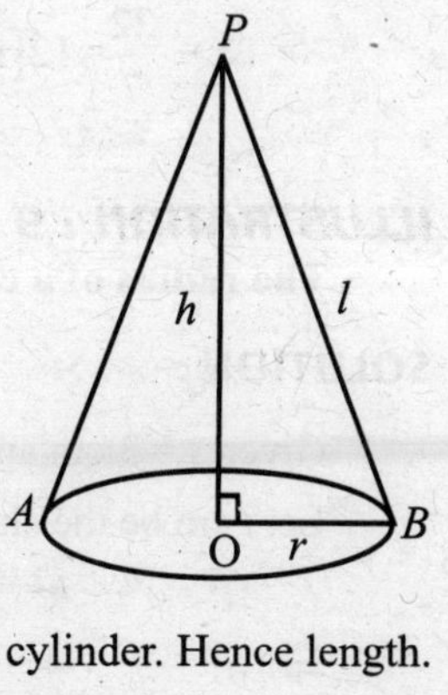

It is solid generated by revolving a right triangular sheet about its one of the perpendicular side.

In the figure, the right circular cone is formed by revolving the Δ *AOP* right angled at O about its one of perpendicular side, say *OP*.

Vertex : The top point *P* is called the vertex of the cone.

Base : A cone has a plane circular end, called the base of the cone.

Axis : The line joining the centre *O* of the base to the vertex *P* is called the axis of the cone. In the right circular cone, axis is perpendicular to the base.

Radius (*r*) : *OA* or *OB* is known as radius of the cone.

Height (*h*) : The distance of the vertex P from the centre O of the base is called height of the right circular cylinder. Hence length. OP is the height in the given figure.

Slant Height (*l*) : The length of the line segment joining the vertex to any point on the circular edge of the base is called slant height In fig. *PB* is the slant height. It is denoted as '*l*'

The slant height = $l = \sqrt{h^2 + r^2}$

NOTE : The angle *OPA* or *OPB* is called the semi-vertical angle of the cone.

Surface Area of a Right Circular Cone

For the given cone of base radius r as shown in fig. (i) the length of the circular edge is $2\pi r$ and area of the plane end (or base) is $2\pi r^2$.

Now suppose, the given cone is hollow and cut the cone along the slant height PA and On spreading out it on a plane surface. You will find that the spread out figure as shown in (ii).

The spread out cone is a sector of a circle of radius equal to the slant height 'l' of the cone and whose arc is equal to the circumference $2\pi r$ of the base of the cone.

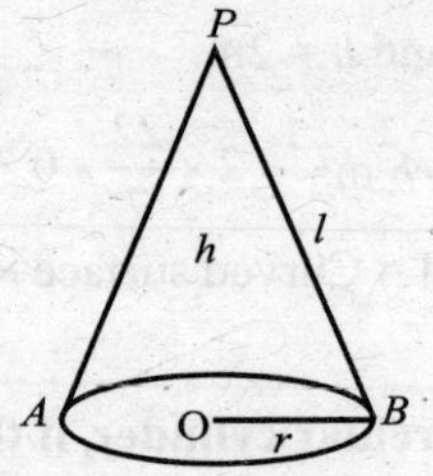

(i) Hollow cone

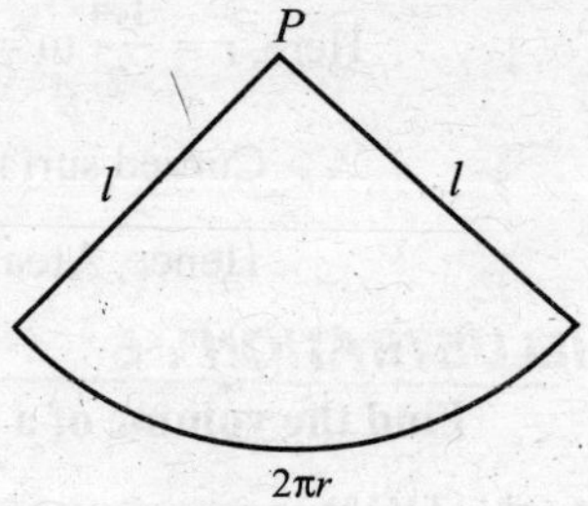

(ii) Spread out figure of the hollow cone

$\therefore$ Curved (or lateral) surface area of the cone $= \pi l^2 \times \dfrac{2\pi r}{2\pi l}$ [Since area of a sector of radius r and arc length l is $\pi r^2 \times \dfrac{l}{2\pi r}$]

$= \pi rl$

Total surface area of the cone = curved surface area + area of the base $= \pi rl + \pi r^2 = \pi r\,(l + r)$

Volume of Right Circular Cone

For this we consider the experiment. Take a conical cup of radius r and height h. Also take a cylindrical jar of radius r and height h. Fill the conical cup with water to the brim and transfer the water to the jar. Repeat the process two times more. You will find that 3 cup of water fill the cylindrical jar completely. Thus, we find that

3(volume of cone of radius r and height h) = (volume of a cylinder or radius r and height h) $= \pi r^2 h$

$\therefore$ Volume of a cone of radius r and height h $= \dfrac{1}{3}\pi r^2 h$

Also, volume of the cone of radius r and height h $= \dfrac{1}{3}(\pi r^2) \times h = \dfrac{1}{3} \times$ (Area of the base) $\times$ height

ILLUSTRATION : 8

The radius of the base of the cone is 12m and its slant height is 9m. Find its total surface area.

SOLUTION :

We know that the total surface area S of a right circular cylinder of radius r and slant height l is given by

$S = \pi r^2 + \pi rl = \pi r\,(r + l)$

Here, $r = 12$ m and $l = 9$ m

$\therefore \quad S = \dfrac{22}{7} \times 12[12+9]\text{m}^2 = 792\text{m}^2$

ILLUSTRATION : 9

The radius of a cone is 3 cm and vertical height is 4 cm. Find its curved surface area

SOLUTION :

Given r = 3 cm and $h = 4$ cm.

Let l cm be the slant height of the cone.

$\therefore \quad l^2 = r^2 + h^2$

$\Rightarrow \quad l^2 = 3^2 + 4^2$

$\Rightarrow \quad l^2 = 25$

$\Rightarrow \quad l = \sqrt{25}\text{cm} = 5\text{cm}$

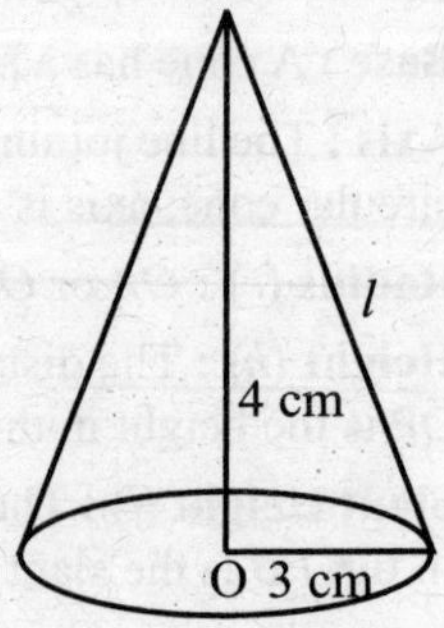

Hence area of the curved surface $= \pi rl = \left(\dfrac{22}{7} \times 4 \times 5\right)\text{cm}^2 = 62.85\text{cm}^2$

ILLUSTRATION : 10

What is the height of the cone if the diameter is 8 cm and volume is 48 π cm³.

SOLUTION :

Let h cm be the height of the cone

D = Diameter of the cone = 8 cm

$\therefore$ r = Radius of the cone = 4cm

Now, Volume of the cone = $48\pi\ cm^3$ [Given]

As we know $V = \frac{1}{3}\pi r^2 h$

$\Rightarrow \frac{1}{3} \times \pi \times 4 \times 4 \times h = 48\pi$

$\Rightarrow h = \frac{48\pi \times 3}{16\pi} cm = 9 cm$

Hence, the height of the cone is 9 cm.

ILLUSTRATION : 11

The volume of a cone is 18480 cm³. If the height of the cone is 40 cm. find the radius of its base.

SOLUTION :

Let the radius of the cone be r cm.

We have, h = Height of the cone = 40 cm and, V = volume of the cone = 18480 cm^3

$\therefore \frac{1}{3} \times \frac{22}{7} \times r^2 \times 40 = 18480$

$\Rightarrow r^2 = \frac{18480 \times 3 \times 7}{22 \times 40} = 441$

$\Rightarrow r = \sqrt{441}\ cm = 21\ cm$

ILLUSTRATION : 12

The base radii of two right circular cones of the same height are in the ratio 3 : 5. Find the ratio of their volumes.

SOLUTION :

Let r_1 and r_2 be the radii of two cones and V_1 and V_2 be their volumes.

Let h be the height of the two cones. Then,

$V_1 = \frac{1}{3}\pi r_1^2 h$ and $V_2 = \frac{1}{3}\pi r_2^2 h$

$\therefore \frac{V_1}{V_2} = \frac{\frac{1}{3}\pi r_1^2 h}{\frac{1}{3}\pi r_2^2 h} = \frac{r_1^2}{r_2^2} = \frac{9}{25}$ $\left[\because \frac{r_1}{r_2} = \frac{3}{5} \text{ (Given), } \therefore \frac{r_1^2}{r_2^2} = \frac{9}{25}\right]$

So, the required ratio of the volumes of two cones is 9 : 25.

ILLUSTRATION : 13

A cone and cylinder are having the same base. Find the ratio of their heights if their volumes are equal.

SOLUTION :

Let the radius of the common base be r. Let h_1 and h_2 be the heights of the cone and cylinder respectively. Then,

Volume of the cone = $\frac{1}{3}\pi r^2 h_1$, volume of the cylinder = $\pi r^2 h_2$

It is given that the cone and the cylinder are of the same volume.

$\therefore \frac{1}{3}\pi r^2 h_1 = \pi r^2 h_2 \Rightarrow \frac{1}{3}h_1 = h_2 \Rightarrow \frac{h_1}{h_2} = \frac{3}{1} \Rightarrow h_1 : h_2 = 3 : 1$

Hence, the ratio of the height of the cone and cylinder is 3:1

SPHERE

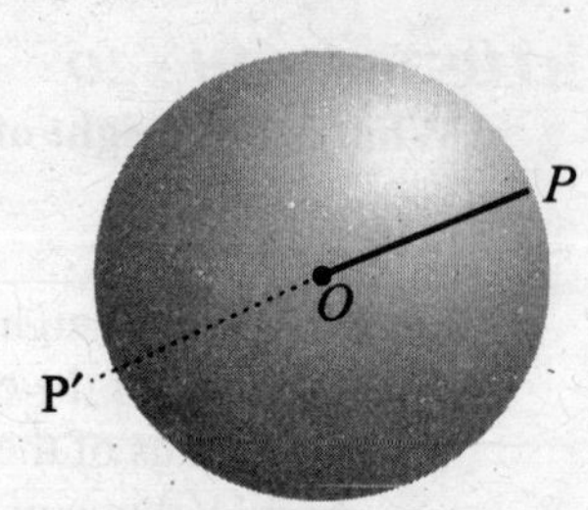

It is the set of all points in space which are at a constant and equal distance from a fixed point. The fixed point is called the centre of the sphere and the fixed distance is called the radius of the sphere.

In the given figure, O is the centre and OP is radius of the sphere.

Diameter : A line segment through the centre of a sphere whose end-points are on the sphere is called the diameter of the sphere. In the given figure PP' is the diameter of the sphere.

HEMISPHERE

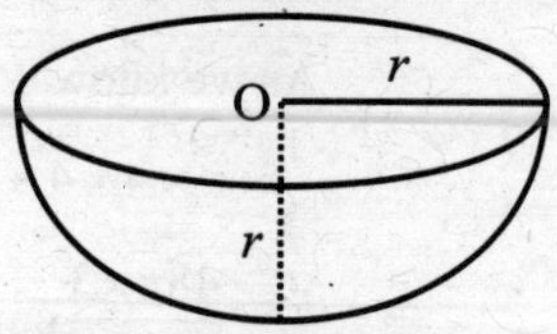

A plane through the centre of a sphere divides the sphere into two equal parts, each of which is called a hemisphere. It is shown in the figure.

SPHERICAL SHELL

The difference of two solid concentric spheres is called a spherical shell. This is shown in the fig. Here r and R is the radius of internal and external spherical surfaces respectively.

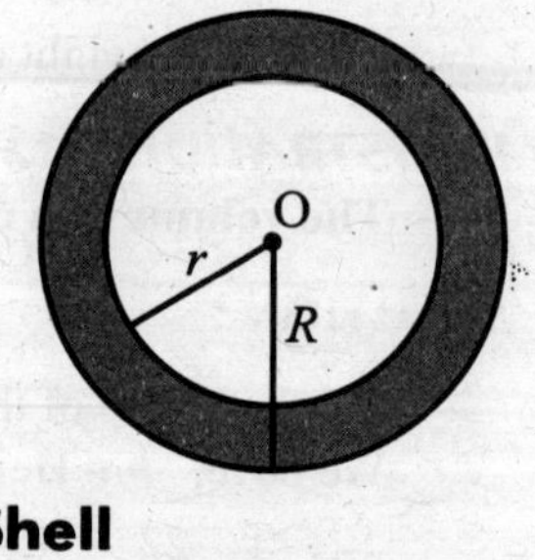

HEMISPHERICAL SHELL

A plane through the centre of a spherical shell divides the spherical shell into two parts, each of which is called a hemispherical shell.

Surface Area of a Sphere, Hemisphere, Spherical Shell and Hemi-spherical Shell

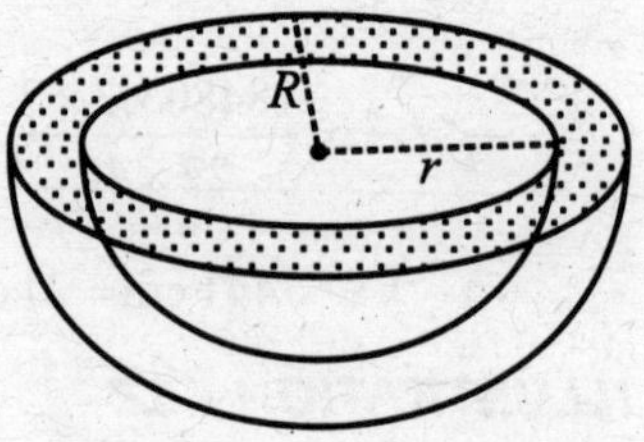

(i) Surface area of a sphere of radius $r = 4\pi r^2$ = curved surface area

(ii) Curved surface area of Hemisphere $= 2\pi r^2$

(iii) Total surface Area of Hemisphere = Curved surface Area + Area of plane circular surface

$$= 2\pi r^2 + \pi r^2 = 3\pi r^2$$

(iv) If R and r be the outer and inner radii of a hemispherical shell then

Outer curved surface area $= 2\pi R^2$

Inner curved surface area $= 2\,\pi r^2$

Surface area of plane ring $= \pi R^2 - \pi r^2 = \pi\,(R^2 - r^2)$

Total surface area = (outer curved surface area) + (inner curved area) + (surface area of plane ring)

$$= 2\pi R^2 + 2\pi r^2 + \pi\,(R^2 - r^2) = \pi\,(3R^2 + r^2)$$

Volume of a Sphere, Hemisphere and a Spherical Shell

(i) Volume of a sphere, $V = \frac{4}{3}\pi r^3$

(ii) Volume of a hemi-sphere, $V = \frac{2}{3}\pi r^3$

(iii) Volume of a spherical shell,

$$V = \text{Outer volume} - \text{Inner volume} = \frac{4}{3}\pi R^3 - \frac{4}{3}\pi r^3 = \frac{4}{3}\pi\,(R^3 - r^3) \text{ cubic units}$$

(iv) Volume of a hemispherical shell = (Outer volume) – (Inner volume) $= \frac{2}{3}\pi R^3 - \frac{2}{3}\pi r^3 = \frac{2}{3}\pi(R^3 - r^3)$

ILLUSTRATION : 14

The radius of the sphere is 7 cm. Find its surface area.

SOLUTION :

We know that the surface area S of a sphere of radius r is given by $S = 4\pi r^2$

Given $r = 7$ cm

$$\therefore \quad S = 4 \times \frac{22}{7} \times 7 \times 7\text{cm}^2 = 616 \text{ cm}^2$$

ILLUSTRATION : 15

Find the surface area and total surface area of a hemisphere of radius 21 cm.

SOLUTION :

We know that the surface area S and total surfaces area S_1 of a hemisphere of radius r are given by
$S = 2\pi r^2$ and, $S_1 = 3\pi r^2$ respectively.
Here, $r = 21$ cm

$\therefore \quad S = 2 \times \frac{22}{7} \times 21 \times 21 \text{ cm}^2$ and $S_1 = 3 \times \frac{22}{7} \times 21 \times 21 \text{ cm}^2$

$\Rightarrow \quad S = 2772 \text{ cm}^2$ and, $S_1 = 4158 \text{ cm}^2$

ILLUSTRATION : 16

The radius of a sphere is 7 cm. Find its volume

SOLUTION :

We know that the volume V of a sphere of radius r is given by

$V = \frac{4}{3}\pi r^3$ cubic units

Here, $r = 7$ cm

$\therefore \quad V = \frac{4}{3} \times \frac{22}{7} \times 7 \times 7 \times 7 \text{cm}^3 = 1437.33 \text{cm}^3$

ILLUSTRATION : 17

Find the volume of hemisphere of radius 3.5 cm

SOLUTION :

$V = \frac{2}{3}\pi r^3$ cubic units

Here, $r = 3.5$ cm

$\therefore \quad V = \frac{2}{3} \times \frac{22}{7} \times \frac{7}{2} \times \frac{7}{2} \times \frac{7}{2} \text{cm}^3 = \frac{11 \times 49}{3 \times 2} \text{cm}^3 = 89.83 \text{cm}^3$

ILLUSTRATION : 18

Find the volume of a sphere whose surface area is 154 square cm.

SOLUTION :

Let the radius of the sphere be r cm. Then,
surface area = 154 cm^2

$\Rightarrow \quad 4\pi r^2 = 154 \Rightarrow 4 \times \frac{22}{7} \times r^2 = 154 \Rightarrow r^2 = \frac{154 \times 7}{4 \times 22} = \frac{49}{4} \Rightarrow r = \frac{7}{2}\text{cm}$

Let V be the volume of the sphere. Then,

$V = \frac{4}{3}\pi r^3 = \frac{4}{3} \times \frac{22}{7} \times \frac{7}{2} \times \frac{7}{2} \times \frac{7}{2} \text{cm}^3 = \frac{1}{3} \times 11 \times 7 \times 7 \text{cm}^3 = 179.66 \text{cm}^3$

MISCELLANEOUS SOLVED EXAMPLES

1. A solid is in the form of a cylinder with hemispherical ends. The total height of the solid is 19 cm and diameter of the cylinder is 7 cm. Find the volume and total surface area of the solid.

Sol.

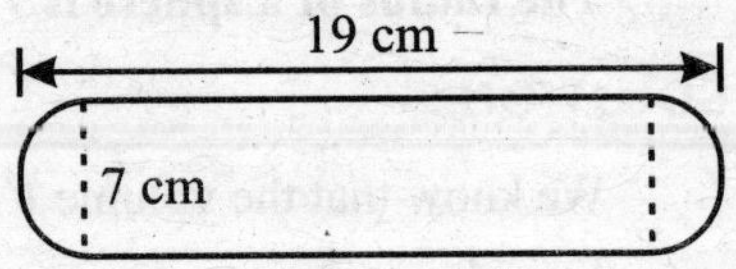

Total height of solid = 19 cm,

Diameter of cylinder = diameter of hemisphere = 7 cm

$\therefore$ Radius of cylinder = radius of hemisphere = 3.5 cm.

Height of cylindrical part = [19 – 2 (radius of hemisphere)] cm.

= 19 – 2 × 3.5 = 12 cm.

Now volume of solid = Volume of cylinder + Volume of two hemispheres

$$\Rightarrow \text{Volume} = \pi r^2 h + 2\times\frac{2}{3}\pi r^3 = \pi r^2\left(h+\frac{4r}{3}\right) = \frac{22}{7}\times(3.5)^2\left[12+\frac{4\times 3.5}{3}\right] = 641.67 \text{ cm}^3$$

Now surface area of solid = Curved surface area of cylinder + curved surface area of two hemisphere

$$\Rightarrow S = 2\pi rh + 2\times 2\pi r^2 = 2\pi r\,(h+2r) = 2\times\frac{22}{7}\times 3.5\,(12+7) = 418 \text{ cm}^2$$

2. The height of a cone is 30 cm. A small cone is cut off at the top by a plane parallel to its base. If its volume be 1/27 of the volume of the give cone, at which height above the base is the section cut ?

Sol. Let OAB be the given cone of height, H = 30 cm, and base radius R cm. Let this cone be cut by the plane CND to obtain the cone OCD with height h cm and base radius r cm

Then, Δ OND ~ Δ OMB

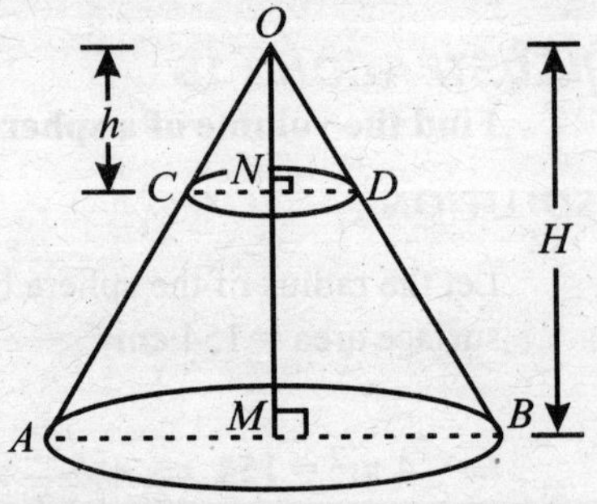

So, $\frac{ND}{MB} = \frac{ON}{OM} \Rightarrow \frac{r}{R} = \frac{h}{30}$ ....(i)

Volume of cone $OCD = \frac{1}{27}$ × Volume of cone OAB (Given)

$\Rightarrow \frac{1}{3}\pi r^2 h = \frac{1}{27}\times\frac{1}{3}\pi R^2\times 30 \Rightarrow \left(\frac{r}{R}\right)^2 = \frac{10}{9h} \Rightarrow \left(\frac{h}{30}\right)^2 = \frac{10}{9h}$ [From (i)]

$\Rightarrow 9h^3 = 9000 \Rightarrow h^3 = 1000 \Rightarrow h = 10$

$\therefore$ Height of the cone OCD = 10 cm.

Hence, the section is cut at the height of (30 – 10) cm, i.e. 20 cm from the base.

3. The surface area of a solid metallic sphere is 1256 cm². It is melted and recast into solid right circular cone of radius 2.5 cm and height 8 cm. Calculate (i) the radius of the solid sphere, (ii) the number of cones recast (Take π = 3.14)

Sol. (i) Let the radius of the sphere be r cm.

Then, its surface area = $(4\pi r^2)$ cm²

$\therefore$ $4\pi r^2 = 1256 \Rightarrow 4\times 3.14\times r^2 = 1256$

$\Rightarrow r^2 = \frac{1256}{4\times 3.14} = \frac{1256}{12.56} = 100 \Rightarrow r = 10$ cm.

Hence, the radius of the sphere = 10 cm.

(ii) Volume of the sphere = $\frac{4}{3}\pi r^3 = \left[\frac{4}{3}\pi\times(10)^3\right]\text{cm}^3 = \left(\frac{4000}{3}\pi\right)\text{cm}^3$

Volume of a cone $= \frac{1}{3}\pi R^2 h = \left[\frac{1}{3}\pi \times (2.5)^2 \times 8\right] \text{cm}^3 = \left(\frac{50}{3}\pi\right) \text{cm}^3$

$\therefore$ Number of cone recast $= \frac{\text{Volume of the sphere}}{\text{Volume of 1 cone}} = \left(\frac{4000}{3}\pi \times \frac{3}{50\pi}\right) = 80$

4. The volume of a rectangular block of stone is 10368 dm³. Its length, breadth and height are in the ratio 3 : 2 : 1. Find its dimensions. Find also the cost of polishing its entire surface at 2 paise per dm².

Sol. Let the length of block = $3x$ dm

breadth of block = $2x$ dm

height of block = dx m

$\therefore$ Volume of the block of stone = $3x \times 2x \times x = 6x^3$ dm³

But the given volume of the stone = 10368 dm³

$\therefore \quad 6x^3 = \frac{10368}{6} = 1728$

$\Rightarrow \quad x = \sqrt[3]{1728} = (12 \times 12 \times 12)^{1/3} = (12^3)^{1/3} = 12$

Hence, the length of the stone = 3 × 12 = 36 dm

breadth of the stone = 2 × 12 = 24 dm.

height of the stone = 1 × 12 = 12 dm.

Surface area of the block of stone = $2(\ell b + bh + h\ell)$

= 2 (36 × 24 + 24 × 12 + 12 × 36)

= 2 (864 + 288 + 432) = 2 × 1584 = 3168 dm²

Total cost of polishing the entire surface at 2 paise per dm²

= ₹ 3168 × 2 = ₹ 6336 = ₹ 63.36

5. An ice-cream cone is the union of a right circular cone and a hemisphere that has the same circular base as the cone. Find the volume of ice cream if the height of the cone is 9 cm and radius of its base is 2.5 cm.

Sol.

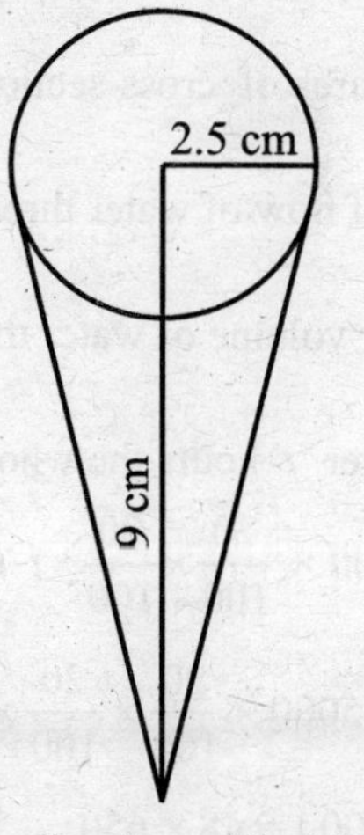

Given height of the cone = 9 cm.

and radius of the base = 2.5 cm = $\frac{5}{2}$ cm.

Volume of the cone $= \frac{1}{3}\pi r^2 h = \frac{1}{3} \times \frac{22}{7} \times \frac{5}{2} \times \frac{5}{2} \times 9 = \frac{11 \times 25 \times 3}{7 \times 2} \text{cm}^3 = \frac{825}{14} \text{cm}^3$

Volume of the hemisphere $= \frac{2}{3}\pi r^3 = \frac{2}{3} \times \frac{22}{7} \times \frac{5}{2} \times \frac{5}{2} \times \frac{5}{2} = \frac{11 \times 125}{42} \text{cm}^3 = \frac{1375}{42} \text{cm}^3$

Volume of the ice cream cone $= \frac{825}{14} + \frac{1375}{42} = \frac{2475 + 1375}{42} = \frac{3850}{42} \text{cm}^3 = 91.66 \text{ cm}^3$

6. The surface area of a sphere of radius 5 cm is five times the curved surface area of a cone of radius 4 cm. Find the height and volume of the cone.

Sol. Radius of the sphere (r) = 5 cm

Radius of the base of cone (r_1) = 4 cm

Let h cm be the height of the cone.

Surface area of sphere = $4\pi r^2 \Rightarrow 4\pi(5)^2 = 100\pi$ cm²

Curved surface area of cone = $\pi r_1 l = 4\pi l$ cm², where l is the slant height of the cone.

According to the question

$100\pi = 5(4\pi l) \qquad \Rightarrow \quad l = 5$ cm

Now, $h^2 = l^2 - r^2 = 5^2 - 4^2 = 3^2 \Rightarrow h = 3$ cm.

$$\therefore \text{ Volume of cone} = \frac{1}{3}\pi r^2 h = \frac{1}{3} \times \frac{22}{7} \times 4^2 \times 3 = \frac{352}{7}\text{cm}^3 = 50.29 \text{ cm}^3 \text{ (Approximately)}$$

7. A sphere and a right circular cylinder of the same radius have equal volumes. By what percentage does the diameter of the cylinder exceeds its height?

Sol. Let the radius of sphere and cylinder be r and h be the height of cylinder.

Then according to the question,

Volume of sphere = Volume of cylinder

$$\Rightarrow \frac{4}{3}\pi r^3 = \pi r^2 h \Rightarrow r = \frac{3}{4}h$$

Diameter of the cylinder $= \frac{3}{2}h$

Difference between the diameter and height of the cylinder $= \frac{3}{2}h - h = \frac{h}{2}$

Percentage by which the diameter exceeds the height of cylinder $= \frac{\frac{h}{2}}{h} \times 100 = \frac{h}{2} \times \frac{1}{h} \times 100 = 50\%$

Thus, the diameter of the cylinder exceeds its height by 50%.

8. Water in a rectangular reservoir having base 80 m by 60 m is 6.5 m deep. In what time can the water be emptied by a pipe of which the cross-section is a square of side 20 cm, if the water runs through the pipe at the rate of 15 km/hr.

Sol. Given : Dimension of the reservoir is 80 m, 60 m and 6.5 m

So, its volume will be

$V = 60 \times 80 \times 6.5 = 48 \times 650 \text{ m}^3$

Now, Dimension of pipe is 20 cm, 20 cm.

So its area of cross-section $= \frac{20}{100} \times \frac{20}{100} \text{ m}^2$

Rate of flow of water through the pipe = 15 km hr^{-1} = 15000 m hr^{-1}

In 1 hr volume of water that flow out through the pipe $= 15000 \times \frac{20}{100} \times \frac{20}{100} \text{ m}^3$

Let after 't' hours the whole reservoir becomes emptied so the volume of water that flows out through the pipe after 't' hours

$= 15000 \times \frac{20}{100} \times \frac{20}{100} \times t \text{ m}^3$

$$\therefore \quad 15000 \times \frac{20}{100} \times \frac{20}{100} \times t = 48 \times 650$$

$600t = 48 \times 650$

$$t = \frac{48 \times 650}{600} = 52 \text{ hr}$$

So the required time will be 52 hours.

9. A lead pencil consists of a cylinder of wood with a solid cylinder of graphite filled into it. The diameter of the pencil is 7mm, the diameter of the graphite is 1 mm and the length of the pencil is 14 cm. Find the: (i) volume of the graphite (ii) volume of the wood (iii) weight of the whole pencil, if the specific gravity of the wood is 0.7 gm/ cm³ and that of the graphite is 2.1 gm /cm³.

Sol. (i) We have,

Diameter of the graphite cylinder = 1 mm = $\frac{1}{10}$ cm

$\therefore$ Radius of the graphite cylinder = $\frac{1}{20}$ cm

Length of the graphite cylinder = 14 cm

V_1 = Volume of the graphite cylinder = $\frac{22}{7}\times\frac{1}{20}\times\frac{1}{20}\times 14\text{cm}^3 = 0.11\text{cm}^3$

(ii) We have,

Diameter of pencil = 7 mm = $\frac{7}{10}$ cm

Radius = $\frac{7}{20}$ cm

$\therefore$ V_2 = Volume of pencil = $\frac{22}{7}\times\frac{7}{20}\times\frac{7}{20}\times 14\text{cm}^3 = 5.39\text{cm}^3$

Volume of wood = $V_2 - V_1 = (5.39 - 0.11)\ \text{cm}^3 = 5.28\ \text{cm}^3$

(iii) We have,

Specific gravity of wood = 0.7 gm/ cm^3

and, specific gravity of wood graphite = 2.1 gm/cm^3

$\therefore$ Weight of the pencil = Volume of wood × Specific gravity of wood + Volume of graphite × Specific gravity of wood graphite

= $(5.28 \times 0.7 + 0.11 \times 2.1)$ gm = 3.927 gm

10. Water flows out through a circular pipe whose internal diameter is 2 cm, at the rate of 6 metres per second into a cylindrical tank. The radius of whose base is 60 cm. Find the rise in the level of water in 30 minutes?

Sol. Internal diameter of the pipe = 2 cm

So its radius = 1 cm = $\frac{1}{100}$ m

Water that flows out through the pipe is 6 ms^{-1}

So volume of water that flows out through the pipe in 1 sec = $\pi\times\left(\frac{1}{100}\right)^2\times 6\ \text{m}^3$

$\therefore$ In 30 minutes, volume of water flow = $\pi\left[\frac{1}{100\times100}\times6\times30\times60\right]\text{m}^3$

This must be equal to the volume of water that rises in the cylindrical tank after 30 min and height up to which it rises say h.

$\therefore$ Radius of tank = 60 cm = $\frac{60}{100}$ m

Volume = $\pi\left(\frac{60}{100}\right)^2 h$

$$\pi\left(\frac{60}{100}\right)^2 h = \pi\times\frac{1}{100\times100}\times6\times30\times60 = \frac{60\times60}{100\times100}h = \frac{6\times30\times60}{100\times100}$$

$$h = \frac{3\times36}{36} = 3\text{ m}$$

So required height will be 3 m.

11. A cylindrical tube, open at both ends, is made of metal. The internal diameter of the tube is 10.4 cm and its length is 25 cm. The thickness of the metal is 8 mm everywhere. Calculate the volume of the metal.

Sol. Internal diameter of the tube = 10.4 cm

Hence internal radius (r) = 5.2 cm

h = length of the tube = 25 cm

Let t = thickness = 8 mm = $\frac{8}{10}$ cm = 0.8 cm

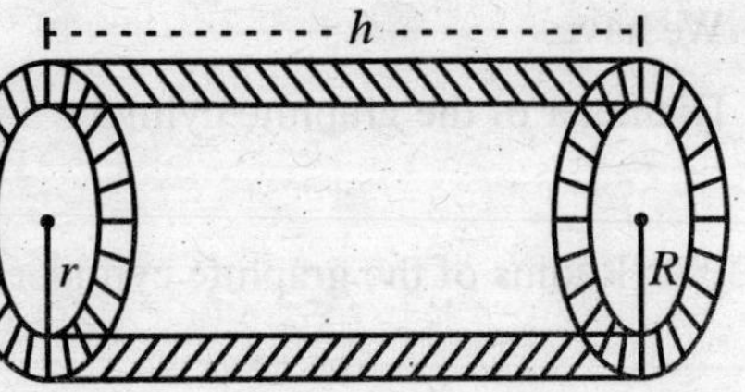

So, external radius (R) = 5.2 + 0.8 = 6 cm

Now, volume of the metal which is the volume of the shaded portion

$= \pi R^2 h - \pi r^2 h = \pi h(R^2 - r^2)$

Putting the values, we get $V = \frac{22}{7} \times 25 \times (6^2 - 5.2^2)$

$= \frac{22}{7} \times 25 \times (6+5.2)(6-5.2) = \frac{22}{7} \times 25 \times 11.2 \times 0.8 = 704 \text{ cm}^3$

12. Monica has piece of Canvas whose area is 551 m². She use it to make a conical tent, with a base radius of 7 m. Assuming that all the stitching margins and wastage incurred while cutting, amounts to approximately 1 m². Find the volume of the tent that can be made with it.

Sol. Surface area of canvas = 551 m^2

Area which wastes while cutting is 1 m^2

so the area remaining = 551 – 1 = 550 m^2

Radius of the base r = 7 m

As the canvas in the form of a cone.

So its surface i.e. its curved surface area will be πrl

$\pi rl = 550 \text{ m}^2$

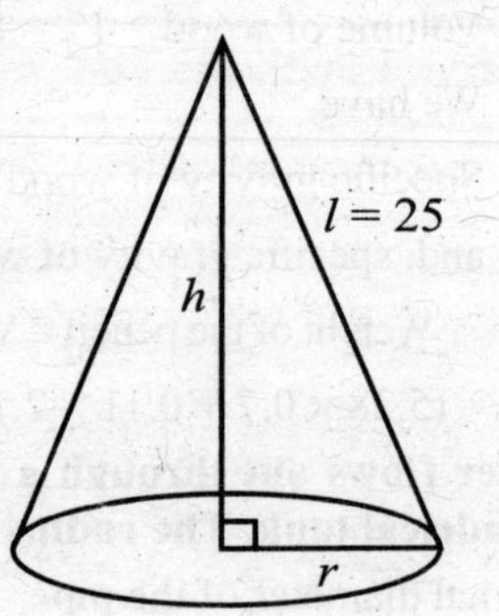

$\frac{22}{7} \times 7 \times l = 550$ [l = Slant height of the cone]

$l = \frac{550}{22} = \frac{55 \times 10}{22} \Rightarrow l = 25$

$h^2 + r^2 = l^2$

$h^2 = l^2 - r^2 = 25^2 - 7^2 = 625 - 49 = 576$

$h = \sqrt{576} = 24$ m

So, the volume of the required tent will be $V = \frac{1}{3}\pi r^2 h$

$= \frac{1}{3} \times \frac{22}{7} \times 7 \times 7 \times 24 = 22 \times 56 = 1232 \text{ m}^3$

13. A toy is in the shape of a right circular cylinder with a hemisphere on one end and a cone on the other. The height and radius of the cylindrical part are 13 cm and 5 cm respectively. The radii of the hemispherical and conical parts are the same as that of the cylindrical part. Calculate the surface area of the toy if height of the conical part is 12 cm.

Sol. Let r cm be the radius and h cm be the height of the cylindrical part. Then,

r = 5 cm and h = 13 cm.

Clearly, radii of the spherical part and base of the conical part are also r cm. Let h_1 cm be the height, l cm be the slant height of the conical part. Then,

$l^2 = r^2 + h_1^2 \Rightarrow l = \sqrt{r^2 + h_1^2} \Rightarrow l = \sqrt{5^2 + 12^2} = 13$ cm [$\because h_1 = 12$ cm, $r = 5$ cm]

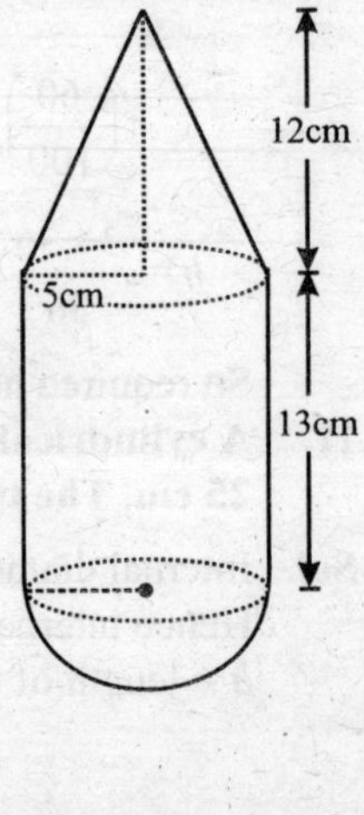

Now,

Surface area of the toy = Curved surface area of the cylindrical part

+ Curved surface area of hemispherical part + Curved surface area of conical part

$= (2\pi rh + 2\pi r^2 + \pi rl) \text{ cm}^2$

$= \frac{22}{7} \times 5 \times (2 \times 13 + 2 \times 5 + 13) \text{ cm}^2$

$= \frac{22}{3} \times 5 \times 39 \text{ cm}^2 = 330 \text{ cm}^2$

14. A cylindrical tub of radius 12 cm contains water to a depth of 20 cm. A spherical ball is dropped into the tub and thus the level of water is raised by 6.75 cm. What is the radius of the ball ?

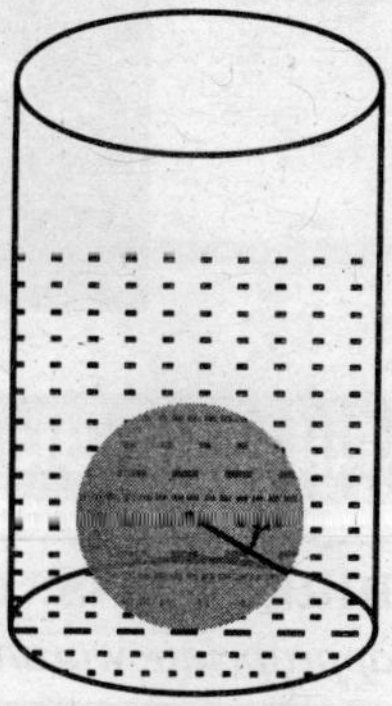

Sol. Given : R = radius of cylindrical tub = 12 cm

H = height of water level = 20 cm

h = level of water which raises = 6.75 cm

Let r = radius of spherical ball

Now, volume of spherical ball = volume of water level raised

$$\frac{4}{3}\pi r^3 = \pi R^2 h$$

$$r^3 = \frac{3}{4} \times 12 \times 12 \times 6.75 = 729$$

$$r = (729)^{1/3} = 9 \text{ cm}$$

15. Three cubes each of side 5 cm are joined end to end. Find the surface area of the resulting cuboid.

Sol. The dimensions of the cuboid so formed are

l = Length = 15 cm, b = Breadth = 5cm, and h = Height = 5 cm.

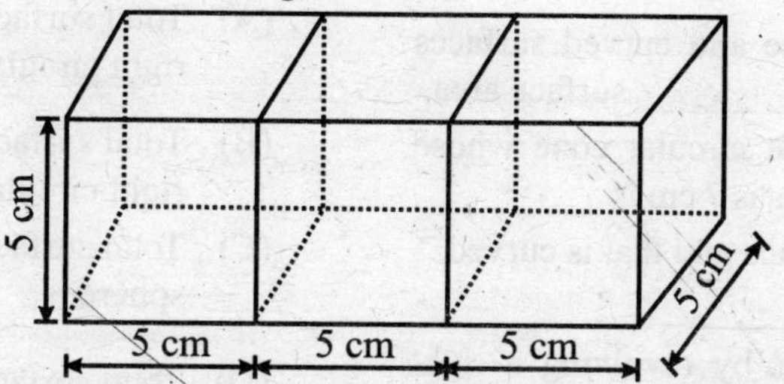

So, surface area of the cuboid = 2 (15×5 + 5× 5 + 15 × 5) cm^2 = 2 (75 + 25 +75) cm^2 = 350 cm^2

1 EXERCISE

Fill in the Blanks :

DIRECTIONS: *Complete the following statements with an appropriate word/term to be filled in the blank space(s).*

1. ___________ of a solid is the amount of space enclosed by the bounding surface.
2. The volume of a rectangular solid measuring 1 m by 50 cm by 0.5 m is ___________ cm^3.
3. The sum of the areas of the plane and curved surfaces (faces) of a solid is called its ___________ surface area.
4. The curved surface area of a right circular cone whose slant height is 10 cm and base radius is 7 cm is ________.
5. A sphere has only _________ surface and that is curved.
6. Cube is a special form of ___________.
7. A right circular cone is generated by revolving a right angled triangle about one of the sides containing the ___________.
8. The solid bounded by two concentric spherical surfaces is called a ___________ .
9. Volume of a cylinder is three times the volume of a ___________ on the same base and of the same height.
10. The volume of a sphere is ___________ to two-thirds the volume of a cylinder of the same height and diameter.

True/False :

DIRECTIONS: *Read the following statements and write your answer as true or false.*

1. If the line joining the centres of circular ends of a cylinder is not perpendicular to the circular ends, then the cylinder is not a right circular cylinder.
2. A solid generated by the revolution of a rectangle about one of its sides is called a right circular cylinder.
3. Each of the circular ends on which the cylinder rests is called its base.
4. The curved surface area of a cone is also called the lateral surface area.
5. A right circular cone is a solid generated by revolving a line segment which passes through a fixed point and which makes a constant angle with a fixed line.
6. In a sphere the number of faces is 2.

Match the Columns :

DIRECTIONS: *Each question contains statements given in two columns which have to be matched. Statements (A, B, C, D, ...) in Column-I have to be Matched with statements (p, q, r, s, ...) in Column-II.*

1.

Column-I	Column-II
(A) Total surface area of right circular cylinder is	(p) $\frac{2}{3}\pi r^3$
(B) Total surface area of right circular cone is	(q) $\frac{4}{3}\pi r^3$
(C) Total surface area of sphere is	(r) $l \times b \times h$
(D) Total surface area of hemisphere is	(s) $\frac{1}{3}\pi r^2 h$
(E) Volume of cuboid is	(t) $\sqrt{l^2+b^2+h^2}$
(F) Volume of cylinder is	(u) $\pi r^2 h$
(G) Diagonal of cuboid is	(v) $3\pi r^2$
(H) Volume of sphere is	(w) $4\pi r^2$
(I) Volume of cone is	(x) $\pi r(l+r)$
(J) Volume of hemisphere is	(y) $2\pi r(r+h)$

Very Short Answer Questions :

DIRECTIONS: *Give answer in one word or one sentence.*

1. Study the figure given below carefully and complete the statements based on it

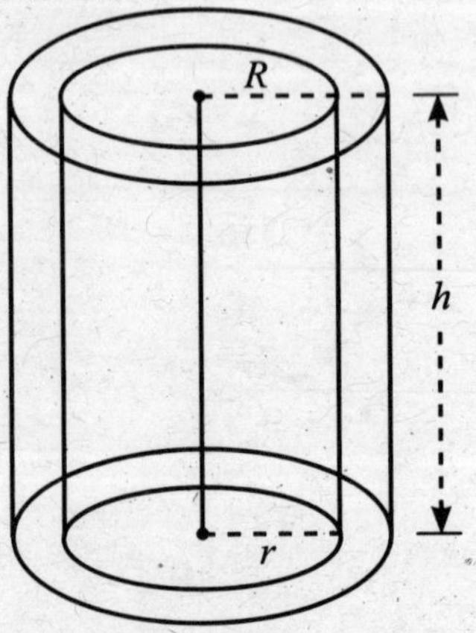

(a) R and r are the ________ and ________ of a hollow cylinder respectively and h is its ________.
(b) Thickness of cylinder is ____________. (formula)
(c) External curved surface area is ________. (formula)
(d) Total surface area = ____________________
________ + ____________________
________ + ____________________
________ = ____________________
____________. (formula)
(e) Area of a cross-section is ____________. (formula)

2. Study the figure given below and fill the blanks based on it.

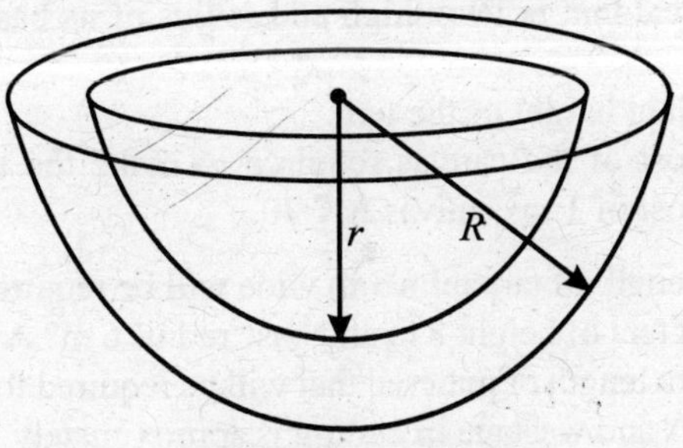

Hemispherical shell

(a) The solid enclosed between two concentric ________ is called a hemispherical shell.
(b) R and r are the radii of the ________ and the ________ hemispheres respectively.
(c) Area of base is ____________. (formula)
(d) Total surface area is ____________. (formula)
(e) Thickness of shell is ____________. (formula)

3. Write the number of surfaces of a right circular cylinder.
4. Write the ratio of total surface area to the curved surface area of a cylinder of radius r and height h.
5. Write the number of surfaces of a cone.
6. Write the area of the curved surface of a cone whose radius is 2r and slant height is $\frac{\ell}{2}$.
7. Write the total surface area of a cone whose radius is $\frac{r}{2}$ and length is $2l$.
8. Find the total surface area of a hemisphere of radius 10 cm. (use $\pi = 3.14$)

Short Answer Questions :

DIRECTIONS: *Give answer in 2-3 sentences.*

1. The total surface area of a cube is 864 cm^2. Find its edge and lateral surface area.
2. A cylindrical pillar is 50 cm in diameter and 3.5 m in height. Find the cost of painting the curved surface of the pillar at the rate of ₹ 12.50 per m^2.
3. In a hot water heating system, there is a cylindrical pipe of length 28 m and diameter 5 cm. Find the total radiating surface in the system.
4. A right circular cylinder just encloses a sphere of radius 7 cm.
   (i) Find the curved surface area of the cylinder and the sphere.
   (ii) What is the ratio of these areas?
5. The total surface area of a cube is 486 cm^2. Find its volume.
6. The total surface area of a cylinder is 231 cm^2 and its curved surface area is $\frac{2}{3}$ of the total surface area. Find the volume of the cylinder.

Long Answer Questions :

DIRECTIONS: *Give answer in four to five sentences.*

1. The diameter of a sphere is decreased by 25%. By what percent does its curved surface area decrease?
2. A dome of a building is in the form of a hemisphere. From inside, it was white-washed at the cost of ₹ 498.96. If the cost of white-washing is ₹ 2.00 per square metre, find the
   (i) inside surface area of the dome
   (ii) volume of the air inside the dome.
3. From a right circular cylinder with height 10 cm and radius of base 6 cm, a right circular cone of the same height and base is removed. Find the volume of the remaining solid.
4. The internal and external diameters of a hollow hemi-spherical vessel are 24 cm and 25 cm respectively. The cost of paint one sq. cm of the surface is 7 paise. Find the total cost to paint the vessel all over (ignore the area of edge).

2 EXERCISE

Text-Book Exercise

1. A plastic box 1.5 m long, 1.25 m wide and 65 cm deep is to be made. It is to be open at the top. Ignoring the thickness of the plastic sheet, determine the area of the sheet, required for making the box.
2. The length, breadth and height of a room are 5 m, 4 m and 3 m respectively. Find the cost of white washing the walls of the room and the ceiling at the rate of ₹ 7.50 per m^2.
3. The paint in a certain container is sufficient to paint an area equal to 9.375 m^2. How many bricks of dimensions 22.5 cm × 10 cm × 7.5 cm can be painted out of this container ?
4. A small indoor greenhouse (herbarium) is made entirely of glass panes (including base) held together with tape. It is 30 cm long, 25 cm wide and 25 cm high.
   (i) What is the area of the glass ?
   (ii) How much of tape is needed for all the 12 edges ?
5. Shanti Sweets Stall was placing an order for making cardboard boxes for packing their sweets. Two sizes of boxes were required. The bigger of dimensions 25 cm × 20 cm × 5 cm and the smaller of dimensions 15 cm × 12 cm × 5 cm. For all the overlaps, 5% of the total surface area is required extra. If the cost of the cardboard is ₹ 4 for 1000 cm^2, find the cost of cardboard required for supplying 250 boxes of each kind.
6. It is required to make a closed cylindrical tank of height 1 m and base diameter 140 cm from a metal sheet. How many square metres of the sheet are required for the same?
7. A metal pipe is 77 cm long. The inner diameter of a cross section is 4 cm, the outer diameter being 4.4 cm. Find its
   (i) inner curved surface area
   (ii) outer curved surface area
   (iii) total surface area
8. The inner diameter of a circular well is 3.5 m. It is 10 m deep. Find
   (i) its inner curved surface area,
   (ii) the cost of plastering this curved surface at the rate of ₹ 40 per m^2.
9. In a hot water heating system, there is a cylindrical pipe of length 28 m and diameter 5 cm. Find the total radiating surface in the system.
10. The students of a Vidyalaya were asked to participate in a competition for making and decorating pen holders in the shape of a cylinder with a base, using cardboard. Each pen holder was to be of radius 3 cm and height 10.5 cm. The Vidyalaya was to supply the competitors with cardboard. If there were 35 competitors, how much cardboard was required to be bought for the competition ?
11. A conical tent is 10 m high and radius of its base is 24 m. Find :
    (i) slant height of the tent.
    (ii) cost of the canvas required to make the tent, if the cost of 1 m^2 canvas is ₹ 70.
12. What length of tarpaulin 3 m wide will be required to make conical tent of height 8 m and base radius 6 m? Assume that the extra length of material that will be required for stitching margins and wastage in cutting is approximately 20 cm. (use $\pi = 3.14$)
13. A joker's cap is in the form of a right circular cone of base radius 7 cm and height 24 cm. Find the area of the sheet required to make 10 such caps.
14. The radius of a spherical balloon increases from 7 cm to 14 cm as air is being pumped into it. Find the ratio of surface areas of the balloon in the two cases.
15. A hemispherical bowl made of brass has inner diameter 10.5 cm. Find the cost of tin-plating it on the inside at the rate of ₹ 16 per 100 cm^2.
16. The diameter of the moon is approximately one fourth of the diameter of the earth. Find the ratio of their surface areas.
17. A right circular cylinder just encloses a sphere of radius r. Find

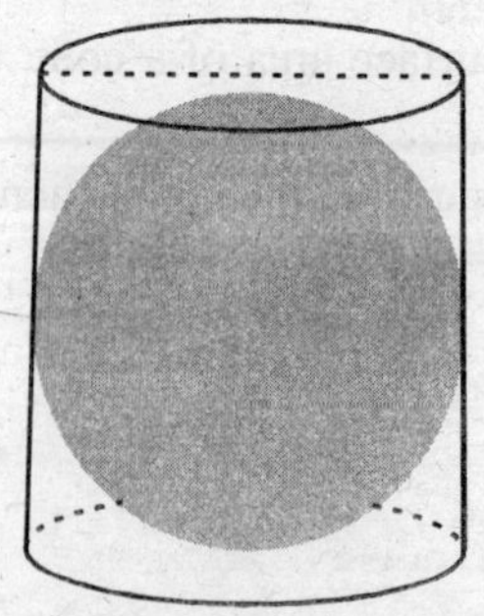

    (i) surface area of the sphere,
    (ii) curved surface area of the cylinder,
    (iii) ratio of the areas obtained in (i) and (ii).
18. A cuboidal vessel is 10 m long and 8 m wide. How high must it be made to hold 380 cubic meters of a liquid?

19. The capacity of a cuboidal tank is 50000 liters of water. Find the breadth of the tank, if its length and depth are respectively 2.5 m and 10 m.

20. A village, having a population of 4000, requires 150 litres of water per head per day. It has a tank measuring 20 m × 15 m × 6 m. For how many days will the water of this tank last ?

21. A solid cube of side 12 cm is cut into eight cubes of equal volume. What will be the side of the new cube ? Also, find the ratio between their surface areas.

22. The inner diameter of a cylindrical wooden pipe is 24 cm and its outer diameter is 28 cm. The length of the pipe is 35 cm. Find the mass of the pipe, if 1 cm^3 of wood has a mass of 0.6 g.

23. A soft drink is available in two packs –
   (i) a tin can with a rectangular base of length 5 cm and width 4 cm, having a height of 15 cm and
   (ii) a plastic cylinder with a circular base of diameter 7 cm and height 10 cm.

   Which container has greater capacity and by how much ?

24. The capacity of a closed cylindrical vessel of height 1 m is 15.4 litres. How many square metres of metal sheet would be needed to make it ?

25. A lead pencil consists of a cylinder of wood with a solid cylinder of graphite filled in the interior. The diameter of the pencil is 7 mm and the diameter of the graphite is 1 mm. If the length of the pencil is 14 cm, find the volume of the wood and that of the graphite.

26. A patient in a hospital is given soup daily in a cylindrical bowl of diameter 7 cm. If the bowl is filled with soup to a height of 4 cm, how much soup the hospital has to prepare daily to serve 250 patients ?

27. A right triangle ABC with sides 5 cm, 12 cm and 13 cm is revolved about the side 12 cm. Find the volume of the solid so obtained.

28. A heap of wheat is in the form of a cone whose diameter is 10.5 m and height is 3 m. Find its volume. The heap is to be covered by canvas to protect it from rain. Find the area of the canvas required.

29. The diameter of a metallic ball is 4.2 cm. What is the mass of the ball, if the density of the metal is 8.9 g per cm^3 ?

30. A hemispherical tank is made up of an iron sheet 1 cm thick. If the inner radius is 1 m, then find the volume of the iron used to make the tank.

31. A dome of a building is in the form of a hemisphere. From inside, it was white-washed at the cost of ₹ 498.96. If the cost of white-washing is ₹ 2.00 per square metre, find the
   (i) inside surface area of the dome,
   (ii) volume of the air inside the dome.

32. Twenty seven solid iron spheres, each of radius r and surface area S are melted to form a sphere with surface area S'. Find the
   (i) radius r' of the new sphere,
   (ii) ratio of S and S'.

33. A wooden bookshelf has external dimensions as follows : Height = 110 cm, Depth = 25 cm, Breadth = 85 cm (see figure). The thickness of the plank is 5 cm everywhere. The external faces are to be polished and the inner faces are to be painted. If the rate of polishing is 20 paise per cm^2 and the rate of painting is 10 paise per cm^2, find the total expenses required for polishing and painting the surface of the bookshelf.

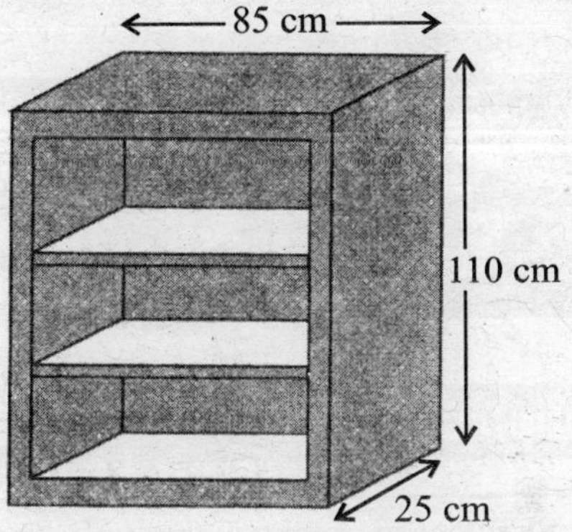

34. The diameter of a sphere is decreased by 25%. By what per cent does its curved surface area decrease?

Exemplar Questions :

1. The surface area of a sphere of radius 5 cm is five times the area of the curved surface of a cone of radius 4 cm. Find the height and the volume of the cone (taking $\pi = \frac{22}{7}$).

2. Rain water which falls on a flat rectangular surface of length 6 m and breadth 4 m is transferred into a cylindrical vessel of internal radius 20 cm. what will be the height of water in the cylindrical vessel if the rain fall is 1 cm. Give your answer to the nearest integer. (Take $\pi = 3.14$)

3. The radius of a sphere is 2r, then its volume will be

   (a) $\frac{4}{3}\pi r^3$ (b) $4\pi r^3$
   (c) $\frac{8\pi r^3}{3}$ (d) $\frac{32}{3}\pi r^3$

4. The total surface area of a cube is 96 cm^2. The volume of the cube is:

   (a) 8 cm^3 (b) 512 cm^3
   (c) 64 cm^3 (d) 27 cm^3

5. In a cylinder, radius is doubled and height is halved, curved surface area will be

   (a) halved (b) doubled
   (c) same (d) four times

6. The total surface area of a cone whose radius is $\frac{r}{2}$ and slant height $2l$ is

(a) $2\pi r(l+r)$ (b) $\pi r\left(l+\frac{r}{4}\right)$

(c) $\pi r(l+r)$ (d) $2\pi rl$

7. The radii of two cylinders are in the ratio of 2 : 3 and their heights are in the ratio of 5 : 3. The ratio of their volumes is:

(a) 10 : 17 (b) 20 : 27

(c) 17 : 27 (d) 20 : 37

Hots Questions :

1. A solid toy is in the form of a hemisphere surrounded by a right circular cone. The height of the cone is 2 cm, diameter of the base is 4 cm. If a right circular cylinder circumscribes the solid, find how much more space it will cover.

2. If h, C and V respectively are the height, the curved surface and volume of cone, prove that $3\pi Vh^3 - C^2h^2 + 9V^2 = 0$.

3. The radius of a sphere is increased by 10%. Prove that the volume will be increased by 33.1% approximately.

3 EXERCISE

Single Option Correct :

DIRECTIONS: *This section contains multiple choice questions. Each questions has 4 choices (a), (b), (c) and (d) out of which ONLY ONE is correct.*

1. If the inner dimensions of a cuboidal box are 50 cm × 40 cm × 30 cm, then the length of the longest rod that can be placed in the box is

(a) 50 cm (b) $50\sqrt{2}$ cm

(c) $50\sqrt{3}$ cm (d) 120 cm

2. A cylindrical pencil of diameter 1.2 cm. has one of its end sharpened into a conical shape of height 1.4 cm. The volume of the material removed is

(a) 1.056 cm^3 (b) 4.224 cm^3

(c) 10.56 cm^3 (d) 42.24 cm^3

3. A small indoor greenhouse is made entirely of glass panes held together with tape. It is 30 cm long, 25 cm wide and 25 cm high. How much of tape is needed for all the 12 edges?

(a) 230 cm (b) 320 cm

(c) 302 cm (d) 203 cm

4. A conical tent has a floor area of 154 sq. m. Its height is 24 m. How much canvas is required for the tent?

(a) 500 sq. m. (b) 550 sq. m.

(c) 700 sq. m. (d) 450 sq. m.

5. If the perimeter of one face of a cube is 20 cm, then its surface area is

(a) 120 cm^2 (b) 150 cm^2

(c) 125 cm^2 (d) 400 cm^2

6. A hemispherical tank of radius 3 cm is full of milk. It is connected to a pipe, through which liquid is emptied at the 1/7 litre per second. The time taken to empty the tank completely?

(a) 0.302 sec (b) 0.396 sec

(c) 0.453 sec (d) 0.492 sec

7. If the radius and height of a right circular cone are 'r' and 'h' respectively, the slant height of the cone is

(a) $(h^2+r^2)^{1/3}$ (b) $(h+r)^{1/3}$

(c) $(h^2+r^2)^{1/2}$ (d) none of these

8. If V is the volume of a cuboid of dimensions a, b, c and A is its surface area, then $\frac{A}{V}$ is

(a) $a^2b^2c^2$ (b) $2\left(\frac{1}{a}+\frac{1}{b}+\frac{1}{c}\right)$

(c) $\frac{1}{abc}$ (d) $\frac{1}{2}\left(\frac{1}{ab}+\frac{1}{bc}+\frac{1}{ca}\right)$

9. If each edge of a cube, of volume V, is doubled, then the volume of the new cube is

(a) 2V (b) 4V

(c) 6V (d) 8V

10. Two cylindrical jars have their diameters in the ratio 3 : 1, but height 1 : 3. Then the ratio of their volumes is

(a) 1 : 3 (b) 3 : 1

(c) 2 : 5 (d) 1 : 4

11. Vertical cross-section of a right circular cylinder is always a

(a) rectangle (b) rhombus

(c) square (d) trapezium

12. Two circular cylinders of equal volume have their heights in the ratio 1 : 2. Ratio of their radii is
(a) $\sqrt{2}:1$ (b) 1 : 2
(c) 1 : 4 (d) $1:\sqrt{2}$

13. The number of surfaces in right cylinder is
(a) 4 (b) 3
(c) 2 (d) 1

14. A rectangular sheet of metal, x cm by y cm has a square of size z cm cut from each corner. The sheet is then bent to form a tray of depth z cm. The volume of the tray is
(a) $z(x-z)(y-z)\ cm^3$
(b) $xyz\ cm^3$
(c) $z(x-2z)(y-2z)\ cm^3$
(d) $(x+y)z\ cm^3$

15. The volumes of two cylinders are as a : b and their heights are as c : d. Find the ratio of their diameters.
(a) $\frac{ad}{bc}$ (b) $\frac{ad^2}{ac^2}$
(c) $\sqrt{\frac{ad}{bc}}$ (d) $\sqrt{\frac{a}{b}\times\frac{c}{d}}$

16. The radius of a sphere is increased by P %. Its surface area increases by
(a) P % (b) P^2%
(c) $\left(2P+\frac{P^2}{100}\right)\%$ (d) $\frac{P^2}{2}\%$

17. The ratio of the volume and surface area of a sphere of unit radius without considering units is
(a) 4 : 3 (b) 3 : 4
(c) 1 : 3 (d) 3 : 1

18. If the volumes of two cones are in the ratio 1 : 4 and their diameters are in the ratio 4 : 5, then the ratio of their heights is
(a) 25 : 64 (b) 5 : 4
(c) 64 : 25 (d) 5 : 16

More than One Option Correct :

DIRECTIONS: *This section contains multiple choice questions. Each question has 4 choices (a), (b), (c) and (d) out of which ONE or MORE may be correct.*

1. A match box measures 4 cm × 2.5 cm × 1.5 cm. The volume of a packet containing 12 such boxes, is
(a) $12 \times 15\ cm^3$ (b) $(12 \times 4 \times 2.5 \times 1.5)\ cm^3$
(c) $180\ cm^3$ (d) $(4 \times 2.5 \times 1.5)\ cm^3$

2. A solid cube is cut into two cuboids of equal volumes. The ratio of the total surface area of the given cube and that of one of the cuboids is
(a) $6a^2 : 4a^2$ (b) $4a^2 : 6a^2$
(c) 3 : 2 (d) 2 : 3

3. The height of a lead pipe is 3.5 m long, if the external diameter of the pipe is 2.4 cm and the thickness of the lead is 2 mm and 1 cubic cm of lead weighs 11 gm, is
(a) (484 × 11) gm (b) 5.324 kgs
(c) 5 kg (d) π(2.2)(0.2)(350)(11) gm

4. The base radii of two right circular cones of the same height are in the ratio 3 : 5. The ratio of their volumes is
(a) $r_2^2 : r_1^2$ (b) $r_1^2 : r_2^2$
(c) 25 : 9 (d) 9 : 25

5. The volume of the two spheres are in the ratio 64 : 27. The difference of their surface areas, if the sum of their radii is 7, is
(a) $28\pi\ cm^2$ (b) $88\ cm^2$
(c) $64\pi\ cm^2$ (d) $36\pi\ cm^2$

Passage Based Questions :

DIRECTIONS: *Study the given paragraph(s) and answer the following questions.*

PASSAGE-I

A cube is a special type of a cuboid whose length, breadth and height are all equal. So, the volume V of a cube of edge 'a' is given by

$$V = a \times a \times a = a^3 = (Edge)^3$$

1. The volume of a cube is $1000\ cm^3$. The edge of a cube is
(a) 100 cm (b) 1000 cm
(c) 10 cm (d) 1 cm

2. Three metal cubes whose edges are 3 cm, 4 cm and 5 cm respectively are melted to form a single cube. Its edge is
(a) 3 cm (b) 4 cm
(c) 5 cm (d) 6 cm

3. If the volumes of two cubes are in the ratio 8 : 1, then the ratio of their edges is
(a) $2\sqrt{2}:1$ (b) 2 : 1
(c) 8 : 1 (d) 1 : 2

PASSAGE-II

A solid bounded by two coaxial cylinders of the same height and different radii is called a hollow cylinder. Solid like iron pipes, rubber tubes etc., are hollow cylinders.

Let R and r be the external and internal radii of a hollow cylinders and h be its height. Then we have

(i) Each base surface area = $\pi(R^2 - r^2)$ sq. units
(ii) Curved surface area = $2\pi h(R + r)$ sq units
(iii) Total surface area = $2\pi(R + r)(h + R - r)$ sq. unit

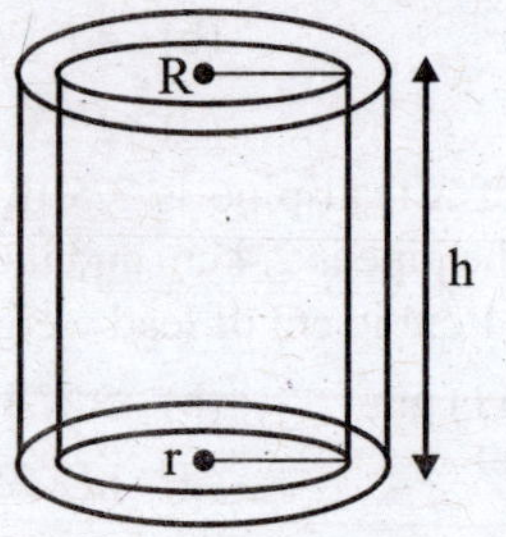

4. An iron pipe 20 cm long has exterior diameter equal to 25 cm. If the thickness of the pipe is 1 cm, then the whole surface of the pipe is
   (a) 3168 cm^2 (b) 6138 cm^2
   (c) 1368 cm^2 (d) 3186 cm^2
5. The volume of a hollow cylinder is
   (a) $\pi(R^2 - r^2)\, h$ (b) $\pi R^2 r^2 h$
   (c) $\pi R^3 r^3$ (d) $\pi(R^2 + r^2)\, h$

Assertion & Reason :

DIRECTIONS: *Each of these questions contains an Assertion followed by Reason. Read them carefully and answer the question on the basis of following options. You have to select the one that best describes the two statements.*

(a) If both **Assertion** and **Reason** are **correct** and Reason is the **correct explanation** of Assertion.
(b) If both **Assertion** and **Reason** are correct, but Reason is **not the correct explanation** of Assertion.
(c) If **Assertion** is **correct** but **Reason** is **incorrect**.
(d) If **Assertion** is **incorrect** but **Reason** is **correct**.

1. **Assertion:** An edge of a cube measures r cm. If the largest possible right circular cone is cut out of this cube, then the volume of the cone is $\frac{1}{6}\pi r^3$.
   Reason: Volume of the cone is given by $\frac{1}{3}\pi r^2 h$, where r is the radius of the base and h is the height of the cone.
2. **Assertion:** In a cylinder, if radius is halved and height is doubled, the volume will be halved.
   Reason: In a cylinder, radius is doubled and height is halved, curved surface area will be same.
3. **Assertion:** The total surface area of a cone whose radius is $\frac{r}{2}$ and slant height $2l$ is $(\pi)r\left(l+\frac{r}{4}\right)$.
   Reason : Total surface area of cone is $\pi r(l+r)$ where r is radius and l is the slant height of the cone.
4. **Assertion:** If the inner dimensions of a cuboidal box are 50 cm × 40 cm × 30 cm, then the length of the longest rod that can be placed in the box is $50\sqrt{2}$ cm.
   Reason: The line joining opposite corners of a cuboid is called its diagonal.
   Also, length of longest rod = length of diagonal.
   $= \sqrt{l^2 + b^2 + h^2}$

Match the Column :

DIRECTIONS : *Following question has four statements (A, B, C and D) given in Column-I and statements (p, q, r, s, ...) in Column-II. Any given statement in Column-I can have correct matching with one or more statement(s) given in Column-II.*

1.

Column - I		Column - II	
(A)	Volume of a cuboid is	(p)	perimeter of the base of the cylinder × h
(B)	Volume of a cube is	(q)	Area of circular base × height
(C)	Volume of a cylinder is	(r)	$(\text{edge})^3$
(D)	Curved surface area of the cylinder is	(s)	base × area × height
		(t)	$2\pi rh$
		(u)	length × breadth × height
		(v)	edge × edge × edge
		(w)	$\pi r^2 h$

Integer Type Questions :

DIRECTIONS : *Answer the following questions. The answer to each of the question is a single digit integer, ranging from 0 to 9.*

1. Water flows out through a circular pipe whose internal diameter is 2 cm, at the rate of 6 metres per second into a cylindrical tank. The radius of whose base is 60 cm. Find the rise in the level of water in 30 minutes.
2. A solid cube of side 12 cm is cut into eight cubes of equal volume. What will be the side of new cube? The ratio between their surface areas is k : 1. Find the value of k.
3. If the inner dimensions of a cuboidal box are 50 cm × 40 cm × 30 cm, then the length of the longest rod that can be placed in the box is 50 $\sqrt{a}$ cm. The value of 'a' is
4. A cylindrical tub of radius 12 cm contains water to a depth of 20 cm. A spherical ball is dropped into the tub and thus the level of water is raised by 6.75 cm, then the radius of the ball is
5. Twenty-seven solid iron spheres, each of radius r and surface area s are melted to form a sphere with surface area s'. The radius r' of the new sphere is k (r). The value of 'k' is
6. Two solid spheres made of the same metal have masses 5920 g and 740 g respectively. Determine the radius of the larger sphere, if the diameter of the smaller sphere is 5 cm.

SOLUTIONS

Brief Explanations of Selected Questions

1 EXERCISE

FILL IN THE BLANKS :

1. Volume
2. 250,000
3. total
4. 220 cm^2
5. One
6. Cuboid
7. right angle
8. Spherical shell
9. cone
10. equal

TRUE/FALSE :

1. True 2. True 3. True 4. True
5. True 6. False, sphere has 1 face.

MATCH THE COLUMNS :

1. (A) → (y); (B) → (x); (C) → (w); (D) → (v); (E) → (r); (F) → (u); (G) → (t); (H) → (q); (I) → (s); (J) → (p)

VERY SHORT ANSWER QUESTIONS :

1. (a) External, Internal, height.
 (b) $R - r$.
 (c) $2\pi Rh$.
 (d) Total surface area = external curved area + internal curved area + area of two ends.
 $= 2\pi Rh + 2\pi rh + 2\pi (R^2 - r^2)$
 $= 2\pi (Rh + rh + R^2 - r^2)$
 (e) $\pi (R^2 - r^2)$.
2. (a) hemispheres
 (b) outer, inner.
 (c) $\pi (R^2 - r^2)$.
 (d) $2\pi R^2 + 2\pi r^2 + \pi (R^2 - r^2) = \pi (3R^2 + r^2)$
 (e) $R - r$.
3. 3
4. Required ratio = h + r : r
5. 2
6. πrl
7. $\pi r\left(\ell + \frac{r}{4}\right)$
8. Radius of the hemisphere r = 10 cm
 Total surface area of the hemisphere
 $= 3\pi r^2 = 3 \times 3.14 \times (10)^2$
 $= 9.42 \times 100 \text{ cm}^2 = 942 \text{ cm}^2$

SHORT ANSWER QUESTIONS :

1. The total surface area of the cube = 864 cm^2
 Let each side of the cube be a cm.
 Then $6a^2 = 864 \text{ cm}^2$
 $a^2 = \frac{864}{6} \text{cm}^2 = 144 \text{ cm}^2$
 ∴ edge $a = \sqrt{144}$ cm = 12 cm
 Lateral surface area of the cube $= 4a^2 = 4 \times (12)^2 \text{ cm}^2$
 $= 4 \times 144 \text{ cm}^2 = 576 \text{ cm}^2$
2. Diameter of the pillar $d = 50$ cm ⇒ $d = 0.50$ m
 radius of the pillar $r = \frac{d}{2} = \frac{0.50}{2}\text{m} = 0.25\text{m}$
 height $h = 3.5$ m
 Curved surface area of the pillar $= 2\pi rh$
 $= 2 \times \frac{22}{7} \times 0.25 \times 3.5 \text{m}^2 = 5.5 \text{ m}^2$
 Cost of painting the pillar at the rate of ₹ 12.50 perm^2
 $= 5.50 \text{ m}^2 \times$ ₹ 12.50 per m^2 = ₹ 68.75.
3. Diameter of the pipe $d = 5$ cm = 0.05 m
 radius $r = \frac{d}{2} = \frac{0.05}{2}$m Length of the pipe $h = 28$ m
 Total radiating surface $= 2\pi rh$
 $= 2 \times \frac{22}{7} \times \frac{0.05}{2} \times 28\text{m}^2 = 4.4 \text{ m}^2$
4. Base radius of the cylinder = radius of the sphere = 7 cm
 Height of the cylinder = h = diameter of the sphere
 $= 2r = 2 \times 7$ cm, $h = 14$ cm
 The curved surface area of the cylinder $= 2\pi rh$

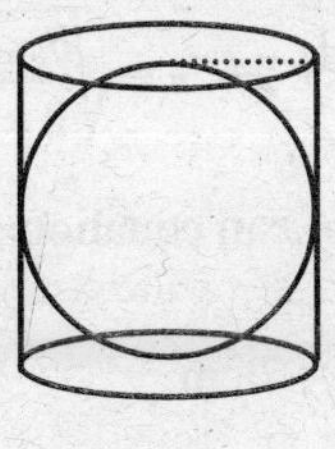

 $= 2 \times \frac{22}{7} \times 7 \times 14 = 616 \text{ cm}^2$
 Curved surface area of the sphere $= 4\pi r^2$
 $= 4 \times \frac{22}{7} \times 7 \times 7 \text{cm}^2 = 616 \text{ cm}^2$
 Ratio of these areas $= \frac{616\text{cm}^2}{616\text{cm}^2} = 1 : 1$

5. Let each side of the cube be a cm.

Total surface area = 486 cm^2

$\Rightarrow \quad 6a^2 = 486\ cm^2$

$\Rightarrow \quad a^2 = \frac{486}{6} cm^2$

$\Rightarrow \quad a^2 = 81\ cm^2$

$\Rightarrow \quad a = \sqrt{81} = 9\,cm$

Volume of the cube = a^3 = 9 × 9 × 9 cm^3 = 729 cm^3

6. Total surface area of the cylinder = 231 cm^2

$2\pi r(h+r) = 231 \Rightarrow 2\times\frac{22}{7}r(h+r) = 231$

$r(h+r) = \frac{231\times 7}{2\times 22}$

$rh + r^2 = \frac{21\times 7}{2\times 2}$ ... (i)

Curved surface area of the cylinder

$= 2\pi rh = \frac{2}{3}\times 231 cm^2$

$2\times\frac{22}{7}r\,h = 154 cm^2 \quad \Rightarrow \quad rh = \frac{154\times 7}{2\times 22}$

$\Rightarrow \quad rh = \frac{7\times 7}{2}$ ...(ii)

Putting the value of rh in equation (i), we get

$\frac{7\times 7}{2} + r^2 = \frac{21\times 7}{2\times 2}$

$\Rightarrow \quad r^2 = \frac{21\times 7}{2\times 2} - \frac{7\times 7}{2} = \frac{7\times 7}{2}\left[\frac{3}{2}-1\right]$

$\Rightarrow \quad r^2 = \frac{7\times 7}{2}\times\frac{1}{2} \quad \Rightarrow r = \sqrt{\frac{7\times 7}{2\times 2}} = \frac{7}{2}cm$

Putting the value of r in equation (ii), we get

$\frac{7}{2}h = \frac{7\times 7}{2} \quad \Rightarrow \ h = 7$ cm

Hence, the volume of the cylinder = $\pi r^2 h$

$= \frac{22}{7}\times\left(\frac{7}{2}\right)^2 \times 7$

$= 22\times\frac{7}{2}\times\frac{7}{2} = \frac{539}{2} = 269.5\,cm^3$

LONG ANSWER QUESTIONS :

1. Let the original diameter of the sphere be $2x$.

Then, original radius of the sphere = x

Original curved surface area = $4\pi x^2$

Decreased diameter of the sphere = $2x$ – 25% of $2x$

$= 2x - \frac{x}{2} = \frac{3}{2}x$

Decreased radius of the sphere = $\frac{3}{4}x$

$\therefore$ Decreased curved surface area = $4\pi\left(\frac{3}{4}x\right)^2 = \frac{9}{4}\pi x^2$

Decrease in area = $4\pi x^2 - \frac{9}{4}\pi x^2 = \frac{7}{4}\pi x^2$

Hence, percentage decrease in area = $\frac{\frac{7}{4}\pi x^2}{4\pi x^2}\times 100\%$

$= \frac{7}{16}\times 100\% = \frac{175}{4}\% = 43.75\%$

2. Let r be the inner radius of the hemispherical dome. Then, inside surface area of the hemispherical dome

$= \frac{\text{Total cost}}{\text{Cost per square metre}}$

$= \frac{498.96}{2}m^2 = 249.48m^2$

Now, $2\pi r^2 = 249.48$

$\Rightarrow r^2 = \frac{249.48\times 7}{2\times 22} = 39.69 \Rightarrow r = \sqrt{39.69} = 6.3$ m

Volume of the air inside the dome = Volume of the hemispherical dome

$= \frac{2}{3}\pi r^3 = \frac{2}{3}\times\frac{22}{7}\times(6.3)^3\ m^3 = 523.908\ m^3$

3. Let V_1 and V_2 be the volumes of the right circular cylinder and cone respectively.

Then,

$V_1 = \frac{22}{7}\times 6\times 6\times 10\ cm^3$ [Using : $V_1 = \pi r^2 h$]

and $V_2 = \frac{1}{3} \times \frac{22}{7} \times 6 \times 6 \times 10 \text{ cm}^3$

$\left[\text{Using} : V_2 = \frac{1}{3}\pi r^2 h\right]$

$\therefore$ Volume of the remaining solid $= V_1 - V_2$

$\Rightarrow$ Volume of the remaining solid

$= \left(\frac{22}{7} \times 6 \times 6 \times 10 - \frac{1}{3} \times \frac{22}{7} \times 6 \times 6 \times 10\right) \text{cm}^3$

$\Rightarrow$ Volume of the remaining solid

$= \frac{22}{7} \times 6 \times 6 \times 10 \times \left(1 - \frac{1}{3}\right) \text{cm}^3$

$\Rightarrow$ Volume of the remaining solid

$= \frac{22}{7} \times 6 \times 6 \times 10 \times \frac{2}{3} \text{cm}^3$

$\Rightarrow$ Volume of the remaining solid $= 754.28 \text{ cm}^3$

4. Let R cm and r cm be respectively the external and internal radii of the hemispherical vessel. Then, R = 12.5 cm, r = 12 cm.

Now,

Internal surface area of the vessel

$= 2\pi R^2 = 2 \times \frac{22}{7} \times (12.5)^2 \text{ cm}^2$

External surface area of the vessel

$= 2\pi r^2 = 2 \times \frac{22}{7} \times (12)^2 \text{ cm}^2$

$\therefore$ Total area to be painted

$= 2 \times \frac{22}{7} \times (12.5)^2 + 2 \times \frac{22}{7} \times 12^2 \text{ cm}^2$

$\Rightarrow$ Total area to be painted

$= 2 \times \frac{22}{7} \times \left\{\left(\frac{25}{2}\right)^2 + 12^2\right\} \text{cm}^2$

$\Rightarrow$ Total area to be painted

$= 2 \times \frac{22}{7} \times \left(\frac{625}{4} + 144\right) \text{cm}^2 = \frac{13211}{7} \text{ cm}^2$

Cost of painting at the rate of 7 paise per sq. cm

$= ₹\frac{13211}{7} \times \frac{7}{100} = ₹132.11$

2 EXERCISE

TEXT-BOOK EXERCISE :

1. Length of the plastic box (l) = 1.5 m

Breadth (b) = 1.25 m

Height (h) = 65 cm $= \frac{65}{100}$ m = 0.65 m $\left[\because 1 \text{ cm} = \frac{1}{100} \text{m}\right]$

Since the box is open at the top.

Therefore the surface area of the sheet required

= Surface area of a cuboid – area of the top

$= 2(l \times b + b \times h + h \times l) - l \times b$

$= 2(1.5 \text{ m} \times 1.25 \text{ m} + 1.25 \text{ m} \times 0.65 \text{ m} + 0.65 \text{ m} \times 1.5 \text{ m}) - 1.5 \text{ m} \times 1.25 \text{ m}$

$= 2(1.875 \text{ m}^2 + 0.8125 \text{ m}^2 + 0.975 \text{ m}^2) - 1.875 \text{ m}^2$

$= 2(3.6625 \text{ m}^2) - 1.875 \text{ m}^2$

$= 7.325 \text{ m}^2 - 1.875 \text{ m}^2 = 5.45 \text{ m}^2$

2. The dimensions of the room are :

Length (l) = 5 m, Breadth (b) = 4 m and

Height (h) = 3 m

Area of the walls and ceiling = Lateral surface area + Area of the ceiling

$= 2(l + b) \times h + l \times b$

$= 2(5 \text{ m} + 4 \text{ m}) \times 3 \text{ m} + 5 \text{ m} \times 4 \text{ m}$

$= 54 \text{ m}^2 + 20 \text{ m}^2 = 74 \text{ m}^2$

The cost of white washing the walls and ceiling at the rate of ₹ 7.50 per m^2

= Surface area of the walls and ceiling × Rate

$= 74 \text{ m}^2 \times ₹ 7.50/\text{m}^2 = ₹ 555.$

3. Dimensions of each brick is

length (l) = 22.5 cm, breadth (b) = 10 cm,

height (h) = 7.5 cm

Surface area of each brick

$= 2(l \times b + b \times h + h \times l)$

$= 2(22.5 \text{ cm} \times 10 \text{ cm} + 10 \text{ cm} \times 7.5 \text{ cm} + 7.5 \text{ cm} \times 22.5 \text{ cm})$

$= 2(225 \text{ cm}^2 + 75 \text{ cm}^2 + 168.75 \text{ cm}^2)$

$= 2 \times 468.75 \text{ cm}^2 = 937.5 \text{ cm}^2$

Let n bricks will be painted.

Then the surface area of n bricks $= 9.375 \text{ m}^2$

$n \times$ area of each brick $= 9.375 \times 10000 \text{ cm}^2$

$\left[\because 1m^2 = 10000cm^2\right]$

$n \times 937.5\ cm^2 = 93750\ cm^2$

$n = \dfrac{93750cm^2}{937.5cm^2} = \dfrac{93750\times10}{937.5\times10}$

$= \dfrac{937500}{9375} = 100$ bricks.

4. Length of the greenhouse (l) = 30 cm

breadth (b) = 25 cm

height (h) = 25 cm

(i) Area of the glass used in the greenhouse,

= Total surface area of the greenhouse

$= 2\ (l \times b + b \times h + h \times l)$

$= 2\ (30\ cm \times 25\ cm + 25\ cm \times 25\ cm + 25\ cm \times 30\ cm)$

$= 2\ (750\ cm^2 + 625\ cm^2 + 750\ cm^2)$

$= 2\ (2125\ cm^2) = 4250\ cm^2$

(ii) Tape needed for all the 12 edges

$= 4\ (l + b + h)$

$= 4\ (30\ cm + 25\ cm + 25\ cm)$

$= 4\ (80\ cm) = 320\ cm$

5. Dimensions of the bigger box

length (l) = 25 cm, breadth (b) = 20 cm,

height (h) = 5 cm

Total surface area of the bigger box

$= 2\ (l \times b + b \times h + h \times l)$

$= 2\ (25\ cm \times 20\ cm + 20\ cm \times 5\ cm + 5\ cm \times 25\ cm)$

$= 2\ (500\ cm^2 + 100\ cm^2 + 125\ cm^2)$

$= 2\ (725\ cm^2) = 1450\ cm^2$

Dimensions of the smaller box

length (l) = 15 cm, breadth (b) = 12 cm,

height (h) = 5 cm

Total surface area of the smaller box

$= 2\ (l\times b + b \times h + h \times l)$

$= 2\ (15\ cm \times 12\ cm + 12\ cm \times 5\ cm + 5\ cm \times 15\ cm)$

$= 2\ (180\ cm^2 + 60\ cm^2 + 75\ cm^2)$

$= 2\ (315\ cm^2) = 630\ cm^2$

Total surface area of both boxes

$= 1450\ cm^2 + 630\ cm^2 = 2080\ cm^2$

Total surface area for making 250 boxes of each kind

$= 2080\ cm^2 \times 250 = 520000\ cm^2$

Area required for all the overlaps

= 5% of the total surface area

$= \dfrac{5\times520000}{100}\ cm^2 = 26000\ cm^2$

Hence total surface area of cardboard required

$= 520000\ cm^2 + 26000\ cm^2 = 546000\ cm^2$

The cost of cardboard at the rate of ₹ 4 per 1000 cm^2

$= 546000cm^2 \times \dfrac{4}{1000\ cm^2} = ₹\ 2184.$

6. Diameter of the cylindrical tank, $d = 140$ cm

radius $r = \dfrac{d}{2} = \dfrac{140}{2}$ cm = 70 cm = 0.70 m

height $h = 1$ m

Sheet required = Total surface area of the cylindrical tank

$= 2\pi r(r + h)$

$= 2\times\dfrac{22}{7}\times0.70(0.70+1)\,m^2$

$= 4.4 \times (1.70)\ m^2 = 7.48\ m^2$

7. (i) Inner diameter $d_1 = 4$ cm

Inner radius $r_1 = \dfrac{d_1}{2} = \dfrac{4}{2}cm = 2cm$

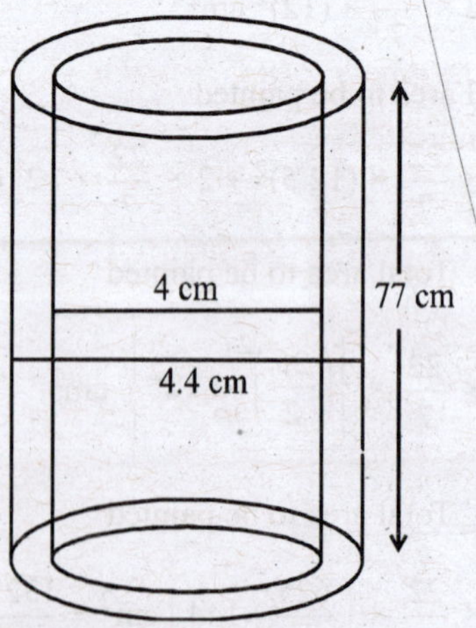

Outer diameter $d_2 = 4.4$ cm

Outer radius $r_2 = \dfrac{d_2}{2} = \dfrac{4.4}{2}cm = 2.2cm$

height $h = 77$ cm

Inner curved surface area

$= 2\pi r_1 h = 2\times\frac{22}{7}\times 2\times 77\,cm^2 = 968\ cm^2$

(ii) Outer curved surface area $= 2\pi r_2 h$

$= 2\times\frac{22}{7}\times 2.2\times 77\,cm^2 = 1064.8\ cm^2$

(iii) Total surface area $= 2\pi(r_1 + r_2)(h + r_2 - r_1)$

$= 2\times\frac{22}{7}(2+2.2)(77+2.2-2)$

$= 2\times\frac{22}{7}(4.2)(77.2) = 2038.08\ cm^2$

8. Inner diameter of the well $d = 3.5$ m

So inner radius of the well $= \frac{d}{2} = \frac{3.5}{2}$ m

depth $h = 10$ m

(i) Inner curved surface area of the well

$= 2\pi rh = 2\times\frac{22}{7}\times\frac{3.5}{2}\times 10 = 110\ m^2$

(ii) The cost of plastering the curved surface area at the rate of ₹ 40 per m^2

$= 110\ m^2 \times$ ₹$40/m^2 =$ ₹ 4400

9. Diameter of the pipe $d = 5$ cm $= 0.05$ m

radius $r = \frac{d}{2} = \frac{0.05}{2}$ m

Length of the pipe $h = 28$ m

Total radiating surface

$= 2\pi rh = 2\times\frac{22}{7}\times\frac{0.05}{2}\times 28\,m^2 = 4.4\ m^2$

10. Radius of the pen holder $= r = 3$ cm

height $h = 10.5$ cm

Cardboard required for one competitor $= 2\pi rh + \pi r^2$

$= 2\times\frac{22}{7}\times 3\times 10.5\,cm^2 + \frac{22}{7}(3)^2 = 198\,cm^2 + \frac{198}{7}cm^2$

Hence the cardboard supplied for 35 competitors

$= 198\times 35\,cm^2 + \frac{198}{7}\times 35\,cm^2$

$= 6930\ cm^2 + 990\ cm^2 = 7920\ cm^2$

11. Here $h = 10$ m and $r = 24$ m

(i) Slant height $l = \sqrt{r^2 + h^2}$

$= \sqrt{24^2 + 10^2}$

$= \sqrt{576+100} = \sqrt{676}$

$l = 26$ m

(ii) Curved surface area of the tent

$= \pi rl = \frac{22}{7}\times 24\times 26\,m^2$

The cost of the canvas required to make the tent at the rate of ₹70 per m^2.

$= \frac{22}{7}\times 24\times 26\,m^2 \times$ ₹$70/m^2 =$ ₹ 137280.

12. The height of the conical tent $h = 8$ m

base radius $r = 6$ m

Slant height $l = \sqrt{r^2 + h^2} = \sqrt{6^2 + 8^2}$ m

$l = \sqrt{36+64} = 10\,m$

Curved surface area of the tent

$= \pi rl = 3.14 \times 6\times 10\ m^2 = 188.40\ m^2$

Let the length of the tarpauline $L = a$ m, width $B = 3$ m

Area $= L \times B = 188.4\ m^2$

$a \times 3\ m = 188.4\ m^2$

$a = 62.8$ m

Extra length for margins = 20 cm = 0.2 m

Hence total length = 62.8 m + 0.2 m = 63 m

13. The base radius of the conical cap $r = 7$ cm

height $h = 24$ cm

Slant height $l = \sqrt{r^2 + h^2} = \sqrt{7^2 + 24^2}$ cm

$= \sqrt{48+576}$ cm

$l = \sqrt{625}$ m $= 25\,cm$

Curved surface area of the cap $= \pi rl$

$= \frac{22}{7}\times 7\times 25\,cm^2 = 550\ cm^2$

Area of the sheet required for making one cap $= 550\ cm^2$

So the area of the sheet required for making 10 such caps

$= 550\ cm^2 \times 10 = 5500\ cm^2$

14. Initial radius of the spherical balloon $r_1 = 7$ cm

Surface area of the balloon $S_1 = 4\pi r_1^2$

$= 4\times\frac{22}{7}\times 7\times 7\,cm^2 = 616\ cm^2$

Increased radius of the balloon $r_2 = 14$ cm

Surface area of $S_2 = 4\pi r_2^2$

$= 4 \times \frac{22}{7} \times 14 \times 14 \text{cm}^2$

$S_2 = 2464 \text{cm}^2$

Ratio $= \frac{S_1}{S_2} = \frac{616 \text{cm}^2}{2464 \text{cm}^2} = \frac{1}{4}$

$S_1 : S_2 = 1 : 4$

15. Inner diameter of the hemispherical bowl = 10.5 cm

Radius $r = \frac{d}{2} = \frac{10.5}{2}$ cm

Inner surface area of the bowl $= 2\pi r^2$

$= 2 \times \frac{22}{7} \times \frac{10.5}{2} \times \frac{10.5}{2} \text{cm}^2$

$= 173.25 \text{ cm}^2$

The cost of tin plating it on the inside at the rate of ₹ 16 per 100 cm^2

$= 173.25 \times$ ₹ 16 per 100 $\text{cm}^2 = \frac{2772}{100} \text{cm}^2$

= 27.72

16. Let the diameter of the earth $D = 2x$ units,

radius $R = \frac{D}{2} = \frac{2x}{2} = x$ units

Diameter of the moon, $d = \frac{1}{4}$ diameter of the earth

$= \frac{1}{4} \times 2x = \frac{x}{2}$ units

radius $r = \frac{d}{2} = \frac{x/2}{2} = \frac{x}{4}$ units.

Surface area of the earth $s = 4\pi R^2 = 4 \times \pi x^2$ sq. units.

Surface area of the moon $S = 4\pi r^2 = 4\pi \left(\frac{x}{4}\right)^2 = \frac{4\pi x^2}{16}$

Ratio of their surface areas $= \frac{S}{s} = \frac{\frac{4\pi x^2}{16}}{4\pi x^2} = \frac{1}{16} = 1 : 16$

17. Radius of the sphere $= r$,

Radius of the cylinder $= r$,

height of the cylinder $h = 2r$

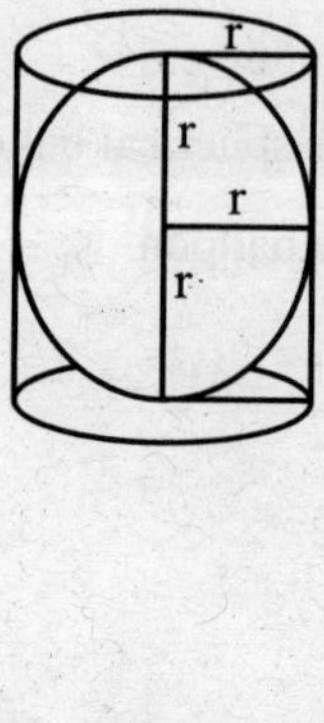

(i) Surface area of the sphere $= 4\pi r^2$

(ii) Curved surface area of the cylinder

$= 2\pi rh = 2\pi r \times 2r = 4\pi r^2$

(iii) Ratio of the areas in (i) and (ii)

$= \frac{4\pi r^2}{4\pi r^2} = 1 : 1$

18. Length of the cuboidal vessel $l = 10$ m, breadth $b = 8$ m

Let height $= h$ m

Volume of the vessel = 380 m^3

$l \times b \times h = 380 \text{ m}^3$

$10 \times 8 \times h = 380 \text{ m}^3$

$h = \frac{380 \text{ m}^3}{10 \times 8 \text{ m}^2} = 4.75 \text{m}$

19. Length of the cuboidal tank $l = 2.5$, depth $h = 10$ m,

Let breadth $= b$ m

Volume of the tank = 50000 litres

$l \times b \times h = \frac{50000}{1000} \text{m}^3$ [$\because 1 \text{m}^3 = 1000$ lit.]

$2.5 \times b \times 10 = 50 \text{m}^3$

$b = \frac{50}{25}$ m

$b = 2$ m

20. Population of the village = 4000

Water required per day = 4000 × 150 liters = 600000 lit.

$= \frac{600000}{1000} \text{m}^3$ [$\because$ 1 m^3 = 1000 l]

= 600 m^3

The volume of the tank $= l \times b \times h$

= 20 m × 15 m × 6 m = 1800 m^3

Hence the water will last for $\frac{1800}{600}$ days

= 3 days.

21. Side of the cube $a = 12$ cm

Volume of the cube = $(\text{side})^3$

$= (12 \text{ cm})^3 = 12 \times 12 \times 12 \text{ cm}^3$

It is divided into 8 cubes

So, volume of each cube $= \frac{12\times12\times12}{8} cm^3$

$(side)^3 = \frac{12\times12\times12}{2\times2\times2} cm^3$

$(side)^3 = 6 \times 6 \times 6\ cm^3$

side $= \sqrt[3]{6\times6\times6}$ cm

side = 6 cm.

Surface area of the first cube $= 6{a_1}^2 = 6 \times (12)^2\ cm^2$

$= 6 \times 12 \times 12\ cm^2$

$S_1 = 6 \times 144\ cm^2$

Surface area of the smaller cube

$S_2 = 6a_2^2 = 6 \times (6\ cm)^2 = 6 \times 6 \times 6\ cm^2$

Ratio between their surface areas $= \frac{S_1}{S_2}$

$= \frac{6\times144\,cm^2}{6\times6\times6\,cm^2} = \frac{4}{1} = 4:1$

22. Inner radius of the cylindrical pipe

$r_1 = \frac{\text{diameter}}{2} = \frac{24}{2} = 12\,cm$

Outer radius $r_2 = \frac{28}{2} cm = 14\,cm$

Length of the pipe $h = 35$ cm

Volume of the wood in the pipe $= \pi h(r_2^2 - r_1^2)$

$= \frac{22}{7}\times35(14^2 - 12^2) = 110\ (14 + 12)\ (14 - 12)$

$= 110 \times 26 \times 2 = 5720\ cm^3$

mass of the pipe = volume × density

$= 5720\ cm^3 \times 0.6$ g per $cm^3 = 3432.0\ g = \frac{3432}{1000}$ kg

= 3.432 kg

23. Length of the rectangular pack (l) = 5 cm

breadth (b) = 4 cm, height (h) = 15 cm

Capacity of the pack $= l \times b \times h = 5 \times 4 \times 15\ cm^3$

$= 300\ cm^3$

Base radius of the cylindrical pack $r = 7$ cm

height $h = 10$ cm

Volume of the cylindrical pack

$= \pi r^2 h = \frac{22}{7}\times\left(\frac{7}{2}\right)^2 \times 10\,cm^3$

$= \frac{22}{7}\times\frac{7\times7}{2\times2}\times10 = 11 \times 35\ cm^3 = 385\ cm^3$

Hence the cylindrical pack has greater capacity by

$385\ cm^3 - 300\ cm^3 = 85\ cm^3$

24. Capacity of a closed cylindrical vessel = 15.4 litres.

height h = 1 m = 100 cm,

$\pi r^2 h = 15.4\times1000\,cm^3$

$\frac{22}{7}r^2\times100 = 15400\,cm^3$

$\Rightarrow\ r^2 = \frac{15400\times7}{22\times100} cm^2$

$\Rightarrow\ r^2 = 7\times7\,cm^2$

$\Rightarrow\ r = \sqrt{7\times7}$ cm $\Rightarrow r = 7$ cm

Metal sheet needed to make it = Total surface area of the cylindrical vessel $= 2\pi r(h + r)$

$= 2\times\frac{22}{7}\times7(100+7) = 44 \times 107\ cm^2 = 4708\ cm^2$

$= \frac{4708}{10000} m^2$ $[\because 1\ m^2 = 10000\ cm^2]$

$= 0.4708\ m^2$

25. The diameter of the graphite $d_1 = 1$ mm,

radius $r_1 = \frac{d_1}{2} = \frac{1}{2}$ mm $= \frac{0.5}{10}$ cm $= 0.05$ cm

The diameter of the pencil $d_2 = 7$ mm,

radius $r_2 = \frac{7}{2}$ mm = 3.5 mm = 0.35 cm

Length of the pencil = h = 14 cm

Volume of the wood

$= \pi r_2^2 h - \pi r_1^2 h = \pi h(r_2^2 - r_1^2) = \frac{22}{7}\times14(0.35^2 - 0.05^2)$

$= 44\ (0.35 + 0.05)\ (0.35 - 0.05)$

$= 44 \times 0.40 \times 0.30 = 5.28\ cm^3$

Volume of the graphite

$= \pi r_1^2 h = \frac{22}{7}\times(0.05)^2\times14 = 44 \times .0025\ cm^3$

$= 0.1100\ cm^3 = 0.11\ cm^3$

26. Diameter of the cylindrical bowl = $d = 7$ cm

Radius of the bowl = $r = \frac{d}{2} = \frac{7}{2}$ cm = 3.5 cm

Height of the soup bowl = $h = 4$ cm

Volume of the soup in 1 bowl = $\pi r^2 h$

$= \frac{22}{7} \times (3.5)^2 \times 4 \text{cm}^3 = \frac{22}{7} \times 3.5 \times 3.5 \times 4 \text{cm}^3$

$= 11.0 \times 14.0 \text{ cm}^3 = 154 \text{ cm}^3$

Volume of the soup for 250 patients

$= 250 \times 154 \text{cm}^3 = 38500 \text{cm}^3$ s

or $= 38.5\, l$ $[\because 1000 \text{ cm}^3 = 1 l]$

27.

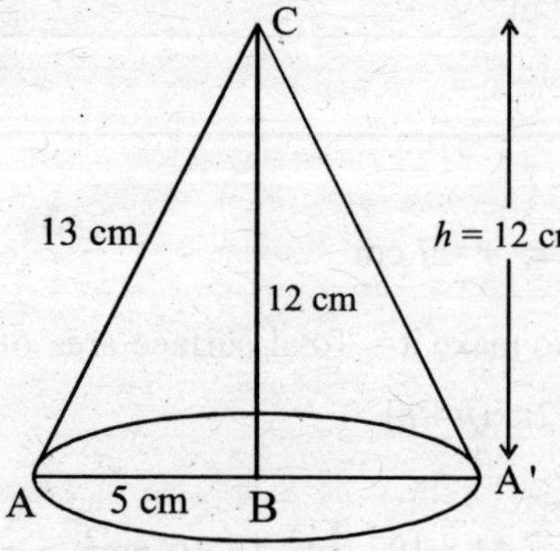

Since the triangle is revolved about the side 12 cm.

So height of the cone so formed $h = 12$ cm

Base radius $r = 5$ cm

So volume of the cone

$= \frac{1}{3}\pi r^2 h = \frac{1}{3} \times \pi \times (5)^2 \times 12 \text{cm}^3 = 100\pi \text{cm}^3$

28. The base diameter of the heap of wheat in the form of a cone $d = 10.5$ m

Base radius $r = \frac{d}{2} = \frac{10.5}{2}$ m = 5.25 m

Height h = 3 m

Volume of the heap

$= \frac{1}{3}\pi r^2 h = \frac{1}{3} \times \frac{22}{7} \times \frac{10.5}{2} \times \frac{10.5}{2} \times 3 \text{m}^3$

$= 86.615 \text{ m}^3$

Area of the canvas required to cover the heap

= Curved surface area of the heap

$= \pi r l = \frac{22}{7} \times \frac{10.5}{2} \times \sqrt{r^2 + h^2}$

$= 11 \times 1.5 \times \sqrt{\left(\frac{10.5}{2}\right)^2 + 3^2}$

$= 16.5\sqrt{27.5625 + 9} = 16.5\sqrt{36.5625}$

$= 16.5 \times 6.04 \text{ m}^2 = 99.66 \text{ m}^2$

29. Diameter of the metalic ball = $d = 4.2$ cm, $r = \frac{4.2}{2}$ cm

Volume of the ball $= \frac{4}{3}\pi r^3$

$= \frac{4}{3} \times \frac{22}{7} \times \frac{4.2}{2} \times \frac{4.2}{2} \times \frac{4.2}{2} = 38.808 \text{ cm}^3$

Mass of the ball = volume × density

$= 38.808 \times 8.9$ g per cm^3 = 345.39 gm (approx)

30. The inner radius of the hemispherical tank,

$r_1 = 1$ m

thickness of the iron sheet = 1 cm = 0.01m

$\therefore$ Outer radius of the tank

$r_2 = 1 + 0.01$m

$r_2 = 1.01$ m

$\therefore$ Volume of the iron used

$= \frac{2}{3}\pi(r_2^3 - r_1^3) = \frac{2}{3} \times \frac{22}{7} \times \left[(1.01)^3 - (1)^3\right]$

$= \frac{44}{21}(1.0303 - 1) = \frac{44}{21} \times 0.0303$

$= 0.0635 \text{ m}^3$ (approx.)

31. (i) The cost of white-washing inside the dome = ₹ 498.96

Rate = ₹ 2.00 per m^2

$\therefore$ Inside surface area of the dome

$= \frac{\text{Cost}}{\text{Rate}} = \frac{₹\, 498.96}{₹\, 2 \text{ per m}^2} = 249.48 \text{ m}^2$

(ii) Surface area of hemispherical dome

$2\pi r^2 = 249.48 \text{m}^2$

$2 \times \frac{22}{7} \times r^2 = 249.48 \text{ m}^2$

$r^2 = \frac{249.48}{2 \times 22} \times 7 \text{m}^2 \Rightarrow r^2 = \frac{11.34 \times 7}{2} \text{m}^2$

$r^2 = 5.67 \times 7 \text{m}^2 \Rightarrow r = \sqrt{39.69}$ m

$r = 6.3\text{m}$

So the inside volume of the dome

$= \frac{2}{3}\pi r^3 = \frac{2}{3} \times \frac{22}{7} \times 6.3 \times 6.3 \times 6.3$

$= 13.2 \times 6.3 \times 6.3 \text{ m}^3 = 523.908 \text{ m}^3$

32. (i) Volume of new sphere $= 27$ volume of small sphere

$\frac{4}{3}\pi r'^3 = 27.\frac{4}{3}\pi r^3$

$r' = \sqrt[3]{27r^3}$

$r' = 3r$

(ii) $S = 4\pi r^2$ and $S' = 4\pi . r'^2$

$= 4\pi.(3r)^2$

$S' = 4\pi.9r^2$

$S : S' = 4\pi r^2 : 4\pi \times 9r^2 = 1 : 9$

33. Surface area to be polished $= [(110 \times 85) + 2\,(110 \times 25) + 2\,(85 \times 25) + 2\,(110 \times 5) + 4\,(75 \times 5)]$

$= (9350 + 5500 + 4250 + 1100 + 1500) \text{ cm}^2$

$= 21700 \text{ cm}^2$

$\therefore$ Expenses required for polishing at the rate 20 paise per $\text{cm}^2 = 21700 \times 20$ paise

$= ₹\, \frac{21700 \times 20}{100} = ₹\,4340$

Now, surface area to be painted

$= [2\,(20 \times 90) + 6\,(75 \times 20) + (75 \times 90)] \text{ cm}^2$

$= (3600 + 9000 + 6750) \text{ cm}^2 = 19350 \text{ cm}^2$

$\therefore$ Required Expenses for painting at the rate 10 paise per cm^2

$= 19350 \times 10$ paise $= ₹\, \frac{19350 \times 10}{100} = ₹\,1935$

$\therefore$ Total expenses for polishing and painting the surface of the bookshelf

$= ₹\,4340 + ₹\,1935 = ₹\,6275.$

34. Let the radius of the sphere be $\frac{r}{2}$ cm.

then its diameter $= 2\left(\frac{r}{2}\right) = r$ cm

[$\because$ Radius = 2 (diameter)]

Curved surface area of the original sphere

$= 4\pi\left(\frac{r}{2}\right)^2 = \pi r^2 \text{ cm}^2$

Since, the diameter of sphere is decreased by 25%.

$\therefore$ New diameter of the sphere $= r - r \times \frac{25}{100}$

$= r - \frac{r}{4} = \frac{3r}{4}$ cm

$\therefore$ Radius of the new sphere $= \frac{1}{2}\left(\frac{3r}{4}\right) = \frac{3r}{8}$ cm

$\therefore$ New curved surface area of the sphere

$= 4\pi\left(\frac{3r}{8}\right)^2 = \frac{9\pi r^2}{16} \text{ cm}^2$

$\therefore$ Decrease in the original curved surface area

$= \pi r^2 - \frac{9\pi r^2}{16} = \frac{7\pi r^2}{16}$

$\therefore$ Decrease in % in surface area

$= \frac{\frac{7\pi r^2}{16}}{\pi r^2} \times 100\% = \frac{700}{16}\% = 43\frac{3}{4}\%$ or 43.75%

Hence, the original curved surface area decreases by $43\frac{3}{4}\%$.

EXAMPLAR QUESTIONS :

1. Surface area of the sphere $= 4\pi \times 5 \times 5 \text{ cm}^2$.

Curved surface area of the cone $= \pi \times 4 \times l \text{ cm}^2$, where l is the slant height of the cone.

According to the statement

$4\pi \times 5 \times 5 = 5 \times \pi \times 4 \times l$

or $l = 5$ cm.

Now, $l^2 = h^2 + r^2$

Therefore, $(5)^2 = h^2 + (4)^2$

where h is the height of the cone

or $(5)^2 - (4)^2 = h^2$

or $(5 + 4)\,(5 - 4) = h^2$

or $9 = h^2$

or $h = 3$ cm

Volume of Cone $= \frac{1}{3}\pi r^2 h$

$= \frac{1}{3} \times \frac{22}{7} \times 4 \times 4 \times 3 \text{ cm}^3$

$= \frac{22 \times 16}{7}$ cm^3

$= \frac{352}{7}$ cm^3 = 50.29 cm^3 (approximately)

2. Let the height of the water level in the cylindrical vessel be h cm

Volume of the rain water = 600 × 400 × 1 cm^3

Volume of water in the cylindrical vessel = $\pi (20)^2 \times h$ cm^3

According to statement

$600 \times 400 \times 1 = \pi (20)^2 \times h$

or $h = \frac{600}{3.14}$ cm = 191 cm

3. (d) Volume of sphere = $\frac{4}{3}\pi (\text{Radius})^3$

$= \frac{4}{3}\pi(2r)^3$

$= \frac{4}{3}\pi(8r^3) = \frac{32}{3}\pi r^3$

4. (c) Let 'a' be the side of a cube

$6a^2 = 96$ (given)

$\Rightarrow a^2 = 16 \Rightarrow a = 4$ cm

Volume of cube = $(4)^3 = 64$ cm^3

5. (c) Given: $r = 2r$

$h = h/2$

$\therefore$ curved surface area of cylinder

$= 2\pi rh = 2\pi(2r)\left(\frac{h}{2}\right) = 2\pi rh$

Hence, when radius is doubled and height is halved, curved surface area will be same.

6. (b) Let $r = \frac{r}{2}, \ell = 2\ell$

T.S.A. of cone = $\pi r(\ell + r) = \pi\frac{r}{2}\left[2\ell + \frac{r}{2}\right]$

$= \pi\left[r\ell + \frac{r^2}{4}\right] = \pi r\left[\ell + \frac{r}{4}\right]$

7. (b) Given: $\frac{r_1}{r_2} = \frac{2}{3}$ and $\frac{h_1}{h_2} = \frac{5}{3}$

Required ratio of volume = $\frac{\pi r_1^2 h_1}{\pi r_2^2 h_2} = \frac{r_1^2 h_1}{r_2^2 h_2}$

$= \frac{4(5)}{9(3)} = \frac{20}{27}$

HOTS QUESTIONS :

1. Let BPC, be the hemisphere and ABC be the cone standing on the base of hemisphere.

Radius BO of hemisphere = $\frac{1}{2} \times 4$ cm = 2 cm.

Now, let the right circular cylinder $EFGH$ circumscribe the given solid.

Radius of base of the right circular cylinder

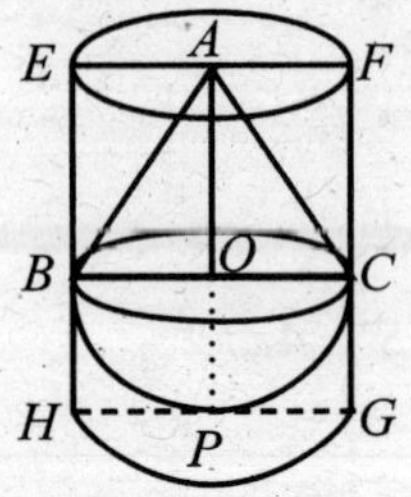

$= HP = BO = 2$ cm.

Height of the cylinder = $AP = AO + OP$

$= 2$ cm + 2 cm = 4 cm.

Now, the volume of the right circular cylinder – volume of the solid

$= \left[\pi \times 2^2 \times 4 - \left(\frac{2}{3} \times \pi \times 2^3 + \frac{1}{3} \times \pi \times 2^3\right)\right]$ cm^3

$= (16\pi - 8\pi)$ cm^3 = 8π cm^3.

Hence, the right circular cylinder covers 8π cm^3 more space than the solid.

2. $V = \frac{1}{3}\pi r^2 h$

$\Rightarrow V^2 = \frac{1}{9}\pi^2 r^4 h^2$

$\Rightarrow 9V^2 = \pi^2 r^2 (\ell^2 - h^2) h^2$

$\Rightarrow 9V^2 = (\pi^2 r^2 \ell^2) h^2 - \pi^2 r^2 h^4$

$\Rightarrow 9V^2 = C^2 h^2 - 3\left(\frac{1}{3}\pi r^2 h\right).\pi h^3$

$\Rightarrow 9V^2 = C^2 h^2 - 3V\pi h^3$

$\Rightarrow 3\pi V h^3 - C^2 h^2 + 9V^2 = 0$

3. The volume of a sphere = $\frac{4}{3}\pi r^3$

10% increase in radius = 10% r

Increased radius = $r + \frac{1}{10}r = \frac{11}{10}r$

The volume of the sphere now becomes

$$\frac{4}{3}\pi\left(\frac{11}{10}r\right)^3 = \frac{4}{3}\pi \times \frac{1331}{1000}r^3 = \frac{4}{3}\pi \times 1.331r^3$$

$$\text{Increase in volume} = \frac{4}{3}\pi \times 1.331r^3 - \frac{4}{3}\pi r^3$$

$$= \frac{4}{3}\pi r^3(1.331-1) = \frac{4}{3}\pi r^3 \times .331$$

Percentage increase in volume

$$= \left[\frac{\frac{4}{3}\pi r^3 \times .331}{\frac{4}{3}\pi r^3} \times 100\right] = 33.1\%$$

3 EXERCISE

SINGLE OPTION CORRECT:

1. (b) Length of longest rod = length of diagonal

$$= \sqrt{\ell^2 + b^2 + h^2} = \sqrt{(50)^2 + (40)^2 + (30)^2} = 50\sqrt{2} \text{ cm}$$

2. (a) Volume of material removed $= \pi r^2 h - \frac{1}{3}\pi r^2 h$

$$= \pi r^2 h\left[\frac{2}{3}\right]$$

$$= \frac{22}{7} \times (0.6)^2 \times 1.4 \times \frac{2}{3}$$

$$= 1.056 \text{ cm}^3$$

3. (b) Length of tape $= (4l + 4b + 4h)$ cm

$= (4 \times 30 + 4 \times 25 + 4 \times 25)$ cm $= 320$ cm

4. (b) Area of base = 154

$$\pi r^2 = 154$$

$$\frac{22}{7} \times r^2 = 154 \Rightarrow r^2 - \frac{154 \times 7}{22}$$

$r = 7$ m

Slant height of cone $= \sqrt{r^2 + h^2}$

$$= \sqrt{7^2 + 24^2}$$

$$= \sqrt{625}$$

$= 25$ m

Curved surface area $= \pi rl$

$$= \frac{22}{7} \times 7 \times 25$$

$= 550 \text{ m}^2$

5. (b) Edge of cube $= \frac{20}{4}$ cm $= 5$ cm,

surface area $= 6 \times 5^2 \text{ cm}^2 = 150 \text{ cm}^2$

6. (b) Radius of the hemisphere

$h = 3$ cm.

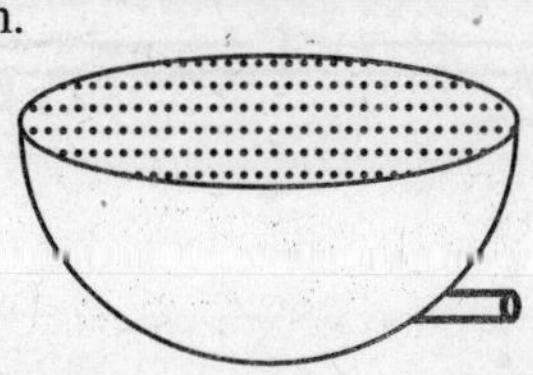

Volume of milk in the sphere $= \frac{2}{3}\pi r^3$

$$= \frac{2}{3}\pi \times 3^3 = \frac{22}{7} \times 2 \times 3^2 \text{ cm}^3$$

$$= \frac{22}{7} \times 2 \times 3^2 \times \frac{1}{1000} \text{ litre.}$$

Flow of liquid through the pipe $= \frac{1}{7}$ litre per second.

Time taken to empty the hemisphere

$$= \frac{22}{7} \times 2 \times 3^2 \times \frac{1}{1000} \times 7 = \frac{396}{1000} \text{sec.}$$

7. (c) $\ell = \sqrt{h^2 + r^2}$

8. (b) $A = 2(ab + bc + ca)$

$V = abc$

$$\therefore \frac{A}{V} = \frac{2(ab + bc + ca)}{abc} = 2\left(\frac{1}{c} + \frac{1}{a} + \frac{1}{b}\right)$$

9. (d) Let 'a' be the edge of cube.

(V) volume of cube $= a^3$

Edge of new cube $= 2a$

Volume of cube $= (2a)^3 = 8a^3$

$= 8(V)$.

10. (b) Required ratio $= \dfrac{\pi\left(\frac{3}{2}\right)^2 .1}{\pi\left(\frac{1}{2}\right)^2 .3}$

$$= \frac{9}{4} \times \frac{4}{3} = \frac{3}{1} \equiv 3:1$$

11. (a) Rectangle

12. (a) Given: $\pi r_1^2 h_1 = \pi r_2^2 h_2$

$$\Rightarrow \pi r_1^2(1) = \pi r_2^2(2)$$

$$\Rightarrow \frac{r_1^2}{r_2^2} = \frac{2}{1} \Rightarrow \frac{r_1}{r_2} = \frac{\sqrt{2}}{1} \equiv \sqrt{2}:1$$

13. (b) No. of surfaces in cylinder = 3.

14. (c) When rectangular sheet is cut at each corner, then length, breadth and height respectively will be

x – 2z, y – 2z, z

∴ Volume of tray = (x – 2z) (y – 2z)z

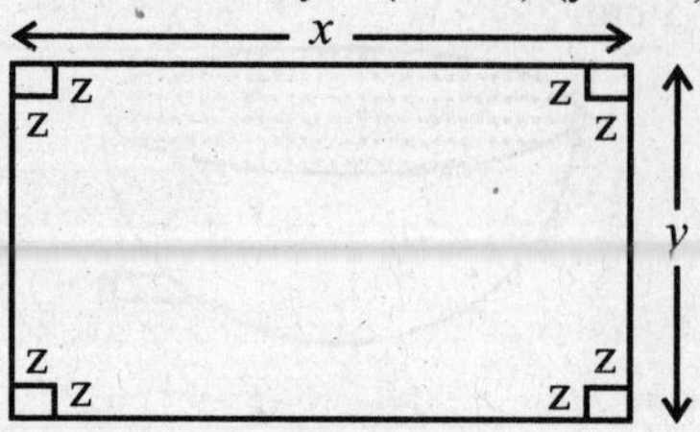

15. (c) Let r_1, r_2 be the radii of the two cylinders respectively. Let the heights of the two cylinders be cK and dK respectively.

$$\therefore \frac{\pi r_1^2 cK}{\pi r_1^2 dk} = \frac{a}{b} \Rightarrow \frac{r_1}{r_2} = \sqrt{\frac{ad}{bc}}$$

16. (c) Let r be radius of the sphere

$$\text{New radius} = \left(r + \frac{P}{100}r\right) = \left(1 + \frac{P}{100}\right)r$$

Original surface area of sphere = $4\pi r^2$

New surface area

$$= 4\pi\left(\left(1+\frac{P}{100}\right)r\right)^2 = 4\pi\left(1+\frac{P}{100}\right)^2 r^2$$

∴ % increase in surface area

$$= \frac{\text{Change in surface area}}{\text{Original surface area}} \times 100$$

$$= \left(\left(1+\frac{P}{(100)}\right)^2 - 1\right) \times 100$$

$$= \left(1 + \frac{P^2}{(100)^2} + \frac{2P}{100} - 1\right) \times 100 = \left(\frac{P^2}{100} + 2P\right)\%$$

17. (c) r = 1 unit (given)

$$\frac{\text{Volume of sphere}}{\text{Surface area of sphere}} = \frac{\frac{4}{3}\pi(1)^3}{4\pi(1)^2} = \frac{1}{3} = 1:3$$

18. (a)

$$\frac{\frac{1}{3}\pi(2)^2 h_1}{\frac{1}{3}\pi\left(\frac{5}{2}\right)^2 h_2} = \frac{1}{4}$$

$$\Rightarrow \frac{4h_1}{\frac{25}{4}h_2} = \frac{1}{4} \Rightarrow \frac{16h_1}{25h_2} = \frac{1}{4}$$

$$\Rightarrow \frac{h_1}{h_2} = \frac{1}{4} \times \frac{25}{16} = \frac{25}{64}$$

MORE THAN ONE OPTION CORRECT :

1. (a, b, c)

Volume of one match box

$= (4 \times 2.5 \times 1.5)\ \text{cm}^3 = 15\ \text{cm}^3$

∴ Required volume = Volume of 12 match boxes

$= 12 \times 15\ \text{cm}^3 = 180\ \text{cm}^3$

2. (a, c)

Let the edge of the solid cube = a

Since, cube is cut into two cuboids of equal volumes.

∴ Length = a, breadth = a, height = $\frac{a}{2}$

Total surface area of cube = $6a^2$ sq. unit

Total surface area of one cuboid

$$= 2\left(a \times a + a \times \frac{a}{2} + \frac{a}{2} \times a\right) = 4a^2 \text{ sq. unit}$$

Required ratio = $6a^2 : 4a^2 = 3 : 2$

3. (a, b, d)

R = external radius of pipe = 1.2 cm

r = internal radius = 1.2 – 0.2 = 1 cm

h = length of pipe = 3.5 m

∴ Volume of lead = $\pi(R^2 - r^2)\,h$

$$= \left[\frac{22}{7}(1.2+1)(1.2-1) \times 350\right] \text{cm}^3$$

$$= \frac{22}{7} \times 2.2 \times 0.2 \times 350\ \text{cm}^3 = 484\ \text{cm}^3$$

Since, one cubic centimeter of lead weighs 11 gm.

∴ Weight of the pipe = (484 × 11) gms

$$= \frac{484 \times 11}{1000}\text{kgs} = 5.324 \text{ kgs}$$

4. (b, d)

Let r_1 and r_2 be the radii of two cones and V_1 and V_2 be their volumes.

Let h be the height of the two cones, then

$$V_1 = \frac{1}{3}\pi r_1^2 h \text{ and } V_2 = \frac{1}{3}\pi r_2^2 h$$

$$\frac{V_1}{V_2} = \frac{\frac{1}{3}\pi r_1^2 h}{\frac{1}{3}\pi r_2^2 h} = \frac{r_1^2}{r_2^2} = \frac{9}{25} \quad (\because\ r_1 : r_2 = 3:5)$$

5. (a, b)

Let the radii of two spheres be r_1 cm and r_2 cm respectively.

Let the volumes be V_1 and V_2 respectively.

Now, $\frac{V_1}{V_2} = \frac{64}{27} \Rightarrow \frac{\frac{4}{3}\pi r_1^3}{\frac{4}{3}\pi r_2^3} = \frac{64}{27} \Rightarrow \frac{r_1}{r_2} = \frac{4}{3}$ ...(i)

Also, given $r_1 + r_2 = 7$ ...(ii)

Using (i) and (ii), we get

$r_1 = 4$ cm and $r_2 = 3$ cm

So, $S_1 - S_2 = 4\pi r_1^2 - 4\pi r_2^2 = 64\pi - 36\pi = 28\ \pi cm^2$

$= 28 \times \frac{22}{7} = 88\ cm^2$

PASSAGE BASED QUESTIONS :

PASSAGE-I

1. (c) Let edge = a cm

$\therefore\ a \times a \times a = 1000 \Rightarrow a^3 = 1000$

$\Rightarrow a = (1000)^{1/3} = 10$ cm

2. (d) Let edge of new cube = x cm

Volume of new cube = Sum of the volume of three cubes

$\Rightarrow x^3 = (3)^3 + (4)^3 + (5)^3 = 216$

$\Rightarrow x = 6$ cm

3. (b) Given : $\frac{a^3}{b^3} = \frac{8}{1}$

where 'a' and 'b' are edges of two cubes respectively

$\Rightarrow \frac{a}{b} = \frac{2}{1}$

Required ratio = 2 : 1

PASSAGE - II

4. (a) R = 12.5 cm, r = (12.5 – 1) = 11.5 cm

h = 20 cm

T.S.A. = $2\pi(R + r)(h + R - r)$

$= 2 \times \frac{22}{7} \times (12.5 + 11.5) \times (20 + 12.5 - 11.5)\ cm^2$

$= 2 \times \frac{22}{7} \times 24 \times 21\ cm^2 = 3168\ cm^2$

5. (a) $V = \pi(R^2 - r^2)h$

ASSERTION & REASON :

1. (d) Assertion is false but reason is correct.
2. (b) Both Assertion and Reason is correct.
3. (a) **Assertion :** T.S.A. = $\pi r(l + r)$

$= \pi \frac{ü}{ü}\left[2ü + —\right] = \pi\left[\ +—\right]$

4. (a) Length of the diagonal is the length of the longest rod that can be placed in the cuboid.

MULTIPLE MATCHING QUESTIONS :

1. (A) → (s), (u); (B) → (r), (v); (C) → (q), (w); (D) → (p), (t)

INTEGER TYPE QUESTIONS :

1. **Ans : 3**

Internal diameter of the pipe = 2 cm

So, its radius = 1 cm = $\frac{1}{100}$ m

Water that flows out through the pipe is 6 ms^{-1}

So, volume of water that flows out through the pipe in 1 sec

$= \pi \times \left(\frac{1}{100}\right)^2 \times 6\ m^3$

$\therefore$ In 30 minutes, volume of water flow

$= \pi \times \frac{1}{100 \times 100} \times 6 \times 30 \times 60\ m^3$

This must be equal to the volume of water that rises in the cylindrical tank after 30 min and height up to which it rises say h.

$\therefore$ Radius of tank = 60 cm = $\frac{60}{100}$ m

Volume = $\pi\left(\frac{60}{100}\right)^2 h$

$\pi\left(\frac{60}{100}\right)^2 h = \pi \times \frac{1}{100 \times 100} \times 6 \times 30 \times 60$

$\frac{60 \times 60}{100 \times 100} h = \frac{6 \times 30 \times 60}{100 \times 100}$

$\Rightarrow h = \frac{üx}{36} = 3$ m

So, required height will be 3 m.

2. **Ans : 4**

Volume of given cube = $a^3 = 12^3 = 12 \times 12 \times 12\ cm^3$

Let the edge of the new cube = x

$\therefore$ Volume of new cube = x^3

Volume of 8 new cubes = $8x^3$

Now, $8x^3 = 12 \times 12 \times 12$

$\Rightarrow x^3 \aleph \frac{12 \times 12 \times 12}{8}\ \ 216\ \ 6^3$

$\Rightarrow \quad x = 6$ cm

$$\frac{\text{Surface area of given cube}}{\text{Surface area of new cubes}} = \frac{6a^2}{6x^2} = \frac{6\times12^2}{6\times6^2}$$

$$= \frac{6\times12\times12}{6\times6\times6} = \frac{4}{1} = 4:1$$

3. Ans : 2

Length of longest rod = Length of diagonal

$$= \sqrt{l^2+b^2+h^2}$$

$$= \sqrt{(50)^2+(40)^2+(30)^2} = 50\sqrt{2} \text{ cm}$$

4. Ans : 9

Given : R = radius of cylindrical tub = 12 cm

H = height of water level = 20 cm

h = level of water which raises = 6.75 cm

Let r = radius of spherical ball

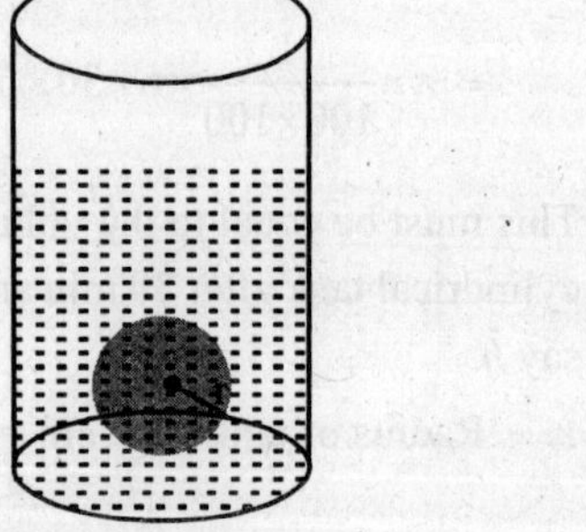

Now, volume of spherical ball = volume of water level raised

$$\frac{4}{3}\pi r^3 = \pi R^2 h$$

$$r^3 = \frac{3}{4}\times12\times12\times6.75 = 729$$

$$r = (729)^{1/3} = 9 \text{ cm}$$

5. Ans : 3

Volume of 27 solid sphere, each of radius,

$$r = 27\times\frac{4}{3}\pi r^3 = 36\pi r^3$$

According to the statement,

Volume of sphere of radius r' = Volume of 27 solid spheres

$$\Rightarrow \frac{4}{3}\pi(r')^3 = 36\pi r^3$$

$$\Rightarrow \quad (r')^3 = 27r^3 = (3r)^3 \Rightarrow r' = 3r$$

6. Ans : 5

Let r and R be the radii of the smaller and larger sphere respectively.

We have, $r = \frac{5}{2}$ cm

Volume of the smaller sphere

$$= \frac{4}{3}\pi r^3 = \frac{4}{3}\pi\left(\frac{5}{2}\right)^3 \text{cm}^3 = \frac{4}{3}\times\pi\times\frac{125}{8}\text{cm}^3$$

$$\text{Density of metal} = \frac{\text{Mass}}{\text{Volume}} = \frac{740}{\frac{4}{3}\times\frac{125}{8}\pi} \quad \text{...... (i)}$$

$$\text{Volume of larger sphere} = \frac{4}{3}\pi R^3$$

$$\text{Density of metal} = \frac{\text{Mass}}{\text{Volume}} = \frac{5920}{\frac{4}{3}\pi R^3} \quad \text{...... (ii)}$$

From (i) and (ii), we have

$$\frac{740}{\frac{4}{3}\times\frac{125}{8}\pi} = \frac{5920}{\frac{4}{3}\pi R^3}$$

$$\Rightarrow \quad R^3 = \frac{5920\times125}{740\times8} = 125$$

$$\Rightarrow \quad R^3 = 5^3 \Rightarrow R = 5 \text{ cm}$$

Chapter 14

Statistics

INTRODUCTION

Statistics is the science which deals with the collection of numerical facts called raw data and classification, tabulation, interpretation of raw data.

Statistics is basically the study of numerical data. It includes methods of collection, classification, presentation, analysis of data and inferences from data.

Expressing facts with the help of a data is of great importance in our day-to-day life just as we collect bricks, stones, rods, cement etc. before construction of a house. Data in fact is the fundamental unit of statistics. We can understand and solve even most complicated problems logically by making proper use of data.

Data as such can be qualitative or quantitative in nature. If one speaks of honesty, beauty, colour etc, the data is qualitative while height, weight, distance, marks etc. are quantitative.

In this chapter, we study the types of data, grouping or classification of data, graphical representation of data and central tendency (i.e. mean, median & mode) of raw data.

DATA

The word 'data' means information in the form of numerical figures or a set of given facts.

For example, the percentage of marks scored by 10 pupils of a class in a test are :

36, 80, 65, 75, 94, 48, 12, 64, 88 and 98. The set of these figures is the data related to the marks obtained by 10 pupils in a class test. Statistical data are of two types (i) Primary, (ii) secondary.

Primary Data : The data which is collected by the investigator with a definite plan or design in mind is called Primary Data.

Secondary Data : When the data is gathered from some sources which already had stored for some purpose, then the data is called secondary data.

UNGROUPED (OR RAW) DATA

The data which is collected for specific purpose and put as it is (without any arrangement) is called raw data or the data obtained in original form are called raw data or ungrouped data. Each entry in raw data is known as an observation.

For example : Runs scored by batsman in a T-20 cricket match are :

17, 20, 15, 42, 25, 17, 23, 18, 5, 15

RANGE OF RAW DATA

The difference between the highest and lowest values of given data is called range. In the above case;

Highest Score = 42, Lowest score = 5

∴ Range = Highest Score – Lowest score = 42 – 5 = 37

FREQUENCY

The number of times a particular observation occurs is called its frequency.

For example : Marks obtained by 20 students of a class in a unit test are:

8, 5, 10, 6, 12, 18, 10, 5, 11, 13, 4, 3, 9, 11, 2, 10, 10, 19, 5, 7

By observation, we can see that 5, 10 and 11 occurs three times, four times and two times respectively. Hence, frequency of 5, 10 and 11 are 3, 4 and 2 respectively.

PRESENTATION OF DATA

Frequency Distribution Table

There are two types of frequency distribution table.

(i) Discrete (or Ungrouped) Frequency Distribution Table

Consider the marks obtained by 20 students in mathematics annual examination of class VIII (Marks are out of 100) :

60, 70, 59, 60, 50, 58, 62, 56, 59, 59, 58, 70, 58, 62, 50, 58, 58, 50, 62, 56

To make the data easily understandable we write it as in the following table.

Marks obtained	50	56	58	59	60	62	70
No. of students (Frequency)	3	2	5	3	2	3	2

The above table is called Discrete (or Ungrouped) Frequency Distribution Table or simply a Frequency Distribution Table.

(ii) Grouped Frequency Distribution Table

When our data is large e.g. we are given marks out of 100 of 60 students. To make the data more sensible, we condense the data into groups like 50 – 55, ..., 90 – 95 (Assuming that our data is from 50 to 92) as given below.

Marks obtained (Groups or class Intervals)	No. of Students (frequency)
50 – 55	8
55 – 60	4
60 – 65	12
65 – 70	5
70 – 75	2
75 – 80	6
80 – 85	8
85 – 90	5
90 – 95	10
Total	60

The above type of table is called Grouped Frequency Distribution Table.

Least number of any class interval is called the lower limit of that class interval. And greatest number of any class interval is called the upper limit of that class interval. For example 50 and 55 are the lower and upper limit respectively of the class interval 50 – 55.

CLASS SIZE

The difference of upper limit and lower limit of any class interval is called class size or class width of the whole grouped frequency distribution. Class size of the above grouped frequency distribution is (55 – 50 = 5).

NOTE : Upper limit of any class is not included in that class. Hence the class inverval 60-65 means 'equal and greater than 60 but less than 65.'

CUMULATIVE FREQUENCY DISTRIBUTION TABLE

There are two types of cumulative frequency distribution table.

(i) Discrete Frequency Distribution

In a discrete frequency distribution, the cumulative frequency of a particular value of the variable is the total of all the frequencies of the values of the variable which are less than or equal to the particular value.

For example : Consider marks obtained by 45 students of class VIII in an assessment is given below:

Marks	0	5	10	14	16	18	20
No. of students (Frequency)	1	4	8	9	12	6	5

From the table we conclude that
1 student secured zero mark
4 students secured 5 marks
8 students secured 10 marks and so on.
Now, how many students secured 10 marks or less
To answer this question we have to add all the students who secured 10 or less marks i.e. (1 + 4 + 8) = 13 students.
13 is termed as cumulative frequency of marks 10. Similarly cumulative frequency of marks 16 is (1 + 4 + 8 + 9 + 12) = 34.
See the following table :

No. of children	No. of families (frequency)	Cumulative frequency
1	5	5
2	6	11 (= 5 + 6)
3	4	15 (= 11 + 4)
4	3	18 (= 15 + 3)
5	2	20 (= 18 + 2)
Total	**20**	

The above table is called Discrete Cumulative Frequency Distribution Table.

(ii) Grouped Frequency Distribution

In a grouped frequency distribution the cumulative frequency of a class is the total of all frequencies up to that particular class. To calculate cumulative frequencies, the classes should be written in ascending order.

For Example : The following table shows the number of patients getting medical treatment in a hospital on a day.

Age (in years) [Class Interval]	No. of Patients [Frequency]	Cumulative Frequency
10 – 20	90	90
20 – 30	50	140 (= 90 + 50)
30 – 40	60	200 (= 140 + 60)
40 – 50	80	280 (= 200 + 80)
50 – 60	50	330 (= 280 + 50)
60 – 70	30	360 (= 330 + 30)
Total	**360**	

The above table showing the cumulative frequency with class interval is called grouped frequency distribution table. The above grouped cumulative frequency distribution table can be presented in two other following ways.

(a) Less Than Type Grouped Cumulative Frequency Distribution Table

Age (in years)	No. of Patients (cumulative frequency)
Less than 20	90
Less than 30	140
Less than 40	200
Less than 50	280
Less than 60	330
Less than 70	360

(b) More Than Type Grouped Frequency Distribution Table

Age (in years)	No. of Patients (cumulative frequency)
Equal and more than 10	360
Equal and more than 20	270 (= 360 – 90)
Equal and more than 30	220 (= 270 – 50)
Equal and more than 40	160 (= 220 – 60)
Equal and more than 50	80 (= 160 – 80)
Equal and more than 60	30 (= 80 – 50)

EXCLUSIVE AND INCLUSIVE CLASS INTERVAL

Class interval of the form 10 – 20, 20 – 30, 30 – 40, ...; in which upper limit of any class interval coincides with the lower limit of the just next class interval, is called **Exclusive class Interval.**

Class interval of the form 10 – 19, 20 – 29, 30 – 39, ...; in which upper limit of any class interval does not coincides with the lower limit of the just next class interval, is called **Inclusive class Interval.** In the inclusive class interval, the difference between lower limit of any class interval and upper limit of just previous class interval is always 1.

To use inclusive class interval frequency or cumulative frequency distribution, first of all we convert it into exclusive class interval frequency distribution. For this, we only decrease the lower limit of each class interval by 0.5 and increase the upper limit of each class interval by 0.5 of inclusive class interval. But frequency or cumulative frequency remains the same.

For Example:

Marks obtained (Inclusive class interval)	No. of students (Frequency)	Cumulative Frequency
10 – 19	5	5
20 – 29	2	7
30 – 39	7	14
40 – 49	3	17
50 – 59	8	25
60 – 69	10	35
70 – 79	5	40
80 – 89	10	50
Total	**50**	

The above table is the inclusive class interval cumulative frequency distribution. Its corresponding exclusive class interval cumulative frequency distribution is given below.

Marks obtained (exclusive class interval)	No. of students (frequency)	Cumulative frequency
9.5 – 19.5	5	5
19.5 – 29.5	2	7
29.5 – 39.5	7	14
39.5 – 49.5	3	17
49.5 – 59.5	8	25
59.5 – 69.5	10	35
69.5 – 79.5	5	40
79.5 – 89.5	10	50
Total	**50**	

CONVERSION OF LESS THAN TYPE GROUPED CUMULATIVE FREQUENCY DISTRIBUTION TABLE INTO GENERAL TYPE

GROUPED CUMULATIVE FREQUENCY DISTRIBUTION.TABLE

Age (in years)	No. of Patients (Cumulative Frequency)
Less than 20	90
Less than 30	140
Less than 40	200
Less than 50	280
Less than 60	330
Less than 70	360

The above table is the less than type grouped cumulative frequency distribution table. Its corresponding general type grouped cumulative frequency distribution table is

Age (in years)	No. of Patients (frequency)	Cumulative frequency
10 – 20	90	90
20 – 30	50 (= 140 – 90)	140
30 – 40	60 (= 200 – 140)	200
40 – 50	80 (= 280 – 200)	280
50 – 60	50 (= 330 – 280)	330
60 – 70	30 (= 360 – 330)	360
Total	**360**	

CONVERSION OF MORE THAN TYPE GROUPED CUMULATIVE FREQUENCY DISTRIBUTION TABLE INTO GENERAL TYPE

GROUPED CUMULATIVE FREQUENCY DISTRIBUTION TABLE

Age (in years)	No. of Patients (cumulative frequency)
Equal and more than 10	360
Equal and more than 20	270
Equal and more than 30	220
Equal and more than 40	160
Equal and more than 50	80
Equal and more than 60	30

The above table is the more than type grouped cumulative frequency distribution table. Its corresponding general type grouped cumulative frequency distribution table is

Age (in years)	No. of Patients (frequency)	Cumulative frequency
10 – 20	90 (= 360 – 270)	90
20 – 30	50 (= 270 – 220)	140
30 – 40	60 (= 220 – 160)	200
40 – 50	80 (= 160 – 80)	280
50 – 60	50 (= 80 – 30)	330
60 – 70	30	360
Total		

GRAPHICAL REPRESENTATION OF DATA

To analyse and draw quick conclusion from the numerical data, data is suitably represented through graphs. The information provided by a numerical frequency distribution is easily understood when represented by diagrams or graphs. The diagrams act as visual aids and leave a lasting impression on the mind. This enables the investigator to make quick conclusions about the distribution.

In this class, we study only three types of graphical representation of data. The three types of graphs are

(A) Bar graph or Bar chart

(B) Histogram and

(C) Frequency polygon

(A) BAR GRAPH

A bar graph is a pictorial representation of the numerical data by a number of bars of uniform width erected horizontally or vertically with equal spacing between them.

Bar graphs is the simple most and popular graph to show ungrouped (or descrete) frequency distribution graphically. To draw bar graph, rectangular bars of uniform width with equal spaces in between them are drawn on a horizontal ray *OX*. Data (or items) are taken on *OX* ray. Each bar represent a data (or items). Height of each bar represents frequency of the corresponding data. Suitable scale of height of bars are shown on a vertical ray *OY*. See the following table :

Years	Expenditure (in 10 lakh of rupees) [frequency]
2004	5
2005	15
2006	25
2007	35
2008	10

The above table is the discrete frequency distribution table, which shows expenditure on health by ABC Pvt. Ltd. during five years (2004 to 2008).

Bar graph of the above discrete frequency distribution is shown below:

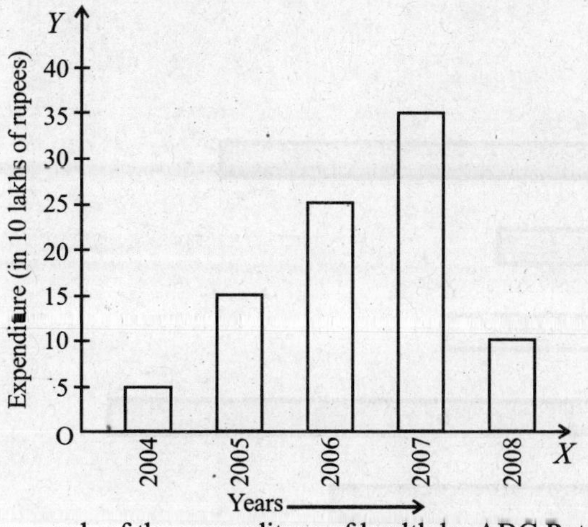

Bar graph of the expenditure of health by ABC Pvt. Ltd.

NOTE : (i) Sometimes for the sake of convenient, to draw bar graph of some discrete frequency distribution, data (or items) are taken on vertical OY-ray and frequency represented by length of the bars are measured on suitable scale on horizontal OX-ray.While constructing bar graphs the following points should be noted.

(ii) While constructing bar graphs the following points should be noted.

(a) The width of the bars should be uniform throughout.

(b) The gap between one bar and another should be uniform another should be uniform throughout.

(c) Bars may be either horizontal or vertical.

The important features of bar graphs are:

(a) It is used to represent unclassified frequency distributions.

(b) Frequency of a value of a variable is represented by a bar (rectangle) whose length (i.e.-height) is equal (proportional) to the frequency.

(c) The breadth of the bar is arbitrary and the breadth of all the bars are equal.The bars may or may not touch each other.

ILLUSTRATION : 1

Represent the following frequency distribution by bar graph :

Value of variable	3	6	9	12	15
Frequency	6	10	4	3	8

SOLUTION:

Either of the following bar graphs (fig (i) or fig (ii)) may be used to represent the above frequency distribution.

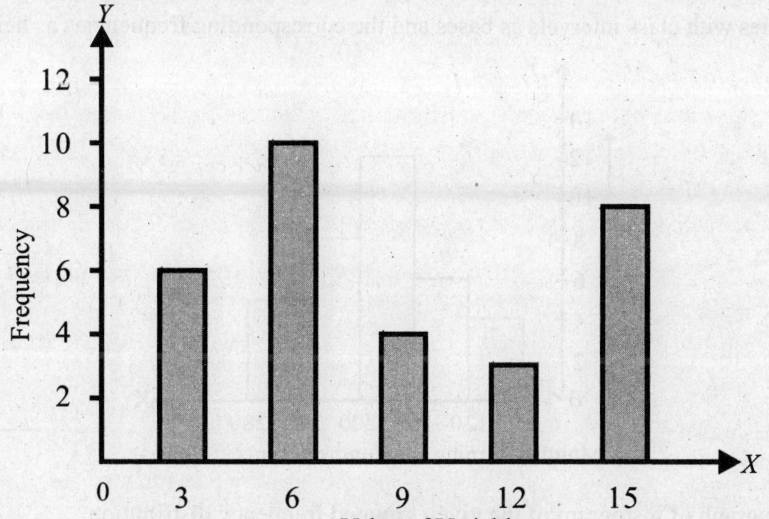

(fig. (i))

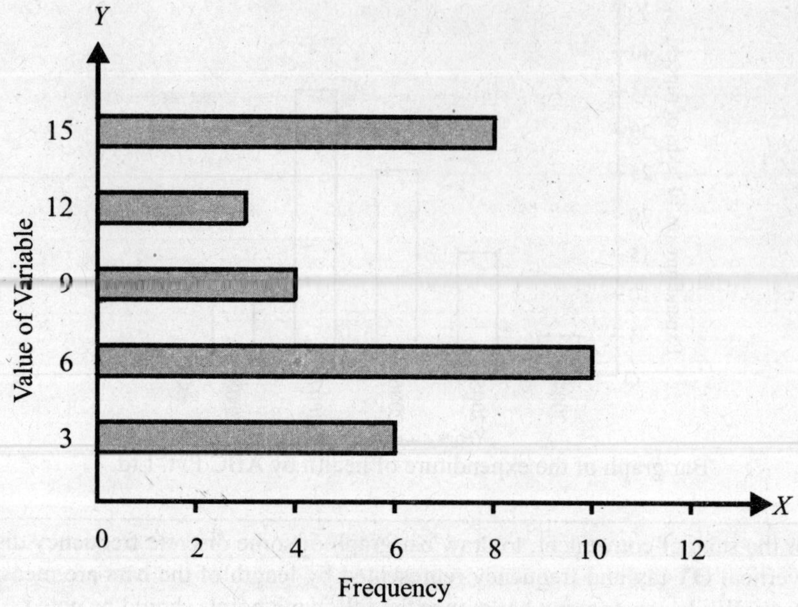

(fig. (ii))

(B) HISTOGRAM

A histogram is a graphical representation of a frequency distribution in the form of rectangles one after the other.

The bases of these rectangles represent the magnitudes of the variables of the class-boundaries. So these are taken along the x-axis. The heights of these represent the frequencies of the corresponding magnitudes of the variable of the class-boundaries.

Monthly Earnings (in hundred rupees)	No. of Workers
80-120	4
120-160	6
160-200	12
200-240	8
240-280	5

To draw the histogram of the above frequency distribution we follow the following steps :

(a) On the horizontal axis, mark the class intervals with a uniform scale.

(b) On the vertical axis mark a scale to measure the height of bars which is equal to the frequencies, with a uniform scale.

(c) Construct rectangles with class intervals as bases and the corresponding frequencies as heights

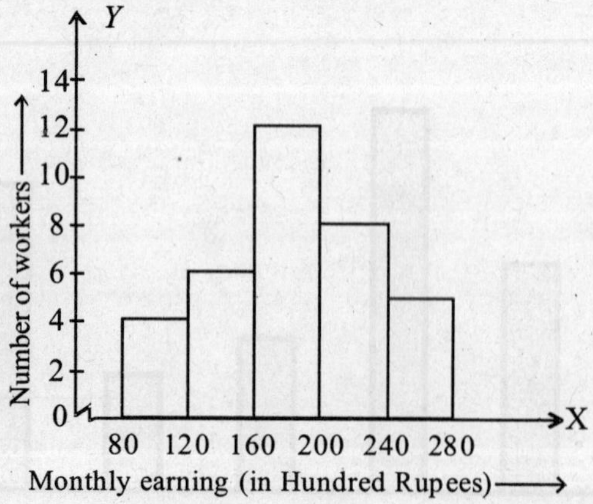

The above graph is the graph of histogram of the given grouped frequency distribution.

Note : Since the first class interval is start from 80 not from 0, hence we use a 'kink' or a break (z) on the x-ray just after 0.

ILLUSTRATION : 2

The following table gives the marks scored by 100 students in an entrance examination.

Mark :	0-10	10-20	20-30	30-40	40-50	50-60	60-70	70-80
No. of students (Frequency)	4	10	16	22	20	18	8	2

Represent this data in the form of a histogram.

SOLUTION:

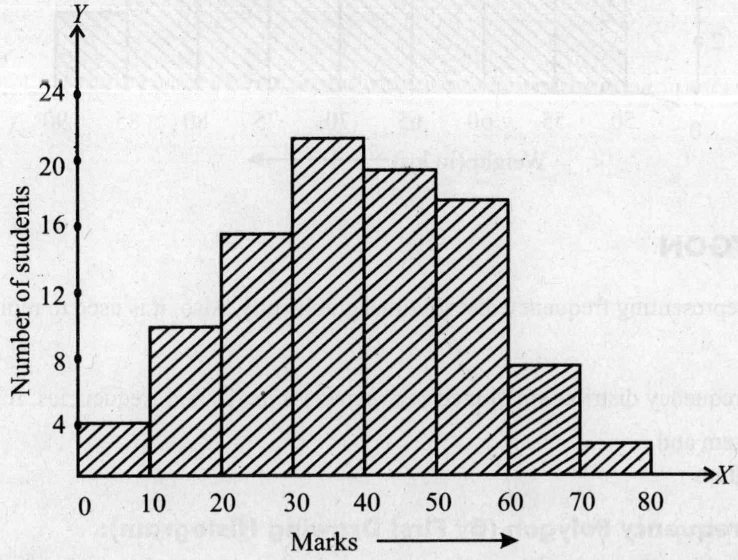

We represent the class limits along X-axis on a suitable scale and the frequencies along Y-axis on a suitable scale.

Taking class-intervals as bases and the corresponding frequencies as heights, we construct rectangles to obtain the histogram of the given frequency distribution as shown in figure.

ILLUSTRATION : 3

The following is the distribution of weights (in kg) of 50 persons:

Weight (in kg) :	50-55	55-60	60-65	65-70	70-75	75-80	80-85	85-90
Number of persons :	12	8	5	4	5	7	6	3

Draw a histogram for the above data.

SOLUTION :

We represent the class limits along X-axis on a suitable scale and the frequencies along Y-axis on a suitable scale.

Since the scale on X-axis starts at 50, a kink (break) is indicated near the origin to signify that the graph is drawn to scale beginning at 50, and not at the origin.

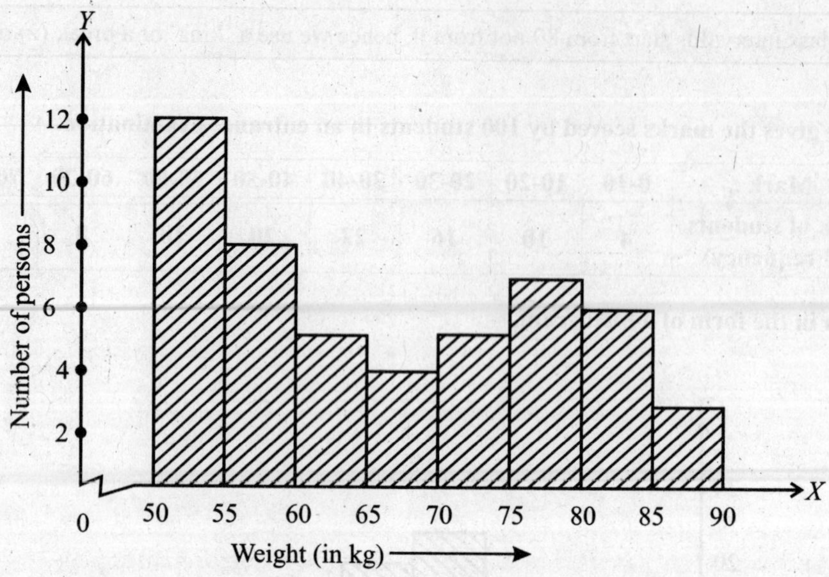

(C) FREQUENCY POLYGON

It is another method of representing frequency distributions graphically. Also, it is used to represent classified or grouped data graphically.

It is a line graph of grouped frequency distribution plotted between class marks and frequencies. It can be obtained in two ways

(a) By first drawing Histogram and
(b) Without drawing Histogram

(a) Steps of Drawing Frequency Polygon (By First Drawing Histogram):

(i) Draw the histogram from the given data
(ii) Obtain the mid-points of the upper horizontal sides of each rectangle.
(iii) Join these mid-points of the adjacent rectangles by dotted line segments.
(iv) Obtain the mid-point of two assumed class intervals of zero frequency. One before the first and other after the last class interval.
(v) Complete the polygon by joining the mid-point of class first to mid-point of its left adjacent class and mid-point of last class intervals to the mid point of its right adjacent class interval.

ILLUSTRATION 4 :

Draw a histogram and a frequency polygon of the following data :

Age in years	0-6	6-12	12-18	18-24	24-30	30-36	36-42
No. of persons	6	11	25	35	18	12	6

SOLUTION :

First we draw histogram of the given data, then we will locate mid-points of top horizontal side of rectangles.

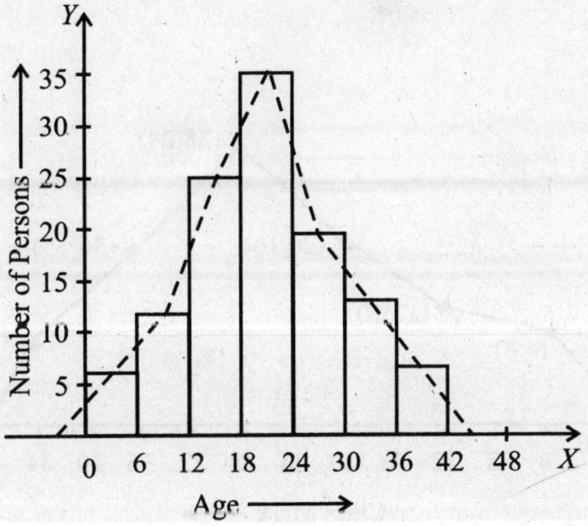

Now, join these mid points by dotted line segments. Complete the polygon by joining the mid points of first interval to the mid-point of its left adjacent assumed class interval of zero frequency and mid-point of last class interval to its adjacent right assumed class interval of zero frequency.

(b) Steps of Drawing Frequency Polygon (Without Drawing Histogram)

(i) First calculate the class marks (mid points) $x_1, x_2, x_3, \ldots, x_n$ of the given class intervals.

(ii) Mark $x_1, x_2, x_3, \ldots, x_n$ along X-axis.

(iii) Mark respective frequencies $f_1, f_2, f_3, \ldots, f_n$ along Y-axis.

(iv) Plot the points $(x_1, f_1), (x_2, f_2), (x_3, f_3), \ldots (x_n, f_n)$

(v) Join points plotted in step (iv) by line segments.

(vi) Take two class intervals of zero frequency, one just before the first and other just after the last class interval given. Locate their mid points.

(vii) Complete the frequency polygon by joining the point (x_1, f_1) to the mid-point of the assumed class interval of zero frequency just before the first class interval and (x_n, f_n) to the assumed class interval of zero frequency just right to the last class interval.

ILLUS ATION 5 :

Construct a frequency polygon for the following data without drawing the histogram:

Class Interval	0-8	8-16	16-24	24-32	32-40	40-48
Frequency	8	10	16	24	15	7

SOLUTION :

Calculate class marks of given frequency distribution

Class Interval	Class Mark (or mid-point)	Frequency
0-8	4	8
8-16	12	10
16-24	20	16
24-32	28	24
32-40	36	15
40-48	44	7

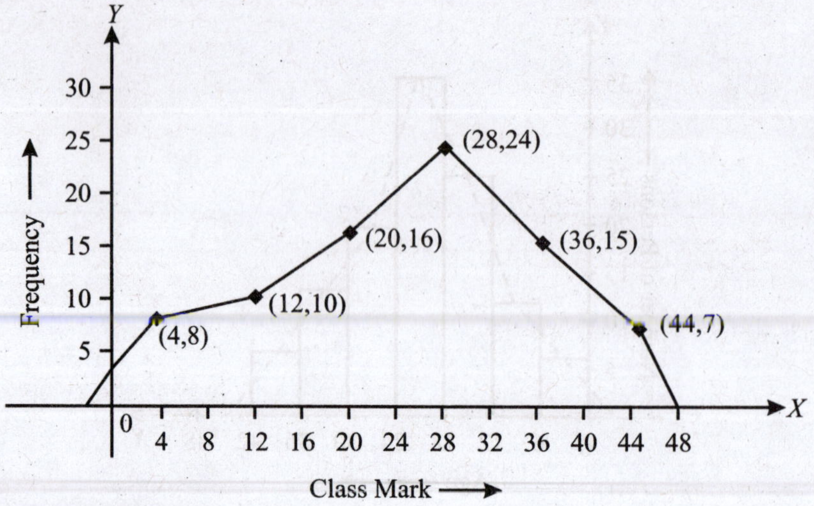

USE OF SUMMATION (Σ) NOTATION

The symbol Σ (read: sigma) means summation. If $x_1, x_2, x_3, ..., x_n$ are the 'n' values of a variable 'x' then their sum $x_1 + x_2 + x_3 + ... + x_n$ is denoted by $\sum_{i=1}^{n} x_i$ or simply Σx.

Similarly the sum $k_1x_1 + k_2x_2 + \cdots\cdots + k_nx_n$ is denoted by $\sum_{i=1}^{n} k_i x_i$ or simply $\sum kx$

: $\sum_{i=1}^{n}(ax_i + b) = a\sum_{i=1}^{n} x_i + nb$

ASURES OF CENTRAL TENDENCY

the data is very large, the user cannot get much information from these data or its associated frequency distribution. In this case, he information contained in data are represented by some numerical values, called averages. These averages are also called measures of central tendency or measures of location because they also give an idea about the concentration of the values in the central part of the distribution of data which describes the characteristics of the entire data or its associated frequency distribution.

The most commonly used averages are

(a) Arithmetic mean simply called mean

(b) Median and

(c) Mode

MEAN

(i) Mean of Ungrouped Data

Mean of a set of observations is their sum divided by number of observations. Mean is denoted by $\overline{x}$. The mean $\overline{x}$ of n observations $x_1, x_2, x_3, ..., x_n$ is given by

$$\overline{x} = \frac{x_1 + x_2 + x_3 + ... + x_n}{n} = \frac{1}{n}\sum_{i=1}^{n} x_i$$

ILLUSTRATION 6 :

Find mean of 21, 22, 24, 26, 32.

SOLUTION:

$$\bar{x} = \frac{x_1 + x_2 + x_3 + x_4 + x_5}{5} = \frac{21 + 22 + 24 + 26 + 32}{5} = \frac{125}{5} = 25$$

ILLUSTRATION 7 :

The mean of 6, 10, x and 12 is 8. Find the value of x.

SOLUTION:

$$\bar{x} = \frac{\sum_{i=1}^{n} x_i}{n} = \frac{6 + 10 + x + 12}{4} = \frac{28 + x}{4} \Rightarrow 8 = \frac{28 + x}{4} \quad (\because \bar{x} = 8)$$

$\Rightarrow 28 + x = 32 \Rightarrow x = 4$, $\therefore$ value of x is 4

Some Important Results About Mean

(i) If each observation is increased by 'a', then the mean is also increased by 'a'. If $\bar{x}$ is the mean of n observations $x_1, x_2, \ldots, x_n$, then the mean of observations $(x_1 + a), (x_2 + a), (x_3 + a), \ldots, (x_n + a)$ is $(\bar{x} + a)$.

(ii) If each observation is decreased by 'a', then mean is also decreased by 'a'. If $\bar{x}$ is the mean of n observations $x_1, x_2, \ldots, x_n$; then mean of observations $(x_1 - a), (x_2 - a), \ldots, (x_n - a)$ is $(\bar{x} - a)$.

(iii) If each observation is multiplied by a non-zero number 'a'. Then, mean is also multiplied by 'a'. If $\bar{x}$ is mean of n observations $x_1, x_2, \ldots, x_n$; then mean of $ax_1, ax_2, \ldots, ax_n$ is $a.\bar{x}$.

(iv) If each observation is divided by a non-zero number 'a', then mean is also divided by the non-zero number 'a'. If $\bar{x}$ is the mean of n observations $x_1, x_2, \ldots, x_n$, then mean of $\frac{x_1}{a}, \frac{x_2}{a}, \ldots, \frac{x_n}{a}$, is $\frac{\bar{x}}{a}$.

(v) If $\bar{x}$ is the mean of n observations $x_1, x_2, \ldots, x_n$, then the algebraic sum of deviations from mean is zero. i.e. $\sum_{i=1}^{n}(x_i - \bar{x}) = 0$

CONNECTING TOPIC

Combined Mean : If $\bar{x}_1, \bar{x}_2, \ldots, \bar{x}_k$ are the mean of k series having number of observations (or data) $n_1, n_2, \ldots, n_k$ respectively then the mean $\bar{x}$ of the composite series is given by

$$\bar{x} = \frac{n_1\bar{x}_1 + n_2\bar{x}_2 + \ldots + n_k\bar{x}_k}{n_1 + n_2 + \ldots + n_k}$$

Weighted Arithmetic Mean :

If $x_1, x_2, \ldots, x_n$ denote n values of the variable x and $w_1, w_2, \ldots, w_n$ denote respectively their weights, then their weighted mean is $\bar{x}_w = \frac{\sum_{i=1}^{n} w_i x_i}{\sum_{i=1}^{n} w_i}$

Note : If the weight of each observation is 1, then weighted mean = arithmetic mean

ILLUSTRATION 8 :

The mean income of a group of persons is ₹ 400. Another group of persons has mean income ₹ 480. If the mean income of all the persons in the two groups together is ₹ 430, then find ratio of the number of persons in the group.

SOLUTION :

$$\bar{x} = \frac{n_1\bar{x}_1 + n_2\bar{x}_2}{n_1 + n_2} \qquad \because \bar{x}_1 = 400,\ \bar{x}_2 = 480,\ \bar{x} = 430$$

$$\therefore\ 430 = \frac{n_1(400) + n_2(480)}{n_1 + n_2} \Rightarrow 30n_1 = 50n_2 \Rightarrow \frac{n_1}{n_2} = \frac{5}{3} \Rightarrow n_1 : n_2 = 5:3$$

Hence, required ratio = 5 : 3

(ii) Mean of Ungrouped (or Discrete) Frequency Distribution

Let $f_1, f_2, f_3, \ldots, f_n$ be the frequencies of $x_1, x_2, x_3, \ldots, x_n$, then

$$\bar{x} = \frac{f_1x_1 + f_2x_2 + f_3x_3 + \ldots + f_nx_n}{f_1 + f_2 + f_3 + \ldots + f_n}$$

or $$\bar{x} = \frac{\sum_{i=1}^{n} f_ix_i}{\sum_{i=1}^{n} f_i} = \frac{1}{N}\sum_{i=1}^{n} f_ix_i \text{ , where } N = \sum_{i=1}^{n} f_i$$

ILLUSTRATION 9 :

Find the mean of the following distribution:

Number (x)	8	10	15	20
Frequency (f)	5	8	8	4

SOLUTION :

x	f	fx
8	5	40
10	8	80
15	8	120
20	4	80
Total	25	320

$$\therefore \quad \bar{x} = \frac{\sum_{i=1}^{n} f_ix_i}{\sum_{i=1}^{n} f_i}$$

$$\bar{x} = \frac{320}{25} = 12.8, \qquad \therefore \quad \text{mean} = 12.8$$

MEDIAN

Median of a distribution is the value of the variable which divides the distribution into two equal parts.

(i) Median of ungrouped data

The median is that value of the given number of observations, which divides it into exactly two parts.
Median of a given number of observations arranged in ascending or descending order, is the middle most observation. If there are two middle most observation, then median is the average of these two observations.

When the data is arranged in ascending or descending order then median is calculated as follows:

(a) When the number of observation (n) is odd, the median is the $\left(\frac{n+1}{2}\right)^{th}$ observation.

For example : If there are 21 observations, then $\left(\frac{21+1}{2}=11\right)^{th}$ observation will be the median of given observations.

(b) If the number of observation (n) is even, then median is the mean of $\left(\frac{n}{2}\right)^{th}$ and $\left(\frac{n}{2}+1\right)^{th}$ observations.

For example if number of observations are 20 then

$$\text{Median} = \frac{\left(\frac{20}{2}\right)^{th}\text{ observation} + \left(\frac{20}{2}+1\right)^{th}\text{ observation}}{2}$$

$$\text{Median} = \frac{10^{th}\text{ observation} + 11^{th}\text{ observation}}{2}$$

ILLUSTRATION 10 :

The monthly salaries (in ₹) of 10 employees of a factory are:
12000, 8500, 9200, 7400, 11300, 12700, 7800, 11500, 10320, 8100. Find the median salary.

SOLUTION:

Arranging the observation in ascending order :
7400, 7800, 8100, 8500, 9200, 10320, 11300, 11500, 12000, 12700
Total number of observations (n) = 10 (even)

$$\therefore \quad \text{median} = \frac{1}{2}\left[\left(\frac{n}{2}\right)^{th}\text{ observation} + \left(\frac{n}{2}+1\right)^{th}\text{ observation}\right]$$

$$= \frac{1}{2}\left[\left(\frac{10}{2}\right)^{th}\text{ observation} + \left(\frac{10}{2}+1\right)^{th}\text{ observation}\right]$$

$$= \frac{1}{2}\left[5^{th}\text{ observation} + 6^{th}\text{ observation}\right]$$

$$\text{Median} = \frac{1}{2}[9200+10320] = \frac{19520}{2} = 9760$$

Median Salary = ₹ 9760

PROPERTIES OF MEDIAN

(i) The median can be calculated graphically, while mean cannot be.

(ii) The sum of the absolute deviations taken from the median is less than the sum of the absolute deviations taken from any other observation is the data.

(iii) Median is not affected by extreme values.

5. The median of a set of 9 distinct observations is 20.5. If each of the largest 4 observation of the set is increased by 2, then the median of the new set

(a) is increased by 2 **(b) is decreased by 2**

(c) is two times the original median **(d) Remains the same as that of the original set**

Sol. (d) Since $n = 9$, then median $= \left(\frac{9+1}{2}\right)^{th} = 5^{th}$ observation

Now, last four observations are increased by 2.

$\because$ The median is 5th observation, which remains unchanged.

$\therefore$ There will be no change in median.

6. A set of numbers consists of three 4's, five 5's, six 6's, eight 8's and seven 10's. The mode of this set of numbers is

(a) 6 **(b) 7** **(c) 8** **(d) 10**

Sol. (c) Mode of the data is 8 as it repeated maximum number of times.

7. Mean of 25 observations was found to be 78.4. But later on it was found that 96 was misread 69. Find the correct mean.

Sol. Mean $\overline{x} = \frac{\Sigma x}{n}$ or $\Sigma x = n\overline{x}$ = Sum of 25 observations

$\Sigma x = 25 \times 78.4 = 1960$

= sum of 25 observations

Sum of 24 obs. + 69 = 1960

As 69 was misread in place of 96

Sum of 24 obs. + 96 = 1960 – 69 + 96

Sum of 25 obs. = 1987

$\therefore$ Correct mean $= \frac{1987}{25} = 79.48$

8. Draw a histogram for the following data :

Class Mark	12.5	17.5	22.5	27.5	32.5	37.5
Frequency	7	13	20	29	10	5

Sol. h = Class-size = Difference between two consecutive class-marks = (17.5 – 12.5) = 5

$\therefore \frac{h}{2} = \frac{5}{2} = 2.5$

$\therefore$ Subtract 2.5 from each class-mark to get lower-limit. And, add 2.5 to the class-mark to get upper-limit.

Thus, the given frequency distribution in exclusive form will be as given below :

Class Interval	Frequency
10-15	7
15-20	13
20-25	20
25-30	29
30-35	10
35-40	5

Now, along x-axis, mark the points 10, 15, 20, 25, 30, 35 and 40 and along y-axis, mark the corresponding points 7, 13, 20, 29, 10, 5.

Construct rectangles with class-intervals as bases and the corresponding frequencies as heights, as shown.

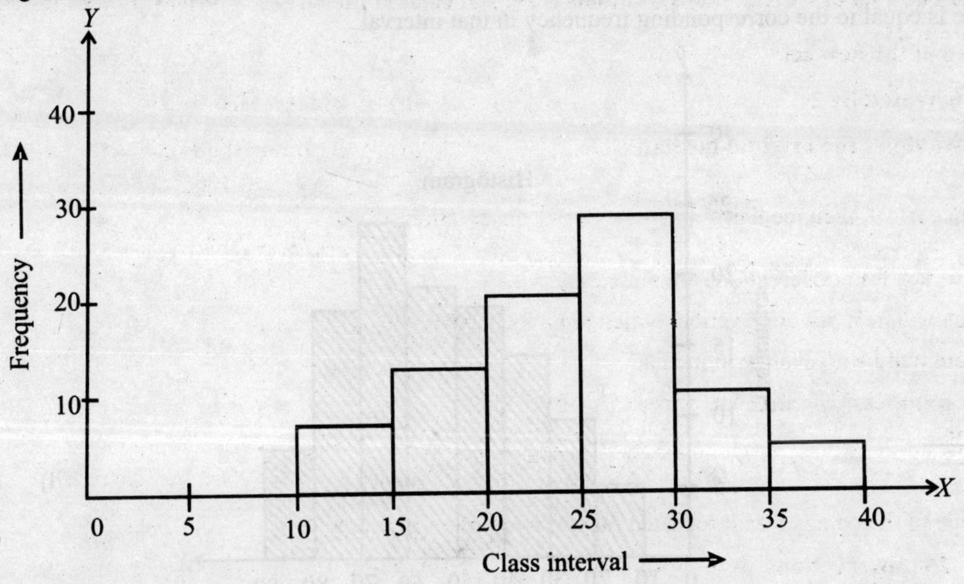

9. The marks obtained by a set of students in an examination are given below :

Marks	5	10	15	20	25	30
No. of Students	6	4	6	12	x	4

If the mean of the above data is 18, calculate the numerical value of x.

Sol. From the above data, we may prepare the table given below :

Marks (x_i)	No. of students (frequency) (f_i)	f_ix_i
5	6	30
10	4	40
15	6	90
20	12	240
25	x	25x
30	4	120
	$\Sigma f_i = (32 + x)$	$\Sigma f_ix_i = (520 + 25x)$

$\therefore$ Mean $= \dfrac{\Sigma f_i x_i}{\Sigma f_i} = \dfrac{(520+25x)}{(32+x)}$ But, mean = 18

$\therefore$ $\dfrac{520+25x}{32+x} = 18 \Rightarrow 520 + 25x = 18\,(32+x) \Rightarrow 7x = 56 \Rightarrow x = 8$, Hence, $x = 8$

10. For the following frequency table, draw a histogram

Class	Frequency
10-20	5
20-30	10
30-40	15
40-50	17
50-60	20
60-70	24
70-80	16
80-90	8

Sol. In the given histogram, class-intervals are taken on the x-axis and the corresponding frequencies on the y-axis. The height of each rectangle is equal to the corresponding frequency in that interval.

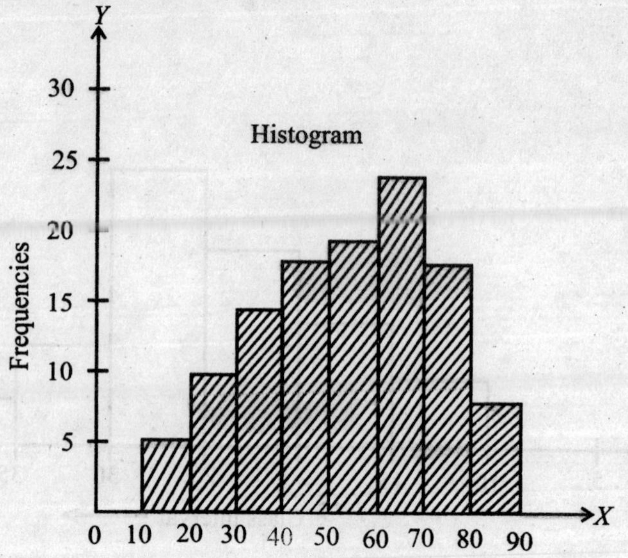

11. Calculate the median score for the following scores :

(a) 2, 27, 15, 10, 8, 13, 30 **(b) 2, 22, 25, 8, 12, 17, 3, 10**

Sol. (a) The scores in ascending order : 2, 8, 10, 13, 15, 27, 30

Since, there are 7 scores

$\therefore$ median = 4th score = 13

(b) The scores in ascending order : 2, 3, 8, 10, 12, 17, 22, 25

Since, there are 8 scores

$\therefore$ median $= \frac{1}{2}$(4th score + 5th score) $= \frac{1}{2}(10 + 12) = 11$

12. Find the value of k from the following data if mean of the given data is 16.

x	5	10	15	20	25
f	2	8	k	10	5

Sol.

x	f	fx
5	2	10
10	8	80
15	k	$15k$
20	10	200
25	5	125
Total	$25 + k$	$415 + 15k$

$$\text{Mean} = \frac{\Sigma fx}{\Sigma f}$$

$$16 = \frac{415+15k}{25+k}$$

$(25 + k)\ 16 = 415 + 15k$

$400 + 16k = 415 + 15k$

$16k - 15k = 415 - 400$

$k = 15$

13. Construct a frequency polygon for the following data:

Age (in years)	0–2	2–4	4–6	6–8	8–10	10–12	12–14	14–16	16–18
Frequency	2	4	6	8	9	6	5	3	1

Sol. First we obtain the class marks as given in the following table:

Age (in years)	Class Marks	Frequency
0–2	1	2
2–4	3	4
4–6	5	6
6–8	7	8
8–10	9	9
10–12	11	6
12–14	13	5
14–16	15	3
16–18	17	1

Now, we plot the points (1, 2), (3, 4), (5, 6), (7, 8), (9, 9), (11, 6), (13, 5), (15, 3), and (17, 1).

Now, we join the plotted points by line segments. The end points (1, 2) and (17, 1) are joined to the mid-points (–1,0) and (19,0) respectively of imagined class-intervals to obtain the frequency polygon.

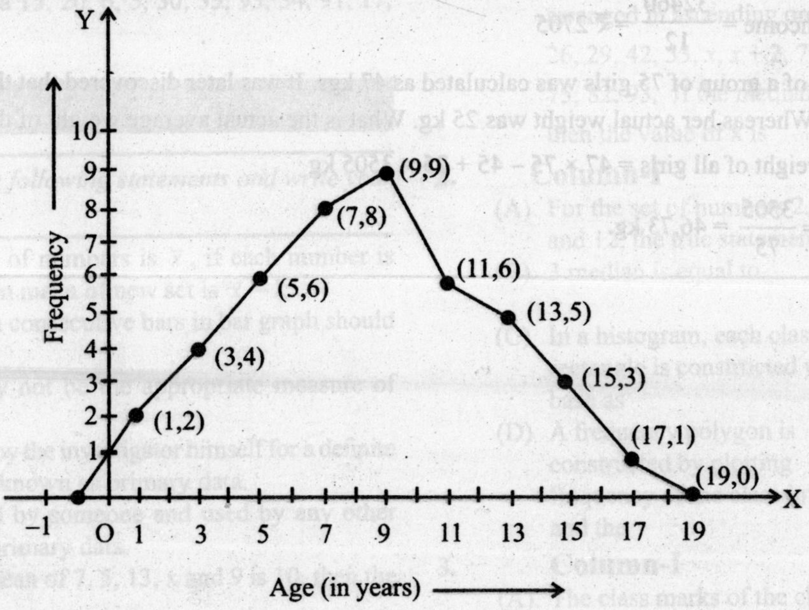

2 EXERCISE

1. Give five examples of data that you can collect from your day-to-day life.
2. Classify the data in Q.1 above as primary or secondary data.
3. The distance (in km) of 40 engineers from their residence to their place of work were found as follows :

5	3	10	20	25	11	13	7	12	31
19	10	12	17	18	11	32	17	16	2
7	9	7	8	3	5	12	15	18	3
12	14	2	9	6	15	15	7	6	12

Construct a grouped frequency distribution table with class size 5 for the data given above taking the first interval as 0–5 (5 not included). What main features do you observe from this tabular representation?

4. The relative humidity (in %) of a certain city for a month of 30 days was as follows :

98.1	98.6	99.2	90.3	86.5	95.3	92.9	96.3	94.2	95.1
89.2	92.3	97.1	93.5	92.7	95.1	97.2	93.3	95.2	97.3
96.2	92.1	84.9	90.2	95.7	98.3	97.3	96.1	92.1	89

(i) Construct a grouped frequency distribution table with classes 84 – 86, 86 – 88, etc.

(ii) Which month or season do you think this data is about?

(iii) What is the range of this data?

5. A study was conducted to find out the concentration of sulphur dioxide in the air in parts per million (ppm) of a certain city. The data obtained for 30 days is as follows :

0.03	0.08	0.08	0.09	0.04	0.17
0.16	0.05	0.02	0.06	0.18	0.20
0.11	0.08	0.12	0.13	0.22	0.07
0.08	0.01	0.10	0.06	0.09	0.18
0.11	0.07	0.05	0.07	0.01	0.04

(i) Make a grouped frequency distribution table for this data with class intervals as 0.00 – 0.04, 0.04 – 0.08, and so on.

(ii) For how many days, was the concentration of sulphur dioxide more than 0.11 parts per million.

6. The value of π upto 50 decimal places is given below :

3.14159265358979323846264338327950288419716939937510

(i) Make a frequency distribution of the digits from 0 to 9 after the decimal point.

(ii) What are the most and the least frequently occurring digits?

7. A company manufactures car batteries of a particular type. The lives (in years) of 40 such batteries were recorded as follows :

2.6	3.0	3.7	3.2	2.2	4.1	3.5	4.5
3.5	2.3	3.2	3.4	3.8	3.2	4.6	3.7
2.5	4.4	3.4	3.3	2.9	3.0	4.3	2.8
3.5	3.2	3.9	3.2	3.2	3.1	3.7	3.4
4.6	3.8	3.2	2.6	3.5	4.2	2.9	3.6

Construct a grouped frequency distribution table for this data, using class intervals of size 0.5 starting from the interval 2–2.5

8. The following data on the number of girls (to the nearest ten) per thousand boys in different sections of the society is given below :

Section	Number of girls per thousand boys
Scheduled Caste (SC)	940
Scheduled Tribe (ST)	970
Non SC/ST	920
Backward districts	950
Non-backward districts	920
Rural	930
Urban	910

(i) Represent the information above by a bar graph.

(ii) In the classroom discuss what conclusion can be arrived from the graph.

9. The length of 40 leaves of a plant are measured correct to one millimetre, and the obtained data is represented in the following table.

Length (in im)	Number of leaves
118–126	3
127–135	5
136–144	9
145–153	12
154–162	5
163–171	4
172–180	2

(i) Draw a histogram to represent the given data.

(ii) Is there any other suitable graphical representation for the same data?

(iii) Is it correct to conclude that the maximum number of leaves are 153 mm long? why?

10. The following table gives the distribution of students of two sections according to the marks obtained by them :

Section A		Section B	
Marks	Frequency	Marks	Frequency
0–10	3	0-10	5
10–20	9	10-20	19
20–30	17	20-30	15
30–40	12	30-40	10
40–50	9	40-50	1

Represent the marks of the students of both the sections on the same graph by two frequency polygons.

From the two polygons compare the performance of the two sections.

11. The runs scored by two teams A and B on the first 60 balls in a cricket match are given below :

Number of balls	Team A	Team B
1–6	2	5
7–12	1	6
13–18	8	2
19–24	9	10
25–30	4	5
31–36	5	6
37–42	6	3
43–48	10	4
49–54	6	8
55–60	2	10

Represent the data of both the teams on the same graph by frequency polygons.

(Hint : First make the class intervals continuous.)

12. A random survey of the number of children of various age groups playing in a park was found as follows:

Age (in years)	Number of Children
1–2	5
2–3	3
3–5	6
5–7	12
7–10	9
10–15	10
15–17	4

Draw a histogram to represent the data above.

13. 100 surnames were randomly picked up from a local telephone directory and a frequency distribution of the number of letters in the English alphabet in the surnames was found as follows :

Number of letters	Number of surnames
1–4	6
4–6	30
6–8	44
8–12	16
12–20	4

(i) Draw a histogram to depict the given information.

(ii) Write the class interval in which the maximum number of surnames lie.

14. In a mathematics test given to 15 students, the following marks (out of 100) are recorded :

41, 39, 48, 52, 46, 62, 54, 40, 96, 52, 98, 40, 42, 52, 60

Find the mean, median and mode of this data.

15. The following observations have been arranged in ascending order. If the median of the data is 63, find the value of x.

29, 32, 48, 50, x, x + 2, 72, 78, 84, 95

16. Find the mode of 14, 25, 14, 28, 18, 17, 18, 14, 23, 22, 14, 18.

17. Find the mean salary of 60 workers of a factory from the following table :

Salary (in ₹)	Number of workers
3000	16
4000	12
5000	10
6000	8
7000	6
8000	4
9000	3
10000	1
Total	60

Exemplar Questions :

1. The marks obtained by 17 students in a mathematics test (out of 100) are given below:

91, 82, 100, 100, 96, 65, 82, 76, 79, 90, 46, 64, 72, 68, 66, 48, 49.

The range of the data is:

(a) 46 (b) 54

(c) 90 (d) 100

2. The class-mark of the class 130-150 is:
(a) 130 (b) 135
(c) 140 (d) 145

3. In a frequency distribution, the mid value of a class is 10 and the width of the class is 6. The lower limit of the class is:
(a) 6 (b) 7
(c) 8 (d) 12

4. The mean of the data:
2, 8, 6, 5, 4, 5, 6, 3, 6, 4, 9, 1, 5, 6, 5
is given to be 5. Based on this information, is it correct to say that the mean of the data:
10, 12, 10, 2, 18, 8, 12, 6, 12, 10, 8, 10, 12, 16, 4
is 10? Give reason.

5. In a histogram, the areas of the rectangles are proportional to the frequencies. Can we say that the lengths of the rectangles are also proportional to the frequencies?

6. Consider the data : 2, 3, 9, 16, 9, 3, 9. Since 16 is the highest value in the observations, is it correct to say that it is the mode of the data ? Give reason.

7. There are 50 numbers. Each number is subtracted from 53 and the mean of the numbers so obtained is found to be –3.5. The mean of the given numbers is:
(a) 46.5 (b) 49.5
(c) 53.5 (d) 56.5

8. For drawing a frequency polygon of a continuous frequency distribution, we plot the points whose ordinates are the frequencies of the respective classes and abcissae are respectively:
(a) upper limits of the classes
(b) lower limits of the classes
(c) class marks of the classes
(d) upper limits of perceeding classes

9. The mean of 100 observations is 50. If one of the observations which was 50 is replaced by 150, the resulting mean will be:
(a) 50.5 (b) 51
(c) 51.5 (d) 52

10. The mean of five numbers is 30. If one number is excluded, their mean becomes 28. The excluded number is:
(a) 28 (b) 30
(c) 35 (d) 38

Hots Questions :

1. The mean of 121 numbers is 59. If each number is multiplied by 4. What will be the new mean?
2. Consider a small unit of a factory where there are 5 employees : a supervisor and four labourers. The labourers draw a salary of ₹ 5,000 per month each while the supervisor gets ₹ 15,000 per month. Calculate the mean, median and mode of the salaries of this unit of the factory.
3. Prove that $\sum_{i=1}^{n}(x_i - \bar{x}) = 0$ where $\bar{x}$ is the mean of the n observations $x_1, x_2, \ldots x_n$
4. In a data, 10 numbers are arranged in ascending order. If the 8th entry is increased by 6, then what will be the change in median.
5. The mean of 10 numbers is 20. If 5 is subtracted from every number, what will be the new mean?
6. The scores of two groups of class IV students on a test of reading ability are given below

Class interval	50-52	47-49	44-46	41-43	38-40	35-37	32-34	Total
Group-A	4	10	15	18	20	12	13	92
Group-B	2	3	4	8	12	17	22	68

Construct a frequency polygon for each of these groups on the same graph.

3 EXERCISE

Single Correct Options :

DIRECTIONS: *This section contains multiple choice questions. Each questions has 4 choices (a), (b), (c) and (d) out of which ONLY ONE is correct.*

1. In a frequency distribution, the mid value of a class is 10 and the width of the class is 6. The lower limit of the class is

(a) 6 (b) 7
(c) 8 (d) 12

2. If the mean of the observations x, $x + 3$, $x + 5$, $x + 7$ and $x + 10$ is 9, the mean of the last three observations is

(a) $10\frac{1}{3}$ (b) $10\frac{2}{3}$
(c) $11\frac{1}{3}$ (d) $11\frac{2}{3}$

3. Let $\bar{x}$ be the mean of $x_1, x_2, \ldots\ldots, x_n$ and $\bar{y}$ the mean of $y_1, y_2, \ldots\ldots, y_n$. If $\bar{z}$ is the mean of $x_1, x_2, \ldots\ldots, x_n, y_1, \ldots y_n$ then $\bar{z}$ is equal to

(a) $\bar{x}+\bar{y}$ (b) $\frac{\bar{x}+\bar{y}}{2}$
(c) $\frac{\bar{x}+\bar{y}}{n}$ (d) $\frac{\bar{x}+\bar{y}}{2n}$

4. If $\bar{x}$ is the mean of $x_1, x_2, \ldots\ldots, x_n$ then for $a \neq 0$, the mean of $ax_1, ax_2, \ldots\ldots, ax_n, \frac{x_1}{a}, \frac{x_2}{a}, \ldots\ldots, \frac{x_n}{a}$ is

(a) $\left(a+\frac{1}{a}\right)\bar{x}$ (b) $\left(a+\frac{1}{a}\right)\frac{\bar{x}}{2}$
(c) $\left(a+\frac{1}{a}\right)\frac{\bar{x}}{n}$ (d) $\frac{\left(a+\frac{1}{a}\right)\bar{x}}{2n}$

5. The mean of 100 observations is 50. If one of the observations which was 50 is replaced by 150, the resulting mean will be

(a) 50.5 (b) 51
(c) 51.5 (d) 52

6. In a morning walk, I took 20 rounds of a park. During this period I came across person A, person B, person C and person D, 11 times, 7 times, 10 times and 5 times respectively. I want to represent this data graphically. Which of the following is the best representation?

(a) Bar graph
(b) Histogram with unequal widths
(c) Histogram with equal widths
(d) Frequency polygon

7. The mean of six numbers is 30. If one number is excluded, the mean of the remaining numbers is 29. The excluded number is

(a) 29 (b) 30
(c) 35 (d) 45

8. Let n be the mid-point and m be the lower limit of a class in a continuous frequency distribution. The upper limit of the class is

(a) n + m (b) n – m
(c) 2n – m (d) 2n + m

9. If each observation of a data is increased by 5, then their mean

(a) is decreased by 5 (b) is increased by 5
(c) becomes 7 times the original mean
(d) remains the same.

10. Tally marks are used to find

(a) class intervals (b) range
(c) upper limits (d) frequency

11. In the class-intervals 30 – 40, 40 – 50 the number 50 is included in

(a) 40 – 50
(b) 30 – 40
(c) Both in 30 – 40 and 40 – 50
(d) Neither in 30 – 40 nor in 40 – 50

12. The mid – value of a class interval is 25 and the class size is 8. The class interval is

(a) 37 – 45 (b) 36.5 – 46.5
(c) 36.5 – 44.5 (d) 21 – 29

13. Given the class-interval 0 – 10, 10 – 20, 20 – 30, ... then 20 is considered in class

(a) 20 – 30 (b) 10 – 20
(c) 10 – 30 (d) 15 – 25

14. A, B, C are three sets of values of x :

A : 2, 3, 7, 1, 3, 2, 3
B : 7, 5, 9, 12, 5, 3, 8
C : 4, 4, 11, 7, 2, 3, 4

Which one of the following statements is correct?

(a) Mean of A = Mode of C

(b) Mean of C = Median of B

(c) Median of B = Mode of A

(d) Mean, Median and Mode of A are equal.

More than One Option Correct :

DIRECTIONS: *This section contains multiple choice questions. Each question has 4 choices (a), (b), (c) and (d) out of which ONE OR MORE may be correct.*

1. Which of the following is/are measure of central tendency?

(a) Mean (b) Median

(c) Variance (d) Mode

2. Given below are the seats won by different political parties in the polling outcome of a state assembly election :

Political party	A	B	C	D
Seats Won	75	55	37	29

The graphical representation will be

(a) a histogram

(b) a vertical bar graph

(c) a horizontal bar graph

(d) a frequency polygon curve

3. A frequency polygon can be

(a) drawn using histogram

(b) drawn using bar graph

(c) drawn independently

(d) drawn using tally marks

4. Measure of central tendency represents

(a) averages

(b) central value

(c) mean, median and mode

(d) None of these

5. Which of the following statement(s) is/are correct ?

(a) Mode can be calculated graphically.

(b) Median is not affected by extreme values.

(c) A frequency polygon is the polygon obtained by joining the mid-points of upper horizontal sides of all the rectangles in a histogram.

(d) None of these.

6. Which of the following statement(s) is/are correct ?

(a) The data obtained in original form are called raw data.

(b) The number of times an observation occurs is called its frequency.

(c) The data collected by the investigator himself/herself is known as primary data.

(d) The data collected by someone, other than the investigator, are known as secondary data.

Passage Based Questions :

DIRECTIONS : *Study the given paragraph(s) and answer the following questions.*

PASSAGE

The following bar graph shows the number of vehicles passing through a road crossing in Delhi in different time intervals on a particular day. Read the bar graph and answer the following questions:

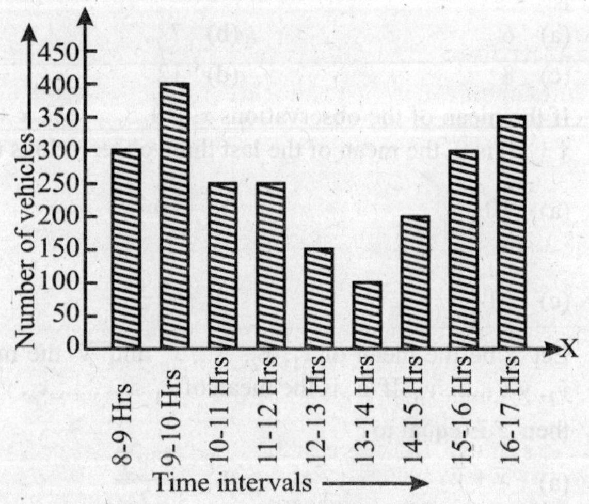

1. The maximum number of vehicles,

(a) 400 (b) 100

(c) 200 (d) 300

2. When is the hourly traffic maximum?

(a) 8 - 9 hrs (b) 9 - 10 hrs

(c) 10 - 11 hrs (d) 11 - 12 hrs

3. What is the total number of vehicles passing through a crossing during a particular day ?

(a) 2305 (b) 2503

(c) 2350 (d) 2530

Assertion & Reason :

DIRECTIONS: *Each of these questions contains an Assertion followed by Reason. Read them carefully and answer the question on the basis of following options. You have to select the one that best describes the two statements.*

(a) If both **Assertion** and **Reason** are **correct** and Reason is the **correct explanation** of Assertion.

(b) If both **Assertion** and **Reason** are correct, but Reason is **not the correct explanation** of Assertion.

(c) If **Assertion** is **correct** but **Reason** is **incorrect**.

(d) If **Assertion** is **incorrect** but **Reason** is **correct**.

1. **Assertion :** Mode of the given data 110, 120, 130, 120, 110, 140, 130, 120, 140, 120, is 120.

Reason : The observation that occurs most frequently, *i.e.*, the observation with maximum frequency is called mode.

2. **Assertion :** Median of the given data 34, 31, 42, 43, 46, 25, 39, 45, 32, is 39.

Reason : When the number of observations (n) is even, the median is the mean of the $\left(\frac{n}{2}\right)^{th}$ and $\left(\frac{n}{2}+1\right)^{th}$ observations.

3. **Assertion :** The difference between the maximum and minimum values of a variable is called its range.

Reason : The number of times a variate (observation) occurs in a given data is called range.

4. **Assertion :** If the median of the given data 26, 29, 42, 53, x, $x + 2$, 70, 75, 82, 93, is 65 then the value of x is 64.

Reason : When the number of observations (n) is odd the median is the value of the $\left(\frac{n+1}{2}\right)^{th}$ observation.

5. **Assertion :** The range of the first 6 multiples of 6 is 9.

Reason : Mean of n observations is

$$\frac{\text{Sum of observations}}{\text{Number of observations}}$$

6. **Assertion :** Mean may or may not be the appropriate measure of central tendency.

Reason : If the number of observations are even then median is $\left(\frac{n+1}{2}\right)^{\text{th}}$ term.

7. **Assertion :** The following is the data of wages per day:

8, 4, 7, 5, 8, 8, 5, 7, 9, 5, 7, 8, 10, 8 then the mode of the data is 8.

Reason : Mode = Highest observation – Lowest observation.

Integer Type Questions :

DIRECTIONS : *Answer the following questions. The answer to each of the question is a single digit integer, ranging from 0 to 9.*

1. If $\bar{x}$ is the mean of n observations $x_1, x_2, \ldots\ldots, x_n$ then the algebraic sum of deviations from mean is

2. The mean of 6, 4, 7, 13 and 10 is

3. If the mean of five observations x, $x + 2$, $x + 4$, $x + 6$, $x + 8$ is 11, then the mean of first three observations is

4. If the mode of scores 3, 4, 3, 5, 4, 6, 6, x is 4, then the value of x is

5. If the median of the scores 1, 2, x, 4, 5 (where $1 < 2 < x < 4 < 5$) is 3, then find the mean of scores.

6. If the ratio of mean and median of a certain data is 2 : 3, then find the sum of ratio of its mode and mean.

4 ADVANCED EXERCISE
BASED ON CONNECTING TOPICS

DIRECTIONS : *This section contains multiple choice questions. Each question has 4 choices (a), (b), (c) and (d) out of which only one is correct.*

1. If the combined mean of two groups is $\frac{40}{3}$ and if the mean of one group with 10 observations is 15, then the mean of the other group with 8 observations is equal to
   (a) $\frac{46}{3}$ (b) $\frac{35}{4}$
   (c) $\frac{45}{4}$ (d) $\frac{41}{4}$

2. The average score of a cricketer in two matches is 27 and in three other matches is 32. Then the average score in all the five matches is
   (a) 30 (b) 27
   (c) 32 (d) 31

3. The average age of students of a class is 15.8 years. The average age of boys in the class is 16.4 years and that of the girls is 15.4 years. The ratio of the number of boys to the number of girls in the class is
   (a) 1 : 2 (b) 2 : 3
   (c) 3 : 4 (d) 3 : 5

4. The average of six numbers is 3.95. The average of two of them is 3.4, while the average of the other two is 3.85. What is the average of the remaining two numbers?
   (a) 4.5 (b) 4.6
   (c) 4.7 (d) 4.8

5. The average weight of 45 students in a class is 52 kg. 5 of them whose average weight is 48 kg leave the class and other 5 students whose average weight is 54 kg join the class. What is the new average weight (in kg) of the class?
   (a) 52.6 (b) $52\frac{2}{3}$
   (c) $52\frac{1}{3}$ (d) None of these

SOLUTIONS

Brief Explanations of Selected Questions

1 EXERCISE

FILL IN THE BLANKS :

1. Median
2. mode
3. Mean
4. Frequency polygon
5. $\left(\frac{n+1}{2}\right)^{th}$
6. mid-point
7. width
8. range
9. size
10. $93 - 5 = 88$

TRUE/FALSE :

1. False. New mean = $\bar{x} + k$.
2. True
3. True
4. True
5. False. It is known as secondary data.
6. True, $\frac{7+5+13+x+9}{5} = 10 \Rightarrow x = 16$
7. True
8. True

MATCH THE COLUMNS :

1. (A) → (s); (B) → (t); (C) → (q); (D) → (r); (E) → (p)

(A) Most occuring observation is 15.

(B) Highest data value is 32 and the lowest is 6

∴ Range = highest value – lowest value

$= 32 - 6 = 26.$

(C) Class-mark $= \frac{90+120}{2} = \frac{210}{2} = 105$

(D) The class corresponding to the class mark 20 is given as $\frac{15+20}{2} = \frac{35}{2} = 17.5$ and $\frac{20+25}{2} = \frac{45}{2} = 22.5$

(E) Since the number of observations is 10 (even)

$\therefore$ Median $= \frac{5^{th}\text{ obs} + 6^{th}\text{ obs}}{2}$

$65 = \frac{x+x+2}{2} = \frac{2x+2}{2} = x+1$

$\Rightarrow x = 64.$

2. $(A) \to r; (B) \to p; (C) \to s; (D) \to q$

(A) Mean $= \frac{2+2+4+5+12}{5} = 5$, Mode = 2

(B) Mode = 3 median – 2 mean

3. $(A) \to s; (B) \to p; (C) \to q; (D) \to r$

(A) $Class - Marks = \frac{145+150}{2} = \frac{295}{2} = 147.5$

(B) Let the upper limit = x

Lower limit = y

$\therefore$ $x - y = 6$ and $\frac{x+y}{2} = 10 \Rightarrow x + y = 20$

On solving both the equations, we get $x = 13$ and $y = 7$

(C) Sum of the 8 obs. = 40 × 8 = 320

Sum of the 7 obs. = 30 × 7 = 210

Excluded obs. is 320 – 210 = 110

(D) Class – width = 20 – 15 = 5

Class mark = 25

$\therefore$ Required class $= \left(25 - \frac{5}{2}\right) - \left(25 + \frac{5}{2}\right)$

$= 22.5 - 27.5$

VERY SHORT ANSWER QUESTIONS :

1. 16 is not the mode of the data. The mode of a given data is the observation with highest frequency and not the observation with highest value.
2. The median is that value of the given number of observations, which divides it into exactly two parts.
3. When the information was collected by the investigator herself or himself with a definite objective, the data obtained is called primary data.
4. The data collected by someone and used by any other person known as secondary data.
5. (i) Heights of students in our class.
   (ii) Number of class-rooms in our school.
   (iii) Water bills of our house for last three years.
   (iv) Election results obtained from television or newspaper.
   (v) Literacy rate figures obtained from educational survey.
6. **Frequency :** It is a number, which tells that how many times does a particular data appear in a given set of data.

   E.g. consider the following set of data :

   1, 2, 0, 3, 2, 1, 5, 4, 3, 2, 1, 2

   In the given set of data, 1 appears 3 times,

   ∴ frequency of 1 is 3.

   Similarly, 2 appears 4 times, therefore frequency of 2 is 4 and so on.
7. Class-mark $= \frac{\text{upper class limit} + \text{lower class limit}}{2}$

8. Class size = 10 – 6 = 4
Class intervals are : 4 – 8, 8 – 12, 12 – 16, 16 – 20, 20 – 24, 24 – 28, 28 – 32.

9. A bar graph is a pictorial representation of the numerical data by a number of bars (rectangles) of uniform width erected horizontally or vertically with equal spacing between them.

10. (i) Mode can be calculated graphically.
(ii) It is not affected by extreme values.
(iii) It can be used for open-ended distribution and qualitative data.

11. We have $x_1 + x_2 = 12$ and $x_1 + x_2 + x_3 = 21$
$\therefore \quad 12 + x_3 = 21 \Rightarrow x_3 = 21 - 12 = 9$

12. (i) The median can be calculated graphically.
(ii) It is not affected by extreme values.

SHORT ANSWER QUESTIONS :

1. Frequency table

x_i	f_i	$f_i x_i$
6	4	24
4	2	8
8	5	40
3	1	3
Total	**12**	**75**

$\therefore$ Required mean $= \dfrac{\sum f_i x_i}{\sum f_i} = \dfrac{75}{12} = 6.25$

2. Required mean $= \dfrac{10 \times 12 + 20 \times 9}{30} = \dfrac{120 + 180}{30} = 10$

3. (i) Given table can be rewritten in modified manner as :
[Minimum class-size = 2]

Number of letters	Number of surnames	Width of the class	Length of the rectangle
1-4	6	3	$\frac{6}{3} \times 2 = 4$
4-6	30	2	$\frac{30}{2} \times 2 = 30$
6-8	44	2	$\frac{44}{2} \times 2 = 44$
8-12	16	4	$\frac{16}{4} \times 2 = 8$
12-20	4	8	$\frac{4}{8} \times 2 = 1$

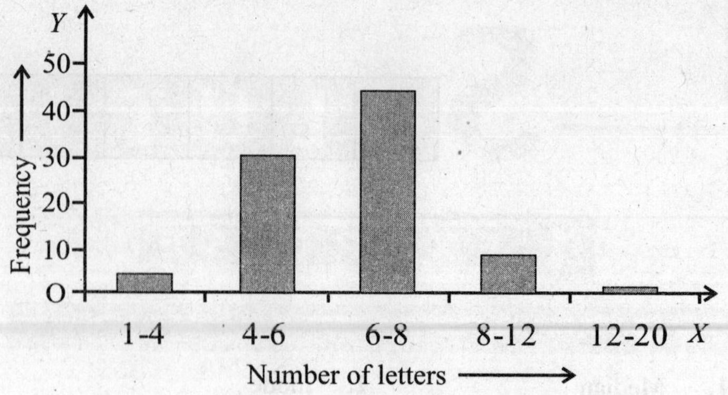

(ii) Maximum number of surnames lie in 6–8 interval.

4. Factors of 12 are 1, 2, 3, 4, 6, 12
Mean $= \dfrac{1+2+3+4+6+12}{6} = \dfrac{28}{6} = \dfrac{14}{3} = 4.66$

5.

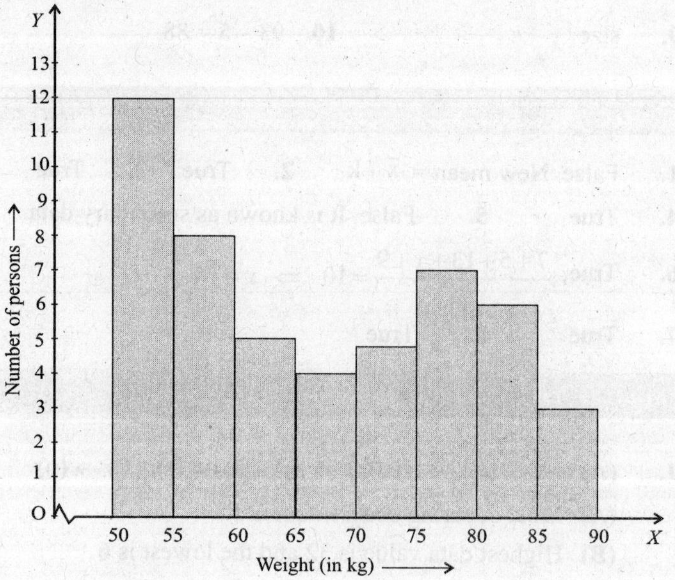

6. (i) Modal score = 4
because 4 occurs seven time.
(ii) Total score = (1 × 3) + (2 × 6) + (3 × 4) + (4 × 7) + (5 × 5)
= 3 + 12 + 12 + 28 + 25
= 80
(iii) Mean score $= \dfrac{80}{25} = 3.2$

7. Let their ages be $4x$,$5x$ and $6x$.
mean age $= \dfrac{4x + 5x + 6x}{3}$

$$15 = \frac{15x}{3} \Rightarrow x = 3$$

So, their ages are 12, 15, 18 year.

8. (i) The given bar graph gives the information about the production of coal in million tonnes in two consecutive years, namely 1992-93 and 1993-94 in various states.

(ii) M.P. and Bihar have same production in 1993-1994.

(iii) U.P. has the same production in both the years.

(iv) U.P.

9. Mean = $\dfrac{\text{Sum of observations}}{\text{Number of observations}}$

Sum = 18 × 5 = 90

New sum = 90 × 2 = 180

$\therefore$ New mean = $\dfrac{180}{18} = 10$

10. Mean = $\dfrac{\text{Sum of observations}}{\text{Number of observations}}$

Sum of the observations = 20 × 30 = 600

New sum when 5 is added in each

20 observations = 600 + 20 × 5 = 700

$\therefore$ New mean = $\dfrac{700}{20} = 35$

11. Since M is the mean of $x_1, x_2, .., x_6$

$\therefore \dfrac{x_1 + x_2 + .. + x_6}{6} = M$

$\Rightarrow x_1 + x_2 + .. + x_6 = 6M$

Consider $(x_1 - M) + (x_2 - M) + (x_3 - M) + (x_4 - M) + (x_5 - M) + (x_6 - M) = (x_1 + ... + x_6) - 6M$

$= 6M - 6M = 0$

12. **Bar graph :** It is the simplest and most widely used graph in which the numerical data is represented by bars (rectangles) of equal width.

Histogram : A histogram is a graphical representation of a frequency distribution in the form of rectangles one after the other.

The bases of these rectangles represent the magnitudes of the variables of the class-boundaries. So these are taken along the x-axis. The heights of these represent the frequencies of the corresponding magnitudes of the variable of the class-boundaries.

Frequency polygon : After drawing the histogram of a frequency distribution, when the mid-points of the respective tops of the rectangles are joined by the line segment, the figure so obtained is known as frequency polygon.

LONG ANSWER QUESTIONS :

1. First we find the class marks and make new table as follows:

Class	Class marks	Section-A (frequency)	Section-B (frequency)
0-10	5	3	5
10-20	15	9	19
20-30	25	17	15
30-40	35	12	10
40-50	45	9	1

Steps to draw frequency polygon:

For Section-A

(1) First plot the points (5,3), (15, 9), (25, 17), (35, 12) and (45, 9) on graph paper.

(2) Join consecutive points by thick line segments.

(3) Join the first end point with the mid-point of class (– 10 to 0) with zero frequency, and join the other end point with the mid-point of class (50 – 60) with zero frequency.

(4) The required frequency polygon is shown by thick line segments in the figure.

For Section-B

(1) First plot the points (5, 5), (15, 19), (25, 15), (35, 10) and (45, 1)

(2) Join consecutive points with dotted line segment.

(3) Join the first end point with the mid-point of class (– 10 to 0) with zero frequency, and join the other end point with the mid-point of class (50 – 60) with zero frequency.

(4) The required frequency polygon is shown by dotted line segments in the same figure.

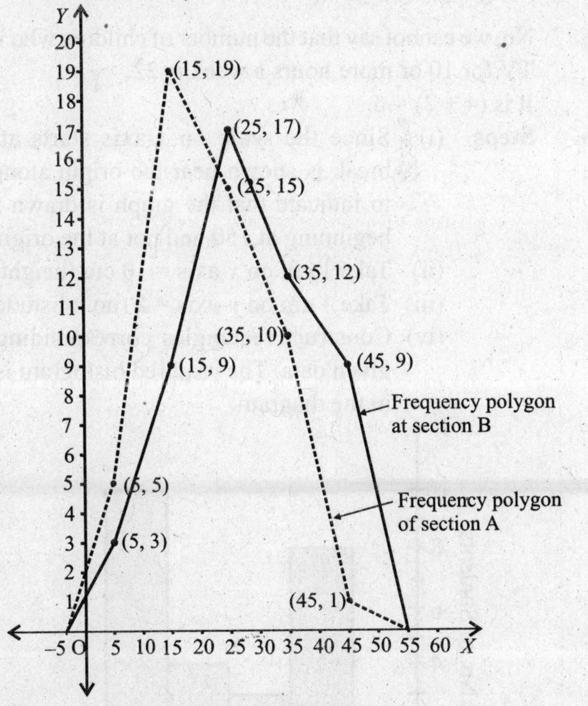

Performance of section A is better than performance of section B.

2. Mean $= \frac{1+7+5+3+4+4}{6} \Rightarrow m = \frac{24}{6} = 4$

Also, $m-1 = \frac{3+2+4+2+3+3+p}{7}$

$\Rightarrow \quad 21 = 17 + p$

$\Rightarrow \quad p = 4$

First we arrange the observations in ascending order.
i.e. 2, 2, 3, 3, 3, 4, 4.
Since, no. of observations is odd

$\therefore$ Median $= \left(\frac{7+1}{2}\right)^{th}$ observation.

$q = 4^{th}$ observation.

$\Rightarrow \quad q = 3.$

3. Mean $= \frac{\Sigma f.x}{\Sigma f} = \frac{30+160+360+200+420+350+50p}{40+p}$

$40.4 = \frac{1520+50p}{40+p} \Rightarrow 9.6\,p = 96 \Rightarrow p = 10$

4. Mean $= \frac{25+27+19+29+21+23+25+33+28+20}{10}$

$= \frac{250}{10} = 25$

Further, required sum

$= (25-25) + (27-25) + (19-25) + (29-25) + (21-25) + (23-25) + (25-25) + (33-25) + (28-25) + (20-25)$

$= 0 + 2 + (-6) + (4) + (-4) + (-2) + 0 + 8 + 3 + (-5)$

$= -6 + 8 + 3 - 5 = 0$

5. No, we cannot say that the number of children who watched TV for 10 or more hours a week is 22.
It is $(4 + 2) = 6$.

6. **Steps** (i) Since the scale on x-axis starts at 150, a break is shown near the origin along x-axis to indicate that the graph is drawn to scale beginning at 150 and not at the origin itself.

(ii) Take 1 cm on x-axis = 10 cm (height)

(iii) Take 1 cm on y-axis = 2 (no. of students)

(iv) Construct rectangles corresponding to the given data. The required histogram is shown in the diagram.

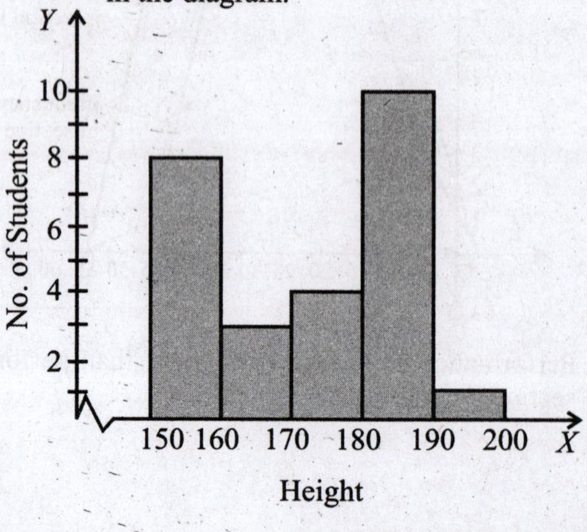

7. (a) 5

(b) 43 (c) 98795

8. Factors of 42 are 1, 2, 3, 6, 7, 14, 21, 42 i.e., 8

Mean $= \frac{1+2+3+6+7+14+21+42}{8} = \frac{96}{8} = 12$

Arrange the data in ascending order, we have 1, 2, 3, 6, 7, 14, 21, 42

Number of term = 8 (even)

For even number of terms is

Median $= \frac{\left(\frac{n}{2}\right)^{th} \text{term} + \left(\frac{n}{2}+1\right)^{th} \text{term}}{2}$

$= \frac{\text{4th term} + \text{5th term}}{2} = \frac{6+7}{2} = 6.5$

Difference between mean and median

$= 12 - 6.5 = 5.5$

9. First 11 multiples of 11 are 11, 22, 33, 44, …. 121

Mean $= \frac{\text{Sum of 11 multiples of 11}}{11}$

$= \frac{11+22+33+44+55+66+77+88+99+110+121}{11}$

$\bar{x} = \frac{726}{11} = 66$

Number of terms = 11 (odd),

For odd number of terms, we have

Median $= \left(\frac{11+1}{2}\right)^{th}$ term i.e., 6th term

$\therefore \quad y = 66$

$\therefore \quad x : y = 66 : 66 = 1 : 1$

2 EXERCISE

TEXT BOOK EXERCISE :

1. (i) Heights of students in our class.

(ii) Number of class-rooms in our school.

(iii) Water bills of our house for last three years.

(iv) Election results obtained from television or newspaper.

(v) Literacy rate figures obtained from educational survey.

2. (i), (ii) and (iii) are primary data. (iv) and (v) are secondary data.

3.

Distance (in km)	Tally marks	Number of engineers (frequency)
0 – 5	𝍸	5
5 – 10	𝍸 𝍸 |	11
10 – 15	𝍸 𝍸 |	11
15 – 20	𝍸 ||||	9
20 – 25	|	1
25 – 30	|	1
30 – 35	||	2
Total		40

Main features from this tabular representation are :

(i) The maximum number of engineers are in the intervals 5 –10 and 10 –15.

(ii) The minimum number of engineers are in the intervals 20 – 25 and 25 – 30 each.

(iii) The frequencies of the intervals 20 – 25 and 25 – 30 are the same. (Each = 1)

4. (i)

Relative humidity (in %)	Tally marks	Number of days (frequency)
84–86	|	1
86–88	|	1
88–90	||	2
90–92	||	2
92–94	𝍸 ||	7
94–96	𝍸 |	6
96–98	𝍸 ||	7
98–100	||||	4
Total		30

(ii) Since, the relative humidity is high.

∴ This data appears to be taken in the rainy season.

(iii) Range = Highest value – Lowest value

$= 99.2 - 84.9 = 14.3$ (in %)

5. (i)

Concentration of sulphur dioxide in the air (ppm)	Tally marks	Number of days (frequency)
0.00 – 0.04	||||	4
0.04 – 0.08	𝍸 ||||	9
0.08 – 0.12	𝍸 ||||	9
0.12 – 0.16	||	2
0.16 – 0.20	||||	4
0.20 – 0.24	||	2
Total		30

(ii) For $2 + 4 + 2 = 8$ days, the cocentration was more than 0.11 parts per million.

6. (i) Frequency distribution is as follows

Digits	Tally maks	Frequency
0	||	2
1	𝍸	5
2	𝍸	5
3	𝍸 |||	8
4	||||	4
5	𝍸	5
6	||||	4
7	||||	4
8	𝍸	5
9	𝍸 |||	8
Total		50

(ii) 3 and 9 are the most frequently occurring digits and the least occurring digit is 0.

7. By taking class-interval of size 0.5, we construct a grouped frequency distribution as follows:

Lives (in years)	Tally maks batteries	Number of batteries (frequency)
2.0 – 2.5	||	2
2.5 – 3.0	𝍸 |	6
3.0 – 3.5	𝍸 𝍸 ||||	14
3.5 – 4.0	𝍸 𝍸 |	11
4.0 – 4.5	||||	4
4.5 – 5.0	|||	3
Total		40

8. (i)

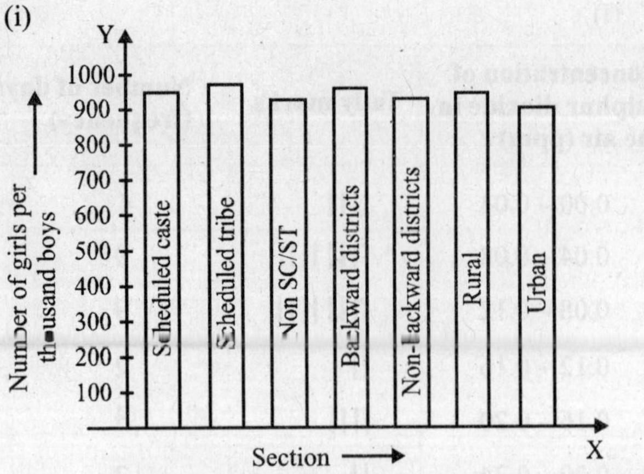

(ii) (a) We conclude from the graph that the number of girls to the nearest ten per thousand boys is maximum in Scheduled Tribe section of the society and minimum in Urban section of the society.

(b) The number of girls to the nearest ten per thousand boys is the same for 'Non SC/ST' and 'Non-backward Districts' sections of the society.

9. (i) **Modified Continuous Distribution**

Length (in mm)	Number of leaves
117.5-126.5	3
126.5-135.5	5
135.5-144.5	9
144.5-153.5	12
153.5-162.5	5
162.5-171.5	4
171.5-180.5	2

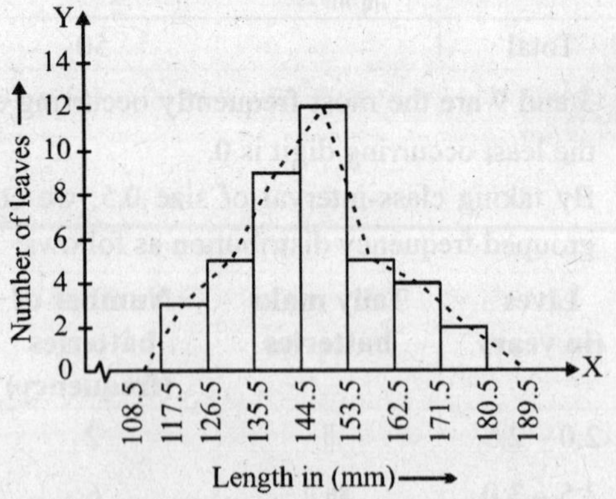

(ii) Other suitable graphical representation is frequency polygon.

(iii) No (∵ the maximum number of leaves have their lengths lying in the interval 145–153.)

10. From the single given table we can make two modified tables for both the sections.

Modified Tables

For section A	For section B	
Classes	**Class-Marks**	**Frequency**
0-10	5	3
10-20	15	9
20-30	25	17
30-40	35	12
40-50	45	9

Classes	Class-Marks	Frequency
0-10	5	5
10-20	15	19
20-30	25	15
30-40	35	10
40-50	45	1

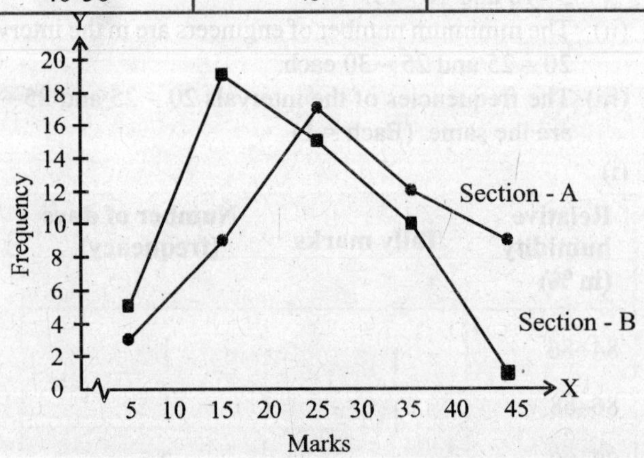

11. By making the class -intervals continuous we get a modified table as

Number of balls	Class-Marks	Team A	Team B
0.5 - 6.5	3.5	2	5
6.5 - 12.5	9.5	1	6
12.5 - 18.5	15.5	8	2
18.5 - 24.5	21.5	9	10
24.5 - 30.5	27.5	4	5
30.5 - 36.5	33.5	5	6
36.5 - 42.5	39.5	6	3
42.5 - 48.5	45.5	10	4
48.5 - 54.5	51.5	6	8
54.5 - 60.5	57.5	2	10

Now, we plot the points on the graph paper of both team.

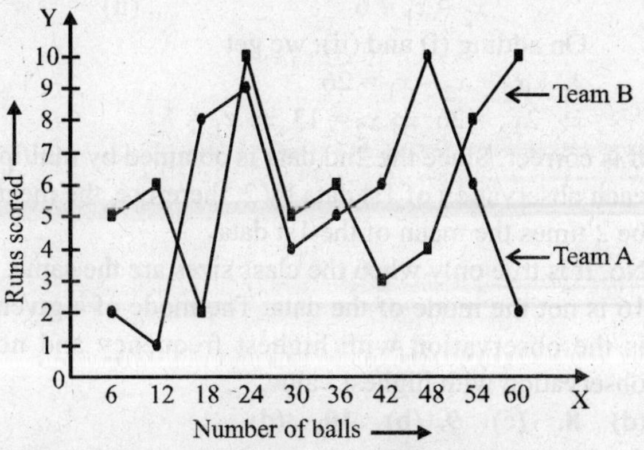

12. Table given in the question can be re-written as

[Minimum class-size = 1]

"Age (in years)"	Number of children (frequency)	Width of the class	Length of the rectangle"
1 - 2	5	1	$\frac{5}{1}\times 1=5$
2 - 3	3	1	$\frac{3}{1}\times 1=3$
3 - 5	6	2	$\frac{6}{2}\times 1=3$
5 - 7	12	2	$\frac{12}{2}\times 1=6$
7 - 10	9	3	$\frac{9}{3}\times 1=3$
10 - 15	10	5	$\frac{10}{5}\times 1=3$
15 - 17	4	2	$\frac{4}{2}\times 1=2$

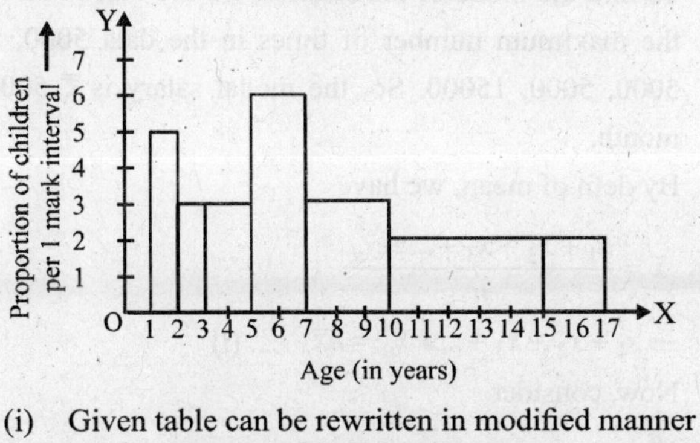

13. (i) Given table can be rewritten in modified manner as :

[Minimum class-size = 2]

Number of letters	Number of surnames	Width of the class	Length of the rectangle
1–4	6	3	$\frac{6}{3}\times 2=4$
4–6	30	2	$\frac{30}{2}\times 2=30$
6–8	44	2	$\frac{44}{2}\times 2=44$
8–12	16	4	$\frac{16}{2}\times 2=8$
12–20	4	8	$\frac{4}{8}\times 2=1$

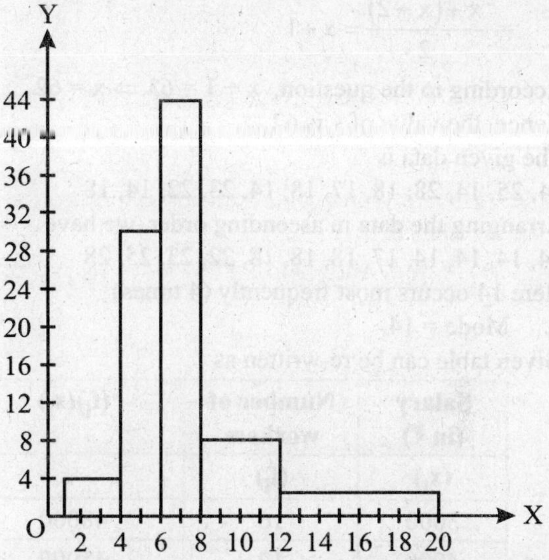

(ii) The maximum number of surnames lie in class interval 6 – 8.

14. (i) By the formula:

$$\text{Mean} = \frac{\text{Sum of all the observations}}{\text{Total numbers of observations}}$$

$$= \frac{41+39+48+52+46+62+54+40+96+52+98+40+42+52+60}{15} = \frac{822}{15} = 54.8$$

(ii) **Median :** By arranging the given data in descending order, we have

98, 96, 62, 60, 54, 52, 52, 52, 48, 46, 42, 41, 40, 40, 39

Number of observations (n) = 15, which is odd.

$\therefore$ Median = $\left(\frac{n+1}{2}\right)^{th}$ observation.

$= \left(\frac{15+1}{2}\right)^{th}$ observation = 8th observation = 52

(iii) **Mode :** By arranging the data in descending order, we have

98, 96, 62, 60, 54, 52, 52, 52, 48, 46, 42, 41, 40, 40, 39

Here, 52 occurs most frequently (3 times)

$\therefore$ Mode = 52.

15. Consider the observations

29, 32, 48, 50, x, x +2, 72, 78, 84, 95.

Total number of observations (n) = 10, which is even

∴ Median

$$= \frac{\left(\frac{n}{2}\right)^{th} \text{observation} + \left(\frac{n}{2}+1\right)^{th} \text{observation}}{2}$$

$$= \frac{\left(\frac{10}{2}\right)^{th} \text{observation} + \left(\frac{10}{2}+1\right)^{th} \text{observation}}{2}$$

$$= \frac{5^{th} \text{ observation} + 6^{th} \text{ observation}}{2}$$

$$= \frac{x+(x+2)}{2} = x+1$$

According to the question, $x + 1 = 63 \Rightarrow x = 62$

Hence, the value of x is 62.

16. The given data is

14, 25, 14, 28, 18, 17, 18, 14, 23, 22, 14, 18

Arranging the data in ascending order, we have

14, 14, 14, 14, 17, 18, 18, 18, 22, 23, 25, 28

Here 14 occurs most frequently (4 times)

∴ Mode = 14.

17. Given table can be re-written as

Salary (in ₹)	Number of workers	$(f_i)(x_i)$
(x_i)	(f_i)	
3000	16	48000
4000	12	48000
5000	10	50000
6000	8	48000
7000	6	42000
8000	4	32000
9000	3	27000
10,000	1	10000
Total	$\sum_{i=1}^{8} f_i = 60$	$\sum_{i=1}^{8} f_i x_i = 305000$

∴ For ungrouped frequency distribution ,

$$\bar{x} = \frac{\sum_{i=1}^{8} f_i x_i}{\sum_{i=1}^{8} f_i} = \frac{305000}{60} = ₹\ 5083.33$$

Hence, the mean salary is ₹ 5083.33

EXAMPLAR QUESTIONS :

1. (b) Range = 100 – 46 = 54

2. (c) Class mark $= \frac{130+150}{2} = 140$

3. (b) Let x_1 be the lower and x_2 be the upper limit.

Given : $x_1 + x_2 = 2 \times 10 = 20$ ...(i)

$x_2 - x_1 = 6$ ...(ii)

On adding (i) and (ii), we get

$x_1 + x_2 + x_2 - x_1 = 26$

$\Rightarrow 2x_2 = 26 \Rightarrow x_2 = 13 \Rightarrow x_1 = 7$

4. It is correct. Since the 2nd data is obtained by multiplying each observation of 1st data by 2, therefore, the mean will be 2 times the mean of the 1st data.

5. No. It is true only when the class sizes are the same.

6. 16 is not the mode of the data. The mode of a given data is the observation with highest frequency and not the observation with highest value.

7. (d) **8.** (c) **9.** (b) **10.** (d)

HOTS SUBJECTIVE QUESTIONS :

1. Here $n = 121$, $\bar{x} = 59$.

∴ The sum of 121 numbers = $n\bar{x}$ = (121 × 59) =7139.

When each number is multiplied by 4,

total = 4 × (previous total) = 4 × 7139 = 28556.

∴ New mean $= \left(\frac{28556}{121}\right) = 236$

2. Mean $= \frac{5000+5000+5000+5000+15000}{5}$

$= \frac{35000}{5} = 7000$

So, the mean salary is ₹ 7000 per month.

To find the median, we arrange the salaries in ascending order :

5000, 5000, 5000, 5000, 15000

Since the number of employees in the factory is 5, the median is given by the $\frac{5+1}{2}$th $= \frac{6}{2}$th = 3rd observation.

Therefore, the median is ₹ 5000 per month.

To find the mode of the salaries, we see that 5000 occurs the maximum number of times in the data 5000, 5000, 5000, 5000, 15000. So, the modal salary is ₹ 5000 per month.

3. By defn of mean, we have

$$\bar{x} = \frac{x_1 + x_2 + x_3 + ... + x_n}{n}$$

$\Rightarrow x_1 + x_2 + x_3 + ... + x_n = n\bar{x}$ ... (i)

Now, consider

$$\sum_{i=1}^{n}(x_i - \bar{x}) = (x_1 - \bar{x}) - (x_2 - \bar{x}) + (x_3 - \bar{x}) + ... + (x_n - \bar{x})$$

$= (x_1 - x_2 + x_3 - ... + x_n) - n\bar{x}$

$= n\bar{x} - n\bar{x} = 0$ [(From (i)]

4. As the median depends only on 5th and 6th entries and there is no change in these entries therefore there is no change in the value of the median.

5. Let $x_1, x_2, ..., x_{10}$ be 10 numbers with their mean equal to 20. Then,

$$\bar{X} = \frac{1}{n}(\Sigma x_i)$$

$$\Rightarrow \quad 20 = \frac{x_1 + x_2 + \cdots + x_{10}}{10}$$

$$\Rightarrow \quad x_1 + x_2 + ... + x_{10} = 200 \qquad ...(i)$$

New numbers are $x_1 - 5, x_2 - 5, ..., x_{10} - 5$.

Let $\bar{X}'$ be the mean of new numbers. Then,

$$\bar{X}' = \frac{(x_1 - 5) + (x_2 - 5) + \cdots + (x_{10} - 5)}{10}$$

$$\bar{X}' = \frac{(x_1 + x_2 + \cdots + x_{10}) - 5 \times 10}{10} = \frac{200 - 50}{10} \qquad \text{[Using (i)]}$$

$$\bar{X}' = 15$$

6. Frequency polygon for groups A and B of class IV students in a test of reading ability.

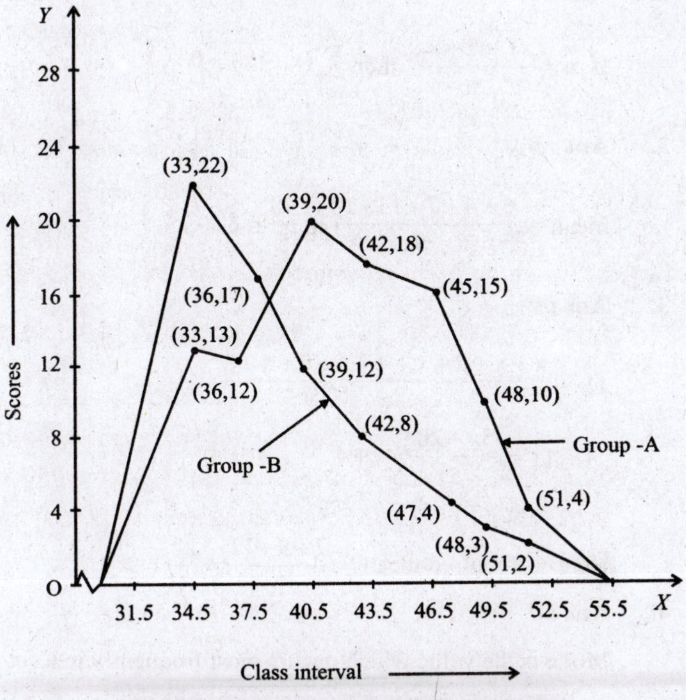

3 EXERCISE

SINGLE OPTION CORRECT :

1. (b) Let x be the upper limit and y be the lower limit.

Since the mid value of the class is 10

$$\therefore \frac{x + y}{2} = 10 \quad \Rightarrow \quad x + y = 20. \qquad ...(i)$$

and $x - y = 6$ (width of the class = 6) ...(ii)

By solving (i) and (ii), we get $y = 7$.

Hence, lower limit of the class is 7.

2. (c) We know, mean $= \dfrac{\text{Sum of all the observations}}{\text{Total no. of observation}}$

$$\Rightarrow \text{Mean} = \frac{x + x + 3 + x + 5 + x + 7 + x + 10}{5}$$

$$9 = \frac{5x + 25}{5} \Rightarrow x = 4$$

So, mean of last three observations is

$$\frac{3x + 22}{3} = \frac{12 + 22}{3} = \frac{34}{3} = 11\frac{1}{3}$$

3. (b) $\dfrac{x_1 + ... + x_n}{n} = \bar{x}$

$$\frac{y_1 + y_2 + ... + y_n}{n} = \bar{y}$$

$$\bar{z} = \frac{\bar{x} + \bar{y}}{2}$$

4. (b) Given $\dfrac{x_1 + ... + x_n}{n} = \bar{x}$ .....(i)

$$\Rightarrow \quad \frac{ax_1 + ... + ax_n}{an} = \bar{x} \Rightarrow \frac{ax_1 + ... + ax_n}{n} = a\bar{x} \qquad .....(ii)$$

Also, from (i), we have

$$\frac{\frac{1}{a}x_1 + ... + \frac{1}{a}x_n}{\frac{1}{a}(n)} = \bar{x}$$

$$\Rightarrow \frac{\frac{x_1}{a} + ... + \frac{x_n}{a}}{n} = \frac{\bar{x}}{a} \qquad .....(iii)$$

So, the mean of $ax_1, ..., ax_n, \dfrac{x_1}{a}, ..., \dfrac{x_n}{a}$

is $\dfrac{a\bar{x} + \dfrac{\bar{x}}{a}}{2} = \dfrac{\bar{x}}{2}\left(a + \dfrac{1}{a}\right)$

5. (b) $\bar{x} = 50$

$$\Rightarrow \frac{\Sigma x_i}{100} = 50 \Rightarrow \Sigma x_i = 5000$$

As, 50 is replaced by 150.

Thus,

New, $\Sigma x_i = 5000 - 50 + 150 = 5100$

New, $= \dfrac{5100}{100} = 51$

6. (a) Bar Graph is the simple most and popular graph to show ungrouped frequency distribution graphically.

7. (c) Sum of 6 numbers = 30 × 6 = 180

Sum of remaining 5 numbers = 29 × 5 = 145

∴ Excluded number = 180 – 145 = 35.

8. (c) mid value = $\frac{\text{lower class limit} + \text{upper class limit}}{2}$

Let upper limit = l

$\therefore \quad n = \frac{m+l}{2} \Rightarrow l = 2n - m$

9. (b) Let $\bar{x} = \frac{x_1 + x_2 + ... + x_n}{n}$

If 5 is added in each observation, then

mean = $\frac{(x_1+5)+(x_2+5)+...+(x_n+5)}{n}$

$= \frac{(x_1 + ... + x_n) + 5n}{n} = \bar{x} + 5$

10. (d)

11. (d) 50 is included in neither in 30 – 40 nor in 40 – 50.

12. (d) Class marks = 25, class size = 8

Class-size = upper class limit – lower class limit

$\Rightarrow \quad l + u = 50 \quad ...(i)$

$u - l = 8 \quad ...(ii)$

On solving (i) and (ii), we get u = 29 and l = 21

13. (a) 20 is considered in class 20 – 30

14. Mean of A = $\frac{2+3+7+1+3+2+3}{7} = \frac{21}{7} = 3$

Median : 1, 2, 2, 3, 3, 3, 7

n = 7 ∴ Median = 4th obs. = 3

Mode = 3

MORE THAN ONE CORRECT :

1. (a, b, d)
Variance is not a measure of central tendency.
2. (b, c) 3. (a, c)
4. (a, b, c)
5. (a, b, c) All the statements given in option *a*, *b* and *c* are correct
6. (a, b, c, d)

PASSAGE BASED QUESTONS :

1. (a) The bar graph represents the number of vehicles passing through a particular crossing of Delhi in different time intervals on a particular day. The maximum number of vehicles is 400.
2. (b) The maximum traffic is between 9 to 10 hours.
3. (c) The total number of vehicles passing through a crossing during a particular day = 300 + 400 + 250 + 250 + 150 + 100 + 200 + 325 + 375 = 2350.

ASSERTION AND REASON :

1. (a) Since the value 120 occurs maximum number of times.
2. (b) Both Assertion and Reason is correct but Reason is not correct explanation for Assertion.
3. (c) Assertion is correct. But reason is false.
The number of times a variate (observation) occurs in a given data is called frequency of that variate.
4. (b) **Assertion :** Given no. of observation is 10 (even)

$\therefore \quad \text{Median} = \frac{x+(x+2)}{2} = \frac{2x+2}{2} = x+1$

$65 = x + 1 \Rightarrow x = 64$

5. (d) Assertion is incorrect. First 6 multiples of 6 = 6, 12, 18, 24, 30, 36. Range = 36 – 6 = 30
6. (c) Asertion is correct and Reason is incorrect.
7. Assertion is correct but Reason is not correct.

INTEGER TYPE QUESTION :

1. **Ans : 0**

If $\bar{x} = \frac{x_1 + ... + x_n}{n}$ then $\sum_{i=1}^{n}(x_i - \bar{x}) = 0$

2. **Ans : 8**

mean = $\frac{6+4+7+13+10}{5} = \frac{40}{5} = 8$

3. **Ans : 9**

$11 = \frac{x+x+2+x+4+x+6+x+8}{5}$

$11 = \frac{5x+20}{5} = x + 4$

$\Rightarrow x = 7$

Hence, Required mean $= \frac{7+9+11}{3} = \frac{27}{3} = 9$

4. **Ans : 4**

Mode is the value which occurs most frequently in a set of observations.

Given mode = 4

∴ x = 4

5. **Ans : 3**

Given observations are 1, 2, x, 4, 5 in ascending order.

since n = 5 (odd) therefore median is equal to the $\left(\frac{n+1}{2}\right)^{th}$ observation.

$\Rightarrow$ median = 3rd observation

$\Rightarrow$ 3 = x

Thus, required mean = $\frac{1+2+3+4+5}{5}=\frac{15}{5}=3$

6. **Ans : 7**

Let mean be 2x and median be 3x

we know

mode = 3 median – 2 mean

= 3(3x) – 2(2x) = 5x

Thus, mode : mean = 5 : 2

sum = 5 + 2 = 7

4 ADVANCE EXERCISE
BASED ON CONNECTING TOPICS

1. (c) Total no. of obs = 18

Combined mean = $\frac{(a_1 \times 10)+(a_2 \times 8)}{18}$

where a_1 and a_2 denote the mean

$a_1 = 15$

$\Rightarrow \frac{40}{3}=\frac{150+8a_2}{18}$

$\Rightarrow a_2=\frac{45}{4}$

2. (a) Average in 5 matches = $\frac{2\times 27+3\times 32}{2+3}=\frac{54+96}{5}$

= 30

3. (b) Let the number of boys in a class be x.

Let the number of girls in a class be y.

$\therefore$ Sum of the ages of the boys = $16.4\,x$

Sum of the ages of the girls = $15.4\,y$

$\therefore$ $15.8\,(x+y) = 16.4\,x + 15.4\,y$

$\Rightarrow 0.6\,x = 0.4\,y \Rightarrow \frac{x}{y}=\frac{2}{3}$

$\therefore$ Required ratio = 2 : 3

4. (b) Sum of the remaining two numbers

= (3.95 × 6) – [(3.4 × 2) + (3.85 × 2)]

= 23.70 – (6.8 + 7.7) = 23.70 – 14.5 = 9.20

$\therefore$ Required average = $\left(\frac{9.2}{2}\right)$ = 4.6.

5. (b) Total weight of 45 students = 45 × 52 = 2340 kg

Total weight of 5 students who leave

= 5 × 48 = 240 kg

Total weight of 5 students who join

= 5 × 54 = 270 kg

Therefore, new total weight of 45 students

= 2340 – 240 + 270 = 2370

$\Rightarrow$ New average weight = $\frac{2370}{45}=52\frac{2}{3}$ kg.

EMPIRICAL PROBABILITY

Let there be *n*-trials of an experiment and E be an event associated to it such that E happens in *m*-trials. Then the empirical probability of happening of event E is denoted by P(E) is given by

$$P(E) = \frac{\text{Number of trials in which the event happens}}{\text{Total number of trials}}$$

$$\Rightarrow \quad P(E) = \frac{m}{n}$$

Clearly, $0 \le m \le n$

$\therefore \quad 0 \le \frac{m}{n} \le 1$

$\Rightarrow$ Probability of any event is equal or greater than 0 (zero) but equal or less than 1. i.e. $0 \le P(E) \le 1$.

For example: On tossing a coin, there are two possibilities either head may come up or tail may come up. Therefore, total no. of possible outcomes = 2.

The number of favorable outcomes for getting a head = 1

$\therefore$ Probability of getting a head, $P(H) = \frac{1}{2}$

Similarly, probability of getting a tail, $P(T) = \frac{1}{2}$

> **NOTE :** (i) The sum of all the probabilities is 1.
> (ii) If P(E) = 1, then E is called a certain event.
> (iii) If P(E) = 0, then E is known as an impossible event.

ILLUSTRATION : 1

Two coins are tossed simultaneously 500 times, and we get
Two heads : 105 times; One head : 275 times;
No head : 120 times
Find the probability of occurrence of each of these events.

SOLUTION :

Let us denote the events of getting two heads, one head and no head by E_1, E_2 and E_3 respectively.

So, $P(E_1) = \frac{105}{500} = 0.21$,

$P(E_2) = \frac{275}{500} = 0.55$,

$P(E_3) = \frac{120}{500} = 0.25$

ILLUSTRATION : 2

Suppose that an integer is picked from among 1 to 20 (both inclusive). What is the probability of picking a prime?

SOLUTION :

There are 20 outcomes of the experiment of picking an integer. The primes between 1 and 20 are 2, 3, 5, 7, 11, 13, 17 and 19 and these are 8 in number. Therefore, 8 are favourable to the event of picking a prime and hence the probability of picking a prime is

$\frac{8}{20} = \frac{2}{5}$

MISCELLANEOUS SOLVED EXAMPLES

1. There are 52 students in class 10th of a school out of which there are 35 girls and 17 boys. The class teacher has to select one student as a class representative. She writes the name of each student on a separate card, the cards being identical. Then she puts the cards in a bag and stirs them thoroughly. She then draws one card from the bag. What is the probability that the name written on the card is the name of (i) a girl? (ii) a boy?

Sol. Total number of cards with different names written on them = 52

The number of the cards on which the names of the girl students written = 35

The number of the cards having boy names = 17

We write G for the event of the card drawn with name of a girl and write B for the event of the card drawn with name of a boy.

35 outcomes favour the event G and 17 outcomes favour the event B.

Then $P(G) = \frac{35}{52}$ and $P(B) = \frac{17}{52}$

2. A bag contains 7 red balls and 6 green balls. A ball is drawn at random from the bag. What is the probability of getting (i) a red ball? (ii) a green ball? (iii) a coloured ball?

Sol. Number of red balls = 7

Number of green balls = 6

Total number of balls in the bag = 7 + 6 = 13

All the 13 balls are coloured balls

No ball in the bag is black.

(i) P (a red ball) = $\frac{7}{13}$ (ii) P (a green ball) = $\frac{6}{13}$

(iii) P (a coloured ball) = $\frac{13}{13} = 1$

3. Cards each marked with one of the numbers 8, 9, 10, 11, 12, ..., 30 are placed in a box and mixed thoroughly. One card is drawn at random from the box. What is the probability of getting (i) an even number? (ii) an odd number? (iii) a prime number? (iv) a number multiple of 5? (v) a number divisible by 3?

Sol. The possible outcomes 8, 9, 10, 11; 12, ..., 30 are in all 23 (total number of possible outcomes)

(i) P (an even number) = P (8, 10, 12, 14, 16, 18, 20, 22, 24, 26, 28, 30) = $\frac{12}{23}$

(ii) P (an odd number) = P (9, 11, 13, 15, ..., 29) = $\frac{11}{23}$

(iii) P (a prime number) = P (11, 13, 17, 19, 23, 29) = $\frac{6}{23}$

(iv) P (a number multiple of 5) = P (10, 15, 20, 25, 30) = $\frac{5}{23}$

(v) P (a number divisible by 3) = P (9, 12, 15, 18, 21, 24, 27, 30) = $\frac{8}{23}$

4. A die is thrown 1000 times with the frequencies for the outcomes 1, 2, 3, 4, 5 and 6 as given in the following table:

Outcome	1	2	3	4	5	6
Frequency	157	175	160	179	145	184

Find the possibility of getting each outcome.

Sol. Total number of trials = 1000

If $E_1, E_2, ...E_6$ denote the events of getting the numbers 1, 2, ..., 6 respectively, then

$$P(E_1) = \frac{157}{1000},\ P(E_2) = \frac{175}{1000} = \frac{7}{40},\ P(E_3) = \frac{160}{1000} = \frac{4}{25},$$

$$P(E_4) = \frac{179}{1000},\ P(E_5) = \frac{145}{1000} = \frac{29}{200},\ P(E_6) = \frac{184}{1000} = \frac{23}{125}.$$

1 EXERCISE

Fill in the Blanks :

DIRECTIONS: *Complete the following statements with an appropriate word / term to be filled in the blank space(s).*

1. An activity which results in a well defined end is called an ______________.

2. Total number of results are called ______________.

3. Probability of an event can be any ______________ from 0 to 1.

4. A ______________ is an action which results in one of several outcomes.

5. Number of favorable outcomes for an event cannot be ______________ than the number of total outcomes.

6. An experiment is called a ______________ experiment if all the possible outcomes are pre-decided.

7. Probability is a measure of ______________.

8. An ______________ for an experiment is the collection of some outcomes of the experiment.

True / False :

DIRECTIONS: *Read the following statements and write your answer as true or false.*

1. If a coin is tossed thrice, the total number of outcomes is 8.

2. Probability of the occurrence of an event always lies between1 and –1.

3. Total number of outcomes in a throw of two dice is 12.

4. The sum of probabilities of occurrence and not occurrence of an event is always equal to 1

5. $P(E) = \dfrac{\text{Total number of trials}}{\text{Number of trials in which } E \text{ has happened}}$

6. The experimental probability of an event is a negative number.

7. The experimental probability of an event is greater than 1.

8. Tossing a coin 50 times is called an experiment.

9. When a die is rolled, the number of outcomes for getting a composite number is 2.

10. When a die is rolled, the probability that the number on the face showing up is greater than 6 is zero.

Match the Columns :

DIRECTIONS: *Each question contains statements given in two columns which have to be matched. Statements (A, B, C, D...) in Column - I have to be matched with statements (p, q, r, s, ...) in Column - II.*

1.

Column - I	Column - II
(A) The probability of getting one or more tails in the toss of two coins simultaneously is	(p) $\frac{2}{13}$
(B) During rainy season of 90 days, it was observed that it rained on 20 days only. Then the probability that it did not rain on a day is	(q) 0.8
(C) The probability of not getting a prime number in a single throw of a die is	(r) $\frac{7}{10}$
(D) In a one-day cricket match Kohli faced 30 balls and hit 9 boundaries. The probability that he did not hit a boundary on a ball is	(s) $\frac{1}{2}$
(E) The sum of all the probabilities is	(t) $\frac{3}{6}$
(F) Probability of getting an even number on a die will be	(u) $\frac{6}{11}$
(G) A bag contains 12 pencils, 3 sharpeners and 7 pens. If we take out one item from the bag at random, probability of drawing a pencil is	(v) $\frac{7}{9}$
(H) In a sample study of 642 people, it was found that 514 people have a high school certificate. If a person is selected at random, the probability that the person has a high school certificate is	(w) $\frac{3}{4}$
(I) The probability of getting a king or a queen, if a card is drawn from a well shuffled pack of cards, is	(x) 1

2.

	Column - I		Column - II
(A)	A trial is	(p)	the possible outcome of an experiment.
(B)	An experiment is	(q)	an action which results in one or several outcomes.
(C)	An event is	(r)	an action which results in some well defined outcomo

Very Short Answer Questions :

DIRECTIONS: *Give answer in one word or one sentence.*

1. A coin is tossed 50 times with 17 head. Find the probability of getting a tail.
2. What is the sum of probabilities of different events in an experiment?
3. Find the probability of drawing a jack or an ace from a pack of playing cards.
4. A die is thrown once. Find the probability that 3 or greater than 3 turns up.
5. A coin is tossed twice. What is the probability that head will appear twice ?

Short Answer Questions :

DIRECTIONS: *Give answer in 2-3 sentences.*

1. If two dice are tossed, find the probability of throwing a total of ten or more.
2. One hundred cards are numbered from 1 to 100. Find the probability that a card chosen at random has the digit 5.

2 EXERCISE

Text-Book Exercise :

1. In a cricket match, a batswoman hits a boundary 6 times out of 30 balls she plays. Find the probability that she did not hit a boundary.

2. 1500 families with 2 children were selected randomly, and the following data were recorded.

Number of girls in a family	2	1	0
Number of families	475	814	211

Compute the probability of a family, chosen at random, having

(i) 2 girls (ii) 1 girl (iii) No girl

Also check whether the sum of these probabilities is 1.

3. In a particular section of Class IX, 40 students were asked about the months of their birth and the following graph was prepared for the data so obtained:

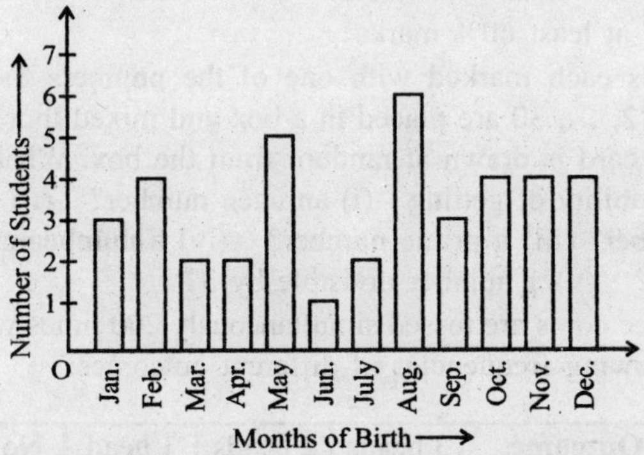

Find the probability that a student of the class was born in August.

4. Three coins are tossed simultaneously 200 times with the following frequencies of different outcomes :

Outcome	3 heads	2 heads	1 head	No head
Frequency	23	72	77	28

If the three coins are simultaneously tossed again, compute the probability of 2 heads coming up.

5. An organisation selected 2400 families at random and surveyed them to determine a relationship between income level and the number of vehicles in a family. The information gathered is listed in the table below:

"Monthly income (in ₹)"	**Vehicles per family**			
	0	1	2	Above 2
Less than 7000	10	160	25	0
7000 – 10000	0	305	27	2
10000 – 13000	1	535	29	1
13000 – 16000	2	469	59	25
16000 or more	1	579	82	88

Suppose a family is chosen. Find the probability that the family chosen is

(i) earning ₹ 10000 – ₹ 13000 per month and owning exactly 2 vehicles.

(ii) earning ₹ 16000 or more per month and owning exactly 1 vehicle.

(iii) earning less than ₹ 7000 per month and does not own any vehicle.

(iv) earning ₹ 13000 – ₹ 16000 per month and owning more than 2 vehicles.

(v) owning not more than 1 vehicle.

6. Read the table and answer the following questions :

Marks	**Number of students**
0 – 20	7
20 – 30	10
30 – 40	10
40 – 50	20
50 – 60	20
60 – 70	15
70 – above	8
Total	90

(i) Find the probability that a student obtained less than 20% in the mathematics test.

(ii) Find the probability that a student obtained marks 60 or above.

7. To know the opinion of the students about the subject statistics, a survey of 200 students was conducted. The data is recorded in the following table.

Opinion	**Number of Students**
like	135
dislike	65

Find the probability that a student chosen at random

(i) likes statistics, (ii) does not like it.

8. The distance (in km) of 40 engineers from their residence to their place of work were found as follows:

5	3	10	20	25	11	13	7	12	31
19	10	12	17	18	11	32	17	16	2
7	9	7	8	3	5	12	15	18	3
12	14	2	9	6	15	15	7	6	12

What is the probability that an engineer lives :

(i) less than 7 km from her place of work?

(ii) more than or equal to 7 km from her place of work?

(iii) within $\frac{1}{2}$ km from her place of work?

9. Eleven bags of wheat flour, each marked 5 kg, actually contained the following weights of flour (in kg) :

4.97 5.05 5.08 5.03 5.00 5.06 5.08
4.98 5.04 5.07 5.00

Find the probability that any of these bags chosen at random contains more than 5 kg of flour.

Exemplar Questions :

1. Here is an extract from a mortality table.

Age (in years)	Number of persons surviving out of a sample of one million
60	16090
61	11490
62	8012
63	5448
64	3607
65	2320

(i) Based on this information, what is the probability of a person 'aged 60' of dying within a year?

(ii) What is the probability that a person 'aged 61' will live for 4 years?

HOTS Questions :

1. In cricket match, a batsman hits a boundary 12 times out of 48 balls he plays. Find the probability that he does not hit a boundary in the next ball.

2. An Insurance company selected 2000 drivers at random in a particular city to find a relationship between age and accidents. The data obtained are given in the following table :

Age of drivers (in years)	Accidents in one year				
	0	1	2	3	over 3
18 – 29	440	160	110	61	35
30 – 50	505	125	60	22	18
Above 50	360	45	35	15	9

Find the probabilities of the following events for a driver chosen at random from the city :

(i) being 18-29 years of age and having exactly 3 accidents in one year.

(ii) being 30-50 years of age and having one or more accidents in a year.

(iii) having no accident in one year.

3. The percentage of marks obtained by a student in monthly unit tests are given below.

Test	I	II	III	IV	V	VI
Percentage of marks	52	60	65	75	80	72

Find the probability that in the next test the student gets

(i) more than 70% marks

(ii) less than 70% marks

(iii) at least 60% marks

4. Cards each marked with one of the numbers 8, 9, 10, 11, 12, ..., 30 are placed in a box and mixed thoroughly. One card is drawn at random from the box. What is the probability of getting (i) an even number? (ii) an odd number? (iii) a prime number? (iv) a number multiple of 5? (v) a number divisible by 3?

5. Three coins are tossed simultaneously 200 times with the following frequencies of different outcomes:

Outcome	3 heads	2 heads	1 head	No head
Frequency	23	72	77	28

Find the probability of getting : (i) three heads (ii) two heads and one tail (iii) at least two heads

3 EXERCISE

Single Option Correct :

DIRECTIONS: *This section contains multiple choice questions. Each question has 4 choices (a), (b), (c) and (d) out of which ONLY ONE is correct.*

1. Probability of an event can be
   (a) -0.7 (b) $\frac{11}{9}$
   (c) 1.001 (d) 0.6
2. In a class of 40 students there are 120% boys. Then the number of boys is
   (a) 48 (b) 24
   (c) 80 (d) None of these
3. A coin is tossed 40 times and it showed tail 24 times. The probability of getting a head was
   (a) $\frac{2}{5}$ (b) $\frac{3}{5}$
   (c) $\frac{1}{2}$ (d) $\frac{17}{40}$
4. A bag contains 10 balls, out of which 4 balls are white and the others are non-white. The probability of getting a non-white ball is
   (a) $\frac{2}{5}$ (b) $\frac{3}{5}$
   (c) $\frac{1}{2}$ (d) $\frac{2}{3}$
5. If E is an event, then
   (a) $0 < P(E) < 1$ (b) $0 \le P(E) < 1$
   (c) $0 \le P(E) \le 1$ (d) $0 < P(E) \le 1$
6. In an experiment, the sum of probabilities of different events is
   (a) 1 (b) 0.5
   (c) -2 (d) 0
7. The probability of happening of an event is 37%. Then probability of the event is.
   (a) 37 (b) 0.037
   (c) 3.7 (d) 0.37
8. If a coin was tossed 100 times, out of which 65 times we got head and 35 times tail. Then the probability of not getting a tail is
   (a) 6.5 (b) 7.5
   (c) .65 (d) 35
9. In rolling a dice, the probability of getting number 8 is
   (a) 0 (b) 1
   (c) -1 (d) $\frac{1}{2}$
10. Two dice are rolled simultaneously. The probability that they show different faces is.
    (a) $\frac{6}{5}$ (b) $\frac{1}{6}$
    (c) $\frac{1}{3}$ (d) $\frac{5}{6}$

More Than One Option Correct :

DIRECTIONS: *This section contains multiple choice questions. Each question has 4 choices (a), (b), (c) and (d) out of which ONE OR MORE may be correct.*

1. Which of the following is/are experiment ?
   (a) Tossing a coin
   (b) Rolling a single 6-sided die
   (c) Choosing a marble from a jar.
   (d) None of these
2. Which of the following is/are not outcome ?
   (a) Rolling a pair of dice.
   (b) Landing on red.
   (c) Choosing two marbles from a jar.
   (d) Tossing a coin.
3. Which of the following is not the sample space when two coins are tossed?
   (a) {H, T, H, T} (b) {H, T}
   (c) {HH, HT, TH, TT} (d) {HH, TT}
4. Which of the following words represent uncertainty
   (a) probability (b) doubt
   (c) sure (d) chances
5. An experiment is performed and probability of an event A is recorded, probability of an event A can be
   (a) 0.001 (b) 0.999
   (c) 1.001 (d) -0.999
6. In an experiment, the sum of probabilities of different events is
   (a) 1 (b) 0.5
   (c) -2 (d) $\frac{15}{15}$

7. Events E_1, E_2, E_3 are the possible events of an experiment and their probabilities are recorded. Mark the possible correct answer

(a) $P(E_1) = 0.3, P(E_2) = 0.4, P(E_3) = 0.3$

(b) $P(E_1) = 0.1, P(E_2) = 0.4, P(E_3) = 0.5$

(c) $P(E_1) = 0.6, P(E_2) = -0.3, P(E_3) = 0.7$

(d) $P(E_1) = 0.4, P(E_2) = 0.2, P(E_3) = 0.3$

Passage Based Questions :

DIRECTIONS : *Study the given paragraph(s) and answer the following questions.*

PASSAGE

Over the past 200 working days, the number of defective parts produced by a machine is given in the following table:

Table-I

No. of defective parts	0	1	2	3	4	5	6	7	8	9	10	11	12	13
No. of days on which the defective parts produce	50	32	22	18	12	12	10	10	10	8	6	6	2	2

Find the probability that tomorrow's output will have

1. no defective part

(a) .25 (b) 2.5

(c) 25 (d) 50

2. at least one defective part

(a) 7.5 (b) .75

(c) 75 (d) 73

3. not more than 5 defective parts

(a) 7.3 (b) 73

(c) .73 (d) 75

4. more than 13 defective parts

(a) 0 (b) 1

(c) –1 (d) None of these

Assertion & Reason :

DIRECTIONS: *Each of these questions contains an Assertion followed by Reason. Read them carefully and answer the question on the basis of following options. You have to select the one that best describes the two statements.*

(a) If both **Assertion** and **Reason** are **correct** and Reason is the **correct explanation** of Assertion.

(b) If both **Assertion** and **Reason** are correct, but Reason **is not the correct explanation** of Assertion.

(c) If **Assertion** is **correct** but **Reason** is **incorrect.**

(d) If **Assertion** is **incorrect** but **Reason** is **correct.**

1. **Assertion :** In a class there are x boys. and y girls, A student is selected at random, then the probability of selecting a girl is $\frac{y}{x}$.

Reason : Probability of an event E of an experiment is ratio of the number of trials in which event E has happened to the total number of trials.

2. **Assertion :** Tossing a coin 50 times is called an event.

Reason : The possible outcomes of an experiment are called events.

3. **Assertion :**If E_1, E_2, ..., E_n are n elementary events associated to a random experiment, then $P(E_1) + P(E_2) + ... + P(E_n) = 1$

Reason : For any event 'A' associated to an experiment, we have $-1 \le P(A) \le 1$

4. **Assertion:** A die is thrown. Let E be the event that number appears on the upper face is less than 1, then $P(E) = \frac{1}{6}$.

Reason: Probability of impossible event is 0.

5. **Assertion:** A coin is tossed two times. Probability of getting at least two heads is $\frac{1}{4}$.

Reason: When a coin is tossed two times, then the sample space is {HH, HT, TH, TT}

Multiple Matching Question :

DIRECTIONS : *Following question has four statements (A, B, C and D) given in Column-I and four statements (p, q, r, s) in Column-II. Any given statement in Column-I can have correct matching with one or more statement(s) given in Column-II.*

1. A NGO selected 2000 families at random and surveyed them to determine number of children in a family. The data is given below:

Number of families	Boy	Girl
400	1	1
600	2	1
300	1	2
500	2	0
200	0	2

If one family is chosen at random then, match the Column-I with their corresponding probabilities in Column-II.

Column - I	Column - II
(A) The probability that the family chosen has 1 boy and 2 girls is	(p) $\frac{1}{10}$
(B) The probability that the family chosen has no boy is	(q) $\frac{3}{10}$
(C) The probability that the family chosen has 1 boy and 1 girl is	(r) $\frac{3}{20}$
(D) The probability that the family chosen has 2 boys and 1 girl is	(s) $\frac{1}{5}$

Integer Type Questions :

DIRECTIONS : *Answer the following questions. The answer to each of the question is a single digit integer, ranging from 0 to 9.*

1. A number from 1 to 11 is chosen at random. The probability of choosing an odd number is $\frac{a}{11}$. The value of '*a*' is
2. The probability of choosing a vowel from the English alphabets is $\frac{m}{n}$. The value of m is
3. Difference between the numerator and denominator of probability of choosing a vowel randomly from the word 'EXAMINATION'.
4. Reema and Anshi playing a game. Reema's winning probability is $\frac{1}{3}$ and sum of their winning probabilities is 1. Numerator of Anshi's winning probability is
5. A bag contains 7 red balls and 6 green balls. A ball is drawn at random from the bag. What is the probability of getting a black ball?

SOLUTIONS

Brief Explanations of Selected Questions

1 EXERCISE

FILL IN THE BLANKS :

1. Experiment
2. Outcomes
3. Fraction
4. Trial
5. Greater
6. Random
7. Uncertainty
8. Event

TRUE/FALSE :

1. True 2. False 3. False 4. True
5. False 6. False 7. False 8. True
9. True 10. True

MATCH THE COLUMNS :

1. (A) → (w); (B) → (v); (C) → (t); (D) → (r); (E) → (x); (F) → (s); (G) → (u); (H) → (q); (I) → (p)

2. (A) →(q) ; (B) → (r) ; (C) → (p)

VERY SHORT ANSWER QUESTIONS :

1. No. of head = 17

$\therefore$ No. of tail = 50 – 17 = 33

Total no. of trials = 50

$\therefore$ Required prob = $\frac{33}{50}$

2. Required sum = 1

3. Total number of cards = 52 as there are four jacks and four aces, the number of favourable cases = 8

$\therefore$ The required probability = $p = \frac{8}{52} = \frac{2}{13}$

4. n = Number of all cases = 6

m = Number of favourable cases = 4

(since the numbers that appear are 3, 4, 5, 6)

$\therefore$ The required probability = $p = \frac{m}{n} = \frac{4}{6} = \frac{2}{3}$

5. Here, the total number of cases = 4 i.e. HH, HT, TH, TT. The number of favourable cases = 1 i.e. HH

$\therefore$ Required probability = $p = \frac{m}{n} = \frac{1}{4}$

SHORT ANSWER QUESTIONS :

1. Here the number of favourable cases, consists of throwing 10,11 or 12 with the two dice. The number of ways in which a sum of 10 can be thrown are (4,6), (5,5), (6,4) i.e. 3 ways.

The number of ways in which a total of 11 can be thrown are (5, 6), (6,5) i.e. 2 ways.

The number of ways in which a total of 12 can be thrown is (6, 6) i.e. 1 way.

m = number of favourable cases = 3 + 2 + 1 = 6

n = Total number of cases = 6 × 6 = 36

$\therefore$ Probability = $p = \frac{m}{n} = \frac{6}{36} = \frac{1}{6}$

2. Total number of cases = n = 100

All the numbers from 50 to 59 have the digit 5. They are 10 in number. Besides these numbers the numbers 5, 15, 25, 35, 45, 65, 75, 85, 95 have the digit 5. These are 9 in number.

Number of favourable cases = m = Number of numbers which have the digit 5 = 10 + 9 = 19

$\therefore$ Probability = $p = \frac{m}{n} = \frac{19}{100}$

2 EXERCISE

TEXT-BOOK EXERCISE :

1. Let A be the event of hitting the boundary. then,

$$P(A) = \frac{\text{Number of times the batswoman hits the boundary}}{\text{Total number of balls she plays}}$$

$$= \frac{6}{30} = \frac{1}{5} = 0.2$$

$\therefore$ Probability of not hitting the boundary = 1 – Probability of hitting the boundary,

= 1 – P(A) = 1 – 0.2 = 0.8.

2. Total number of families = 475 + 814 + 211 = 1500

(i) Let A be the event of choosing the family having 2 girls.

$$\therefore\ P(A) = \frac{\text{Number of family having 2girls}}{\text{Total no. of family}}$$

$$= \frac{475}{1500} = \frac{19}{60}$$

(ii) Let B be the event of choosing the family, having 1 girl

$$\therefore\ P(B) = \frac{814}{1500} = \frac{407}{750}$$

(iii) Let C be the event of choosing the family, having no girl

$$\therefore\ P(C) = \frac{211}{1500}$$

Now, sum of these probabilities

$$=\frac{19}{60}+\frac{407}{750}+\frac{211}{1500}=\frac{475+814+211}{1500}=\frac{1500}{1500}=1$$

Hence, the sum is checked

3. From the bar chart we have

total number of students born in the year

$= 3 + 4 + 2 + 2 + 5 + 1 + 2 + 6 + 3 + 4 + 4 + 4 = 40$

Again from the bar graph we observe that the Number of students born in August = 6

Let C be the event that student was born in August.

$$\therefore\ P(C)=\frac{6}{40}=\frac{3}{20}.$$

4. Total number of times the three coins are tossed = 200

From the given data we have number of times when 2 heads appear = 72

Let A be the event of getting 2 heads.

$$\therefore\ P(A)=\frac{72}{200}=\frac{9}{25}.$$

5. Total number of families selected = 2400

(i) From the given table we have no. of families earning ₹ 10,000 – ₹13000 per month and owning exactly 2 vehicles = 29

Let A be the event of choosing a family which earns ₹ 10000 – ₹13000 per month and owning exactly 2 vehicles.

$$\therefore\ P(A)=\frac{29}{2400}.$$

(ii) Number of families earning ₹ 16000 or more per month and owning exactly 1 vehicle = 579

Let B be the event of choosing a family which earns ₹ 16000 or more per month and owning exactly 1 vehicle

$$\therefore\ P(B)=\frac{579}{2400}=\frac{193}{800}.$$

(iii) From the table number of families earning less than ₹ 7000 per month and does not own any vehicle = 10

Let C be the event of choosing a family which earns less than ₹ 7000 per month and does not own any vehicle

$$\therefore\ P(C)=\frac{10}{2400}=\frac{1}{240}.$$

(iv) From the table Number of families earning ₹ 13000 – 16000 per month and owning more than 2 vehicles = 25

Let D be the event of choosing a family which earns ₹ 13000 – 16000 per month and owning more than 2 vehicles.

$$\therefore\ P(D)=\frac{25}{2400}=\frac{1}{96}.$$

(v) Number of families owning not more than 1 vehicle

= Number of families owning 0 vehicle + Number of families owning 1 vehicle

$=(10+0+1+2+1)+(160+305+535+469+579)$

$= 14 + 2048 = 2062$

∴ Probability that the family chosen owns not more than 1 vehicle $=\frac{2062}{2400}=\frac{1031}{1200}$.

6. From the table, it is given that total number of students = 90

(i) It is clear from the table that number of students obtaining less than 20% in the mathematics test = 7

Let A be the event that a student obtained less than 20% in mathematics test

$$\therefore\ P(A)=\frac{7}{90}$$

(ii) It is clear from the table that number of students obtaining marks 60 or above = 15 + 8 = 23

Let B be the event that a student obtained marks 60 or above

$$\therefore\ P(B)=\frac{23}{90}.$$

7. Given total number of students = 200

(i) Given in the table, number of students who like statistics = 135

∴ Probability (a student likes statistics) $=\frac{135}{200}=\frac{27}{40}$.

(ii) Again, from the table, we have

Number of students who do not like statistics = 65

∴ Probability (a student does not like it) $=\frac{65}{200}=\frac{13}{40}$.

8. Given total number of female engineers = 40

(i) Number of female engineers whose distance (in km) from their residence to their place of work is less than 7 km = 9.

∴ Probability (engineer lives less than 7 km from place of work) $=\frac{9}{40}$.

(ii) Number of female engineers whose distance (in km) from their residence to their place of work is more than or equal to 7 km = 31.

∴ Probability (engineer lives more than or equal to 7 km from her place of work) $=\frac{31}{40}$.

(iii) Number of female engineers whose distance (in km) from their residence to their place of work is within $\frac{1}{2}$ km = 0.

∴ Required probability $=\frac{0}{40}=0.$

9. Given Total number of bags of wheat flour = 11.
From the given data, total number of bags of wheat flour which contains more than 5 kg of flour = 7.

$\therefore$ Required probability $= \frac{7}{11}$.

EXEMPLAR QUESTIONS :

1. (i) We see that 16090 persons aged 60, (16090-11490), i.e., 4600 died before reaching their 61st birthday.
Therefore, P(a person aged 60 die within a year)

$= \frac{4600}{16090} = \frac{460}{1609}$

(ii) Number of person aged 61 years = 11490

Number of person surviving for 4 years = 2320

P(a person aged 61 will live for 4 years)

$= \frac{2320}{11490} = \frac{232}{1149}$

HOTS QUESTIONS :

1. Let E be the event 'the batsman hits a boundary'.
Then, $\bar{E}$ is the event 'the batsman does not hit a boundary'.

$\therefore \quad P(E) = \frac{12}{48} = \frac{1}{4}$

$\Rightarrow \quad P(\bar{E}) = 1 - P(E) = 1 - \frac{1}{4} = \frac{3}{4}$

2. Total number of drivers = 2000

(i) Number of drivers who are 18-29 years old and have exactly 3 accidents in one year is 61

So, P (driver is 18-29 years old with exactly 3 accidents) $= \frac{61}{2000} = 0.0305 \approx 0.031$

(ii) Number of drivers having 30-50 years of age and having one or more accidents in one year.

= 125 + 60 + 22 + 18 = 225

So, P (driver is 30-35 years of age and having one or more accidents) $= \frac{225}{2000} = 0.1125 = 0.113$

(iii) Number of drivers having no accident in one year = 440 + 505 + 360 = 1305

So, P (drivers with no accident)

$= \frac{1305}{2000} = 0.6525 = 0.653$

3. (i) Number of tests in which the student scored more than 70% marks = 3

$\therefore$ P (more than 70% marks) $= \frac{3}{6} = \frac{1}{2}$

(ii) Number of tests in which the student scored less than 70% marks = 3

$\therefore$ P (more than 70% marks) $= \frac{3}{6} = \frac{1}{2}$

(iii) Number of tests in which the student scored at least 60% marks = 5

$\therefore$ P (at least 60% marks) $= \frac{5}{6}$

4. The possible outcomes 8, 9, 10, 11, 12, ..., 30 are in all 23 (total number of possible outcomes)

(i) P (an even number)

$= P(8, 10, 12, 14, 16, 18, 20, 22, 24, 26, 28, 30) = \frac{12}{23}$

(ii) P (an odd number)

$= P(9, 11, 13, 15, \ldots, 29) = \frac{11}{23}$

(iii) P (a prime number)

$= P(11, 13, 17, 19, 23, 29) = \frac{6}{23}$

(iv) P (a number multiple of 5)

$= P(10, 15, 20, 25, 30) = \frac{5}{23}$

(v) P (a number divisible by 3)

$= P(9, 12, 15, 18, 21, 24, 27, 30) = \frac{8}{23}$

5. Let us define the following events:

A = Getting three heads
B = Getting two head and one tail
C = Getting at least two heads

We have, total number of trials = 200

Number of trials in which we get three heads i.e. in which event A happens = 23

Number of trials in which we get two heads and one tail i.e. in which event B happens = 72

Number of trials in which we get either two heads and one tails or all heads i.e. in which event C happens = 72 + 23 = 95

Hence, $P(A) = \frac{23}{200} = 0.165, P(B) = \frac{72}{200} = 0.36$

and $P(C) = \frac{95}{200} = 0.475$

3 EXERCISE

SINGLE OPTION CORRECT :

1. (d) Probability of an event always lies between 0 and 1. (both inclusive)

2. (d) 120% is not valid.

3. (a) P (getting a head) = $\frac{40-24}{40}=\frac{16}{40}=\frac{2}{5}$

4. (b) Total no. of balls = 10

No. of white balls = 4

No. of non-white balls = 10 – 4 = 6

So, Required prob = $\frac{6}{10}=\frac{3}{5}$

5. (c) $0 \le P(E) \le 1$

6. (a) In an experiment, the sum of probabilities of different events is 1.

7. (d) Required prob = 37% = $\frac{37}{100}=.37$

8. (c) Required probability $=\frac{100-35}{100}=\frac{65}{100}=.65$

9. (a) Required probability is zero because number 8 does not appear on a dice.

10. (d)

More Than One Option Correct :

1. (a, b, c)
2. (a, c, d)
3. (a, b, d)
4. (a, b, d)
5. (a, b)
6. (a, d)
7. (a, b)

Passage Based Questions :

1. (a) P (no defective part) $=\frac{50}{200}=\frac{1}{4}=.25$

2. (b) P (at least one defective part)

$= P(1) + P(2) + P(3) + P(4) + P(5) + P(6) + P(7) + P(8) + P(9) + P(10) + P(11) + P(12) + P(13)$

$=\frac{32+22+18+12+12+10+10+10+8+6+6+2+2}{200}$

$=\frac{150}{200}=\frac{3}{4}=.75$

3. (c) P (not more than 5 defective parts)

$= P(0) + P(1) + P(2) + P(3) + P(4) + P(5)$

$=\frac{50+32+22+18+12+12}{200}=\frac{146}{200}=.73$

4. (a) P (more than 13 defective parts) = 0

Assertion & Reason :

1. (d) Assertion is false.

P (selecting a girl) = $\frac{y}{x+y}$

2. (d) Assertion is false. Tossing a coin 50 times is called an experiment.

3. (c) Assertion is correct but Reason is incorrect.

4. (d) When a die is thrown, then number of outcomes are 1, 2, 3, 4, 5, 6

P(number appear on the upper face is less than 1) = 0

Assertion is false and Reason is true.

5. (b) Number of total outcomes when a coin is tossed 2 times {HH, HT, TH, TT} = 4

P(getting at least two heads) = $\frac{1}{4}$

Assertion and Reason both are true, but Reason is not the correct explanation of Assertion.

Multiple Matching Question :

1. A → r; B → p; C → s; D → q

(A) Let E be the event that chosen family has 1 boy and 2 girls ∴ n(E) = 300

P(E) = $\frac{300}{2000}=\frac{3}{20}$

(B) Let F be the event that chosen family has no boy n(F) = 200

P(F) = $\frac{200}{2000}=\frac{1}{10}$

(C) Let G be the event that chosen family has 1 boy and 1 girl ∴ n(G) = 400

P(G) = $\frac{400}{2000}=\frac{1}{5}$

(D) Let H be event that chosen family has 2 boys and 1 girl ∴ n(H) = 600

P(H) = $\frac{600}{2000}=\frac{3}{10}$

Integer Type Questions :

1. **Ans : 6**

Total numbers = 11

∴ n(sample space) = n(S) = 11

E = odd numbers = 1, 3, 5, 7, 9, 11

∴ n(E) = 6

⇒ P(E) = $\frac{6}{11}$ Hence, '*a*' = 6

2. **Ans : 5**

Number of alphabets = 26

∴ n(S) = 26

E = number of vowels = 5

∴ n(E) = 5

⇒ P(E) = $\frac{5}{26}=\frac{m}{n}$

Hence, m = 5

3. Ans : 5

Number of letter in word EXAMINATION = 11 = n(S)

Number of vowels in word EXAMINATION = 6

Let E be the event of chosing a vowel

$\Rightarrow$ n(E) = 6

$$P(E) = \frac{n(E)}{n(S)} = \frac{6}{11}$$

Difference between numerator and denominator

= 11 − 6 = 5

4. Ans : 2

Reema's winning probability $= \frac{1}{3}$

$\Rightarrow$ Anshi's winning probability $= 1 - \frac{1}{3} = \frac{2}{3}$

Numerator of Anshi's winning probability is 2.

5. Ans : 0

Number of red balls = 7

Number of green balls = 6

Total number of balls = 7 + 6 = 13

$$P \text{ (a black ball)} = \frac{0}{13} = 0$$

Chapter 16

Linear Inequalities

INTRODUCTION

When we compare two quantities in day-to-day situations, it is more likely that the two quantities are unequal rather than equal. A student may not write a three hour examination paper in exactly three hours. He may finish it in less time or more time. It rarely happens as planned.

The distance shown on a railway ticket from one station to other is either little less or a little more. Thus, in reality inequalities occur quite frequently in practical life, so it is natural to expect that their study is important in mathematics too.

Inequality, in mathematics, states that a mathematical expression is less than or greater than some other expression. An inequality is not a specific as an equation but it does contain information about the expression involved.

INEQUALITY (INEQUATIONS)

A statement involving variable(s) and the sign of inequality viz >, <, ≥ or ≤ is called an inequation or an inequality.
For examples : $5 < 7$, $x \geq 3$, $x < 5$, $3 < x \leq 8$, $ax + b > 0$, $2x + y \geq 0$ are inequality.

> **NOTE :** An inequation may contain one or more variables. Also, it may be linear or quadratic or cubic etc.

Important Points to be Remember

(i) Sign of inequality does not change when equal numbers added to (or subtracted from) both sides of an inequality.

Example : If $x \geq 3$, then $x + 2 \geq 5$. Also if $y < 8$, then $y - 2 < 6$

(ii) Sign of inequality does not change when both sides of an inequality can be multiplied (or divided) by the same positive number.

Example : If $x > -4$ then $2x > -8$. Also if $y \leq 8$, then $\frac{y}{2} \leq 4$

(iii) But when both sides are multiplied or divided by a negative number, then the sign of inequality is reversed.

Example : If $x > 3$, then $-2x < -6$. Also, if $x \leq 12$, then $-\frac{x}{3} \geq -4$

Types of Inequalities

1. Numerical Inequalities (Literal Inequalities)

Inequalities which does not contain any variable are called numerical, inequalities. $8 > 6$, $-7 < 0$, etc.

2. An inequality may contain more than one variable. For examples $2xy < 8$, $x + 3y \geq 20$, etc.

3. An inequality in one variable may be linear, quadratic or cubic etc. For examples $2x + 5 < 10$, $x^2 + 4x + 3 \geq 0$, $-x^3 + 2x^2 - 4 \leq 8$, etc.

4. Strict Inequalities :

Inequalities involving the symbol '>' or '<' are called strict inequalities.

5. Slack Inequalities :

Inequalities involving the symbol '≥' or '≤' are called slack inequalities.

$a \geq b$ means $a > b$ or $a = b$

$a \leq b$ means $a < b$ or $a = b$

> **NOTE :** Simultaneous relation between any three different quantities a, b and c will be either $a < b < c$, $a < b \leq c$, $a \leq b < c$ or $a \leq b \leq c$

ALGEBRAIC SOLUTION OF LINEAR INEQUALITIES IN ONE VARIABLE AND THEIR GRAPHICAL REPRESENTATION ON THE NUMBER LINE

(i) A solution of an inequation is the values of the variable which make it a true statement.

(ii) To represent the solution $x < a$ (or $x > a$) on a number line, put a very small blank circle on the number a and dark the line to the left (or right) of the number a. In the inequality $x < a$ or $x > a$ the point $x = a$ on the number line is not included in the solutions of the inequality.

(iii) To represent the solution $x \leq a$ (or $x \geq a$) on a number line, put a very small filled dark circle on the number a and dark the line to the left (or right) of the number a.
In the inequality $x \leq a$ or $x \geq a$, the point $x = a$ on the number line is included in the solutions.

SOLUTION SET

The set of all possible solutions of an inequation is known as its solution set.

ILLUSTRATION : 1

Solve the inequality $3(x-1) \geq 2(x-3)$ and represent the solution on the number line

SOLUTION :

$3(x-1) \geq 2(x-3)$

$\Rightarrow \quad 3x-3 \geq 2x-6$ ...(i)

Subtracting $2x$ from both sides of inequality '≥' of (i), we get

$3x-3-2x \geq 2x-6-2x$

$\Rightarrow \quad x-3 \geq -6$ ...(ii)

Add 3 on both sides

we get

$x-3+3 \geq -6+3$

$x \geq -3$

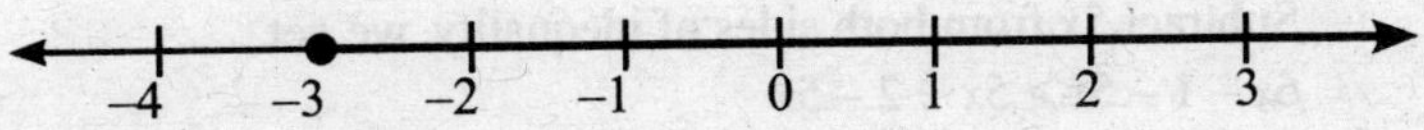

ILLUSTRATION : 2

Solve the inequality $\frac{2x}{3} < \frac{x}{2} + 1$ and represent the solution on the number line.

SOLUTION :

$\frac{2x}{3} < \frac{x}{2} + 1$ ...(i)

Subtract $\frac{x}{2}$ from both sides

$\frac{2x}{3} - \frac{x}{2} < \frac{x}{2} + 1 - \frac{x}{2}$

$\Rightarrow \quad \frac{2x}{3} - \frac{x}{2} < 1$ ...(ii)

Multiply by 6 (L.C.M. of 3 and 2) on both sides of inequality, we get

$6 \times \frac{2x}{3} - 6 \times \frac{x}{2} < 6$

$\Rightarrow \quad 4x - 3x < 6$

$\Rightarrow \quad x < 6$

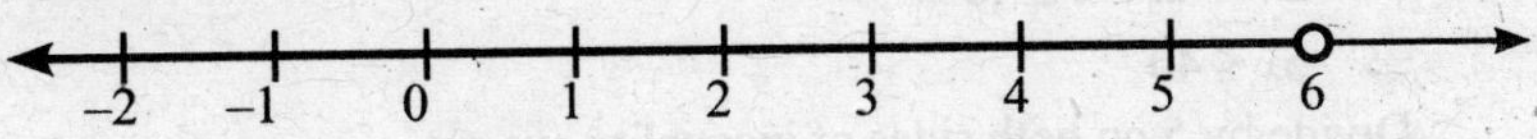

ILLUSTRATION : 3

Solve the inequality $-\frac{x}{3} - 5x > 8$ and repersent the solution on the number line

SOLUTION :

$-\frac{x}{3} - 5x > 8$ ...(i)

Multiply by –3 on both sides of inequality (i), we get

$(-3) \times \left(-\frac{x}{3}\right) - (-3) \times 5x < (-3) \times 8$

$\Rightarrow \quad x + 15x < -24$

$\Rightarrow \quad 16x < -24$ ...(ii)

Divide by 16 on both sides of inequality (ii), we get

$\frac{16x}{16} < \frac{-24}{16}$

$\Rightarrow \quad x < -\frac{3}{2}, \quad \Rightarrow \quad x < -1\frac{1}{2}$

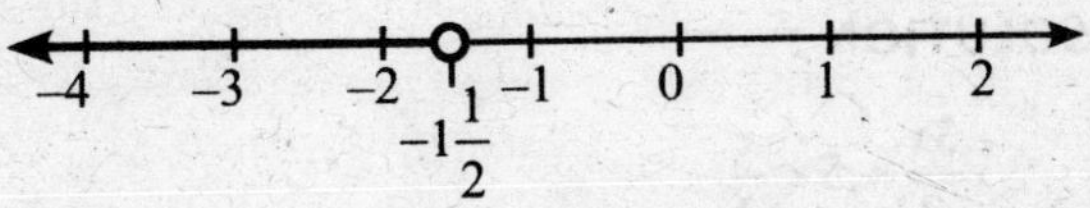

ALGEBRAIC SOLUTION OF A SYSTEM OF LINEAR INEQUALITIES IN ONE VARIABLE

The common algebraic solution of all the solutions of individual inequality in one variable of the system is the algebraic solutions of the given system of linear inequalities in one variable.

ILLUSTRATION : 4

Solve the given system of inequalities: $6x - 1 > 5x + 2$, $\frac{x}{2} + x \le \frac{x}{4} + 10$ and repersent the solution on the number line.

SOLUTION :

$6x - 1 > 5x + 2$ ...(i)

Subtract 5x from both sides of inequality, we get

$6x - 1 - 5x > 5x + 2 - 5x$

$\Rightarrow x - 1 > 2$ ...(ii)

Add 1 on both sides of inequality, we get

$x - 1 + 1 > 2 + 1$

$\Rightarrow x > 3$ ...(iii)

Now $\frac{x}{2} + x \le \frac{x}{4} + 10$ ...(iv)

Subtract $\frac{x}{4}$ from both side of inequality, we get

$\frac{x}{2} + x - \frac{x}{4} \le \frac{x}{4} + 10 - \frac{x}{4}$

$\Rightarrow \frac{x}{2} + x - \frac{x}{4} \le 10$ ...(v)

Multiply by 4 (L.C.M of 2 and 4) on both sides of inequality, we get

$4 \times \frac{x}{2} + 4x - 4 \times \frac{x}{4} \le 4 \times 10$

$\Rightarrow 2x + 4x - x \le 40$

$\Rightarrow 5x \le 40$ ...(vi)

Divide by 5 on both sides of inequality, we get

$\frac{5x}{5} \le \frac{40}{5}$

$\Rightarrow x \le 8$ ...(vii)

From (iii) and (vii), we get

$3 < x \le 8$

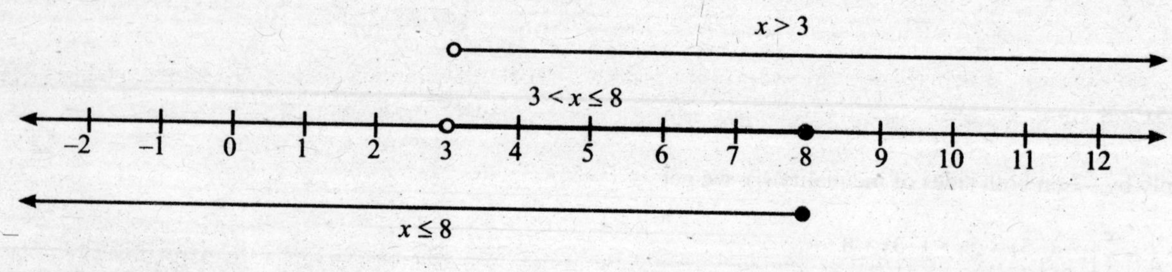

ILLUSTRATION : 5

Solve the following system of inequalities $\frac{3x}{2} + 5 < \frac{x}{2}$, $x - \frac{5x}{3} > -8$

SOLUTION :

$\frac{3x}{2} + 5 < \frac{x}{2}$ ...(i)

Subtracting $\frac{x}{2}$ from both sides of inequality, we get

$$\frac{3x}{2}+5-\frac{x}{2}<\frac{x}{2}-\frac{x}{2}$$

$$\Rightarrow \frac{3x}{2}-\frac{x}{2}+5<0 \quad \text{...(ii)}$$

Subtracting 5 from both sides of inequality, we get

$$\frac{3x}{2}-\frac{x}{2}+5-5<0-5$$

$$\Rightarrow \frac{3x}{2}-\frac{x}{2}<-5 \quad \text{...(iii)}$$

Multiply by 2 (L.C.M. of 2 and 2) on both sides of inequality, we get

$$\frac{3x}{2}\times 2-\frac{x}{2}\times 2<-5\times 2$$

$$\Rightarrow 3x-x<-10$$

$$\Rightarrow 2x<-10 \quad \text{...(iv)}$$

Divide by 2 on both sides of inequality, we get

$$x<-\frac{10}{2}$$

$$\Rightarrow x<-5 \quad \text{...(v)}$$

$$\text{And } x-\frac{5x}{3}>-8 \quad \text{...(vi)}$$

Multiply by 3 on both sides of inequality, we get

$$3x-3\times\frac{5x}{3}>3\times(-8)$$

$$\Rightarrow 3x-5x>-24$$

$$\Rightarrow -2x>-24 \quad \text{...(vii)}$$

Divide by –2 on both sides of inequality, we get

$$\frac{-2x}{-2}>\frac{-24}{-2}$$

$$\Rightarrow x>12 \quad \text{...(viii)}$$

There is no value of x which satisfies (v) and (viii) i.e., there is no common solution of the given two inequalities. Hence there is no solution of the given system of inequalities.

GRAPH OF A LINEAR EQUATION

(i) To draw the graph of a linear equation containing both x and y, find the point on the x-axis (by putting $y = 0$ in the equation) and on the y-axis (by putting $x = 0$ in the equation). Draw a line by joining these two points. This line is the graph of the given linear equation.

(ii) The graph of the equation $x = a$ (or $y = b$) is a straight line perpendicular to the x-axis at $x = a$ (or y-axis at $y = b$) where 'a' and 'b' are any real number.

ILLUSTRATION : 6

Draw the graph of $2x - y + 1 = 0$

SOLUTION :

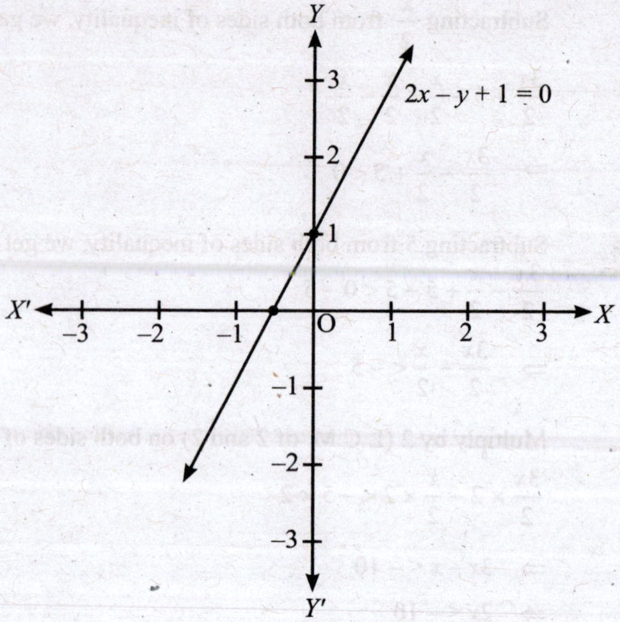

Consider $2x - y + 1 = 0$ ...(i)

Put $y = 0$ in equation (i), we get

$2x = -1 \Rightarrow x = -\frac{1}{2}$

Put $x = 0$ in equation (i), we get

$2 \times 0 - y + 1 = 0 \Rightarrow y = 1$

x	$-\frac{1}{2}$	0
y	0	1

ILLUSTRATION : 7

Draw the graph of (i) $x = -3$ (ii) $y = \frac{7}{2}$

SOLUTION :

(i)

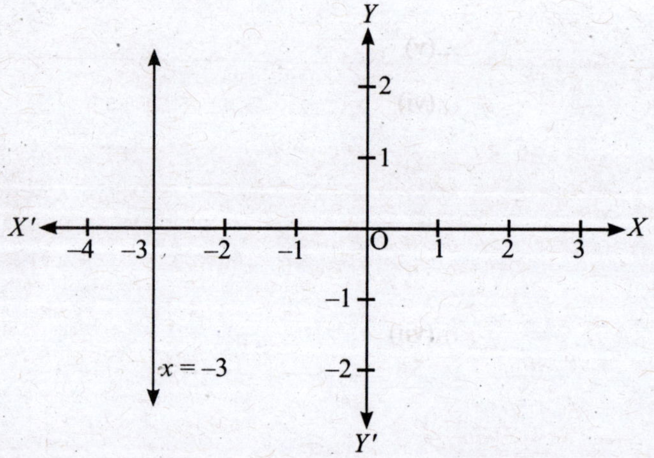

(ii)

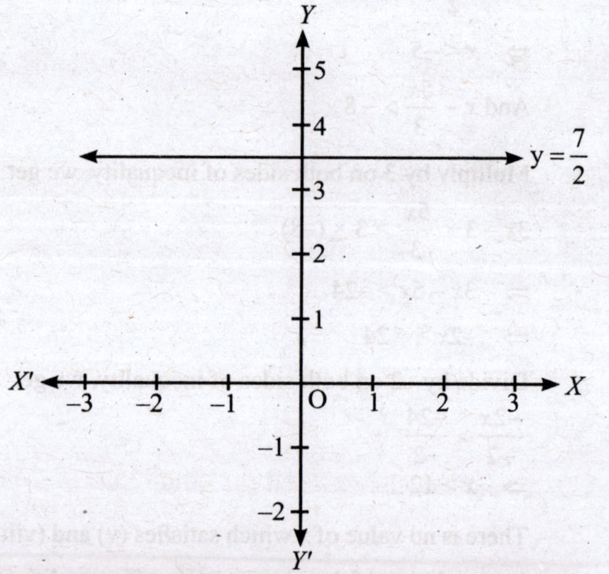

TO FIND THE GRAPHICAL SOLUTION OF A LINEAR INEQUALITY IN TWO VARIABLES IN A CARTESIAN PLANE

(i) Draw the graph of the linear equation in two variables corresponding to the linear inequalities in two variables.

(ii) The line drawn in step (i) divide the cartesian plane in two half planes.

(iii) Take any point on either side of the line drawn in step (i), if co-ordinate of this point satisfy the linear inequality, then the half plane containing this point is the solution region of the inequality of the form $ax + by > c$ or $ax + by < c$

Hence to show the solution region of this form of inequality we shade the solution region. The point on the line $ax + by = c$ are not included in the solution region. So, the line drawn in step (i) should be broken or dotted, which means line is not included in the solution region.

If the inequality of the form $ax + by \geq c$ or $ax + by \leq c$, then the solution region is the half plane satisfy $ax + by > c$ or $ax + by < c$ containing all the points on the line $ax + by = c$. Hence to show the solution region of this form of inequality, we shade and dark the line drawn in step (i), which shows the solution region is the shaded half plane containing the line.

ILLUSTRATION : 8

Solve the following inequations graphically $2x - y \geq 1$

SOLUTION :

Converting the given inequation into equation, we obtain $2x - y = 1$. This line meets x and y-axes at $A(1/2, 0)$ and $B(0,-1)$ respectively. Joining these points by a thick line we obtain the line passing through A and B as shown in Fig. This line divides the xy-plane into two regions viz. one lying above it and the other lying below it. Consider the point $O(0,0)$. Clearly, (0,0) does not satisfy the inequation $2x - y \geq 1$. So, the region not containing the origin is represented by the given inequation as shown in Fig. Clearly it represents the solution set of the given inequation.

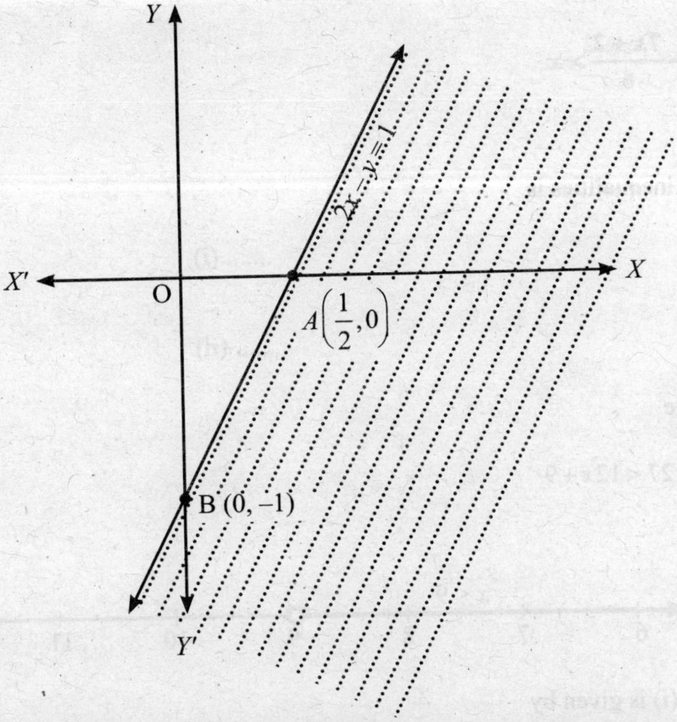

GRAPHICAL SOLUTION OF SYSTEM OF LINEAR INEQUALITIES IN TWO VARIABLES

(i) Shade the solution region of each linear inequality in different ways.

(ii) The common shaded region of all the regions of linear inequalities of the given system of linear inequalities in two variables is the solution region.

ILLUSTRATION : 9

Draw the graph of the solution set of the system of linear inequations $3x + 4y \geq 12, y \geq 1, x \geq 0$

SOLUTION :

Converting the inequations into equations, we get

$3x + 4y = 12, y = 1, x = 0$

Region Represented by $3x + 4y \geq 12$: The line $3x + 4y = 12$ meets the coordinate axes at $A(0, 4)$ and $B(0, 3)$ joining these points by a thick line we get the graph of $3x + 4y = 12$. Since (0, 0) does not satisfy the inequation $3x+4y \geq 12$. So, the half plane on the right side of the line repersented by $3x+4y=12$ including the line is represented by the inequation $3x + 4y \geq 12$.

Region Represented by $y \geq 1$: The line $y = 1$ is parallel to x-axis at a unit distance from it. Since (0, 0) does not satisfy the inequation $y \geq 1$. So, the region lying above and including the line $y = 1$ is represented by $y \geq 1$.

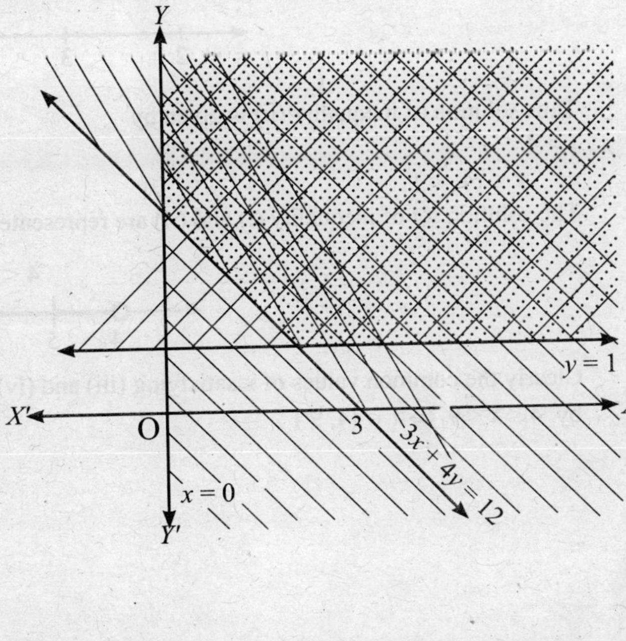

Region Represented by $x \geq 0$: Clearly, $x \geq 0$ represents the region lying on the right side of y-axis including y-axis. The solution set of the given system of linear equations is the intersection of the above regions as shown in Figure.

SOME APPLICATIONS OF LINEAR INEQUATIONS IN ONE VARIABLE

In this section, we shall use the knowledge of solving linear inequations in one variable in solving different problems from various fields. Following illustrations will be helpful to understand this.

ILLUSTRATION : 10

Find the solution of the following system of linear inequalities.

$$\frac{4x}{3}-\frac{9}{4}<x+\frac{3}{4},\quad \frac{7x-1}{3}-\frac{7x+2}{6}>x$$

SOLUTION :

The given system of linear inequalities is

$$\frac{4x}{3}-\frac{9}{4}<x+\frac{3}{4} \quad \text{....... (i)}$$

$$\frac{7x-1}{3}-\frac{7x+2}{6}>x \quad \text{....... (ii)}$$

From inequality (i), we have

$$\frac{16x-27}{12}<\frac{4x+3}{4} \Rightarrow 16x-27<12x+9$$

$$\Rightarrow \quad 4x<36 \Rightarrow x<9$$

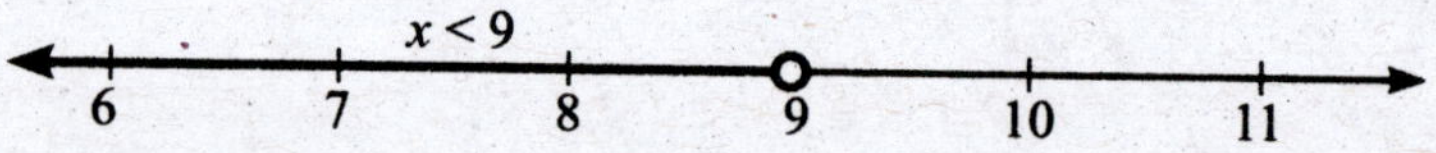

Thus solution of inequality (i) is given by

$x<9$ .... (iii)

$\Rightarrow \quad x \in (-\infty, 9)$

From inequality (ii), we get

$$\frac{14x-2}{6}-\frac{7x+2}{6}>x \Rightarrow 14x-2-7x-2>6x$$

$$\Rightarrow \quad 7x-4>6x \Rightarrow x>4 \Rightarrow x \in (4, \infty)$$

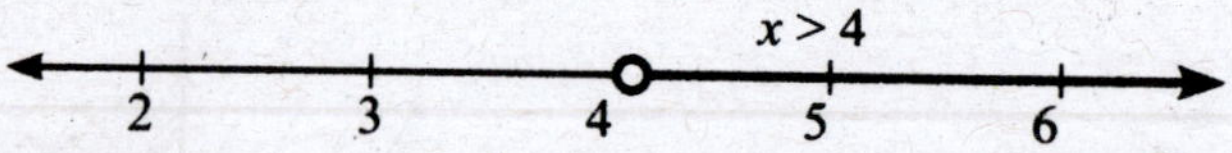

Thus solution of inequality (ii) is given by

$x>4$ .... (iv)

$\Rightarrow \quad x \in (4, \infty)$

The solution set of inequality (i) and (ii) are represented graphically on real line :

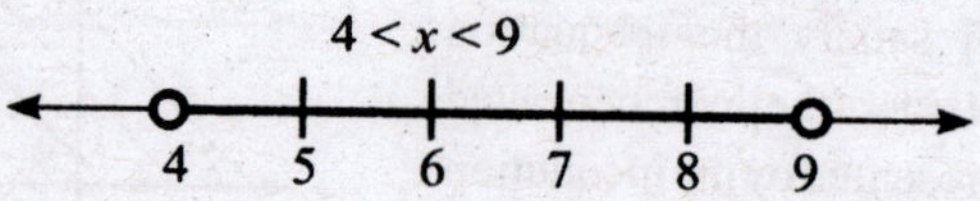

Clearly the common values of x satisfying (iii) and (iv), lie between 4 and 9. Hence the solution of the given system is given by $4<x<9 \Rightarrow x \in (4, 9)$

ILLUSTRATION : 11

Ravi obtained 70 and 75 marks in first two unit test. Find the number if minimum marks he should get in the third test to have an average of at least 60 marks.

SOLUTION :

Let Ravi get x marks is third unit test

$\therefore$ Average marks obtained by Ravi $= \dfrac{70+75+x}{3}$

He is obtained atleast 60 marks

$\therefore \quad \dfrac{70+75+x}{3} \geq 60 \Rightarrow \dfrac{145+x}{3} \geq 60$

Multiplying by 3, $145+x \geq 60 \times 3 = 180$

Transposing 145 to RHS $\Rightarrow x \geq 180-145 = 35$

$\therefore$ Ravi should got atleast 35 marks in the third unit test.

ILLUSTRATION : 12

A man wants to cut three lengths from a single piece of board of length 91 cm, the second length is to be 3cm longer than the shortest and the third length is to be twice as long as the shortest. What are the possible lengths of the shortest board if the third piece is to be at least 5cm longer than the second ?

SOLUTION :

Let x be the length of the shortest board, then $x + 3$ is the second length and $2x$ is the third length. Thus,

$x + (x + 3) + 2x \leq 91 \quad \Rightarrow \quad 4x + 3 \leq 91 \quad \Rightarrow \quad 4x \leq 88 \quad \Rightarrow \quad x \leq 22$

According to the problem,

$2x \geq (x + 3) + 5 \quad \Rightarrow \quad x \geq 8$

At least 8 cm long but not more than 22 cm long.

EXERCISE

Single Option Correct :

DIRECTIONS: *This section contains multiple choice questions. Each questions has 4 choices (a), (b), (c) and (d) out of which ONLY ONE is correct.*

1. Which of the following representation of the solution set of the inequation $12+1\frac{5}{6}x \le 5+3x,\ x \in R$ on a number line is correct?

(a) 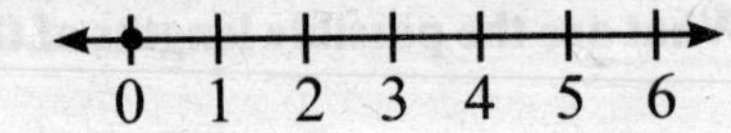

(b) 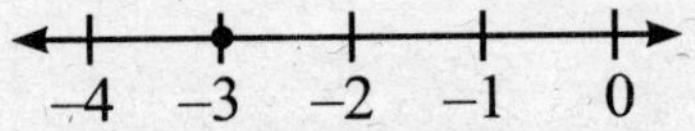

(c) 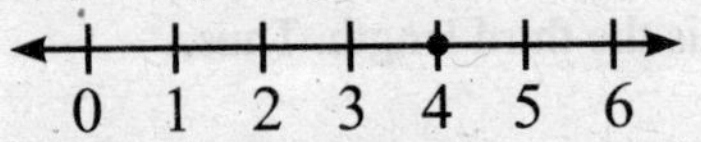

(d) 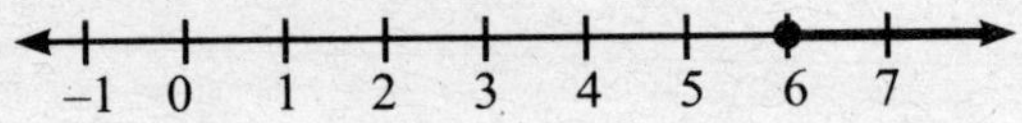

2. If $7 \le \frac{3x+11}{2} \le 11$, then

(a) $1 < x < \frac{11}{3}$ (b) $x = 1$

(c) $1 \le x \le \frac{11}{3}$ (d) $-1 \le x \le \frac{-11}{3}$

3. In the diagram below, the unshaded region R is defined by three inequalities, one of which is $x \ge 0$. The other two inequalities are:

(a) $x + y \le 3, y \ge 1$ (b) $x + y \ge 3, y \le 1$
(c) $x - y \le 3, x \le 1$ (d) $x - y \ge 3, x \ge 1$

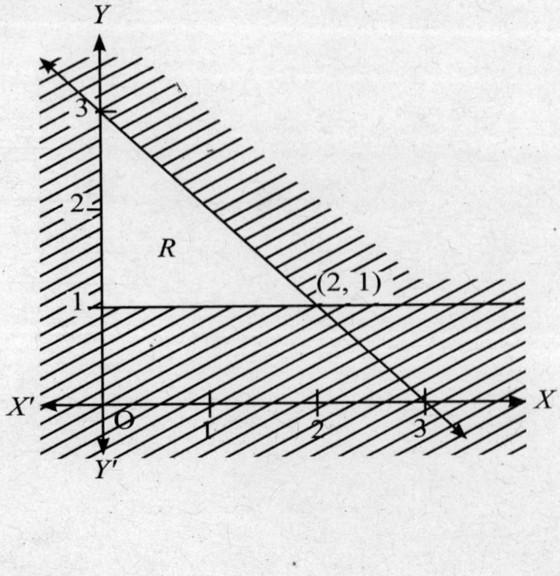

4. To receive grade 'A' in a course, one must obtain an average of 90 marks or more in five examinations (each of 100 marks). If Sunita's marks in first four examination are 87, 92, 94 and 95. The minimum marks that Sunita must obtain in fifth examination to get grade 'A' in the course, is

(a) 82 (b) 83
(c) 85 (d) 90

5. If $\frac{x+3}{x-3} < 1$, then which of the following cannot be the value of x ?

(a) 0 (b) 1
(c) 2 (d) 4

6. If $0 < \frac{2x-5}{2} < 7$ and x is an integer, then the sum of the greatest and least value of x is

(a) 9 (b) 10
(c) 6 (d) 12

7. The common solution set of the inequations $5 \le 2x + 7 \le 8$ and $7 \le 3x + 5 \le 9$ is

(a) $\frac{2}{3} \le x \le \frac{4}{3}$ (b) $-1 \le x \le \frac{4}{3}$

(c) $\frac{2}{3} \le x \le \frac{1}{2}$ (d) Null set

8. Set of solution for :
$(x+5) - 7(x-2) \ge 4x + 9$ and
$2(x-3) - 7(x+5) \le 3x - 9$ is

(a) $[-4, 1]$ (b) $[1, 1]$
(c) $[2, 1]$ (d) $[-3, 1]$

9. If x and y are any two positive real numbers, then $x > y$ implies,

(a) $-x < -y$ (b) $-x > -y$

(c) $\frac{1}{x} > \frac{1}{y}$ (d) $\frac{-1}{x} > \frac{1}{y}$

10.

Column-I (Inequalities)	**Column-II (Solution Set)**
(A) $-11 \le 4x - 3 \le 13$	(1) $[2, 4]$
(B) $3x - 6 \ge 0$ and $4x - 10 \le 0$	(2) $(-\infty, -3]$
(C) $4x - 12 \ge 0$	(3) $(3, \infty)$
(D) $7x + 9 > 30$	(4) $[3, \infty)$
(E) $3x + 17 \le 2(1 - x)$	(5) $[-2, 4]$

A B C D E

(a) 5 1 4 3 2
(b) 1 5 4 3 2
(c) 4 3 2 1 5
(d) 3 4 2 1 5

More than One Option Correct :

DIRECTIONS: *This section contains multiple choice questions. Each question has 4 choices (a), (b), (c) and (d) out of which ONE or MORE may be correct.*

1. All pairs of consecutive odd positive integers, both of which are smaller than 18, such that their sum is more than 20, are
   (a) (11, 13) (b) (13, 15)
   (c) (15, 17) (d) None of these

Integer Type Questions :

DIRECTIONS : *Answer the following questions. The answer to each of the question is a single digit integer, ranging from 0 to 9.*

1. Solution of the following system of linear inequalities : $x + 2 > 11$; $2x \le 20$ is (a, 10]. The value of 'a' is
2. The longest side of a triangle is 3 times the shortest side and the third side is 2 cm shorter than the longest side. If the perimeter of the triangle is at least 61 cm, find the minimum length of the shortest side.
3. Solve: $-3 \le 4 - \frac{7x}{2} \le 18$. Solution is $[-4, b]$. Find value of *b*.
4. Solve: $-15 < \frac{3(x-2)}{5} \le 0$, $x \in (-23, b)$. Find *b*.

SOLUTIONS

Brief Explanations of Selected Questions

EXERCISE

SINGLE OPTION CORRECT :

1. (d) We have $12 + 1\frac{5}{6}x \le 5 + 3x \Rightarrow 12 + \frac{11}{6}x \le 5 + 3x$

$\Rightarrow$ $72 + 11x \le 30 + 18x$
[Multiplying both sides by 6]
$\Rightarrow$ $11x \le 18x - 42$
[Adding –72 on both sides]
$\Rightarrow$ $-7x \le -42$ [Adding $-18x$ on both sides]
$\Rightarrow$ $x \ge 6$
[Dividing both sides by –7]

$\therefore$ Solution set $= \{x : x \ge 6, x \in R\}$

2. (c) Multiplying by 2, we get $7 \times 2 \le \frac{3x+11}{2} \times 2 \le 11 \times 2$

$\Rightarrow 14 \le 3x + 11 \le 22$
Subtracting by 11
$14 - 11 \le 3x + 11 - 11 \le 22 - 11 \Rightarrow 3 \le 3x \le 11$

Dividing by 3, $1 \le x \le \frac{11}{3}$ or $x \in \left[1, \frac{11}{3}\right]$

i.e., x is greater than or equal to 1 and less than or equal to $\frac{11}{3}$

3. (a) Other two inequalities are $x + y \le 3$ and $y \ge 1$.
4. (a) Let Sunita obtain x marks in the fourth examination.
$\therefore$ Average of marks of 5 examinations.

$$= \frac{87 + 92 + 94 + 95 + x}{5} = \frac{368 + x}{5}$$

This average must be atleast equal to 90

$\Rightarrow$ $\frac{368 + x}{5} \ge 90$

$\Rightarrow$ $368 + x \ge 5 \times 90 = 450$

$\Rightarrow$ $x \ge 450 - 368 = 82$

i.e. She should obtain atleast 82 marks in the fifth examination.

5. (d) Given, $\frac{x+3}{x-3} < 1$

Subtract 1 on both side, $\frac{x+3}{x-3} - 1 < 1 - 1$

$\Rightarrow$ $\frac{x+3-x+3}{x-3} < 0$

$\Rightarrow$ $\frac{6}{x-3} < 0$

$\Rightarrow$ x cannot be equal to 4.

6. (d) Given, $0 < \frac{2x-5}{2} < 7$

Multiply by 2 on each side, $0 < 2x - 5 < 14$

Add 5 on each side,

$0+5<2x-5+5<14+5$

$\Rightarrow 5<2x<19$

$\Rightarrow \frac{5}{2}<x<\frac{19}{2}$

So, Required sum $=\frac{5}{2}+\frac{19}{2}=\frac{24}{2}=12$

7. (d) Consider $5\le 2x+7\le 8$

$\Rightarrow -2\le 2x\le 1$

$\Rightarrow -1\le x\le \frac{1}{2}$

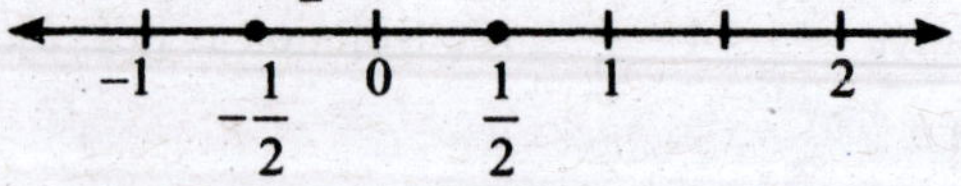

Consider $7\le 3x+5\le 9$

$\Rightarrow 2\le 3x\le 4$

$\Rightarrow \frac{2}{3}\le x\le \frac{4}{3}$

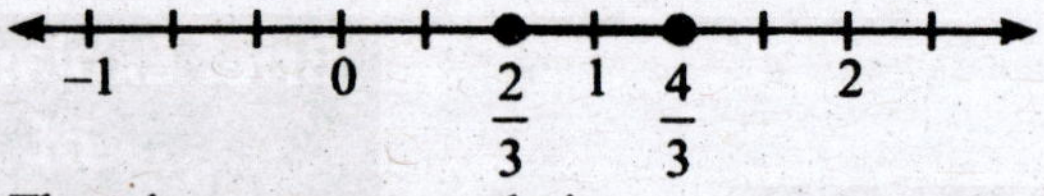

There is no common solution set.

8. (a) $(x+5)-7(x-2)\ge 4x+9$

$\Rightarrow 19-6x\ge 4x+9$

$\Rightarrow 10\ge 10x$

$\Rightarrow x\le 1$ .....(i)

$2(x-3)-7(x+5)\le 3x-9$

$\Rightarrow -5x-41\le 3x-9$

$\Rightarrow -8x-41\le -9$

$\Rightarrow x\ge -4$ ....(ii)

Thus, from (i) and (ii)

$-4\le x\le 1$

9. (a) $x>y \Rightarrow -x<-y$

10. (a)

MORE THAN ONE OPTION CORRECT :

1. (a, b, c)

Let x be the smaller of the two consecutive odd positive integers. Then, the other odd integer is x + 2. It is given that both the integers are smaller than 18 and their sum is more than 20.

Therefore,

$x+2<18$ and, $x+(x+2)>20$

$\Rightarrow x<16$ and $2x+2>20$

$\Rightarrow x<16$ and $2x>18$

$\Rightarrow x<16$ and $x>9$

$\Rightarrow 9<x<16$

$\Rightarrow x=11, 13, 15$ [$\because$ x is an odd integer]

Hence, the required pairs of odd integers are (11, 13), (13, 15) and (15, 17).

INTEGER BASED QUESTIONS :

1. **Ans : 9**

The given system of inequalities is

$x+2>11$ .... (i)

$2x\le 20$ ... (ii)

Now, $x+2>11 \Rightarrow x>11-2$

$\Rightarrow x>9 \Rightarrow x\in(9,\infty)$

$\therefore$ Solution of inequality (i) is $x>9$ ... (iii)

and $2x\le 20 \Rightarrow x\le 10 \Rightarrow x\in(-\infty, 10]$

$\therefore$ Solution of inequality (ii) is $x\le 10$ ... (iv)

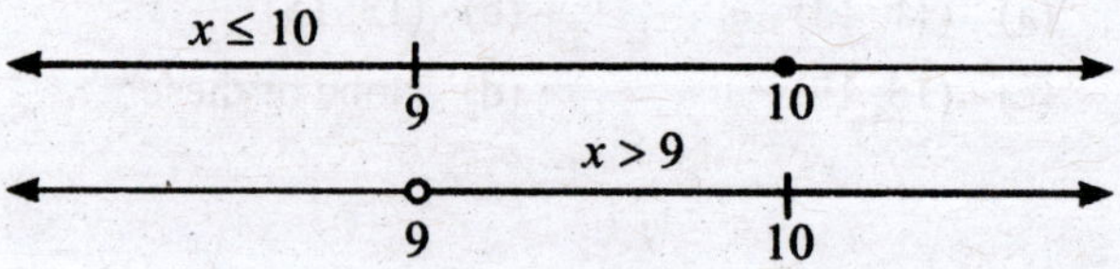

Hence, the solution of the given system is given by $9<x\le 10 \Rightarrow x\in(9, 10]$

2. **Ans : 9**

Let shortest side measure x cm. Therefore the longest side will be $3x$ cm and third side will be $(3x-2)$ cm

According to the problem,

$x+3x+3x-2\ge 61 \Rightarrow 7x-2\ge 61$

or $7x\ge 63 \Rightarrow x\ge 9$cm

Hence, the minimum length of the shortest side is 9 cm and the other sides measure 27 cm and 25 cm.

3. **Ans : 2**

Subtract 4, we get

$-3-4\le 4-\frac{7x}{2}-4\le 18-4 \Rightarrow -7\le -\frac{7x}{2}\le 14$

Dividing by $\frac{-7}{2}$, $-7\times\frac{-2}{7}\ge -\frac{7x}{2}\times\frac{-2}{7}\ge 14\times\frac{-2}{7}$

$\Rightarrow 2\ge x\ge -4 \Rightarrow x\in[-4, 2]$

$\therefore$ x is less than or equal to 2 and greater than or equal to –4.

4. **Ans : 2**

Multiplying by 5,

$-15\times 5<\frac{3(x-2)}{5}\times 5\le 0\times 5 \Rightarrow -75<3(x-2)\le 0$

$\Rightarrow \frac{-75}{3}<x-2\le\frac{0}{3}$ (Divide by 3)

or $-25<x-2\le 0$

Adding 2, we get

$-25+2<x-2+2\le 0+2 \Rightarrow -23<x\le 2$

Hence, x is less than or equal to 2 and greater than – 23 i.e. $x\in(-23, 2)$

Chapter 17

PERMUTATIONS AND COMBINATIONS

INTRODUCTION

In this chapter, you will study how to arrange several things (which are distinct or non-distinct) in some specific order and number of ways in which the specific things arranged in some given order. You will also study in this chapter that how many groups are formed from the given various things, when specific thing can be selected in the groups.

Also, the study of permutations and combinations is concerned with determining the number of different ways of arranging and selecting objects out of a given number of objects without actually listing them.

FUNDAMENTAL PRINCIPLES OF COUNTING

(a) Principle of Addition

If an event can occur in 'm' ways and another event can occur in 'n' ways independent of the first event, then either of the two events can occur in $(m + n)$ ways.

ILLUSTRATION : 1

In a class there are 10 boys and 8 girls. The class teacher wants to select a student for monitor of the class. In how many ways the class teacher can make this selection ?

SOLUTION:

The teacher can select a student for monitor in two exclusive ways

(i) Select a boy among 10 boys, which can be done in 10 ways OR

(ii) Select a girl among 8 girls, which can be done in 8 ways.

Hence, by the fundamental principle of addition, either a boy or a girl can be selected in $10 + 8 = 18$ ways.

(b) Principle of Multiplication

If there are two jobs such that one of them can be completed in m ways and when it has been completed in any one of these m ways, second job can be completed in n ways; then the two jobs in succession can be completed in $m \times n$ ways.

ILLUSTRATION : 2

In a class there are 10 boys and 8 girls. The teacher wants to select a boy and a girl to represent the class in a function. In how many ways can the teacher make this selection?

SOLUTION:

The teacher has to perform two jobs :

(i) To select a boy among 10 boys, which can be done in 10 ways.

(ii) To select a girl, among 8 girls, which can be done in 8 ways.

Hence, the required number of ways = $10 \times 8 = 80$.

FACTORIALS

$n!$ or $\lfloor n$ is read as n factorial, where n is a whole number (or non-negative integer) and $n! = n.(n-1).(n-2) \ldots 3.2.1$

Examples :

(i) $8! = 8 \times 7 \times 6 \times 5 \times 4 \times 3 \times 2 \times 1$

(ii) $5! = 5 \times 4 \times 3 \times 2 \times 1$

(iii) $11! = 11 \times 10 \times 9 \times 8!$

(iv) $1! = 1 = 0!$

(v) $8! + 5! = 8 \times 7 \times 6 \times 5! + 5!$

$= 5! \times (8 \times 7 \times 6 + 1)$

$= 5! \times 337$

(vi) $8! - 5! = 8 \times 7 \times 6 \times 5! - 5!$

$= 5! \times (8 \times 7 \times 6 - 1)$

$= 5! \times 335$

(vii) $\dfrac{5}{8!} + \dfrac{3}{6!} = \dfrac{5 + (8 \times 7) \times 5}{8!}$

(viii) $\dfrac{5!}{9!} = \dfrac{5!}{9 \times 8 \times 7 \times 6 \times 5!} = \dfrac{1}{9 \times 8 \times 7 \times 6}$

(ix) $5! \times 3! \neq 15!$

> **NOTE :** L.C.M of $a!$ and $b!$ is $a!$, if $a > b$

ILLUSTRATION : 3

If $\dfrac{1}{6!} + \dfrac{1}{7!} = \dfrac{x}{8!}$, find x.

SOLUTION:

$$\frac{1}{6!} + \frac{1}{7!} = \frac{1}{6 \times 5 \times 4 \times 3 \times 2 \times 1} + \frac{1}{7 \times 6 \times 5 \times 4 \times 3 \times 2 \times 1}$$

$$= \frac{7+1}{7\times6\times5\times4\times3\times2\times1} = \frac{8}{7\times6\times5\times4\times3\times2\times1} \quad \frac{8\times8}{8\times7\times6\times5\times4\times3\times2\times1} = \frac{64}{8!}$$

$$\Rightarrow \frac{64}{8!} = \frac{x}{8!} \Rightarrow x = 64$$

PERMUTATIONS AND COMBINATIONS

(a) Permutations

Each of the arrangements, which can be made by taking some or all of a number of things is called a permutation.

(b) Combinations

Each of the different selections that can be made with a given number of objects taken some or all of them is called a combination.

DIFFERENCE BETWEEN PERMUTATION AND COMBINATION

To understand the difference between permutation and combinations clearly consider the following example.
If we have 4 objects A, B, C and D the possible selection (or combination) and arrangements (or permutations) of 3 objects out of 4 are given below.

Selection (Combination)	Arrangement (Permutation)
ABC	ABC, ACB, BAC, BCA, CAB, CBA
ABD	ABD, ADB, BAD, BDA, DAB, DBA
ACD	ACD, ADC, CAD, CDA, DAC, DCA
BCD	BCD, BDC, CBD, CDB, DBC, DCB
No. of combinations = 4	No. of permutations = 24

NUMBER OF PERMUTATIONS OF n ELEMENTS

(a) The number of permutations of n different things taken all at a time when repetition is not allowed is given by

$n\,.\,(n-1)\,.\,.\,.\,4\,.\,3\,.\,2\,.\,1 = n!$

(b) The number of permutations of n different things taken r at a time, where repetition is not allowed, is denoted by ^nP_r [or $P(n, r)$] and is given by $^nP_r = \dfrac{n!}{(n-r)!}$, where $0 \le r \le n$.

(c) The number of permutations of n different things, taken r at a time, where repetition is allowed, is $(n)^r$.

(d) The number of permutations of n objects taken all at a time, where p_1 objects are of first kind, p_2 objects are of the second kind, ..., p_k objects are of the kth kind and rest, if any, are all different is $\dfrac{n!}{p_1!\,p_2!\ldots\ldots p_k!}$.

(e) The number of circular permutations of n different things taken all at a time is $\dfrac{^nP_n}{n} = (n-1)\,!$, if clockwise and anticlockwise orders are taken as different.

(f) Arrangements of beads or flowers (all different) around a circular necklace or garland:

The number of circular permutations of 'n' different things taken all at a time is $\dfrac{1}{2}(n-1)!$, if clockwise and anticlockwise orders are taken to be same.

ILLUSTRATION : 4

Find n if $^{n-1}P_3 : {}^nP_4 = 1 : 9$

SOLUTION:

$$\frac{^{n-1}P_3}{^nP_4} = \frac{1}{9} \text{ or } \frac{(n-1)(n-2)(n-3)}{n(n-1)(n-2)(n-3)} = \frac{1}{9}$$

$$\frac{1}{n} = \frac{1}{9} \text{ or } n = 9$$

NUMBER OF COMBINATION OF *n* ELEMENTS

(a) The number of combinations of n different things taken r at a time, denoted by ^nC_r [or $C(n, r)$], is given by

$$^nC_r = \frac{n!}{r!(n-r)!} \frac{n(n-1)(n-2)...(n-r+1)}{r!}, \; 0 \le r \le n$$

(b) The total number of selections of r things from n different things when each thing may be repeated any number of times is $^{n+r-1}C_r$.

ILLUSTRATION : 5

How many words with or without meaning, each of 2 vowels and 3 consonants can be formed from the letters of the word DAUGHTER?

SOLUTION:

The word DAUGHTER consists of 3 vowels and 5 consonants

2 vowels and 3 consonants may be selected in $^3C_2 \times {}^5C_3$ ways

$$= {}^3C_1 \times {}^5C_2 \text{ ways} = \frac{3}{1} \times \frac{5 \times 4}{1 \times 2} = 30 \text{ ways}$$

5 letters can be arranged in 5! ways or in $5 \times 4 \times 3 \times 2 \times 1 = 120$ ways

Number of words formed by 2 vowels and 3 consonants which are selected from the word DAUGHTER = $30 \times 120 = 3600$

ILLUSTRATION : 6

In how many ways can a student choose a programme of 5 courses if 9 courses are available and two courses are compulsory for every students?

SOLUTION:

Out of available nine courses, two are compulsory

Hence, the student is free to select 3 courses out of 7 remaining courses. If P is the number of ways of selecting 3 courses out of 7 courses, then

$$P = C(7, 3) = \frac{7!}{3!(7-3)!} = \frac{7!}{3!4!} = \frac{7 \times 6 \times 5 \times 4!}{3 \times 2 \times 1 \times 4!} = 7 \times 5 = 35 \text{ ways}$$

Notations : $^nC_0 = C_0 = 1, \; ^nC_1 = C_1 = n, \; ^nC_2 = C_2 = \frac{n(n-1)}{2!}, ...$

Remarks :

(i) $^nC_n = 1$

(ii) $^nC_0 = 1$

(iii) $^nC_r = \frac{^nP_r}{r!}, \; 0 < r \le n.$

(iv) $^nC_r = {}^nC_{n-r}, (1 < r < n)$

(v) $^nC_r = \frac{n}{r}\, {}^{n-1}C_{r-1} = \frac{n}{r} \cdot \frac{n-1}{r-1}\, {}^{n-2}C_{r-2} = ...$

(vi) $n\left({}^{n-1}C_{r-1}\right) = (n-r+1)\; {}^nC_{r-1}$

(vii) If $^nC_r = {}^nC_{r'}$, then either $r = r'$ or $r + r' = n$

(viii) $^nC_r + {}^nC_{r-1} = {}^{n+1}C_r$

(ix) $^nC_1 + {}^nC_2 + {}^nC_3 + ... + {}^nC_n = 2^n - 1$

(x) $^nC_0 + {}^nC_1 + {}^nC_2 + {}^nC_3 + ... + {}^nC_n = 2^n \; (\because \; {}^nC_0 = 1)$

NOTE : (i) $^nC_r = {}^nC_{n-r}$; if $1 < r < n$

(ii) $^nC_r = {}^nC_{r-1} = {}^{n+1}C_r$

(iii) $^nC_r + {}^nC_{r-1} = {}^{n+1}C_r$

EXERCISE

Single Option Correct :

DIRECTIONS : *This section contains multiple choice questions. Each question has 4 choices (a), (b), (c) and (d) out of which ONLY ONE is correct.*

1. Number of different permutations, each containing all letters of the word "STATESMAN" is
(a) 90720 (b) 45360
(c) 22680 (d) None of these

2. The total number of 9 digit numbers, which have all different digits is
(a) 9! (b) 8!
(c) $9 \times 9!$ (d) None of these

3. Number of 6-digit telephone numbers, which can be constructed with digits 0, 1, 2, 3, 4, 5, 6, 7, 8, 9, if each number starts with 35 and no digit appears more than once is
(a) 1680 (b) 8!
(c) 6! (d) 6.6 !

4. If ${}^nC_9 = {}^nC_8$, what is the value of ${}^nC_{17}$?
(a) 1 (b) 0
(c) 3 (d) 17

5. If ${}^{10}C_x = {}^{10}C_{x+4}$, then the value of x, is
(a) 5 (b) 4
(c) 3 (d) 2

6. What is the value of ${}^nP_0$?
(a) 0 (b) 1
(c) ∞ (d) $\frac{1}{2}$

7. What is the value of ${}^nC_n$?
(a) 0 (b) ∞
(c) r (d) 1

8. What is the value of ${}^nC_0$?
(a) 0 (b) ∞
(c) 1 (d) None of these

9. Six persons A, B, C, D, E and F are to be seated at a circular table. The number of ways, this can be done if A must have either B or C on his right and B must have either C or D on his right is
(a) 36 (b) 12
(c) 24 (d) 18

10. Given five line segments of length 2, 3, 4, 5, 6 units. Then the number of triangles that can be formed by joining these lines is
(a) ${}^5C_3 - 3$ (b) ${}^5C_3 - 1$
(c) ${}^5C_3$ (d) ${}^5C_3 - 2$

11. Find n if ${}^{n-1}P_3 : {}^nP_4 = 1 : 9$
(a) 9 (b) 1
(c) 8 (d) 7

12. How many chords can be drawn through 21 points on a circle?
(a) 120 (b) 210
(c) 102 (d) 21

13. Compute $\frac{8!}{6! \times 2!}$
(a) 82 (b) 28
(c) 22 (d) 56

14. If ${}^nC_8 = {}^nC_2$. Find ${}^nC_2$.
(a) 45 (b) 46
(c) 47 (d) 48

15. A box contains two white balls, three black balls and four red balls. No. of ways can three balls be drawn from the box if atleast one black ball is to be included in the draw is
(a) 129 (b) 84
(c) 64 (d) None of these

16. The number of ways in which four letters of the word MATHEMATICS can be arranged is given by
(a) 136 (b) 192
(c) 1680 (d) 2454

More Than One Option Correct :

DIRECTIONS : *This section contains multiple choice questions. Each question has 4 choices (a), (b), (c) and (d) out of which ONE OR MORE may be correct.*

1. Which among the following is/ are correct ?
(a) If an operation can be performed in 'm' different ways and a second operation can be performed in 'n' different ways, then both of these operations can be performed in '$m \times n$' ways together.
(b) The number of arrangements of n different objects taken all at a time is $n!$.
(c) The number of permutations of n different things taken r at a time, when each thing may be repeated any number of times is n^r.
(d) The number of circular permutations of 'n' different things taken all at a time is $\frac{1}{2}(n-1)!$, if clockwise and anticlockwise orders are taken as different.

2. $C(8, 3) = ?$

(a) $\frac{P(8,3)}{3!}$ (b) $C(8, 5)$

(c) 56 (d) $P(8, 5)$

3. To fill up 12 vacancies, there are 25 candidates of which 5 are from SC. If 3 of these vacancies are reserved for SC candidates while the remaining are open to all then the number of ways in which the selection can be made is

(a) ${}^5C_2 \times {}^{22}C_{13}$ (b) ${}^5C_3 \times {}^{22}C_9$

(c) ${}^5C_3 \times {}^{23}C_8$ (d) ${}^8C_5 \times {}^{21}C_7$

4. ${}^{10}P_0$ corresponds to which value of the following given options.

(a) 0 (b) ${}^{10}C_0$

(c) 1 (d) 10

5. Which of the following is/are not correct?

(a) ${}^6C_2 + {}^6C_1 = {}^7C_2$ (b) ${}^6C_1 + {}^6C_2 = {}^6C_2$

(c) ${}^6C_2 + {}^6C_1 = {}^7C_1$ (d) ${}^6C_2 - {}^6C_1 = {}^7C_2$

6. The number of ways in which a team of eleven players can be selected from 22 players, always including 2 of them and excluding 4 of them is

(a) ${}^{16}C_{11}$ (b) ${}^{16}C_7$

(c) ${}^{16}C_9$ (d) ${}^{20}C_9$

Passage Based Questions :

DIRECTIONS : *Study the given paragraph(s) and answer the following questions.*

PASSAGE - I

There are 4 candidates for a Natural science scholarship, 2 for a classical and 6 for a Mathematical scholarship.

1. No. of ways these scholarships can be awarded is

(a) 48 (b) 12

(c) 24 (d) 8

2. No. of ways one of these scholarship can be awarded is

(a) 6 (b) 10

(c) 48 (d) 12

PASSAGE - II

In how many ways can a cricket eleven be chosen out of a batch of 15 players if

3. there is no restriction on the selection;

(a) ${}^{15}C_0$ (b) ${}^{15}C_1$

(c) ${}^{15}C_{11}$ (d) None of these

4. a particular player is always chosen;

(a) ${}^{14}C_4$ (b) ${}^{14}C_1$

(c) ${}^{14}C_{13}$ (d) None of these

5. a particular player is never chosen?

(a) ${}^{14}C_3$ (b) ${}^{14}C_0$

(c) ${}^{14}C_{14}$ (d) None of these

Assertion & Reason :

DIRECTIONS : *Each of these questions contains an Assertion followed by Reason. Read them carefully and answer the question on the basis of following options. You have to select the one that best describes the two statements.*

(a) If both **Assertion** and **Reason** are **correct** and Reason is the **correct explanation** of Assertion.

(b) If both **Assertion** and **Reason** are correct, but Reason is **not the correct explanation** of Assertion.

(c) If **Assertion** is **correct** but **Reason** is **incorrect**.

(d) If **Assertion** is **incorrect** but **Reason** is **correct**.

1. **Assertion :** The maximum number of points of intersection of 8 circles of unequal radii is 56.

Reason : The maximum number of points into which 4 circles of unequal radii and 4 non coincident straight lines intersect, is 50.

2. Consider the word 'SMALL'

Assertion : Total number of 3 letter words from the letters of the given word is 13.

Reason : Number of words having all the letters distinct = 4 and number of words having two are alike and third different = 9

3. **Assertion :** The number of ways of selecting 5 students from 12 students (of which six are boys and six are girls), such that in the selection there are at least three girls is ${}^6C_3\ {}^9C_2$.

Reason : If a work has two independent parts, of which first part can be done in *m* way and for each choice of first part, the second part can be done in *n* ways, then the work can be completed in $m \times n$ ways.

4. **Assertion :** A polygon has 44 diagonals and number of sides are 11.

Reason : From *n* distinct objects *r* objects can be selected in ${}^nC_r$ ways.

Multiple Matching Question :

DIRECTIONS : *Following question has four statements (A, B, C and D) given in Column-I and four statements (p, q, r and s) in Column-II. Any given statement in Column-I can have correct matching with one or more statement(s) given in Column-II.*

1.

Column-I	Column-II
(A) ${}^{20}C_{19}$	(p) 20!
(B) ${}^{20}P_{19}$	(q) ${}^{20}C_1$
(C) ${}^6C_3 - {}^6C_2$	(r) 5
(D) P (5, 1)	(s) $\frac{P(20,19)}{19!}$

Integer Type Questions :

DIRECTIONS : *Answer the following questions. The answer to each of the question is a single digit integer, ranging from 0 to 9.*

1. If $^9P_5 + 5.\,^9P_4 = {}^{10}P_r$, then find *r*.
2. If $^{2n+1}P_{n-1} : {}^{2n-1}P_n = 3 : 5$, find *n*.
3. Determine n if $^{2n}C_3 : {}^nC_3 = 11 : 1$
4. A bag contain 5 black and 6 red balls. The number of ways in which 2 black and 3 red balls can be selected is '*a*'. Find the value of $a \div 100$.
5. 6-digit numbers can be formed from the digits 0, 1, 3, 5, 7 and 9 which will divisible by 10 and no digit is repeated are '*a*'. Find the value of $a \div 60$.

SOLUTIONS

Brief Explanations of Selected Questions

EXERCISE

SINGLE OPTION CORRECT :

1. (b) "STATESMAN"
Total number of letters = 9,
Number of S's = 2, Number of T's = 2,
Number of A's = 2
$\therefore$ Required number of permutations
$$= \frac{9!}{(2)!\,(2)!\,(2)!} = 45360$$

2. (c) Total number of digits is 10, i.e., 0, 1, 2, 3, 4, 5, 6, 7, 8, 9.
In order to find the total number of 9 digit numbers we have to find the number of ways of filling up 9 places out of these 10 digits, but 0 cannot be in the first place. Out of the remaining 9 digits any one can be put in the first place.
$\therefore$ The first place can be filled in 9 ways.
The remaining 8 places can be filled by any eight of the remaining 9 digits which can be done in ${}^9P_8$ ways.
Hence, the total number of 9 digit numbers are
$9 \times {}^9P_8 = 9 \times 9!$

3. (a) Since, each number consisting of 6 digits starts with 35, 3 and 5 are fixed in the first and second places.
The other four places can be filled up with remaining 8 digits in ${}^8P_4$ ways $= 8 \times 7 \times 6 \times 5 = 1680$ ways.
Hence, the required number of telephone numbers is 1680.

4. (a) $\frac{n!}{9!\,(n-9)!} = \frac{n!}{8!\,(n-8)!}$
$$\Rightarrow \frac{1!}{9 \times 8!(n-9)!} = \frac{1!}{8!\,(n-8)(n-9)!}$$
$$\Rightarrow \frac{1}{9} = \frac{1}{(n-8)} \Rightarrow 9 = n-8$$
$$\Rightarrow 9 + 8 = n \Rightarrow n = 17$$
$\therefore {}^nC_{17} = {}^{17}C_{17} = 1 \qquad [\because {}^nC_n = 1]$

5. (c) We have ${}^{10}C_x = {}^{10}C_{x+4}$
$\Rightarrow x + x + 4 = 10 \Rightarrow 2x = 6 \Rightarrow x = 3$

6. (b) ${}^nP_0 = \frac{n!}{(n-0)!} = \frac{n!}{n!} = 1$

7. (d) ${}^nC_n = \frac{n!}{n!(n-n)!} = \frac{n!}{n!\,0!}$
$= \frac{n!}{n!} = 1\;[\because n \times 0 = n]$

8. (c) ${}^nC_0 = \frac{n!}{0!\,(n-0)} = \frac{n!}{0!\,n!} = \frac{n!}{n!} = 1$

9. (d) When A has B or C to his right we have the order :
AB or AC ...(i)
When B has C or D to his right, we have the order :
BC or BD ...(ii)
Taking these two possibilities together, we must have ABC or ABD or AC and BD.
For ABC, D, E, F to arrange along a circle, number of way = 3 ! = 6, where three persons A,B,C together are treated as single.
For ABD, C, E, F, the number of ways = 6.
For AC, BD, E,F the number of ways = 6.
Hence, total number of ways = 18.

10. (a) We know that in any triangle the sum of two sides is always greater than the third side.
$\therefore$ The triangle will not be formed if we select segments of length (2, 3, 5), (2, 3, 6) or (2, 4, 6).
Hence, number of triangles formed = ${}^5C_3 - 3$.

11. (a) $\frac{{}^{n-1}P_3}{{}^nP_4} = \frac{1}{9} \Rightarrow \frac{{}^{n-1}P_3}{n.{}^{n-1}P_3} = \frac{1}{9}$
$$\Rightarrow \frac{1}{n} = \frac{1}{9} \text{ or } n = 9$$

12. (b) We get a chord by joining two points
If P is the number of chords from 21 points, then
$$P = C(21, 2) = \frac{21!}{2!(21-2)!} = \frac{21!}{2!19!}$$
$$= \frac{21 \times 20(19!)}{2 \times (19!)} = 21 \times 10 = 210 \text{ chords}$$

13. (b) $\frac{8!}{6! \times 2!} = \frac{8 \times 7 \times 6 \times 5 \times 4 \times 3 \times 2 \times 1}{(6 \times 5 \times 4 \times 3 \times 2 \times 1) \times (2 \times 1)}$
$$= \frac{8 \times 7}{2 \times 1} = 28$$

14. (a) We have
${}^nC_r = {}^nC_{n-r}$
${}^nC_2 = {}^nC_{n-2}$
${}^nC_8 = {}^nC_{n-2} \Rightarrow n - 2 = 8$ or $n = 10$
$${}^nC_2 = {}^{10}C_2 = \frac{10 \times 9}{1 \times 2} = 45$$

15. (c) At least one black ball can be drawn in the following ways:
(i) one black and two other colour balls
(ii) two black and one other colour balls, and
(iii) all the, three black balls
Therefore the required number of ways is
$^3C_1 \times {^6C_2} + {^3C_2} \times {^6C_1} + {^3C_3} = 64$.

16. (d) Two pairs of identical letters can be arranged in $^3C_2 \dfrac{4!}{2!2!}$ ways. Two identical letters and two different letters can be arranged in $^3C_1 \times {^7C_2} \times \dfrac{4!}{2!}$ ways. All different letters can be arranged in $^8P_4$ ways.
∴ Total no. of arrangements
$= {^3C_2}\dfrac{4!}{2!2!} + {^3C_1} \times {^7C_2} \times \dfrac{4!}{2!} + \dfrac{8!}{4!} = 2454.$

MORE THAN ONE OPTION CORRECT :

1. (a, b, c)
2. (a, b, c)
3. (a, b)
3 vacancies for *SC* candidates can be filled up from 5 candidates in $^5C_3$ ways.
After this for remaining $12 - 3 = 9$ vacancies, there will be 32 candidates. These vacancies can be filled up in $^{22}C_9$ ways.
Hence, required number of ways $= {^5C_3} \times {^{22}C_9}$
or $^5C_3 \times {^{22}C_9} = {^5C_{5-3}} \times {^{22}C_{22-9}} = {^5C_2} \times {^{22}C_{13}}$
4. (b, c)
5. (b, c, d)
6. (b, c)

PASSAGE BASED QUESTIONS :

1. (a) Natural science scholarship can be awarded to any one of the four candidates. So, there are 4 ways of awarding the natural science scholarships.
Similarly, mathematical and classical scholarships can be awarded in 2 and 6 ways respectively. Hence, by fundamental principle of multiplication, number of ways of awarding these scholarships = 4×2×6 = 48

2. (d) By fundamental principle of addition, number of ways of awarding one of the three scholarships
$= 4 + 2 + 6 = 12$

3. (c) The total number of ways of selecting 11 players out of 15 is
$^{15}C_{11}$

4. (a) If a particular player is always chosen. This means that 10 players are selected out of the remaining 14 players.
∴ Required number of ways
$= {^{14}C_{10}} = {^{14}C_{14-10}} = {^{14}C_4}$

5. (a) If a particular player is never chosen. This means that 11 players are selected out of the remaining 14 players.
∴ Required number of ways $= {^{14}C_{11}} = {^{14}C_{14-11}}$
$= {^{14}C_3}$

ASSERTION & REASON :

1. (b) Two circles intersect in 2 points.
∴ Maximum number of points of intersection
= 2 × number of selections of two circles from 8 circles
$= 2 \times {^8C_2} = 2 \times 28 = 56$
Statement 2 : 4 lines intersect each other in $^4C_2 = 6$ points
4 circles intersect each other in $2 \times {^4C_2} = 12$ points.
Further, one lines and one circle intersect in two points.
So 4 lines will intersect four circles in 32 points.
Maximum number of points = 6 + 12 + 32 = 50

2. (a) Number of words having all the letters distinct $= {^4P_1} = 4$
Number of words having two are alike and third different
$= {^1C_1} \cdot {^3C_1} \cdot \dfrac{3!}{2!} = 9$

3. (d) Reason is true, known as the rule of product.
Assertion is not true, as the two parts of the work are not independent. Three girls can be chosen out of six girls in $^6C_3$ ways, but after this choosing 3 students out of remaining nine students depends on the first part.

4. (a) Let number of sides are *n*.
$^nC_2 - n = 44$
$\Rightarrow n = -8$ or $11 \Rightarrow n = 11$.

MULTIPLE MATCHING QUESTION :

1. (A) → (q, s); (B) → (p); (C) → (r); (D) → (r)

INTEGER TYPE QUESTIONS :

1. **Ans : 5**
We have,
$^9P_5 + 5.{^9P_4} = {^{10}P_r}$
$\Rightarrow \dfrac{9!}{(9-5)!} + 5.\dfrac{9!}{(9-4)!} = \dfrac{10!}{(10-r)!}$
$\Rightarrow \dfrac{9!}{4!} + 5.\dfrac{9!}{5!} = \dfrac{10!}{(10-r)!}$
$\Rightarrow \dfrac{9!}{4!} + \dfrac{9!}{4!} = \dfrac{10!}{(10-r)!}$
$\Rightarrow 2 \times \dfrac{9!}{4!} = \dfrac{10!}{(10-r)!}$

$\Rightarrow \dfrac{5\times2\times9!}{5\times4!}=\dfrac{10!}{(10-r)!}$

$\Rightarrow \dfrac{10\times9!}{5!}=\dfrac{10!}{(10-r)!}$

$\Rightarrow \dfrac{10!}{5!}=\dfrac{10!}{(10-r)!}$

$\Rightarrow (10-r)! = 5! \Rightarrow 10-r=5 \Rightarrow r=5$

2. Ans : 1

We have,

$^{2n+1}P_{n-1} : {}^{2n-1}P_n = 3:5$

$\Rightarrow \dfrac{^{2n+1}P_{n-1}}{^{2n-1}P_n}=\dfrac{3}{5}$

$\Rightarrow \dfrac{(2n+1)!}{(n+2)!}\times\dfrac{(n-1)!}{(2n-1)!}=\dfrac{3}{5}$

$\Rightarrow \dfrac{(2n+1)(2n)(2n-1)!}{(n+2)(n+1)n\,(n-1)!}\times\dfrac{(n-1)!}{(2n-1)!}=\dfrac{3}{5}$

$\Rightarrow \dfrac{2(2n+1)}{(n+2)\,(n+1)}=\dfrac{3}{5}$

$\Rightarrow 10(2n+1)=3(n+2)(n+1)$

$\Rightarrow 3n^2+9n+6=20n+10$

$\Rightarrow 3n^2-11n-4=0$

$\Rightarrow (n-4)(3n+1)=0 \Rightarrow n=4 \qquad [\because n \neq -\frac{1}{3}]$

3. Ans : 6

$^{2n}C_3 : {}^{n}C_3 = 11:1$

or $\dfrac{2n(2n-1)(2n-2)}{1.2.3}\div\dfrac{n(n-1)(n-2)}{1.2.3}=\dfrac{11}{1}$

or $\dfrac{4n(n-1)(2n-1)}{6}\times\dfrac{6}{n(n-1)(n-2)}=\dfrac{11}{1}$

or $\dfrac{4(2n-1)}{n-2}=11$

$4(2n-1)=11(n-2)$ or $8n-4=11n-22$

or $3n=18 \quad \therefore n=6$

4. Ans : 2

The number of ways in which 2 black and 3 red balls can be selected $= {}^5C_2\times{}^6C_3$

$=\dfrac{5\times4}{1\times2}\times\dfrac{6\times5\times4}{1\times2\times3}=10\times20=200$

Hence, $a\div100=200\div100=2$

5. Ans : 2

A number is divisible by 10 if zero occurs at the units place. Now, we have to fill up 5 place with the digits 1, 3, 5, 7 and 9.

This can be done in $5! = 120$ ways

$\therefore$ Required number $= 120$

Hence, $a\div60=120\div60=2$

Chapter 18

Limits

INTRODUCTION

Consider a function, f (x) = 2x + 3

x approaches 4 from left → 4 ← *x* approaches 4 from right

x	2	3.6	3.9	3.99	3.999		4.001	4.01	4.1	4.8	5
***f*(x)**	7	10.2	10.8	10.98	10.998		11.002	11.02	11.2	12.6	13

$f(x)$ approaches 11 from left → 11 ← $f(x)$ approaches 11 from right

In the above table, we see that when the value of x approaches 4 (but not equal to 4) from left, the value of $f(x)$ approaches 11 and when the value of x approaches 4 (but not equal to 4) from right, the value of $f(x)$ even then approaches to 11.

Here, 11 is said to be the limit of $f(x)$ as x approaches 4 (but not equal to 4) from either side. We can abbreviate this statement as $\lim_{x \to 4} f(x) = 11$ or $\lim_{x \to 4} (2x+3) = 11$. Thus in general, if $y = f(x)$ be a function of x and the value of the function tends to a definite unique value 'l' as x tends to a particular value 'a' (either from left or right), then the value 'l' is called the limit of $f(x)$ at $x = a$ and we write it as $\lim_{x \to a} f(x) = l$.

MEANING OF '$x \to a$'

Let x be a variable and a be a constant. If x assumes values nearer and nearer to 'a', then we can say 'x tends to a' and we write '$x \to a$'.

It should be noted that $x \to a$ means :

(i) x assumes values nearer and nearer to 'a' and we are not specify any manner in which x should approach to a. x may approaches to 'a' from left or right as shown in the figure.

(ii) $x \neq a$

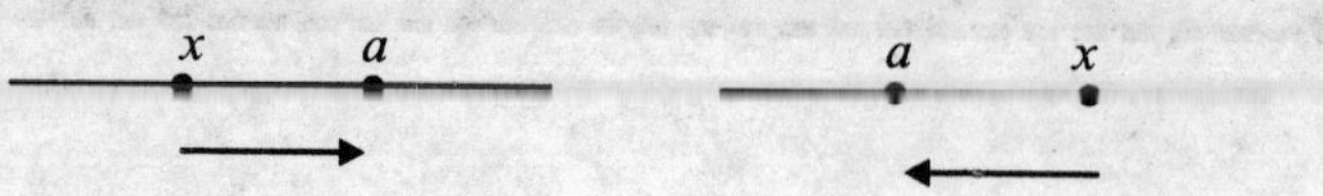

x approaches 'a' from left x approaches 'a' from right

EVALUATION OF LEFT HAND AND RIGHT HAND LIMITS (i.e. ONE SIDED LIMIT)

The statement $x \to a^-$ means that x is tending to 'a' from the left hand side, i.e. x is a number less than 'a' but very close to a.
Therefore $x \to a^-$ is equivalent to $x = a - h$ where $h > 0$ such that $h \to 0$.
Similarly, $x \to a^+$ is equivalent to $x = a + h$ where $h > 0$ such that $h \to 0$.
Thus, we have the following algorithms for finding left hand and right hand limits of a function at $x = a$.

ALGORITHM FOR FINDING LEFT HAND LIMIT (L.H.L)

To evaluate LHL of $f(x)$ at $x = a$, i.e. $\lim\limits_{x \to a^-} f(x)$ we proceed as follows :

(i) Write $\lim\limits_{x \to a^-} f(x)$

(ii) Put $x = a - h$ in $f(x)$ and replace $x \to a^-$ by $h \to 0$ to obtain $\lim\limits_{h \to 0} f(a-h)$.

(iii) Simplify $\lim\limits_{h \to 0} f(a-h)$ by using the formula for the given function.

(iv) The value obtain in step (iii) is the LHL of $f(x)$ at $x = a$.

ALGORITHM FOR FINDING RIGHT HAND LIMIT (R.H.L)

To evaluate RHL of $f(x)$ at $x = a$, i.e. $\lim\limits_{x \to a^+} f(x)$ we proceed as follows :

(i) Write $\lim\limits_{x \to a^+} f(x)$

(ii) Put $x = a + h$ in $f(x)$ and replace $x \to a^+$ by $h \to 0$ to obtain $\lim\limits_{h \to 0} f(a+h)$

(iii) Simplify $\lim\limits_{h \to 0} f(a+h)$ by using the formula for the given function.

(iv) The value obtained in step (iii) is the RHL of $f(x)$ at $x = a$.

ILLUSTRATION : 1

Evaluate the left hand and right hand limits of the function defined by

$$f(x) = \begin{cases} 1 + x^2, \text{ if } 0 \\ 2 - x, \text{ if } x > 1 \end{cases} \quad \text{at } x = 1$$

Also, show that $\lim\limits_{x \to 1} f(x)$ does not exist.

SOLUTION :

We have,

(LHL of $f(x)$ at $x = 1$) $= \lim\limits_{x \to 1^-} f(x) = \lim\limits_{h \to 0} f(1-h)$

$$= \lim_{h \to 0} 1 + (1-h)^2 = \lim_{h \to 0} 2 - 2h + h^2 = 2$$

and, (RHL of $f(x)$ at $x = 1$) $= \lim\limits_{x \to 1^+} f(x) = \lim\limits_{h \to 1^+} f(1+h)$

$= \lim_{h\to 0} 2-(1+h) = \lim_{h\to 0} 1-h = 1$

Clearly, $\lim_{x\to 1^-} f(x) \neq \lim_{x\to 1^+} f(x)$

So, $\lim_{x\to 1} f(x)$ does not exist.

EXISTENCE OF LIMIT (i.e. LIMIT FROM BOTH SIDES) OF A FUNCTION AT A POINT

The limit of a function at some point exists only when its left-hand limit & right hand limit at that point exist and are equal. If the limit of a function exists then limit of the function is equal to the left/right hand limit. Thus, $\lim_{x\to a} f(x)$ exists and equal if

$$\lim_{x\to a^-} f(x) = \lim_{x\to a^+} f(x) = l$$

where l is called the limit of the function.

ILLUSTRATION : 2

Find $\lim_{x\to 0} f(x)$, where $f(x) = \begin{cases} \frac{x}{|x|}, & x \neq 0 \\ 0, & x = 0 \end{cases}$

SOLUTION :

When $x < 0, |x| = -x$

$\therefore \lim_{x\to 0^-} f(x) = \lim_{x\to 0^-} \frac{x}{|x|} = \lim_{x\to 0^-} \left(\frac{x}{-x}\right) = -1$

When $x > 0, |x| = x$

$\therefore \lim_{x\to 0^+} f(x) = \lim_{x\to 0^+} \frac{x}{|x|} = \lim_{x\to 0^+} \frac{x}{x} = 1$

$\therefore \lim_{x\to 0^-} f(x) \neq \lim_{x\to 0^+} f(x)$

$\therefore \lim_{x\to 0} f(x)$ does not exist.

THE ALGEBRA OF LIMITS

(i) $\lim_{x\to a} (f \pm g)(x) = \lim_{x\to a} f(x) \pm \lim_{x\to a} g(x)$

(ii) $\lim_{x\to a} (f(x) \cdot g(x)) = \lim_{x\to a} f(x) \cdot \lim_{x\to a} g(x)$

(iii) $\lim_{x\to a} \frac{f(x)}{g(x)} = \frac{\lim_{x\to a} f(x)}{\lim_{x\to a} g(x)}$, provided that $\lim_{x\to a} g(x) \neq 0$

(iv) $\lim_{x\to a} kf(x) = k. \lim_{x\to a} f(x)$, where k is a constant

(v) $\lim_{x\to a} [f(x)+k] = \lim_{x\to a} f(x) + k$, where k is a constant

(vi) $\lim_{x\to a} |f(x)| = |\lim_{x\to a} f(x)|$

(vii) $\lim_{x\to a} (f(x))^{g(x)} = \left(\lim_{x\to a} f(x)\right)^{\lim_{x\to a} g(x)}$

EVALUATION OF ALGEBRAIC LIMITS

In order to evaluate algebraic limits we have the following methods :

(i) Direct Substitution Method :

ILLUSTRATION : 3

Find the value of the following :

$$\lim_{x\to 3} \frac{x^2+11}{x^2-4}$$

SOLUTION :

$$\lim_{x\to 3}\frac{x^2+11}{x^2-4}=\frac{\lim_{x\to 3}(x^2+11)}{\lim_{x\to 3}(x^2-4)}=\frac{(3)^2+11}{(3)^2-4}=\frac{20}{5}=4$$

(ii) Factorisation Method :

ILLUSTRATION : 4

Find the value of the following : $\lim_{x\to 4}\dfrac{x^2-16}{x^2-2x-8}$

SOLUTION :

$$\lim_{x\to 4}\frac{x^2-16}{x^2-2x-8}=\lim_{x\to 4}\frac{(x+4)(x-4)}{(x+2)(x-4)}=\lim_{x\to 4}\frac{x+4}{x+2}$$

$$=\frac{\lim_{x\to 4}(x+4)}{\lim_{x\to 4}(x+2)}=\frac{4+4}{4+2}=\frac{4}{3}$$ [limit of polynomial functions]

ILLUSTRATION : 5

Evaluate : $\lim_{x\to 2}\dfrac{x^2-3x+2}{x^2+x-6}$

SOLUTION :

$$\lim_{x\to 2}\frac{x^2-3x+2}{x^2+x-6}=\lim_{x\to 2}\frac{(x-2)(x-1)}{(x-2)(x+3)}=\frac{2-1}{2+3}=\frac{1}{5}$$

(iii) Rationalisation Method :

ILLUSTRATION : 6

Find the value of $\lim_{x\to 5}\dfrac{1-\sqrt{x-4}}{x-5}$

SOLUTION :

$$\lim_{x\to 5}\frac{1-\sqrt{x-4}}{x-5}=\lim_{x\to 5}\frac{1-\sqrt{x-4}}{x-5}\cdot\frac{1+\sqrt{x-4}}{1+\sqrt{x-4}}=\lim_{x\to 5}\frac{1-x+4}{(x-5)(1+\sqrt{x-4})}=\lim_{x\to 5}\frac{-(x-5)}{(x-5)(1+\sqrt{x-4})}$$

$$=\lim_{x\to 5}\frac{-1}{(1+\sqrt{x-4})}=\frac{-1}{(1+\sqrt{5-4})}=\frac{-1}{2}$$

ILLUSTRATION : 7

Evaluate : $\lim_{x\to 0}\dfrac{\sqrt{1+x+x^2}-1}{x}$

SOLUTION :

$$\lim_{x\to 0}\frac{\sqrt{1+x+x^2}-1}{x}=\lim_{x\to 0}\frac{\sqrt{1+x+x^2}-1}{x}\cdot\frac{\sqrt{1+x+x^2}+1}{\sqrt{1+x+x^2}+1}=\lim_{x\to 0}\frac{1+x+x^2-1}{x\left(\sqrt{1+x+x^2}+1\right)}=\lim_{x\to 0}\frac{x(1+x)}{x\left(\sqrt{1+x+x^2}+1\right)}$$

$$=\lim_{x\to 0}\frac{1+x}{\sqrt{1+x+x^2}+1}=\frac{1}{2}$$

(iv) By Using Some Standard Limits for any positive 'a'

(i) $\lim\limits_{x\to a}\dfrac{x^n-a^n}{x-a}=na^{n-1}$ (ii) $\lim\limits_{x\to 0}\sin x=0$

(iii) $\lim\limits_{x\to 0}\cos x=\lim\limits_{x\to 0}\left(\dfrac{1}{\cos x}\right)=1$ (iv) $\lim\limits_{x\to 0}\dfrac{\sin x}{x}=\lim\limits_{x\to 0}\dfrac{x}{\sin x}=1$

(v) $\lim\limits_{x\to 0}\tan x=0$ (vi) $\lim\limits_{x\to 0}\dfrac{\tan x}{x}=\lim\limits_{x\to 0}\dfrac{x}{\tan x}=1$

ILLUSTRATION : 8

Evaluate : $\lim\limits_{x\to a}\dfrac{(x+2)^{5/3}-(a+2)^{5/3}}{x-a}$.

SOLUTION :

$$\lim_{x\to a}\frac{(x+2)^{5/3}-(a+2)^{5/3}}{x-a}=\lim_{x\to a}\frac{(x+2)^{5/3}-(a+2)^{5/3}}{(x+2)-(a+2)}$$

$$=\lim_{y\to b}\frac{y^{5/3}-b^{5/3}}{y-b}\text{, where } x+2=y,\ a+2=b \text{ and when } x\to a,\ y\to b$$

$$=\frac{5}{3}b^{5/3-1}=\frac{5}{3}b^{2/3}=\frac{5}{3}(a+2)^{2/3}.$$

ILLUSTRATION : 9

Evaluate : $\lim\limits_{x\to 0}\dfrac{\tan x-\sin x}{\sin^3 x}$

SOLUTION :

$$\lim_{x\to 0}\frac{\tan x-\sin x}{\sin^3 x}=\lim_{x\to 0}\frac{\frac{\sin x}{\cos x}-\sin x}{\sin^3 x}=\lim_{x\to 0}\frac{\sin x(1-\cos x)}{\cos x\sin^3 x}$$

$$=\lim_{x\to 0}\frac{1-\cos x}{\cos x\sin^2 x}=\lim_{x\to 0}\frac{1-\cos x}{\cos x(1-\cos^2 x)}$$

$$=\lim_{x\to 0}\frac{1-\cos x}{\cos x(1+\cos x)(1-\cos x)}=\lim_{x\to 0}\frac{1}{\cos x(1+\cos x)}=\frac{1}{2}$$

EXERCISE

Single Option Correct :

DIRECTIONS: *This section contains multiple choice questions. Each questions has 4 choices (a), (b), (c) and (d), out of which ONLY ONE is correct.*

1. Limit of difference of two functions is ________ of the limits of the functions.

(a) difference (b) sum
(c) multiplication (d) division

2. $\lim_{x\to a}\frac{f(x)}{g(x)}=$ ________

(a) $\lim_{x\to a} f(x)$ (b) $\lim_{x\to a} g(x)$

(c) $\lim_{x\to a} f(x)\cdot \lim_{x\to a} g(x)$ (d) $\frac{\lim_{x\to a} f(x)}{\lim_{x\to a} g(x)}$

3. For any positive integer n, $\lim_{x\to a}\frac{x^n-a^n}{x-a}=$ ________

(a) $n.a^{n-1}$ (b) $\frac{n}{a^{n-1}}$

(c) $n+a^{n-1}$ (d) $n-a^{n-1}$

4. $\lim_{x\to 0}\frac{\sin 4x}{\sin 2x}=$ ________

(a) 0 (b) 1
(c) 2 (d) 4

5. Value of the following limits:

$\lim_{x\to 3}\left(\frac{x^4-81}{2x^2-5x-3}\right)$ is

(a) 7 (b) $\frac{7}{108}$

(c) $\frac{108}{7}$ (d) 108

6. Value of the following limits

$\lim_{x\to -2}\frac{\frac{1}{x}+\frac{1}{2}}{x+2}$ is

(a) $-\frac{1}{4}$ (b) $\frac{1}{4}$

(c) 4 (d) 1

7. Evaluate : $\lim_{x\to 2}\frac{\sin 5x}{2x}$

(a) $\frac{5}{2}$ (b) $\frac{2}{5}$

(c) 5 (d) 2

8. Value of $\lim_{x\to 0}\frac{(1-x)^n-1}{x}$ is

(a) n (b) $-n$
(c) 1 (d) -1

9. If $\lim_{x\to -a}\frac{x^9+a^9}{x+a}=9$, then the value of 'a' is

(a) 9 (b) -9
(c) ± 1 (d) ± 8

10. Value of $\lim_{x\to 0}\frac{\sin 3x}{x}$ is

(a) 3 (b) -3
(c) 1 (d) 9

11. Value of $\lim_{x\to 0}\frac{\sin^2 3x}{x^2}$ is

(a) 9 (b) -9
(c) 1 (d) -1

12. Value of $\lim_{x\to 9}\frac{x^{3/2}-27}{x-9}$ is

(a) $\frac{2}{9}$ (b) $\frac{9}{2}$

(c) $\frac{3}{2}$ (d) $\frac{2}{3}$

More Than One Option Correct :

DIRECTIONS: *This section contains multiple choice questions. Each question has 4 choices (a), (b), (c) and (d), out of which ONE OR MORE may be correct.*

1. Which of the following statement(s) is/are incorrect ?

(a) $\lim_{x\to a}(f\pm g)(x)\neq \lim_{x\to a} f(x)\pm \lim_{x\to a} g(x)$

(b) $\lim_{x\to a} f(x).g(x)\neq \lim_{x\to a} f(x).\lim_{x\to a} g(x)$

(c) $\lim_{x \to a} k.f(x) = k.\lim_{x \to a} f(x)$, where k is a constant

(d) $\lim_{x \to a} |f(x)| \neq \left|\lim_{x \to a} f(x)\right|$

2. Which of the following limits is/are correct ?

(a) $\lim_{x \to 0} \frac{\sin x}{x} = 1$ (b) $\lim_{x \to 0} \frac{x}{\tan x} = 1$

(c) $\lim_{x \to 0} \frac{x}{\sin x} \neq 1$ (d) $\lim_{x \to 0} \frac{\tan x}{x} = 1$

Passage Based Questions :

DIRECTIONS: *Study the given paragraph(s) and answer the following questions.*

PASSAGE

If $\lim_{x \to a} \frac{f(x)}{g(x)}$ attains $\frac{0}{0}$ form, then x – a must be a factor of numerator and denominator which can be cancelled out.

For example.

$\lim_{x \to 2} \frac{x^2 + 3x - 10}{x^2 - 5x + 6}$. It is $\frac{0}{0}$ form, hence $(x - 2)$ must be a factor of numerator as well as denominator

$= \lim_{x \to 2} \frac{(x-2)(x+5)}{(x-2)(x-3)} = \lim_{x \to 2} \frac{x+5}{x-3} = -7$

1. Value of $\lim_{x \to 2} \frac{x^2 - 5x + 6}{x^2 - 4}$ is

(a) $\frac{-1}{4}$ (b) $\frac{1}{4}$

(c) 4 (d) – 4

2. Value of $\lim_{x \to 1} \frac{x^3 - 1}{x - 1}$ is

(a) –3 (b) 3

(c) 6 (d) – 6

3. Value of $\lim_{x \to \frac{1}{2}} \frac{8x^3 - 1}{16x^4 - 1}$ is

(a) $\frac{4}{3}$ (b) $\frac{1}{2}$

(c) $\frac{-4}{3}$ (d) $\frac{3}{4}$

Assertion & Reason :

DIRECTIONS: *Each of these questions contains an Assertion followed by Reason. Read them carefully and answer the question on the basis of following options. You have to select the one that best describes the two statements.*

(a) If both **Assertion** and **Reason** are **correct** and Reason is the **correct explanation** of Assertion.

(b) If both **Assertion** and **Reason** are correct, but Reason is **not the correct explanation** of Assertion.

(c) If **Assertion** is **correct** but **Reason** is **incorrect.**

(d) If **Assertion** is **incorrect** but **Reason** is **correct.**

1. **Assertion :** If $\lim_{x \to 1} \frac{x^4 - 1}{x - 1} = \lim_{x \to k} \frac{x^3 - k^3}{x^2 - k^2}$, then the value of k is $\frac{8}{3}$.

Reason : For any positive integer n, $\lim_{x \to a} \frac{x^n - a^n}{x - a} = n.a^{n-1}$

[n can be any rational number also]

2. **Assertion :** Value of $\lim_{x \to 0} \frac{\sin 2x + \sin 3x}{2x + \sin 3x}$ is 1.

Reason : $\lim_{x \to 0} \frac{\sin x}{x} = 1$ and $\lim_{x \to 0} \frac{x}{\sin x} = 1$

Integer Type Questions :

DIRECTIONS: *Answer the following questions. The answer to each of the question is a single digit integer, ranging from 0 to 9.*

1. If $\lim_{x \to 2} \frac{x^n - 2^n}{x - 2} = 80$ and $n \in N$, then find n.

2. Evaluate : $\lim_{x \to 0} \frac{1 - \cos 2x}{x}$

3. Evaluate the following limit :

$\lim_{x \to 0} \frac{(x+1)^5 - 1}{x}$

SOLUTIONS

Brief Explanations of Selected Questions

EXERCISE

SINGLE OPTION CORRECT :

1. (a) difference

2. (d) $\dfrac{\lim\limits_{x\to a} f(x)}{\lim\limits_{x\to a} g(x)}$

3. (a) $n.a^{n-1}$

4. (c) 2

5. (c) $\lim\limits_{x\to 3}\left(\dfrac{x^4-81}{2x^2-5x-3}\right)=\lim\limits_{x\to 3}\dfrac{(x-3)(x+3)(x^2+9)}{(x-3)(2x+1)}$

$=\lim\limits_{x\to 3}\dfrac{(x+3)(x^2+9)}{2x+1}=\dfrac{6\times 18}{7}=\dfrac{108}{7}$

6. (a) $\lim\limits_{x\to -2}\dfrac{\frac{1}{x}+\frac{1}{2}}{x+2}=\lim\limits_{x\to -2}\dfrac{2+x}{2x}\div(x+2)$

$=\lim\limits_{x\to -2}\dfrac{2+x}{2x}\times\dfrac{1}{(x+2)}$

$=\lim\limits_{x\to -2}\left(\dfrac{1}{2x}\right)=-\dfrac{1}{4}$

7. (a) $\lim\limits_{x\to 2}\dfrac{\sin 5x}{2x}=\lim\limits_{x\to 2}\left(\dfrac{5}{5}.\dfrac{\sin 5x}{2x}\right)$

$=\dfrac{5}{2}\lim\limits_{x\to 0}\dfrac{\sin 5x}{5x}=\dfrac{5}{2}(1)=\dfrac{5}{2}\quad\left[\because \lim\limits_{x\to 0}\dfrac{\sin 5x}{5x}=1\right]$

8. (b) $\lim\limits_{x\to 0}\dfrac{(1-x)^n-1}{x}\quad \lim\limits_{x\to 0}\dfrac{(1-x)^n-1}{x\quad 1-1}$

$=-\lim\limits_{x\to 0}\dfrac{(1-x)^n-1}{(1-x)-1}=-n(1)^{n-1}=-n$

9. (c) $\lim\limits_{x\to -a}\dfrac{x^9-(-a)^9}{x-(-a)}=9\Rightarrow 9.(-a)^{9-1}=9$

$\Rightarrow\ 9.a^8=9\Rightarrow a^8=1\Rightarrow a=\pm 1$

10. (a) $\lim\limits_{x\to 0}\dfrac{\sin 3x}{x}=\lim\limits_{x\to 0}\dfrac{3\sin 3x}{3x}$

$=3.\lim\limits_{3x\to 0}\dfrac{\sin 3x}{3x}=3.1=3$

11. (a) $\lim\limits_{x\to 0}\dfrac{\sin^2 3x}{x^2}=\lim\limits_{x\to 0}\dfrac{9\sin^2 3x}{9.x.x}$

$=9\lim\limits_{x\to 0}\dfrac{\sin^2 3x}{9x^2}=9\times 1=9$

12. (b) $\lim\limits_{x\to 9}\dfrac{x^{3/2}-27}{x-9}=\lim\limits_{x\to 9}\dfrac{x^{\frac{3}{2}}-9^{\frac{3}{2}}}{x-9}$

$=\dfrac{3}{2}.(9)^{\frac{3}{2}-1}=\dfrac{3}{2}(9)^{\frac{1}{2}}=\dfrac{3}{2}\times 3=\dfrac{9}{2}$

MORE THAN ONE OPTION CORRECT :

1. (a, b, d) 2. (a, b, d)

PASSAGE BASED QUESTIONS :

1. (a) $\lim\limits_{x\to 2}\dfrac{x^2-5x+6}{x^2-4}=\lim\limits_{x\to 2}\dfrac{(x-2)(x-3)}{(x+2)(x-2)}$

$=\lim\limits_{x\to 2}\dfrac{x-3}{x+2}=\dfrac{2-3}{2+2}=\dfrac{-1}{4}$

2. (b) $\lim\limits_{x\to 1}\dfrac{x^3-1}{x-1}=\lim\limits_{x\to 1}\dfrac{(x-1)(x^2+x+1)}{(x-1)}$

$=\lim\limits_{x\to 1}(x^2+x+1)=1^2+1+1=3$

3. (d) $\lim\limits_{x\to\frac{1}{2}}\dfrac{8x^3-1}{16x^4-1}=\lim\limits_{x\to\frac{1}{2}}\dfrac{(2x)^3-1^3}{(4x^2)^2-1^2}$

$=\lim\limits_{x\to\frac{1}{2}}\dfrac{(2x-1)(4x^2+2x+1)}{(4x^2+1)(2x-1)(2x+1)}$

$=\lim\limits_{x\to\frac{1}{2}}\dfrac{4x^2+2x+1}{(4x^2+1)(2x+1)}=\dfrac{3}{4}$

ASSERTION & REASON :

1. **(a)** L.H.S $=\lim\limits_{x\to 1}\dfrac{x^4-1}{x-1}=4(1)^3=4$

RHS $=\lim\limits_{x\to k}\dfrac{x^3-k^3}{(x-k)}.\dfrac{(x-k)}{(x^2-k^2)}=\dfrac{3k^2}{2k}=\dfrac{3k}{2}$

LHS = RHS $\Rightarrow 4=\dfrac{3k}{2}\Rightarrow k=\dfrac{8}{3}$

2. (a) $\lim\limits_{x\to 0}\dfrac{\sin 2x+\sin 3x}{2x+\sin 3x}=\lim\limits_{x\to 0}\dfrac{\dfrac{2x\sin 2x}{2x}+\dfrac{3x\sin 3x}{3x}}{2x+3x\dfrac{\sin 3x}{3x}}$

$N^r=\lim\limits_{x\to 0}2x.\lim\limits_{x\to 0}\dfrac{\sin 2x}{2x}+\lim\limits_{x\to 0}3x.\lim\limits_{x\to 0}\dfrac{\sin 3x}{3x}$

$=\lim\limits_{x\to 0}2x+\lim\limits_{x\to 0}3x \qquad \left(\because \lim\limits_{x\to 0}\dfrac{\sin x}{x}=1\right)$

$=\lim\limits_{x\to 0}(2x+3x)=\lim\limits_{x\to 0}5x$

$D^r=\lim\limits_{x\to 0}2x+\lim\limits_{x\to 0}3x.\lim\limits_{x\to 0}\dfrac{\sin 3x}{3x}$

$=\lim\limits_{x\to 0}(2x+3x)=\lim\limits_{x\to 0}5x$

Now, $\dfrac{N^r}{D^r}=\lim\limits_{x\to 0}\dfrac{5x}{5x}=\lim\limits_{x\to 0}1=1$

INTEGER TYPE QUESTIONS :

1. **Ans : 5**

$\lim\limits_{x\to 2}\dfrac{x^n-2^n}{x-2}=80$

$\Rightarrow n\,.\,2^{n-1}=80\Rightarrow n\,.\,2^n=160.\ 2^5.5 \Rightarrow n=5.$

2. **Ans : 0**

$\lim\limits_{x\to 0}\dfrac{1-\cos 2x}{x}=\lim\limits_{x\to 0}\dfrac{2\sin^2 x}{x}$

$=2\lim\limits_{x\to 0}\left(\dfrac{\sin x}{x}.\sin x\right)=2\left(\lim\limits_{x\to 0}\dfrac{\sin x}{x}\right)\left(\lim\limits_{x\to 0}\sin x\right)$

$=2\,(1)\,(0)=0$

3. **Ans : 5**

$\lim\limits_{x\to 0}\dfrac{(x+1)^5-1}{x}=\lim\limits_{x\to 0}\dfrac{\left(1+5x+\dfrac{5.\ 4}{1.\ 2}x^2+.....+x^5\right)-1}{x}$

$=\lim\limits_{x\to 0}\dfrac{5x+10x^2+.......+x^5}{x}$

$=\lim\limits_{x\to 0}(5+10x+.....+x^4)=5$